Conversations

CONVERSATIONS
Readings for Writing
third edition

Jack Selzer
The Pennsylvania State University

ALLYN AND BACON

Boston   London   Toronto   Sydney   Tokyo   Singapore

Vice President: Eben W. Ludlow
Editorial Assistant: Liz Egan
Marketing Manager: Lisa Kimball
Production Administrator: Rowena Dores
Editorial-Production Service: Lauren Green Shafer
Art Director: Linda Knowles
Cover Designer: Susan Paradise
Composition Buyer: Linda Cox
Manufacturing Buyer: Megan Cochran

Library of Congress Cataloging-in-Publication Data
Conversations : readings for writing / [compiled by] Jack Selzer. —
    3rd ed.
        p.   cm.
    Includes index.
    ISBN 0-205-19694-2
    1. College readers.   2. English language—Rhetoric.   I. Selzer,
Jack.
PE1417.C6545 1996
808'.0427—dc20
                                                            96–18433
                                                                CIP

Credits

PART I
Pages 21–23: From "Education" from *One Man's Meat* by E. B. White.
Copyright 1939 by E. B. White. Copyright renewed. Reprinted by permis-
sion of HarperCollins Publishers, Inc.
Pages 23–27: From John Chubb and Terry Moe, "The Private vs. Public
Debate," *The Wall Street Journal,* July 25, 1991. Reprinted with permission
of The Wall Street Journal. © 1991 Dow Jones & Company, Inc. All rights
reserved.

*Credits continued on page 1083, which constitutes an extension of the
copyright page.*

Printed in the United States of America

10 9 8 7 6 5 4 3 2   99 98 97 96

For Molly and Maggie:
Their Book

Contents

What's College For?   **74**

II. LANGUAGE

Is English Sexist?   245

III. RACE AND GENDER

In their quest for a "raceless" society, in their
efforts to reconceive of the concept of race itself,
are some African American intellectuals undermining Black consciousness and Black identity?
Is there a postmodern conspiracy to explode
racial identity?

A leading Afrocentrist analyzes "the race to
leave the race" by leading African American
postmodernists.

"The days of an essential Black are definitely over
for me. I've had enough suppressing so-called
lesser issues such as gender and class. . . . Black
racial essences are but mirror images of white
racial essences, the very foundation of white
supremacy."

"The concept of race as we commonly use it . . . is
merely the slaveholders' expedient for defining
a segment of the population into permanent
subordination."

Our second president and his wife debate the place
of women in the new republic of the United States.

Is Single Parenthood a Problem?   486

Who "Owns" This Child?   **544**

V. CIVIL LIBERTIES AND CIVIL RIGHTS

Should Abortion Be Legal?   **736**

Gay, Lesbian, and Bisexual Rights   **761**

VI. CRIME AND PUNISHMENT

Contents

Should Drugs Be Legalized?

VII. SCIENCE AND SOCIETY

Rhetorical Contents

Description and Narration

Argument: Evaluation

Argument: Proposal

Argument: Refutation

Preface

Imagine that you enter a parlor. You come late. When you arrive, others have long preceded you, and they are engaged in a heated discussion, a discussion too heated for them to pause and tell you exactly what it is about. In fact, the discussion had already begun long before any of them got there, so that no one present is qualified to retrace for you all the steps that had gone before. You listen for a while, until you decide that you have caught the tenor of the argument; then you put in your oar. Someone answers; you answer him; another comes to your defense; another aligns himself against you, to either the embarrassment or gratification of your opponent, depending upon the quality of your ally's assistance.

This well-known passage from Kenneth Burke's *Philosophy of Literary Form* explains the basic metaphor and the orientation of this anthology of readings for first-year college composition courses. *Conversations* contains conversations: public discourse on contemporary issues that is calculated to engage students' interests, to encourage and empower their own contributions to contemporary civic discussions, and to represent a broad cross-section of the kinds of conversational styles and genres that are available to writers at the end of the twentieth century.

What's Different about *Conversations?*

Conversations encourages student writing on important current civic issues. The premise of this reader is that writing is less a private act of making personal meaning out of thin air than it is a public and social act of making meaning within a specific rhetorical situation—a specific situation that guides and shapes the meaning-making activity. To put the matter more simply, writing emerges from other writing, other discourse. Though nearly every anthology claims to encourage student responses, those anthologies just as often actually intimidate students because they present only one or two authoritative voices on a given issue and because those voices are given little context outside the anthology; the student reads an essay by Quindlen or Baldwin or Woolf or some other eloquent writer and says to himself or herself, "Gee, that sure seems right to me. How could I disagree with such an expert?" By contrast, instead of one or two authoritative items on an issue or topic, this reader contains "conversations" on public issues or topics, conversations-with-contexts that will seem less intimidating and therefore invite student responses.

In fact, the book will encourage students to adopt a social and rhetorical model—a "conversation model"—for their own writing. Instead of seeing writing merely as private or as point-counterpoint debate, students should sense from *Conversations* that "people are talking about this issue—and I'd like to get in on the talk somewhere." The conversation metaphor does not mean that students should "write like they talk" (since conversational informality is not always appropriate in public discourse); rather, the metaphor simply implies that students should see writing as a response to other writing or to other forms of discourse, a response that students make after considering the implications and importance of what they have read and heard. Students should be encouraged to cooperate as well as to compete with other writers, to address subissues as well as the main chance, to seek consensus and new syntheses as often as victory.

Thus, *Conversations* is organized around focused, topical, contemporary public issues (e.g., censorship, what to do about public education, affirmative action, legalization of drugs, abortion, gun control), each within seven larger thematic groupings (education, language, race and gender, family matters, civil liberties and civil rights, crime and punishment, and science and society) that lend additional historical and conceptual perspective to those contemporary issues. *Intertextuality* would be the buzzword from contemporary critical theory: The book includes items that "talk to each other" both directly and indirectly. Some pieces speak directly and explicitly to each other (as in the case of the four-way discussion of single parenthood, or Milton Friedman's exchange with William Bennett about the legalization of drugs, or the e-mail discussion of electronic censorship, or the controversy on the meaning of "race" from the pages of *Black Scholar*). Some pieces refer only indirectly to others, as in the sections on education, genetic engineering, and affirmative action. And still other items comment on selections in other sections of *Conversations:* for example, selections on education comment on those on language and race; the section on pornography is informed by the sections on gender and the causes of crime; the items on gay, lesbian, and bisexual rights are related to the section on AIDS and same-sex marriage. And so forth. There is certainly no reason why the selections in this anthology cannot be read individually as they are in other books, without reference to other selections, especially since the headnotes orient readers to each item. And there is certainly no reason why the selections could not be read in some other order than the order in which they are presented here. Nevertheless, *Conversations* does give students a particular incentive to write because it establishes contexts for writing.

The conversation model should make the book suitable to a range of writing courses. There is plenty of expository prose here: comparisons of all kinds; a careful analysis of the language of men and women by Deborah Tannen; Tom Regan's analysis of the religious grounds for animal rights; Karen Grigsby Bates's overview of interracial adoption; cool descriptions of schools and school choice, men and women, the internet, campus politics, single parenthood, and a hanging; expositions of the reasons why women are excluded from science and why people commit crimes; etc.—lots of et cetera. The "modes of exposition" are illustrated by numerous selections, as the alternate table of contents makes clear. But *Conversations* will also accommodate courses with an argumentative edge, for this book includes a fair proportion of explicitly or implicitly argumentative writing and tends to encourage a broadly argumentative approach to all discourse. In short, the conversation metaphor implies an inclusive approach to prose, one that subsumes and includes exposition as well as argument, dialogue as well as dialectic. *Conversations* includes not only Jonathan Kozol's prescriptions for the high school classroom, but Theodore Sizer's descriptions as well; not only partisan arguments for and against gun control, but also a careful analysis of the issue by Leonard Kriegel; and not only impassionate pro and con arguments on capital punishment, abortion, animal rights, and the "men's movement," but also dispassionate analyses of language issues, child custody laws, multiculturalism, the internet, and more.

Consequently—and this is another notable feature of *Conversations*—this anthology includes a very broad range of genres and tries to represent as fully as possible the full spectrum of the "universe of discourse." True, essays are prominent in *Conversations*—familiar and formal essays, academic as well as nonacademic ones—because the essay is a common and important genre and because the form has important correspondences with other genres (e.g., the letter, the sermon, the report, the news story). But essays are not so prominent here as to exclude other genres. Students will find other ways of engaging in public discourse as well: through fiction, poetry, drama, letters of various kinds, internet postings, public oratory, posters, congressional hearings and reports, cartoons, advertisements, journals, and more. The occasions for public discourse are many and various. Students and their teachers will find news stories and book reviews, rhetorical analyses and studies of cultural artifacts, parodies and satires, letters to the editor and counter-responses, laws and proposed laws.

And they will hear a range of voices as well. *Conversations* assumes that students are ready, willing, and able to engage in civic, public discourse, but that does not preclude the possibility for personal inventiveness. Indeed, *Conversations* is committed to the proposition that there are many possible rhetorical stances, that there is no one "correct" way to address a reader. This anthology therefore exposes students to as many rhetorical choices as possible—from the studied erudition of John Simon to the semiformal, "objective" voice associated with the academy; from the conversational informality of E. B. White, Garrison Keillor, and Deborah Tannen to satiric invective by Judy Syfers and Lewis Grizzard; from the thrilling oratory of Sojourner Truth to the careful reasoning of Iris Young; from *Rolling Stone, Ms., Mother Jones,* and *The Village Voice* to *Esquire, The New Yorker,* and *The American Scholar;* from Jamaica Kincaid, Stephen Jay Gould, Adrienne Rich, and James Baldwin to George Orwell, bell hooks, Richard Rodriguez, Molefi Asante, and Andrea Dworkin. Students will encounter mainstream texts and dissenting views, conventional rhetorical maneuvers and startlingly inventive ones. They will hear from famous professional writers and anonymous but eloquent fellow citizens; from public figures and fellow students (a dozen or so contributions by students are included); from women and men, gays and heterosexuals; from majority and minority voices. *Conversations* gives students a better chance to find their own voices because they've experienced a full range of possible voices in their reading.

"A rhetorician," says Kenneth Burke in his essay "Rhetoric—Old and New," "is like one voice in a dialogue. Put several such voices together, with each voicing its own special assertion, let them act upon one another in co-operative competition, and you get a dialectic that, properly developed, can lead to views transcending the limitations of each." Fostering that "co-operative competition" is the aim of *Conversations*.

Editorial Apparatus

Substantial editorial assistance has been provided to the users of *Conversations*. The book's Introduction orients students to social motives for writing and domesticates for them the metaphor of conversation. It also introduces students to the notion of critical or rhetorical reading, so that they might have a practical means of approaching every item in *Conversations*—and so that they might better understand how careful reading habits can reinforce effective writing habits. In addition, a headnote is provided for each selection so that students can orient themselves to the rhetoric of each piece. The headnotes provide background on the author (especially when prior knowledge about the author affects one's response to an item), on the topic of the selection (when the matter requires any explanation), and on the specific occasion for the piece (especially on when and where it was originally published). The assumption of most anthologies is that the original context of an essay or story—or whatever—doesn't matter much, or that the anthology itself comprises the context. *Conversations* assumes instead that careful reading must take into account the original circumstances that prompted a given piece of writing. Writing, after all, most often emerges from other writing, so situating each item by means of the headnotes is essential to the concept of *Conversations*. Finally, each of the seven major parts of the book includes an introductory overview of the particular issues under discussion in that part. In sum, the editorial apparatus ensures that the selections in *Conversations* can be used in any order that a teacher or student might wish.

Otherwise, the text of *Conversations* assumes that students are already quite capable readers. On the grounds that students and teachers can handle things on their own and can appropriate readings to their own ends, the book includes no selection questions, no suggestions for writing assignments or class discussions, no exercises, and limited footnotes. Space that might have been devoted to those matters is given instead to additional selections so that teachers might have as many selections as possible from which to choose.

Instructor's Manual

Teachers who do want additional background on unfamiliar readings or specific suggestions for making the most of *Conversations* will find plenty of help in the detailed Instructor's Manual I compiled with Robert S. Davis of Clark University. The manual contains further information on writers, overviews of the parts and discussions of each selection, some suggestions for further reading, and ideas for discussion and writing. It also offers pointers for teaching each "conversation"—for how particular selections can be used with other selections. Together, the editorial apparatus and the Instructor's Manual are designed to help *Conversations* engage the intelligence and passion of students and teachers, without getting in the way of either.

Acknowledgments

There may be only one name cited on the cover of *Conversations,* but this book too is the product of conversation—many conversations, in fact—with a number of people who collaborated in one way or another on its development and production. My greatest debt is to those who assisted me in finding appropriate selections. Anneliese Watt (Penn State), Rosa Eberly (now at the University of Texas), Dawn Keetley (now of the University of Wisconsin), and Jay Shuchter (Penn State) deserve special mention. But

many others affected the outcome: Tom Miller and Tilly
Warnock (University of Arizona); Deborah Kirkman (University
of Kentucky); Paul Klemp (University of Wisconsin—Eau
Claire); David Randall (Bloomsburg University);
Tom Buckley and Linda Ferreira-Buckley (University of
Texas); Tony O'Keeffe (Bellarmine College); Debra Journet
(University of Louisville); Dominic Delli Carpini (St.
Ambrose University); Cynthia Miecznikowski Sheard (University
of Kentucky); and Jim Brasfield, Bob Burkholder,
Deb Clarke, Christopher Clausen, Mel DeYoung, Claudia
Limbert, Steve Mastrofski, Jeff Purvis, Umeeta Sadarangani,
Blake Scott, and Linda Selzer (all of Penn State). Several
reviewers of previous editions of the book made
excellent suggestions: Eugene Antonio, Georgia Institute of
Technology; Philip Auslander, Georgia Institute of Technology;
Margaret T. Banocy-Payne, Tallahassee Community
College; Stephen Behrendt, University of Nebraska; John
Bodnar, Prince George's Community College; Vivian R.
Brown, Laredo Junior College; Wyeth O. Burgess, Georgia
Institute of Technology; Christine Cetrulo, University of
Kentucky; John Cooper, University of Kentucky; Kitty Dean,
Nassau Community College; John Dick, University of Texas
at El Paso; Jack Dodds, Harper College; Lester Faigley, University
of Texas at Austin; Robert Funk, Eastern Illinois University;
Ann George, Penn State University; Paula Gillespie,
Marquette University; JoEllen Hall, California State College,
Chico; Doug Hess, Illinois State University; Dona Hickey,
University of Richmond; Missy James, Tallahassee Community
College; Keith Kroll, Kalamazoo Valley Community College;
Lia Kushnir, University of New Orleans; Robert
Lesman, Northern Virginia Community College; Gerald
Levin, University of Akron; Steve Lynn, University of South
Carolina–Columbia; Margaret Mahoney, Iowa State University;
James May, Penn State University, Dubois Campus;
James C. McDonald, University of Southwestern Louisiana;
Robert Miedel, La Salle University; George Otte, Baruch College,
CUNY; Gordon M. Pradl, New York University; David
Ragsdale, Kingwood College; Gerald Richman, Suffolk University;
Patricia Roberts, University of North Carolina at
Greensboro; Joan Samuelson, Kingwood College; Sheila
Schwartz, Cleveland State University; Carol Senf, Georgia
Institute of Technology; Carolyn H. Smith, University of
Florida; Scott Stoddard, Nova University; Gloria Underwood,
University of South Carolina–Columbia; Richard

Vela, Pembroke State University; and Richard Zbaracki,
Iowa State University. The third edition in particular prof-
ited from advice from Patsy Callaghan of Central Washing-
ton University; Douglas Catron of Iowa State University;
Rosa Eberly of the University of Texas at Austin; Christy
Friend of the University of Texas at Austin; Gregory Glau of
Arizona State University; Ronald L. Pitcock of the University
of Kentucky; Richard Raymond, then of Armstrong State
College and now of the University of Arkansas; and Judith P.
Schiffbauer of the University of Kentucky. Other colleagues
across the country and at Penn State—particularly Don Bia-
lostosky, Davida Charney, Sharon Crowley, Rich Doyle,
Christina Haas, John Harwood, Nancy Lowe, Marie Secor,
and Jeff Walker—stimulated my thinking on a daily basis.
Janet Zepernick, Peggy Keating, and Suzanne Marcum
worked diligently to secure permissions, and Todd Post,
Anneliese Watt, and Keith Waddle did research for some of
the headnotes. And twenty teachers at Penn State tested a
prototype of the first edition in their classes during the 1989
fall semester.

   Thanks too to those on the production end of things. Kim
Witherite Keller, Sam Gunderson, and especially Kathy
Leitzell efficiently and cheerfully produced much of the
manuscript; they helped me out of a thousand small scrapes
to boot. Another thousand that I don't even know about
were taken care of by Liz Egan, Rowena Dores, and Lauren
Shafer. Eben Ludlow has been an ideal editor: full of excellent suggestions, encouraging without ever being overbear-
ing, supportive at every turn. His confidence in this project
brought it into being and has sustained it now for nearly a
decade.

Introduction

Why Write?

Why do people write?

For many reasons, of course. Sometimes the impulse to write derives from a personal need. The motive to write can come from within. Everyone needs to sort out feelings at one time or another or to make some personal sense of the world and its parts, and a good way to do such sorting is by writing. If you keep a diary or journal, or if you've shared your most intimate feelings through correspondence with a trusted friend, or if you've written essays—or notes toward an essay—in order to explore possible explanations for things, then you know what it means to write for personal reasons. (A root meaning of the word *essay* is "to try out, to experiment.") People do need a means of expressing powerful feelings and personal insights, and writing seems to provide just the tranquility required for a gathering of thoughts.

Other times the world itself motivates a writer. We seem to have a need to note our observations about the world, especially if those observations are indeed noteworthy—if they seem special or unique in some way. Sometimes this process of "taking note" is relatively formalized, as when a scientist records observations in a log of some kind or when the president at the end of a day records significant details for future reference or when you keep score at a baseball game or when a reporter transcribes "just the facts" into a news article. But just as often it is something less formal—when you take notes for a course, for instance, or when I write something in my journal about the life and times of my two children. The drive "to hold the mirror up to nature," as Hamlet called it, to record our understanding about the way of the world,

1

accounts for much of the prose we encounter and produce
each day.

The motive to write can also derive from one's vocation. In
other words, some people write because it's their life's work.
They are professional writers—poets, news reporters, novelists, technical writers, screenwriters. And they are semipro-
fessional writers, people who don't think of themselves as
writers but who indeed spend a large amount of their time
writing—police officers, engineers, college professors, lawyers, physicians, corporate managers, teachers, and so forth.
(You'd be surprised at how much time such people spend on
the writing required by their jobs.) Professional writers and
professionals who write sometimes put words onto paper for
the reasons named in the previous paragraphs—to express
personal feelings or ideas, or to record their impressions or
interpretations of their workaday worlds. But they also often
think in terms of a particular kind of writing—a genre—when
they compose: Newspaper employees think of themselves as
writing news stories or editorials; poets set out to write
poems; engineers or police officers think of the reports they
have to turn in; lawyers have to produce those legal briefs
next week. Their sense of completing a particular genre can
sometimes take precedence over other motives.

Of course all these motives to write are legitimate, and seldom do these motives exist in a pure state. It is probably better to think of motives to write, instead of *a* motive, and to
think of primary and secondary motives, instead of a single,
all-consuming aim. When John Milton wrote *Paradise Lost*,
for instance, he was certainly out to record his assessment of
the nature of things and to express his most personal
thoughts—and to write an epic. When Henry David Thoreau
wrote *Walden*, he certainly had personal motives—the book
originated in his daily journals—but he wanted "to hold the
mirror up to nature" as well. (The very title of *Walden* suggests that Thoreau was attempting to record his close observations of nature.)

But *Walden* and *Paradise Lost* are "public" documents,
too—attempts to sway public opinion and public behavior.
Thoreau advertised *Walden*, after all, as his attempt to "brag
as lustily as Chanticleer [the rooster] in the morning, if only
to wake my neighbor up." He wanted to awaken his fellow citizens to nature and to persuade them to renew their own lives
after his own example and experience. Milton's stated purpose—"to justify the ways of God to man"—was just as social.
He wanted to change how people conceive of their relation to

God, and to detail his vision of the heroic life to be lived by every wayfaring Christian. Writing to persuade, to have an effect on the thinking of others, does not preclude writing to discover or writing to record or writing in a particular genre. Indeed, writing to persuade nearly always means writing *about something* in a *particular genre* for reasons that are *intensely personal.* But writing to persuade does mean writing something that has designs on the hearts or minds (or both) of particular readers. It is writing that is calculated to have an effect on a real reader. This goes for John Milton and Anna Quindlen, and it goes for you, too.

For though a writer may work in private, a writer is never really alone. A writer out "to wake people up" or "to justify the ways of God" to men and women is obviously anything but working privately, for the writer out to persuade is inherently social. But every other kind of writing is social as well. The engineer who writes a report on a project is out to influence the project's managers. A physician's report on a patient is used by other caregivers in the short run and long run to direct medical attention in a specific way. The lawyer's brief is meant to sway judges. The movie reviewer's account is designed to direct people to (or away from) the film. Even private writing is often quite public in fact. The letters in which you pour out your feelings get read by sympathetic and responsive friends. The essays you write to discover your version of the truth become written attempts to convert readers to that version. Even journal entries that no one but you will read are shaped to an extent by what society considers to be noteworthy and by what a different "you" will want to read a few years from now; and the very words you choose to use reflect a vocabulary you share with others and learn from others. Writing is a social act. It is a primary means for touching others, and reading what others have written is a primary way of being touched in turn. The words you read and write are surrounded and shaped by the words and attitudes and beliefs of the many people who share your society, your "social context." People may write to express themselves, or to complete a particular kind of writing, or to say something about their world—or some combination of these—but in some sense they do so in order to have an effect on someone else.

In fact, usually writing emerges quite specifically in response to other writing. When you write, your reasons for writing are nearly always related to the people around you and what they have said or written themselves. A friend expects a letter; a supervisor at work has asked for a report; a professor assigns a paper; a job is advertised that requires a written application; a story or an editorial is printed in a local paper or national magazine that arouses your ire; an encouraging teacher or a moving story inspires you to write a journal entry or your own story. That is why this book is titled *Conversations*. It assumes that your writing emerges from other writing or from other speech, and that other writing is likely to follow in response to your own. You want to stay in touch, answer a friend's questions, ask your own questions, and maybe gossip or otherwise entertain along the way, so you return a friend's letter; you expect a response in a week or two. You've listened to a controversy or witnessed some expression of confusion in one of your classes, so you write a paper to straighten things out; you anticipate an argument, a counterresponse (or assent and praise) in turn. You want the person who takes your job to have an easier time than you did, so you rewrite the directions on how to do it; you figure the next person will make further revisions next year. Your cousin asks you how you like your school, so you write to encourage her to join you there next year; you end by asking her to let you know if she needs more information. Writing is engaging in conversation. To get in on it, you have to know what others have said about the matter at hand, and you must be able to anticipate possible responses.

This collection of readings comprises "public conversations"—conversations on public issues that concern American society (in general and within your local community) in the last years of the twentieth century. Not every burning issue is represented here, of course; that would be impossible. But this book does include conversations—give-and-take discussions—on many matters that concern you and your community today. What do you want to get out of your years in college? What kind of experience should your college or university be providing? What changes ought to be made to improve American secondary schools? Should English be our official or semiofficial national language? What does it (or should it) mean to be a woman or a man these days? Is affirmative action legitimate? Should women be treated differently on the job? Should we be doing something to strengthen the American family? Should pornography be banned or regulated? Should certain books be kept out of the curriculum? Should abortion remain legal? Should the ownership of handguns be restricted? What are the causes and cures of crime? Is capital punishment ever justified? Should drugs be legalized? Do animals have rights? Is mercy killing ever legitimate? How should we fight AIDS? And so forth. This book assumes that you'll want to get in on some of those conversations, that you'll want to contribute to resolving some of those questions either nationally or within your own community.

For while there is plenty of discussion of these matters in the national media, there is plenty of local discussion as well. What you read here about the reform of secondary education or the control of the curriculum probably frames in many ways discussions of particular school matters in your local community. What you read here about race or animal rights probably is relevant to what is happening someplace on your own campus. What you read here about gender issues will be relevant to your campus (do many women major in science or engineering at your school?), your community (does your town have adequate child-care facilities?), your job (how are women treated where you work?), even your own family (are family chores apportioned in stereotypical ways?). Sometimes you will want to be involved in a debate over The Larger Issue—for instance, should pornography be banned? Other times you'll want to take up more local concerns or subissues: Should X-rated films be shown on your campus? Does pornography demean women—or men? Is a particular item really pornographic? How might pornography be defined? Democracy can be seen as a sometimes messy but always spirited exchange of ideas on how we should conduct ourselves as a society and as individual communities. The readings here are designed to introduce you to public conversations going on in our democracy, and to encourage you to contribute in some way to those conversations yourself. Even if these particular issues do not always engage you personally, they should provide you with models of how to engage in public discussions when an issue does concern you.

There are plenty of ways to make such contributions. The contents to follow will introduce you to many different genres, many different kinds of writing. Essays are most prominent because the essay is a common genre and because the essay (or article) has important analogs with other forms, like the letter, the sermon, the report, or the editorial. But you will see other ways of engaging in public discourse as well—through fiction, poetry, speeches, plays, interviews, e-mail exchanges, cartoons, and advertisements, for instance. There are news stories and movie reviews, personal letters and letters to the editor and counterresponses, parodies and satires, explanations and analyses and outright arguments. As you think about what to contribute to discussions going on around you, you'll need to think about how to contribute, too—in what form, in what manner.

Indeed, there are as many ways of addressing issues as reasons for doing so. Do you want to be formal, less formal, or downright intimate with your reader? Do you want to present yourself as something of an expert on the matter in question, or as someone on the same level as your readers? Do you want to speak dispassionately, or do you want to let your feelings show? Do you want to be explicit in stating your purpose, or less direct? Do you want to compose sentences that are careful and complex and qualified, or ones that are direct and emphatic? You'll see a broad range of tactics illustrated in the following pages, a broad range that will represent the possible ways of engaging in public discourse. You'll encounter mainstream, classic items—and dissenting views. You'll see conventional presentations and startlingly inventive ones. You'll see how famous professional writers earned their fame, and you'll hear from anonymous but just-as-eloquent fellow citizens and fellow students. You'll hear from women as well as men, from majority as well as minority voices. The idea is to give you a better chance of finding your voice in a given circumstance by exposing you to a full range of possible voices in your reading. The idea is to empower you to engage in civic discourse—now, today—on the issues that concern you and your community.

How to Read This Book—And an Example

As the previous section explains, an answer to the question "Why write?" ultimately depends on several factors: on the writer's personal needs and motives, on the state of the world or issues within our world, on a genre or form of writing that a writer may be drawn or compelled toward, and on a reader or a community of readers that the writer wants to influence. Many times all those factors, in combination, are involved in the decision to write.

All those factors, in combination, are also involved in decisions on *how* to write. Effective writers consider what they want to accomplish (aim), on what subject or issue, in what genre, for which particular readers. A writer's decisions on those matters compose what rhetoricians call a writer's "rhetorical stance"—what *you* decide to say to *someone* on a given *issue* in a particular *genre*. But the matter might be put more simply: Your decisions about how to write at a given time are colored by the *occasion* for that writing and your attitude toward that occasion. A football coach will prepare his team for a game by considering the opponent's strengths and weaknesses (audience), by thinking about his own aims (to win, of course, but also perhaps "to establish our running game" or "to get some experience for our younger players"), by assessing his own team's strengths, and so forth. Writers devise their own game plans as well, based on aim, issue, genre, and audience.

But what does all of that have to do with reading—with reading in general and reading this book in particular? When you read this book, try to distinguish between two kinds of reading that in practice usually go on together whenever you engage yourself with a particular document.

In the first kind of reading, think of yourself as part of each writer's intended audience—as someone who the writer actually hoped would read and respond to his or her message. In other words, in this first kind of reading, read as you normally read the things that are directed to you every day: as you would read a newspaper or an article in your favorite magazine or a personal letter from a friend. Read as if the writer has written just for you, and react accordingly. In most cases this will be quite easy to do, for most of the items in *Conversations* (e.g., the articles on abortion by Sallie Tisdale and Mike Royko, the exchange on pornography between John Irving and Andrea Dworkin) are directed to the American public—people like you—and were written quite recently in magazines and newspapers that you read yourself. In some other cases you will feel more remote from an article because it was written some time ago (e.g., Clarence Darrow's address to the prisoners in Cook County Jail or Martin Luther King Jr.'s "Letter from Birmingham Jail") or because it is not on a topic that has interested you, but even then you can behave as a member of the writer's intended audience and react to the selection as if the piece were written directly to you.

In the second kind of reading—let's call it "critical reading" or "rhetorical reading"—you read a document not as the intended reader but as a student of it, as someone studying it to understand and appreciate its tactics. Since you are probably reading this book as part of a writing course, as a critical reader encountering the selections in *Conversations* you should remember your role as student and try to use the readings to advance your sophistication as a writer and an analyst of writing. Although you normally read as a writer's intended audience, when you read critically you try to get some distance on the experience; it's almost as if you are eavesdropping on what someone is saying to someone else, with the purpose of understanding better how it is said. When you read critically you not only react to the message, but you also appreciate *how* the writer is conveying that message to his or her intended audience, whether that intended audience includes you or not. For example, as a critical reader you try to consider how Sallie Tisdale's content, arrangement, and style advance her aims, or how Martin Luther King Jr. and Clarence Darrow adapted their presentations to the particular situations in which they found themselves. Again, let me emphasize that normally in the act of reading you read critically as well as for content, and the two activities aren't really separable. But for the sake of your progress in writing, here in this introduction to *Conversations* it is important to emphasize critical reading.

Critical readers—readers committed to understanding how prose works—must attend to the same matters that writers attend to: shaping an idea to an audience in a particular form for a specific purpose. When you read each item in this book, therefore, read with those matters in mind. Read the headnotes carefully, for the headnotes are designed to orient you to the original situation in which the writers found themselves: You'll hear about the writer's audience in the headnote, you'll learn more about the writer (especially when the writer is well-known enough that prior reputation affects the reading experience), and you'll learn anything else necessary to orient you to the original occasion of each selection. That way, you'll be in a position to read critically. When you do, consider the issue of course; consider what the writer has to offer on a given subject. But also consider the writer's purpose, the limitations (or opportunities) that a given genre exerts, and the way the item is adapted by the writer to specific readers' knowledge, attitudes, and needs. Consider how those matters affect *what* is said (what rhetoricians call "invention"—the art of discovering what information and arguments will affect readers), in what *order* it is said (or arrangement), and *how* it is said (style and tone). Reading, like writing, is a social and rhetorical activity. It involves not simply passively decoding a message but actively understanding the designs the message has for the reader and how it is calculated to achieve its effects.

Let me offer an extended example of critical reading. The first item in this book is E. B. White's short essay, "Education." What is its purpose? (If you haven't read "Education" yet, take five minutes to do so now; that way, you can more easily follow the rest of this introduction.) White wrote the essay half a century ago, but you probably find it to be interesting still, in part at least because it concerns a perennial American question: What should our schools be like? Is education better carried out in large, fully equipped, but relatively impersonal settings, or in smaller but intensely personal, teacher-dominated schools? Which should count for more: the efficiencies of an educational system that is "progressive" (the word comes from paragraph two), or the personal traits of the individual classroom teacher? The essay is a personal one, in that it is the education of his son that White is "worried about"; yet it is a public matter, too. After all, as the headnote indicates, White published it in *The New Yorker*, a magazine with a readership wide and influential and far more national than its name implies.

What is White's position on the issue? At first it might seem that the author takes no side, that he simply wants to describe objectively the two alternatives and to record his son's experiences in each circumstance. He gives equal time to each school, he spends the same amount of space on concrete details about each, and he seems in firm control of his personal biases ("I have always rather favored public schools"). Through his light and comic tone White implies that all will be well for his son—and our children—in either circumstance, that the two schools each are to be neither favored nor feared by us. "All one can say is that the situation is different" (paragraph four), not better, in the two places.

Or is it? Many readers—myself among them—contend that "Education" is less an objective, neutral appraisal than it is a calculated argument that subtly favors the country school. To such readers, White's objective pose is only that—a created pose, an attempt to create a genial, sympathetic, and trustworthy speaker. By caring so obviously for his son (final paragraph), by confessing his biases, and by treating both schools with distance and detachment and reliable detail, White creates what rhetoricians call "ethos"—that quality of a piece of writing that persuades through the character of the speaker or writer. By poking gentle humor at just about everything—his son "the scholar"; his wife the prim graduate of Miss Winsor's private schools; himself "the victim of a young ceramist"; and, of course, both schools—White makes himself seem enormously sympathetic and trustworthy: fair-minded and unflappable, balanced and detached.

But is this reliable speaker arguing or describing? Those who see the essay as an argument for the ways of the country

school can point to the emotional aspects of the essay—to its
pathos, in other words. The image of the one-room schoolhouse, for instance, is imprinted in positive terms on the
American psyche, and White exploits that image for his argumentative purposes. The "scholar" walks miles through the
snow to get his education; like the schoolhouse itself, he has
the self-reliance and weather-resistance to care for himself
and to fit into a class with children both younger and older;
and he learns a practical curriculum—there is "no time at all
for the esoteric"—"just as fast and as hard as he can." It is all
Abraham Lincoln and "The Waltons," isn't it? And the teacher
who presides over the country school appeals to the reader's
emotions as only The Fairy Tale Mother can. This teacher-
mother is not only "a guardian of their health, their clothes,
their habits . . . and their snowball engagements," but "she has
been doing this sort of Augean task for twenty years, and is
both kind and wise. She cooks for the children on the stove
that heats the room, and she can cool their passions or warm
their soup with equal competence."

No such individual Fairy Tale Mother presides over the city
school. Instead, that school is presided over by a staff of Educational Professionals—a bus driver, half a dozen anonymous
teachers, a nurse, an athletic instructor, dietitians. The school
itself is institutional, regimented, professionalized. There the
scholar is "worked on," "supervised," "pulled." Like the one-
room schoolhouse, the regimented institution is ingrained in
the American psyche. But in this case the emotional appeal is
negative, for "The System" is something that Americans
instinctively resist. True, the city school is no prison, and
true, the scholar in this school learns "to read with a gratifying discernment." But the accomplishments remain rather
abstract. Faced with such an education, such a school, no
wonder the students literally become ill. At least that is the
implication of the end of paragraph three, where the account
of the city school is concluded with an account of the networks of professional physicians that discuss diseases that
never seem to appear in the country schools.

For these reasons many readers see "Education" as an
argument against the city school and an endorsement of the
country one. They see the essay as a comparison with an aim
like most comparison essays: to show a preference. The evaluative aim is carried out by reference to specific criteria,
namely that schools are better if they are less structured and
if they make students want to attend (because motivated students learn better); a structured, supervised curriculum and

facilities are inferior to a personalized, unstructured environment that makes students love school. Days at the country school pass "just like lightning"; to attend the country school the boy is willing literally to walk through snowdrifts, while to get to the city school he must be escorted to the bus stop— or be "pulled" there. The country school is full of "surprises" and "individual instruction," while the city school is full of supervision; there are no surprises in the "progressive" school. In a real sense, therefore, White persuades not only by the force of his personality or through emotional appeals but also through hard evidence, what rhetoricians call "logos." "Education" amounts to an argument by example wherein the single case—the boy scholar—stands for many such cases. This case study persuades like other case studies: by being presented as representative. White creates through his unnamed son, who is described as typical in every way, a representative example that stands for the education of Everychild. The particular details provided in the essay become not mere "concrete description" but hard evidence, good reasons, summoned to support White's implicit thesis. The logic of the piece seems to go something like this: "Country schools are a bit superior to city ones. They make up for what they lack in facilities with a more personal, less authoritarian atmosphere that children respond to."

E. B. White, then, wins his reader's assent by means of ethos, pathos, and logos. But the country-school approach is also reinforced by the essay's arrangement. Notice, for example, that the essay begins and ends with favorable accounts of the country school. In other words, the emphatic first and final positions of the essay are reserved for the virtues of country schools, while the account of the city school is buried in the unemphatic middle of the essay. The article could easily have begun with the second paragraph (wouldn't sentence two of paragraph two have made a successful opener?), but such a strategy would have promoted the value of the city school. By choosing to add the loving vignette of the Fairy Tale Teacher in his opening paragraph, White disposes his readers to favor country schools from the very start. Notice too that the comparison of the two schools in the body of "Education" proceeds from city to country. Again, it didn't have to be so; White could have discussed the country school first, or he could have gone back and forth from city to country more often (adopting what some handbooks call an "alternating" method of comparison as opposed to the "divided" pattern that White actually did use). By choosing to deal first with the city school, all in one lump, and then to present the country school in another lump, White furthered his persuasive aim. After all, most "preference comparisons" move from the inferior item to the superior one. In other words, writers of comparisons usually move from "this one is good" to "but this other one is even better," rather than vice versa. So when White opts to deal first with the city schools, he subtly reinforces his persuasive end through very indirect means. White's arrangement serves his purpose in two ways, then: it permits him to end with the item he wishes to prefer; and it permits him to add an introductory paragraph that places his country school in that favorable spot as well.

Even the arrangement of details within White's individual paragraphs serves his goals. It appears that the central paragraphs (three, four, and five) are arranged chronologically, that details in those paragraphs are arranged according to the rhythm of the school day. But a closer examination shows that paragraph three closes on a note of sickness. That detail could have come earlier in the paragraph, but White places the negative detail in the emphatic final position. Similarly, the two paragraphs on the country school are manipulated for rhetorical ends. Why does White divide the account of the country school into two paragraphs? (After all, he dealt with the city school in one paragraph.) By doing so he is able to give special emphasis to the first sentence of one of his paragraphs, "There is no supervised play," highlighting thereby a key difference between the two schools.

A critical reading of "Education" must also consider expression, those sentence and word choices that are sometimes equated with the style of a particular essay or author. Like most rhetoricians, I personally resist the idea that "style is the person"—that style is something inherent in a writer, that it amounts to a sort of genetic code or set of fingerprints that are idiosyncratic to each person, that it is possible to speak generically of Anna Quindlen's style or Martin Luther King's style or E. B. White's style. It has always seemed to me more appropriate to think of style as characteristic of a particular *occasion* for writing, as something that is as appropriate to reader and subject and genre as it is to a particular author. Words and sentences are chosen in response to rhetorical and social circumstances, and those words and sentences change as the occasion changes. If it is possible to characterize E. B. White's style or Hemingway's style in general (and I'm not sure even of that), then it is so only with respect to certain kinds of writing that they did again and again and again. For when those writers found themselves writing outside *The New Yorker* (in White's case) or outside fiction (in Hemingway's), they did indeed adopt different stylistic choices. It is probably wiser to focus not on the apparent idiosyncrasies associated with a Quindlen or a King or a Hemingway or an E. B. White, but on the particular word and sentence choices at work in a particular rhetorical situation.

Take the case at hand. What stylistic choices are worthy of note in "Education"? How has White chosen particular sentence patterns and words in order to further the aims of his essay?

The sentences of White's essay are certainly appropriate for public discourse. There are roughly a thousand words and fifty sentences in "Education," so average sentence length comes to about twenty words. Many are shorter than twenty words, though (the shortest is five words), and only one forty-three-word sentence seems particularly long. The result is that this essay can probably be readily comprehended by most adults, without its sentences creating the impression of superficiality or childishness. (The sentences in White's book for children *Charlotte's Web*, by contrast, have an average length of about twelve words.)

Moreover, White's sentences are unpretentious. They move in conventional ways—from subjects and verbs to objects and modifiers. There are no sentence inversions (violations of the normal subject/verb/object order), few distracting interrupters (the parentheses and the "I suspect" in that one long sentence in paragraph two are exceptions), and few lengthy opening sentence modifiers that keep us too long from subjects and verbs. Not only that, the sentences are simple and unpretentious in another sense: White comparatively rarely uses subordinate (or modifying) clauses—clauses containing a subject and verb and beginning with "who" or "although" or "that" or "because" or the like. I count only two such modifying (or dependent) clauses in the first and third paragraphs, for instance, and just five in the second; if you don't think that is a low number, compare it to a six-hundred-word sample of your own prose. When White does add length to a sentence, he does it not by adding complex clauses that modify other clauses, but by adding independent clauses (ones that begin with "and" or "but") and by adding phrases and modifiers in parallel series. Some examples? The children's teacher is a guardian "of their health, their clothes, their habits, their mothers, and their snowball engagements"; the boy "learned fast, kept well, and we were satisfied"; the bus "would sweep to a halt, open its mouth, suck the boy in, and spring away." And so forth. The "ands" make White's essay informal and conversational, never remote or scholarly or full of disclaimers and qualifiers.

White uses relatively simple sentence patterns in "Education," then, but his prose is still anything but simple. Some of his sentences are beautifully parallel: "she can cool their passions or warm their soup"; "she conceives their costumes, cleans up their noses, and shares their confidences"; "in a cinder court he played games supervised by an athletic instructor, and in a cafeteria he ate lunch worked out by a dietitian"; "when the snow is deep or the motor is dead"; "rose hips in fall, snowballs in winter." These precise, mirror-image parallel structures are known as isocolons to rhetoricians. White delights in them and in the artful informality they create. He uses parallel structures and relentless coordination—"and" after "and" after "and"—to make his prose accessible to a large audience of appreciative readers. And he uses those lists of specific items in parallel series to give his writing its remarkably concrete, remarkably vivid quality.

That brings us to White's word choices. They too contributed to White's purposes. Remember the sense of detachment and generosity in White's narrative voice, the ethos of involvement and detachment apparent in the speaker? In large measure that is the result of White's word choices. For instance, White has the ability to attach mock-heroic terminology to his descriptions so that he comes across as balanced and wise, as someone who doesn't take himself or his world too seriously. The boy is a "scholar" who "sallied forth" on a "journey" to school or to "make Indian weapons of a semi-deadly nature." The gentle hyperbole fits in well with the classical allusion inherent in the word "Augean" (one of Hercules' labors was to clean the Augean stables): there is a sophistication and worldly wisdom in the speaker's voice that qualifies him to speak on this subject. And remember the discussion of whether White's aim was purely descriptive or more argumentative in character? White's metaphors underscore his argumentative aim: the city school bus "was as punctual as death," a sort of macabre monster that "would sweep to a halt, open its mouth, suck the boy in, and spring away with an angry growl"; or it is "like a train picking up a bag of mail." At the country school, by contrast, the day passes "just like lightning." If the metaphors do not provide enough evidence of White's persuasive aim, consider the connotations of words—their emotional charges, that is—that are associated with the city school: "regimented," "supervised," "worked on," "uniforms," "fevers." And then compare these with the connotation of some words White associates with the country school: "surprises," a "bungalow," "weather-resistant," "individual instruction," "guardian," and so forth. The diction and sentence choices made by White indeed do reinforce his argumentative purpose.

This analysis by no means exhausts the full measure of rhetorical sophistication that E. B. White brings to the composition of "Education." You may have noticed other tactics at work, or you may disagree with some of the generalizations presented here. But the purpose of this discussion is not to detail the rhetoric of White's "Education." It is merely to illustrate a method of critical reading that you might employ as you read the selections in this book and the public rhetoric that you encounter in your life each day. The point has been to encourage you to read not just for *what* is said—though this is crucial—but for *how* it is said as well. For reading is as "rhetorical" an activity as is writing. It depends on an appreciation of how writer, subject, and reader are all "negotiated" through a particular document.

If you read for "how" as well as "what," the distinction between the two may begin to shorten for you. Appreciation of the rhetoric of public discourse can make you more skeptical of the arguments presented to you and to other citizens. It can make you a reader less likely to be won over on slender grounds, more likely to remain the doubter than the easy victim or trusting soul who accepts all arguments at face value. Therefore, whether or not you decide to take part in any of the particular "conversations" captured in this book, your thinking can be stimulated by critical reading.

Not only that, you'll find yourself growing as a writer; if you read critically, you'll begin to adopt and adapt for your own purposes the best rhetorical maneuvers on display in this book and elsewhere. What is a particular writer's real aim? What evidence is used to win the assent of readers? How does a particular writer establish credibility? What kind of emotional and logical appeals are at work in a given circumstance? How does the arrangement of a presentation influence its reception? How can sentence style and word choices sustain a writer's aim? By asking and answering questions like these, you can gain confidence as reader and writer. By becoming better able to understand and appreciate the conversations going on around you, you'll learn to make more powerful and sophisticated contributions to the discussions that most engage you personally. Critical reading of the selections in this book can make you a better writer, a better citizen.

I.

EDUCATION

Introduction

Americans have always been passionate about issues
related to education. Why? For one thing, education issues
affect every American in a personal way. True, there is a
strong anti-intellectual strain in American life; but it is also
true that Americans pursue with a passion the ideal of "education for all" both as a means of self-improvement and as the
source of the enlightened citizenry required by democratic
institutions. For another thing, education issues are decided
locally and immediately. The relatively decentralized nature
of our educational "system" (American education is hardly as
monolithic as the term "system" implies) encourages continuing and passionate public discussion among citizens interested in shaping the policies and practices of local schools.
(About 93 percent of the money spent on primary and secondary education in the United States in 1995 came from
state and local governments. Incidentally, Americans spend
more per capita on education than all but three other Western
nations.)

Portions of three current discussions related to education
are included in this part of *Conversations*. (In addition, education issues are taken up more tangentially elsewhere in the
book, in the parts on Language, Race and Gender, Family Matters, and Civil Liberties.) The first—"What to Do about the
Schools"—concerns proposals for improving public education, particularly secondary education. In the past decade,
particularly in response to the economic crises of the early
1980s and early 1990s, a number of committees and commis-
sions launched well-publicized reform efforts aimed at everything from teacher education and school governance to
classroom climate and the curriculum—at everything from
competency testing and conduct codes to the size of schools
and the wisdom of "tracking." Presidents Bush and Clinton
also promoted reform efforts that they believed would invigo-
rate U.S. education. Those calls for reform can be seen in the
selections included here. Should schools be large, central-
ized, efficient, and comprehensive? Or should they be smaller
and more personal—have all the advantages of small size? Is
discipline a major problem in the schools, and (if so) how can
it be improved? Or does an overemphasis on discipline make
schools confining and constricting—places that value order
and conformity over independence and freedom of inquiry?
What about the curriculum—should it emphasize mastery of
bodies of knowledge, "what every educated person needs to

know"? Or instead should it emphasize learning skills—problem-solving ability, flexibility, independent thinking, and resourcefulness? Should the way schools are funded be reconsidered, to even out differences between the "haves" and the "have nots"? Or would that undermine a cornerstone of our educational tradition, local control? Should schools be "privatized"? Should citizens have more choice over which schools to attend? Could citizens through some sort of voucher system be given more choices over which school to attend? Or would that tend to widen the gap in educational opportunities now available to rich and poor? Does the concept of "charter schools," one that in a handful of states permits private companies or groups of teachers and parents, or nonprofit organizations to operate schools—hold promise? And finally, what about the teachers? Should they be given better pay and more responsibility for what goes on in the classroom? Or should we continue to honor top-down administrative mechanisms for ensuring competency and consistency and currency?

The second set of readings addresses the question, "What Is College For?" No doubt on your own campus you have listened in on discussions of this topic in one form or another, and no doubt you have given your own educational goals considerable thought. In broad terms, the question can be posed this way: Is college an opportunity for personal growth and general intellectual development? Or is it a means to economic advancement? If college should foster both general education and professional specialization, then in what proportions should it do so? And through what means? Is college designed for the intellectual elite who are sophisticated enough to pursue truly advanced learning, or is it something that ought to be within the reach of most high school graduates? Does college offer a critical perspective on our institutions and habits? Or is it merely a way of socializing students into willing servants of the status quo?

That last question introduces the final group of readings, on the question of so-called "political correctness." Political correctness is usually used to denote efforts of various kinds to create a more hospitable atmosphere on campus for women and minorities—people whose presence on campus has been increasingly visible in the past few decades. Such efforts may take the form of conduct codes, curricular reforms (for example, insistence that course syllabi reflect the experiences of women and minorities, or perhaps a requirement that students take some kind of course that investigates

issues related to ethnic diversity or gender or multiculturalism), or other efforts to encourage toleration and awareness
on campus. But in its effort to encourage "doing the right
thing" on campus and in society, especially on issues of race
and gender, are universities going too far? Are the first-
amendment right to free speech and the university's avowed
openness to diverse opinions and free exchange being dampened by political proselytizing on behalf of women and
minorities? Is that what is going on—political proselytizing,
rather than teaching? Are curricular changes long overdue, or
are they politically motivated assaults on mainstream culture? Is "political correctness" a bad thing, merely a liberal
fashion, or is it a code word used by conservatives to undermine the efforts of those who simply wish to mitigate the
oppression and repression experienced by racial minorities,
women, and homosexuals?

Some of these ideas are developed further in Part III of
Conversations, which considers issues of race and gender, and
in Part V, which takes up issues of civil liberties and civil
rights. But in this part, the emphasis is on education in general and college education in particular. The readings you
encounter should give you a better understanding of the
issues that you and your classmates are grappling with right
now. As you read, remember that the perennial nature of
debates about education can be frustrating, especially to educational leaders. But the very relentlessness of the debates
probably brings out the best feature of a democratic society:
the freedom of citizens to shape policy through open and
public exchange.

WHAT TO DO ABOUT THE SCHOOLS?

E. B. White
Education

E. B. White (1899–1985), who contributed regularly to The New Yorker *and whose work has been collected into several books, was perhaps America's most popular essayist. You may also know him as the author of the children's classic* Charlotte's Web *(1952). First published in 1939 in* Harper's *and in White's* One Man's Meat, *the following comparison of two educational philosophies remains relevant half a century later.*

I have an increasing admiration for the teacher in the country school where we have a third-grade scholar in attendance. She not only undertakes to instruct her charges in all the subjects of the first three grades, but she manages to function quietly and effectively as a guardian of their health, their clothes, their habits, their mothers, and their snowball engagements. She has been doing this sort of Augean task for twenty years, and is both kind and wise. She cooks for the children on the stove that heats the room, and she can cool their passions or warm their soup with equal competence. She conceives their costumes, cleans up their messes, and shares their confidences. My boy already regards his teacher as his great friend, and I think tells her a great deal more than he tells us.

The shift from city school to country school was something we worried about quietly all last summer. I have always rather favored public school over private school, if only because in public school you meet a greater variety of children. This bias of mine, I suspect, is partly an attempt to justify my own past (I never knew anything but public schools) and partly an involuntary defense against getting kicked in the shins by a young ceramist on his way to the kiln. My wife was unacquainted with public schools, never having been exposed (in her early life) to anything more public than the washroom of Miss Winsor's. Regardless of our backgrounds, we both knew that the change in schools was something that

21

concerned not us but the scholar himself. We hoped it would work out all right. In New York our son went to a medium-priced private institution with semi-progressive ideas of education, and modern plumbing. He learned fast, kept well, and we were satisfied. It was an electric, colorful, regimented existence with moments of pleasurable pause and giddy incident. The day the Christmas angel fainted and had to be carried out by one of the Wise Men was educational in the highest sense of the term. Our scholar gave imitations of it around the house for weeks afterward, and I doubt if it ever goes completely out of his mind.

3   His days were rich in formal experience. Wearing overalls and an old sweater (the accepted uniform of the private seminary), he sallied forth at morn accompanied by a nurse or a parent and walked (or was pulled) two blocks to a corner where the school bus made a flag stop. This flashy vehicle was as punctual as death: seeing us waiting at the cold curb, it would sweep to a halt, open its mouth, suck the boy in, and spring away with an angry growl. It was a good deal like a train picking up a bag of mail. At school the scholar was worked on for six or seven hours by half a dozen teachers and a nurse, and was revived on orange juice in mid-morning. In a cinder court he played games supervised by an athletic instructor, and in a cafeteria he ate lunch worked out by a dietitian. He soon learned to read with gratifying facility and discernment and to make Indian weapons of a semi-deadly nature. Whenever one of his classmates fell low of a fever the news was put on the wires and there were breathless phone calls to physicians, discussing periods of incubation and allied magic.

4   In the country all one can say is that the situation is different, and somehow more casual. Dressed in corduroys, sweatshirt, and short rubber boots, and carrying a tin dinner pail, our scholar departs at the crack of dawn for the village school, two and a half miles down the road, next to the cemetery. When the road is open and the car will start, he makes the journey by motor, courtesy of his old man. When the snow is deep or the motor is dead or both, he makes it on the hoof. In the afternoons he walks or hitches all or part of the way home in fair weather, gets transported in foul. The schoolhouse is a two-room frame building, bungalow type, shingles stained a burnt brown with weather-resistant stain. It has a chemical toilet in the basement and two teachers above the stairs. One takes the first three grades, the other the fourth, fifth, and sixth. They have little or no time for individ-

ual instruction, and no time at all for the esoteric. They teach what they know themselves, just as fast and as hard as they can manage. The pupils sit still at their desks in class, and do their milling around outdoors during recess.

There is no supervised play. They play cops and robbers   5
(only they call it "Jail") and throw things at one another—snowballs in winter, rose hips in fall. It seems to satisfy them. They also construct darts, pinwheels, and "pick-up-sticks" (jackstraws), and the school itself does a brisk trade in penny candy, which is for sale right in the classroom and which contains "surprises." The most highly prized surprise is a fake cigarette, made of cardboard, fiendishly lifelike.

The memory of how apprehensive we were at the beginning   6
is still strong. The boy was nervous about the change too. The tension, on that first fair morning in September when we drove him to school, almost blew the windows out of the sedan. And when later we picked him up on the road, wandering along with his little blue lunch-pail, and got his laconic report "All right" in answer to our inquiry about how the day had gone, our relief was vast. Now, after almost a year of it, the only difference we can discover in the two school experiences is that in the country he sleeps better at night—and *that* probably is more the air than the education. When grilled on the subject of school-in-country vs. school-in-city, he replied that the chief difference is that the day seems to go so much quicker in the country. "Just like lightning," he reported.

John Chubb and Terry Moe
The Private vs. Public Debate

Chubb, a fellow at the Brookings Institute (an officially neutral but politically liberal Washington, DC, research institute devoted to the study of public-policy issues), and Moe, a professor at Stanford University with a special interest in education, contributed this essay to The Wall Street Journal *in July 1991. They are the authors of several books, including* Politics, Markets, and America's Schools, *published by the Brookings Institute in 1990. That book recommends fundamental institutional changes in America's schools—in particular, a greater reliance on choice and free-market mechanisms for the schools.*

1   The Bush administration wants Congress to enact legislation to encourage state and local authorities to provide parents with choice among and between public and private
schools. Opponents of the administration's proposal generally
accept the expansion of public school choice but vehemently
oppose public support for private school options. Most of the
reasons for this opposition are familiar—private schools are
said to succeed, for example, through selective admissions
and expulsions. But in recent days, opponents have come up
with a fresh justification: Private schools are no better than
public schools—so why add private schools to the public educational menu?

2   This is an important argument—indeed, far more important than its proponents seem to realize—for if there are no
differences between public and private schools, there is little
reason to support educational choice of any kind, private or
public. Private schools, subject to the daily discipline of
parental choice, are the best test of the argument that choice
enhances school performance. If private schools fail this test,
why subject public schools to the same ineffective discipline?

3   The test that private schools (religious and nonreligious)
are now said to have failed is the mathematics exam of the
recent National Assessment of Educational Progress. Testifying before the House Education and Labor Committee, Al
Shanker, president of the American Federation of Teachers,
charged that students in private schools performed scarcely
better than students in public schools: both need great
improvement. Mr. Shanker is right about the widespread
need for improvement but wrong about the differences
between public and private performance—on the NAEP and
in general.

Dropout Rates

4   Public and private math scores on the NAEP are close only
in the 12th grade, after public schools have lost a large portion of their least successful students as dropouts and gained
a large number of students from private elementary and middle schools (one-third of whose students go to public high
schools). Among fourth- and eighth-graders, scores are not
close. Private schools place 10 to 15 percentage points more
students at grade-appropriate levels than public schools do.

5   Some may say that these differences are not large, but the
NAEP is but one measure of how schools perform. Consider

dropout rates. According to a recent national survey, the sophomore-to-senior-year dropout rate is 24% in public schools vs. 12% in private schools. Or take the results of college admissions testing. A little over a third of all public school seniors take the SAT: In 1990 they had an average score of 896. About two-thirds of all private school seniors take the SAT; yet this more inclusive group scored an average 932—12 percentiles higher than the score for public school students.

Experiences after high school are also revealing. Public   6
high schools send fewer than 30% of their graduates directly on to four-year colleges. Six years later, only about 13% of public school graduates have earned bachelor's degrees; among black and Hispanic graduates, only about 9%. Private schools send roughly half of their graduates directly to four-year colleges; 31% of all of their graduates and more than a quarter of their black and Hispanic graduates hold bachelor's degrees six years later.

To be sure, private schools have certain advantages over   7
public schools. Nearly twice as many private school students as public school students come from families that are college educated, and less than half as many private school students come from families that are financially poor. Private schools also get to select their students (though most are not very selective) and can expel students more easily than public schools can (though public schools actually lose or get rid of more problem students). In light of all this, it is somewhat surprising to note that private schools are more likely than public schools to be racially mixed.

Some will argue that school composition—students and   8
parents—rather than school quality can account for any and all differences between the outcomes of public and private schooling. However, there are lots of differences between public and private schools not easily explained by differences between students. For example, teachers in private schools seem to work with more dedication: A recent survey found that 40% of private school teachers go a whole semester without missing a day of school; only 20% of the teachers in public schools have the same exemplary record. Teachers in private schools also report spending about 15% more time outside of school preparing lessons, helping students, meeting with parents, and otherwise trying to do a good job.

Private schools, which generally have smaller budgets   9
than public schools, spend relatively more of their financial resources directly on instruction. Public schools spend

relatively more of theirs on administration. Private schools are far more successful at encouraging students to take academic track coursework: An average student is twice as likely to be placed in a "college prep" program in a private school as in a public school. Private schools also do a much better job of promoting parent involvement. Indeed, private schools get more participation out of parents of lower socioeconomic status than public schools get out of parents of higher socioeconomic status—even though participation rapidly increases with socioeconomic status.

10   Private schools, in short, do many of the things that school reformers believe are important for school success: They emphasize academic instruction and achievement, get teachers and students to work hard, and get parents involved. The question that should be on the minds of policy makers is not *whether* private schools do these things but *why* they do them—or, more precisely, why they are more likely than public schools to do them.

11   In a recent study of 500 high schools, we concluded that the differences between public and private schools have a lot to do with the differences between politics and markets—especially with the absence or presence of choice. Private educators, trying to succeed in a market where parents can take or leave their schools, are compelled to organize their schools in ways that are most sensitive to and most effective in meeting parent and student demands.

12   Generally, this means concentrating resources at the school level, where they can make the most difference. It means vesting greater authority in teachers, who are in the best position to understand the diverse needs of families and students, and who can be expected to work with greater dedication if trusted to do so. It also means focusing sharply on the tangible results, like academic achievement, and involving parents—who, after all, are doing the choosing—deeply in the school.

Market Pressures

13   Public educators have their schools organized for them by federal, state, and local authorities pressured by countless groups with legitimate but conflicting interest in school policy. Generally, these conflicts are resolved through bureaucratic solutions that, despite the best intentions of everyone concerned, tend to rob schools of critical authority, divert schools from their core academic mission, discourage bold

leadership from principals, make a mockery of teacher professionalism, drive a wedge between schools and parents (who become just another political interest), and provide accountability for following rules—not for producing results.

Public schools could—and would—do things differently if they were subject to different pressures. The lesson of public-private comparisons is not that private schools are better than public schools. It is that market pressures encourage the development of better schools than political pressures do.   14

Choice, then, is essential. However, the issue that Congress and the administration should be worrying about is not whether choice should include private schools (though with appropriate ground rules, private school participation would enhance market pressures). The key issue is whether choice plans provide all schools—be they public or private—the political autonomy and economic interest to focus, reorganize, compete and improve.   15

David L. Kirp

What School Choice Really Means

David L. Kirp, a professor of public policy at the University of California–Berkeley, has published over two dozen books on a range of social issues, most of them related in one way or another to education. He also writes regularly for a number of magazines, including The Atlantic Monthly, *where the following essay appeared in November 1992. The Atlantic is a respected forum, mildly liberal in its outlook, that carries book and movie reviews, original poetry and fiction, and commentary on current events and issues.*

On standard-issue maps of Manhattan, Ninety-sixth Street on the Upper East Side is shown slightly thicker than the lines representing neighboring streets, to signify that traffic on it runs both east and west. There is no hint of a border on these maps, no intimation that Ninety-sixth Street marks a division between two dramatically different worlds.   1

2   South of Ninety-sixth Street lie some of New York City's most fashionable addresses. The continuing collapse of the city's economy has touched even these streets, of course, and now there are empty stores, unsellable condominiums. But nannies still push strollers along Fifth Avenue and in Central Park, and adolescents still stream forth from private schools. Lawyers and investment bankers still look as if they had stepped straight out of the display windows at Talbot's or Brooks Brothers. Almost the only nonwhite faces to be seen belong to the help.

3   To the north of Ninety-sixth Street lies East Harlem. On its two hundred square blocks many of the brownstones are empty, boarded up, covered with barbed wire and jagged bits of glass to keep out the vagrants and drug addicts. Half of East Harlem's population of 120,000 is Hispanic, and almost all the rest is African-American. New arrivals come mostly from dirt-poor Caribbean and Central American countries. By all the standard social measures, East Harlem is among the worst-off neighborhoods in the city.

4   Yet every school-day morning brings a remarkable sight, as a thousand or so children from elsewhere in the city, many of them from families that could easily afford private academies, negotiate the buses and subways with practiced cool to join the 14,000 Hispanic and black children who attend East Harlem's elementary and junior high schools. These students come to East Harlem not because some official issued an integration order or redrew a school-district boundary but because their families have chosen to send them here. Remarkably, in some of the battered school buildings of this neighborhood, where these children attend classes with the children of the barrio, an exemplary education can be had. East Harlem's schools have, in fact, become famous, at least among educators, for their quality—relative to that of other inner-city schools, anyway—and the story of the transformation of these schools has by now acquired the status of an oft-told legend.

5   In 1970, when each of New York City's elementary and junior high schools was assigned to one of thirty-two community school districts, with powerful elected school boards that had the right to pick the local superintendent, East Harlem's schools, which make up District Four, were widely regarded as the city's worst. In 1974 the children scored thirty-second—dead last—on standardized reading tests. Absenteeism was chronic among teachers as well as students. Gangs had turned junior high corridors into battlegrounds, school bathrooms into drug bazaars. And yet scarcely a decade later

this prototypical blackboard jungle had come to be hailed as something of a model for urban education. The most widely cited measure of its accomplishment is the reported improvement in reading achievement: by the mid-1980s East Harlem's scores had risen from the very worst citywide to a level approximating the citywide average.

Behind this change, East Harlem's boosters say, lies the   6 simple but revolutionary fact that parents in East Harlem are now allowed to choose their children's schools—thereby introducing the salutary effects of competition into institutions dispirited by inertia, red tape, and the chaos of the surrounding community. These changes are not unique to East Harlem. Across the country, public school choice has been one of the most widely adopted reforms of the past decade, and enthusiasts for one or another version of school choice span the political spectrum. But what does make East Harlem special, and so worth paying attention to, is that it came first—and that New York has just decided to make a school-choice program citywide. In District Four choice has been sustained as a guiding philosophy for nearly two decades—a geological epoch in the faddish world of education policy. Moreover, the system of choice has been implemented in a city where the difficulties of making *anything* happen are well known, and in a neighborhood characterized by deep social pathology. And it is undeniable that much of the education in East Harlem is better than what was available twenty years ago. But did choice make the difference? And how much difference has actually been made?

These are important questions, the answers to which have   7 implications for schools around the country—because even as legions of defenders hold up East Harlem as a national model, critics assail some of what has happened there as a triumph of public relations. Yes, they say, many East Harlem mini-schools may get a silk-stocking trade, and may offer instruction that is as good as in the better private schools, but just a few corridors away are classrooms with no middle-class students and all the familiar woes of inner-city education. And, they say, the way the system labeled "choice" works in practice makes such disparities inevitable.

The Revolution Begins

During the mid-1950s the novelist Dan Wakefield, then a   8 young reporter, lived in Spanish Harlem for six months and delivered a savage indictment of official neglect, especially in the public schools. "[The schools] have been of little help to the children of Spanish Harlem in escaping the realities of its streets, or...changing those realities to something like the promise of the posters that smile from the classrooms," Wakefield wrote in *Island in the City*. "The schools, in fact, have blocked out the possibilities of the world beyond even more profoundly than the tenement buildings around them." The situation only deteriorated in 1968, when black and radical white parents and teachers throughout the city fought the teachers' union and the education bureaucracy for greater local control over schools. They got it in 1970, after several bitter teachers' strikes, but the aftermath brought infighting of every kind among the board members of the thirty-two newly created school districts.

9   Things began to improve in District Four in 1973, when an insurgent slate was elected to the school board. Robert Rodriguez, an East Harlem native who headed the slate and directed the East Harlem Neighborhood Manpower Service Center, was only twenty-one at the time. The new board chairman was committed to running a clean enterprise, in which educational priorities didn't get confused with personal agendas and board members didn't push pet programs or hand out patronage jobs to friends. Keeping fellow board members and local leaders from meddling in the details of personnel and programs didn't prove easy, however, and tensions ran so high that police officers were sometimes present at board meetings to assure order.

10   When Rodriguez came to power, the district superintendent was seen by many in the community as symbolizing the old, unresponsive regime. The superintendent was quickly forced out, and the board chose as his successor Anthony Alvarado, a charismatic thirty-year-old Puerto Rican from East Harlem. His fast-track career had taken him from Fordham University to half a dozen jobs in education, including running an experimental preschool and heading up a bilingual elementary school.

11   As the District Four superintendent, Alvarado brought in new black and Hispanic principals—a good idea in itself, and certainly also a way of fending off potential local critics. He also pushed an agenda that included alternative schools, bilingual schools (which now enroll 2,000 of the district's students), a district-wide reading program, and major infusions of federal and state dollars.

12   The alternative schools have gotten the most attention, yet they began almost accidentally. In 1974 Alvarado approached

Deborah Meier, a longtime teacher on Manhattan's Upper West Side and a pedagogical reformer committed to bringing open classrooms to city schools, and asked if she would be interested in running her own elementary school. Meier jumped at the chance. In the school she had in mind, classrooms would have places to build things, quiet spaces for reading, and corners for painting. Teachers would move around, offering individual help. Classes would be small by city standards, and teachers would come to know their students well, because they would spend two years with the same children. The new school would depend for its survival on parents' willingness to accept the risks of an unfamiliar kind of education for their children, and also on teachers' willingness to surrender their lunch hours to students and their after-school hours to meetings that ran as long as in socialist heaven. The school had to start small, Meier argued, one grade at a time, with no set curriculum—"If the teacher cared a lot [about a topic] and the kids cared a lot, that was a good topic"—and no guaranteed results.

Although classes like this have been routine for half a century in the best progressive private academies, the school Meier and Alvarado proposed to create was a deviant institution in New York City public schools, where teachers typically stood at the front of the classroom talking at rows of nodding heads and covering a prescribed curriculum. Central Park East, as Meier's elementary school was called, started out in the fall of 1974 on two floors of P.S. 171, a run-down elementary school with which it would be competing for students and resources. Many of the Puerto Rican parents living in the neighborhood, whose memories of their own education led them to equate quality with order, were suspicious of a white Jewish woman and her permissive ideas. Some community activists wanted a school rooted more in the language and struggles of the barrio than in the theories of John Dewey and Jean Piaget. But the school attracted students, and after a troubled first few years its reputation as a good place to learn began to spread. Soon there were more applicants than spaces, with many of the applications coming from outside East Harlem.

The same year that Central Park East opened its doors, two other alternative schools opened, to serve grades five through nine: the East Harlem Performing Arts School and the BETA ("better education through alternatives") School, which took rejects from other schools, where they had made teachers' lives hell (the BETA School would close in 1990).

15   In 1976 Alvarado hired Seymour Fliegel, who had been a
teacher and administrator in Harlem for two decades, to
oversee the existing alternative schools and help create many
new ones. By 1982 two new primary schools, Central Park
East II and River East, were launched to meet a rising
demand for open classrooms. Though they began as spinoffs
of Central Park East, and took students from a common pool
of applicants, the new academies gradually developed their
own identities. From the outset, places in these schools were
much sought-after, and soon educators with other dreams
appeared at Fliegel's doorstep. Alan Sofferman, who had
taught fifth and sixth grades at P.S. 96, and who eventually
became its assistant principal, imagined a School of Science
and Humanities, as tradition-oriented as any parochial
school. Students would wear uniforms, and silence would be
observed as orderly ranks of pupils passed by one another in
the corridors. Leonard Bernstein, a science teacher, designed
the Isaac Newton School with the intention of exposing the
brightest youngsters from the ghetto to state-of-the-art
instruction in science and math. Beryl Epton, who had taught
at the BETA School, wanted a chance to work with younger
children who had troubled histories. She started the Children's Workshop, the smallest of East Harlem's alternative
schools, a one-room second-through-fourth-grade class for
children who had been or were likely to be held back because
of behavioral problems. New schools opened almost every
year, each one trying to find its special niche. Their names
reveal the range of aspirations: the Academy of Environmental Science, the Maritime School, the East Harlem Career
Academy, the Talented and Gifted School.

16   While every other district in the city was pleading poverty,
East Harlem usually found the money to do what it wanted.
For one thing, its administrators came to realize that because
the notion of choice pushed the right buttons at Ronald
Reagan's Department of Education, Washington after 1980
would be forthcoming with cash. At one point during the
1980s District Four received more federal money per student
than any other school district in the country. The Republicans
from Washington and the liberal Democrats from Spanish
Harlem have made strange bedfellows, and there are those
who say that the district was manipulated. Yet in the cutthroat world of New York City school politics, Washington's
support bought East Harlem a measure of protection.

17   District Four was also prepared to fend for itself. For years
it engaged heavily in the risky business of deficit financing,

and it outmaneuvered the dozing downtown bureaucrats. The alternative schools, with their tiny staffs, could not live with the seniority system that reigned in every other city district. So the principals (called directors) of the alternative schools recruited teachers mainly by word of mouth, and turned to Fliegel to slip the new teachers onto the payroll regardless of seniority.

The teachers' unions initially protested about all the rules   18
East Harlem was breaking. But they backed off when they saw members volunteering to swap protections won through collective bargaining for the rewards of professionalism. (Today the New York City teachers' contract specifies that with a three-quarters-majority vote the teachers at any school can waive rules about class size and teachers' schedules.)

"I could say, 'We had a long-range plan: we envisioned a   19
choice program ten years down the line,'" Fliegel says. "But things don't work that way. It developed organically." Slowly, if haphazardly, with a sizable dose of what Fliegel calls "creative noncompliance" with the rules, an alternative system parallel to the regular schools emerged, with a handful of alternative elementary schools and a somewhat larger number of junior highs—twenty-two alternative schools in all by 1982, offering a wide range of options. By then there were enough options to enable every sixth-grade student in East Harlem to have at least *some* choice, although competition for places at the most popular schools was sufficiently intense that the schools, not the parents and students, ended up doing most of the picking. Still, by 1982 half of East Harlem's junior high students were attending one of the alternative schools, and by that year East Harlem had moved from thirty-second to fifteenth in the city in reading scores. District Four began getting national attention.

The Numbers Game

East Harlem officials focus on District Four's dramatically   20
improved test scores when trumpeting their success. In 1974, they note only 15.3 percent of the district's students could read at or above grade level; by 1988 the proportion had quadrupled, to 62.5 percent.

This fact is always seized on by those who would com-   21
mend the East Harlem experience to other school systems. Yet those statistics, while technically correct, are somewhat misleading, and a close look at them begins to reveal some

other realities of the East Harlem experience. The biggest improvements in reading scores occurred in 1975 (13 percentage points), when the choice program was just getting started, and in 1986 (9.5 percentage points), when New York City switched to a different test. In those two years reading levels improved substantially all across the city.

22   Moreover, in 1988 the city was using a test whose norms—the criteria for what should be expected by way of performance—had been set a decade earlier. But in the interim there had been a marked increase in basic-skills levels, and so the norms were out-of-date. It's as if a high-jump bar had remained at a certain height even as the jumpers had grown taller. After new national norms were established, in 1989, the proportion of youngsters performing at grade level dropped to 42 percent in East Harlem (as against 48 percent citywide). This doesn't mean that things weren't getting better in East Harlem, but it does mean that the statistical gain is not as fantastically large as is commonly claimed. Nor have matters changed much since then. Last year 43 percent of students in East Harlem (as compared with 49 percent of students citywide) were doing grade-level work.

23   Comparisons with other districts do show that from 1978, when norms were previously established, to 1989 District Four's reading scores rose by 14.2 percent, as compared with 2.3 percent for the city as a whole. That was the second-biggest improvement recorded in all of the city's districts. (The biggest improvement, 14.5 percent, occurred in Bedford-Stuyvesant, a Brooklyn district that is 98 percent black and Hispanic, whose school system combines choice at the junior high level with a strong emphasis on scholastic drills and testing.) Performance on the mathematics test has been far weaker. Since 1986, when the current citywide test for mathematics was adopted, District Four has fallen from twentieth to twenty-seventh place.

24   It is hard to know how much of the improvement in reading scores to attribute to choice. For one thing, much of the gain has been recorded in neighborhood elementary schools, where choice has not been as widely available as in the junior highs. For another, the district-wide data conceal variations as great as can be found among public schools anywhere in America. In 1991 at least 75 percent of the students at the most elite East Harlem schools, including the Talented and Gifted School (TAG) for elementary students and Manhattan East and Isaac Newton for junior high students, scored at or above grade level. At Central Park East Secondary School,

with a more diverse student body, more than half of the junior high school students read at grade level. Until recently these schools received special funding from the federal magnet-schools program, and they have attracted most of the students who come from outside East Harlem. TAG, for example, is 40 percent white.

The question of who is attending which East Harlem schools goes to the heart of the system of choice. In its publicity brochures District Four describes its schools as "Schools That Dare to Compete," but the fact is that in many cases it is not the schools but the students that are competing—competing for the schools. A mother visiting New York Prep while I was there was eager to persuade its director at the time, Brian Spears, that her daughter, who was shyly tagging along, should be admitted.

"Why do you want to send your daughter here?" Spears asked.

"You've got computers and a good reading program," the mother said. "It's a safe school. I've got a younger daughter downstairs in the elementary school, and the principal there says it's good."

"There are two hundred and fifty applications for seventy places," Spears replied, and then added, "The fact that you've come down, shown an interest, that's very important."

Sometimes parents treat the selection process as casually as if they were selecting a brand of cereal. Other parents— ones considering elementary schools in particular—base their decisions on factors like proximity and the safety of the neighborhood, which are important but only indirectly related to the quality of the education their children will receive. And for the many youngsters who are characterized by district officials as "at risk"—including children with young mothers strung out on crack, children who have worn thin the patience of their grandmothers, children living in group homes or on the streets—there is no responsible adult to make a choice.

Choice is a tool wielded less decisively by parents than by the school directors, the most adept of whom, like Spears, seek out students they think will succeed in their schools. Five alternative junior highs recruit many of their best students from elementary schools located in the same building that they themselves occupy. Until the past few years others ran their own early-admissions programs, effectively picking students before most parents had a chance to apply. It is largely because of this hidden selection process—which screens both for levels of skill and for traits of character—that some very good schools have been created in East Harlem.

31   A hierarchy has emerged, reflecting the extent to which schools can be selective. At the top are the so-called elite schools, which the ablest East Harlem children and most of the youngsters from outside neighborhoods attend. The highly selective sixth-through-eighth-grade school Manhattan East, which offers what it calls "a rigorous classical academic program," attracts as many as eighty of its 215 students from the world outside District Four; this integration would be less likely to occur if the school had less say over who gets in from the world *inside* District Four. The junior high school New York Prep, in the middle of the academic pecking order but with four applicants for every place, can also fill up with good children and reject all likely troublemakers. At the bottom of the heap are schools that virtually none of each year's 1,400 prospective seventh-graders in District Four would choose. These get the hundreds of children who are left over after the more successful schools have made their picks.

32   In theory, unsuccessful schools in a competitive system would be shut down and replaced with more-popular alternatives. That can be hard to arrange, though, when one reason that a school is unsuccessful is that it has been saddled with the least-promising and most-disruptive students—a change of name, director, and educational philosophy can accomplish only so much. It's also hard to arrange in the real world, where a teachers'-union contract guarantees job security and where many among the poor are possessive even of terrible schools, because these happen to be *their* schools. In nearly two decades only three alternative schools have been shut down in East Harlem. For all these reasons, a substantial proportion of elementary and junior high students wind up in schools that remain largely unaffected by the improvements in District Four.

An East Harlem Sampler

33   Diversity is just an abstraction until you walk into the East 109th Street building that a decade ago was a conventional junior high for 1,300 students. At that time it was a school with a reputation for student violence and dead-end teaching. Now the building houses four alternative elementary and junior high schools: the Harbor Performing Arts School, the Talented and Gifted School, the East Harlem Career Academy,

and the Key School. Pedagogically these places are worlds apart, though they are separated physically by no more than a staircase or a fire door.

A visitor must sign in at a guard's desk before entering—a reminder that trouble is always possible from the crack dealers or the bullying high schoolers who hang around. When I visited the building, the guard was a young woman from the neighborhood, a recent high school graduate who returned to a book of word puzzles when no visitors were in sight. She carried no weapon and would have scared no one, but she offered at least the illusion of protection.

The Talented and Gifted School's name is no mere euphemism. Prospective TAG students take a battery of intelligence and psychological tests, and submit to interviews. The school rejects six children for every one it accepts. In one classroom I saw, pre-kindergartners age four were already beginning to write. A first-grade classroom was filled with stuffed dolls, likenesses of themselves that the children had crafted. "I'm Leslie," the writing on one doll proclaimed. "My puppy sleeps in my bed." "I'm Jenna," said the words on another. "I went to Florida." There was an "Artists' Touch" corner and an "Our Pets" corner. On the wall were cartoon figures demonstrating "angry," "afraid," and "frustrated." I asked the teacher's aide whether "frustrated" wasn't too sophisticated a concept for these six-year-olds, but she assured me that they get it. One of the kids volunteered, "It's the feeling I have when I can't do what I want."

Two floors away, at the Harbor Performing Arts School, with 210 seventh- through ninth-graders, a dance teacher led a dozen girls through a routine. The girls stood poised at the bar. "First position and stop and step back and step forward— don't use your arm, use your entire body... first position three, down on four... Please stop fidgeting. Don't give me third, Ebony—we're in fifth." A sign hanging in the room read, IF YOU'RE NOT WORKING ON YOURSELF, YOU'RE NOT WORKING, and intensity was sketched on the girls' straining faces. From down the hall came the sounds of a choir practicing a medley of songs. In a month the Harbor School's singers and dancers would begin rehearsing their major school production, a Broadway musical. The director at the time, Leslie Moore, told me that these classes build self-esteem. "If teenagers who are having trouble in math or English can succeed in singing or dancing," she said, "with all the discipline that that demands, they don't walk away defeated; they'll stay in school, maybe catch on to academic work. There's also some direct carry-over, since students in music or drama have to make sense of words."

37   Four hundred students apply for the seventy openings in the seventh grade at Harbor. Some will go on to La Guardia High School of Music and Art and Performing Arts—in 1990 ten of the twelve who applied there were admitted—and more will attend prep schools or the city's selective high schools. A handful of alumni are celebrated, among them Amani A. W.-Murray, who has released a saxophone album to bravo reviews, and Carlos Guity, a boy from the slums of the southeast Bronx who became an acrobat with the Big Apple Circus.

38   A typical junior high teacher with 150 students to teach over five periods can't be expected to remember all the students' names, let alone know very much about them. The intimate scale of some of the East Harlem junior high schools invites teachers to invest themselves, much like coaches, in their students' futures. On my initial visit to New York Prep, which occupies the fifth floor of an old elementary school, a boy whom I will call Jaime Morelia, home on vacation after his first term at a Connecticut prep school, came in to check up on his former teachers and see his friends. Jaime's natural ease made him seem more like a college freshman than a fifteen-year-old. He appeared to have made the transition from Harlem to an elite private academy without difficulty. His grades were decent and his confidence was intact. "It's different there," he said. "The work isn't so easy. And it's quiet. I'm used to noise. But we had good preparation for it, and the school is small enough so you can become close to everybody."

39   Christina Giammalva, who until recently divided her time between teaching history at New York Prep and placing her students at prep schools, believed that Jaime would make it at prep school. Although there were students with stronger academic records and better test scores, Jaime was clear-headed, a survivor. When his father disappeared from the family picture, Jaime, then thirteen, became the man of the house. All during his time at New York Prep he had to juggle the heavy and sometimes conflicting demands of home and school.

40   In terms of overall reading scores, New York Prep isn't impressive: in 1991 only 35 percent of the students there were reading at or above grade level. But typically eight or nine of the seventy ninth-graders at New York Prep, many of whom have lived lives at least as hard as Jaime's, will go on to private schools. Student programs involving Scarsdale High and Princeton University, and field trips to places like Boston and

Washington, D.C., show New York Prep's students something of the world beyond the ghetto. One or two afternoons after school every week, 120 of the 210 students spend nearly an hour getting to Columbia University, where they are tutored by law-school and business-school students. Those accepted by private schools take an intensive summer course to hone their academic skills and prepare them psychologically for what's ahead. Almost all will go on to college. Don't pay too much attention to the test scores, the teachers at New York Prep write in their recommendation letters, because we know this student. We won't hide the weaknesses, but we will tell you why they're manageable. In ordinary junior highs in inner cities this degree of involvement in the lives of students is largely unheard of.

The teachers' predictions cannot be infallible, of course,   41
because few among us live perfectly mapped-out and predictable lives. Certainly not most fifteen-year-olds—they believe in their own immortality, and their eyes are on many prizes all at once.

We know how treacherous the passage from ghetto to pri-   42
vate school can be from stories like that of Edmund Perry, whose journey from Harlem to Phillips Exeter Academy ended in robbery and death. Jaime's story is not so tragic, only shadowed and human. During his first year at prep school he was caught cheating—in Spanish, of all subjects—and placed on probation. This past spring, at the end of his junior year, he used a teacher's telephone calling card to phone his mother and his friends in East Harlem. He was found out—how could it have been otherwise?—and expelled. Now he is enrolled in a New York City public high school.

What Jaime Morelia did was plainly wrong, and his moral   43
compass was calibrated finely enough for him to know that. The deeper puzzle is why he behaved as he did. Christina Giammalva speculates that for Jaime the psychological distance may have been too great, the demands to conform to prep-school mores too imposing. Perhaps, Giammalva says, he made those phone calls to invite rejection, rather than be forced to do the rejecting.

Jaime's failure cannot be chalked up entirely to adolescent   44
acting-out, because the school's insensitivity is pertinent too. When Jaime first got into trouble, his prep-school mentors never called his mother to enlist her support, and the first she heard of her son's expulsion was after the fact. Nor is the school's attitude unusual—and this makes the success stories even more special. Another graduate of New York Prep, a boy

I'll call Jamail Robinson, was almost kept from returning to a private school where he had spent two years because his mother, a security guard raising two children, owed the school $1,000. School officials were ready to bounce Jamail without even talking to his mother; it took several anxious phone calls from Giammalva to get him reinstated. This past June, when Jamail graduated from a private school (one of half a dozen or so New York Prep alumni to do so), he was picked by both the faculty and the students as the senior who best embodied their school's ideals.

45   The Key School, which occupies the basement of the same building that houses the Talented and Gifted School and the Harbor School for the Performing Arts, is a school that reflects the underside of reform in East Harlem. None of the Key School's 120 seventh- through ninth-graders chose to be there. The places in this school are filled by youngsters who can't make it elsewhere, and enrollment at Key keeps climbing. Desperate administrators of other alternative schools plead with its director, Iris Novak, to take one more hard-to-handle adolescent, one more kid that nobody else wants. The last arrival had stolen $600 collected for a school dinner from a teacher's handbag at his old school. Since the BETA School closed, there are almost no other schools in the district for problem students. Those who can't make it here may be sent to special-education classes for the emotionally disabled, where about one East Harlem child in fifteen winds up.

46   The Key School is a dark place, out of sight, with none of the amenities of the more elite schools. Its ceilings vibrate whenever students from the Harbor School are playing basketball or practicing their ballet movements in the gym upstairs. Its name could be a metaphor for opening up new opportunities or, perhaps more fittingly, for locking a jail cell.

47   As I talked with Novak, students came and went, pleading for the key to the bathroom, a privilege granted at the absolute discretion of the director. It's an emergency, each of them insisted. A burly ninth-grader stormed in, demanding the return of his hat, which Novak had confiscated earlier in the day. "Gimme back my fuckin' hat," he screamed at Novak. "You think I'm a nice kid but I'm not. I'm mean." Novak wrote it all down, and then silenced the kid with a look and a rumbling voice that comes from having trained for the stage. "I'm not your mother or sister or girlfriend or grandmother. I'm the director of this school. I demand to be treated with respect. There will be no 'fuck, fuck' here. You are suspended."

The day before, after one student had held up another at gunpoint on the sidewalk, security guards were called in; they put the suspect up against the wall and frisked him.

Only nine percent of the students at the Key School are   48
reading at grade level. This isn't surprising, given the composition of the school. Even among East Harlem schools that are not designated as repositories for problem children, more than a few have only one youngster in five—if that—making the grade, and have experienced a decline in performance levels during the past decade. The worst of these schools was Music 13, which until June of 1990 (when it was shut down) coped with seventh- through ninth-graders.

"If you're interested in music, a strong academic back-   49
ground, and high standards," the brochure given to parents bravely announced, "Music 13 is the place to be." The name of Music 13 was intended to reveal its special focus, and there was an able music teacher, Luis Rosa, on the premises. But nobody really chose to attend Music 13, and by the end few at the school cared much about music anymore. The "13" in its name turned out to be more significant than the "Music."

The building that housed it was formerly Junior High   50
School 13, and when two of Deborah Meier's schools were moved there in 1985, some neighborhood parents rebelled. We want to keep our *own* school, they insisted—even though the junior high had been such a misery that most parents had stopped sending their children there years before. A number of teachers also wanted to stay on, and a grandfather clause in the union contract entitled them to do so. Some of the half dozen who remained—"the grandfathers"—epitomized much of what has gone wrong with many big-city schools. During my visit to the school one teacher read *The New York Times* while students chattered, another shouted desperately for order, and a third delivered a by-the-book lesson to a class of uninterested ninth-graders. Often the teachers didn't bother to show up, or else let the director know a day ahead of time that they felt "a sickness coming on." Music 13 had become a school in name but not intention, a place of last resort.

Students like an eighth-grader I'll call Kevin Jones were   51
stuck. "Kevin is intelligent and articulate, with a real talent for science and basketball," Ira Lyons, the third director Music 13 had had in five years, told me. "He has more brains than I do." Kevin first attended Isaac Newton, but was kicked out after being accused of smashing the headlights of the director's car. He has had fights with other students at Music 13. Family conferences came to nothing when the boy's elderly

and deeply religious grandmother insisted that he was no
trouble at home. "High-ability kickouts don't mesh with low-
ability kids," Lyons said. "He belongs in a school that would
challenge him." But no other school was interested.

52   Every urban school district has its Kevin Joneses, and
they're probably no worse off at a place like Music 13 than at
some run-down junior high in the Bronx. That reality points
to the expedient bargain that has in effect been struck in East
Harlem among those who have worked for reform. The deal
is essentially this: Through the mechanism called choice—a
mechanism that gives some options to parents and students
but at the same time is rigged to give even more options to
school directors—we can greatly improve the situation for
about a third of our students, offering them a far better education than they could otherwise have had in one of the most
battered neighborhoods in America. Perhaps we can even
offer something useful to another third of our students. But
the bottom third will be virtually abandoned—as they would
have been anyway.

School by School by School

53   Confronted with crumbling buildings and daily episodes of
violence, with splintered families and refractory bureaucrats—problems that elsewhere might in themselves suck up
all the energy of school leaders—East Harlem has transformed a number of its schools. Elsewhere, initiatives are frequently abandoned when their champions leave, but the
alternative schools in East Harlem have survived the departure of Alvarado and Fliegel, the entrepreneurs who launched
the plan. They have survived a procession of chancellors at
110 Livingston Street, most of whom have been cool to what
the district is doing. They weathered a 1988 financial scandal
that brought down Alvarado's successor, cast suspicion on
Fliegel's successor as director of alternative schools (who was
later exonerated), and for a while left East Harlem's schools
in the hands of an acting superintendent who made no secret
of her dislike for the alternative-schools program. Whether
any further progress is possible in District Four—and
whether other New York City districts will be able to proceed
with plans for similar restructuring depends on the impact of
the continuing fiscal crisis in the New York City schools.

54   East Harlem, with all its problems, has built a far better
school system than I have seen in any comparable neighborhood. For all the hype about reading-test scores, what's more

impressive is the students' generally clearer writing and focused thinking, their greater self-confidence and understanding, and their willingness and ability to enter the world beyond the ghetto in high school and afterward. Graduates from junior highs in East Harlem *are* making it out of the barrio. In the intensely competitive environment of New York City's elite high schools, sorting is nearly as rigid as it was under the old British eleven-plus exam system. The four examination schools—Bronx High School of Science, Stuyvesant High, La Guardia High School, and Brooklyn Technical High School—are among the very best high schools in the nation. Another handful, including Aviation High and East Harlem's Manhattan Center for Science and Mathematics, enroll the next tier of students. The nonselective schools get the leftovers. In the mid-1970s fewer than ten of East Harlem's junior high graduates were accepted by the examination high schools. By 1987 things had radically changed. East Harlem sent 139 youngsters, or ten percent of the district's graduating class that year, to those elite high schools—double the citywide average. An additional 13 percent enrolled at four other high schools that also screen their students—a rate four times as high as the city average. That same year at least thirty-six students from East Harlem received scholarships to private schools, including some of the best ones in the country.

Some of the students who travel to East Harlem from   55 other parts of the city volunteered to me that for the first time in their lives they are being treated with respect by teachers. Teachers reported that the smallness and autonomy of the alternative schools enable them to identify a distinctive voice in each of their children and to respond in kind. In the corridors and directors' offices where teachers congregate, the talk is mainly about what works in the classroom and what doesn't, not about Macy's sales and last night's Knicks game. Not all the schools are as innovative as those that Deborah Meier founded, for there are, after all, only a handful of such educators. But as the history of good urban parochial schools suggests, educational innovation isn't essential to success. What *is* essential is that the school take the time to shape an identity that seems right to those who inhabit the premises, and that this effort be sustained by teachers and administrators who have a measure of independence, a feeling of being driven, and a capacity to know each of their charges. If the idea of intimate enclaves in factory-like city schools is going to take hold, it must happen not by treating East Harlem as a model to be mechanically applied, and certainly not by taking literally the misleading metaphor of the schools as a market-place. Instead, it must happen as an approach adapted to the particularities of place.

56   Schools like those in East Harlem are being asked to accomplish the impossible—to challenge the highly achieving and rescue those who otherwise would drop out, to ease racial separation and reduce inequity in schooling, and all the while to function as the cutting edge of educational innovation. In truth, there are no easy paths even to modest progress. What's needed can be as time-consuming and undramatic as meticulous planning, into-the-wee-hours sessions with anxious school-board members, months of meetings with teachers and school directors to give content to the dreams, and then endless reassurances to parents troubled by what is new and untried. And even then, as District Four shows, there may well remain a large portion of the student population for whom reform might just as well never have occurred.

57   It is essential to risk the mistakes that so often accompany newness and to resist overpromising. Each school will have to find its own way, because everywhere the talents and the possibilities are different, but out of the process something of real value can emerge. This much, at least, East Harlem has to teach the rest of America, as the nation quietly but unmistakably embarks on the great experiment of remaking its schools, one by one.

Jonathan Kozol

A Tale of Two Schools: How Poor Children Are Lost to the World

The following article was published in the Los Angeles Times *in October 1991; it amounts to an excerpt from Kozol's polemical book* Savage Inequalities: Children in America's Schools, *published in the same year. In 1964, Kozol, a teacher at the time at an inner-city school in Boston, had described in* Death at an Early Age *the terrible conditions that he found in schools in poor neighborhoods.* Savage Inequalities *emerged from his visits twenty-five years later to similar schools in places like Camden, NJ; Bronx, NY; East St. Louis, IL; and Washington, DC—and from his conviction that the gap between schools for*

the rich and those for the poor in America has only been widen-
ing, not narrowing.

New Trier's physical setting might well make the students 1
of Du Sable High School envious. The Chicago suburb school
is, says a student, "a maple land of beauty and civility." While
Du Sable is sited on one crowded Chicago city block, New
Trier students have the use of 27 acres. While Du Sable's science students have to settle for makeshift equipment, New
Trier's students have superior labs and up-to-date technology.
One wing of the school, a physical-education center that
includes three separate gyms, also contains a fencing room, a
wrestling room and studios for dance instruction. In all, the
school has seven gyms as well as an Olympic pool.

"This is a school with a lot of choices," says one student at 2
New Trier; and this hardly seems an overstatement if one
studies the curriculum. Courses in music, art and drama are
so varied and abundant that students can virtually major in
these subjects in addition to their academic programs. The
modern and classical language department offers Latin and
six other foreign languages. In a senior literature class, students are reading Nietzsche, Darwin, Plato, Freud and Goethe.

Average class size is 24 children; classes for slower learners 3
hold 15.

The wealth of New Trier's geographical district provides 4
$340,000 worth of taxable property for each child; Chicago's
property wealth affords only one-fifth this much. Nonetheless, *Town and Country*, which profiled the school, gives New
Trier's parents credit for a "willingness to pay enough...in
taxes" to make this one of the state's best-funded schools.
New Trier, according to the magazine, is "a striking example
of what is possible when citizens want to achieve the best for
their children." Families move here "seeking the best," and
their children "make good use" of what they're given. Both
statements may be true, but *Town and Country* flatters the
privileged for having privilege but terms it aspiration.

"Competition is the lifeblood of New Trier," *Town and* 5
Country writes. But there is one kind of competition that
these children will not need to face. They will not compete
against the children who attended Du Sable.

Conditions at Du Sable High School, which I visited in 6
1990, seem in certain ways to be improved. Improvement,
however, is a relative term. Du Sable is better than it was
three or four years ago. It is still a school that would be
shunned—or, probably, shut down—if it were serving a white

middle-class community. The building, a three-story Tudor structure, is in fairly good repair and, in this respect, contrasts with its immediate surroundings, which are almost indescribably despairing. The school, whose student population is 100% black, has no campus and no schoolyard, but there is at least a full-sized playing field and track. Overcrowding is not a problem. Much to the reverse, it is uncomfortably empty. Built in 1935 and holding some 4,500 students in past years, its student population is now fewer than 1,600. Of these students, according to data provided by the school, 646 are "chronic truants."

7   The graduation rate is 25%. Of those who get to senior year, only 17% are in a college-preparation program. Twenty percent are in the general curriculum, a stunning 63% in vocational classes.

8   A vivid sense of loss is felt by standing in the cafeteria in early spring, when students file in to choose their courses for the following year. "These are the ninth graders," says a supervising teacher; but, of the official freshman class of some 600 children, only 350 fill the room. An hour later the 11th graders come to choose their classes: I count at most 170 students.

9   The faculty includes some excellent teachers, but there are others, says the principal, who don't belong in education. "I can't do anything with them but I'm not allowed to fire them," he says.

10   In a 12th-grade English class, the students are learning to pronounce a list of words. The words are not derived from any context; they are simply written on a list. A tall boy struggles to read "fastidious," "gregarious," "auspicious," "fatuous." When he struggles to pronounce "egregious," I ask him if he knows its meaning. It turns out that he has no idea. The teacher never asks the children to write the words or use them in a sentence. The lesson baffles me. It may be that these are words that will appear on a required test that states impose now in the name of "raising standards," but it all seems dreamlike and surreal.

11   After lunch, I talk with a group of students who are hoping to go on to college but do not seem sure of what they'll need to do to make this possible. Only one out of five seniors in the group has filed an application, and it is already April. Pamela, the one who did apply, however, tells me she neglected to submit her grades and college-entrance test results and therefore has to start again. The courses she is taking seem to rule out application to a four-year college. She tells me she is taking

Spanish, literature, physical education, Afro-American history and a class she terms "job strategy." When I ask her what this is, she says, "It teaches how to dress and be on time and figure your deductions." She's a bright, articulate student, and it seems quite sad that she has not had any of the richness of curriculum that would have been given to her at a high school like New Trier.

The children in the group seem not just lacking in impor-   12
tant, useful information that would help them to achieve their dreams, but, in a far more drastic sense, cut off and disconnected from the outside world. In talking of some recent news events, they speak of Moscow and Berlin, but all but Pamela are unaware that Moscow is the capital of the Soviet Union or that Berlin is in Germany. Several believe that Jesse Jackson is the mayor of New York City. Listening to their guesses and observing their confusion, I am thinking of the students at New Trier High. These children live in truly separate worlds. What do they have in common? Yet the kids before me seem so innocent and spiritually clean and also— most of all—so vulnerable. It's as if they have been stripped of all the armament—the reference points, the facts, the reasoning, the elemental weapons—that suburban children take for granted.

"It took an extraordinary combination of greed, racism,   13
political cowardice and public apathy," writes James D. Squires, the former editor of the Chicago Tribune, "to let the public schools in Chicago get so bad." He speaks of the schools as a costly result of "the political orphaning of the urban poor... daytime warehouses for inferior students... a bottomless pit."

The results of these conditions are observed in thousands   14
of low-income children in Chicago, who are virtually disjoined from the worldview, even from the basic reference points, of the American experience. A 16-year-old girl who has dropped out discusses her economic prospects with a TV interviewer.

"How much money would you like to make in a year?" asks   15
the reporter.

"About $2,000," she replies.   16

The reporter looks bewildered by this answer. This teen-   17
age girl, he says, "has no clue that $2,000 a year isn't enough to survive anywhere in America, not even in her world."

John Gatto

I May Be a Teacher,
But I'm Not an Educator

John Gatto had just been named Teacher of the Year in the state of New York (by the State Education Department) when he contributed the following essay to The Wall Street Journal *in July 1991.*

1   I've taught public school for 26 years but I just can't do it anymore. For years I asked the local school board and superintendent to let me teach a curriculum that doesn't hurt kids, but they had other fish to fry. So I'm going to quit, I think.

2   I've come slowly to understand what it is I really teach: a curriculum of confusion, class position, arbitrary justice, vulgarity, rudeness, disrespect for privacy, indifference to quality, and utter dependency. I teach how to fit into a world I don't want to live in.

3   I just can't do it anymore. I can't train children to wait to be told what to do; I can't train people to drop what they are doing when a bell sounds; I can't persuade children to feel some justice in their class placement when there isn't any; and I can't persuade children to believe teachers have valuable secrets they can acquire by becoming our disciples. That isn't true.

4   Government schooling is the most radical adventure in history. It kills the family by monopolizing the best times of childhood and by teaching disrespect for home and parents.

5   An exaggeration? Hardly. Parents aren't meant to participate in our form of schooling, rhetoric to the contrary. My orders as schoolteacher are to make children fit an animal training system, not to help each find his or her personal path.

6   The whole blueprint of school procedure is Egyptian, not Greek or Roman. It grows from the faith that human value is a scarce thing, represented symbolically by the narrow peak of a pyramid.

7   That idea passed into American history through the Puritans. It found its "scientific" presentation in the bell curve, along which talent supposedly apportions itself by some Iron Law of biology.

8   It's a religious idea and school is its church. New York City hires me to be a priest. I offer rituals to keep heresy at bay. I provide documentation to justify the heavenly pyramid.

Socrates foresaw that if teaching became a formal profes-   9
sion something like this would happen. Professional interest
is best served by making what is easy to do seem hard; by subordinating laity to priesthood. School has become too vital a
jobs project, contract-giver and protector of the social order,
to allow itself to be "re-formed." It has political allies to guard
its marches.

That's why reforms come and go—without changing much.   10
Even reformers can't imagine school much different.

David learns to read at age four; Rachel, at age nine. In   11
normal development, when both are 13, you can't tell which
one learned first—the five-year spread means nothing at all.
But in school I will label Rachel "learning disabled" and slow
David down a bit, too.

For a paycheck, I adjust David to depend on me to tell him   12
when to go and stop. He won't outgrow that dependency. I
identify Rachel as discount merchandise, "special education."
After a few months she'll be locked into her place forever.

In 26 years of teaching rich kids and poor I almost never   13
met a "learning disabled" child; hardly ever met a "gifted and
talented" one, either. Like all school categories, these are
sacred myths, created by the human imagination. They derive
from questionable values we never examine because they preserve the temple of schooling.

That's the secret behind short-answer tests, bells, uniform   14
time blocks, age grading, standardization, and all the rest of
the school religion punishing our nation.

There isn't a right way to become educated; there are as   15
many ways as fingerprints. We don't need state-certified
teachers to make education happen—that probably guarantees it *won't*.

How much more evidence is necessary? Good schools   16
don't need more money or a longer year; they need real free-
market choices, variety that speaks to every need and runs
risks. We don't need a national curriculum, or national testing
either. Both initiatives arise from ignorance of how people
learn, or deliberate indifference to it.

I can't teach this way any longer. If you hear of a job where   17
I don't have to hurt kids to make a living, let me know. Come
fall I'll be looking for work, I think.

Theodore Sizer
Horace's Compromise

*Born in 1932, Theodore Sizer now chairs the education depart-
ment at Brown University. His book* Horace's Compromise:
The Dilemma of the American High School, *published in
1984, offers a program of reform for America's high schools;
the book describes the frustrations (and their sources) of a fictional but representative English teacher, Horace Smith, who
is forced to compromise his best educational instincts in the
face of a fragmented and fragmenting high school system. In
1992, Mr. Sizer wrote* Horace's School, *which proposes a series
of solutions to Horace's problems and those of his fictional
Franklin High School. Sizer has pioneered the Coalition of
Essential Schools, which now has over eight hundred member
schools. Following is the first chapter from* Horace's School.

1   Meet Horace Smith, fifty-nine, a veteran English teacher at
Franklin High. Among parents and graduates, he is widely
considered a star faculty member of this inner suburban high
school of 1350 pupils. Certainly he is respected by his colleagues; they find him the professional's professional, even to
a fault. While many of the faculty who are his age are already
considering retirement, thanks to the state's generous annuity
plan, Horace is not. He believes—perversely, he often
thinks—that Franklin High is not nearly what it could be. He
wants to stay on and make it better.

2   The good light in which the community sees the school is
not deserved, he feels. Franklin is a caring place, but the kids
worry Horace. Many are lively, well intentioned, and adept at
cranking out acceptable test scores, but they are without the
habits of serious thought, respectful skepticism, and curiosity
about much of what lies beyond their immediate lives. They
lack assurance, skill, and interest in confronting the stuff of
Franklin's curriculum and committing their God-given minds
to strenuous use.

3   Sure, they rack up lists of "extracurriculars" to dazzle university admissions officers, but even when they show a dash
of substance, too many of them lack style, that gossamer
quality which separates the interesting person from the conventional one. They get top grades on the English Advanced
Placement exams, but never read a serious piece of fiction
outside or beyond school. They score high on the social stud-

ies tests, but later will vote for political candidates on
impulse, if they vote at all.

The kids play a game with school, making deals with us,   4
striking bargains. What will be on the test, Mr. Smith? Will
this count in the grade, Mr. Smith? How many pages must
this be, Mr. Smith? When do we have to read this by, Mr.
Smith? If we do this, will you ease up on that? They all ought
to be ambassadors, Horace thinks, wheeler-dealers striking
bargains and making treaties. However, the treaties will be
ones to lessen work, lessen the pain of thinking anew, lessen
anything that may get into the way of having a happy time
after school. Treaties to protect the Good Life. Horace snorts
at himself: What a cynic I am. Aren't we adults that way too,
excessively so? What are all of us coming to?

Many of Horace's colleagues find his criticism harsh, but   5
he persists. We do not know the half of what these kids can
do, he contends. But, his friends retort, can one school turn
them around? The whole society is soft. The kids' culture is
defined by MTV and cravings created by national merchandise. Even their parents do not want the school to change
much. Get Susie into a good college, they say. And if we do,
they love us. If we do not, they blame us. But *style?* Come on,
Horace.

Horace understands the familiar lament. And he knows   6
that Franklin hasn't many of the searing problems swamping
the nearby city schools. For kids in those schools, there's not
even a question of developing style; sheer survival is their
task. He also remembers the exceptional kids he taught who
did have fresh, inquiring, informed minds, and thoughtful
hearts too. Why can't we have more kids like those, he wonders. Schools can help shape them, or at the least encourage
those happy tendencies. Why must schooling, and its typical
products, be so mindless? It need not be so. And though the
culture out there may be inattentive, the school—even Franklin High School—can do something about it.

That, Horace knows, is a presumption. Who are teachers   7
to set standards? Who says that they have a corner on wisdom? Horace worries about this. The schools should reflect
what the culture wants, and if the culture is careless, then the
school can be careless.

But, then, what is the role of the teacher? Merely to be the   8
agent of the culture? No, Horace says, we must try to be better than that. And, contrary to conventional wisdom, most
parents are our allies. What they want, at heart, is more than
a ticket for their offspring to a prestigious college. They want

that, yes, but they want more; and it is by an alliance of aware and demanding teachers, parents, and adolescents that a better school can be molded, a thoughtful place to teach thoughtful young citizens.

9   A thoughtful place. Horace hesitates on this, because he knows from decades of experience that Franklin is, if nothing else, unexamined. Like most high schools, it just rolls on, fettered by routines of long standing. The result is a cacophony of jumbled practices, orchestrated only by a complex computer-driven schedule whose instrument is a bell system and whose ushers are assistant principals.

10   The faculty itself, he muses, is hardly thoughtful about its own situation. The status quo is never challenged. We have curriculum committees that talk only about revising the accepted subjects, never pondering what the curriculum could be. We have committees on schedule changes that never ask the basic questions about the uses of time. We "restructure" while assuming that all the existing building materials and architectural commitments—physical and intellectual—will remain as they are.

11   Horace knows that the status quo *is* the problem. It forces him to compromise in ways that cripple his teaching, his ability to create thoughtful students. Compromises are always necessary in the real world, Horace admits; and the issue, then, is which compromises will serve the students best. Only by examining the existing compromises, however painful that may be, and moving beyond them to better compromises, can one form a more thoughtful school. And only in thoughtful schools can thoughtful students be hatched.

12   Horace's complaints are many and fundamental. It would be easier if the system were basically sound, but the lamentable truth is that it is not, and that the complex routines of schools are all related. Question one, and you question all.

13   Take Horace's student load. Officially it should be 120, five classes of twenty-four students each, the "contract ratio" for English teachers. This year it is 132. Horace's courses are popular, and he has difficulty saying no to eager kids, particularly those who have studied with him before. Horace knows that he should insist on a writing assignment from every one of those youngsters every day, or at least every other day, and that he should promptly read, comment on, and return these papers. But with 120? Impossible. Spending just five out-of-class minutes per week looking at the work of each student and, at least once a month, talking privately with the youngster would total ten hours—ten hours of enervating work, two

hours every evening, Monday through Friday, week after week. And this in addition to all the rest he has to do outside those contact hours in class with the kids, not to mention his evening work at the family's liquor store to help meet the household bills. So, like most English teachers, he does not do the careful reading and criticizing he knows is so valuable for students.

Accordingly, Horace recognizes that he does not know   14
many of his kids well enough to understand really how their minds work, how and why they make mistakes, what motivates them, what stars they seek to reach or whether each hankers after a star at all. Yes, most are acquaintances; they hail him in the hallways. But does he know them well enough to teach them powerfully, know the ways of their minds and moods? No, not even close. Horace compromises. He gets to know a few students well, usually those who interest him especially or who press themselves to his attention. The kids in the middle remain a genial blur. Indeed, Horace wryly admits most of them cherish their anonymity. If Mr. Smith really knows me, then he'd find out that....

During the school day, the students come to Horace by   15
"classes," ninth grade, tenth grade, and the rest. A student is in a particular class on the basis of her or his birthday. To be out of step, sixteen in the ninth grade or fourteen in the eleventh grade, is cause for comment, usually contemptuous. Dummy. Nerd. One of *those* kids. The assumption behind the system is that kids of the same age are essentially alike, more or less teachable in the same ways and properly held to similar standards. Franklin High School splits each grade into three lumps, honors, college prep, and regular, as well as special needs. But the prevailing, and overwhelming, characterization of students is by grade level. Teachers ask, *What's your name? What grade are you in?* The answers provide the two critical labels. Because all the kids in each grade have experienced, it is presumed, the same number of hours of schooling, they should, save at the extremes, all know the same things.

Horace knows better. Young people grow intellectually,   16
physically, and socially at different rates, often with mysterious spurts and stops along the way. Some kids excel at language and flounder in mathematics; the hotshot in one area is not necessarily great in another. Further, not all kids pay attention at school at any given moment, for benign or deplorable reasons. So by their high school years the youngster's potential and actual school performance often diverge:

"ninth grade" is an administratively useful concept, but one
that tells a teacher far less about a student's intellectual and
emotional development than the grouping would suggest.

17   One copes, however, largely by not being careful, by deliberately not attending to the record and specialness and stage
of growth and disposition of each youngster. They are all
ninth-graders. Treat them the same—same curriculum, same
textbook, same pedagogy, same tests, same standards, same
everything.

18   It defies common sense, Horace knows. Age grading hurts
some kids, swelling the heads of those who appear, for whatever obvious or mysterious reasons, to be "swift" and humiliating the "slow." Pigeonholing honors, regular, and special
needs students sets up the self-fulfilling prophecies. *Oh no,
Mr. Smith, I couldn't take AP English. I'm not an honors
student....* Every year Horace sees the swift kid who plugs
hard, with the confidence of being perceived as honors quality, and the slow youngster who ignores his talents, giving up,
acting up, not caring, finding school a place of unrelieved and
anticipated failure.

19   Franklin High School uses plenty of public relations talk
about "taking each child individually," but the school's practices belie the boast. For example, there is virtually no
attempt, Horace ruefully recalls, to get thorough information
to a student's new teacher about the youngster's history in
school. Students do have files someplace, Horace knows.
Teachers don't read them, though, and are not encouraged to
do so. In any event, there are too many to absorb. May as well
treat 'em all the same. Or accept someone else's judgment
about how swift a kid is, and go with it. Expect more, or
expect less. Compromise with your common sense: the kids
are different, but we can't admit it, even to ourselves.

20   The curriculum does not help. Franklin High School has a
statement of goals, but it is as vague as it is hortatory and
conventional. The goals connect only rhetorically with the
formal Course of Study. The latter is laid out by course and
grade and is usually cast as a list of ideas, classics to be read,
facts, skills, procedures, and qualities of character to be
admired, opportunities to stock one's mind. Simply, the curriculum, however artfully described, is a listing of what the
teachers will do, what "things" the kids will be "exposed" to.
The students remain invisible, lumped in their age-graded
cohorts, ready to watch the teachers' parade of things.

21   Horace knows this is backward. What counts is what the
students do, as Horace has learned from the Theater Club

plays he directs. The members know what the "target" is. Others find targets in some of the more imaginative Advanced Placement courses. But there are few such compelling ends in view in the core curriculum; the destinations are clearly cast in terms of what the students should be able to do. Except for aiming to help students pass the tests, the formal Course of Study Guide says little about what the material *means*. We teachers are "to cover" the Lake poets, and the students should then be able to answer questions about them. How the students are to *use* the experience is not addressed. This is as depressing as it is confusing, but Horace continues to compromise. We will all read *Hamlet* during the spring term, and there will be one test for all eleventh-graders. . . .

Franklin's "goal statement" talks of graduates able to   22
"function in society and the economy as useful citizens."
Horace would put that as "making sense of the world." Either way, it assumes that Franklin alumni will see which issues are of consequence to themselves and others, will be competent to analyze these situations, to sort them out, and will be both able and disposed to do something about them. Some would say that this means that graduates should be interested in learning and practiced in teaching themselves, able to figure out their world and motivated to do something about it.

Fine, Horace thinks. But how is the school's curriculum   23
organized? By subjects, most of which are poorly defined and each of which is planned in almost total isolation from the others. The stuff of these subjects is offered up to students in fifty-two-minute slivers of time, rapid fire.

Horace wonders whether this gives kids practice in making   24
sense of the world. Even the teachers in the English Department can't agree on what their subject really is; the mathematics sequence has no planned connection with science courses; and the teachers of literature, art, music, and drama pay attention only to each art separately. Making sense is tough even for adults; despite its goal statement, Franklin gives students little practice in the craft. Indeed, the high school's presentation of the curriculum guarantees superficiality.

These realities sting Horace, but he goes along. He com-   25
promises. The faculty doesn't like to hear any sort of fundamental criticism. We're tired of being the butt of all the griping, they say. Furthermore, this list of subjects is what the colleges want. A likely story, Horace thinks. Do the colleges want kids schooled in intellectual chaos?

Give a little, get along, compromise. Yes, sometimes there   26
is electricity in the classrooms, but not often enough. The

kids compromise too, taking what is offered, observing that to which they are exposed, more or less cranking out the tests, and then forgetting most of it. Feeling good is important, not only about oneself but also about the school. Franklin Pride.

27   Horace remembers a devilish experiment that a visiting consultant recently suggested: give students a test they took twelve to fifteen months earlier, and see how they perform. What had they retained? Horace winces at the thought. Kids forget so much so quickly. It is better that school accentuate the immediate, the stuff of the last unit, rather than instill intellectual habits. Horace plays the game too. Last year's English is expected to be gone, and if we hold a student responsible for it, we are "unfair." And so we stress the immediate.

28   All this is agonizing for Horace. He resents his compromises, and derides himself for making them. Some respected colleagues share his frustration, but they know that an honest evaluation of the school's compromises will open a Pandora's box. Everything in the school affects everything else. That finely tuned complexity which is the daily schedule cannot withstand more than trivial adjustments, and more than trivial adjustments are needed to improve Franklin High. The ultimate frustration for Horace is that even if a corps of like-minded, risk-taking colleagues evolved an ambitious, sensible new plan for Franklin, they would not have the authority to act on it. The major elements of schooling are controlled outside the teachers' world. The state, or its contractor firms, writes the tests. The state mandates when each subject is to be taught; it and the district control that key coinage of school, the time of teachers and students. Evaluations of school and teachers, the union contract, the departmental divisions, all run according to traditional formulas.

29   Horace knows that he has limited control over his own destiny. Others would have to affirm his intention to teach with better compromises, to organize his and the students' work along more sensible lines. Obviously, they don't trust us, Horace thinks. The folk higher up are sure they know better. We always have to ask permission. Teachers with hall passes not to the bathroom but to better schools, he snorts to himself. Of all Horace's feelings about his work, this is the most bitter.

David P. Gardner et al.
A Nation at Risk

In 1981, Secretary of Education T. H. Bell created the National Commission on Excellence in Education and directed it to report within eighteen months on the quality of education in American schools. Sparked by a widespread public perception that "something is wrong" with our educational system, the Commission (chaired by David P. Gardner, president of the University of California, and comprising eighteen teachers, school administrators, university presidents, and distinguished public officials and business leaders) created a national stir with its final report, "A Nation at Risk," reprinted (with some small omissions) below. More than a decade later the report continues to provide a context for discussions of educational reform in the United States.

Our Nation is at risk. Our once unchallenged preeminence in commerce, industry, science, and technological innovation is being overtaken by competitors throughout the world. This report is concerned with only one of the many causes and dimensions of the problem, but it is the one that undergirds American prosperity, security, and civility. We report to the American people that while we can take justifiable pride in what our schools and colleges have historically accomplished and contributed to the United States and the well-being of its people, the educational foundations of our society are presently being eroded by a rising tide of mediocrity that threatens our very future as a Nation and a people. What was unimaginable a generation ago has begun to occur—others are matching and surpassing our educational attainments. 1

If an unfriendly foreign power had attempted to impose on America the mediocre educational performance that exists today, we might well have viewed it as an act of war. As it stands, we have allowed this to happen to ourselves. We have even squandered the gains in student achievement made in the wake of the Sputnik challenge. Moreover, we have dismantled essential support systems which helped make those gains possible. We have, in effect, been committing an act of unthinking, unilateral educational disarmament. 2

Our society and its educational institutions seem to have lost sight of the basic purposes of schooling, and of the high expectations and disciplined effort needed to attain them. 3

This report, the result of 18 months of study, seeks to generate reform of our educational system in fundamental ways and to renew the Nation's commitment to schools and colleges of high quality throughout the length and breadth of our land.

4   That we have compromised this commitment is, upon reflection, hardly surprising, given the multitude of often conflicting demands we have placed on our Nation's schools and colleges. They are routinely called on to provide solutions to personal, social, and political problems that the home and other institutions either will not or cannot resolve. We must understand that these demands on our schools and colleges often exact an educational cost as well as a financial one.

5   On the occasion of the Commission's first meeting, President Reagan noted the central importance of education in American life when he said: "Certainly there are few areas of American life as important to our society, to our people, and to our families as our schools and colleges." This report, therefore, is as much an open letter to the American people as it is a report to the Secretary of Education. We are confident that the American people, properly informed, will do what is right for their children and for the generations to come.

The Risk

6   History is not kind to idlers. The time is long past when America's destiny was assured simply by an abundance of natural resources and inexhaustible human enthusiasm, and by our relative isolation from the malignant problems of older civilizations. The world is indeed one global village. We live among determined, well-educated, and strongly motivated competitors. We compete with them for international standing and markets, not only with products but also with the ideas of our laboratories and neighborhood workshops. America's position in the world may once have been reasonably secure with only a few exceptionally well-trained men and women. It is no longer.

7   The risk is not only that the Japanese make automobiles more efficiently than Americans and have government subsidies for development and export. It is not just that the South Koreans recently built the world's most efficient steel mill, or that American machine tools, once the pride of the world, are being displaced by German products. It is also that these developments signify a redistribution of trained capability

throughout the globe. Knowledge, learning, information, and skilled intelligence are the new raw materials of international commerce and are today spreading throughout the world as vigorously as miracle drugs, synthetic fertilizers, and blue jeans did earlier. If only to keep and improve on the slim competitive edge we still retain in world markets, we must dedicate ourselves to the reform of our educational system for the benefit of all—old and young alike, affluent and poor, majority and minority. Learning is the indispensable investment required for success in the "information age" we are entering.

Our concern, however, goes well beyond matters such as industry and commerce. It also includes the intellectual, moral, and spiritual strengths of our people which knit together the very fabric of our society. The people of the United States need to know that individuals in our society who do not possess the levels of skill, literacy, and training essential to this new era will be effectively disenfranchised, not simply from the material rewards that accompany competent performance, but also from the chance to participate fully in our national life. A high level of shared education is essential to a free, democratic society and to the fostering of a common culture, especially in a country that prides itself on pluralism and individual freedom. 8

For our country to function, citizens must be able to reach some common understandings on complex issues, often on short notice and on the basis of conflicting or incomplete evidence. Education helps form these common understandings, a point Thomas Jefferson made long ago in his justly famous dictum: 9

> I know no safe depository of the ultimate powers of the society but the people themselves; and if we think them not enlightened enough to exercise their control with a wholesome discretion, the remedy is not to take it from them but to inform their discretion.

Part of what is at risk is the promise first made on this continent: All, regardless of race or class or economic status, are entitled to a fair chance and to the tools for developing their individual powers of mind and spirit to the utmost. This promise means that all children by virtue of their own efforts, competently guided, can hope to attain the mature and informed judgment needed to secure gainful employment and to manage their own lives, thereby serving not only their own interests but also the progress of society itself. 10

Indicators of the Risk

11   The educational dimensions of the risk before us have been amply documented in testimony received by the Commission. For example:

- International comparisons of student achievement, completed a decade ago, reveal that on 19 academic tests American students were never first or second and, in comparison with other industrialized nations, were last seven times.
- Some 23 million American adults are functionally illiterate by the simplest tests of everyday reading, writing, and comprehension.
- About 13 percent of all 17-year-olds in the United States can be considered functionally illiterate. Functional illiteracy among minority youth may run as high as 40 percent.
- Average achievement of high school students on most standardized tests is now lower than 26 years ago when Sputnik was launched.
- Over half the population of gifted students do not match their tested ability with comparable achievement in school.
- The College Board's Scholastic Aptitude Tests (SAT) demonstrate a virtually unbroken decline from 1963 to 1980. Average verbal scores fell over 50 points and average mathematics scores dropped nearly 40 points.
- College Board achievement tests also reveal consistent declines in recent years in such subjects as physics and English.
- Both the number and proportion of students demonstrating superior achievement on the SATs (i.e., those with scores of 650 or higher) have also dramatically declined.
- There was a steady decline in science achievement scores of U.S. 17-year-olds as measured by national assessments of science in 1969, 1973, and 1977.
- Between 1975 and 1980, remedial mathematics courses in public 4-year colleges increased by 72 percent and now constitute one-quarter of all mathematics courses taught in those institutions.
- Average tested achievement of students graduating from college is also lower.

- Business and military leaders complain that they are required to spend millions of dollars on costly remedial education and training programs in such basic skills as reading, writing, spelling, and computation. The Department of the Navy, for example, reported to the Commission that one-quarter of its recent recruits cannot read at the ninth grade level, the minimum needed simply to understand written safety instructions. Without remedial work they cannot even begin, much less complete, the sophisticated training essential in much of the modern military.

These deficiencies come at a time when the demand for 12
highly skilled workers in new fields is accelerating rapidly.
For example:

- Computers and computer-controlled equipment are penetrating every aspect of our lives—homes, factories, and offices.
- One estimate indicates that by the turn of the century millions of jobs will involve laser technology and robotics.
- Technology is radically transforming a host of other occupations. They include health care, medical science, energy production, food processing, construction, and the building, repair, and maintenance of sophisticated scientific, educational, military, and industrial equipment.

Analysts examining these indicators of student perfor- 13
mance and the demands for new skills have made some chilling observations. Educational researcher Paul Hurd concluded at the end of a thorough national survey of student achievement that within the context of the modern scientific revolution, "We are raising a new generation of Americans that is scientifically and technologically illiterate." In a similar vein, John Slaughter, a former Director of the National Science Foundation, warned of "a growing chasm between a small scientific and technological elite and a citizenry ill-informed, indeed uninformed, on issues with a science component."

But the problem does not stop there, nor do all observers 14
see it the same way. Some worry that schools may emphasize such rudiments as reading and computation at the expense of other essential skills such as comprehension, analysis, solving

problems, and drawing conclusions. Still others are concerned that an over-emphasis on technical and occupational
skills will leave little time for studying the arts and humanities that so enrich daily life, help maintain civility, and
develop a sense of community. Knowledge of the humanities,
they maintain, must be harnessed to science and technology
if the latter are to remain creative and humane, just as the
humanities need to be informed by science and technology if
they are to remain relevant to the human condition. Another
analyst, Paul Copperman, has drawn a sobering conclusion.
Until now, he has noted:

> Each generation of Americans has outstripped its parents in
> education, in literacy, and in economic attainment. For the
> first time in the history of our country, the educational skills
> of one generation will not surpass, will not equal, will not
> even approach, those of their parents.

15   It is important, of course, to recognize that *the average citizen* today is better educated and more knowledgeable than
the average citizen of a generation ago—more literate, and
exposed to more mathematics, literature, and science. The
positive impact of this fact on the well-being of our country
and the lives of our people cannot be overstated. Nevertheless, *the average graduate* of our schools and colleges today is
not as well-educated as the average graduate of 25 or 35 years
ago, when a much smaller proportion of our population completed high school and college. The negative impact of this
fact likewise cannot be overstated.

Hope and Frustration

16   Statistics and their interpretation by experts show only the
surface dimension of the difficulties we face. Beneath them
lies a tension between hope and frustration that characterizes
current attitudes about education at every level.

17   We have heard the voices of high school and college students, school board members, and teachers; of leaders of
industry, minority groups, and higher education; of parents
and State officials. We could hear the hope evident in their
commitment to quality education and in their descriptions of
outstanding programs and schools. We could also hear the
intensity of their frustration, a growing impatience with
shoddiness in many walks of American life, and the com-

plaint that this shoddiness is too often reflected in our schools and colleges. Their frustration threatens to overwhelm their hope.

What lies behind this emerging national sense of frustra- 18 tion can be described as both a dimming of personal expectations and the fear of losing a shared vision for America.

On the personal level the student, the parent, and the car- 19 ing teacher all perceive that a basic promise is not being kept. More and more young people emerge from high school ready neither for college nor for work. This predicament becomes more acute as the knowledge base continues its rapid expansion, the number of traditional jobs shrinks, and new jobs demand greater sophistication and preparation.

On a broader scale, we sense that this undertone of frustra- 20 tion has significant political implications, for it cuts across ages, generations, races, and political and economic groups. We have come to understand that the public will demand that educational and political leaders act forcefully and effectively on these issues. Indeed, such demands have already appeared and could well become a unifying national preoccupation. This unity, however, can be achieved only if we avoid the unproductive tendency of some to search for scapegoats among the victims, such as the beleaguered teachers.

On the positive side is the significant movement by politi- 21 cal and educational leaders to search for solutions—so far centering largely on the nearly desperate need for increased support for the teaching of mathematics and science. This movement is but a start on what we believe is a larger and more educationally encompassing need to improve teaching and learning in fields such as English, history, geography, economics, and foreign languages. We believe this movement must be broadened and directed toward reform and excellence throughout education.

Excellence in Education

We define "excellence" to mean several related things. At 22 the level of the *individual learner,* it means performing on the boundary of individual ability in ways that test and push back personal limits, in school and in the workplace. Excellence characterizes a *school or college* that sets high expectations and goals for all learners, then tries in every way possible to help students reach them. Excellence characterizes a *society* that has adopted these policies, for it will then be prepared through the education and skill of its people to respond to the challenges of a rapidly changing world. Our Nation's people and its schools and colleges must be committed to achieving excellence in all these senses.

23   We do not believe that a public commitment to excellence and educational reform must be made at the expense of a strong public commitment to the equitable treatment of our diverse population. The twin goals of equity and high-quality schooling have profound and practical meaning for our economy and society, and we cannot permit one to yield to the other either in principle or in practice. To do so would deny young people their chance to learn and live according to their aspirations and abilities. It also would lead to a generalized accommodation to mediocrity in our society on the one hand or the creation of an undemocratic elitism on the other.

24   Our goal must be to develop the talents of all to their fullest. Attaining that goal requires that we expect and assist all students to work to the limits of their capabilities. We should expect schools to have genuinely high standards rather than minimum ones, and parents to support and encourage their children to make the most of their talents and abilities.

25   The search for solutions to our educational problems must also include a commitment to life-long learning. The task of rebuilding our system of learning is enormous and must be properly understood and taken seriously: Although a million and a half new workers enter the economy each year from our schools and colleges, the adults working today will still make up about 75 percent of the workforce in the year 2000. These workers, and new entrants into the workforce, will need further education and retraining if they—and we as a Nation—are to thrive and prosper.

The Learning Society

26   In a world of ever-accelerating competition and change in the conditions of the workplace, of ever-greater danger, and of ever-larger opportunities for those prepared to meet them, educational reform should focus on the goal of creating a Learning Society. At the heart of such a society is the commitment to a set of values and to a system of education that affords all members the opportunity to stretch their minds to full capacity, from early childhood through adulthood, learning more as the world itself changes. Such a society has as a basic foundation the idea that education is important not only because of what it contributes to one's career goals but

also because of the value it adds to the general quality of one's life. Also at the heart of the Learning Society are educational opportunities extending far beyond the traditional institutions of learning, our schools and colleges. They extend into homes and workplaces; into libraries, art galleries, museums, and science centers; indeed, into every place where the individual can develop and mature in work and life. In our view, formal schooling in youth is the essential foundation for learning throughout one's life. But without life-long learning, one's skills will become rapidly dated.

In contrast to the ideal of the Learning Society, however, we find that for too many people education means doing the minimum work necessary for the moment, then coasting through life on what may have been learned in its first quarter. But this should not surprise us because we tend to express our educational standards and expectations largely in terms of "minimum requirements." And where there should be a coherent continuum of learning, we have none, but instead an often incoherent, outdated patchwork quilt. Many individual, sometimes heroic, examples of schools and colleges of great merit do exist. Our findings and testimony confirm the vitality of a number of notable schools and programs, but their very distinction stands out against a vast mass shaped by tensions and pressures that inhibit systematic academic and vocational achievement for the majority of students. In some metropolitan areas basic literacy has become the goal rather than the starting point. In some colleges maintaining enrollments is of greater day-to-day concern than maintaining rigorous academic standards. And the ideal of academic excellence as the primary goal of schooling seems to be fading across the board in American education. 27

Thus, we issue this call to all who care about America and its future: to parents and students; to teachers, administrators, and school board members; to colleges and industry; to union members and military leaders; to governors and State legislators; to the President; to members of Congress and other public officials; to members of learned and scientific societies; to the print and electronic media; to concerned citizens everywhere. America is at risk. 28

Recommendations

In light of the urgent need for improvement, both immediate and long term, this Commission has agreed on a set of recommendations that the American people can begin to act 29 on now, that can be implemented over the next several years, and that promise lasting reform. The topics are familiar; there is little mystery about what we believe must be done. Many schools, districts, and States are already giving serious and constructive attention to these matters, even though their plans may differ from our recommendations in some details.

30   We wish to note that we refer to public, private, and parochial schools and colleges alike. All are valuable national resources. Examples of actions similar to those recommended below can be found in each of them.

31   We must emphasize that the variety of student aspirations, abilities, and preparation requires that appropriate content be available to satisfy diverse needs. Attention must be directed to both the nature of the content available and to the needs of particular learners. The most gifted students, for example, may need a curriculum enriched and accelerated beyond even the needs of other students of high ability. Similarly, educationally disadvantaged students may require special curriculum materials, smaller classes, or individual tutoring to help them master the material presented. Nevertheless, there remains a common expectation: We must demand the best effort and performance from all students, whether they are gifted or less able, affluent or disadvantaged, whether destined for college, the farm, or industry.

32   Our recommendations are based on the beliefs that everyone can learn, that everyone is born with an *urge* to learn which can be nurtured, that a solid high school education is within the reach of virtually all, and that life-long learning will equip people with the skills required for new careers and for citizenship.

33   *Recommendation A: Content.* **We recommend** *that State and local high school graduation requirements be strengthened and that, at a minimum, all students seeking a diploma be required to lay the foundations in the Five New Basics by taking the following curriculum during their 4 years of high school: (a) 4 years of English; (b) 3 years of mathematics; (c) 3 years of science; (d) 3 years of social studies; and (e) one-half year of computer science. For the college-bound, 2 years of foreign language in high school are strongly recommended in addition to those taken earlier.*

34   *Recommendation B: Standards and Expectations.* **We recommend** *that schools, colleges, and universities adopt more rigorous and measurable standards, and higher expectations,*

for academic performance and student conduct, and that 4-year colleges and universities raise their requirements for admission. This will help students do their best educationally with challenging materials in an environment that supports learning and authentic accomplishment.

Recommendation C: Time. **We recommend** *significantly more time be devoted to learning the New Basics. This will require more effective use of the existing school day, a longer school day, or a lengthened school year.* 35

Recommendation D: Teaching. **This recommendation** *consists of seven parts. Each is intended to improve the preparation of teachers or to make teaching a more rewarding and respected profession. Each of the seven stands on its own and should not be considered solely as an implementing recommendation.* 36

1. Persons preparing to teach should be required to meet high educational standards, to demonstrate an aptitude for teaching, and to demonstrate competence in an academic discipline. Colleges and universities offering teacher preparation programs should be judged by how well their graduates meet these criteria.

2. Salaries for the teaching profession should be increased and should be professionally competitive, market-sensitive, and performance-based. Salary, promotion, tenure, and retention decisions should be tied to an effective evaluation system that includes peer review so that superior teachers can be rewarded, average ones encouraged, and poor ones either improved or terminated.

3. School boards should adopt an 11-month contract for teachers. This would ensure time for curriculum and professional development, programs for students with special needs, and a more adequate level of teacher compensation.

4. School boards, administrators, and teachers should cooperate to develop career ladders for teachers that distinguish among the beginning instructor, the experienced teacher, and the master teacher.

5. Substantial nonschool personnel resources should be employed to help solve the immediate problem of the shortage of mathematics and science teachers.

Qualified individuals including recent graduates with mathematics and science degrees, graduate students, and industrial and retired scientists could, with appropriate preparation, immediately begin teaching in these fields. A number of our leading science centers have the capacity to begin educating and retraining teachers immediately. Other areas of critical teacher need, such as English, must also be addressed.

6. Incentives, such as grants and loans, should be made available to attract outstanding students to the teaching profession, particularly in those areas of critical shortage.

7. Master teachers should be involved in designing teacher preparation programs and in supervising teachers during their probationary years.

America Can Do It

37   Despite the obstacles and difficulties that inhibit the pursuit of superior educational attainment, we are confident, with history as our guide, that we can meet our goal. The American educational system has responded to previous challenges with remarkable success. In the 19th century our land-grant colleges and universities provided the research and training that developed our Nation's natural resources and the rich agricultural bounty of the American farm. From the late 1800s through mid-20th century, American schools provided the educated workforce needed to seal the success of the Industrial Revolution and to provide the margin of victory in two world wars. In the early part of this century and continuing to this very day, our schools have absorbed vast waves of immigrants and educated them and their children to productive citizenship. Similarly, the Nation's Black colleges have provided opportunity and undergraduate education to the vast majority of college-educated Black Americans.

38   More recently, our institutions of higher education have provided the scientists and skilled technicians who helped us transcend the boundaries of our planet. In the last 30 years, the schools have been a major vehicle for expanded social opportunity, and now graduate 75 percent of our young people from high school. Indeed, the proportion of Americans of college age enrolled in higher education is nearly twice that of Japan and far exceeds other nations such as France, West

Germany, and the Soviet Union. Moreover, when international comparisons were last made a decade ago, the top 9
percent of American students compared favorably in achievement with their peers in other countries.

In addition, many large urban areas in recent years report   39
that average student achievement in elementary schools is
improving. More and more schools are also offering advanced
placement programs and programs for gifted and talented students, and more and more students are enrolling in them.

We are the inheritors of a past that gives us every reason to   40
believe that we will succeed.

A Final Word

This is not the first or only commission on education, and   41
some of our findings are surely not new, but old business that
now at last must be done. For no one can doubt that the
United States is under challenge from many quarters.

Children born today can expect to graduate from high   42
school in the year 2000. We dedicate our report not only to
these children, but also to those now in school and others to
come. We firmly believe that a movement of America's
schools in the direction called for by our recommendations
will prepare these children for far more effective lives in a far
stronger America.

Our final word, perhaps better characterized as a plea, is   43
that all segments of our population give attention to the implementation of our recommendations. Our present plight did
not appear overnight, and the responsibility for our current
situation is widespread. Reform of our educational system will
take time and unwavering commitment. It will require equally
widespread, energetic, and dedicated action. For example, we
call upon the National Academy of Sciences, National Academy of Engineering, Institute of Medicine, Science Service,
National Science Foundation, Social Science Research Council, American Council of Learned Societies, National Endowment for the Humanities, National Endowment for the Arts,
and other scholarly, scientific, and learned societies for their
help in this effort. Help should come from students themselves; from parents, teachers, and school boards; from colleges and universities; from local, State, and Federal officials;
from teachers' and administrators' organizations; from industrial and labor councils; and from other groups with interest in
and responsibility for educational reform.

44   It is their America, and the America of all of us, that is at
risk; it is to each of us that this imperative is addressed. It is
by our willingness to take up the challenge, and our resolve to
see it through, that America's place in the world will be either
secured or forfeited. Americans have succeeded before and so
we shall again.

Charles Dickens
What Is a Horse?

*Was Charles Dickens (1812–1870) the greatest English novel-
ist? This selection from the opening pages of* Hard Times
*(1854) illustrates Dickens's satiric edge; designed as a com-
mentary on a "mechanical" system of education devised during
the industrial revolution, it may also offer perspective on the
schools of today.*

1   Thomas Gradgrind, sir. A man of realities. A man of fact
and calculations. A man who proceeds upon the principle
that two and two are four, and nothing over, and who is not to
be talked into allowing for anything over. Thomas Gradgrind,
sir—peremptorily Thomas—Thomas Gradgrind. With a rule
and a pair of scales, and the multiplication table always in his
pocket, sir, ready to weigh and measure any parcel of human
nature, and tell you exactly what it comes to. It is a mere
question of figures, case of simple arithmetic. You might
hope to get some other nonsensical belief into the head of
George Gradgrind, or Augustus Gradgrind, or John Gradgrind, or Joseph Gradgrind (all suppositious, nonexistent persons), but into the head of Thomas Gradgrind—no sir!

2   In such terms Mr Gradgrind always mentally introduced
himself, whether to his private circle of acquaintance, or to
the public in general. In such terms, no doubt, substituting
the words 'boys and girls', for 'sir', Thomas Gradgrind now
presented Thomas Gradgrind to the little pitchers before him,
who were to be filled so full of facts.

3   Indeed, as he eagerly sparkled at them from the cellarage
before mentioned, he seemed a kind of cannon loaded to the
muzzle with facts, and prepared to blow them clean out of the
regions of the childhood at one discharge. He seemed a galva-

nizing apparatus, too, charged with a grim mechanical substitute for the tender young imaginations that were to be
stormed away.

'Girl number twenty,' said Mr Gradgrind, squarely pointing   4
with his square forefinger, 'I don't know that girl. Who is that
girl?'

'Sissy Jupe, sir,' explained number twenty, blushing, stand-   5
ing up, and curtseying.

'Sissy is not a name,' said Mr Gradgrind. 'Don't call your-   6
self Sissy. Call yourself Cecilia.'

'It's father as calls me Sissy, sir,' returned the young girl in   7
a trembling voice, and with another curtsey.

'Then he has no business to do it,' said Mr Gradgrind. 'Tell   8
him he mustn't. Cecilia Jupe. Let me see. What is your father?'

'He belongs to the horse-riding, if you please, sir.'   9

Mr Gradgrind frowned, and waved off the objectionable   10
calling with his hand.

'We don't want to know anything about that, here. You   11
mustn't tell us about that, here. Your father breaks horses,
don't he?'

'If you please, sir, when they can get any to break, they do   12
break horses in the ring, sir.'

'You mustn't tell us about the ring, here. Very well, then.   13
Describe your father as a horsebreaker. He doctors sick
horses, I dare say?'

'Oh yes, sir.'   14

'Very well, then. He is a veterinary surgeon, a farrier and   15
horsebreaker. Give me your definition of a horse.'

(Sissy Jupe thrown into the greatest alarm by this   16
demand.)

'Girl number twenty unable to define a horse!' said Mr   17
Gradgrind, for the general behoof of all the little pitchers.
'Girl number twenty possessed of no facts, in reference to one
of the commonest of animals! Some boy's definition of a
horse. Bitzer, yours.'

The square finger, moving here and there, lighted suddenly   18
on Bitzer, perhaps because he chanced to sit in the same ray
of sunlight which, darting in at one of the bare windows of the
intensely whitewashed room, irradiated Sissy. For, the boys
and girls sat on the face of the inclined plane in two compact
bodies, divided up the centre by a narrow interval; and Sissy,
being at the corner of a row on the sunny side, came in for the
beginning of a sunbeam, of which Bitzer, being at the corner
of a row on the other side, a few rows in advance, caught the
end. But, whereas the girl was so dark-eyed and dark-haired,

that she seemed to receive a deeper and more lustrous colour from the sun when it shone upon her, the boy was so light-eyed and light-haired that the self-same rays appeared to draw out of him what little colour he ever possessed. His cold eyes would hardly have been eyes, but for the short ends of lashes which, by bringing them into immediate contrast with something paler than themselves, expressed their form. His short-cropped hair might have been a mere continuation of the sandy freckles on his forehead and face. His skin was so unwholesomely deficient in the natural tinge, that he looked as though, if he were cut, he would bleed white.

19   'Bitzer,' said Thomas Gradgrind. 'Your definition of a horse.'

20   'Quadruped. Graminivorous. Forty teeth, namely twenty-four grinders, four eye-teeth, and twelve incisive. Sheds coat in the spring; in marshy countries, sheds hoofs, too. Hoofs hard, but requiring to be shod with iron. Age known by marks in mouth.' Thus (and much more) Bitzer.

21   'Now girl number twenty,' said Mr Gradgrind. 'You know what a horse is.'

Jerome Stern

What They Learn in School

Jerome Stern teaches English at Florida State University. This "monologue" aired March 17, 1989, on National Public Radio's "All Things Considered." It was later reprinted in Harper's *magazine.*

1   In the schools now, they want them to know all about marijuana, crack, heroin, and amphetamines,

2   Because then they won't be interested in marijuana, crack, heroin, and amphetamines,

3   But they don't want to tell them anything about sex because if the schools tell them about sex, then they will be interested in sex,

4   But if the schools don't tell them anything about sex,

5   Then they will have high morals and no one will get pregnant, and everything will be all right,

And they do want them to know a lot about computers so 6
    they will outcompete the Japanese,

But they don't want them to know anything about real sci- 7
    ence because then they will lose their faith and become
    secular humanists,

And they do want them to know all about this great land of 8
    ours so they will be patriotic,

But they don't want them to learn about the tragedy and 9
    pain in its real history because then they will be critical
    about this great land of ours and we will be passively
    taken over by a foreign power,

And they want them to learn how to think for themselves so 10
    they can get good jobs and be successful,

But they don't want them to have books that confront them 11
    with real ideas because that will confuse their values,

And they'd like them to be good parents, 12

But they can't teach them about families because that takes 13
    them back to how you get to be a family,

And they want to warn them about how not to get AIDS 14

But that would mean telling them how not to get AIDS, 15

And they'd like them to know the Constitution, 16

But they don't like some of those amendments except when 17
    they are invoked by the people they agree with,

And they'd like them to vote, 18

But they don't want them to discuss current events because 19
    it might be controversial and upset them and make them
    want to take drugs, which they already have told them all
    about,

And they want to teach them the importance of morality, 20

But they also want them to learn that Winning is not every- 21
    thing—it is the Only Thing,

And they want them to be well-read, 22

But they don't want them to read Chaucer or Shakespeare 23
    or Aristophanes or Mark Twain or Ernest Hemingway or
    John Steinbeck, because that will corrupt them,

And they don't want them to know anything about art 24
    because that will make them weird,

But they do want them to know about music so they can 25
    march in the band,

And they mainly want to teach them not to question, not to 26
    challenge, not to imagine, but to be obedient and behave
    well so that they can hold them forever as children to
    their bosoms as the second millennium lurches toward
    its panicky close.

WHAT'S COLLEGE FOR?

Alice Walker

Everyday Use

for your grandmama

Alice Walker (born 1944) is an essayist, poet, feminist, and activist, but she is best known for her Pulitzer Prize–winning third novel The Color Purple *(1982). Asked why she writes, she once explained, "I'm really paying homage to people I love, the people who are thought to be dumb and backward but who were the ones who first taught me to see beauty." "Everyday Use" appeared in her acclaimed collection of stories,* In Love and Trouble, *published in 1973.*

1   I will wait for her in the yard that Maggie and I made so clean and wavy yesterday afternoon. A yard like this is more comfortable than most people know. It is not just a yard. It is like an extended living room. When the hard clay is swept clean as a floor and the fine sand around the edges lined with tiny, irregular grooves anyone can come and sit and look up into the elm tree and wait for the breezes that never come inside the house.

2   Maggie will be nervous until after her sister goes: she will stand hopelessly in corners homely and ashamed of the burn scars down her arms and legs, eyeing her sister with a mixture of envy and awe. She thinks her sister has held life always in the palm of one hand, that "no" is a word the world never learned to say to her.

3   You've no doubt seen those TV shows where the child who has "made it" is confronted, as a surprise, by her own mother and father, tottering in weakly from backstage. (A pleasant surprise, of course: What would they do if parent and child came on the show only to curse out and insult each other?) On TV mother and child embrace and smile into each other's

faces. Sometimes the mother and father weep, the child wraps them in her arms and leans across the table to tell how she would not have made it without their help. I have seen these programs.

Sometimes I dream a dream in which Dee and I are sud-   4
denly brought together on a TV program of this sort. Out of a dark and soft-seated limousine I am ushered into a bright room filled with many people. There I meet a smiling, gray, sporty man like Johnny Carson who shakes my hand and tells me what a fine girl I have. Then we are on the stage and Dee is embracing me with tears in her eyes. She pins on my dress a large orchid, even though she has told me once that she thinks orchids are tacky flowers.

In real life I am a large, big-boned woman with rough,   5
man-working hands. In the winter I wear flannel nightgowns to bed and overalls during the day. I can kill and clean a hog as mercilessly as a man. My fat keeps me hot in zero weather. I can work outside all day, breaking ice to get water for wash-ing; I can eat pork liver cooked over the open fire minutes after it comes steaming from the hog. One winter I knocked a bull calf straight in the brain between the eyes with a sledge hammer and had the meat hung up to chill before nightfall. But of course all this does not show on television. I am the way my daughter would want me to be: a hundred pounds lighter, my skin like an uncooked barley pancake. My hair glistens in the hot bright lights. Johnny Carson has much to do to keep up with my quick and witty tongue.

But that is a mistake. I know even before I wake up. Who   6
ever knew a Johnson with a quick tongue? Who can even imagine me looking a strange white man in the eye? It seems to me I have talked to them always with one foot raised in flight, and my head turned in whichever way is farthest from them. Dee, though. She would always look anyone in the eye. Hesitation was no part of her nature.

"How do I look, Mama?" Maggie says, showing just enough   7
of her thin body enveloped in pink skirt and red blouse for me to know she's there, almost hidden by the door.

"Come out into the yard," I say.   8

Have you ever seen a lame animal, perhaps a dog run over   9
by some careless person rich enough to own a car, sidle up to someone who is ignorant enough to be kind to him? That is the way my Maggie walks. She has been like this, chin on chest, eyes on ground, feet in shuffle, ever since the fire that burned the other house to the ground.

10   Dee is lighter than Maggie, with nicer hair and a fuller figure. She's a woman now, though sometimes I forget. How
long ago was it that the other house burned? Ten, twelve
years? Sometimes I can still hear the flames and feel Maggie's
arms sticking to me, her hair smoking and her dress falling
off her in little black papery flakes. Her eyes seemed stretched
open, blazed open by the flames reflected in them. And Dee. I
see her standing off under the sweet gum tree she used to dig
gum out of: a look of concentration on her face as she
watched the last dingy gray board of the house fall in toward
the red-hot brick chimney. Why don't you do a dance around
the ashes? I'd wanted to ask her. She hated the house that
much.

11   I used to think she hated Maggie, too. But that was before
we raised the money, the church and me, to send her to
Augusta to school. She used to read to us without pity; forcing words, lies, other folks' habits, whole lives upon us two,
sitting trapped and ignorant underneath her voice. She
washed us in a river of make-believe, burned us with a lot of
knowledge we didn't necessarily need to know. Pressed us to
her with the serious way she read, to shove us away at just the
moment, like dimwits, we seemed about to understand.

12   Dee wanted nice things. A yellow organdy dress to wear to
her graduation from high school; black pumps to match a
green suit she'd made from an old suit somebody gave me.
She was determined to stare down any disaster in her efforts.
Her eyelids would not flicker for minutes at a time. Often I
fought off the temptation to shake her. At sixteen she had a
style of her own: and knew what style was.

13   I never had an education myself. After second grade the
school was closed down. Don't ask me why: in 1927 colored
asked fewer questions than they do now. Sometimes Maggie
reads to me. She stumbles along good-naturedly but can't see
well. She knows she is not bright. Like good looks and money,
quickness passed her by. She will marry John Thomas (who
has mossy teeth in an earnest face) and then I'll be free to sit
here and I guess just sing church songs to myself. Although I
never was a good singer. Never could carry a tune. I was
always better at a man's job. I used to love to milk till I was
hooked in the side in '49. Cows are soothing and slow and
don't bother you, unless you try to milk them the wrong way.

14   I have deliberately turned my back on the house. It is three
rooms, just like the one that burned, except the roof is tin;
they don't make shingle roofs anymore. There are no real

windows, just some holes cut in the sides, like the portholes in a ship, but not round and not square, with rawhide holding the shutters up on the outside. This house is in a pasture, too, like the other one. No doubt when Dee sees it she will want to tear it down. She wrote me once that no matter where we "choose" to live, she will manage to come see us. But she will never bring her friends. Maggie and I thought about this and Maggie asked me, "Mama, when did Dee ever *have* any friends?"

She had a few. Furtive boys in pink shirts hanging about   15
on washday after school. Nervous girls who never laughed. Impressed with her they worshiped the well-turned phrase, the cute shape, the scalding humor that erupted like bubbles in lye. She read to them.

When she was courting Jimmy T she didn't have much   16
time to pay to us, but turned all her faultfinding power on him. He *flew* to marry a cheap gal from a family of ignorant flashy people. She hardly had time to recompose herself.

When she comes I will meet—but there they are!   17

Maggie attempts to make a dash for the house, in her shuf-   18
fling way, but I stay her with my hand. "Come back here," I say. And she stops and tries to dig a well in the sand with her toe.

It is hard to see them clearly through the strong sun. But   19
even the first glimpse of leg out of the car tells me it is Dee. Her feet were always neat-looking, as if God himself had shaped them with a certain style. From the other side of the car comes a short, stocky man. Hair is all over his head a foot long and hanging from his chin like a kinky mule tail. I hear Maggie suck in her breath. "Uhnnnh," is what it sounds like. Like when you see the wriggling end of a snake just in front of your foot on the road. "Uhnnnh."

Dee next. A dress down to the ground, in this hot weather.   20
A dress so loud it hurts my eyes. There are yellows and oranges enough to throw back the light of the sun. I feel my whole face warming from the heat waves it throws out. Ear-rings gold, too, and hanging down to her shoulders. Bracelets dangling and making noises when she moves her arm up to shake the folds of the dress out of her armpits. The dress is loose and flows, and as she walks closer, I like it. I hear Mag-gie go "Uhnnnh" again. It is her sister's hair. It stands straight up like the wool on a sheep. It is black as night and around the edges are two long pigtails that rope about like small liz-ards disappearing behind the ears.

21   "Wa-su-zo-Tean-o!" she says, coming on in that gliding way
the dress makes her move. The short stocky fellow with the
hair to his navel is all grinning and he follows up with "Asalamalakim, my mother and sister!" He moves to hug Maggie
but she falls back, right up against the back of my chair. I feel
her trembling there and when I look up I see the perspiration
falling off her chin.

22   "Don't get up," says Dee. Since I am stout it takes something of a push. You can see me trying to move a second or
two before I make it. She turns, showing white heels through
her sandals, and goes back to the car. Out she peeks next
with a Polaroid. She stoops down quickly and lines up picture after picture of me sitting there in front of the house
with Maggie cowering behind me. She never takes a shot
without making sure the house is included. When a cow
comes nibbling around the edge of the yard she snaps it and
me and Maggie *and* the house. Then she puts the Polaroid in
the back seat of the car, and comes up and kisses me on the
forehead.

23   Meanwhile Asalamalakim is going through the motions
with Maggie's hand. Maggie's hand is as limp as a fish, and
probably as cold, despite the sweat, and she keeps trying to
pull it back. It looks like Asalamalakim wants to shake hands
but wants to do it fancy. Or maybe he don't know how people
shake hands. Anyhow, he soon gives up on Maggie.

24   "Well," I say. "Dee."

25   "No, Mama," she says. "Not 'Dee,' Wangero Leewanika
Kemanjo!"

26   "What happened to 'Dee'?" I wanted to know.

27   "She's dead." Wangero said. "I couldn't bear it any longer
being named after the people who oppress me."

28   "You know as well as me you was named after your aunt
Dicie," I said. Dicie is my sister. She named Dee. We called
her "Big Dee" after Dee was born.

29   "But who was *she* named after?" asked Wangero.

30   "I guess after Grandma Dee," I said.

31   "And who was she named after?" asked Wangero.

32   "Her mother," I said, and saw Wangero was getting tired.
"That's about as far back as I can trace it," I said. Though, in
fact, I probably could have carried it back beyond the Civil
War through the branches.

33   "Well," said Asalamalakim, "there you are."

34   "Uhnnnh," I heard Maggie say.

35   "There I was not," I said, "before 'Dicie' cropped up in our
family, so why should I try to trace it that far back?"

He just stood there grinning, looking down on me like   36
somebody inspecting a Model A car. Every once in a while he
and Wangero sent eye signals over my head.

"How do you pronounce this name?" I asked.   37

"You don't have to call me by it if you don't want to," said   38
Wangero.

"Why shouldn't I?" I asked. "If that's what you want us to   39
call you, we'll call you."

"I know it might sound awkward at first," said Wangero.   40

"I'll get used to it," I said. "Ream it out again."   41

Well, soon we got the name out of the way. Asalamalakim   42
had a name twice as long and three times as hard. After I
tripped over it two or three times he told me to just call him
Hakim-a-barber. I wanted to ask him was he a barber, but I
didn't really think he was, so I didn't ask.

"You must belong to those beef-cattle peoples down the   43
road," I said. They said "Asalamalakim" when they met you,
too, but they didn't shake hands. Always too busy: feeding the
cattle, fixing the fences, putting up salt-lick shelters, throwing
down hay. When the white folks poisoned some of the herd
the men stayed up all night with rifles in their hands. I walked
a mile and a half just to see the sight.

Hakim-a-barber said, "I accept some of their doctrines, but   44
farming and raising cattle is not my style." (They didn't tell
me, and I didn't ask, whether Wangero [Dee] had really gone
and married him.)

We sat down to eat and right away he said he didn't eat col-   45
lards and pork was unclean. Wangero, though, went on
through the chitlins and corn bread, the greens and everything else. She talked a blue streak over the sweet potatoes.
Everything delighted her. Even the fact that we still used the
benches her daddy made for the table when we couldn't
afford to buy chairs.

"Oh, Mama!" she cried. Then turned to Hakim-a-barber. "I   46
never knew how lovely these benches are. You can feel the
rump prints," she said, running her hands underneath her
and along the bench. Then she gave a sigh and her hand
closed over Grandma Dee's butter dish. "That's it!" she said. "I
knew there was something I wanted to ask you if I could
have." She jumped up from the table and went over in the
corner where the churn stood, the milk in it clabber by now.
She looked at the churn and looked at it.

"This churn top is what I need," she said. "Didn't Uncle   47
Buddy whittle it out of a tree you all used to have?"

"Yes," I said.   48

49   "Uh huh," she said happily. "And I want the dasher, too."
50   "Uncle Buddy whittle that, too?" asked the barber.
51   Dee (Wangero) looked up at me.
52   "Aunt Dee's first husband whittle the dash," said Maggie so
low you almost couldn't hear her. "His name was Henry, but
they called him Stash."
53   "Maggie's brain is like an elephant's," Wangero said, laughing. "I can use the churn top as a centerpiece for the alcove
table," she said, sliding a plate over the churn, "and I'll think
of something artistic to do with the dasher."
54   When she finished wrapping the dasher the handle stuck
out. I took it for a moment in my hands. You didn't even have
to look close to see where hands pushing the dasher up and
down to make butter had left a kind of sink in the wood. In
fact, there were a lot of small sinks; you could see where
thumbs and fingers had sunk into the wood. It was beautiful
light yellow wood, from a tree that grew in the yard where Big
Dee and Stash had lived.
55   After dinner Dee (Wangero) went to the trunk at the foot of
my bed and started rifling through it. Maggie hung back in
the kitchen over the dishpan. Out came Wangero with two
quilts. They had been pieced by Grandma Dee and then Big
Dee and me had hung them on the quilt frames on the front
porch and quilted them. One was in the Lone Star pattern.
The other was Walk Around the Mountain. In both of them
were scraps of dresses Grandma Dee had worn fifty and more
years ago. Bits and pieces of Grandpa Jarrell's Paisley shirts.
And one teeny faded blue piece, about the size of a penny
matchbox, that was from Great Grandpa Ezra's uniform that
he wore in the Civil War.
56   "Mama," Wangero said sweet as a bird. "Can I have these
old quilts?"
57   I heard something fall in the kitchen, and a minute later
the kitchen door slammed.
58   "Why don't you take one or two of the others?" I asked.
"These old things was just done by me and Big Dee from
some tops your grandma pieced before she died."
59   "No," said Wangero. "I don't want those. They are stitched
around the borders by machine."
60   "That'll make them last better," I said.
61   "That's not the point," said Wangero. "These are all pieces
of dresses Grandma used to wear. She did all this stitching by
hand. Imagine!" She held the quilts securely in her arms,
stroking them.

"Some of the pieces, like those lavender ones, come from 62
old clothes her mother handed down to her," I said, moving up
to touch the quilts. Dee (Wangero) moved back just enough so
that I couldn't reach the quilts. They already belonged to her.

"Imagine!" she breathed again, clutching them closely to 63
her bosom.

"The truth is," I said, "I promised to give them quilts to 64
Maggie, for when she marries John Thomas."

She gasped like a bee had stung her. 65

"Maggie can't appreciate these quilts!" she said. "She'd 66
probably be backward enough to put them to everyday use."

"I reckon she would," I said. "God knows I been saving 'em 67
for long enough with nobody using 'em. I hope she will!" I
didn't want to bring up how I had offered Dee (Wangero) a
quilt when she went away to college. Then she had told me
they were old-fashioned, out of style.

"But they're *priceless!*" she was saying now, furiously; for 68
she has a temper. "Maggie would put them on the bed and in
five years they'd be in rags. Less than that!"

"She can always make some more," I said. "Maggie knows 69
how to quilt."

Dee (Wangero) looked at me with hatred. "You just will not 70
understand. The point is these quilts, *these* quilts!"

"Well," I said, stumped. "What would *you* do with them?" 71

"Hang them," she said. As if that was the only thing you 72
could do with quilts.

Maggie by now was standing in the door. I could almost 73
hear the sound her feet made as they scraped over each other.

"She can have them, Mama," she said, like somebody used 74
to never winning anything, or having anything reserved for
her. "I can 'member Grandma Dee without the quilts."

I looked at her hard. She had filled her bottom lip with 75
checkerberry snuff and it gave her face a kind of dopey, hang-
dog look. It was Grandma Dee and Big Dee who taught her
how to quilt herself. She stood there with her scarred hands
hidden in the folds of her skirt. She looked at her sister with
something like fear but she wasn't mad at her. This was Maggie's portion. This was the way she knew God to work.

When I looked at her like that something hit me in the top 76
of my head and ran down to the soles of my feet. Just like
when I'm in church and the spirit of God touches me and I get
happy and shout. I did something I never had done before:
hugged Maggie to me, then dragged her on into the room,
snatched the quilts out of Miss Wangero's hands and dumped

them into Maggie's lap. Maggie just sat there on my bed with her mouth open.

77   "Take one or two of the others," I said to Dee.

78   But she turned without a word and went out to Hakim-a-barber.

79   "You just don't understand," she said, as Maggie and I came out to the car.

80   "What don't I understand?" I wanted to know.

81   "Your heritage," she said. And then she turned to Maggie, kissed her, and said, "You ought to try to make something of yourself, too, Maggie. It's really a new day for us. But from the way you and Mama still live you'd never know it."

82   She put on some sunglasses that hid everything above the tip of her nose and her chin.

83   Maggie smiled; maybe at the sunglasses. But a real smile, not scared. After we watched the car dust settle I asked Maggie to bring me a dip of snuff. And then the two of us sat there just enjoying, until it was time to go in the house and go to bed.

bell hooks

Pedagogy and Political Commitment: A Comment

bell hooks teaches at Oberlin College in Ohio. You will learn more about her by reading the following essay, which is a chapter in her book Talking Back: Thinking Feminist, Thinking Black *(1989), one of her nine books on race, gender, politics, and culture. (A second essay by bell hooks appears elsewhere in this book, on page 216.)*

1   Education is a political issue for exploited and oppressed people. The history of slavery in the United States shows that black people regarded education—book learning, reading, and writing—as a political necessity. Struggle to resist white supremacy and racist attacks informed black attitudes toward education. Without the capacity to read and write, to think critically and analytically, the liberated slave would remain forever bound, dependent on the will of the oppressor.

No aspect of black liberation struggled in the United States has been as charged with revolutionary fervor as the effort to gain access to education at all levels.

From slavery to the present, education has been revered in   2
black communities, yet it has also been suspect. Education represented a means of radical resistance but it also led to caste/class divisions between the educated and the uneducated, as it meant the learned black person could more easily adopt the values and attitudes of the oppressor. Education could help one assimilate. If one could not become the white oppressor, one could at least speak and think like him or her, and in some cases the educated black person assumed the role of mediator—explaining uneducated black folks to white folks.

Given this history, many black parents have encouraged   3
children to acquire an education while simultaneously warning us about the danger of education. One very real danger, as many black parents traditionally perceived it, was that the learned black person might lose touch with the concrete reality of everyday black experience. Books and ideas were important but not important enough to become barriers between the individual and community participation. Education was considered to have the potential to alienate one from community and awareness of our collective circumstance as black people. In my family, it was constantly emphasized that too much book learning could lead to madness. Among everyday black folks, madness was deemed to be any loss of one's ability to communicate effectively with others, one's ability to cope with practical affairs.

These ambivalent attitudes toward education have made it   4
difficult for black students to adapt and succeed in educational settings. Many of us have found that to succeed at the very education we had been encouraged to seek would be most easily accomplished if we separated ourselves from the experience of black folk, the underprivileged experience of the black underclass that was our grounding reality. This ambivalent stance toward education has had a tremendous impact on my psyche. Within the working-class black community where I grew up, I learned to be suspicious of education and suspicious of white folks. I went for my formative educational years to all-black schools. In those schools, I learned about the reality of white people but also about the reality of black people, about our history. We were taught in those schools to be proud of ourselves as black people and to work for the uplift of our race.

5   Experiencing as I did an educational environment struc-
     tured to meet our needs as black people, we were deeply
     affected when those schools ceased to exist and we were com-
     pelled to attend white schools instead. At the white school, we
     were no longer people with a history, a culture. We did not
     exist as anything other than primitives and slaves. School was
     no longer the place where one learned how to use education
     as a means to resist white-supremacist oppression. Small
     wonder that I spent my last few years of high school
     depressed about education, feeling as though we had suffered
     a grave loss, that the direction had shifted, the goals had
     changed. We were no longer taught by people who spoke our
     language, who understood our culture; we were taught by
     strangers. And further, we were dependent on those strangers
     for evaluation, for approval. We learned not to challenge their
     racism since they had power over us. Although we were told
     at home that we were not to openly challenge whites, we were
     also told not to learn to think like them.

6   Within this atmosphere of ambivalence toward education,
     I, who had been dubbed smart, was uncertain about whether
     or not I wanted to go to college. School was an oppressive
     drag. Yet the fate of smart black women had already been
     decided; we would be schoolteachers. At the private, mostly
     white women's college where I spent my first year, I was an
     outsider. Determined to stay grounded in the reality of south-
     ern black culture, I kept myself aloof from the social practices
     of the white women with whom I lived and studied. They, in
     their turn, perceived me as hostile and alien. I, who had
     always been a member of a community, was now a loner. One
     of my white teachers suggested to me that the alienation I
     experienced was caused by being at a school that was not
     intellectually challenging, that I should go to Stanford where
     she had gone.

7   My undergraduate years at Stanford were difficult ones.
     Not only did I feel myself alienated from the white people
     who were my peers and teachers, but I met black people who
     were different, who did not think the way I did about black
     culture or black life—who seemed in some ways as strange to
     me as white people. I had known black people from different
     classes in my hometown, but we still experienced much the
     same reality, shared similar world views. It was different at
     Stanford. I was in an environment where black people's class
     backgrounds and their values were radically different than
     my own.

To overcome my feelings of isolation, I bonded with work- 8
ers, with black women who labored as maids, as secretaries.
With them I felt at home. During holiday break, I would stay
in their homes. Yet being with them was not the same as
being home. In their houses I was an honored guest, someone
to be looked up to, because I was getting a college education.
My undergraduate years at Stanford were spent struggling to
find meaning and significance in education. I had to succeed.
I could not let my family or the race down. And so I graduated in English. I had become an English major for the same
reason that hundreds of students of all races become English
majors: I like to read. Yet I did not fully understand that the
study of literature in English departments would really mean
the study of works by white males.

It was disheartening for me and other non-white students 9
to face the extent to which education in the university was
not the site of openness and intellectual challenge we had
longed for. We hated the racism, the sexism, the domination.
I began to have grave doubts about the future. Why was I
working to be an academic if I did not see people in that environment who were opposing domination? Even those very
few concerned professors who endeavored to make courses
interesting, to create a learning atmosphere, rarely acknowledged destructive and oppressive aspects of authoritarian rule
in and outside the classroom. Whether one took courses from
professors with feminist politics or marxist politics, their presentations of self in the classroom never differed from the
norm. This was especially so with marxist professors. I asked
one of these professors, a white male, how he could expect students to take his politics seriously as a radical alternative to a
capitalist structure if we found marxist professors to be even
more oppressively authoritarian than other professors. Everyone seemed reluctant to talk about the fact that professors
who advocated radical politics rarely allowed their critique of
domination and oppression to influence teaching strategies.
The absence of any model of a professor who was combining a
radical politic opposing domination with practice of that politic in the classroom made me feel wary about my ability to do
differently. When I first began to teach, I tried not to emulate
my professors in any way. I devised different strategies and
approaches that I felt were more in keeping with my politics.
Reading the work of Paulo Freire greatly influenced my sense
that much was possible in the classroom setting, that one did
not simply need to conform.

10   In the introduction to a conversation with Paulo Freire
published in *idac,* emphasis is placed on an educative process
that is not based on an authoritarian, dominating model
where knowledge is transferred from a powerful professor to
a powerless student. Education, it was suggested, could be a
space for the development of critical consciousness, where
there could be dialogue and mutual growth of both student
and professor:

> If we accept education in this richer and more dynamic sense
> of acquiring a critical capacity and intervention in reality, we
> immediately know that there is no such thing as neutral edu-
> cation. All education has an intention, a goal, which can only
> be political. Either it mystifies reality by rendering it impene-
> trable and obscure—which leads people to a blind march
> through incomprehensible labyrinths—or it unmasks the eco-
> nomic and social structures which are determining the rela-
> tionships of exploitation and oppression among persons,
> knocking down labyrinths and allowing people to walk their
> own road. So we find ourselves confronted with a clear
> option: to educate for liberation or to educate for domination.

In retrospect, it seems that my most radical professors were
still educating for domination. And I wondered if this was so
because we could not imagine how to educate for liberation
in the corporate university. In Freire's case, he speaks as a
white man of privilege who stands and acts in solidarity with
oppressed and exploited groups, especially in their efforts to
establish literacy programs that emphasize education for critical consciousness. In my case, as a black woman from a
working-class background, I stand and act as a member of an
oppressed, exploited group who has managed to acquire a
degree of privilege. While I choose to educate for liberation,
the site of my work has been within the walls of universities
peopled largely by privileged white students and a few non-
white students. Within those walls, I have tried to teach literature and Women's Studies courses in a way that does not
reinforce structures of domination: imperialism, racism, sexism, and class exploitation.

11   I do not pretend that my approach is politically neutral, yet
this disturbs students who have been led to believe that all
education within the university should be "neutral." On the
first day of classes, I talk about my approach, about the ways
the class may be different from other classes as we work to
create strategies of learning to meet our needs—and of course

we must discover together what those needs are. Even though I explain that the class will be different, students do not always take it seriously. One central difference is that all students are expected to contribute to class discussion, if not spontaneously, then through the reading of paragraphs and short papers. In this way, every student makes a contribution, every student's voice is heard. Despite the fact that this may be stated at the onset of class, written clearly on the syllabus, students will complain and whine about having to speak. It is only recently that I have begun to see much of the complaining as "change back" behavior. Students and teachers find it hard to shift their paradigms even though they have been longing for a different approach.

Struggling to educate for liberation in the corporate university is a process that I have found enormously stressful. Implementing new teaching strategies that aim to subvert the norm, to engage students fully, is really a difficult task. Unlike the oppressed or colonized, who may begin to feel as they engage in education for critical consciousness a newfound sense of power and identity that frees them from colonization of the mind, that liberates, privileged students are often downright unwilling to acknowledge that their minds have been colonized, that they have been learning how to be oppressors, how to dominate, or at least how to passively accept the domination of others. This past teaching year, a student confronted me (a black male student from a middle-class urban experience) in class with the question of what I expected from them (like his tone of voice was: did I have the right to expect anything). Seriously, he wanted to know what I wanted from them. I told him and the class that I thought the most important learning experience that could happen in our classroom was that students would learn to think critically and analytically, not just about the required books, but about the world they live in. Education for critical consciousness that encourages all students—privileged or non-privileged—who are seeking an entry into class privilege rather than providing a sense of freedom and release, invites critique of conventional expectations and desires. They may find such an experience terribly threatening. And even though they may approach the situation with great openness, it may still be difficult, and even painful.

This past semester, I taught a course on black women writers in which students were encouraged to think about the social context in which literature emerges, the impact of politics of domination—racism, sexism, class exploitation—on the writing. Students stated quite openly and honestly that reading the literature in the context of class discussion was making them feel pain. They complained that everything was changing for them, that they were seeing the world differently, and seeing things in that world that were painful to face. Never before had a group of students so openly talked about the way in which learning to see the world critically was causing pain. I did not belittle their pain or try to rationalize it. Initially, I was uncertain about how to respond and just asked us all to think about it. Later, we discussed the way in which all their comments implied that to experience pain is bad, an indication that something is wrong. We talked about changing how we perceive pain, about our society's approach to pain, considering the possibility that this pain could be a constructive sign of growth. I shared with them my sense that the experience should not be viewed as static, that at another point the knowledge and new perspectives they had might lead to clarity and a greater sense of well-being.

14   Education for liberation can work in the university setting but it does not lead students to feel they are enjoying class or necessarily feeling positive about me as a teacher. One aspect of radical pedagogy that has been difficult for me is learning to cope with not being seen positively by students. When one provides an experience of learning that is challenging, possibly threatening, it is not entertainment, or necessarily a fun experience, though it can be. If one primary function of such a pedagogy is to prepare students to live and act more fully in the world, then it is usually when they are in that context, outside the classroom, that they most feel and experience the value of what they have shared and learned. For me, this often means that most positive feedback I receive as a teacher comes after students have left the class and rarely during it.

15   Recently talking with a group of students and faculty at Duke University, we focussed on the issue of exposure and vulnerability. One white male professor, who felt his politics to be radical, his teaching to be an education for liberation, his teaching strategies subversive, felt it was important that no one in the university's bureaucratic structure know what was happening in the classroom. Fear of exposure may lead teachers with radical visions to suppress insight, to follow set norms. Until I came to teach at Yale, no one outside my classes had paid much attention to what was going on inside them. At Yale, students talked a lot outside about my classes, about what happens in them. This was very difficult for me as I felt both exposed and constantly scrutinized. I was certainly

subjected to much critical feedback both from students in my classes and faculty and students who heard about them. Their responses forced recognition of the way in which teaching that is overtly political, especially if it radically challenges the status quo, requires acknowledgement that to choose education as the practice of freedom is to take a political stance that may have serious consequences.

Despite negative feedback or pressures, the most reward-   16
ing aspect of such teaching is to influence the way students mature and grow intellectually and spiritually. For those students who wish to try to learn in a new way but who have fears, I try to reassure them that their involvement in different types of learning experiences need not threaten their security in other classes; it will not destroy the backing system of education, so they need not panic. Of course, if all they can do is panic, then that is a sign that the course is not for them. My commitment to education as the practice of freedom is strengthened by the large number of students who take my courses and, by doing so, affirm their longing to learn in a new way. Their testimony confirms that education as the practice of liberation does take place in university settings, that our lives are transformed there, that there we do meaningful radical political work.

Adrienne Rich
Claiming an Education

"Claiming an Education" is the transcript of a talk first given to new students at Douglass College, the Women's College of Rutgers University, on September 6, 1977; later it was included in Adrienne Rich's book On Lies, Secrets, and Silence. *Rich (born 1929) is a noted teacher, essayist, and feminist who won the National Book Award for poetry in 1974.*

For this convocation, I planned to separate my remarks   1
into two parts: some thoughts about you, the women students here, and some thoughts about us who teach in a women's college. But ultimately, those two parts are indivisible. If university education means anything beyond the processing of

human beings into expected roles, through credit hours, tests, and grades (and I believe that in a women's college especially it *might* mean much more), it implies an ethical and intellectual contract between teacher and student. This contract must remain intuitive, dynamic, unwritten; but we must turn to it again and again if learning is to be reclaimed from the depersonalizing and cheapening pressures of the present-day academic scene.

2   The first thing I want to say to you who are students is that you cannot afford to think of being here to *receive* an education; you will do much better to think of yourselves as being here to *claim* one. One of the dictionary definitions of the verb "to claim" is: *to take as the rightful owner; to assert in the face of possible contradiction.* "To receive" is *to come into possession of; to act as receptacle or container for; to accept as authoritative or true.* The difference is that between acting and being acted-upon, and for women it can literally mean the difference between life and death.

3   One of the devastating weaknesses of university learning, of the store of knowledge and opinion that has been handed down through academic training, has been its almost total erasure of women's experience and thought from the curriculum, and its exclusion of women as members of the academic community. Today, with increasing numbers of women students in nearly every branch of higher learning, we still see very few women in the upper levels of faculty and administration in most institutions. Douglass College itself is a women's college in a university administered overwhelmingly by men, who in turn are answerable to the state legislature, again composed predominantly of men. But the most significant fact for you is that what you learn here, the very texts you read, the lectures you hear, the way your studies are divided into categories and fragmented one from the other—all this reflects, to a very large degree, neither objective reality, nor an accurate picture of the past, nor a group of rigorously tested observations about human behavior. What you can learn here (and I mean not only at Douglass but any college in any university) is how *men* have perceived and organized their experience, their history, their ideas of social relationships, good and evil, sickness and health, etc. When you read or hear about "great issues," "major texts," "the mainstream of Western thought," you are hearing about what men, above all white men, in their male subjectivity, have decided is important.

4   Black and other minority people have for some time recognized that their racial and ethnic experience was not

accounted for in the studies broadly labeled human; and that even the sciences can be racist. For many reasons, it has been more difficult for women to comprehend our exclusion, and to realize that even the sciences can be sexist. For one thing, it is only within the last hundred years that higher education has grudgingly been opened up to women at all, even to white, middle-class women. And many of us have found ourselves poring eagerly over books with titles like: *The Descent of Man; Man and His Symbols; Irrational Man; The Phenomenon of Man; The Future of Man; Man and the Machine; From Man to Man; May Man Prevail?; Man, Science and Society;* or *One-Dimensional Man*—books pretending to describe a "human" reality that does not include over one-half the human species.

Less than a decade ago, with the rebirth of a feminist 5 movement in this country, women students and teachers in a number of universities began to demand and set up women's studies courses—to *claim* a woman-directed education. And, despite the inevitable accusations of "unscholarly," "group therapy," "faddism," etc., despite backlash and budget cuts, women's studies are still growing, offering to more and more women a new intellectual grasp on their lives, new understanding of our history, a fresh vision of the human experience, and also a critical basis for evaluating what they hear and read in other courses, and in the society at large.

But my talk is not really about women's studies, much as I 6 believe in their scholarly, scientific, and human necessity. While I think that any Douglass student has everything to gain by investigating and enrolling in women's studies courses, I want to suggest that there is a more essential experience that you owe yourself, one which courses in women's studies can greatly enrich, but which finally depends on you, in all your interactions with yourself and your world. This is the experience of *taking responsibility toward yourself.* Our upbringing as women has so often told us that this should come second to our relationships and responsibilities to other people. We have been offered ethical models of the self-denying wife and mother; intellectual models of the brilliant but slapdash dilettante who never commits herself to anything the whole way, or the intelligent woman who denies her intelligence in order to seem more "feminine," or who sits in passive silence even when she disagrees inwardly with everything that is being said around her.

Responsibility to yourself means refusing to let others do 7 your thinking, talking, and naming for you; it means learning to respect and use your own brains and instincts; hence, grappling with hard work. It means that you do not treat your body as a commodity with which to purchase superficial intimacy or economic security; for our bodies and minds are inseparable in this life, and when we allow our bodies to be treated as objects, our minds are in mortal danger. It means insisting that those to whom you give your friendship and love are able to respect your mind. It means being able to say, with Charlotte Brontë's *Jane Eyre:* "I have an inward treasure born with me, which can keep me alive if all the extraneous delights should be withheld or offered only at a price I cannot afford to give."

8   Responsibility to yourself means that you don't fall for shallow and easy solutions—predigested books and ideas, weekend encounters guaranteed to change your life, taking "gut" courses instead of ones you know will challenge you, bluffing at school and life instead of doing solid work, marrying early as an escape from real decisions, getting pregnant as an evasion of already existing problems. It means that you refuse to sell your talents and aspirations short, simply to avoid conflict and confrontation. And this, in turn, means resisting the forces in society which say that women should be nice, play safe, have low professional expectations, drown in love and forget about work, live through others, and stay in the places assigned to us. It means that we insist on a life of meaningful work, insist that work be as meaningful as love and friendship in our lives. It means, therefore, the courage to be "different"; not to be continuously available to others when we need time for ourselves and our work; to be able to demand of others—parents, friends, roommates, teachers, lovers, husbands, children—that they respect our sense of purpose and our integrity as persons. Women everywhere are finding the courage to do this, more and more, and we are finding that courage both in our study of women in the past who possessed it, and in each other as we look at other women for comradeship, community, and challenge. The difference between a life lived actively, and a life of passive drifting and dispersal of energies, is an immense difference. Once we begin to feel committed to our lives, responsible to ourselves, we can never again be satisfied with the old, passive way.

9   Now comes the second part of the contract. I believe that in a women's college you have the right to expect your faculty to take you seriously. The education of women has been a matter of debate for centuries, and old, negative attitudes

about women's role, women's ability to think and take leadership, are still rife both in and outside the university. Many male professors (and I don't mean only at Douglass) still feel that teaching in a women's college is a second-rate career. Many tend to eroticize their women students—to treat them as sexual objects—instead of demanding the best of their minds. (At Yale a legal suit [*Alexander* v. *Yale*] has been brought against the university by a group of women students demanding a stated policy against sexual advances toward female students by male professors.) Many teachers, both men and women, trained in the male-centered tradition, are still handing the ideas and texts of that tradition on to students without teaching them to criticize its antiwoman attitudes, its omission of women as part of the species. Too often, all of us fail to teach the most important thing, which is that clear thinking, active discussion, and excellent writing are all necessary for intellectual freedom, and that these require *hard work*. Sometimes, perhaps in discouragement with a culture which is both anti-intellectual and antiwoman, we may resign ourselves to low expectations for our students before we have given them half a chance to become more thoughtful, expressive human beings. We need to take to heart the words of Elizabeth Barrett Browning, a poet, a thinking woman, and a feminist, who wrote in 1845 of her impatience with studies which cultivate a "passive recipiency" in the mind, and asserted that "women want to be made to *think actively:* their apprehension is quicker than that of men, but their defect lies for the most part in the logical faculty and in the higher mental activities." Note that she implies a defect which can be remedied by intellectual training, *not* an inborn lack of ability.

I have said that the contract on the student's part involves   10 that you demand to be taken seriously so that you can also go on taking yourself seriously. This means seeking out criticism, recognizing that the most affirming thing anyone can do for you is demand that you push yourself further, show you the range of what you *can* do. It means rejecting attitudes of "take-it-easy," "why-be-so-serious," "why-worry-you'll-probably-get-married-anyway." It means assuming your share of responsibility for what happens in the classroom, because that affects the quality of your daily life here. It means that the student sees herself engaged *with* her teachers in an active, ongoing struggle for real education. But for her to do this, her teachers must be committed to the belief that women's minds and experience are intrinsically valuable and indispensable to any

civilization worthy of the name; that there is no more exhila-
rating and intellectually fertile place in the academic world
today than a women's college—*if* both students and teachers
in large enough numbers are trying to fulfill this contract.
The contract is really a pledge of mutual seriousness about
women, about language, ideas, methods, and values. It is our
shared commitment toward a world in which the inborn
potentialities of so many women's minds will no longer be
wasted, raveled-away, paralyzed, or denied.

Garry B. Trudeau
Doonesbury

*Garry B. Trudeau (born 1948) is one of America's most influen-
tial (and controversial) political and social commentators. His
vehicle is the comic strip "Doonesbury," which appears in more
than 850 newspapers and whose audience may top 100 million
readers. An example of his work relevant to the topic of education follows; another related cartoon appears on page 161. For
other examples of Trudeau's commentary, see page 976.*

DOONESBURY COPYRIGHT 1985 G. B. Trudeau. Reprinted with permission of Universal Press Syndicate. All rights reserved.

The ad for Hofstra University on this page appeared in several magazines and newspapers in 1989 and 1990; the ad for Adelphi University on the next page appeared in the same places in 1994 and 1995. What does each ad imply about the purpose of a college education?

What does it take to be the best?

Determination and hard work, at any age, can lead to being the best. Hofstra University, just 50 years old, is already among the top ten percent of American colleges and universities in almost all academic criteria and resources.

Professionally accredited programs in such major areas as business, engineering, law, psychology and education.

A library with over 1.1 million volumes *on campus*—a collection larger than that of 95% of American universities.

Record enrollments with students from 31 states and 59 countries— with a student-faculty ratio of only 17 to 1.

The largest, most sophisticated non-commercial television facility in the East. A high technology undergraduate teaching resource with broadcast-quality production capability.

A ranking in *Barron's Guide to the Most Prestigious Colleges*—one of only 262 colleges and universities chosen from almost 4,000.

At Hofstra, determination, inspiration and hard work are qualities our faculty demands in itself and instills in our students. These qualities are what it takes to be the best. In anything.

HOFSTRA UNIVERSITY
WE TEACH SUCCESS.

50th Anniversary
Hempstead, L.I., New York 11550

Aram Bakshian Jr.
Just Say No to College

Aram Bakshian Jr. (born 1944) is a member of the National Council for the Humanities; he served as a communications expert in the Reagan administration. You'll learn more about him and his background when you read the following essay, which appeared in The American Spectator *(a monthly magazine that reviews politics and current affairs from a resolutely conservative perspective) in November 1991.*

1   Few things in life are worth standing in line for, especially on a sweltering summer day in Washington, D.C. Higher education certainly didn't seem like one of them in September of 1963, when, overcome by the dinginess of George Washington University's downtown campus, and the industrial-strength effluvium issuing from long queues of nervous, sweaty registering freshmen, I made what may well have been the defining choice of my life. Anticipating Nancy Reagan by twenty years, I "just said no"—in my case, to that most mind-bending of hallucinogens, a second-rate liberal arts degree. It meant chucking a generously apportioned yet unappetizing academic scholarship, but my mind was made up: rather than go to college, I would get an education.

2   More immediately, I decided to abandon campus and walk a few blocks to the old Circle Theatre on Pennsylvania Avenue. By happy chance, Lucino Visconti's exquisite film adaptation of Giuseppe di Lampedusa's *The Leopard* was playing and the erratic air conditioning system was working that afternoon; two auspicious omens in a row convinced me that I had made the right decision. As I watched the world-weary patrician hero turning his back on the gilded sham of *risorgimento* Italy, I felt a smug kinship, excusable, perhaps, in one still in his teens.

3   From elementary school onward, I had always learned more from independent reading and conversation than from the standard gruel dispensed in class, taking to heart the Shakespearean admonition that

> No profit grows where is no pleasure ta'en; in brief, sir, study what you most affect . . . .

and agreeing with Sydney Smith (to the aggravation of innumerable family members over the years) that there is "no furniture so charming as books." So much so that, from junior high school onward, I regularly played hooky to visit the vast, fusty second-hand bookstores that still dotted the Washington landscape in the 1950s and 1960s. Nearly all of them, Lowdermilk's, Pearlman's, Estate, Savile, and Park Books, are gone now.

Today's book fanciers, usually forced to choose between 4 overpriced antiquarian dealers and chain retailers limited to standard current titles, would be amazed at how far—and wide—a few dollars could go in those literary old curiosity shops. Nicely bound broken sets of the collected works of Voltaire could be bought for all of seventy-five cents a volume, and Homer, Plato, Thucydides, Xenophon, Le Sage, Clarendon, Cervantes, Marcus Aurelius, Gibbon, Macaulay, Carlyle, Thackeray, Dickens, Sterne, Smollett, Daudet, de Maupassant, Surtees, Suetonius, Sheridan, Aristophanes, Chaucer, Emerson, Parkman, Pascal, Molière, Madame de Sévign, St. Simon, Pepys, Pope, Johnson, Boswell, Montaigne, Dryden, Goldsmith, Goethe, Byron, Tennyson, Kipling, de Ligne, Luther, and Dante, not to mention more recent and routine titles, could be had for a song, sometimes in morocco or calf.

"Good as it is to inherit a library, it is better to collect one," 5 wrote Augustine Birrell, and at that time, even a newspaper carrier turned copyboy like myself could afford to start. The very act of working to pay for each volume seemed to quicken one's appetite for reading it, a principle that probably applies to students who have to work for their tuition. Serving as a copyboy, first at the (now-defunct) *National Observer* and then at the (now-unrecognizable) *U.S. News & World Report,* also meant access to good reference libraries and interesting conversation with the less stuffy writers and editors. One of the earliest pleasures of my own writing career came when, a few years after I had left the *National Observer,* I appeared in its pages as a book critic and was able to renew earlier acquaintances on a more equal footing.

Reading, writing, and intelligent discussion are the keys to 6 a good liberal arts education in academia; I simply sought, and was lucky enough to find, the same essentials in the outside world without being subjected to the nuisance of gym, the irrelevance of Geology I, and the forced purchase of dozens of badly written textbooks, as expensive as they were worthless.

7   This is *not* to say that I owe nothing to formal education. Several inspiring elementary and secondary school teachers tolerated my maverick streak and encouraged my interests in history and literature. As a day student at a cozy if somewhat down-at-the-heels little academy called Woodward Prep, I even learned the elements of real, as opposed to apparent, political power: control communications and law enforcement and it doesn't matter who is president. This is as true of countries as of student councils, as I would later observe in the Nixon and Ford White Houses before becoming director of speechwriting for Ronald Reagan, a President who knew a thing or two about communicating.

8   Editing the school newspaper and literary supplement and commanding the hall monitors meant real power and real rewards: extensive writing on the topics of one's choosing, more free time and fewer scheduled classes, and the ability to slip out for an illicit beer (I was tall for my age) with the connivance of one's subordinate hall monitors.

9   At the same time, a curriculum that still included Latin meant an early grounding in the fundamental structure of languages that would make later acquisition of rudimentary French and German easier. How Latin came to be dropped by some high schools as "irrelevant" baffles me to this day; it is the most practical subject many secondary school students will ever study. Given a little Latin, years later you will be able to get the gist of street signs, simple news clips, and broadcasts in Spanish, Italian, Portuguese, and in a pinch, even Romanian.

10   This is particularly true in my case, since Don Manuel Castello, Woodward Prep's Latin and French master, taught both languages with a thick Spanish accent. When asked about this, the headmaster's wife dismissed the matter with a phrase echoed thirty years later by Sybil Fawlty explaining the foibles of another Manuel, this time a waiter: "It's all right. He's from Barcelona."

11   Unlike the author of a recent best-seller, I do not claim that everything I needed to know I had already learned in kindergarten. But I can honestly say that everything I needed to learn—in school, that is—I knew by the twelfth grade. While my own curiosity deserves some of the credit, so does a motley but worthy crew of teachers, not one of whom was an education major.

12   They included a deaf, dentured retired colonel, Merritt Booth, who taught algebra and geometry with the logic and precision they deserved; a dedicated young English teacher

named Bill Gaull who, while working his way through law school, took the trouble to encourage bright students to read non-syllabus authors like Fielding and Tolstoy; a one-legged Seventh Day Adventist history master named Donald F. Haynes who, although somewhere to the right of the John Birch Society, graded fairly and taught passionately; and a wonderful 76-year-old chemistry teacher, "Doc" Valaer, whose enthusiasm for his subject was such that, although a teetotaler, he had written a book entitled *Wines of the World*, painstakingly analyzing their chemical compositions without tasting any of them.

My graduate and post-graduate teachers, while more   13
famous, have all been untenured and unofficial: editors, authors, politicians, journalists, artists, and a widening circle of interesting friends. We didn't need classrooms; sometimes we didn't even need face-to-face meetings. One of my earliest literary mentors was the late Frank Meyer, who edited the arts and manners section of *National Review* from the magazine's founding until his death in the early 1970s. Although we struck up a strong intellectual friendship during hundreds of hours of phone conversations, we never met. The only time we were in the same room together was at his funeral in Woodstock, New York, yet Frank's disembodied voice during our long-distance dialogues on everything from the ideals of the Founding Fathers to the foibles of King Farouk was an important part of my education.

A twenty-year association with the British magazine *His-*   14
tory Today, beginning with its founding editors, poet-biographer Peter Quennell and the late Alan Hodge who, among other things, was one of the two ghostwriters for Winston Churchill, I've been lucky enough to know, has been an unending source of new ideas, friendships, and interests. Similarly, collaborating with Viennese composer Robert Stolz (1880–1975) on his memoirs was the equivalent of several years of post-graduate study on the musical, theatrical, intellectual, political, and social history of *Mitteleuropa* under a man who had known or met everyone from the last two Hapsburg emperors to Brahms, Bruckner, Johann and Richard Strauss, Lehar, and Puccini to Charlie Chaplin, Albert Einstein, Eleanor Roosevelt, Marshal Tito, Marlene Dietrich, and Marilyn Monroe, a rather fascinating mixed bag.

The odds are that I would have missed out on most of these   15
opportunities if I had kept my scholarship at George Washington University and followed the oft-trodden rut of academia,

where as early an observer as William Penn remarked that "much reading is an oppression of the mind, and extinguishes the natural candle, which is the reason of so many useless scholars in the world." At the very worst, I might have ended up as a tenured, politically correct hack...perhaps even a registered Democrat.

16   Just thinking about *that* makes me shudder. Fortunately, all I had to do was just say no.

W. D. Snodgrass
The Examination

W. D. Snodgrass (born 1926), educated at Geneva College and the University of Iowa, teaches at the University of Delaware. His book of poetry Heart's Needle *won the Pulitzer Prize in 1960.*

1 Under the thick beams of that swirly smoking light,
       The black robes are clustering, huddled in together.
   Hunching their shoulders, they spread short, broad sleeves
          like night-
       Black grackles' wings; then they reach bone-yellow

2 leathery fingers, each to each. And are prepared. Each turns
       His single eye—or since one can't discern their eyes,
   That reflective single, moon-pale disc which burns
       Over each brow—to watch this uncouth shape that lies

3 Strapped to their table. One probes with his ragged nails
       The slate-sharp calf, explores the thigh and the lean thews
   Of the groin. Others raise, red as piratic sails,
       His wing, stretching, trying the pectoral sinews.

4 One runs his finger down the whet of that cruel
       Golden beak, lifts back the horny lids from the eyes,
   Peers down in one bright eye malign as a jewel,
       And steps back suddenly. "He is anaesthetized?"

"He is. He is. Yes. Yes." The tallest of them, bent   5
   Down by the head, rises: "This drug possesses powers
Sufficient to still all gods in this firmament.
   This is Garuda who was fierce. He's yours for hours.

"We shall continue, please." Now, once again, he bends   6
   To the skull, and its clamped tissues. Into the cran-
ial cavity, he plunges both of his hands
   Like obstetric forceps and lifts out the great brain,

Holds it aloft, then gives it to the next who stands   7
   Beside him. Each, in turn, accepts it, although loath,
Turns it this way, that way, feels it between his hands
   Like a wasp's nest or some sickening outsized growth.

They must decide what thoughts each part of it must think;   8
   They tap at, then listen beside, each suspect lobe;
Next, with a crow's quill dipped into India ink,
   Mark on its surface, as if on a map or globe,

Those dangerous areas which need to be excised.   9
   They rinse it, then apply antiseptics to it;
Now silver saws appear which, inch by inch, slice
   Through its ancient folds and ridges, like thick suet.

It's rinsed, dried, and daubed with thick salves. The smoky   10
   saws
   Are scrubbed, resterilized, and polished till they gleam.
The brain is repacked in its case. Pinched in their claws,
   Glimmering needles stitch it up, that leave no seam.

Meantime, one of them has set blinders to the eyes,   11
   Inserting light packing beneath each of the ears,
And calked the nostrils in. One, with thin twine, ties
   The genitals off. With long wood-handled shears,

Another chops pinions out of the scarlet wings.   12
   It's hoped that with disuse he will forget the sky
Or, at least, in time, learn, among other things,
   To fly no higher than his superiors fly.

Well; that's a beginning. The next time, they can split   13
   His tongue and teach him to talk correctly, can give
Him opinions on fine books and choose clothing fit
   For the integrated area where he'll live.

14   Their candidate may live to give them thanks one day.
         He will recover and may hope for such success.
     He might return to join their ranks. Bowing away,
         They nod, whispering, "One of ours; one of ours. Yes. Yes."

Louis Menand

What Are Universities For?

*Louis Menand teaches English at Queens College and at the
Graduate Center of the City University of New York. The winner of prestigious fellowships and an expert on English and
American writers of the first half of the twentieth century, he
often writes articles on current cultural affairs such as the following one, which appeared in* Harper's *magazine (a prestigious forum for discussions of American politics and culture)
in December 1991. The article appeared in the same issue as
the one by Rosa Ehrenreich that appears on page 170.*

1   Several times in the last few years I have taught a course
called Introduction to Poetry. The class was always overenrolled; I usually spent the beginning of the first few meetings turning students away. Its popularity had nothing to do
with me—I was one of many instructors, teaching one of
many sections, and all the sections were overenrolled. Introduction to Poetry was popular because it happened to satisfy
three requirements: It was a prerequisite for English department courses; it could be used as the final installment in a
sequence of composition courses all students had to take;
and, as a "humanities" elective, it satisfied a college-wide distribution requirement.

2   There are 18,000 students at my school, which is one campus of a public university. Most of them are pursuing careers
in fields remote from literature; many know English only as a
second language. These students approach a course on poetry
with the same sense of dread with which most English majors

might approach an advanced course in statistics. Other students, though, are eager to take an English course—not because they hope to acquire an appreciation of poetry, but because they believe it will enhance their communications skills and help them get into law school. And there are a few students who want to become English majors because English literature is their primary academic interest.

All of these types of students have turned up in every section of Introduction to Poetry, so I found myself trying to teach some of my students how to write a grammatical sentence, to introduce others to the academic study of literature, and to give the rest of them—though most were essentially unacquainted with serious literary culture—exposure to the best that has been thought and said in the world. For the majority of the students, of course (as they were not shy about making me aware), the principal object was to secure the passing grade needed to fulfill whatever requirement happened to apply in their case. You could walk away from a session of Introduction to Poetry feeling that whatever the current public debate over the university was about—"political correctness," deconstruction, "multiculturalism," the canon—what you had just spent the last hour or so doing had very little to do with it. Ideology was about as remote a presence in an Introduction to Poetry classroom as leather bindings.

In all the uproar over the academy—which entered the mainstream of public debate in 1987 with Allan Bloom's bestselling *The Closing of the American Mind,* and which has produced, more recently, Roger Kimball's *Tenured Radicals,* Dinesh D'Souza's *Illiberal Education* (also a bestseller), cover stories in almost every news and opinion magazine of note, and even some observations in a commencement address last spring by President Bush—no one has bothered to ask what practical effect the so-called politicization of the humanities has actually had on the undergraduate mind. Seventy-four percent of the nation's freshman class last year described themselves, in a poll conducted by the American Council on Education, as politically middle-of-the-road or conservative. When they were asked why they chose to attend college, the most popular answer, picked by 78 percent, was to "get a better job" followed by to "make more money" (73 percent). Asked to name an objective they considered "essential or very important," 74 percent chose "being very well-off financially"; second place went to "raising a family," named by 70 percent (an answer almost equally popular among male and female students).

5   There is no evidence I know of to suggest that in four years
spent trying to win the grades and recommendations needed
for jobs or for admission to graduate or professional school,
these students become radicalized, or are in any way
deflected from the social mainstream, by the few humanities
courses they are required to take. Students enrolled in Introduction to Poetry would learn just as much about poetry from
a professor who thought Milton was a sexist as they would
from one who didn't—which is to say, in either case, that they
would have had to read and talk for a few hours about a
writer of whom they would otherwise remain essentially
ignorant. The professor's political slant, if it can be ferreted
out, makes a difference to most students only insofar as it
might determine the kind of questions likely to turn up on an
exam. The effect the course might have on those students'
good opinion of Milton—or of any other poet they are likely
to be required to read—is a microscopic influence, rapidly
diminishing to zero as college recedes behind them, on their
ultimate sense of things.

6   The educational ethos is different at a selective, residential,
private college. There students are likely to be better primed
to become personally engaged with the course material; they
are also likely to feel the loss of income higher education represents less acutely, which enables them to enter into the
spirit of their instruction with their eyes a little less fixed on
the bottom line. Students at elite colleges identify much more
strongly with their professors: They want to argue the
nuances and to pick up the insights. But in the end the practical impact is much the same. Anyone who has taught literature at such a school knows the phenomenon: The brightest
students happily learn the most advanced styles of contemporary critical theory, with all of their radical political implications, and then they apply, with equal good cheer, to business
school. Whatever subversiveness they have ingested has
mostly served to give them a kind of superior intellectual
sophistication that they are right to feel is not in the least bit
incompatible with professional success on Wall Street or
Madison Avenue.

7   Academic thought may have been heading left in the last
ten years or so, in other words, but college students themselves have been heading straight into the mainstream. Even
comfortably middle-class students feel an economic imperative almost unknown to middle-class students of twenty years
ago. When I was a freshman, in 1969, I didn't have a thought
in my head about how I was eventually going to support

myself. I suppose I imagined that I would just hitchhike around the country with my guitar (which I didn't know how to play) reciting my poetry (which I didn't know how to write).

In the 1990s, though, young people in the middle class are 8 perfectly alive to the fact that they go to college because they have to; young people not in the middle class continue to go to college for the reason they always have, which is to get into the middle class. It seems to me that there is every good reason to challenge these students for a semester or two to think with a little balanced skepticism about the conventional wisdom of the society they are so anxious to join. But whether they're being taught skepticism or not, literature classes are the last places students are likely to be getting their values. Madonna has done more to affect the way young people think about sexuality than all the academic gender theorists put together. Perhaps D'Souza should write a book about her.

It's easier, of course, to attack Catharine Stimpson, the 9 former dean of graduate school at Rutgers and former president of the Modern Language Association, who has become one of the point persons in the defense of new academic trends. Stimpson doesn't appear on MTV, so there isn't a tidal wave of popular sentiment to overcome before one can take her to task. But the lack of a mass following ought to be a clue to the extent of Stimpson's, or any other academic's, real influence on the culture at large. A group of literature professors calling themselves Teachers for a Democratic Culture has come together this fall to launch a counteroffensive against the attack on "political correctness." I suspect that it's a little late in the day for a counteroffensive: The cen- ter on this issue has already been grabbed. But one of the arguments this new group wants to make is that the whole situation has been exaggerated. I think it's a just complaint.

It isn't hard to guess the motives behind the controversy in 10 its present melodramatic mode. It is always tempting to blame bad conditions on bad ideas, and it must seem to conservatives that since liberal and leftist thinking has been driven out of nearly every other part of American life, the pitiful remnant of left-wing ideology that has taken refuge in university literature departments must be the reason social problems so disobligingly persist. It is the good fortune of conservatives that this is a view that meets exactly the belief of some of the professors being attacked, which is that they are in possession of the one ground—the humanities curriculum of American colleges—on which real social change might be accomplished. The American media, for their rather inflammatory part, are always happy to find an occasion not to appear too liberal, and the excesses of "political correctness" are the perfect thing to get noisily to the right of. The whole controversy is marvelously apt in a country that no longer shows any interest in publicly funded social programs; for whichever political faction wins control of the undergraduate reading list, no taxpayer dollars will have been spent.

11   This doesn't mean that there's not a crisis. But the issue is not whether (in the words of some of the demonstrators against Stanford's core curriculum a few years ago) Western culture's got to go. Western culture, whether it's in good odor at the Modern Language Association these days or not, we're stuck with. The real issue concerns the role of higher education in American life. Too many people are fighting over how much T. S. Eliot versus how much Alice Walker young minds ought to be exposed to, and not enough people are asking why undergraduate English courses should be bearing the load of this debate in the first place. What is it we are expecting colleges to do that makes the particular mix of the reading lists in literature courses seem to spell the difference between— well, between culture and anarchy?

12   Matthew Arnold is, indeed, the name most frequently associated with the traditional idea of liberal arts education that the new wave of "politicization" in the academy is supposed to be wrecking. But the liberal arts component of higher education belongs to what is in some ways the least salient of the university's social functions. In fact, the Arnoldian program of using humanistic studies as a means of moral instruction, far from being the most venerable of the university's activities, entered the modern university almost as an afterthought.

13   The modern university in America is defined by two features, both of which date from the late nineteenth century: the existence of an elective curriculum for undergraduates and the existence of a graduate school, which trains the people who teach the undergraduates. The elective system was not designed to disseminate culture. When Charles William Eliot instituted the first elective system, at Harvard in 1883, his idea was to allow college students to "track" themselves in the direction of their future careers—not to acquire a common culture, but to specialize according to individual needs. Eliot believed that college ought to play a vocational role, to serve a frankly utilitarian function. His faith in the real-world utility of academic studies was great enough, in fact, to allow

him, in 1901, to praise the assembled scholars of the Modern Language Association, virtually all of whom were philologists, by telling them that their work enjoyed "a vital connection with the industrial and commercial activities of the day."

At the same time, Eliot saw the need to provide specialists   14
to train college students, and in 1890 he established the Harvard Graduate School of Arts and Sciences, modeled on the first research institution in the country, Johns Hopkins (founded in 1876). The principal function of the graduate school is the production of teachers, whom it certifies with the doctoral degree, to staff the modern college; but it also produces scholarly research, and the research ideal is expressly nonutilitarian. The researcher cannot be influenced by what the world will find profitable: The goal is knowledge for its own sake, without regard for "the industrial and commercial activities of the day."

So there was already in the modern university, as Eliot and   15
the other late-nineteenth-century pioneers of higher education helped to create it, a contradiction between what professors do, which is to follow their research interests, and what their students do, which is to prepare for careers outside the academy—to pursue "education for experience," as Eliot called it. There is no reason, of course, as William James complained in 1903 in an essay called "The Ph.D. Octopus," why the possession of a doctorate, earned by scholarship, should serve as a credential for teaching undergraduates; yet these separate functions were made to complement each other, and by the end of the nineteenth century the ideals of research and of vocational training had achieved such an ascendancy in American universities that a reaction against them occurred on behalf of what was called, by many of its champions, "liberal culture." This reaction is the origin of the idea that college is the place of future social leaders to be exposed to, in Arnold's phrase, "the study of perfection." The liberal arts "tradition" that the new scholarship is accused of trashing, in other words, is not even a century old.

The "true aim of culture," wrote Hiram Corson, the chair-   16
man of the Cornell English department and a proponent of "liberal culture," in 1894, is "to induce soul states or conditions, soul attitudes, to attune the inward forces to the idealized forms of nature and of human life produced by art, and not to make the head a cockloft for storing away the trumpery of barren knowledge." This ideal is both anti-utilitarian and anti-research, and the reaction on its behalf was successful enough to lead, in 1909, to Eliot's replacement as president of

Harvard by A. Lawrence Lowell—a member of the faculty who, many years before, had opposed the institution of the elective system. Thus emerged the third mission of the modern academy: the liberalization, through exposure to art, literature, and philosophy, of the undergraduate mind.

17   Although no school was ever purely one type or another, universities before 1910 could be distinguished according to their leading educational ideals: Harvard was utilitarian, for example; Johns Hopkins, Clark, and Chicago were research institutions. Schools like Princeton and Yale tended to resist both these trends. But after 1910 (as Laurence Veysey explains in *The Emergence of the American University*) there was a shift. Educators stopped arguing about ideals; the various versions of what properly constituted higher education were no longer regarded as conflicting. The university learned to accommodate divergent views of its purpose, and the goal of the people who administered universities became not the defense of an educational philosophy but the prosperity of the institution. And the prosperity of the institution depended on its being, to as great an extent as it found possible, all things to all people.

18   This is how a pedagogical portmanteau like Introduction to Poetry could come into being—a single course on a specific subject expected to serve, all at the same time, a utilitarian function (by training students how to read and write), a research function (by preparing future English majors for the scholarly study of literature), and a liberal arts function (by exposing students to the leavening influence of high culture).

19   Even at schools where there is no actual Introduction to Poetry course, the overall effect of the undergraduate curriculum is the same. Students in the humanities are expected to major in a field—French, say, or religion—that will provide them with a lot of knowledge most of which will be useful only in the unlikely event they decide to enter graduate school and become professors themselves. At the same time, they are required to fulfill "distribution" requirements designed to expose them to smatterings of learning in every major area—with the vague idea that this contributes to something approximating genuine well-roundedness, and thus serves a "liberalizing" function. And there is the expectation, now almost universal, that beyond college lies professional school, for which some practical training will be useful.

20   It's possible to argue that these three educational functions—scholarly, vocational, and liberalizing—are only

three ways of looking at the same thing, which is the exposure to knowledge. For higher education in any field certainly
can serve, simultaneously, all three purposes: pure speculation, practical application, and general enlightenment. Even
so, there needs to be a consensus that these benefits are
worth pursuing, and that the traditional structure of the university provides the best means of doing so, in order for the
system to work effectively. Three recent developments, none
of them having to do explicitly with politics—illiberal or
not—seem to me to have undermined this consensus.

The first is the major demographic change in the under-   21
graduate population over the last twenty years, a change that
reflects both a significant increase in the proportion of people
who attend college (from 1970 to 1988, the percentage of
Americans who had completed four years of college doubled)
and a significant increase on most campuses in the proportion
of students who are not white or not male. This means that the
average college class is not the relatively homogeneous group,
culturally and socio-economically speaking, it once was: The
level of preparation among students differs more widely, and
their interests and assumptions differ as well.

Since the whole idea of liberal arts education is to use liter-   22
ature and philosophy as a way of learning how to value one's
interests and assumptions, it is (or it ought to be) obviously
absurd to insist that books that served this function when the
audience was predominantly made up of young middle-class
white men can serve the same function now that the audience
is more diverse. When Columbia College admitted women for
the first time, in 1983, it was suddenly realized by the faculty
that the reading list for Humanities A, the famous great books
course required of all students, had never included a book by
a woman. Though for years it had been advertised as representing the best that the educated person needed to know, the
list was changed: Sappho and Jane Austen became great writers. It took some fancy rhetoric to explain why this adjustment didn't amount to a confession that "the great books" is
really just a grand name for "the books that will expose students to ideas we want them at the moment to be talking
about." And that is part of the problem; for since so much has
been emotionally (and, I think, mistakenly) invested in the
traditional great books curriculum, changes can't happen
without resentment and reaction.

The second development putting pressure on tradi-   23
tional educational ideals is the spread of critical theory as a
kind of interdisciplinary currency in university humanities

departments. For contemporary critical theory—in particular post-structuralist theories, emphasizing the indeterminacy of meaning, and ideological theories, emphasizing the social construction of values—rejects precisely the belief on which the professional apparatus of the university (graduate exams, dissertation defenses, tenure review, publication in refereed journals, and so forth) depends: the belief that the pursuit of knowledge is a disinterested activity whose results can be evaluated objectively by other trained specialists in one's field. "What's really going on" in the production of knowledge is now regarded, by these new theoretical lights, as not a disinterested enterprise at all but an effort to make the views of a particular class of people prevail.

24   This rejection of the positivistic model of knowledge production has helped to turn the system of professional rewards, always an arena for academic politics, into an arena for real-world politics as well. Critical theorists whose work attacks the traditional premises of scholarship are invited into humanities departments for the good marketing reason that their work is where the action is today: Every graduate program wants a prominent profile. But the system whose principles those professors teach one another to regard with skepticism remains, except that it has been thoroughly corrupted. It is now regarded as legitimate by some professors to argue that the absence of a political intention or multicultural focus in another professor's work constitutes a prima facie disqualification for professional advancement. And why not, if all scholarship is at bottom political anyway?

25   Finally, there has been a change in the role of college in the preparation of young people for careers outside the academy. Although the number of bachelor's degrees awarded each year has been increasing steadily—by 28 percent between 1970 and 1989—the number of professional degrees has been increasing at a much greater rate. The material value of a B.A. is a function of supply: The greater the number of people who have one, the less a B.A. is worth in the marketplace. Particularly for students interested in "being very well-off financially" (74 percent, according to the American Council of Education survey), it has now become imperative not to stop with the B.A. but to proceed to professional school; and the number of M.B.A.'s awarded between 1970 and 1989 therefore increased by 239 percent, the number of M.D.'s by 88 percent, the number of law degrees by 143 percent. Increases in advanced degrees in architecture, engineering, and a number of other nonacademic professional fields were similarly dramatic.

This wave of professionalism has transformed the experi- 26 ence of college. The academic demands on undergraduates are in a sense now more real, since good grades are essential for getting over the hurdle to the next degree program; but the content is somehow less real, since most students now perceive that the education that matters to them will take place after college is finished. This helps to explain the phenomenon of the undergraduate whiz in Foucauldian analysis who goes merrily on to a career in corporate finance.

These various challenges to the established design of higher 27 education present difficulties that have little to do with politics. Perhaps the university will find a way to muddle through them, but muddling alone is not likely to be very effective. For it is not only a philosophical idea about education that is being thrown into doubt by these recent developments. It is also the institutional structure of the university itself.

I happen to think, for example—and without putting any 28 political valuation on the judgment—that contemporary theoretical skepticism about the positivistic nature of "knowledge" in fields like literature is perfectly justified. It is absurd to treat literary criticism as a species of scientific inquiry; the professional system of rewards in the humanistic disciplines is essentially bogus and leads mostly to intellectual conformity, predictable "demonstrations" of theoretical points, and a panicky desire to please one's elders and superiors. But what university is about to tear down the bureaucratic system of professional advancement in the humanities? How would departments administer themselves without the fiction that they were engaged in the production of real knowledge about real specialities?

Similarly, the undergraduate major seems to me an institu- 29 tion that is at best pedagogically inefficient (why should students going on to law school have to pass a course of what amounts to pre-professional training for graduate school in English or some other academic discipline?) and at worst a contributor to the perpetuation of a fundamentally arbitrary definition of knowledge. The modern academic discipline is only as old as the modern university: Before the 1800s, no one imagined that history, political science, economics, anthropology, and sociology constituted distant areas of study, each with its own theoretical and methodological traditions. Nor was it imagined by most people that "literature" was a discriminable area of human endeavor that must be talked about exclusively in literary-critical (as opposed to sociological or ethical or theological) terms.

30   But these distinctions have become institutionalized in the form of academic departments; the people who work in those departments have professionalized themselves to keep out "unqualified" practitioners; and the professions run the fields, monopolizing both instruction and scholarship. It seems to me that a college student today might want, in four years, to acquire knowledge about American culture, about American politics and law, and about capitalism. What a student who bothers to seek out knowledge in these areas is likely to get are courses introducing him or her to the academic specialities of American studies, political science, and economics. Though there is no reason why every undergraduate should not receive it, a practical introduction to the law or to business must usually wait until law school or business school, since that is where the specialists are. Because there are no instructors who are not certified members of an academic discipline, there is very little genuinely general education going on in American colleges.

31   These problems are severe enough, but they don't explain completely why the university is in such a bad way right now. Questions about educational philosophy must eventually have educational answers; the contemporary university, though, has reached beyond the purview of education, and it has thereby become entangled in problems it lacks the means to resolve. Universities can decide the things people ought to know, and they can decide how those things should be taught. But universities cannot arbitrate disputes about democracy and social justice, or govern the manner in which people relate socially to one another, or police attitudes; and that is what they are being asked to do today.

32   To some extent this overreaching is the fault of the society as a whole, which is happy to turn over to educators problems it lacks the will (and, it believes, the means) to address politically. It is easier to integrate a reading list, or even a dormitory, than it is to integrate a suburban neighborhood. But to some extent it is the consequence of the university's own indiscriminate appetite, whose history begins in the 1960s.

33   The contention that the current problems in the academy are the natural outcome of Sixties radicalism is common to many of the recent attacks on higher education—it can be found in Bloom's, Kimball's, and D'Souza's books. I think the claim is basically false, and that (as Camille Paglia argued in a long diatribe on the subject last spring in the journal *Arion*) the humorless ethos of the politically correct humanities

department could not be more antithetical to the spirit of the 1960s. Even the most callow radicalism of that era has nothing to do with the sort of doctrinaire political attitudes critics of the contemporary academy complain about. Are the people who are so eager to censor "fighting words" on campus today the same people who went around in 1968 calling anyone wearing a uniform or a necktie a "pig"? If they are the same people, they've left their radicalism behind.

There is one thing, however, that the present situation does   34
owe to the 1960s, and that is the belief that the university is a miniature reproduction of the society as a whole. That idea dominates, for example, the Port Huron Statement, the manifesto of the New Left drafted by Tom Hayden and endorsed by the Students for a Democratic Society in 1962. But it is not only a leftist idea; for the postwar university has always been eager to incorporate every new intellectual and cultural development that has come its way.

The university is, in fact, expressly designed to do this: It   35
can accommodate almost any interest by creating a new course, a new program, a new studies center. It has managed, for instance, to institutionalize activities like painting and creative writing, not traditionally thought to require academic preparation, by devising M.F.A. programs—which, in turn, provide a place on university faculties for practicing painters and writers. When new scholarly movements emerged—Third World Studies, Women's Studies—the university was quick to establish research centers and institutes to house them. Degrees are now offered in almost everything. There are few intellectual activities left that do not have an academic incarnation.

The problems begin when this process of absorption   36
extends beyond the intellectual realm. In the late 1960s, serious attention began to be paid by university administrators to the quality of campus life. This, too, was in part a response to student protest: Everyone agreed, for example, that one of the lessons of the crisis that led to the shutdown of Columbia in 1968 was that the college had to become less like a corporation and more like a community. But it was also natural that, as higher education became accessible to (and desired by) a greater variety of people in the postwar boom years, the university would evolve in this direction of its own accord.

This development of the university as a social microcosm   37
has been guided in most places by the view (which originated with the students themselves) that there should be available within the walls of the academy the full range of experiences

available (or ideally available) outside. The initial break-
through was a purely middle-class phenomenon: the liberalization of parietal restrictions. (In the late 1960s, to give an
idea of the magnitude of the change that has taken place, a
student at Barnard, a sophisticated school in a sophisticated
city, was expelled for sharing an apartment with her boyfriend *off campus.*) The eventual abandonment of regulations
governing relations between the sexes was followed by the
sexual integration of many traditionally single-sex schools
(Princeton, Yale, Dartmouth, Vassar), and by the recruitment
of ethnic minorities in the interest (among other things) of
social diversity on campus.

38   This enormous and successful engulfment of intellectual
and social variety, coming on top of the shocks to the system's
academic identity, is what has given the university its present
headache. The university has become, at last, too many
things to too many people. It now reproduces all the conflicts
of the culture at large; but it reproduces them, as it were, in
vitro. For unlike the society it simulates, the university is
unequipped, both administratively and philosophically, to
deal with conflicts that cannot be treated simply as conflicts
of ideas. It has the machinery needed to arbitrate the sorts of
disagreements that arise naturally in the pursuit of the university's traditional educational goals; but it is not designed to
arbitrate among antagonistic interest groups, or to discover
ways of correcting inequities and attitudes that persist in the
society as a whole.

39   The reason is that the university is required, by its accom-
modationist philosophy, to give equal protection to every idea
and point of view anyone chooses to express. This is, of
course, an indispensable principle of intellectual freedom.
But when the issue is political, when it involves the distribution of power, accommodationism fails. For power is a zero-
sum game. In the real world, interest groups vie against one
another for resources in the knowledge that one group gains
by taking from other groups. Political and legal institutions
exist to mediate these struggles.

40   In the university, though, no one has ever needed to cede
ground to someone else, since conflict has always been
avoided by expanding the playing field. But this strategy
doesn't work when the stakes are not simply intellectual. As
long as the activities of the Gay Student Alliance and the
Bible Study Group remain merely academic, they can coexist.
Once those groups become versions of their real-world counterparts—once they become actively political—there is no

way to keep both of them happy. But who in the university wants to have to choose between them? In the nonacademic world, pluralism means a continual struggle over the distribution of a single pie. In the academic world (and the Democratic Party), it means trying to give every group a pie of its own.

Yet somehow it is expected that, once they are relocated to 41 a campus, differences that have proved intractable elsewhere will be overcome, both in the classroom and in the student union. This insistence, on the part of academics and nonacademics alike, on making higher education the site for political and social disputes of all types, and on regarding the improvement of social relations and the mediation of political differences as one of higher education's proper functions, has produced ridiculous distortions. Thus we have a debate, for example, in which the economic rights of women are argued about in terms of reading lists for introductory literature courses—as though devoting fewer class hours to male authors might be counted a blow against discrimination in the workplace. And outside the classroom, in the dorms and the dean's office, the university has managed to become a laboratory for the study and cure of social problems like date rape.

There are as well the notorious speech codes and disciplin- 42 ary procedures aimed at enforcing campus "'civility." These are mostly the results of hasty attempts to jury-rig disciplinary systems whose need had not been felt until it became commonly assumed that how students addressed one another was a matter college administrators ought to be concerned about. That the president of the university should have become the leading figure and spokesperson in the incident in which a Brown undergraduate was expelled for drunkenly shouting insults at no one in particular is an indication not only that the university doesn't know how seriously it is supposed to be taking these sorts of "problems" but that it has no appropriate administrative apparatus for dealing with them either.

And there is, to take a final example, the notion—much 43 less prevalent than the critics of political correctness claim, but present nonetheless—that the undergraduate curriculum should include courses whose purpose is, in effect, to cheerlead for civil and sexual rights. There is no doubt that many civil and sexual rights remain to be secured in this country; there is no doubt that scandalous inequities persist unattended to. But English professors are not experts on these matters. They are taught how to identify tropes, not how to eliminate racist attitudes. To turn their courses into classes on (say) Post-Colonial Literature with the idea of addressing with some degree of insight the problem of ethnocentrism is to ask someone equipped to catch butterflies to trap an elephant.

44   This is done, usually, by pretending the butterfly is an elephant—by loading up a poem with so much ideological baggage that it can pass for an instrument of oppression. Poems won't bear the weight; most works of literature are designed to deflect exactly this kind of attention and to confute efforts to assign them specific political force. If literature is taught honestly from an ideological perspective—if what a book seems to say about the relations of power among people is made the focus of classroom discussion—students are just being led around the mulberry bush. It's not that the spirit of great literature is being dishonored, for literature can surely be talked about ideologically; it's that a false impression is being created among students that unhappiness whose amelioration lies in real-world political actions is being meaningfully addressed by classroom debates about the representation of the Other in the work of Herman Melville.

45   Professors should not be regarded as the people in possession of the "correct" views on subjects of public concern. But the idea that they ought to be has become an illusion shared by academics and their critics alike. When George Will wrote last spring in *Newsweek* that the task faced by Secretary of Defense Dick Cheney was less urgent than the one confronting his wife, Lynne, who is the director of the National Endowment for the Humanities, he sounded clearly the note of hysteria that has come to dominate debate about higher education in America. Mrs. Cheney, Will suggested, "is secretary of domestic defense. The foreign adversaries her husband, Dick, must keep at bay are less dangerous, in the long run, than the domestic forces with which she must deal. Those forces are fighting against the conservation of the common culture that is the nation's social cement."

46   This is witch-hunt talk; but it repeats an error found in less partisan writing as well, which is that the care of "the common culture" is the responsibility of college professors. Professors are people trained to *study* culture, not to *conserve* it (whatever that would mean). Their purview is limited by the kind of work, always highly specialized and narrowly defined, professionals in their disciplines have traditionally done. It is no favor to these people to regard them as the guardians of

our culture or as experts on ministering to its self-inflicted wounds. Nor is it a favor to the culture to hand it over to academics for its nourishment and protection.

Social and political controversies have swamped the academy for two reasons: because universities, unwilling to define their mission in specific terms and eager to accommodate everything that comes along, could not find a rationale for keeping those controversies at bay; and because there has been so little serious intellectual debate in the rest of American society in the last ten years. There have been no real ideas argued in American politics, for instance, since Ronald Reagan showed that ideas were overrated. And intellectual journalism has become dominated by position-taking—the point-counterpoint syndrome, which permits just two points of view to every pre-packaged "issue." 47

It is almost certain that one of the effects of the public scrutiny of what professors do will be to turn the academy into another bastion of intellectual predictability. I'm not sure that hasn't happened already. But if not, the only way to prevent it is for the university to renounce the role of model community and arbiter of social disputes that it has assumed, to ignore the impulse to regulate attitudes and expressions that are the epiphenomena of problems far outside the college walls, to stop trying to set up academic housing for every intellectual and political interest group that comes along, and to restrict itself to the business of imparting some knowledge to the people who need it. 48

POLITICAL CORRECTNESS

Eugene Genovese
Heresy, Yes—Sensitivity, No

Eugene Genovese (born in 1930 in Brooklyn, New York) is Distinguished Scholar-in-Residence at the University Center in Georgia; he has been on the faculty at Rutgers, Yale, Columbia, Rochester, and other universities. Frequently honored for his outstanding scholarship in history, he has dedicated his career to a better understanding of slavery in America. Among his many books are Roll, Jordan, Roll: The World the Slaves Made *(1976), the product of a decade of scholarship, and his recent* The Slaveholders' Dilemma: Freedom and Progress in Southern Political Thought *(1991). The following book review (and more than a book review) of Dinesh D'Souza's* Illiberal Education *appeared in* The New Republic, *a magazine of public affairs considered middle of the road in outlook, in April 1991.*

1   Were today's universities the places of higher education that they jocularly pretend to be, we would have had a vigorous debate on the issues raised by Allan Bloom's *The Closing of the American Mind*. Instead, with some notable exceptions, the left settled for the denunciations and the right for hosannas. Now we have another chance. Dinesh D'Souza's *Illiberal Education* recounts, in a manner both responsible and chilling, the atrocities that ravage our campuses. Whatever your politics, read it.

2   A domestic policy adviser in the Reagan White House and a frequent contributor to *National Review* and other satanic organs, D'Souza speaks from the right. He also speaks for sanity, and, rare among right-wingers, he displays a deep appreciation of the travails of black students. Nothing comes through this powerful yet restrained book more clearly than its protest against the betrayal of black youth by the demagogues who claim to support them. D'Souza shows that blacks are paying the highest price for the degradation of our campuses and the prostitution of higher education. Thus he

pointedly exposes what few right-wingers wish to notice: the increase in flagrantly racist assaults, physical and other, on black students.

The atrocities documented here include the silencing of 3 professors accused of "insensitivity" because they dare to ask students to read racist material in appropriate courses. (By extension, a professor ought not to assign *Mein Kampf* in a course on Nazi Germany since it might offend the sensibilities of Jewish students.) And they include the repression of professors and students who take unpopular stands against quotas, affirmative action, busing, abortion, homosexuality, and much else. Clearly, they have no right to present views offensive to those who accept the reigning pieties in universities committed to "diversity." D'Souza's account makes stomach-turning reading. And I have a suspicion that he is pulling his punches, lest he be accused of exaggeration.

As one who saw his professors fired during the McCarthy 4 era, and who had to fight, as a pro-Communist Marxist, for his own right to teach, I fear that our conservative colleagues are today facing a new McCarthyism in some ways more effective and vicious than the old. Are conservatives only getting, then, a dose of their own medicine? In fact, they are not. The right did not rule our campuses during the McCarthy era. Most of the purges of those years were conducted by administrators and faculties who loudly proclaimed their own liberalism—by the same kind of people, that is, who are enforcing "political correctness" today. Yet few of the culprits were then, or are now, "liberals."

The principled liberals on our campuses constitute about 5 the same proportion of the center as principled people do of the left and the right. All political camps have principled people, careerists, and thugs. D'Souza seems to appreciate this distinction. He largely avoids liberal-bashing and appeals instead to honest people across the spectrum to stand up for the principles that they profess in common. He warns of the few who have a totalitarian agenda, but wisely he concentrates his fire on those who appease them.

In these matters, as in others, Harvard, led by Derek Bok, 6 strives mightily to be No. 1. Harvard seems determined to lead in high comedy, too, though Stephan Thernstrom and other members of its faculty who have been savaged for political incorrectness in the classroom may be forgiven if they do not appreciate the humor. To wit: dining hall workers held a "Back to the Fifties Party," and a dean denounced them for being nostalgic about a decade in which segregation still prevailed.

A professor assigned a film in which a black maid appeared, and he was forced to cancel its screening, since blacks should not be shown in such jobs. A new president at Radcliffe declined to identify herself as a feminist, and local feminists, disgracing an admirable cause, denounced her for "doing violence to herself."

7   The Harvard administration more or less upheld Thernstrom's academic freedom; it did not fire him for having introduced pro-slavery and racist documents in his course on "The Peopling of America," which he co-taught with the distinguished historian Bernard Bailyn. Significantly, the students who complained about Thernstrom's "racial insensitivity" did not bother to confront him, as academic protocol, not to mention common courtesy, would require. Instead, they took their complaint to the administration and the press. In the event, the dean of the college, without mentioning Thernstrom by name, gravely announced his stern disapproval of "prejudice, harassment, and discrimination," and warned professors to watch their mouths, lest they offend the sensibilities of their students. In effect, the Harvard administration acknowledged Thernstrom's right to behave in a manner that embarrassed the university and ought to make him ashamed of himself. No doubt Bok and most of his deans disapprove of the excesses that accompany the struggle for diversity, sensitivity, and a radiant future for the peoples. They are merely doing their best to create an atmosphere in which professors who value their reputations and their perquisites learn to censor themselves.

8   The manner in which some of the administrators of our universities choose to fight racial discrimination is marvelous to behold. Having decided that a democratic admissions policy required roughly proportionate representation of blacks, Hispanics, and whites, the University of California, Berkeley, coolly discriminated against Asians. Nearly 30 percent of the Asian high school graduates from California qualified for admission to Berkeley, compared with about 15 percent of the whites, 6 percent of the Hispanics, and 4 percent of the blacks. Yet according to Berkeley's own weighted index, blacks were admitted with scores of 4800 out of 8000, whereas whites needed at least 7000. Asians needed at least 7000 just to have a 50 percent chance of admission.

9   But Asian students, as is well known, offend the sensibilities of true egalitarians and democrats by displaying a passion for hard work, and by having strong and supportive

families. Could America have been built if it had relied on such perverse people? Or more precisely, it must have relied on such people, which would explain its emergence as a racist, sexist, homophobic, imperialist country. Either way, a sensitive person must see that the fight against racism demands the exclusion of Asians in favor of people with safer credentials. How could we demonstrate that Asians are no better motivated and self-disciplined than the rest of us if we let them demonstrate that they are? And if we let them demonstrate that they are better motivated, how could we ever be sure that they are not also smarter?

The Asian community counterattacked and forced Berkeley   10
to modify its policies. Still, three trifles must be noted. First, the administrators, with little or no protest from the faculty, repeatedly lied about their discriminatory policy until they were caught red-handed, and then they solemnly announced that they were shocked to learn of their own "insensitivity" to Asians. Second, nobody has yet explained how, if discrimination against Asians were necessary to fight white racism (never mind the blatant imbecility of the proposition), the university could eliminate such discrimination without succumbing to precisely that white racism. Third, how could the university now admit more Asians without further reducing the quota for white students, including deserving poor and working-class white students?

To right old wrongs, our leading universities are now try-   11
ing to buy black students and professors, of whom there are demonstrably not enough qualified ones to go around, even in Afro-American history. In consequence, they accept some who could not compete on merit, but who might do well at a university of the second rank; and the universities of the second rank accept those who belong in universities of the third rank; and the universities of the third rank accept available warm bodies. At all levels, many black students who cannot compete receive passing grades while being treated with contempt. And so frustration, resentment, and anger build among them, and among the white students, too, who have been shunted aside to facilitate this charade. The dropout rate for black students would rank as a scandal, if anything any longer ranked as a scandal.

At all levels, moreover, qualified black students and profes-   12
sors are made to look like charity cases. A number of blacks today rank among the finest American historians in the country, and many are honored for their achievements. But those

well-deserved honors often stick in the craw of their recipients, who can never be sure that the honors are not merely awarded to fill quotas. And if mature and accomplished professors suffer from this outrage, how must gifted black students feel about their situation?

13   Does affirmative action, then, undermine academic standards? Not necessarily, according to D'Souza, who sharply attacks its present form, and offers an alternative to which we shall return. Affirmative action cannot explain the decline in academic standards, which began well before it. The damning indictment of the long-practiced discrimination against women and blacks, moreover, properly focused on the lowering of academic standards made inevitable by a talent pool restricted to white males. By insisting that qualified women and blacks be given due consideration, affirmative action properly implemented ought to replace mediocre professors with superior ones.

14   Unfortunately D'Souza sidesteps this larger issue. Still, it will emerge quickly if his book receives the attention it deserves. The decline in academic standards has proceeded in tandem with the radical egalitarian conviction that everyone is fit for, and has a right to, a college education. As a consequence of this conviction, even our finest colleagues have had to struggle constantly to do more than teach at a high school level, since most of their students are certainly unprepared and probably unqualified. We have transformed our colleges from places of higher learning into places for the technical training of poorly prepared young men and women who need a degree to get a job in a college-crazy society. An example: the "democratization" of the history curriculum has led to the abolition of required courses in Western civilization and, in American history, of the introductory courses that serve as prerequisites for ostensibly advanced courses on, say, the Civil War. Which means that every such course must be reduced to an introductory course, since the professor cannot assume that his students know the difference between John C. Calhoun and Henry Clay, or know about Nullification and the Wilmot Proviso, or about anything else for that matter.

15   D'Souza recognizes as ghastly the conditions that are keeping blacks off the fabled "level playing field," but he sensibly insists that universities cannot do much to correct those conditions without pointlessly ruining themselves. Still, D'Souza himself continues to preach "equality of opportunity," even though conservatives like Richard Weaver and M. E. Bradford, not to mention a few liberals, have exploded it as a cruel

hoax. If, as should be obvious, some people, black or white, begin with less cultural advantage, less preparation, and less talent than others, "equality of opportunity" can only result in the perpetuation of the initial levels of inequality.

The problems posed by D'Souza range well beyond the horror stories and lead directly to the essential purposes of liberal education, and to the alarming assault on Western civilization—on the civilization, not just on the courses on the civilization. D'Souza, a man of color born in India, is no mindless celebrant of Western virtues and values. He advocates a curriculum that includes attention to the rest of the world. And he argues well that those who denigrate the Western also denigrate the non-Western: they have no interest in teaching the *Analects*, the Ramayana, or the Koran, but prefer instead to peddle what usually turns out to be little more than recent non-Western versions of their favorite radical Western ideologies. 16

The point deserves pausing over. It is almost always the case that those who denigrate Western civilization do not tolerate those who teach the entire truth about Asia and Africa, about Hinduism and Islam, which have also had a history of racism, sexism, class exploitation, imperialism, and murderous violence. It does not occur to them (or does it?) that they thereby rob their Asian and African American students of a chance to learn the specifics, and the complexities, of the history of their own forebears. They leave their Asian and African American students bereft of a full appreciation of the glory and the shame, the virtue and the vice, that go into the making of everything human. 17

The campaign for "political correctness" invites ugly tactics that could never be sustained, however, without the complicity of the very administrators and the very faculty members at whom they are directed. At Stanford, students seized the office of President Donald Kennedy, making demands, some constructive and some preposterous. Kennedy bravely announced: "The university will not negotiate on issues of substance in response to unlawful coercion." The next day under unlawful coercion, he entered into negotiations, and he caved in to the demands. (Come to think of it, did he mean that he might negotiate on issues of procedure under unlawful coercion? Did he mean to endorse lawful coercion? Never mind: we don't expect university presidents to speak English these days.) 18

19   Administrators capitulate to terrorists primarily because
they are damage control experts obsessed with the smart
move. When terrorists threaten to trash them as racists, sexists, homophobes, and enemies of the people, the smart move
is to capitulate, for the administrators have nothing to lose
save honor; and since the poststructuralists on their faculties
have nicely deconstructed honor, they need pay it no mind.
Who could blame administrators for not wanting to face
demonstrators who denounce them as criminals? Besides,
the national academic establishments and most of the media
will commend them for their statesmanship in defusing confrontation, for opening new lines of communication, for
showing compassion and sensitivity.

20   A university president who negotiates with storm troopers
who have occupied any part of his campus, much less his
own office, should be fired. But first we must do our best to
save all such quivering time-servers from themselves. To that
end, I offer the Law of Liberation through Counterterror: *In
every such political struggle, honorable men and women can
defeat terrorism only by unleashing counterterrorism against
cowardly administrators and their complicit faculty.* Of course,
we must obey this law in a humane spirit, for the purpose of
liberating these benighted souls to realize their own inner
wills. Like loving parents, we must accept the disagreeable
duty to inflict excruciating pain on ourselves by whipping our
errant children for their own good.

21   After all, our campus heroes do not wish to face demonstrators of another kind: those who, closer to the truth, trash them
as front men for a new McCarthyism, as hypocrites who
preach diversity and practice totalitarianism, as cowards,
whores, and rogues. Let us, then, drive into their brains the
terrifying recognition that counterterrorists will (figuratively)
draw their blood for every concession made to terrorists; that
administrators who deftly avoid calls for their ouster from the
one side will face such calls from the other side; that, whatever
they do, they will suffer hard blows; and that, despite every
smart move known to God and man, they will find no place to
hide from any war that the terrorists unleash. All, again, for
their own good. By raising the price of sleaziness as high as the
price of a staunch defense of their campuses, we shall liberate
administrators to stand on their own professed principles,
secure in the knowledge that they have nothing left to lose.

22   The surrender of the administrators is not hard to understand, at least in one respect. Who wants to be accused of

insensitivity? The answer is, those who recognize "sensitivity" as a code word for the promulgation of a demagogic political program. At Brooklyn College, which I attended in the late 1940s, everyone took for granted that students ought to challenge their professors and each other. Professors acted as if they were paid to assault their students' sensibilities, to offend their most cherished values. The classroom was an ideological war zone. And self-respecting students returned the blows. In this way we had a chance to acquire a first-rate education, that is, to learn to sustain ourselves in combat against dedicated but overworked professors who lacked the time and the "tolerance" to worry about our "feelings."

I learned my lessons well, and so I routinely assign books   23
that contradict the point of view presented in my own classroom. I insist only that students challenge my point of view in accordance with the canons of (Southern) courtesy, and in obedience to a rule: lay down plausible premises, argue logically, appeal to evidence. If they say things that offend others, the offended ones are invited to reply, fiercely but in accordance with the same courtesy and in obedience to the same rule. I know no other way to show students, white or black, male or female, the respect that ought to be shown in a place of intellectual and ideological contention. Thus I submit the First Law of College Teaching: *Any professor who, subject to the restraints of common sense and common decency, does not seize every opportunity to offend the sensibilities of his students is insulting and cheating them, and is no college professor at all.*

*   *   *

Illiberal Education pays much less attention to gender than   24
to race, and displays less knowledge of the issues, the personalities, and the circumstances of women's studies in this country. Yet a larger problem affects D'Souza's treatment of both race and gender: he falls into the trap of condemning black studies and women's studies programs out of hand. D'Souza simply ignores the record of the best of those programs in enriching the college curriculum. He acknowledges excellent scholarship in black studies, but he wrongly asserts that it emanates from scholars in traditional departments. His assertion is anyway beside the point.

The demand for separate programs arose because the tra-   25
ditional departments were ignoring, and even condemning, significant subject matter. In this respect, the history of these programs does not differ markedly from the history of area

studies, religious studies, Jewish studies, or film studies, some of which also arose in response to political pressures. In principle, we should emphatically welcome black studies and women's studies programs or departments as a legitimate means of promoting scholarship about valuable subjects long and stupidly ignored. In practice, moreover, some of these programs have functioned admirably, as have such centers for the promotion of scholarship as the Carter Woodson Center at the University of Virginia, which offers scholars in black studies an opportunity to pursue their research in an institution that upholds high standards and is open to diverse viewpoints. I very much doubt that D'Souza's blanket condemnation of these academic innovations would apply, after careful investigation, to the women's studies program at Emory University, say, or to a number of other black studies and women's studies programs.

26   If many such programs have little intellectual merit and are principally engaged in political indoctrination, there are exceptions, and they prove that the result is not fated. D'Souza is right to charge that the culpable programs arose from the cynicism (not to mention the racism and the sexism) of administrations and faculties that refused to hold them to proper academic standards. As a result, large numbers of excellent professors in black studies programs and women's studies programs have been left to the mercies of campus politicians who are uninterested in academic standards and hostile to academic freedom.

27   I know of no women's studies program that has a conservative or anti-feminist faculty member, although I know of at least one such program that would like to. The problem is not only that many programs are run by professors who, supported by administrators, apply ideological standards in the recruitment of faculty. The problem is also that professors of a more conservative disposition whose work includes subject matter appropriate to women's studies normally want nothing to do with programs that they view as inescapably political. Accepting exclusion, they do not fight for their right to participate and to teach from their own point of view.

28   When has a conservative or an anti-feminist professor applied for a job in a women's studies program? Such an applicant would be rejected in most places. But if that is the case, then the issue of "discrimination" ought to be joined precisely on grounds of a commitment to "diversity." No university should tolerate a program or a department of any kind that applies political and ideological criteria in hiring and

promotions (as many history departments now do). I do not underestimate the magnitude of the task that faces those who would fight this battle. Still, if principled liberals and leftists do inhabit our campuses, as we must hope that they do, then surely they can be rallied to the defense of the academic freedom of their conservative colleagues.

In discussing present trends, D'Souza presents two explanations that, while not mutually exclusive, coexist uneasily. He excoriates administrators for succumbing to pressure from those who have sectarian agendas, but he also argues that administrators are imposing their own ideological agendas. He shows that "a revolution from above" is occurring at such leading universities as Harvard, Berkeley, Stanford, and Wisconsin, and that it is spreading; but the burden of his evidence suggests that the greater problem remains the general capitulation to destructive political pressures.   29

The capitulation has some high-minded alibis. D'Souza mentions them, but he does not probe adequately. The principal alibi stresses the moral imperative of submission to the will of "the community," which is necessary, it is claimed, for the maintenance of a democratic society. The university, this song goes, has no right to exist as an ivory tower, oblivious to the needs and the aspirations of a democratic people. None can object, of course, when the choice is posed so starkly, though it might be recalled that Southern universities long justified segregation as an accommodation to the prevailing sentiments of their communities. To pose it so starkly, however, is to talk nonsense.   30

Intellectual work in general, and higher education in particular, depend upon academic freedom, which depends upon a wide swath of autonomy, of detachment, for the university. The university must be ready, therefore, to stand against the community, and to protect those who challenge the attitudes and the sensibilities that prevail in the community. Neither academic freedom nor the autonomy of the university should be defended as absolutes. Some measure of accommodation to the larger society is always necessary and proper, and the gray area will always be a battleground. Still, a university worthy of the name must, so far as practicable, recognize its duty to protect those who defy the political consensus of the moment.   31

That is, it must recognize itself as an institution in constant and principled tension with the community in which it resides. When the New Left of the 1960s demanded that the universities become responsive to the community, it ironically   32 advanced the work begun by its Establishment enemies. Long before the hysterical response to Sputnik, the universities had been under pressure to serve the interests of communities attuned to the government and big business. All that the New Left did was to define "community" to suit its own ideas and interests. Like its enemies, it insisted on an engaged academy and poured contempt on the ideal of the university as an autonomous institution.

33   D'Souza's book contains telling quotations from campus zealots on the problem of "politicization." The universities have always been political, they argue. Indeed, everything has a political dimension—and so the only issue is what kind of politics are to be imposed. There is a grain of truth here, but carried to its logical conclusion it would transform every institution into an instrument of political correctness. And that, to speak precisely, is totalitarianism.

34   D'Souza makes too many concessions to democratic and egalitarian dogmas for my taste. He responds to these arguments weakly, by arguing that the politicization of the universities is leading to their domination by coalitions of ideological minorities. No doubt it is. But the danger would be even greater if the universities were to succumb to an ideological majority. The hard truth is that academic freedom— the real work of scholarship—requires a willingness to set limits to the claims of democracy. It requires a strong dose of hierarchical authority within institutions that must be able to defy a democratic consensus. Sooner or later we shall have to face this fact, or be defeated by those who seek the total politicization of our campuses.

35   D'Souza ends his book constructively, with three proposals to promote academic standards and academic freedom and simultaneously to do justice to genuinely disadvantaged youth. His first, and most significant, is his call for "nonracial affirmative action." With this idea, he risks the ire of many on the right. He notes that the rising tide of white racism among students is being fueled by discrimination against qualified white students in favor of less qualified black students who receive financial support despite coming from affluent families. Recognizing that most qualified black students, like many qualified white students, need financial support, he proposes to subsidize according to a combination of demonstrated merit and need. An advocate of "individualism," D'Souza insists that his program promotes "equality of opportunity" and rejects categorization by group. Surely he

jests. For his program implies a collectivism that merely replaces "race" with "class." At least it promises to attack racial injustice, since the correlation of race and lower class among blacks is, as he takes pains to show, strikingly high.

His second proposal is for "choice without separation." It's   36
not exactly clear what this slogan means. It originates in a critique of black separatism that I find sadly wrongheaded. D'Souza, fearful of ghettoization and the institutionalization of racial oppression in a new form, seems alarmed at the very idea of separate black professional and extracurricular organizations. He lashes out, therefore, at everything that hints of black separatism, of any kind of separatism. But he is uncritically assimilating the black experience in America to the general "ethnic" experience, and he is thereby missing its uniqueness. Blacks did not bring a distinct culture from Africa as, say, Italian-Americans or Polish-Americans did from their homelands; they forged a new and powerful culture of their own. Afro-American culture has grown out of a forced emigration from Africa, out of resistance to slavery, and out of enforced segregation, and for those reasons it has imparted to many black people a sense of being "a nation within a nation," to invoke a term that dates from early colonial times and was popularized by W. E. B. DuBois. The attendant problems of analysis, not to mention politics, are extraordinarily complex. And for just that reason they ought long ago to have been made the center of discussion on our campuses, in and out of black studies programs.

D'Souza's third proposal offers an intriguing curriculum   37
reform that would expose students "to the basic issues of equality and human difference, through a carefully chosen set of classic texts that deal powerfully with those issues." Briefly, he aims at grounding American students in the Western experience that has constituted the foundation of our society and culture, but in a way that promotes comparison and contrast with the civilizations of the rest of the world and appreciates their contribution to our own national development. This proposal is unobjectionable, but it is not very original. In fact, an increasing number of principled professors are in fact promoting "World Civilization" in the manner D'Souza recommends—that is, by introducing African, Asian, and Latin American cultural studies without denigrating Western civilization.

Illiberal Education invites cooperation in a common effort   38
in defense of the campus. Occasionally D'Souza descends into

biased and irritating attacks on the left and center, with
sweeping and one-sided characterizations of Marxism and
Marxists, liberalism and liberals. (He does not do justice to
the literary critic Henry Louis Gates, Jr. or the historian Linda
Kerber, among others.) Yet on the whole he makes a good
effort to be fair, to focus on issues, to avoid ad hominem
attacks, and to check his own political passions. He acknowledges, however grudgingly, the commitment of certain Marxists, feminists, proponents of black studies, and others to
academic freedom and to scholarly integrity. This book could
open a salutary national debate. But the cause it champions
will go down, unless it is supported by a substantial portion of
the left and the center.

39   For this is not an issue only of the right, not least for a
practical reason: there are not nearly enough conservatives
on our campuses to do more than fight a rearguard action.
Indeed, the predicament of the right should give many on the
left a sense of déjà vu, and a good laugh. Opposition to campus atrocities attracts two kinds of right-wingers: those who
defend academic freedom and academic standards on principle, and those interested in using the issue as a "transmission
belt" for recruitment into their "movement." The former, I
mean the principled defenders of the academy, understand
that they must cooperate with those whom they oppose on
other issues. The latter, I mean the sectarians, do everything
possible to identify the academic cause with their own partisan politics and slander all liberals and leftists as complicit in
the new wave of campus barbarism. Looking beyond the
immediate struggle, they fear nothing so much as the dissolution of the reigning isms, and the redrawing of political lines
in a manner that brings together the healthiest elements of
long-warring political camps.

40   The sectarians are correct to fear the consecration of the
campuses to a vigorous political debate under conditions of
real mutual respect and genuine academic freedom. Such a
debate would undermine all the sectarianisms. It would
encourage new political formations to meet the challenges of
a new era. And so it should: the defense of academic freedom
requires an all-out counterattack by a coalition that cuts
across all the lines of politics, race, and gender. It is time to
close ranks.

John Taylor

Are You Politically Incorrect?

John Taylor writes frequently for New York *magazine; indeed, he is a contributing editor for it.* New York *magazine could be described as a sort of* Time *or* Newsweek *for New Yorkers: Published weekly, it covers the current events and contemporary cultural affairs that are particularly interesting to people in the New York metropolitan area. The following article appeared in* New York *in January 1991.*

"Racist."   1

"Racist!"   2

"The man is a racist!"   3

"A *racist!*"   4

Such denunciations, hissed in tones of self-righteousness   5
and contempt, vicious and vengeful, furious, smoking with
hatred—such denunciations haunted Stephan Thernstrom
for weeks. Whenever he walked through the campus that
spring, down Harvard's brick paths, under the arched gates,
past the fluttering elms, he found it hard not to imagine the
pointing fingers, the whispers. Racist. There goes *the racist.* It
was hellish, this persecution. Thernstrom couldn't sleep. His
nerves were frayed, his temper raw. He was making his family
miserable. And the worst thing was that he didn't know who
was calling him a racist, or why.

Thernstrom, 56, a professor at Harvard University for 25   6
years, is considered one of the preeminent scholars of the history of race relations in America. He has tenure. He has won
prizes and published numerous articles and four books and
edited the *Harvard Encyclopedia of American Ethnic Groups.*
For several years, Thernstrom and another professor, Bernard Bailyn, taught an undergraduate lecture course on the
history of race relations in the United States called "Peopling
of America." Bailyn covered the Colonial era. Thernstrom
took the class up to the present.

Both professors are regarded as very much in the academic   7
mainstream, their views grounded in extensive research on
their subject, and both have solid liberal democratic credentials. But all of a sudden, in the fall of 1987, articles began to
appear in the *Harvard Crimson* accusing Thernstrom and Bailyn of "racial insensitivity" in "Peopling of America." The

sources for the articles were anonymous, the charges vague, but they continued to be repeated, these ringing indictments.

8   Finally, through the intervention of another professor, two students from the lecture course came forward and identified themselves as the sources for the articles. When asked to explain their grievances, they presented the professors with a six-page letter. Bailyn's crime had been to read from the diary of a southern planter without giving equal time to the recollections of a slave. This, to the students, amounted to a covert defense of slavery. Bailyn, who has won two Pulitzer Prizes, had pointed out during the lecture that no journals, diaries, or letters written by slaves had ever been found. He had explained to the class that all they could do was read the planter's diary and use it to speculate about the experience of slaves. But that failed to satisfy the complaining students. Since it was impossible to give equal representation to the slaves, Bailyn ought to have dispensed with the planter's diary altogether.

9   Thernstrom's failures, according to the students, were almost systematic. He had, to begin with, used the word *Indians* instead of *Native Americans*. Thernstrom tried to point out that he had said very clearly in class that *Indian* was the word most Indians themselves use, but that was irrelevant to the students. They considered the word racist. Thernstrom was also accused of referring to an "Oriental religion." The word *Oriental*, with its imperialist overtones, was unacceptable. Thernstrom explained that he had used the word as an adjective, not as a noun, but the students weren't buying any wriggling, sophistic evasions like that.

10   Even worse, they continued, Thernstrom had assigned a book to the class that mentioned that some people regarded affirmative action as preferential treatment. That was a racist opinion. But most egregiously, Thernstrom had endorsed, in class, Patrick Moynihan's emphasis on the breakup of the black family as a cause of persistent black poverty. That was a racist idea.

11   All of these words and opinions and ideas and historical approaches were racist. *Racist!* They would not be tolerated.

12   The semester was pretty much over by then. But during the spring, when Thernstrom sat down to plan the course for the following year, he had to think about how he would combat charges of racism should they crop up again. And they assuredly would. All it took was one militant student, one word like *Oriental* taken out of context, one objection that a professor's

account of slavery was insufficiently critical or that, in discussing black poverty, he had raised the "racist" issue of welfare dependency. And a charge of racism, however unsubstantiated, leaves a lasting impression. "It's like being called a Commie in the fifties," Thernstrom says. "Whatever explanation you offer, once accused, you're always suspect."

He decided that to protect himself in case he was mis-   13
quoted or had comments taken out of context, he would need to tape all his lectures. Then he decided he would have to tape his talks with students in his office. He would, in fact, have to tape everything he said on the subject of race. It would require a tape-recording system worthy of the Nixon White House. Microphones everywhere, the reels turning constantly. That was plainly ridiculous. Thernstrom instead decided it would be easier just to drop the course altogether. "Peopling of America" is no longer offered at Harvard.

The New Fundamentalism

When the Christian-fundamentalist uprising began in the   14
late seventies, Americans on the left sneered at the Bible thumpers who tried to ban the teaching of evolution in public schools, at the troglodtyes who wanted to remove *The Catcher in the Rye* from public libraries. They heaped scorn on the evangelists who railed against secular humanism and the pious hypocrites who tried to legislate patriotism and Christianity through school prayer and the Pledge of Allegiance. This last effort was considered particularly heinous. Those right-wing demagogues were interfering with individual liberties! They were trying to indoctrinate the children! It was scandalous and outrageous, and unconstitutional too.

But curiously enough, in the past few years, a new sort of   15
fundamentalism has arisen precisely among those people who were the most appalled by Christian fundamentalism. And it is just as demagogic and fanatical. The new fundamentalists are an eclectic group; they include multiculturalists, feminists, radical homosexuals, Marxists, New Historicists. What unites them—as firmly as the Christian fundamentalists are united in the belief that the Bible is the revealed word of God—is their conviction that Western culture and American society are thoroughly and hopelessly racist, sexist, oppressive. "Racism and sexism are pervasive in America and fundamentally present in all American institutions," declares a draft report on "race and gender enrichment" at Tulane University. A 1989 report by a

New York State Board of Education task force was even more sweeping: "Intellectual and educational oppression...has characterized the culture and institutions of the United States and the European American world for centuries."

16   The heart of the new fundamentalists' argument is not just that, as most everyone would agree, racism and sexism historically have existed within political systems designed to promote individual liberties. They believe that the doctrine of individual liberties *itself* is inherently oppressive. At the University of Pennsylvania, an undergraduate on the "diversity education committee" wrote a memo to committee members describing her "deep regard for the individual and my desire to protect the freedoms of all members of society." The tone was earnest and sincere. The young woman clearly considered herself an idealist of the Jeffersonian persuasion. Individual freedom, she seemed to indicate, was a concept to be cherished above all else.

17   But in the prevailing climate, Thomas Jefferson and all the Founding Fathers are in disrepute. (The Constitution, according to the 1989 New York State report, is "the embodiment of the White Male with Property Model.") One college administrator had no patience with the young woman's naïve and bourgeois sentiments. He returned her memo with the word *individual* underlined. "This is a 'RED FLAG' phrase today, which many consider RACIST," the administrator wrote. "Arguments that champion the individual over the group ultimately privilege the 'INDIVIDUALS' belonging to the largest or dominant group."

18   Defenders of Western culture try to point out that other civilizations—from the Islamic and the Hindu to the Confucian and the Buddhist—are rife with racism and sexism. They find it odd that while Eastern Europeans are rushing to embrace Western democracy, while the pro-democracy movement in China actually erected a replica of the Statue of Liberty in Tiananmen Square, this peculiar intellectual cult back in the States continues to insist that Western values are the source of much of the world's evil.

19   But one of the marvels of the new fundamentalism is the rationale it has concocted for dismissing all dissent. Just as Christian fundamentalists attack nonbelievers as agents of Satan, so the politically correct dismiss their critics as victims of, to use the famous Marxist phrase, "false consciousness." Anyone who disagrees is simply too soaked in the oppressors' propaganda to see the truth. "Racism and sexism are subtle and, for the most part, subconscious or at least subsurface,"

the Tulane report continues. "It is difficult for us to see and overcome racism and sexism because we are all a product of the problem, i.e., we are all the progeny of a racist and sexist society."

This circular reasoning enables the new fundamentalists to 20 attack not just the opinions of their critics but the right of their critics to disagree. Alternate viewpoints are simply not allowed. Though there was little visible protest when Louis Farrakhan was invited to speak at the University of Wisconsin, students at the University of Northern Colorado practically rioted when Linda Chavez, a Hispanic member of the Reagan administration who opposes affirmative action and believes immigrants should be encouraged to learn English, was asked to talk. The invitation was withdrawn. Last February, Patrick Moynihan declared during a lecture at Vassar that America was "a model of a reasonably successful multi-ethnic society." Afterward, he got into an argument with a black woman who disagreed with him, and when she claimed the senator had insulted her, militant students occupied a school building until Moynihan returned his lecture fee. "The disturbing factor in the success of totalitarianism is...the true selflessness of its adherents," Hannah Arendt wrote in *The Origins of Totalitarianism.* "The fanaticized members can be reached by neither experience nor argument."

It is this sort of demand for intellectual conformity, 21 enforced with harassment and intimidation, that has led some people to compare the atmosphere in universities today to that of Germany in the thirties. "It's fascism of the left," says Camille Paglia, a professor at the University of the Arts in Philadelphia and the author of *Sexual Personae.* "These people behave like the Hitler Youth."

It reminds others of America in the fifties. "This sort of 22 atmosphere, where a few highly mobilized radical students can intimidate everyone else, is quite new," Thernstrom says. "This is a new McCarthyism. It's more frightening than the old McCarthyism, which had no support in the academy. Now the enemy is within. There are students and faculty who have no belief in freedom of speech."

And it reminds still others of China during the Cultural 23 Revolution of the sixties, when thought criminals were paraded through towns in dunce caps. "In certain respects, the University of Pennsylvania has become like the University of Peking," says Alan Kors, a professor of history.

Indeed, schools like Berkeley and Carleton require courses 24 in race relations, sometimes called "oppression studies." A

proposed course book for a required writing seminar at the
University of Texas contains, instead of models of clarity like
E. B. White, essays such as "is not so gd [*sic*] to be born a girl,"
by Ntozake Shange. Many schools—including Stanford, Pennsylvania, and the University of Wisconsin—have adopted
codes of conduct that require students who deviate from politically correct thinking to undergo thought reform. When a
student at the University of Michigan read a limerick that
speculated jokingly about the homosexuality of a famous athlete, he was required to attend gay-sensitivity sessions and
publish a piece of self-criticism in the student newspaper
called "Learned My Lesson."

25   But is any of this so awful? In the minds of its advocates,
thought reform is merely a well-intentioned effort to help
stop the spread of the racial tensions that have proliferated in
universities in recent years. "I don't know of any institution
that is saying you have to adore everyone else," says
Catharine Stimpson, dean of the graduate school at Rutgers.
"They are saying you have to learn to live with everyone. They
are taking insulting language seriously. That's a good thing.
They're not laughing off anti-Semitic and homophobic graffiti."

26   After all, it is said, political indoctrination of one sort or
another has always taken place at universities. Now that process is simply being made overt. And anyway, all these people
complaining about the loss of academic freedom and the
decline in standards are only trying to disguise their own
efforts to retain power. "The attack on diversity is a rhetorical
strategy by neoconservatives who have their own political
agenda," says Stimpson. "Under the guise of defending objectivity and intellectual rigor, which is a lot of mishmash, they
are trying to preserve the cultural and political supremacy of
white heterosexual males."

Everything Is Political

27   If the debate over what students should be taught has
become an openly political power struggle, that is only
because, to the politically correct, *everything* is political. And
nothing is more political, in their view, than the humanities,
where much of the recent controversy has been centered.

28   For most of the twentieth century, professors in the
humanities modeled themselves on their counterparts in the
natural sciences. They thought of themselves as specialists in

the disinterested pursuit of the truth. Their job, in the words of T. S. Eliot, was "the elucidation of art and the correction of taste," and to do so they concentrated on what Matthew Arnold called "the best that has been thought and written."

That common sense of purpose began to fracture in the sixties. The generation of professors now acquiring prominence and power at universities—Elaine Showalter, the head of the English department at Princeton; Donna Shalala, chancellor of the University of Wisconsin; James Freedman, the president of Dartmouth—came of age during that period. They witnessed its upheavals and absorbed its political commitments.

And by and large, they have retained them. Which means that, though much of the country subsequently rejected the political vision of the sixties, it has triumphed at the universities. "If the undergraduate population has moved quietly to the right in recent years, the men and women who are paid to introduce students to the great works and ideas of our civilization have by and large remained true to the emancipationist ideology of the sixties," writes Roger Kimball in his book, *Tenured Radicals*. The professors themselves eagerly admit this. "I see my scholarship as an extension of my political activism," said Annette Kolodny, a former Berkeley radical and now the dean of the humanities faculty at the University of Arizona.

In the view of such activists, the universities were hardly the havens of academic independence they pretended to be. They had hopelessly compromised their integrity by accepting contracts from the Pentagon, but those alliances with the reviled "military-industrial Establishment" were seen as merely one symptom of a larger conspiracy by white males. Less obviously, but more insidiously, they had appointed themselves guardians of the culture and compiled the list of so-called Great Books as a propaganda exercise to reinforce the notion of white-male superiority. "The canon of great literature was created by high-Anglican ass----s to underwrite their social class," Stanley Hauerwas, a professor at Duke's Divinity School, put it recently.

Several schools of French critical theory that became fashionable during the seventies provided the jargon for this critique. Semiotics and Lacanian psychoanalysis argued that language and art conveyed subliminal cultural prejudices, power configurations, metaphoric representations of gender. Deconstruction declared that texts, to use the preferred word, had no meaning outside themselves. "There is no such thing

29

30

31

32

as literal meaning…there is no such thing as intrinsic merit," wrote Stanley Fish, the head of Duke's English department.

33   That being the case, any attempt to assign meaning to art, literature, or thought, to interpret it and evaluate it, was nothing more than an exercise in political power by the individual with the authority to impose his or her view. It then followed that the only reason to require students to read certain books is not to "correct taste" or because the books were "the best that has been thought or written" but because they promoted politically correct viewpoints. That ideological emphasis also applied to scholarship generally. "If the work doesn't have a strong political thrust, I don't see how it matters," said Eve Sedgwick, a professor of English at Duke and the author of such papers as "Jane Austen and the Masturbating Girl."

34   This agenda can produce a rather remarkable, not to say outré, reading list. Catharine Stimpson has declared that her ideal curriculum would contain the little-known book *Stars in My Pocket Like Grains of Sand*. "Like many contemporary speculative fictions," Stimpson wrote, *"Stars in My Pocket* finds conventional heterosexuality absurd. The central characters are two men, Rat Korga and Marq Dyeth, who have a complex but ecstatic affair. Marq is also the product of a rich 'nurture stream.' His ancestry includes both humans and aliens. His genetic heritage blends differences. In a sweet scene, he sees three of his mothers."

Ethnic and Ideological Purity

35   The multicultural and ethnic-studies programs now in place at most universities tend to divide humanity into five groups—whites, blacks, Native Americans, Hispanics, and Asians. (Homosexuals and feminists are usually included on the grounds that, though they are not a distinct ethnic group, they, too, have been oppressed by the "whitemale," to use the neologism of black literature professor Houston Baker, and prevented from expressing their "otherness.") These are somewhat arbitrary categories, and, in fact, the new fundamentalists have two contradictory views about just what constitutes an ethnic group and who can belong.

36   On the one hand, there is a reluctance to confer ethnic status on certain groups. At the University of Washington, a student-faculty Task Force on Ethnicity denied Jews, Italians, and Irish-Americans certification as ethnic groups. Status as an oppressed ethnic group is guarded even more jealously.

The Washington task force also decided that a required ethnic-studies program exploring the pervasiveness of racism in America would not take up the subject of anti-Semitism. The reason, *Commentary* quoted professor Johnnella Butler as having said, was that "anti-Semitism is not institutionalized in this country."

At the same time, the racial credentials of people aspiring   37
to membership in the officially sanctioned ethnic categories are examined with an attention to detail associated with apartheid. Recently, a Hispanic who had been turned down for an affirmative-action promotion in the San Francisco fire department filed a complaint because the person who got the job instead was from Spain rather than Latin America. Colleges are becoming equally obsessed with such distinctions. Three years ago, the faculty at Hampshire College in Amherst began interviewing candidates for a professorship in Latin American literature. The professor, of course, needed to be Latin. *Pure* Latin. One woman who applied for the job was turned down because, though she was Argentine, she had, like many Argentines, Jewish and Italian blood, and thus her Third World ethnicity was considered insufficiently pure. Her heritage made her, in the words of one faculty member, "Eurocentric."

But even as these standards become increasingly exacting,   38
more and more groups are clamoring for oppressed status. While supporters of American involvement in the Vietnam War were denounced as "war criminals" at the University of Michigan in the sixties, the school now counts Vietnam veterans as an oppressed group. In fact, the politically correct have concluded that virtually *any*one with *any* sort of trait, anxiety, flaw, impediment, or unusual sexual preference qualifies for membership in an oppressed group. This past fall, a handout from the Office of Student Affairs at Smith College explained that many people are *unaware* they are oppressed, though with help they are finding out: "As groups of people begin the process of realizing that they are oppressed, and why, new words tend to be created to express the concepts that the existing language cannot."

This obsessive tendency to see oppression everywhere is   39
creating a sort of New Age caste system. The Smith handout listed various categories of oppression that ranged from "classism" and "ageism" to "ableism" (identified as "oppression of the differently abled by the temporarily able") and "lookism," which was revealed to be "the construction of a standard for beauty/attractiveness; and oppression through

stereotypes and generalizations of both those who do not fit
that standard and those who do." Heightism may be next. In
a joke now making the rounds, short people are demanding
to be known as "the vertically challenged."

40   But joking isn't allowed! Even the most harmless, light-
hearted remarks can lead to virulent denunciations. In October, Roderick Nash, a professor at the University of California
at Santa Barbara, pointed out during a lecture on environmental ethics that there is a movement to start referring to
pets as animal companions. (Apparently, domesticated animals are offended by the word *pet*.) Nash then made some
sort of off-the-cuff observation about how women who pose
for *Penthouse* are still called Pets (and not *Penthouse* Animal
Companions). Inevitably, several female students filed a formal sexual-harassment complaint against him. Susan Rode,
one of the signers, said, "Maybe this will make more people
aware in other classes and make other faculty watch what
they say."

41   Indeed, making people *watch what they say* is the central
preoccupation of politically correct students. Stephan Thernstrom is not the only professor who has been forced to give
up a course on race relations. Reynolds Farley, one of the
leading scholars on race relations, dropped a course he had
taught for nearly ten years at the University of Michigan after
he was accused of racial insensitivity for reading Malcolm X's
description of himself as a pimp and a thief and for discussing the southern defense of slavery. "Given the climate at
Michigan," Farley said, "I could be hassled for anything I do
or don't say in that class."

42   *Watch what you say:* And it's not enough just to avoid racism. One must display absolute ideological purity. The search
committee at Hampshire College also considered a highly
qualified Chicano candidate for the Latin American–literature
post. Unfortunately for him, in his dissertation on Chicano literature he drew parallels between Shakespeare and Mexican
writers. This demonstrated dangerous "Eurocentric" tendencies. Certain faculty members, doubting the candidate's ethnic purity as well, wondered whether someone of Mexican
heritage was *really* Latin American. They thought a Puerto
Rican might be better. He didn't get the job.

43   It was finally offered to Norman Holland, who seemed
both ethnically and ideologically pure. But this past summer,
Holland's contract was not renewed, and Holland claims it is
because he also was branded "Eurocentric." Though the
school's official position is that Holland was an ineffective

teacher, two of the professors who reviewed his work insinuated that he had a European bias. Holland, one professor declared, had "focused mainly on Western Europe to the exclusion of cultural issues Third World students perceive as uniquely relevant." "I suppose I committed certain kinds of sins," says Holland. "When I was teaching *One Hundred Years of Solitude,* I would talk about colonial rape, but I would also talk about how the novel originated in Europe and how García Márquez was working in that tradition and addressing ideas in Proust and Joyce. I didn't limit myself to considering it as a sociological document."

The Gender Feminists and Date Rape

"Misogynistic!"   44
"Patriarchal!"   45
"Gynophobic!"   46
"Phallocentric!"   47
Last fall, Camille Paglia attended a lecture by a "feminist   48
theorist" from a large Ivy League university who had set out
to "decode" the subliminal sexual oppressiveness in fashion
photography. The feminist theorist stood at the front of the
room showing slides of fashion photography and cosmetics
ads and exposing, in the style of Lacanian psychoanalysis,
their violent sexism. She had selected a Revlon ad of a woman
with a heavily made-up face who was standing up to her chin
in a pool of water. When it came up on the screen, she
exclaimed, "Decapitation!"

She showed a picture of a black woman who was wearing   49
aviator goggles and had the collar of her turtleneck sweater
pulled up. "Strangulation!" she shouted. "Bondage!"

It went on like this for the entire lecture. When it was over,   50
Paglia, who considers herself a feminist, stood up and made
an impassioned speech. She declared that the fashion photography of the past 40 years is great art, that instead of decapitation she saw the birth of Venus, instead of strangulation she saw references to King Tut. But political correctness has achieved a kind of exquisitely perfect rigidity among the group known as the gender feminists, and she was greeted, she says, "with gasps of horror and angry murmuring. It's a form of psychosis, this slogan-filled machinery. The radical feminists have contempt for values other than their own, and they're inspiring in students a resentful attitude toward the world."

51   Indeed, the central tenet of gender feminism is that Western society is organized around a "sex/gender system." What
defines the system, according to Sandra Harding, a professor
of philosophy at the University of Delaware and one of its
exponents, is "male dominance made possible by men's control of women's productive and reproductive labor."

52   The primary arena for this dominance is, of course, the
family, which Alison Jaggar, a professor at the University of
Cincinnati and the head of the American Philosophical Association's Committee on the Status of Women in Philosophy,
sees as "a cornerstone of women's oppression." The family, in
Jaggar's view, "enforces heterosexuality" and "imposes the
prevailing masculine and feminine character structures on
the next generation."

53   This position makes gender feminists, as Christina Sommers has written in an article in *Public Affairs Quarterly,* from
which some of these quotes were taken, "oddly unsympa-
thetic to the women whom they claim to represent." But that
poses no problem. Women who have decided to get married
and raise families, women who want to become mothers, are,
naturally, victims of false consciousness. The radical feminists are fond of quoting Simone de Beauvoir, who said, "No
woman should be authorized to stay at home and raise
children...precisely because if there is such a choice, too
many women will make that one."

54   Jaggar, for one, would like to abolish the family altogether
and create a society where, with the aid of technology, "one
woman could inseminate another,...men...could lactate,...
and fertilized ova could be transferred into women's or even
men's bodies." All that is preventing this, according to the
gender feminists, is "phallocentricity" and "androcentricity,"
the view that society is organized around the male and his
sexual organs. The feminists, ablaze with revolutionary rhetoric, have set out to overthrow this system. "What we feminists
are doing," the philosopher Barbara Minnich has said, "is
comparable to Copernicus shattering our geocentricity, Darwin shattering our species-centricity. We are shattering
androcentricity, and the change is as fundamental, as dangerous, as exciting."

55   But unlike the pre-Copernican view that the Earth was at
the center of the universe, androcentricity is not, in the view
of the gender feminists, merely a flawed theory. It is a moral
evil, dedicated to the enslavement of women. And since most
of Western culture, according to this view, has been a testament to "male power and transcendence," it is similar to evil

and must be discarded. This includes not only patriarchal books like the Bible and sexist subjects like traditional history, with its emphasis on great men and great deeds, but also the natural sciences and even the very process of analytical thinking itself. "To know is to f---" has become a radical-feminist rallying cry. Indeed, scientific inquiry itself is seen as "the rape of nature." A project sponsored by the state of New Jersey to integrate these views into college campuses has issued a set of "feminist scholarship guidelines" that declares "mind was male. Nature was female, and knowledge was created as an act of aggression—a passive nature had to be interrogated, unclothed, penetrated, and compelled by man to reveal her secrets."

To certain women, however, this is just a veiled restate-   56
ment of the old idea that women don't make good scientists. "As a liberal feminist, I encourage women to study science," says Christina Sommers. "I'm not impugning science itself as hostile to the female sensibility."

But it is not just the coldly analytical and dualistic struc-   57
tures of male thinking that the gender feminists find so contemptible. It is males themselves, or at least heterosexual males. After all, heterosexuality is responsible for the subjugation of women, and so, in the oppressive culture of the West, any woman who goes on a date with a man is a prostitute. "Both man and woman might be outraged at the description of their candlelight dinner as prostitution," Jaggar has written. "But the radical feminist argues this outrage is simply due to the participants' failure or refusal to perceive the social context in which the dinner occurs." In other words, they are victims of—what else?—false consciousness.

This eagerness to see all women as victims, to describe all   58
male behavior with images of rape and violation, may shed some light on the phenomenon of date rape, a legitimate issue that has been exaggerated and distorted by a small group with a specific political agenda. As with the hysteria a few years ago over the sexual abuse of children, endless talk shows, television news stories, and magazine articles have been devoted to date rape, often describing it as "an epidemic" that, as the Chicago *Tribune* put it, "makes women campus prisoners" and forces them, as at Brown, to list supposed rapists on bathroom walls.

Much of this discussion starts off with the claim that one   59
in four female students is raped by a date. The figure seems staggeringly high, and debate tends to focus on whether actual rape or merely the reporting of rape is on the rise. But

the journalist Stephanie Gutmann has pointed out in *Reason* magazine the gross statistical flaws in the survey of date rape that produced this figure. According to Gutmann, "the real story about campus date rape is not that there's been any significant increase of rape on college campuses, at least of the acquaintance type, but that the word *rape* is being stretched to encompass any type of sexual interaction."

60   In fact, rape under the new definition does not have to involve physical assault at all. Andrea Parrot, a professor at Cornell who has promoted the idea of the date-rape epidemic, has declared that "any sexual intercourse without mutual desire is a form of rape." In other words, a woman is being raped if she has sex when not in the mood, even if she fails to inform her partner of that fact. As a former director of Columbia's date-rape-education program told Gutmann, "Every time you have an act of intercourse, there must be explicit consent, and if there's no explicit consent, then it's rape.... Stone silence throughout an entire physical encounter with someone is not explicit consent." And rape is no longer limited to actual intercourse. A training manual at Swarthmore College states that "acquaintance rape...spans a spectrum of incidents and behaviors ranging from crimes legally defined as rape to verbal harassment and inappropriate innuendo."

61   It is no surprise then that Catherine Nye, a University of Chicago psychologist interviewed by Gutmann, found that 43 percent of the women in a widely cited rape study "had not realized they had been raped." In other words, they were victims of, yes, false consciousness. But by the definition of the radical feminists, all sexual encounters that involve any confusion or ambivalence constitute rape. "Ordinary bungled sex—the kind you regret in the morning or even during—is being classified as rape," Gutmann says. "Bad or confused feelings after sex become someone else's fault." Which is fine with the feminists. "In terms of making men nervous or worried about overstepping their bounds, I don't think that's a bad thing," Parrot said. Indeed, since it encourages a general suspicion of all men, it's a good thing. As Parrot has put it, "Since you can't tell who has the potential for rape simply by looking, be on your guard with every man."

Afrocentrism

62   For all their fury, the gender feminists are surpassed in ideological rage by an even more extreme wing of the politi-

cally correct: the Afrocentrists. Afrocentrists argue that not only is Western culture oppressive, it isn't even really *Western*. Key accomplishments, from mathematics and biology to architecture and medicine, were in fact the work of Africans. "Very few doctors, African-American or otherwise in America, are aware of the fact that when they take their medical oath, the hypocratic [*sic*] oath, they actually swear to Imhotep, the African God of Medicine," Asa Hilliard, a professor of Afro-American history at Georgia State, has written.

63   The theory that Africa was the true source of Western civilization hinges on the claim that the ancient Egyptians were black. "The first 12 dynasties plus dynasties 18 and 25 were native-black-African dynasties," Hilliard has asserted. Traditional Egyptologists generally believe that while blacks, from Nubia to the south, were active in Egyptian society, ancient Egyptians, like their contemporary counterparts, tended to be of Semitic stock. But to the Afrocentrists, that explanation is merely part of the long-running conspiracy by Western whites to deny the African contribution to civilization.

64   The conspiracy began, in the Afrocentric view, when the ancient Greeks "stole" African philosophy and science from the Egyptians. To claim European credit for these discoveries, Romans and, later, Christians burned the library of Alexandria in Egypt. The conspiracy has continued ever since. Napoleon's soldiers shot off the nose and lips of the Sphinx to obliterate its Negroid features. Beethoven and Robert Browning were actually blacks whose ethnicity has been hidden. "African history has been lost, stolen, destroyed, and suppressed," Hilliard maintains.

65   Leonard Jeffries, chairman of the black-studies department at City College and one of the most extreme exponents of Afrocentrism, has worked up a sort of anthropological model to explain why Europeans have oppressed Africans. The human race, according to Jeffries, is divided into the "ice people" and the "sun people." The ethnic groups descended from the ice people are materialistic, selfish, and violent, while those descended from the sun people are nonviolent, cooperative, and spiritual. In addition, blacks are biologically superior to whites, Jeffries maintains, because they have more melanin, and melanin regulates intellect and health.

66   Despite the spiritual benevolence one might expect from a "sun person," Jeffries is known for making the sort of hostile denunciations that, if he were at the other end of the political spectrum, would no doubt provoke howls of indignation. According to Fred Rueckher, a white student who took his

course, Jeffries attacked black males for succumbing to the "white pussy syndrome," that is, pursuing white women. He called Diana Ross an "international whore" for her involvement with white men. And he applauded the destruction of the Challenger space shuttle because it would deter white people from "spreading their filth throughout the universe."

67   Jeffries's wild remarks are excused by the politically correct on the grounds that to be a racist, you have to have "institutional power," and since blacks do not have "institutional power," they cannot be considered racist. The somewhat flimsy propositions of Afrocentrism are excused with equal finesse. First of all, since everything is political, there has never been disinterested scholarship, only power plays by various groups to justify their own claims. And even if there are some holes in Afrocentrism, the approach is useful because it raises the "self-esteem" of black students.

68   Such was the reasoning of the New York State Board of Education's Task Force on Minorities, to which Leonard Jeffries was a consultant. Its report suggested that "all curricular materials [including math and science] be prepared on the basis of multicultural contributions." As a result, the report said, children from minority cultures "will have higher self-esteem and self-respect, while children from European cultures will have a less arrogant perspective." The notion has already been put into effect in public schools in Portland, Indianapolis, and Washington, D.C., where students are taught subjects like Yoruba mathematics and ancient-Egyptian astronomy.

69   The idea that the "self-esteem" of students—rather than historical relevance—should be the basis for including material in textbooks does have its critics. Among the most prominent is Diane Ravitch, who has said the idea "that children can learn only from the experiences of people from the same race" represents a sort of "racial fundamentalism." The success of Chinese students in math is due not to numbers but to hard work. If the "self-esteem" model had any validity, Italian-American students—the descendants of Caesar and Michelangelo—would excel in school, but in fact they have the highest dropout rate of any white group in New York City schools. By promoting a brand of history "in which everyone is either a descendant of victims or oppressors," Ravitch has declared, "ancient hatreds are fanned and re-created in each new generation."

70   Ravitch naturally was branded a racist for this position. Participants at a recent Afrocentrism conference in Atlanta

derided her as "Miss Daisy." She has been attacked in the *City Sun* and on black television and radio programs. As a result, she has received so many threats that when we first agreed to meet, she was afraid to tell me where she lived. "They've written saying things like 'We're going to get you, bitch. We're going to beat your white ass.'"

Moonies in the Classroom

The supreme irony of the new fundamentalism is that   71
the generation that produced the free-speech movement in Berkeley and rebelled against the idea of *in loco parentis*—that university administrators should act as surrogate parents—is now trying to restrict speech and control the behavior of a new generation of students. The enterprise is undertaken to combat racism, of course, and it is an article of faith among the politically correct that the current climate of racial hostility can be traced to the Reagan and Bush presidencies, to conservative-Republican efforts to gut civil-rights legislation and affirmative-action programs. However true that may be, scholars like Shelby Steele, a black essayist and English professor, have also argued that the separatist movements at universities—black dorms, Native-American student centers, gay-studies programs, the relentless harping on "otherness"—have heightened tensions and contributed to the culture of victimization. "If you sensitize people from day one to look at everything in terms of race and sex, eventually they will see racism and sexism at the root of everything," says Alan Kors. "But not all the problems and frustrations in life are due to race and gender."

Furthermore, they say, instead of increasing self-esteem,   72
schools that offer an Afrocentric education will only turn out students who are more resentful, and incompetent, than ever. Indeed, while the more rabid Afrocentrics have claimed that crack and AIDS are conspiracies by whites to eliminate blacks, it could just as easily be argued that white indulgence of Afrocentric education represents a conspiracy to provide blacks with a useless education that will keep them out of the job market.

Of course, to make such a statement is invariably to pro-   73
voke a charge of racism. But part of the problem with this reaction is that it trivializes the debate. In fact, it makes debate impossible. But that is just as well, according to the new fundamentalists. Debate, and the analytic thinking it

requires, is oppressive. It's logocentric. It favors the articulate at the expense of the inarticulate. It forces people to make distinctions, and since racism is the result of distinctions, they should be discouraged. "I have students tell me they don't need to study philosophy because it's patriarchal and logocentric," says Christina Sommers. "They're unteachable and scary. It's like having a Moonie in the classroom."

74   Resistance to this sort of robotic sloganeering is beginning. "Today, routinized righteous indignation has been substituted for rigorous criticism," Henry Louis Gates, a black English professor at Duke, recently declared. Some professors are actually arguing that colleges should begin to emphasize what whites, homosexuals, minorities, and women have in common rather than dwelling constantly on "difference." In November, writing in the *Stanford Daily* about a proposal to require Stanford students to take a course in diversity, David Kennedy, chairman of American studies at Stanford and previously a champion of multiculturalism, said, "I worry that the proposal will add to the already considerable weight that Stanford culture places on racial and ethnic divisiveness, rather than shared participation. I question whether this is socially wise and, further, whether it is intellectually true to the lived experience of members of this society."

75   A few emboldened administrators are actually suggesting that it is not unreasonable for Western culture to enjoy a certain prominence at American colleges. In an address to incoming Yale students in September, Donald Kagan, dean of the college, encouraged them to center their undergraduate studies around Western culture. He argued that the West "has asserted the claims of the individual against those of the state, limiting its power and creating a realm of privacy into which it cannot penetrate." The West's tradition of civil liberties has produced "a tolerance and respect for diversity unknown in most cultures."

76   But many of the Yale freshmen—or "freshpeople," as the *Yale Daily News* puts it—considered the dean's statements "quite disturbing." And the dean was denounced with the obligatory mind-numbing litany.

77   "Paternalistic!"
78   "Racist!"
79   "Fascist!"

Campus Speech Code

In the late 1980s, hundreds of colleges and universities enacted speech codes for their campuses, codes that spell out disciplinary measures appropriate for students and faculty who use racist or discriminatory language. Such codes are widely defended as ensuring hospitable environments for minorities (and hence reinforcing the Constitution's fourteenth-amendment guarantee of equal protection under the law). But they have also been widely criticized (particularly for restraining first-amendment guarantees of free speech). Here is one such code, enacted by the University of Connecticut. Its wording, influenced by an earlier version that was challenged in court, was collaboratively written by a federal judge, the university's attorney, and a representative of the American Civil Liberties Union.

An action which disrupts or impairs the purposes of the   1
University and its community is subject to penalty under the
Student Conduct Code. This is the *general principle* for determining whether a violation has occurred even if the action
does not violate criminal law. Behaviors which violate the
Student Conduct Code may also violate criminal or civil law
and as such be subject to proceedings under the legal system.

Students at The University of Connecticut are subject to   2
the provisions of the *Student Conduct Code* while on University premises or University-related premises or when involved
with off-campus University activities. A student who is found
guilty of misconduct or is found guilty of being an accessory
to misconduct shall be subject to the penalties authorized by
this Code:

Students alleged to have committed the following acts are   3
subject to disciplinary procedures of this Code:

1. Academic Misconduct. (See Section XI of this Code
   for penalties and procedures related to academic
   misconduct.)
2. Disruption of Classes, Seminars, Research Projects,
   or Activities of the University.
3. Actual or Threatened Physical Assault or Injury to
   Persons.
4. Actual or Threatened Sexual Assault—This includes,
   but is not limited to, unwanted sexual touching even
   between acquaintances.

5. Harassment and/or Intimidation—Engaging in conduct which threatens to cause physical harm to persons or damage to their property; making unwelcome sexual advances or requests for sexual favors. This also covers harassment or intimidation of persons involved in a University disciplinary hearing and of persons in authority who are in the process of discharging their responsibilities.

   The face-to-face use of "fighting words" by students to harass any person(s) on University property or on other property to which the *Student Conduct Code* applies is prohibited. "Fighting words" are those personally abusive epithets which, when directly addressed to any ordinary person are, in the context used and as a matter of common knowledge, inherently likely to provoke an immediate violent reaction, whether or not they actually do so. Such words include, but are not limited to, those terms widely recognized to be derogatory references to race, ethnicity, religion, sex, sexual orientation, disability, and other personal characteristics.

6. Disorderly Conduct—Conduct causing inconvenience and/or annoyance which includes any action which can reasonably be expected to disturb the academic pursuits or to interfere with or infringe upon the privacy, rights, privileges, health or safety of members of the University community.

7. Manufacture, Distribution, Sale, Use, Offer for Sale, or Possession of Drugs or Narcotics, or Drug Paraphernalia—The manufacture, distribution, sale, use, offer for sale, or possession of drug paraphernalia or of any illegal drug or narcotic, including barbiturates, hallucinogens, amphetamines, cocaine, opium, heroin, marijuana, or any other substance not chemically distinguishable from them except as authorized by medical prescription.

8. Behavior or Activity Which Endangers the Safety of Oneself or Others....

Punkaj Srivastava
Multiculturalism: Politics and Paranoia?

Punkaj Srivastava wrote the following essay for a first-year composition course at the University of Arizona in 1994. The essay was designed for an assignment on persuasive writing (the audience for the piece was the general public as well as students and teachers), but as you will see, it also emerged from his personal experiences as an Indian student on campus. The essay was later included in A Student's Guide to First-Year Composition, *a collection of student writing and other pedagogical materials used in writing courses at Arizona.*

Take a stroll down the campus of one of our nation's most   1
prestigious universities, and you may find something peculiar
taking place. Sweeping through is a new idea, one that it is
taking the university by storm. The concept is called "multiculturalism." Ask what it means, and you'll probably be told
that it stands for the "recognition and cultivation" of the
diverse ethnic identities that make up the student body. And
you'll discover that along with this statement come a stock of
strategies, ideologies, and policies that are advocated. Naturally, such an extravagant undertaking merits some investigation. These are our *finest* universities, after all. And
universities are often the forefront of social change; in many
ways they serve as a sort of microcosm of the larger society.
What happens at Berkeley and Yale has a good chance of
being reflected in our homes, offices, and public quarters.

So the question to be asked by any calm and rational per-   2
son is: why is "multiculturalism" necessary and how is it helpful? As it turns out, the movement, although stressing that it
aims to promote racial tolerance, has some serious draw-
backs. According to the theory, once the "modifications" proposed by multiculturalists are adopted, a more tolerant,
educated, and higher quality society will result. Unfortunately, in real life, most of the proposed strategies don't help,
some have opposite effects, and others are just plain unfair.

The goals on the multiculturalist agenda are numerous   3
when it comes to the university; overall, however, there are two
major concepts that proponents feel are important. The first is
the belief that there needs to be a certain amount of "diversity"
in the classroom. In other words, all ethnic groups must be

present in certain ratios, and measures need to be enforced to ensure that such a thing happens. Second, the curriculum needs to reflect equally the background of each of these minority groups. Rather than a Western Civilization requirement, colleges should offer courses which present a "diversity of perspectives" from different cultures, especially to combat the debilitating effects of "Eurocentrism."

4   Let's begin by examining what is happening today with admissions policies. If you were to discover that your child's admission to Harvard was dependent on his skin color, what would you say? Many would be upset with such a notion; some would go so far as to call it "racist." Yet this is precisely what is happening at some of our most celebrated schools. It used to be that admissions criteria were pretty straight-forward and objective; nowadays, however, they are fast becoming a caste system. Consider what is happening at Berkeley. In *Illiberal Education*, Dinesh D'Souza describes the phenomenon in detail. Suppose that a student has a 3.5 grade point average and an S.A.T. score of 1200, two critical factors in assessing if a student has what it takes to thrive in a high-powered educational environment. According to a study by D'Souza, the chance of admittance of a Black applicant with these scores is 100 percent. For an Asian-American applicant, however, the chances are less than 5 percent (D'Souza 3). Why? Racial quotas, pure and simple. A ceiling has to be imposed on Asians to make room for underrepresented Blacks. Statistically, Blacks and Hispanics generally score lower on standardized tests (such as the S.A.T.) compared to whites and Asians (Glazer 19). The truth of the matter is that if you rack up the scores and resumes side by side, you end up with a lot of Asians and whites and fewer Blacks and Hispanics getting in. Schools such as Harvard have traditionally been merit-based; the A's are given out to the most effective students, who receive the highest scores on tests by virtue of their knowledge, and go to the best colleges by virtue of their effort. However, multiculturalists propose forcing an artificial equilibrium on this dynamic; a caste system has developed, with Blacks and Hispanics at the top receiving preferential treatment, and whites and Asians at the bottom receiving stringent restraints. The result: the sacrifice of academic merit on the altar of political appeasement.

5   The problems compound themselves. The Black student who was admitted with leniency because of his ethnic background now finds himself in an intense academic situation he is not prepared for and is not used to; the dropout rates of

such students is alarming. In 1987, only eighteen percent of Blacks and twenty-two percent of Hispanics admitted through Affirmative Action graduated within five years (D'Souza 39). Meanwhile, Asians with excellent records who would make prime Berkeley material find themselves settling for a college with lower standards and frustrated by the ineffectiveness of their academic efforts. Such situations have caused an uproar in the Asian community, who feel discriminated against, while pressure from the Black community keeps college administrators at bay (D'Souza 25).

6   The question we need to ask ourselves is what we truly want from our universities in terms of *education*, their primary function. A mix of ethnic groups is certainly wanted, but should we try and *force* this situation? At what expense? As it stands now, the unfortunate result is supporting "quotas over quality." This we don't need, considering how American students are already hideously lagging behind those in other industrialized nations. As Charles Krauthammer points out in "Education: Doing Bad and Feeling Good," American students are already too absorbed in a "self-esteem" curriculum whereby they are told they are performing well when in relation to the rest of the industrialized world they are actually not (78). This is exactly what is happening when we let less qualified students into the university to fill racial quotas. To make them feel "included" we must make the mistake of telling them that they're academically ready for what they're not. This leads us into the dark pits of disaster.

7   When it comes to excellence, there is no room for politics. To those who side with the multiculturalist, let me say this: let all barriers be removed but let no constraints be added. Real academic excellence can only be determined through free competition that is blind to skin color and racial background. I have been through all the levels of American schools and I was hard-pressed to come across any barriers "oppressing" me because of my ethnic background, certainly none which were insurmountable. So why add constraints? Free competition is one of the basics of democracy; thousands of people have come to this country just to enjoy this principle.

8   One often raised point among multiculturalists is that a hodgepodge of minorities in the classroom is necessary for giving us "diverse" perspectives in education. This is a fascinating theory. Apparently, to follow this argument, one would have to believe that certain "perspectives" are inherent in people by virtue of their skin color. What are we to make of this? If we were really interested in "diverse perspectives," perhaps

we ought to poll applicants for their political, philosophical, moral, and scientific views and then pick the ones who disagree the most. Instead of an individual thing, however, multiculturalists subscribe to the view that race and skin color are critical factors. This does not make sense. Even if true, it would make admissions policies a nightmare. We would have to "dehomogenize" every ethnic group to make sure that we were true to form. "Asian Americans" would need to be split into Chinese, Japanese, Indians, Persians, Filipinos, etc., since it makes sense that by definition students who have ancestry from each of these cultures will harbor special perspectives. This is an invitation to stereotyping; it claims that one Korean is likely to have the same views as the next. If you admit that this is not necessarily the case, you have to accept that perspective is more precisely an *individual* thing rather than a cultural factor. Rather than assuming that ethnic diversity equals a liberal education, I agree more with D'Souza, who offers that "the primary form of diversity which universities should try to foster is diversity of the mind" (230). When it comes down to basics, there are only minds and ideas; recognizing that each mind has equal potential and that ideas transcend race and culture is true equality. Slapping skin color onto every idea and accomplishment is a demeaning concept.

9   If the admissions policy crises hasn't stirred up enough antagonism among the ethnic groups, the argument over a "diverse curriculum" certainly has. On the campus of Stanford, irate students chanted the slogan "Hey, hey, ho, ho, Western culture's got to go" (D'Souza 59). Amazingly enough, they have been surprisingly successful in convincing the faculty that the core curriculum needs to be revolutionized in the name of multiculturalism. The questions are: what exactly do they mean, and why is it better?

10   Some say that a "global perspective" needs to be adopted. But is this what is really meant? As educator Diane Ravitch points out, "when educators argue about multiculturalism, they are usually not talking about disciplined study of another culture. They refer instead to American culture" (A44). More specifically, multiculturalists advocate classes extolling the virtues of Afro-, Asian-, and Mexican-American cultures to boost morale. If we were truly adopting the philosophy to teach ideas from a global perspective, it makes sense that we should include in the requirement classes like Tibetan Literature 112 and Islamic Fundamentalism 218. But this is not what is in mind. If we are to have a class on African soci-

ety, then it makes sense, in the interest of education, to reveal all aspects of African society, negative as well as positive. In Western Civilization, for example, it is urged that events such as the slavery, subjugation, and inward and racially unjust treatments of other peoples be revealed in explicit detail. However, it is unlikely that a "multicultural" course on Africans will mention the selling of slaves or cannibalism; although such things have historically taken place, they are not to be mentioned. As D'Souza reports, "the university leadership often discourages faculty from presenting factual material that may provoke or irritate minority students" (5).

Instead, it appears that the primary purpose of the new   11
"multicultural curriculum" is to raise minority self-esteem. As Ravitch describes them, such courses embrace "fundamentalist notions of racial and ethnic purity," whereby students are encouraged to believe that something in their blood or race or memory or their cultural D.N.A. defines who they are and what they may achieve" (A44). Ravitch likens such "education" to preaching a religious faith: "Students are taught to believe in the subject, to immerse themselves in its truths, and to champion them against skeptics. They are taught to believe, not doubt or criticize" (A44). This is unusual, considering that universities are infamous for being places where doubt, skepticism, analysis, mad non-conformity abound, and thankfully so.

Adopting a non-Western curriculum of which Western civi-   12
lization is just a small part causes its own paradoxes and moral dilemmas. As D'Souza explains, "The basic difficulty [of a non-Western curriculum] is that, by and large, non-Western cultures have no developed tradition of racial equality. Not only do they violate equality in practice, but the very principle is alien to them, regarded by many with suspicion and contempt" (79). He also points out how views of male superiority are inherent in many non-Western cultures, as well as considerably hostile or antipathetic treatment towards homosexuals. Clearly, non-Western viewpoints would introduce a lot of old ideas which multiculturalists would shudder at. On one hand, multiculturalists wish to censor any ideas that might suggest male superiority, religious fundamentalism, intolerance to "alternative lifestyles," notions of racial superiority, or non-democratic ideals. But all of these ideas are parts of the history and cultures of a vast number of non-Western civilizations. In fact, the only civilization that comes close to not being totally ingrained with such "dangerous" ideas is Western civilization. But of course, the multicultural curriculum is

built around the idea that non-Western cultures need to be emphasized. In light of these complications, the option that has received support is to provide a nicely tailored one-sided curriculum. In other words, we stretch the truth and glorify the positive aspects of the minority culture to make minorities "look good" all around. "Looking good" and "feeling good" are the primary motivations behind this kind of thinking, after all. But this is no longer education as we know it; it is politics and psycho-therapy.

13   One of the major arguments used to back a "multicultural curriculum" is that the regular curriculum, indeed, our very institutions, are harmfully and woefully "Eurocentric," meaning that they naturally subjugate and "push out" minorities. Paul Gray makes an interesting comment: "In what person or doctrine can Eurocentrism be defined? Savonarola? Jane Austen? Deism? Communism? Insofar as it means anything specific, Eurocentric looks suspiciously like a code word for 'white'" (16). The point here is to bring forth the true nature of the issue. The fact that this argument has roots in resentment is typified by the various extremes, especially Afrocentrism. The Afrocentric view is a popular way Blacks account for academic difficulty: "Black children are being miseducated and they're resisting it by not wanting to go to school, so genocide takes place" (Innert F10). So says a member of the National Black United Front, a group crusading for "Black power" (qtd. in Glazer 19). Reading between the lines of such statements, I can't help but feel that this is some sort of political and emotional backlash, a backlash that justifies itself by resurrecting feelings of prejudice and injustice from previous discriminations and allegations of inferiority. Nathan Glazer is convinced that the multicultural movement was invented by Black educators; he goes on to say that "were it not for the pattern of poor achievement among Blacks in the schools, the multicultural movement would lose much of its force" (19).

14   In any case, the proposals made by such activists seem odd. They are the same type of claims that argue that if the S.A.T. reading essays are written about a Black political leader, Blacks will be more likely to understand the material. In effect, they will seem smarter because the article is about someone they like. I find this especially bewildering; not only is there little proof that such an approach will "tune up" the ability level, it doesn't explain why Asian Americans, who are rarely mentioned in tests and books, generally manage to excel on such tests to the point where they often outperform the white majority.

I can't help but think that this is yet another example of   15
one of our most grievous and disempowering faults—our propensity to find someone to blame for our problems. In America we enjoy this so much that we would rather do it than
look for viable solutions to our problems. Once told that it is
"white" science, "white" philosophy, and "white" values that
are holding them back, minorities are often both surprised
and delighted (D'Souza 244). Although it is difficult to explain
how "Eurocentrism" is applied to science and mathematics,
frustrated minorities somehow manage to conclude that the
reason they are making the B- in history or philosophy is
because "white" men wrote and developed these ideas. To
make matters worse, universities are encouraging this type of
thinking: that cultural medium is the overriding factor in
intellectual understanding. *This* is a truly limited perspective;
that our universities can condone such ideology is disturbing.

In the final analysis, I can understand the emotional   16
human motivations for preaching multiculturalism; but
rationally, I must disagree with its precepts. One has only to
look to the effects multiculturalism is already producing to
see its weakness. At Berkeley, good students are denied
admission on the grounds of their race, while others less
qualified are admitted because of theirs. Racial stress and
tension have swept over Stanford, where the consensus is
that "people can say pretty much anything they want about
white males or religious fundamentalists, but woe betide the
individual who does something deemed offensive to the
oppressed: women, homosexuals...or people of color"
(Stafford 15). At Yale, undergraduate dean Paul Kagan was
charged with racism after making a speech emphasizing the
importance of Western thought and culture (Stafford 15). At
the University of Connecticut, censorship regulations call for
penalties ranging from reprimand to expulsion for any
remarks deemed to be offensive to women or minorities,
characterized by anything from "the use of derogatory
names" to "misdirected laughter" (D'Souza 9). At Duke University, incoming freshmen are required to take an examination to ensure correct "attitudes" towards women and
minorities (Siegel 34). In too many cases to mention, tension
and discord have proliferated among the ethnic divisions as
they continue to alienate themselves through concepts of
"political correctness" and censor each other vigorously
under allegations of "racism." Indeed, rather than peace, harmony, and equality, we have engendered hostility, separatism,
and paranoia.

17   And yet, somewhere in the nebula of multiculturalism I see an especially bright star that shines through. Despite being swept up in the maelstrom of misguided theories and politics, most normal people interested in multiculturalism have somewhere in their hearts a noble motive: the commitment to improving the quality of human interaction. But I've always thought that human interaction should be guided by love and wisdom, not politics and resentment. I've always thought that a school should be a place where excellence is molded and brought forth, not where it is corrupted by factionalism. I've always thought that one's worth should be determined by individual character, not calculated on the basis of racial background. Perhaps it is old-fashioned, but I still believe in looking past appearances rather than emphasizing them.

18   It's time to seek new alternatives. Affirmative Action? Why not do as D'Souza suggests and make it based on socioeconomic factors rather than racial ones (251)? As for curriculum? How about selecting texts which illustrate the ins and outs of cultural frameworks? An intelligent education makes students understand that history is interpreted from the "winner's" perspective, rather than simply telling them the current opinion of who the "winners" and "losers" are. Philosophy is more enlightening than policy. University clubs and facilities? Dedicate them to a cause, or leader, if you wish. But not to a special group or culture.

19   Together, students and faculty must work to discover real solutions to the problems of diversity and politics. Quick fixes may keep pressure off administrators in the short run, but it is the long run that determines if our universities are really first-rate. In a spirit not unlike Abraham Lincoln, or Martin Luther King, Jr., or Ghandi, we must press on to a higher, more noble vision. We must raise our standards in our goals of achieving true harmony and equality. If we believe in *true* equality, and a *truly* liberal education, then we have no choice.

For information on Trudeau and more examples of his comic strip, see pages 94–95 and 976.

DOONESBURY   BY GARRY TRUDEAU

Emily Tsao

Thoughts of an Oriental Girl

Emily Tsao was a sophomore at Yale University when she contributed the following essay to the Washington Post *(the most important daily newspaper published in our nation's capital) in September 1991.*

1   I am an Oriental girl. Excuse me, I forgot to use my politically correct dictionary. Let me rephrase that, I am an Asian-American woman. Yes, that sounds about right. Excuse me again; I mean politically correct.

2   When I first stepped onto the campus scene last year, I, like many other anxious freshmen, wanted to fit in. I wanted to wear the right clothes, carry the right bookbag and, most important, say the right things. Speaking to upperclassmen, however, I realized that I had no command of the proper "PC" language.

3   Girls, it became clear, were to be called women. Freshmen who were girls were to be called freshwomen. Mixed groups of both sexes were to be labeled freshpeople, and upperclassmen were to be referred to as upperclasspeople. Orientals were to be called Asian Americans, blacks were to be called African Americans and Hispanics Latinos.

4   To me, most of this seemed pointless. Being called a girl doesn't bother me. I'm 18 years old. My mom is a woman. I'm her kid. I don't expect her to refer to me as a woman.

5   I have always referred to my female friends as girls, and still do. I want my boyfriend to call me his girlfriend, not his woman friend.

6   My friends and I refer to the male students at college as boys or guys. Never men. Kevin Costner and Robert Redford are men. Men don't drink themselves sick at keg parties every weekend, ask Dad for money, or take laundry home to Mom.

7   For 12 years of high school and grade school, the female students were always girls and the males were boys. Why does going to college with these same peers suddenly make me a woman and the boys men? I certainly don't feel much older or wiser than I did last year. When people refer to me as a woman, I turn around to see who might be standing behind me.

Another fad now is for people to spell women with a "y" in   8
place of the "e"—"womyn." These people want to take the
"men" out of "women." Next perhaps they'll invent "femyle."

I've always been gender conscious with my language when   9
it seemed logical. In third grade I referred to the mailman as
a mailperson because our mail was sometimes delivered by a
woman. I don't think I ever said mailwoman, though, because
it just didn't sound right.

From elementary through high school, I told people I was   10
Chinese, and if I wanted to refer to all Asians, I used the word
"Orientals." I guess I was young and foolish and didn't know
any better.

At college I was told that the proper label for me was Asian   11
American, that "Oriental" was a word to describe furniture,
not people. But what is the difference? All Asians are still
being clumped together, even though each group—Chinese,
Korean, Japanese, Indians, Vietnamese and Filipinos, to
name just a few—comes from a different country with a different language and culture.

The new "PC" term to describe Asian Americans and all   12
other minorities is "people of color." The reason, I am told, is
that the "minority" population has grown to be the majority.
But even if that's true, the phrase seems contradictory. Since
many African Americans no longer want to be referred to as
blacks, why should the term for minorities once again refer to
skin color? The same is true for Asians, most of whom find
the label "yellow" more offensive than Oriental. And isn't
white also a color?

As long as we're throwing out all the old labels, why not   13
replace "white" with "European American." Wasps could be
EAASPS (European-American Anglo Saxon Protestants).
Well, maybe not. Minority groups want new labels to give
themselves a more positive image, but unless the stereotypes
disappear as well, is it really going to help very much?

Look at the word "sophomore," which comes from Greek   14
roots meaning "wise fool." PC-conscious sophomores ought
to revolt against this offensive phrase. I, however, will not be
among them. Changing the world won't make me any
smarter, humbler or wiser.

Richard Goldstein
The Politics of Political Correctness

Richard Goldstein, an executive editor for The Village Voice, *wrote the following analysis in June 1991. The* Village Voice *is a weekly newspaper for New Yorkers that has a decidedly liberal and irreverent tone. It reports on current events (national and local) and very thoroughly covers contemporary culture—films, books, music, dance, and so forth.*

1   When Carol Iannone, a frequent contributor to *Commentary*, was nominated to head the National Endowment for the Humanities, senators Edward Kennedy and Claiborne Pell put the appointment on hold. They were concerned about a piece in which Iannone called praise for Alice Walker's *The Color Purple* "less a recognition of literary achievement than some official act of reparation." Instead of defending the nominee's views on minority cultures—surely a valid issue for someone who would be dispensing federal grants to scholars—the current NEH chair, Lynn Cheney, chose to rail against "a classic example of political correctness—to oppose someone's ideological position, and then make inflammatory and irresponsible charges." The *New York Post* soon joined in, with an editorial excoriating "Literature's PC cops": "It's clear enough what is going on here. Various liberal groups are trying to chill discussion about a number of issues in the country by imposing a standard of 'political correctness.'"

2   The phrase has given conservatives, neo and trad, an excuse to avoid hard questions about race and gender. Now they can obscure all sorts of bigotry by accusing the left of practicing a new form of McCarthyism. And opponents of affirmative action have a new basis for defending hiring policies that exclude women and minorities: they're resisting intimidation. When Robert Brustein, artistic director of the American Repertory Theater, was attacked by *The Boston Globe* for running a largely white institution, he responded in *The New Republic* by deriding "the context of contemporary political correctness," which leads to inappropriate "inquiries into the racial, religious, political, and sexual background" of personnel. "To play this numbers game is to distract attention from the primary purpose of cultural institutions, which is to create works of art with high standards," Brustein writes. This from the man who once suggested (also in *The New*

Republic) that Harvey Fierstein got a Tony Award for *Torch Song Trilogy* because he won "the AIDS sympathy vote."

In this incarnation, politically correct stands for an undue   3
attention to racial and gender parity. But the phrase has also become a way to chill any discussion of racism or sexism in cultural works. Congressional conservatives erupted last month over an exhibition of frontier art at the Smithsonian that included interpretive texts analyzing the racial and sexual politics of these familiar images. Though he defended the show's right to federal funding, *New York Times* critic Michael Kimmelman derided "art-historical revisionism of the kind that has given rise to the phrase political correctness." Kimmelman doesn't say whether he objects to the excesses of this approach or to any attempt at all to elucidate the politics of culture, especially when doing so might tread on hallowed ground, such as the American West. The p.c. label lets this critic off the hook. Is there racism in the representation of Indians? P.c. renders the question moot.

A handy phrase, indeed—as John Taylor demonstrated in   4
his recent *New York* article, which featured the face of a bemused preppy, obscured by the question: "Are you politically correct?" For Taylor, the term describes everything about race and sex that would terrify the "young traditionalists" who are that magazine's demographic base. The proliferation of "oppression studies," campus codes against offensive speech, references to masturbation in academic papers, and "the phenomenon of date rape" all come under Taylor's fire. To deflect doubts about his authority to make such charges, he invokes the sacred name of Camille Paglia, whose book, *Sexual Personae,* is a tribute to the traditional view of gender as destiny. It is Paglia who tells the readers of *New York* that "radical feminists have contempt for values other than their own, and they're inspiring in students a resentful attitude toward the world."

Op-editors can count on Paglia to rail against p.c. But most   5
of the other attacks have come from straight white males. Many are straight white *liberal* males. Indeed, the attack on p.c. has brought men of the left and right together in a new Popular Front. Just think: in *The New Republic,* Eugene Genovese, the Marxist historian of slavery, marches hand in hand with Dinesh D'Souza, former editor of the race-baiting *Dartmouth Review.* It was during D'Souza's tenure that the *Review* ran an interview with an ex-official of the Ku Klux Klan, illustrated by a staged photo of a black student hanging from a tree. D'Souza also ran a fictional colloquium in which an

affirmative-action candidate declared: "Now we be comin' to Dartmut and be up over our 'fros in studies, but we still be graduatin' Phi Beta Kappa."

6   Perhaps Genovese can be forgiven his myopia, since none of this is revealed in D'Souza's *Illiberal Education,* the book that put political correctness on the think-tank agenda. Nor does the scant jacket blurb explain that the author, during his tenure as a domestic policy analyst at the Reagan White House, came up with the bright idea of shifting federal funds from abortion clinics to adoption services. These biases are masked by D'Souza's background (Genovese calls him "a man of color who was born in India"), and by his insistence on referring to his ideas as "liberal." Neocons often use that word, in its Burkean sense, to describe politics that predate by centuries contemporary standards of social justice. Many white liberals have become incapable of seeing beneath the surface of this claim to the churning waters that often lie beneath.

7   Which is why, I suspect, Genovese can remark in his review of D'Souza's book that the author "displays a deep appreciation of the travails of black students." Though he chides D'Souza for his "sweeping and one-sided characterizations of Marxism and Marxists, liberalism and liberals," Genovese is otherwise glad to join in the bashing. Having asserted that "the campaign for 'political correctness'" is a threat to the integrity of universities, he calls on "honorable men and women [to] defeat terrorism ... by unleashing counterterrorism against cowardly administrators and complicit faculty.... The hard truth is that academic freedom ... requires a strong dose of hierarchical authority within institutions that must be able to defy a democratic consensus." To achieve this goal, Genovese envisions "the redrawing of political lines in a manner that brings together the healthiest elements of long-warring political camps."

8   Healthy elements? Hierarchical authority? These buzz-words reveal more about the mindset of many men on the left than any politically correct analysis can. Examining Genovese's discourse, one can glimpse the enduring rigidities of orthodox Marxism, with its insistence that class is the only valid basis of struggle. This fear of racial and sexual pluralism, built into Marxism by its founder's hostility toward Jews and homosexuals (not to mention social democrats), persists on the left, fueling the ongoing struggle between political and cultural radicals. Ever since the '60s, the New Left has battled against its elders to broaden the base of progressive politics,

and over the past 20 years feminism and gay liberation have sharpened that conflict. By now, a social conservative like Genovese has more in common with Dinesh D'Souza (who proposes that affirmative action programs be organized around class rather than race) than he does with radical feminists.

"What a pity we cannot...restore a genuine core curriculum to our schools," Genovese wrote last year in *Commentary*. "For then we might be able to require a four-semester sequence in Christian theology or at least in common decency and good sense. As it is, the rot deepens; we are being overwhelmed by drugs; mass-homelessness; the poisoning of our children with pornography, perversion, and impossible aspirations." So much for bread and roses.   9

The movement for cultural and sexual pluralism has forced liberals and leftists alike to make a choice between the old politics of dialectical materialism and new, often foreboding, modes of discourse and analysis—not to mention behavior. A similar challenge has gone out to men and women in all walks of society—and a similar backlash is the result. The sexist tropes of metal and rap, the rise of the psychokiller in movies and lately literature; these are the cultural components of a male revanchism that finds its political expression in the current conservative hegemony.   10

Liberals, of course, are not one of Poppy's constituencies. But they have an infinitely greater capacity than even Republicans to hide their sexual and racial fears behind a patina of high principle. When the consequences of that denial are identified as bigotry, liberals explode. Twenty years of such pent-up fury is being unleashed in the attack on political correctness. That's why this right-wing critique has such broad appeal. A similar gap between ideals and anxieties is what has driven so many blue-collar voters into the arms of the Republicans. It's a bromide of the '80s that "a neoconservative is a liberal who's been mugged," and this group of affluent intellectuals perceives the emergence of racial and sexual minorities in precisely such threatening terms.   11

"A new McCarthyism, in some ways more effective and vicious than the old," Genovese cries. But as he might well remember, it was precisely the willingness of liberals to form an alliance with the right that enabled anticommunists to purge the universities of political radicals in the '50s. McCarthy could not have prevailed without the complicity of the left, and it's entirely possible that history will repeat itself in the current attack on p.c. This time around, the temptation to   12 purge radicals may be even greater, because the "threat" involves nothing so tangible as communism, but regions of the psyche where one's nightmares about sexual and racial otherness abide.

13   The straight white male is being asked to give up the power to mistake his perceptions for reality. To forgo pleasure in a culture that glorifies his own image at everyone else's expense. To suffer the intrusion of otherness into what was once his exclusive representational domain. To question all practices that express dominance over any living thing. Meanwhile, Poppy says to those weary—or wary—of this herculean task: Make war, eat meat, be free. This conflation of liberty with the preservation of privilege is a secret weapon in the right's arsenal, far more tempting—even to many liberals—than the left's insistence on self-restraint in the name of justice.

14   The line between civility and oppression will always be argued, even among the politically correct. But the current critique—encompassing everything from multicultural curricula to date rape, from affirmative action to gay dances—is an assault on diversity itself. This attack announces a new alignment in American politics, between social conservatives of the left and right.

15   There's nothing new about male bonding, of course. But in the past, *all* politics was male, and alliances were forged by class, region, or religious affinities. Only now is it possible to construct an alignment of threatened men that transcends the old categories of the cold war. What is currently referred to as "the gender gap" may actually signal the emergence of a white male voting bloc, as an inevitable reaction to the autonomy of women, gays, and people of color. This is a powerful force, and its claim to reason and rectitude is made with all the authority men are so skillful at mustering. Yet underlying its morality of freedom and individuality is terror of a world where endlessly changing affinities and alliances determine social reality—not a simple consensus among dudes.

16   To understand the fear of pluralism is also to see D'Souza's program for what it is. On the op-ed page of the *Wall Street Journal,* he recently called for a return to "liberal education." His formula for achieving that is revealing: "Universities should [refuse] to recognize or fund any group that is racially separatist." Sounds progressive, until D'Souza gets into particulars. "Universities would not permit a Black Students Association, but they would permit a W. E. B. Du Bois Society based on interest in [his] writings.... This principle could extend

beyond race, so that universities would decline to fund a homosexual association, but would fund a Sappho Society." His rationale: "The consolidation of identity based on race or sexuality may be a project that some students ardently seek, but it is not always consistent with the mission of universities."

Here is a program to intrude on the autonomy of universi-   17
ties in the name of academic freedom. No longer would students be invited to form their own campus societies. No longer would administrators be empowered to hire faculty on the basis of racial, sexual, or ideological balance. Tampering with the curriculum, so that it includes contemporary works by women, gays, and people of color, would be tantamount to treason against the West. D'Souza suggests introducing students to the *classical* tradition in other cultures, but no attempt would be made to convey current reality—especially in regard to groups whose experience was unaddressed in literature until this generation. And no course of study would explore the mass culture that is so powerful a determinant of values in American life. The university would return to the hermetic state it occupied in the '50s, when men were men, women were women, and everyone was white or stayed out of sight.

The restoration of America as a peaceable kingdom run by   18
straight white males (and administered by those who identify with them) is a goal many might embrace if it were presented in more "progressive" terms. Which is what the attack on political correctness achieves. Its appeal to liberals reflects the perception that the right is less threatening than radical feminists, queer nationals, black separatists, and animal liberationists. In reality, of course, the fundamental threat to freedom comes *from* the right. And once you size up Poppy against p.c., the choice becomes clear. Even at its most ridiculous, political correctness stems from the impulse to create an etiquette of relations among people of difference. And even at its most tempting, political incorrectness is the liberalism of fools.

Rosa Ehrenreich
What Campus Radicals?

*Rosa Ehrenreich completed her studies at Harvard in 1991,
just before she published the following essay in* Harper's, *a
monthly magazine on American politics and culture. (The
essay appeared in the same issue as the one by Louis Menand,
on page 104.)*

1   A national survey of college administrators released last
summer found that "political correctness" is not the campus
issue it has been portrayed to be by pundits and politicians of
the political right. During the 1990–91 academic year, according to the survey's findings, faculty members complained of
pressure from students and fellow professors to alter the
political and cultural content of their courses at only 5 *percent*
of all colleges. So much for the influence of the radicals, tenured or otherwise.

2   The survey's findings came as no real surprise to me. The
hegemony of the "politically correct" is not a problem at Harvard, where I've just completed my undergraduate education,
or at any other campus I visited during my student years. But
then none among those who have escalated the P.C. debate in
the past year—Dinesh D'Souza and Roger Kimball, George
Will and George Bush, *Time* and *New York* magazines—is
actually interested in what is happening on the campuses. In
all the articles and op-ed pieces published on P.C., multiculturalism, etc., very few student voices have been heard. To be
a liberal arts student with progressive politics today is at once
to be at the center of a raging national debate and to be completely on the sidelines, watching others far from campus
describe you and use you for their own ends.

3   For instance: During the spring semester of my freshman
year at Harvard, Stephen Thernstrom, an American history
professor, was criticized by several black students for making
"racially insensitive" comments during lectures. The incident
made the *Harvard Crimson* for a few days, then blew over
after a week or so and was quickly forgotten by most students. It continued a kind of mythic afterlife, however, in the
P.C. debate. Here is how it was described last January in a
New York magazine cover story by John Taylor on, in the
author's words, the "moonies in the classroom" propagating
the "new fundamentalism":

"Racist." "Racist!" "The man is a racist!" "A *racist!*"

Such denunciations, hissed in tones of self-righteousness and contempt, vicious and vengeful, furious, smoking with hatred—such denunciations haunted Stephen Thernstrom for weeks. Whenever he walked through the campus that spring, down Harvard's brick paths, under the arched gates, past the fluttering elms, he found it hard not to imagine the pointing fingers, the whispers.

The operative word here is "imagine." Taylor seriously dis-   4
torted what actually happened. In February of 1988, several black female students told classmates that they had been disturbed by some "racially insensitive" comments made by Professor Thernstrom. Thernstrom, they said, had spoken approvingly of Jim Crow laws, and had said that black men, harboring feelings of inadequacy, beat their female partners. The students, fearing for their grades should they anger Professor Thernstrom by confronting him with their criticisms— this is not an unusual way for college students to think things through, as anyone who's been an undergraduate well knows—never discussed the matter with him. They told friends, who told friends, and the *Crimson* soon picked up word of the incident and ran an article.

Professor Thernstrom, understandably disturbed to learn of   5
the matter in the *Crimson,* wrote a letter protesting that no student had ever approached him directly with such criticisms. He also complained that the students' vague criticisms about "racial insensitivity" had "launched a witchhunt" that would have "chilling effect[s] upon freedom of expression." Suddenly, Professor Thernstrom was to be understood as a victim, falsely smeared with the charge of racism. But no one had ever accused him of any such thing. "I do not charge that [Thernstrom] is a racist," Wendi Grantham, one of the students who criticized Thernstrom, wrote to the *Crimson* in response to his letter. Grantham believed the professor gave "an incomplete and over-simplistic presentation of the information.... I am not judging [his] character; I am simply asking questions about his presentation of the material...." As for the professor's comment that the criticisms were like a "witch-hunt," Grantham protested that Thernstrom had "turned the whole situation full circle, proclaimed himself victim, and resorted to childish name-calling and irrational comparisons.... 'witch-hunt' [is] more than a little extreme...." But vehement, even hysterical language is more and more used to demonize students who question and comment. Terms like "authoritarian"

and "Hitler youth" have been hurled at students who, like Grantham, dare to express any sort of criticism of the class-room status quo.

6   In my four years as a student at Harvard, I found few signs of a new fascism of the left. For that matter, there are few signs of the left at all. The Harvard-Radcliffe Democratic Socialists Club collapsed due to lack of members, as did the left-wing newspaper, the *Subterranean Review*. As to the neo-conservative charge that the traditional political left has been supplanted by a feminist-gay-multicultural left: In my senior year the African-American Studies department and the Women's Studies committee each had so few faculty that the same woman served as chair of both. I got through thirty-two courses at Harvard, majoring in the history and literature of England and America, without ever being required to read a work by a black woman writer, and of my thirty-two profes-sors only two were women. I never even *saw* a black or His-panic professor. (Fewer than 10 percent of tenured professors at Harvard are women, and fewer than 7 percent are mem-bers of minorities.)

7   Perhaps, as some conservatives have maintained, even a few radical professors can reach hundreds of students, bend-ing their minds and sending them, angry and politicized, out into society upon graduation. To cure such fears, drop by Harvard's Office of Career Services. Most staffers there spend their days advising those who would be corporate execs, financial consultants, and investment bankers. Nearly 20 per-cent of the class of 1990 planned to go to law school. This compares with 10 percent who claimed that they would even-tually go into government or one of what Career Services calls the "helping professions."

8   President Bush, speaking at the University of Michigan's commencement exercises last spring, went on about radical extremists on campus. It would be interesting to know how he calculated this rise in radicalism. Two thirds of Harvard students wholeheartedly supported the Gulf War, according to one *Crimson* poll. That's more support for the war than was found in the country at large. And during my years at Har-vard I found that most women on campus, including those who consider themselves politically liberal, would not will-ingly identify themselves as feminists.

9   The very notion of "politicization" makes most Harvard students nervous. I discovered this in the fall of 1989, when I was elected president of Harvard's community service organi-

zation, Phillips Brooks House Association. I had been reckless enough to suggest that volunteers would benefit from having some awareness of the social and political issues that affected the communities in which they did their volunteer work. I was promptly attacked in the *Crimson* for trying to inappropriately "politicize" public service. The paper also suggested that under my leadership volunteer training might mimic a "party line," with Brooks House as a "central planning office." This used to be called red-baiting. (So much for the liberal campus media.)

Meanwhile—and unremarked upon by D'Souza, et al.—the campus right thrives nationally. Two new right-wing vehicles have popped up on Harvard's campus in recent years. The Association Against Learning in the Absence of Religion and Morality (AALARM) initially made a splash with its uninhibited gay-bashing. The magazine *Peninsula*, closely tied to AALARM, bears an uncanny editorial resemblance to the notorious *Dartmouth Review*, claims to uphold Truth, and has a bizarre propensity for centerfold spreads of mangled fetuses. And older, more traditional conservative groups have grown stronger and more ideological. The Harvard Republican Club, once a stodgy and relatively inactive group, suffered a rash of purges and resignations as more moderate members were driven out by the far right. It is inactive no more. 10

There *are* those on the left who are intolerant and who could stand to lighten up a bit—these are the activists whom *progressive* and *liberal* students mockingly called "politically correct" years before the right appropriated the term, with a typical lack of irony. But on the whole, intolerance at Harvard—and, I suspect, elsewhere—is the province mostly of extreme conservatism. Posters put up at Harvard by the Bisexual, Gay and Lesbian Students Association are routinely torn down. I don't recall any Republican Club posters being ripped up or removed. 11

The day after the bombing started in Iraq, I went to an event advertised as "a non-partisan rally to support our troops," sponsored by the Republican Club. After the scheduled speakers—and several other non-scheduled speakers—had finished, I tried to speak. The rally organizers promptly turned off the microphone. I kept speaking, saying that I supported the troops but not the war. I added that I had been disturbed to hear it said by rally organizers—and applauded by the audience—that the time for debate was over. In a democracy, I said, the time for debate is never over. 12

13   I would have gone on, but at this point a group of men in the audience felt the need to demonstrate their conviction that there should be no debate. They began to loudly chant "victory" over and over, quite effectively drowning me out. By way of contrast, supporters of the war were listened to in polite silence by the crowd at an anti-war rally the next day.

14   In the classroom, too, right-wing political views are heard without disruption. One of Harvard's largest core courses, taken by nearly half of all undergraduates while I was there, is Social Analysis 10, Principles of Economics. It was taught, during my undergrad years, by two of President Reagan's top economic advisers, Martin Feldstein and Larry Lindsay. Students did not rise up *en masse* to protest the course's right-wing political bias; instead, they sat scribbling feverishly in their notebooks: Ec-10 had a notoriously steep grading curve. (No one seemed worried that each year some 750 innocent Harvard students were being lectured to by the engineers of what George Bush, in one of his more forthright moments, once referred to as "voodoo economics.")

15   There are many other politically conservative professors at Harvard whose courses are quite popular—Richard Pipes on Russian history and Samuel P. Huntington on modern democracy, to name two of the most prominent—and in their classrooms, as in all undergrad classrooms I was in, free and open discussion did quite well. I took many classes in which fearless conservatives rushed to take part in entirely civil discussions about the efficacy and justice of affirmative action, about whether books like *Uncle Tom's Cabin* and Frederick Douglass's autobiography are "really *literature*," as opposed to just interesting historical documents, and about whether it's at all fair or even interesting to condemn Jefferson for owning slaves even as he decried slavery. These are all valid questions, and all sides deserve a hearing—which, in my experience, is exactly what they always got.

16   And my experience was not unique. Most other Harvard students seemed to agree that there's no such thing as a cadre of P.C. thought police. Last winter the Republican Club laid huge sheets of poster board across several dining-hall tables and put up a sign asking students to scribble down their responses to the question "Is there free speech at Harvard?" The vast majority of students wrote things like "What's the big deal? Of course there's free speech here." And the lively, cheerful discussion going on among the students gathered around the tables attested to that fact.

Conservatives like D'Souza and Kimball charge that tradi- 17
tional Western culture courses barely exist anymore at
schools like Harvard, because of some mysterious combination of student pressure and the multiculturalist, post-structuralist tendencies of radical professors. Writing in the
Atlantic Monthly last year, Caleb Nelson, a former editor of
the conservative *Harvard Salient*, complained that in the
1989–90 Harvard course catalogue:

> No core Literature and Arts course lists any of the great nine-
> teenth-century British novelists among the authors studied,
> nor does any list such writers as Virgil, Milton, and Dosto-
> evsky. In the core's history areas even students who...took
> every single course would not focus on any Western history
> before the Middle Ages, nor would they study the history of
> the Enlightenment, the Renaissance, the American Civil War,
> or a host of other topics that one might expect a core to cover.

Nelson's major complaint is that Harvard is not properly 18
educating all of its students. I agree with him here; in Caleb
Nelson, Harvard has let us all down by producing a student so
poorly educated that he's unable even to read the course catalogue. I have the 1989–90 catalogue in front of me as I write,
and a quick sampling of some of the entries gives us, from the
Literature and Arts and the Historical Study sections of the
core curriculum, the following courses: Chaucer, Shakespeare, The Bible and Its Interpreters, Classical Greek Literature and 5th-Century Athens, The Rome of Augustus, The
British Empire, The Crusades, The Protestant Reformation.
Perhaps Chaucer and Shakespeare are somehow, to Caleb
Nelson, not "such writers" as Milton and Dostoevsky and the
Protestant Reformation is a historically trivial topic.

Nelson also worries that students will have "no broad look 19
at . . . philosophy"—by which he really means Western philosophy. Yet in the Moral Reasoning section of the core, seven of
the ten courses listed have at least four of the following
authors on their primary reading lists: Plato, Aristotle, Thucydides, Machiavelli, Locke, Kant, Rousseau, Hume, Mill,
Nietzsche, Marx, and Weber. There is one course devoted to a
non-Western philosopher: Confucius. The remaining two
Moral Reasoning courses focus, respectively, on the writings
of "Aristotle...[and] Maimonides," and of "Jesus as presented in the Gospels."

These courses are far more representative of those taken 20
by most Harvard undergraduates than the titillating and

much denounced 1991 English course on Cross-Dressing and Cultural Anxiety—a graduate seminar listed in the course catalogue but ultimately never held. But then, if you are a right-winger looking for something to replace the commies on campus—remember them?—you aren't going to sell books or raise funds or win votes complaining about undergrads studying Confucian Humanism and Moral Community.

21   Many of the loudest complainers about P.C. thought police are those who are doing their best to curb free expression in other areas. It doesn't appear to bother Dinesh D'Souza that the word "abortion" cannot be uttered at a federally funded family clinic. More broadly, the brouhaha about political conformity on campus serves as a perfect smoke screen, masking from Americans—from ourselves—the rigid political conformity *off* campus: the blandness of our political discourse, the chronic silence in Washington on domestic matters, the same faces returned to office each year, the bipartisanship that keeps problems from becoming issues. During the Gulf War, the number of huge yellow bouquets in public places rivaled the number of larger-than-life photos of Saddam Hussein displayed on Iraqi billboards. Patriotically correct.

22   The campuses are no more under siege by radicals than is the society at large. It has been clever of the Kimballs and D'Souzas to write as if it were so. It is always clever of those in ascendance to masquerade as victims. Rebecca Walkowitz, the newly elected president of the *Harvard Crimson*, understands perfectly how this dynamic works. Referring to the 1988 incident involving Professor Thernstrom and several of his black students, Walkowitz has said: "People call the *Crimson* and ask what we 'did to that man.' It's important to remember who has the power here, because it's not students. Who would dare criticize a professor for political reasons now? In addition to fearing for your grade, you'd fear being pilloried in the national press."

II.

LANGUAGE

Introduction

People used to think of language as being ideologically neutral—as a sort of transparent window through which ideas are conveyed. Now many people agree that language is not transparent but colored by ideological and cultural biases. Far from being neutral, language is a product (as well as a producer) of culture. As such, it inevitably reflects (as well as shapes) that particular culture. The three issues explored in this part of *Conversations*—"Should There Be . . . A 'Standard' English?"; "Should We Have a National Language?"; and "Is English Sexist?"—share the assumption that language is culture-bound, that social issues inevitably mingle with language issues.

The first section includes six items that explore relationships between language and power, particularly about the ideology of standard American English. Is Black English a robust dialect that proceeds according to normal conventions of sound and structure? Or is it (especially in its written form) a substandard dialect that impedes communication and clouds thinking? Do Black English and other "nonstandard" dialects empower their users as fully as any other language, or do they undermine literacy, discourage the chances of their users for success in the main streams of American life, and keep their users politically and socially marginalized?

The next section includes two items that are generally related to those in the previous section, items that consider language against the backdrop of America's ethnic diversity. (These readings also relate closely to the pieces in the sections on political correctness and defining race reprinted elsewhere in *Conversations*.) Should public policies enforce English as our national language and discourage the use of other tongues? For many years federal, state, and local governments, for instance, have supported the policy of giving students schoolwork in their native languages—English for most, but Spanish and Chinese and many other languages as well—so that students with limited proficiency in English would not fall behind in other subjects while they mastered English "as a second language." In 1974, Congress required schools to promote knowledge of students' native languages and cultures as well as to promote growth in English. But in the past decade the policy of bilingual education has come under fire. Some educators have contended that bilingual programs do not work well or that they are too expensive. Other critics, noting the importance of English as a unifying force in American society, contend that bilingual programs—because they interfere with students' mastery of English—prevent non-English-speaking citizens from assuming a central role in life in the United States. As a result, some citizens in over two dozen states have even advocated, and in some cases passed, laws designating English as "the official language" of the United States. They argue partly on the grounds of cost (bilingual education, bilingual ballots, bilingual forms and signs and menus all cost money), partly to promote a more unified nation, partly to avoid the possibility that states in the Southwest might become Spanish-speaking "American Quebecs." (You probably remember that in 1995 the predominantly French-speaking Canadian province of Quebec nearly approved a resolution to secede from Canada.) Opponents contend that creating English as an official language would foster intolerance and bigotry, would compromise the civil rights of citizens who have not mastered English, and would undermine the richness of our nation's ethnic diversity.

Power is also at the heart of feminist critiques of the English language. As the three selections and cartoon printed in this part on sexist language disclose, the English language can favor some groups at the expense of others—particularly men at the expense of women. To what extent does English, as the product of a culture dominated by males, demean and delimit women? To what extent does English perpetuate outworn cultural assumptions about women? In other words, to what extent is English itself sexist? And what can be done about it? Those are the questions taken up in this final section.

Most citizens in this country have been proud of the metaphor of America as a melting pot—a place where immigrants are assimilated into the fabric of American life and American language. Recently, another metaphor has been proposed: America as salad bowl, as a place where immigrant citizens become American but still retain their unique cultural flavor even as they contribute to the mix. Whatever the metaphor, language will continue to be an area where differences between individuals and their society are negotiated, where conflicts between "American society" and its diverse individuals are adjudicated. In other words, language itself will remain an issue.

SHOULD THERE BE—OR CAN THERE BE—A "STANDARD" ENGLISH?

Barbara Mellix

From Outside, In

You will learn a lot about Barbara Mellix from reading the following essay, which was published in The Georgia Review *in the summer of 1987, just after Mellix completed her master's degree in creative writing at the University of Pittsburgh. The* Georgia Review *is a quarterly journal of arts and letters that includes scholarly articles, fiction, poetry, and book reviews.*

1   Two years ago, when I started writing this paper, trying to bring order out of chaos, my ten-year-old daughter was suffering from an acute attack of boredom. She drifted in and out of the room complaining that she had nothing to do, no one to "be with" because none of her friends were at home. Patiently I explained that I was working on something special and needed peace and quiet, and I suggested that she paint, read, or work with her computer. None of these interested her. Finally, she pulled up a chair to my desk and watched me, now and then heaving long, loud sighs. After two or three minutes (nine or ten sighs), I lost my patience. "Looka here, Allie," I said, "you too old for this kinda carryin' on. I done told you this is important. You wronger than dirt to be in here haggin' me like this and you know it. Now git on outta here and leave me off before I put my foot all the way down."

2   I was at home, alone with my family, and my daughter understood that this way of speaking was appropriate in that context. She knew, as a matter of fact, that it was almost inevitable; when I get angry at home, I speak some of my finest, most cherished black English. Had I been speaking to my daughter in this manner in certain other environments, she would have been shocked and probably worried that I had taken leave of my sense of propriety.

3   Like my children, I grew up speaking what I considered two distinctly different languages—black English and stan-

180

dard English (or as I thought of them then, the ordinary everyday speech of "country" coloreds and "proper" English) —and in the process of acquiring these languages, I developed an understanding of when, where, and how to use them. But unlike my children, I grew up in a world that was primarily black. My friends, neighbors, minister, teachers—almost everybody I associated with every day—were black. And we spoke to one another in our own special language: *That sho is a pretty dress you got on. If she don't soon leave me off I'm gon tell her head a mess. I was so mad I could'a pissed a blue nail. He all the time trying to low-rate somebody. Ain't that just about the nastiest thing you ever set ears on?*

Then there were the "others," the "proper" blacks, trans-   4
planted relatives and one-time friends who came home from the city for weddings, funerals, and vacations. And the whites. To these we spoke standard English. "Ain't?" my mother would yell at me when I used the term in the presence of "others." "You *know* better than that." And I would hang my head in shame and say the "proper" word.

I remember one summer sitting in my grandmother's   5
house in Greeleyville, South Carolina, when it was full of the chatter of city relatives who were home on vacation. My parents sat quietly, only now and then volunteering a comment or answering a question. My mother's face took on a strained expression when she spoke. I could see that she was being careful to say just the right words in just the right way. Her voice sounded thick, muffled. And when she finished speaking, she would lapse into silence, her proper smile on her face. My father was more articulate, more aggressive. He spoke quickly, his words sharp and clear. But he held his proud head higher, a signal that he, too, was uncomfortable. My sisters and brothers and I stared at our aunts, uncles, and cousins, speaking only when prompted. Even then, we hesitated, formed our sentences in our minds, then spoke softly, shyly.

My parents looked small and anxious during those occa-   6
sions, and I waited impatiently for leave-taking when we would mock our relatives the moment we were out of their hearing. "Reeely," we would say to one another, flexing our wrists and rolling our eyes, "how dooo you stan' this heat? Chile, it just too hy*ooo*-mid for words." Our relatives had made us feel "country," and this was our way of regaining pride in ourselves while getting a little revenge in the bargain. The words bubbled in our throats and rolled across our tongues, a balming.

7   As a child I felt this same doubleness in uptown Greeleyville where the whites lived. "Ain't that a pretty dress you're
wearing!" Toby, the town policeman, said to me one day when
I was fifteen. "Thank you very much," I replied, my voice
barely audible in my own ears. The words felt wrong in my
mouth, rigid, foreign. It was not that I had never spoken that
phrase before—it was common in black English, too—but I
was extremely conscious that this was an occasion for proper
English. I had taken out my English and put it on as I did my
church clothes, and I felt as if I were wearing my Sunday best
in the middle of the week. It did not matter that Toby had not
spoken grammatically correct English. He was white and
could speak as he wished. I had something to prove. Toby did
not.

8   Speaking standard English to whites was our way of demonstrating that we knew their language and could use it.
Speaking it to standard-English-speaking blacks was our way
of showing them that we, as well as they, could "put on airs."
But when we spoke standard English, we acknowledged (to
ourselves and to others—but primarily to ourselves) that our
customary way of speaking was inferior. We felt foolish,
embarrassed, somehow diminished because we were ashamed
to be our real selves. We were reserved, shy in the presence of
those who owned and/or spoke *the* language.

9   My parents never set aside time to drill us in standard
English. Their forms of instruction were less formal. When my
father was feeling particularly expansive, he would regale us
with tales of his exploits in the outside world. In almost flaw-
less English, complete with dialogue and flavored with gestures and embellishment, he told us about his attempt to get a
haircut at a white barbershop; his refusal to acknowledge one
of the town merchants until the man addressed him as "Mis-
ter"; the time he refused to step off the sidewalk uptown to let
some whites pass; his airplane trip to New York City (to visit a
sick relative) during which the stewardesses and porters—recognizing that he was a "gentleman"—addressed him as "Sir." I
did not realize then—nor, I think, did my father—that he was
teaching us, among other things, standard English and the
relationship between language and power.

10   My mother's approach was different. Often, when one of us
said, "I'm gon wash off my feet," she would say, "And what
will you walk on if you wash them off?" Everyone would
laugh at the victim of my mother's "proper" mood. But it was
different when one of us children was in a proper mood. "You
think you are so superior," I said to my oldest sister one day

when we were arguing and she was winning. "Superior!" my sister mocked. "You mean I'm acting 'biggidy'?" My sisters and brothers sniggered, then joined in teasing me. Finally, my mother said, "Leave your sister alone. There's nothing wrong with using proper English." There was a half-smile on her face. I had gotten "uppity," had "put on airs" for no good reason. I was at home, alone with the family, and I hadn't been prompted by one of my mother's proper moods. But there was also a proud light in my mother's eyes; her children were learning English very well.

Not until years later, as a college student, did I begin to understand our ambivalence toward English, our scorn of it, our need to master it, to own and be owned by it—an ambivalence that extended to the public school classroom. In our school, where there were no whites, my teacher taught standard English but used black English to do it. When my grammar-school teachers wanted us to write, for example, they usually said something like, "I want y'all to write five sentences that make a statement. Anybody git done before the rest can color." It was probably almost those exact words that led me to write these sentences in 1953 when I was in the second grade:

> The white clouds are pretty.
> There are only 15 people in our room.
> We will go to gym.
> We have a new poster.
> We may go out doors.

Second grade came after "Little First" and "Big First," so by then I knew the implied rules that accompanied all writing assignments. Writing was an occasion for proper English. I was not to write in the way we spoke to one another: The white clouds pretty; There ain't but fifteen people in our room; We going to gym; We got a new poster; We can go out in the yard. Rather I was to use the language of "other": clouds *are*, there *are*, we *will*, we *have*, we *may*.

My sentences were short, rigid, perfunctory, like the letters my mother wrote to relatives:

> Dear Papa,
>
> How are you? How is Mattie? Fine I hope. We are fine. We will come to see you Sunday. Cousin Ned will give us a ride.
>> Love,
>> Daughter

11

12

The language was not ours. It was something from outside us, something we used for special occasions.

13   But my coloring on the other side of that second-grade paper is different. I drew three hearts and a sun. The sun has a smiling face that radiates and envelopes everything it touches. And although the sun and the world are enclosed in a circle, the colors I used—red, blue, green, purple, orange, yellow, black—indicate that I was less restricted with drawing and coloring than I was with writing standard English. My valentines were not just red. My sun was not just a yellow ball in the sky.

14   By the time I reached the twelfth grade, speaking and writing standard English had taken on new importance. Each year, about half of the newly graduated seniors of our school moved to large cities—particularly in the North—to live with relatives and find work. Our English teacher constantly corrected our grammar: "Not 'ain't,' but 'isn't.'" We seldom wrote papers, and even those few were usually plot summaries of short stories. When our teacher returned the papers, she usually lectured on the importance of using standard English: "I *am;* you *are;* he, she, or it *is,*" she would say, writing on the chalkboard as she spoke. "How you gon git a job talking about 'I is,' or 'I isn't' or 'I ain't'?"

15   In Pittsburgh, where I moved after graduation, I watched my aunt and uncle—who had always spoken standard English when in Greeleyville—switch from black English to standard English to a mixture of the two, according to where they were or who they were with. At home and with certain close relatives, friends, and neighbors, they spoke black English. With those less close, they spoke a mixture. In public and with strangers, they generally spoke standard English.

16   In time, I learned to speak standard English with ease and to switch smoothly from black to standard or a mixture, and back again. But no matter where I was, no matter what the situation or occasion, I continued to write as I had in school:

Dear Mommie,

How are you? How is everybody else? Fine I hope. I am fine. So are Aunt and Uncle. Tell everyone I said hello. I will write again soon.
            Love,
            Barbara

At work, at a health insurance company, I learned to write letters to customers. I studied form letters and letters written by co-workers, memorizing the phrases and the ways in which they were used. I dictated:

> Thank you for your letter of January 5. We have made the changes in your coverage you requested. Your new premium will be $150 every three months. We are pleased to have been of service to you.

In a sense, I was proud of the letters I wrote for the company: they were proof of my ability to survive in the city, the outside world—an indication of my growing mastery of English. But they also indicate that writing was still mechanical for me, something that didn't require much thought.

Reading also became a more significant part of my life during those early years in Pittsburgh. I had always liked reading, but now I devoted more and more of my spare time to it. I read romances, mysteries, popular novels. Looking back, I realize that the books I liked best were simple, unambiguous: good versus bad and right versus wrong with right rewarded and wrong punished, mysteries unraveled and all set right in the end. It was how I remembered life in Greeleyville.   17

Of course I was romanticizing. Life in Greeleyville had not become very uncomplicated. Back there I had been—first as a child, then as a young woman with limited experience in the outside world—living in a relatively closed-in society. But there were implicit and explicit principles that guided our way of life and shaped our relationships with one another and the people outside—principles that a newcomer would find elusive and baffling. In Pittsburgh, I had matured, become more experienced. I had worked at three different jobs, associated with a wider range of people, married, had children. This new environment with different prescripts for living required that I speak standard English much of the time and slowly, imperceptibly, I had ceased seeing a sharp distinction between myself and "others." Reading romances and mysteries, characterized by dichotomy, was a way of shying away from change, from the person I was becoming.   18

But that other part of me—that part which took great pride in my ability to hold a job writing business letters—was increasingly drawn to the new developments in my life and the attending possibilities, opportunities for even greater change. If I could write letters for a nationally known business, could I not also do something better, more challenging, more important? Could I not, perhaps, go to college and become a school teacher? For years, afraid and a little embarrassed, I did no   19

more than imagine this different me, this possible me. But
sixteen years after coming north, when my youngest daughter
entered kindergarten, I found myself unable—or unwilling—
to resist the lure of possibility. I enrolled in my first college
course: Basic Writing, at the University of Pittsburgh.

20   For the first time in my life, I was required to write exten-
sively about myself. Using the most formal English at my
command, I wrote these sentences near the beginning of the
term:

> One of my duties as a homemaker is simply picking up after
> others. A day seldom passes that I don't search for a mislaid
> toy, book, or gym shoe, etc. I change the Ty-D-Bol, fight "ring
> around the collar," and keep our laundry smelling "April
> fresh." Occasionally, I settle arguments between my children
> and suggest things to do when they're bored. Taking tele-
> phone messages for my oldest daughter is my newest (and
> sometimes most aggravating) chore. Hanging the toilet
> paper roll is my most insignificant.

My concern was to use "appropriate" language, to sound as
if I belonged in a college classroom. But I felt separate from
the language—as if it did not and could not belong to me. I
couldn't think and feel genuinely in that language, couldn't
make it express what I thought and felt about being a
housewife. A part of me resented, among other things, being
judged by such things as the appearance of my family's
laundry and toilet bowl, but in that language I could only
imagine and write about a conventional housewife.

21   For the most part, the remainder of the term was a period
of adjustment, a time of trying to find my bearings as a student in a college composition class, to learn to shut out my
black English whenever I composed, and to prevent it from
creeping into my formulations; a time for trying to grasp the
language of the classroom and reproduce it in my prose; for
trying to talk about myself in that language, reach others
through it. Each experience of writing was like standing naked
and revealing my imperfection, my "otherness." And each new
assignment was another chance to make myself over in language, reshape myself, make myself "better" in my rapidly
changing image of a student in a college composition class.

22   But writing became increasingly unmanageable as the
term progressed, and by the end of the semester, my sentences sounded like this:

> My excitement was soon dampened, however, by what
> seemed like a small voice in the back of my head saying that
> I should be careful with my long awaited opportunity. I felt
> frustrated and this seemed to make it difficult to concentrate.

There is a poverty of language in these sentences. By this
point, I knew that the clichéd language of my Housewife
essay was unacceptable, and I generally recognized trite
expressions. At the same time, I hadn't yet mastered the language of the classroom, hadn't yet come to see it as belonging to me. Most notable is the lifelessness of the prose, the
apparent absence of a person behind the words. I wanted
those sentences—and the rest of the essay—to convey the
anguish of yearning to, at once, become something more
and yet remain the same. I had the sensation of being split
in two, part of me going into a future the other part didn't
believe possible. As that person, the student writer at that
moment, I was essentially mute. I could not—in the process
of composing—use the language of the old me, yet I couldn't
imagine myself in the language of "others."

I found this particularly discouraging because at mid-   23
semester I had been writing in a much different way. Note the
language of this introduction to an essay I had written then,
near the middle of the term:

> Pain is a constant companion to the people in "Footwork."
> Their jobs are physically damaging. Employers are insensi-
> tive to their feelings and in many cases add to their problems.
> The general public wounds them further by treating them
> with disgrace because of what they do for a living. Although
> the workers are as diverse as they are similar, there is a defi-
> nite link between them. They suffer a great deal of abuse.

The voice here is stronger, more confident, appropriating
terms like "physically damaging," "wounds them further,"
"insensitive," "diverse"—terms I couldn't have imagined
using when writing about my own experience—and shaping
them into sentences like, "Although the workers are as
diverse as they are similar, there is a definite link between
them." And there is the sense of a personality behind the
prose, someone who sympathizes with the workers: "The
general public wounds them further by treating them with
disgrace because of what they do for a living."

24   What caused these differences? I was, I believed, explaining other people's thoughts and feelings, and I was free to move about in the language of "others" so long as I was speaking *of* others. I was unaware that I was transforming into my best classroom language my own thoughts and feelings about people whose experiences and ways of speaking were in many ways similar to mine.

25   The following year, unable to turn back or let go of what had become something of an obsession with language (and hoping to catch and hold the sense of control that had eluded me in Basic Writing), I enrolled in a research writing course. I spent most of the term learning how to prepare for and write a research paper. I chose sex education as my subject and spent hours in libraries, searching for information, reading, taking notes. Then (not without messiness and often-demoralizing frustration) I organized my information into categories, wrote a thesis statement, and composed my paper—a series of paraphrases and quotations spaced between carefully constructed transitions. The process and results felt artificial, but as I would later come to realize I was passing through a necessary stage. My sentences sounded like this:

> This reserve becomes understandable with examination of who the abusers are. In an overwhelming number of cases, they are people the victims know and trust. Family members, relatives, neighbors and close family friends commit seventy-five percent of all reported sex crimes against children, and parents, parent substitutes and relatives are the offenders in thirty to eighty percent of all reported cases. While assault by strangers does occur, it is less common, and is usually a single episode. But abuse by family members, relatives and acquaintances may continue for an extended period of time. In cases of incest, for example, children are abused repeatedly for an average of eight years. In such cases, "the use of physical force is rarely necessary because of the child's trusting, dependent relationship with the offender. The child's cooperation is often facilitated by the adult's position of dominance, an offer of material goods, a threat of physical violence, or a misrepresentation of moral standards."

26   The completed paper gave me a sense of profound satisfaction, and I read it often after my professor returned it. I know now that what I was pleased with was the language I used and the professional voice it helped me maintain. "Use better

words," my teacher had snapped at me one day after reading the notes I'd begun accumulating from my research, and slowly I began taking on the language of my sources. In my next set of notes, I used the word "vacillating"; my professor applauded. And by the time I composed the final draft, I felt at ease with terms like "overwhelming number of cases," "single episode," and "reserve," and I shaped them into sentences similar to those of my "expert" sources.

If I were writing the paper today, I would of course do some   27
things differently. Rather than open with an anecdote—as my teacher suggested—I would begin simply with a quotation that caught my interest as I was researching my paper (and which I scribbled, without its source, in the margin of my notebook): "Truth does not do so much good in the world as the semblance of truth does evil." The quotation felt right because it captured what was for me the central idea of my essay—an idea that emerged gradually during the making of my paper—and expressed it in a way I would like to have said it. The anecdote, a hypothetical situation I invented to conform to the information in the paper, felt forced and insincere because it represented—to a great degree—my teacher's understanding of the essay, *her* idea of what in it was most significant. Improving upon my previous experiences with writing, I was beginning to think and feel in the language I used, to find my own voices in it, to sense that how one speaks influences how one means. But I was not yet secure enough, comfortable enough with the language to trust my intuition.

Now that I know that to seek knowledge, freedom, and   28
autonomy means always to be in the concentrated process of becoming—always to be venturing into new territory, feeling one's way at first, then getting one's balance, negotiating, accommodating, discovering one's self in ways that previously defined "others"—I sometimes get tired. And I ask myself why I keep on participating in this highbrow form of violence, this slamming against perplexity. But there is no real futility in the question, no hint of that part of the old me who stood outside standard English, hugging to herself a disabling mistrust of a language she thought could not represent a person with her history and experience. Rather, the question represents a person who feels the consequence of her education, the weight of her possibilities as a teacher and writer and human being, a voice in society. And I would not change that person, would not give back the good burden that accompanies my growing expertise, my increasing power to shape myself in language and share that self with "others."

29   "To speak," says Frantz Fanon, "means to be in a position to use a certain syntax, to grasp the morphology of this or that language, but it means above all to assume a culture, to support the weight of a civilization."* To write means to do the same, but in a more profound sense. However, Fanon also says that to achieve mastery means to "get" to a position of power, to "grasp," to "assume." This, I have learned—both as a student and subsequently as a teacher—can involve tremendous emotional and psychological conflict for those attempting to master academic discourse. Although as a beginning student writer I had a fairly good grasp of ordinary spoken English and was proficient at what Labov calls "code switching" (and what John Baugh in *Black Street Speech* terms "style shifting"), when I came face to face with the demands of academic writing, I grew increasingly self-conscious, constantly aware of my status as a black and a speaker of one of the many black English vernaculars, a traditional outsider. For the first time, I experienced my sense of doubleness as something menacing, a built-in enemy. Whenever I turned inward for salvation, the balm so available during my childhood, I found instead this new fragmentation which spoke to me in many voices. It was the voice of my desire to prosper, but at the same time it spoke of what I had relinquished and could not regain: a safe way of being, a state of powerlessness which exempted me from responsibility for who I was and might be. And it accused me of betrayal, of turning away from blackness. To recover balance, I had to take on the language of the academy, the language of "others." And to do that, I had to learn to imagine myself a part of the culture of that language, and therefore someone free to manage that language, to take liberties with it. Writing and rewriting, practicing, experimenting, I came to comprehend more fully the generative power of language. I discovered—with the help of some especially sensitive teachers—that through writing one can continually bring new selves into being, each with new responsibilities and difficulties, but also with new possibilities. Remarkable power, indeed. I write and continually give birth to myself.

---

* *Black Skin, White Masks* (1952, rpt. New York: Grove Press, 1967), pp. 17–18.

Rachel L. Jones
What's Wrong with Black English

Rachel L. Jones contributed this essay to the "My Turn" column in Newsweek *in 1982, while she was a sophomore at Southern Illinois University. She currently writes for the* River Front Times, *a weekly newspaper in St. Louis.*

William Labov, a noted linguist, once said about the use of black English, "It is the goal of most black Americans to acquire full control of the standard language without giving up their own culture." He also suggested that there are certain advantages to having two ways to express one's feelings. I wonder if the good doctor might also consider the goals of those black Americans who have full control of standard English but who are every now and then troubled by that colorful grammar-to-the-winds patois that is black English. Case in point—me.

I'm a 21-year-old black born to a family that would probably be considered lower-middle class—which in my mind is a polite way of describing a condition only slightly better than poverty. Let's just say we rarely if ever did the winter-vacation thing in the Caribbean. I've often had to defend my humble beginnings to a most unlikely group of people for an even less likely reason. Because of the way I talk, some of my black peers look at me sideways and ask, "Why do you talk like you're white?"

The first time it happened to me I was nine years old. Cornered in the school bathroom by the class bully and her sidekick, I was offered the opportunity to swallow a few of my teeth unless I satisfactorily explained why I always got good grades, why I talked "proper" or "white." I had no ready answer for her, save the fact that my mother had from the time I was old enough to talk stressed the importance of reading and learning, or that L. Frank Baum and Ray Bradbury were my closest companions. I read all my older brothers' and sisters' literature textbooks more faithfully than they did, and even lightweights like the Bobbsey Twins and Trixie Belden were allowed into my bookish inner circle. I don't remember exactly what I told those girls, but I somehow talked my way out of a beating.

I was reminded once again of my "white pipes" problem while apartment hunting in Evanston, Illinois, last winter. I doggedly made out lists of available places and called all around. I would immediately be invited over—and immediately turned down. The thinly concealed looks of shock when the front door opened clued me in, along with the flustered instances of "just getting off the phone with the girl who was ahead of you and she wants the rooms." When I finally found a place to live, my roommate stirred up old memories when she remarked a few months later, "You know, I was surprised when I first saw you. You sounded white over the phone." Tell me another one, sister.

5   I should've asked her a question I've wanted an answer to for years: how does one "talk white"? The silly side of me pictures a rabid white foam spewing forth when I speak. I don't use Valley Girl jargon, so that's not what's meant in my case. Actually, I've pretty much deduced what people mean when they say that to me, and the implications are really frightening.

6   It means that I'm articulate and well-versed. It means that I can talk as freely about John Steinbeck as I can about Rick James. It means that "ain't" and "he be" are not staples of my vocabulary and are only used around family and friends. (It is almost Jekyll and Hyde-ish the way I can slip out of academic abstractions into a long, lean, double-negative-filled dialogue, but I've come to terms with that aspect of my personality.) As a child, I found it hard to believe that's what people meant by "talking proper"; that would've meant that good grades and standard English were equated with white skin, and that went against everything I'd ever been taught. Running into the same type of mentality as an adult has confirmed the depressing reality that for many blacks, standard English is not only unfamiliar, it is socially unacceptable.

7   James Baldwin once defended black English by saying it had added "vitality to the language," and even went so far as to label it a language in its own right, saying, "Language [i.e., black English] is a political instrument" and a "vivid and crucial key to identity." But did Malcolm X urge blacks to take power in this country, "any way y'all can"? Did Martin Luther King Jr. say to blacks, "I has been to the mountaintop, and I done seed the Promised Land"? Toni Morrison, Alice Walker and James Baldwin did not achieve their eloquence, grace and stature by using only black English in their writing. Andrew Young, Tom Bradley and Barbara Jordan did not acquire political power by saying, "Y'all crazy if you ain't gon vote for me." They all have full command of standard

English, and I don't think that knowledge takes away from their blackness or commitment to black people.

I know from experience that it's important for black people, stripped of culture and heritage, to have something they can point to and say, "This is ours, *we* can comprehend it, *we* alone can speak it with a soulful flourish." I'd be lying if I said that the rhythms of my people caught up in "some serious rap" don't sound natural and right to me sometimes. But how heartwarming is it for those same brothers when they hit the pavement searching for employment? Studies have proven that the use of ethnic dialects decreases power in the marketplace. "I be" is acceptable on the corner, but not with the boss.   8

Am I letting capitalistic, European-oriented thinking fog the issue? Am I selling out blacks to an ideal of assimilating, being as much like whites as possible? I have not formed a personal political ideology, but I do know this: it hurts me to hear black children use black English, knowing that they will be at yet another disadvantage in an educational system already full of stumbling blocks. It hurts me to sit in lecture halls and hear fellow black students complain that the professor "be tripping dem out using big words dey can't understand." And what hurts most is to be stripped of my own blackness simply because I know my way around the English language.   9

I would have to disagree with Labov in one respect. My goal is not so much to acquire full control of both standard and black English, but to one day see more black people less dependent on a dialect that excludes them from full participation in the world we live in. I don't think I talk white, I think I talk right.   10

Geneva Smitherman

White English in Blackface, or Who Do I Be?

Geneva Smitherman is a professor of linguistics at Michigan State University. Her contention, printed here, that Black English is not slang but an English dialect that follows careful rules first appeared in The Black Scholar *in 1973.*

1   Bin nothin in a long time lit up the English teaching profession like the current hassle over Black English. One finds beaucoup sociolinguistic research studies and language projects for the "disadvantaged" on the scene in nearly every sizable black community in the country.[1] And educators from K-Grad. School bees debating whether: (1) blacks should learn and use only standard white English (hereafter referred to as WE); (2) blacks should command both dialects, i.e., be bidialectal (hereafter BD); (3) blacks should be allowed (??????) to use standard Black English (hereafter BE or BI). The appropriate choice having everything to do with American political reality, which is usually ignored, and nothing to do with the educational process, which is usually claimed. I say without qualification that we cannot talk about the Black Idiom apart from Black Culture and the Black Experience. Nor can we specify educational goals for blacks apart from considerations about the structure of (white) American society.

2   And we black folks is not gon take all that weight, for no one has empirically demonstrated that linguistic/stylistic features of BE impede educational progress in communication skills, or any other area of cognitive learning. Take reading. It's don been charged, but not actually verified, that BE interferes with mastery of reading skills.[2] Yet beyond pointing out

---

[1]For examples of such programs see *Non-Standard Dialect*, Board of Education of the City of New York (National Council of Teachers of English, 1968); San-Su C. Lin, *Pattern Practices in the Teaching of Standard English with a Non-Standard Dialect* (USOE Project 1339, 1965); Arno Jewett, Joseph Mersand, Doris Gunderson, *Improving English Skills of Culturally Different Youth in Large Cities* (U.S. Department of Health, Education and Welfare, 1964); *Language Programs for the Disadvantaged* (NCTE, 1965).

[2]See, for example, Joan Baratz and Roger Shuy, eds., *Teaching Black Children to Read* (Center for Applied Linguistics, 1969); A. L. Davis, ed., *On the Dialects of Children* (NCTE, 1968); Eldonna L. Evertts, ed., *Dimensions of Dialect* (NCTE, 1967).

the gap between the young brother/sistuh's phonological and syntactical patterns and those of the usually-middle-class-WE-speaking-teacher, this claim has not been validated. The distance between the two systems is, after all, short and is illuminated only by the fact that reading is taught *orally.* (Also get to the fact that preceding generations of BE-speaking folks learned to read, despite the many classrooms in which the teacher spoke a dialect different from that of their students.)

For example, a student who reads *den* for *then* probably   3 pronounces initial /th/ as /d/ in most words. Or the one who reads *doing* for *during* probably deletes intervocalic and final /r/ in most words. So it is not that such students can't read, they is simply employing the black phonological system. In the reading classrooms of today, what we bees needin is teachers with the proper attitudinal orientation who thus can distinguish actual reading problems from mere dialect differences. Or take the writing of an essay. The only percentage in writing a paper with WE spelling, punctuation, and usage is in maybe eliciting a positive *attitudinal* response from a pre-scriptivist middle-class-aspirant-teacher. Dig on the fact that sheer "correctness" does not a good writer make. And is it any point in dealing with the charge of BE speakers being "nonverbal" or "linguistically deficient" in oral communication skills—behind our many Raps who done disproved that in living, vibrant colors?[3]

What linguists and educators need to do at this juncture is   4 to take serious cognizance of the Oral Tradition in Black Culture. The uniqueness of this verbal style requires a language competence/performance model to fit the black scheme of things. Clearly BI speakers possess rich communication skills (i.e., are highly *competent* in using language), but as yet there bees no criteria (evaluative, testing, or other instrument of measurement), based on black communication patterns, wherein BI speakers can demonstrate they competence (i.e., *performance*). Hence brothers and sisters fail on language performance tests in English classrooms. Like, to amplify on what Nikki [Giovanni] said, that's why we always lose, not only cause we don't know the rules, but it ain't even our game.

[3]For the most racist and glaring of these charges, see Fred Hechinger, ed., *Pre-School Education Today* (Doubleday, 1966); for an excellent rebuttal, see William Labov, *Nonstandard English* (NCTE, 1970); for a complete overview of the controversy and issues involved as well as historical perspective and rebuttal to the non-verbal claim, see my "Black Idiom and White Institutions," *Negro American Literature Forum,* Fall 1971.

5   We can devise a performance model only after an analysis
of the components of BI. Now there do be linguists who supposedly done did this categorization and definition of BE.[4]
But the descriptions are generally confining, limited as they
are to discrete linguistic units. One finds simply ten to fifteen
patterns cited, as for example, the most frequently listed one,
the use of *be* as finite verb, contrasting with its deletion:
(a) *The coffee be cold* contrasts with (b) *The coffee cold*, the
former statement denoting a continuing state of affairs, the
latter applying to the present moment only. (Like if you the
cook, (a) probably get you fired, and (b) only get you talked
about.) In WE no comparable grammatical distinction exists
and *The coffee is cold* would be used to indicate both meanings. However, rarely does one find an investigation of the
total vitality of black expressive style, a style inextricable
from the Black Cultural Universe, for after all, BI connects
with Black Soul and niggers is more than deleted copulas.[5]

6   The Black Idiom should be viewed from two important
perspectives: linguistic and stylistic. The linguistic dimension
is comprised of the so-called nonstandard features of phonol-
ogy and syntax (patterns like *dis heah* and *The coffee be cold*),
and a lexicon generally equated with "slang" or hip talk. The
stylistic dimension has to do with *rapping, capping, jiving,*
etc., and with features such as cadence, rhythm, resonance,
gestures, and all those other elusive, difficult-to-objectify elements that make up what is considered a writer or speaker's
"style." While I am separating linguistic and stylistic features,
I have done so only for the purpose of simplifying the discussion since the BI speaker runs the full gamut of both dimensions in any given speech event.

7   I acknowledge from the bell that we's dealing with a dialect
structure which is a subsystem of the English language; thus
BE and WE may not appear fundamentally different. Yet,
though black folks speak English, it do seem to be an entirely
different lingo altogether. But wherein lies the uniqueness?

---

[4]The most thorough and scholarly of these, though a bit overly technical, is Walter Wolfram, *Detroit Negro Speech* (Center for Applied Linguistics, 1969).

[5]Kochman is one linguist who done gone this route; see for instance his
"Rapping in the Black Ghetto," *Trans-action* February 1969. However, he
makes some black folks mad because of what one of my students called his
"superfluity," and others shame cause of his exposure of our "bad" street
elements. Kochman's data: jam up with mutafuckas and pussy-copping
raps collected from Southside Chicago.

Essentially in language, as in other areas of Black Culture, we have the problem of isolating those elements indigenous to black folks from those cultural aspects shared with white folks. Anthropologist Johnnetta Cole suggests that Black Culture has three dimensions: (1) those elements shared with mainstream America; (2) those elements shared with all oppressed peoples; (3) those elements peculiar to the black condition in America.[6] Applying her concepts to language, I propose the accompanying schematic representation.

Referring to the first column, contemporary BE is simply   8 one of the many dialects of contemporary American English, and it is most likely the case that the linguistic patterns of BE differ from those of WE in surface structure only. There's no essential linguistic difference between *dis heah* and *this here*, and from a strictly linguistic point of view, *God don't never change* can be written *God doesn't ever change* (though definitely not from a socio-cultural/political perspective, as Baraka quite rightly notes).[7] Perhaps we could make a case for deep structure difference in the BE use of *be* as finite verb (refer to *The coffee be cold* example above), but we be hard pressed to find any other examples, and even in this case, we could posit that the copula exists in the deep structure, and is simply deleted by some low-level phonological deletion rule, dig: The coffee is cold . . . The coffee's cold . . . The coffee cold. My conclusion at this point is that despite the claims of some highly respected Creole linguists (with special propers to bad Sistuh Beryl Bailey),[8] the argument for deep structure differences between contemporary BE and WE syntax cannot pass the test of rigorous transformational analysis.

Referring to the second column, we note the psychologi-   9 cal tendency of oppressed people to adopt the modes of behavior and expression of their oppressors (also, during the African slave trade, the functional necessity of pidginized forms of European language). Not only does the conqueror force his victims into political subjugation, he also coerces them into adopting his language and doles out special rewards to those among the oppressed who best mimic his

[6]Johnnetta B. Cole, "Culture: Negro, Black and Nigger," *The Black Scholar,* June 1970.

[7]Imamu Baraka, "Expressive Language," *Home,* pp. 166–172.

[8]See her "Toward a New Perspective in Negro English Dialectology," *American Speech* (1965); and "Language and Communicative Styles of Afro-American Children in the United States," *Florida FL Reporter 7* (Spring-Summer 1969).

FEATURES SHARED WITH MAINSTREAM AMERICA	FEATURES SHARED WITH ALL OPPRESSED PEOPLES	FEATURES UNIQUE TO BLACK AMERICANS
Linguistic	*Linguistic*	*Linguistic*
1. British/ American English lexicon 2. Most aspects of British/ American English phonology and syntax	1. Superimpositions of dominant culture's language on native language, yielding 2. Pidginized form of dominant culture's language, subject to becoming extinct, due to 3. Historical evolution, linguistic leveling out in direction of dominant culture's dialect	Unique meanings attributed to certain English lexical items *Stylistic* Unique communication patterns and rhetorical flourishes

language and cultural style. In the initial language contact stage, the victims attempt to assemble the new language into their native linguistic mold, producing a linguistic mixture that is termed *pidgin*. In the next stage, the pidgin may develop into a Creole, a highly systematic, widely used mode of communication among the oppressed, characterized by a substratum of patterns from the victim's language with an overlay of forms from the oppressor's language. As the oppressed people's identification with the victor's culture intensifies, the pidgin/Creole begins to lose its linguistic currency and naturally evolves in the direction of the victor's language. Reconstructing the linguistic history of BE, we theorize that it followed a similar pattern; due to the radically different condition of black oppression in America, the process of *de-creolization* is nearly complete and has been for perhaps over a hundred years.

10   The most important features of BI are, of course, those referred to in column three, for they point us toward the linguistic uniqueness and cultural significance of the Oral Tradition in the Black Experience. It should be clear that all along I been talkin about that Black Experience associated with the

grass-roots black folks, the masses, the sho-nuff niggers—in short, all those black folks who do not aspire to white middle-class American standards.

Within this tradition, language is used as a teaching/social- 11
izing force and as a means of establishing one's reputation via his verbal competence. Black talk is never meaningless cock-tail chit-chat but a functional dynamic that is simultaneously a mechanism for acculturation and information-passing and a vehicle for achieving group recognition. Black communica-tion is highly verbal and highly stylized; it is a performance before a black audience who become both observers and par-ticipants in the speech event. Whether it be through a slap-ping of hands ("giving five" or "giving skin"), Amen's, or Right on's, the audience influences the direction of a given rap and at the same time acknowledges or withholds its approval, depending on the linguistic skill and stylistic ingenuity of the speaker. I mean like a Brother is only as bad as his rap bees.

I. Toward a Black Language Model: Linguistic

While we concede that black people use the vocabulary of 12
the English language, certain words are always selected out of that lexicon and given a special black semantic slant. So though we rappin bout the same language, the reality refer-ents are different. As one linguist has suggested, the proper question is not what do words mean but what do the users of the words mean? These words may be associated with and more frequently used in black street culture but not necessar-ily. *Muthafucka* has social boundaries, but not *nigger*.

Referring to the lexicon of BI, then, the following general 13
principles obtain:

1. The words given the special black slant exist in a 14
dynamic state. The terms are discarded when they move into the white mainstream. (Example: One no longer speaks of a "hip" brother; now he is a "togetha" brother.) This was/is necessitated by our need to have a code that was/is undeci-pherable by foreigners (i.e., whites).

2. In BI, the concept of denotation vs. connotation does 15
not apply.

3. What does apply is shades of meaning along the conno- 16
tative spectrum. For example, depending on contextual envi-ronment, the word *bad* can mean extraordinary; beautiful; good; versatile; or a host of other terms of positive value. Dig

it; after watching a Sammy Davis performance, a BI speaker testified: "Sammy sho did some *bad* stuff," i.e., extraordinary stuff. Or upon observing a beautiful sister: "She sho is *bad*," i.e., beautiful, pretty, or good-looking. Or, noticing how a brother is dressed: "You sho got on some *bad* shit," i.e., *good* shit = attractively dressed.

17   Note that the above examples are all in the category of *approbation*. It is necessary to rap about *denigration* as well, since certain words in the black lexicon can frequently be used both ways. Consider the word *nigger*, for instance. "He's my main nigger" means my best friend (hence, approbation); "The nigger ain't shit," means he's probably lazy, trifling, scheming, wrong-doing, or a host of other *denigrating* terms, depending on the total context of the utterance.

18   4. Approbation and denigration relate to the semantic level; we can add two other possible functions of the same word on the grammatical level: *intensification* and *completion*. Slide back to *nigger* for a minute, and dig that often the word is void of real meaning and simply supplies the sentence with a subject. "Niggers was getting out of there left and right, then the niggers was running, and so the niggers said ..." etc., etc., my main point being that a steady stream of overuse means neither denigration nor approbation. Some excellent illustrations of this function of the word are to be found in *Manchild in the Promised Land*, where you can observe the word used in larger contexts.

19   To give you a most vivid illustration, consider the use of what WE labels "obscenities." From the streets of Detroit: (a) "That's a bad *muthafucka*." Referring to a Cadillac Eldorado, obviously indicating approval. (b) "He's a no-good *muthafucka*." Referring to a person who has just "put some game" on the speaker, obviously indicating disapproval. (c) "You *muthafuckin* right I wasn't gon let him do that." Emphasizing how correct the listener's assessment is, obviously using the term as a grammatical intensifier, modifying "right." (d) "We wasn't doin nothing, just messing round and *shit*." Though a different "obscenity," the point is nonetheless illustrated, "shit" being used neutrally, as an expletive (filler) to complete the sentence pattern; semantically speaking, it is an empty word in this contextual environment.

20   Where I'm comin from is that the lexicon of BI, consisting of certain specially selected words, requires a unique scheme of analysis to account for the diverse range and multiplicity of

meanings attributed to these words. While there do be some dictionaries of Afro-American "slang," they fail to get at the important question: what are the psycho-cultural processes that guide our selection of certain words out of the thousands of possible words in the Anglo-Saxon vocabulary? Like, for instance, Kochman[9] has suggested that we value action in the black community, and so those words that have action implied in them, we take and give positive meanings to, such as *swing, game, hip, hustle,* etc.; whereas words of implied stasis are taken and given negative connotations, such as *lame, square, hung-up, stiffin and jivin,* etc. At any rate, what I've tried to lay here are some suggestions in this particular linguistic dimension; the definitive word on black lexicon is yet to be given.

I shall go on to discuss the stylistic dimension of black   21
communication patterns, where I have worked out a more definitive model.

II. Toward a Black Language Model: Stylistic

Black verbal style exists on a sacred-secular continuum, as   22
represented by the accompanying scheme. The model allows us to account for the many individual variations in black speech, which can all be located at some point along the continuum.

The sacred style is rural and Southern. It is the style of the   23
black preacher and that associated with the black church tradition. It tends to be more emotive and highly charged than the secular style. It is also older in time. However, though I've called it "sacred," it abounds in secularisms. Black church service tends to be highly informal, and it ain't nothin for a preacher to get up in the pulpit and, say, show off what he's wearing: "Y'all didn't notice the new suit I got on today, did y'all? Ain the Lord good to us...."

The secular style is urban and Northern, but since it probably had its beginnings in black folk tales and proverbs, its   24
roots are Southern and rural. This is the street culture; the style found in barbershops and on street corners in the black

[9]See Thomas Kochman, "The Kinetic Element in Black Idiom," paper read at the American Anthropological Association Convention, Seattle, Washington, 1968; also his *Rappin' and Stylin' Out: Communication in Urban Black America.*

SACRED	SECULAR
Political Rap Style	*Political Rap Style*
Examples: Jesse Jackson	*Examples:* Malcom X
Martin Luther King	Rap Brown
Political Literary Style	*Political Literary Style*
Examples: Barbara Ann Teer's	*Examples:* Don Lee
National Black Theater	Last Poets
Nikki Giovanni's "Truth	
Is on Its Way"	

ghettos of American cities. It tends to be more cool, more emotionally restrained than sacred style. It is newer and younger in time and only fully evolved as a distinct style with the massive wave of black migration to the cities.

25   Both sacred and secular styles share the following characteristics:

26   1. *Call and Response.*   This is basic black oral tradition. The speaker's solo voice alternates or is intermingled with the audience's response. In the sacred style, the minister is urged by the congregation's Amen's, That's right, Reverend's, or Preach Reverend's. One also hears occasional Take your time's when the preacher is initiating his sermon, the congregation desiring to savor every little bit of this good message they bout to hear. (In both sacred and secular political rap styles, the "Preach Reverend" is transposed to "Teach Brother.") In the secular style, the response can take the form of a back-and-forth banter between the speaker and various members of the audience. Or the audience might manifest its response in giving skin (fives) when a really down verbal point is scored. Other approval responses include laughter and phrases like "Oh, you mean, nigger," "Get back, nigger," "Git down, baby," etc.

27   2. *Rhythmic Pattern.*   I refer to cadence, tone, and musical quality. This is a pattern that is lyrical, sonorous, and generally emphasizing sound apart from sense. It is often established through repetition, either of certain sounds or words. The preacher will get a rhythm going, conveying his message through sound rather than depending on sheer semantic import. "I-I-I-I-I-Oh-I-I-Oh, yeah, Lord-I-I-heard the

voice of Jesus saying. . . ." Even though the secular style is characterized by rapidity, as in the toasts (narrative tales of bad niggers and they exploits like Stag-O-Lee, or bad animals and they trickeration, like the Signifying Monkey), the speaker's voice tone still has that rhythmic, musical quality, just with a faster tempo.

3. *Spontaneity*. Generally, the speaker's performance is [28] improvisational, with the rich interaction between speaker and audience dictating and/or directing the course and outcome of the speech event. Since the speaker does not prepare a formal document, his delivery is casual, nondeliberate, and uncontrived. He speaks in a lively, conversational tone, and with an ever-present quality of immediacy. All emphasis is on process, movement, and creativity of the moment. The preacher says "Y'all don wont to hear dat, so I'm gon leave it lone," and his audience shouts, "Naw, tell it Reverend, tell it!," and he does. Or, like, once Malcolm [X] mentioned the fact of his being in prison, and sensing the surprise of his audience, he took advantage of the opportunity to note that all black people were in prison: "That's what American means: prison."

4. *Concreteness*. The speaker's imagery and ideas center [29] around the empirical world, the world of reality, and the contemporary Here and Now. Rarely does he drift off into esoteric abstractions; his metaphors and illustrations are commonplace and grounded in everyday experience. Perhaps because of his concreteness, there is a sense of identification with the event being described or narrated, as in the secular style where the toast-teller's identity merges with that of the protagonist of his tale, and he becomes Stag-O-Lee or Shine; or when the preacher assumes the voice of God or the personality of a Biblical character. Even the experience of being saved takes on a presentness and rootedness in everyday life: "I first met God in 1925. . . ."

5. *Signifying*. This is a technique of talking about the [30] entire audience or some member of the audience either to initiate verbal "war" or to make a point hit home. The interesting thang bout this rhetorical device is that the audience is not offended and realizes—naw, expects—the speaker to launch this offensive to achieve this desired effect. "Pimp, punk, prostitute, Ph.D.—all the P's—you still in slavery!" announces the Reverend Jesse Jackson. Malcolm puts down the nonviolent movement with: "In a revolution, you swinging, not singing." (Notice the characteristic rhythmic pattern in the above examples—the alliterative poetic effect of Jackson's statement and the rhyming device in Malcolm's.)

31   An analysis of black expressive style, such as presented
here, should facilitate the construction of a performance
instrument to measure the degree of command of the style of
any given BI speaker. Linguists and educators sincerely interested in black education might be about the difficult, complex
business of devising such a "test," rather than establishing
linguistic remediation programs to correct a nonexistent
remediation. Like in any other area of human activity, some
BI rappers are better than others, and today's most effective
black preachers, leaders, politicians, writers are those who
rap in the black expressive style, appropriating the ritual
framework of the Oral Tradition as vehicle for the conveyance
of they political ideologies. Which brings me back to what I
said from Jump Street. The real heart of this language controversy relates to/is the underlying political nature of the American educational system. Brother Frantz Fanon is highly
instructive at this point. From his "Negro and Language," in
Black Skin, White Masks:

> I ascribe a basic importance to the phenomenon of lan-
> guage.... To speak means ... above all to assume a culture, to
> support the weight of a civilization.... Every dialect is a way
> of thinking.... And the fact that the newly returned [i.e.,
> from white schools] Negro adopts a language different from
> that of the group into which he was born is evidence of a dis-
> location, a separation....

In showing why the "Negro adopts such a position ... with
respect to European languages," Fanon continues:

> It is because he wants to emphasize the rupture that has now
> occurred. He is incarnating a new type of man that he
> imposes on his associates and his family. And so his old
> mother can no longer understand him when he talks to her
> about his *duds*, the family's *crummy joint*, the *dump*... all of
> it, of course, tricked out with the appropriate accent.
>   In every country of the world, there are climbers, 'the ones
> who forget who they are,' and in contrast to them, 'the ones
> who remember where they came from.' The Antilles Negro
> who goes home from France expresses himself in the dialect
> if he wants to make it plain that nothing has changed.

32   As black people go moving on up toward separation and
cultural nationalism, the question of the moment is not
which dialect, but which culture, not whose vocabulary but
whose values, not *I am* vs. *I be*, but WHO DO I BE?

John Simon

Why Good English Is Good for You

John Simon (born 1925) has reviewed theater and film for several magazines. An eloquent—and sometimes merciless—critic of the misuse of language, for many years he wrote a language column for Esquire. *Several of those columns were collected in* Paradigms Lost, *a book about the "decline of literacy." This essay is from that 1980 collection.*

What's good English to you that . . . you should grieve for it?   1
What good is correct speech and writing, you may ask, in an age in which hardly anyone seems to know, and no one seems to care? Why shouldn't you just fling bloopers, bloopers riotously with the throng, and not stick out from the rest like a sore thumb by using the language correctly? Isn't grammar really a thing of the past, and isn't the new idea to communicate in *any* way as long as you can make yourself understood?

The usual, basic defense of good English (and here, again,   2
let us not worry about nomenclature—for all I care, you may call it "Standard English," "correct American," or anything else) is that it helps communication, that it is perhaps even a *sine qua non* of mutual understanding. Although this is a crude truth of sorts, it strikes me as, in some ways, both more and less than the truth. Suppose you say, "Everyone in their right mind would cross on the green light" or "Hopefully, it won't rain tomorrow"; chances are very good that the person you say this to will understand you, even though you are committing obvious solecisms or creating needless ambiguities. Similarly, if you write in a letter, "The baby has finally ceased it's howling" (spelling *its* as *it's*), the recipient will be able to figure out what was meant. But "figuring out" is precisely what a listener or reader should not have to do. There is, of course, the fundamental matter of courtesy to the other person, but it goes beyond that: why waste time on unscrambling simple meaning when there are more complex questions that should receive our undivided attention? If the many cooks had to worry first about which out of a large number of pots had no leak in it, the broth, whether spoiled or not, would take forever to be ready.

It is, I repeat, only initially a matter of clarity. It is also a   3
matter of concision. Space today is as limited as time. If you have only a thousand words in which to convey an important

message, it helps to know that "overcomplicated" is correct and "overly complicated" is incorrect. Never mind the grammatical explanations; the two extra characters and one space between words are reason enough. But what about the more advanced forms of word-mongering that hold sway nowadays? Take redundancy, like the "hopes and aspirations" of Jimmy Carter, quoted by Edwin Newman as having "a deeply profound religious experience"; or elaborate jargon, as when Charles G. Walcutt, a graduate professor of English at CUNY, writes (again as quoted by Newman): "The colleges, trying to remediate increasing numbers of...illiterates up to college levels, are being high-schoolized"; or just obfuscatory verbiage of the pretentious sort, such as this fragment from a letter I received: "It is my impression that effective interpersonal verbal communication depends on prior effective intra-personal verbal communication." What this means is that if you think clearly, you can speak and write clearly—except if you are a "certified speech and language pathologist," like the writer of the letter I quote. (By the way, she adds the letters Ph.D. after her name, though she is not even from Germany, where *Herr* and *Frau Doktor* are in common, not to say, vulgar, use.)

4   But except for her ghastly verbiage, our certified language pathologist (whatever that means) is perfectly right: there is a close connection between the ability to think and the ability to use English correctly. After all, we think in words, we conceptualize in words, we work out our problems inwardly with words, and using them correctly is comparable to a craftsman's treating his tools with care, keeping his materials in good shape. Would you trust a weaver who hangs her wet laundry on her loom, or lets her cats bed down in her yarn? The person who does not respect words and their proper relationships cannot have much respect for ideas—very possibly cannot have ideas at all. My quarrel is not so much with minor errors that we fall into from time to time even if we know better as it is with basic sloppiness or ignorance or defiance of good English.

5   Training yourself to speak and write correctly—and I say "training yourself" because nowadays, unfortunately, you cannot depend on other people or on institutions to give you the proper training, for reasons I shall discuss later—training yourself, then, in language, means developing at the very least two extremely useful faculties: your sense of discipline and your memory. Discipline because language is with us always, as nothing else is: it follows us much as, in the old morality play, Good Deeds followed Everyman, all the way to the

grave; and, if the language is written, even beyond. Let me explain: if you can keep an orderly apartment, if you can see to it that your correspondence and bill-paying are attended to regularly, if your diet and wardrobe are maintained with the necessary care—good enough; you are a disciplined person.

But the preliminary discipline underlying all others is nev- 6 ertheless your speech: the words that come out of you almost as frequently and—if you are tidy—as regularly as your breath. I would go so far as to say that, immediately after your bodily functions, language is first, unless you happen to be an ascetic, an anchorite, or a stylite; but unless you are a styl*ite*, you had better be a styl*ist*.

Most of us—almost all—must take in and give out lan- 7 guage as we do breath, and we had better consider the seriousness of language pollution as second only to air pollution. For the linguistically disciplined, to misuse or mispronounce a word is an unnecessary and unhealthy contribution to the surrounding smog. To have taught ourselves not to do this, or—being human and thus also imperfect—to do it as little as possible, means deriving from every speaking moment the satisfaction we get from a cap that snaps on to a container perfectly, an elevator that stops flush with the landing, a roulette ball that comes to rest exactly on the number on which we have placed our bet. It gives us the pleasure of hearing or seeing our words—because they are abiding by the rules—snapping, sliding, falling precisely into place, expressing with perfect lucidity and symmetry just what we wanted them to express. This is comparable to the satisfaction of the athlete or ballet dancer or pianist finding his body or legs or fingers doing his bidding with unimpeachable accuracy.

And if someone now says that "in George Eliot's lesser nov- 8 els, she is not completely in command" is perfectly comprehensible even if it is ungrammatical, the "she" having no antecedent in the nominative (*Eliot's* is a genitive), I say, "Comprehensible, perhaps, but lopsided," for the civilized and orderly mind does not feel comfortable with that "she"—does not hear that desired and satisfying click of correctness— unless the sentence is restructured as "George Eliot, in her lesser novels, is not..." or in some similar way. In fact, the fully literate ear can be thrown by this error in syntax; it may look for the antecedent of that "she" elsewhere than in the preceding possessive case. Be that as it may, playing without rules and winning—in this instance, managing to communicate without using good English—is no more satisfactory than winning in a sport or game by accident or by disregarding the rules: which is really cheating.

9   The second faculty good speech develops is, as I have mentioned before, our memory. Grammar and syntax are partly
logical—and to that extent they are also good exercisers and
developers of our logical faculty—but they are also partly
arbitrary, conventional, irrational. For example, the correct
"compared to" and "contrasted with" could, from the logical
point of view, just as well be "contrasted to" and "compared
with" ("compared with," of course, is correct, but in a different sense from the one that concerns us here, namely, the
antithesis of "contrasted with"). And, apropos *different*, logic
would have to strain desperately to explain the exclusive correctness of "different from," given the exclusive correctness of
"other than," which would seem to justify "different than,"
jarring though that is to the cultivated ear.

10   But there it is: some things are so because tradition, usage,
the best speakers and writers, the grammar books and dictionaries have made them so. There may even exist some hidden
historical explanation: something, perhaps, in the Sanskrit,
Greek, Latin, or other origins of a word or construction that
you and I may very easily never know. We can, however, mem-
orize; and memorization can be a wonderfully useful thing—
surely the Greeks were right to consider Mnemosyne (memory) the mother of the Muses, for without her there would be
no art and no science. And what better place to practice one's
mnemonic skills than in the study of one's language?

11   There is something particularly useful about speaking correctly and precisely because language is always there as a
foundation—or, if you prefer a more fluid image, an under-
current—beneath what is going on. Now, it seems to me that
the great difficulty of life lies in the fact that we must almost
always do two things at a time. If, for example, we are walking and conversing, we must keep our mouths as well as feet
from stumbling. If we are driving while listening to music, we
must not allow the siren song of the cassette to prevent us
from watching the road and the speedometer (otherwise the
less endearing siren of the police car or the ambulance will
follow apace). Well, it is just this sort of bifurcation of attention that care for precise, clear expression fosters in us. By
learning early in life to pay attention to both what we are saying and to how we are saying it, we develop the much-needed
life skill of doing two things simultaneously.

12   Put another way, we foster our awareness of, and ability to
deal with, form and content. If there is any verity that modern
criticism has fought for, it is the recognition of that indissolu-
bility of content and form. Criticism won the battle, won it so

resoundingly that this oneness has become a contemporary commonplace. And shall the fact that form *is* content be a platitude in all the arts but go unrecognized in the art of self-expression, whether in conversation or correspondence, or whatever form of spoken or written utterance a human being resorts to? Accordingly, you are going to be judged, whether you like it or not, by the correctness of your thinking; there are some people to whose ear bad English is as offensive as gibberish, or as your picking your nose in public would be to their eyes and stomachs. The fact that people of linguistic sensibilities may be a dying breed does not mean that they are wholly extinct, and it is best not to take any unnecessary chances.

To be sure, if you are a member of a currently favored   13
minority, many of your linguistic failings may be forgiven you—whether rightly or wrongly is not my concern here. But if you cannot change your sex or color to the one that is getting preferential treatment—Bakke case or no Bakke case— you might as well learn good English and profit by it in your career, your social relations, perhaps even in your basic self-confidence. That, if you will, is the ultimate practical application of good English; but now let me tell you about the ultimate impractical one, which strikes me as being possibly even more important.

Somewhere in the prose writings of Charles Péguy, who   14
was a very fine poet and prose writer—and, what is perhaps even more remarkable, as good a human being as he was an artist—somewhere in those writings is a passage about the decline of pride in workmanship among French artisans, which, as you can deduce, set in even before World War I, wherein Péguy was killed. In the passage I refer to, Péguy bemoans the fact that cabinetmakers no longer finish the backs of furniture—the sides that go against the wall—in the same way as they do the exposed sides. What is not seen was just as important to the old artisans as what is seen—it was a moral issue with them. And so, I think, it ought to be with language. Even if no one else notices the niceties, the precision, the impeccable sense of grammar and syntax you deploy in your utterances, you yourself should be aware of them and take pride in them as in pieces of work well done.

Now, I realize that there are two possible reactions among   15
you to what I have said up to this point. Some of you will say to yourselves: what utter nonsense! Language is a flexible, changing, living organism that belongs to the people who speak it. It has always been changed according to the ways in

which people chose to speak it, and the dictionaries and books on grammar had to, and will have to, adjust themselves to the people and not the other way around. For isn't it the glory of language that it keeps throwing up new inventions as surf tosses out differently polished pebbles and bits of bottle glass onto the shore, and that in this inexhaustible variety, in this refusal to kowtow to dry-as-dust scholars, lies its vitality, its beauty?

16   Others among you, perhaps few in number, will say to yourselves: quite so, there is such a thing as Standard English, or purity of speech, or correctness of expression— something worth safeguarding and fostering; but how the devil is one to accomplish that under the prevailing conditions: in a democratic society full of minorities that have their own dialects or linguistic preferences, and in a world in which television, advertising, and other mass media manage daily to corrupt the language a little further? Let me try to answer the first group first, and then come back to the questions of the second.

17   Of course language is, and must be, a living organism to the extent that new inventions, discoveries, ideas enter the scene and clamor rightfully for designations. Political, social, and psychological changes may also affect our mode of expression, and new words or phrases may have to be found to reflect what we might call historical changes. It is also quite natural for slang terms to be invented, become popular, and, in some cases, remain permanently in the language. It is perhaps equally inevitable (though here we are on more speculative ground) for certain words to become obsolescent and obsolete, and drop out of the language. But does that mean that grammar and syntax have to keep changing, that pronunciations and meanings of words must shift, that more complex or elegant forms are obliged to yield to simpler or cruder ones that often are not fully synonymous with them and not capable of expressing certain fine distinctions? Should, for instance, "terrestrial" disappear entirely in favor of "earthly," or are there shades of meaning involved that need to remain available to us? Must we sacrifice "notwithstanding" because we have "in spite of" or "despite"? Need we forfeit "jettison" just because we have "throw overboard"? And what about "disinterested," which is becoming a synonym for "uninterested," even though that means something else, and though we have no other word for "disinterested"?

18   "Language has *always* changed," say these people, and they might with equal justice say that there has always been war

or sickness or insanity. But the truth is that some sicknesses that formerly killed millions have been eliminated, that some so-called insanity can today be treated, and that just because there have always been wars does not mean that someday a cure cannot be found even for that scourge. And if it cannot, it is only by striving to put an absolute end to war, by pretending that it can be licked, that we can at least partly control it. Without such assumptions and efforts, the evil would be so widespread that, given our current weaponry, we would no longer be here to worry about the future of language.

But we are here, and having evolved linguistically this far,   19 and having the means—books of grammar, dictionaries, education for all—to arrest unnecessary change, why not endeavor with might and mind to arrest it? Certain cataclysms cannot be prevented: earthquakes and droughts, for example, can scarcely, if at all, be controlled; but we can prevent floods, for which purpose we have invented dams. And dams are precisely what we can construct to prevent floods of ignorance from eroding our language, and, beyond that, to provide irrigation for areas that would otherwise remain linguistically arid.

For consider that what some people are pleased to call lin-   20 guistic evolution was almost always a matter of ignorance prevailing over knowledge. There is no valid reason, for example, for the word *nice* to have changed its meaning so many times—except ignorance of its exact definition. Had the change never occurred, or had it been stopped at any intermediate stage, we would have had just as good a word as we have now and saved some people a heap of confusion along the way. But if *nice* means what it does today—and it has two principal meanings, one of them, as in "nice distinction," alas, obsolescent—let us, for heaven's sake, keep it where it is, now that we have the means with which to hold it there.

If, for instance, we lose the accusative case *whom*—and we   21 are in great danger of losing it—our language will be the poorer for it. Obviously, "The man, whom I had never known, was a thief" means something other than "The man who I had never known was a thief." Now, you can object that it would be just as easy in the first instance to use some other construction; but what happens if *this* one is used incorrectly? Ambiguity and confusion. And why should we lose this useful distinction? Just because a million or ten million or a billion people less educated than we are cannot master the difference? Surely it behooves us to try to educate the ignorant up to our level rather than to stultify ourselves down to theirs.

Yes, you say, but suppose they refuse to or are unable to learn? In that case, I say, there is a doubly good reason for not going along with them. Ah, you reply, but they are the majority, and we must accept their way or, if the revolution is merely linguistic, lose our "credibility" (as the current parlance, rather confusingly, has it) or, if the revolution is political, lose our heads. Well, I consider a sufficient number of people to be educable enough to be capable of using *who* and *whom* correctly, and to derive satisfaction from this capability—a sufficient number, I mean, to enable us to preserve *whom*, and not to have to ask "for who the bell tolls."

22   The main problem with education, actually, is not those who need it and cannot get it, but those who should impart it and, for various reasons, do not. In short, the enemies of education are the educators themselves: miseducated, underpaid, overburdened, and intimidated teachers (frightened because, though the pen is supposed to be mightier than the sword, the switchblade is surely more powerful than the ferule), and professors who—because they are structural linguists, democratic respecters of alleged minority rights, or otherwise misguided folk—believe in the sacrosanct privilege of any culturally underprivileged minority or majority to dictate its ignorance to the rest of the world. For, I submit, an English improvised by slaves and other strangers to the culture—to whom my heart goes out in every human way—under dreadfully deprived conditions can nowise equal an English that the best literary and linguistic talents have, over the centuries, perceptively and painstakingly brought to a high level of excellence.

23   So my answer to the scoffers in this or any audience is, in simplest terms, the following: contrary to popular misconception, language does not belong to the people, or at least not in the sense in which *belong* is usually construed. For things can rightfully belong only to those who invent or earn them. But we do not know who invented language: is it the people who first made up the words for *father* and *mother*, for *I* and *thou*, for *hand* and *foot;* or is it the people who evolved the subtler shadings of language, its poetic variety and suggestiveness, but also its unambiguousness, its accurate and telling details? Those are two very different groups of people and two very different languages, and I, as you must have guessed by now, consider the latter group at least as important as the former. As for *earning* language, it has surely been earned by those who have striven to learn it properly, and here even economic and social circumstances are but an imperfect excuse for bad

usage; history is full of examples of people rising from humble origins to learn, against all kinds of odds, to speak and write correctly—even brilliantly.

Belong, then, should be construed in the sense that parks, national forests, monuments, and public utilities are said to belong to the people: available for properly respectful use but not for defacement and destruction. And all that we propose to teach is how to use and enjoy the gardens of language to their utmost aesthetic and salubrious potential. Still, I must now address myself to the group that, while agreeing with my aims, despairs of finding practical methods for their implementation.   24

True enough, after a certain age speakers not aware of Standard English or not exceptionally gifted will find it hard or impossible to change their ways. Nevertheless, if there were available funds for advanced methods in teaching; if teachers themselves were better trained and paid, and had smaller classes and more assistants; if, furthermore, college entrance requirements were heightened and the motivation of students accordingly strengthened; if there were no structural linguists and National Councils of Teachers of English filling instructors' heads with notions about "Students' Rights to Their Own Language" (they have every right to it as a *second* language, but none as a *first*); if teachers in all disciplines, including the sciences and social sciences, graded on English usage as well as on specific proficiencies; if aptitude tests for various jobs stressed good English more than they do; and, above all, if parents were better educated and more aware of the need to set a good example to their children, and to encourage them to learn correct usage, the situation could improve enormously.   25

Clearly, to expect all this to come to pass is utopian; some of it, however, is well within the realm of possibility. For example, even if parents do not speak very good English, many of them at least can manage an English that is good enough to correct a very young child's mistakes; in other words, most adults can speak a good enough four-year-old's idiom. They would thus start kids on the right path; the rest could be done by the schools.   26

But the problem is what to do in the most underprivileged homes: those of blacks, Hispanics, immigrants from various Asian and European countries. This is where day-care centers could come in. If the fathers and mothers could be gainfully employed, their small children would be looked after by day-care centers where—is this asking too much?—good English   27 could be inculcated in them. The difficulty, of course, is what to do about the discrepancy the little ones would note between the speech of the day-care people and that of their parents. Now, it seems to me that small children have a far greater ability to learn things, including languages, than some people give them credit for. Much of it is indeed rote learning, but, where languages are concerned, that is one of the basic learning methods even for adults. There is no reason for not teaching kids another language, to wit, Standard English, and turning this, if desirable, into a game: "At home you speak one way; here we have another language," at which point the instructor can make up names and explanations for Standard English that would appeal to pupils of that particular place, time, and background.

28   At this stage of the game, as well as later on in school, care should be exercised to avoid insulting the language spoken in the youngsters' homes. There must be ways to convey that both home and school languages have their validity and uses and that knowing both enables one to accomplish more in life. This would be hard to achieve if the children's parents were, say, militant blacks of the Geneva Smitherman sort, who execrate Standard English as a weapon of capitalist oppression against the poor of all races, colors, and religions. But, happily, there is evidence that most black, Hispanic, and other non-Standard English–speaking parents want their children to learn correct English so as to get ahead in the world.

29   Yet how do we defend ourselves against the charge that we are old fogeys who cannot emotionally adjust to the new directions an ever-living and changing language must inevitably take? Here I would want to redefine or, at any rate, clarify, what "living and changing" means, and also explain where we old fogeys stand. Misinformed attacks on Old Fogeydom, I have noticed, invariably represent us as people who shudder at a split infinitive and would sooner kill or be killed than tolerate a sentence that ends with a preposition. Actually, despite all my travels through Old Fogeydom, I have yet to meet one inhabitant who would not stick a preposition onto the tail of a sentence; as for splitting infinitives, most of us O.F.'s are perfectly willing to do that, too, but tactfully and sparingly, where it feels right. There is no earthly reason, for example "to dangerously live," when "to live dangerously" sounds so much better; but it does seem right to say (and write) "What a delight to sweetly breathe in your sleeping lover's breath"; that sounds smoother, indeed sweeter, than

"to breathe in sweetly" or "sweetly to breathe in." But infinitives begging to be split are relatively rare; a sensitive ear, a good eye for shades of meaning will alert you whenever the need to split arises; without that ear and eye, you had better stick to the rules.

About the sense in which language is, and must be, alive, let me speak while donning another of my several hats—actually it is not a hat but a cap, for there exists in Greenwich Village an inscription on a factory that reads "CRITIC CAPS." So with my drama critic's cap on, let me present you with an analogy. The world theater today is full of directors who wreak havoc on classic plays to demonstrate their own ingenuity, their superiority, as it were, to the author. These directors—aborted playwrights, for the most part—will stage productions of *Hamlet* in which the prince is a woman, a flaming homosexual, or a one-eyed hunchback.

Well, it seems to me that the same spirit prevails in our approach to linguistics, with every newfangled, ill-informed, know-nothing construction, definition, pronunciation enshrined by the joint efforts of structural linguists, permissive dictionaries, and allegedly democratic but actually demagogic educators. What really makes a production of, say, *Hamlet* different, and therefore alive, is that the director, while trying to get as faithfully as possible at Shakespeare's meanings, nevertheless ends up stressing things in the play that strike him most forcefully; and the same individuality in production design and performances (the Hamlet of Gielgud versus the Hamlet of Olivier, for instance—what a world of difference!) further differentiates one production from another, and bestows on each its particular vitality. So, too, language remains alive because each speaker (or writer) can and must *within the framework of accepted grammar, syntax, and pronunciation*, produce a style that is his very own, that is as personal as his posture, way of walking, mode of dress, and so on. It is such stylistic differences that make a person's—or a nation's—language flavorous, pungent, alive, and all this without having to play fast and loose with the existing rules.

But to have this, we need, among other things, good teachers and, beyond them, enlightened educators. I shudder when I read in the *Birmingham* (Alabama) *Post-Herald* on October 6, 1978, an account of a talk given to eight hundred English teachers by Dr. Alan C. Purves, vice-president of the National Council of Teachers of English. Dr. Purves is quoted as saying things like "We are in a situation with respect to reading where . . . ," and culminating in the following truly horrifying sentence: "I am going to suggest that when we go back to the basics, I think what we should be dealing with is our charge to help students to be more proficient in producing meaningful language—language that says what it means." Notice all the deadwood, the tautology, the anacoluthon in the first part of that sentence; but notice especially the absurdity of the latter part, in which the dubious word "meaningful"—a poor relation of "significant"—is thought to require explaining to an audience of English teachers.

33   Given such leadership from the N.C.T.E., the time must be at hand when we shall hear—not just "Don't ask for who the bell rings" (*ask not* and *tolls* being, of course, archaic, elitist language), but also "It rings for you and I."

bell hooks

Teaching New Worlds/ New Words

You can learn quite a bit about bell hooks from reading her well-known essays, which usually mix intensely personal elements with carefully considered conclusions. (For more on bell hooks and for another example of her prose, see her essay on college classrooms in Part I, "Education," page 82.) This particular essay appeared in 1994 as a chapter of her book Teaching to Transgress: Education as the Practice of Freedom.

1   Like desire, language disrupts, refuses to be contained within boundaries. It speaks itself against our will, in words and thoughts that intrude, even violate the most private spaces of mind and body. It was in my first year of college that I read Adrienne Rich's poem, "The Burning of Paper Instead of Children." That poem, speaking against domination, against racism and class oppression, attempts to illustrate graphically that stopping the political persecution and torture of living beings is a more vital issue than censorship, than burning books. One line of this poem that moved and disturbed something within me: "This is the oppressor's language yet I need it to talk to you." I've never forgotten it. Per-

haps I could not have forgotten it even if I tried to erase it from memory. Words impose themselves, take root in our memory against our will. The words of this poem begat a life in my memory that I could not abort or change.

When I find myself thinking about language now, these   2
words are there, as if they were always waiting to challenge and assist me. I find myself silently speaking them over and over again with the intensity of a chant. They startle me, shaking me into an awareness of the link between languages and domination. Initially, I resist the idea of the "oppressor's language," certain that this construct has the potential to disempower those of us who are just learning to speak, who are just learning to claim language as a place where we make ourselves subject. *"This is the oppressor's language yet I need it to talk to you."* Adrienne Rich's words. Then, when I first read these words, and now, they make me think of standard English, of learning to speak against black vernacular, against the ruptured and broken speech of a dispossessed and displaced people. Standard English is not the speech of exile. It is the language of conquest and domination; in the United States, it is the mask which hides the loss of so many tongues, all those sounds of diverse, native communities we will never hear, the speech of the Gullah, Yiddish, and so many other unremembered tongues.

Reflecting on Adrienne Rich's words, I know that it is not   3
the English language that hurts me, but what the oppressors do with it, how they shape it to become a territory that limits and defines, how they make it a weapon that can shame, humiliate, colonize. Gloria Anzaldúa reminds us of this pain in *Borderlands/La Frontera* when she asserts, "So, if you want to really hurt me, talk badly about my language." We have so little knowledge of how displaced, enslaved, or free Africans who came or were brought against their will to the United States felt about the loss of language, about learning English. Only as a woman did I begin to think about these black people in relation to language, to think about their trauma as they were compelled to witness their language rendered meaningless with a colonizing European culture, where voices deemed foreign could not be spoken, were outlawed tongues, renegade speech. When I realize how long it has taken for white Americans to acknowledge diverse languages of Native Americans, to accept that the speech their ancestral colonizers declared was merely grunts and gibberish was indeed *language,* it is difficult not to hear in standard English always the sound of slaughter and conquest. I think now of

the grief of displaced "homeless" Africans, forced to inhabit a
world where they saw folks like themselves, inhabiting the
same skin, the same condition, but who had no shared language to talk with one another, who needed "the oppressor's
language." *"This is the oppressor's language yet I need it to talk
to you."* When I imagine the terror of Africans on board slave
ships, on auction blocks, inhabiting the unfamiliar architecture of plantations, I consider that this terror extended
beyond fear of punishment, that it resided also in the anguish
of hearing a language they could not comprehend. The very
sound of English had to terrify. I think of black people meeting one another in a space away from the diverse cultures and
languages that distinguished them from one another, compelled by circumstance to find ways to speak with one
another in a "new world" where blackness or the darkness of
one's skin and not language would become the space of bonding. How to remember, to reinvoke this terror. How to
describe what it must have been like for Africans whose deepest bonds were historically forged in the place of shared
speech to be transported abruptly to a world where the very
sound of one's mother tongue had no meaning.

4   I imagine them hearing spoken English as the oppressor's
language, yet I imagine them also realizing that this language
would need to be possessed, taken, claimed as a space of
resistance. I imagine that the moment they realized the
oppressor's language, seized and spoken by the tongues of the
colonized, could be a space of bonding was joyous. For in
that recognition was the understanding that intimacy could
be restored, that a culture of resistance could be formed that
would make recovery from the trauma of enslavement possible. I imagine, then, Africans first hearing English as "the
oppressor's language" and then re-hearing it as a potential
site of resistance. Learning English, learning to speak the
alien tongue, was one way enslaved Africans began to reclaim
their personal power within a context of domination. Possessing a shared language, black folks could find again a way to
make community, and a means to create the political solidarity necessary to resist.

5   Needing the oppressor's language to speak with one
another they nevertheless also reinvented, remade that language so that it would speak beyond the boundaries of conquest and domination. In the mouths of black Africans in the
so-called "New World," English was altered, transformed, and
became a different speech. Enslaved black people took broken bits of English and made of them a counter-language.

They put together their words in such a way that the colonizer had to rethink the meaning of the English language. Though it has become common in contemporary culture to talk about the messages of resistance that emerged in the music created by slaves, particularly spirituals, less is said about the grammatical construction of sentences in these songs. Often, the English used in the song reflected the broken, ruptured world of the slave. When the slaves sang "nobody knows de trouble I see—" their use of the word "nobody" adds a richer meaning than if they had used the phrase "no one," for it was the slave's *body* that was the concrete site of suffering. And even as emancipated black people sang spirituals, they did not change the language, the sentence structure, of our ancestors. For in the incorrect usage of words, in the incorrect placement of words, was a spirit of rebellion that claimed language as a site of resistance. Using English in a way that ruptured standard usage and meaning, so that white folks could often not understand black speech, made English into more than the oppressor's language.

An unbroken connection exists between the broken   6
English of the displaced, enslaved African and the diverse black vernacular speech black folks use today. In both cases, the rupture of standard English enabled and enables rebellion and resistance. By transforming the oppressor's language, making a culture of resistance, black people created an intimate speech that could say far more than was permissible within the boundaries of standard English. The power of this speech is not simply that it enables resistance to white supremacy, but that it also forges a space for alternative cultural production and alternative epistemologies—different ways of thinking and knowing that were crucial to creating a counter-hegemonic worldview. It is absolutely essential that the revolutionary power of black vernacular speech not be lost in contemporary culture. That power resides in the capacity of black vernacular to intervene on the boundaries and limitation of standard English.

In contemporary black popular culture, rap music has   7
become one of the spaces where black vernacular speech is used in a manner that invites dominant mainstream culture to listen—to hear—and, to some extent, be transformed. However, one of the risks of this attempt at cultural translation is that it will trivialize black vernacular speech. When young white kids imitate this speech in ways that suggest it is the speech of those who are stupid or who are only interested in entertaining or being funny, then the subversive power of

speech is undermined. In academic circles, both in the sphere of teaching and that of writing, there has been little effort made to utilize black vernacular—or, for that matter, any language other than standard English. When I asked an ethnically diverse group of students in a course I was teaching on black women writers why we only hear standard English spoken in the classroom, they were momentarily rendered speechless. Though many of them were individuals for whom standard English was a second or third language, it had simply never occurred to them that it was possible to say something in another language, in another way. No wonder, then, that we continue to think "This is the oppressor's language yet I need it to talk to you."

8   I have realized that I was in danger of losing my relationship to black vernacular speech because I too rarely use it in the predominantly white settings that I am most often in, both professionally and socially. And so I have begun to work at integrating into a variety of settings the particular Southern black vernacular speech I grew up hearing and speaking. It has been hardest to integrate black vernacular in writing, particularly for academic journals. When I first began to incorporate black vernacular in critical essays, editors would send the work back to me in standard English. Using the vernacular means that translation into standard English may be needed if one wishes to reach a more inclusive audience. In the classroom setting, I encourage students to use their first language and translate it so they do not feel that seeking higher education will necessarily estrange them from that language and culture they know most intimately. Not surprisingly, when students in my Black Women Writers class began to speak using diverse language and speech, white students often complained. This seemed to be particularly the case with black vernacular. It was particularly disturbing to the white students because they could hear the words that were said but could not comprehend their meaning. Pedagogically, I encouraged them to think of the moment of not understanding what someone says as a space to learn. Such a space provides not only the opportunity to listen without "mastery," without owning or possessing speech through interpretation, but also the experience of hearing non-English words. These lessons seem particularly crucial in a multicultural society that remains white supremacist, that uses standard English as a weapon to silence and censor. June Jordan reminds us of this in *On Call* when she declares:

I am talking about majority problems of language in a democratic state, problems of a currency that someone has stolen
and hidden away and then homogenized into an official
"English" language that can only express non-events involving nobody responsible, or lies. If we lived in a democratic
state our language would have to hurtle, fly, curse, and sing,
in all the common American names, all the undeniable and
representative participating voices of everybody here. We
would not tolerate the language of the powerful and, thereby,
lose all respect for words, per se. We would make our language conform to the truth of our many selves and we would
make our language lead us into the equality of power that a
democratic state must represent.

That the students in the course on black women writers   9
were repressing all longing to speak in tongues other than
standard English without seeing this repression as political
was an indication of the way we act unconsciously, in complicity with a culture of domination.

Recent discussion of diversity and multiculturalism tend   10
to downplay or ignore the question of language. Critical feminist writings focused on issues of difference and voice have
made important theoretical interventions, calling for a recognition of the primacy of voices that are often silenced, censored, or marginalized. This call for the acknowledgement
and celebration of diverse voices, and consequently of diverse
language and speech, necessarily disrupts the primacy of
standard English. When advocates of feminism first spoke
about the desire for diverse participation in women's movement, there was no discussion of language. It was simply
assumed that standard English would remain the primary
vehicle for the transmission of feminist thought. Now that the
audience for feminist writing and speaking has become more
diverse, it is evident that we must change conventional ways
of thinking about language, creating spaces where diverse
voices can speak in words other than English or in broken,
vernacular speech. This means that at a lecture or even in a
written work there will be fragments of speech that may or
may not be accessible to every individual. Shifting how we
think about language and how we use it necessarily alters
how we know what we know. At a lecture where I might use
Southern black vernacular, the particular patois of my region,
or where I might use very abstract thought in conjuction with
plain speech, responding to a diverse audience, I suggest that
we do not necessarily need to hear and know what is stated in

its entirety, that we do not need to "master" or conquer the narrative as a whole, that we may know in fragments. I suggest that we may learn from spaces of silence as well as spaces of speech, that in the patient act of listening to another tongue we may subvert that culture of capitalist frenzy and consumption that demands all desire must be satisfied immediately, or we may disrupt that cultural imperialism that suggests one is worthy of being heard only if one speaks in standard English.

11   Adrienne Rich concludes her poem with this statement:

> I am composing on the typewriter late at night, thinking of today. How well we all spoke. A language is a map of our failures. Frederick Douglass wrote an English purer than Milton's. People suffer highly in poverty. There are methods but we do not use them. Joan, who could not read, spoke some peasant form of French. Some of the sufferings are: it is hard to tell the truth; this is America; I cannot touch you now. In America we have only the present tense. I am in danger. You are in danger. The burning of a book arouses no sensation in me. I know it hurts to burn. There are flames of napalm in Cantonsville, Maryland. I know it hurts to burn. The typewriter is overheated, my mouth is burning, I cannot touch you and this is the oppressor's language.

12   To recognize that we touch one another in language seems particularly difficult in a society that would have us believe that there is no dignity in the experience of passion, that to feel deeply is to be inferior, for within the dualism of Western metaphysical thought, ideas are always more important than language. To heal the splitting of mind and body, we marginalized and oppressed people attempt to recover ourselves and our experiences in language. We seek to make a place for the intimacy. Unable to find such a place in standard English, we create the ruptured, broken, unruly speech of the vernacular. When I need to say words that do more than simply mirror or address the dominant reality, I speak black vernacular. There, in that location, we make English do what we want it to do. We take the oppressor's language and turn it against itself. We make our words a counter-hegemonic speech, liberating ourselves in language.

Gary Larson grew up in Tacoma, Washington, and graduated from Washington State University. Though Larson no longer publishes new cartoons, "The Far Side" continues to be one of America's most popular (and offbeat) cartoons.

THE FAR SIDE   By GARY LARSON

"Ha! The idiots spelled 'surrender' with only one 'r'!"

SHOULD WE HAVE A NATIONAL LANGUAGE?

Richard Rodriguez

Aria: A Memoir of a Bilingual Childhood

Richard Rodriguez, born in 1944 into a Spanish-speaking, Mexican American family, was educated at Stanford, Columbia, and Berkeley. Many of his eloquent essays—like the ones in his 1992 book Days of Obligation: An Argument with My Mexican Father—*mix memoir and argument, and many measure the gains and losses that result when English replaces Spanish that is spoken at home. This essay, first published in the magazine* The American Scholar *(1981), was incorporated into his acclaimed book* Hunger of Memory *(1982).*

1   I remember, to start with, that day in Sacramento, in a California now nearly thirty years past, when I first entered a classroom—able to understand about fifty stray English words. The third of four children, I had been preceded by my older brother and sister to a neighborhood Roman Catholic school. But neither of them had revealed very much about their classroom experiences. They left each morning and returned each afternoon, always together, speaking Spanish as they climbed the five steps to the porch. And their mysterious books, wrapped in brown shopping-bag paper, remained on the table next to the door, closed firmly behind them.

2   An accident of geography sent me to a school where all my classmates were white and many were the children of doctors and lawyers and business executives. On that first day of school, my classmates must certainly have been uneasy to find themselves apart from their families, in the first institution of their lives. But I was astonished. I was fated to be the "problem student" in class.

3   The nun said, in a friendly but oddly impersonal voice: "Boys and girls, this is Richard Rodriguez." (I heard her sound it out: *Rich-heard Road-ree-guess.*) It was the first time

I had heard anyone say my name in English. "Richard," the nun repeated more slowly, writing my name down in her book. Quickly I turned to see my mother's face dissolve in a watery blur behind the pebbled-glass door.

Now, many years later, I hear of something called "bilingual education"—a scheme proposed in the late 1960s by Hispanic-American social activists, later endorsed by a congressional vote. It is a program that seeks to permit non-English-speaking children (many from lower class homes) to use their "family language" as the language of school. Such, at least, is the aim its supporters announce. I hear them, and am forced to say no: It is not possible for a child, any child, ever to use his family's language in school. Not to understand this is to misunderstand the public uses of schooling and to trivialize the nature of intimate life.   4

Memory teaches me what I know of these matters. The boy reminds the adult. I was a bilingual child, but of a certain kind: "socially disadvantaged," the son of working-class parents, both Mexican immigrants.   5

In the early years of my boyhood, my parents coped very well in America. My father had steady work. My mother managed at home. They were nobody's victims. When we moved to a house many blocks from the Mexican-American section of town, they were not intimidated by those two or three neighbors who initially tried to make us unwelcome. ("Keep your brats away from my sidewalk!") But despite all they achieved, or perhaps because they had so much to achieve, they lacked any deep feeling of ease, of belonging in public. They regarded the people at work or in crowds as being very distant from us. Those were the others, *los gringos*. That term was interchangeable in their speech with another, even more telling: *los americanos*.   6

I grew up in a house where the only regular guests were my relations. On a certain day, enormous families of relatives would visit us, and there would be so many people that the noise and the bodies would spill out to the backyard and onto the front porch. Then for weeks no one would come. (If the doorbell rang, it was usually a salesman.) Our house stood apart—gaudy yellow in a row of white bungalows. We were the people with the noisy dog, the people who raised chickens. We were the foreigners on the block. A few neighbors would smile and wave at us. We waved back. But until I was seven years old, I did not know the name of the old couple living next door or the names of the kids living across the street.   7

8   In public, my father and mother spoke a hesitant, accented, and not always grammatical English. And then they would have to strain, their bodies tense, to catch the sense of what was rapidly said by *los gringos*. At home, they returned to Spanish. The language of their Mexican past sounded in counterpoint to the English spoken in public. The words would come quickly, with ease. Conveyed through those sounds was the pleasing, soothing, consoling reminder that one was at home.

9   During those years when I was first learning to speak, my mother and father addressed me only in Spanish; in Spanish I learned to reply. By contrast, English (*inglés*) was the language I came to associate with gringos, rarely heard in the house. I learned my first words of English overhearing my parents speaking to strangers. At six years of age, I knew just enough words for my mother to trust me on errands to stores one block away—but no more.

10   I was then a listening child, careful to hear the very different sounds of Spanish and English. Wide-eyed with hearing, I'd listen to sounds more than to words. First, there were English (gringo) sounds. So many words still were unknown to me that when the butcher or the lady at the drugstore said something, exotic polysyllabic sounds would bloom in the midst of their sentences. Often the speech of people in public seemed to me very loud, booming with confidence. The man behind the counter would literally ask, "What can I do for you?" But by being so firm and clear, the sound of his voice said that he was a gringo; he belonged in public society. There were also the high, nasal notes of middle-class American speech—which I rarely am conscious of hearing today because I hear them so often, but could not stop hearing when I was a boy. Crowds at Safeway or at bus stops were noisy with the birdlike sounds of *los gringos*. I'd move away from them all—all the chirping chatter above me.

11   My own sounds I was unable to hear, but I knew that I spoke English poorly. My words could not extend to form complete thoughts. And the words I did speak I didn't know well enough to make distinct sounds. (Listeners would usually lower their heads to hear better what I was trying to say.) But it was one thing for *me* to speak English with difficulty; it was more troubling to hear my parents speaking in public: their high-whining vowels and guttural consonants; their sentences that got stuck with "eh" and "ah" sounds; the confused syntax; the hesitant rhythm of sounds so different from the way gringos spoke. I'd notice, moreover, that my

parents' voices were softer than those of gringos we would meet.

I am tempted to say now that none of this mattered. (In adulthood I am embarrassed by childhood fears.) And, in a way, it didn't matter very much that my parents could not speak English with ease. Their linguistic difficulties had no serious consequences. My mother and father made themselves understood at the county hospital clinic and at government offices. And yet, in another way, it mattered very much. It was unsettling to hear my parents struggle with English. Hearing them, I'd grow nervous, and my clutching trust in their protection and power would be weakened.   12

There were many times like the night at a brightly lit gasoline station (a blaring white memory) when I stood uneasily hearing my father talk to a teenage attendant. I do not recall what they were saying, but I cannot forget the sounds my father made as he spoke. At one point his words slid together to form one long word—sounds as confused as the threads of blue and green oil in the puddle next to my shoes. His voice rushed through what he had left to say. Toward the end, he reached falsetto notes, appealing to his listener's understanding. I looked away at the lights of passing automobiles. I tried not to hear any more. But I heard only too well the attendant's reply, his calm, easy tones. Shortly afterward, headed for home, I shivered when my father put his hand on my shoulder. The very first chance that I got, I evaded his grasp and ran on ahead into the dark, skipping with feigned boyish exuberance.   13

But then there was Spanish: *español,* the language rarely heard away from the house; *español,* the language which seemed to me therefore a private language, my family's language. To hear its sounds was to feel myself specially recognized as one of the family, apart from *los otros.* A simple remark, an inconsequential comment could convey that assurance. My parents would say something to me and I would feel embraced by the sounds of their words. Those sounds said: *I am speaking with ease in Spanish. I am addressing you in words I never use with los gringos. I recognize you as someone special, close, like no one outside. You belong with us. In the family. Ricardo.*   14

At the age of six, well past the time when most middle-class children no longer notice the difference between sounds uttered at home and words spoken in public, I had a different experience. I lived in a world compounded of sounds. I was a child longer than most. I lived in a magical world, surrounded   15 by sounds both pleasing and fearful. I shared with my family a language enchantingly private—different from that used in the city around us.

16   Just opening or closing the screen door behind me was an important experience. I'd rarely leave home all alone or without feeling reluctance. Walking down the sidewalk, under the canopy of tall trees, I'd warily notice the (suddenly) silent neighborhood kids who stood warily watching me. Nervously, I'd arrive at the grocery store to hear there the sounds of the gringo, reminding me that in this so-big world I was a foreigner. But if leaving home was never routine, neither was coming back. Walking toward our house, climbing the steps from the sidewalk, in summer when the front door was open, I'd hear voices beyond the screen door talking in Spanish. For a second or two I'd stay, linger there listening. Smiling, I'd hear my mother call out, saying in Spanish, "Is that you, Richard?" Those were her words, but all the while her sounds would assure me: *You are home now. Come closer inside. With us.* "Sí," I'd reply.

17   Once more inside the house, I would resume my place in the family. The sounds would grow harder to hear. Once more at home, I would grow less conscious of them. It required, however, no more than the blurt of the doorbell to alert me all over again to listen to sounds. The house would turn instantly quiet while my mother went to the door. I'd hear her hard English sounds. I'd wait to hear her voice turn to soft-sounding Spanish, which assured me, as surely as did the clicking tongue of the lock on the door, that the stranger was gone.

18   Plainly it is not healthy to hear such sounds often. It is not healthy to distinguish public from private sounds so easily. I remained cloistered by sounds, timid and shy in public, too dependent on the voices at home. And yet I was a very happy child when I was at home. I remember many nights when my father would come back from work, and I'd hear him call out to my mother in Spanish, sounding relieved. In Spanish, his voice would sound the light and free notes that he never could manage in English. Some nights I'd jump up just hearing his voice. My brother and I would come running into the room where he was with our mother. Our laughing (so deep was the pleasure!) became screaming. Like others who feel the pain of public alienation, we transformed the knowledge of our public separateness into a consoling reminder of our intimacy. Excited, our voices joined in a celebration of sounds. *We are speaking now the way we never speak out in public—we are together,* the sounds told me. Some nights no one seemed will-

ing to loosen the hold that sounds had on us. At dinner we invented new words that sounded Spanish, but made sense only to us. We pieced together new words by taking, say, an English verb and giving it Spanish endings. My mother's instructions at bedtime would be lacquered with mock-urgent tones. Or a word like *sí*, sounded in several notes, would convey added measures of feeling. Tongues lingered around the edges of words, especially fat vowels, and we happily sounded that military drum roll, the twirling roar of the Spanish *r*. Family language, my family's sounds: the voices of my parents and sisters and brother. Their voices insisting: *You belong here. We are family members. Related. Special to one another. Listen!* Voices singing and sighing, rising and straining, then surging, teeming with pleasure which burst syllables into fragments of laughter. At times it seemed there was steady quiet only when, from another room, the rustling whispers of my parents faded and I edged closer to sleep.

Supporters of bilingual education imply today that students 19 like me miss a great deal by not being taught in their family's language. What they seem not to recognize is that, as a socially disadvantaged child, I regarded Spanish as a private language. It was a ghetto language that deepened and strengthened my feeling of public separateness. What I needed to learn in school was that I had the right, and the obligation, to speak the public language. The odd truth is that my first-grade class-mates could have become bilingual, in the conventional sense of the word, more easily than I. Had they been taught early (as upper middle-class children often are taught) a "second language" like Spanish or French, they could have regarded it simply as another public language. In my case, such bilingual-ism could not have been so quickly achieved. What I did not believe was that I could speak a single public language.

Without question, it would have pleased me to have heard 20 my teachers address me in Spanish when I entered the class-room. I would have felt much less afraid. I would have imag-ined that my instructors were somehow "related" to me; I would indeed have heard their Spanish as my family's lan-guage. I would have trusted them and responded with ease. But I would have delayed—postponed for how long?—having to learn the language of public society. I would have evaded—and for how long?—learning the great lesson of school: that I had a public identity.

Fortunately, my teachers were unsentimental about their 21 responsibility. What they understood was that I needed to speak public English. So their voices would search me out, asking me questions. Each time I heard them I'd look up in surprise to see a nun's face frowning at me. I'd mumble, not really meaning to answer. The nun would persist. "Richard, stand up. Don't look at the floor. Speak up. Speak to the entire class, not just to me!" But I couldn't believe English could be my language to use. (In part, I did not want to believe it.) I continued to mumble. I resisted the teacher's demands. (Did I somehow suspect that once I learned this public language my family life would be changed?) Silent, waiting for the bell to sound, I remained dazed, diffident, afraid.

22   Because I wrongly imagined that English was intrinsically a public language and Spanish was intrinsically private, I easily noted the difference between classroom language and the language at home. At school, words were directed to a general audience of listeners. ("Boys and girls...") Words were meaningfully ordered. And the point was not self-expression alone, but to make oneself understood by many others. The teacher quizzed: "Boys and girls, why do we use that word in this sentence? Could we think of a better word to use there? Would the sentence change its meaning if the words were differently arranged? Isn't there a better way of saying much the same thing?" (I couldn't say. I wouldn't try to say.)

23   Three months passed. Five. A half year. Unsmiling, ever watchful, my teachers noted my silence. They began to connect my behavior with the slow progress my brother and sisters were making. Until, one Saturday morning, three nuns arrived at the house to talk to our parents. Stiffly they sat on the blue living-room sofa. From the doorway of another room, spying on the visitors, I noted the incongruity, the clash of two worlds, the faces and voices of school intruding upon the familiar setting of home. I overheard one voice gently wondering, "Do your children speak only Spanish at home, Mrs. Rodriguez?" While another voice added, "That Richard especially seems so timid and shy."

24   *That Rich-heard!*

25   With great tact, the visitors continued, "Is it possible for you and your husband to encourage your children to practice their English when they are home?" Of course my parents complied. What would they not do for their children's well-being? And how could they question the Church's authority which those women represented? In an instant they agreed to give up the language (the sounds) which had revealed and accentuated our family's closeness. The moment after the visitors left, the change was observed. *"Ahora,* speak to us only *en inglés,"* my father and mother told us.

At first, it seemed a kind of game. After dinner each night, the family gathered together to practice "our" English. It was still then *inglés,* a language foreign to us, so we felt drawn to it as strangers. Laughing, we would try to define words we could not pronounce. We played with strange English sounds, often overanglicizing our pronunciations. And we filled the smiling gaps of our sentences with familiar Spanish sounds. But that was cheating, somebody shouted, and everyone laughed.

In school, meanwhile, like my brother and sisters, I was required to attend a daily tutoring session. I needed a full year of this special work. I also needed my teachers to keep my attention from straying in class by calling out, *"Rich-heard"*—their English voices slowly loosening the ties to my other name, with its three notes, *Ri-car-do.* Most of all, I needed to hear my mother and father speak to me in a moment of seriousness in "broken"—suddenly heartbreak-ing—English. This scene was inevitable. One Saturday morn-ing I entered the kitchen where my parents were talking, but I did not realize that they were talking in Spanish until, the moment they saw me, their voices changed and they began speaking English. The gringo sounds they uttered startled me. Pushed me away. In that moment of trivial misunder-standing and profound insight, I felt my throat twisted by unsounded grief. I simply turned and left the room. But I had no place to escape to where I could grieve in Spanish. My brother and sisters were speaking English in another part of the house.

Again and again in the days following, as I grew increas-ingly angry, I was obliged to hear my mother and father encouraging me: "Speak to us *en inglés.*" Only then did I deter-mine to learn classroom English. Thus, sometime afterward it happened: one day in school, I raised my hand to volunteer an answer to a question. I spoke out in a loud voice and I did not think it remarkable when the entire class understood. That day I moved very far from being the disadvantaged child I had been only days earlier. Taken hold at last was the belief, the calming assurance, that I *belonged* in public.

Shortly after, I stopped hearing the high, troubling sounds of *los gringos.* A more and more confident speaker of English, I didn't listen to how strangers sounded when they talked to me. With so many English-speaking people around me, I no longer heard American accents. Conversations quickened. Listening to persons whose voices sounded eccentrically pitched, I might note their sounds for a few seconds, but then

26

27

28

29

I'd concentrate on what they were saying. Now when I heard someone's tone of voice—angry or questioning or sarcastic or happy or sad—I didn't distinguish it from the words it expressed. Sound and word were thus tightly wedded. At the end of each day I was often bemused, and always relieved, to realize how "soundless," though crowded with words, my day in public had been. An eight-year-old boy, I finally came to accept what had been technically true since my birth: I was an American citizen.

30   But diminished by then was the special feeling of closeness at home. Gone was the desperate, urgent, intense feeling of being at home among those with whom I felt intimate. Our family remained a loving family, but one greatly changed. We were no longer so close, no longer bound tightly together by the knowledge of our separateness from *los gringos*. Neither my older brother nor my sisters rushed home after school any more. Nor did I. When I arrived home, often there would be neighborhood kids in the house. Or the house would be empty of sounds.

31   Following the dramatic Americanization of their children, even my parents grew more publicly confident—especially my mother. First she learned the names of all the people on the block. Then she decided we needed to have a telephone in our house. My father, for his part, continued to use the word gringo, but it was no longer charged with bitterness or distrust. Stripped of any emotional content, the word simply became a name for those Americans not of Hispanic descent. Hearing him, sometimes, I wasn't sure if he was pronouncing the Spanish word *gringo*, or saying gringo in English.

32   There was a new silence at home. As we children learned more and more English, we shared fewer and fewer words with our parents. Sentences needed to be spoken slowly when one of us addressed our mother or father. Often the parent wouldn't understand. The child would need to repeat himself. Still the parent misunderstood. The young voice, frustrated, would end up saying, "Never mind"—the subject was closed. Dinners would be noisy with the clinking of knives and forks against dishes. My mother would smile softly between her remarks; my father, at the other end of the table, would chew and chew his food while he stared over the heads of his children.

33   My mother! My father! After English became my primary language, I no longer knew what words to use in addressing my parents. The old Spanish words (those tender accents of sound) I had earlier used—*mamá* and *papá*—I couldn't use

any more. They would have been all-too-painful reminders of how much had changed in my life. On the other hand, the words I heard neighborhood kids call their parents seemed equally unsatisfactory. "Mother" and "father," "ma," "papa," "pa," "dad," "pop" (how I hated the all-American sound of that last word)—all these I felt were unsuitable terms of address for *my* parents. As a result, I never used them at home. Whenever I'd speak to my parents, I would try to get their attention by looking at them. In public conversations, I'd refer to them as my "parents" or my "mother" and "father."

My mother and father, for their part, responded differently,   34
as their children spoke to them less. My mother grew restless, seemed troubled and anxious at the scarceness of words exchanged in the house. She would question me about my day when I came home from school. She smiled at my small talk. She pried at the edges of my sentences to get me to say something more. ("What . . . ?") She'd join conversations she overheard, but her intrusions often stopped her children's talking. By contrast, my father seemed to grow reconciled to the new quiet. Though his English somewhat improved, he tended more and more to retire into silence. At dinner he spoke very little. One night his children and even his wife helplessly giggled at his garbled English pronunciation of the Catholic "Grace Before Meals." Thereafter he made his wife recite the prayer at the start of each meal, even on formal occasions when there were guests in the house.

Hers became the public voice of the family. On official   35
business it was she, not my father, who would usually talk to strangers on the phone or in stores. We children grew so accustomed to his silence that years later we would routinely refer to his "shyness." (My mother often tried to explain: both of his parents died when he was eight. He was raised by an uncle who treated him as little more than a menial servant. He was never encouraged to speak. He grew up alone—a man of few words.) But I realized my father was not shy whenever I'd watch him speaking Spanish with relatives. Using Spanish, he was quickly effusive. Especially when talking with other men, his voice would spark, flicker, flare alive with varied sounds. In Spanish he expressed ideas and feelings he rarely revealed when speaking English. With firm Spanish sounds he conveyed a confidence and authority that English would never allow him.

The silence at home, however, was not simply the result of   36
fewer words passing between parents and children. More profound for me was the silence created by inattention to

sounds. At about the time I no longer bothered to listen with care to the sounds of English in public, I grew careless about listening to the sounds made by the family when they spoke. Most of the time I would hear someone speaking at home and didn't distinguish his sounds from the words people uttered in public. I didn't even pay much attention to my parents' accented and ungrammatical speech—at least not at home. Only when I was with them in public would I become alert to their accents. But even then their sounds caused me less and less concern. For I was growing increasingly confident of my own public identity.

37   I would have been happier about my public success had I not recalled, sometimes, what it had been like earlier, when my family conveyed its intimacy through a set of conveniently private sounds. Sometimes in public, hearing a stranger, I'd hark back to my lost past. A Mexican farm worker approached me one day downtown. He wanted directions to some place. *"Hijito,..."* he said. And his voice stirred old longings. Another time I was standing beside my mother in the visiting room of a Carmelite convent, before the dense screen which rendered the nuns shadowy figures. I heard several of them speaking Spanish in their busy, singsong, overlapping voices, assuring my mother that yes, yes, we were remembered, all our family was remembered, in their prayers. Those voices echoed faraway family sounds. Another day a dark-faced old woman touched my shoulder lightly to steady herself as she boarded a bus. She murmured something to me I couldn't quite comprehend. Her Spanish voice came near, like the face of a never-before-seen relative in the instant before I was kissed. That voice, like so many of the Spanish voices I'd hear in public, recalled the golden age of my childhood.

38   Bilingual educators say today that children lose a degree of "individuality" by becoming assimilated into public society. (Bilingual schooling is a program popularized in the seventies, that decade when middle-class "ethnics" began to resist the process of assimilation—the "American melting pot.") But the bilingualists oversimplify when they scorn the value and necessity of assimilation. They do not seem to realize that a person is individualized in two ways. So they do not realize that, while one suffers a diminished sense of *private* individuality by being assimilated into public society, such assimilation makes possible the achievement of *public* individuality.

Simplistically again, the bilingualists insist that a student 39
should be reminded of his difference from others in mass society, of his "heritage." But they equate mere separateness with
individuality. The fact is that only in private—with intimates—
is separateness from the crowd a prerequisite for individuality; an intimate "tells" me that I am unique, unlike all others,
apart from the crowd. In public, by contrast, full individuality
is achieved, paradoxically, by those who are able to consider
themselves members of the crowd. Thus it happened for me.
Only when I was able to think of myself as an American, no
longer an alien in gringo society, could I seek the rights and
opportunities necessary for full public individuality. The
social and political advantages I enjoy as a man began on the
day I came to believe that my name is indeed *Rich-heard Road-
ree-guess.* It is true that my public society today is often impersonal; in fact, my public society is usually mass society. But
despite the anonymity of the crowd, and despite the fact that
the individuality I achieve in public is often tenuous—because
it depends on my being one in a crowd—I celebrate the day
I acquired my new name. Those middle-class ethnics who
scorn assimilation seem to me filled with decadent self-pity,
obsessed by the burden of public life. Dangerously, they
romanticize public separateness and trivialize the dilemma of
those who are truly socially disadvantaged.

If I rehearse here the changes in my private life after my 40
Americanization, it is finally to emphasize a public gain. The
loss implies the gain. The house I returned to each afternoon
was quiet. Intimate sounds no longer greeted me at the door.
Inside there were other noises. The telephone rang. Neighborhood kids ran past the door of the bedroom where I was
reading my schoolbooks—covered with brown shopping-bag
paper. Once I learned the public language, it would never
again be easy for me to hear intimate family voices. More and
more of my day was spent hearing words, not sounds. But
that may only be a way of saying that on the day I raised my
hand in class and spoke loudly to an entire roomful of faces,
my childhood started to end.

Victor Villanueva Jr.

Whose Voice Is It Anyway?
Rodriguez' Speech in Retrospect

Victor Villanueva Jr., on the faculty at Northern Arizona University until 1995, now teaches English at Washington State University. In 1993, he published the award-winning Bootstraps: From an American Academic of Color, *a personal and intellectual narrative of his own encounter with language issues in the United States in general and in the academy in particular. Villanueva also reveals a lot about himself in the following essay, which he wrote in 1987 for* English Journal, *a professional magazine directed to high school and elementary school English teachers.*

1   During the 1986 annual conference of the NCTE (National Council of Teachers of English) I attended a luncheon sponsored by the secondary section. Richard Rodriguez, author of *Hunger of Memory,* was the guest speaker. He spoke of how he came to be an articulate speaker of this standard dialect, and he spoke of the conclusions concerning language that his experiences had brought him to. He was impressive. I was taken by his quiet eloquence. His stage presence recalled Olivier's Hamlet. He spoke well. But for all his eloquence and his studied stage presence, I was nevertheless surprised by the audience's response, an enthusiastic, uncritical acceptance, marked by a long, loud standing ovation. I was surprised because he had blurred distinctions between language and culture, between his experiences and those more typical of the minority in America, between the history of the immigrant and that of the minority, in a way that I had thought would raise more than a few eyebrows. Yet all he raised was the audience to its feet.

2   In retrospect, I think I can understand the rave reception. The message he so softly delivered relieved us all of some anxiety. Classroom teachers' shoulders stoop under the weight of the paper load. They take 150 students through writing and grammar, spelling and punctuation. Within those same forty-five-minute spurts they also work on reading: drama, poetry, literature, the great issues in literature. After that, there's the writers' club or the school paper or the yearbook, coaching volleyball or producing the school play. And throughout it all, they are to remain sensitive to the language of the nonstand-

ard or non-English speaker. They are not really told how—just "be sensitive," while parents, the media, sometimes it seems the whole world, shake their fingers at them for not doing something about America's literacy problems. Richard Rodriguez told the teachers to continue to be sensitive but to forget about doing anything special. The old ways may be painful, but they really are best. There is a kind of violence to the melting pot, he said, but it is necessary. He said that this linguistic assimilation is like alchemy, initially destructive perhaps but magical, creating something new and greater than what was. Do as you have always done. And the teachers sighed.

Richard Rodriguez is the authority, after all: a bilingual   3 child of immigrant parents, a graduate of two of the nation's more prestigious schools, Stanford and Berkeley, an English teacher, the well-published author of numerous articles and a well-received, well-anthologized book. He knows. And he says that the teachers who insisted on a particular linguistic form can be credited with his fame. But what is it, really, that has made him famous? He is a fine writer; of that there can be no doubt. But it is his message that has brought him fame, a message that states that the minority is no different than any other immigrant who came to this country not knowing its culture or its language, leaving much of the old country behind to become part of this new one, and in becoming part of America subtly changing what it means to be American. The American who brought his beef and pudding from England became the American of frankfurter, the bologna sandwich, pizza. Typically American foods—like typical Americans—partake of the world.

At the luncheon, Richard Rodriguez spoke of a TV ad for   4 Mexican-style Velveeta, "the blandest of American cheeses," he called it, now speckled with peppers. This cultural contrast, said Rodriguez, demonstrated how Mexico—no less than England or Germany—is part of America.

But I think it shows how our times face a different kind of   5 assimilation. Let's put aside for the moment questions as to why, if Mexicans really are being assimilated, they have taken so much longer than other groups, especially since Mexicans were already part of the West and Southwest when the West and Southwest became part of America. Let's look, rather, at the hyphen in Mexican-Velveeta. Who speaks of a German-American sausage, for instance? It's a hot dog. Yet tacos remain ethnic, sold under a mock Spanish mission bell or a sombrero. You will find refried beans under "ethnic foods" in the supermarket, not among other canned beans, though items as foreign-sounding as sauerkraut are simply canned vegetables. Mexican foods, even when Americanized as the taco salad or Mexican-Velveeta, remain distinctly Mexican.[1]

6   And like the ethnic food, some ethnic minorities have not been assimilated in the way the Ellis Islanders were. The fires of the melting pot have cooled. No more soup. America's more a stew today. The difference is the difference between the immigrant and the minority, a difference having to do with how each, the immigrant and the minority, came to be Americans, the difference between choice and colonization. Those who emigrated from Europe chose to leave unacceptable conditions in search of better. Choice, I realize, is a tricky word in this context: religious persecution, debtor's prison, potato famine, fascism, foreign takeover, when compared with a chance at prosperity and self-determination, don't seem to make for much of a choice; yet most people apparently remained in their homelands despite the intolerable, while the immigrants did leave, and in leaving chose to sever ties with friends and families, created a distance between themselves and their histories, cultures, languages. There is something heroic in this. It's a heroism shared by the majority of Americans.

7   But choice hardly entered into most minorities' decisions to become American. Most of us recognize this when it comes to Blacks or American Indians. Slavery, forcible displacement, and genocide are fairly clear-cut. Yet the circumstances by which most minorities became Americans are no less clear-cut. The minority became an American almost by default, as part of the goods in big-time real estate deals or as some of the spoils of war. What is true for the Native American applies to the Alaska Native, the Pacific Islander (including the Asian), Mexican-Americans, Puerto Ricans. Puerto Rico was part of Christopher Columbus' great discovery, Arawaks and Boriquens among his "Indians," a real-estate coup for the Queen of Spain. Then one day in 1898, the Puerto Ricans who had for nearly four hundred years been

---

[1]Mexican food is not the only ethnic food on the market, of course. Asian and Mediterranean foods share the shelves. But this too is telling, since Asians alone had had restricted access to the US before the country ended its Open Door Immigration Policy. When the US closed its doors in 1924, it was to regulate the flow of less desirable "new immigrants"—the Eastern and Southern Europeans who remain "ethnic" to this day. See Oscar Handlin's *Race in American Life*, New York, Anchor, 1957.

made proud to be the offspring of Spain, so much so that their native Arawak and Boricua languages and ways were virtually gone, found themselves the property of the United States, property without the rights and privileges of citizenship until—conveniently—World War I. But citizenship notwithstanding, Puerto Rico remains essentially a colony today.[2]

One day in 1845 and in 1848 other descendants of Spain who had all but lost their Indian identities found themselves Americans. These were the long-time residents and land-owners of the Republic of Texas and the California Republic: the area from Texas to New Mexico, Arizona, Utah, and California. Residents in the newly established US territories were given the option to relocate to Mexico or to remain on their native lands, with the understanding that should they remain they would be guaranteed American Constitutional rights. Those who stayed home saw their rights not very scrupulously guarded, falling victim over time to displacement, dislocation, and forced expatriation. There is something tragic in losing a long-established birthright, tragic but not heroic—especially not heroic to those whose ancestors had fled their homelands rather than acknowledge external rule.   8

The immigrant gave up much in the name of freedom—and for the sake of dignity. For the Spanish-speaking minority in particular, the freedom to be American without once again relinquishing one's ancestry is also a matter of dignity.   9

This is not to say that Richard Rodriguez forfeited his dignity in choosing not to be Ricardo. The Mexican's status includes not only the descendants of the West and Southwest, Spanish-speaking natives to America, but also immigrants and the descendants of immigrants. Richard Rodriguez is more the immigrant than the minority. His father, he told us, had left his native Mexico for Australia. He fell in love along the way, eventually settling with wife and family in Sacramento. America was not his father's first choice for a new home perhaps, but he did choose to leave his homeland in much the same way European immigrants had. The Rodriguezes no doubt felt the immigrants' hardships, the drive to assimilate, a drive compounded perhaps by the association in their and others' minds between them and the undocumented migrant worker or between them and the minority.   10

---

[2]Nor is it a simple matter of Puerto Rico's deciding whether it wants to remain a commonwealth, gaining statehood, or independence. The interests of US industry, of the US military, and the social and economic ramifications of Puerto Rico's widespread poverty complicate matters.

11   And it is this confusion of immigrant and minority in Richard Rodriguez with which we must contend. His message
rings true to the immigrant heritage of his audience because
it happens to be the immigrant's story. It is received as if it
were a new story because it is confused with this story of the
minority. The complexities of the minority are rendered simple—not easy, but easily understood.

12   Others tell the story of the minority. I think, for instance, of
Piri Thomas and Tato Laviera, since theirs are stories of
Puerto Ricans. My own parents had immigrated to New York
from Puerto Rico, though not in the way of most. My mother,
an American, a US citizen like all Puerto Ricans, fair-skinned
and proud of her European descent, had been sold into servi-
tude to a wealthy Chicago family. My father, recently discharged from the US Army, followed my mother, rescued his
sweetheart, and together they fled to New York. I was born a
year later, 1948.

13   My mother believed in the traditional idea of assimilation.
She and my father would listen to the radio shows in English
and try to read the American newspapers. They spoke to me
in two languages from the start. The local parochial school's
tuition was a dollar a month, so I was spared PS 168. Rodriguez tells of nuns coming to his home to suggest that the
family speak English at home. For Rodriguez this was something of a turning point in his life; intimacy lost, participation
in the public domain gained. A public language would dominate, the painful path to his assimilation, the path to his eventual success. A nun spoke to my parents, too, when I was in
kindergarten. I spoke with an accent, they were told. They
should speak to me in English. My mother could only laugh:
my English was as it was *because* they spoke to me in English.
The irony reinforced our intimacy while I continued to learn
the "public language."

14   There is more to assimilating than learning the language. I
earned my snacks at the Saturday matinee by reading the
credits on the screen. I enjoyed parsing sentences, was good at
it too. I was a Merriam-Webster spelling bee champ. I was an
"A" student who nevertheless took a special Saturday course
on how to do well on the standardized test that would gain me
entry to the local Catholic high school. I landed in the public
vo-tech high school, slotted for a trade. Jarapolk, whose parents had fled the Ukraine, made the good school; so did Marie
Engels, the daughter of German immigrants. Lana Walker, a
Black girl whose brains I envied, got as far as the alternate list.
I don't recall any of the Black or Puerto Rican kids from my

class getting in. I never finished high school, despite my being a bright boy who knew the public language intimately.

I don't like thinking minorities were intentionally excluded from the better school. I would prefer to think minorities didn't do as well because we were less conscious than the immigrants of the cultural distances we had to travel to be truly Americans. We were Americans, after all, not even seeing ourselves as separated by language by the time most of us got to the eighth grade. I spoke Spanglish at home, a hybrid English and Spanish common to New York Puerto Ricans; I spoke the Puerto Rican version of Black English in the streets, and as far as I knew, I spoke something close to the standard dialect in the classroom. We thought ourselves Americans, assimilated. We didn't know about cultural bias in standardized tests. I still don't do well on standardized tests.

A more pointed illustration of the difference between the minority and the immigrant comes by way of a lesson from my father. I was around ten. We went uptown one day, apartment hunting. I don't recall how he chose the place. He asked about an apartment in his best English, the sounds of a Spanish speaker attempting his best English. No vacancies. My father thanked the man, then casually slipped into the customary small talk of the courteous exit. During the talk my father mentioned our coming from Spain. By the end of the chat a unit became available. Maybe my father's pleasing personality had gained us entry. More likely, Puerto Rican stereotypes had kept us out. The immigrant could enter where the minority could not. My father's English hadn't improved in the five minutes it had taken for the situation to change.

Today I sport a doctorate in English from a major university, study and teach rhetoric at another university, do research in and teach composition, continue to enjoy and teach English literature. I live in an all-American city in the heart of America. And I know I am not quite assimilated. In one weekend I was asked if I was Iranian one day and East Indian the next. "No," I said. "You have an accent," I was told. Yet tape recordings and passing comments throughout the years have told me that though there is a "back East" quality to my voice, there isn't much of New York to it anymore, never mind the Black English of my younger years or the Spanish of my youngest. My "accent" was in my not sounding midwestern, which does have a discernible, though not usually a pronounced, regional quality. And my "accent," I would guess, was in my "foreign" features (which pale alongside the brown skin of Richard Rodriguez).

18   Friends think I make too much of such incidents. Minority
hypersensitivity, they say. They desensitize me (and display
their liberal attitudes) with playful jabs at Puerto Ricans:
greasy hair jokes, knife-in-pocket jokes, spicy food jokes (and
Puerto Ricans don't even eat hot foods, unless we're eating
Mexican or East Indian foods). If language alone were the
secret to assimilation, the rate of Puerto Rican and Mexican
success would be greater, I would think. So many Mexican-
Americans and Puerto Ricans remain in the barrios—even
those who are monolingual, who have never known Spanish.
If language alone were the secret, wouldn't the secret have
gotten out long before Richard Rodriguez recorded his memoirs? In fact, haven't we always worked with the assumption
that language learning—oral and written—is the key to parity,
even as parity continues to elude so many?

19   I'm not saying the assumption is wrong. I think teachers
are right to believe in the potential power of language. We
want our students to be empowered. That's why we read professional journals. That's why we try to accommodate the pronouncements of linguists. That's why we listen to the likes of
Richard Rodriguez. But he spoke more of the English
teacher's power than the empowerment of the student. "Listen to the sound of my voice," he said. He asked the audience
to forget his brown skin and listen to his voice, his "unac-
cented voice." "This is your voice," he told the teachers. Better
that we, teachers at all levels, give students the means to find
their own voices, voices that don't have to ask that we ignore
what we cannot ignore, voices that speak of their brown or
yellow or red or black skin with pride and without need for
bravado or hostility, voices that can recognize and exploit the
conventions we have agreed to as the standards of written
discourse—without necessarily accepting the ideology of
those for whom the standard dialect is the language of home
as well as commerce, for whom the standard dialect is as private as it is public, to use Rodriguez' terms.

20   Rodriguez said at the luncheon that he was not speaking
of pedagogy as much as of ideology. He was. It is an ideology
which grew out of the memoirs of an immigrant boy
confronting contrasts, a child accommodating his circumstances. He remembers a brown boy in a white middle-class
school and is forced to say no to bilingual education. His
classmates were the descendants of other immigrants, the
products of assimilation, leading him to accept the traitional
American ideology of a multiculturalism that manifests as
one new culture and language, a culture and language which

encompasses and transcends any one culture. I remember a brown boy among other brown boys and girls, blacks, and olives, and variations on white, and must agree with Richard that bilingualism in the classroom would have been impractical. But my classmates were in the process of assimilation—Polish, German, Ukrainian, and Irish children, the first of their families to enter American schools; my classmates were also Black and Puerto Rican. It seemed to this boy's eyes that the immigrants would move on but the minority would stay, that the colonized do not melt. Today I do not hear of the problems in educating new immigrants, but the problems of Black literacy continue to make the news. And I hear of an eighty per cent dropout rate among Puerto Ricans in Boston, of Mexicans in the Rio Grande Valley where the dropout rate exceeds seventy per cent, of places where English and the education system do not address the majority—Spanish speakers for whom menial labor has been the tradition and is apparently the future. I must ask how *not* bilingual education in such situations. One person's experiences must remain one person's, applicable to many others, perhaps, but not all others. Simple, monolithic, universal solutions simply can't work in a complex society.

When it comes to the nonstandard speaker, for instance, 21 we are torn between the findings of linguists and the demands of the marketplace. Our attempts at preparing students for the marketplace only succeed in alienating nonstandard speakers, we are told. Our attempts at accommodating their nonstandard dialects, we fear, only succeed in their being barred from the marketplace. So we go back to the basics. Or else we try to change their speech without alienating them, in the process perhaps sensing that our relativism might smack of condescension. Limiting the student's language to the playground and home still speaks of who's right and who's wrong, who holds the power. I would rather we left speaking dialects relatively alone (truly demonstrating a belief in the legitimacy of the nonstandard). The relationship between speaking and writing is complex, as the debate sparked by Thomas Farrell has made clear. My own research and studies, as well as my personal experiences, suggest that exposure to writing and reading affects speaking. My accent changes, it seems, with every book I read. We don't have to give voices to students. If we give them pen and paper and have them read the printed page aloud, no matter what their grade, they'll discover their own voices.

22   And if we let the printed page offer a variety of world
views, of ideologies, those voices should gather the power we
wish them to have. Booker T. Washington, Martin Luther
King, Jr., W. E. B. DuBois all wrote with eloquence. Each presents a different world view. Maxine Hong Kingston's "voice"
resounds differently from Frank Chin's. Ernesto Galarza saw
a different world than Richard Rodriguez. Rodriguez' is only
one view, one voice. Yet it's his voice which seems to resound
the loudest. Rodriguez himself provided the reason why this
is so. He said at the luncheon that the individual's story, the
biography or autobiography, has universal appeal because it
strikes at experiences we have in common. The immigrant's
story has the most in common with the majority.

23   Rodriguez implied that he didn't feel much kinship to
minority writers. He said he felt a special bond with D. H.
Lawrence. It seems appropriate that Rodriguez, who writes
of his alienation from family in becoming part of the mainstream, would turn to Lawrence. Lawrence, too, was a
teacher turned writer. Lawrence, too, felt alienated from his
working-class background. It was Lawrence who argued, in
"Reflections on the Death of the Porcupine," that equality is
not achievable; Lawrence who co-opted, left the mastered to
join the masters. Is this what we want for our minority students? True, Lawrence's mastery of the English language cannot be gainsaid. I would be proud to have a Lawrence credit
me with his voice, would appreciate his accomplishment. But
I would rather share credit in a W. B. Yeats, Anglo and Irish,
assimilated but with a well-fed memory of his ancestry, master of the English language, its beauty, its traditions—and
voice of the colony.

IS ENGLISH SEXIST?

Beverly Gross

Bitch

Salmagundi, *a quarterly magazine of the humanities and social sciences that is produced at Skidmore College, carries poetry, fiction, critical essays, and social analyses on a variety of issues. In the summer of 1994, it published the following meditation on language by Beverly Gross, a professor of English at City University of New York.*

We were discussing Mary McCarthy's *The Group* in a course called Women Writers and Literary Tradition. McCarthy's biographer Carol Gelderman, I told the class, had been intrigued by how often critics called Mary McCarthy a bitch. I read a few citations. "Her novels are crammed with cerebration and bitchiness" (John Aldridge). "Her approach to writing [is] reflective of the modern American bitch" (Paul Schlueter). Why McCarthy? a student asked. Her unrelenting standards, I ventured, her tough-minded critical estimates—there was no self-censoring, appeasing Angel in the House of Mary McCarthy's brain. Her combativeness (her marital battles with Edmund Wilson became the stuff of academic legend). Maybe there were other factors. But the discussion opened up to the more inclusive issue of the word bitch itself. What effect does that appellation have on women? What effect might it have had on McCarthy? No one ever called Edmund Wilson a bitch. Do we excuse, even pay respect when a man is critical, combative, assertive? What is the male equivalent of the word bitch, I asked the class. 1

"Boss," said Sabrina Sims. 2

This was an evening class at a branch of the City University 3
of New York. Most of the students are older adults trying to fit a college education into otherwise busy lives. Most of them have fulltime jobs during the day. Sabrina Sims works on Wall Street, is a single mother raising a ten year old daughter, is black, and had to take an Incomplete in the course because she underwent a kidney transplant in December.

4   Her answer gave us all a good laugh. I haven't been able to get it out of my mind. I've been thinking about bitch, watching how it is used by writers and in conversation, and have explored its lexical history. "A name of reproach for a woman" is how Doctor Johnson's Dictionary dealt with the word in the eighteenth century, as though anticipating the great adaptability of this particular execration, a class of words that tends toward early obsolescence. Not bitch, however, which has been around for a millennium, outlasting a succession of definitions. Its longevity is perhaps attributable to its satisfying misogyny. Its meaning matters less than its power to denounce and subjugate. Francis Grose in *A Classical Dictionary of the Vulgar Tongue* (1785) considered bitch "the most offensive appellation that can be given to an English woman, even more provoking than that of whore." He offered as evidence "a low London woman's reply on being called a bitch" in the late eighteenth century: "I may be a whore but can't be a bitch!" The meaning of bitch has changed over the centuries but it remains the word that comes immediately to the tongue, still "the most offensive appellation" the English language provides to hurl at a woman.

5   The *Oxford English Dictionary* records two main meanings for the noun bitch up through the nineteenth century:

> 1. The female of the dog
>
> 2. Applied opprobriously to a woman; strictly a lewd or sensual woman. Not now in decent use.

6   It was not until the twentieth century that bitch acquired its opprobrious application in realms irrespective of sensuality. The Supplement to the *OED* (1972) adds:

> 2a: "In mod. use, esp. a malicious or treacherous woman."

Every current desk dictionary supplies some such meaning:

> A spiteful, ill-tempered woman [*World Book Dictionary*]
>
> A malicious, unpleasant, selfish woman, esp. one who stops at nothing to reach her goal. [*Random House Dictionary*]

But malice and treachery only begin to tell the story. The informal questionnaire that I administered to my students and a number of acquaintances elicited ample demonstration of the slippery adaptability of bitch as it might be used these days:

a conceited person, a snob

a self-absorbed woman

a complainer

a competitive woman

a woman who is annoying, pushy, possibly underhanded (in short, a man in a woman's body)

someone rich, thin and free!

"A word used by men who are threatened by women" was   7
one astute response. Threat lurks everywhere: for women the
threat is in being called a bitch. "Someone whiny, threatening, crabby, pestering" is what one woman offered as her definition. "Everything I try hard not to be," she added, "though
it seeps through." I offer as a preliminary conclusion that
bitch means to men whatever they find threatening in a
woman and it means to women whatever they particularly
dislike about themselves. In either case the word functions as
a misogynistic club. I will add that the woman who defined
bitch as everything she tries hard not to be when asked to free
associate about the word came up immediately with
"mother." That woman happens to be my sister. We share the
same mother, who was often whiny and crabby, though I
would never have applied the word bitch to her, but then
again, I don't consider whiny, crabby and pestering to be
prominent among my own numerous flaws.

Dictionaries of slang are informative sources, in touch as   8
they are with nascent language and the emotive coloration of
words, especially words of abuse. A relatively restrained definition is offered by the only female lexicographer I consulted
for whom bitch is "a nasty woman" or "a difficult task" (Anita
Pearl, *Dictionary of Popular Slang*). The delineations of bitch
by the male lexicographers abound with such cascading hostility that the compilers sometimes seem to be reveling in
their task. For example, Howard Wentworth and Stuart Berg
Flexner in *Dictionary of American Slang:*

A woman, usu., but not necessarily, a mean, selfish, malicious, deceiving, cruel, or promiscuous woman.

Eugene E. Landy's *The Underground Dictionary* (1971)
offers:

1. Female who is mean, selfish, cruel, malicious, deceiving.
a.k.a. cunt.

2. Female. See Female.

9   I looked up the entry for "Female" (Landy, by the way, provides no parallel entry for "Male"):

> beaver, bird, bitch, broad, bush, cat, chick, crack, cunt,
> douche, fish, fox, frail, garbage can, heffer, pussy, quail, ruca,
> scag, snatch, stallion, slave, sweet meat, tail, trick, tuna. See
> GIRLFRIEND; WIFE.

Richard A. Spear's *Slang and Euphemism* comments on the
derivative adjective:

> bitchy 1. pertaining to a mood wherein one complains inces-
> santly about anything. Although this applies to men or
> women, it is usually associated with women, especially when
> they are menstruating. Cf. DOG DAYS

10   Robert L. Chapman's definition in *Thesaurus of American
Slang* starts off like a feminist analysis:

> bitch. 1 n. A woman one dislikes or disapproves of.
> Followed, however, by a sobering string of synonyms:
> "broad, cunt, witch."

And then this most interesting note:

> Female equivalents of the contemptuous terms for men,
> listed in this book under "asshole," are relatively rare. Con-
> tempt for females, in slang, stresses their putative sexual pro-
> miscuity and weakness rather than their moral vileness and
> general odiousness. Some terms under "asshole," though,
> are increasingly used of women.

11   "See ball-buster." Chapman suggests under his second definition for bitch ("anything arduous or very disagreeable"). I
looked up "ball-buster":

> n. Someone who saps or destroys masculinity.
> ball-whacker
> bitch
> nut-cruncher.

Some*thing* has become some*one*. The ball-buster is not a   12
disagreeable thing but a disagreeable (disagreeing?) person.
A female person. "A woman one dislikes or disapproves of."
For someone so sensitive to the nuances of hostility and verbal putdown, Chapman certainly takes a circuitous route to
get to the underlying idea that no other dictionary even
touches: Bitch means ball-buster.

What one learns from the dictionaries: there is no classifi-   13
able thing as a bitch, only a label produced by the act of
name-calling. The person named is almost always a female.
The name-calling refers to alleged faults of ill-temper, selfishness, malice, cruelty, spite, all of them faults in the realm of
interpersonal relating—women's faults: it is hard to think of a
put-down word encompassing these faults in a man. "Bas-
tard" and even "son of a bitch" have bigger fish to fry. And an
asshole is an asshole in and of himself. A bitch is a woman
who makes the name-caller feel uncomfortable. Presumably
that name-caller is a man whose ideas about how a woman
should behave toward him are being violated.

"Women," wrote Virginia Woolf, "have served all these cen-   14
turies as looking-glasses possessing the magic and delicious
power of reflecting the figure of man at twice its natural size."
The woman who withholds that mirror is a bitch. Bitchiness
is the perversion of womanly sweetness, compliance, pleas-
antness, ego-building. (Male ego-building, of course, though
that is a virtual tautology; women have egos but who builds
them?) If a woman is not building ego she is busting balls.

Ball-buster? The word is a nice synecdoche (like asshole)   15
with great powers of revelation. A ball-buster, one gathers, is
a demanding bitch who insists on overexertion from a man to
satisfy her sexual or material voraciousness. "The bitch is
probably his wife. But balls also bust when a disagreeable
woman undermines a guy's ego and "saps or destroys masculinity." The bitch could be his wife, but also his boss, Gloria
Steinem, the woman at the post office, the woman who
spurns his advances. The familiar Freudian delineation of the
male-female nexus depicts male sexuality as requiring the
admiration, submission and subordination of the female. The
ultimate threat of (and to) the back-talking woman is male
impotence.

Bitch, the curse and concept, exists to insure male potency   16
and female submissiveness. Men have deployed it to defend
their power by attacking and neutralizing the upstart. "Bitch"
is admonitory, like "whore," like "dyke." Borrowing something

from both words, "bitch" is one of those verbal missiles with the power of shackling women's actions and impulses.

17   The metamorphosis of bitch from the context of sexuality (a carnal woman, a promiscuous woman) to temperament (an angry woman, a malicious woman) to power (a domineering woman, a competitive woman) is a touchstone to the changing position of women through this century. As women have become more liberated, individually and collectively, the word has taken on connotations of aggressive, hostile, selfish. In the old days a bitch was a harlot; nowadays she is likely to be a woman who won't put out. Female sensuality, even carnality, even infidelity, have been supplanted as what men primarily fear and despise in women. Judging by the contemporary colorations of the word bitch, what men primarily fear and despise in women is power.

18   Some anecdotes:
1) Barbara Bush's name-calling of Geraldine Ferraro during the 1984 presidential election: "I can't say it but it rhymes with 'rich.'"

19   How ladylike of the future First Lady to avoid uttering the unmentionable. The slur did its dirty work, particularly among those voters disturbed by the sudden elevation of a woman to such unprecedented political heights. In what possible sense did Barbara Bush mean that Geraldine Ferraro is a bitch? A loose woman? Hardly. A nasty woman? Not likely. A pushy woman? Almost certainly. The unspoken syllable was offered as a response to Ferraro's lofty ambitions, potential power, possibly her widespread support among feminists. Imagine a woman seeking to be vice-president instead of vice-husband.

20   The ascription of bitchery seems to have nothing to do with Ferraro's bearing and behavior. Certainly not the Ferraro who wrote about the event in her autobiography:

> Barbara Bush realized what a gaffe she had made...
>
> "I just want to apologize to you for what I said," she told me over the phone while I was in the middle of another debate rehearsal. "I certainly didn't mean anything by it."
>
> "Don't worry about it," I said to her. "We all say things at times we don't mean. It's all right."
>
> "Oh," she said breathlessly. "You're such a lady."

All I could think of when I hung up was: Thank God for my convent school training.

2) Lady Ashley at the end of *The Sun Also Rises:* "It makes 21 one feel rather good, deciding not to be a bitch." The context here is something like this: a bitch is a woman who ruins young heroic bullfighters. A woman who is propelled by her sexual drive, desires and vanity. The fascination of Brett Ashley is that she lives and loves like a man: her sexuality is unrepressed and she doesn't care much for monogamy. (Literary critics until the 1960s commonly called her a nymphomaniac.) She turns her male admirers into women—Mike becomes a self-destructive alcoholic, Robert a moony romantic, Pedro a sacrificial virgin, and Jake a frustrated eunuch. At her entrance in the novel she is surrounded by an entourage of twittering fairies. Lady Ashley is a bitch not because she is nasty, bossy or ill-tempered (she has lovely manners and a terrific personality). And perhaps not even because of her freewheeling, strident sexuality. She is a bitch because she overturns the male/female nexus. What could be a more threatening infraction in a Hemingway novel?

2a) Speaking of Hemingway: After his falling out with Gertrude Stein who had made unflattering comments about his 22 writing in *The Autobiography of Alice B. Toklas,* Hemingway dropped her off a copy of his newly published *Death in the Afternoon* with the handwritten inscription, "A bitch is a bitch is a bitch."
[Q.] Why was Gertrude Stein a bitch?
[A.] For no longer admiring Hemingway. A bitch is a woman who criticizes.

3) "Ladies and gentlemen. I don't believe Mrs. Helmsley is 23 charged in the indictment with being a tough bitch" is how her defense lawyer Gerald A. Feffer addressed the jury in Leona Helmsley's trial for tax fraud and extortion. He acknowledged that she was "sometimes rude and abrasive," and that she "may have overcompensated for being a woman in a hard-edged men's business world." Recognizing the difficulty of defending what the New York *Post* called "the woman that everyone loves to hate," his tactic was to preempt the prosecution by getting there first with "tough bitch." He lost.

24   4) *Esquire* awarded a Dubious Achievement of 1990 to Victor Kiam, owner of the New England Patriots football team,
for saying "he could never have called Boston *Herald*
reporter Lisa Olson 'a classic bitch' because he doesn't use
the word classic." Some background on what had been one
of that year's most discussed controversies: Olson aroused
the ire of the Patriots for showing up in their locker room
with the male reporters after a game. Members of the Patriots, as *Esquire* states, surrounded her, "thrusting their genitals in her face and daring her to touch them."

25   Why is Lisa Olson a bitch? For invading the male domain
of sports reportage and the male territory of the locker room?
For telling the world, instead of swallowing her degradation,
pain and anger? The club owner's use of "bitch" seems meant
to conjure up the lurking idea of castrating female. Seen in
that light the Patriots' act of "thrusting their genitals in her
face" transforms an act of loutishness into a position of innocent vulnerability.

26   5) Bumper sticker observed on back of pickup truck:

> Impeach Jane Fonda, American Traitor Bitch

The bumper sticker seemed relatively new and fresh. I
observed it a full two decades after Jane Fonda's journey to
North Vietnam which is the event that surely inspired this
call to impeachment (from what? aerobics class?). Bitch
here is an expletive. It originates in and sustains anger. Calling Jane Fonda a "traitor" sounds a bit dated in the 1990s,
but adding "bitch" gives the accusation timelessness and
does the job of rekindling old indignation.

27   6) Claude Brown's account in *Manchild in the Promised
Land* of how he learned about women from a street-smart
older friend:

> Johnny was always telling us about bitches. To Johnny, every
> chick was a bitch. Even mothers were bitches. Of course
> there were some nice bitches, but they were still bitches. And
> a man had to be a dog in order to handle a bitch.
>   Johnny said once, "If a bitch ever tells you she's only got a
> penny to buy the baby some milk, take it. You take it, 'cause
> she's gon git some more. Bitches can always git some
> money." He really knew about bitches. Cats would say, "I saw

your sister today, and she is a fine bitch." Nobody was offended by it. That's just the way things were. It was easy to see all women as bitches.

Bitch in black male street parlance seems closer to its orig- 28
inal meaning of a female breeder—not a nasty woman and not a powerful woman, but the biological bearer of litters. The word is likely to be used in courting as well as in anger by males seeking the sexual favor of a female, and a black female addressed as bitch by an admirer is expected to feel not insulted but honored by the attention. (Bitch signifies something different when black women use it competitively about other black women.) But even as an endearment, from male to female, there is no mistaking the lurking contempt.

A Dictionary of Afro-American Slang compiled by Clarence 29
Major (under the imprint of the leftist International Publishers) provides only that bitch in black parlance is "a mean, flaunting homosexual," entirely omitting any reference to its rampant use in black street language as the substitute word for woman. A puzzling omission. Perhaps the word is so taken for granted that its primary meaning is not even recognized as black vernacular.

Bitch, mama, motherfucker—how frequently motherhood 30
figures in street language. Mothers are the object of insults when playing the dozens. The ubiquitous motherfucker simultaneously strikes out at one's immediate foe as well as the sanctity of motherhood. Mama, which Clarence Major defines as—a pretty black girl," is an endearment that a man might address to a sexy contemporary. "Hey mama" is tinged with a certain sweetness. "Hey bitch" has more of an edge, more likely to be addressed to a woman the man no longer needs to sweet-talk. It is hard to think of white males coming on by evoking motherhood or of white women going for it. A white male addressing a woman as bitch is not likely to be expecting a sexual reward. She will be a bitch behind her back and after the relationship is over or didn't happen.

The widespread use of bitch by black men talking to black 31
women, its currency in courting, and its routine acceptance by women are suggestive of some powerful alienation in male-female relations and in black self-identity. Although there may be the possibility of ironic inversion, as in calling a loved one nigger, a black man calling a loved one bitch is expressing contempt for the object of his desire with the gratuitous fillip of associative contempt for the woman who gave him life. Bitch, like motherfucker, bespeaks something threatening to the

male sense of himself, a furious counter to emasculation in a world where, as the young Claude Brown figured out, mothers have all the power. It is not hard to see that the problem of black men is much more with white racism than it is with black women. Whatever the cause, however, the language sure doesn't benefit the women. Here is still one more saddening instance of the victim finding someone even more hapless to take things out on. (Does this process explain why Clarence Major's only reference for bitch is to the "mean, flaunting homosexual"?)

32   7) "Do you enjoy playing that role of castrating bitch" is a question put to Madonna by an interviewer for *The Advocate*. Madonna's answer: "I enjoy expressing myself. . . ."

33   A response to another question about the public's reaction to her movie *Truth or Dare:* "They already think I'm a cunt bitch, they already think I'm Attila the Hun. They already compare me to Adolf Hitler and Saddam Hussein."

34   Bitch has lost its power to muzzle Madonna. Unlike other female celebrities who have cringed from accusations of bitchiness (Joan Rivers, Imelda Marcos, Margaret Thatcher, Nancy Reagan), Madonna has made her fortune by exploiting criticism. Her career has skyrocketed with the media's charges of obscenity and sacrilege; she seems to embrace the bitch label with the same eager opportunism.

35   "I enjoy expressing myself" is not merely the explanation for why Madonna gets called bitch; "I enjoy expressing myself" is the key to defusing the power of bitch to fetter and subdue. Madonna has appropriated the word and turned the intended insult to her advantage. This act of appropriation, I predict, will embolden others with what consequences and effects it is impossible to foresee.

Lewis Grizzard

Women Will Be Womyn

Lewis Grizzard (pronounced Griz-ZARD) was a columnist for the Atlanta Constitution, *where, until his death from heart disease in 1994 at the age of forty-seven, he regularly published a widely syndicated column that sometimes delighted and sometimes enraged his readers. A humorist and fiercely proud Southerner whose columns often mimicked redneck values, Grizzard took special pleasure in satirizing Northerners, feminists, and liberals. The following column appeared in 1991.*

The new-for-the-90s Webster's Collegiate Dictionary is out   1
and wouldn't you know it. There are now different ways to
spell certain words so as to accommodate the feminists.

There's even a new way to spell woman, according to the   2
new dictionary. It may now be spelled "womyn," so there's
no longer any need to use those awful three letters that spell
m-a-n.

There's more. HIStory. That's for guys. The new word is   3
HER-story, as in, "Joan Rivers was the worst morning television show hostess in all of *herstory.*"

The report I read concerning the new dictionary did not,   4
however, tell of how certain other words, akin to the ones
above, can be altered in order to rid them of any sexist connotations.

I did some guessing, though. Here's some examples of   5
other changes:

- HERSTERECTOMY: Whoever heard of a man going
  through that type of operation?
- HERMALAYAS: Womyn should have a mountain
  range of their very own.
- HERSTERICAL: "Wanda was *hersterical* when she
  found out Bob had taken Bernice on a trip to the Hermalayas."
- HERMNS: Womyn sing in church, too.
- HERSY: "Bernice threw a *hersy* when she found out
  Wanda had found out about her trip to the Hermalayas with Bob."

You get my drift.   6

7   But let us take this a step further. Even if you spell woman "womyn," it still sounds the same. What womyn need in order to throw off the yoke of sexism when it comes to calling themselves something is an entirely new word.

8   Female doesn't work for obvious reasons. Changing that to fe-MULE would only encourage too many sexists to make remarks about the stereotypical tendency of a womyn to be stubborn.

9   I even thought it might work to turn women around backward. They would become "nemows," as in, "Boy, you should have seen the *nemows* in Ralph's last night."

10   But nemows still includes n-e-m, men spelled backward, a reminder of just how backward many of them still are despite all the efforts to teach them not to say, "You should have seen the chicks in Ralph's last night."

11   I did some thinking on this matter as well and came upon a few ideas of something new to call womyn.

- GIRL PERSONS: Too juvenile? You're right.
- LADIES: Some men name their dogs Lady, and there's that awful sexist joke that goes: "Who was that lady I saw you with last night?"
  "That was no lady. That was my wife."

12   Forget ladies.

- ADNOFENAJS: (Pronounced ad-NOFEN-ajuhs). That's Jane Fonda spelled backward, but it's a little cumbersome to say, "That adnofenaj should have been hanged for treason."
- EELADNERBS: (Pronounced eel-LADNER-buh). That's Brenda Lee spelled backward. I like Brenda Lee a lot more than Jane Fonda, but I guess most '90s womyn wouldn't.
- CHICKS: Just kidding.
- RALPHETTES: As in, "You shoulda seen the two Ralphettes we met last night at Ralph's."

13   Sorry, I just can't seem to get untracked here.

- PLAINTIFFS: That's got some possibilities. Like the guy said, "I've been divorced so many times, I just refer to all my ex-wives as Plaintiff."

I think that is probably as far as I should go here. The feminist hate mail will pour in for weeks as it is.   14

Oops! did I say "mail"?   15

This cartoon appeared in The New Yorker, *famous for its very funny and rather sophisticated cartoons. Is the cartoon just for fun, or does it make a serious point?*

"You'll just love the way he handles."

Drawing by Bernard Schoenbaum; © 1991 The New Yorker Magazine, Inc.

Deborah Tannen
CrossTalk

Deborah Tannen, a professor of linguistics at Georgetown University in Washington, DC, published You Just Don't Understand: Women and Men in Conversation *in 1990. An exploration of the complexities of communication between men and women, it became a national best-seller. The following selection from that book has been printed elsewhere as a self-contained piece.*

1   A woman who owns a bookstore needed to have a talk with the store manager. She had told him to help the bookkeeper with billing, he had agreed, and now, days later, he still hadn't done it. Thinking how much she disliked this part of her work, she sat down with the manager to clear things up. They traced the problem to a breakdown in communication.

2   She had said, "Sarah needs help with the bills. What do you think about helping her out?" He had responded, "OK," by which he meant, "OK, I'll think about whether or not I want to help her." During the next day, he thought about it and concluded that he'd rather not.

3   This wasn't just an ordinary communication breakdown that could happen between any two people. It was a particular sort of breakdown that tends to occur between women and men.

4   Most women avoid giving orders. More comfortable with decision-making by consensus, they tend to phrase requests as questions, to give others the feeling they have some say in the matter and are not being bossed around. But this doesn't mean they aren't making their wishes clear. Most women would have understood the bookstore owner's question, "What do you think about helping her out?" as assigning a task in a considerate way.

5   The manager, however, took the owner's words literally. She had asked him what he thought; she hadn't told him to *do* anything. So he felt within his rights when he took her at her word, thought about it and decided not to help Sarah.

6   Women in positions of authority are likely to regard such responses as insubordination: "He knows I am in charge, and he knows what I want; if he doesn't do it, he is resisting my authority."

There may be a kernel of truth in this view—most men are   7
inclined to resist authority if they can because being in a subordinate position makes them intensely uncomfortable. But
indirect requests that are transparent to women may be genuinely opaque to men. They assume that people in authority
will give orders if they really want something done.

These differences in management styles are one of many   8
manifestations of gender differences in how we talk to one
another. Women use language to create connection and rapport; men use it to negotiate their status in a hierarchical
order. It isn't that women are unaware of status or that men
don't build rapport, but that *the genders tend to focus on different goals.*

The Source of Gender Differences

These differences stem from the way boys and girls learn   9
to use language while growing up. Girls tend to play indoors,
either in small groups or with one other girl. The center of a
girl's social life is her best friend, with whom she spends a
great deal of time sitting, talking and exchanging secrets. It is
the telling of secrets that makes them best friends. Boys tend
to play outdoors, in larger groups, usually in competitive
games. It's doing things together that makes them friends.

Anthropologist Marjorie Harness Goodwin compared boys   10
and girls at play in a black innercity neighborhood in Philadelphia. Her findings, which have been supported by
researchers in other settings, show that the boys' groups are
hierarchical: high-status boys give orders, and low-status
boys have to follow them, so they end up being told what to
do. Girls' groups tend to be egalitarian: girls who appeared
"better" than others or gave orders were not countenanced
and in some cases were ostracized.

So while boys are learning to fear being "put down" and   11
pushed around, girls are learning to fear being "locked out."
Whereas high-status boys establish and reinforce their
authority by giving orders and resisting doing what others
want, girls tend to make suggestions, which are likely to be
taken up by the group.

Cross-Gender Communication in the Workplace

The implications of these different conversational habits   12
and concerns in terms of office interactions are staggering.

Men are inclined to continue to jockey for position, trying to resist following orders as much as possible within the constraints of their jobs.

13   Women, on the other hand, are inclined to do what they sense their bosses want, whether or not they are ordered to. By the same token, women in positions of authority are inclined to phrase their requests as suggestions and to assume they will be respected because of their authority. These assumptions are likely to hold up as long as both parties are women, but they may well break down in cross-gender communication.

14   When a woman is in the position of authority, such as the bookstore owner, she may find her requests are systematically misunderstood by men. And when a woman is working for a male boss, she may find that her boss gives bald commands that seem unnecessarily imperious because most women would prefer to be asked rather than ordered. One woman who worked at an all-male radio station commented that the way the men she worked for told her what to do made her feel as if she should salute and say, "Yes, boss."

15   Many men complain that a woman who is indirect in making requests is manipulative: she's trying to get them to do what she wants without telling them to do it. Another common accusation is that she is insecure: she doesn't know what she wants. But if a woman gives direct orders, the same men might complain that she is aggressive, unfeminine or worse.

16   Women are in a double bind: *If we talk like women, we are not respected. If we talk like men, we are not liked.*

17   We have to walk a fine line, finding ways to be more direct without appearing bossy. The bookstore owner may never be comfortable by directly saying, "Help Sarah with the billing today," but she might find some compromise such as, "Sarah needs help with the billing. I'd appreciate it if you would make some time to help her out in the next day or two." This request is clear, while still reflecting women's preferences for giving reasons and options.

18   What if you're the subordinate and your boss is a man who's offending you daily by giving you orders? If you know him well enough, one potential solution is "metacommunication"—that is, talk about communication. Point out the differences between women and men, and discuss how you could accommodate to each other's styles. (You may want to give him a copy of this article or my book.)

19   But if you don't have the kind of relationship that makes metacommunication possible, you could casually, even jok-

ingly, suggest he give orders another way. Or just try to remind yourself it's a cross-cultural difference and try not to take his curtness personally.

How to Handle a Meeting

There are other aspects of women's styles that can work against us in a work setting. Because women are most comfortable using language to create rapport with someone they feel close to, and men are used to talking in a group where they have to prove themselves and display what they know, a formal meeting can be a natural for men and a hard nut to crack for women. Many women find it difficult to speak up at meetings; if they do, they may find their comments ignored, perhaps later to be resuscitated by a man who gets credit for the idea. Part of this is simply due to the expectation that men will have more important things to contribute.   20

But the way women and men tend to present themselves can aggravate this inequity. At meetings, men are more likely to speak often, at length and in a declamatory manner. They may state their opinions as fact and leave it to others to challenge them.   21

Women, on the other hand, are often worried about appearing to talk too much—a fear that is justified by research showing that when they talk equally, women are perceived as talking more than men. As a result, many women are hesitant to speak at a meeting and inclined to be succinct and tentative when they do.   22

Developing Options

Working on changing your presentational style is one option; another is to make your opinions known in private conversation with the key people before a meeting. And if you are the key person, it would be wise to talk personally to the women on your staff rather than assuming all participants have had a chance to express themselves at the meeting.   23

Many women's reticence about displaying their knowledge at a meeting is related to their reluctance to boast. They find it more humble to keep quiet about their accomplishments and wait for someone else to notice them. But most men learn early on to display their accomplishments and skills. And women often find that no one bothers to ferret out their   24

25 achievements if they don't put them on display. Again, a woman risks criticism if she talks about her achievements, but this may be a risk she needs to take, to make sure she gets credit for her work.

26 I would never want to be heard as telling women to adopt men's styles across the board. For one thing, there are many situations in which women's styles are more successful. For example, the inclination to make decisions by consensus can be a boon to a woman in a managerial position. Many people, men as well as women, would rather feel they have influence in decision-making than be given orders.

27 Moreover, recommending that women adopt men's styles would be offensive, as well as impractical, because women are judged by the norms for women's behavior, and doing the same thing as men has a very different, often negative, effect.

A Starting Point

28 Simply knowing about gender differences in conversational style provides a starting point for improving relations with the women and men who are above and below you in a hierarchy.

29 The key is *flexibility;* a way of talking that works beautifully with one person may be a disaster with another. If one way of talking isn't working, try another, rather than trying harder to do more of the same.

30 Once you know what the parameters are, you can become an observer of your own interactions, and a style-switcher when you choose.

III.

RACE AND GENDER

Introduction

One of the stunning social developments of the twentieth century has been the economic and political and cultural emergence of women and people of color. Beginning with the success of the women's suffrage movement early in the century and continuing through the civil rights movement and a series of legal and legislative victories in the past quarter of a century, the women's movement and the movement for civil rights for nonwhite Americans have largely achieved the goal of political equality in the United States—at least on paper. But that has not closed discussion of women's concerns and of the means of combating racism, of course, because social, economic, and political parity between women and men and between African Americans and Anglo Americans remains incomplete and because the specific terms of social and economic liberation have not yet been agreed on. In fact, discussion of racial issues and gender issues has intensified in the past decade as race and gender concerns continue to be negotiated through public discourse. This part of *Conversations* barely begins to capture the range of issues currently under debate, but it does present discussions of six general issues: How do you define race? How do you define gender? Should affirmative action policies continue? What do you make of the men's movement? Are women's brains, are the ways women reason, different somehow from men's? And how should we as a society address sexual harassment? (In addition, issues of race and gender are taken up elsewhere in this book, most notably—but not only—in Part II, "Language," in Part IV, "Family Matters," and the sections in Part V on pornography, civil disobedience, and abortion.)

In the midst of all the discussions related to race in the United States, it is inevitable that the question of the nature of race itself would be raised as an issue. Is race something that is biologically determined? If so, what features distinguish one race from another—skin color? The shape of one's eyes or nose? Or what? What happens to the concept of race when people of different "races" intermarry and have children? Is it reasonable to consider someone "black" if only one of that person's grandparents was African American, or does that merely perpetuate the outdated thinking of antimiscegenation laws? How and why do people think of themselves in one or another racial or ethnic category? Although people in the past assumed that racial designations corresponded to particular physical traits, now many argue that racial identities derive from social and historical forces, that those designations can vary over time—and that such designations are now being reconsidered in the United States. In this decade, since multicultural and multiethnic considerations have been pressed, since immigration from Latin America and Asia have created new citizens less easily categorized than in the past, since interracial marriage has become more common, and since some vestiges of segregation have become less virulent, it seems that racial categories are particularly being reconsidered. To many people, Americans have taken a too "binary" approach to race; while other nations (rightly or wrongly) often recognize gradations of color in their citizens, Americans often persist in thinking of race as an either-or proposition. While in one sense, Black-White antagonisms have persisted in the face of challenges to affirmative action and the continuation of social inequities in our society, in another sense those antagonisms seem somehow anachronistic as Americans shift their views of race in the face of a social interrogation of the concept of race itself. Consequently, the first section of this part considers definitions of race—especially the question of whether or not inherited notions of race profit our national community.

The concept of race is not the only thing that is being redefined right now. Until very recently it was men who defined women, mostly in a misogynist (women-hating) tradition that is deeply seated in Western cultures. But the fact that women are now involved in defining gender roles has not effaced that tradition of misogyny, nor has it ended discussion of the nature of those roles. Just what form will the feminist revolution take? Just what is it that defines the essential natures of women and men? Beyond reproductive differences, are there inevitable distinctions between the sexes in terms of emotions, sexuality, physiology, morals, values, and so forth? Or are all such distinctions the result of social conditioning— social conditioning that might be altered? That is the basic issue under discussion in the second section of this part. A half dozen or so selections of various kinds describe, explain, dramatize, or argue for various positions on the question of the "essential natures" of women and men and the extent to which history and culture and environment determine those natures. The selections also illustrate the range of voices that can be summoned in support of a discussion of gender roles. While most of the selections address women's concerns directly, each one has direct and indirect implications for men as well. And in the final years of this century those implications must be faced each day.

Gender issues and race issues have been emphasized in a central document of the civil rights movement, the Civil Rights Act of 1964. which attempted to eradicate discrimination from a range of public institutions in America. Part of Title VII of that act prohibited discrimination on the job because of race, color, religion, sex, or national origin:

> It shall be an unlawful employment practice for an employer...to fail or refuse to hire or to discharge any individual, or otherwise to discriminate against any individual with respect to his compensation, terms, conditions, or privileges of employment, because of such individual's race, color, religion, sex, or national origin.... It shall be an unlawful employment practice for any employer, labor organization, or joint labor-management committee controlling apprenticeship or other training or retraining, including on-the-job training programs, to discriminate against any individual because of his race, color, religion, sex, or national origin in admission to, or employment in, any program established to provide apprenticeship or other training.... If the court finds that the respondent has intentionally engaged in an unlawful employment practice...the court may enjoin the respondent from engaging in such unlawful employment practice, and order such affirmative action as may be appropriate.

Title VII thus initiated a period of "affirmative action" to redress past injustices and to establish for everyone the possibility of equal opportunity.

But just what should affirmative action mean? Should it be a means of ensuring that everyone has a chance to compete on equal terms for jobs and education? Or should it denote a more active process of ensuring equal results, especially for people who arrive at jobs and schools with disadvantages that arise from past inequality? For some people, affirmative action means the former; in the words of the late Hubert Humphrey, nothing in Title VII should "give any power to the [Civil Rights] Commission or any court to require hiring, firing, or promotion of employees in order to meet a racial quota." For others, however, affirmative action means action: active measures (at least in the short run) such as goals, timetables, guidelines, and quotas designed to promote balanced results.

Are such actions fair? Is affirmative action a legitimate, short-term measure for breaking up a rigid caste system and for ameliorating the long-term effects of Jim Crow laws, sexist traditions, and inequitable education policies? Or is it inherently unfair? Has the "short-term" expired by now? Can we now justify passing over someone or favoring someone else because of the group that person is born into? Is the goal of affirmative action the reduction of social injustice or proportional representation of all races and both sexes? Is affirmative action inefficient, in that it favors racial and gender factors over job performance? Or is it more efficient, in that it speeds the progress of women and minorities and therefore allows those people a chance, at last, to show their right stuff? Does affirmative action damage self-esteem or promote it? Should colleges and universities eliminate racial and gender preferences in admissions decisions? Finally, would affirmative action make better sense if it were administered on a class-wide basis instead of on the basis of race or gender? Those sensitive questions are discussed in the selections reprinted here on affirmative action.

Speaking of people excluded from certain occupations: It is not hard to notice that, historically, women have rarely distinguished themselves in fields related to science and mathematics. But why? That question is the topic in the fifth section. Are there somehow sex differences in mathematical reasoning ability? Do women actually *think* any differently than men do? Are women disadvantaged by their sex from excelling at math and science? Or, are any such apparent differences the result of social conditioning? How can more women be encouraged to enter scientific and technical fields? What barriers discourage women from careers in science and engineering? Perhaps those questions have concrete implications on your campus or in your own life.

This part of *Conversations* concludes with a set of readings that deals with the conditions women face at work. What happens—on the job and at home—when women enter professions and institutions traditionally dominated by men? How can women cope with unfriendly circumstances? Is it possible to keep unequal power relations at work from affecting personal relationships? In short: What about the question of sexual harassment at work—what is it, and what can be done about it? Should sexual harassment be defined broadly or very specifically? Are men as frequently as women the victims of harassment? Even before Anita Hill accused Supreme Court Justice Clarence Thomas of sexual harassment during Thomas's confirmation hearings in 1991, these questions were being discussed in our country; the three readings in this section offer a range of answers, a range that will likely force you to rethink your own positions.

So where do you stand on these questions of race and gender? The selections in this part are designed to provoke further discussion, not to close it off. In fact, a premise of this part on race and gender is that by engaging in open, public discourse on these complex questions, writers can hasten the day when the effects of racial and sexual polarization—perhaps racial and sexual polarization itself—might be minimized and when codes of personal behavior might be more freely chosen, to the benefit of everyone.

DEFINING RACE

Sharon Begley
Three Is Not Enough

The following essay was published as a Newsweek *magazine story on February 13, 1995. Since the cover of* Newsweek *that day posed the question, "What Color Is Black?," this was one of several essays in the magazine that discussed one or another aspect of the issue of defining race: one considered biracial children and interracial marriage; another looked at affirmative action; still another was a historical analysis of definitions of race in America. Sharon Begley is a senior writer for* Newsweek, *where her work often appears.*

To most Americans race is as plain as the color of the nose   1
on your face. Sure, some light-skinned blacks, in some neighborhoods, are taken for Italians, and some Turks are confused with Argentines. But even in the children of biracial couples, racial ancestry is writ large—in the hue of the skin and the shape of the lips, the size of the brow and the bridge of the nose. It is no harder to trace than it is to judge which basic colors in a box of Crayolas were combined to make tangerine or burnt umber. Even with racial mixing, the existence of primary races is as obvious as the existence of primary colors.

Or is it? C. Loring Brace has his own ideas about where   2
race resides, and it isn't in skin color. If our eyes could perceive more than the superficial, we might find race in chromosome 11: there lies the gene for hemoglobin. If you divide humankind by which of two forms of the gene each person has, then equatorial Africans, Italians and Greeks fall into the "sickle-cell race"; Swedes and South Africa's Xhosas (Nelson Mandela's ethnic group) are in the healthy-hemoglobin race. Or do you prefer to group people by whether they have epicanthic eye folds, which produce the "Asian" eye? Then the !Kung San (Bushmen) belong with the Japanese and Chinese. Depending on which trait you choose to demarcate races, "you won't get anything that remotely tracks conventional

[race] categories," says anthropologist Alan Goodman, dean
of natural science at Hampshire College.

3   The notion of race is under withering attack for political
and cultural reasons—not to mention practical ones like what
to label the child of a Ghanaian and a Norwegian. But scientists got there first. Their doubts about the conventional
racial categories—black, white, Asian—have nothing to do
with a sappy "we are all the same" ideology. Just the reverse.
"Human variation is very, very real," says Goodman. "But
race, as a way of organizing [what we know about that varia-
tion], is incredibly simplified and bastardized." Worse, it does
not come close to explaining the astounding diversity of
humankind—not its origins, not its extent, not its meaning.
"There is no organizing principle by which you could put 5
billion people into so few categories in a way that would tell
you anything important about humankind's diversity," says
Michigan's Brace, who will lay out the case against race at the
annual meeting of the American Association for the Advancement of Science.

4   About 70 percent of cultural anthropologists, and half of
physical anthropologists, reject race as a biological category,
according to a 1989 survey by Central Michigan University
anthropologist Leonard Liebermnan and colleagues. The
truths of science are not decided by majority vote, of course.
Empirical evidence, woven into a theoretical whole, is what
matters. The threads of the argument against the standard
racial categories:

5   • **Genes:** In 1972, population biologist Richard Lewontin
of Harvard University laid out the genetic case against race.
Analyzing 17 genetic markers in 168 populations such as Aus-
trians, Thais and Apaches, he found that there is more genetic
difference within one race than there is between that race and
another. Only 6.3 percent of the genetic differences could be
explained by the individuals' belonging to different races. That
is, if you pick at random any two "blacks" walking along the
street, and analyze their 23 pairs of chromosomes, you will
probably find that their genes have less in common than do
the genes of one of them with that of a random "white" person.
Last year the Human Genome Diversity Project used 1990s
genetics to extend Lewontin's analysis. Its conclusion: genetic
variation from one individual to another of the same "race"
swamps the average differences between racial groupings. The
more we learn about humankind's genetic differences, says
geneticist Luca Cavalli-Sforza of Stanford University, who

chairs the committee that directs the biodiversity project, the more we see that they have almost nothing to do with what we call race.

• **Traits:** As sickle-cell "races" and epicanthic-fold "races"   6 show, there are as many ways to group people as there are traits. That is because "racial" traits are what statisticians call non-concordant. Lack of concordance means that sorting people according to *these* traits produces different groupings than you get in sorting them by *those* (equally valid) traits. When biologist Jared Diamond of UCLA surveyed half a dozen traits for a recent issue of *Discover* magazine, he found that, depending on which traits you pick, you can form very surprising "races." Take the scooped-out shape of the back of the front teeth, a standard "Asian" trait. Native Americans and Swedes have these shovel-shaped incisors, too, and so would fall in the same race. Is biochemistry better? Norwegians, Arabians, north Indians and the Fulani of northern Nigeria, notes Diamond, fall into the "lactase race" (the lactase enzyme digests milk sugar). Everyone else—other Africans, Japanese, Native Americans—forms the "lactase-deprived race" (their ancestors did not drink milk from cows or goats and hence never evolved the lactase gene). How about blood types, the familiar A, B and O groups? Then Germans and New Guineans, populations that have the same percentages of each type, are in one race; Estonians and Japanese comprise a separate one for the same reason, notes anthropologist Jonathan Marks of Yale University. Depending on which traits are chosen, "we could place Swedes in the same race as either Xhosas, Fulani, the Ainu of Japan or Italians," writes Diamond.

• **Subjectivity:** If race is a valid biological concept, any-   7 one in any culture should be able to look at any individual and say, Aha, you are a . . . It should not be the case, as French tennis star Yannick Noah said a few years ago, that "in Africa I am white, and in France I am black" (his mother is French and his father is from Cameroon). "While biological traits give the impression that race is a biological unit of nature," says anthropologist George Armelagos of Emory University, "it remains a cultural construct. The boundaries between races depends on the classifier's own cultural norms."

• **Evolution:** Scholars who believe in the biological valid-   8 ity of race argue that the groupings reflect human pre-history. That is, populations that evolved together, and separately from others, constitute a race. This school of thought holds that blacks should all be in one race because they are descended from people who stayed on the continent where humanity began. Asians, epitomized by the Chinese, should be another race because they are the children of groups who walked north and east until they reached the Pacific. Whites of the pale, blond variety should be another because their ancestors filled Europe. Because of their appearance, these populations represent the extremes, the archetypes, of human diversity—the reds, blues and yellows from which you can make every other hue. "But if you use these archetypes as your groups you have classified only a very tiny proportion of the world's people, which is not very useful," says Marks, whose incisive new book "Human Biodiversity" deconstructs race. "Also, as people walked out of Africa, they were differentiating along the way. Equating 'extreme' with 'primordial' is not supported by history."

9   Often, shared traits are a sign of shared heritage—racial heritage. "Shared traits are not random," says Alice Brues, an anthropologist at the University of Colorado. "Within a continent, you of course have a number of variants [on basic traits], but some are characteristic of the larger area, too. So it's natural to look for these major divisions. It simplifies your thinking." A wide distribution of traits, however, makes them suspect as evidence of a shared heritage. The dark skin of Somalis and Ghanaians, for instance, indicates that they evolved under the same selective force (a sunny climate). But that's all it shows. It does *not* show that they are any more closely related, in the sense of sharing more genes, than either is to Greeks. Calling Somalis and Ghanaians "black" therefore sheds no further light on their evolutionary history and implies—wrongly—that they are more closely related to each other than either is to someone of a different "race." Similarly, the long noses of North Africans and northern Europeans reveal that they evolved in dry or cold climates (the nose moistens air before the air reaches the lungs, and longer noses moisten more air). The tall, thin bodies of Kenya's Masai evolved to dissipate heat; Eskimos evolved short, squat bodies to retain it. Calling these peoples "different races" adds nothing to that understanding.

10   Where did the three standard racial divisions come from? They entered the social, and scientific, consciousness during the Age of Exploration. Loring Brace doesn't think it's a coincidence that the standard races represent peoples who, as he puts it, "lived at the end of the Europeans' trade routes"—in Africa and China—in the days after Prince Henry the Navigator set sail. Before Europeans took to the seas, there was little

perception of races. If villagers began to look different to an Englishman riding a horse from France to Italy and on to Greece, the change was too subtle to inspire notions of races. But if the English sailor left Lisbon Harbor and dropped anchor off the Kingdom of Niger, people looked so different he felt compelled to invent a scheme to explain the world—and, perhaps, distance himself from the Africans.

This habit of sorting the world's peoples into a small num- 11
ber of groups got its first scientific gloss from Swedish taxon-
omist Carolus Linnaeus. (Linnaeus is best known for his system of classifying living things by genus and species—*Escherichia coli, Homo sapiens* and the rest.) In 1758 he declared that humanity falls into four races: white (Europe-ans), red (Native Americans), dark (Asians) and black (Afri-cans). Linnaeus said that Native Americans (who in the 1940s got grouped with Asians) were ruled by custom. Africans were indolent and negligent, and Europeans were inventive and gentle, said Linnaeus. Leave aside the racist undertones (not to mention the oddity of ascribing gentleness to the group that perpetrated the Crusades and Inquisition): that alone should not undermine its validity. More worrisome is that the notion and the specifics of race predate genetics, evolutionary biol-ogy and the science of human origins. With the revolutions in those fields, how is it that the 18th-century scheme of race retains its powerful hold? Consider these arguments:

• **If I parachute into Nairobi, I know I'm not in Oslo:** 12
Colorado's Alice Brues uses this image to argue that denying the reality of race flies in the face of common sense. But the parachutists, if they were familiar with the great range of human diversity, could also tell that they were in Nairobi rather than Abidjan—east Africans don't look much like west Africans. They could also tell they were in Istanbul rather than Oslo, even though Turks and Norwegians are both called Caucasian.

• **DOA, male, 5'11"...black:** When U.S. police call in a 13
forensic anthropologist to identify the race of a skeleton, the scientist comes through 80 to 85 percent of the time. If race has no biological validity, how can the sleuths get it right so often? The forensic anthropologist could, with enough infor-mation about bone structure and genetic markers, identify the region from which the corpse came—south and west Africa, Southeast Asia and China, Northern and Western Europe. It just so happens that the police would call corpses from the first two countries black, from the middle two Asian, and the last pair white. But lumping these six distinct populations into

three groups of two serves no biological purpose, only a social convention. The larger grouping may reflect how society views humankind's diversity, but does not explain it.

14   • **African-Americans have more hypertension:** If race is not real, how can researchers say that blacks have higher rates of infant mortality, lower rates of osteoporosis and a higher incidence of hypertension? Because a social construct can have biological effects, says epidemiologist Robert Hahn of the U.S. Centers for Disease Control and Prevention. Consider hypertension among African-Americans. Roughly 34 percent have high blood pressure, compared with about 16 percent of whites. But William Dressler finds the greatest incidence of hypertension among blacks who are upwardly mobile achievers. "That's probably because in mundane interactions, from the bank to the grocery store, they are treated in ways that do not coincide with their self-image as respectable achievers," says Dressler, an anthropologist at the University of Alabama. "And the upwardly mobile are more likely to encounter discriminatory white culture." Lab studies show that stressful situations—like being followed in grocery stores as if you were a shoplifter—elevate blood pressure and lead to vascular changes that cause hypertension. "In this case, race captures social factors such as the experience of discrimination," says sociologist David Williams of the University of Michigan. Further evidence that hypertension has more to do with society than with biology: black Africans have among the lowest rates of hypertension in the world.

15   If race is not a biological explanation of hypertension, can it offer a biological explanation of something as complex as intelligence? Psychologists are among the strongest proponents of retaining the three conventional racial categories. It organizes and explains their data in the most parsimonious way, as Charles Murray and Richard Herrnstein argue in "The Bell Curve." But anthropologists say that such conclusions are built on a foundation of sand. If nothing else, argues Brace, every ethnic group evolved under conditions where intelligence was a requirement for survival. If there are intelligence "genes," they must be in all ethnic groups equally: differences in intelligence must be a cultural and social artifact.

16   Scientists who doubt the biological meaningfulness of race are not nihilists. They just prefer another way of capturing, and explaining, the great diversity of humankind. Even today most of the world's peoples marry within their own group. Intramarriage preserves features—fleshy lips, small ears,

wide-set eyes—that arose by a chance genetic mutation long ago. Grouping people by geographic origins—better known as ethnicity—"is more correct both in a statistical sense and in understanding the history of human variation," says Hampshire's Goodman. Ethnicity also serves as a proxy for differences—from diet to a history of discrimination—that can have real biological and behavioral effects.

In a 1942 book, anthropologist Ashley Montagu called race "Man's Most Dangerous Myth." If it is, then our most ingenuous myth must be that we sort humankind into groups in order to understand the meaning and origin of humankind's diversity. That isn't the reason at all; a greater number of smaller groupings, like ethnicities, does a better job. The obsession with broad categories is so powerful as to seem a neurological imperative. Changing our thinking about race will require a revolution in thought as profound, and profoundly unsettling, as anything science has ever demanded. What these researchers are talking about is changing the way in which we see the world—and each other. But before that can happen, we must do more than understand the biologist's suspicions about race. We must ask science, also, why it is that we are so intent on sorting humanity into so few groups—us and Other—in the first place.

Jon Michael Spencer

Trends of Opposition to Multiculturalism

In the winter/spring 1993 issue of Black Scholar *(a magazine that bills itself as "the journal of the black experience . . . for college intellectuals, street academicians, and movement leaders," particularly from the Left), Jon Michael Spencer contributed the following meditation on race and multiculturalism and their relation to the possibility of cultural equality in the United States. The essay raises the possibility that certain Black theorists and advocates of multiculturalism in their quest for a "raceless democracy," are losing along the way a sense of a distinctively Black identity and consciousness.*

(Spencer, the author of a number of books, is editor of Black Sacred Music: A Journal of Theomusicology *and associate professor of African and Afro-American Studies at the University of North Carolina, Chapel Hill.)*

The essay obviously touched a nerve because the next issue of Black Scholar *included a special Reader's Forum section with ten elaborate and thoughtful responses to Spencer written by prominent academicians. Here in* Conversations, *we offer three of those responses, by Molefi Asante, Patricia Hill Collins, and David Lionel Smith. Asante is the controversial chair of Temple University's department of African American Studies; in part as a result of his publication in 1987 of* The Afrocentric Idea, *he is often considered the leader of the Afrocentric Movement, which emphasizes specifically Black consciousness, cultural and philosophical affinities with Africa, and the sense that imitation of whites can only be disastrous to African Americans. Hill Collins, who teaches sociology and African American Studies at the University of Cincinnati, is a feminist scholar who has argued that the belief in an essential Black identity has compromised the possibilities of African American women. Her most recent book is* Fighting Words: Black Feminist Thought and the Search for Meaningful Social Theory. *Smith, an essayist and poet, is a professor of English at Williams College in Massachusetts.*

1   The March 29,1993 issue of *Newsweek* magazine has the feature title "White Male Paranoia: Are They the Newest Victims—or Just Bad Sports?" In the feature article, the essayist David Gates says: "Suddenly white American males are surrounded by feminists, multiculturalists, P.C. policepersons, affirmative-action employers, rap artists, Native Americans, Japanese tycoons, Islamic fundamentalists and Third World dictators, all of them saying the same thing: You've been a bad boy."[1] Although the article conveys the message that white males are still very much in control of this country— economically, politically, and, of course, educationally—it also makes room for white males to feel that their alleged victimization warrants their being granted the moral clout that underdog status carries. What this moral clout entails is white males being better able to oppose myriad efforts aimed at challenging their traditional status as the lords of western civilization.

2   This situation may be one trend in the search for strategies to oppose multiculturalism. But there is another trend, perhaps more menacing, about which we should be cognizant.

There is today a pattern in our public discourse that is aimed in part at reversing the impetus to implement multicultural education. Much of this kind of discourse is coming from intellectuals involved in what I call *the postmodern conspiracy to explode racial identity.* This conspiracy is the postmodern equivalent to the earlier "melting pot" theory, which postulated that all Americans should melt into a single cultural identity. What makes the postmodern version just as disturbing as its "melting pot" precursor is that it too seeks to leave black people and other peoples of colors with no alternative but to fulfill Frantz Fanon's prophecy in *Black Skin, White Masks.* "However painful it may be for me to accept this conclusion," prophesies Fanon, "I am obliged to state it. For the black man there is only one destiny. And it is white."[2]

Religion professor Alton Pollard concurs with my assessment that the postmodernists seem eager to rush us toward this singular destiny. In his essay titled "The Last Great Battle of the West: W. E. B. Du Bois and the Struggle for African America's Soul," Pollard says: 3

> The belief in "color-blindness" is largely a post-Du Bois condition among African Americans, a quality or approach to establishing a sense of self or identity that implies certain rites (and rights) of social entry without regard to race. For many if not all adherents to this position, rainbow declarations of a "color-full" society (the postmodern recognition of otherness, social heterogeneity, cultural difference, distinctive gender views and so on) are highly suspect, an odious and irrational deception.... The new breed of "color-blind" African American sings a refrain that is distressingly as simple as it is symptomatic: "Rather than cast our lot with the race, we race to leave the caste."[3]

I have in mind, as I think Pollard does, such adherents to   4
this position as Shelby Steele, Stephen Carter, Glenn Loury, and Stanley Crouch. What makes these blacks deserving of careful critique is that they have been touted as "authorities" on black concerns by whites who then refer to their writings to support arguments against multiculturalism.

In addition to the above four writers, we especially must   5
beware of the arguments made by the Ghanaian philosopher at Harvard University, Kwame Anthony Appiah. In his book *In My Father's House: Africa in the Philosophy of Culture* (1992), Appiah contends that the time has passed for black racialism—that is, black identity based on the concept of race—to be

an intelligent reaction to white racism. He simply does not
believe that people of African ancestry can or even should create alliances based on the concept of the black person.[4] But for
whom, we should ask, has the time passed? If we read Appiah
carefully, the time has passed for intellectuals for whom inconsistency in belief is a sign of irrationality. That is to say, the
time has passed for intellectuals who hold up Rationality as
the object of requisite faith. In this respect Appiah says:

> Rationality is best conceived of as an ideal, both in the sense
> that it is something worth aiming for and in the sense that it
> is something we are incapable of realizing. It is an ideal that
> bears an important internal relation to that other great cog-
> nitive ideal, Truth. And, I suggest, we might say that rational-
> ity in belief consists in being disposed so to react to evidence
> and reflection that you change your beliefs in ways that
> make it more likely that they are true.[5]

Appiah concludes that while we cannot change the world by
evidence and reasoning alone, we certainly cannot expect to
change the world without these things.[6]

6   While Appiah presents evidence that the old gods of African traditional religions have not always served Africans well
and that literal belief in spirits has often resulted in tragic
consequences which Rationality could have prevented, he
withholds evidence regarding the myriad failures of the new
gods, Rationality and Truth. I contend that the idea of Rationality and Truth completely replacing the mythologies and
mystifications of African or black identity is an idea whose
time has not yet come. Appiah is considering neither the global evidence that human beings are still fundamentally religious human beings nor the cultural pattern that the
oppressed require mythologies and mystifications to fend off
the theologies of the powerful. In not considering this, it is
understandable that Appiah would state in a negative rather
than positive connotation that African Americans need Africa
as a source of validation. Despite the fact that all peoples seek
self-knowledge as one source of group validation, Appiah's
comment is one that we find being reiterated by such anti-
multiculturalists as Arthur Schlesinger, Jr.

7   Appiah, in sum, rejects the prospect that racism can be
countered by accepting the category of race. So does Henry
Louis Gates, who says that when we attempt to appropriate
the idea of race as a way of pointing to some kind of essence

we yield the great possibility of a common humanity.[7] I contend, however, that race is not an essence but rather a metaphor pointing to cultural and historical differences. These differences have arisen largely from whites and African peoples having existed for centuries at the opposite ends in the master-slave dialectic. But my concession that I refer not to racial essentialism probably would not satisfy Appiah or Gates because they find the word "race" itself to be fraught with implications too inseparable from the traditional hierarchical stratifying of the races.

Certainly the discourse coming from Appiah and Gates   8
sounds very humanistic. But, in terms of the quest for multiculturalism, we must be cautious of the oppositional uses of their quest for the human consciousness to be post-race. In this regard, Houston Baker's response to Appiah's arguments is equally a response to Gates:

> In the presence of Appiah's essay, one wants to exclaim, "He is teaching us! He is teaching us!" But depression quickly sets in when one realizes that what Appiah—in harmony with his privileged evolutionary biologists—discounts as mere "gross" features of hair, bone, and skin are not, in fact, discountable. In a world dramatically conditioned both by the visible and by a perduring discursive formation of "old"(and doubtless mistaken) racial enunciative statements, such gross features always make a painfully significant difference—perhaps, *the only* significant difference where life and limb are concerned in a perilous world.
>
> In short, Appiah's eloquent shift to the common ground of subtle academic discourse is instructive but, ultimately, unhelpful in a world where New York cab drivers scarcely ever think of mitochondria before refusing to pick me up.[8]

Appiah's reaction to this response proceeds into the sphere   9
that we would expect of a philosopher: He edifies the ideals of Truth and Rationality. In Appiah's estimation, people who do not hold to his Enlightenment faith have given into temptation and fallen into intellectual apostasy: "One temptation..., for those who see the centrality of these fictions in our lives, is to leave reason behind: to celebrate and endorse those identities that seem at the moment to offer the best hope of advancing our other goals, and to keep silence about the lies and the myths. But... intellectuals do not easily neglect the truth."[9]

Actually, history shows that intellectuals reveal only part of   10
truth, often only enough truth to camouflage the mythologies

of race, gender, class, and empire that stablize their privilege. The reality regarding Appiah's assumption that truth predicated in the academy trickles down in the form of national policy to fashion increasing quality of life for the masses is that only *some* of the truth trickles down. Perhaps the most important truths are guarded by intellectuals who have ideological agendas to protect.

11   Certainly Appiah is correct that our societies profit from the academic institutionalization of the imperative that truth not be neglected: This should be our central argument for multicultural education. But the quest for truth has obviously only left us with the question "Whose truth?" In the meantime, while the powerful and privileged maintain their favored truths that are undergirded with deeply set mythologies, we cannot expect the unprivileged and oppressed to unbridle themselves in favor of these truths that belong to someone else. That is, we cannot expect the unprivileged and oppressed to discard their mythologies and mystifications regarding race and the essential blessings of their particular race until the privileged and powerful discard their mythologies and mystifications of this sort.

12   Here is where I disagree even further with those postmodern co-conspirators who seek to explode racial identity. Stanley Crouch, who is one of them, informs us that he is at odds with "the patronizing idea that Negroes are somehow so incapable of existing as adults in the contemporary world that they should always be handled like extremely fragile children who must be fed the myths that 'make them feel good about themselves.' "[10] I am arguing, contrariwise, that the best defenses for the oppressed are religious ones, without which we would stand unguarded to fend off the wicked truths that rush at us from other worlds. Until the powerful and privileged permit multicultural education, which can begin to level the historical and intellectual playing field, we cannot expect the unprivileged and the uneducated to discard "overly romantic" notions of history, race, and Africa.

13   My propositions will still sound unintelligible to the debunkers of multiculturalism, such as Arthur Schlesinger, who use the postmodern petition for anti-racialism as their oppositional strategy. I think the principal reason that such black anti-racialists as Glenn Loury, Shelby Steele, and Stephen Carter will find it necessary to reject my proposition is because they each tend to suffer from what Shelby Steele calls "racial fatigue" in his book *The Content of Our Character.*

This fatigue, which Steele says especially plagues the black middle-class, results from their having always to be burdened with "things racial" when race is allegedly no longer the obstacle it once was prior to the 1960s. At the root of the postmodernists' fatigue over "things racial" lies the burden of their feeling that their individual identities must succumb to the group or racial identity of blacks. Steele, for instance, would prefer that blacks interact only when there are reasons beyond the mere fact of racial similarity.[11] His erroneous premise is, however, that the historical and intellectual playing field was leveled by the gains brought on by the civil rights movement.

Stephen Carter reveals in his book *Reflections of an Affirmative Action Baby* (1991) that he too is racially fatigued. He is fatigued by the notion that blacks in positions of prominence are expected always to be representatives of their race: 14

> Black people who have attained a measure of success in the white world are assumed—and, indeed, expected—always and everywhere to represent the race, not in the traditional and still important senses of serving as role models for those who will come later or opening doors by proving their worth, but in a strange new sense of bringing excluded voices into the corridors of power, thereby articulating the interests of a constituency.[12]

But what is so new or strange about blacks who have gleaned a measure of prominence—say, in the corridors of academe—giving voice to those who suffer the most from socially induced misery (misery that miseducation contributes to)? Cornel West says in his book *Race Matters* that his basic aim in life is "to speak the truth to power with love so that the quality of everyday life for ordinary people is enhanced and white supremacy is stripped of its authority and legitimacy." In anticipation of the postmodernist reflex to this position, West adds that a love ethic has nothing to do with "sentimental feelings of tribal connections" but rather is "a last attempt at generating a sense of agency among a downtrodden people."[13] I think multicultural education is a means to this end, despite what is said by blacks suffering from "racial fatigue." Those of us who favor this means of historical reconciliation and intellectual redemption should beware of opponents who use the arguments of racially fatigued blacks to contest multiculturalism.   15

Those of us who wish to generate a sense of agency among our downtrodden by nurturing a self-reconciliatory sense of   16 racial pride via multicultural education, will also be accused of something else. We will be accused by those who draw from the arguments of Shelby Steele as suffering from what Steele calls "integration shock" and "inferiority anxiety." Integration shock is, according to Steele, the shock of our suddenly being individually accountable when integrated into mainstream society. This shock allegedly leads to an anxiety that makes black people maintain the discourse of race, racial pride, and even multiculturalism as a means of camouflaging our alleged individual incapacities.[14] In this respect, Stanley Crouch provides the most pernicious claim against blacks. He suggests that blacks shocked by integration might actually long for the days when we were really oppressed so that we do not have to contend with our anxiety of feeling inferior to whites. In asking why blacks continue to talk of race and racial pride in the way that Du Bois did at the beginning of the century, Crouch answers:

> Is it because those ideas remove Negroes from the weights of modern life as they fall upon everyone? Is it because those turn-of-the-century ideas allow for the avoidance of individual responsibility and make it possible to see Negroes in something akin to a pure state, or at least a state in which all is very simply white and black, Western and Third World, oppressor and oppressed? Today... there might even be nostalgia for those times, or at least for the simpler ideas those times allowed.[15]

17   The only nostalgia felt by those who are pro-multiculturalism is a nostalgia for an understanding of the whole historical story, not just a part of it told to bolster the status and security of those who have been this country's physical conquerors and ideological rulers. We suffer from no "integration shock" or "inferiority anxiety" in wanting to see a reconciliation of American and world history. For us to succomb to the postmodern conspiracy to explode racial identity—for us to transcend the notion of race—when the quest for racial equity is a central motivating factor in multiculturalism, is to undermine this historical movement.

Notes

1. David Gates, "White Male paranoia," *Newsweek* 29 March 1993, 48.
2. Frantz Fanon, *Black Skin, White Masks*, trans. Charles Lam Markmann (New York: Grove, 1967), 10.

3. Alton B. Pollard III, "The Last Great Battle of the West: W. E. B. DuBois and the Struggle for African America's Soul," in Gerald Early, ed., *Lure and Loathing: Essays on Race, Identity, and the Ambivalence of Assimilation* (New York: Penguin, 1993), 47.
4. Kwame Anthony Appiah, *In My Father's House: Africa in the Philosophy of Culture* (New York: Oxford University Press, 1992), 176.
5. Appiah, 116.
6. Appiah, 179.
7. Henry Louis Gates, Jr., "Editor's Introduction: Writing 'Race' and the Difference It Makes," *"Race," Writing, and Difference* (Chicago: University of Chicago Press, 1986), 13.
8. Houston A. Baker, Jr., "Caliban's Triple Play," in Henry Louis Gates, ed., *"Race," Writing, and Difference*, 384–85.
9. Appiah, 179.
10. Stanley Crouch, "Who Are We? Where Did We Come From? Where Are We Going?" in Early, ed., *Lure and Loathing*, 93.
11. Shelby Steele, *The Content of Our Character: A New Vision of Race* (New York: HarperCollins, 1990), 23.
12. Stephen L. Carter, *Reflections of an Affirmative Action Baby* (New York: Basic Books, 1991), 32–33.
13. Cornel West, *Race Matters* (Boston; Beacon, 1993), x.
14. Steele, 23–24.
15. Crouch, 88.

Molefi Asante

Racing to Leave the Race:
Black Postmodernists Off-Track

Response to Spencer

This race to leave the race on the part of the new breed of [1] African American post-modernists identified by Jon Michael Spencer in "Trends of Opposition to Multiculturalism" is directly related to psychological and cultural dislocation, that is, to an anti-historical or ahistorical view of reality in the United States. I would argue that this "conspiracy to explode racial identity" is rooted in three principal elements of what Alton Pollard calls the "post-Du Bois condition." They are self-hatred, political fear, and intellectual defeatism.

2   One cannot read magazines like *New People* and *Interrace* without getting the idea that self-hatred among some African Americans is at an all time high. Both of these magazines, founded by interracial couples and appealing most to interracial families, see themselves as the vanguard to explode racial identity by claiming to be a third race in addition to African and European. Of course, in the context of a racist society the white parent wishes for his/her offspring the same privileges that he/she has enjoyed often at the expense of Africans. However, the offspring is considered by tradition, custom, appearances and history to be black. In a white racist society blackness is considered a negative attribute which carries with it the burden of history and discrimination. Thus, the *New People* and the *Interrace* group attempt to minimize the effects of blackness by claiming that they are neither white nor black, but colored. The nonsense in this position is seen when we consider the fact that nearly seventy per cent of all African Americans are genetically mixed with either Native Americans or whites. The post-Du Bois, and perhaps more accurately, the post–Martin Luther King, Jr. phenomenon of seeking to explode racial identity has two prongs: one is white guilt and the other is black self-hatred. In the case of interracial families one often sees the urgent need to provide the offspring with a race other than that defined by custom, tradition, appearances, and history.

3   Many African or African American males who are either in interracial relations or are the products of such families often speak out of their own dislocations. Kwame Appiah's book *In My Father's House: Africa in the Philosophy of Culture* might better have been titled "In My Mother's House" because he essentially criticizes his Ghanaian father's family and traditions while favoring in his analyses his British mother's family and traditions. Appiah is not alone in his dislocation. One cannot really accept that he speaks for Africans but rather for Europeans when he writes; otherwise there would be no need to explode racial identity.

4   Spencer has finally raised the issue that must be confronted by African intellectuals, that is, what loyalties, commitments, histories must be brought to bear on questions of Africa and African people? How do we evaluate and locate the positions of those whose aim is to explode racial identity even while they parade before audiences as if they are speaking out of an African reality or interest?

5   This is why I say one of the elements in this attack on racial identity is political fear. It is a conservative's agenda to

construct a post-modernist web of a multiplicity of identities in order to befuddle the real issue. In my opinion, the opposition to multiculturalism, and more specifically, to Afrocentricity, the quality of giving agency to African people, is based on the fear of African agency which might mean African solidarity and African self-determination. But it is an old fear, one which has always been a part of our reality in this nation. Of course, if you confuse the issue of racial identity or seek to explode it, you minimize the possibility of collective action. One does not see other ethnic or racial communities clamoring to explode their racial identity because they recognize that it is not fundamental to national cohesion and citizenship responsibilities that people give up their racial identities. Only those who feel that they have no future even dream of exploding racial identity.

In my judgment the list of individuals (all males) mentioned in Jon Michael Spencer's article (Steele, Carter, Loury, Crouch, Gates and Appiah) are victims of intellectual defeatism. They are careerists like most of us in the universities but what they seem to seek, unlike many of us, is the approval of whites. They have already accepted Fanon's prediction about the white destiny and they are rushing as fast as they can to divorce themselves from the modern baggage of race, more precisely, the baggage, as they see it, of the African race. One does not find whites seeking to divest themselves of their whiteness because they do not feel that their destiny is black. The intellectual defeatism that is promoted in the postmodern quest for racial transcendence is bound to fail because it is unconnected to the reality of the people I see here in North Philadelphia on Broad Street.   6

To ask post-modernist blacks to present the agency of Africans is to ask the impossible because they have come to believe that there are neither Africans nor Europeans, these are mere essentialist conceptions which ought to be avoided at all costs. Thus, they have adopted the intellectual defeatism that is inherent in all slave societies or, at least in the lives and activities of those who have abandoned their own history for the illusions of transcending race. No group of whites that I know of has expressed the desire to transcend race. The reason they have not taken this step is because they recognize that race is not merely a biological fact but a cultural and historical fact. People operate on the basis of this fact, create institutions, raise children, develop industries, practice rituals, and produce literature. This is not to say that race should consume our thinking, only that Africans cannot allow others   7 to dictate the nature of our discourse about race or, for that matter, any other subject.

8   Our writers and thinkers must write so that the people can understand the conditions and possibilities of victory. Any understanding on the part of the African masses is a revolt against the Eurocentric imposition on African people. This means that we cannot merely see ourselves as successors to whites in the literary, philosophical, or sociological fields. We must view ourselves as agents for transformation of the power relationships existing between black and white people in this country. To fudge the lines and claim that there are no black people and no white people is to attempt to fool white people into believing that Africans are merely dark-skinned whites. The power reality does not permit this easy slide into facile logic. As Jon Michael Spencer understands so clearly the "conspiracy to explode racial identity" is an indication of the degree to which some of us have been dislocated psychologically and culturally.

9   What is problematic, then, for a discourse on identity is the fact that we often have those with little psychological attachment to their African identity speaking as if they are African when in fact they can only speak for the few black-looking people who claim no cultural attachment to the African culture. Such a group as they represent has no historical, social or cultural depth; it is merely a group which seeks the demonization of African identity, not, I remind the reader, the demonization of identity. In fact, one can sum up the black post-modernist approach to cultural identity as follows:

Thou shalt not accept an African origin

Thou shalt not mock the white man

Thou shalt not threaten the cultural imperialist

Thou shalt not identify with any Africans

Thou shalt not despise the legacy of the white slave owner

Thou shalt not speak evil of Thomas Jefferson and George Washington

Thou shalt not praise other African men and women

Thou shalt not seek to create values for African survival

Thou shalt not work to develop an African identity

Thou shalt not allow anyone to call you African

Thus, this group of black post-modernists is out of its   10
mind. To say that they do not want to claim their African
identity is to say that they want to claim some other identity
since we cannot divest ourselves of some identity or the
other. No great person has ever been frightened of his or her
race. I think Langston Hughes was correct when he wrote
that the mountain standing in the way of the African in
America was "this urge within the race toward whiteness, the
desire to pour racial individuality into the mould of American standardization."

Patricia Hill Collins

Setting Our Own Agenda

Response to Spencer

In his essay "Trends of Opposition to Multiculturalism,"   1
Jon Michael Spencer raises two important interrelated questions for contemporary African Americans who want a new
agenda for Black intellectual and political activism. I will
consider each issue in turn by exploring Spencer's treatment
of the issue and offering some reflections of my own.

First, Spencer directly questions the utility of postmodern-   2
ist discourse for Black political practice. Spencer quite rightly
questions whether the shift toward postmodernism by Black
intellectuals is a good idea for Black people. Intellectuals who
participate in "the postmodern conspiracy to explode racial
identity," as Spencer puts it, form one group challenging the
significance of multiculturalism. In this area of Spencer's
argument, my issue is not with the significance of the question. I, too, think that the difficulties of using some postmodernist ideas, especially their treatment of race and Black
identity, as the basis for Black political practice is something
about which we must think long and hard. Rather, my concern
lies with Spencer's presentation of this issue. To me, by focusing on multiculturalism instead of Black political practice he
sends us off in the wrong direction. Moreover, he misreads

African American use of postmodernist discourse while over-
looking some real negatives.

3   I, for one, do not see postmodernism as a plot to unseat
multiculturalism. Rather, I see both multiculturalism and
postmodernism as complementary outgrowths of struggles
by people of color as part of our decolonization efforts and
efforts to dismantle structures of white supremacy. Postmodernist ideas theoretically work well with what most people
would identify as multiculturalism.

4   Let me offer a brief interpretation. I suggest that what we
are now calling postmodernism is an academic theoretical
orientation that was stimulated in large part by challenges
made by Africans, African Americans and other people of
color to structures of colonialism, imperialism, de jure segregation, and apartheid. Part of these struggles for political
power was a corresponding challenge to the notion of white
centers of any type, whether imperial centers of empire from
former colonial powers, or the centers of white power in the
United States organized around white superiority. With the
belief in the "center" shaken, conceptual space was created in
academic circles to challenge centers of all types, including
categories like race. Postmodernist discourse itself introduces
concepts such as decentering, difference and deconstruction,
all terms that challenge the notion that any one group has a
best view of the world and that this best view entitles them to
rule everyone else. Multiculturalism in the United States is
the domestic version of these types of power struggles as they
affect school curriculum and, to a lesser extent, scholarly
research. In brief, multiculturalism challenges the conceptual
center of whiteness in the curriculum with different versions
of multiculturalism suggesting varying methods of decentering the curriculum.

5   Within academic postmodernist circles, the origins of multiculturalism in the political struggles of oppressed peoples
seem to be increasingly forgotten today. What's becoming
more "in" today are decontextualized discussions of concepts
such as multiplicity, diversity, and difference in abstract
terms that increasingly appear to have little effect on real people's lives. We are all different, reality is shifting, and everything is multiple, postmodernist chic posits. Some
postmodernist scholars seem overly attached to the concepts
of postmodernism without realizing the very real political
struggles that created the conceptual space in which they
work or the political implications of the work that they produce. Some versions of multiculturalism appear to provide

conceptual space for Black people to be "human" just like everyone else, with us all coexisting in a happy multicultural family.

But can African Americans ground a politics in such a worldview? I suspect that this is the version of postmodernism and multiculturalism to which Spencer is opposed. It's not that Spencer thinks that postmodernism is a threat to multiculturalism, but rather that the politics of how postmodernism is being used and done now pose a very real threat to Black political practice. This is the issue that Spencer does not pursue but one that is implicit in his argument. [6]

Spencer knows that a real danger lurks in postmodernist discourse, namely, that its diffuse nature makes it a very slippery entity when it comes to the area of politics. Unlike Marxist social thought, liberal bourgeois reformism, Black cultural nationalism, or most of what we think of as political programs backed by distinctive intellectual perspectives, postmodernist discourse appears to lack a political program and therefore appears to be apolitical. (This doesn't mean that a politics isn't there, just that thinkers typically don't own up to it.) It's like trying to grasp at the air—how do you organize such a group as this? [7]

Unfortunately, Spencer never confronts this question of the political utility of postmodernism for Black political practice. Instead, he paints postmodernism in broad brush strokes by substituting a discussion of the ideas of selected black postmodernist intellectuals for hard hitting analysis of the politics of such a position. And it is at this point that Spencer gets into trouble. [8]

Take, for example, Spencer's claim that a postmodern "conspiracy" exists to explode racial identity. The reams of postmodernist discourse that I have waded through indicate no such conspiracy. In fact, one of the major problems of postmodernist discourse as I see it is that its participants can barely talk to each other, let alone make some of the ideas comprehensible to the rest of us. This hardly places postmodernist thinkers in a position to launch a conspiracy against anybody. [9]

In fact, the lack of a center among postmodernist intellectuals is itself a reflection of one key tenet of postmodernism. There can be no "center," they proclaim, no set of universal standards that apply to everyone. More ominously, searching for overarching theories about racism, sexism or class exploitation are passé—such "metanarratives" are features of a [10] worldview in decline. Organizations of any type, built upon rules, laws, and standards are to be "interrogated." In other words, it seems to me that there is an inherent political limitation built into postmodernist discourse. By questioning everything, including their own discourse and practices, postmodernist discourse offers few avenues for action of any type, including conspiracies. Without a "center" of some type, how do you organize people?

11   Spencer's claim that intellectuals implicated in the postmodern conspiracy want to "explode racial identity" as we know it leads to the second significant question raised by his essay, namely the issue of an essential Black identity as the foundation for Black political practice. In brief, I think that there is a difference between thinkers who aim to explode racial identity in order to further their own careers (Shelby Steele and Clarence Thomas come to mind), and thinkers who wish to explode racial identity as we know it in order to develop political practice more suitable to the racism that Black people face today. Spencer confines his analysis to the former group. I find the latter to be much more interesting.

12   Many Black intellectuals draw upon many of the useful ideas of postmodernism, ideas that themselves were first raised by people of color, in framing contemporary scholarship. bell hooks, for example, is well grounded in the language and ideas of postmodernist discourse, yet hooks demonstrates no such predelection to eliminate race so that she can just "be herself." In philosophy, Cornel West offers a powerful alternative to the ideas of Kwame Anthony Appiah. West challenges prevailing notions of race yet I suspect is supportive of versions of multiculturalism that represent real redistributions of power to people of color. Within law, a group of critical legal theorists, among them Mari Matsuda, Patricia Williams, Richard Delgado, and Charles Lawrence in varying ways use the decentering premise upon which postmodernist discourse is grounded to take on putatively racist dimensions of law.

13   Postmodernist perspectives on Blackness challenge the elevation of Blackness as a master status that supersedes all other parts of Black identity. Worldviews that produced scientific racism and religious justifications for white supremacy have come under the assault of postmodernist scrutiny. There is no center, especially one organized around race, claim postmodernist thinkers. The spirit of such a position has been to challenge the main ideas of scientific racism and the concept of race that we have inherited from this intellectual

framework. Scientific racist thinking argued that race was a master status and made race central to the distribution of power and privilege. Such thinking claimed that whites were "essentially" superior to Black people and that whiteness was a master status that made all white people better than all Black people.

Faced with such a worldview, it made sense to organize 14 Black people around a comparable oppositional version of racial essence or Blackness. With whites operating as a group to exclude, impoverish and kill Black people, what sense would it have made for Black people to say things like "race isn't really real" or "I'm an individual—race forms only one part of my multiple identities?" Essential racial identity appeared to be a necessary part of racial solidarity and of Black political practice.

Black people knew how to fight the battle against a racist 15 center. One simply proclaimed a new Black center, organized everybody under the banner of racial solidarity, and fought back. The old ways of organizing around an essential Black identity within African American communities for the result of racial solidarity and unity certainly worked. In any political movement, there must be one agenda that guides political practice. (Here is another point where postmodernism and I part ways.) But how do you organize under the banner of multiplicity, context and change?

While presenting a unified front to an external enemy is 16 important, constructing an essential Black identity necessarily leads to exclusionary politics within African American communities. Something must be at the center as being "essentially Black" and everything else becomes measured in relation to this implicit center or norm. In the past, one group within the African American community elevated its experiences as being most important, its views as being those around which Black identity, racial solidarity, and thus Black political practice should be organized. In a sense, the type of racial thinking introduced by the dominant group—whites in the center, and everything and everybody else defined in relationship to their experiences and their needs—has been duplicated within African American communities and Black intellectual and political practice.

The costs of this approach have been high for different seg- 17 ments within African American communities. The manipulation of the idea of an essential black identity around which we must all rally has been used to foster both racial solidarity and as a method of controlling African Americans. Consider, for example, the effects of subordinating Black women's issues to the concerns of Black men. Issues of grave importance to African American communities are minimized or eliminated because men are deemed more important than women in drafting solutions to the social issues confronting African American communities. Racial solidarity is achieved, but on the backs of Black women.

18   Similarly, homophobia within African American communities and the elevation of an essential Blackness deemed to be heterosexual deprives African American communities of the talents and leadership of Black gays, lesbians, and bisexuals who deeply care about African American people. More ominously, once aware of the attachment that many Black people have to this notion of the essential Black identity, the dominant group can use this knowledge to manipulate Black communities. Consider, for example, the suppression of the economic needs issues of poor Black people to the economic and political agenda of Black conservatives via the construction of Clarence Thomas as the new essential Black in the confirmation hearings. Thomas fit the bill. He was the image of the essential Black—male, dark, heterosexual, and from a poor background—and African Americans may pay for the oversight of backing a racial solidarity based on this version of the essential Black for some time to come.

19   The days of an essential Black are definitely over for me. I've had enough of suppressing so-called lesser issues such as gender and class for the greater good of racial solidarity defined as a Black normative identity. Our politics erode if we cannot take into account heterogeneity within African American communities. Black racial essences are but mirror images of white racial essences, the very foundation of white supremacy. While grounding politics in a Black essence may definitely win short-term battles, as a long-term strategy, it is doomed to be bankrupt because we remain locked in a dialogue with white supremacy on its own terms. Isn't there a better way of holding a community together than defining its center by excluding the many at its margins?

20   But despite the problems of racial solidarity organized around an essential Black identity, thus far, this approach has been virtually the only game in town. Along comes postmodernism, which questions this very way of organizing the world, a challenge that itself offers no real alternatives. Spencer sees this danger yet never pursues the arguments beyond raising the legitimate concern that postmodernist discourse

is itself a problem for Black people in that it challenges the premises upon which Black political practice are based. He clearly does not believe in an essentialized Black identity, one where genetics and physical features are markers of consciousness and behavior. He definitely sees racial identity as being historically and socially constituted. But, like so many of us, he does not take the next logical step of questioning how the postmodern challenge might transform how we currently organize Black identity and the types of politics that grow from it. Instead, he argues that the only away to achieve racial solidarity necessary for Black political activism is to continue doing business as usual. In the absence of seeing an alternative, he advises us to hold on to what we already have.

But while this approach is the best choice for now, I suspect that it is unlikely to get us where we want to go in the long run. To me, the challenge facing Black intellectuals and Black activists consists of producing alternatives that avoid the limitations of the politics of exclusion growing from racial solidarity as we know it, and the very real dangers of throwing our lot in with a seemingly apolitical postmodernist intellectual framework. In brief, how we might build racial solidarity that informs Black political practice without resorting to an essentialized, exclusionary Black identity? Until we answer this question, we will never know whether African American agendas are our own, or merely reactions to those of more powerful groups.

David Lionel Smith
Let Our People Go

Response to Spencer

1   All modern culture is multicultural. The real issue is what
we understand this to entail. In the 1970s Ishmael Reed
began to use the term "multi-cultural artist" to describe a
phenomenon that was developing in the San Francisco Bay
area with himself as its leading voice. "Multi-culturalism"
referred to the attitudes and practices of artists whose works
drew upon various cultural traditions and who collaborated
with and learned from each other in a spirit of egalitarian fellowship. Defined in opposition to the monoculturalist, Euro-
chauvinist Eastern literary establishment, this group of
artists—at least as described by Reed—rejected the exclusionary, hierarchical aesthetic values of the Eurochauvinists and
regarded each other's traditions and works with mutual
respect. They formed the Before Columbus Foundation and
published in *Yardbird Reader*. Though they represented various ethnic and racial groups, what defined these artists as
multi-cultural was their commitment to an egalitarian, cooperative cultural pluralism.

2   Now multi-culturalism has lost its hyphen and it struts
lewdly wherever liberals thrive: campuses, professional asso-
ciations, publishing houses, educational bureaucracies, etc.
Unfortunately, this new multiculturalism is not the one that
Reed described two decades ago. Even if his description idealized a less perfect reality, it specified an interactive, pro-
tean, mutually respectful set of attitudes that contrasts
sharply with the dogmatic self-aggrandizing of the current
identity politics, which so often uses pluralist rhetoric to
advance selfish agendas. When we are accosted by "multiculturalists," we might be wise to run a background check and
ascertain what, exactly, we are about to embrace.

3   The word "multiculturalism" purveys something for everybody. Universal and specific, inclusive and exclusive, democratic and despotic, sublime and ridiculous, empirically real
and really theoretical, "multiculturalism" embraces everything
and precludes nothing. Its promiscuous circulation carica-
tures perfectly the befuddled liberalism of the Clinton era:
progressive in rhetoric, regressive in practice. Part euphemism, part shibboleth, and entirely mystification, the word

"multiculturalism" yields itself equally to its reactionary detractors and its radical celebrants. Lacking any content of its own, this empty signifier has become an expedient receptacle for the passionate investments of various malcontents. Thus, "multiculturalism" is simultaneously hailed as either the subversion or the salvation of "Western civilization." Taking this "contention" into account, it does not seem accurate to portray postmodern theorists as enemies of "multiculturalism." Such theorists, after all, have deconstructed old-fashioned binary oppositions into clamoring pluralities. Thus, we should understand "multiculturalism" as a logical expression of postmodernity.

Jon Michael Spencer's "Trends of Opposition to Multiculturalism," though illuminating as both a reflection of and a reflection upon the current multiculturalism debate, misses this important point. Indeed, Professor Spencer's essay overburdens itself by finding enemies in virtually every camp—so much so that it lapses inevitably into a rhetoric of paranoia, decrying *"the postmodern conspiracy to explode racial identity."* [His italics.] Ironically, most of the thinkers whom he identifies under this heading seem improperly identified as "postmodern theorists," while others whom he enlists as allies, such as Cornel West and Houston Baker, are quite clearly "postmodern theorists." To quibble over philosophical definitions, however, is not the point of this essay, nor is it intended as a critique of Spencer's thoughtful article. Instead, I want to challenge its defense of racial identity and, more broadly, of multiculturalism. I want to suggest that the fundamental political and cultural interests of most black Americans are ill served by the notions of race and multiculturalism.

The concept of race as we commonly use it, which classifies so many white-looking people as "black," is merely the slaveholders' expedient for defining a segment of the population into permanent subordination. After the abolition of slavery, race continued to maintain the social relations mandated by slavery. Judging from the relative social and economic status of the black and white populations, race continues to do its work quite effectively. There is nothing obvious about "black" as a definition of identity. Enslaved Africans certainly remembered their diverse tribal and cultural origins; and though we have forgotten this now, Euro-Americans recognized this diversity, too. In fact, there is massive evidence demonstrating that right up through the early nineteenth century, whites distinguished among the physical, cultural, and behavioral traits of slaves from various tribal

backgrounds and had clear preferences among them. Over
the course of American history, our notions of race have actually grown narrower, more ideological and less empirical.

6   This is worth remembering when one argues for maintaining the category of racial identity as if it were somehow "natural." The argument by Kwame Anthony Appiah, Henry
Louis Gates, and others that race is socially constructed is
absolutely true. What's legitimately at issue is not the truth of
this claim but rather what follows from it. For a very tiny elite
of African Americans, rejecting racial identity is a real though
perhaps a self-deluded option. If people like Shelby Steele
want to secede from the race, why should we not celebrate
their departure? Their claim to speak authoritatively for
other black people, not their self-defeating attempts to escape
the cage of race, are what we ought to challenge. There are
perfectly legitimate political, social, cultural, and emotional
reasons why others of us may elect to identify with the majority of black people, nor do we require any specious claims
about "racial identity" in order to do so. This act of commitment, not the "fact" of race, is what ought to be at issue.
Social groups are already constituted, regardless of our theories, and whether they have a valid basis or not is an academic question. Within the academy, we ought to pursue that
inquiry assiduously. As a political point, however, we would
be wise to focus our attention on questions of allegiance, leaving notions of inherent identity alone.

7   The vague rubric "multiculturalism" will not advance the
interests of African Americans unless it brings us new and
committed allies. This seems unlikely. On the contrary, it
will enable an endless assortment of "identity" factions to
claim for themselves the moral authority achieved by the
hard-fought struggles of the Civil Rights and Black Power
Movements—just to name the recent manifestations of our
political tradition. Obviously, many of these groups have
legitimate claims of their own, and we should respect those
claims. Nevertheless, to conflate blackness into "multiculturalism" alongside miscellaneous other forms of identity is to
obfuscate an understanding taught to us through long, bitter
experience. In America, race matters, but blackness matters
in more detailed ways. "Black" was created to be a special
case, and it remains one. If we allow our fellow Americans to
ignore this fact, they will hasten to do so. "Multiculturalism"
offers them a perfect diversion. At the same time, Negro-
phobes will not hesitate to assault multiculturalism, espe-

cially, its more dubious forms, as an indirect means of hammering African Americans.

Practically speaking, the term "multiculturalism" is so flex-   8
ibly inclusive that it might best be understood as attitudinal rather than denotative. It implies an embracing of traditions and groups that have been suppressed by the dominant culture. In actual usage, its meaning is even more generalized than this. Proponents of multiculturalism tend to focus on their own preferred groups, while using the "multicultural" rubric to represent themselves as egalitarians rather than partisans. Ultimately, however, the umbrella of multiculturalism is so broad that no ethnic group or lifestyle faction can be excluded from it, including those which constitute the so-called "dominant" group. In this respect, a loosely defined conception of multiculturalism is self-defeating, because its lack of distinctions causes it to include even what it intends to oppose. Eventually, the conservatives who oppose multiculturalism will recognize this paradox and respond by declaring themselves multiculturalists too, thereby turning the movement on its head. At that point, the alleged coalition of oppressed versus oppressors will collapse, leaving the plethora of factions to fend for themselves. Such conditions will not be conducive to generosity, and the groups that began with the strongest power base (i.e., white men) will continue to command the greatest strategic advantages.

Some members of the new black elite are blind to both the   9
unabated racism of American society and to the continuing vitality of African American culture. Obtuseness does not become respectable just because it is loudly or arrogantly asserted. Theoretically, race is an indefensible category; practically, it is an inescapable aspect of American social reality. This is the paradox that we as African American intellectuals must endeavor to understand. If certain individuals wish to cross over into some fancied raceless paradise, we must let our people go. When the river parts to let them pass, perhaps we will follow them to the promised land. For now, however, we need not pack our bags.

DEFINING GENDER

John Adams and Abigail Adams
Letters

Here are two letters and part of a third written by John Adams of Massachusetts, one of America's Founding Fathers (and later the second president of the United States), and his wife Abigail Adams (a formidable person as well) in the spring of 1776—while the nation was considering declaring its freedom from British rule. The first was sent by Abigail to John while he was in Philadelphia debating with his colleagues the merits of a declaration of independence: Note how Abigail uses the occasion to press her husband to "remember the ladies" in his discussions about freedom from tyranny. She was probably thinking not of suffrage—too radical an idea—but of fairer laws regarding inheritance, wifebeating, and so forth. The second is John's response to that letter. The third, John Adams's letter to James Sullivan (who had proposed that one's power at the ballot box should be proportional to one's financial worth), indicates that John Adams understood all too well the probable long-term implications of what was being written in the Declaration.

Letter from Abigail Adams to John Adams, March 31, 1776

1   I long to hear that you have declared an independancy—and by the way in the new Code of Laws which I suppose it will be necessary for you to make I desire you would Remember the Ladies, and be more generous and favourable to them than your ancestors. Do not put such unlimited power into the hands of the Husbands. Remember all Men would be tyrants if they could. If perticuliar care and attention is not paid to the Laidies we are determined to foment a Rebelion, and will not hold ourselves bound by any Laws in which we have no voice, or Representation.

That your Sex are Naturally Tyrannical is a Truth so thor- 2
oughly established as to admit of no dispute, but such of you
as wish to be happy willingly give up the harsh title of Master for the more tender and endearing one of Friend. Why
then, not put it out of the power of the vicious and the Lawless to use us with cruelty and indignity with impunity. Men
of Sense in all Ages abhor those customs which treat us only
as the vassals of your Sex. Regard us then as Beings placed
by providence under your protection and in immitation of
the Supreem Being make use of that power only for our
happiness.

Letter from John Adams to Abigail Adams, April 14, 1776

As to Declarations of Independency, be patient. Read our 3
Privateering Laws, and our Commercial Laws. What signifies
a Word.

As to your extraordinary Code of Laws, I cannot but laugh. 4
We have been told that our Struggle has loosened the bands
of Government every where. That Children and Apprentices
were disobedient—that schools and Colledges were grown
turbulent—that Indians slighted their Guardians and Negroes
grew insolent to their Masters. But your Letter was the first
Intimation that another Tribe more numerous and powerfull
than all the rest were grown discontented.—This is rather too
coarse a Compliment but you are so saucy, I wont blot it out.

Depend upon it, We know better than to repeal our Mascu- 5
line systems. Altho they are in full Force, you know they are
little more than Theory. We dare not exert our Power in its
full Latitude. We are obliged to go fair, and softly, and in Practice you know We are the subjects. We have only the Name of
Masters, and rather than give up this, which would com-
pleatly subject Us to the Despotism of the Peticoat, I hope
General Washington, and all our brave Heroes would fight. I
am sure every good Politician would plot, as long as he would
against Despotism, Empire, Monarchy, Aristocracy, Oligar-
chy, or Ochlocracy.—A fine Story indeed. I begin to think the
Ministry as deep as they are wicked. After stirring up Tories,
Landjobbers, Trimmers, Bigots, Canadians, Indians, Negroes,
Hanoverians, Hessians, Russians, Irish Roman Catholicks,
Scotch Renegadoes, at last they have stimulated the[m] to
demand new Priviledges and threaten to rebell.

Letter from John Adams to James Sullivan, May 26, 1776

6   ... The same reasoning which will induce you to admit all men who have no property, to vote, with those who have, for those laws which affect the person, will prove that you ought to admit women and children; for, generally speaking, women and children have as good judgments, and as independent minds, as those men who are wholly destitute of property; these last being to all intents and purposes as much dependent upon others, who will please to feed, clothe, and employ them, as women are upon their husbands, or children on their parents.

7   As to your idea of proportioning the votes of men, in money matters, to the property they hold, it is utterly impracticable. There is no possible way of ascertaining, at any one time, how much every man in a community is worth; and if there was, so fluctuating is trade and property, that this state of it would change in half an hour....

8   Depend upon it, Sir, it is dangerous to open so fruitful a source of controversy and altercation as would be opened by attempting to alter the qualifications of voters; there will be no end of it. New claims will arise; women will demand a vote; lads from twelve to twenty-one will think their rights not enough attended to; and every man who has not a farthing, will demand an equal voice with any other, in all acts of state. It tends to confound all distinctions, and prostrate all ranks to one common level.

Sojourner Truth

Ain't I a Woman?

Sojourner Truth's story is fascinating and moving. Born in Ulster County, New York, into slavery around 1797 and given the name Isabella, she was sold three times before she turned twelve. Raped by one of her masters, she fled to freedom in 1827, a year before slavery was outlawed in New York. In New York City she worked as a domestic and fell in with an evangelical preacher who encouraged her efforts to convert prostitutes. In 1843, inspired by mystical visions, she took the name Sojourner Truth and set off alone and undeterred by her illiteracy to preach and sing about religion and the abolition of slavery. By 1850, huge crowds were coming to witness the oratory of the ex-slave with the resounding voice and message. During the Civil War she was presented to President Lincoln at the White House. After the war she spoke out for women's suffrage, but she never gave up her spiritual and racial themes—or her humor and exuberance. She continued to lecture until near her death in Battle Creek, Michigan, in 1883.

Sojourner Truth accepted neither the physical inferiority of women nor the idea that they should be placed on pedestals; nor did she subordinate women's rights to the pursuit of racial equality. At a religious meeting in May 1851, Sojourner Truth rose extemporaneously to rebut speakers who had impugned the rights and capabilities of women. According to an eyewitness who recorded the scene in his diary, this is what she said:

Well, children, where there is so much racket there must 1
be something out of kilter. I think that 'twixt the negroes of the South and the women at the North, all talking about rights, the white men will be in a fix pretty soon. But what's all this here talking about?

That man over there says that women need to be helped 2
into carriages, and lifted over ditches, and to have the best place everywhere. Nobody ever helps me into carriages, or over mud-puddles, or gives me any best place! And ain't I a woman? Look at me! Look at my arm! I have ploughed and planted, and gathered into barns, and no man could head me! And ain't I a woman? I could work as much and eat as much as a man—when I could get it—and bear the lash as well! And ain't I a woman? I have borne thirteen children, and seen them most all sold off to slavery, and when I cried out with

my mother's grief, none but Jesus heard me! And ain't I a woman?

3   Then they talk about this thing in the head; what's this they call it? [Intellect, someone whispers.] That's it, honey. What's that got to do with women's rights or negro's rights? If my cup won't hold but a pint, and yours holds a quart, wouldn't you be mean not to let me have my little half-measure full?

4   Then that little man in black there, he says women can't have as much rights as men, 'cause Christ wasn't a woman! Where did your Christ come from? Where did your Christ come from? From God and a woman! Man had nothing to do with Him.

5   If the first woman God ever made was strong enough to turn the world upside down all alone, these women together ought to be able to turn it back, and get it right side up again! And now they is asking to do it, the men better let them.

6   Obliged to you for hearing on me, and now old Sojourner ain't got nothing more to say.

Susan Glaspell

Trifles

Susan Glaspell (1882–1948), an Iowan by birth and educa-tion, moved east in 1911. A Pulitzer Prize–winning dramatist and a prolific fiction writer, she cofounded the Provincetown Playhouse on Cape Cod in 1915, which became a center for experimental and innovative drama. In 1916 she wrote Trifles, *the one-act play reprinted here; then she adapted it a few months later into the story "A Jury of Her Peers."*

Characters

GEORGE HENDERSON, *County Attorney*
HENRY PETERS, *Sheriff*
LEWIS HALE, *A Neighboring Farmer*
MRS. PETERS
MRS. HALE

SCENE

The kitchen in the now abandoned farmhouse of JOHN WRIGHT, *a*   1
gloomy kitchen, and left without having been put in order—
unwashed pans under the sink, a loaf of bread outside the
breadbox, a dish towel on the table—other signs of incompleted
work. At the rear the outer door opens and the SHERIFF *comes in*
followed by the COUNTY ATTORNEY *and* HALE. *The* SHERIFF *and* HALE
are men in middle life, the COUNTY ATTORNEY *is a young man; all*
are much bundled up and go at once to the stove. They are fol-
lowed by two women—the SHERIFF'S *wife first; she is a slight wiry*
woman, a thin nervous face. MRS. HALE *is larger and would ordi-*
narily be called more comfortable looking, but she is disturbed
now and looks fearfully about as she enters. The women have
come in slowly, and stand close together near the door.

COUNTY ATTORNEY. [*Rubbing his hands.*] This feels good. Come   2
    up to the fire, ladies.
MRS. PETERS. [*After taking a step forward.*] I'm not—cold.   3
SHERIFF. [*Unbuttoning his overcoat and stepping away from the*   4
    stove as if to mark the beginning of official business.] Now,
    Mr. Hale, before we move things about, you explain to Mr.
    Henderson just what you saw when you came here yester-
    day morning.
COUNTY ATTORNEY. By the way, has anything been moved? Are   5
    things just as you left them yesterday?
SHERIFF. [*Looking about.*] It's just the same. When it dropped   6
    below zero last night I thought I'd better send Frank out
    this morning to make a fire for us—no use getting pneu-
    monia with a big case on, but I told him not to touch any-
    thing except the stove—and you know Frank.
COUNTY ATTORNEY. Somebody should have been left here   7
    yesterday.
SHERIFF. Oh—yesterday. When I had to send Frank to Morris   8
    Center for that man who went crazy—I want you to know I
    had my hands full yesterday. I knew you could get back
    from Omaha by today and as long as I went over every-
    thing here myself—
COUNTY ATTORNEY. Well, Mr. Hale, tell just what happened when   9
    you came here yesterday morning.
HALE. Harry and I had started to town with a load of potatoes.   10
    We came along the road from my place and as I got here I
    said, "I'm going to see if I can't get John Wright to go in
    with me on a party telephone." I spoke to Wright about it
    once before and he put me off, saying folks talked too
    much anyway, and all he asked was peace and quiet—I

guess you know about how much he talked himself; but I thought maybe if I went to the house and talked about it before his wife, though I said to Harry that I didn't know as what his wife wanted made much difference to John—

11 COUNTY ATTORNEY. Let's talk about that later, Mr. Hale. I do want to talk about that, but tell now just what happened when you got to the house.

12 HALE. I didn't hear or see anything; I knocked at the door, and still it was all quiet inside. I knew they must be up, it was past eight o'clock. So I knocked again, and I thought I heard somebody say, "Come in." I wasn't sure, I'm not sure yet, but I opened the door—this door [*Indicating the door by which the two women are still standing*] and there in that rocker—[*Pointing to it.*] sat Mrs. Wright. [*They all look at the rocker.*]

13 COUNTY ATTORNEY. What—was she doing?

14 HALE. She was rockin' back and forth. She had her apron in her hand and was kind of—pleating it.

15 COUNTY ATTORNEY. And how did she—look?

16 HALE. Well, she looked queer.

17 COUNTY ATTORNEY. How do you mean—queer?

18 HALE. Well, as if she didn't know what she was going to do next. And kind of done up.

19 COUNTY ATTORNEY. How did she seem to feel about your coming?

20 HALE. Why, I don't think she minded—one way or other. She didn't pay much attention. I said, "How do, Mrs. Wright, it's cold, ain't it?" And she said, "Is it?"—and went on kind of pleating at her apron. Well, I was surprised; she didn't ask me to come up to the stove, or to set down, but just sat there, not even looking at me, so I said, "I want to see John." And then she—laughed. I guess you would call it a laugh. I thought of Harry and the team outside, so I said a little sharp: "Can't I see John?" "No," she says, kind o' dull like. "Ain't he home?" says I. "Yes," says she, "he's home." "Then why can't I see him?" I asked her, out of patience. " 'Cause he's dead," says she. "*Dead?*" says I. She just nodded her head, not getting a bit excited, but rockin' back and forth. "Why—where is he?" says I, not knowing what to say. She just pointed upstairs—like that [*Himself pointing to the room above.*] I got up, with the idea of going up there. I walked from there to here—then I says, "Why, what did he die of?" "He died of a rope round his neck," says she, and just went on pleatin' at her apron. Well, I went out and called Harry. I thought I might—need help. We went upstairs and there he was lyin'—

COUNTY ATTORNEY. I think I'd rather have you go into that   21
upstairs, where you can point it all out. Just go on now
with the rest of the story.

HALE. Well, my first thought was to get that rope off. It   22
looked... [*Stops, his face twitches*]...but Harry, he went up
to him, and he said, "No, he's dead all right, and we'd better not touch anything." So we went back down stairs.
She was still sitting that same way. "Has anybody been
notified?" I asked. "No," says she, unconcerned. "Who did
this, Mrs. Wright?" said Harry. He said it businesslike—
and she stopped pleatin' of her apron. "I don't know," she
says. "You don't *know?*" says Harry. "No," says she.
"Weren't you sleepin' in bed with him?" says Harry. "Yes,"
says she, "but I was on the inside." "Somebody slipped a
rope round his neck and strangled him and you didn't
wake up?" says Harry. "I didn't wake up," she said after
him. We must 'a looked as if we didn't see how that could
be, for after a minute she said, "I sleep sound." Harry was
going to ask her more questions but I said maybe we
ought to let her tell her story first to the coroner, or the
sheriff, so Harry went fast as he could to Rivers' place,
where there's a telephone.

COUNTY ATTORNEY. And what did Mrs. Wright do when she knew   23
that you had gone for the coroner?

HALE. She moved from that chair to this one over here [*Point-   24
ing to a small chair in the corner.*] and just sat there with
her hands held together and looking down. I got a feeling
that I ought to make some conversation, so I said I had
come in to see if John wanted to put in a telephone, and at
that she started to laugh, and then she stopped and looked
at me—scared. [*The* COUNTY ATTORNEY, *who has had his notebook out, makes a note.*] I dunno, maybe it wasn't scared. I
wouldn't like to say it was. Soon Harry got back, and then
Dr. Lloyd came, and you, Mr. Peters, and so I guess that's
all I know that you don't.

COUNTY ATTORNEY. [*Looking around.*] I guess we'll go upstairs   25
first—and then out to the barn and around there. [*To the*
SHERIFF] You're convinced that there was nothing important
here—nothing that would point to any motive.

SHERIFF. Nothing here but kitchen things.   26

[*The* COUNTY ATTORNEY, *after again looking around the kitchen,
opens the door of a cupboard closet. He gets up on a chair
and looks on a shelf. Pulls his hand away, sticky.*]

COUNTY ATTORNEY. Here's a nice mess.   27

[*The women draw nearer.*]

28   MRS. PETERS. [*To the other woman.*] Oh, her fruit; it did freeze. [*To the* COUNTY ATTORNEY] She worried about that when it turned so cold. She said the fire'd go out and her jars would break.

29   SHERIFF. Well, can you beat the women! Held for murder and worryin' about her preserves.

30   COUNTY ATTORNEY. I guess before we're through she may have something more serious than preserves to worry about.

31   HALE. Well, women are used to worrying over trifles. [*The two women move a little closer together.*]

32   COUNTY ATTORNEY. [*With the gallantry of a young politician.*] And yet, for all their worries, what would we do without the ladies? [*The women do not unbend. He goes to the sink, takes a dipperful of water from the pail and pouring it into a basin, washes his hands. Starts to wipe them on the roller towel, turns it for a cleaner place.*] Dirty towels! [*Kicks his foot against the pans under the sink.*] Not much of a housekeeper, would you say, ladies?

33   MRS. HALE. [*Stiffly.*] There's a great deal of work to be done on a farm.

34   COUNTY ATTORNEY. To be sure. And yet [*With a little bow to her*] I know there are some Dickson county farmhouses which do not have such roller towels.
      [*He gives it a pull to expose its full length again.*]

35   MRS. HALE. Those towels get dirty awful quick. Men's hands aren't always as clean as they might be.

36   COUNTY ATTORNEY. Ah, loyal to your sex, I see. But you and Mrs. Wright were neighbors. I suppose you were friends, too.

37   MRS. HALE. [*Shaking her head.*] I've not seen much of her of late years. I've not been in this house—it's more than a year.

38   COUNTY ATTORNEY. And why was that? You didn't like her?

39   MRS. HALE. I liked her all well enough. Farmers' wives have their hands full, Mr. Henderson. And then—

40   COUNTY ATTORNEY. Yes—?

41   MRS. HALE. [*Looking about.*] It never seemed a very cheerful place.

42   COUNTY ATTORNEY. No—it's not cheerful. I shouldn't say she had the homemaking instinct.

43   MRS. HALE. Well, I don't know as Wright had, either.

44   COUNTY ATTORNEY. You mean that they didn't get on very well?

45   MRS. HALE. No, I don't mean anything. But I don't think a place'd be any cheerfuller for John Wright's being in it.

46   COUNTY ATTORNEY. I'd like to talk more of that a little later. I want to get the lay of things upstairs now.
      [*He goes to the left, where three steps lead to a stair door.*]

SHERIFF. I suppose anything Mrs. Peters does'll be all right. She   47
was to take in some clothes for her, you know, and a few little things. We left in such a hurry yesterday.

COUNTY ATTORNEY. Yes, but I would like to see what you take,   48
Mrs. Peters, and keep an eye out for anything that might be
of use to us.

MRS. PETERS. Yes, Mr. Henderson.   49
[*The women listen to the men's steps on the stairs, then look
about the kitchen.*]

MRS. HALE. I'd hate to have men coming into my kitchen,   50
snooping around and criticising.
[*She arranges the pans under sink which the* COUNTY ATTORNEY
had shoved out of place.]

MRS. PETERS. Of course it's no more than their duty.   51

MRS. HALE. Duty's all right, but I guess that deputy sheriff that   52
came out to make the fire might have got a little of this on.
[*Gives the roller towel a pull.*] Wish I'd thought of that
sooner. Seems mean to talk about her for not having things
slicked up when she had to come away in such a hurry.

MRS. PETERS. [*Who has gone to a small table in the left rear corner   53
of the room, and lifted one end of a towel that covers a pan.*]
She had bread set.
[*Stands still.*]

MRS. HALE. [*Eyes fixed on a loaf of bread beside the breadbox,   54
which is on a low shelf at the other side of the room. Moves
slowly toward it.*] She was going to put this in there. [*Picks
up loaf, then abruptly drops it. In a manner of returning to
familiar things.*] It's a shame about her fruit. I wonder if it's
all gone. [*Gets up on the chair and looks.*] I think there's
some here that's all right, Mrs. Peters. Yes—here; [*Holding
it toward the window.*] this is cherries too. [*Looking again.*]
I declare I believe that's the only one. [*Gets down, bottle in
her hand. Goes to the sink and wipes it off on the outside.*]
She'll feel awful bad after all her hard work in the hot
weather. I remember the afternoon I put up my cherries
last summer.
[*She puts the bottle on the big kitchen table, center of the
room. With a sigh, is about to sit down in the rocking-chair.
Before she is seated realizes what chair it is; with a slow look
at it, steps back. The chair which she has touched rocks back
and forth.*]

MRS. PETERS. Well, I must get those things from the front room   55
closet. [*She goes to the door at the right, but after looking
into the other room, steps back.*] You coming with me, Mrs.
Hale? You could help me carry them.

[*They go in the other room; reappear,* MRS. PETERS *carrying a dress and skirt,* MRS. HALE *following with a pair of shoes.*]

56   MRS. PETERS. My, it's cold in there.

[*She puts the clothes on the big table, and hurries to the stove.*]

57   MRS. HALE. [*Examining her skirt.*] Wright was close. I think maybe that's why she kept so much to herself. She didn't even belong to the Ladies Aid. I suppose she felt she couldn't do her part, and then you don't enjoy things when you feel shabby. She used to wear pretty clothes and be lively, when she was Minnie Foster, one of the town girls singing in the choir. But that—oh, that was thirty years ago. This all you was to take in?

58   MRS. PETERS. She said she wanted an apron. Funny thing to want, for there isn't much to get you dirty in jail, goodness knows. But I suppose just to make her feel more natural. She said they was in the top drawer in this cupboard. Yes, here. And then her little shawl that always hung behind the door. [*Opens stair door and looks.*] Yes, here it is.

[*Quickly shuts door leading upstairs.*]

59   MRS. HALE. [*Abruptly moving toward her.*] Mrs. Peters?

60   MRS. PETERS. Yes, Mrs. Hale?

61   MRS. HALE. Do you think she did it?

62   MRS. PETERS. [*In a frightened voice.*] Oh, I don't know.

63   MRS. HALE. Well, I don't think she did. Asking for an apron and her little shawl. Worrying about her fruit.

64   MRS. PETERS. [*Starts to speak, glances up, where footsteps are heard in the room above. In a low voice.*] Mr. Peters says it looks bad for her. Mr. Henderson is awful sarcastic in a speech and he'll make fun of her sayin' she didn't wake up.

65   MRS. HALE. Well, I guess John Wright didn't wake when they was slipping that rope under his neck.

66   MRS. PETERS. No, it's strange. It must have been done awful crafty and still. They say it was such a—funny way to kill a man, rigging it all up like that.

67   MRS. HALE. That's just what Mr. Hale said. There was a gun in the house. He says that's what he can't understand.

68   MRS. PETERS. Mr. Henderson said coming out that what was needed for the case was a motive; something to show anger, or—sudden feeling.

69   MRS. HALE. [*Who is standing by the table.*] Well, I don't see any signs of anger around here. [*She puts her hand on the dish towel which lies on the table, stands looking down at table, one half of which is clean, the other half messy.*] It's wiped to here. [*Makes a move as if to finish work, then turns and looks at loaf of bread outside the breadbox. Drops towel. In*

that voice of coming back to familiar things.] Wonder how
they are finding things upstairs. I hope she had it a little
more red-up up there. You know, it seems kind of *sneaking.*
Locking her up in town and then coming out here and trying to get her own house to turn against her!

MRS. PETERS. But Mrs. Hale, the law is the law.   70

MRS. HALE. I s'pose 'tis. [*Unbuttoning her coat.*] Better loosen up   71
your things, Mrs. Peters. You won't feel them when you go
out.

[MRS. PETERS *takes off her fur tippet, goes to hang it on hook at*
back of room, stands looking at the under part of the small
corner table.]

MRS. PETERS. She was piecing a quilt.   72

[*She brings the large sewing basket and they look at the*
bright pieces.]

MRS. HALE. It's log cabin pattern. Pretty, isn't it? I wonder if she   73
was goin' to quilt it or just knot it?

[*Footsteps have been heard coming down the stairs. The*
SHERIFF *enters followed by* HALE *and the* COUNTY ATTORNEY.]

SHERIFF. They wonder if she was going to quilt it or just knot it!   74

[*The men laugh; the women look abashed.*]

COUNTY ATTORNEY. [*Rubbing his hands over the stove.*] Frank's fire   75
didn't do much up there, did it? Well, let's go out to the
barn and get that cleared up.

[*The men go outside.*]

MRS. HALE. [*Resentfully.*] I don't know as there's anything so   76
strange, our takin' up our time with little things while
we're waiting for them to get the evidence. [*She sits down*
at the big table smoothing out a block with decision.] I don't
see as it's anything to laugh about.

MRS. PETERS. [*Apologetically.*] Of course they've got awful   77
important things on their minds.

[*Pulls up a chair and joins* MRS. HALE *at the table.*]

MRS. HALE. [*Examining another block.*] Mrs. Peters, look at this   78
one. Here, this is the one she was working on, and look at
the sewing! All the rest of it has been so nice and even. And
look at this! It's all over the place! Why, it looks as if she
didn't know what she was about!

[*After she has said this they look at each other, then start to*
glance back at the door. After an instant MRS. HALE *has pulled*
at a knot and ripped the sewing.]

MRS. PETERS. Oh, what are you doing, Mrs. Hale?   79

MRS. HALE. [*Mildly.*] Just pulling out a stitch or two that's not   80
sewed very good. [*Threading a needle.*] Bad sewing always
made me fidgety.

81   MRS. PETERS. [*Nervously.*] I don't think we ought to touch
      things.

82   MRS. HALE. I'll just finish up this end. [*Suddenly stopping and
      leaning forward.*] Mrs. Peters?

83   MRS. PETERS. Yes, Mrs. Hale?

84   MRS. HALE. What do you suppose she was so nervous about?

85   MRS. PETERS. Oh—I don't know. I don't know as she was ner-
      vous. I sometimes sew awful queer when I'm just tired.
      [MRS. HALE *starts to say something, looks at* MRS. PETERS, *then
      goes on sewing.*] Well, I must get these things wrapped up.
      They may be through sooner than we think. [*Putting apron
      and other things together.*] I wonder where I can find a piece
      of paper, and string.

86   MRS. HALE. In that cupboard, maybe.

87   MRS. PETERS. [*Looking in cupboard.*] Why, here's a birdcage.
      [*Holds it up.*] Did she have a bird, Mrs. Hale?

88   MRS. HALE. Why, I don't know whether she did or not—I've not
      been here for so long. There was a man around last year
      selling canaries cheap, but I don't know as she took one;
      maybe she did. She used to sing real pretty herself.

89   MRS. PETERS. [*Glancing around.*] Seems funny to think of a bird
      here. But she must have had one, or why would she have a
      cage? I wonder what happened to it.

90   MRS. HALE. I s'pose maybe the cat got it.

91   MRS. PETERS. No, she didn't have a cat. She's got that feeling
      some people have about cats—being afraid of them. My cat
      got in her room and she was real upset and asked me to
      take it out.

92   MRS. HALE. My sister Bessie was like that. Queer, ain't it?

93   MRS. PETERS. [*Examining the cage.*] Why, look at this door. It's
      broke. One hinge is pulled apart.

94   MRS. HALE. [*Looking too.*] Looks as if someone must have been
      rough with it.

95   MRS. PETERS. Why, yes.
      [*She brings the cage forward and puts it on the table.*]

96   MRS. HALE. I wish if they're going to find any evidence they'd be
      about it. I don't like this place.

97   MRS. PETERS. But I'm awful glad you came with me, Mrs. Hale.
      It would be lonesome for me sitting here alone.

98   MRS. HALE. It would, wouldn't it? [*Dropping her sewing.*] But I
      tell you what I do wish, Mrs. Peters. I wish I had come over
      sometimes when *she* was here. I—[*Looking around the
      room.*]—wish I had.

99   MRS. PETERS. But of course you were awful busy, Mrs. Hale—
      your house and your children.

MRS. HALE. I could've come. I stayed away because it weren't 100
cheerful—and that's why I ought to have come. I—I've never
liked this place. Maybe because it's down in a hollow and
you don't see the road. I dunno what it is but it's a lonesome
place and always was. I wish I had come over to see Minnie
Foster sometimes. I can see now—[*Shakes her head.*]

MRS. PETERS. Well, you mustn't reproach yourself, Mrs. Hale. 101
Somehow we just don't see how it is with other folks
until—something comes up.

MRS. HALE. Not having children makes less work—but it makes 102
a quiet house, and Wright out to work all day, and no company when he did come in. Did you know John Wright,
Mrs. Peters?

MRS. PETERS. Not to know him; I've seen him in town. They say 103
he was a good man.

MRS. HALE. Yes—good; he didn't drink, and kept his word as 104
well as most, I guess, and paid his debts. But he was a hard
man, Mrs. Peters. Just to pass the time of day with him—
[*Shivers.*] Like a raw wind that gets to the bone. [*Pauses,
her eye falling on the cage.*] I should think she would'a
wanted a bird. But what do you suppose went with it?

MRS. PETERS. I don't know, unless it got sick and died. [*She 105
reaches over and swings the broken door, swings it again.
Both women watch it.*]

MRS. HALE. You weren't raised round here, were you? [MRS. 106
PETERS *shakes her head.*] You didn't know—her?

MRS. PETERS. Not till they brought her yesterday. 107

MRS. HALE. She—come to think of it, she was kind of like a bird 108
herself—real sweet and pretty, but kind of timid and—fluttery. How—she—did—change. [*Silence; then as if struck by
a happy thought and relieved to get back to every day things.*]
Tell you what, Mrs. Peters, why don't you take the quilt in
with you? It might take up her mind.

MRS. PETERS. Why, I think that's a real nice idea, Mrs. Hale. 109
There couldn't possibly be any objection to it, could there?
Now, just what would I take? I wonder if her patches are in
here—and her things.

[*They look in the sewing basket.*]

MRS. HALE. Here's some red. I expect this has got sewing things 110
in it. [*Brings out a fancy box.*] What a pretty box. Looks like
something somebody would give you. Maybe her scissors
are in here. [*Opens box. Suddenly puts her hand to her
nose.*] Why—[MRS. PETERS *bends nearer, then turns her face
away.*] There's something wrapped up in this piece of silk.

MRS. PETERS. Why, this isn't her scissors. 111

112 MRS. HALE. [*Lifting the silk.*] Oh, Mrs. Peters—its—[MRS. PETERS *bends closer.*]

113 MRS. PETERS. It's the bird.

114 MRS. HALE. [*Jumping up.*] But, Mrs. Peters—look at it! Its neck! Look at its neck! It's all—other side *to.*

115 MRS. PETERS. Somebody—wrung—its—neck.

[*Their eyes meet. A look of growing comprehension, of horror. Steps are heard outside.* MRS. HALE *slips box under quilt pieces, and sinks into her chair. Enter* SHERIFF *and* COUNTY ATTORNEY. MRS. PETERS *rises.*]

116 COUNTY ATTORNEY. [*As one turning from serious things to little pleasantries.*] Well, ladies, have you decided whether she was going to quilt it or knot it?

117 MRS. PETERS. We think she was going to—knot it.

118 COUNTY ATTORNEY. Well, that's interesting, I'm sure. [*Seeing the birdcage.*] Has the bird flown?

119 MRS. HALE. [*Putting more quilt pieces over the box.*] We think the—cat got it.

120 COUNTY ATTORNEY. [*Preoccupied.*] Is there a cat?

[MRS HALE *glances in a quick covert way at* MRS. PETERS.]

121 MRS. PETERS. Well, not *now.* They're superstitious, you know. They leave.

122 COUNTY ATTORNEY. [*To* SHERIFF PETERS, *continuing an interrupted conversation.*] No sign at all of anyone having come from the outside. Their own rope. Now let's go up again and go over it piece by piece. [*They start upstairs.*] It would have to have been someone who knew just the—[MRS. PETERS *sits down. The two women sit there not looking at one another, but as if peering into something and at the same time holding back. When they talk now it is in the manner of feeling their way over strange ground, as if afraid of what they are saying, but as if they can not help saying it.*]

123 MRS. HALE. She liked the bird. She was going to bury it in that pretty box.

124 MRS. PETERS. [*In a whisper.*] When I was a girl—my kitten—there was a boy took a hatchet, and before my eyes—and before I could get there—[*Covers her face an instant.*] If they hadn't held me back I would have—[*Catches herself, looks upstairs where steps are heard, falters weakly.*]—hurt him.

125 MRS. HALE. [*With a slow look around her.*] I wonder how it would seem never to have had any children around. [*Pause.*] No, Wright wouldn't like the bird—a thing that sang. She used to sing. He killed that, too.

126 MRS. PETERS. [*Moving uneasily.*] We don't know who killed the bird.

MRS. HALE. I knew John Wright.   127

MRS. PETERS. It was an awful thing was done in this house that   128
night, Mrs. Hale. Killing a man while he slept, slipping a
rope around his neck that choked the life out of him.

MRS. HALE. His neck. Choked the life out of him.   129
[Her hand goes out and rests on the birdcage.]

MRS. PETERS. [With rising voice.] We don't know who killed him.   130
We don't know.

MRS. HALE. [Her own feeling not interrupted.] If there'd been   131
years and years of nothing, then a bird to sing to you, it
would be awful—still, after the bird was still.

MRS. PETERS. [Something within her speaking.] I know what still-   132
ness is. When we homesteaded in Dakota, and my first
baby died—after he was two years old, and me with no
other then—

MRS. HALE. [Moving.] How soon do you suppose they'll be   133
through, looking for the evidence?

MRS. PETERS. I know what stillness is. [Pulling herself back.] The   134
law has got to punish crime, Mrs. Hale.

MRS. HALE. [Not as if answering that.] I wish you'd seen Minnie   135
Foster when she wore a white dress with blue ribbons and
stood up there in the choir and sang. [A look around the
room.] Oh, I wish I'd come over here once in a while! That
was a crime! That was a crime! Who's going to punish
that?

MRS. PETERS. [Looking upstairs.] We mustn't—take on.   136

MRS. HALE. I might have known she needed help! I know how   137
things can be—for women. I tell you, it's queer, Mrs. Peters.
We live close together and we live far apart. We all go
through the same things—it's all just a different kind of the
same thing. [Brushes her eyes; noticing the bottle of fruit,
reaches out for it.] If I was you I wouldn't tell her her fruit
was gone. Tell her it ain't. Tell her it's all right. Take this in
to prove it to her. She—she may never know whether it was
broke or not.

MRS. PETERS. [Takes the bottle, looks about for something to wrap   138
it in; takes petticoat from the clothes brought from the other
room, very nervously begins winding this around the bottle.
In a false voice.] My, it's a good thing the men couldn't hear
us. Wouldn't they just laugh! Getting all stirred up over a
little thing like a—dead canary. As if that could have anything to do with—with—wouldn't they laugh!
[The men are heard coming down stairs.]

MRS. HALE. [Under her breath.] Maybe they would—maybe they   139
wouldn't.

140   COUNTY ATTORNEY. No, Peters, it's all perfectly clear except a rea-
      son for doing it. But you know juries when it comes to
      women. If there was some definite thing. Something to
      show—something to make a story about—a thing that
      would connect up with this strange way of doing it—[*The
      women's eyes meet for an instant. Enter* HALE *from outer door.*]
141   HALE. Well, I've got the team around. Pretty cold out there.
142   COUNTY ATTORNEY. I'm going to stay here a while by myself. [*To
      the* sheriff.] You can send Frank out for me, can't you? I
      want to go over everything. I'm not satisfied that we can't
      do better.
143   SHERIFF. Do you want to see what Mrs. Peters is going to take
      in? [*The* COUNTY ATTORNEY *goes to the table, picks up the apron,
      laughs.*]
144   COUNTY ATTORNEY. Oh, I guess they're not very dangerous things
      the ladies have picked out. [*Moves a few things about, dis-
      turbing the quilt pieces which cover the box. Steps back.*] No,
      Mrs. Peters doesn't need supervising. For that matter, a
      sheriff's wife is married to the law. Ever think of it that way,
      Mrs. Peters?
145   MRS. PETERS. Not—just that way.
146   SHERIFF. [*Chuckling.*] Married to the law. [*Moves toward the
      other room.*] I just want you to come in here a minute,
      George. We ought to take a look at these windows.
147   COUNTY ATTORNEY. [*Scoffingly.*] Oh, windows!
148   SHERIFF. We'll be right out, Mr. Hale.
      [HALE *goes outside. The* SHERIFF *follows the* COUNTY ATTORNEY
      into the other room. Then MRS. HALE *rises, hands tight
      together, looking intensely at* MRS. PETERS, *whose eyes make a
      slow turn, finally meeting* MRS. HALE's. *A moment* MRS. HALE
      *holds her, then her own eyes point the way to where the box
      is concealed. Suddenly* MRS. PETERS *throws back quilt pieces
      and tries to put the box in the bag she is wearing. It is too big.
      She opens box, starts to take bird out, cannot touch it, goes
      to pieces, stands there helpless. Sound of a knob turning in
      the other room.* MRS. HALE *snatches the box and puts it in the
      pocket of her big coat. Enter* COUNTY ATTORNEY *and* SHERIFF.]
149   COUNTY ATTORNEY. [*Facetiously.*] Well, Henry, at least we found
      out that she was not going to quilt it. She was going to—
      what is it you call it, ladies?
150   MRS. HALE. [*Her hand against her pocket.*] We call it—knot it,
      Mr. Henderson.

CURTAIN

Diane Wakoski

Belly Dancer

Diane Wakoski (born 1937) has spent much of her life in New York, though she was born in Whittier, California, and edu-cated at Berkeley. She now teaches at Michigan State University. This poem is from Trilogy *(1966), one of several collections of her poetry.*

Can these movements which move themselves   1
be the substance of my attraction?
Where does this thin green silk come from that covers my
  body?
Surely any woman wearing such fabrics
would move her body just to feel them touching every part of
  her.

Yet most of the women frown, or look away, or laugh stiffly.   2
They are afraid of these materials and these movements in
  some way.
The psychologists would say they are afraid of themselves,
  somehow.
Perhaps awakening too much desire—
that their men could never satisfy?

So they keep themselves laced and buttoned and made up   3
in hopes that the framework will keep them stiff enough not
  to feel
the whole register.
In hopes that they will not have to experience that un-quench-
  able desire for rhythm and contact.

If a snake glided across this floor   4
most of them would faint or shrink away.
Yet that movement could be their own.
That smooth movement frightens them—
awakening ancestors and relatives to the tips of the arms and
  toes.

So my bare feet   5
and my thin green silks
my bells and finger cymbals
offend them—frighten their old-young bodies.

While the men simper and leer—
glad for the vicarious experience and exercise.
They do not realize how I scorn them:
or how I dance for their frightened,
unawakened, sweet
women.

Jamaica Kincaid

Girl

*Born in St. Johns, on the Caribbean island of Antigua (the sub-
ject and setting of her 1988 book* Small Place*), Jamaica
Kincaid now lives with her family in Vermont. She is the
author of a number of books of fiction, most of them derived
from her own personal experiences, including* At the Bottom of
the River *(1983), which contains the following chapter, titled
"Girl." "Girl" also stands quite well on its own, however: Indeed,
it first appeared on its own in the pages of* The New Yorker, *a
monthly review of arts, letters, and public affairs that has a
reputation for publishing outstanding writing and writers.*

Wash the white clothes on Monday and put them on the
stone heap; wash the color clothes on Tuesday and put them
on the clothesline to dry; don't walk barehead in the hot sun;
cook pumpkin fritters in very hot sweet oil; soak your little
clothes right after you take them off; when buying cotton to
make yourself a nice blouse, be sure that it doesn't have gum
on it, because that way it won't hold up well after a wash;
soak salt fish overnight before you cook it; is it true that you
sing benna in Sunday school?; always eat your food in such a
way that it won't turn someone else's stomach; on Sundays try
to walk like a lady and not like the slut you are so bent on
becoming; don't sing benna in Sunday school; you mustn't
speak to wharf-rat boys, not even to give directions; don't eat
fruits on the street—flies will follow you; *but I don't sing
benna on Sundays at all and never in Sunday school;* this is
how to sew on a button; this is how to make a buttonhole for
the button you have just sewed on; this is how to hem a dress

when you see the hem coming down and so to prevent yourself from looking like the slut I know you are so bent on
becoming; this is how you iron your father's khaki shirt so
that it doesn't have a crease; this is how you iron your father's
khaki pants so that they don't have a crease; this is how you
grow okra—far from the house, because okra tree harbors red
ants; when you are growing dasheen, make sure it gets plenty
of water or else it makes your throat itch when you are eating
it; this is how you sweep a corner; this is how you sweep a
whole house; this is how you sweep a yard; this is how you
smile to someone you don't like too much; this how you smile
to someone you don't like at all; this is how you smile to
someone you like completely; this is how you set a table for
tea; this is how you set a table for dinner; this is how you set
a table for dinner with an important guest; this is how you set
a table for lunch; this is how you set a table for breakfast; this
is how to behave in the presence of men who don't know you
very well, and this way they won't recognize immediately the
slut I have warned you against becoming; be sure to wash
every day, even if it is with your own spit; don't squat down to
play marbles—you are not a boy, you know; don't pick people's flowers—you might catch something; don't throw stones
at blackbirds, because it might not be a blackbird at all; this is
how to make a bread pudding; this is how to make doukona;
this is how to make pepper pot; this is how to make a good
medicine for a cold; this is how to make a good medicine to
throw away a child before it even becomes a child; this is how
to catch a fish; this is how to throw back a fish you don't like,
and that way something bad won't fall on you; this is how to
bully a man; this is how a man bullies you; this is how to love
a man, and if this doesn't work there are other ways, and if
they don't work don't feel too bad about giving up; this is how
to spit up in the air if you feel like it and this is how to move
quick so that it doesn't fall on you; this is how to make ends
meet; always squeeze bread to make sure it's fresh; *but what if
the baker won't let me feel the bread?;* you mean to say that
after all you are really going to be the kind of woman who the
baker won't let near the bread?

Judy Syfers Brady
Why I Want a Wife

*Judy Syfers Brady (born in 1937), active in support of women's
causes, was educated at the University of Iowa. She now lives
in San Francisco. This well-known essay appeared in the very
first issue of* Ms. *in 1972.*

1   I belong to that classification of people known as wives. I
am A Wife. And, not altogether incidentally, I am a mother.

2   Not too long ago a male friend of mine appeared on the
scene fresh from a recent divorce. He had one child, who is,
of course, with his ex-wife. He is looking for another wife. As
I thought about him while I was ironing one evening, it suddenly occurred to me that I, too, would like to have a wife.
Why do I want a wife?

3   I would like to go back to school so that I can become economically independent, support myself, and, if need be, support those dependent upon me. I want a wife who will work
and send me to school. And while I am going to school I want
a wife to take care of my children. I want a wife to keep track
of the children's doctor and dentist appointments. And to
keep track of mine, too. I want a wife to make sure my children eat properly and are kept clean. I want a wife who will
wash the children's clothes and keep them mended. I want a
wife who is a good nurturant attendant to my children, who
arranges for their schooling, makes sure that they have an
adequate social life with their peers, takes them to the park,
the zoo, etc. I want a wife who takes care of the children
when they are sick, a wife who arranges to be around when
the children need special care, because, of course I cannot
miss classes at school. My wife must arrange to lose time at
work and not lose the job. It may mean a small cut in my
wife's income from time to time, but I guess I can tolerate
that. Needless to say, my wife will arrange and pay for the
care of the children while my wife is working.

4   I want a wife who will take care of *my* physical needs. I
want a wife who will keep my house clean. A wife who will
pick up after my children, a wife who will pick up after me. I
want a wife who will keep my clothes clean, ironed, mended,
replaced when need be, and who will see to it that my personal things are kept in their proper place so that I can find
what I need the minute I need it. I want a wife who cooks the

meals, a wife who is a *good* cook. I want a wife who will plan the menus, do the necessary grocery shopping, prepare the meals, serve them pleasantly, and then do the cleaning up while I do my studying. I want a wife who will care for me when I am sick and sympathize with my pain and loss of time from school. I want a wife to go along when our family takes a vacation so that someone can continue to care for me and my children when I need a rest and a change of scene.

I want a wife who will not bother me with rambling complaints about a wife's duties. But I want a wife who will listen to me when I feel the need to explain a rather difficult point I have come across in my course of studies. I want a wife who will type my papers for me when I have written them.   5

I want a wife who will take care of the details of my social life. When my wife and I are invited out by my friends, I want a wife who will take care of the babysitting arrangements. When I meet people at school that I like and want to entertain, I want a wife who will have the house clean, will prepare a special meal, serve it to me and my friends, and not interrupt when I talk about things that interest me and my friends. I want a wife who will have arranged that the children are fed and ready for bed before my guests arrive so that the children do not bother us. I want a wife who takes care of the needs of my guests so that they feel comfortable, who makes sure that they have an ashtray, that they are passed the hors d'oeuvres, that they are offered a second helping of the food, that their wine glasses are replenished when necessary, that their coffee is served to them as they like it. And I want a wife who knows that sometimes I need a night out by myself.   6

I want a wife who is sensitive to my sexual needs, a wife who makes love passionately and eagerly when I feel like it, a wife who makes sure that I am satisfied. And, of course, I want a wife who will not demand sexual attention when I am not in the mood for it. I want a wife who assumes the complete responsibility for birth control, because I do not want more children. I want a wife who will remain sexually faithful to me so that I do not have to clutter up my intellectual life with jealousies. And I want a wife who understands that *my* sexual needs may entail more than strict adherence to monogamy. I must, after all, be able to relate to people as fully as possible.   7

If, by chance, I find another person more suitable as a wife than the wife I already have, I want the liberty to replace my present wife with another one. Naturally, I will expect a fresh, new life; my wife will take the children and be solely responsible for them so that I am left free.   8

9   When I am through with school and have a job, I want my
wife to quit working and remain at home so that my wife can
more fully and completely take care of a wife's duties.

10   My God, who *wouldn't* want a wife?

Kurt Fernsler

Why I Want a Husband

*Kurt Fernsler (born in 1969) grew up in State College, Pennsyl-
vania, and graduated in 1992 from Penn State with a degree in
finance. He is planning a career in law. The following essay
was written in 1988 for a class of fellow student writers, all of
whom had read Judy Syfers's essay "Why I Want a Wife."*

1   I am not a husband. I am, however, a male, and have a
father who is a husband. I am also fortunate enough to know
a great many men who are husbands and will probably
become a husband myself someday.

2   I recently read Judy Syfers' essay "Why I Want a Wife" and
decided a reply was in order. Though not the most qualified
author for such an undertaking, I felt it my duty to make an
effort. For I now realize that just as Judy Syfers wants a wife,
I want a husband.

3   I want a husband who brings home the bacon. I mean
really rakes in the bucks. After all, I certainly can't have anything less than the best. My husband must be driven to succeed; he must climb the corporate ladder quickly and
efficiently. He must make every payroll and meet every deadline. Anything less would be completely unacceptable.

4   And I want a husband who bears the burden of being the
wage earner without complaint. He must deal with the
stresses of his job without bringing his problems home from
the office so as not to upset me. I want a husband who deals
patiently and lovingly with screaming, fighting kids even after
a tough day. I want a husband who, for fairness sake, does the
dishes (even sometimes the wash) for me so that I can put my
feet up after dinner. And, I want a husband who will leave the

office during a busy day of work to check on a sick child while I'm out on the town shopping.

I want a husband who will gladly eat cold leftovers for a 5 week while I am relaxing with a friend in sunny California. My husband will have to sit through boring PTA meetings and ice-cream socials after a rough day at work. My husband must, of course, be courteous and kind to meddling gossiping friends. (After all, I am entitled to my friends, too.) I want a husband who listens patiently to my panic about the over-sudsing washing machine while he silently sweats about the thousands of dollars he just borrowed from the bank.

I want a husband who keeps the house and lawn looking 6 beautiful in his spare time. He must be willing to spend his Saturday afternoons weeding my garden, and he must give up that tee time with the guys when I decide the grass is a little too long. I want one who makes sure the car is fixed (engines are so complicated and dirty!) and takes care of all the "little" chores around the house—raking leaves in the fall, shoveling snow in the winter, painting the house in spring. And I want one who will take out the garbage. When he's done with these chores, he can take the kids to the zoo or the park or the ballgame because these are things a father should share with his children.

I want a husband who gladly pays for his wife's shopping 7 sprees without ever asking her where all the money goes. He will understand that women need to spend time with their friends. I want a husband who will watch the kids on vacation so my wife can shop and work on her tan. (He must accept the fact that after traveling so many miles, a shopping trip is the only way to wind down.)

And I want my husband to be completely receptive to my 8 sexual needs. He must completely understand when I have a "headache." He will be sensitive to my problems and respect my private life. I want a husband who understands that I must have my freedom. He will be ready to accept the possibility that I may need to "find myself" and may walk out at any time. He will understand, of course, that I will take half of everything we own. He would keep the kids, however, because I would need to start a brand new life for myself.

I want a husband who will do all these things for me for- 9 ever or until I decide we have enough money to retire, or until he has a heart attack and collapses in a heap. Yes, I want a husband.

How could anyone live without one?   10

AFFIRMATIVE ACTION

Shelby Steele

A Negative Vote
on Affirmative Action

A professor of English at San Jose State University, Shelby Steele frequently writes essays on the topic of race in America—particularly on the causes of (and potential cures for) the friction between Black and White Americans. He collected many of those essays (including the one printed here) in his 1990 book The Content of Our Character. *The article first appeared in* The New York Times Magazine *in 1990.*

1   In a few short years, when my two children will be applying to college, the affirmative-action policies by which most universities offer black students some form of preferential treatment will present me with a dilemma. I am a middle-class black, a college professor, far from wealthy, but also well removed from the kind of deprivation that would qualify my children for the label "disadvantaged." Both of them have endured racial insensitivity from whites. They have been called names, have suffered slights and have experienced first hand the peculiar malevolence that racism brings out of people. Yet they have never experienced racial discrimination, have never been stopped by their race on any path they have chosen to follow. Still, their society now tells them that if they will only designate themselves as black on their college applications, they will probably do better in the college lottery than if they conceal this fact. I think there is something of a Faustian bargain in this.

2   Of course many blacks and a considerable number of whites would say that I was sanctimoniously making affirmative action into a test of character. They would say that this small preference is the meagerest recompense for centuries of unrelieved oppression. And to these arguments other very obvious facts must be added. In America, many marginally competent or flatly incompetent whites are hired every day—

some because their white skin suits the conscious or unconscious racial preference of their employers. The white children of alumni are often grandfathered into elite universities in what can only be seen as a residual benefit of historic white privilege. Worse, white incompetence is always an individual matter, but for blacks it is often confirmation of ugly stereotypes. Given that unfairness cuts both ways, doesn't it only balance the scales of history, doesn't this repair, in a small way, the systematic denial under which my children's grandfather lived out his days?

In theory, affirmative action certainly has all the moral   3
symmetry that fairness requires. It is reformist and corrective, even repentent and redemptive. And I would never sneer at these good intentions. Born in the late 1940's in Chicago, I started my education (a charitable term, in this case) in a segregated school, and suffered all the indignities that come to blacks in a segregated society. My father, born in the South, made it only to the third grade before the white man's fields took permanent priority over his formal education. And though he educated himself into an advanced reader with an almost professorial authority, he could only drive a truck for a living, and never earned more than $90 a week in his entire life. So yes, it is crucial to my sense of citizenship, to my ability to identify with the spirit and the interests of America, to know that this country, however imperfectly, recognizes its past sins and wishes to correct them.

Yet good intentions can blind us to the effects they gener-   4
ate when implemented. In our society affirmative action is, among other things, a testament to white good will and to black power, and in the midst of these heavy investments its effects can be hard to see. But after 20 years of implementation I think that affirmative action has shown itself to be more bad than good and that blacks—whom I will focus on in this essay—now stand to lose more from it than they gain.

In talking with affirmative-action administrators and with   5
blacks and whites in general, I found that supporters of affirmative action focus on its good intentions and detractors emphasize its negative effects. It was virtually impossible to find people outside either camp. The closest I came was a white male manager at a large computer company who said, "I think it amounts to reverse discrimination, but I'll put up with a little of that for a little more diversity." But this only makes him a half-hearted supporter of affirmative action. I think many people who don't really like affirmative action support it to one degree or another anyway.

6   I believe they do this because of what happened to white and black Americans in the crucible of the 1960's, when whites were confronted with their racial guilt and blacks tasted their first real power. In that stormy time white absolution and black power coalesced into virtual mandates for society. Affirmative action became a meeting ground for those mandates in the law. At first, this meant insuring equal opportunity. The 1964 civil-rights bill was passed on the understanding that equal opportunity would not mean racial preference. But in the late 60's and early 70's, affirmative action underwent a remarkable escalation of its mission from simple anti-discrimination enforcement to social engineering by means of quotas, goals, timetables, set-asides and other forms of preferential treatment.

7   Legally, this was achieved through a series of executive orders and Equal Employment Opportunity Commission guidelines that allowed racial imbalances in the workplace to stand as proof of racial discrimination. Once it could be assumed that discrimination explained racial imbalances, it became easy to justify group remedies to presumed discrimination rather than the normal case-by-case redress.

8   Even though blacks had made great advances during the 60's without quotas, the white mandate to achieve a new racial innocence and the black mandate to gain power, which came to a head in the very late 60's, could no longer be satisfied by anything less than racial preferences. I don't think these mandates, in themselves, were wrong, because whites clearly needed to do better by blacks and blacks needed more real power in society. But as they came together in affirmative action, their effect was to distort our understanding of racial discrimination. By making black the color of preference, these mandates have reburdened society with the very marriage of color and preference (in reverse) that we set out to eradicate.

9   When affirmative action grew into social engineering, diversity became a golden word. Diversity is a term that applies democratic principles to races and cultures rather than to citizens, despite the fact that there is nothing to indicate that real diversity is the same thing as proportionate representation. Too often the result of this, on campuses for example, has been a democracy of colors rather than of people, an artificial diversity that gives the appearance of an educational parity between black and white students that has not yet been achieved in reality. Here again, racial preferences allow society to leapfrog over the difficult problem of developing blacks to parity with whites and into a cosmetic diversity that covers the blemish of

disparity—a full six years after admission, only 26 to 28 percent of blacks graduate from college.

Racial representation is not the same thing as racial development. Representation can be manufactured; development is always hard earned. But it is the music of innocence and power that we hear in affirmative action that causes us to cling to it and to its distracting emphasis on representation. The fact is that after 20 years of racial preferences the gap between median incomes of black and white families is greater than it was in the 1970's. None of this is to say that blacks don't need policies that insure our right to equal opportunity, but what we need more of is the development that will let us take advantage of society's efforts to include us. 10

I think one of the most troubling effects of racial preferences for blacks is a kind of demoralization. Under affirmative action, the quality that earns us preferential treatment is an implied inferiority. However this inferiority is explained—and it is easily enough explained by the myriad deprivations that grew out of our oppression—it is still inferiority. There are explanations and then there is the fact. And the fact must be borne by the individual as a condition apart from the explanation, apart even from the fact that others like himself also bear this condition. In integrated situations in which blacks must compete with whites who may be better prepared, these explanations may quickly wear thin and expose the individual to racial as well as personal self-doubt. (Of course whites also feel doubt, but only personally, not racially.) 11

What this means in practical terms is that when blacks deliver themselves into integrated situations they encounter a nasty little reflex in whites, a mindless, atavistic reflex that responds to the color black with negative stereotypes, such as intellectual ineptness. I think this reflex embarrasses most whites today and thus it is usually quickly repressed. On an equally atavistic level, the black will be aware of the reflex his color triggers and will feel a stab of horror at seeing himself reflected in this way. He, too, will do a quick repression, but a lifetime of such stabbings is what constitutes his inner realm of racial doubt. Even when the black sees no implication of inferiority in racial preferences, he knows that whites do, so that—consciously or unconsciously—the result is virtually the same. The effect of preferential treatment—the lowering of normal standards to increase black representation—puts blacks at war with an expanded realm of debilitating doubt, so that the doubt itself becomes an unrecognized preoccupation 12

that undermines their ability to perform, especially in integrated situations.

13   I believe another liability of affirmative action comes from
the fact that it indirectly encourages blacks to exploit their
own past victimization. Like implied inferiority, victimization
is what justifies preference, so that to receive the benefits of
preferential treatment one must, to some extent, become
invested in the view of one's self as a victim. In this way, affirmative action nurtures a victim-focused identity in blacks
and sends us the message that there is more power in our
past suffering than in our present achievements.

14   When power itself grows out of suffering, blacks are
encouraged to expand the boundaries of what qualifies as
racial oppression, a situation that can lead us to paint our victimization in vivid colors even as we receive the benefits of
preference. The same corporations and institutions that give
us preference are also seen as our oppressors. At Stanford
University, minority group students—who receive at least the
same financial aid as whites with the same need—recently
took over the president's office demanding, among other
things, more financial aid.

15   But I think one of the worst prices that blacks pay for preference has to do with an illusion. I saw this illusion at work
recently in the mother of a middle-class black student who was
going off to his first semester of college: "They owe us this, so
don't think for a minute that you don't belong there." This is
the logic by which many blacks, and some whites, justify affirmative action—it is something "owed," a form of reparation.
But this logic overlooks a much harder and less digestible reality, that it is impossible to repay blacks living today for the historic suffering of the race. If all blacks were given a million
dollars tomorrow it would not amount to a dime on the dollar
for three centuries of oppression, nor would it dissolve the res-
idues of that oppression that we still carry today. The concept
of historic reparation grows out of man's need to impose on
the world a degree of justice that simply does not exist. Suffering can be endured and overcome, it cannot be repaid. To
think otherwise is to prolong the suffering.

16   Several blacks I spoke with said they were still in favor of
affirmative action because of the "subtle" discrimination
blacks were subject to once they were on the job. One photo-
journalist said, "They have ways of ignoring you." A black
female television producer said: "You can't file a lawsuit when
your boss doesn't invite you to the insider meetings without
ruining your career. So we still need affirmative action." Oth-

ers mentioned the infamous "glass ceiling" through which blacks can see the top positions of authority but never reach them. But I don't think racial preferences are a protection against this subtle discrimination; I think they contribute to it.

In any workplace, racial preferences will always create two-tiered populations composed of preferreds and unpreferred. In the case of blacks and whites, for instance, racial preferences imply that whites are superior just as they imply that blacks are inferior. They not only reinforce America's oldest racial myth but, for blacks, they have the effect of stigmatizing the already stigmatized. 17

I think that much of the "subtle" discrimination that blacks talk about is often (not always) discrimination against the stigma of questionable competence that affirmative action marks blacks with. In this sense, preferences make scapegoats of the very people they seek to help. And it may be that at a certain level employers impose a glass ceiling, but this may not be against the race so much as against the race's reputation for having advanced by color as much as by competence. This ceiling is the point at which corporations shift the emphasis from color to competency and stop playing the affirmative-action game. Here preference backfires for blacks and becomes a taint that holds them back. Of course one could argue that this taint, which is after all in the minds of whites, becomes nothing more than an excuse to discriminate against blacks. And certainly the result is the same in either case— blacks don't get past the glass ceiling. But this argument does not get around the fact that racial preferences now taint this color with a new theme of suspicion that makes blacks even more vulnerable to discrimination. In this crucial yet gray area of perceived competence, preferences make whites look better than they are and blacks worse, while doing nothing whatever to stop the very real discrimination that blacks may encounter. I don't wish to justify the glass ceiling here, but only suggest the very subtle ways that affirmative action revives rather than extinguishes the old rationalizations for racial discrimination. 18

I believe affirmative action is problematic in our society because we have demanded that it create parity between the races rather than insure equal opportunity. Preferential treatment does not teach skills, or educate, or instill motivation. It only passes out entitlement, by color, a situation that in my profession has created an unrealistically high demand for black professors. The social engineer's assumption is that this high demand will inspire more blacks to earn Ph.D's and join 19 the profession. In fact, the number of blacks earning Ph.D's has declined in recent years. Ph.D's must be developed from preschool on. They require family and community support. They must acquire an entire system of values that enables them to work hard while delaying gratification.

20   It now seems clear that the Supreme Court, in a series of recent decisions, is moving away from racial preferences. It has disallowed preferences except in instances of "identified discrimination," eroded the precedent that statistical racial imbalances are prima facie evidence of discrimination, and, in effect, granted white males the right to challenge consent decrees that use preference to achieve racial balances in the workplace. Referring to this and other Supreme Court decisions, one civil-rights leader said, "Night has fallen . . . as far as civil rights are concerned." But I am not so sure. The effect of these decisions is to protect the constitutional rights of everyone rather than to take rights away from blacks. Night has fallen on racial preferences, not on the fundamental rights of black Americans. The reason for this shift, I believe, is that the white mandate for absolution from past racial sins has weakened considerably in the 1980's. Whites are now less willing to endure unfairness to themselves in order to grant special entitlements to blacks, even when those entitlements are justified in the name of past suffering. Yet the black mandate for more power in society has remained unchanged. And I think part of the anxiety many blacks feel over these decisions has to do with the loss of black power that they may signal.

21   But the power we've lost by these decisions is really only the power that grows out of our victimization. This is not a very substantial or reliable power, and it is important that we know this so we can focus more exclusively on the kind of development that will bring enduring power. There is talk now that Congress may pass new legislation to compensate for these new limits on affirmative action. If this happens, I hope the focus will be on development and antidiscrimination, rather than entitlement, on achieving racial parity rather than jerry-building racial diversity.

22   But if not preferences, what? The impulse to discriminate *is* subtle and cannot be ferreted out unless its many guises are made clear to people. I think we need social policies that are committed to two goals: the educational and economic development of disadvantaged people regardless of race and the eradication from our society—through close monitoring and severe sanctions—of racial, ethnic or gender discrimination. Preferences will not get us to either of these goals,

because they tend to benefit those who are not disadvantaged—middle-class white women and middle-class blacks—and attack one form of discrimination with another. Preferences are inexpensive and carry the glamour of good intentions—change the numbers and the good deed is done. To be against them is to be unkind. But I think the unkindest cut is to bestow on children like my own an undeserved advantage while neglecting the development of those disadvantaged children in the poorer sections of my city who will most likely never be in a position to benefit from a preference. Give my children fairness; give disadvantaged children a better shot at development—better elementary and secondary schools, job training, safer neighborhoods, better financial assistance for college and so on. A smaller percentage of black high school graduates go to college today than 15 years ago; more black males are in prison, jail or in some other way under the control of the criminal-justice system than in college. This despite racial preferences.

The mandates of black power and white absolution out of   23
which preferences emerged were not wrong in themselves. What was wrong was that both races focused more on the goals of those mandates than on the means to the goals. Blacks can have no real power without taking responsibility for their own educational and economic development. Whites can have no racial innocence without earning it by eradicating discrimination and helping the disadvantaged to develop. Because we ignored the means, the goals have not been reached and the real work remains to be done.

Roger Wilkins

Racism Has Its Privileges

The Case for Affirmative Action

The Nation, *a highly respected weekly magazine of current public affairs that is liberal in its orientation, published the following essay on March 27, 1995. Roger Wilkins, a member of the editorial board at* The Nation, *is also professor of history at George Mason University in northern Virginia.*

1   The storm that has been gathering over affirmative action for the past few years has burst. Two conservative California professors are leading a drive to place an initiative on the state ballot in 1996 that will ask Californians to vote affirmative action up or down. Since the state is beloved in political circles for its electoral votes, advance talk of the initiative has put the issue high on the national agenda. Three Republican presidential contenders—Bob Dole, Phil Gramm and Lamar Alexander—have already begun taking shots at various equal opportunity programs. Congressional review of the Clinton Administration's enforcement of these programs has begun. The President has started his own review, promising adherence to principles of nondiscrimination and full opportunity while asserting the need to prune those programs that are unfair or malfunctioning.

2   It is almost an article of political faith that one of the major influences in last November's election was the backlash against affirmative action among "angry white men," who are convinced it has stacked the deck against them. Their attitudes are shaped and their anger heightened by unquestioned and virtually uncheckable anecdotes about victimized whites flooding the culture. For example, *Washington Post* columnist Richard Cohen recently began what purported to be a serious analysis and attack on affirmative action by recounting that he had once missed out on a job someplace because they "needed a woman."

3   Well, I have an anecdote too, and it, together with Cohen's, offers some important insights about the debate that has flared recently around the issues of race, gender and justice. Some years ago, after watching me teach as a visiting professor for two semesters, members of the history department at George Mason University invited me to compete for a full pro-

fessorship and endowed chair. Mason, like other institutions in Virginia's higher education system, was under a court order to desegregate. I went through the appropriate application and review process and, in due course, was appointed. A few years later, not long after I had been honored as one of the university's distinguished professors, I was shown an article by a white historian asserting that he had been a candidate for that chair but that at the last moment the job had been whisked away and handed to an unqualified black. I checked the story and discovered that this fellow had, in fact, applied but had not even passed the first threshold. But his "reverse discrimination" story is out there polluting the atmosphere in which this debate is taking place.

Affirmative action, as I understand it, was not designed to   4
punish anyone; it was, rather—as a result of a clear-eyed look at how America actually works—an attempt to enlarge opportunity for *everybody*. As amply documented in the 1968 Kerner Commission report on racial disorders, when left to their own devices, American institutions in such areas as college admissions, hiring decisions and loan approvals had been making choices that discriminated against blacks. That discrimination, which flowed from doing what came naturally, hurt more than blacks: It hurt the entire nation, as the riots of the late 1960s demonstrated. Though the Kerner report focused on blacks, similar findings could have been made about other minorities and women.

Affirmative action required institutions to develop plans   5
enabling them to go beyond business as usual and search for qualified people in places where they did not ordinarily conduct their searches or their business. Affirmative action programs generally require some proof that there has been a good-faith effort to follow the plan and numerical guidelines against which to judge the sincerity and the success of the effort. The idea of affirmative action is *not* to force people into positions for which they are unqualified but to encourage institutions to develop realistic criteria for the enterprise at hand and then to find a reasonably diverse mix of people qualified to be engaged in it. Without the requirements calling for plans, good-faith efforts and the setting of broad numerical goals, many institutions would do what they had always done: assert that they had looked but "couldn't find anyone qualified," and then go out and hire the white man they wanted to hire in the first place.

Affirmative action has done wonderful things for the United   6
States by enlarging opportunity and developing and utilizing a

far broader array of the skills available in the American population than in the past. It has not outlived its usefulness. It was
never designed to be a program to eliminate poverty. It has not
always been used wisely, and some of its permutations do have
to be reconsidered, refined or, in some cases, abandoned. It is
not a quota program, and those cases where rigid numbers are
used (except under a court or administrative order after a specific finding of discrimination) are a bastardization of an otherwise highly beneficial set of public policies.

7   President Clinton is right to review what is being done
under present laws and to express a willingness to eliminate
activities that either don't work or are unfair. Any program
that has been in place for thirty years should be reviewed.
Getting rid of what doesn't work is both good government
and good politics. Gross abuses of affirmative action provide
ammunition for its opponents and undercut the moral
authority of the entire effort. But the President should
retain—and strengthen where required—those programs necessary to enlarge social justice.

8   What makes the affirmative action issue so difficult is that
it engages blacks and whites exactly at those points where
they differ the most. There are some areas, such as rooting for
the local football team, where their experiences and views are
virtually identical. There are others—sometimes including
work and school—where their experiences and views both
overlap and diverge. And finally, there are areas such as affirmative action and inextricably related notions about the presence of racism in society where the divergences draw out
almost all the points of difference between the races.

This Land Is My Land

9   Blacks and whites experience America very differently.
Though we often inhabit the same space, we operate in very
disparate psychic spheres.

10   Whites have an easy sense of ownership of the country;
they feel they are entitled to receive all that is best in it. Many
of them believe that their country—though it may have some
faults—is superior to all others and that, as Americans, they
are superior as well. Many of them think of this as a white
country and some of them even experience it that way. They
think of it as a land of opportunity—a good place with a lot of
good people in it. Some suspect (others *know*) that the presence of blacks messes everything up.

To blacks there's nothing very easy about life in America,   11
and any sense of ownership comes hard because we encounter so much resistance in making our way through the ordinary occurrences of life. And I'm not even talking here about
overt acts of discrimination but simply about the way whites
intrude on and disturb our psychic space without even thinking about it.

A telling example of this was given to me by a black college   12
student in Oklahoma. He said whites give him looks that say:
"What are *you* doing here?"

"When do they give you that look?" I asked.   13

"Every time I walk in a door," he replied.   14

When he said that, every black person in the room nodded,   15
and smiled in a way that indicated recognition based on thousands of such moments in their own lives.

For most blacks, America is either a land of denied oppor-   16
tunity or one in which the opportunities are still grudgingly
extended and extremely limited. For some—that one-third
who are mired in poverty, many of them isolated in dangerous ghettos—America is a land of desperadoes and despera-
tion. In places where whites see a lot of idealism, blacks see,
at best, idealism mixed heavily with hypocrisy. Blacks accept
America's greatness but are unable to ignore ugly warts that
many whites seem to need not to see. I am reminded here
of James Baldwin's searing observation from *The Fire Next
Time:*

> The American Negro has the great advantage of having never
> believed that collection of myths to which white Americans
> cling: that their ancestors were all freedom-loving heroes,
> that they were born in the greatest country the world has
> ever seen, or that Americans are invincible in battle and wise
> in peace, that Americans have always dealt honorably with
> Mexicans and Indians and all other neighbors or inferiors,
> that American men are the world's most direct and virile,
> that American women are pure.

It goes without saying, then, that blacks and whites   17
remember America differently. The past is hugely important
since we argue a lot about who we are on the basis of who we
think we have been, and we derive much of our sense of the
future from how we think we've done in the past. In a nation
in which few people know much history these are perilous
arguments, because in such a vacuum, people tend to weave
historical fables tailored to their political or psychic needs.

18   Blacks are still recovering the story of their role in America, which so many white historians simply ignored or told in ways that made black people ashamed. But in a culture that batters us, learning the real history is vital in helping blacks feel fully human. It also helps us understand just how deeply American we are, how richly we have given, how much has been taken from us and how much has yet to be restored. Supporters of affirmative action believe that broad and deep damage has been done to American culture by racism and sexism over the whole course of American history and that they are still powerful forces today. We believe that minorities and women are still disadvantaged in our highly competitive society and that affirmative action is absolutely necessary to level the playing field.

19   Not all white Americans oppose this view and not all black Americans support it. There are a substantial number of whites in this country who have been able to escape our racist and sexist past and to enter fully into the quest for equal justice. There are other white Americans who are not racists but who more or less passively accept the powerful suggestions coming at them from all points in the culture that whites are entitled to privilege and to freedom from competition with blacks. And then there are racists who just don't like blacks or who actively despise us. There are still others who may or may not feel deep antipathy, but who know how to manipulate racism and white anxiety for their own ends. Virtually all the people in the last category oppose affirmative action and some of them make a practice of preying upon those in the second category who are not paying attention or who, like the *Post*'s Richard Cohen, are simply confused.

The Politics of Denial

20   One of these political predators is Senate majority leader Bob Dole. In his offhandedly lethal way, Dole delivered a benediction of "let me now forgive us" on *Meet the Press* recently. After crediting affirmative action for the 62 percent of the white male vote garnered by the Republicans, he remarked that slavery was "before we were born" and wondered whether future generations ought to have to continue "paying a price" for those ancient wrongs.

21   Such a view holds that whatever racial problems we once may have had have been solved over the course of the past thirty years and that most of our current racial friction is

caused by racial and gender preferences that almost invariably work to displace some "qualified" white male. Words and
phrases like "punish" or "preference" or "reverse discrimination" or "quota" are dropped into the discourse to buttress
this view, as are those anecdotes about injustice to whites.
Proponents of affirmative action see these arguments as dis-
ingenuous but ingenious because they reduce serious and
complex social, political, economic, historical and psychological issues to bumper-sticker slogans designed to elicit Pavlov-
ian responses.

The fact is that the successful public relations assault on   22
affirmative action flows on a river of racism that is as broad,
powerful and American as the Mississippi. And, like the Mississippi, racism can be violent and deadly and is a permanent
feature of American life. But while nobody who is sane denies
the reality of the Mississippi, millions of Americans who are
deemed sane—some of whom are powerful and some even
thought wise—deny, wholly or in part, that racism exists.

It is critical to understand the workings of denial in this   23
debate because it is used to obliterate the facts that created the
need for the remedy in the first place. One of the best examples
of denial was provided recently by the nation's most famous
former history professor, House Speaker Newt Gingrich.
According to *The Washington Post,* "Gingrich dismissed the
argument that the beneficiaries of affirmative action, commonly African Americans, have been subjected to discrimination over a period of centuries. 'That is true of virtually every
American,' Gingrich said, noting that the Irish were discriminated against by the English, for example."

That is breathtaking stuff coming from somebody who   24
should know that blacks have been on this North American
continent for 375 years and that for 245 the country permitted slavery. Gingrich should also know that for the next hundred years we had legalized subordination of blacks, under a
suffocating blanket of condescension and frequently enforced
by nightriding terrorists. We've had only thirty years of something else.

That something else is a nation trying to lift its ideals out of   25
a thick, often impenetrable slough of racism. Racism is a hard
word for what over the centuries became second nature in
America—preferences across the board for white men and,
following in their wake, white women. Many of these men
seem to feel that it is un-American to ask them to share anything with blacks—particularly their work, their neighborhoods or "their" women. To protect these things—apparently

essential to their identity—they engage in all forms of denial. For a historian to assert that "virtually every American" shares the history I have just outlined comes very close to lying.

26   Denial of racism is much like the denials that accompany addictions to alcohol, drugs or gambling. It is probably not stretching the analogy too much to suggest that many racist whites are so addicted to their unwarranted privileges and so threatened by the prospect of losing them that all kinds of defenses become acceptable, including insistent distortions of reality in the form of hypocrisy, lying or the most outrageous political demagogy.

"Those People" Don't Deserve Help

27   The demagogues have reverted to a new version of quite an old trick. Before the 1950s, whites who were busy denying that the nation was unfair to blacks would simply assert that we didn't deserve equal treatment because we were *inferior*. These days it is not permissible in most public circles to say that blacks are inferior, but it is perfectly acceptable to target the *behavior* of blacks, specifically poor blacks. The argument then follows a fairly predictable line: The behavior of poor blacks requires a severe rethinking of national social policy, it is said. Advantaged blacks really don't need affirmative action anymore, and when they are the objects of such programs, some qualified white person (unqualified white people don't show up in these arguments) is (as Dole might put it) "punished." While it is possible that color-blind affirmative action programs benefiting all disadvantaged Americans are needed, those (i.e., blacks) whose behavior is so distressing must be punished by restricting welfare, shriveling the safety net and expanding the prison opportunity. All of that would presumably give us, in William Bennett's words, "what we want—a color-blind society," for which the white American psyche is presumably fully prepared.

28   There are at least three layers of unreality in these precepts. The first is that the United States is not now and probably never will be a color-blind society. It is the most color-conscious society on earth. Over the course of 375 years, whites have given blacks absolutely no reason to believe that they can behave in a color-blind manner. In many areas of our lives—particularly in employment, housing and education— affirmative action is required to counter deeply ingrained racist patterns of behavior.

Second, while I don't hold the view that all blacks who 29
behave badly are blameless victims of a brutal system, I do
believe that many poor blacks have, indeed, been brutalized
by our culture, and I know of *no* blacks, rich or poor, who
haven't been hurt in some measure by the racism in this
country. The current mood (and, in some cases like the
Speaker's, the cultivated ignorance) completely ignores the
fact that some blacks never escaped the straight line of
oppression that ran from slavery through the semislavery of
sharecropping to the late mid-century migration from Southern farms into isolated pockets of urban poverty. Their families have always been excluded, poor and without skills, and
so they were utterly defenseless when the enormous American economic dislocations that began in the mid-1970s
slammed into their communities, followed closely by deadly
waves of crack cocaine. One would think that the double-digit
unemployment suffered consistently over the past two
decades by blacks who were *looking for work* would be a permanent feature of the discussions about race, responsibility,
welfare and rights.

But a discussion of the huge numbers of black workers who 30
are becoming economically redundant would raise difficult
questions about the efficiency of the economy at a time when
millions of white men feel insecure. Any honest appraisal of
unemployment would reveal that millions of low-skilled white
men were being severely damaged by corporate and Federal
Reserve decisions; it might also refocus the anger of those
whites in the middle ranks whose careers have been shattered
by the corporate downsizing fad.

But people's attention is kept trained on the behavior of 31
some poor blacks by politicians and television news shows,
reinforcing the stereotypes of blacks as dangerous, as threats,
as unqualified. Frightened whites direct their rage at pushy
blacks rather than at the corporations that export manufacturing operations to low-wage countries, or at the Federal
Reserve, which imposes interest rate hikes that slow down
the economy.

Who Benefits? We All Do

There is one final denial that blankets all the rest. It is that 32
only society's "victims"—blacks, other minorities and women
(who should, for God's sake, renounce their victimological out-
looks)—have been injured by white male supremacy. Viewed

in this light, affirmative action remedies are a kind of zero-sum game in which only the "victims" benefit. But racist and sexist whites who are not able to accept the full humanity of other people are themselves badly damaged—morally stunted—people. The principal product of a racist and sexist society is damaged people and institutions—victims and victimizers alike. Journalism and education, two enterprises with which I am familiar, provide two good examples.

33   Journalistic institutions often view the nation through a lens that bonds reality to support white privilege. A recent issue of *U.S. News & World Report* introduced a package of articles on these issues with a question on its cover: "Does affirmative action mean NO WHITE MEN NEED APPLY?" The words "No white men need apply" were printed in red against a white background and were at least four times larger than the other words in the question. Inside, the lead story was illustrated by a painting that carries out the cover theme, with a wan white man separated from the opportunity ladders eagerly being scaled by women and dark men. And the story yielded up the following sentence: "Affirmative action poses a conflict between two cherished American principles: the belief that all Americans deserve equal opportunities and the idea that hard work and merit, not race or religion or gender or birthright, should determine who prospers and who does not."

34   Whoever wrote that sentence was in the thrall of one of the myths that Baldwin was talking about. The sentence suggests—as many people do when talking about affirmative action—that America is a meritocratic society. But what kind of meritocracy excludes women and blacks and other minorities from all meaningful competition? And even in the competition among white men, money, family and connections often count for much more than merit, test results (for whatever they're worth) and hard work.

35   The *U.S. News* story perpetuates and strengthens the view that many of my white students absorb from their parents: that white men now have few chances in this society. The fact is that white men still control virtually everything in America except the wealth held by widows. According to the Urban Institute, 53 percent of black men aged 25-34 are either unemployed or earn too little to lift a family of four from poverty.

36   Educational institutions that don't teach accurately about why America looks the way it does and why the distribution of winners and losers is as it is also injure our society. Here is another anecdote.

A warm, brilliant young white male student of mine came   37
in just before he was to graduate and said that my course in
race, law and culture, which he had just finished, had been
the most valuable and the most disturbing he had ever taken.
I asked how it had been disturbing.

"I learned that my two heroes are racists," he said.   38
"Who are your heroes and how are they racists?" I asked.   39
"My mom and dad," he said. "After thinking about what I   40
was learning, I understood that they had spent all my life
making me into the same kind of racists they were."

Affirmative action had brought me together with him   41
when he was 22. Affirmative action puts people together in
ways that make that kind of revelation possible. Nobody is a
loser when that happens. The country gains.

And that, in the end, is the case for affirmative action. The   42
arguments supporting it should be made on the basis of its
broad contributions to the entire American community. It is
insufficient to vilify white males and to skewer them as the
whiners that journalism of the kind practiced by *U.S. News*
invites us to do. These are people who, from the beginning of
the Republic, have been taught that skin color is destiny and
that whiteness is to be revered. Listen to Jefferson, writing in
the year the Constitution was drafted:

> The first difference that strikes us is that of colour. . . . And is
> the difference of no importance? Is it not the foundation of a
> greater or less share of beauty in the two races? Are not the
> fine mixtures of red and white . . . in the one, preferable to that
> eternal monotony, which reigns in the countenances, that
> immoveable veil of black which covers all the emotions of the
> other race? Add to these, flowing hair, a more elegant symme-
> try of form, their own judgment in favor of the whites,
> declared by their preference for them, as uniformly as is the
> preference of the Oran-ootan for the black women over those
> of his own species. The circumstance of superior beauty, is
> thought worthy attention in the propagation of our horses,
> dogs, and other domestic animals; why not in that of man?

In a society so conceived and so dedicated, it is understandable that white males would take their preferences as a matter of natural right and consider any alteration of that a
primal offense. But a nation that operates in that way aban-
dons its soul and its economic strength, and will remain
mired in ugliness and moral squalor because so many people

are excluded from the possibility of decent lives and from forming any sense of community with the rest of society.

43   Seen only as a corrective for ancient wrongs, affirmative action may be dismissed by the likes of Gingrich, Gramm and Dole, just as attempts to federalize decent treatment of the freed slaves were dismissed after Reconstruction more than a century ago. Then, striking down the Civil Rights Act of 1875, Justice Joseph Bradley wrote of blacks that "there must be some stage in the progress of his elevation when he takes the rank of a mere citizen, and ceases to be the special favorite of the laws, and when his rights, as a citizen or a man, are to be protected in the ordinary modes by which other men's rights are protected."

44   But white skin has made some citizens—particularly white males—*the special favorites of the culture.* It may be that we will need affirmative action until most white males are really ready for a color-blind society—that is, when they are ready to assume "the rank of a mere citizen." As a nation we took a hard look at that special favoritism thirty years ago. Though the centuries of cultural preference enjoyed by white males still overwhelmingly skew power and wealth their way, we have in fact achieved a more meritocratic society as a result of affirmative action than we have ever previously enjoyed in this country.

45   If we want to continue making things better in this society, we'd better figure out ways to protect and defend affirmative action against the confused, the frightened, the manipulators and, yes, the liars in politics, journalism, education and wherever else they may be found. In the name of longstanding American prejudice and myths and in the service of their own narrow interests, power-lusts or blindness, they are truly victimizing the rest of us, perverting the ideals they claim to stand for and destroying the nation they pretend to serve.

Migdia Chinea-Varela
My Life as a "Twofer"

Migdia Chinea-Varela contributed this essay to Newsweek *on December 26, 1988.*

This Christmas I'll be celebrating my 10th anniversary as a   1
card-carrying member of the film industry's Writers Guild. Ten
brain-numbing years and a debilitating employment lull during the five-month-long writers' strike have taken their toll.
Last week I'd awakened in what can only be described as profound financial melancholia and was taking inventory of my
career alternatives when the phone rang. The caller was a
friend at the Writers Guild of America, West. Great news, he
said. Several production companies were starting "access"
programs for minorities, women, the elderly and the disabled.
They'd requested a sampler of scripts ASAP from which to fish
out two, maybe *three* writers for free-lance assignments. It
could even lead to staff jobs, he said.

My imagination flashes to a TV scene in which I grab the   2
lifeline and submit my best script. I subsequently get chosen
for a plum writing assignment that quickly turns into a staff
position, where I do such a bang-up job that I become the
show's producer and an Emmy award winner as well. In real
life, however, I thank the guide rep for his good-faith efforts
and tell him that my answer is no. Though I helped found and
then chaired the Latino writer's committee, I don't want to
send in my scripts.

Why? Why would anyone pass up such a sweet deal? Every-   3
one knows how tough the film and television industry is. Yet
contacts are everything, the insiders say. It helps if you have an
agent with hot connections who believes in you and is willing
to put in the time required to promote your career. It helps if
you attended the "right" film school. It's a matter of timing. It's
difficult for everyone. Yes, but consider this—if you're a member of a minority group, the equation should be multiplied by
10; and if you're a minority woman, then add 30 more points.

So what's my problem? Why not take advantage of every   4
opportunity that comes my way? The answer is: I've been in
this situation before and I don't like the way it makes me feel.
There's something almost insulting about these well-meaning
affirmative-action searches. In the past I'd always rationalized my participation partly because I needed the break and

even more because I needed the money. And as fate would have it, whenever a film- or TV-production company saw fit to round up minorities for a head count, I always came out on top. But the truth is that I've never felt good about it.

5   I've asked myself the obvious questions. Am I being picked for my writing ability, or to fulfill a quota? Have I been selected because I'm a "twofer"—a female Hispanic—or because they were enthralled with my deftly drawn characters and strong, original story line? My writing career, it appears, has taken a particularly tortuous course. I've gone from being a dedicated writer to dedicated *minority* writer, which seems limiting for someone who was first inspired by Woody Allen.

6   Truth is, that even with the aid of special programs, job assignments for writers who fit the "minority" category are inexplicably few and far between. The sad employment statistics reveal that ethnic minorities comprise less than 3 percent of our guild. Those who work do so less frequently and for a lot less money, yet the publicity harvested by the special programs creates the illusion of equal opportunity where very little exists. I don't want to seem overly gloomy. Nevertheless, my work's almost always seen on shows that have a minority star like "The Facts of Life," "What's Happening Now!" and "Punky Brewster."

7   Except for "The Cosby Show," minorities are not being taken seriously enough to write about their real lives outside of the ghetto. Though few of us will admit to it—for fear of speaking out or being tagged as ungrateful—we're reminded of our status in not-so-subtle ways. I remember the time I was waiting for a story meeting where I wanted to pitch several ideas. As I chatted with the production secretary, an aspiring writer herself, I could hear laughter coming from inside the conference room. Finally, the executive in charge stepped outside, followed by five young men. Judging by the look of satisfaction on their faces, it had probably been a profitable session. The executive greeted me effusively by saying, as he turned to the rest of the group, "Meet M-I-G-D-I-A V-A-R-R-R-R-E-L-A. She's one of our minority writers." This comment drew a tight smile from my lips, as one and all present reacted with extravagant expressions of support. Somehow I knew right then and there that my project would be down for the count. KO'd with kindness.

8   ***Killer sharks:*** More recently, I was spilling my guts to a friend with a recognizable name whose uncle was a famous writer. After sharing my woes and commiserating as fellow

writers often do, we parted with that old cliché: "We're in the same boat." Suddenly it dawned on me that hell *no*, we're not even close. We're no doubt on the same ocean, but hardly in the same boat. From where I sit, my friend's being attended to on a luxury liner while I'm all alone paddling a canoe, surrounded by killer sharks and in the midst of a typhoon.

I'd like to think that after 10 years of paying my dues as a   9
professional writer that I've earned the right to walk through the front door. After so many years, it's depressing to feel that I have to tag myself a minority as an incentive to those who may hire me. Why can't I get a job on my own merits? Am I destined to spend the rest of my writing career hooked up to these kinds of life-support systems?

I'm painfully aware that affirmative action, what little   10
there is of it, may be the only way minorities are given a chance to compete. However, for me, it has become a stigma of sorts. In my view, there can be no affirmative action without segregation—nor any end to the segregation if our names must be kept on separate lists. I'd like to propose instead a simple scenario: a fair job market where employment is commensurate with ability regardless of gender, racial or ethnic background. I make a pitch, they like my story, I get the job. Why not?

Richard Kahlenberg
Class, Not Race

Richard Kahlenberg has completed a book on class-based affirmative action. On April 3, 1995, he contributed the following to The New Republic, *a politically middle-of-the-road publication on current affairs.*

In an act that reflected panic as much as cool reflection,   1
Bill Clinton said recently that he is reviewing all federal affirmative action programs to see "whether there is some other way we can reach [our] objective without giving a preference by race or gender." As the country's mood swings violently against affirmative action, and as Republicans gear up to use the issue to bludgeon the Democratic coalition yet again in

1996, the whole project of legislating racial equality seems suddenly in doubt. The Democrats, terrified of the issue, are now hoping it will just go away. It won't. But at every political impasse, there is a political opportunity. Bill Clinton now has a chance, as no other Democrat has had since 1968, to turn a glaring liability for his party into an advantage—without betraying basic Democratic principles.

2   There is, as Clinton said, a way "we can work this out." But it isn't the *"Bakke* straddle," which says yes to affirmative action (race as a factor) but no to quotas. It isn't William Julius Wilson's call to "emphasize" race-neutral social programs, while downplaying affirmative action. The days of downplaying are gone; we can count on the Republicans for that. The way out—an idea Clinton hinted at—is to introduce the principle of race neutrality and the goal of aiding the disadvantaged into affirmative action preference programs themselves: to base preferences, in education, entry-level employment and public contracting, on class, not race.

3   Were Clinton to propose this move, the media would charge him with lurching to the right. Jesse Jackson's presidential campaign would surely soon follow. But despite its association with conservatives such as Clarence Thomas, Antonin Scalia and Dinesh D'Souza, the idea of class-based affirmative action should in fact appeal to the left as well. After all, its message of addressing class unfairness and its political potential for building cross-racial coalitions are traditional liberal staples.

4   For many years, the left argued not only that class was important, but also that it was more important than race. This argument was practical, ideological and politic. An emphasis on class inequality meant Robert Kennedy riding in a motorcade through cheering white and black sections of racially torn Gary, Indiana, in 1968, with black Mayor Richard Hatcher on one side, and white working-class boxing hero Tony Zale on the other.

5   Ideologically, it was clear that with the passage of the Civil Rights Act of 1964, class replaced caste as the central impediment to equal opportunity. Martin Luther King Jr. moved from the Montgomery Boycott to the Poor People's Campaign, which he described as "his last, greatest dream," and "something bigger than just a civil rights movement for Negroes." RFK told David Halberstam that "it was pointless to talk about the real problem in America being black and white, it was really rich and poor, which was a much more complex subject."

Finally, the left emphasized class because to confuse class   6
and race was seen not only as wrong but as dangerous. This
notion was at the heart of the protest over Daniel Patrick
Moynihan's 1965 report, *The Negro Family: The Case for
National Action*, in which Moynihan depicted the rising rates
of illegitimacy among poor blacks. While Moynihan's critics
were wrong to silence discussion of illegitimacy among
blacks, they rightly noted that the title of the report, which
implicated all blacks, was misleading, and that fairly high
rates of illegitimacy also were present among poor whites—a
point which Moynihan readily endorses today. (In the wake of
the second set of L.A. riots in 1992, Moynihan rose on the
Senate floor to reaffirm that family structure "is not an issue
of race but of class.... It is class behavior.")

The irony is that affirmative action based on race violates   7
these three liberal insights. It provides the ultimate wedge to
destroy Robert Kennedy's coalition. It says that despite civil
rights protections, the wealthiest African American is more
deserving of preference than the poorest white. It relentlessly
focuses all attention on race.

In contrast, Lyndon Johnson's June 1965 address to   8
Howard University, in which the concept of affirmative action
was first unveiled, did not ignore class. In a speech drafted by
Moynihan, Johnson spoke of the bifurcation of the black
community, and, in his celebrated metaphor, said we needed
to aid those "hobbled" in life's race by past discrimination.
This suggested special help for disadvantaged blacks, not all
blacks; for the young Clarence Thomas, but not for Clarence
Thomas's son. Johnson balked at implementing the thematic
language of his speech. His Executive Order 11246, calling for
"affirmative action" among federal contractors, initially
meant greater outreach and required hiring without respect
to race. In fact, LBJ rescinded his Labor Department's proposal to provide for racial quotas in the construction industry
in Philadelphia. It fell to Richard Nixon to implement the
"Philadelphia Plan," in what Nixon's aides say was a conscious effort to drive a wedge between blacks and labor.
(Once he placed racial preferences on the table, Nixon
adroitly extricated himself, and by 1972 was campaigning
against racial quotas.)

The ironies were compounded by the Supreme Court. In   9
the 1974 case *DeFunis v. Odegaard*, in which a system of
racial preferences in law school admissions was at issue, it
was the Court's liberal giant, William O. Douglas, who argued
that racial preferences were unconstitutional, and suggested

instead that preferences be based on disadvantage. Four years later, in the *Bakke* case, the great proponent of affirmative action as a means to achieve "diversity" was Nixon appointee Lewis F. Powell Jr. Somewhere along the line, the right wing embraced Douglas and Critical Race Theory embraced Powell.

10   Today, the left pushes racial preferences, even for the most advantaged minorities, in order to promote diversity and provide role models for disadvantaged blacks—an argument which, if it came from Ronald Reagan, the left would rightly dismiss as trickle-down social theory. Today, when William Julius Wilson argues the opposite of the Moynihan report— that the problems facing the black community are rooted more in class than race—it is Wilson who is excoriated by civil rights groups. The left can barely utter the word "class," instead resorting to euphemisms such as "income groups," "wage earners" and "people who play by the rules."

11   For all of this, the left has paid a tremendous price. On a political level, with a few notable exceptions, the history of the past twenty-five years is a history of white, working-class Robert Kennedy Democrats turning first into Wallace Democrats, then into Nixon and Reagan Democrats and ultimately into today's Angry White Males. Time and again, the white working class votes its race rather than its class, and Republicans win. The failure of the left to embrace class also helps turn poor blacks, for whom racial preferences are, in Stephen Carter's words, "stunningly irrelevant," toward Louis Farrakhan.

12   On the merits, the left has committed itself to a goal— equality of group results—which seems highly radical, when it is in fact rather unambitious. To the extent that affirmative action, at its ultimate moment of success, merely creates a self-perpetuating black elite along with a white one, its goal is modest—certainly more conservative than real equality of opportunity, which gives blacks and whites and other Americans of all economic strata a fair chance at success.

13   The priority given to race over class has inevitably exacerbated white racism. Today, both liberals and conservatives conflate race and class because it serves both of their purposes to do so. Every year, when SAT scores are released, the breakdown by race shows enormous gaps between blacks on the one hand and whites and Asians on the other. The NAACP cites these figures as evidence that we need to do more. Charles Murray cites the same statistics as evidence of intractable racial differences. We rarely see a breakdown of scores

by class; which would show enormous gaps between rich and poor, gaps that would help explain the differences in scores by race.

On the legal front, it once made some strategic sense to emphasize race over class. But when states moved to the remedial phrase—and began trying to address past discrimination—the racial focus became a liability. The strict scrutiny that struck down Jim Crow is now used, to varying degrees, to curtail racial preferences. Class, on the other hand, is not one of the suspect categories under the Fourteenth Amendment, which leaves class-based remedies much less assailable.   14

If class-based affirmative action is a theory that liberals should take seriously, how would it work in practice? In this magazine, Michael Kinsley has asked, "Does Clarence Thomas, the sharecropper's kid, get more or fewer preference points than the unemployed miner's son from Appalachia?" Most conservative proponents of class-based affirmative action have failed to explain their idea with any degree of specificity. Either they're insincere—offering the alternative only for tactical reasons—or they're stumped.   15

The former is more likely. While the questions of implementation are serious and difficult, they are not impossible to answer. At the university level, admissions committees deal every day with precisely the type of apples-and-oranges question that Kinsley poses. Should a law school admit an applicant with a 3.2 GPA from Yale or a 3.3 from Georgetown? How do you compare those two if one applicant worked for the Peace Corps but the other had slightly higher LSATs?   16

In fact, a number of universities already give preferences for disadvantaged students in addition to racial minorities. Since 1989 Berkeley has granted special consideration to applicants "from socioeconomically disadvantaged backgrounds . . . regardless of race or ethnicity." Temple University Law School has, since the 1970s, given preference to "applicants who have overcome exceptional and continuous economic deprivation." And at Hastings College of Law, 20 percent of the class is set aside for disadvantaged students through the Legal Equal Opportunity Program. Even the U.C.-Davis medical program challenged by Allan Bakke was limited to "disadvantaged" minorities, a system which Davis apparently did not find impossible to administer.   17

Similar class-based preference programs could be provided by public employers and federal contractors for high school graduates not pursuing college, on the theory that at   18 that age their class-based handicaps hide their true potential and are not at all of their own making. In public contracting, government agencies could follow the model of New York City's old class-based program, which provided preferences based not on the ethnicity or gender of the contractor, but to small firms located in New York City which did part of their business in depressed areas or employed economically disadvantaged workers.

19   The definition of class or disadvantage may vary according to context, but if, for example, the government chose to require class-based affirmative action from universities receiving federal funds, it is possible to devise an enforceable set of objective standards for deprivation. If the aim of class-based affirmative action is to provide a system of genuine equality of opportunity, a leg up to promising students who have done well despite the odds, we have a wealth of sociological data to devise an obstacles test. While some might balk at the very idea of reducing disadvantage to a number, we currently reduce intellectual promise to numbers—SATs and GPAs— and adding a number for disadvantage into the calculus just makes deciding who gets ahead and who does not a little fairer.

20   There are three basic ways to proceed: with a simple, moderate or complex definition. The simple method is to ask college applicants their family's income and measure disadvantage by that factor alone, on the theory that income is a good proxy for a whole host of economic disadvantages (such as bad schools or a difficult learning environment). This oversimplified approach is essentially the tack we've taken with respect to compensatory race-based affirmative action. For example, most affirmative action programs ask applicants to check a racial box and sweep all the ambiguities under the rug. Even though African Americans have, as justice Thurgood Marshall said in *Bakke,* suffered a history "different in kind, not just degree, from that of other ethnic groups," universities don't calibrate preferences based on comparative group disadvantage (and, in the Davis system challenged by Bakke, two-thirds of the preferences went to Mexican-Americans and Asians, not blacks). We also ignore the question of when an individual's family immigrated in order to determine whether the family was even theoretically subject to the official discrimination in this country on which preferences are predicated.

21   "Diversity" was supposed to solve all this by saying we don't care about compensation, only viewpoint. But, again, if

universities are genuinely seeking diversity of viewpoints, they should inquire whether a minority applicant really does have the "minority viewpoint" being sought. Derrick Bell's famous statement—"the ends of diversity are not served by people who look black and think white"—is at once repellent and a relevant critique of the assumption that all minority members think alike. In theory, we need some assurance from the applicant that he or she will in fact interact with students of different backgrounds, lest the cosmetic diversity of the freshman yearbook be lost to the reality of ethnic theme houses.

The second way to proceed, the moderately complicated calculus of class, would look at what sociologists believe to be the Big Three determinants of life chances: parental income, education and occupation. Parents' education, which is highly correlated with a child's academic achievement, can be measured in number of years. And while ranking occupations might seem hopelessly complex, various attempts to do so objectively have yielded remarkably consistent results—from the Barr Scale of the early 1920s to Alba Edwards' Census rankings of the 1940s to the Duncan Scores of the 1960s. 22

The third alternative, the complex calculus of disadvantage, would count all the factors mentioned, but might also look at net worth, the quality of secondary education, neighborhood influences and family structure. An applicant's family wealth is readily available from financial aid forms, and provides a long-term view of relative disadvantage, to supplement the "snap-shot" picture that income provides. We also know that schooling opportunities are crucial to a student's life chances, even controlling for home environment. Some data suggest that a disadvantaged student at a middle-class school does better on average than a middle-class student at a school with high concentrations of poverty. Objective figures are available to measure secondary school quality—from per student expenditure, to the percentage of students receiving free or reduced-price lunches, to a school's median score on stan-dardized achievement tests. Neighborhood influences, mea-sured by the concentration of poverty within Census tracts or zip codes, could also be factored in, since numerous studies have found that living in a low-income community can adversely, affect an individual's life chances above and beyond family income. Finally, everyone from Dan Quayle to Donna Shalala agrees that children growing up in single-parent homes have a tougher time. This factor could be taken into account as well. 23

24   The point is not that this list is the perfect one, but that it *is* possible to devise a series of fairly objective and verifiable factors that measure the degree to which a teenager's true potential has been hidden. (As it happens, the complex definition is the one that disproportionately benefits African Americans. Even among similar income groups, blacks are more likely than whites to live in concentrated poverty, go to bad schools and live in single-parent homes.) It's just not true that a system of class preferences is inherently harder to administer than a system based on race. Race only seems simpler because we have ignored the ambiguities. And racial preferences are just as easy to ridicule. To paraphrase Kinsley, does a new Indian immigrant get fewer or more points than a third-generation Latino whose mother is Anglo?

25   Who should benefit? Mickey Kaus, in "Class Is In," (Times Review of Books, March 27) argued that class preferences should be reserved for the underclass. But the injuries of class extend beyond the poorest. The offspring of the working poor and the working class lack advantages, too, and indeed SAT scores correlate lockstep with income at every increment. Unless you believe in genetic inferiority, these statistics suggest unfairness is not confined to the underclass. As a practical matter, a teenager who emerges from the underclass has little chance of surviving at an elite college. At Berkeley, administrators found that using a definition of disadvantaged, under which neither parent attended a four-year college and the family could not afford to pay $1,000 in education expenses, failed to bring in enough students who were likely to pass.

26   Still, there are several serious objections to class-based preferences that must be addressed.

27   1. *We're not ready to be color-blind because racial discrimination continues to afflict our society.* Ron Brown says affirmative action "continues to be needed not to redress grievances of the past, but the current discrimination that continues to exist." This is a relatively new theory, which conveniently elides the fact that preferences were supposed to be temporary. It also stands logic on its head. While racial discrimination undoubtedly still exists, the Civil Rights Act of 1964 meant to address prospective discrimination. Affirmative action—discrimination in itself—makes sense only to the extent that there is a current-day legacy of *past* discrimination which new prospective laws cannot reach back and remedy.

28   In the contexts of education and employment, the Civil Rights Act already contains powerful tools to address inten-

tional and unintentional discrimination. The Civil Rights Act of 1991 reaffirmed the need to address unintentional discrimination—by requiring employers to justify employment practices that are statistically more likely to hurt minorities—but it did so without crossing the line to required preferences. This principle also applies to Title VI of the Civil Rights Act, so that if, for example, it can be shown that the SAT produces an unjustified disparate impact, a university can be barred from using it. In addition, "soft" forms of affirmative action, which require employers and universities to broaden the net and interview people from all races are good ways of ensuring positions are not filled by word of mouth, through wealthy white networks.

We have weaker tools to deal with discrimination in other areas of life—say, taxi drivers who refuse to pick up black businessmen—but how does a preference in education or employment remedy that wrong? By contrast, there is nothing illegal about bad schools, bad housing and grossly stunted opportunities for the poor. A class preference is perfectly appropriate. 29

2. *Class preferences will be just as stigmatizing as racial* 30 *preferences.* Kinsley argues that "any debilitating self-doubt that exists because of affirmative action is not going to be mitigated by being told you got into Harvard because of your 'socioeconomic disadvantage' rather than your race."

But class preferences are different from racial preferences 31 in at least two important respects. First, stigma—in one's own eyes and the eyes of others—is bound up with the question of whether an admissions criterion is accepted as legitimate. Students with good grades aren't seen as getting in "just because they're smart." And there appears to be a societal consensus—from Douglas to Scalia—that kids from poor backgrounds deserve a leg up. Such a consensus has never existed for class-blind racial preferences.

Second, there is no myth of inferiority in this country 32 about the abilities of poor people comparable to that about African Americans. Now, if racial preferences are purely a matter of compensatory justice, then the question of whether preferences exacerbate white racism is not relevant. But today racial preferences are often justified by social utility (bringing different racial groups together helps dispel stereotypes) in which case the social consequences are highly relevant. The general argument made by proponents of racial preferences—that policies need to be grounded in social reality, not ahistorical theory—cuts in favor of the class category.

Why? Precisely because there is no stubborn historical myth for it to reinforce.

33   Kaus makes a related argument when he says that class preferences "will still reward those who play the victim." But if objective criteria are used to define the disadvantaged, there is no way to "play" the victim. Poor and working-class teenagers are the victims of class inequality not of their own making. Preferences, unlike, say, a welfare check, tell poor teenagers not that they are helpless victims, but that we think their long-run potential is great, and we're going to give them a chance—if they work their tails off—to prove themselves.

34   3. *Class preferences continue to treat people as members of groups as opposed to individuals.* Yes. But so do university admissions policies that summarily reject students below a certain SAT level. It's hard to know what treating people as individuals means. (Perhaps if university admissions committees interviewed the teachers of each applicant back to kindergarten to get a better picture of their academic potential, we'd be treating them more as individuals.) The question is not whether we treat people as members of groups—that's inevitable—but whether the group is a relevant one. And in measuring disadvantage (and hidden potential) class is surely a much better proxy than race.

35   4. *Class-based affirmative action will not yield a diverse student body in elite colleges.* Actually, there is reason to believe that class preferences will disproportionately benefit people of color in most context—since minorities are disproportionately poor. In the university context, however, class-based preferences were rejected during the 1970s in part because of fear that they would produce inadequate numbers of minority students. The problem is that when you control for income, African American students do worse than white and Asian students on the SAT—due in part to differences in culture and linguistic patterns, and in part to the way income alone as a measurement hides other class-based differences among ethnic groups.

36   The concern is a serious and complicated one. Briefly, there are four responses. First, even Murray and Richard Herrnstein agree that the residual racial gap in scores has declined significantly in the past two decades, so the concern, though real, is not as great as it once was. Second, if we use the sophisticated definition of class discussed earlier—which reflects the relative disadvantage of blacks vis-à-vis whites of the same income level—the racial gap should close further.

Third, we can improve racial diversity by getting rid of unjustified preferences— for alumni kids or students from underrepresented geographic regions—which disproportionately hurt people of color. Finally, if the goal is to provide genuine equal opportunity, not equality of group result, and if we are satisfied that a meritocratic system which corrects for class inequality is the best possible approximation of that equality, then we have achieved our goal.

5. *Class-based affirmative action will cause as much resentment among those left out as race-based affirmative action.* 37 Kinsley argues that the rejected applicant in the infamous Jesse Helms commercial from 1990 would feel just as angry for losing out on a class-based as a race-based preference, since both involve "making up for past injustice." The difference, of course, is that class preferences go to the actual victims of class injury, mooting the whole question of intergenerational justice. In the racial context, this was called "victim specificity." Even the Reagan administration was in favor of compensating actual victims of racial discrimination.

The larger point implicit in Kinsley's question is a more 38 serious one: that any preference system, whether race- or class-based, is "still a form of zero-sum social engineering." Why should liberals push for class preferences at all? Why not just provide more funding for education, safer schools, better nutrition? The answer is that liberals should do these things; but we cannot hold our breath for it to happen. In 1993, when all the planets were aligned—a populist Democratic president, Democratic control of both Houses of Congress—they produced what *The New York Times* called "A BUDGET WORTHY OF MR. BUSH." Cheaper alternatives, such as preferences, must supplement more expensive strategies of social spending. Besides, to the extent that class preferences help change the focus of public discourse from race to class, they help reforge the coalition needed to sustain the social programs liberals want.

Class preferences could restore the successful formula on 39 which the early civil rights movement rested: morally unassailable underpinnings and a relatively inexpensive agenda. It's crucial to remember that Martin Luther King Jr. called for special consideration based on class, not race. After laying out a forceful argument for the special debt owed to blacks, King rejected the call for a Negro Bill of Rights in favor of a Bill of Rights for the Disadvantaged. It was King's insight that there were nonracial ways to remedy racial wrongs, and that the injuries of class deserve attention along with the injuries of race.

40   None of this is to argue that King would have opposed affirmative action if the alternative were to do nothing. For Jesse Helms to invoke King's color-blind rhetoric now that it is in the interests of white people to do so is the worst kind of hypocrisy. Some form of compensation is necessary, and I think affirmative action, though deeply flawed, is better than nothing.

41   But the opportunity to save affirmative action of any kind may soon pass. If the Supreme Court continues to narrow the instances in which racial preferences are justified, if California voters put an end to affirmative action in their state and if Congress begins to roll back racial preferences in legislation which President Clinton finds hard to veto—or President Phil Gramm signs with gusto—conservatives will have less and less reason to bargain. Now is the time to call their bluff.

Ellen Willis
Race, Class, and the State

The following essay by Ellen Willis appeared in The Village Voice *in the middle of May 1995, a month or so after the previous essay by Richard Kahlenberg was published.* The Village Voice *is a weekly newspaper for New Yorkers that has a decidedly liberal and irreverent tone. It reports on current events (national and local) and very thoroughly covers contemporary culture—films, books, music, dance, and so forth. (Another essay by Willis is in the Family Matters part of* Conversations, *page 517. She is a journalism professor at New York University and author of* No More Nice Girls: Countercultural Essays *[1992].)*

1   "Class, Not Race" is the title of a recent *New Republic* article by Richard Kahlenberg, which argues that affirmative action should be based on economic disadvantage. Those words could as easily be the bumper sticker for a larger political strategy long favored by liberals and populists distressed at the defection of working-class whites from the New Deal

coalition. As Kahlenberg wistfully puts it, "An emphasis on class inequality meant Robert Kennedy riding in a motorcade through cheering white and black sections of racially torn Gary, Indiana, in 1968, with black Mayor Richard Hatcher on one side, and white working-class boxing hero Tony Zale on the other."

I've never bought this formulation; to me it has always   2
sounded suspiciously like "Economics Not Culture," a way of dismissing not only racial but sexual conflict. Anyway, I disagree with its basic assumption—I think the coalition was ultimately derailed less by race, per se, than by the "War on Poverty" approach to class politics, which pitted the poor against the working and lower-middle classes instead of focusing on their common interest in extending public services and universal social benefits financed by a progressive tax system. And now that Kahlenberg and other liberal commentators are applying this slogan to the affirmative action debate, it strikes me as a nice, progressive-sounding way to make an end run around a messy issue.

The original point of affirmative action, as I argued in an   3
earlier column, was to tackle forms of reflexive, unconscious cultural discrimination against minorities and women that could not be attributed to individuals with provable intent. As an inherently modest strategy for integrating the middle class, it made sense only insofar as it reflected a social consensus that such forms of discrimination actually exist and are a serious problem. That consensus has now eroded to the point where even proponents of affirmative action justify it as reparations and "diversity"—i.e., representation—rather than as a remedy for ongoing discrimination. At the heart of anti–affirmative action resentment is the belief that blacks (the main target at the moment) are falsely blaming their condition on racism rather than on their own inferiority.

In the context of this history, "class not race" is something   4
of a non sequitur. For one thing, while there is certainly cultural discrimination based on class, this is insult added to a more basic injury: unlike skin color or gender, class is inherently a vehicle of social stratification. And unlike racial minorities, Kahlenberg's proposed constituency, "the offspring of the working poor and the working class," are undoubtedly a majority of the population of their age group, and one that's growing all the time. To give working-class kids "genuine equal opportunity"—Kahlenberg's professed goal—would mean significantly curtailing the opportunities of the middle class and undermining the most basic function of the present

educational system, which is to serve as a gatekeeper protecting middle- and upper-class privilege.

5   Needless to say, Kahlenberg has nothing this radical in
mind. Since actually doing away with class hierarchy is currently beyond the pale of serious political discussion, what
passes for debate about class in America generally boils down
to an argument between Darwinian meritocrats and advocates of mitigating class differences with social democratic
measures (including free or cheap higher education). And we
all know who's winning that argument these days. Under the
circumstances, Kahlenberg opts for Darwinian meritocracy
with a human face. "Why should liberals push for class preferences at all?" he asks. "Why not just provide more funding
for education, safer schools, better nutrition? The answer is
that liberals should do these things; but we cannot hold our
breath for it to happen." Instead, let's give "a leg up to promising students who have done well despite the odds."

6   Aside from his charming suggestion that the disadvantage
of coming from a single-parent home should be considered
when deciding who gets a leg up (don't single mothers have
enough problems without being accused of staying unmarried so they can get their kids into Harvard?), Kahlenberg is
probably right in thinking that working- and middle-class
whites will not resent this attempt to help Horatio Alger along
in the same way that they resent the competition of "unqualified" blacks. But that's because giving a little help to the certi-
fiably deserving poor rocks no social boats; on the contrary it
bolsters an increasingly shaky American myth (hard work
will get you anywhere, etc.), without raising any disturbing
challenges to received ideas of who deserves what. Tellingly,
Kahlenberg focuses entirely on education and doesn't consider how "class preferences" might be applied to the workplace, though markers of class—dress, accent, cultural
references, and so on—figure prominently and prejudicially
in hiring decisions. Adapting affirmative action to confront
such prejudices, far from defusing the issue, would merely
extend conflict about multiculturalism into complicated new
arenas.

7   I began working on this piece shortly before Oklahoma
City. After the bombing—which looks more and more like one
of those watershed events that give shape to a murky period
of history and reframe public debate—it occurred to me that
I was missing an important point about affirmative action,
probably because it was so obvious: the campaign against a.a.

is among other things a linchpin of the right's attack on federal authority. At present, the U.S. government remains the chief source of whatever institutional power (as distinct from cultural influence) egalitarian social movements have managed to achieve since the New Deal. This fact has made the feds an unambiguous object of fear and loathing on the right; the welfare state has more or less replaced Communism as the catalyst of an alliance between restless post–Cold War capitalists and America's latest cultural antihero: the post–civil rights, post-Vietnam, postfeminist white guy out to prove life is a Michael Douglas movie. At the same time, the equation of social welfare with government is by no means unproblematic for the left.

The problem starts with the ongoing soul-search about 8 why said white guys, most of whom are being royally screwed by said capitalists, nonetheless persist in seeing blacks/women/liberals/government as the enemy rather than the banks and the corporations. Liberal abdication on class issues is no doubt part of the answer, and so is the displacement of anger from rich and powerful targets to poor and vulnerable ones. But in my view, the most profound reason for this seeming contradiction is that economic motives are secondary to people's need for freedom and for satisfying sexual and emotional lives—and that when those needs are thwarted, enjoying power over others feels like a matter of psychic survival.

It follows from this perspective that opposing the right's 9 assault on egalitarian social policies is hardly a simple matter of defending the welfare state. The state is, after all, an authoritarian institution. Its chief function is enforcing the existing social order; for the most part it serves the interests of other powerful institutions, from the corporation to the church. True, democratic ideology, various constitutional rights and liberties, and the electoral system make the American state and its agencies more vulnerable to public pressure than the corporation, the church, or any other "private" institution. Within limits, social movements have been able to influence and even participate in government, to correct private injustices and promote a vital public life. When such movements are powerful and potentially disruptive, the state will accommodate them because its ultimate imperative is maintaining social stability. But it's important to remember—and the left seems to have a hard time with this—that movements, not the state itself, are responsible for every hard-won egalitarian measure on the books.

10   Now that conservative movements are ascendant, the state is rapidly throwing off its social welfare baggage. Since the right seems determined to wreck the entire existing infrastructure of public services and amenities, from support for the poor and the aged to schools, hospitals, libraries, transit systems, environmental protections—you name it—those of us who oppose this destructive, indeed barbaric, impulse have no choice, in the short run, but to defend government. Yet without an alternative vision of how a genuinely free society might organize collective activity for the common good, the left will always be caught in a contradiction: in a statist system, social cooperation comes packaged with oppression, which gives it a bad name.

11   Affirmative action reflects this dilemma. It was invented to address the question "How can we placate minorities and women in a way that will be as inexpensive and disturb the social structure as little as possible?" The answer, in effect, has been state-managed scarcity—giving "underrepresented groups" a bit more of a shot at the decreasing number of decent jobs and at educational opportunities less and less likely to lead to decent jobs. If the white guys feel had by this—well, we're all being had. The issue is what to do about it other than rush headlong toward fascism. Ignoring race (or sex, for that matter) won't help.

Kurt Vonnegut Jr.

Harrison Bergeron

After graduating from Cornell University, Kurt Vonnegut Jr. (born in 1922 in Indianapolis) worked in journalism and public relations. Then he started publishing best-selling novels that often feature imaginary (yet all too real) settings, a satiric edge, and his characteristic narrative voice. Among them are Cat's Cradle, Slaughterhouse-Five, Breakfast of Champions, *and* Jailbird. *"Harrison Bergeron" was published as part of his collection of stories titled* Welcome to the Monkey House *(1961).*

1   The year was 2081, and everybody was finally equal. They weren't only equal before God and the law. They were equal

every which way. Nobody was smarter than anybody else. Nobody was better looking than anybody else. Nobody was stronger or quicker than anybody else. All this equality was due to the 211th, 212th, and 213th Amendments to the Constitution, and to the unceasing vigilance of agents of the United States Handicapper General.

Some things about living still weren't quite right, though. April, for instance, still drove people crazy by not being springtime. And it was in that clammy month that the H-G men took George and Hazel Bergeron's fourteen-year-old son, Harrison, away. 2

It was tragic, all right, but George and Hazel couldn't think about it very hard. Hazel had a perfectly average intelligence, which meant she couldn't think about anything except in short bursts. And George, while his intelligence was way above normal, had a little mental handicap radio in his ear. He was required by law to wear it at all times. It was tuned to a government transmitter. Every twenty seconds or so, the transmitter would send out some sharp noise to keep people like George from taking unfair advantage of their brains. 3

George and Hazel were watching television. There were tears on Hazel's cheeks, but she'd forgotten for the moment what they were about. 4

On the television screen were ballerinas. 5

A buzzer sounded in George's head. His thoughts fled in panic, like bandits from a burglar alarm. 6

"That was a real pretty dance, that dance they just did," said Hazel. 7

"Huh?" said George. 8

"That dance—it was nice," said Hazel. 9

"Yup," said George. He tried to think a little about the ballerinas. They weren't really very good—no better than anybody else would have been, anyway. They were burdened with sashweights and bags of birdshot, and their faces were masked, so that no one, seeing a free and graceful gesture or a pretty face, would feel like something the cat drug in. George was toying with the vague notion that maybe dancers shouldn't be handicapped. But he didn't get very far with it before another noise in his ear radio scattered his thoughts. 10

George winced. So did two out of the eight ballerinas. 11

Hazel saw him wince. Having no mental handicap herself, she had to ask George what the latest sound had been. 12

"Sounded like somebody hitting a milk bottle with a ball peen hammer," said George. 13

14   "I'd think it would be real interesting, hearing all the different sounds," said Hazel, a little envious. "All the things they think up."

15   "Um," said George.

16   "Only, if I was Handicapper General, you know what I would do?" said Hazel. Hazel, as a matter of fact, bore a strong resemblance to the Handicapper General, a woman named Diana Moon Glampers. "If I was Diana Moon Glampers," said Hazel, "I'd have chimes on Sunday—just chimes. Kind of in honor of religion."

17   "I could think, if it was just chimes," said George.

18   "Well—maybe make 'em real loud," said Hazel. "I think I'd make a good Handicapper General."

19   "Good as anybody else," said George.

20   "Who knows better'n I do what normal is?" said Hazel.

21   "Right," said George. He began to think glimmeringly about his abnormal son who was now in jail, about Harrison, but a twenty-one-gun salute in his head stopped that.

22   "Boy!" said Hazel, "that was a doozy, wasn't it?"

23   It was such a doozy that George was white and trembling, and tears stood on the rims of his red eyes. Two of the eight ballerinas had collapsed to the studio floor, [and] were holding their temples.

24   "All of a sudden you look so tired," said Hazel. "Why don't you stretch out on the sofa, so's you can rest your handicap bag on the pillows, honeybunch." She was referring to the forty-seven pounds of birdshot in a canvas bag, which was padlocked around George's neck. "Go on and rest the bag for a little while," she said. "I don't care if you're not equal to me for a while."

25   George weighed the bag with his hands. "I don't mind it," he said. "I don't notice it any more. It's just a part of me."

26   "You been so tired lately—kind of wore out," said Hazel. "If there was just some way we could make a little hole in the bottom of the bag, and just take out a few of them lead balls. Just a few."

27   "Two years in prison and two thousand dollars fine for every ball I took out," said George. "I don't call that a bargain."

28   "If you could just take a few out when you came home from work," said Hazel. "I mean—you don't compete with anybody around here. You just set around."

29   "If I tried to get away with it," said George, "then other people'd get away with it—and pretty soon we'd be right back

to the dark ages again, with everybody competing against everybody else. You wouldn't like that, would you?"

"I'd hate it," said Hazel.   30

"There you are," said George. "The minute people start 31 cheating on laws, what do you think happens to society?"

If Hazel hadn't been able to come up with an answer to this 32 question George couldn't have supplied one. A siren was going off in his head.

"Reckon it'd fall all apart," said Hazel.   33

"What would?" said George blankly.   34

"Society," said Hazel uncertainly. "Wasn't that what you 35 just said?"

"Who knows?" said George.   36

The television program was suddenly interrupted for a 37 news bulletin. It wasn't clear at first as to what the bulletin was about, since the announcer, like all announcers, had a serious speech impediment. For about half a minute, and in a state of high excitement, the announcer tried to say, "Ladies and gentlemen—"

He finally gave up, handed the bulletin to a ballerina to 38 read.

"That's all right—" Hazel said of the announcer, "he tried. 39 That's the big thing. He tried to do the best he could with what God gave him. He should get a nice raise for trying so hard."

"Ladies and gentlemen—" said the ballerina, reading the 40 bulletin. She must have been extraordinarily beautiful, because the mask she wore was hideous. And it was easy to see that she was the strongest and most graceful of all the dancers, for her handicap bags were as big as those worn by two-hundred-pound men.

And she had to apologize at once for her voice, which was 41 a very unfair voice for a woman to use. Her voice was a warm, luminous, timeless melody. "Excuse me—" she said, and she began again, making her voice absolutely uncompetitive.

"Harrison Bergeron, age fourteen," she said in a grackle 42 squawk, "has just escaped from jail, where he was held on suspicion of plotting to overthrow the government. He is a genius and an athlete, is under-handicapped, and should be regarded as extremely dangerous."

A police photograph of Harrison Bergeron was flashed on 43 the screen upside down, then sideways, upside down again, then right side up. The picture showed the full length of Harrison against a background calibrated in feet and inches. He was exactly seven feet tall.

44 The rest of Harrison's appearance was Halloween and hardware. Nobody had ever borne heavier handicaps. He had outgrown hindrances faster than the H-G men could think them up. Instead of a little ear radio for a mental handicap, he wore a tremendous pair of earphones, and spectacles with thick wavy lenses. The spectacles were intended to make him not only half blind, but to give him whanging headaches besides.

45 Scrap metal was hung all over him. Ordinarily, there was a certain symmetry, a military neatness to the handicaps issued to strong people, but Harrison looked like a walking junkyard. In the race of life, Harrison carried three hundred pounds.

46 And to offset his good looks, the H-G men required that he wear at all times a red rubber ball for a nose, keep his eyebrows shaved off, and cover his even white teeth with black caps at snaggle-tooth random.

47 "If you see this boy," said the ballerina, "do not—I repeat, do not—try to reason with him."

48 There was the shriek of a door being torn from its hinges.

49 Screams and barking cries of consternation came from the television set. The photograph of Harrison Bergeron on the screen jumped again and again, as though dancing to the tune of an earthquake.

50 George Bergeron correctly identified the earthquake, and well he might have—for many was the time his own home had danced to the same crashing tune. "My God—" said George, "that must be Harrison!"

51 The realization was blasted from his mind instantly by the sound of an automobile collision in his head.

52 When George could open his eyes again, the photograph of Harrison was gone. A living, breathing Harrison filled the screen.

53 Clanking, clownish, and huge, Harrison stood in the center of the studio. The knob of the uprooted studio door was still in his hand. Ballerinas, technicians, musicians, and announcers cowered on their knees before him, expecting to die.

54 "I am the Emperor!" cried Harrison. "Do you hear? I am the Emperor! Everybody must do what I say at once!" He stamped his foot and the studio shook.

55 "Even as I stand here—" he bellowed, "crippled, hobbled, sickened—I am a greater ruler than any man who ever lived! Now watch me become what I *can* become!"

Harrison tore the straps of his handicap harness like wet   56
tissue paper, tore straps guaranteed to support five thousand
pounds.

Harrison's scrap-iron handicaps crashed to the floor.   57

Harrison thrust his thumbs under the bar of the padlock   58
that secured his head harness. The bar snapped like celery.
Harrison smashed his headphones and spectacles against the
wall.

He flung away his rubber-ball nose, revealed a man that   59
would have awed Thor, the god of thunder.

"I shall now select my Empress!" he said, looking down on   60
the cowering people. "Let the first woman who dares rise to
her feet claim her mate and her throne!"

A moment passed, and then a ballerina arose, swaying like   61
a willow.

Harrison plucked the mental handicap from her ear,   62
snapped off her physical handicaps with marvelous delicacy.
Last of all, he removed her mask.

She was blindingly beautiful.   63

"Now—" said Harrison, taking her hand, "shall we show   64
the people the meaning of the word dance? Music!" he
commanded.

The musicians scrambled back into their chairs, and Har-   65
rison stripped them of their handicaps, too. "Play your best,"
he told them, "and I'll make you barons and dukes and earls."

The music began. It was normal at first—cheap, silly, false.   66
But Harrison snatched two musicians from their chairs,
waved them like batons as he sang the music as he wanted it
played. He slammed them back into their chairs.

The music began again and was much improved.   67

Harrison and his Empress merely listened to the music for   68
a while—listened gravely, as though synchronizing their
heartbeats with it.

They shifted their weights to their toes.   69

Harrison placed his big hands on the girl's tiny waist, let-   70
ting her sense the weightlessness that would soon be hers.

And then, in an explosion of joy and grace, into the air they   71
sprang!

Not only were the laws of the land abandoned, but the law   72
of gravity and the laws of motion as well.

They reeled, whirled, swiveled, flounced, capered, gam-   73
boled, and spun.

They leaped like deer on the moon.   74

The studio ceiling was thirty feet high, but each leap   75
brought the dancers nearer to it.

76   It became their obvious intention to kiss the ceiling.

77   They kissed it.

78   And then, neutralizing gravity with love and pure will, they remained suspended in air inches below the ceiling, and they kissed each other for a long, long time.

79   It was then that Diana Moon Glampers, the Handicapper General, came into the studio with a double-barreled ten-gauge shotgun. She fired twice, and the Emperor and the Empress were dead before they hit the floor.

80   Diana Moon Glampers loaded the gun again. She aimed it at the musicians and told them they had ten seconds to get their handicaps back on.

81   It was then that the Bergerons' television tube burned out.

82   Hazel turned to comment about the blackout to George. But George had gone out into the kitchen for a can of beer.

83   George came back in with the beer, paused while a handicap signal shook him up. And then he sat down again. "You been crying?" he said to Hazel.

84   "Yup," she said.

85   "What about?" he said.

86   "I forget," she said. "Something real sad on television."

87   "What was it?" he said.

88   "It's all kind of mixed up in my mind," said Hazel.

89   "Forget sad things," said George.

90   "I always do," said Hazel.

91   "That's my girl," said George. He winced. There was the sound of a riveting gun in his head.

92   "Gee—I could tell that one was a doozy," said Hazel.

93   "You can say that again," said George.

94   "Gee—" said Hazel, "I could tell that one was a doozy."

THE MEN'S MOVEMENT

Andrew Kimbrell

A Time for Men to Pull Together

A former concert pianist and music teacher, Andrew Kimbrell is now an attorney and lobbyist who lives and works in the Washington, DC, area. Among other things, he sees himself as one spokesman for the so-called "men's movement," an effort to liberate people from the notion that men must remain rational, unemotional, competitive, efficient breadwinners. He published the following essay in the May/June issue of the Utne Reader, *a magazine that bills itself as "the best of the alternative press" because it republishes articles on public affairs from other publications—somewhat in the tradition of* Reader's Digest, *except that* Reader's Digest *is quite traditional whereas* Utne Reader *articles reflect a more liberal and exploratory perspective.*

> *"Our civilization is a dingy ungentlemanly business; it drops so much out of a man."*
> —Robert Louis Stevenson

Men are hurting—badly. Despite rumors to the contrary, 1
men as a gender are being devastated physically and psychically by our socioeconomic system. As American society continues to empower a small percentage of men—and a smaller but increasing percentage of women—it is causing significant confusion and anguish for the majority of men.

In recent years, there have been many impressive analyses 2
documenting the exploitation of women in our culture. Unfortunately, little attention has been given to the massive disruption and destruction that our economic and political institutions have wrought on men. In fact, far too often, men as a gender have been thought of as synonymous with the power elite.

But thinking on this subject is beginning to change. Over 3
the last decade, men have begun to realize that we cannot

365

properly relate to one another, or understand how some of us in turn exploit others, until we have begun to appreciate the extent and nature of our dispossessed predicament. In a variety of ways, men across the country are beginning to mourn their losses and seek solutions.

4   This new sense of loss among men comes from the deterioration of men's traditional roles as protectors of family and the earth (although not the sole protectors)—what psychologist Robert Mannis calls the *generative* potential of men. And much of this mourning also focuses on how men's energy is often channeled in the direction of destruction—both of the earth and its inhabitants.

5   The mission of many men today—both those involved in the men's movement and others outside it—is to find new ways that allow men to celebrate their generative potential and reverse the cycle of destruction that characterizes men's collective behavior today. These calls to action are not abstract or hypothetical. The oppression of men, especially in the last several decades, can be easily seen in a disturbing upward spiral of male self-destruction, addiction, hopelessness, and homelessness.

6   While suicide rates for women have been stable over the last 20 years, among men—especially white male teenagers—they have increased rapidly. Currently, male teenagers are five times more likely to take their own lives than females. Overall, men are committing suicide at four times the rate of women. America's young men are also being ravaged by alcohol and drug abuse. Men between the ages of 18 and 29 suffer alcohol dependency at three times the rate of women of the same age group. More than two-thirds of all alcoholics are men, and 50 percent more men are regular users of illicit drugs than women. Men account for more than 90 percent of arrests for alcohol and drug abuse violations.

7   A sense of hopelessness among America's young men is not surprising. Real wages for men under 25 have actually declined over the last 20 years, and 60 percent of all high school dropouts are males. These statistics, added to the fact that more than 400,000 farmers have lost their land in the last decade, account in part for the increasing rate of unemployment among men, and for the fact that more than 80 percent of America's homeless are men.

8   The stress on men is taking its toll. Men's life expectancy is 10 percent shorter than women's, and the incidence of stress-related illnesses such as heart disease and certain cancers remains inordinately high among men.

And the situation for minority men is even worse. One out   9
of four black men between the ages of 20 and 29 is either in
jail, on probation, or on parole—ten times the proportion for
black women in the same age range. More black men are in
jail than in college, and there are 40 percent more black
women than black men studying in our nation's colleges and
universities. Homicide is the leading cause of death among
black males ages 15 to 24. Black males have the lowest life
expectancy of any segment of the American population. Statistics for Native American and Hispanic men are also grim.

Men are also a large part of the growing crisis in the Amer-   10
ican family. Studies report that parents today spend 40 percent less time with their children than did parents in 1965,
and men are increasingly isolated from their families by the
pressures of work and the circumstances of divorce. In a
recent poll, 72 percent of employed male respondents agreed
that they are "torn by conflict" between their jobs and the
desire to be with their families. Yet the average divorced
American man spends less than two days a month with his
children. Well over half of black male children are raised
without fathers. While the trauma of separation and divorce
affects all members of a family, it is especially poignant for
sons: Researchers generally agree that boys at all ages are
hardest hit by divorce.

The Enclosure of Men

The current crisis for men, which goes far beyond statis-   11
tics, is nothing new. We have faced a legacy of loss, especially
since the start of the mechanical age. From the Enclosure
Acts, which forced families off the land in Tudor England, to
the ongoing destruction of indigenous communities throughout the Third World, the demands of the industrial era have
forced men off the land, out of the family and community,
and into the factory and office. The male as steward of family
and soil, craftsman, woodsman, native hunter, and fisherman
has all but vanished.

As men became the primary cog in industrial production,   12
they lost touch with the earth and the parts of themselves that
needed the earth to survive. Men by the millions—who long
prided themselves on their husbandry of family, community,
and land—were forced into a system whose ultimate goal was
to turn one man against another in the competitive "jungle"
of   industrialized   society.   As   the   industrial   revolution

advanced, men lost not only their independence and dignity, but also the sense of personal creativity and responsibility associated with individual crafts and small-scale farming.

13   The factory wrenched the father from the home, and he often became a virtual nonentity in the household. By separating a man's work from his family, industrial society caused the permanent alienation of father from son. Even when the modern father returns to the house, he is often too tired and too irritable from the tensions and tedium of work in the factory or corporation to pay close attention to his children. As Robert Bly, in his best-selling book *Iron John* (1990, Addison-Wesley), has pointed out, "When a father, absent during the day, returns home at six, his children receive only his temperament, and not his teaching." The family, and especially sons, lose the presence of the father, uncle, and other male role models. It is difficult to calculate the full impact that this pattern of paternal absence has had on family and society over the last several generations.

14   While the loss of fathers is now beginning to be discussed, men have yet to fully come to terms with the terrible loss of sons during the mechanized wars of this century. World War I, World War II, Korea, and Vietnam were what the poet Robert Graves called "holocausts of young men." In the battlefields of this century, hundreds of millions of men were killed or injured. In World Wars I and II—in which more than 100 million soldiers were casualties—most of the victims were teenage boys, the average age being 18.5 years.

15   Given this obvious evidence of our exploitation, it is remarkable that so few men have acknowledged the genocide on their gender over the last century—much less turned against those responsible for this vast victimization. Women have increasingly identified their oppression in society; men have not. Thankfully, some men are now working to create a movement, or community, that focuses on awareness and understanding of men's loss and pain as well as the potential for healing. Because men's oppression is deeply rooted in the political and economic institutions of modern society, it is critical that awareness of these issues must be followed by action: Men today need a comprehensive political program that points the way toward liberation. Instead of grieving over and acting on our loss of independence and generativity, modern men have often engaged in denial—a denial that is linked to the existence of a "male mystique." This defective mythology of the modern age has created a "new man." The male mystique recasts what anthropologists have identified

as the traditional male role throughout history—a man, whether hunter-gatherer or farmer, who is steeped in a creative and sustaining relationship with his extended family and the earth household. In the place of this long-enduring, rooted masculine role, the male mystique has fostered a new image of men: autonomous, efficient, intensely self-interested, and disconnected from community and the earth.

The male mystique was spawned in the early days of the   16
modern age. It combines Francis Bacon's idea that "knowledge is power" and Adam Smith's view that the highest good is "the individual exerting himself to his own advantage." This power-oriented, individualistic ideology was further solidified by the concepts of the survival of the fittest and the ethic of efficiency. The ideal man was no longer the wise farmer, but rather the most successful man-eater in the Darwinian corporate jungle.

The most tragic aspect of all this for us is that as the male   17
mystique created the modern power elite, it destroyed male friendship and bonding. The male mystique teaches that the successful man is competitive, uncaring, unloving. It celebrates the ethic of isolation—it turns men permanently against each other in the tooth and claw world of making a living. As the Ivan Boesky-type character in the movie *Wall Street* tells his young apprentice, "If you need a friend, get a dog."

The male mystique also destroys men's ties to the earth. It   18
embodies the view of 17th century British philosopher John Locke that "[l]and that is left wholly to nature is called, as indeed it is, waste." A sustainable relationship with the earth is sacrificed to material progress and conspicuous consumption.

Ironically, men's own sense of loss has fed the male mys-   19
tique. As men become more and more powerless in their own lives, they are given more and more media images of excessive, caricatured masculinity with which to identify. Men look to manufactured macho characters from the Wild West, working-class America, and modern war in the hope of gaining some sense of what it means to be a man. The primary symbols of the male mystique are almost never caring fathers, stewards of the land, or community organizers. Instead, over several decades these aggressively masculine figures have evolved from the Western independent man (John Wayne, Gary Cooper) to the blue-collar macho man (Sly Stallone and Robert DeNiro) and finally to a variety of military and police figures concluding with the violent revelry of *Robocop*.

20   Modern men are entranced by this simulated masculinity—
they experience danger, independence, success, sexuality, idealism, and adventure as voyeurs. Meanwhile, in real life most
men lead powerless, subservient lives in the factory or
office—frightened of losing their jobs, mortgaged to the gills,
and still feeling responsible for supporting their families.
Their lauded independence—as well as most of their basic
rights—disappear the minute they report for work. The disparity between their real lives and the macho images of masculinity perpetrated by the media confuses and confounds
many men. In his book *The Men from the Boys*, Ray Raphael
asks, "But is it really that manly to wield a jackhammer, or
spend one's life in the mines? Physical labor is often mindless,
repetitive, and exhausting.... The workers must be subservient while on the job, and subservience is hard to reconcile
with the masculine ideal of personal power."

21   Men can no longer afford to lose themselves in denial. We
need to experience grief and anger over our losses and not
buy into the pseudo-male stereotypes propagated by the male
mystique. We are not, after all, what we are told we are.

22   At the same time, while recognizing the pervasive victimization of women, we must resist the view of some feminists
that maleness itself, and not the current systems of social
control and production, is primarily responsible for the
exploitation of women. For men who are sensitive to feminist
thinking, this view of masculinity creates a confusing and
debilitating double bind: We view ourselves as oppressors yet
experience victimization on the personal and social level.
Instead of blaming maleness, we must challenge the defective
mythology of the male mystique. Neither the male mystique
nor the denigration of maleness offers hope for the future.

23   Fortunately, we may be on the verge of a historic shift in
male consciousness. Recently, there has been a rediscovery
of masculinity as a primal creative and generative force
equal to that of the recently recognized creative and nurturing power of the feminine. A number of thinkers and activists are urging men to substitute empathy for efficiency,
stewardship for exploitation, generosity for the competitive-
ness of the marketplace.

24   At the forefront of this movement have been poet Robert
Bly and others working with him: psychologist James Hillman,
drummer Michael Meade, Jungian scholar Robert Moore. Bly
has called for the recognition and reaffirmation of the "wild"
man. As part of Bly's crusade, thousands of men have come
together to seek a regeneration of their sexuality and power, as

they reject the cerebral, desiccated world of our competitive corporate culture. Another compelling analysis is that of Jungian therapist Robert Mannis, who has called for a renewal of the ethic of "husbandry," a sense of masculine obligation involved with generating and maintaining a stable relationship to one's family and to the earth itself. And a growing number of men are mounting other challenges to the male mystique. But so far, the men's movement has remained primarily therapeutic. Little effort has been made to extend the energy of male self-discovery into a practical social and political agenda.

As many of us come to mourn the lost fathers and sons of   25
the last decades and seek to re-establish our ties to each other and to the earth, we need to find ways to change the political, social, and economic structures that have created this crisis. A "wild man" weekend in the woods, or intense man-to-man discussions, can be key experiences in self-discovery and personal empowerment. But these personal experiences are not enough to reverse the victimization of men. As the men's movement gathers strength, it is critical that this increasing sense of personal liberation be channeled into political action. Without significant changes in our society there will only be continued hopelessness and frustration for men. Moreover, a coordinated movement pressing for the liberation of men could be a key factor in ensuring that the struggle for a sustainable future for humanity and the earth succeeds.

What follows is a brief political platform for men, a short   26
manifesto with which we can begin the process of organizing men as a positive political force working for a better future. This is the next step for the men's movement.

Fathers and Children

Political efforts focusing on the family must reassert   27
men's bonds with the family and reverse the "lost father" syndrome. While any long-term plan for men's liberation requires significant changes in the very structure of our work and economic institutions, a number of intermediate steps are possible: We need to take a leadership role in supporting parental leave legislation, which gives working parents the right to take time from work to care for children or other family members. And we need to target the Bush administration for vetoing this vital legislation. Also needed is pro-child tax relief such as greatly expanding the young child tax credit, which would provide income relief and tax

breaks to families at a point when children need the most parental care and when income may be the lowest.

28   We should also be in the forefront of the movement pushing for changes in the workplace including more flexible hours, part-time work, job sharing, and home-based employment. As economic analyst William R. Mattox Jr. notes, a simple step toward making home-based employment more viable would be to loosen restrictions on claiming home office expenses as a tax deduction for parents. Men must also work strenuously in the legal arena to promote more liberal visitation rights for non-custodial parents and to assert appropriateness of the father as a custodial parent. Non-traditional family structures should also be given more recognition in our society, with acknowledgment of men's important roles as stepfathers, foster fathers, uncles, brothers, and mentors. We must seek legislative ways to recognize many men's commitments that do not fit traditional definitions of family.

Ecology as Male Politics

29   A sustainable environment is not merely one issue among others. It is the crux of all issues in our age, including men's politics. The ecological struggles of our time offer a unique forum in which men can express their renewed sense of the wild and their traditional roles as creators, defenders of the family, and careful stewards of the earth.

30   The alienation of men from their rootedness to the land has deprived us all of what John Muir called the "heart of wilderness." As part of our efforts to re-experience the wild in ourselves, we should actively become involved in experiencing the wilderness first hand and organize support for the protection of nature and endangered species. Men should also become what Robert Bly has called "inner warriors" for the earth, involving themselves in non-violent civil disobedience to protect wilderness areas from further destruction.

31   An important aspect of the masculine ethic is defense of family. Pesticides and other toxic pollutants that poison our food, homes, water, and air represent a real danger, especially to children. Men need to be adamant in their call for limitations on the use of chemicals.

32   Wendell Berry has pointed out that the ecological crisis is also a crisis of agriculture. If men are to recapture a true sense of stewardship and husbandry and affirm the "seedbearing," creative capacity of the male, they must, to the extent possible, become involved in sustainable agriculture and organic farm-

ing and gardening. We should also initiate and support legislation that sustains our farming communities.

Men in the Classrooms and Community

In many communities, especially inner cities, men are 33
absent not only from homes but also from the schools. Men
must support the current efforts by black men's groups
around the country to implement male-only early-grade
classes taught by men. These programs provide role models
and a surrogate paternal presence for young black males. We
should also commit ourselves to having a far greater male
presence in all elementary school education. Recent studies
have shown that male grade school students have a higher
level of achievement when they are taught by male teachers.
Part-time or full-time home schooling options can also be
helpful in providing men a great opportunity to be teachers—
not just temperaments—to their children.

We need to revive our concern for community. Commu- 34
nity-based boys' clubs, scout troops, sports leagues, and big
brother programs have achieved significant success in helping fatherless male children find self-esteem. Men's groups
must work to strengthen these organizations.

Men's Minds, Men's Bodies, and Work

Men need to join together to fight threats to male health 35
including suicide, drug and alcohol abuse, AIDS, and stress
diseases. We should support active prevention and education
efforts aimed at these deadly threats. Most importantly, men
need to be leaders in initiating and supporting holistic and
psychotherapeutic approaches that directly link many of these
health threats to the coercive nature of the male mystique and
the current economic system. Changes in diet, reduction of
drug and alcohol use, less stressful work environments,
greater nurturing of and caring for men by other men, and
fighting racism, hopelessness, and homelessness are all important, interconnected aspects of any male health initiative.

Men without Hope or Homes

Men need to support measures that promote small busi- 36
ness and entrepreneurship, which will allow more people to
engage in crafts and human-scale, community-oriented
enterprises. Also important is a commitment to appropriate,

human-scale technologies such as renewable energy sources. Industrial and other inappropriate technologies have led to men's dispossession, degradation—and increasingly to unemployment.

37   A related struggle is eliminating racism. No group of men is more dispossessed than minority men. White men should support and network with African-American and other minority men's groups. Violence and discrimination against men because of their sexual preference should also be challenged.

38   Men, who represent more than four-fifths of the homeless, can no longer ignore this increasing social tragedy. Men's councils should develop support groups for the homeless in their communities.

The Holocaust of Men

39   As the primary victims of mechanized war, men must oppose this continued slaughter. Men need to realize that the traditional male concepts of the noble warrior are undermined and caricatured in the technological nightmare of modern warfare. Men must together become prime movers in dismantling the military-industrial establishment and redistributing defense spending toward a sustainable environment and protection of family, school, and community.

Men's Action Network

40   No area of the men's political agenda will be realized until men can establish a network of activists to create collective action. A first step might be to create a high-profile national coalition of the men's councils that are growing around the country. This coalition, which could be called the Men's Action Network (MAN), could call for a national conference to define a comprehensive platform of men's concerns and to provide the political muscle to implement those ideas.

A Man Could Stand Up

41   The current generation of men face a unique moment in history. Though often still trapped by economic coercion and

psychological co-optation, we are beginning to see that there is a profound choice ahead. Will we choose to remain subservient tools of social and environmental destruction or to fight for rediscovery of the male as a full partner and participant in family, community, and the earth? Will we remain mesmerized by the male mystique, or will we reclaim the true meaning of our masculinity?

There is a world to gain. The male mystique, in which   42
many of today's men—especially the most politically powerful—are trapped, is threatening the family and the planet with irreversible destruction. A men's movement based on the recovery of masculinity could renew much of the world we have lost. By changing types of work and work hours, we could break our subordination to corporate managers and return much of our work and lives to the household. We could once again be teaching, nurturing presences to our children. By devoting ourselves to meaningful work with appropriate technology, we could recover independence in our work and our spirit. By caring for each other, we could recover the dignity of our gender and heal the wounds of addiction and self-destruction. By becoming husbands to the earth, we could protect the wild and recover our creative connections with the forces and rhythms of nature.

Ultimately we must help fashion a world without the daily   43
frustration and sorrow of having to view each other as a collection of competitors instead of a community of friends. We must celebrate the essence and rituals of our masculinity. We can no longer passively submit to the destruction of the household, the demise of self-employment, the disintegration of family and community, and the desecration of our earth.

Shortly after the First World War, Ford Madox Ford, one of   44
this century's greatest writers, depicted 20th century men as continually pinned down in their trenches, unable to stand up for fear of annihilation. As the century closes, men remain pinned down by an economic and political system that daily forces millions of us into meaningless work, powerless lives, and self-destruction. The time has come for men to stand up.

Robert Bly
Naïveté

The following article is an excerpt from Robert Bly's 1990 best-
seller Iron John *(subtitled* A Book about Men*). In the process*
of offering an elaborate explanation of each phase of a Grimm
fairy tale called "Iron John"—the story of a wild man impris-
oned in a cage who escapes and teaches a young boy the secrets
of manhood—the book discusses changes in the modern Amer-
ican view of manhood and attempts to redefine the world of
work and the whole notion of "masculinity." Bly (born 1926)
is a native and resident of rural Minnesota who attempts in
his poetry to articulate archetypal myths, to celebrate primal
emotions, and to explore relations among people and the ele-
mental forces of nature. His many books of poetry have estab-
lished him as a major poetic voice in the United States.

1   We see more and more passivity in men, but also more and
more naïveté. The naïve man feels a pride in being attacked.
If his wife or girlfriend, furious, shouts that he is "chauvinist," a "sexist," a "man," he doesn't fight back, but just takes it.
He opens his shirt so that she can see more clearly where to
put the lances. He ends with three or four javelins sticking
out of his body, and blood running all over the floor. If he
were a bullfighter, he would remain where he was when the
bull charges, would not even wave his shirt or turn his body,
and the horn would go directly in. After each fight friends
have to carry him on their shoulders to the hospital.

2   He feels, as he absorbs attacks, that he is doing the brave
and advanced thing; he will surely be able to recover somewhere in isolation. A woman, so mysterious and superior, has
given him some attention. To be attacked by someone you
love—what could be more wonderful? Perhaps the wounds
may pay for some chauvinistic act, and so allow him to
remain special still longer.

3   The naïve man will also be proud that he can pick up the
pain of others. He particularly picks up women's pain. When
at five years old he sat at the kitchen table, his mother may
have confided her suffering to him, and he felt flattered to be
told of such things by a grown-up, even if it showed his father
up poorly. He becomes attracted later to women who "share
their pain." His specialness makes him, in his own eyes,
something of a doctor. He is often more in touch with

women's pain than with his own, and he will offer to carry a
woman's pain before he checks with his own heart to see if
this labor is proper in the situation. In general, I think each
gender drops its own pain when it tries to carry the pain of
the other gender. I don't mean that men shouldn't listen. But
hearing a woman's pain and carrying it are two different
things. Women have tried for centuries to carry men's pain,
and it hasn't worked well.

The word special is important to the naïve man, and he has   4
special relationships with certain people. We all have some
special relationships, but he surrounds the special person
with a cloying kind of goodwill. The relationship is so special
that he never examines the dark side of the person, which
could be a son, a daughter, a wife, a male friend, a girlfriend.
He accepts responses that are way off, conspires somehow
with their dark side. "Some people are special," he says.

We might say that if he doesn't investigate his son's or   5
daughter's dark side, perhaps they will not investigate his. He
may also have a secret and special relationship with a
wounded little boy inside himself. If so, he won't challenge
the little boy, nor will he point out his self-pity, nor actually
listen to the boy either. He will simply let the boy run his life.

Sincerity is a big thing with him. He assumes that the per-   6
son, stranger, or lover he talks with is straightforward, good-
willed, and speaking from the heart. He agrees with
Rousseau and Whitman that each person is basically noble
by nature, and only twisted a little by institutions. He puts a
lot of stock in his own sincerity. He believes in it, as if it were
a horse or a city wall. He assumes that it will, and should,
protect him from consequences that fall to less open people.
He may say, "It's true that I betrayed you with your best
friend while you were away, and even after you were back,
but I was frank with you and told about it. So why should
you be angry with me?"

A naïve man acts out strange plays of self-isolation. For   7
example, when an angry woman is criticizing him, he may
say, quite sensibly, "You're right. I had no right to do that." If
her anger turns to rage, he bends his head and says, "I've
always been this way." In the third act, he may implicate his
father. "He was never there; he never gave me any support."
Her rage continues and he bends over still farther. He is losing ground rapidly, and in the fourth act he may say: "All men
are shits." He is now many more times isolated than he was a
few minutes ago. He feels rejected by the woman and he is
now isolated from all other men as well. One man I knew

went through this play every time he had a serious fight with a woman, about once a week.

8   The naïve man will lose what is most precious to him because of a lack of boundaries. This is particularly true of the New Age man, or the man seeking "higher consciousness." Thieves walk in and out of his house, carrying large bags, and he doesn't seem to notice them. He tells his "white light" experiences at parties; he confides the contents of last night's dream to a total stranger. Mythologically, when he meets the giant he tells him all his plans. He rarely fights for what is his; he gives away his eggs, and other people raise the chicks. We could say that, unaware of boundaries, he does not develop a good container for his soul, nor a good container for two people. There's a leak in it somewhere. He may break the container himself when he sees an attractive face. As an artist he improvises; as a poet his work lacks meter and shape. Improvisation is not all wrong, but he tends to be proud of his lack of form because he feels suspicious of boundaries. The lack of boundaries will eventually damage him.

9   The naïve man tends to have an inappropriate relation to ecstasy. He longs for ecstasy at the wrong time or in the wrong place, and ignores all masculine sources of it. He wants ecstasy through the feminine, through the Great Mother, through the goddess, even though what may be grounding for the woman ungrounds him. He uses ecstasy to be separated from grounding or discipline.

10   The naïve man will sink into a mood as if into a big hole. Some women, we notice, are able to get around a mood. If a woman has a bad mood before a party, for example, she may walk around the mood, detach it, and get rid of it, at least for a time. But the naïve man's mood seems attached as if to a mountain. He can't separate it. If he feels hurt, or in a low mood, he identifies with the mood, and everyone around him has to go down into the hole. In his mood-trance, he is not present to wife, children, friends.

11   The man without limitations may also specialize in not telling. If, for example, he and others decide that some chairs should be arranged before a performance, and he is assigned to do that, he will probably not tell anyone that he has decided to leave the chairs as they are. The people involved, usually older, immediately get mad and shout. Basically he has tricked them into carrying the anger, and its heaviness. He is clean and light, and wonders why other people get angry so often.

The naïve man often doesn't know that there is a being in 12
him that wants to remain sick. Inside each man or woman
there is a sick person and a well person: and one needs to
know which one is talking at any moment. But awareness of
the sick being, and knowledge of how strong he is, is not part
of the naïve man's field of perceptions.

The naïve man often lacks what James Hillman has called 13
"natural brutality." The mother hawk pushes the younglings
out of the nest one day; we notice the father fox drives the
cubs away in early October. But the ascender lets things go on
too long. At the start of a relationship, a few harsh words of
truth would have been helpful. Instead he waits and waits,
and then a major wounding happens farther down the line.

His timing is off. We notice that there will often be a miss- 14
ing beat a second or so after he takes a blow, verbal or physical. He will go directly from the pain of receiving the blow to
an empathetic grasp of the reason why it came, skipping over
the anger entirely. Misusing Jesus' remark, he turns the missing cheek.

As a final remark about naïveté, we might mention that 15
there is something in naïveté that demands betrayal. The
naïve man will have a curious link to betrayal, deceit, and
lies. Not only will he betray others easily, being convinced his
motives are always good, but when a woman lives with a truly
naïve man for a while, she feels impersonally impelled to
betray him. When there is too much naïveté around, the universe has no choice but to crystallize out some betrayal.

The New Warrior
Training Adventure

*Following is the copy for a promotional brochure that is
designed to attract men to the training that it describes. For a
commentary on the New Warrior Training Adventure, see the
next essay by Doug Stanton.*

> "The real accomplishment (in life) is the art of being
> a warrior, which is the only way to balance the terror
> of being a man with the wonder of being a man."
> *Carlos Castaneda*

Who is the New Warrior?

1   MEN HAVE BEEN WARRIORS since the beginning of time and
every man has his warrior side. But social forces pressure many to
repress this part of themselves. They unconsciously substitute a distorted shadow for the healthy warrior energy so essential to sustaining
individual and communal balance.

2   The New Warrior is a man who has confronted this destructive
"shadow" form and has achieved hard-won ownership of the highly
focused, aggressive energy that empowers and shapes the inner masculine self. Sustained by this new energy, the New Warrior is at once
tough and loving, wild and gentle, fierce and tolerant. He lives passionately and compassionately, because he has learned to live his mission with integrity, and without apology.

What happens in the training?

3   THE NEW WARRIOR TRAINING ADVENTURE is a process of
initiation and self-examination that is crucial to the development of a
healthy and mature male self. It is the "hero's journey" of classical literature and myth—the process of moving away from the comforting
embrace of the mother's feminine energy and safely into the masculine kingdom. It is a journey of the soul during which men confront
their dependence on women, their mistrust of other men and their
need to be special.

> "The truth is, I was afraid of this training. Even though
> I've written about men and worked with men for many
> years, the fact is—as I discovered on the Weekend—I
> didn't really trust men. I'm glad I overcame my fear.
> This was the most powerful training I've ever done, and
> the changes it started in me have been both deep and
> positive."   *Mark Gerzon, author of "A Choice of
> Heroes"*

Who runs the training?

4   THE NEW WARRIOR NETWORK, a national not-for-profit corporation, has assembled a highly motivated, experienced staff to lead the
training programs. Most staff members are volunteers, and because all
have experienced the initiation process themselves, they have a compelling sense of male initiation and authentic self-examination.

In the final analysis, however, you run your own training through   5
the responses and decisions you make along your journey. The staff
serve as your guides and mentors, but you choose your own level of
commitment, and you decide how far you will explore the inner ter-
rain of your life, to discover the treasures and obstacles buried within
your self.

How do I register?

YOU WILL FIND AN ENROLLMENT FORM enclosed with this   6
brochure. Only you can decide if you are ready to participate in the
New Warrior Training Adventure. Because training sessions are
booked far in advance, it may take some time before you are admitted.

Who comes to the training?

DURING YOUR TRAINING you will stand shoulder to shoulder   7
with an immensely rich mix of masculinity, with occupations and
ages as wide as masculinity itself. Whether they're corporate executives or high school students, all come to share a common understanding that their lives as men can be empowered with greater focus
and direction, and that this personal initiation into manhood is crucial
to their full development as men.

Am I ready?

WE DO NOT RECOMMEND this training for every man. We urge   8
you not to apply to this program without serious forethought, and not
to enroll simply at the urging of a spouse or friend.

To participate in this training, you must be in reasonably good   9
physical condition and willing to face the prospect of transformative
change in your life. You must be highly committed to your life, and
ready to participate fully in all training activities, many of which
encourage you to take a hard look at yourself, your deepest fears,
your wounds from the past, and the specific ways in which your life is
not working for you. We choose to work only with men who are
ready and willing to do this initiatory work with us.

What happens after the training?

SEVERAL DAYS AFTER you have completed your initiation into   10
manhood, you are welcomed back into the community of your families, friends and fellow Warriors at a graduation ceremony. There, you
will join a small voluntary team called an Integration Group, which
will help you integrate the training into your life. These Integration
Groups have proven as valuable as the training itself, so we urge each
graduate to join one.

What will I get out of this?

"Previous cultures throughout history always intended authentic masculine initiation. But their vision and their cultural context of the world was necessarily limited. Since the first earthrise photograph from outer space, we have entered a new mythological era. For the first time in human history, we have before us the possibility of authentic masculine initiation—an initiation into the global brotherhood."   *Dr. Robert Moore, Coauthor of "King, Warrior, Magician, Lover"*

"New Warrior training is an authentic initiation into the cauldron of mature masculinity. I recommend it highly to deeply committed men. The NW staff are loving, generous, and deep-intentioned men who will evoke the very best within you."   *Forrest Craver, Convener of the North American Confederation of Men's Councils*

"The New Warrior Training Adventure is the finest experience I've ever had in all my years of men's work. I support it one hundred percent, and I know in my heart that it is critical to our lives, our longevity, our brotherhood, and our health."   *Asa Baber, Men's Columnist for* Playboy *magazine*

"In 1983, I wrote *The Secrets that Men Keep.* After experiencing the New Warrior Training I'm rewriting that book. It's the most important men's work occurring in the U.S., and perhaps in the world, today."   *Dr. Ken Druck, psychologist, consultant, author*

New Warrior Training Center, Director, Phone & Address

For training dates, write or call a center near you.

Tuition—$550 covers complete training, including room and
   board
Deposit—$100 (non-refundable) reserves your space. Payment plans and some scholarships are available. Make checks payable, and clip and mail the Enrollment Form below, to the Training Center of your choice. Visa and Mastercard accepted at most Centers.

Doug Stanton

Inward Ho!

This commentary on the New Warrior Training Adventure weekend (see the previous selection) appeared in the October 1991 issue of Esquire, *a mass-circulation magazine on contemporary culture that appeals mainly to men. That particular* Esquire, *billed as a Special Issue on "the state of masculinity," included a report on Robert Bly and* Iron John *as well as a half dozen other articles on one or another aspect of masculinity. Doug Stanton tells you a bit about himself in the article.*

This is a story about a descent, a gut-chilling, moaning, puking belly flop into grief. The eyes pop, the man's face streams with tears, he busts out giggling. He is hugged, he whispers I love you to the man hugging him. Twenty-fours hours earlier, these two men, a dentist and an accountant, were total strangers. The question nobody seems to be asking is, *Aren't they still?* 1

The Kenosha, Wisconsin, twilight was lovely, casting a yellow, antique tint over the rental car, over the farm fields laid out in the dusk like photos of the night sky. 2

So, naturally, this seemed like the last place I'd expect to be kidnapped. The last place I'd see a real estate agent kiss his dead father goodbye. The last place I'd watch a naked insurance salesman on a plastic lawn-chair cushion smoking a cigar and juggling a double-headed dildo, the giant ends bobbing up and down as he confessed, "I too, have a short dick." 3

The New Warrior Training Adventure Weekend, founded in 1984 by psychotherapist Bill Kauth, ex-Marine and industrial engineer Rich Tosi, and personal-growth aficionado Ron Hering, boasts training compounds in Wisconsin, Minnesota, California, and Illinois (with expansion planned in four more states). Thus far, the self-help empire has graduated an estimated 1,500 New Warriors: Nineties Real Men who growl and yodel to protect what's theirs (their balls, among other things), weep and moan over what they've lost (their minds, it seems), and kick the world's ass without apology while smiling at feminists. They walk softly, wave huge inner swords, and carry honest-to-God New Warrior calling cards embossed with their animal *nommes de change* (Harley "Mountain 4

Goat" Faunteleroy) and the trademarked New Warrior logo,
which looks like a pissed-off finch choking on a twig.

5   Traditional, macho roles have failed us, they murmur, and
after twenty years of feminism, they feel more receptive to
women's needs and emotions than their own—true enough.
And by drumming their brains out and chanting their lips off,
the men try to reclaim an inner, primal, ruddy Natural Man,
the Wildman—the New Warrior's hairy mentor—who lum-
bers through Robert Bly's best-selling book *Iron John* (based
on a Grimm Brothers fairy tale) like an absentminded bigfoot
with a degree in social work.

6   Joke: How many fairy tales did it take to make a woman a
senator?

7   To talk about the men's movement is to talk about how
American men—white, educated American men—are spending money to make themselves feel good. Therapy and economics, psychologist James Hillman points out, are now
America's leading ideologies. The men's movement seems
mostly a therapeutic circus of monied fellows who sometime
over the last twenty years lost their souls either on Wall Street
or during a feminist march. The men's movement is like the
1970s revisited, except now it's the We Decade: men in one big
flock taking one giant leap inward to ask, "Who am I as a
man?"

8   "Most of the men are from white Middle America—
professors, computer programmers, in their middle thirties
to fifties," said Marvin Allen of the Austin Men's Center, the
country's largest clubhouse for wounded males. "Twenty-five
to thirty percent are therapists, and forty to fifty percent are
in some kind of twelve-step recovery program," constituting
not what you'd call a demographic sweep of the country.

9   Allen estimated, however, that a quarter million men have
attended some kind of men's event similar to the Wildman
gatherings organized by the Austin Men's Center. Indeed,
publications like *Man* and *Wingspan*, which boasts a world-
wide circulation of 120,000, advertise things like Holotropic
Breathwork and workshops on how to "encounter your inner
shadow." Or you can ship yourself off to a men's sacred initiation, a men's "spirit camp" (to "track your feelings"), a men's
canoe passage ("mask-making and mischief" included), a
men's desert vision quest, or a "Quest for Survival." If you
can't actually go anywhere, the gents on the phone at Ally
Press Center or the Sounds True Catalog will slap some cassette tapes on your Gold Card, turning your Volvo into a rolling woodlot of weeping, chanting men.

In all, the men's movement is like one big manly travel   10
agency, delivering you to undiscovered corners of your
psyche. Last May, the movement moved into America's living
room when Hugh Downs and *20 20* showed up at one of
Allen's Wildman gatherings.

"God, I feel sorry for those guys," said my wife while our   11
television swarmed with men screaming around a bonfire.

Hugh Downs murmured into the camera about how so far   12
everything was impressive and interesting.

"Turn around, Hugh," my wife said. *"There's a guy beating*   13
up a tree."

The wiry goon with the walkie-talkie running security for   14
the weekend stepped boldly into our rental car's path and
raised his clipboard.

"Halt!" he yelled.   15

You're joking, I thought. Dressed in black pants, black sweat   16
shirt, his jaunty green beret floating above his ash-smudged
face, he looked like a Boy Scout who'd earned a badge in modern art. He leaned in to my window larger than a bad made-
for-TV-movie terrorist and peered solemnly.

Without asking my name, he checked it off a list of twenty-   17
three mostly white-collar hombres who'd already arrived
from as far away as Colorado and North Carolina for a rite of
passage into manhood, which is how the brochure, dainty as
a vegetarian menu, described this $550 men-only retreat.

Charlie Boy Scout was feeling out the brotherhood between   18
us, but his eyes were saying, *The others all arrived ON TIME.*

This was true, but hadn't I read that a New Warrior is a   19
"man without apology?" Leaving the Milwaukee airport, I'd
picked up Tom Daly (the registration packet had reminded
me that carpooling is a good "opportunity for men to be with
each other") and had driven to Kenosha by first going to Madison, which is like driving to New York via Los Angeles. It was
a weird road to Warrior City and I had wanted to check in
early before all the finger paints were gone.

"When you made that one turn back there..." Tom said   20
quietly. And then, as if blinking an inner eye, "I haven't been
trusting my *instinct.*"

"Kind of embarrassing for two would-be Warriors," I said   21
and laughed. Tom didn't. Tom's a mover and shaker in the
men's movement, which means he doesn't have much of a
sense of humor. He's active in the Rocky Mountain Men's Center, and director of the Men's Council Project in Boulder,
where he spends his days "body-and-soul wrestling" and

"power dancing." He's a helluva nice guy, even if he does sleep with his homemade spear and take it for jogs through the park, as he explained in *Wingspan. Harper's* reprinted Tom's meditation and managed, with little effort, to make it sound like the most ridiculous thing since the *last* time a guy ran through a park with a spear.

22   "Did that bother you?" I asked.

23   "No. They completely missed the point."

24   When you spend any time around the Men, you learn one thing: Everyone knows everyone in the movement and no one who isn't, and those outsiders are usually *missing the point.*

25   Bill Kauth suddenly slid, smiling like Kenny Rogers, into the rental car, tapped me mystically, and whispered, "Drive!" I was being taken hostage to manhood, New Warrior style.

26   He ordered me to lock the car and led me in a trot to the Haimowoods Conference Center, a concrete-and-rafter bunker in the middle of the woods. "Go, *go*," he whispered like an urgent wizard, trotting off before I could ask him why everyone in the men's movement wore a beard. My Rite o' Passage had begun.

27   As I nudged the door open with my briefcase, I expected to bust in on turtlenecked men sitting cross-legged and speaking urgently about what it's like to be turtlenecked men. Instead, facing me was an ash-smudged guy in black commando gymwear biting on a Tiparillo and blowing clouds of smoke in my face. I'll call him Sergeant Wolf.

28   "Are *you* ready?" he boomed.

29   *Are you kidding?* I thought. "Yes." I said.

30   "Why have you come?"

31   "Curiosity."

32   Wolfman cocked his head.

33   "Curiosity *as a man*," I quickly added. This pleased him.

34   "Are you ready to challenge yourself in every aspect, to meet your shadow?"

35   "Sure," I said.

36   Mr. Wolf studied my resolve, our noses nearly touching. "Step ahead, *now*."

37   A screech zipped down the candle-lit hallway. "Get your shit together and put it down here!" This was Mr. Peepers (not his real animal name). He was a short, unhappy-looking male, another one of the weekend's staff members. I tried stepping around him, then spied a roomful of fellows just like him waiting for me to make my move. I put my shit down.

38   Sitting at a card table was another little male in somber clothes eyeing me down the beam of his cigar. He pointed to a

name tag on the table. "Turn it over!" I did. "You're Number Twenty-one now." He shoved a piece of paper at me. "Read this and sign it!"

I read it: "I agree not to publicly discuss or write about   39
what I'm about to experience." Something to that effect. The light was bad. I signed it: At my feet lay a briefcase with all my notes for this story, including the transcript of one interview with Sergeant Wolf, whose voice I recognized from our earlier phone conversation, when he said: "We want the whole symphony of your manhood at your disposal, *not just the brass section, or the timpani.*"

So now I'm waiting for my briefcase of notes to spring   40
open and fly around the room, sparking a New Warrior riot.

"Number Twenty-one, give my your wallet, your watch,   41
rings, weapons, your electrical devices, medications, your drugs, and tobacco," keened Mr. Cliff Swallow, which seemed to be his real animal name. He held out a Ziploc bag.

I gave him my wallet and watch. Kill me for the rest.   42
"You may go," he said, waving me on.   43
Heh, heh, so long, I thought. And then I walked into a room   44
where a bank of thousand-watt lightbulbs immediately blew a part in my hair, gave me skin cancer, and tattooed me with the thought that everything happening was still manageable, which signaled, I knew, greater weirdness to come. The goons stood in a solemn line behind a conference table, longing to be badasses, squinting through a curtain of cheap cigar smoke. Next to the table sat a black-and-white television vibrating with static and snow.

What was going on here? On the phone, Bill Kauth had   45
deflected my preweekend questions, and now I knew why: I wouldn't have shown up. You could have more fun spending $550 in an emergency room.

"We create a container wherein men can completely rede-   46
fine themselves," Kauth did say over the phone.

"Completely?" I asked.   47
"Absolutely."   48
The rite of passage, he said, is about finding one's authen-   49
ticity. "It's a dive into the essential self and soul beyond masks. We talk a great deal of building this container where men can dive into their hearts, guts, and balls. We find incredible brotherhood in this."

Why not run into the woods and throw down a sleeping   50
bag for adventure? I wondered. It's a lot easier and nobody has to dress up.

51   Kauth supposed you could find yourself by getting lost in the woods, but it might take months.

52   "So what's the difference?"

53   "We do it in two days. Take your pick."

54   The Microwave Ritual! Because in the kingdom of the New Warrior, you haven't got time for the pain.

55   I picked up my suitcase and dumped my shit onto the big, pink table and watched while the goons pawed and sifted.

56   "What's *this*?" Brother Marmot was holding up a hair dryer.

57   "A hair dryer."

58   "No! *This* is an electrical device!"

59   "And we guess you won't be needing this *nail file!*" said Brother Earth Pig.

60   "My wife's, it's her suitcase...."

61   "And this Tampax! Hah!"

62   Marmot held up the Tampax so Earth Pig could look at it, and it must have been the funniest goddamned thing ever to come across the table because they grinned like drunken pirates.

63   "Empty your pockets." Out came my pens, notebooks, car keys, tape recorder, camera, compass, and lucky jackknife.

64   "A weapon!" someone yelled. "In the interest of your safety and the safety of others, do I have your permission to frisk you?"

65   The goons confiscated everything but my haircut, missing the notes that would have triggered a fair imitation of truth or dare at the Manson house.

66   This was my rite of passage? In five minutes I'd been bush-whacked by a gang of merchants in the therapy trade dressed up like Boy Scouts on steroids. I stunk with sweat, my eyes burned, and the scripted interrogation was a comic opera call for Big Daddy. *Kick my ass! Help my get my shit together! Teach me to be a man!* The whole room seemed seized not only in a crisis of male identity but in a crisis of imagination: Are cigars and theatrical snarls the best we fellows can offer each other? "Know deeply who you are as a man," the brochure had urged me. "Reclaim your power as a man. Realize you are not alone." These interesting challenges to the soul were reduced to a Three Stooges skit.

67   Bill Kauth explained the greeting, as he called it, another way: "We're saying, 'We're the Elders, the grandfathers.' We're saying, 'Surrender and trust us.'"

68   After the interrogation, we'd been led to a dark basement and ordered to shut up, sit on our luggage, and wait. Soon, a

furious, awkward drumming thrummed overhead and the
goons solemnly led us upstairs into something that resembled
Barney Rubble's living room. They stood chewing their cigars
and farting and burping like a choir of barn animals, while
we, a tribe of white middle-class guys, rustled anxiously in
flannel shirts, jeans, dress slacks, and snappy sportswear.

And then, from a darkened hallway, strode an honest-to-   69
God bearded Elder who leaned down from the stone ledge
and shook an honest-to-God walking staff like Moses on angel
dust.

Surrender! This was it! We were KO'd flat on our asses.   70

"Number Thirteen, stand up and tell these men why you   71
didn't bring *food to feed them!*" boomed Senor Elder.

The poor chump in penny loafers and blue Patagonia   72
jacket cockily rose and said, "It wasn't mentioned in the *original* agreement I signed." Also, for five hundred bucks who'd
think you'd have to bring a dish to pass?

"Are you a fucking lawyer, Number Thirteen?"   73
"Yes."   74

"How will you apologize to these men for not feeding   75
them?"

Number Thirteen shrugged.   76
Senor Elder barked, *"You could massage their feet!"*   77
The chump's eyes widened in fear.   78
"Do you want to tell me to fuck off, Number Thirteen?"   79
Blink. "No."   80

You could feel our communal Pit o' Grief rise up on its ten- 81
nis shoes and Tony Lamas to beat Senor Elder with his own
stick.

"I think you do."   82
Surrender!   83

"Fuck you! Fuck you! Fuck you!" screamed Number Thir-   84
teen. It blew out of his mouth in a steaming, raging spray that
had been festering in his soul ever since the chimp at the door
blew cigar smoke in his face. His chest heaved, he blinked
dumbly.

"Again!"   85

"Fuck fuck fuck YOU!" On and on the rage came, spewing   86
and splashing around the room, men ducking their heads,
closing their eyes. "FUCK you, FUCK you, you fucking motherFUCKER!" flew the bile, springing from deeper sources
now, hitting his father, his boss, his wife, smack in the face,
whap! The room was silent.

"How do you feel?"   87
Quietly: "Better. I feel better."   88

89   Number Seven suddenly erupted, "I'm afraid I'm an ass-hole, I don't wanna be an asshole any longer! Let's get the ball rolling, Jack! Fuckin' A, let's get on with the weekend, I don't wanna be an asshole anymore!" It was breathtaking, like attending a Rotary meeting in a lifeboat.

90   "Ho!" barked Scowling Beaver, silencing us with the Native American expression meaning "I understand."

91   He opened a manila folder and read a typed sacred page describing Manhood, *our* Manhood, tracing its lineage far back into a distant mythic forest rippling in the fuzz of his prose, where, he assured us, our grandfathers had emoted to beat the band and worked at fulfilling jobs in something that resembled a gold-roofed arts-and-crafts barn, making spears and shit, and living happy, happy, manly lives.

92   But then, he explained, shaking his finger, the Industrial Revolution came along and cut down the forest—*bad* Industrial Revolution! And Grandpa Zeus and Uncle Odysseus were forced from the manly forest into the city, where they found *un*fulfilling jobs as trailer-park managers and chemical engineers. Aha. This is why we've paid $550—enough money to support a family with two malnourished children for a *month*—to gather as educated white men for whom the world is an unfulfilling place.

93   And we want our mythic forest back!

94   "Ho!" shouted some fellows.

95   "What! Have! You! Come! Here! To! *Learn?*" thundered Senor Elder.

96   "I want to know why I fear women!" shouted a pilgrim.

97   "Women can shame the *fuck* out of us!" Sergeant Wolf shouted back. The Pit o' Grief swelled with fellow feeling, *splash!* Our lives were crossing paths, *wham!* Here we were, strangers in a strange land, instantly cutting the bullshit and diving willy-nilly into our balls and shouting out our fear, our joys. Glances caromed through the room. *Who really really really am I as a man? Are you my brother?* The thrill of discovery pinned us to one big heartbeat. We were charging into the mythic forest!

98   Next we played a ritual bonding game of Capture the Flag, crashing through muddy farm fields and inch-long thorns that shredded our clothes and delivered us wheezing like rag salesmen back at the Pit, where we immediately discussed how the game *felt*.

99   "It felt kind of stupid," I said, diving into my heart in this container of fellows with whom I'd just bonded. "I mean, it's not like we were really raising the emotional ante out there."

My fellow pilgrims murmured cautiously. The staff just   100
stared. The thing about the Rite of Passage, apparently, was
that you could tell everybody to fuck off, but you couldn't get
personal.

Scowling Beaver finally pierced the silence with his cry,   101
"Men, it's time to meet the Wildman!"

Let us begin the guided visualization!   102

Out through the stereo squirted new age music. And while   103
Scowling Beaver narrated the Wildman tale (which I can't
divulge due to my vow of secrecy), urging us downward into
our fiercest selves, we closed our eyes and howled like cross-
eyed mutts in a humane society kennel on Euthanasia Friday.
Beyond the conference center, the world glimmered like an
irrelevant outpost. I lay there biting the carpet, my voice
wrecked by mythic snarling.

The fellows stood up sheepishly, glanced around.   104

"You've done good *work* here tonight, men. You really   105
have," said a pleased Scowling Beaver.

"You now have sixty seconds to find your room. In the   106
morning, you'll have sixty seconds to take a cold shower.
Each of you has a sink in your room. In other words, each of
you has a urinal. You'll need your energy tomorrow, so no sex
tonight! *No jurkin' uff!*"

No one even blinked; by the end of our first night together, 107
we'd *surrendered 'To the Grandfathers.'*

"Sometimes I think our leadership in this country is noth-   108
ing more than an attempt to prove it's not a wimp," Betty
Friedan railed on the phone. "What does it prove that we can
bomb with smart bombs and still not solve our nation's problems, like homelessness?

"The men's movement does tap into a yearning for the   109
father who was distant because of the bipolar nature of the
family. And there is also a yearning for a more authentic,
masculine self. But! These Wildman and Warrior gatherings
are an attempt to *rigidify* the machismo mask that actually
may or may not have aided the original caveman in his survival. The authenticity of masculinity has to rest on firmer
ground."

(Wait a minute! "I think she called Robert Bly an *asshole* 110
publicly!" said *Wingspan* publisher Bob Frenier. "When she
hears Wildman, she sees John Wayne. I'm all for feminism,
but if she hadn't spent twenty years bashing men, if she had
more testosterone, she might see what we're talking about!
She's! . . . She's! . . . She's a Warrior herself, you know!")

111   Friedan railed on: "If the women's movement was anything, it was an affirmation of the authenticity of womanhood, an attempt to break constricting masks that I called the
feminine mystique. I really object to the implication that this
Warrior stuff is a male version of the women's movement. The
men's movement is a dangerous constriction of masculinity,
an invalid reaction to the women's movement. The promise of
an *authentic* men's movement is the thought that men would
not have to put on these false masks."

112   Maybe not a joke: How many women *would* be senators if
during the Sixties one of them had cooked up a Betty
Crocker-from-Hell Weekend replete with Terminal PMS
Scream and a Ritual Torture Kitchen, in which Bitchy Betty
flogged paying housewives with the Mythic Cake Pan of Fem-
ininity while ratty wenches in chain-mail aprons fogged the
air with clouds of Pam?

113   The mood next morning as we mill around the Pit is somewhere between a slaughterhouse and a moonwalk.

114   We woke up tired, pissed in our sinks, munched on bowls
of industrial-grade oatmeal, and chatted nervously:

115   "So, what's your Shadow?"

116   "How 'bout them Red Sox!"

117   "I don't know about you, but I didn't jerk off last night."

118   We received our animal names. Hi, I'm Fox.

119   And we also distilled our life "missions" and "affirmations"
on scratch paper ("As a man among men, I show strength!"
Or "As a man among men, I give love!") and mused about our
"dicks, women, and rage" while filling out a questionnaire
that resembled a therapist's intake form.

120   Now we glance nervously at absent watches, cinch up
sweat pants. The staff emerges from a secret back-room meeting where they've been planning our next ritual. Something is
different this morning, but what? It's the staff! They're smiling at us! And they're not burping and farting this morning:
They're hugging!

121   So even before Scowling Beaver ceremoniously unrolls a
dirty yellow rug and calls it a "magic carpet," we know something's up. In fact, this is our invitation to run screaming into
the brotherhood of mythic forest, the weekend's central
moment, the creme of the Rite of Passage.

122   "This is an exploration of your Shadow!" Scowling Beaver
announces, "your deepest self, your darkest fears and secrets.
This is the Hero's Journey. And the hero continues on even
when facing certain annihilation."

Birdman, a long-haired fellow in his twenties, steps boldly   123
from our circle and onto the carpet. We clap, we cheer, we
don't know what the hell we're doing.

"Repeat your life affirmation three times, and really mean   124
it" says Scowling Beaver.

"As a man among men, I am a recycler of aluminum!" Or   125
something. He beams, waiting for permission to rejoin our
circle.

"You don't seem very convinced of yourself," Scowling   126
Beaver says. "He didn't convince us—did he, men?"

"No!" a few shout.   127

Mr. Peepers joins in: "Birdman, how do you feel now?"   128

"Scared. I feel scared. I feel alone. I feel like an idiot."   129

"Thanks," says Mr. Peepers, exhaling, as if he just invented   130
the word. *"Thanks* for sharing that."

Birdman drops his head, his chin bobbing on big chest.   131

"And what are you feeling *now*, Birdman? That twitching in   132
your shoulder? Yes, *that* movement—what is it? Go with it!"

Birdman's chest heaves.   133

"Fear?" he croaks.   134

"Fear of what?"   135

"Of not being a recycler of aluminum."   136

"Follow the feeling, the trembling," Scowling Beaver   137
coaxes. "Are you scared because your dad said you'd never be
a *real* recycler of aluminum?"

"No, no, no . . ."   138

"That's it—isn't it, Birdman?"   139

Birdman rises slowly on his toes, his rigid face juts upward   140
at the infinite sky on the other side of the ceiling, his chest
heaves, his fists clench. He hovers trembling at the edge of
the forest, at the lip of the abyss where the sunlight ends and
the Shadow begins.

And then: *"AAAARRRRGGGG. GOD HELP MEEEE!"* he   141
howls in a long, spiraling descent.

He implodes in his tennis shoes, his face screwing up into   142
a gooey mask of fear, incomprehension, and rage. Long, deep
bellows pour forth in operatic jets, shaking him to the magic
carpet, where he lies weeping his death song. Ten minutes
ago, he'd stood smiling at us, a hotel desk clerk from Chicago.
Now he's a mess.

He sobs with oceanic force, ripping himself apart. The staff   143
urgently kneels at his side, guiding him to his Shadow, allowing
him to taste it, touch it—inhabit it! Even afterward, nothing
else will seem as horrible as this minute, this meeting with his
unexplored self, what Carl Jung called "the dark side of our

nature." Birdman is sticking his nose in every sour, vile impulse, every nagging odor of insecurity, and it isn't killing him!

144   But it's putting the hurt on everyone in the Pit of Grief. The place explodes. Eight other men begin to shake and weep, yelling at dads, at horrible childhoods, at domineering mothers.

145   Who will freak out next? Those who haven't imploded, like me, nervously pace the carpet, fighting tears, pausing to stare at the contortions of our brethren. Where are my tears coming from? Is this what I've always wanted, to spew my guts all over the walls?

146   Suddenly the man next to me, Jackrabbit, commences growling. Scowling Beaver stands and juggles two oranges.

147   "I want me balls back, Mother!" Jackrabbit howls at Scowling Beaver. Jackrabbit flicks his head side to side, his wild eyes fixed on the oranges' orbit.

148   Scowling Beaver quickly orders us to stand in a barricade around him.

149   "Give 'em to me, you bitch!" Jackrabbit screams. He crashes into us with a sweaty *whump,* reaching for the oranges, blood draining from his face. We stop him. He backs up, rockets ahead again.

150   "I can't go on," he groans.

151   "You can *do* it!" we yell.

152   "MOTHER OF GOD!" He's never felt this strong before! He's always been an accountant, and now the Wildman's energy beats in his heart, his guts, his balls! No, wait, not his balls, his mother has his balls. She turned him into a wimp, always told him to be a good boy, never let him piss in the sink. He raises his left hand—*his sword!*—and charges, panting like a plow horse, busting through the knot of men, emerging on the other side.

153   He halts, stunned, spins on his feet, and stares murderously at his oranges, like a psychopath in a fruit market. Scowling Beaver hands over the fruit, what he's paid $550 for at the door.

154   "I got'em back! I got'em back!" Jackrabbit shouts gleefully.

155   He hops to the stone ledge, sticks a plastic baseball bat between his legs, and waves his new weenie at us, his exhausted face streaming with joy. Brother Marmot ceremoniously dips a soup ladle in a spaghetti pot filled with tap water and delivers it to Jackrabbit, who drinks deep, like a prince.

156   This is the most amazing thing I've ever seen, and it refuses to stop happening—ten, eleven hours of men biting blankets in half, men puking awful childhood memories of Mom and Dad into aluminum bowls, men beating pillows with tennis

rackets, men kissing dead fathers goodbye. The sun sets in the woods beyond the windows, the room goes dark, time stops, the world dies, but in the Pit a new world is rising up, bucking and writhing like a giant gray sponge oozing grief. Time is measured in screams, grunts, and howls as the men crawl, raising swords, fighting their battles, all night dropping down, down. . . .

"This is men's work, Fox," Mr. Peepers says, gliding up to 157 me. He looks deeply in my eyes, urging me to implode. I'm the only one who hasn't. My ears are jelly, my eyes ragged holes. I'm speaking in tongues and wearing my hair backwards. It's like being locked in a dumpster.

Other men are huddled around the spaghetti pot, slurping 158 their Hero's Drink, hugging and smiling blissfully at vanishing points in each other's eyes.

"Men need to grieve, and they never do enough of it," Mr. 159 Peepers tells me. And then he urges me, "*Feed on male milk,* Fox. There really is such a thing, you know."

Male milk! Yuck!   160

Nearby, two weeping men leap up, a dentist and an 161 accountant, striding from the separate seas of their loneliness, filled now with unspoken understanding of the other's grief and embrace:

"I love you, Water Buffalo," the first says.   162

"And I love you, Zebra," says the other.   163

Bingo! They are basking in the mythic forest's brotherhood! 164

"We have not finished with the moment of truth," Scowling 165 Beaver announces. "You've done good work here tonight, men. The work of warriors. Any man who hasn't had his opportunity to see his Shadow, please step forward and get it."

All eyes turn to me. I don't step forward and for the rest of 166 the weekend my newfound pals are guarded strangers. So much for brotherhood.

So now the men are strangers to each other no longer, 167 emoting freely like Grandpa Zeus and Uncle Odysseus. But what did these men really know about each other? Can you make a credo, a community, out of a roomful of screams? We wouldn't see each other again, most of us. If we were pets, some of us would've been left behind at a rest stop. The emotions dripping down the walls were murderously authentic, but at any moment Mr. Peepers could snap his fingers, tell us to knock it off, and the wailing would have shut down as if on a valve. We were inside a psychodramatic process, and Mr. Peepers wanted us all inside with him. Me, I wanted to be outdoors, looking at a tree.

168   This leap inward seemed like a giant leap backward, into the monarchy of self, therapy's cathedral. Life is a democracy of sunlight, wind, people, birds, rivers—*out there*. With enough bad food, sleep deprivation, cigars, and drums, anyone can be made to cry, but this is not the same as being made to think. Or to imagine a new way to live *out there* in the big world's bloody maw.

169   We'd plunked down our money to stand around like schoolboys waiting for the order to cry, to go fetch our souls. There is no good reason, however, to explain why a man who feels incomplete should solve this problem by paying someone to tell him he can cry. If you want to weep, weep. Who told us it would be easy? If you want to hug your father, spend your $550 on a plane ticket to his door. Our rite of passage seemed not a cure for a passionless grip on life, but rather a symptom.

170   "Tonight is a good night to die!" Brother Marmot whoops, rips off my blindfold, slaps me on my bare ass, and over the thunderous drumming yells, "Go dance!"

171   This is the weekend's crowning dollop, our irritation ceremony. It's nearly four in the morning, the magic carpet is rolled up in the corner like a dirty yellow rug, and the Pit o' Grief is now awhir with naked, yodeling men beating their chests and prancing with weenies akimbo around a bonfire of patio candles. It's actually even less picturesque than it sounds—it's like standing in a poorly lit room surrounded by twenty-two pink refrigerators.

172   The drumming halts and we plop down cross-legged around the fire. Brother Marmot blesses a talisman—sage and stones in a red leather pouch—in the pungent smoke of a burning sage stick.

173   "Brother Water Buffalo! Smelly, fat, hard of hearing! Men have run very far to get away from you. And, now, YOU R-UH WARYORE." Delivered with a ceremonial slap on the cheek, as if to a mosquito, and the anointing of the talisman around the neck.

174   "Brother Fox! Sly, elusive. Men have peered far into the forest to glimpse your beauty," Brother Marmot peers, slaps. "Get into trouble, Fox! That's what men do! AND NOW YOU R-UH WARYORE!"

175   GRANDFATHER, WE'RE NEW WARRIORS!

176   We stand, join hands, our talismans flouncing on our puffed-out chests. Exhausted, mushy smiles crease our faces. Silence.

We're brothers now, strangers no longer, the men nod, burp-   177
ing in the candlelight.

The next day, Brother Water Buffalo, a dentist from nearby   178
farm country, goes home to his wife, a schoolteacher who
spent the weekend working a fundraiser at a children's hospital. She reports that her husband "looked miserable, walking
through the door with beady red eyes, hair sticking straight
up, flames coming out of his ears. He looked like he could've
lifted up the house if he wanted."

He feels that way because that's how he felt the night   179
before, dancing around the fire. The room seemed like a cave,
and the drumming went to work on him. Now he's going to
build his own drum—imagine that, a dentist with a tom-tom,
practically overnight. He'd been seeing a counselor who told
him, "We can work here for months, or you can get with the
Warrior weekend."

"The problem is," says his wife, "now when I say some-   180
thing that offends him, he *snorts*. Now it's: 'I'm a man, I've
said my piece.' He even announced that we're going to leave
the toilet seat *up!* I've talked to the staff's children, too, and
they tell me that when dad comes home from his weekend,
he's weird for a week."

Her girlfriend's husband, Badger, became a Warrior, too,   181
and they commiserate. Her girlfriend spent the weekend worrying. "I was pacing, I was almost ill. When he walked
through the door, I thought he'd say he didn't want to live
here anymore." Hadn't that happened to a couple they knew,
some man Badger had met through his insurance business?

"But it's changed me," she say. "I'm more in touch with his   182
emotions because he is."

"I was ripe," says Zebra, a physiology teacher and Vietnam   183
vet. "I'd been in counseling and I was ready." His wife went to
Europe, he went to Warrior City. "I feel I'm strong and soft at
the same time. It feels good to be whole. But let me tell you, I
jumped back sixteen years to the jungle that first night. I was
back in survival mode, I was ready to slit the guy's throat. . . .
I'll never meet all my shadows, but knowing that they're there
is empowering."

I didn't talk to the guy who showed up, peeked in the front   184
door and slammed it on Sergeant Wolf's cigar. Or to another
guy, Boar, who left after the first night, murmuring, "It's not
for me, it's not for me." Marvin Allen told me, "One of my people from the Men's Center went to a Warrior weekend, and he
found it boring, monotonous, and repetitive"

185   The weekend was like medicine: The brethren didn't like *being* there, but liked having *been* there. If the twenty-three of us wimps had pooled our registration fees, we could've thrown one helluva $13,500 party, replete with some *real* Wildman activity.

186   Tacked to my office wall is a yellow certificate in a plastic sheath which tells the world I "completed and survived" the New Warrior Training Adventure Weekend. It reminds me of one of those I FOUGHT MIKE TYSON T-shirts. I imagine that Grandpa Zeus and Uncle Odysseus, reposed in the shade of the mythic forest, are laughing. In the old days, you didn't become a man just by showing up.

187   The certificate bears the illustration of a man in a business suit running into a tunnel, his umbrella raised like a sword, his briefcase swinging like a shield. Why is he running into the tunnel? There's nobody in there. Anyway, good luck.

188   I'm the other guy, running the other way, fast as I can.

Ursula K. Le Guin
Limberlost

Ursula K. Le Guin (born 1929) is one of the most respected science fiction and fantasy writers in America: perhaps you have read her children's books or poetry or short fiction or one of her many novels—maybe The Left Hand of Darkness *(1969) or* The Dispossessed *(1974) or one of the pieces of her Earthsea Trilogy. A resident of Portland, Oregon, a conservationist, and a passionate devotee of the western United States, she has received a National Book Award and a host of other prizes for her work. In 1992, she contributed her story "Limberlost" to a book of readings called* Women Respond to the Men's Movement, *edited by Kay Leigh Hagan and containing contributions by many prominent feminists. In an afterword, Le Guin notes that although the story is presented as fiction, nothing except its title is invented: the events depicted actually took place in 1985. Le Guin had been invited to a conference on "The Great Mother" in order to read from her novel* Always Coming Home, *which celebrates a society where gender issues have been resolved, when she experienced something akin to the events fictionalized here.*

The poet revolved slowly counterclockwise in the small, 1
dark, not very deep pool. The novelist sat on the alder log that
dammed the creek to make the pool. Also on the log were the
poet's clothes, except his underpants. Coming upstream to the
swimming hole, they had passed a naked nut-brown maid,
beached and frontal to the sun; but she was young and they
were not; and the poet was not Californian. "You don't mind if
I'm old-fashioned about modesty?" he had asked, disarmingly.
The novelist, although a Californian, did not mind. The poet's
massive body was impressive enough as it was. Age, slacking
here and tightening there what had been all smooth evenness
in youth, gave pathos and dignity to that strong beast turning
in the dark water. Among roots and the dark shadows of the
banks, the hands and arms shone white. The novelist's bare
feet, though tanned, also gleamed pallid under the water, as
she sat rather less than comfortably on the log, wondering
whether she should have pulled off shirt and jeans and joined
the poet in his pool. She had been at his conference less than
an hour and did not know the rules. Did he want a companion, or a spectator? Did it matter? She splashed the water
with her feet and deplored her inability to do, to know, what
she wanted herself—fifty-five years old and sitting in adolescent paralysis, a bump on a log. Should I swim? I don't want
to. I want to. Should I? Which underpants am I wearing? This
is like the first day of summer camp. I want to go home. I
ought to swim. Ought I? Now?

The poet spared her further debate by hauling out on the 2
far end of the log. He was shivering. The log was in sunlight,
but the air was cool. Discovering that he would not soon get
dry in wet boxer shorts, he did then remove them, but very
modestly, back turned, sitting down again quickly. He spread
his underpants out on the log to dry, and conversed with his
guest.

An expansive gesture as he described the events of the first 3
week of the conference swept his socks into the water. He
caught one, but the current took the other out of reach. It
sank slowly He mourned; the novelist commiserated. He dismissed the sock.

"The Men have raised a Great Phallus farther up the river," 4
he said, smiling. "It was their own idea. I'd show you, but it's
off limits to the Women. A temenos. Very interesting, some of
the ritual that has developed this week! I am hearing men
talk—not sports scores and business, but talk—"

Impressed and interested, the novelist listened, trying to 5
ignore a lesser fascination: the sock. It had reemerged, all the

way across the sun-flecked water, under a muddy, rooty bank. It was now moving very slowly but apparently—yes—definitely clockwise in a circle that would bring it back toward the log. The novelist sought and found a broken branch and held it ready, idly teasing the water with it. Housewife, she thought, ashamed. Fixated on socks. Prose writer!

6   The poet, sensitive and alert even when talking of his concerns, observed, and asked what she was fishing for.

7   "Your sock is coming back," she said.

8   In a silence of complete fellow feeling, they both watched the stately progress of the floating sock coming round unhurried in the fullness of time, astronomically certain, till the current brought it within branch reach. It was lifted dripping on the forked end. In quiet triumph the novelist turned the branch to the poet, presenting the sock to its owner, who removed it from the branch and squeezed it thoughtfully.

9   Soon after this he dressed, and they returned downstream to the conference center and the scattered cabins under the redwoods.

10   The food was marvelous. Infinitely imaginatively vegetarian, eclectic but not hodgepodge: the chilis hot, the salads delicate, the curries fragrant. The kitchen staff who produced these wonders were unlike the other people at the conference, though in fact several of them were members of the conference working out their fees. When they came out front and listened to the lecture on the Hero, they disappeared into the others and she could not recognize them; but in the crowded, hot, flashing kitchen, each of them seemed almost formidably individual, laughing more than anyone else here, talking differently, moving with deft purpose, so that the onlooker felt superfluous and inferior, not because the cooks meant to impress or to exclude but only because, being busy with the work in hand, they were quite unconscious of doing so.

11   After dinner on the second day, in honey-colored evening sunlight, crossing the broad wooden bridge across the creek between the main hall and her set of cabins, the novelist stopped and set her hands on the rough railing. I have been here before! I know this creek, this bridge, that trail going up into the trees—Such moments were a familiar accompaniment to tension and self-consciousness. She had felt them waiting to be asked to dance in dancing class at twelve, and at fifty in a hotel room in a city she had never seen before. Sometimes they justified themselves as a foresight remembered, bringing with them a queer double-exposure effect of

that place where she had foreseen being in this place. But this time the experience was one of pure recognition, unexplainable but not uncanny, though solemnized by the extraordinary grandeur of the setting.

For the creek ran and the path led from fog-softened golden light into a darkness under incredible trees. It was always dark under them, and silent, and bare, for their huge community admitted little on a smaller scale. In the open clearings weeds and brambles and birds and bugs made the usual lively mess and tangle; under the big trees the flash of a scrub jay's wing startled as it would in the austere reaches of a Romanesque church. To come under the trees was as definite a transition as entering a building, but a building the size of a county.   12

Yet in among those immense living trunks there were also some black, buttressed objects that confused the sense of scale still further, for though squat, they were bigger than the cabins—much bigger. In bulk and girth, they were bigger than the trees. They were ruins. Tree ruins, the logged and burned-over stumps of the original forest. With effort, the novelist comprehended that the sequoias so majestically towering their taper bulk and gracile limbs all around here were second growth, not even a century old, mere saplings, shoots, scions of the great presences that had grown here in a length of silence now altogether and forever lost.   13

All the same, it was very quiet under the trees, and still quieter at night. There were refinements of the absence of sound, which the novelist had never before had the opportunity to observe. The cabins of her group straggled along, one every ten or twenty yards, unlighted, above the creek, which ran shallow but almost soundless, as if obeying the authority of the redwoods, their counsel of silence. There was no wind. Fog would mosey in over the hills from the sea before dawn to hush what was hushed already. Far away one small owl called once. Later, one mosquito shrilled hopelessly for a moment at the screen.   14

The novelist lay in darkness on her narrow board bunk in her sleeping bag listening to nothing and wondering if this was the bag her daughter had been using when she got the flu camping last summer and how long flu germs might live in the dark, warm, moist medium of a zippered sleeping bag. Her thoughts ran on such matters because she was acutely uncomfortable. Sometimes she thought it was diarrhea, sometimes a bladder infection, sometimes a coward spirit. Whatever it was, would it force her yet again to leave the germy warmth of the sleeping bag and take her flashlight and   15 try to find the evasive path up that ominous hiss to the all too communal, doorless, wet-floored toilets, praying that nobody would join her in her misery? Yes. No, maybe not. She heard a screen door creak, a cabin or two downstream, and almost immediately after, a soft, rushing noise: a man pissing off his cabin porch onto the dark, soft, absorbent ground of redwood leaf and twig and bark. O lucky Men, who need not crouch and straddle! Her bladder twinged, remorseless. "I do not have to go pee," she told herself, unconvinced. "I am not sick." She listened to the terrific silence. Nothing lived. But there, deep in the hollow darkness, a soft, lively sound: a little fart. And, now that she was all ears, presently another fart, louder, from a cabin on higher ground. The beans with chilis would probably explain it. Or did it need explanation, did people like cattle add nightly to the methane in the atmosphere, had those who had slept in longhouses by this creek been accustomed to this soft concert? For it was pleasing, almost melodious, this sparse pattern of a snore here—a long efflatus there—a little sigh—against the black and utter stillness.

16   When she was nearly asleep, she heard voices far upstream, male voices, chanting, as if from the dawn of history. Deep, primeval. The Men were performing the rituals of manhood. But the little farts in the night were nearer and dearer.

17   The Women sat in a circle on the sand, about thirty of them. Nearby the shallow river widened to the sea. Soft, fog-paled sunshine of the north coast lay beautifully on low breakers and dunes. The Women passed an ornamented wooden wand from hand to hand; who held the wand, spoke; the others listened. It did not seem quite right to the novelist. A good thing, but not the right one. Men wanted wands, women did not, she thought. These women had dutifully accepted the wand, but left to themselves they might have preferred some handwork and sat talking round and about like a flock of sparrows. Sparrows are disorderly, don't take turns, don't shut up to listen to the one with the wand, peck and talk at the same time. The wind blew softly, the wand passed. A woman in her twenties who wore an emblem of carved wood and feathers on a chain round her neck read a manuscript poem in a trembling voice half lost in the distant sound of the breakers. "My arms are those wings," she read, her voice shaken by fear and passion till it broke. The wand passed. A blond, fine-boned woman in her forties spoke of the White Goddess, but the novelist had ceased to listen, nervously rehearsing what she would say, should she say it?

should she not? The wand passed to her. "It seems to me, coming in from outside, into the middle of this, you know, just for a couple of days, but perhaps just because of that I can be useful, anyhow it seems to me that to some extent some of the women here are sort of looking for a, for something actually to sort of *do*. Instead of kind of talking mostly in a sort of derivative way," she sod in a harsh, chirping voice like a sparrow's. Shaking, she passed the wand. After the circle broke up, several women told her with enthusiasm about the masked dancing last Wednesday night, when the Women had acted out the female archetype of their choice. "It got wild," one said cheerfully. Another woman told her that this leader of the Women had quarreled with that one and personalities were destroying harmony. Several of them started making a large dragon out of wet sand, and while doing so told her that this year was different from earlier years, before the Men and the Women were separated, and that the East Coast meetings were always more spiritual than the West Coast meetings, or vice versa. They all chattered till the Men came back from their part of the beach, some with faces marked splendidly with charcoal.

The fine-boned blond whom the novelist had not listened to rode beside her in the car going back inland, a long, rough road through the logged-out coast range. "I've been coming to this place all my life," she said with a laugh. "It was a summer camp. I started coming when I was ten. Oh, it was wonderful then! I still meet people who came to Limberlost."   18

"Limberlost!" said the novelist.   19

"It was Camp Limberlost," said the other woman, and laughed again, affectionately.   20

"But I went there," said the novelist. "I went to Camp Limberlost. You mean this is it? Where the conference is? But I was wondering, earlier this year, I realized I had no idea where it was, or how to find out. I didn't know where it was when I went there. It was in the redwoods, that's literally all I knew. We all got into a bus downtown, and talked for six hours, you know, and then we were there—you know how kids are, they don't *notice*—but it was a Girl Reserve camp then. The YW ran it. I had to join the Girl Reserves to come."   21

"The city took it over after the war," the other woman said, her eyes merry and knowing. "This really is it. This is Limberlost."   22

"But I don't remember it," the novelist said in distress.   23

"The conference is in the old Boys Camp. The Girls Camp was upstream about a mile. Maybe you never came down here."   24

25   Yes. The novelist remembered that Jan and Dorothy had cut Camp Fire one evening and sneaked out of camp and down the creek to Boys Camp. They had hidden across the creek behind stumps and shrubs in the twilight, they had hooted and bleated and meowed until the Boys began coming out of their cabins, and then a counselor had come out, and Jan and Dorothy had run away, and got back after dark, muddy and triumphant, madly giggling in the jammed cabin after Lights Out, reciting their adventure, counting coup....

26   But she had not gone with them. There was no way she could have remembered that bridge across the creek, the trail going up out of the evening light.

27   Still, how could she not have recognized the place as a whole—the forest, the cabins? Two weeks of three summers she had lived here, at twelve and thirteen and fourteen, and had she never noticed the silence? the size of the redwoods? the black, appalling, giant stumps?

28   It was forty years; the trees might have grown a good deal—and now as she thought it did seem that she and Jan had actually climbed one of the stumps one day, to sit and talk, cutting Crafts, probably. But they hadn't thought anything about the stump but that it was climbable, a place to talk in privacy. No sense of what that huge wreck meant, except (like those who had cut the tree) to their own convenience; no notion of what it was in relation to anything else, or where it was, or where they were. They were here. Despairingly homesick the first night, thereafter settled in. At home in the world, as cheekily indifferent to cause and effect as sparrows, as ignorant of death and geography as the redwoods.

29   She had envied Jan and Dorothy their exploit, knowing them to be a good deal braver than she was. They had agreed to take her back to Boys Camp with them, and hoot and meow, or just hide and watch, but they never got around to it. They all went to Camp Fire and sang lonesome cowboy songs instead. So she had never seen Boys Camp until she came here and sat on the log and watched the poet circle slowly in the pool, and what would she and Jan and Dorothy, fourteen, merciless, have thought of *that?* "Oh, Lord!" she said involuntarily.

30   The woman beside her in the car laughed, as if in sympathy. "It's such a beautiful place," she said. "It's wonderful to be able to come back. What do you think of the conference?"

31   "I like the drumming," the novelist replied, after a pause, with fervor. "The drumming is wonderful. I never did that

before." Indeed she had found that she wanted to do nothing else. If only there weren't a lecture tonight and they could drum again after dinner, thirty or forty people each with a drum on or between their knees, the rhythm set and led by a couple of drummers who knew what they were doing and kept the easy yet complex beat and pattern going, going, going till there was nothing in consciousness but that and nothing else needed, no words at all.

The lecture was on the Wild Man. That night she woke up in the pitch dark and went out without using her flashlight and pissed beside her cabin, almost noiselessly. She heard no local breaking of wind, but guessed that many of the cabins were still empty; the Men had all gone off upstream, off limits, after the lecture, and now she heard them not chanting but yelling and roaring, a wild noise, but so far away that it didn't make much of a dent on the silence here. Here at Limberlost. 32

In the low, cold mist of morning, the poet came from cabin to cabin. The novelist heard him coming, chanting and making animal sounds, banging the screen doors of the cabins. He wore a dramatic animal mask, a gray, snarling, hairy snout. "Up! Up! Daybreak! The old wolf's at the door! The wolf, the wolf!" he chanted entering a cabin in a predatory crouch. Sleepy voices protested laughingly. The novelist was already up and dressed and had performed t'ai chi. She had stayed inside the screened cabin instead of going out on its spacious porch, because she was self-conscious, because doing t'ai chi was just too damn much the kind of thing you did here and yet didn't fit at all with what they were doing here and anyhow she was going home today and would damn well do t'ai chi in the broom closet if that's where she felt like doing it. 33

The poet approached her cabin and paused. "Good morning!" he said politely and incongruously through his staring, hairy muzzle. "Good morning," said the novelist from behind her screens, feeling a surge of snobbish irritation at the silly poet parading his power to wake everybody up, but *she* was up already!—and at the same time yearning to be able to go out and pat the wolf, to call him brave, to play the game he wanted so much to play, or at least to offer him something better than a wet sock on a stick. 34

DO WOMEN AND MEN
THINK DIFFERENTLY?

Anne Moir and David Jessel
Brain Sex

The Introduction to Anne Moir and David Jessel's book Brain
Sex *(published in 1991) states that "men are different from
women...because their brains are different." Since the book
was published in 1991, Moir and Jessel have extended their
ideas—perhaps most notably in a series of television shows on
the Discovery channel in 1992. This "abstract" of their book,
published as Chapter 2, appeared in a slightly different form in
the* Washington Post *in May 1991.*

1   A hundred years ago, the observation that men were different from women, in a whole range of aptitudes, skills, and
abilities, would have been a leaden truism, a statement of the
yawningly obvious.

2   Such a remark, uttered today, would evoke very different
reactions. Said by a man, it would suggest a certain social
ineptitude, a *naïveté* in matters of sexual politics, a sad deficiency in conventional wisdom, or a clumsy attempt to be
provocative. A woman venturing such an opinion would be
scorned as a traitor to her sex, betraying the hard-fought 'victories' of recent decades as women have sought equality of
status, opportunity and respect.

3   Yet the truth is that virtually every professional scientist
and researcher into the subject has concluded that the brains
of men and women are different. There has seldom been a
greater divide between what intelligent, enlightened opinion
presumes—that men and women have the same brain—and
what science knows—that they do not.

4   When a Canadian psychologist entitled an academic paper
'Are men's and women's brains really different?' she acknowledged that the answer to the question was self-evident:

Yes, of course. It would be amazing if men's and women's brains were not different, given the gross morphological [structural] and often striking behavioural differences between men and women.

Most of us intuitively sense that the sexes are different. But this has become a universal, unshared, guilty secret. We have ceased to trust our common sense.

The truth is that for virtually our entire tenancy of the planet, we have been a sexist species. Our biology assigned separate functions to the male and female of *Homo sapiens*. Our evolution strengthened and refined those differences. Our civilisation reflected them. Our religion and our education reinforced them.

Yet we both fear, and defy, history. We fear it, because we are afraid of seeming to be in complicity with the centuries-old crimes of sexual prejudice. We defy it, because we want to believe that mankind has at last achieved escape velocity, released from the muddy gravity of our animal past and neanderthal assumptions.

In the last thirty years a small but influential collection of well-intentioned souls have tried to persuade us to adopt this new defiant appreciation. They have discovered that the religions and the education were a male plot to maintain the subordinate status of women. The discovery is probably correct. They have found that our so-called civilisations are founded on male aggression and dominance. That's probably true as well. So far so good.

The problem comes when you look for an explanation of why this happened. If men and women are identical, and always have been, in the degree and manner in which they use their identical brains, how did the male sex manage so successfully, in virtually every culture and society in the world, to contrive a situation where the female was subordinate? Was it just men's greater musculature and body-weight that have made the realm of womanhood an occupied country for the past scores of thousands of years? Was it the fact that until recent centuries women were pregnant most of the time? Or is it more likely—as the facts suggest—that the differences between the male and the female brain are at the root of the society we have and the people we are? There are some biological facts of life that, with the best, and most sexually liberated will in the world, we just cannot buck; would it not be better, rather than rage impotently against the differences between the sexes, to acknowledge, understand, exploit, and even enjoy them?

9   For the last hundred years, scientists have tried to explain those differences—although it has to be said that the first science of brain sex differences began with a methodology as crude as its assumptions. Simple measurement of the brain apparently proved that women lacked the necessary cerebral endowment to claim an equality of intellect. The Germans were particularly obsessed with this tape-measure scholarship. Bayerthal found it a minimum requirement for a professor of surgery that he have a head circumference of 52–53 centimetres: 'Under 52 cms you cannot expect an intellectual performance of any significance, while under 50.5 cms no normal intelligence can be expected.' In this connection he also observed, 'We do not have to ask for the head circumference of women of genius—they do not exist.'

10   The French scientist Gustave Le Bon, noting that many Parisian women had brains closer in size to those of gorillas than of men, concluded that female inferiority was 'so obvious that no one can contest it for a moment'. And he warned, forebodingly, of

> the day when, misunderstanding the inferior occupations which nature has given her, women leave the home and take part in our battles; on that day a social revolution will begin and everything that maintains the sacred ties of the family will disappear.

That social revolution has been with us for some time; there has also been a revolution in the science of brain differences. Many—perhaps most—of the mysteries of how the brain works have yet to be unravelled, but the differences between the brains of males and females—and the processes by which they become different—are now clear. There is more to be known, more detail and qualification perhaps to add—but the nature and cause of brain differences are now known beyond speculation, beyond prejudice, and beyond reasonable doubt.

11   But now, just at the very moment when science can tell us what the differences are, and where they spring from, we are asked to banish the assumption of difference as if it were a guilty thought.

12   Recent decades have witnessed two contradictory processes: the development of scientific research into the differ-

ences between the sexes, and the political denial that such differences exist. These two intellectual currents are, understandably, not on speaking terms. Science knows it dabbles in matters of sexual differences at its risk: at least one researcher into the field of gender differences was refused a grant on the grounds that 'this work ought not to be done'. Another told us that he had given up his work because 'the political pressure—the pressure on the truth' had become too much. On the other hand, some of those working in the field of sex differences seem to evince an almost wanton disregard for scientific findings, blinkering themselves against findings whose implications they might find too uncomfortable to recognise.

The first systematic tests to explore sex differences were   13
conducted in 1882 by Francis Gatton at the South Kensington Museum in London. He purported to have identified significant sex differences favouring men in strength of grip, sensitivity to shrill whistle sounds, and ability to work under pressure. Women were observed to be more sensitive to pain.

Ten years later, in the United States, studies discovered   14
that women could hear better than men, had a more conventional vocabulary, and preferred blue to red. Men preferred red to blue, used more adventurous vocabulary, and had a preference for abstract and general thought, while women preferred practical problems, and individual tasks.

Havelock Ellis's *Man and Woman*, published in 1894,   15
aroused immediate interest and ran into eight editions. Among the differences he chronicled were women's superiority over men in memory, cunning, dissimulation, compassion, patience, and tidiness. The work of female scientists was found to be more precise than that of men, but 'perhaps a little lacking in breadth and initiative, though admirable within a limited range.' A woman genius seemed to need the close support of a man; Ellis gave the example of Madame Curie, who was the wife of an already distinguished scientist, and pointed out that Mrs. Browning's finest poems were all written after she had the good fortune to meet Mr. Browning. Ellis found that women disliked the essentially intellectual process of analysis—'They have the instinctive feeling that analysis may possibly destroy the emotional complexes by which they are largely moved and which appeal to them.'

These observations would have remained mere curiosities   16
of scholarship were it not for the development, beginning in the 1960s, of new scientific research into the brain. Paradoxically, the finding of gender differences corresponded with the

period when the political denial that any differences existed was at its most vocal.

17   Paradoxically, too, interest in these differences grew out of an original scientific motive to suppress them. The problem arose from IQ tests. Researchers noticed consistent differences favouring one sex over the other in some of the abilities tested. This did not result in a chorus of eureka from the scientific community. In fact, it was regarded as something of a nuisance, muddying the waters of accurate measurement of intelligence. In the 1950s Dr. D. Wechsler, an American scientist who developed the IQ test most commonly used today, found that over thirty tests 'discriminated' in favour of one or the other sex. The very use of the word suggests that the tests themselves were somehow to blame for the fact that different sexes achieved different success rates.

18   Wechsler, among others, sought to resolve the problem by eliminating all those tests which resulted in findings of significant sex differences. When it still proved difficult to produce 'sex-neutral' results, they deliberately introduced 'male-slanted' or 'female-slanted' items to arrive at approximately equal scores. It is an odd way of conducting a scientific study; if you don't like the result you get from an experiment, you fix the data to produce a more palatable conclusion. The sporting equivalent would be to handicap Olympic pole-vaulters with lead weights, or poles of different length, to ensure that the desired truth prevails: that all pole-vaulters, regardless of prowess or agility, are created equal.

19   Even so, sex differences stubbornly emerged, like recalcitrant dandelions in a chemically treated lawn. Wechsler even came to the conclusion from a series of sub-tests that it might be possible to demonstrate a measurable superiority of women over men in general intelligence. On the other hand, out of 105 tests assessing skills in solving maze-puzzles, involving the most heterogeneous populations throughout the world, ranging from the most primitive to the most highly civilised, 99 showed an incontrovertible male superiority. Perhaps the safest and least controversial synthesis of these findings would have been that girls are too intelligent to bother with anything as silly as a maze-puzzle test.

20   Preoccupied with finding sex-neutral IQ techniques, Wechsler regarded the evidence that the sexes *were* different as a mere nuisance. Rather as Columbus might have regarded his discovery of America as something of an irrelevance, since, after all, he was looking for the East Indies, Wechsler observed, almost parenthetically,

> Our findings do confirm what poets and novelists have often
> asserted, and the average person long believed, namely, that
> men not only behave, but 'think' differently from women.

What an early British pioneer of sex differences has called 'a
conspiracy of silence surrounding the topic of human sex
differences' was soon drowned in a babble of sociological
explanations. Children, it was argued, were born psychosex-
ually neutral; then parents, teachers, employers, politicians,
and all the wicked fairies of society got to work on the innocent virginity of the mind. The main group championing the
neutrality theory was led by Dr. John Money, of Johns Hopkins University in the USA.

> Sexuality is undifferentiated at birth and . . . it becomes dif-
> ferentiated as masculine or feminine in the various experi-
> ences of growing up.

So, if men and women were different, it must be the result
of social conditioning. Society was to blame, which, in the
view of sociology, it usually is.

If there is still a dispute about how sex differences arise   21
there is now no argument in the scientific community that
such differences exist. It cannot be stressed often enough that
this essay concerns itself with the *average* man and the *average* woman. In the same way, we might say that men are taller
than women. Look across any crowded room and this will be
obvious. Of course some women will be taller than some
men, and the tallest woman may possibly be taller than the
tallest man. But statistically men are on average 7 per cent
taller, and the tallest person in the world, rather than in the
room, is certainly a man.

The statistical variations in sex differences which we will   22
explore, in skills, aptitudes or abilities, are much greater than
they are in relation to height; there will always be the exception to the average, the person with exceptional 'wrong-sex'
skills, but the exception does not invalidate the general, average rule. These differences have a practical, social relevance.
On measurements of various aptitude tests, the difference
between the sexes in average scores on these tests can be as
much as 25 per cent. A difference of as little as 5 per cent has
been found to have a marked impact on the occupations or
activities at which men or women will, on average, excel.

23   The area where the biggest differences have been found lies
in what scientists call 'spatial ability'. That's being able to picture things, their shape, position, geography and proportion,
accurately in the mind's eye—all skills that are crucial to the
practical ability to work with three-dimensional objects or
drawings. One scientist who has reviewed the extensive literature on the subject concludes, 'The fact of the male's superiority in spatial ability is not in dispute.' It is confirmed by
literally hundreds of different scientific studies.

24   A typical test measures the skill of men and women in the
assembly of a three-dimensional, mechanical apparatus. Only
a quarter of the women could perform the task better than
the average male. At the top end of the scale of mechanical
aptitude there will be twice as many men as women.

25   From school age onwards, boys will generally outperform
girls in areas of mathematics involving abstract concepts of
space, relationships, and theory. At the very highest level of
mathematical excellence, according to the biggest survey ever
conducted, the very best boys totally eclipse the very best
girls. Dr. Julian Stanley and Dr. Camilla Benbow, two American psychologists, worked with highly gifted students of both
sexes. Not only did they find that the best girl never beat the
best boy—they also discovered a startling sex ratio of mathematical brilliance: for every exceptional girl there were more
than thirteen exceptional boys.

26   Scientists know that they walk on social eggshells when
they venture any theory about human behaviour. But
researchers into sex differences are increasingly impatient
with the polite attempt to find a social explanation for these
differences. As Camilla Benbow now says of her studies showing a male superiority in mathematically gifted children, 'After
15 years looking for an environmental explanation and getting
zero results, I gave up.' She readily admitted to us her belief
that the difference in ability has a biological basis.

27   Boys also have the superior hand-eye co-ordination necessary for ball sports. Those same skills mean that they can
more easily imagine, alter, and rotate an object in their mind's
eye. Boys find it easier than girls to construct block buildings
from two-dimensional blueprints, and to assess correctly how
the angle of the surface level of water in a jug would change
when the jug was tilted to different angles.

28   This male advantage in seeing patterns and abstract relationships—what could be called general strategic rather than
the detailed tactical thinking—perhaps explains the male
dominance of chess, even in a country like the USSR, where

the game is a national sport played by both sexes. An alternative explanation, more acceptable to those who would deny the biological basis of sex differences, is that women have become so conditioned to the fact of male chess-playing superiority that they subconsciously assign themselves lower expectations; but this is a rather wilful rejection of scientific evidence for the sake of maintaining a prejudice.

The better spatial ability of men could certainly help to   29
explain that male superiority in map-reading we noted earlier. Here again, the prejudice of male motorists is confirmed by experiment; girls and boys were each given city street maps and, without rotating the map, asked to describe whether they would be turning left or right at particular intersections as they mentally made their way across town and back. Boys did better. More women than men like to turn the map round, physically to match the direction in which they are traveling when they are trying to find their way.

While the male brain gives men the edge in dealing with   30
things and theorems, the female brain is organised to respond more sensitively to all sensory stimuli. Women do better than men on tests of verbal ability. Females are equipped to receive a wider range of sensory information, to connect and relate that information with greater facility, to place a primacy on personal relationships, and to communicate. Cultural influences may reinforce these strengths, but the advantages are innate.

The differences are apparent in the very first hours after   31
birth. It has been shown that girl babies are much more interested than boys in people and faces; the boys seem just as happy with an object dangled in front of them.

Girls say their first words and learn to speak in short sen-   32
tences earlier than boys, and are generally more fluent in their pre-school years. They read earlier, too, and do better in coping with the building blocks of language like grammar, punctuation and spelling. Boys outnumber girls by 4 : 1 in remedial reading classes. Later, women find it easier to master foreign languages, and are more proficient in their own, with a better command of grammar and spelling. They are also more fluent: stuttering and other speech defects occur almost exclusively among boys.

Girls and women hear better than men. When the sexes are   33
compared, women show a greater sensitivity to sound. The dripping tap will get the woman out of bed before the man has even woken up. Six times as many girls as boys can sing in tune. They are also much more adept at noticing small

changes in volume, which goes some way to explaining women's superior sensitivity to that 'tone of voice' which their male partners are so often accused of adopting.

34   Men and women even see some things differently. Women see better in the dark. They are more sensitive to the red end of the spectrum, seeing more red hues there than men, and have a better visual memory.

35   Men see better than women in bright light. Intriguing results also show that men tend to be literally blinkered; they see in a narrow field—mild tunnel vision—with greater concentration on depth. They have a better sense of perspective than women. Women, however, quite literally take in the bigger picture. They have wider peripheral vision, because they have more of the receptor rods and cones in the retina, at the back of the eyeball, to receive a wider arc of visual input.

36   The differences extend to the other senses. Women react faster, and more acutely, to pain, although their overall resistance to long-term discomfort is greater than men's. In a sample of young adults, females showed 'overwhelmingly' greater sensitivity to pressure on the skin on every part of the body. In childhood and maturity, women have a tactile sensitivity so superior to men's that in some tests there is no overlap between the scores of the two sexes; in these, the least sensitive woman is more sensitive than the most sensitive man.

37   There is strong evidence that men and women have different senses of taste—women being more sensitive to bitter flavours like quinine, and preferring higher concentrations and greater quantities of sweet things. Men score higher in discerning salty flavours. Overall, however, the evidence strongly suggests a greater female delicacy and perception in taste. Should more great chefs be women? Or do many great male chefs have more than their share of feminine sensibilities?

38   Women's noses, as well as their palates, are more sensitive than men's; a case in point is their perception of exaltolide, a synthetic musk-like odour associated with men, but hardly noticeable to them. Women found the smell attractive. Interestingly, this superior sensitivity increases just before ovulation; at a critical time of her menstrual cycle, the biology of a woman makes her more sensitive to man.

39   This superiority in so many of the senses can be clinically measured—yet it is what accounts for women's almost supernatural 'intuition'. Women are simply better equipped to notice things to which men are comparatively blind and deaf. There is no witchcraft in this superior perception—it is extrasensory only in terms of the blunter, male senses. Women are

better at picking up social cues, picking up important
nuances of meaning from tones of voice or intensity of
expression. Men sometimes become exasperated at a
woman's reaction to what they say. They do not realise that
women are probably 'hearing' much more than what the man
himself thinks he is 'saying'. Women tend to be better judges
of character. Older females have a better memory of names
and faces, and a greater sensitivity to other people's preferences.

Sex differences have been noted in the comparative mem-   40
ory of men and women. Women can store, for short periods
at least, more irrelevant and random information than men;
men can only manage the trick when the information is organised into some coherent form, or has a specific relevance to
them.

So men are more self-centered—so what else is new?   41
What's new is that the folklore of gender, which is always vulnerable to dismissive, politically motivated, fashionable opinion, is now shown to have a basis in scientific fact.

Le Anne Schreiber

The Search for His
and Her Brains

This essay by Le Anne Schreiber appeared in Glamour, *a magazine with a predominantly female readership, in April 1993.
Schreiber's work appears frequently in that magazine.*

Many researchers are trying to answer such basic questions   1
as how the brain develops, acquires language, stores memories, retrieves information and repairs itself after damage. To
date, however, the line of research that has been most widely
publicized is the one devoted to that most debatable of questions: What makes men and women different? A *Time* cover
story, "Sizing Up the Sexes," the three-part Discovery Channel
series *Brain Sex* and a segment called "Different Strokes" on
PrimeTime Live suggest the eagerness of the popular media to
broadcast the notion that, as one scientist declared, "the entire
brain is a sex difference."

2   This emphasis on gender in current brain research makes
some people nervous, and with good reason. In every other
period of the history of science, the search for sex differences
in the brain has been a search for female deficiencies. Today's
researchers are quick to assert that they take it as given that
male and female brains are *different but equal,* not better and
worse. But the fact that the female brain has been referred to
as a "default brain" in current sex-difference literature does
not inspire confidence. Neither does the fact that current
research is frequently cited as evidence for allegedly innate
male talents in such areas as science, mathematics, architecture and engineering. Since math achievement is the filter that
determines access to many higher-paying occupations, such
biological handicapping is a high-stakes issue for women.

3   "It feels as though we have time traveled backward to a
period of extreme biological determinism," says Anne Fausto-
Sterling, Ph.D., a developmental geneticist at Brown University. "It's easy for us to see how racial and sexual attitudes
affected earlier generations of scientists, but it's harder for
people to see that beliefs about sexual differences are still so
strong that few scientists can move outside them."

4   Blindness to the implications of brain-gender theories can
be costly, according to Dr. Fausto-Sterling, whose recently
updated book, *Myths of Gender,* offers an extremely thorough
and cogent critique of recent biological theories of sex difference. "Jobs and education—that's what it's really all about,"
she says. "About whether boys and girls should attend separate schools, about job and career choices and, as always,
about money—how much employers will have to pay to
whom. These issues form an unbroken bridge spanning the
length of the century."

5   The gist of current brain-gender theory is this: Although
both males and females produce the class of hormones called
androgens, males produce higher levels of them early in fetal
life, when the developing testes start secreting testosterone—
the major androgen. This hormonal surge supposedly washes
over the developing male brain, producing structural differences that determine the degree to which an individual exhibits masculine characteristics later in life. The corollary of this
theory is that men and women who do not conform to gender
stereotypes in their behavior, interests, abilities or temperament were exposed to abnormally low or high levels of androgens in the womb. Although supported only by scant and
inconclusive evidence, this theory is often presented as
proven fact in the popular press.

The *Washington Post*, for instance, used the following information to introduce a multiple-choice quiz titled "How Female Is Your Brain?" "What gives us a male or female brain is the degree to which our embryonic brains are exposed to male hormone. The die is cast *in utero;* after that the luggage of our bodies, and society's expectations of us, merely supplement this biological fact of life." 6

So what gives? Is the brain really a sex organ, as structurally different in men and women as more visible parts of our anatomy? Are men and women really born with differing abilities to read maps and find socks? Are men innately better mathematicians and architects? Are women innately better at...well, let's see...spelling, smelling and reading emotions? Since proponents of brain-gender theories claim to be uncovering the biological bases of our possibilities and limits, it is crucial that we pay close attention to what they are asserting—and on what grounds they base these assertions. 7

The current interest in brain-gender research was sparked in 1982, when Nobel Prize–winning neurobiologist Roger Sperry, Ph.D., demonstrated what others had suspected: that the left and right hemispheres of the human brain house different mental abilities. The left side, for instance, seems to be the locus of certain verbal abilities, and the right side, of certain visual-spatial abilities, which are in turn thought to be related to certain mathematical skills. Dr. Sperry himself did not associate the separate functions of the two halves of the brain with gender; in fact, he emphasized that each person's brain network was vastly more individualized than fingerprints. But other scientists found the possibility of neat differences too tempting to ignore. The hunt for the gendered brain was on. 8

Since there were no apparent sex differences in the size or shape of the two hemispheres, scientists began to look for differences in the corpus callosum, a thick bundle of nerve fibers that connects the two hemispheres. There were two main working hypotheses. One was that the two hemispheres of the female brain are *less* strongly linked than those of the male's, making the female brain less integrated and less endowed with, for example, mathematical ability. The other was that the female brain's hemispheres are *more* strongly linked than the male's, making it, therefore, less specialized and less endowed with, for example, mathematical ability. When it comes to female brains, the less-equals-less or more-equals-less formulation is a staple of sex-difference research. 9

The first widely reported finding of a sex difference in the corpus callosum was published in 1982 in *Science*, the 10 prestigious weekly journal that plays an inordinately large role in setting the agenda for science coverage in the popular press. After performing autopsies on nine male and five female brains, physical anthropologist Ralph Holloway and cell biologist Christine de Lacoste-Utamsing claimed to have found a dramatic difference in the shape of the tail end of the corpus callosum. They reported that this section of the corpus callosum, called the splenium, was so much wider in females than in males that it deserved to be regarded as an anatomical sex difference second only to the reproductive organs.

11   Although there was no clinical evidence that a wider splenium creates stronger communication between the two brain hemispheres, proponents of brain gender nonetheless used this finding to support the notion that male brains are more specialized, and this theory of "brain specialization" was then offered as an explanation for a host of supposed male mental superiorities, particularly in mathematically related areas. The female's wider splenium, however, was thought to cause more "cross talk" between the two hemispheres—a kind of over-the-fence brain chat that just might be the source of female intuition. It was suggested, for instance, that if the emotions are primarily registered in the right hemisphere and verbal ability resides in the left, then it is innately easier for women to express emotion than it is for men, whose brains store words and emotions more separately.

12   In the past ten years there have been 16 attempts by various scientists, using both autopsies and magnetic resonance imaging (MRI) technology on much larger samples of both children and adults, to confirm the initial finding of a dramatic sex difference in the corpus callosum. Ten of the sixteen studies revealed no sex differences in the shape or size of any part of the corpus callosum. Five studies resulted in mixed or statistically insignificant findings. The most recent study claimed to find a sex-linked difference in the shape of the adult splenium, but also found out that if you tried to guess the sex of a subject by looking at his or her splenium, you would be wrong more than half of the time. Several researchers emphasized that variations in the size and shape of the corpus callosum were greater *among* members of the same sex than *between* the sexes.

13   At present, any claims about sex differences in the corpus callosum are highly questionable at best. Furthermore, scientists don't claim to know very much about how the corpus callosum works. Jonathan Beckwith, Ph.D., professor of microbiology and molecular genetics at Harvard Medical

School, puts it this way: "Even if they found differences, there is absolutely no way at this point that they can make a connection between any differences in brain structure and any particular behavior pattern or any particular aptitude."

Equally hypothetical is the notion that these alleged structural brain differences are caused by fetal testosterone. This theory, like the early findings on the corpus callosum, was first reported in *Science* in 1982 and from there was widely disseminated in the popular press. What got lost in translation was the fact that there is *no* clinical support for this thesis. 14

The basis of the theory is this: In 1982, Harvard neurologist Norman Geschwind, M.D., suggested that there was a statistical correlation between left-handedness—which is more common in boys—and a whole host of afflictions, including immune-system disorders, autism, dyslexia, myopia and stuttering. He speculated that all these conditions might have a single cause—fetal exposure to excess testosterone. And since left-handedness is associated with right-brain dominance, he further hypothesized in a 1983 *Science* interview that testosterone might cause the fetal male brain to produce "superior right-hemisphere talents, such as artistic, musical or mathematical talent." 15

To bolster his speculations, Dr. Geschwind cited two studies conducted by other scientists. One was on rat brains, in which parts of the right cortex of male rats were found to be 3 percent thicker than the corresponding parts of the left cortex. This difference was not found in female rats. The other, which involved human fetal brains, found that two convolutions of the right hemisphere develop slightly earlier than those on the left. Dr. Geschwind chose not to mention that the right brain convolutions developed earlier in *both* male and female fetuses, and therefore could not be caused by hormones from fetal testes. 16

And yet the unproven theory that men and women have innately different mental abilities, which rests upon the unproven theory of different brain structures, which rests upon a string of unproven theories about how those structures function, is making its way into the mass media and therefore into the public consciousness as fact. "In science, it's not unreasonable to make hypotheses based on slim data," says Dr. Beckwith, "but one runs into problems when those hypotheses, represented as fact or near fact, affect people's attitudes and even social policy. I think scientists should be much more careful than they are in communicating their ideas to the press." 17

18   The late Ruth Bleier, M.D., a neuroscientist at the University of Wisconsin in Madison, was blunter. Writing in her book *Science and Gender*, she said, "Scientists attempting to establish the biological basis for sex differences in some human behavior will frequently pool the results of a number of inconclusive, ill-controlled, and often contradictory studies (of rodents, primates, and humans) and conclude that despite the inconclusiveness and inadequacies of *each* of them, *together* they make a case simply because there are so many of them. This is like claiming that if you add three zeros together, you get zero, but if you add enough zeros together, say 25, then you'll get 25. But you don't. You still have nothing."

19   If research on sex differences in the brain is so shaky, how has it been able to establish such a firm footing in the media? Why are voices like Anne Fausto-Sterling's, Ruth Bleier's and Jonathan Beckwith's so seldom heard in the press, or heard only as whispers of caution tucked away in final paragraphs, outshouted by headlines blaring "Sex and the Brain" (*USA Today*), "Why Are Men and Women Different?" (*Time*), and "Math Genius May Have Hormonal Basis" (*Science*)?

20   In part, the problem is one intrinsic to the nature of scientific investigation. Almost by definition, scientists look for differences, and if they find one, however slight, they have an easier time getting their research published. Or, as Dr. Bleier succinctly put it, "There is no field of sex similarities."

21   "It's called 'the problem of negative evidence,'" explains Dr. Fausto-Sterling. "If you hypothesize no difference and find no difference, you never know if you've just not looked in the right place. The only time a finding of no difference is considered significant is when you are trying to replicate experiments that have found a difference, but even then it is difficult to get negative evidence published." As a result, an original finding of difference, however faulty or flimsy, is likely to receive much more widespread publicity than subsequent failures to confirm that finding.

22   When it comes to sex-difference research, this problem is often compounded by an eagerness on the part of the press and the public to embrace findings that confirm commonly held beliefs. "I think many people have a major investment in believing there are very basic differences between men and women that are responsible for the differences in our status in society," says Ruth Hubbard, Ph.D., Harvard professor of biology emerita and author of *The Politics of Women's Biology*. "It is well to be suspicious when 'objective science' confirms long-standing prejudices."

After all, the starting point of all sex-difference research is   23
the observation that men and women differ—in their behavior, roles, status, and achievements as well as their anatomy. Much of the brain research discussed above is devoted to finding biological explanations for alleged sex differences in mathematical ability. This alleged math gap is in turn used to help account for very observable sex differences in occupational and financial status.

Ironically, research into the biological basis of alleged male   24
mathematical superiority began in the early 1980s, when a decade of social changes had already narrowed the gender gap. In 1990, psychologist Janet Hyde, Ph.D., and colleagues at the University of Wisconsin in Madison used a statistical technique called meta-analysis to assess the results of 100 studies that looked for gender differences in the mathematical performance of more than three million American students.

Their conclusion: Averaged over 30 years, standardized   25
tests show a slight female superiority in math performance at the elementary and middle-school level. There was no gender difference at any age in tests that measured understanding of mathematical concepts, but a moderate male superiority in problem solving did emerge in high school and continued through college and adulthood. Most important, in studies published after 1973, the gender difference was half what it had been in previous years. Differences in course selection beginning in high school account for some but not all of the male advantage in performance on standardized tests in high school and college. Less measurable influences—like parent, teacher and peer encouragement of math achievement—are also a factor.

What does Dr. Hyde think of biological arguments for a   26
math gap? "The bottom line is that they are constructing biological models to explain a nondifference. The math gap is basically zero."

Although Hyde's findings are well-known among sex-   27
difference researchers, they have received less prominent exposure in the popular press than those of psychologist Camilla Benbow, Ed.D., whose research is frequently cited as evidence of innate male mathematical superiority. For 20 years, first at Johns Hopkins University with colleague Julian Stanley and now at Iowa State University in Ames, Dr. Benbow has conducted nationwide searches for gifted children to participate in a program called Study of Mathematically Precocious Youth. Seventh and eighth graders who scored in the top few percentiles on junior high standardized achievement tests are

invited to take high-school-level SATs; if they score high enough, they can enroll in accelerated college math courses.

28   Year after year, Dr. Benbow finds that the best boys out-perform the best girls by a significant margin on the math portion of the SAT. Fewer girls than boys choose to enter the talent search and of those who qualify for the accelerated courses, even fewer enroll in them. When Dr. Benbow's results were first published in *Science* in 1980, she was quoted there and elsewhere as favoring a biological explanation for her findings. In a 1983 *Science* article, she was portrayed as an enthusiastic supporter of Dr. Geschwind's testosterone theory of male mathematical superiority.

29   "What astounds me about Benbow's interpretation of her results," says Dr. Beckwith, "is that there really isn't much research to support the possible biological basis of the differences in math ability between men and women. But if you look at the research on possible environmental factors, it probably outweighs the biological research tenfold."

30   Dozens of studies that document the importance of parental attitude and other factors upon a child's math performance have not swayed Dr. Benbow from her conviction that males are innately superior in math. She also dismisses as unimportant studies showing that, despite their lower scores on standardized tests, female students get better math grades than males at all levels, including graduate school.

31   There is evidence that grades are often the only recognition female students receive in the math classroom. Several studies document that in high school and college, boys get significantly more attention from both male and female math teachers. Boys are spoken to more, called on more and receive more corrective feedback, social interaction, individual instruction, praise and encouragement. There is one form of attention bestowed more frequently on girls: In one study of ten high school geometry classes, girls received 84 percent of the discouraging comments.

32   Psychologist Jacquelynne Eccles, Ph.D., director of the Achievement Research Lab at the University of Michigan in Ann Arbor, studies the impact of parents' attitudes on children's school performance. Several studies document how parents tend to overestimate their sons' math ability and underestimate their daughters'. In 1980, she and colleague Janis Jacobs, Ph.D., found this tendency grew stronger in mothers, particularly in mothers of daughters, who had seen media coverage of Dr. Benbow's findings of male math superiority.

The impact of such distortions is heightened by Dr. 33
Eccles's surprising finding that how parents perceive their
children's abilities has an even greater influence on children's
self-assessment than the children's previous performance.
Given these interlocking factors, it is not surprising that in a
1991 study of sixth through eleventh graders, Dr. Jacobs
found that boys had more confidence in their math abilities
than girls did, despite the girls' having consistently higher
grades.

Math professor Harvey Keynes, Ph.D., of the University of 34
Minnesota in Minneapolis knows how crucial social factors
are to math performance. Like Dr. Benbow, he works with
mathematically precocious children, and for ten years, he, like
Dr. Benbow, found a significant gender gap between the
brightest boys and girls. Presuming the problems resided in
the learning environment and not the children's brains, he
introduced certain social supports for the girls and found that
the achievement gap disappeared within five years.

But, however one chooses to assess mathematical achieve- 35
ment, the differences in performance that exist between
American boys and girls are minuscule compared with the differences that exist between American and foreign students. In
a study made public by the Educational Testing Service last
year, American 9-year-old students ranked ninth out of 10
industrialized nations in math and 13-year-olds ranked thirteenth out of 15 industrialized nations. Firm evidence of foreign superiority is seldom followed, however, by government
funding for biological research into its causes. Calls for curriculum reform are more likely.

What, finally, are we to make of the current direction of 36
sex-difference research? It was between 1980 and 1983—that
distinct period of time when the pendulum of research interest and funding began to swing from an emphasis on social
explanations of difference to an emphasis on biological explanations—that three hypotheses were put forward by three
independent sets of researchers working in separate areas:
that there was a dramatic sex difference in the corpus callosum, that testosterone organizes male and female brains differently, and that males have an innate mathematical
superiority.

All three hypotheses were given prominent coverage in one 37
publication, *Science*, whose partiality for biological explanations is uncritically accepted by the popular press. The evidence supporting each of the three theories was slight, but
when combined, as they frequently were in the pages of that

journal, they seemed to prop one another up in a way that made the whole look much more solid than its wobbly parts. In the years since, an enormous castle of research and specu- lation has been built upon that shaky foundation.

38   Now, already well into the third year of the Decade of the Brain, with increased funding and publicity for all types of brain research, we are repeatedly induced to accept this many-turreted castle of speculation as a fortress of established fact. The Discovery Channel runs footage of little boys playing with toy trucks and girls with dolls—while an invisible voice of authority explains that their brains were "wired" in the womb to enjoy these activities. "The more we know about the male brain and the more we know about the female brain," a consulting anthropologist explains, "the more we can apply these things in our daily lives with our friends and our lovers, in our educational system, in our political system, in our busi- ness contacts around the world."

39   Another voice, not to be heard on the Discovery Channel, is that of Harvard's Dr. Ruth Hubbard, who warns: "To try to find the biological basis of our social roles or to sort people by sex when it comes to strength, ability to do math, or other intellectual or social attributes is a political exercise, not a scientific one."

Stephen Jay Gould
Women's Brains

Gould, born in 1941, teaches biology, geology, and the history of science at Harvard, but he is best known as an essayist and as the author of a number of books on scientific issues and controversies. He has won many awards and honors for collec- tions of essays such as Ever Since Darwin *(1977),* The Fla- mingo's Smile *(1985), and* The Panda's Thumb *(1980), and for books such as* Time's Arrow, Time's Cycle *(1987),* Wonder- ful Life *(1989), and* The Mismeasure of Man *(1981). The fol- lowing essay appeared in* The Panda's Thumb *and, in somewhat different form, in a section of* The Mismeasure of Man—*a book about both the abuses of intelligence testing and the social influences on science.*

In the prelude to *Middlemarch,* George Eliot lamented the 1
unfulfilled lives of talented women:

> Some have felt that these blundering lives are due to the
> inconvenient indefiniteness with which the Supreme Power
> has fashioned the natures of women: if there were one level
> of feminine incompetence as strict as the ability to count
> three and no more, the social lot of women might be treated
> with scientific certitude.

Eliot goes on to discount the idea of innate limitation, but 2
while she wrote in 1872, the leaders of European anthropometry were trying to measure "with scientific certitude" the
inferiority of women. Anthropometry, or measurement of the
human body, is not so fashionable a field these days, but it
dominated the human sciences for much of the nineteenth
century and remained popular until intelligence testing
replaced skull measurement as a favored device for making
invidious comparisons among races, classes, and sexes. Cran-
iometry, or measurement of the skull, commanded the most
attention and respect. Its unquestioned leader, Paul Broca
(1824–80), professor of clinical surgery at the Faculty of Medicine in Paris, gathered a school of disciples and imitators
around himself. Their work, so meticulous and apparently
irrefutable, exerted great influence and won high esteem as a
jewel of nineteenth-century science.

Broca's work seemed particularly invulnerable to refuta- 3
tion. Had he not measured with the most scrupulous care and
accuracy? (Indeed, he had. I have the greatest respect for
Broca's meticulous procedure. His numbers are sound. But
science is an inferential exercise, not a catalog of facts. Numbers, by themselves, specify nothing. All depends upon what
you do with them.) Broca depicted himself as an apostle of
objectivity, a man who bowed before facts and cast aside
superstition and sentimentality. He declared that "there is no
faith, however respectable, no interest, however legitimate,
which must not accommodate itself to the progress of human
knowledge and bend before truth." Women, like it or not, had
smaller brains than men and, therefore, could not equal them
in intelligence. This fact, Broca argued, may reinforce a common prejudice in male society, but it is also a scientific truth.
L. Manouvrier, a black sheep in Broca's fold, rejected the inferiority of women and wrote with feeling about the burden
imposed upon them by Broca's numbers:

Women displayed their talents and their diplomas. They also invoked philosophical authorities. But they were opposed by *numbers* unknown to Condorcet or to John Stuart Mill. These numbers fell upon poor women like a sledge hammer, and they were accompanied by commentaries and sarcasms more ferocious than the most misogynist imprecations of certain church fathers. The theologians had asked if women had a soul. Several centuries later, some scientists were ready to refuse them a human intelligence.

4   Broca's argument rested upon two sets of data: the larger brains of men in modern societies, and a supposed increase in male superiority through time. His most extensive data came from autopsies performed personally in four Parisian hospitals. For 292 male brains, he calculated an average weight of 1,325 grams; 140 female brains averaged 1,144 grams for a difference of 181 grams, or 14 percent of the male weight. Broca understood, of course, that part of this difference could be attributed to the greater height of males. Yet he made no attempt to measure the effect of size alone and actually stated that it cannot account for the entire difference because we know, a priori, that women are not as intelligent as men (a premise that the data were supposed to test, not rest upon):

> We might ask if the small size of the female brain depends exclusively upon the small size of her body. Tiedemann has proposed this explanation. But we must not forget that women are, on the average, a little less intelligent than men, a difference which we should not exaggerate but which is, nonetheless, real. We are therefore permitted to suppose that the relatively small size of the female brain depends in part upon her physical inferiority and in part upon her intellectual inferiority.

5   In 1873, the year after Eliot published *Middlemarch*, Broca measured the cranial capacities of prehistoric skulls from L'Homme Mort cave. Here he found a difference of only 99.5 cubic centimeters between males and females, while modern populations range from 129.5 to 220.7. Topinard, Broca's chief disciple, explained the increasing discrepancy through time as a result of differing evolutionary pressures upon dominant men and passive women:

The man who fights for two or more in the struggle for existence, who has all the responsibility and the cares of tomorrow, who is constantly active in combating the environment
and human rivals, needs more brain than the woman whom
he must protect and nourish, the sedentary woman, lacking
any interior occupations, whose role is to raise children,
love, and be passive.

In 1879, Gustave Le Bon, chief misogynist of Broca's   6
school, used these data to publish what must be the most
vicious attack upon women in modern scientific literature (no
one can top Aristotle). I do not claim his views were representative of Broca's school, but they were published in France's
most respected anthropological journal. Le Bon concluded:

In the most intelligent races, as among the Parisians, there
are a large number of women whose brains are closer in size
to those of gorillas than to the most developed male brains.
This inferiority is so obvious that no one can contest it for a
moment; only its degree is worth discussion. All psychologists who have studied the intelligence of women, as well as
poets and novelists, recognize today that they represent the
most inferior forms of human evolution and that they are
closer to children and savages than to an adult, civilized
man. They excel in fickleness, inconstancy, absence of
thought and logic, and incapacity to reason. Without doubt
there exist some distinguished women, very superior to the
average man, but they are as exceptional as the birth of any
monstrosity, as, for example, of a gorilla with two heads;
consequently, we may neglect them entirely.

Nor did Le Bon shrink from the social implications of his   7
views. He was horrified by the proposal of some American
reformers to grant women higher education on the same
basis as men:

A desire to give them the same education, and, as a consequence, to propose the same goals for them, is a dangerous
chimera.... The day when, misunderstanding the inferior
occupations which nature has given her, women leave the
home and take part in our battles; on this day a social revolution will begin, and everything that maintains the sacred ties
of the family will disappear.

Sound familiar?*

8   I have reexamined Broca's data, the basis for all this derivative pronouncement, and I find his numbers sound but his
interpretation ill-founded, to say the least. The data supporting his claim for increased difference through time can be
easily dismissed. Broca based his contention on the samples
from L'Homme Mort alone—only seven male and six female
skulls in all. Never have so little data yielded such far ranging
conclusions.

9   In 1888, Topinard published Broca's more extensive data
on the Parisian hospitals. Since Broca recorded height and
age as well as brain size, we may use modern statistics to
remove their effect. Brain weight decreases with age, and
Broca's women were, on average, considerably older than his
men. Brain weight increases with height, and his average
man was almost half a foot taller than his average woman. I
used multiple regression, a technique that allowed me to
assess simultaneously the influence of height and age upon
brain size. In an analysis of the data for women, I found that,
at average male height and age, a woman's brain would weigh
1,212 grams. Correction for height and age reduces Broca's
measured difference of 181 grams by more than a third, to
113 grams.

10   I don't know what to make of this remaining difference
because I cannot assess other factors known to influence
brain size in a major way. Cause of death has an important
effect: degenerative disease often entails a substantial diminution of brain size. (This effect is separate from the decrease
attributed to age alone.) Eugene Schreider, also working with
Broca's data, found that men killed in accidents had brains
weighing, on average, 60 grams more than men dying of
infectious diseases. The best modern data I can find (from
American hospitals) records a full 100-gram difference
between death by degenerative arteriosclerosis and by violence or accident. Since so many of Broca's subjects were very
elderly women, we may assume that lengthy degenerative disease was more common among them than among the men.

*When I wrote this essay, I assumed tht Le Bon was a marginal, if color-
ful, figure. I have since learned that he was a leading scientist, one of the
founders of social psychology, and best known for a seminal study on
crowd behavior, still cited today (La psychologie des foules, 1895), and for
his work on unconscious motivation.

More importantly, modern students of brain size still have   11
not agreed on a proper measure for eliminating the powerful
effect of body size. Height is partly adequate, but men and
women of the same height do not share the same body build.
Weight is even worse than height, because most of its variation reflects nutrition rather than intrinsic size—fat versus
skinny exerts little influence upon the brain. Manouvrier took
up this subject in the 1880s and argued that muscular mass
and force should be used. He tried to measure this elusive
property in various ways and found a marked difference in
favor of men, even in men and women of the same height.
When he corrected for what he called "sexual mass," women
actually came out slightly ahead in brain size.

Thus, the corrected 113-gram difference is surely too large;   12
the true figure is probably close to zero and may as well favor
women as men. And 113 grams, by the way, is exactly the
average difference between a 5 foot 4 inch and a 6 foot 4 inch
male in Broca's data. We would not (especially us short folks)
want to ascribe greater intelligence to tall men. In short, who
knows what to do with Broca's data? They certainly don't permit any confident claim that men have bigger brains than
women.

To appreciate the social role of Broca and his school, we   13
must recognize that his statements about the brains of
women do not reflect an isolated prejudice toward a single
disadvantaged group. They must be weighed in the context of
a general theory that supported contemporary social distinctions as biologically ordained. Women, blacks, and poor people suffered the same disparagement, but women bore the
brunt of Broca's argument because he had easier access to
data on women's brains. Women were singularly denigrated
but they also stood as surrogates for other disenfranchised
groups. As one of Broca's disciples wrote in 1881: "Men of the
black races have a brain scarcely heavier than that of white
women." This juxtaposition extended into many other realms
of anthropological argument, particularly to claims that, ana-
tomically and emotionally, both women and blacks were like
white children—and that white children, by the theory of
recapitulation, represented an ancestral (primitive) adult
stage of human evolution. I do not regard as empty rhetoric
the claim that women's battles are for all of us.

Maria Montessori did not confine her activities to educa-   14
tional reform for young children. She lectured on anthropology for several years at the University of Rome, and wrote an
influential book entitled *Pedagogical Anthropology* (English

edition, 1913). Montessori was no egalitarian. She supported most of Broca's work and the theory of innate criminality proposed by her compatriot Cesare Lombroso. She measured the circumference of children's heads in her schools and inferred that the best prospects had bigger brains. But she had no use for Broca's conclusions about women. She discussed Manouvrier's work at length and made much of his tentative claim that women, after proper correction of the data, had slightly larger brains than men. Women, she concluded, were intellectually superior, but men had prevailed heretofore by dint of physical force. Since technology has abolished force as an instrument of power, the era of women may soon be upon us: "In such an epoch there will really be superior human beings, there will really be men strong in morality and in sentiment. Perhaps in this way the reign of women is approaching, when the enigma of her anthropological superiority will be deciphered. Woman was always the custodian of human sentiment, morality and honor."

15   This represents one possible antidote to "scientific" claims for the constitutional inferiority of certain groups. One may affirm the validity of biological distinctions but argue that the data have been misinterpreted by prejudiced men with a stake in the outcome, and that disadvantaged groups are truly superior. In recent years, Elaine Morgan has followed this strategy in her *Descent of Woman,* a speculative reconstruction of human prehistory from the woman's point of view— and as farcical as more famous tall tales by and for men.

16   I prefer another strategy. Montessori and Morgan followed Broca's philosophy to reach a more congenial conclusion. I would rather label the whole enterprise of setting a biological value upon groups for what it is: irrelevant and highly injurious. George Eliot well appreciated the special tragedy that biological labeling imposed upon members of disadvantaged groups. She expressed it for people like herself—women of extraordinary talent. I would apply it more widely—not only to those whose dreams are flouted but also to those who never realize that they may dream—but I cannot match her prose. In conclusion, then, the rest of Eliot's prelude to *Middlemarch:*

> The limits of variation are really much wider than anyone would imagine from the sameness of women's coiffure and the favorite love stories in prose and verse. Here and there a cygnet is reared uneasily among the ducklings in the brown pond, and never finds the living stream in fellowship with its

own oary-footed kind. Here and there is born a Saint Theresa, foundress of nothing, whose loving heartbeats and sobs after an unattained goodness tremble off and are dispersed among hindrances instead of centering in some long-recognizable deed.

SEXUAL HARASSMENT

Kati Marton

An All Too Common Story

Kati Marton, a writer and formerly a network correspondent, contributed the following commentary to Newsweek *on October 21, 1991, just after the Clarence Thomas/Anita Hill controversy over sexual harassment.*

1   Is there a woman in the American workplace for whom Prof. Anita Hill's painful revelations regarding sexual harassment do not resonate? For me, her recollections revived an incident I had suppressed for more than a decade and a half. Unlike Professor Hill's experience, my memory of sexual harassment will not leave a deep imprint on the nation's psyche. Mine is but one woman's story. The professor and I are products of vastly different cultures and professions: she an Oklahoma farm girl; I, Budapest-born and -raised, a relative newcomer to this land. In common we had this: both of us were determined to succeed in highly competitive and conspicuously male-dominated professions: hers the law, mine the media. Yet, listening to her testimony, I was struck by how similarly she and I, different in almost every way, responded to sexual pressures in our professional lives. In the wake of Anita Hill's searing memories, I now see my own experience as part of a sad, pervasive pattern of sexual blackmail in offices across the land.

2   I was 25 years old at the time, the same age as Professor Hill when she worked for Judge Clarence Thomas at the Equal Employment Opportunity Commission. I was only six months into my job as an on-air reporter for a network affiliate in Philadelphia. Like Professor Hill, I, too, lacked a résumé. I, too, loved my job. On the day in question, a station news executive and I traveled by train to New York so that I could receive a George Foster Peabody Award for my work on a documentary on the Philadelphia Orchestra's visit to China. I delivered an earnest and self-conscious acceptance speech

to the media heavyweights gathered in the gold-trimmed room. At one point, I momentarily lost my composure and my newly acquired American accent when I mentioned that only a few years before, I did not even speak English. But through it all I basked in the warm glow of my peers' approval. It should have been a proud day for a neophyte reporter. It did not turn out that way.

My executive escort, seemingly bristling with pride (it was 3 the first time a local Philadelphia television reporter had won the coveted Peabody), invited me and a childhood friend from Budapest to the Russian Tea Room to toast the event. The hours passed in a happy haze. "Isn't it time we headed for the Metroliner back to Philadelphia?" I asked the executive around nightfall. Having said goodnight to my friend, we walked to the limousine my colleague had hired for the occasion. But the car did not follow the familiar route to Penn Station. Without a word of prompting, the limo pulled up in front of the Hilton hotel. Too astonished and too intimidated to muster anything like a firm protest, I found myself following the executive into the hotel elevator. "I only want to get to know you better," he explained. "To talk to you."

And talk I did, with the feverish urgency of a drowning per- 4 son clinging to a life raft. I saw talk as my only escape from certain disaster, a compromise between humiliating the man to whom I owed my career and my own revulsion at the situation he had placed me in. So I talked about my childhood, embellishing and dramatizing, in the manner of a stand-up comic auditioning for the big time. By midnight I had run out of steam and stories so I prodded him to talk about his life, his troubles. It was the most exhausting tap dance of my life, but it was the only way I could think of to deflect this man from pursuing what I assumed to be his own objectives. There was no time to even wonder how in God's name he presumed this was where I wanted to spend the proudest night of my short career. What gave a man with whom I had exchanged one handshake—and that on the day I was hired— this right? He assumed that right. I, loving my job, thinking I got it only by a stroke of luck, became his accomplice by not walking out, by not even voicing outrage. I did not have the nerve.

At dawn, he finally drifted off to sleep and I made my 5 bleary-eyed way to the train and to Philadelphia. Toward evening, as I faced the bright lights of the studio cameras, I saw him just arriving to work. He looked much more rested than I. By then all memories of the previous day's brief moment of glory had been supplanted by other memories. Irrational feelings of guilt regarding my conduct began to nag at me. Had I given the wrong signals? He seemed such a nice, square sort of family man. And why had I not walked out on him? The minute a woman decides to stay and stay silent, in her own mind at least, she loses the moral edge. Like thousands of women in newsrooms, offices and factories, I had swapped the moral edge for job security. I did not think I had the luxury of choice in the matter.

6   I suppose the executive felt sure I would never talk about his abortive attempt at seduction. He was right. I never have, until now. Nor have I let myself take much pride in that hard-won Peabody Award, fearing that the other memories would rush in beside them. But hearing Professor Hill's taut recitation, accompanied by the belittling comments of certain members of the gentleman's club on Capitol Hill, forced me to mentally revisit that room in the Hilton. Professor Hill's dignity did not mask the lasting humiliation that is the inevitable residue of such moments.

7   There is more than personal catharsis at stake in owning up to this long-suppressed incident. I am writing this not only because the memory would not let go. I am writing because Professor Hill's voice moved me to do so. I wanted to say to the Senate panel, "Look, I know why she stayed on with the man who insulted her. So many of us have been there, not liked ourselves for it, but have stayed." And there is another impulse to my speaking out now. If men and women alike pronounce such degrading episodes unacceptable, perhaps our daughters might be spared similar choices in their professional lives. No one should have to purchase job security at so high a price.

Frederic Hayward

Sexual Harassment—From a Man's Perspective

Frederic Hayward was executive director of Men's Rights, Inc., a not-for-profit corporation that raises awareness on men's issues, when (in October 1990) he contributed the following essay to The Business Journal, *a publication that discusses issues of general interest to businesspeople in the Sacramento, California, area.*

The newcomer approaches a second man and snarls, "Hey, pal, you got a problem?" "No." "Well, I don't like the way you're lookin' at me." Typical macho behavior? Women are above that sort of thing? 1

Not exactly. It is at the insistence of women that simply looking at a woman "the wrong way" is banned by government. 2

On the surface, Freedom of Vision seems like a more fundamental right even than Freedom of Speech. Yet, just as laws against pornography can prohibit a man from looking at a naked woman, laws against sexual harassment can prohibit him from looking at a clothed woman while imagining her naked. 3

If you stare at a man and he doesn't like it, you risk a punch in the jaw. If you stare at a woman and she doesn't like it, you risk a megabuck financial settlement and/or a ruined career. 4

The problem is not, of course, that we make too much of sexual harassment; rather, the problem is that our perspective is biased by narrow, sexist, political interests. 5

A less-biased look at sexual harassment reveals, among other things, a host of women and men who are victimized by female abuse of sexual power. Ignore the immensity of that power at your peril. 6

Before our gender consciousness was raised by feminism, men had most of the political-economic power, while women had most of the sexual power. The traditional male-female relationship was based on the exchange of these two power imbalances. The traditional male-female contract consisted of the man tapping his source of power to give physical and financial security to the woman while she, in return, tapped her sexual power to give him access to her body. 7

8   Recent events hint at the enormous sexual power that can
be unleashed. Gary Hart gambled and lost the presidency in
order to have sex with a woman. Jim Bakker gambled and
lost a multimillion-dollar ministry in order to have sex with a
woman. In the American embassy in Moscow, Sgt. Clayton
Lonetree sacrificed our nation's security in order to have sex
with a woman. If a man would trade away the highest office,
the greatest prestige and the deepest loyalty in order to have
sex with a woman, only the most dogmatic could deny that he
would trade away a letter of recommendation.

9   Feminist protestations of women's powerlessness (hence,
innocence) notwithstanding, most of us personally know of
women who have used and abused their sexual power. Questions arise: If I or a woman do not get into graduate school
because a female competitor has more A's from sleeping with
more professors (Ilene F. was the notorious but proud example from my own university) then what are we victims of? If I
or a woman do not get a job because a female competitor displays more enticing cleavage, then what are we victims of? If I
or a woman do not get a promotion because a female competitor has an affair with our boss, then what are we victims of?

10   We do not even have a name for it, let alone a law against it.
Any analysis of sexual office politics that ignores this component might be "politically correct," but is woefully inadequate.

11   Furthermore, the sexual harassment for which we do have
a name has a silent, twin brother.

12   In essence, sexual harassment means requiring a person to
carry out a traditional sex role as a subcondition for employment. Since a main component of the traditional female role
is to provide sexual gratification, women usually find themselves caught in the well-publicized trap of providing sex as
part of a job.

13   A main component of the traditional male role, on the
other hand, is to bear physical risk and undertake heavy
labor. The twin brother of sexual harassment, then, entails
the primary assumption of dangerous and beast-of-burden
tasks as a condition for a man's employment.

14   A people-based definition of sexual harassment would
probably include as many male as female victims. Not surprisingly, a frequent complaint of male security officers is
that equally paid female co-workers are routinely given less
than equally risky assignments. Male sales agents complain
that they are forced into front-line duty when potentially violent customers appear. The federal Equal Employment

Opportunity Commission and state agencies are singularly unresponsive to male "crybabies."

The bottom line is that men suffer a disproportionate share of work-related accidents. The male-centered form of sexual "harassment" kills. Indeed, *USA Today* reports that men, who comprise about half the work force, suffer 95 percent of at-work fatalities and 82 percent of at-work murders! (In a telling comment on the media's deflection of attention away from male victimization, however, the article was simply headlined: "732 women were murdered on the job.") 15

This is not to say, of course, that there are no male victims of the female-centered definition of sexual harassment, in which sexual favors become a condition of employment. 16

Since women are just as human as men, they are just as likely to abuse power. There are cases where men incur sexual pressure from female (and gay male) bosses. 17

But for men, sex has historically been a reward for money and power, while for women, sex has been a means to money and power. Again, the traditional contract acknowledged that women start with sexual power and need not trade for it. 18

The so-called shortage of eligible men, a common complaint in women's magazines, attests to the continuing expectation that a man is not "eligible" if he stands below the woman on the ladder of success. The reason a female vice president is less likely to sexually harass her male secretary, therefore, has nothing to do with her higher standard of behavior. It is simply that she is conditioned to prefer an affair with the president. 19

Even when the concern is limited to only-female victims of only-female defined sexual harassment, moreover, the male perspective needs to be included before effective solutions can be developed. Blaming one gender exclusively (men) is as politically popular as it is specious. Women do play a role in perpetrating the harassment ethic. 20

Not unusually, my own sexual harassment training was at the hands of a woman. When I was young, I did not believe the peers and movie characters who encouraged me to never take "no" for an answer. The person who finally convinced me was Jane B. She was mercifully blunt about why her initial romantic interest in me had dissipated into a platonic friendship. I was too much of a gentleman, she informed me. Before making decisions, I had naively asked for her input. Worst of all, when getting sexual, I had foolishly waited for permission. "Be a man!" was her closing advice. 21

22   I tested her sexual harassment encouragement on a succession of women and found that it worked. The consistent romantic failure that had been my reward for treating women with "respect" was replaced by consistent romantic success.

23   Popular wisdom has it backward: Sexist conditioning has not left most women ill-prepared to say an assertive "no." Rather, it has left most women ill-prepared to give assertive "yesses." That is, most men already assume that if a woman means "no," she says "no." But experience has taught us that when a woman means "yes," we cannot count on hearing it clearly.

24   Before men can unlearn harassing behavior, we need to experience female initiative. Until then, the game of romance will continue to have men playing the actor/predator and women playing the object/prey. Until then, men will never be sure whether a particular "no" means "No, I'm not interested at all," or "No, I'm not ready now, but I might be ready later, so you better try again because that is the only way you will find out," or "Yes, but I don't want you to lose respect for me by sounding too easy."

25   To make matters worse, since women are comparatively passive when it comes to initiating, men become conditioned to responding to visual cues. Indeed, some women in my workshops assert that giving visual cues is the female version of initiating. The problem, however, is that men cannot always read the visual signals they receive.

26   If a woman dresses to kill, for example, hoping to arouse the interest of those men she likes, non-targeted men receive many of the same visual cues. More and more men are, in fact, complaining that provocative dress constitutes sexual harassment against them.

27   Furthermore, sexual harassment is not necessarily a physical attack; it can even be an unwanted glance. Yet, the only purpose of showing cleavage is to have people admire it; can we really place all the blame on the man for looking?

28   Recently, I accompanied an attorney on her way to interview a potential client, a woman who felt she was unfairly fired. The attorney explained that she did not yet know what the actual complaint would be because she did not yet know the gender of the boss. If the boss was male, he would be charged with sexual harassment. In other words, his actual conduct was irrelevant; if there is a conflict between a male boss and a female employee, the charge is sexual harassment. It's automatic.

Indeed, a personnel director at one of the nation's largest   29
computer firms expressed his dismay to me at how many
good male executives he has lost from accusations (and even
simple threats of accusations) of sexual harassment.

As homely Henry Kissinger remarked, power is the ulti-   30
mate aphrodisiac. For every executive who chases his secretary around the desk, there is a secretary who dreams of
marrying an executive and not having to be a secretary any
more.

Given the bitterness that can attend a broken love affair   31
and the bitterness that can plague office politics, combining
the two can be a powerful motivation to reach for any available weapon. The same safeguards that protect an innocent
victim of sexual harassment are a potent arsenal in the hands
of a bitter colleague/ex-lover.

Statistics do not tell us, therefore, how prevalent the prob- 32
lem is. We know only that the problem is serious. We also
know that the problem will persist as long as we turn a deaf
ear and a blind eye to the male perspective.

Susan Squire
Office Intercourse

*The following essay about sexual harassment appeared in the
October 1994 issue of* Harper's Bazaar, *a magazine with articles and features particularly intended for women. For another
example of the work of Susan Squire, who writes often for*
Harper's Bazaar, Redbook, *and similar publications for
women, see page 544.*

The dubious Paula Jones notwithstanding, most men (even   1
politicians, who often seem compelled to behave more crudely
than the rest of their gender) are not in the habit of dropping
their trousers and commanding a female underling to "kiss it."
Nor do most women file a sexual-harassment lawsuit whenever the guy down the hall offers to buy lunch. For every
alleged victim and every accused perp, there are several million people, male and female, doing their best to keep the
workplace safe for business and for its related small pleasures.

Such as the no-big-deal flirtatious repartee that makes going to the office more fun than communicating with it from home by modem.

2   "There's a sense of commitment on the part of both genders to maintaining a certain level of frivolity in the workplace," insists Stanley Bing, author of *Crazy Bosses,* who tracks office manners and mores regularly as an *Esquire* columnist. "It's the only way to keep it human."

3   After all, sexual harassment in its true form has nothing to do with complimenting one's secretary/boss/client/colleague on their dress/tie/shoes/haircut, and everything to do with abuse of power by a superior against a subordinate. It's threatening to fire, promising to hire, or denying a raise or promotion based on the delivery of specified sexual favors; nothing ambiguous about it. It's a superstar lawyer accused of grabbing his secretary and demanding to know which of her breasts is larger—as has recently been alleged in a sensational San Francisco case involving the prominent firm Baker & McKenzie.

4   But such ham-fisted aggression is rare. Most of what passes for sex play in the office is far more... playful. And wide open to interpretation—depending on who's involved. "If a cute V.P. with a Harvard M.B.A. asks you to have a drink after work, it's a date," says Patricia, a 32-year-old Los Angeles account executive. "If he's old, fat, balding, *and* he's higher up than you are in the organization, it harassment." More seriously, she adds, "It strikes me as grossly unfair to men because these judgments are so subjective."

5   Enter Deborah Tannen, the linguistics expert and Georgetown University professor whose megaseller, *You Just Don't Understand,* analyzed what men and women really mean when they talk to each other in their private lives. Tannen's new book, *Talking from 9 to 5* (William Morrow), focuses on how gender differences shape office behavior and communication. Tannen's timing—given the apparently unisex confusion over what is and what isn't acceptable discourse in the workplace—couldn't be better.

6   Twenty years ago as Tannen confides in *Talking from 9 to 5,* she was a graduate student writing her first book. Her older male editor was in town on business. He wanted to discuss her manuscript—in his hotel room. Tannen felt a bit uneasy, but being young, unpublished, and intimidated by his position, did as he asked. When they finished their talk, the editor stood up. He said he was going to change his clothes, and immediately began to strip!

The point is not what happened next (nothing: She turned   7
her back and pretended to be engrossed in her manuscript
until he was done), but how far to the other extreme we've
moved since then. "I doubt it would have occurred to this
man that I might be offended or scared in any way, or that he
was making himself vulnerable to accusation," says Tannen,
now 49. "But today a man would have to be living in a bubble
for that not to occur to him."

Ever since the Thomas/Hill hearings brought sexual   8
harassment to the forefront of public consciousness, we've
been in a "period of overcompensation," according to Tannen. "My impression is that, in some sense, women and men
are not getting each other. Men don't get the inchoate, lurking
fear of violence that women live with, and women don't get
men's fear of false accusation." Both sexes, she feels, could
stand to give the other some slack. "It would be great if
women could tell men they're uncomfortable in a way that
doesn't sound like an attack, and it would be great if men
could accept that women have been made uncomfortable by
something they've said or done without feeling insulted or
outraged."

This mutual lack of comprehension develops from early   9
patterns of socialization, Tannen points out. She cites studies
that demonstrate how boys are raised—to challenge others
without worrying about their feelings—while girls are taught
to weigh their own needs, and how they are expressed,
against how the other person might react to them. "A woman
assumes that if a man talks to her in a way that makes her
uncomfortable, he must want to make her uncomfortable,"
Tannen says. "But I think a man just talks the way he talks,
without thinking about how it will affect her. If she doesn't
object he figures it must be okay."

What offends one women in the workplace might amuse,   10
or not even be noticed by, another. Think of two male bosses
who each send flowers to their female assistants for working
all weekend. One of the women feels appreciated and
respected. The other feels that the gift was inappropriate,
more suggestive of romance than gratitude for a job well
done. A raise, a bonus, a glowing notation in her file, would,
she thinks, have been more suitable. Who's right? Both and
neither, says Tannen. "Subjectivity is built into this scenario,
because our rituals for courtship and for courtesy are inter-
twined. A boss who sends flowers may have intended to be
courteous, but the recipient might misunderstand his intention, or vice versa. You can never come up with guidelines

about what is acceptable and what isn't, because everyone
has their own sense of where to draw the line."

11   Tannen believes that such differences in sensibility among
women are rooted in what was considered normal behavior
in the environment we grew up in. "As a culture," she says,
"we jump far too quickly to psychological explanations, when
a lot of it is simply what you've been exposed to—habitual
ways of talking that seem appropriate."

12   Elizabeth, a 36-year-old executive with a chemical-sales
company, grew up with three older brothers, an experience
that has made her uniquely well suited to success in her male-
dominated industry. "I've always been comfortable with
men," she says. "My brothers taught me how they think and
how to look out for myself." Married and a mother of two, she
travels frequently for work and is accustomed to "staving off
flirtation" while on the road, which she takes in stride as "a
fact of life for any businesswoman." Elizabeth is a pragma-
tist: In gauging her response to a man who hustles her, one of
her primary considerations is how important he is to her
career. The more important, the more delicately she turns
him down.

13   Sometimes it's enough just to feign a Pollyannaish naïveté
about his proposition. "In my experience," Elizabeth says,
"the come-on is usually pretty understated, because no man
wants to be rejected." However, if he persists, Elizabeth
doesn't care who he is or how he can affect her career: "For
me, it's gray until it becomes black, and once it's black—once
he says, 'fuck me or I'll fire you'—I'd take legal action. No
question about it, I'd nail the guy to the wall." In the end,
Elizabeth's brothers taught her well. She knows where her
boundaries lie, and she allows no one to cross them.

14   Jennie, 28, is a trader in a Chicago investment bank. She
doesn't have brothers but does have a "very high tolerance"
for obnoxious male behavior. A tomboy growing up, she was
"always trying to be one of the guys," and that kind of acceptance is still very important to her, possibly at her own
expense. Being less savvy, less sure of herself, and more eager
to please than Elizabeth, Jennie can be—not coincidentally—
foggy about what she will and will not accept in others. As
a result, she sometimes sends mixed messages to male
colleagues.

15   All of her work takes place on the trading floor with the
same bunch of (mostly) men, who tend to be young, single,
and aggressive, like Jennie herself. There's plenty of inter-
office flirting, swearing, joking, and drinking, in which she

more or less fully participates. She could do without the girlie pictures some of the men tape to their computer monitors, but tells herself that she's just "dealing with little boys who have a new toy." The last thing she wants is to come across as "some uptight feminist." But there was one recent incident that truly offended her.

A male trader was turning 30. Two of his buddies arranged   16
for a stripper, dressed in a business suit, to come to the office under the pretense that she was there to be interviewed by the birthday boy. All the offices are glass-walled, so everyone could see the "interview" plainly. "I didn't like the connection between business suit and stripping," Jennie admits. Later she told one of her colleagues (in a joking manner, so that "he wouldn't hate me") that she thought this gag had gone a bit too far. He was bewildered by her reaction.

Why, he asked, did the stripper antic strike Jennie as   17
demeaning to women when the jokes and pinups and sexual teasing didn't? "His confusion was honest," Jennie sighs. "He wanted clearcut rules to follow, and I didn't have any. I'm still making them up as I go along."

As American business culture continues to have its con-   18
sciousness raised, repositioning the line of the permissible between the boorish and the boring, certain new limits have been established. The sexually suggestive joke, told expressly to embarrass or humiliate women, has gone the way of the racial slur in corporate America: out the window. And the workplace is far less hospitable to power moves masquerading as sexual overtures.

"These limits are good," says Stanley Bing, "because they   19
allow us to flush out the wackos on both ends of the spectrum: the guy who can't stop telling the completely unfunny dirty joke, and the incompetent woman who claims everyone's out to get her just because she's a woman. There's still plenty of flirting, but less room to abuse power—and less room to be a jerk."

IV.

FAMILY MATTERS

Introduction

During the 1992 presidential campaign, both George Bush and Bill Clinton promised to sustain vigorous efforts to protect the American family—one indication of just how broad concern about the family has become in the United States during the 1990s. That concern emerged again during the 1996 election campaign, as candidates from both major parties offered one after another solution to The Family Problem—whatever that may be. No doubt you have heard the general concerns mentioned again and again—concerns about the state of the family during a time of increasing divorce and out-of-wedlock births; concerns about child support that ought to be honored by absent spouses, but isn't; concerns about teenage crime, suicide, pregnancy, substance abuse, and truancy that seem to be associated with broken homes; concerns about the effectiveness of day care, education, and children's health; concerns about child abuse. Moreover, you have probably also heard discussions in the media about new family matters that have come about as a result of new social customs and developments in reproductive technology—about who should have custody of children in cases of divorce, about whether or not single-sex couples should share in the benefits and responsibilities of marriage, about controversial adoption cases of one kind or another. Consequently, this part of *Conversations* takes up several topics related to the family, most of which are related to each other in some way.

The first section offers four readings on broad questions about the current condition of the American family. Is the family indeed in trouble in our country? Does it require some sort of repair—or is our society simply experiencing understandable and temporary pains associated with a transition from the traditional, two-parent home to less monolithic, less misogynist, more varied, and ultimately healthier versions of the family? Are children in our society being routinely damaged by broken homes, absent fathers, and general neglect of the family, or are those problems the result of other social factors, mostly associated with poverty? Would tougher child support laws help to amend the family? (Currently only 67 percent of child support is being paid by absent spouses.) Should we make it more difficult to divorce in our society? More difficult to reproduce outside marriage? More difficult to retain children born out of wedlock or living in abusive households? Do we need more stringent laws to discourage deadbeat fathers and mothers?

Those questions also lead to the next section, which takes up the specific issue of single parenthood. As you may know, during the past two decades the number of single-parent households in America has increased dramatically, as divorce and illegitimacy rates have increased. Since 1950, the number of American children living in mother-only families has quadrupled, from about 5 million to about 20 million, and since 1970, the number of single parents has tripled, from about 4 million to about 12 million. Ten percent of all live births in the United States are to mothers under 18. In 1995, 30 percent of all American children under 18 lived with one parent (26 percent with the mother, 4 percent with the father), compared with 12 percent in 1970. As a result, Senator Daniel Patrick Moynihan (a Democrat) and former Vice President Dan Quayle (a Republican) have made well-publicized attempts to draw attention to the problem of single parenthood: Moynihan through congressional hearings and reports, Quayle through his much publicized charges that television's Murphy Brown was glamorizing unwed motherhood.

But is it a problem? Is single parenthood the cause of social ills? Or are single parents, especially if they work, the victim of difficult circumstances and unrealistic expectations, particularly if their spouses offer insufficient child support? And if single parenthood is a problem, what should be done about it? Can and should the federal government play a role in this matter at a time when many Americans are suspicious about the federal government's role in their lives? In 1995, Newt Gingrich introduced the Personal Responsibility Act, which would have eliminated welfare benefits for children born to unwed mothers under the age of 18 and would have required mothers to establish paternity as a condition for receiving welfare: Is such an act a good idea? *Conversations* presents a spirited exchange among five women concerning all these questions.

Single parenthood is closely related, of course, to custody issues, the subject of the third section in this part. New reproductive technologies, increased interracial marriage, and new customs associated with divorce and adoption are making custody issues knottier every day. The courts in the United States have traditionally sided with mothers in matters of custody, at least since the middle of the last century, when maternal preference began to replace fathers' common law right to custody; but recently new, gender-neutral laws and the consequent pressure on domestic courts to consider "the best interests of the child" are requiring judges to think more carefully about custody. As a result, an increasing number of children of divorced parents live with dads—13 percent, as opposed to 9 percent in 1970. Women's groups contend that the courts are sometimes holding mothers to a higher standard of parental responsibility than they do men, particularly if the woman holds a job, while men's rights advocates are demanding joint custody arrangements as well as the awarding of primary custody to fathers in an increasing number of cases. What are the rights (and responsibilities of mothers and fathers? Is joint custody (now available as an option in forty-three states) in the best interests of the children of divorced parents, or does it merely exacerbate tensions between divorced parents who act out their disagreements with their children? What exactly does "child support" mean—is it simply a matter of finances? What are the rights of a supportive but absent parent in decisions affecting children, and what should be the penalty for insufficient support? Should visitation rights be tied to child support payments? And what are the rights of adoptive parents? Should African American or mixed-race couples have preference when it comes to the adoption of children of African American or mixed descent?

This part of *Conversations* closes with a discussion of same-sex marriage at a time when many states are considering legislation that would permit it. Should such matches be sanctioned by our laws so that same-sex couples can enjoy the civic benefits associated with marriage—that is, health benefits tied to family membership, tax benefits, the right to adopt children, the right to inherit money, and so forth? Would recognizing same-sex partners as lawfully married somehow undermine the family? Or would it put unwelcome pressure on same-sex couples to conform to an institution that many people find ill-suited to same-sex couples?

If this introduction has focused more on questions than on answers, that is because the discussion of family matters in this country is so problematic right now. The selections in this part will give you the opportunity to confront some of the most vexing questions in our culture—and an opportunity to have your own say during a time when people are particularly interested in reading about these questions.

CAN THE FAMILY BE SAVED?

Roger Rosenblatt

The Society That Pretends
to Love Children

Roger Rosenblatt (born 1940) is a writer and editor at Time
magazine; he is also a frequent contributor to the New York
Times Magazine, *a publication on current events that is
enclosed with every Sunday* Times. *The following essay
appeared in a special issue of the* New York Times Magazine
(October 8, 1995) on childhood in America.

Henry will not face me. We sit close together on small plas-   1
tic chairs in a classroom at P.S. 314, an elementary school in
the Sunset Park area of Brooklyn, where he works with small
children in a summer camp. Our knees, drawn high because
we are sitting on the low chairs, almost touch. Still, Henry
angles his body so that he shows me only his profile. If he
turns toward me briefly and catches my eye, he immediately
turns away again and gazes out the large schoolroom window
at kids on a stoop across the street.

His neighborhood, Sunset Park, consists of approximately   2
110,000 people, most of them poor, with a per capita income of
$11,115. A quarter of the residents have incomes below the
poverty line. They represent a variety of backgrounds—Puerto
Rican, African-American, Dominican, Mexican, Jordanian,
Pakistani, Chinese, Korean and Vietnamese. These groups are
the latest to populate Sunset Park. They follow the Irish, Finns,
Swedes, Norwegians, Poles and Italians of the late 19th century, and the Greeks, Russians and Jews of the early 20th. The
first area residents were the Dutch and the English, who
established farms where the Canarsie Indians had lived.

A little over a mile wide and 2.6 miles long, the area lies   3
between middle-class Bay Ridge to the south and gentrified
Park Slope to the north. The rectangle of the neighborhood

slopes down from the high ridge at Eighth Avenue to the east to Upper New York Bay, where the Statue of Liberty rises. At the top of the ridge is Sunset Park itself—an 18-acre public park with old trees and a W.P.A. swimming pool. On the grid of narrow streets and wide avenues between the ridge and the bay lie two- and three-story brownstones with attractive cornices; brick-and-masonry houses with little gardens in the front, where corn is sometimes grown, and many rows of drab no-color tenements. Henry lives in one of these. His home is near Third Avenue, which is close to the water, and is shadowed by the Gowanus Expressway, one of the highways built by Robert Moses to carry white people away from places like Sunset Park.

4   Henry is 16, tall for his age at about 6 foot 1. His skin is a dull dark brown; antiperspirant under his arms foams white against it. His hair is spun into curlicues. He rarely smiles, though when he does, he looks warm and welcoming—in contrast to his usual self-concealing blankness. He is sleepy this morning. He yawns frequently, and fully, his mouth wide open like a baby's.

5   "What else have you seen?" I ask him. He is talking about life on the streets.

6   "I saw a man throw a telephone out the window," he says. "It hit a baby in a carriage. It nearly killed her. So her father ran up the stairs, and he grabbed the man who threw the phone, and he cut him." He traces a line across his throat with his index finger. "He lived, but he's got this necklace now."

7   "Did you know the men involved?" I ask him.

8   "I knew the man who threw the phone," he says. "He's my mother's boyfriend."

9   "Why did he do that?"

10   "He was drunk, crazy." He shrugs to indicate that the behavior is normal for his mother's boyfriend.

11   "What did you do when the baby's father slit his throat?" I ask.

12   "I was happy," Henry says. "I laughed when he did it. I even testified against the boyfriend in court. My mother was mad. She's always mad at me." He gives me a glance, then turns his head to the side. "That was when things really blew up at home. So I went to the Center for Family Life and told Jennifer. She's been everything to me." He says this without emotion. "She makes me think about what I do."

13   "What about your mother?"

14   "She screams. Says I'm the Devil. Calls me stupid and retarded. She says I'm bad. I *am* bad." He holds his head

down. "I hang out. I write up—you know?—do graffiti. I fight,
maybe less now, but I used to fight all the time. When I start
fighting, it's like seek and destroy. You start with me and
you're the enemy. Nobody else in sight. You my spotlight, my
way out. You the exit door."

"The exit door from what?" He does not answer. "Are other   15
grown-ups in your life good to you? Teachers?"

"Some are O.K.," he says. "I had a teacher tell me: 'I don't   16
care if you come to class or not. I get paid anyway.'"

"Police?"   17

"When I got arrested for writing up, a woman cop told me   18
she hopes they send me to jail."

"Ministers? Priests?" I ask.   19

He shakes his head. "I don't have religion."   20

"The Mayor? The Governor? The President?" I am speak-   21
ing a foreign language. "Are there any grown-ups who help
you?"

"Jennifer," he says softly. "People at the center."   22

I ask him: "Henry, do you think that your mother loves   23
you?"

"She pretends to love me," he says.   24

The fact that Henry is poor and black, and that he lives in   25
violent circumstances, makes him an unusually dramatic and
sadly familiar example of the mistreatment of American children. But, for what he represents, he could be any child, anywhere in the country. I could have the wrong Henry. Henry is
not a kid from Sunset Park, Brooklyn. He is a rich, white, 16-
year-old senior at Groton, who has just cheated on his Greek
exam because his father, a true-blue Yalie, yells at him constantly for being stupid and retarded and for not being good
enough to get into Yale.

No, that isn't Henry, either. Henry is a 12-year-old girl from 26
Corpus Christi, Tex., who is trying to get pregnant "to have
love in my life." Or the boy whose father set him on fire to
strike back at his wife in a custody case. Or those teen-agers
who made a suicide pact in New Jersey. Henry is a 14-year-old
girl from Aspen, Colo., who wears all that oversize clothing
and who heads for the ladies' room immediately after meals.
He is the toddler in Los Angeles whose grandmother punished him by holding a pillow over his head and squeezing
him between a table and a sofa. His last words were "Me no
breathe."

Here's Henry now. That's his key in the door. His folks are   27
both at work and will be out till midnight. He has the house

to himself. He pours himself a Coors, calls his girlfriend to come over and plunks down in front of the TV to watch the Jenny Jones show bring him a picture of America.

28   Actually, the Henry of Sunset Park is a bit luckier than the tens of millions of American children, of all economic classes, races and regions, whom the country pretends to love. At least this Henry has an effective local social service agency— the Center for Family Life to which he has been referred— that is devoted to his well-being.

29   In 1993, according to several child interest groups like the Children's Defense Fund, an estimated three million children were reported to public social service agencies to be suffering from abuse or neglect. Some 1,300 of them died. Approximately half a million children are in foster care or similar substitute homes, an increase of 250,000 since 1986. About 14 million live in poverty. About 100,000 children are homeless. The welfare bill passed overwhelmingly by the Senate last month, ending guaranteed assistance to poor families, should add significantly to the number of children in need.

30   The American Humane Association reports that since 1988 American teen-age boys are more likely to die from gunshot wounds than from all natural causes combined. Studies of teen-age pregnancy in Seattle and Chicago show that two-thirds of teen-age mothers reported having been sexually abused. Figures on sexual abuse have been disputed as being too high, but even if the true figures are only half of those reported, they are still considerable.

31   While poor children, black and white, suffer a disproportionate share of ills, the increasing affliction of the American child occurs in rural regions as well as in the cities, and among the middle and upper classes, too. Responses to a survey of girls in grades 6 through 12 in mainly Midwestern states, in 111 communities with populations under 100,000, indicated that by grade nine, one in five girls had been sexually abused. By grade 10, the number was still one in five, but one in three girls had been abused physically, sexually or both. The survey defined physical abuse as an adult causing a scar, bruises, welts, bleeding or a broken bone and sexual abuse as a family member or "someone else" imposing sexual behavior on the child. In 1993, there were 19,466 incidents of child abuse reported to the Iowa Department of Human Services. The advocacy organization, Girls Inc. in Omaha, states that sexual abuse of girls reported in Nebraska (3 in a class of 25) is that of the national average. The abuse of boys is more rarely reported, so the numbers are probably comparable.

Statistics on poor families, like Henry's, are more available   32
than those on better-off families; welfare agencies rarely
invade the homes of the rich. But the mistreatment of children is also a middle-class problem. A random sampling of
adolescents in Minnesota found that 6 percent of middle- or
middle-to-high-income families had at least one child in alcohol or drug treatment programs by ages 14 to 17. Adolescents
in an additional 5 percent of families were using as much
alcohol and drugs as the kids who were in treatment.

Middle-class whites like to think that kids with guns are a   33
black or Latino inner-city menace exclusively. But William C.
Haynes, juvenile justice director of the Tennessee Commission
on Children and Youth, reports that groups of middle-class
white kids in Antioch had a gunfight armed with 9-millimeter
semiautomatic pistols. Richard Louv, the author of "Childhood's Future," notes that the shooting programs of the 4-H
Clubs drew at least 100,000 kids at the end of the 1980's, a
tenfold increase since the mid-1980's.

Two middle-class parents who work full time will, natu-   34
rally, spend less time with their children. In 1976, according
to the economist Sylvia Ann Hewlett, author of "When the
Bough Breaks," 11 percent of children under the age of 1 year
had mothers in the work force. By 1994, the number had
risen to 54.5 percent. Another economist, Victor Fuchs, contends that children have lost 10 to 12 hours a week of parental
time since 1960 because of the added number of hours that
both parents work. The Bureau of Labor Statistics reports
that the average work week was 43.3 hours in 1994, with professional people working an average of 43.8.

At an exhibit of children's artwork at Christie's in New York   35
City last year, paintings were displayed depicting "Images of
Mothers and Fathers." One, showing a man with his hands
held up in surrender and surrounded by clocks, carried the
caption: "This is my father." A ninth grader drew a picture of
her mother *as* a clock.

Neglect is a varied form of abuse and is difficult to pin   36
down. Martha Farrell Erickson of the Children, Youth and
Family Consortium at the University of Minnesota reports that
45 percent of child-abuse cases are officially cited as neglect,
but "it seems likely that the actual incidence is much higher."
Erickson also notes that many neglected children are infants:
"Given that neglect is often chronic rather than episodic, these
children may grow up thinking this is the way life is."

Violent and destructive behavior by middle-class and upper-   37
middle-class kids—generally considered to be a consequence

of neglect—is a daily news story. In the placid seaport town of Dartmouth, Mass., in 1993, three teen-agers burst into a high-school classroom, beat a freshman over the head with a baseball bat and stabbed him to death. In Williamson County, Tenn., the richest county in the state, a boy driving the new car that his parents had just bought him shot and killed a horse in a field—for the fun of it. High-school kids go on destructive binges in Montana and Vermont. In 1989, ABC's television news program, "20/20," ran a piece on high-living teenagers in wealthy Pacific Palisades, Calif., who were lost to drugs and drink. Last year, the network news shows broadcast a video of middle-class teenagers in Florida on a rampage. They tore apart elegant homes, tortured a dog and cooked a goldfish in the microwave. The teenagers made the video themselves.

38   Divorce is not always a destructive event in a child's life, but it is more often so than the divorcing parents care to admit. Fully 40 percent of children living with their mothers do not see their fathers after the breakup. Of the 58 percent of divorced fathers ordered to pay child support, less than two-thirds actually pay in full. One father explained that he could not pay child support because he needed the money to board his two Doberman pinschers. Even when both parents maintain contact with the children, the children can pay penalties. The headmaster of one of New York's distinguished private schools tells of an afternoon when he was summoned to the school lobby, where two parents were shouting and fighting. Each had thought that the coming weekend was the one in which he or she was to take their child. When the headmaster arrived on the scene, the parents were yanking at the child's arms, stretching him between them.

39   If some wealthier parents are not looking out for their children, they are looking out for themselves. Many young couples simply do not have children, even if they are able to, because a child will cut into their income and their time for self-interested pursuits. Many who do have kids did not really want the responsibility of rearing a human being; they wanted another witty, charming, urbane adult in the house. So neglect was built into their vision of the child in the first place. And, of course, when the child turned out not to be the delightful companion the parents originally had in mind, they abandoned it to "independence."

40   In "Habits of the Heart," Robert Bellah points out that since 1965, Americans have been hooked on the therapeutic mentality. The social critic Christopher Lasch also concluded that therapy has replaced religion in American adult lives. A

guidance counselor in Alabama tells me that a reason many parents do not come home at night to their children is that they are taking therapy classes to help them be better parents.

The neglect and abuse of children is hardly new in American history. One may go back through the 350 years represented by the different inhabitants of Sunset Park alone, starting with the Puritans, and discover an unbroken pattern of beating children, psychologically tormenting children, imposing one or another form of miseducation on them, forcing them into labor, giving them too little freedom, or giving them too much. Every major intellectual influence on American children, from Locke to Spock, has wound up distorting their lives. In 1646, "stubborn child laws" were enacted (though never enforced) in Massachusetts, which provided the death penalty for a rebellious son. In the 1850's, the Rev. Samuel Arnold of Ossipee, N.H., nearly beat his adopted son to death because the boy failed to pronounce the words "utter" and "gutter" to the reverend's satisfaction. In 1985, a Sunset Park father, who wanted to show off how smart his 6-year-old son was, forced him to stand and read aloud from a book. When the boy mispronounced the word "bite" as "bit," his father slammed his fist on the kitchen table and made him read the book from the beginning.   41

The difference between past and present abuses is that today's children are not assaulted by one or two destructive forces. They are assaulted by everything, all at once. Individual parents may love their kids, but the society seems to wish the children disappeared. It is as if children are seen as interfering with life, rather than as contributing to it or perpetuating it. Modern living is too difficult, too much to handle or to bear. Children get in the way of one's pleasure or of one's survival. They compete for one's money, resources and affections. Worse, like Henry, they remind adults of their incapacity to love them.   42

"What is to be done?" I ask Mary Paul and Geraldine, the two Sisters of the Good Shepherd who founded the Center for Family Life 17 years ago. The center, which is a lay institution, addresses all sources of difficulty for children, works with the family members involved, and embraces every facet of life in the neighborhood. Besides counseling, it provides an employment agency, an emergency food program, advocacy and legal services, a theater program, a literacy program, summer camps like the one in which Henry works, day care for school-age children and a neighborhood foster-care program. The foster   43 families are selected within the community of the original family, so that the children do not lose touch with their homes.

44   "Better ask what is *not* to be done," Mary Paul says. "People do have positive goals in regard to children. But somehow these goals become subverted because, paradoxically, they become overcommitted to whatever they are doing. Life ceases to be an adaptation and an exchange with an outside environment. We become mere doers. We do and we do and we do, and we grow to be more narrowly focused and more narrowly driven. Soon we lose energy and we fail. It's the law of entropy."

45   "Does that happen in education?" I ask.

46   "Absolutely," she says. "A few years ago, schools in places like New York started out being attentive to the needs of children in a multicultural environment. Perfectly sensible, given all the new immigrant groups who were coming in. Then people became overcommitted to that one goal of multiculturalism. They forgot about what else was worthwhile in education. They thought that education was about self-esteem. They came up with the idea of teaching bilingualism, which serves no useful purpose at all for children trying to make it in American society. In Sunset Park, bilingualism is promoted solely to get patronage jobs for Spanish teachers."

47   "The reason we instituted neighborhood foster care," says Geraldine, "is that child welfare in this country—the Child Welfare Administration in particular—focuses only on the well-being of the child."

48   "The aim is to remove the child from the original family as far away as possible," Mary Paul says. "Often the taking of children is done abruptly. The C.W.A. will take a child from school because it's easier than confronting the mother. Sometimes children are removed in the middle of the night, with the police in attendance. They'll use even more coercive methods. I cannot stand the violence of it."

49   Geraldine breaks in. "This is why we began neighborhood foster care in Sunset Park. We've been doing this seven years now, and sometimes we succeed and sometimes not. But even the failures can be a partial success. A child whom we placed in foster care here has a mother who is seriously mentally ill. The woman will stand in the street and scream up at the windows of the little girl's foster parents' house. She will sit in the hallway and bang on the door with her fists all night. And she will not go for treatment. And still the little girl—because she has been allowed to remain close to her mother—sees the dis-

ease for what it is. She understands. It doesn't make the mother well but it helps the *girl*."

"Everyone suffers from tunnel vision," says Mary Paul. "We are in an economic depression right now. All one reads is how strapped city, state and Federal budgets are. Politicians win points by coming up with ways to save the country money. 'We have to reduce the deficit. We have to reduce the national debt.' For whose benefit should we rescue the economy? It is always the children and the grandchildren. Yet how should we save the economy?" 50

"Take money away from children," Geraldine offers, and laughs. 51

"Exactly," says Mary Paul. "Take the money from the children even though you are focusing on the children as the reason for rescuing the economy. By this logic, you will amass a fortune as a legacy and, at the same time, kill off the legatees." 52

"When parents fail their children," says Geraldine, "it is almost always because of an excessive commitment to one or another pursuit. Henry's mother yells at him and degrades him because she thinks that's how to make him toe the mark. And naturally, Henry is angry at her. He's in a constant rage. And he takes out his rage in street fights." 53

"This is a poor neighborhood," says Mary Paul. "Money drives much of people's behavior. The rage of parents who have sacrificed so much and invested so much and then nothing works...they begin to see the child as a repudiation of their capacity for giving." 54

"What happens when a parent assaults or kills a child?" I ask. 55

"You know," Mary Paul says, "the feeling that one has to love a child can be overwhelming, especially for those—and there are many—who do not. And then the child reminds you every day of your inability to build a world for it. It calls forth something that the parent cannot give. 56

"A Mexican mother in this neighborhood killed her child by repeated beatings. It said in the papers that the family 'somehow made its way from Mexico to Sunset Park.' Somehow made its way! Can you imagine what commitment it took to get from Mexico to here, what ambitions for a new life they had? They wind up in a situation where all forms of love and rationality are abandoned to that dream, which had at its center the children, after all. And then one day the child becomes a noise. And the noise has to be stilled. 57

"We have to remind the child that it belongs to a community. We have to do that for adults, too. Adults are yesterday's children." 58

59   "A client of ours killed her daughter," says Geraldine. "The girl was about 3½. She had diabetes and she was always thirsty. So she would go to the refrigerator again and again for juice. The mother, who was unaware that the child had diabetes, was very poor. She had so little food. She told the girl not to keep going to the refrigerator, but the girl kept going anyway. So the mother hit her in the head, the child went into a coma and eventually died. The mother did not want to kill her little girl, of course. She was thinking about the juice."

60   Jennifer, the social worker who has been counseling Henry, says: "We spend so much time protecting ourselves from the realities because we can't bear to see what we are doing to our kids. How could we live with ourselves if we really knew what we are creating?"

61   She started working with Henry after the incident involving his mother's boyfriend. She had seen him around the center but had no idea of the trouble in his life until he approached her the day he testified against the boyfriend in court. His mother was shutting him out. "'I need to talk to you,' he told me." Then he burst into tears.

62   "The situation was terrible in the beginning. It is getting a bit better now. But with his mother at that time, my God! She did not speak to him for three whole months. The afternoon that Geraldine and I first went over to their house, the mother pulled a kitchen knife on Henry. He stood there helplessly, repeating, 'I don't want to hurt you.' And she kept screaming at him.

63   "Henry has a very tender heart. He is struggling with the question of whether it is possible to feel something without being hurt. Once he came to me and said. 'I saw something in the park today that almost made me tear. A mother and her daughter were sitting on a bench. The mother said, I love you. And the daughter said, I love *you*. I thought: Can people really be that way? And then I thought: Nah.'

64   "He is very gentle. He's wonderful with little kids in the summer camp. He would never harm a smaller child. But if an older person attacks or offends him, he is livid beyond control. He is so deeply hurt that the slightest thing sets him off. Fighting is a power issue for him. He tells me, 'When I'm in a fight, I think of my mother and it gives me the energy.'

65   "This graffiti business, this 'writing up.' I've said to him so many times: 'Please. Explain it to me. I want to understand.'

Because he keeps getting arrested for these petty offenses, and they're building up to a point where a prosecutor will want to put him away. One time he was arrested for writing up two days in a row. I get a call and I go down to the 68th Precinct, and there he is—no shoes on, handcuffed to the bench. The cop was awful. She said: 'I hope you go to jail because that's where you deserve to be.' So I wind up being on Henry's side, even though I want to confront him for doing the wrong thing.

"And the third day, there is Henry *again,* down at the sta-   66
tion house, handcuffed to the bench. I said to him: 'Look. If you want to spend time with me, just say so. We'll go do something. You don't need to get arrested to get my attention.' He said, in that glum way of his, 'Very funny, Jennifer.' But on the way out, he leans down and tells me: 'You shouldn't help me. You should help someone else. It's past my time already.' He was 15."

Sitting with Henry in the P.S. 314 classroom, I ask him   67
what he thinks about when he's alone.

"I think about the future, about getting out of here. I'd like   68
to live somewhere else, upstate maybe. I wouldn't want to grow up and have a kid and live in this neighborhood. It's too dangerous.

"A man held a gun to my head one time, 'cause he wanted   69
my fronts." Fronts are gold caps that kids wear on their teeth for show. I said, 'I won't take 'em off for you or anybody.'"

"Why not give him the fronts?" I ask.   70

"It's the way I am."   71

"Did you think he would shoot you?" He shrugs. "How   72
would you treat a kid of your own?"

"I wouldn't hit him. I'd never hit him. If you hit a kid, he   73
cries at first. Then he stops crying after a while and he doesn't care. You can hit him forever and it won't matter."

"Have people hit you?" He nods. "What for?"   74

"Writing up."   75

"Why do you keep doing it?"   76

"I don't know," he says. "I know it gets me into trouble, but   77
I just can't stop."

"What do you write?"   78

"TM1," he says. "Everywhere I see some open space I write   79
it. TM1. In the hallways, on the buildings, I just have to see it."

"What does TM1 mean?"   80

He looks me in the eye for the first time. "The Magnificent   81
One," he says.

Joseph Shapiro and Joanne Schrof
Honor Thy Children

On February 27, 1995, U.S. News & World Report *published
the following "Special Report" on the family in America.
Joseph Shapiro and Joanne Schrof are regular contributors to*
U.S. News, *a weekly newsmagazine, competing with* Time *and*
Newsweek, *that has a conservative editorial stance. (*U.S.
News *staffers Mike Tharp and Dorian Friedman also contrib-
uted to the essay.)*

1   Dad is destiny. More than virtually any other factor, a biological father's presence in the family will determine a child's
success and happiness. Rich or poor, white or black, the children of divorce and those born outside marriage struggle
through life at a measurable disadvantage, according to a
growing chorus of social thinkers. And their voices are more
urgent because an astonishing 38 percent of all kids now live
without their biological fathers—up from just 17.5 percent in
1960. More than half of today's children will spend at least
part of childhood without a father.

2   These new critics challenge the view that external forces
like street crime, lousy schools and economic stress lie behind
the crisis in families. The revised thinking is that it's the breakdown of families that feeds social ills. "Fatherlessness is the
most destructive trend of our generation," argues David Blankenhorn, author of a provocative new book, *Fatherless America: Confronting Our Most Urgent Social Problem.*

3   The absence of fathers is linked to most social nightmares—from boys with guns to girls with babies. No welfare
reform plan can cut poverty as thoroughly as a two-parent
family. Some 46 percent of families with children headed by
single mothers live below the poverty line, compared with 8
percent of those with two parents. Raising marriage rates will
do far more to fight crime than building prisons or putting
more cops on the streets. Studies show that only 43 percent of
state prison inmates grew up with both parents and that a
missing father is a better predictor of criminal activity than
race or poverty. Growing up with both parents turns out to be
a better antidote to teen pregnancy than handing out condoms. Sociologists Sara McLanahan and Gary Sandefur say
in their recent book, *Growing Up With a Single Parent,* that
young women who were reared in disrupted families are

twice as likely to become teen mothers. Social scientists have made similar links between a father's absence and his child's likelihood of being a dropout, jobless, a drug addict, a suicide victim, mentally ill and a target of child sexual abuse.

Bringing the issue into sharp focus are some brutal reali-   4
ties. Only 51 percent of kids still live with both biological parents. There were some 1.2 million divorces last year, about 53 percent of which involved minor children. In addition, 68 percent of black children and 30 percent of all kids are born outside of marriage. There are places in America where fathers—usually the best hope to socialize boys—are so rare that bedlam engulfs the community. Teachers, ministers, cops and other substitute authority figures fight losing battles in these places against gang members to present role models to preteen and teenage boys. The result is often an astonishing level of violence and incomprehensible incidents of brutality.

Americans know this and increasingly yearn for children   5
to have more protection. Fully 71 percent of those surveyed by U.S. News said it is "very important" for "every child to have his or her father living at home" and nearly 8 in 10 think both fathers and mothers should spend more time with their kids. Some 58 percent say it should be harder for couples with children to get a divorce. That's a position Vice President Al Gore wouldn't endorse. But in an interview with U.S. News, the administration's leading spokesman on the fatherhood issue laments the number of parents who won't "tough out" troubled marriages.

Most Americans reject the harshest solution advocated by   6
some conservatives: encouraging unwed mothers to put their children up for adoption by two-parent families. Seventy percent of those in the U.S. News survey said that when children are born to single mothers, it is "preferable for them to be raised by their mothers" than in a two-parent adoptive family.

It seems simple enough to say every child needs a father.   7
But must Daddy be a biological, married and in-residence paterfamilias, as Blankenhorn and his allies insist? These "new traditionalists" argue that the odds are overwhelming against a divorced dad or a father substitute. For proof, they argue that 18 million children should be entitled to $34 billion more in child support from noncustodial parents (about 90 percent of whom are fathers). Even the lucky child who sees his or her dad at least once a week—just 1 child in 6—often winds up with a "treat dad" for weekend movies, not a father to offer constant guidance and discipline.

8   It even turns out that the fairy tales contain germs of truth about stepparents. Youngsters in stepfamilies do no better, and often fare even worse, than children in homes headed by a single parent, according to several recent studies. Stepparents often bring needed income, but that advantage is offset by the emotional rivalries among parents and children in stepfamilies.

9   Finally, the new traditionalists dispute the idea that kids are worse off when stuck in their parents' lousy marriages. Divorce can increase an adult's happiness, but it is devastating to a child, says psychologist Judith Wallerstein, who has studied her child clients since 1971. One third report moderate or severe depression five years after a divorce. The hurt may remain hidden for years. They often grow up wary of love, marriage and family, and over a third have little or no ambition 10 years after their parents part. "Divorce is not just an episode in a child's life," notes Wallerstein. "It's like a natural disaster that really changes the whole trajectory of a child's life."

10   Blankenhorn, founder of the New York-based Institute for American Values, says action must be taken to slow family breakups. The "logic" of his argument, he says, may lead to steps like ending no-fault divorce and encouraging more single mothers to give up children for adoption. (Adoptive parents are the exception to his preference for biological ones.) He also urges that access to sperm banks be denied to unmarried women.

11   Blankenhorn and his allies are struggling against another group—call them fatherhood "reinventors"—who say it is wrongheaded to stigmatize absent fathers. Millions try to be good dads. And most children of divorce, despite the added risks, turn out fine. Besides, reinventors argue, high divorce rates result from irreversible cultural shifts that are best to accommodate rather than battle—like the economic independence of working women who no longer get stuck in abusive marriages. Reinventors say the solution is to build a network of support to help all fathers, including separated fathers or father figures, be involved in children's lives. Family-friendly workplaces, parenting classes and wider visitation rights are among the answers. Says Richard Louv, author of *FatherLove:* "We need all the fathers we can get."

12   These skirmishes show that fatherhood itself is in transition. Inside marriage, there is confusion as fathers are no longer a family's clear-cut breadwinner, the traditional role of a patriarch. Some blame "feminism," like the evangelical

Christian Promise Keepers, a burgeoning grass-roots movement that wants to bring a million men to Washington next
year to proclaim their desire to be "godly" leaders of their
families. Yet, others thank feminism for showing them a
more satisfying model of parenting.

Unfortunately, even the most earnest attempts to strengthen   13
fatherhood, whether they come from traditionalists or reinventors, seem destined for limited success. A close look at such
efforts suggests just how hard it will be to find policies to
decrease divorce or to make AWOL fathers less distant.

Can We Reconnect Fathers?

In Cleveland's Hough neighborhood, social worker Charles   14
Ballard meets young men who have attended scores of funerals but few, if any, weddings. There are children, he says, who
grow up not knowing the proper finger for wearing a wedding
ring. But the 58-year-old Ballard—abandoned by his own
father at age 3 and a father himself at 17—has overcome
inner-city Cleveland's bleak economic and emotional landscape to teach poor fathers that the key to being a man is to
be a good father.

Since 1982, Ballard's Institute for Responsible Fatherhood   15
and Family Revitalization has worked to reconnect over 2,000
absent fathers with their children. Ballard does it through an
intensive social-work approach—visiting the homes of his clients and referring them to parenting classes, drug abuse
programs or GED courses. But Ballard's approach is also
radical. He turns on its head the usual assumption that men
cannot be responsible parents if they cannot find jobs. Convince young men first of the importance of being good
fathers, Ballard argues, and they are then motivated to finish
school and find work. Social workers have long known that
teen mothers are most likely to complete school, get off
drugs or find a job when they see it as a way of protecting
their child.

Alonzo Warren proves the point. The unemployed 31-   16
year-old father of six children by six different women was
referred to Ballard when he went to the county seeking custody of his 9-year-old son, who was in the care of a relative.
Although Warren's new job, cooking hamburgers at a nearby
fast-food restaurant, pays just the minimum wage, his
steady source of income puts him in a stronger position to
persuade county social workers to allow him overnight visi-

tations with his son as well as to do more to support his other young children. "All the guys I know, even though we're not living with our kids, not a single day goes by when we don't worry about them," says Warren. "Even with our faults, they need us."

17   A study by Case Western Reserve University political science professors G. Regina Nixon and Anthony King shows that Ballard's one-on-one program, which lets fathers take the initiative in solving their own problems, gets some often astonishing results. Ninety-seven percent of the men began providing financial support for their children; 71 percent did not have any more children outside of marriage; only 12 percent had full-time work when they entered, but 62 percent found such work and 12 percent got part-time jobs. There was one glaring shortcoming: The program had less impact on marriage rates. Just 1 in 5 of the participants married. Although the study sample was small, the results persuaded the Ford Foundation to give Ballard a $400,000 grant to try to replicate his success in 14 other cities later this year.

18   Still, there are questions as to whether what works in Cleveland will work elsewhere. Ballard is a charismatic visionary whose day-to-day presence may be decisive. And other localities may balk at Ballard's insistence that his staffers neither drink nor smoke nor be homosexual.

19   Other experiments around the country show that it is not easy to match scarce jobs to unskilled workers. Parents' Fair Share, a multimillion-dollar federal demonstration program that began in nine cities in 1992, requires noncustodial fathers of children on welfare to attend employment training when they cannot afford to pay child support. Early results showed that, overall, only 22 percent of those referred to the program reported any employment. But peer support training sessions did appear to rekindle the fathers' desire to do right by their kids.

20   Other fathers similarly yearn for more of a role in their kids' lives. Many men, particularly those in fathers' rights groups, push for joint custody. Although these arrangements remain rare, 90 percent of fathers in them pay child support, which is about triple the national average. Men who feel they have a significant role in the lives of their sons and daughters spend more time with them and pay more child support. Still, three quarters of mothers oppose joint custody, which complicates their own parenting by giving ex-husbands decision-making power.

Should Divorce Be Harder?

It is still a mystery why divorce rates doubled in the decade after the early 1960s. But Illinois State Rep. Bernard Pedersen blames the introduction of no-fault divorce laws that let an unhappy spouse end a marriage unchallenged. So Pedersen, wed 45 years himself, proposed a law that would let marrying couples choose to put fault back in divorce. The effort failed. So did attempts in states like Florida and Washington, indicating that although it might cut the number of divorces, Americans have no interest in returning to the days when wives hired private detectives or even a surrogate blond to catch philandering husbands.   21

Instead, most efforts have focused on teaching divorcing parents to get along for the sake of the kids. In a soft voice, 8-year-old Kaitlyn talks of her pain when her parents separated. "I felt really sad because I thought it was something that happened to other people," she says, nervously swinging her legs, which do not reach the hotel ballroom floor under her chair. She is one of several children, ages 8 to 28, who tell their stories to groups of Maryland parents seeking divorce. Often the soft sobbing of a parent is the only other sound in the room.   22

The sessions are a part of the most popular trend in family courts today: parenting courses for divorcing adults. Not intended to stop divorce, the classes simply show parents how to put their children's needs first. Connecticut and Utah require them for all divorcing adults, and more than 100 courts elsewhere do the same. (One Chicago court, however, ruled it unconstitutional to force unwilling parents to attend.) Studies show that parents come away more aware of divorce's impact on their youngsters, but there is no proof yet that fathers increase the frequency of their visits or support payments.   23

And courses that typically last two to six hours can do little to change a lifetime of problems, notes psychologist Sanford Braver. "They do a good job of selling the idea that for the sake of the children, it's important to get along," says the Arizona State University professor, who surveyed such programs. "But getting parents to put aside hurts and jealousies and carry it off is another matter." Divorced dad Ed Cushman, 52, and his daughter Lora, 24, tell parents to "never give up" trying to get along. Ed dropped by the pizza parlor where Lora worked every week for a year until she would open up to a reconciliation. Both agree their relationship is better now than before the divorce. Still, father and daughter, who   24 participate in panels sponsored by the Children of Separation and Divorce Center in Columbia, Md., repaired their relationship only after years of counseling.

25   Edwin Smithers of Connecticut says a similar class improved his parenting, too. However, his wife and three daughters moved across country and now, Smithers says, it is his stepsons who benefit from his new skills. He thinks the same classes, earlier, might have saved his marriage. "Parent training should be required, the way we require driver's training before you get a driver's license," he says.

Can Marriage Be Taught?

26   "God hates divorce," says Michael McManus, citing Scripture (Malachi 2:16). Churches, says the author of *Marriage Savers*, can best take the lead in reversing the divorce rate. McManus has persuaded ministers in 28 cities to require engaged couples to undergo lengthy relationship counseling before marriage—three quarters of Americans marry in churches—and to train older couples to mentor the younger ones about how to resolve conflict. Amy and Jeff Olson took the marriage preparation course McManus runs at the Fourth Presbyterian Church in Bethesda, Md., and credit it with getting their marriage off to a firm start by resolving their differences over money management.

27   The Catholic Church has long practiced such premarital counseling. And it prohibits divorce. So it is not surprising that Massachusetts, the second-most-heavily-Catholic state, has the lowest divorce rate. McManus thinks the fact that some 75 Peoria, Ill., ministers adopted his idea has something to do with the fact that the number of divorces there fell from 1,210 in 1991 to 984 in 1994. But he notes that couples in Peoria often avoid such counseling by going to a minister who does not require it. Churches can also help long-married couples strengthen relationships. Yet the Marriage Encounter weekend retreats, which once attracted 100,000 couples a year, now get only 15,000. McManus attributes that to spouses' reluctance to probe trouble spots in their marriages.

28   Conservatives tend not to trust schools to teach family values. Largely unnoticed, however, is that high schools have become the new academies of parent training. Such classes are already a graduation requirement in at least eight states, including California, Delaware, Michigan, New Jersey, New York, Tennessee, Vermont and Virginia, notes Jan Bowers of

the Home Economics Education Association. And, another surprise, it is being taught in home economics classes. Home ec, now called family and consumer science, is not cooking and sewing anymore. Nor is it just for girls: Boys make up 42 percent of the students.

Two years ago, rural Anna, Ohio (population 1,164), made parenting class a requirement for high school students. Although these boys may be many years from fatherhood, teacher Joanne Ansley notes that lessons in discipline or child development come in handy to the basketball star who coaches a youth team or the 16-year-old whose baby brother asks so many annoying questions.   29

Small-town Anna has its share of big-town problems. Town ministers welcomed the parenting curriculum, in part, to stop early pregnancies. Students get a smack of reality when drawing up family budgets or visiting the nearby Wilson Memorial Hospital, to watch a film on childbirth. "A lot of people in Anna marry and have kids right out of high school, but the course helped me realize just how big of a responsibility fatherhood is," says Tony Albers, 17, who says he now plans to finish college and wait "at least until I'm 25" to start a family.   30

Blankenhorn, however, doubts that fatherhood can be taught. It is a complicated, lifelong endeavor. "Parenting is not like plumbing or carpentering," he says. "It's not a set of techniques. It depends on a human identity." Some boys seem too young to take the lessons seriously and there is a good deal of adolescent horseplay on any given day in class. Moreover, precedents are not encouraging. Sex education was also intended to change behavior. But classroom lessons, no matter how well taught, are often forgotten in real-life situations, as is clear from rising teen pregnancy rates.   31

Can We Support Fatherhood?

Valente Jimenez knows plenty about machines. He is a mechanic who fixes air-conditioning units for the Los Angeles Department of Water and Power. After his wife gave birth, a company nurse instructed Jimenez how to work a device he didn't know much about: a breast pump. The company lent the electric breast pump, one of 90 it bought for its employees—80 percent of whom are men.   32

"Management sees this as an investment, as a good business strategy," notes company work-family specialist Kimberlee Vandenakker. She cites reduced job turnover and absenteeism   33 since LADWP began its fathering program. Among other services to dads: LADWP lends beepers to expectant fathers working on power lines and other remote job sites; it sets up mentoring sessions with other fathers; it started a child-care center and offers unpaid paternity leave.

34   Most companies remain reluctant to offer such programs to mothers, much less to fathers. And men are even more reluctant to ask for father-friendly policies, says James Levine of the Families and Work Institute, who calls LADWP's program "the single best" for dads. Under the new federal family leave law, many working fathers are eligible for 12 weeks of unpaid parental leave, but it is the rare man who takes it. Moms usually prefer to be the one to take off, Levine says, because it is expected, they need to recover physically or breast-feed, or because their husbands bring home bigger paychecks.

35   At LADWP, most who take advantage of the fathers' policies come from white-collar jobs. Supervisors have more flexible schedules, and there is still the "macho" factor for some blue-collar workers. Jimenez's family was surprised when he agreed to care for his baby while his wife, Jeanne, took a four-day trip to visit family in Texas. Jimenez said the example of other fathers at work convinced him. "I come from a Hispanic family, and we didn't do that kind of stuff," he says. "But this program has opened my eyes."

36   Virtually all sides in the debate now agree that such changes in attitudes are the first and best hope for repairing fatherhood. The campaign to fight fatherlessness will be waged over a long period, much the same way campaigns worked to convince drivers that they should not drink or smokers that cigarettes ruin health. Government programs won't have nearly the impact as numberless one-on-one encounters over a lifetime between men and kids. Both the White House and House Republicans, for example, want to give parents a $500-per-child tax credit. While money helps, most family experts say there is no evidence that such policies directly influence decisions as personal as marriage and childbearing. Of course, there are partisan stakes in this fight. The *U.S. News* poll found that Americans trust Republicans more than Democrats—37 to 32 percent—to help make families stronger.

37   But most see the issue in transcendent terms. As Hillary Rodham Clinton told *U.S. News* last week: "It's difficult for fathers to put aside their own aspirations about their own lives," but one who can "put his child first...is giving a great

gift to a child." Real progress will come only when there is renewed conviction, as Blankenhorn argues, that "being a loving father and a good husband is the best part of being a man."

Don Browning and Ian Evison
The Family Debate: A Middle Way

Don Browning is a professor of religion and psychological studies at the prestigious University of Chicago Divinity School, where Ian Evison coordinates research for the Religion, Culture, and Family Project. They contributed the following analysis to Christian Century *in mid-July 1993.* Christian Century, *which calls itself "an ecumenical weekly," has been publishing news and commentary of particular interest to well-educated Christians for the past one hundred years.*

A great debate is taking place over the condition and prospects of the American family. This debate reflects the fact that Americans are worried about the family. Republicans had hard evidence during the 1992 presidential campaign on the extent of this concern. The Wirthlin Group, which does most of the national polling for the Republicans, published an article in the *Reader's Digest* (May 1992) which in effect outlined the Republican campaign strategy. It demonstrated that one of the largest and most cohesive voting blocs is married couples with children. According to this article, they are "a political powerhouse, a voting block of about 92 million people, 57 percent of all Americans over 25." They are surprisingly conservative on cultural values and family issues, more conservative than either singles or older couples whose children have left the nest—a point which the church should note.

The Republicans tried to win the election by appealing to this group, but they overplayed their hand. They used the family issue to single out scapegoats (single mothers and inner-city residents), and they avoided talking about the economy and failed to develop meaningful and practical family programs.

3   Although the Republicans were wrong in how they used
the family issue, they were right in recognizing that it is
vitally important. The family debate is far from over. Note the
countless articles and op-ed pieces on single parenthood, the
pros and cons of professional day care, the state of children's
health, family-friendly industry, parental leaves, and the sins
of absent fathers. Consider the tremendous response to the
Atlantic article (April 1993) in which Barbara Dafoe Whitehead argued that the two-parent family is better on the whole
for child-rearing than are single parents and stepfamilies.
This was followed by sociologist James Q. Wilson's almost
identical argument in his *Commentary* (April 1993) article,
"The Family-Values Debate."

4   Voices from the mainline Protestant churches have been
strangely absent from this debate. As James Davison Hunter
suggests in *Culture Wars,* churches have been paralyzed by a
division between orthodox and progressive parties that see
the family issue—as they see abortion, homosexuality, education and popular culture—in vastly different ways. Mainline
churches need to say something relevant to the family debate.
Before speaking up, however, they need to face squarely the
disturbing trends in family life that are fueling the debate.

5   1. *Families are in crisis.* The central evidence is the deterioration of the physical and emotional well-being of children.
Economists Victor Fuchs and Diane Reklis say bluntly,
"American children are in trouble. Not all children, to be
sure, but many observers consider today's children to be
worse off than their parents' generation in several important
dimensions of physical, mental, and emotional well-being."
From 1960 to 1988 standardized test scores fell significantly,
teenage suicide and homicide rates more than doubled and
obesity increased by 50 percent. In 1970, 15 percent of children were in poverty, but by the late 1980s nearly 20 percent
were on or below the poverty line. An authoritative report
prepared for the U.S. Department of Health and Human Services by Nicholas Zill and Charlotte Schoenborn provides
more discouraging statistics. Twenty percent of children ages
3 to 17 have a developmental, learning or behavioral disorder.
By ages 12 to 17, one in four adolescents suffers from at least
one of these disorders. One in three teenage boys has one of
these problems.

6   2. *Changes in cultural values as well as changes in the economy have contributed to the crisis in families.* Changes in values may even be the key factor. Fuchs and Reklis demonstrate

that children's well-being began to worsen before the economy turned sour.

> Between 1960 and 1970 the fall in test scores, the doubling of teenage suicide and homicide rates, and the doubling share of births to unwed mothers cannot be attributed to economic adversity. During that decade purchases of goods and services for children by government rose very rapidly, as did real household income per child, and the poverty rate of children plummeted. Thus, we must seek explanations for the rising problems of that period in the cultural realm.

The cultural changes that Fuchs and Reklis have in mind   7
are increasing individualism, growing preoccupation with individual fulfillment, wider tolerance for divorce as a solution to marital problems, and more general acceptance at all social levels of the high rates of out-of-wedlock births and single parenthood. These shifts in values preceded and now interact with worsening economic conditions.

3. *Changing values have interacted with worsening eco-*   8
nomic conditions to create increasing numbers of poor women and children. Much of this poverty is associated with single parents, most of whom are women, and is produced by divorce and out-of-wedlock births. The divorce rate has been increasing for a century. It rose from 7 percent in 1860 to over 50 percent today. Furthermore, demographer Larry Bumpass says that "life table estimates suggest that 17 percent of white women and 70 percent of black women will have a child while unmarried if recent levels persist." According to the Census Bureau, the proportion of children born to unmarried women has doubled since 1970 to 28 percent in 1990. Bumpass estimates that 44 percent of all children born between 1970 and 1984 will spend some of their youth in a single-parent home. Frank Furstenberg and Andrew Cherlin say in *Divided Families* (1991) that if present trends continue, that "figure could reach 60 percent."

It is now more frequently admitted that single parent-   9
hood, on the whole, is a disadvantage for raising children. This is true even when single-parent families are not poor, although they frequently are. We have been slow to acknowledge this because we do not want to stigmatize single mothers who are often heroic, frequently quite successful as parents, and may be single for a wide variety of reasons. But in avoiding moralism we should not neglect the truth of the situation. Whitehead and Wilson, in the articles mentioned,

summarize well the social science data on this point. Children of single-parent families are far more likely even when they are not poor to do badly in school, get in trouble with the law, have poor mental and physical health, and have marital difficulties later in life.

10   4. *The single most important trend in American families today is the increasing absence of fathers and the feminization of kinship.* By feminization of kinship we mean that the families of children are increasingly composed of women—the mothers, grandmothers and aunts who do the child care. Men are increasingly absent from families and their children. Social scientists report that fathers of out-of-wedlock children and divorced fathers give surprisingly little economic or emotional support to their biological children. There are exceptions. There are the good fathers who do everything they can to give financial and relational support to their children born from former unions. But a large number of these fathers gradually give less and less of either. Furstenberg and Cherlin report that a recent national survey found that after divorce "only one child in six saw his or her father as often as once a week on average. Close to half had not visited with their fathers in the 12 months preceding the survey. Another sixth had seen them less often than once a month." Monetary payments by divorced fathers to their children are low. Fathers of children born out of wedlock visit and pay even less.

11   5. *Families in our society are simultaneously undergoing both deinstitutionalization and coercive reinstitutionalization.* Marriage is losing its normative status. By deinstitutionalization we mean not only that fewer couples ask the church to bless their unions, but that many are not even asking the state to make their families official. The proportion of first marriages that were preceded by cohabitation increased from 8 percent in the late 1960s to 49 percent by the mid-'80s. The average duration of cohabitation is short—a median of 1.5 years. Forty percent of these unions split before marriage.

12   Our point is not to moralize about cohabitation but to raise a more complex issue. The deinstitutionalization of marriage and family has led to a new brand of coercive, state-enforced regulation of the family. For example, the state of California requires fathers of out-of-wedlock births to pay the same rate of support as divorced fathers. But such a requirement tremendously expands government control over private lives. Most young men have not awakened to this. One thoughtless sexual adventure can lead to a lifetime responsi-

bility—enforced by the strong arm of the state. A man can avoid marriage, but he is less likely to avoid the courts and their collection agencies. Even the newly developing category of "domestic partnerships" invites coercive state intrusion. Determining the validity of domestic partnerships will entail some investigation by employers and the state into the private lives of couples. Nothing comes free; red tape and public declarations of one kind or another may be required for all those who want government protections and benefits.

6. *Family law is diverging sharply from the inherited traditions of the church.* For centuries family law in Western industrial societies either reflected or was highly consistent with church teachings. Historian James Brundage and legal historian John Witte have described how Catholic canon law of the Middle Ages was used to a significant extent by both the Protestant Reformation and much of secular family law in Western society. This is why the law until the 1960s resisted or delayed divorce, gave a privileged status to monogamous marriage and upheld the need for public commitments of a mutually consenting man and woman as the ground for the formation of legal families. Now most if not all of these traditional commitments of secular family law are up for grabs. We are likely to hear talk soon of legalizing polygamy, extending marriage privileges to the unmarried, and possibly even abolishing marriage, as the moderator of a conference on "Law and Nature" at Brown University recently proposed.

Family issues will be the dominant ones facing the churches in the 1990s and possibly into the next century. They will be hotter than issues of race, or of investment in South Africa, or of involvement in Central America. Family issues hit people in their innermost beings.

After several decades of ignoring or neglecting families, mainline churches will have to decide which of three pro-family strategies to adopt. The first strategy, the most popular in many liberal churches and denominations, will be simply to accept the new pluralism of the family. According to this view, churches must accept openly and without prejudice the full range of single families, stepfamilies, co-habiting families and same-sex families that modern societies are evolving. This position believes that churches also should pressure the government to extend the range of economic and social supports so that these changing families and their children will not become poor. The church in this view should aim in its

474

ministry to provide the psychological and communal supports that help families maintain their dignity and self-esteem.

16   The second pro-family strategy is that of the Christian Right. Some of the mainline churches will move in this direction for want of a better strategy. They will resist family pluralism. In emphasizing the centrality of the intact two-parent family, the conservative reaction probably will continue to emphasize traditional gender roles (even if gently) and to advocate aggressive antihomosexual policies. This approach regards the problems of families as primarily cultural, the result of a decline of values. This strategy distrusts most governmental and legal intrusions. It would cure the problems of families with a triumphalist spread of Christian values into the lives of Christians and non-Christians alike and into all corners of public policy.

17   The third pro-family strategy, the one we advocate, is to try to reconstruct the church's ethics of families while advocating selected governmental and market supports for families. This approach recognizes that the family crisis is caused both by cultural changes and by social-systemic developments in areas of work, economics, child care and gender inequality. This view recognizes, along with the conservative voices, that unfettered individualism and its drive for adult fulfillment at the expense of children presents a real threat to the family. But this third strategy sees the drive toward individualism as partially good. It supports, for example, the push toward more equality for women. Aspects of individualism can be included with integrity in those interpretations of Christian love which see it as commanding a strenuous equal regard for both self and other. This view tries to hold individual fulfillment and regard for the other, be it spouse or children or both, in rigorous balance. Although the Jesus movement and Pauline Christianity never completely freed themselves from the patriarchy of the ancient world, they went far in replacing Greco-Roman male honor-shame patterns and related aristocratic forms of masculine dominance with servanthood models of male responsibility. Furthermore, they pushed the rule of neighbor love and the egalitarianism of the Galatian 3:28 baptismal formula ("there is neither male nor female; for you are all one in Christ Jesus") to the point of threatening patriarchal patterns both within and outside the early Christian ecclesia. This third pro-family approach affirms gender equality even as it both affirms and criticizes aspects of modern individualism.

Mainline churches must recapture their interest in chil-   18
dren. For 30 years mainline denominations have tended to
see the problems of children and families as privatistic issues.
They have held that if the church could help society establish
economic and racial justice, the welfare of families and children would automatically follow. The above analysis shows
how inadequate this view has proved to be. It failed to anticipate the tremendous shifts in cultural values that have preoccupied adults and undermined the well-being of children and
youth. Today, support for family programs, for developing
family theory and family theology, and for local initiatives on
behalf of families should be top denominational priorities.

Churches should be skeptical, however, of programs that   19
treat children as if they were not a part of families, thereby
undermining family solidarity and parental responsibility. Furthermore, they should resist becoming a tool or agent of government programs that have no interest in the unique values
and mission of the church. Churches should attempt to find
their own voice, their own style, their own message and their
own programs, making all other necessary collaborations, even
with the state, fit with integrity into their unique identities.

To put children first, mainline churches need to resist easy   20
talk about the new family pluralism. Without becoming moralistic or harsh, they need to recognize that not all family
forms are equal for the task of raising children. Intact families have, on the whole, more emotional and material
resources for this task. We need to recognize that family pluralism has too often meant exempting men from their responsibilities in raising children, leaving women to do the job.
Some people do not believe that fathers are very important
for families. For instance, Judge Richard Posner in *Sex and
Reason* (1991) argues that there is no convincing evidence,
other things being equal, that outside of their procreative
functions fathers are necessary for the well-being of their
children. In contrast to this view, we believe that the Christian
tradition, common sense and the recent social-science evidence summarized by Whitehead, Wilson and others make a
strong case for the importance of the educative and moral
role of fathers with children, in addition to their procreative
and financial contributions. Even if it were possible to
replace fathers with government supports, better-paying jobs
for single mothers, day care and elaborate social and
extended-family networks, it would be unhealthy for both
men and society to have increasing numbers of single men
adrift without connections to families.

21   While the churches should promote the egalitarian, intact
mother-father partnership as the center of its family ethic, it
also must recognize that a pluralism of family forms is a part
of modern life, including church life. There is much that
churches can do to ease the burden of single parents and
stepfamilies and help them do better jobs of raising children.
Some churches—mainly large evangelical and some black
churches—have outstanding programs for a wide range of
family types. They give special emphasis to the two-parent
family and at the same time deal realistically, nonjudgmen-
tally and helpfully with all families. Some of these churches
have strong programs in marriage preparation and marriage
and family enrichment, as well as strong support groups for
single parents, divorced people and stepfamilies. They preach
and teach regularly about family issues. Some run day-care
programs, after-school programs, parental training groups,
and sometimes even home visitation programs which assist
families with their daily interactions. Some have special programs for men and young boys. Many black churches have
programs designed to prepare young men for responsible
marriage and parenting. Many conservative churches are able
to maintain the tension between their ideals about families
and realistic support for where families actually are. But
many otherwise excellent programs in conservative and fundamentalist churches are marred by rigid gender distinctions
and oppressive male authority. The liberal, mainline churches
would do well to imitate the energy of some of the conservative churches on family matters, while finding a new language and new ethic to guide their programs.

22   If liberal churches are to help reverse the trends toward
family decline, their youth programs should emphasize preparation for life in the egalitarian, postmodern family. This
family will be "postmodern" because it will not idealize the
rigid distinctions between public and private, work and
home, breadwinner father and domestic mother that characterized the family that adapted to early industrial society.
Since one of the major trends of family life in America is the
absence of fathers and the feminization of kinship, boys and
young men should be a major target for the church's family
programs. If all family forms were equal for raising children,
then young men could be ignored. They would not be needed.
But if intact mother-father teams are generally better for children, then serious work with young men about parenting ideals and skills should be part of the church's mission.

With regard to trends in family law, mainline churches   23
must live with ambivalence. They must realize that family law
may continue to diverge from inherited Christian morality on
family matters. The law may grant legal status to more forms
of domestic partnership. It may continue to ease divorce proceedings through no-fault settlements. It may protect the
rights of youth to make moral decisions about abortion and
contraception without the knowledge, and against the moral
guidance, of their parents.

But mainline churches would be wise not to adopt these   24
legal developments as their basic morality. Churches should
forge their own unique position on family and sexual ethics
and help their members live by it. At the same time, churches
must realize that some of the new trends in family law may
make some sense; it is the primary function of law to regulate
behavior, not necessarily to project the moral ideal. Project-
ing the ideal is the task of culture-making institutions such as
the church. This does not mean that churches should be
entirely passive before the law. They have the right to influence the law, just like any other group in our society. One part
of the law worth influencing, for instance, is divorce laws.
Here the task may not be to make divorce more difficult to
obtain; rather, the task may be to require divorcing parents to
make better long-term financial plans for their children,
plans which the courts could enforce.

Finally, the church must understand that there is a place   25
for government family supports in complex postindustrial
societies. But they should not petition government to solve
those problems that only churches and other voluntary organizations can successfully address. Since the days of their
successes in the civil rights movement, mainline churches
have tended to think they are fulfilling their mission when
they lobby government for worthwhile programs. The first
obligation of the churches is to discern their own message,
their own values, their own programs; only after these are
established should they work to influence government policy.

Nevertheless, government policies are important. Some   26
government programs build families; others tear them down.
Some undermine family authority and put control in the
hands of experts outside the family. Others build family
coherence and deliver real assistance. One such proposal,
which has gained support from political right and left, is to
increase personal federal income tax exemptions for dependent children. It was first proposed by the Progressive Policy

Institute. It recommends increasing the exemption that parents can claim for dependent children from $2,300 to $6,000 or $7,000 for each child. This would make exemptions for dependents equal in value to the original $600 per child that families received in 1948, the year the IRS first allowed the exemptions. The Rockefeller Report titled *Beyond Rhetoric* (1991) went in a slightly different direction; it recommended a $1,000 tax credit for each child. These kinds of legislation help families without causing dependency and without putting family functions into the hands of government. They expand the income of parents and make it possible, for instance, to purchase day care or provide the child care themselves.

27   Our aim has not been to offer a comprehensive profamily strategy, but to suggest what a coherent strategy might look like. If nothing more, we have tried to show that a middle road exists and that in the long run it may offer the best course to follow both for the church and for society.

Shere Hite
Bringing Democracy Home

In the spring of 1995, Ms. *magazine carried the following excerpt from Shere Hite's book* The Hite Report on the Family: Growing Up under Patriarchy *(1995), the product of her study of several thousand families. Hite has made a reputation not only on this report but also on her books* The Hite Report: A Nationwide Study of Female Sexuality *(1976) and* The Hite Report: A Study of Male Sexuality *(1981)—both controversial, widely discussed titles.*

1   Love and anger, love and obedience, love and power, love and hate. These are all present in family relationships. It's easy to say that they are inevitable, that stresses and strains are unavoidable, given "human nature." To some extent this is true, but these stresses and strains are exaggerated by a tense and difficult family system that is imposed upon our emotions and our lives, structuring them to fit its own specified goals.

Is the family as we have known it for so long the only way   2
to create safe, loving, and caring environments for people?
The best way? To understand the family in Western tradition,
we must remember that much of what we see, say, and think
about it is based on the archetypal family that is so pervasive
in our society—Jesus, Mary, and Joseph. There is no daughter
icon. This is the "holy family" model that we are expected, in
one way or another, to live up to. But is this model really the
right one for people who believe in equality and justice? Does
it teach a good understanding of love and the way to make
relationships work when we become adults?

One constantly hears that the family is in trouble, that it   3
doesn't work anymore, that we must find ways to help it. If
the family doesn't work, maybe there is something wrong
with its structure. People must have reasons for fleeing
the nuclear family: human rights abuses and the battering of
women are well documented in many governments' statistics.

The family is changing because only in recent decades has   4
the process of democratization, which began in Western
political life more than two centuries ago, reached private
life. Although John Stuart Mill wrote in favor of women's
rights in the egalitarian democratic theory he helped develop,
the family and women's role in the world were left out of most
discussions of democracy, left in the "sacred" religious
domain. Women and nonproperty owners, as well as "minorities," did not have the vote when democracy first began. Men
made a fatal mistake. The democracy they thought they could
make work in the public sphere would not really work without democracy in private life.

Some people, of course, are alarmed by changes in the   5
family. Reactionary fundamentalist groups have gone on the
offensive to try to stop this process. Yet most people are happier with their personal lives today than people were 50 years
ago. Women especially have more choices and freedom than
they did in the past. There is a positive new diversity springing up in families and relationships today in Western society.
This pluralism should be valued and encouraged: far from
signaling a breakdown of society, it is a sign of a new, more
open and tolerant society springing up, a new world being
born out of the clutter of the old.

Democracy could work even better if we changed the   6
aggressive personality that is being created by the patriarchal
family system. Children brought up with choice about whether
to accept their parents' power are more likely to be confident
about believing in themselves and their own ideas, less docile

or habituated to bending to power. Such a population would create and participate in public debate very differently. And there are many more advances we are on the threshold of achieving: naming and eliminating emotional violence, redefining love and friendship, progressing in the areas of children's rights and in men's questioning of their own lives.

7   My work salutes the gentler and more diverse families that seem to be arising. They are part of a system that does not keep its members in terror: fathers in terror lest they not be "manly" and able to support it all; mothers in terror lest they be beaten in their own bedrooms and ridiculed by their children; children in terror of being forced to do things against their will and having absolutely no recourse, no door open to them for exit.

8   What I am offering is a new interpretation of relationships between parents and children, a new theory of the family. My interpretation of the data from my questionnaires takes into account not only the individual's unique experiences, as is done in psychology, but also the cultural backdrop—the canvas of social "approval" or "disapproval" against which children's lives are lived. This interdisciplinary theory also takes into account the historical ideology of the family; those who took part in my research are living in a world where perception of "family" is filtered through the Christian model of the "holy family" with its reproductive icons of Jesus, Mary, and Joseph. But no matter how beautiful it appears (especially in its promise of "true love"), this family model is an essentially repressive one, teaching authoritarian psychological patterns, meekness in women, and a belief in the unchanging rightness of male power. In this hierarchical family, love and power are inextricably linked, a pattern that has damaging effects not only on all family members but on the politics of the wider society. How can there be successful democracy in public life if there is an authoritarian model in private life?

9   So used have we become to these symbols that we continue to believe—no matter what statistics we see in the newspapers about divorce, violence in the home, mental breakdown—that the icons and the system they represent are right, fair, and just. We assume without thinking that this model is the only "natural" form of family, and that if there are problems it must be the individual who is at fault, not the institution.

10   We need a new interpretation of what is going on. We may be at one of the most important turning points of the Western world, the creation of a new social base that will engender an advanced and improved democratic political structure.

What Is the Family All About?

Creating new, more democratic families means taking a   11
clear and rational look at our institutions. We tend to forget
that the family was created in its current form in early patriarchy for political, not religious, reasons. The new political
order had to solve a a specific problem: How could lineage or
inheritance flow through men (and not women as it had previously) if men do not bear children?

The modern patriarchal family was created so that each   12
man would "own" a woman who would reproduce for him.
He then had to control the sexuality of "his" woman, for how
else could he be sure that "his" child was really his? Restrictions were placed on women's lives and bodies by men;
women's imprisonment in marriage was made a virtue, for
example, through the later archetype of the self-sacrificing
Mary, who was happy to be of service, never standing up for
herself or her own rights. Mary, it is important to note, is a
later version of a much earlier Creation Mother goddess. In
her earlier form, she had many more aspects, more like the
Indian goddess Kali than the "mother" whom the Christian
patriarchal system devised.

Fortunately, the family is a human institution: humans   13
made it and humans can change it. My research indicates
that the extreme aggression we see in society is not a characteristic of biological "human nature" (as Freud concluded),
nor a result of hormones. "Human nature" is a psychological
structure that is carefully implanted in our minds—for life—
as we learn the love and power equations of the family. Power
and love are combined in the family structure: in order to
receive love, most children have to humiliate themselves, over
and over again, before power.

In our society, parents have the complete legal, economic,   14
and social "right" to control children's lives. Parents' exclusive
power over children creates obedience. Children are likely to
take on authoritarian emotional, psychological, and sexual
patterns, and to see power as one of the central categories of
existence.

Love is at the heart—so to speak—of our belief in the   15
importance of the family. The desire for love is what keeps us
returning to the icons. Even when they don't seem to work in
our lives, we try and try again. We are told that we will never
find love if we don't participate in the family. We hear repeatedly that the only place we will ever be able to get security,
true acceptance, and understanding is in the family; that we

are only "half a family" or a "pretend family" if we create any
other human group; that without being a member of the family we will be forever "left out," lonely, or useless. No one
would want to deny the importance of love, or of lasting relationships with other people. But the violent, distorted definitions of love created by the patriarchal family make it
difficult for love to last, and to be as profound as it could be.

16   How confusing it is for children, the idea of being loved!
They are so often told by their parents, "Of course we love
you, why do you even ask?" It is easy for children to believe
that the emotion they feel when faced with a powerful person
is "love"—or that the inscrutable ways of a person who is
sometimes caring and friendly, and other times punitive and
angry, are loving. The problem then is that, since the parents
are still the providers and "trainers" of the children, legally
and economically the "owners" of the children, they exercise
incredible power over the children—the very power of survival itself.

17   Children must feel gratitude, and so, in their minds, this
gratitude is mixed with love. How much of the love they feel
is really supplication before the power of the parents? How
will they define love later in life? Won't they be highly confused by passion (either emotional or physical) and what it
means, unable to connect it with other feelings of liking and
concern? Of course, long-term caring for others is something
positive that can also be learned in families, but it can be
learned in other kinds of families, not just the nuclear model.

Does "Love" Include Sex? The Body?

18   And what definition of love do children learn from the way
their parents relate physically? Isn't it strange to think of your
parents having sex? Finding parents in any kind of physical
embrace comes as a fascinating shock to most children: 83
percent of children in my research say their parents seem
completely asexual.

19   It would be logical if children drew the conclusion that
"real love" is never sexual, or even physically affectionate. But
isn't affection a great part of what love is? If parents don't hug
and kiss each other, is the definition of adult "love" different?
And if so, what is it? Why do parents feel that they shouldn't
touch each other in front of the children? Because the children would be jealous? Because it would give the children
sexual feelings and ideas? Or, do many parents really not

want to touch each other? Children wonder, if the parents don't want to be affectionate, why exactly are they together? If they are only together "for the sake of the children," this puts an awfully big burden on the children to be "worth it" or to "make their parents happy," thus confusing the definitions of love even further.

Another way children learn that power and domination are 20 part of love is through observing the relationship of their parents. Gender tension and especially second-class treatment of the mother by the father is reported by the majority of people from two-parent families in this study. Girls in particular find this gender inequality mixed with "love" confusing, even psychologically violent and terrifying. Why? Because for girls it means coming to terms with what this power relationship will mean for them: Will they inherit this gender inequality? Can they avoid being considered lesser beings when they become women? How can they love a father who represents this system? Or a mother who lets herself participate in it?

Are Single-Parent Families Bad for Children?

There are very few carefully controlled studies of the 21 effects of single-parent families on children. Today, much popular journalism assumes that the two-parent family is better for children. My data show that there are beneficial effects for the majority of children living in single-parent families. It is more positive for children not to grow up in an atmosphere poisoned by gender inequality.

Do girls who grow up with "only" their mother have a better 22 relationship with her? According to my study, 49 percent of such girls felt that it was a positive experience; 20 percent did not like it; and the rest had mixed feelings. Mothers in one-parent families are more likely to feel freer to confide in daughters because no "disloyalty to the spouse" is implied. Daughters in such families are less likely to see the mother as a "wimp"—she is an independent person.

Boys who grow up with "only" their mother experience less 23 pressure to demonstrate contempt for things "feminine" and for nonaggressive parts of themselves. In *The Hite Report on Men and Male Sexuality,* I was surprised to find that boys who grew up with their mother alone were much more likely to have good relationships with women in their adult lives: 80 percent of men from such families had formed strong, lasting ties with women (in marriage or long-term relationships), as opposed to only 40 percent from two-parent families. This does not mean that the two-parent family cannot be reformed so that it provides a peaceful environment for children— indeed this is part of the ongoing revolution in the family in which so many people today are engaged.

24   Single-parent families are mostly headed by mothers, yet there is an increasing number of single-father families. Many single fathers don't take much part in child care but instead hire female nannies or ask their mothers, sisters, or girl-friends to take care of the children. Men could change the style of families by taking more part domestically, and by opening up emotionally and having closer contact with chil-dren. My research highlights men's traumatizing and enforced split from women at puberty. . . .

25   Healing this is the single most important thing we as a society could do to bridge the distance men feel from "family."

Democracy of the Heart: A New Politics

26   If you listen to people talk about their families, it becomes clear that we must give up on the outdated notion that the only acceptable families are nuclear families. We should not see the new society that has evolved over the last 40 years as a disaster simply because it is not like the past.

27   The new diversity of families is part of a positive pluralism, part of a fundamental transition in the organization of soci-ety that calls for open-minded brainstorming by all of us: What do we believe "love" and "family" are? Can we accept that the many people fleeing the nuclear family are doing so for valid reasons? If reproduction is no longer the urgent pri-ority that it was when societies were smaller, before industri-alization took hold, then the revolt against the family is not surprising. Perhaps it was even historically inevitable. It is not that people don't want to build loving, family-style rela-tionships, it is that they do not want to be forced to build them within one rigid, hierarchical, heterosexist, reproduc-tive framework. Diversity in family forms can bring joy and enrichment to a society: new kinds of families can be the basis for a renaissance of spiritual dignity and creativity in political as well as personal life.

28   Continuing this process of bringing private life into an eth-ical and egalitarian frame of reference will give us the energy and moral will to maintain democracy in the larger political

sphere. We can create a society with a new spirit and will—but politics will have to be transformed. We can use the interactive frame of reference most often found today in friendships between women. Diversity in families can form the basic infrastructure for a new and advanced type of political democracy to be created, imagined, developed—a system that suits the massive societies that communications technology today has made into one "global village."

One cannot exaggerate the importance of the current 29 debate: there has been fascism in societies before; it could certainly emerge again, alongside fascism in the family. If we believe in the democratic, humanist ideals of the last 200 years, we have the right, almost the duty, to make our family system a more just one; to follow our democratic ideals and make a new, more inclusive network of private life that will reflect not a preordained patriarchal structure, but our belief in justice and equality for all—women, men, and children. Let's continue the transformation, believe in ourselves, and go forward with love instead of fear. In our private lives and in our public world, let's hail the future and make history.

IS SINGLE PARENTHOOD A PROBLEM?

Barbara Dafoe Whitehead
Dan Quayle Was Right

The Atlantic Monthly, *a respected left-of-center magazine of current affairs and opinion, received more letters in response to the following excerpted essay by Barbara Dafoe Whitehead than it has ever received in response to an article. When it was published in April 1993, its title was alluding to former Vice President Dan Quayle's controversial opposition to the family arrangements of TV character Murphy Brown. Whitehead, a native of Wisconsin (born 1944) and a research associate at the Institute for American Values, a nonpartisan, New York City organization devoted to issues of the family, in part defends a position that she expressed in an earlier article in the* Washington Post, *which helped motivate the vice president to make family issues central to the 1992 presidential campaign.*

1   Divorce and out-of-wedlock childbirth are transforming the lives of American children. In the postwar generation more than 80 percent of children grew up in a family with two biological parents who were married to each other. By 1980 only 50 percent could expect to spend their entire childhood in an intact family. If current trends continue, less than half of all children born today will live continuously with their own mother and father throughout childhood. Most American children will spend several years in a single-mother family. Some will eventually live in stepparent families, but because stepfamilies are more likely to break up than intact (by which I mean two-biological-parent) families, an increasing number of children will experience family breakup two or even three times during childhood.

2   According to a growing body of social-scientific evidence, children in families disrupted by divorce and out-of-wedlock birth do worse than children in intact families on several measures of well-being. Children in single-parent families are six times as likely to be poor. They are also likely to stay poor

longer. Twenty-two percent of children in one-parent families will experience poverty during childhood for seven years or more, as compared with only two percent of children in two-parent families. A 1988 survey by the National Center for Health Statistics found that children in single-parent families are two to three times as likely as children in two-parent families to have emotional and behavioral problems. They are also more likely to drop out of high school, to get pregnant as teenagers, to abuse drugs, and to be in trouble with the law. Compared with children in intact families, children from disrupted families are at a much higher risk for physical or sexual abuse.

Contrary to popular belief, many children do not "bounce back" after divorce or remarriage. Difficulties that are associated with family breakup often persist into adulthood. Children who grow up in single-parent or stepparent families are less successful as adults, particularly in the two domains of life—love and work—that are most essential to happiness. Needless to say, not all children experience such negative effects. However, research shows that many children from disrupted families have a harder time achieving intimacy in a relationship, forming a stable marriage, or even holding a steady job.   3

Despite this growing body of evidence, it is nearly impossible to discuss changes in family structure without provoking angry protest. Many people see the discussion as no more than an attack on struggling single mothers and their children: Why blame single mothers when they are doing the very best they can? After all, the decision to end a marriage or a relationship is wrenching, and few parents are indifferent to the painful burden this decision imposes on their children. Many take the perilous step toward single parenthood as a last resort, after their best efforts to hold a marriage together have failed. Consequently, it can seem particularly cruel and unfeeling to remind parents of the hardships their children might suffer as a result of family breakup. Other people believe that the dramatic changes in family structure, though regrettable, are impossible to reverse. Family breakup is an inevitable feature of American life, and anyone who thinks otherwise is indulging in nostalgia or trying to turn back the clock. Since these new family forms are here to stay, the reasoning goes, we must accord respect to single parents, not criticize them. Typical is the view expressed by a Brooklyn woman in a recent letter to *The New York Times:* "Let's stop moralizing or blaming single parents   4

and unwed mothers, and give them the respect they have
earned and the support they deserve."

5   Such views are not to be dismissed. Indeed, they help to
explain why family structure is such an explosive issue for
Americans. The debate about it is not simply about the social-
scientific evidence, although that is surely an important part
of the discussion. It is also a debate over deeply held and often
conflicting values. How do we begin to reconcile our long-
standing belief in equality and diversity with an impressive
body of evidence that suggests that not all family structures
produce equal outcomes for children? How can we square traditional notions of public support for dependent women and
children with a belief in women's right to pursue autonomy
and independence in childbearing and child-rearing? How do
we uphold the freedom of adults to pursue individual happiness in their private relationships and at the same time
respond to the needs of children for stability, security, and permanence in their family lives? What do we do when the interests of adults and children conflict? These are the difficult
issues at stake in the debate over family structure.

6   In the past these issues have turned out to be too difficult
and too politically risky for debate. In the mid-1960s Daniel
Patrick Moynihan, then an assistant secretary of labor, was
denounced as a racist for calling attention to the relationship
between the prevalence of black single-mother families and
the lower socioeconomic standing of black children. For
nearly twenty years the policy and research communities
backed away from the entire issue. In 1980 the Carter Administration convened a historic White House Conference on
Families, designed to address the growing problems of children and families in America. The result was a prolonged,
publicly subsidized quarrel over the definition of "family." No
President since has tried to hold a national family conference.
Last year, at a time when the rate of out-of-wedlock births
had reached a historic high, Vice President Dan Quayle was
ridiculed for criticizing Murphy Brown. In short, every time
the issue of family structure has been raised, the response has
been first controversy, then retreat, and finally silence.

7   Yet it is also risky to ignore the issue of changing family
structure. In recent years the problems associated with family
disruption have grown. Overall child well-being has declined,
despite a decrease in the number of children per family, an
increase in the educational level of parents, and historically
high levels of public spending. After dropping in the 1960s
and 1970s, the proportion of children in poverty has

increased dramatically, from 15 percent in 1970 to 20 percent in 1990, while the percentage of adult Americans in poverty has remained roughly constant. The teen suicide rate has more than tripled. Juvenile crime has increased and become more violent. School performance has continued to decline. There are no signs that these trends are about to reverse themselves.

If we fail to come to terms with the relationship between   8
family structure and declining child well-being, then it will be increasingly difficult to improve children's life prospects, no matter how many new programs the federal government funds. Nor will we be able to make progress in bettering school performance or reducing crime or improving the quality of the nation's future work force—all domestic problems closely connected to family breakup. Worse, we may contribute to the problem by pursuing policies that actually increase family instability and breakup.

From Death to Divorce

Across time and across cultures, family disruption has   9
been regarded as an event that threatens a child's well-being and even survival. This view is rooted in a fundamental biological fact: unlike the young of almost any other species, the human child is born in an abjectly helpless and immature state. Years of nurture and protection are needed before the child can achieve physical independence. Similarly, it takes years of interaction with at least one but ideally two or more adults for a child to develop into a socially competent adult. Children raised in virtual isolation from human beings, though physically intact, display few recognizably human behaviors. The social arrangement that has proved most successful in ensuring the physical survival and promoting the social development of the child is the family unit of the biological mother and father. Consequently, any event that permanently denies a child the presence and protection of a parent jeopardizes the life of the child.

The classic form of family disruption is the death of a par-   10
ent. Throughout history this has been one of the risks of childhood. Mothers frequently died in childbirth, and it was not unusual for both parents to die before the child was grown. As recently as the early decades of this century children commonly suffered the death of at least one parent. Almost a quarter of the children born in this country in 1900

lost one parent by the time they were fifteen years old. Many of these children lived with their widowed parent, often in a household with other close relatives. Others grew up in orphanages and foster homes.

11   The meaning of parental death, as it has been transmitted over time and faithfully recorded in world literature and lore, is unambiguous and essentially unchanging. It is universally regarded as an untimely and tragic event. Death permanently severs the parent-child bond, disrupting forever one of the child's earliest and deepest human attachments. It also deprives a child of the presence and protection of an adult who has a biological stake in, as well as an emotional commitment to, the child's survival and well-being. In short, the death of a parent is the most extreme and severe loss a child can suffer.

12   Because a child is so vulnerable in a parent's absence, there has been a common cultural response to the death of a parent: an outpouring of support from family, friends, and strangers alike. The surviving parent and child are united in their grief as well as their loss. Relatives and friends share in the loss and provide valuable emotional and financial assistance to the bereaved family. Other members of the community show sympathy for the child, and public assistance is available for those who need it. This cultural understanding of parental death has formed the basis for a tradition of public support to widows and their children. Indeed, as recently as the beginning of this century widows were the only mothers eligible for pensions in many states, and today widows with children receive more generous welfare benefits from Survivors Insurance than do other single mothers with children who depend on Aid to Families With Dependent Children.

13   It has taken thousands upon thousands of years to reduce the threat of parental death. Not until the middle of the twentieth century did parental death cease to be a commonplace event for children in the United States. By then advances in medicine had dramatically reduced mortality rates for men and women.

14   At the same time, other forms of family disruption—separation, divorce, out-of-wedlock birth—were held in check by powerful religious, social, and legal sanctions. Divorce was widely regarded both as a deviant behavior, especially threatening to mothers and children, and as a personal lapse: "Divorce is the public acknowledgment of failure," a 1940s sociology textbook noted. Out-of-wedlock birth was stigmatized, and stigmatization is a powerful means of regulating

behavior, as any smoker or overeater will testify. Sanctions against nonmarital childbirth discouraged behavior that hurt children and exacted compensatory behavior that helped them. Shotgun marriages and adoption, two common responses to nonmarital birth, carried a strong message about the risks of premarital sex and created an intact family for the child.

Consequently, children did not have to worry much about   15
losing a parent through divorce or never having had one because of nonmarital birth. After a surge in divorces following the Second World War, the rate leveled off. Only 11 percent of children born in the 1950s would by the time they turned eighteen see their parents separate or divorce. Out-of-wedlock childbirth barely figured as a cause of family disruption. In the 1950s and early 1960s, five percent of the nation's births were out of wedlock. Blacks were more likely than whites to bear children outside marriage, but the majority of black children born in the twenty years after the Second World War were born to married couples. The rate of family disruption reached a historic low point during those years.

A new standard of family security and stability was estab-   16
lished in postwar America. For the first time in history the vast majority of the nation's children could expect to live with married biological parents throughout childhood. Children might still suffer other forms of adversity—poverty, racial discrimination, lack of educational opportunity—but only a few would be deprived of the nurture and protection of a mother and a father. No longer did children have to be haunted by the classic fears vividly dramatized in folklore and fable—that their parents would die, that they would have to live with a stepparent and stepsiblings, or that they would be abandoned. These were the years when the nation confidently boarded up orphanages and closed foundling hospitals, certain that such institutions would never again be needed. In movie theaters across the country parents and children could watch the drama of parental separation and death in the great Disney classics, secure in the knowledge that such nightmare visions as the death of Bambi's mother and the wrenching separation of Dumbo from his mother were only make-believe.

In the 1960s the rate of family disruption suddenly began   17
to rise. After inching up over the course of a century, the divorce rate soared. Throughout the 1950s and early 1960s the divorce rate held steady at fewer than ten divorces a year per 1,000 married couples. Then, beginning in about 1965,

the rate increased sharply, peaking at twenty-three divorces per 1,000 marriages by 1979. (In 1974 divorce passed death as the leading cause of family breakup.) The rate has leveled off at about twenty-one divorces per 1,000 marriages—the figure for 1991. The out-of-wedlock birth rate also jumped. It went from five percent in 1960 to 27 percent in 1990. In 1990 close to 57 percent of births among black mothers were nonmarital, and about 17 percent among white mothers. Altogether, about one out of every four women who had a child in 1990 was not married. With rates of divorce and nonmarital birth so high, family disruption is at its peak. Never before have so many children experienced family breakup caused by events other than death. Each year a million children go through divorce or separation and almost as many more are born out of wedlock.

18   Half of all marriages now end in divorce. Following divorce, many people enter new relationships. Some begin living together. Nearly half of all cohabiting couples have children in the household. Fifteen percent have new children together. Many cohabiting couples eventually get married. However, both cohabiting and remarried couples are more likely to break up than couples in first marriages. Even social scientists find it hard to keep pace with the complexity and velocity of such patterns. In the revised edition (1992) of his book *Marriage, Divorce, Remarriage,* the sociologist Andrew Cherlin ruefully comments: "If there were a truth-in-labeling law for books, the title of this edition should be something long and unwieldy like *Cohabitation, Marriage, Divorce, More Cohabitation, and Probably Remarriage.*"

19   Under such conditions growing up can be a turbulent experience. In many single-parent families children must come to terms with the parent's love life and romantic partners. Some children live with cohabiting couples, either their own unmarried parents or a biological parent and a live-in partner. Some children born to cohabiting parents see their parents break up. Others see their parents marry, but 56 percent of them (as compared with 31 percent of the children born to married parents) later see their parents' marriages fall apart. All told, about three quarters of children born to cohabiting couples will live in a single-parent home at least briefly. One of every four children growing up in the 1990s will eventually enter a stepfamily. According to one survey, nearly half of all children in stepparent families will see their parents divorce again by the time they reach their late teens. Since 80 percent of divorced fathers remarry, things get even more complicated when the romantic or marital history of

the noncustodial parent, usually the father, is taken into account. Consequently, as it affects a significant number of children, family disruption is best understood not as a single event but as a string of disruptive events: separation, divorce, life in a single-parent family, life with a parent and live-in lover, the remarriage of one or both parents, life in one stepparent family combined with visits to another stepparent family; the breakup of one or both stepparent families. And so on. This is one reason why public schools have a hard time knowing whom to call in an emergency.

Given its dramatic impact on children's lives, one might 20 reasonably expect that this historic level of family disruption would be viewed with alarm, even regarded as a national crisis. Yet this has not been the case. In recent years some people have argued that these trends pose a serious threat to children and to the nation as a whole, but they are dismissed as declinists, pessimists, or nostalgists, un-willing or unable to accept the new facts of life. The dominant view is that the changes in family structure are, on balance, positive.

A Shift in the Social Metric

There are several reasons why this is so, but the fundamen- 21 tal reason is that at some point in the 1970s Americans changed their minds about the meaning of these disruptive behaviors. What had once been regarded as hostile to children's best interests was now considered essential to adults' happiness. In the 1950s most Americans believed that parents should stay in an unhappy marriage for the sake of the children. The assumption was that a divorce would damage the children, and the prospect of such damage gave divorce its meaning. By the mid-1970s a majority of Americans rejected that view. Popular advice literature reflected the shift. A book on divorce published in the mid-1940s tersely asserted: "Children are entitled to the affection and *association* of two parents, not one." Thirty years later another popular divorce book proclaimed just the opposite: "A two-parent home is not the only emotional structure within which a child can be happy and healthy.... The parents who take care of themselves will be best able to take care of their children." At about the same time, the long-standing taboo against out-of-wedlock childbirth also collapsed. By the mid-1970s three fourths of Americans said that it was not morally wrong for a woman to have a child outside marriage.

22 Once the social metric shifts from child well-being to adult well-being, it is hard to see divorce and nonmarital birth in anything but a positive light. However distressing and difficult they may be, both of these behaviors can hold out the promise of greater adult choice, freedom, and happiness. For unhappy spouses, divorce offers a way to escape a troubled or even abusive relationship and make a fresh start. For single parents, remarriage is a second try at marital happiness as well as a chance for relief from the stress, loneliness, and economic hardship of raising a child alone. For some unmarried women, nonmarital birth is a way to beat the biological clock, avoid marrying the wrong man, and experience the pleasures of motherhood. Moreover, divorce and out-of-wedlock birth involve a measure of agency and choice; they are man- and woman-made events. To be sure, not everyone exercises choice in divorce or nonmarital birth. Men leave wives for younger women, teenage girls get pregnant accidentally—yet even these unhappy events reflect the expansion of the boundaries of freedom and choice.

23 This cultural shift helps explain what otherwise would be inexplicable: the failure to see the rise in family disruption as a severe and troubling national problem. It explains why there is virtually no widespread public sentiment for restigmatizing either of these classically disruptive behaviors and no sense—no public consensus—that they can or should be avoided in the future....

Dinosaurs Divorce

24 It is true that many adults benefit from divorce or remarriage. According to one study, nearly 80 percent of divorced women and 50 percent of divorced men say they are better off out of the marriage. Half of divorced adults in the same study report greater happiness. A competent self-help book called *Divorce and New Beginnings* notes the advantages of single parenthood: single parents can "develop their own interests, fulfill their own needs, choose their own friends and engage in social activities of their choice. Money, even if limited, can be spent as they see fit." Apparently, some women appreciate the opportunity to have children out of wedlock. "The real world, however, does not always allow women who are dedicated to their careers to devote the time and energy it takes to find—or be found by—the perfect husband and father wanna-be," one woman said in a letter to *The Washington Post*. A mother and chiropractor from Avon, Connecticut, explained

her unwed maternity to an interviewer this way: "It is selfish, but this was something I needed to do for me."

There is very little in contemporary popular culture to contradict this optimistic view. But in a few small places another perspective may be found. Several racks down from its divorce cards, Hallmark offers a line of cards for children—To Kids With Love. These cards come six to a pack. Each card in the pack has a slightly different message. According to the package, the "thinking of you" messages will let a special kid "know how much you care." Though Hallmark doesn't quite say so, it's clear these cards are aimed at divorced parents. "I'm sorry I'm not always there when you need me but I hope you know I'm always just a phone call away." Another card reads: "Even though your dad and I don't live together anymore, I know he's still a very special part of your life. And as much as I miss you when you're not with me, I'm still happy that you two can spend time together." 25

Hallmark's messages are grounded in a substantial body of well-funded market research. Therefore it is worth reflecting on the divergence in sentiment between the divorce cards for adults and the divorce cards for kids. For grown-ups, divorce heralds new beginnings (A HOT NEW SINGLE). For children, divorce brings separation and loss ("I'm sorry I'm not always there when you need me"). 26

An even more telling glimpse into the meaning of family disruption can be found in the growing children's literature on family dissolution. Take, for example, the popular children's book *Dinosaurs Divorce: A Guide for Changing Families* (1986), by Laurene Krasny Brown and Marc Brown. This is a picture book, written for very young children. The book begins with a short glossary of "divorce words" and encourages children to "see if you can find them" in the story. The words include "family counselor," "separation agreement," "alimony," and "child custody." The book is illustrated with cartoonish drawings of green dinosaur parents who fight, drink too much, and break up. One panel shows the father dinosaur, suitcase in hand, getting into a yellow car. 27

The dinosaur children are offered simple, straightforward advice on what to do about the divorce. *On custody decisions:* "When parents can't agree, lawyers and judges decide. Try to be honest if they ask you questions; it will help them make better decisions." *On selling the house:* "If you move, you may have to say good-bye to friends and familiar places. But soon your new home will feel like the place you really belong." *On the economic impact of divorce:* "Living with one parent 28 almost always means there will be less money. Be prepared to give up some things." *On holidays:* "Divorce may mean twice as much celebrating at holiday times, but you may feel pulled apart." *On parents' new lovers:* "You may sometimes feel jealous and want your parent to yourself. Be polite to your parents' new friends, even if you don't like them at first." *On parents' remarriage:* "Not everyone loves his or her stepparents, but showing them respect is important."

29   These cards and books point to an uncomfortable and generally unacknowledged fact: what contributes to a parent's happiness may detract from a child's happiness. All too often the adult quest for freedom, independence, and choice in family relationships conflicts with a child's developmental needs for stability, constancy, harmony, and permanence in family life. In short, family disruption creates a deep division between parents' interests and the interests of children.

30   One of the worst consequences of these divided interests is a withdrawal of parental investment in children's well-being. As the Stanford economist Victor Fuchs has pointed out, the main source of social investment in children is private. The investment comes from the children's parents. But parents in disrupted families have less time, attention, and money to devote to their children. The single most important source of disinvestment has been the widespread withdrawal of financial support and involvement by fathers. Maternal investment, too, has declined, as women try to raise families on their own and work outside the home. Moreover, both mothers and fathers commonly respond to family breakup by investing more heavily in themselves and in their own personal and romantic lives.

31   Sometimes the tables are completely turned. Children are called upon to invest in the emotional well-being of their parents. Indeed, this seems to be the larger message of many of the children's books on divorce and remarriage. *Dinosaurs Divorce* asks children to be sympathetic, understanding, respectful, and polite to confused, unhappy parents. The sacrifice comes from the children: "Be prepared to give up some things." In the world of divorcing dinosaurs, the children rather than the grown-ups are the exemplars of patience, restraint, and good sense.

Three Seventies Assumptions

32   As it first took shape in the 1970s, the optimistic view of family change rested on three bold new assumptions. At that

time, because the emergence of the changes in family life was
so recent, there was little hard evidence to confirm or dispute
these assumptions. But this was an expansive moment in
American life.

The first assumption was an economic one: that a woman   33
could now afford to be a mother without also being a wife.
There were ample grounds for believing this. Women's workforce participation had been gradually increasing in the postwar period, and by the beginning of the 1970s women were a
strong presence in the workplace. What's more, even though
there was still a substantial wage gap between men and
women, women had made considerable progress in a relatively short time toward better-paying jobs and greater
employment opportunities. More women than ever before
could aspire to serious careers as business executives, doctors, lawyers, airline pilots, and politicians. This circumstance, combined with the increased availability of child care,
meant that women could take on the responsibilities of a
breadwinner, perhaps even a sole breadwinner. This was particularly true for middle-class women. According to a highly
regarded 1977 study by the Carnegie Council on Children,
"The greater availability of jobs for women means that more
middle-class children today survive their parents' divorce without a catastrophic plunge into poverty."

Feminists, who had long argued that the path to greater   34
equality for women lay in the world of work outside the
home, endorsed this assumption. In fact, for many, economic
independence was a stepping-stone toward freedom from
both men and marriage. As women began to earn their own
money, they were less dependent on men or marriage, and
marriage diminished in importance. In Gloria Steinem's mem-
orable words, "A woman without a man is like a fish without
a bicycle."

This assumption also gained momentum as the meaning of   35
work changed for women. Increasingly, work had an expressive as well as an economic dimension: being a working
mother not only gave you an income but also made you more
interesting and fulfilled than a stay-at-home mother. Consequently, the optimistic economic scenario was driven by a
cultural imperative. Women would achieve financial independence because, culturally as well as economically, it was the
right thing to do.

The second assumption was that family disruption would   36
not cause lasting harm to children and could actually enrich
their lives. *Creative Divorce: A New Opportunity for Personal*

Growth, a popular book of the seventies, spoke confidently to this point: "Children can survive any family crisis without permanent damage—and grow as human beings in the process. . . ." Moreover, single-parent and stepparent families created a more extensive kinship network than the nuclear family. This network would envelop children in a web of warm and supportive relationships. "Belonging to a stepfamily means there are more people in your life," a children's book published in 1982 notes. "More sisters and brothers, including the step ones. More people you think of as grandparents and aunts and uncles. More cousins. More neighbors and friends. . . . Getting to know and like so many people (and having them like you) is one of the best parts of what being in a stepfamily. . . is all about."

37   The third assumption was that the new diversity in family structure would make America a better place. Just as the nation has been strengthened by the diversity of its ethnic and racial groups, so it would be strengthened by diverse family forms. The emergence of these brave new families was but the latest chapter in the saga of American pluralism.

38   Another version of the diversity argument stated that the real problem was not family disruption itself but the stigma still attached to these emergent family forms. This lingering stigma placed children at psychological risk, making them feel ashamed or different; as the ranks of single-parent and stepparent families grew, children would feel normal and good about themselves.

39   These assumptions continue to be appealing, because they accord with strongly held American beliefs in social progress. Americans see progress in the expansion of individual opportunities for choice, freedom, and self-expression. Moreover, Americans identify progress with growing tolerance of diversity. Over the past half century, the pollster Daniel Yankelovich writes, the United States has steadily grown more open-minded and accepting of groups that were previously perceived as alien, untrustworthy, or unsuitable for public leadership or social esteem. One such group is the burgeoning number of single-parent and stepparent families.

The Education of Sara McLanahan

40   In 1981 Sara McLanahan, now a sociologist at Princeton University's Woodrow Wilson School, read a three-part series by Ken Auletta in *The New Yorker.* Later published as a book

titled *The Underclass,* the series presented a vivid portrait of the drug addicts, welfare mothers, and school dropouts who took part in an education-and-training program in New York City. Many were the children of single mothers, and it was Auletta's clear implication that single-mother families were contributing to the growth of an underclass. McLanahan was taken aback by this notion. "It struck me as strange that he would be viewing single mothers at that level of pathology."

"I'd gone to graduate school in the days when the politically correct argument was that single-parent families were just another alternative family form, and it was fine," McLanahan explains, as she recalls the state of social-scientific thinking in the 1970s. Several empirical studies that were then current supported an optimistic view of family change. (They used tiny samples, however, and did not track the well-being of children over time.)   41

One, *All Our Kin,* by Carol Stack, was required reading for thousands of university students. It said that single mothers had strengths that had gone undetected and unappreciated by earlier researchers. The single-mother family, it suggested, is an economically resourceful and socially embedded institution. In the late 1970s McLanahan wrote a similar study that looked at a small sample of white single mothers and how they coped. "So I was very much of that tradition."   42

By the early 1980s, however, nearly two decades had passed since the changes in family life had begun. During the intervening years a fuller body of empirical research had emerged: studies that used large samples, or followed families through time, or did both. Moreover, several of the studies offered a child's-eye view of family disruption. The National Survey on Children, conducted by the psychologist Nicholas Zill, had set out in 1976 to track a large sample of children aged seven to eleven. It also interviewed the children's parents and teachers. It surveyed its subjects again in 1981 and 1987. By the time of its third round of interviews the eleven-year-olds of 1976 were the twenty-two-year-olds of 1987. The California Children of Divorce Study, directed by Judith Wallerstein, a clinical psychologist, had also been going on for a decade. E. Mavis Hetherington, of the University of Virginia, was conducting a similar study of children from both intact and divorced families. For the first time it was possible to test the optimistic view against a large and longitudinal body of evidence.   43

It was to this body of evidence that Sara McLanahan turned. When she did, she found little to support the optimis-   44 tic view of single motherhood. On the contrary. When she published her findings with Irwin Garfinkel in a 1986 book, *Single Mothers and Their Children,* her portrait of single motherhood proved to be as troubling in its own way as Auletta's.

45   One of the leading assumptions of the time was that single motherhood was economically viable. Even if single mothers did face economic trials, they wouldn't face them for long, it was argued, because they wouldn't remain single for long: single motherhood would be a brief phase of three to five years, followed by marriage. Single mothers would be economically resilient: if they experienced setbacks, they would recover quickly. It was also said that single mothers would be supported by informal networks of family, friends, neighbors, and other single mothers. As McLanahan shows in her study, the evidence demolishes all these claims.

46   For the vast majority of single mothers, the economic spectrum turns out to be narrow, running between precarious and desperate. Half the single mothers in the United States live below the poverty line. (Currently, one out of ten married couples with children is poor.) Many others live on the edge of poverty. Even single mothers who are far from poor are likely to experience persistent economic insecurity. Divorce almost always brings a decline in the standard of living for the mother and children.

47   Moreover, the poverty experienced by single mothers is no more brief than it is mild. A significant number of all single mothers never marry or remarry. Those who do, do so only after spending roughly six years, on average, as single parents. For black mothers the duration is much longer. Only 33 percent of African-American mothers had remarried within ten years of separation. Consequently, single motherhood is hardly a fleeting event for the mother, and it is likely to occupy a third of the child's childhood. Even the notion that single mothers are knit together in economically supportive networks is not borne out by the evidence. On the contrary, single parenthood forces many women to be on the move, in search of cheaper housing and better jobs. This need-driven restless mobility makes it more difficult for them to sustain supportive ties to family and friends, let alone other single mothers.

48   Single-mother families are vulnerable not just to poverty but to a particularly debilitating form of poverty: welfare dependency. The dependency takes two forms: First, single mothers, particularly unwed mothers, stay on welfare longer than other welfare recipients. Of those never-married moth-

ers who receive welfare benefits, almost 40 percent remain on the rolls for ten years or longer. Second, welfare dependency tends to be passed on from one generation to the next. McLanahan says, "Evidence on intergenerational poverty indicates that, indeed, offspring from [single-mother] families are far more likely to be poor and to form mother-only families than are offspring who live with two parents most of their pre-adult life." Nor is the intergenerational impact of single motherhood limited to African-Americans, as many people seem to believe. Among white families, daughters of single parents are 53 percent more likely to marry as teenagers, 111 percent more likely to have children as teenagers, 164 percent more likely to have a premarital birth, and 92 percent more likely to dissolve their own marriages. All these intergenerational consequences of single motherhood increase the likelihood of chronic welfare dependency.

McLanahan cites three reasons why single-mother families   49
are so vulnerable economically. For one thing, their earnings are low. Second, unless the mothers are widowed, they don't receive public subsidies large enough to lift them out of poverty. And finally, they do not get much support from family members—especially the fathers of their children. In 1982 single white mothers received an average of $1,246 in alimony and child support, black mothers an average of $322. Such payments accounted for about 10 percent of the income of single white mothers and for about 3.5 percent of the income of single black mothers. These amounts were dramatically smaller than the income of the father in a two-parent family and also smaller than the income from a second earner in a two-parent family. Roughly 60 percent of single white mothers and 80 percent of single black mothers received no support at all.

Until the mid-1980s, when stricter standards were put in   50
place, child-support awards were only about half to two-thirds what the current guidelines require. Accordingly, there is often a big difference in the living standards of divorced fathers and of divorced mothers with children. After divorce the average annual income of mothers and children is $13,500 for whites and $9,000 for nonwhites, as compared with $25,000 for white nonresident fathers and $13,600 for nonwhite nonresident fathers. Moreover, since child-support awards account for a smaller portion of the income of a high-earning father, the drop in living standards can be especially sharp for mothers who were married to upper-level managers and professionals.

51   Unwed mothers are unlikely to be awarded any child support at all, partly because the paternity of their children may not have been established. According to one recent study, only 20 percent of unmarried mothers receive child support.

52   Even if single mothers escape poverty, economic uncertainty remains a condition of life. Divorce brings a reduction in income and standard of living for the vast majority of single mothers. One study, for example, found that income for mothers and children declines on average about 30 percent, while fathers experience a 10 to 15 percent increase in income in the year following a separation. Things get even more difficult when fathers fail to meet their child-support obligations. As a result, many divorced mothers experience a wearing uncertainty about the family budget: whether the check will come in or not; whether new sneakers can be bought this month or not; whether the electric bill will be paid on time or not. Uncertainty about money triggers other kinds of uncertainty. Mothers and children often have to move to cheaper housing after a divorce. One study shows that about 38 percent of divorced mothers and their children move during the first year after a divorce. Even several years later the rate of moves for single mothers is about a third higher than the rate for two-parent families. It is also common for a mother to change her job or increase her working hours or both following a divorce. Even the composition of the household is likely to change, with other adults, such as boyfriends or babysitters, moving in and out.

53   All this uncertainty can be devastating to children. Anyone who knows children knows that they are deeply conservative creatures. They like things to stay the same. So pronounced is this tendency that certain children have been known to request the same peanut-butter-and-jelly sandwich for lunch for years on end. Children are particularly set in their ways when it comes to family, friends, neighborhoods, and schools. Yet when a family breaks up, all these things may change. The novelist Pat Conroy has observed that "each divorce is the death of a small civilization." No one feels this more acutely than children.

54   Sara McLanahan's investigation and others like it have helped to establish a broad consensus on the economic impact of family disruption on children. Most social scientists now agree that single motherhood is an important and growing cause of poverty, and that children suffer as a result. (They continue to argue, however, about the relationship between family structure and such economic factors as income ine-

quality, the loss of jobs in the inner city, and the growth of low-wage jobs.) By the mid-1980s, however, it was clear that the problem of family disruption was not confined to the urban underclass, nor was its sole impact economic. Divorce and out-of-wedlock childbirth were affecting middle- and upper-class children, and these more privileged children were suffering negative consequences as well. It appeared that the problems associated with family breakup were far deeper and far more widespread than anyone had previously imagined.

The Missing Father

Judith Wallerstein is one of the pioneers in research on the   55
long-term psychological impact of family disruption on children. The California Children of Divorce Study, which she
directs, remains the most enduring study of the long-term
effects of divorce on children and their parents. Moreover, it
represents the best-known effort to look at the impact of
divorce on middle-class children. The California children
entered the study without pathological family histories.
Before divorce they lived in stable, protected homes. And
although some of the children did experience economic insecurity as the result of divorce, they were generally free from
the most severe forms of poverty associated with family
breakup. Thus the study and the resulting book (which
Wallerstein wrote with Sandra Blakeslee), *Second Chances:
Men, Women, and Children a Decade After Divorce* (1989), provide new insight into the consequences of divorce which are
not associated with extreme forms of economic or emotional
deprivation.

When, in 1971, Wallerstein and her colleagues set out to   56
conduct clinical interviews with 131 children from the San
Francisco area, they thought they were embarking on a short-
term study. Most experts believed that divorce was like a bad
cold. There was a phase of acute discomfort, and then a short
recovery phase. According to the conventional wisdom, kids
would be back on their feet in no time at all. Yet when Wallerstein met these children for a second interview more than a
year later, she was amazed to discover that there had been no
miraculous recovery. In fact, the children seemed to be doing
worse.

The news that children did not "get over" divorce was not   57
particularly welcome at the time. Wallerstein recalls, "We got
angry letters from therapists, parents, and lawyers saying we

were undoubtedly wrong. They said children are really much better off being released from an unhappy marriage. Divorce, they said, is a liberating experience." One of the main results of the California study was to overturn this optimistic view. In Wallerstein's cautionary words, "Divorce is deceptive. Legally it is a single event, but psychologically it is a chain— sometimes a never-ending chain—of events, relocations, and radically shifting relationships strung through time, a process that forever changes the lives of the people involved."

58   Five years after divorce more than a third of the children experienced moderate or severe depression. At ten years a significant number of the now young men and women appeared to be troubled, drifting, and underachieving. At fifteen years many of the thirtyish adults were struggling to establish strong love relationships of their own. In short, far from recovering from their parents' divorce, a significant percentage of these grownups were still suffering from its effects. In fact, according to Wallerstein, the long-term effects of divorce emerge at a time when young adults are trying to make their own decisions about love, marriage, and family. Not all children in the study suffered negative consequences. But Wallerstein's research presents a sobering picture of divorce. "The child of divorce faces many additional psychological burdens in addition to the normative tasks of growing up," she says.

59   Divorce not only makes it more difficult for young adults to establish new relationships. It also weakens the oldest primary relationship: that between parent and child. According to Wallerstein, "Parent-child relationships are permanently altered by divorce in ways that our society has not anticipated." Not only do children experience a loss of parental attention at the onset of divorce, but they soon find that at every stage of their development their parents are not available in the same way they once were. "In a reasonably happy intact family," Wallerstein observes, "the child gravitates first to one parent and then to the other, using skills and attributes from each in climbing the developmental ladder." In a divorced family, children find it "harder to find the needed parent at needed times." This may help explain why very young children suffer the most as the result of family disruption. Their opportunities to engage in this kind of ongoing process are the most truncated and compromised.

60   The father-child bond is severely, often irreparably, damaged in disrupted families. In a situation without historical precedent, an astonishing and disheartening number of American fathers are failing to provide financial support to their

children. Often, more than the father's support check is missing. Increasingly, children are bereft of any contact with their fathers. According to the National Survey of Children, in disrupted families only one child in six, on average, saw his or her father as often as once a week in the past year. Close to half did not see their father at all in the past year. As time goes on, contact becomes even more infrequent. Ten years after a marriage breaks up, more than two thirds of children report not having seen their father for a year. Not surprisingly, when asked to name the "adults you look up to and admire," only 20 percent of children in single-parent families named their father, as compared with 52 percent of children in two-parent families. A favorite complaint among Baby Boom Americans is that their fathers were emotionally remote guys who worked hard, came home at night to eat supper, and didn't have much to say to or do with the kids. But the current generation has a far worse father problem: many of their fathers are vanishing entirely.

Even for fathers who maintain regular contact, the pattern 61 of father-child relationships changes. The sociologists Andrew Cherlin and Frank Furstenberg, who have studied broken families, write that the fathers behave more like other relatives than like parents. Rather than helping with homework or carrying out a project with their children, nonresidential fathers are likely to take the kids shopping, to the movies, or out to dinner. Instead of providing steady advice and guidance, divorced fathers become "treat" dads.

Apparently—and paradoxically—it is the visiting relation- 62 ship itself, rather than the frequency of visits, that is the real source of the problem. According to Wallerstein, the few children in the California study who reported visiting with their fathers once or twice a week over a ten-year period still felt rejected. The need to schedule a special time to be with the child, the repeated leave-takings, and the lack of connection to the child's regular, daily schedule leaves many fathers adrift, frustrated, and confused. Wallerstein calls the visiting father a parent without portfolio.

The deterioration in father-child bonds is most severe 63 among children who experience divorce at an early age, according to a recent study. Nearly three quarters of the respondents, now young men and women, report having poor relationships with their fathers. Close to half have received psychological help, nearly a third have dropped out of high school, and about a quarter report having experienced high levels of problem behavior or emotional distress by the time they became young adults.

Long-Term Effects

64   Since most children live with their mothers after divorce,
one might expect that the mother-child bond would remain
unaltered and might even be strengthened. Yet research
shows that the mother-child bond is also weakened as the
result of divorce. Only half of the children who were close to
their mothers before a divorce remained equally close after
the divorce. Boys, particularly, had difficulties with their
mothers. Moreover, mother-child relationships deteriorated
over time. Whereas teenagers in disrupted families were no
more likely than teenagers in intact families to report poor
relationships with their mothers, 30 percent of young adults
from disrupted families have poor relationships with their
mothers, as compared with 16 percent of young adults from
intact families. Mother-daughter relationships often deteriorate as the daughter reaches young adulthood. The only
group in society that derives any benefit from these weakened
parent-child ties is the therapeutic community. Young adults
from disrupted families are nearly twice as likely as those
from intact families to receive psychological help.

65   Some social scientists have criticized Judith Wallerstein's
research because her study is based on a small clinical sample and does not include a control group of children from
intact families. However, other studies generally support and
strengthen her findings. Nicholas Zill has found similar long-
term effects on children of divorce, reporting that "effects of
marital discord and family disruption are visible twelve to
twenty-two years later in poor relationships with parents,
high levels of problem behavior, and an increased likelihood
of dropping out of high school and receiving psychological
help." Moreover, Zill's research also found signs of distress in
young women who seemed relatively well adjusted in middle
childhood and adolescence. Girls in single-parent families
are also at much greater risk for precocious sexuality, teenage
marriage, teenage pregnancy, nonmarital birth, and divorce
than are girls in two-parent families.

66   Zill's research shows that family disruption strongly affects
school achievement as well. Children in disrupted families are
nearly twice as likely as those in intact families to drop out of
high school; among children who do drop out, those from disrupted families are less likely eventually to earn a diploma or a
GED. Boys are at greater risk for dropping out than girls, and
are also more likely to exhibit aggressive, acting-out behaviors.
Other research confirms these findings. According to a study

by the National Association of Elementary School Principals, 33 percent of two-parent elementary school students are ranked as high achievers, as compared with 17 percent of single-parent students. The children in single-parent families are also more likely to be truant or late or to have disciplinary action taken against them. Even after controlling for race, income, and religion, scholars find significant differences in educational attainment between children who grow up in intact families and children who do not. In his 1992 study *America's Smallest School: The Family,* Paul Barton shows that the proportion of two-parent families varies widely from state to state and is related to variations in academic achievement. North Dakota, for example, scores highest on the math-proficiency test and second highest on the two-parent-family scale. The District of Columbia is second lowest on the math test and lowest in the nation on the two-parent-family scale.

Zill notes that "while coming from a disrupted family significantly increases a young adult's risks of experiencing social, emotional or academic difficulties, it does not foreordain such difficulties. The majority of young people from disrupted families have successfully completed high school, do *not* currently display high levels of emotional distress or problem behavior, and enjoy reasonable relationships with their mothers." Nevertheless, a majority of these young adults do show maladjustment in their relationships with their fathers. 67

These findings underscore the importance of both a mother and a father in fostering the emotional well-being of children. Obviously, not all children in two-parent families are free from emotional turmoil, but few are burdened with the troubles that accompany family breakup. Moreover, as the sociologist Amitai Etzioni explains in a new book, *The Spirit of Community,* two parents in an intact family make up what might be called a mutually supportive education coalition. When both parents are present, they can play different, even contradictory, roles. One parent may goad the child to achieve, while the other may encourage the child to take time out to daydream or toss a football around. One may emphasize taking intellectual risks, while the other may insist on following the teacher's guidelines. At the same time, the parents regularly exchange information about the child's school problems and achievements, and have a sense of the overall educational mission. However, Etzioni writes, 68

> The sequence of divorce followed by a succession of boy or girlfriends, a second marriage, and frequently another divorce

and another turnover of partners often means a repeatedly disrupted educational coalition. Each change in participants involves a change in the educational agenda for the child. Each new partner cannot be expected to pick up the previous one's educational post and program.... As a result, changes in parenting partners mean, at best, a deep disruption in a child's education, though of course several disruptions cut deeper into the effectiveness of the educational coalition than just one....

Poverty, Crime, Education

69   Family disruption would be a serious problem even if it affected only individual children and families. But its impact is far broader. Indeed, it is not an exaggeration to characterize it as a central cause of many of our most vexing social problems. Consider three problems that most Americans believe rank among the nation's pressing concerns: poverty, crime, and declining school performance.

70   More than half of the increase in child poverty in the 1980s is attributable to changes in family structure, according to David Eggebeen and Daniel Lichter, of Pennsylvania State University. In fact, if family structure in the United States had remained relatively constant since 1960, the rate of child poverty would be a third lower than it is today. This does not bode well for the future. With more than half of today's children likely to live in single-parent families, poverty and associated welfare costs threaten to become even heavier burdens on the nation.

71   Crime in American cities has increased dramatically and grown more violent over recent decades. Much of this can be attributed to the rise in disrupted families. Nationally, more than 70 percent of all juveniles in state reform institutions come from fatherless homes. A number of scholarly studies find that even after the groups of subjects are controlled for income, boys from single-mother homes are significantly more likely than others to commit crimes and to wind up in the juvenile justice, court, and penitentiary systems. One such study summarizes the relationship between crime and one-parent families in this way: "The relationship is so strong that controlling for family configuration erases the relationship between race and crime and between low income and crime. This conclusion shows up time and again in the literature." The nation's mayors, as well as police officers, social

workers, probation officers, and court officials, consistently
point to family breakup as the most important source of rising rates of crime.

Terrible as poverty and crime are, they tend to be concen-   72
trated in inner cities and isolated from the everyday experience
of many Americans. The same cannot be said of the problem
of declining school performance. Nowhere has the impact of
family breakup been more profound or widespread than in the
nation's public schools. There is a strong consensus that the
schools are failing in their historic mission to prepare every
American child to be a good worker and a good citizen. And
nearly everyone agrees that the schools must undergo dramatic reform in order to reach that goal. In pursuit of that
goal, moreover, we have suffered no shortage of bright ideas or
pilot projects or bold experiments in school reform. But there
is little evidence that measures such as curricular reform,
school-based management, and school choice will address, let
alone solve, the biggest problem schools face: the rising number of children who come from disrupted families.

The great educational tragedy of our time is that many   73
American children are failing in school not because they are
intellectually or physically impaired but because they are
emotionally incapacitated. In schools across the nation principals report a dramatic rise in the aggressive, acting-out
behavior characteristic of children, especially boys, who are
living in single-parent families. The discipline problems in
today's suburban schools—assaults on teachers, unprovoked
attacks on other students, screaming outbursts in class—outstrip the problems that were evident in the toughest city
schools a generation ago. Moreover, teachers find many children emotionally distracted, so upset and preoccupied by the
explosive drama of their own family lives that they are unable
to concentrate on such mundane matters as multiplication
tables.

In response, many schools have turned to therapeutic   74
remediation. A growing proportion of many school budgets is
devoted to counseling and other psychological services. The
curriculum is becoming more therapeutic: children are taking courses in self-esteem, conflict resolution, and aggression
management. Parental advisory groups are conscientiously
debating alternative approaches to traditional school discipline, ranging from teacher training in mediation to the introduction of metal detectors and security guards in the schools.
Schools are increasingly becoming emergency rooms of the
emotions, devoted not only to developing minds but also to

repairing hearts. As a result, the mission of the school, along
with the culture of the classroom, is slowly changing. What
we are seeing, largely as a result of the new burdens of family
disruption, is the psychologization of American education.

75   Taken together, the research presents a powerful challenge to the prevailing view of family change as social
progress. Not a single one of the assumptions underlying
that view can be sustained against the empirical evidence.
Single-parent families are not able to do well economically
on a mother's income. In fact, most teeter on the economic
brink, and many fall into poverty and welfare dependency.
Growing up in a disrupted family does not enrich a child's
life or expand the number of adults committed to the child's
well-being. In fact, disrupted families threaten the psychological well-being of children and diminish the investment of
adult time and money in them. Family diversity in the form
of increasing numbers of single-parent and stepparent families does not strengthen the social fabric. It dramatically
weakens and undermines society, placing new burdens on
schools, courts, prisons, and the welfare system. These new
families are not an improvement on the nuclear family, nor
are they even just as good, whether you look at outcomes for
children or outcomes for society as a whole. In short, far
from representing social progress, family change represents
a stunning example of social regress.

The Two-Parent Advantage

76   All this evidence gives rise to an obvious conclusion: growing up in an intact two-parent family is an important source
of advantage for American children. Though far from perfect
as a social institution, the intact family offers children greater
security and better outcomes than its fast-growing alternatives: single-parent and stepparent families. Not only does the
intact family protect the child from poverty and economic
insecurity; it also provides greater noneconomic investments
of parental time, attention, and emotional support over the
entire life course. This does not mean that all two-parent families are better for children than all single-parent families. But
in the face of the evidence it becomes increasingly difficult to
sustain the proposition that all family structures produce
equally good outcomes for children.

77   Curiously, many in the research community are hesitant to
say that two-parent families generally promote better out-

comes for children than single-parent families. Some argue that we need finer measures of the extent of the family-structure effect. As one scholar has noted, it is possible, by disaggregating the data in certain ways, to make family structure "go away" as an independent variable. Other researchers point to studies that show that children suffer psychological effects as a result of family conflict preceding family breakup. Consequently, they reason, it is the conflict rather than the structure of the family that is responsible for many of the problems associated with family disruption. Others, including Judith Wallerstein, caution against treating children in divorced families and children in intact families as separate populations, because doing so tends to exaggerate the differences between the two groups. "We have to take this family by family," Wallerstein says.

Some of the caution among researchers can also be attributed to ideological pressures. Privately, social scientists worry that their research may serve ideological causes that they themselves do not support, or that their work may be misinterpreted as an attempt to "tell people what to do." Some are fearful that they will be attacked by feminist colleagues, or, more generally, that their comments will be regarded as an effort to turn back the clock to the 1950s—a goal that has almost no constituency in the academy. Even more fundamental, it has become risky for anyone—scholar, politician, religious leader—to make normative statements today. This reflects not only the persistent drive toward "value neutrality" in the professions but also a deep confusion about the purposes of public discourse. The dominant view appears to be that social criticism, like criticism of individuals, is psychologically damaging. The worst thing you can do is to make people feel guilty or bad about themselves.   78

When one sets aside these constraints, however, the case against the two-parent family is remarkably weak. It is true that disaggregating data can make family structure less significant as a factor, just as disaggregating Hurricane Andrew into wind, rain, and tides can make it disappear as a meteorological phenomenon. Nonetheless, research opinion as well as common sense suggests that the effects of changes in family structure are great enough to cause concern. Nicholas Zill argues that many of the risk factors for children are doubled or more than doubled as the result of family disruption. "In epidemiological terms," he writes, "the doubling of a hazard is a substantial increase.... the increase in risk that dietary cholesterol poses for cardiovascular disease, for example, is   79 far less than double, yet millions of Americans have altered their diets because of the perceived hazard."

80   The argument that family conflict, rather than the breakup of parents, is the cause of children's psychological distress is persuasive on its face. Children who grow up in high-conflict families, whether the families stay together or eventually split up, are undoubtedly at great psychological risk. And surely no one would dispute that there must be societal measures available, including divorce, to remove children from families where they are in danger. Yet only a minority of divorces grow out of pathological situations; much more common are divorces in families unscarred by physical assault. Moreover, an equally compelling hypothesis is that family breakup generates its own conflict. Certainly, many families exhibit more conflictual and even violent behavior as a consequence of divorce than they did before divorce.

81   Finally, it is important to note that clinical insights are different from sociological findings. Clinicians work with individual families, who cannot and should not be defined by statistical aggregates. Appropriate to a clinical approach, moreover, is a focus on the internal dynamics of family functioning and on the immense variability in human behavior. Nevertheless, there is enough empirical evidence to justify sociological statements about the causes of declining child well-being and to demonstrate that despite the plasticity of human response, there are some useful rules of thumb to guide our thinking about and policies affecting the family.

82   For example, Sara McLanahan says, three structural constants are commonly associated with intact families, even intact families who would not win any "Family of the Year" awards. The first is economic. In intact families, children share in the income of two adults. Indeed, as a number of analysts have pointed out, the two-parent family is becoming more rather than less necessary, because more and more families need two incomes to sustain a middle-class standard of living.

83   McLanahan believes that most intact families also provide a stable authority structure. Family breakup commonly upsets the established boundaries of authority in a family. Children are often required to make decisions or accept responsibilities once considered the province of parents. Moreover, children, even very young children, are often expected to behave like mature adults, so that the grown-ups in the family can be free to deal with the emotional fallout of the failed relationship. In some instances family disruption

creates a complete vacuum in authority; everyone invents his or her own rules. With lines of authority disrupted or absent, children find it much more difficult to engage in the normal kinds of testing behavior, the trial and error, the failing and succeeding, that define the developmental pathway toward character and competence. McLanahan says, "Children need to be the ones to challenge the rules. The parents need to set the boundaries and let the kids push the boundaries. The children shouldn't have to walk the straight and narrow at all times."

Finally, McLanahan holds that children in intact families [84] benefit from stability in what she neutrally terms "household personnel." Family disruption frequently brings new adults into the family, including stepparents, live-in boyfriends or girlfriends, and casual sexual partners. Like stepfathers, boyfriends can present a real threat to children's, particularly to daughters', security and well-being. But physical or sexual abuse represents only the most extreme such threat. Even the very best of boyfriends can disrupt and undermine a child's sense of peace and security, McLanahan says. "It's not as though you're going from an unhappy marriage to peacefulness. There can be a constant changing until the mother finds a suitable partner."

McLanahan's argument helps explain why children of wid- [85] ows tend to do better than children of divorced or unmarried mothers. Widows differ from other single mothers in all three respects. They are economically more secure, because they receive more public assistance through Survivors Insurance, and possibly private insurance or other kinds of support from family members. Thus widows are less likely to leave the neighborhood in search of a new or better job and a cheaper house or apartment. Moreover, the death of a father is not likely to disrupt the authority structure radically. When a father dies, he is no longer physically present, but his death does not dethrone him as an authority figure in the child's life. On the contrary, his authority may be magnified through death. The mother can draw on the powerful memory of the departed father as a way of intensifying her parental authority: "Your father would have wanted it this way." Finally, since widows tend to be older than divorced mothers, their love life may be less distracting.

Regarding the two-parent family, the sociologist David [86] Popenoe, who has devoted much of his career to the study of families, both in the United States and in Scandinavia, makes this straightforward assertion:

Social science research is almost never conclusive. There are always methodological difficulties and stones left unturned. Yet in three decades of work as a social scientist, I know of few other bodies of data in which the weight of evidence is so decisively on one side of the issue: on the whole, for children, two-parent families are preferable to single-parent and step-families.

The Regime Effect

87   The rise in family disruption is not unique to American society. It is evident in virtually all advanced nations, including Japan, where it is also shaped by the growing participation of women in the work force. Yet the United States has made divorce easier and quicker than in any other Western nation with the sole exception of Sweden—and the trend toward solo motherhood has also been more pronounced in America. (Sweden has an equally high rate of out-of-wedlock birth, but the majority of such births are to cohabiting couples, a long-established pattern in Swedish society.) More to the point, nowhere has family breakup been greeted by a more triumphant rhetoric of renewal than in America.

88   What is striking about this rhetoric is how deeply it reflects classic themes in American public life. It draws its language and imagery from the nation's founding myth. It depicts family breakup as a drama of revolution and rebirth. The nuclear family represents the corrupt past, an institution guilty of the abuse of power and the suppression of individual freedom. Breaking up the family is like breaking away from Old World tyranny. Liberated from the bonds of the family, the individual can achieve independence and experience a new beginning, a fresh start, a new birth of freedom. In short, family breakup recapitulates the American experience.

89   This rhetoric is an example of what the University of Maryland political philosopher William Galston has called the "regime effect." The founding of the United States set in motion a new political order based to an unprecedented degree on individual rights, personal choice, and egalitarian relationships. Since then these values have spread beyond their original domain of political relationships to define social relationships as well. During the past twenty-five years these values have had a particularly profound impact on the family.

90   Increasingly, political principles of individual rights and choice shape our understanding of family commitment and

solidarity. Family relationships are viewed not as permanent or binding but as voluntary and easily terminable. Moreover, under the sway of the regime effect the family loses its central importance as an institution in the civil society, accomplishing certain social goals such as raising children and caring for its members, and becomes a means to achieving greater individual happiness—a lifestyle choice. Thus, Galston says, what is happening to the American family reflects the "unfolding logic of authoritative, deeply American moral-political principles."

One benefit of the regime effect is to create greater equality   91
in adult family relationships. Husbands and wives, mothers and fathers, enjoy relationships far more egalitarian than past relationships were, and most Americans prefer it that way. But the political principles of the regime effect can threaten another kind of family relationship—that between parent and child. Owing to their biological and developmental immaturity, children are needy dependents. They are not able to express their choices according to limited, easily terminable, voluntary agreements. They are not able to act as negotiators in family decisions, even those that most affect their own interests. As one writer has put it, "a newborn does not make a good 'partner.'" Correspondingly, the parental role is antithetical to the spirit of the regime. Parental investment in children involves a diminished investment in self, a willing deference to the needs and claims of the dependent child. Perhaps more than any other family relationship, the parent-child relationship—shaped as it is by patterns of dependency and deference—can be undermined and weakened by the principles of the regime.

More than a century and a half ago Alexis de Tocqueville   92
made the striking observation that an individualistic society depends on a communitarian institution like the family for its continued existence. The family cannot be constituted like the liberal state, nor can it be governed entirely by that state's principles. Yet the family serves as the seedbed for the virtues required by a liberal state. The family is responsible for teaching lessons of independence, self-restraint, responsibility, and right conduct, which are essential to a free, democratic society. If the family fails in these tasks, then the entire experiment in democratic self-rule is jeopardized.

To take one example: independence is basic to successful   93
functioning in American life. We assume that most people in America will be able to work, care for themselves and their families, think for themselves, and inculcate the same traits of independence and initiative in their children. We depend

on families to teach people to do these things. The erosion
of the two-parent family undermines the capacity of families
to impart this knowledge; children of long-term welfare-
dependent single parents are far more likely than others to be
dependent themselves. Similarly, the children in disrupted
families have a harder time forging bonds of trust with others
and giving and getting help across the generations. This, too,
may lead to greater dependency on the resources of the state.

94   Over the past two and a half decades Americans have been
conducting what is tantamount to a vast natural experiment
in family life. Many would argue that this experiment was
necessary, worthwhile, and long overdue. The results of the
experiment are coming in, and they are clear. Adults have
benefited from the changes in family life in important ways,
but the same cannot be said for children. Indeed, this is the
first generation in the nation's history to do worse psychologically, socially, and economically than its parents. Most poi-
gnantly, in survey after survey the children of broken families
confess deep longings for an intact family.

95   Nonetheless, as Galston is quick to point out, the regime
effect is not an irresistible undertow that will carry away the
family. It is more like a swift current, against which it is possible to swim. People learn; societies can change, particularly
when it becomes apparent that certain behaviors damage the
social ecology, threaten the public order, and impose new
burdens on core institutions. Whether Americans will act to
overcome the legacy of family disruption is a crucial but as
yet unanswered question.

Ellen Willis

Why I'm Not "Pro-Family"

Ellen Willis, author of No More Nice Girls: Countercultural
Essays *(1992), teaches journalism at NYU. The article published here originally appeared in* Glamour *(October 1994), a
national magazine devoted to fashions, cultural matters,
careers, nutrition, and civic issues interesting to women.
(Another essay by Willis appears in the section of* Conversations *on affirmative action, page 354.)*

In 1992, "Family Values" bombed in Houston. Right-wing-   1
ers at the Republican convention, sneering at career women
and single mothers, turned voters off. Now the Democrats are
in power—yet ironically, the family issue has reemerged,
more strongly than ever. Last year New York's influential
Democratic senator, Daniel Patrick Moynihan, suggested that
in relaxing the stigma against unmarried childbearing, we
had laid the groundwork for the burgeoning crime rate. Then
The Atlantic published a cover story provocatively titled: "Dan
Quayle Was Right." Its author, social historian Barbara Dafoe
Whitehead, invoked recent research to argue that high rates
of divorce and single parenthood hurt children and underlie
"many of our most vexing social problems."

The article hit a nerve. It provoked an outpouring of mail,   2
was condensed for *Reader's Digest* and won an award from
the National Women's Political Caucus. Commentators both
conservative and liberal praised it in newspapers across the
country. Together, Moynihan's and Whitehead's salvos
launched a national obsession with "the decline of the family." President Clinton joined the bandwagon: "For 30 years,"
he declared in his State of the Union message, "family life in
America has been breaking down."

The new advocates of the family seem more sympathetic to   3
women than their right-wing precursors. They know women
are in the workforce to stay; they are careful to talk about
the time pressures faced by "parents"—not "mothers"—with
jobs, and they put an unaccustomed emphasis on men's family obligations, such as contributing their fair share of child
support. Some advocate liberal reforms ranging from anti-
poverty programs to federally funded child care to abortion
rights, arguing that such measures are pro-family because

they help existing families. (A recent Planned Parenthood fund-raising letter proclaims, "Pro-choice is pro-family.")

4   I'm all for reforms that make it easier to give children the care they need, and I'm certainly in favor of men's equal participation in childrearing. My quarrel is with the underlying terms of the discussion, especially the assumption that anyone who cares about children must be "pro-family." I grew up in the fifties, in a family with two committed parents—the kind of home the pro-familists idealize. I had security; I had love. Yet like many of my peers, especially women, I saw conventional family life as far from ideal and had no desire to replicate it. It wasn't only that I didn't want to be a housewife like my mother; I felt that family life promoted self-abnegation and social conformity while stifling eroticism and spontaneity. I thought the nuclear family structure was isolating, and that within it, combining childrearing with other work would be exhausting, even if both parents shared the load—impressions I can now confirm from experience.

5   To me the alternative that made the most sense was not single parenthood—we needed *more* parents, not fewer, to share the daily responsibilities of childrearing and homemaking. In the seventies, a number of people I knew were bringing up children in communal households, and I imagined someday doing the same. But by the time my companion and I had a child ten years ago, those experiments and the counterculture that supported them were long gone.

6   From my perspective, the new champions of the family are much like the old. They never consider whether the current instability of families might signal that an age-old institution is failing to meet modern needs and ought to be reexamined. The idea that there could be other possible structures for domestic life and childrearing has been excluded from the conversation—so much so that cranks like me who persist in broaching the subject are used to getting the sort of tactful and embarrassed reaction accorded, say, people who claim to have been kidnapped by aliens. And the assumption that marriage is the self-evident solution to single parents' problems leads to impatience and hostility toward anyone who can't or won't get with the nuclear-family program.

7   Consider the hottest topic on the pro-family agenda: the prevalence of unwed motherhood in poor black communities. For Moynihan and other welfare reformers, the central cause of inner-city poverty and crime is not urban economic collapse, unemployment or racism, but fatherless households. Which means the solution is to bring back the stigma of "ille-

gitimacy" and restrict or eliminate welfare for single mothers. Clinton has proposed requiring welfare recipients to leave the rolls after two years and look for work, with temporary government jobs as a backup (where the permanent jobs are supposed to come from, in an economy where massive layoffs and corporate shrinkage are the order of the day, is not explained).

As the reformers profess their concern for poor children (while proposing to make them even poorer), the work ethic (as jobs for the unskilled get even scarcer) and the overburdened taxpayer, it's easy to miss their underlying message— that women have gotten out of hand. They may pay lip service to the idea that men too should be held responsible for the babies they father. But in practice there is no way to force poor, unemployed men to support their children or to stigmatize men as well as women for having babies out of wedlock. This is, after all, still a culture that regards pregnancy as the woman's problem and childrearing as the woman's job. And so, predictably, women are the chief targets of the reformers' punitive policies and rhetoric. It's women who will lose benefits; women who stand accused of deliberately having babies as a meal ticket; women who are (as usual) charged with the social failures of their sons. Given the paucity of decently paying jobs available to poor women or the men they're likely to be involved with, demanding that they not have children unless they have jobs or husbands to support them is tantamount to demanding that they not have children at all. (Note the logic: Motherhood is honorable work if supported by a man but parasitic self-indulgence if supported by the public.) Put that demand together with laws restricting abortion for poor women and teenagers, and the clear suggestion is that they shouldn't have sex either.

While this brand of misogyny is specifically aimed at poor black women, it would be a mistake to think the rest of us are off the hook. For one thing (as Whitehead and other profamilists are quick to remind us), it's all too easy in this age of high divorce and unemployment rates for a woman who imagined herself securely middle-class to unexpectedly become an impoverished single mother. Anyway, there is a thin line between fear and loathing of welfare mothers and moral distaste for unmarried mothers per se. Secretary of Health and Human Services Donna Shalala, a feminist and one of the more liberal members of the Clinton cabinet, has said, "I don't like to put this in moral terms, but I do believe that having children out of wedlock is just wrong." The language the welfare reformers use—the vocabulary of *stigma*

8

9

and *illegitimacy*—unnervingly recalls the repressive moral climate of my own teenage years.

10   I can't listen to harangues about illegitimacy without getting posttraumatic flashbacks. Let's be clear about what the old stigma meant: a vicious double standard of sexual morality for men and women; the hobbling of female sexuality with shame, guilt and inhibition; panic over dislodged diaphragms and late periods; couples trapped into marriages one or both never wanted; pregnant girls barred from school and hidden in homes for unwed mothers; enormous pressure on women to get married early and not be too picky about it.

11   Is it silly to worry that in the post–*Roe* v. *Wade*, post-Pill nineties some version of fifties morality could reassert itself? I don't think so. Activists with a moral cause can be very persuasive. Who would have imagined a few years ago that there would be a public debate about restricting cigarettes as an addictive drug? Abortion may still be legal, but its opponents have done a good job of bringing back its stigma (ironically, this is one reason a lot of pregnant teenagers decide to give birth).

12   Many pro-familists, above all those who call themselves communitarians, are openly nostalgic for a sterner moral order. They argue that we have become a society too focused on rights instead of duties, on personal freedom and happiness instead of sacrifice for the common good. If the welfare reformers appeal to people's self-righteousness, the communitarians tap an equally potent emotion—guilt. In our concern for our own fulfillment, they argue, we are doing irreparable harm to our children.

13   Whitehead's *Atlantic* article cites psychologist Judith Wallerstein and other researchers to support her contention that while adults have benefited from the freedom to divorce and procreate outside marriage, children have suffered. Children in single-parent families, Whitehead warns, are not only at great risk of being poor but are more likely to have emotional and behavioral problems, drop out of school, abuse drugs. She calls on Americans to recognize that our experiment with greater freedom has failed and to "act to overcome the legacy of family disruption."

14   I don't doubt that the fragility of today's family life is hard on kids. It doesn't take a social scientist to figure out that a lone parent is more vulnerable than two to a host of pressures, or that children whose familial world has just collapsed need support that their parents, depleted by the struggle to get their own lives in order, may not be able to give. But

Whitehead's response, and that of communitarians generally, amounts to lecturing parents to pull up their socks, stop being selfish, and do their duty. This moralistic approach does not further a discussion of what to do when adults' need for satisfying relationships conflicts with children's need for stability. It merely stops the conversation.

Women, of course, are particularly susceptible to guilt   15 mongering: If children are being neglected, if marriages are failing, whose fault can it be but ours? And come on now, who is that "parent" whose career is really interfering with family life? (Hint: It's the one who gets paid less.) While the children Judith Wallerstein interviewed were clearly miserable about their parents' breakups, she made it equally clear that the parents weren't self-indulgent monsters, only people who could no longer stand the emotional deadness of their lives. Are we prepared to say that it's too bad, but their lives simply don't matter?

This is the message I get from David Blankenhorn, coeditor   16 of a pro-family anthology and newsletter, who exhorts us to "analyze the family *primarily* through the eyes of children" (my emphasis). I think this idea is profoundly wrongheaded. Certainly we need to take children seriously, which means empathizing with their relatively powerless perspective and never unthinkingly shifting our burdens to their weaker backs. On the other hand, children are more narcissistic than most adults ever dream of being—if my daughter had her way, I'd never leave the house. They too have to learn that other people's needs and feelings must be taken into account.

Besides, children are the next generation's adults. There's   17 something tragic about the idea that parents should sacrifice their own happiness for the sake of children who will grow up to sacrifice in turn (in my generation, that prospect inspired pop lyrics like, "Hope I die before I get old"). Instead of preaching sacrifice, we should be asking what it is about our social structure that puts adults and children at such terrible odds, and how we might change this. Faced with a shortage of food, would we decide parents have to starve so their kids can eat—or try to figure out how to increase food production?

Intelligent social policy on family issues has to start with a   18 deeper understanding of why marriage and the two-parent family are in trouble: not because people are more selfish than they used to be but because of basic—and basically desirable—changes in our culture. For most of history, marriage has not been primarily a moral or an emotional commitment but an economic and social contract. Men supported women and children and had unquestioned authority as head of the household. Women took care of home, children, and men's personal and sexual needs. Now that undemocratic contract, on which an entire social order rested, is all but dead. Jobs and government benefits, along with liberalized sexual mores, allow women and their children to survive (if often meagerly) outside marriage; as a result, women expect more of marriage and are less willing to put up with unsatisfying or unequal relationships. For men, on the other hand, traditional incentives to marry and stay married have eroded.

19   What's left when the old contract is gone is the desire for love, sexual passion, intimate companionship. But those desires are notoriously inadequate as a basis for domestic stability. Human emotions are unpredictable. People change. And in the absence of the social compulsion exerted by that contract, moral platitudes about sacrifice count for little. Nor is it possible to bring back the compulsion with restoring inequality as well. Restrict divorce? Men who want out will still abandon their families as they did in the past; it's women with young children and less earning power who are likely to be trapped. Punish single parenthood? Women will bear the brunt.

20   The dogmatic insistence that only the two-parent family can properly provide for children is a self-fulfilling prophecy. As even some pro-familists recognize, the larger society must begin to play an active part in meeting the economic and social needs the family once fulfilled. This means, first of all, making a collective commitment to the adequate support of every child. Beyond that, it means opening our minds to the possibility of new forms of community, in which children have close ties with a *number* of adults and therefore a stable home base that does not totally depend either on one vulnerable parent or on one couple's emotional and sexual bond.

21   Of course, no social structure can guarantee permanence: In earlier eras, families were regularly broken up by death, war and abandonment. Yet a group that forms for the specific purpose of cooperative child-rearing might actually inspire more long-term loyalty than marriage, which is supposed to provide emotional and sexual fulfillment but often does not. The practical support and help parents would gain from such an arrangement—together with the greater freedom to pursue their own personal lives—would be a strong incentive for staying in it, and the inevitable conflicts and incompatibilities among the group members would be easier to tolerate than the intense deprivation of an unhappy marriage.

It's time, in other words, to think about what has so long 22
been unthinkable, to replace reflexive dismissiveness with
questions. What, for instance, can we learn from the kib-
butz—how might some of its principles be adapted to Americans' very different circumstances? What worked and didn't
work about the communal experiments of the sixties and seventies? What about more recent projects, like groups of old
people moving in together to avoid going to nursing homes?
Or the "co-housing" movement of people who are buying land
in the suburbs or city apartment buildings and dividing the
space between private dwellings and communal facilities
such as dining rooms and child-care centers?

I'm not suggesting that there's anything like an immediate 23
practical solution to our present family crisis. What we can
do, though, is stop insisting on false solutions that scapegoat
women and oversimplify the issues. Perhaps then a real discussion—worthy of Americans' inventiveness and enduring
attraction to frontiers—will have a chance to begin.

Iris Marion Young
Making Single
Motherhood Normal

*Iris Marion Young, a philosopher by trade and a leading femi-
nist who now teaches at the University of Pittsburgh, has written* Throwing Like a Girl and Other Essays in Feminist
Philosophy and Social Theory *(1990) and* Justice and the Politics of Difference *(1990). She contributed the following essay
in the winter of 1994 to* Dissent, *a very liberal bimonthly journal
of public affairs. A few months later her essay was answered in*
Dissent *by Jean Bethke Elshtain, a prominent political scientist
from Vanderbilt who has a particular interest in family issues,
as you can see from her other essay in this book (see page 585)
and in other publications. (For instance, she contributed an
essay on the family to the same issue of* Christian Century *that
carried Don Browning and Ian Evison's article published in the
previous section of* Conversations.) *Margaret O'Brien Steinfels,
the editor of* Commonweal *magazine (a liberal publication on*

public affairs loosely associated with Catholicism—and another place where Elshtain also places some of her work), also responded in the same issue of Dissent to Young's essay, right after Elshtain's piece. Iris Young then responded to both Elshtain and Steinfels. Their entire exchange is reprinted here.

1   When Dan Quayle denounced Murphy Brown for having a baby without a husband in May 1992, most liberals and leftists recognized it for the ploy it was: a Republican attempt to win an election by an irrational appeal to "tradition" and "order." To their credit, American voters did not take the bait. The Clinton campaign successfully turned the family values rhetoric against the GOP by pointing to George Bush's veto of the Family and Medical Leave Act and by linking family well-being to economic prosperity.

2   Nonetheless, family values rhetoric has survived the election. Particularly disturbing is the fact that the refrain has been joined by people who, by most measures, should be called liberals, but who can accept only the two-parent heterosexual family. Communitarians are leading the liberal chorus denouncing divorce and single motherhood. In *The Spirit of Community*, Amitai Etzioni calls for social measures to privilege two-parent families and encourage parents to take care of young children at home. Etzioni is joined by political theorist William Galston—currently White House adviser on domestic policy—in supporting policies that will make divorce more difficult. Jean Bethke Elshtain is another example of a social liberal—that is, someone who believes in state regulation of business, redistributive economic policies, religious toleration and broad principles of free speech—who argues that not all kinds of families should be considered equal from the point of view of social policy or moral education. William Julius Wilson, another academic who has been close to Democratic party policy makers, considers out-of-wedlock birth to be a symptom of social pathology and promotes marriage as one solution to problems of urban black poverty.

3   Although those using family values rhetoric rarely mention gays and lesbians, this celebration of stable marriage is hardly good news for gay and lesbian efforts to win legitimacy for their lives and relationships. But I am concerned here with the implications of family values rhetoric for another despised and discriminated-against group: single mothers. Celebrating marriage brings a renewed stigmatization of these women, and makes them scapegoats for social

ills of which they are often the most serious victims. The only antidote to this injustice is for public policy to regard single mothers as normal, and to give them the social supports they need to overcome disadvantage.

Most people have forgotten another explicit aim of Dan 4 Quayle's appeal to family values: to "explain" the disorders in Los Angeles in May 1992. Unmarried women with children lie at the source of the "lawless social anarchy" that sends youths into the streets with torches and guns. Their "welfare ethos" impedes individual efforts to move ahead in society.

Liberal family values rhetoric also finds the "breakdown" 5 of "the family" to be a primary cause of all our social ills. "It is not an exaggeration," says Barbara Dafoe Whitehead in the *Atlantic* (April 1993) "to characterize [family disruption] as a central cause of many of our most vexing social problems, including poverty, crime, and declining school performance." Etzioni lays our worst social problems at the door of self-indulgent divorced or never-married parents. "Gang warfare in the streets, massive drug abuse, a poorly committed workforce, and a strong sense of entitlement and a weak sense of responsibility are, to a large extent, the product of poor parenting." Similarly, Galston attributed fearsome social consequences to divorce and single parenthood. "The consequences of family failure affect society at large. We all pay for systems of welfare, criminal justice, and incarceration, as well as for physical and mental disability; we are all made poorer by the inability or unwillingness of young adults to become contributing members of society; we all suffer if our society is unsafe and divided."

Reductionism in the physical sciences has faced such dev- 6 astating criticism that few serious physicists would endorse a theory that traced a one-way causal relationship between the behavior of a particular sort of atom and, say, an earthquake. Real-world physical phenomena are understood to have many mutually conditioning forces. Yet here we have otherwise subtle and intelligent people putting forward the most absurd social reductionism. In this simplistic model of society, the family is the most basic unit, the first cause that is itself uncaused. Through that magical process called socialization, families cause the attitudes, dispositions, and capacities of individual children who in turn as adults cause political and economic institutions to work or not work.

The great and dangerous fallacy in this imagery, of course, 7 is its implicit assumption that non-familial social processes do not cause family conditions. How do single-mother families "cause" poverty, for example? Any sensible look at some of these families shows us that poverty is a cause of their difficulties and failures. Doesn't it make sense to trace some of the conflicts that motivate divorce to the structure of work or to the lack of work? And what about all the causal influences on families and children over which parents have very little control—peer groups, dilapidated and understaffed schools, consumer culture, television and movie imagery, lack of investment in neighborhoods, cutbacks in public services? Families unprotected by wide networks of supportive institutions and economic resources are bound to suffer. Ignoring the myriad social conditions that affect families only enables the government and the public to escape responsibility for investing in the ghettos, building new houses and schools, and creating the millions of decent jobs that we need to restore millions of people to dignity.

8   Family-values reductionism scapegoats parents, and especially single parents, and proposes a low-cost answer to crime, poverty, and unemployment: get married and stay married.

9   Whitehead, Galston, Etzioni, and others claim that there is enough impressive evidence that divorce harms children emotionally to justify policies that discourage parents from divorcing. A closer look at the data, however, yields a much more ambiguous picture. One meta-analysis of ninety-two studies of the effects of divorce on American children, for example, finds statistically insignificant differences between children of divorced parents and children from intact families in various measures of well-being. Many studies of children of divorce fail to compare them to children from "intact" families, or fail to rule out predivorce conditions as causes. A ten-year longitudinal study released in Australia last June found that conflict between parents—whether divorced or not—is a frequent cause of emotional distress in children. This stress is mitigated, however, if the child has a close supportive relationship with at least one of the parents. Results also suggest that Australia's stronger welfare state and less adversarial divorce process may partly account for differences with U.S. findings.

10   Thus the evidence that divorce produces lasting damage to children is ambiguous at best, and I do not see how the ambiguities can be definitively resolved one way or the other. Complex and multiple social causation makes it naive to think we can conclusively test for a clear causal relationship between divorce and children's well-being. Without such certainty, how-

ever, it is wrong to suggest that the liberty of adults in their personal lives should be restricted. Galston and Etzioni endorse proposals that would impose a waiting period between the time a couple applied for divorce and the beginning of divorce proceedings. Divorce today already often drags on in prolonged acrimony. Children would likely benefit more from making it easier and less adversarial.

Although many Americans agree with me about divorce,   11 they also agree with Quayle, Wilson, Galston, and others that single motherhood is undesirable for children, a deviant social condition that policy ought to try to correct. Etzioni claims that children of single parents receive less parental supervision and support than do children in two-parent families. It is certainly plausible that parenting is easier and more effective if two or more adults discuss the children's needs and provide different kinds of interactions for them. It does not follow, however, that the second adult must be a live-in husband. Some studies have found that the addition of any adult to a single-mother household, whether a relative, lover, or friend, tends to offset the tendency of single parents to relinquish decision making too early. Stephanie Coontz suggests that fine-tuned research on single-parent families would probably find that they are better for children in some respects and worse in others. For example, although adults in single-parent families spend less time supervising homework, single parents are less likely to pressure their children into social conformity and more likely to praise good grades.

Much less controversial is the claim that children in single-   12 parent families are more often poor than those in two-parent families. One should be careful not to correlate poverty with single-parenthood, however; according to Coontz, a greater part of the increase in family poverty since 1979 has occurred in families with both spouses present, with only 38 percent concentrated in single-parent families. As many as 50 percent of single-parent families are likely to be poor, which is a shocking fact, but intact two-parent families are also increasingly likely to be poor, especially if the parents are in their twenties or younger.

It is harder to raise children alone than with at least one   13 other adult, and the stresses of doing so can take their toll on children. I do not question that children in families that depend primarily on a woman's wage-earning ability are often disadvantaged. I do question the conclusion that getting single mothers married is the answer to childhood disadvantage.

14   Conservatives have always stated a preference for two-parent families. Having liberals join this chorus is disturbing because it makes such preference much more mainstream, thus legitimizing discrimination against single mothers. Single mothers commonly experience credit and employment discrimination. Discrimination against single mothers in renting apartments was legal until 1988, and continues to be routine in most cities. In a study of housing fairness in Pittsburgh in which I participated, most people questioned said that rental housing discrimination is normal in the area. Single mothers and their children also face biases in schools.

15   There is no hope that discrimination of this sort will ever end unless public discourse and government policy recognize that female-headed families are a viable, normal, and permanent family form, rather than something broken and deviant that policy should eradicate. Around one-third of families in the United States are headed by a woman alone; this proportion is about the same world-wide. The single-mother family is not going to fade away. Many women raise children alone because their husbands left them or because lack of access to contraception and abortion forced them to bear unwanted children. But many women are single mothers by choice. Women increasingly initiate divorces, and many single mothers report being happier after divorce and uninterested in remarriage, even when they are poorer.

16   Women who give birth out of wedlock, moreover, often have chosen to do so. Discussion of the "problem" of "illegitimate" births commonly assumes the image of the irresponsible and uneducated teenager (of color) as the unwed mother. When citing statistics about rising rates of out-of-wedlock birth, journalists and scholars rarely break them down by the mother's age, occupation, and so on. Although the majority of these births continue to be to young mothers, a rising proportion are to mid-life women with steady jobs who choose to have children. Women persist in such choices despite the fact that they are stigmatized and sometimes punished for them.

17   In a world where it can be argued that there are already too many people, it may sometimes be wrong for people to have babies. The planned birth of a third child in a stable two-parent family may be morally questionable from this point of view. But principles of equality and reproductive freedom must hold that there is nothing *more* wrong with a woman in her thirties with a stable job and income having a baby than with a similar married couple.

If teen pregnancy is a social problem, this is not because   18
the mothers are unmarried, but because they are young. They
are inexperienced in the ways of the world and lack the skills
necessary to get a job to support their children; once they
become parents, their opportunities to develop those skills
usually decrease. But these remain problems even when the
women marry the young men with whom they have conceived children. Young inexperienced men today are just as ill
prepared for parenting and just as unlikely to find decent
jobs.

Although many young unmarried women who bear chil-   19
dren do so because they are effectively denied access to abortions, many of these mothers want their babies. Today the
prospects for meaningful work and a decent income appear
dim to many youth, and especially to poor youth. Having a
baby can give a young woman's life meaning, earn her
respectful attention, make her feel grown up, and give her an
excuse to exit the "wild" teenager scene that has begun to
make her uncomfortable. Constructing an education and
employment system that took girls as seriously as boys, that
trained girls and boys for meaningful and available work
would be a far more effective antidote to teen birth than rep-
rimanding, stigmatizing, and punishing these girls.

Just as we should examine the assumption that something   20
is wrong with a mid-life woman having a child without a husband, so we ought to ask a more radical question: just what *in
principle* is *more* wrong in a young woman's bearing a child
without a husband than in an older woman's doing so? When
making their reproductive decisions, everyone ought to ask
whether there are too many people in the world. Beyond that,
I submit that we should affirm an unmarried young woman's
right to bear a child as much as any other person's right.

There is reason to think that much of the world, including   21
the United States, has plural childbearing cultures. Recently I
heard a radio interview with an eighteen-year-old African
American woman in Washington, D.C. who had recently
given birth to her second child. She affirmed wanting both
children, and said that she planned to have no more. She lives
in a subsidized apartment and participates in a job training
program as a condition for receiving AFDC. She resisted the
interviewer's suggestion that there was something morally
wrong or at least unfortunate with her choices and her life.
She does not like being poor, and does not like having uncertain child care arrangements when she is away from her children. But she believes that in ten years, with hard work,

social support, and good luck, she will have a community college degree and a decent job doing something she likes, as does her mother, now thirty-four.

22   There is nothing in principle wrong with such a pattern of having children first and getting education and job training later. Indeed, millions of white professional women currently in their fifties followed a similar pattern. Most of them, of course, were supported by husbands, and not state subsidy, when they stayed home to take care of their young children. Our racism, sexism, and classism are only thinly concealed when we praise stay-at-home mothers who are married, white, and middle class, and propose a limit of two years on welfare to unmarried, mostly non-white, and poor women who do the same thing. From a moral point of view, is there an important difference between the two kinds of dependence? If there is any serious commitment to equality in the United States, it must include an equal respect for people's reproductive choices. In order for children to have equal opportunities, moreover, equal respect for parents, and especially mothers, requires state policies that give greater support to some than others.

23   If we assume that there is nothing morally wrong with single-mother families, but that they are often disadvantaged by lack of child care and by economic discrimination and social stigma, then what follows for public policy? Some of the answers to this question are obvious, some not so obvious, but in the current climate promoting a stingy and punitive welfare state, all bear discussion. I will close by sketching a few proposals.

24   1. *There is nothing in principle any more wrong with a teenage woman's choice to have a child than with anyone else's.* Still, there is something wrong with a society that gives her few alternatives to a mothering vocation and little opportunity for meaningful job training. If we want to reduce the number of teenage women who want to have babies, then education and employment policies have to take girls and women much more seriously.

25   2. *Whether poor mothers are single because they are divorced or because they never married, it is wrong for a society to allow mothers to raise children in poverty and then tell them that it's their fault when their children have deprived lives.* Only if the economy offered women decent-paying jobs, moreover, would forcing welfare women to get jobs lift them out of poverty. Of course, with good job opportunities most of them

would not need to be forced off welfare. But job training and employment programs for girls and women must be based on the assumption that a large proportion of them will support children alone. Needless to say, there is a need for massive increases in state support for child care if these women are to hold jobs. Public policy should, however, also acknowledge that taking care of children at home is work, and then support this work with unstigmatized subsidy where necessary to give children a decent life.

3. *The programs of schools, colleges, and vocational and professional training institutions ought to accommodate a plurality of women's life plans, combining childbearing and childrearing with other activities.* They should not assume that there is a single appropriate time to bear and rear children. No woman should be disadvantaged in her education and employment opportunities because she has children at age fifteen, twenty-five, thirty-five, or forty-five (for the most part, education and job structures are currently such that each of these ages is the "wrong time"). 26

4. *Public policy should take positive steps to dispel the assumption that the two-parent heterosexual nuclear family is normal and all other family forms deviant.* For example, the state should assist single-parent support systems, such as the "mothers' houses" in some European countries that provide spaces for shared child minding and cooking while at the same time preserving family privacy. 27

5. *Some people might object that my call for recognizing single motherhood as normal lets men off the hook when it comes to children.* Too many men are running out on pregnant women and on the mothers of their children with whom they have lived. They are free to seek adventure, sleep around, or start new families, while single mothers languish in poverty with their children. This objection voices a very important concern, but there are ways to address it other than forcing men to get or stay married to the mothers of their children. 28

First, the state should force men who are not poor themselves to pay child support for children they have recognized as theirs. I see nothing wrong with attaching paychecks and bank accounts to promote this end. But the objection above requires more than child support. Relating to children is a good thing in itself. Citizens who love and are committed to some particular children are more apt than others to think of the world in the long term, and to see it from the perspective of the more vulnerable people. Assuming that around one-third of households will continue to be headed by women 29 alone, men should be encouraged to involve themselves in close relationships with children, not necessarily their biological offspring.

30   6. *More broadly, the American public must cease assuming that support and care for children are the responsibility of their parents alone, and that parents who require social support have somehow failed.* Most parents require social support, some more than others. According to Coontz, for a good part of American history this fact was assumed. I am not invoking a Platonic vision of communal childrearing; children need particular significant others. But non-parents ought to take substantial economic and social responsibility for the welfare of children.

31   After health care, Clinton's next big reform effort is likely to be aimed at welfare. Condemning single mothers will legitimate harsh welfare reforms that will make the lives of some of them harder. The left should press instead for the sorts of principles and policies that treat single mothers as equal citizens.

Jean Bethke Elshtain

Single Motherhood

A Response to Iris Young

1   What I found most surprising in Iris Young's analysis ("Making Single Motherhood Normal," Winter 1994) is the radical disconnection between her policy proposals and the constraints and possibilities of our current situation. She calls for "massive increases in state support for child care" when state budgets are strapped, cutbacks are being ordered across the board, and new initiatives in health care will gobble up whatever additional revenues are available. (Presumably she supports universal health care and favors moves in that direction.) She calls for "public policy" to dispel any notion of "normality" in family structure. But, surely, we have already conducted that experiment and it has failed. It has failed for the very people it was designed to help—single mothers and

their children. I will offer up evidence on this score—evidence
Young systematically overlooks.

   She calls for states to "force men" to "pay child support for   2
children they have recognized as theirs." She claims men
shouldn't be let off the hook where their responsibilities are
concerned. But her formulation continues to put the onus for
child-rearing and child "recognition," if you will, on women.
In fact, startlingly, her argument is a call for a return to a particularly rigid form of "separate spheres," something I
thought feminists had a strong stake in criticizing and
reforming. Once again we are in a world of "women and children only," where a woman can do it all by herself, thank you.
A man could easily bypass Young's requirement by refusing to
recognize a child as "his." Who is to compel this recognition
if the institutional framework within which it has taken place
historically—the two-parent family—has been entirely dismantled as a "norm" or "ideal" of any sort? There are no
"fathers" or "daddies" in Young's universe with direct, daily
responsibility for child care and family sustenance, something not reducible to a paycheck. Still, Young would
"encourage" men to "involve themselves in close relationships
with children, not necessarily their biological offspring."
How? Why? What institutional forms will nurture and sustain such relationships? Are we to see forlorn bands of disconnected men roaming neighborhoods, knocking on doors,
and asking if there is a baby inside they can "bond" with for a
few hours? Young's rhetorical demolition of what she takes to
be onerous tradition combined with her wholly abstract,
vague pleas for connection and responsibility shows us again
that politics of denunciation and sentimentalism that undermined much of 1960s radicalism. (I know: I was there.)

   Let's enter the real world. For Young misses altogether   3
what is at stake in the travail of the present moment. She
reverts to the claim that "poverty" is the cause of all other
troubles. This is curious because Young thrashes reductionism before rapidly moving to her own reductionist formula,
namely, that any "sensible look" at the plight of poor families
reveals that "poverty" is the cause of, well, being poor. Here
she reproduces the very "one-way" causal claims she attacked
just a few sentences earlier. The problem, of course, is that
matters are far more complex than this. The mountain of evidence now available from reputable scholars tells us that cultural changes—alterations in norms and values—are not
mere epiphenomenal foam on the causal sea but are themselves vectors of economic trouble. We know that poverty is

associated with single parents. This means mothers, often very young mothers (those "babies having babies" Jesse Jackson talks about) in a father-absent situation. We also know, from the National Commission on Children, the Center for the Study of Social Policy, the U.S. Department of Health and Human Services, and dozens of other reliable sources that children growing up in single-parent households are at greater risk on every index of well-being (crime, violence, substance abuse, mental illness, dropping out of school, and so on).

4   But mark this: there is no compelling evidence that a decline in government spending accounts for the past several decades' burgeoning litany of risks to children. Economists Victor Fuchs and Diane Reklis have shown that the well-being of children worsened in a period when "purchases of goods and services for children by government rose very rapidly, as did real household income per child, and the poverty rate of children plummeted. Thus, we must seek explanations for the rising problems of that period in the cultural realm." The period to which Fuchs and Reklis refer is the 1960–1970 decade. If you continue to track direct government expenditures per child up to the present moment you find no compelling correlation between government support and child well-being per se. Indeed, we are spending more for children today in the public sphere than ever before. The sad truth is that our public investment in children is being outstripped by "private disinvestment," in other words, the breakup of the two-parent home. If you control for all other factors, *including* economic status, you learn that father absence is the single most important risk factor for children, whether one is talking about poor health or poverty or behavioral problems (the latter being a euphemistic way of gesturing toward drug addiction, being the victim or perpetrator of violence, adolescent out-of-wedlock birth, and so on). Do we change all of this by making a one-parent family suddenly "normal"? That won't stop children from suffering. That won't help a child find security and trust and safety. Of course, we should do our best for all children. But that means doing our best to create situations that do best for children, not continuing to try to patch things up when we *know*, because the evidence is in, that some familial arrangements are better for children than others.

5   The *Kids Count Data Book*, published by the liberal Center for the Study of Social Policy, one of the most widely accepted scholarly sources in this area, offers up annual "Profiles of Child Well-Being." The most recent profile included the fol-

lowing startling information. Researchers looked at two groups and compared them: couples who completed high school, married, and waited until age twenty to have their first child against couples who did none of the above—they neither married nor finished school, and in which the girl gave birth before age twenty. In the first group, the number of children who fell below the poverty line was 8 percent. In the second group, the number of children who fell below the poverty line was a startling 79 percent. What this suggests is that marriage, somewhat delayed child-bearing, and high school completion—cultural and educational factors—fuel economic outcomes. It is high time we set aside economic reductionism of the sort Young oddly endorses and looked to the dissolution of the fabric of families and communities, a tragedy entangled with the repudiation of those "norms" for male and female responsibility for children that Young finds oppressive because they "stigmatize" single mothers. The stigma attached to single motherhood has virtually disappeared, if we trust the survey data, but the problems associated with the children of single parents do not go away so readily.

If we are to see investment "in the ghettos," the building of   6 new houses and schools, the creation of "millions of decent jobs," no less, we need people capable of holding jobs; we need secure social institutions; we need children who are compelled by parents to stay in school; we need all the things Young blithely ignores. The most successful organizing for change over the past fifty years has come from poor and working-class communities who form broad-based coalitions to work for housing, jobs, schools, in the most devastated urban areas—from Brownsville to San Antonio. I have in mind, for example, the activities of the Industrial Areas Foundation. If Young wants to see revitalization of communities in action she should check out the work of the East Brooklyn Congregations (EBC) and their Nehemiah Homes project or Baltimoreans United in Leadership Development (BUILD), a group that has made significant strides in school reform in the inner city. There are dozens and dozens of such examples. The organizing base is families and churches—the remnants of intact institutions—for you cannot make lasting, meaningful change of any kind outside institutions.

Civic philosophy dies when academics, in the name of rad-   7 icalism, in the name, heaven help us, of that democratic socialism for which this journal has traditionally stood, endorse values that erode the only possible bases for creating and sustaining community institutions over time—calling for more individualism (hence Young's celebration of an individual woman's "choice" to have a baby whether she is thirteen years old or fifty, as if that choice and not any consideration of the child's well-being were the only value at stake); more vast government projects, hence more clientage; normlessness as a norm; and on and on. It is depressing to see these old nostrums refurbished as radical or reformist when they could scarcely be more conformist—to the naively anti-institutionalist, hyper-individualist tendencies of our time, with a heavy dollop of "separate spheres with a feminist face" thrown in for good measure.

Margaret O'Brien Steinfels
Rights and Responsibilities
A Response to Iris Young

1　　Fully achieved, Iris Young's proposals would be a disaster for women and children, probably for men too, and certainly for liberal and left politics.

2　　She is wrong on three points, at least: single mothers are *not* despised; liberals don't view single mothers as the sole source of our social ills; liberalism has *not* abandoned its heritage by rallying to the two-parent family.

3　　If only *Time* magazine had made Marla Maples—an unwed mother—the woman of the year, we would fully realize that a mother's unwedded state is no bar to celebrity or social lionizing—and a kiss on the cheek from (former) Mayor David Dinkins. The press and television treat single motherhood as a variant of the American family. I suspect that teachers, principals, social workers, acquaintances, and neighbors don't ask and don't care. That changes when the individual choice of single motherhood becomes a collective responsibility. It is women who have children that they can't support or get fathers to support that exercise tax-paying Americans, at least some of whom are single-mother families themselves! Plain and simple, the problem is not single mothers but single mothers who depend on the rest of us to support them and their children.

The Reagan administration and accompanying pundits   4
convinced the American electorate that the welfare system
now functions as a dowry system for adolescent girls, who,
becoming pregnant, are launched into motherhood and
adulthood with food stamps, child support, housing allow-
ances, and Medicaid long before they are ready to be good
mothers. And it doesn't end there, the critics go on: rather
than supporting people in need until they can get back on
their feet, the system is failing children and undermining
young men's sense of responsibility for their children. Conservatives think that welfare is hurting poor people. Among others, a lot of poor people agree with them.

This analysis has penetrated the thinking of Democrats   5
and other liberals. Some speak of job training, of community
service in return for welfare. Some speak of two-year limits;
others of withholding aid for infants born when a woman is
already on welfare; all stand behind that once unthinkable
policy of dunning delinquent dads for court-ordered child
support. Even Wisconsin, with its tradition of progressive
politics, is bailing out of the federal welfare system in order to
limit and control in its own expenditures.

Should these be counted traitors to the liberal cause?   6

Those old enough to remember will recall that liberals cre-   7
ated the welfare system to keep families together, to help tide
over those in temporary trouble, and to help widows maintain a household. Aid to Families with Dependent Children
(AFDC) and other welfare measures were never meant to support teenage moms or help their boyfriends elude the responsibilities of fatherhood; nor were they intended to make up
for missing child-support payments. The system has been
adapted to meet these needs on the assumption that women
with children often have no other recourse. Often they do not.
When, however, the system itself seems to encourage unwed
motherhood or male abandonment and to contribute to family breakdown, reasonable people ask their politicians why.
To their credit some liberals are reconsidering the merits of
the two-parent family. Were two-parent families to come back
into vogue, our social ills would not disappear. But there is
reason to expect that children would have saner, more secure,
and—boys especially—more disciplined upbringings. These
would be a good in themselves.

Iris Young wants us to assume that "there is nothing mor-   8
ally wrong with single-mother families." What does she
mean? Women of any age, educational attainment, income

level, or marital status should be able to bear and raise a child. I agree. At least I agree that no one else—the state, the father, the woman's relatives—has a right to force a woman to get an abortion if she is pregnant. Or force her to use contraception. Or, barring abusive or seriously neglectful behavior, take her child from her. In that sense the mother-child relationship is sacrosanct; the right to conceive and bear a child is basic.

9   But not every exercise of a "right" adds up to a moral good. Nations have a right to protect their sovereignty; not every act in pursuit of that right is moral. Individuals in our society have a right to free speech; not every sentence uttered in exercising that right constitutes a moral good. The analogy applies to childbearing decisions: it may be a right, but that does not make it a moral good. Single motherhood—though not wrong in and of itself—can undermine the well-being of others.

10   First, there is the child and his or her need for care, comfort, and stability—constant attention as an infant and consistent attention as a child and adolescent. Even with two (or more) adults, this is an arduous undertaking spanning more than two decades. Can single-mother families really meet this responsibility? Many do; many others do not.

11   Then, consider alternative child-care support systems. There is the woman's own family, which may be her surest recourse. But what if this, too, is a single-mother family? or siblings need attention? or husband and wife both work? A single mother's need may be great, but families have limits. Other child-caring facilities—day-care centers, schools, camps—are available, but they may be overwhelmed with the needs of materially and emotionally deprived children. Young believes more money and more personnel are the answer. But can a single mother (or father) act on the assumption that they are? And from where do these additional and abundant new resources come?

12   This brings us to the question of the common good and the implicit social contract on which it rests. Young refers to the "state" and the "welfare state" as if these were entities capable of delivering goods and services at will. The United States is a democracy that eventually comes to reflect—if only imperfectly—the views of its citizens. Underlying at least some of the critical views of welfare—which Young thinks stingy—is a sense of quid pro quo: Social responsibility ought to encourage individual responsibility, not undermine or replace it. Is that unreasonable? The reservoirs of social responsibility that Young wants to draw upon will be swiftly depleted in a society

whose citizens, women and men alike, do not habitually feel and exercise responsibility for themselves and their families.

Our social experiment in single motherhood over the last twenty-five years is failing great numbers of women and children while corroding the bonds that tie men to familial responsibilities. In the name of reform, we should not take from them the admittedly meager resources provided by the current system. But neither can opinion makers, academics, or intellectual elites, feminist and otherwise, go on arguing that this situation is normal, and will be made even "more normal" by increased welfare payments and better support systems. 13

The communitarians have a slogan that we might all take to heart: strong rights entail strong responsibilities—that goes for the right to bear and raise children. 14

Iris Marion Young
Response to Elshtain and Steinfels

Jean Elshtain and Margaret Steinfels and I agree at least on one thing: too many children are poor, badly educated, at risk of being un- or underemployed, becoming substance dependent, criminal, or dead. What we disagree on are the solutions to these problems. Indeed, for all their strong language, I find neither offering any action. Calls for "secure institutions," restoring the "fabric of families," and living up to "strong responsibilities" are empty exhortations unless we specify just who should take responsibility to do what. The form of the rhetoric, moreover, leaves the impression that it's "they" and not "we" who have shirked responsibilities. This vague rhetoric seems to function as an excuse not only for doing nothing, but for not even thinking about what to do. 1

Elshtain and Steinfels both claim that "we" have undertaken a "social experiment" in single motherhood that has "failed." What odd phrasing! Who are "we" who designed such a cruel "experiment"? But, of course, no one designed the patchwork of plural family living arrangements in the United States today. In some respects, it has always been with 2

us. There is no question, however, that the last two decades
have seen more divorce and less marriage, though the rate of
teenage pregnancy has not in fact increased.

3   What do Elshtain and Steinfels propose that we do about
the lives of children? We should, in the words of Elshtain,
"create situations that do best for children," that is, promote
intact two-parent families. But how shall we do that? It is
hard to believe that Elshtain and Steinfels would forbid
divorce. Perhaps they favor making divorce more difficult, as
some recommend, with a waiting period. This assumes that
couples now rush into divorce without thinking, which is for
the most part not so. Since divorce in the United States is
already painful and costly, especially when there are children,
making divorce more difficult is not likely to reduce apprecia-
bly the number of divorces.

4   And what shall we do about women who give birth without
being married? Again, Elshtain and Steinfels would not force
abortions, and I suspect that they would not force men to
marry and live with the women they have impregnated.
Would they recommend punishing women who give birth out
of wedlock as a deterrent to others, or punishing fathers who
do not marry them? This alternative is frighteningly close to
the minds of some people in the current debate, but it doesn't
sound like Elshtain or Steinfels. Perhaps the carrot is a better
idea: cash awards and medals for couples who get and stay
married.

5   The most that Elshtain's and Steinfels's calls for restoration
of family values and responsibilities can mean practically is
that public discussion promote the idea that intact two-parent families are better than other families; churches, schools,
community groups, perhaps occasional television ad campaigns should send out this message. If such a society-wide
educational campaign were implemented, it might indeed
have some measurable impact on marriage and divorce rates,
but I submit not very much. Thus I find Elshtain and Steinfels recommending virtually no social action to improve the
lives of children.

6   Their insistence that although women have a "right" to parent alone, their family lives are less valuable, moreover, is an
affront to the worth and dignity of women who have tried
marriage and found it wanting, are out on their own with their
children, and are not interested in a new husband. Is a liberal
society really to condemn these women, and if it does can it
claim it is respecting them as equal citizens?

With the communitarian refrain, "strong rights entail   7
strong responsibilities," Steinfels suggests that it's about time
the parents of those children did something, instead of sitting
around waiting for handouts from the state. Elshtain, too,
suggests a kind of quid pro quo: if we are to see investment in
dilapidated neighborhoods, building of new schools and
houses, we need secure social institutions and children who
are compelled by their parents to stay in school. Once parents
get off their duffs and build these institutions and discipline
their children, then maybe we can talk about social support.

Are Elshtain and Steinfels really suggesting that single   8
mothers (not all of whom are poor) or poor people (not all of
whom are in families with one parent) are, as a group, more
irresponsible than other people? When middle-class, married
couples refuse to support the local school system through a
tax increase, complain about the quality of the schools, and
enroll their kids in private school, are they behaving responsibly? When bank executives refuse to make loans to home-
owners and businesses in poor neighborhoods and invest
instead in risky tourism ventures on the other side of the
country, are they behaving responsibly? I submit that irre-
sponsibility is randomly distributed across race, class, gender, and family form, and I agree that there is far too much of
it. But I also submit that most people most of the time are trying to meet their responsibilities to their families, friends,
and coworkers. Less often, perhaps, do people think about
and meet their responsibilities to distant strangers, but here
responsibility increases with social privilege. We live in a time
of a "responsibility deficit," some say, but I don't know the
measure of responsibility levels. If the measure for single
mothers is the income level of their children and the state of
the schools, health clinics, and parks in the neighborhoods
where they live, then this is a most unforgivable example of
blaming the victims.

I completely agree with Elshtain that a vigorous and just   9
society depends on the active participation of citizens in civic
institutions of their own making, either not connected or only
loosely connected to the state—neighborhood cleanup crews,
parent councils in schools, volunteer social services, community arts and culture centers, cooperatives, political advocacy
organizations. Despite communitarian complaints, I find no
evidence that this sort of volunteer community organizing
and service provision has waned in the United States in the
last two decades. The heroic activities of organizations like
the Industrial Areas Foundation or the Cabrini Green Tenants

Association, which Elshtain applauds, are very often led by single mothers. Other such volunteer civic activities are led by the "forlorn bands of disconnected men" Elshtain imagines "roaming neighborhoods." Many men run athletic and cultural programs for children, or volunteer in tutoring centers, drug-prevention, and skills-building workshops. Despite what I regard as a healthy level of civic activity in the United States among people of both genders and all races and classes, there is certainly need for more. Public expenditures on street lighting and better transportation, along with private corporate decisions to reduce working hours without reducing pay, might enable more people to engage in more self-defined civic activities to improve their lives and their neighborhoods.

10   It is Elshtain and Steinfels who have their heads in the sand if they think that "private disinvestment" in the two-parent family has destroyed our schools and taken jobs away from the neighborhoods. American society has been severely damaged by three decades of private and public disinvestment in basic manufacturing, new and rehabilitated housing, bridges and rail lines, public education, adult retraining, and social services such as preventive health care and libraries. Volunteers can only barely begin to fill these gaping holes in the American dream.

11   Elshtain and Steinfels write as though I have called for more of the same tired old welfare policies in order to respond to the stresses of single motherhood and the economic disadvantage many children suffer. But my policy principles call for social *investment* (this word that Elshtain seems to find so hyperbolic), not draining handouts. Private industry should bear as much responsibility for this investment, moreover, as government does. Elshtain suggests that a condition for the creation of decent jobs is that children be motivated to stay in school. Only a little reflection should suggest that precisely the reverse is true. She accuses me of resuscitating a separate spheres ideology that would keep women at home caring for children, yet scoffs at my call for the massive increases in state support for child care that would enable more mothers—and fathers—to work outside the home and volunteer, knowing that their children were cared for. Steinfels suggests that parents cannot assume that more money and personnel will make quality child care more available and affordable. I do not understand why we cannot assume that it would help a great deal.

Neither Elshtain nor Steinfels mentions the single most   12
important cause of the economic disadvantage in which children of many single mothers live: low wages for women's
work. Coupled with the scarcity or expense of child care, low
wages make it rational for many women to stay on welfare.
Millions of single mothers nevertheless take jobs that enable
them and their children only barely to escape poverty, if that.
We do not have to accept as given the sex segregation of
women's work that helps keep those wages low. It is simple
sexism to decide that the only way to pull the children of single mothers out of poverty is to get them live-in fathers; it is
also an unrealistic expectation, since male unemployment
rates have been steadily rising in the last decade, and male
wage rates have been falling. Public and private programs
should be devoted to training women for higher wage jobs and
raising the wages of traditionally female jobs. This is not a
wasteful handout; it is justice.

Decent schools, housing, infrastructure, decent jobs for all   13
able to work, wage equalization, and affordable child care
can come about only through significant levels of public
spending combined with both coerced and voluntary efforts
of private capital. Elshtain and Steinfels throw up their hands
at the absurdity of such a statement in these days "when state
budgets are strapped, cutbacks are being ordered across the
board." Are these facts of nature? If caring progressives treat
them as such, then we are certainly doomed. Americans must
engage in a serious and prolonged discussion of public and
private spending and taxation, with the aim of shifting
resources from waste and quick profits to investment in people and neighborhoods.

Topping the agenda for such discussion must be the fat pub-   14
lic larder where we still see very little in the way of cutbacks:
military spending. According to the Center for Defense Information, Clinton's 1994 budget contains $340 billion in military
spending, only $10 billion lower than Bush's 1993 budget.
Compare this to $54 billion for education and social services,
or $11 billion for community and regional development. In his
State of the Union Address, Clinton vowed not to cut another
dime from military spending. Surely this is madness. I
wouldn't say that we should leave ourselves defenseless, or
even unable to fight one imperialist war at a time; let's just take
half of that $340 billion over the next five years and rechannel
it into job-creating schools, day-care centers, new houses and
apartments, steel, clean trains, parks, libraries, bridges and
roads, and, yes, community organizing clearinghouses.

WHO "OWNS" THIS CHILD?

Susan Squire

Anatomy of a Custody Case

The following essay appeared in the March 1995 issue of Harper's Bazaar, *a magazine with articles and features particularly intended for women. Susan Squire writes often for the magazine, as you can see from the other example of her work in* Conversations, *on page 439.*

1   It was not, the judge remembers, an easy call: Here were a mother and a father, both with careers, both involved with their two young sons, both "clearly fit" parents—yet he had to pick one over the other.

2   No custody decision is easy, of course, especially if you do it the way New York Supreme Court Justice Lewis R. Friedman does—orally, from the bench, just after testimony is concluded. You've got to look both people in the eye and make one of them deeply unhappy, and for that you need a strong stomach and a hell of a lot of faith in your own instincts.

3   In six days of testimony enough had been said to fill some 1300 pages of transcript. The father, who initiated the custody suit, spoke first, followed by the older boy's kindergarten teacher. Then came the court-appointed psychiatrist, Myles Schneider, the family housekeeper, and some 15 other witnesses. The mother, as the defendant, testified on the last day, September 13, 1993.

4   Lewis Friedman is a garrulous, twice-married man just the slightest bit smug about his own amicable divorce. He has a tart, flippant wit and a maverick air. In reaching his custody decisions, he says, he relies heavily on his personal observations of the warring spouses. Using himself as a reality check, Friedman explains, gives him "insight into whether the psychiatrist is 'OTL'"—out to lunch—"or is making sense."

5   Friedman didn't go for Schneider's negative emphasis on the wife's "demanding career goals" as opposed to the husband's: "Whether a more active, more dynamic career is bet-

ter or worse for the children is simply not a psychiatrist's place to resolve," the judge stated, adding that "the children will do well with either of them...." But the school year was starting, and the children needed a primary residence. Would it be with their father in the Manhattan loft (known in court papers as "the marital residence")? Or with their mother in the Montclair, NJ, house that was supposed to—but now would never—be the family home?

In the end, Friedman concurred with Schneider's recom-   6
mendation. He awarded sole legal and physical custody of five-year-old Maxx and three-year-old Myles to their father, Ron Brawer, a 50-year-old music director of the soap opera *Another World*. The 31-year-old mother, Tonya Pinkins, had lost, resoundingly. She is a Tony Award–winning actress (for her performance as Sweet Anita in *Jelly's Last Jam*) and until recently played attorney Livia Frye-Cudahy on the soap opera *All My Children*. (Livia, as it happens, occasionally litigated child-custody cases and was a black woman married to a white man—like Tonya Pinkins.)

Pinkins had nursed her sons, organized their parties,   7
taught them hopscotch, hired babysitters, researched pre-schools, made photographic collages for each year of their lives. Her dressing room at *All My Children* was outfitted with *Aladdin* wallpaper, Legos, and Ninja Turtle costumes to amuse the boys when they visited. Yet as of September 1993 she would be their "noncustodial" parent, her access to them limited by Friedman's visitation order (alternate weekends and holidays, half of each summer, one or two midweek sup-pers). And her customary involvement in parental decision-making would now be denied her. "Ms. Pinkins shall not obtain medical, dental nor psychiatric care, consultations or testing for the children without Mr. Brawer's prior written consent," the judge ordered.

Why did this mother lose and this father win?   8

All contested custody cases share a few elements: enor-   9
mous financial expense, byzantine (sometimes reprehensible) legal tactics, and a willingness on the part of both spouses to engage in mutual psychic torture. But that's about it. The idiosyncrasies far outnumber the similarities.

Still, it's tempting to indulge in trend-spotting. In Septem-   10
ber 1994, a year after Friedman's decision in *Brawer* v. *Pinkins*, a Washington, DC, lawyer named Sharon Prost lost her two sons to her former husband, Kenneth Greene, the assistant executive director of the American Federation of Television and Radio Artists. According to news reports, the

judge perceived Prost as "a driven workaholic" and Greene as "a doting father."

11   Some who watch the legal scoreboard have already insisted that *Greene* v. *Prost* and *Brawer* v. *Pinkins* are examples of working mothers being punished not just for working, but for being more successful, more ambitious, even for having more "demanding career goals" than their spouses. But if women want the option to pursue power, fame, and fat paychecks in a society free of gender bias, can they also continue to expect the automatic edge in a custody dispute?

12   The answer, these days, is no.

13   It is apparent from the court record that Ron Brawer and Tonya Pinkins, married six years, had adjusted to parenthood as many urban dual-career couples do. Which is to say that the father's life remains essentially unchanged while the mother makes countless adjustments. For Tonya Pinkins, this included biking home between performances to nurse a new baby and arranging to show up at the theater a half hour later than everyone else in the *Jelly's Last Jam* cast so she could spend more time with her sons.

14   Not that Tonya was an ideal mother—whatever that means. She could be impatient with the boys; sometimes she even yelled at them. (The housekeeper testified that Ron never got impatient, never yelled.) Tonya could be maddeningly irresponsible, sometimes dangerously so ("Our children," Ron faxed her in November 1993, *"must not* be allowed to roam at will in the cargo area of your station wagon..."). At times she exercised bad judgment (calling her husband "a stupid motherfucker" within earshot of Maxx and Myles). But Tonya's greatest failing, it seems, is that her imperfections were right there, in plain sight, readily available for the opposing counsel to exploit.

15   Was Ron Brawer chosen because he leads a structured, predictable life? Because he appears, in Friedman's words, "laid back"? Was Tonya Pinkins rejected because she lives more chaotically, with more emotional intensity? Judges do tend to place young children in the more ordered environment and with the less volatile parent. But in his decision, Friedman said only that Brawer "is at this moment better able to provide both emotional and intellectual guidance and quality of life that is consistent with the best interests of these children"; he did not offer details. A year later, in his chambers in downtown Manhattan, the judge shrugs when I ask him for specifics. "There was nothing about either of them that strikes you as being terrific," Friedman says. "He was the

better choice of the two because"—long pause. "There's not a single 'because' that fits. It's a matter of totality. . . ."

The "totality," drawn from an analysis of the court record 16 and interviews with the principals, seems to consist of this: Tonya Pinkins is an angry woman, and angry women should not get custody because. . . .

There's not a single "because" that fits.   17

Tonya Pinkins, raised Christian on Chicago's South Side, 18 has been a professional actress and singer since she was 14. She was hired for her first Broadway show during Christmas break of her freshman year at Carnegie Mellon. When the play opened that fall, she dropped out of school.

Ron Brawer was 18 years her senior, born into a middle- 19 class Jewish family on the Upper West Side of Manhattan. He graduated from the University of Wisconsin at Madison in 1964, then did the hippie thing—bummed around Europe as a troubadour, got busted for drugs, learned leatherwork. As an adult he continued to dabble: He wrote music and poetry and fiction, had a mobile DJ company, occasionally worked for a family-owned health club. Then he decided to try record producing. In early 1986 Procter & Gamble music director Jill Diamond, who happened to be Ron's ex-lover, suggested he audition this 23-year-old black singer she knew.

Tonya walked into Ron's loft on West 22nd Street to find a 20 striking, enigmatic man awaiting her. ("Attractive," Diamond had warned her, "in an unusual way.") From that moment on, Tonya says, she was madly in love. Ron describes it as "definitely a chemical shock" when they met.

Tonya did not get the job, but by June, Ron had rented his 21 loft and moved into her six-room riverview apartment in Washington Heights. Less than a year later, on February 10, 1987, they became husband and wife. It was his first marriage, her second. (She and her first husband had recently parted—childlessly and amicably—after two years.)

Tonya and Ron tried to overcome their problems, which 22 had been apparent ever since they moved in together, through couples counseling. But the differences between them were vast—in age, background, temperament, and of course, race. (That she was black and he was white, possibly posing identity problems for their two children in years to come, was an issue raised by Tonya's trial attorney, Ellen Gesmer, but was dismissed by Friedman as not "central" to the case.)

There were smaller differences, too, the ones that over 23 time can make marriage a quotidian hell. Housekeeping style, for instance: "He hates clutter," Tonya says, with her usual self-revealing frankness, "and I'm a total pig." And dietary preferences: Ron favored an austere regimen of ricotta, fruit, and lettuce; she preferred home fries and grits. (Tonya described under oath his prohibition against her bringing meat into the house and how, whenever she would dare to cook anything in his presence, "he would sneer over me... and tell me that I was poisoning our children.")

24   On November 15, 1987, Maxx was born at home, in the West 22nd Street loft, in the big copper Wisconsin cheese vat that served as the family bathtub. Ron and a midwife assisted Tonya in her labor. Tonya, who wasn't working then, claims she spent all her time in those early postpartum months with Maxx, while Ron, ignoring wife and baby, locked himself in his study for hours, working on a detective novel. Ron, meanwhile, says that while he was indeed hard at work on a novel, Maxx was always with him: "He virtually lived in a Snugli strapped to my chest."

25   Soon after Tonya gave birth to Myles—in the same copper cheese vat on June 19, 1990—she began planning to move the family out of the city. She and Ron ultimately decided on Montclair, a racially balanced community with excellent schools, and close to midtown Manhattan. In January 1992 they bought a house there and began renovations, while they continued living in the loft. On May 31, she won the Tony. The subsequent blitz of media attention focused on Tonya further strained the marriage.

26   The house was ready by early November, when Ron took the boys on a weeklong vacation to Jamaica. He says the purpose of the trip was so that Tonya could move out of the loft and into the house, thus paving the way for their mutually-agreed-upon separation without exposing the children to undue stress. Tonya says she had no inkling of the purported separation and that the purpose of the trip to Jamaica was to relieve Ron of the tedious business of moving, which he told her he hated; she had volunteered to do the work while the rest of the family was away.

27   An upsetting tug-of-war occurred on November 16, when Tonya insisted, against her older son's tearful protests, on taking both kids to the New Jersey house. The episode led Ron to believe that she'd already been advised by a lawyer to get the boys into her possession. "At that point," Ron says, "I thought I had better speak to an attorney." Miraculously, although it was already 9:00 P.M. on a Monday and Ron says he had never thought about lawyers until that moment, he managed to

reach the canny matrimonial attorney Patricia Hennessey (who is particularly adept at navigating the new byways of fathers' rights). She just happened to be in her office.

Then, on the 21st, as Tonya was leaving a matinee performance of *Jelly*, a process server thrust the divorce papers into her hand. She says she was stunned. Ron says he's stunned that she was stunned, since they'd already agreed to divorce. 28

The kids were with Tonya in Montclair during Thanksgiving week. Ron visited the children often that week; on Thanksgiving and the day after he brought his mother along, too. On that Friday, Tonya recalled at the trial, she and Ron agreed that the kids would spend the next day at the loft and then the whole family would have dinner there. After this cozy plan was made, her mother-in-law handed her a writ of habeas corpus—an aggressive legal maneuver alleging that Ron was being denied access to his children and knowledge of their whereabouts. 29

It was the preemptive strike in the battle of custody that would culminate, 10 months later, in Judge Friedman's decision. 30

Once upon a time, judges generally subscribed to the "tender years" doctrine, which held that mothers (barring bizarre behavior that rendered them unfit guardians) had a presumptive right to their young children. In the last two decades cultural notions of paternal and maternal rights have been practically upended. Today, although the matrimonial courtroom is supposed to represent a level playing field, it increasingly seems that all a father has to do to be looked upon favorably in a custody battle is make dinner for the kids a few nights a week and hire a killer lawyer. 31

Presumably, judges assign custody based on the best interests of the child. There are recognized guidelines for what constitutes "best interests," but these are often applied subjectively. "Is there a degree of arbitrariness?" Friedman asks, then answers the question himself: "Probably." 32

There is "the friendly parent" rule: The parent who appears most able or willing to encourage the child's relationship with the other parent has an edge in a custody fight. Judges also look for "the altruistic parent," who shapes his or her life around the child; for "the primary caretaker," who arranges play dates and doctors' visits and stays home when the kid is sick; and for "the psychological parent"—"the one the child wants when he's throwing up," as one lawyer puts it. 33

But establishing the identity of the better custodial parent (especially, as in *Brawer* v. *Pinkins*, when both mother and 34 father are deemed fit, and both have careers) is increasingly a matter of lawyerly strategy and of spin control.

35   Harriet N. Cohen of Cohen Hennessey & Bienstock says this about her firm's client Ron Brawer: "He's like the gold standard.... His parenting style is like mothering. Now when people come in here [seeking representation], we have the following test: Is he a Ron?" Cohen's partner Patricia Hennessey, who litigated the case for Ron, is more specific. "He did what women classically did: went to part-time work. So that if a kid is sick at school you can go and pick the kid up." Of course, the court record shows that Ron Brawer did *not* go to part-time work out of commitment to his children. He worked part-time because he was *already* working part-time. But the facts don't matter if they can be shrewdly made to fit the image that the lawyer and client have chosen to project.

36   Anyway, here were these two fit-enough parents who each, being human, left something to be desired. Friedman, far from seeing Ron as "the gold standard" of parenthood, refers to him as "a very strange duck." And Tonya, it seems, was too intense for the judge on just about every level. Would she have triumphed if she'd seemed more submissive—more like the classic female victim? Not with this judge, says Lewis Friedman. "The joke is, if you were going to psychoanalyze me, you'd find that the stronger a woman is the more I'd like her." But likability, Friedman insists, has nothing to do with rendering a decision unless it pertains to custody issues. Such as? "They haven't taken a shower in a month.... That may have some bearing," he says.

37   Poor hygiene wasn't Tonya Pinkins' problem—her problem was anger. Or maybe it was Friedman's problem. The judge certainly referred to it again and again. As he said on September 13, 1993: "If one would miss [her anger] during the course of this hearing one would have to be blind." In his visitation order three weeks later, he mentioned "[the] wife's...palpably obvious anger...." And in a March 1994 court document, he said: "[The] wife's papers continue to demonstrate the extreme anger and hostility that permeated the courtroom."

38   Yet there is no discernible evidence of her anger in 1300 pages of transcript—no outbursts, no dirty words, not even a sarcastic aside. What then was it about Tonya Pinkins' anger that was so palpable, so permeating, so... *angry?*

39   "You'd have to have been there," Friedman says. It was her "body language, tone...the way she'd react to words that [Brawer] said while he was on the stand...." Still, Friedman acknowledges that "some of what [Brawer] was doing was

designed to provoke her kind of overreaction.... Everyone
wants to give the other a hard time."

By "overreaction" Friedman is presumably referring to   40
Tonya's dramatic moves during the summer of 1993. She
managed to get Ron arrested twice—on the first occasion
because, she claimed, he defied a court order requiring him
to leave the loft during her scheduled visits with the children;
on the second because Ron changed the lock on the loft door.
(The cops, whose response was curiously aggressive for this
kind of marital dispute, even had Ron spend a night in jail.)

Why was Friedman perturbed by Tonya's anger and her   41
subsequent act of calling the police, yet not by Ron's anger,
expressed passively by changing the lock? Friedman seems to
think it was Tonya's fault that the cops were so zealously protective of her. ("You know," he says disdainfully, "stars get different treatment than you and I do.") But why doesn't he see
both spouses' maneuvers as examples of everyone wanting
"to give the other a hard time"?

And there is the disturbing "Maxx script." Friedman "didn't 42
know what to make of it." So, he made of it nothing at all.

It's a horror-movie screenplay, which Tonya testified was   43
Ron's gift to her while she was pregnant with Myles. The
characters include a man named Ron, who eats ricotta and
fruit for breakfast, his pregnant wife named Tonya, who eats
home fries and grits, and their toddler named Maxx. And
there is another couple: Jill (the name of Ron's real-life ex-
girlfriend, Jill Diamond) and her husband, Don (the name of
the real-life Jill's real-life husband). By the end of the script,
which takes place at Jill and Don's country house (the real Jill
and Don do have a country house) with all five characters
present, the character Ron has had alfresco sex with the character Jill, and everyone (except the character Maxx) dies,
killed by each other, including the Tonya character's newborn
baby, who is killed by the character Maxx....

Ron admitted under oath that he did write it, that he gave   44
it to Tonya when she was pregnant with Myles, and that
Tonya "didn't like it." When asked about the script recently, he
says, "It was just a tempest in a teapot.... These were ideas
we were all kicking around." Later he calls to say, "It wasn't
even my idea."

No one's suggesting that the Maxx script is the literal   45
expression of Ron's wishes. But since Friedman took into
account such subjective measures as Tonya's tone of voice
and body language in gauging her level of anger and hostility
toward her spouse (and therefore her capacity to be the

custodial parent), shouldn't this judge, a man who so prides himself on the veracity of his gut reactions, have made *something* of the Maxx script?

46   Ron Brawer's thick curtain of hair is a major statement: It has a shielding effect. Samson-like armor against intruders. He wears mostly black and is very slender, very tall, very still, with large hands and perfectly clean, unbitten nails. Although he never taps his foot or evinces other nervous mannerisms, he seems tightly wound.

47   Ron and I talk in his attorney Patricia Hennessey's office, at her suggestion. Ron, often glancing at her, says all the right things, as if programmed. (Q: "How are the boys adjusting?" A: "Very well. Maxx is in second grade now, reading on a sixth-grade level, and. . . .") He attributes both boys' serenity, in part, to a children's self-help book called *Dinosaurs Divorce.* Helpfully, Hennessey produces this book from the shelf behind her desk as soon as Ron mentions the title.

48   "At first," Ron continues, "they didn't want to read the whole thing. So every once in a while I'd pick it up and say, 'Do you want to read a little more?' until we got through it." Then he produces from his briefcase, without being asked, a small photo album: his candids of the boys cavorting on the beach, and more formal portraits, some including Ron, by a professional children's photographer.

49   Tonya does not carry pictures of her sons around with her, although there are shots of Maxx and Myles in her car and other photographs mounted on the walls of her rented house in Vancouver, where she is currently shooting a TV series called *University Hospital.*

50   It is nearly Thanksgiving 1994, and Tonya is back in New York for a visit. She proposes we meet in a beauty salon on Lexington near 29th Street, where she sits with gunky foil in her hair, eating Chinese food from paper cartons. Dressed in Levi's and a white waffle-weave T-shirt, she's full of beans and wisecracks, anything but tightly wound. Perhaps because she seems less programmed than Ron Brawer, she also seems more flawed and more vulnerable.

51   Ask her how the boys are adjusting and she says, "I think okay. Maxx is having more trouble than Myles. He's more disassociated; he says he doesn't have feelings."

52   Friedman excoriated her in the visitation order for her "demonstrated falsehoods from the witness stand" (though nothing was conclusively demonstrated) and says later, informally, that "she made some stuff up." He also says that Ron

"may have made stuff up, too.... Somewhere between the two is the truth."

Yet it is Tonya who seems the more candid of the pair—to her detriment. It didn't help her with Friedman to testify that, in media interviews, she tries to "invent entertaining stories" with "a grain of truth" and that her quotes to the press represent "a performance...not reality." It's hard to imagine Ron Brawer saying anything so recklessly forthright.

Maybe it all came down to a difference in style: She exaggerates, he downplays. Both are ways of shading the truth. Why was his way judged to be more appropriate for a custodial parent?

Now it is early in the New Year, and Tonya Pinkins feels blessed. Just before Christmas she flew to New York to pick up Maxx and Myles for a five-day vacation in Los Angeles, and promptly came down with a terrible flu. Sick as she was, she had a "glorious" time. "My biggest fear," she says, "was that they'd forget me if I wasn't there every day, [that] I wouldn't be important in their lives anymore. They taught me that wasn't true."

She read aloud to them from Madeleine L'Engle's *A Wrinkle in Time,* and the boys fought over who could sit next to her and hold her hand, just like they always had, and they asked questions about God and told her their prayers even though, Tonya marvels, "their daddy says there is no God.... That they still pray and believe in God amazes me because I'm not there to influence them that way."

She's not so scared anymore about time passing, or about being forgotten. "It seems they love him and they love me," she says, "and somehow they've made their peace with all of it."

The legal skirmishes between Ron and Tonya continue, however. There are, among other pending matters, Tonya's appeal of the custody decision; Ron's $6-million federal lawsuit against Tonya, the city of New York, and several police officers for infringement of his civil rights, and Tonya's countersuit against Friedman and Ron's lawyers; the continuing squabbles over child-support payments. And these two aren't even divorced yet.

"When love goes bad" is how Friedman, sounding a bit like a romance novelist, sums up this whole painful, crazy, ambiguous process. When love goes bad and children are at issue, lawyers manipulate and judges decide matters of the heart that ideally should never have left the purview of the people whose hearts are actually involved. In the disintegrating family unit that is now known as *Brawer* v. *Pinkins*—as in all disintegrating family units that come before all matrimonial courts—the decision hinged not so much on truth, because there were too many competing truths; or even on the best interests of the children, because such assessments are always to some degree arbitrary.

60   So what did it hinge on? It came down to one judge's gut feeling, which ultimately is as valid as it is fallible. Maybe, for all the wrong reasons, Lewis Friedman made the right decision.

61   And then again, maybe not.

Ted Fishman
Redefining Fatherhood

"Redefining Fatherhood" appeared as an essay in Playboy, *which calls itself a "men's entertainment magazine." Although Ted Fishman is not a regular contributor, he did submit this item to the Forum section of the March 1995 issue.*

1   In 1973 the Supreme Court established the reproductive rights of women, ruling that a woman has sole control of her body, with the right to choose if and when to bear a child. Subsequent decisions elaborated: She could terminate an unwanted pregnancy without consulting the biological father.

2   Now, a generation later, a woman's power of choice is near absolute. Not only may women leave men out of the decision to abort, they may also leave men out of the decision to become parents. Last year 1.2 million single women had children; only a third of them named the fathers on birth certificates.

3   Fathers go unnamed for lots of reasons: a sense of privacy, shame, ignorance, rage, contempt, convenience. One brand of feminist consciousness-raising has not just tolerated but has encouraged single motherhood. There are support groups for women who are single parents, straight and gay, and support groups for women who are considering pregnancy. More validation comes on daytime talk shows, on soaps, and famously

in prime time on *Murphy Brown*. Empowerment aside, the message is simply this: Dads don't matter.

Yet at the same time, politicians and the media condemn 4 the absentee father, who is typically depicted as an uncaring lout ready to abandon responsibility and disappear. Lawmakers contemplate ways to go after deadbeat dads, to enforce their concept of parental responsibility. But when it comes to the rights of fathers who refuse to be deadbeats, who demand a place in their children's lives, the language is often the same: Unwed fathers deserve nothing.

Not all unwed mothers claim parenthood as their right 5 and/or responsibility. Some 53,000 of them put their babies up for adoption each year. States have passed laws that expedite adoption, trying to get the newborn into a two-parent home as quickly and as permanently as possible. Under a model law known as the Uniform Adoption Act, the unwed father has just 30 days to claim a relationship with his offspring or to challenge the adoption. Not many try. It isn't hard to see why.

Look at what the courts consider improper in a father. In 6 Nebraska, a young woman got pregnant and told her boyfriend that she was going to have an abortion and that she never wanted to see him again. She moved to a distant city and gave birth. When the young man tried to claim a parental right, the judge called him unfit. The evidence? He had made no effort to determine whether or not his former girlfriend had gone through with the abortion. His mistake was in taking his girlfriend's word that she was exercising a right he had no recourse to stop. It is, after all, a federal crime to get in the way of a woman's right to abort.

And in Illinois there's the battle over "Baby Richard." It 7 is a bizarre case. Man meets woman. Man impregnates woman and then, for the course of the pregnancy, supports her and makes plans for marriage. He leaves the country to attend to an ailing grandmother. An aunt in the old country calls the mother-to-be to report—falsely—that the man is seeing an old flame. The mother-to-be moves out of her apartment and offers no forwarding address. She leaves word for the man to get lost. When she gives birth, she refuses to put the father's name on the birth certificate. She instructs her uncle to tell the father that his baby is dead. Taking the advice of her beauty school supervisor, the mother offers the child for adoption. The transfer is made in the maternity ward.

The adoptive parents, legally bound to notify the biological 8 father, decide not to do so. Telling him would have been easy (he still lived at the old address). Instead, their lawyer submitted the papers, claiming that the father is unknown.

9   The father calls hospitals and politicians to determine if there is a death certificate. He goes through the mother's garbage looking for baby items and sends friends to give her money. After a two-month search, he finally learns that his child lives with a family of strangers. The news sends him immediately to court to challenge the legality of the adoption.

10   Two lower courts ruled that the man, Otakar Kirchner, was an unfit father because he did not file within the 30-day limit, and because he never spoke with the mother directly about the birth or death of the baby.

11   The courts focused on the best interests of the child and suggested that an unwed man who sincerely believes that he was "one of the sexual partners to the physiological formation of a child" could file a lawsuit to determine legally whether he is the father and assert his parental rights before the child is born. Filing suit as a fatherly act is what law schools teach instead of the facts of life.

       Kirchner set out to do the right thing. He forgave the mother and married her. He fought the lower court decision with every resource he had.

12   The fight has reached the Illinois Supreme Court twice. After a three-and-a-half-year battle, Kirchner appeared to have won. The justices said that he deserved custody of Baby Richard and that nothing had been said or done that established him as an unfit father. For his efforts, Kirchner got public jeers and anonymous death threats.

13   *Dateline* and *20/20* ran segments on the fight for Baby Richard. Nationally syndicated columnist Bob Greene spewed indignation for weeks, raising high the best-interests-of-the-child banner.

14   Illinois governor Jim Edgar, in the midst of a reelection campaign, echoed public sentiment, calling the birth father's victory "a dark day for justice and human decency. This is not just another lawsuit," he said. "It is about a young boy whom the court has decreed should be brutally, tragically torn away from the only parents he has ever known—parents who by all accounts loved and nurtured him from the second he joined the family."

15   But the Illinois Supreme Court saw something it could not sanction: In effect, Baby Richard had been stolen from Kirchner at birth. The child's adoptive parents and their lawyer were party—along with Baby Richard's biological mother—to

the deception. Together, they usurped Kirchner's right to have a relationship with his son.

If a couple stole your child from a shopping cart and it   16
took police three years to find them, would you expect the court to allow those otherwise loving parents to keep your son or daughter, in the best interests of the child?

Justice James Heiple, writing for the Illinois Supreme   17
Court, outlined the trail of blame: "The fault here lies initially with the mother, who fraudulently tried to deprive the father of his rights, and secondly with the adoptive parents and their attorney, who proceeded with the adoption when they knew that a real father was out there who had been denied knowledge of his baby's existence."

The case continues to drag through the courts. And   18
bizarrely, even though the U.S. Supreme Court refused to reverse the Illinois ruling, Baby Richard stays with the couple who took him, though legally their "adoption" no longer stands. Kirchner once asked for photos of his son. The couple refused. Laws rushed through the Illinois legislature let Baby Richard's keepers make a case for custody, which under the law is a separate issue from parenthood. Kirchner has appealed again to the courts to stop a custody hearing.

We understand the anguish of those who ask, "How do you   19
explain this situation to a child who has known only one home?" But consider the alternative: How would the adoptive parents explain to the child they call their son that his real father fought long and hard to be allowed to raise him and that they did everything they could to keep the two apart?

And someday the judges who have helped keep would-be   20
fathers from their children will have to explain their rulings that fathers aren't parents at all.

Dads Discuss Custody

This excerpt from an e-mail conversation on child custody issues comes from an exchange that took place in August 1995. Dave Bates began the discussion on two "newsgroups" organized on the Internet, one called "child-support" and the other "dad's rights," both of which maintain a lively interchange concerning custody issues. Bates received responses from Carl Wilson, Ben Gardner, and Paul Fraser, as well as from a number of others not included here. (Bates, Wilson, Gardner, and Fraser are all pseudonyms. All spelling and other errors are retained from the original Internet postings.)

1   I know that 50/50 custody is supposed to be best for the children, according to all the experts these days. But it just doesn't feel like the best thing from my point of view. My wife is likely to file for divorce totally against my wishes and totally unjustified. She is the one breaking up our family. I would love to get primary custody, but living in a no-fault state (FL) and the fact that she is a great mother make primary custody for me nigh unto impossible.

2   I would rather have one of the following 2 options, neither of which is in vogue:

3   A) We split our 2 kids: I get one M-F and she gets the other. On weekends, the kids are together, alternating parents. I like this better than the standard 50/50 because I at least get to have primary responsibility for *something*—one of my children. The standard 50/50 leaves me no time to start a new life, yet I still don't feel like I'm with the kids enough.

4   B) She becomes the primary parent and I get the kids every other weekend and Wed. eves. IOW, the old "father's visitation" schedule. I know, this is supposed to be terrible for the kids. But I'm not a very good parent unless I feel like I have some control of my life. This way, I can start a new life and am still young enough (35) to find someone who can actually keep their commitments. Then maybe I can try again to have a whole family. My kids will always be mine, they will love me, and they will be in good hands with their mother.

5   Comments?

Dave Bates

Dear Mr. Bates,

With this type of attitude, no fathers would ever get cus- 1
tody of their children. As for splitting the kids up as you
describe, no judge would find this arrangement feasible.

Let me ask a question. How much do you *LOVE* your 2
children? I will be the first person to tell you to work things
out, but it seems to me that you love yourself more than your
children. I don't mean to be brash, but a lot of fathers here are
fighting what you are willing to concede to. Never give up a
GOD GIVEN RIGHT! You should be entitled to 100% access
to your children at all times. You will always be able to make
a new start in romance. But you cannot make a new start
with your children! (In the sense of always being in their presence.) If you need support you will find it here. If you are
looking for pre-condolences, you would have to look elsewhere. IMHO, I think you should do a little soul searching
before you decide that a divorce is inevitable in your future.
Maybe you should reconsider and seek council. Best of all
luck!

Carl Wilson

Dave—

I'm not sure why you feel 50/50 custody is not the way, but 1
whatever it is I hope you will listen to my expierence before
making any final decision.

I am a two-time loser, both with children involved, both in 2
Florida. My first divorce was in the mid-70's. At that time the
best divorced fathers could expect was the alternating weekend routine. The result was a total loss of bonding with my
oldest daughter and eventually I gave her up to adoption by
her new stepfather. Thus, I ended up missing out on all the
great expierences of raising her and the pleasures of watching
her grow up and become an adult. This is not to say that I
didn't love her or want to do all these things, just that the
weekend routine did not give me substantial grounds to
develop a meaningful relationship with her. Only a token one.
I was fortunate because when she did become an adult and
went out on her own, she did take the time to seek me out and
renew our relationship. Most men never have that second
chance.

3 My second divorce took place in the early 90's and I found (thanks to equal rights) that I too had more rights and decided to go for them. I ended up with 50/50 custody where my youngest son lives six months with his mom and new stepfather and then six months with me. Whoever does not have the primary custody gets the alternating weekend routine. This is all primarily possible because our son does not have to change schools while jocking between my ex and me. As it works, neither of us get less than about 10 days a month, and each has equal opportunities for bonding with our son and participating in his development. There are many other benefits I find in this solution. For one thing even though I have not to date asked for child support from her for my six months of primary care, I still have that option at any time and she knows it. That is a great buffer. I also immediately reduced my child support in half because I do not pay except for the six months of her primary care. Anyway the differences between two divorces are like night and day. Thank God for women's equal rights, because in diguise it gives me rights I never had before.

4 The decision you are faced with is a great one and only you can make it. What you need to remember at this time is that it is easier to get all you want now, rather than deciding later to try to change it after the final judgment comes down. Later it will be much easier to give up a few rights than to get them back. Look deep and decide what you want and go for it all now!

5 Also, don't forget the little things that most attorneys will not advise you on unless you ask such as (1) alternating tax deductions (2) insurance payments and (3) college savings fund, just to mention a few. Remember if your ex is working she too has an equal responsibility in these areas and can be made to compensate for them.

6 I hope I have given you some good food for thought. My mailbox is open anytime—

Ben Gardner

Dave:

1 I am not at all convinced that 50/50 custody is always or even mostly best for the children. I can see where something approaching 50/50 in time spent with each parent is indeed healthy, but important life decisions must still be made, and

in my estimation unless both parents are on the same wave-length and very cooperative, those decisions should rest with a final responsible decision-maker, a primary custodian, and not left to a coin toss or be allowed to fall through the cracks...

I'm currently in perhaps a similar situation as yours where   2 my wife also dropped the bomb, out of the blue and against my wishes, in order to further an affair she'd started (with a person of questionable character, unemployed and with an unsupported child of his own), blatantly lied about, and con-tinues to lie about. She has demonstrated what I believe to be both irresponsible and irrational behavior both toward myself, and more important, with respect to the futures of our three young children. I currently have 4 day-night/week shared custody per temporary orders and already see the inherent problems in having to deal with her (on decisions, not necessarily personally) over the next 15 years.

Am I simply to be satisfied with this arrangement for no   3 other reason than that she is the mother and as such may have some practical legal advantage? Hell no. Not when she has also been working 40-hour weeks, and I have been entrusted with their care over nights and weekends since infancy. I feel the same way as you do, that she is the one breaking up the family, and that she is the one trying to take something away from our children, and from me. I'm not going to take any chances with their futures and live the rest of my life second-guessing myself. Whatever she walks away with, she is going to have to fight me for. If the system is indeed biased or corrupt, I guess I'll have to learn that lesson the hard way. I'm in this to the bitter, bloody end. It's too important.

If you feel strongly enough about it, this is my opinion on   4 the course of action you should take...

Paul Fraser

Karen Grigsby Bates

Are You My Mother?

Karen Grigsby Bates is a freelance journalist whose essays appear in many magazines and newspapers and whom you may have heard on National Public Radio's newsprogram All Things Considered. *She also tells you more about herself in the following piece, which appeared in* Essence *magazine in April 1991.* Essence *is a mass-circulation magazine designed to appeal to African American women. Like its peers—*Cosmopolitan, Vogue, Glamour, Redbook, *and the like—it emphasizes articles on fashion, beauty, careers, and civic issues of special concern to women.*

1   The MacLaren Children's Center near Los Angeles is a large facility designed to house temporarily children who have been abandoned, abused, and neglected. In theory, MacLaren's is a place where children can be sheltered and cared for until they are placed in a foster home or, if they are lucky, adopted. In practice, a child could live at MacLaren's for years.

2   Seven-month-old Gracie, a "failure-to-thrive baby," had been at MacLaren since she was 4 months old. She was dehydrated and malnourished and had a detached retina that gave her a "wandering eye." Although infants are usually the first to be claimed by prospective adoptive parents, the caretakers at MacLaren were afraid that Gracie would be with them for a very long time. Developmentally she was months behind a normal infant and her special needs and increasing age made her a poor prospect for adoption.

3   But Gracie was lucky: Somebody wanted her. Tracie Hotchner, a Los Angeles screenwriter who had done volunteer work at MacLaren for two years, had fallen in love with the baby. She felt that many of Gracie's problems could be minimized with personal, one-on-one care which she and her mate, film producer Frank Yablans, were anxious to give. Hotchner approached the Los Angeles County Children's Services Department, which put her in touch with its adoption division. But there Hotchner was told in no uncertain terms that she was considered unsuitable for consideration as a foster mother. Hotchner is white; Gracie is Black.

4   Hotchner persisted, threatening court action, and Gracie was placed with her as a foster child, pending adoption, for

four months. Despite doctor's expectations, Gracie's weight increased and her health improved during those months. But then the system caught up with them. Gracie was taken from Hotchner, ostensibly to be reunited with her brothers—from whom she'd been separated at infancy—and with a distant aunt who said she wasn't able to care for her.

At this writing, Gracie is still in foster care. She was never sent to her aunt (who told court officials Hotchner should keep the baby), and she wasn't allowed to stay with the foster mother who wanted to adopt her. Today Gracie is one of six foster children who are being boarded in a foster home an hour's drive from Los Angeles.   5

Does a person's color make her an unfit mother? Should Black children be placed only with Black families? Proponents and opponents of transracial adoption—adoption across racial lines—have been arguing these questions for nearly two decades now. The arguments are just as heated today as they were in 1972, when the National Association of Black Social Workers (NABSW) issued a statement at a conference on adoption that changed adoption policy and still reverberates throughout the adoption world.   6

In their statement the Black social workers took "a vehement stand against the placement of Black children in white homes for any reason." They further affirmed the "inviolable position of Black children in Black families, where they belong physically, psychologically, and culturally, in order to receive the total sense of themselves and develop a sound projection of their future." The NABSW reaffirmed the belief in their statement two years ago.   7

The Black social workers' stand and subsequent activism effectively stopped the practice of state-funded transracial adoption, which, prompted by child-welfare activists' desire to improve the quality of life for poor children, had been going on at modest but steady rates across the country. Although some critics branded them as racist and tunnel-visioned, the Black social workers were asking important questions. What happens to Black babies when they grow up in white families that are totally cut off from the larger Black community? Would these adopted Black children identify with other Black people? Would they *want* to?   8

The Black social workers also feared that Black children were being adopted by childless white couples for the wrong reason—namely because the well of available white babies was drying up. Along with adorable children from Korea, South America and parts of Southeast Asia, adorable   9

Black children were quietly being absorbed into white
homes, a practice many people assumed existed only in the
environs of prime-time TV, where cuddly Emmanuel Lewis
(*Webster*) and saucy Gary Coleman (*Diff'rent Strokes*) had
doting white parents, but were treated, to some extent, like
family pets.

10   In many ways in the 1970's these two pop-culture icons
embodied the fears of the Black social workers: Both children
knew they were Black, but that knowledge was seldom reinforced by their adoptive parents, who preferred to rear them
in a color-blind fashion. These social workers maintained
that because the world is not color-blind, teaching Black children that color is unimportant is inappropriate. Society can
be—and often is—hostile to people of color, and failure to
prepare Black children for life in a racist society can be painfully damaging to them later on.

11   The experiences of John Raible, a biracial young adult who
was adopted by white parents as a toddler, support the stand
of the Black social workers. "I wasn't *told* I was Black. My dad
is a Unitarian minister, and my parents believed in the color-
blind approach—but it was clear to me I wasn't white. We
would be stared at when we went out as a family," he remembers. "I stuck out because I was different."

12   The Raibles lived in an all-white neighborhood, and Raible's
only contact with Blacks were, he says dryly, "what I saw on
television, in the movies and in the paper. For a long time I
thought all Black folks were poor, on welfare and violent." He
changed his mind when, as a teenager, he became close to
another Black youngster. But it wasn't until college that he
really began to meet a wide spectrum of African-Americans.

13   According to Dr. Ruth G. McRoy of the University of Texas
at Austin, that kind of reaction from Black children raised in
white families is not unusual. A study completed by McRoy
on the identity and self-esteem of transracially adopted Black
children found that those youngsters raised by white parents
who sought regular, ongoing contact with African-Americans
fared far better than those who grew up as the only Black person in a white world. "Some of the transracially adopted
Black children who had no contact with Blacks in their neighborhood or school characterized Blacks as 'poor' and 'militant' and said, 'They use bad English,'" McRoy observed. Her
findings echo John Raible's experience.

14   But sensitive white parents can make a difference if they
understand the important of race in this society. Dr. Joyce A.
Ladner, sociologist and author of *Mixed Families: Adopting*

Across Racial Boundaries (Anchor Press Doubleday, 1977), warns that white parents of Black children must make serious adjustments in their lives if their children are to make successful adjustments. In her research, in which 80 percent of the families lived in the suburbs and the kids went to suburban schools, there was much "naïveté" about the realities of raising Black children in a racist society."

"[White parents] were very sensitive to this identity issue   15
after the NABSW's verdict," Ladner remembers. "It was a sobering reality for most of them." The thoughtful ones reacted by seeking out more integrated neighborhoods and schools, so their Black children would not feel culturally isolated.

The children of adoptive parents who took Ladner's   16
research seriously are faring well, according to a recent study by Dr. Rita James Simon, coauthor (with Howard Altstein) of *Transracial Adopters and Their Families: A Study of Identity and Commitment* (Praeger, 1987). Simon's long-term study of transracial placements found that after nearly two decades the children who were now young adults were doing well. Of the "problem cases" in the study, Simon says, "in virtually every case, those problems were related to the broader issue of having been adopted ('Where is my birth mother? Why didn't she keep me?'), *not* to race."

Samantha Davidge, an attractive, articulate 26-year-old,   17
feels that part of the reason she didn't suffer the agonies that John Raible and other transracially adopted children experienced was because her mother was sensitive to the issues of adoption and race. "My mom has been a foster parent for years; there have always been different races of kids staying with us," Davidge observes. "She's always been open about discussing race—not just with me, but with all of us."

Davidge, who grew up in a virtually all-white suburb of Los   18
Angeles, said she was aware of both overt and subtle prejudice, but that her mother gave her such a strong sense of self-esteem she was rarely wounded by racism. "Sometimes people would point when we'd be out at the mall and I'd be talking with my mother. They'd hear me call her 'Mom,' and their heads would whip around. But my mother always told me that there was nothing wrong with us—it was the people who were pointing who had a problem," she says.

Davidge, who is currently completing work on a master's   19
degree in social work at the University of Southern California, clearly sees herself as an African-American woman. "It's what I am," she says simply.

Finding Black Homes

20   Today the sheer number of Black children needing permanent homes has reached crisis proportions. Thanks to factors
all too familiar—crack, AIDS, rampant poverty, family disintegration—more children of color than ever before are lan-
guishing in institutions and in sequential foster care. It has
been 20 years since the Black social workers took their controversial stand, and nearly everyone seems to agree that the
needs of children must come first. But the question remains:
How can this best be accomplished?

21   Some Black adoption experts assert that African-
Americans should look toward themselves. They maintain
that the Black community can and will take a larger role in
providing homes for its children—if it is allowed to. Gerald K.
Smith, current president of the National Association of Black
Social Workers, insists that "adoption *per se* really isn't the
issue. Whenever there have been healthy Black infants and
special aggressive programs to find Black parents, Black parents have adopted at four times the rate of whites given equal
income," he says.

22   Zena F. Oglesby, Jr., a social worker with two decades'
worth of adoption experience and the executive director of
the Institute for Black Parenting, strongly agrees with Smith.
"There's this mythology out there that says Black families
don't adopt," says Oglesby. "This gives rise to the assumption
that there are not sufficient Black homes for Black children."
Oglesby and the Institute have managed to combat that
notion with an astonishing placement rate: more than 200
children in two years of operation.

23   How did the Institute, which is one of six or so private
Black adoption agencies in the country, manage such stunning success? "It's simple," Oglesby says. "Everything public
agencies do, we don't. We send Black social workers to Black
homes to interview these families. We send them at night and
on weekends, when it's convenient for working people. We
don't charge money for adoptions (most private agencies do).
And we try to place a child within a few months (usually two
to eight) and not the year and a half to three years it takes
public agencies to place them."

24   Sydney Duncan, president of Homes for Black Children in
Detroit, is convinced that even more Black children could be
placed if more of an effort were made. "An agency that can
bring children and families together is the answer," Duncan
suggests. "This effort would require a national network of sup-

porting organizations—and it could be done. If one national Black organization with a membership of more than 1 million members would just add one extra dollar to its dues and set that money aside to be used solely for placing Black children in Black homes, there could be a tremendous difference."

Finding more Black homes for Black children would   25 reduce the number of Black children available to white families wishing to adopt them, and that wouldn't disturb Tracie Hotchner at all. "I'm hesitant to comment on my particular case further, because the whole issue of transracial adoption is very divisive," Hotchner observes. "It's often couched in terms that pit Black against white, and it shouldn't be. The foremost point in all of this is that each child, *every* child, is entitled to a home. That's a basic right." Samantha Davidge concurs, "Children's needs must be the absolute first priority. We all agree that, all other things being equal, a Black home is best for Black children. But what about the children who *don't* get Black homes? What happens to them?"

That's the hard question, and a satisfactory consensus may   26 be a long time in coming. And meanwhile, oblivious to ideology, the children wait.

Randall Kennedy

Orphans of Separation:
The Politics of Transracial Adoption

Randall Kennedy, a professor at Harvard Law School, offered the following to The American Prospect *magazine in the spring of 1994. It is an excerpt from his book* Orphans of Separatism: The Painful Politics of Transracial Adoption. *The essay also appeared in the October 1994* Current, *a journal that republishes essays of special note on civic and political issues, both domestic and international.*

No issue more highlights feelings of ambivalence over the   1 proper place of racial distinctions in American life than the delicate matter of transracial adoptions. Opponents of such adoptions insist that allowing white adults to raise black children is at worst tantamount to cultural genocide and at best a naive experiment doomed to failure. In most states, custom reflects and reinforces these beliefs; public policy, formally or informally, discourages cross-racial adoptions or foster placements, to the point where thousands of children are denied placement in loving homes.

2   Now one of the Senate's leading liberals is compounding the damage with a well-intentioned but badly misguided bill titled the Multiethnic Placement Act. Senator Howard Metzenbaum of Ohio sees his bill as a deft compromise. On the one hand, the bill prohibits state agencies or agencies that receive funds from the federal government from completely barring or unduly delaying transracial child placements, either for adoptions or foster care. This aspect of the bill has provoked the opposition of those who strongly favor racial matching, the policy that seeks to place children of a given race with foster parents of the same race. On the other hand, the bill evinces a preference for racial matching by explicitly stating that race may be taken into account in prohibiting *undue* delays caused by efforts at racial matching (thereby implicitly authorizing some delay). This preference stems from Metzenbaum's own belief that "every child who is eligible for adoption has the right to be adopted by parents of the same race," and that "teaching a child self love and to embrace their racial and cultural heritage is more easily accomplished when parents and children are of the same race or ethnic group."

3   Metzenbaum thus embraces *moderate* racial matching. While he does not favor barring transracial child placements altogether, he views such arrangements as distinctly less desirable than racially matched child placements. Many intelligent, caring, thoughtful people of good will agree with Senator Metzenbaum. His legislation is supported by Marian Wright Edelman's Children's Defense Fund and is echoed by an editorial in the *New York Times,* which declared that while total prohibition of transracial adoptions is unwise, "Clearly, matching adoptive parents with children of the same race is a good idea."

4   These good people are wrong. To understand why and the stakes involved in their error, one must confront three overlapping social disasters.

Social Disasters

5   The first is the fact that increasingly large numbers of children bereft of functioning parents are flooding social welfare

agencies. Agencies are charged with maintaining these young refugees from destroyed families and either placing them in the temporary care of foster parents or the permanent care of adoptive parents. According to Metzenbaum, the number of such children has exploded from 276,000 in 1986 to 450,000 in 1992—a vivid and concrete manifestation of what happens when poverty, crime, and substance abuse tear families apart.

Like most social catastrophes in the United States, this one weighs most heavily upon racial minority communities: the percentage of minority children in need of foster care or adoptive homes is far greater than their percentage of the population. In Massachusetts, approximately 5 percent of the population is black, yet black children constitute nearly half of the children in need of foster care or adoptive homes. In New York City, 75 percent of the nearly 18,000 children awaiting adoption are black. Nationwide, there are about 100,000 children eligible for adoption; 40 percent are black. While two years and eight months is the median length of time that children in general wait to be adopted, the wait for black children is often twice that long. 6

Conceiving of the deprivations suffered by children without parents is both easy and difficult. It is easy because some of the things that we expect parents to do are so obviously important. We expect parents to protect the interests of their children in a singular fashion, to show a degree of loyalty that cannot be bought, to demonstrate a mysterious allegiance deeper than professional duty. It is difficult because of the enormity of even attempting to calibrate the manifold, subtle, perhaps even unknowable losses borne by parentless children. There is one thing, however, about which we can be sure: it is a tragic condition indeed for a child to be condemned to the limbo of parentlessness, to suffer the loneliness of having no one to call "mother" or "father," to be exposed to the anxiety of having no family that is permanently and intimately one's own. 7

A second social disaster compounds the first. It is the disaster of racial matching itself. Racial matching policies can vary in intensity, from absolute prohibitions against transracial child placements to temporary preferences for same-race placements. Examples of the former are state laws in the segregationist Jim Crow South that forbade adoption across the race line and, more recently, the position of the National Association of Black Social Workers, which categorically opposes transracial adoptions involving black children and white parents. Examples of the latter include the customary 8 practices of many social workers around the country and statutes like the ones in California, Minnesota, and Arkansas which require that social workers spend a given amount of time—90 days in California—seeking a same-race adoption for children before they are made available to prospective adoptive parents of a different race.

9   Racial matching is a disastrous social policy both in how it affects children and in what it signals about our current attitudes regarding racial distinctions. In terms of immediate consequences, strong forms of racial matching block some parentless children from access to adults who would otherwise be deemed suitable as parents except that they are disqualified on the grounds that they are of the "wrong" race. In some jurisdictions, the relevant decisionmakers simply refuse to permit child placements across the color line. In others, authorities will permit foster care across racial lines but then remove the child if they move to deepen the relationship from mere temporary foster care to permanent adoption. In still other jurisdictions, social welfare agencies delay placing children with adoptive parents of the "wrong" race until efforts are undertaken to place the child with adoptive parents of the "right" race. Delay of any length is, of course, a cost in and of itself. While three months might seem like a negligible delay from the perspective of adults, such delays are lengthy indeed from the perspective of infants. Moreover, for many adults, children become less attractive as adoptees as they age. What seems at first like mere delay may obliterate the chance of some youngsters for adoption at all; prospective adoptive parents willing to adopt a child of six months may not be willing to adopt the same child at one year.

10   Furthermore, given that racial matching mirrors and reinforces the belief that same race child placements are better and therefore preferable to transracial arrangements, some adults seeking to become foster or adoptive parents are likely to steer clear of transracial parenting. Some adults who would be willing to raise a child regardless of racial differences find themselves unwilling to do so in the face of social pressures that stigmatize transracial adoption as anything from second-best to cultural genocide. What this means in practice is that racial matching narrows the pool of prospective parents, which in turn either delays or prevents transmission of children in need of parents to adults able and willing to serve as parents. How much misery this adds to our pained country is difficult to calibrate. That racial matching adds a substantial amount of misery, however, is inescapable.

The other level on which racial matching is disastrous has   11
to do with its diffuse, long-term moral and political
consequences. Racial matching reinforces racialism. It
strengthens the baleful notion that race is destiny. It but-
tresses the notion that people of different racial backgrounds
really are different in some moral, unbridgeable, permanent
sense. It affirms the notion that race should be a cage to
which people are assigned at birth and from which people
should not be allowed to wander. It belies the belief that love
and understanding are boundless and instead instructs us
that our affections are and should be bounded by the color
line regardless of our efforts.

When he introduced the Multiethnic Placement Act, Sena-   12
tor Metzenbaum railed against the strongest versions of
racial matching. "Some agencies," he noted disapprovingly,
"prevent the adoption of children by prospective parents of a
different race, even after the child and parents have bonded
after years of living together in a loving foster care home." He
stated that his bill would "make it clear that race, national
origin or color cannot be the only consideration in making
foster care and adoptive placements." Note, however, that he
attacks only the most extreme version of racial matching, that
which wholly prevents transracial child placements. He
leaves alone and indeed authorizes less extreme or obvious
versions of racial matching.

This suggests a third social disaster: the mixture of confu-   13
sion and weakness that disables many people of good will
from combating as fully as they might deeply ingrained
racialist impulses. Metzenbaum's position not only reflects
this failing but compounds it. True he is a *moderate* racial
matcher. There are, as noted above, more fervent and rigid
supporters of racial matching who oppose Metzenbaum's
proposed legislation because, in their view, it fails to go far
enough in the defense of racial matching. But he apparently
does accept the premises of racial matching, preferring same-
race child placements so long as they can be accomplished
without too high a cost.

What the senator and those who support his legislation   14
have failed to appreciate sufficiently is that, under our law,
the drawing of racial distinctions, particularly by government
officials, is and should be presumptively illegitimate. Federal
constitutional law, for instance, establishes that when government officials use racial criteria in their decision-making, they
bear a heavy burden of justification. This aversion to racial
criteria stems from our long and bitter history with them, an

experience that includes slavery, open, invidious racial distinctions, and *de jure* segregation. This history suggests that
far more often than not, there exists no good reason to draw
racial distinctions.

15   This does not mean that all racial criteria are illegitimate,
only that all are presumptively illegitimate. Therefore, if
racial criteria are to be used, the burden of persuasion rests
on those in favor of using such criteria. Thus, in this context,
the burden of persuasion rests not upon those who object to
the use of racial criteria in making child placement decisions
but rather upon those who wish to use such criteria. The burden of persuasion properly rests upon the proponents of
racial matching, not those who contend, as I do, that race
ought to play no part in child placement decisions.

Racial Stereotypes

16   There is no rationale sufficiently compelling to justify preferring same-race child placements over transracial placements. One asserted reason for favoring same-race
placements (at least in terms of black children) is that African-American parents can, on average, better equip African-
American children with what they will need to know in order
to survive and prosper in a society that remains, in significant
degree, a pigmentocracy. This rationale is doubly faulty.

17   First, it rests upon a racial generalization, a racial stereotype, regarding the relative abilities of white and black adults
in terms of raising African-American children. Typically (and
the exception does not apply here), our legal system rightly
prohibits authorities from making decisions on the basis of
racial generalizations, even if the generalizations are accurate. Our legal system demands that people be given individualized consideration to reflect and effectuate our desire to
accord to each person respect as a unique and special individual. Thus, if an employer used whiteness as a criteria to prefer white candidates for a job on the grounds that, on
average, white people have more access to education than
black people, the employer would be in violation of an array
of state and federal laws even if the generalization used by the
employer is accurate. We demand as a society a more exacting process, one more attentive to the surprising possibilities
of individuals than the settled patterns of racial groups. Thus,
even if one believes that, on average, black adults are better
able than white adults to raise black children effectively, it

would still be problematic to disadvantage white adults, on the basis of their race, in the selection process.

Second, there is no evidence that black foster or adoptive   18
parents, on average, do better than white foster or adoptive parents in raising black children. The empirical basis for this claim is suspect; there are no serious, controlled, systematic studies that support it. Nor is this claim self-evidently persuasive. Those who confidently assert this claim rely on the hunch, accepted by many, that black adults, as victims of racial oppression, will generally know more than others about how best to instruct black youngsters on overcoming racial bias. A counter-hunch, however, with just as much plausibility, is that white adults, as insiders to the dominant racial group in America, will know more than racial minorities about the inner world of whites and how best to maneuver with and around them in order to advance one's interests in a white-dominated society.

To substantiate the claim that black adults will on average   19
be better than white adults in terms of raising black children, one must stipulate a baseline conception of what constitutes correct parenting for a black child—otherwise, one will have no basis for judging who is doing better than whom. Metzenbaum and other moderate proponents of racial matching imply that white foster or adoptive parents will be, on average, less capable of instilling within a black child an appropriate sense of self worth and an appropriate racial identity. There exists, however, no consensus on how best to raise a black child (or, for that matter, any other sort of child) or on what constitutes a proper sense of self worth or on what constitutes an appropriate racial identity or on how one would go about measuring any of these things. Is an appropriate sense of blackness evidenced by celebrating Kwanza, listening to rap, and seeking admission to Morehouse College? What about celebrating Christmas, listening to Mahalia Jackson and seeking admission to Harvard? And what about believing in atheism, listening to Mozart, and seeking admission to Bard? Are any of these traits more or less appropriately black? And who should do the grading on what constitutes racial appropriateness? Louis Farrakhan? Jesse Jackson? Clarence Thomas?

Some moderate proponents of racial matching contend   20
that, on average, white adults seeking foster or adoptive children will be less able than similarly situated black adults to tell these children how best to meet the racial impediments they will surely face. But what is the best advice to give?

Blacks do not agree. Nor do whites. Again the key point is that there exists no consensus on how best to raise a black child or any other child.

21   In light of this lack of consensus, the tenuousness of our information regarding the relationship of racial status to social knowledge, the ever-growing complexity of our multi-cultural society, and our well-taken aversion to official racial distinctions in the absence of clear, strong justifications for them, our government should reject any scheme that engages expressly in racial steering on the basis of a hunch that certain people—because of their race, color, or national origin—will know better how to raise a child than other people of a different race, color, or national origin. If officials are satisfied that adults seeking foster or adoptive children are safe, sober folk, they should have to pass no racial screening. What parentless children need are not "white," "black," "yellow," "brown," or "red" parents but *loving* parents.

22   Yet another reason advanced in favor of moderate racial matching is that it may serve to save a child from placement in a transracial family setting in which the child will be made to feel uncomfortable by a disapproving surrounding community. It would be a regrettable concession, however, to allow bigotry to shape our law. One of the asserted justifications of segregation was that it protected blacks from the wrath of those whites who would strongly object to transracial public schooling and transracial accommodations in hotels and restaurants. When the *New York Times* editorializes today that "clearly, matching adoptive parents with children of the same race is a good idea," we should recall that not very long ago it was believed in some parts of this nation that "clearly" it was a good idea to match people of the same race in separate but equal parks, hospitals, prisons, cemeteries, telephone booths, train cars, and practically every other place one can imagine—all for the asserted purpose of accommodating the underlying racial sentiments of those who opposed "racial mixing."

Legal Developments

23   Some of the most admirable rulings in the history of the Supreme Court have involved rejections of just this sort of accommodation—first, in striking down *de jure* segregation in *Brown v. Board of Education* and, second, in refusing to allow racialist opposition to nullify its ruling. In 1958 some of

the white people of Little Rock vociferously, and even violently, protested the admission of black children into a formerly all-white public high school. In response, the local school board decided to suspend its efforts to desegregate the school. But in the same year, in *Cooper v. Aaron*, the Supreme Court ruled against the school board and ordered that the desegregation plan be reinstated. "The constitutional rights of [the black school children] are not to be sacrificed or yielded," the court declared, "to violence and disorder." More recently, in 1984 in *Palmore v. Sidoti*, the Supreme Court faced a situation in which a Florida state court judge awarded custody of a child to her white natural father when the child's white natural mother married a black man. The Florida judge stated that it would be in the best interest of the child to be raised in a racially homogeneous household given the ostracism she was likely to face if she continued to live with her mother in a transracial household. Again the Supreme Court reversed the judgment of the local authorities. Echoing *Cooper*, the Court maintained in *Palmore* that racialist opposition to transracial living arrangements should not be used as a basis for using racial criteria in making child placement decisions.

There are a growing number of cases in which courts have given relief to children and adults who have been kept apart by officials who, on racial grounds, have clearly prevented transracial foster care or adoption. But significant obstacles impede bringing unlawful conduct to the attention of judges. The government agencies that are supposed to advance the best interests of the children under their care are all too often directed by people who either favor racial matching (particularly its moderate version) or fear confronting those who do. Furthermore, adults who are separated by racial matching from children they might otherwise parent face the bitter reality that, even when the law is on your side, litigation is expensive, time-consuming, nerve-wrenching, and uncertain. If a social welfare official offers a non-racial, pretextual reason for making a child placement decision, it will often be difficult to prove that an illicit racial reason animated the decision. This is especially so in the area of child welfare, where courts typically defer even more than they normally do to the presumed expertise of social welfare professionals. 24

The Multiethnic Placement Act raises a somewhat different legal issue: the status of a legislative directive that openly instructs officials that they may take race into account in making child placement decisions so long as race is not the only factor considered in determining what placement to 25 make in the best interest of a child. There are, as noted above, strong reasons to believe that the Multiethnic Placement Act should be found to be in violation of the Equal Protection Clause of the Constitution. On the other hand, it is at least thinkable that the Supreme Court would reject a challenge to the act. First, the court typically grants more deference to racial distinctions made by Congress than to racial distinctions made by the states. Second, by authorizing the use of a racial criterion only in conjunction with other factors, the sponsors of the Multiethnic Placement Act resort to a formula that the Supreme Court has used to justify racial criteria in the affirmative action context. In his decisive 1976 opinion in *University of California at Davis* v. *Bakke,* Justice Lewis Powell gave his blessing to affirmative action programs in which race is used along with other considerations in selecting candidates for admission to institutions of higher education. Last year, in *Shaw* v. *Reno,* which involved the constitutionality of using racial criteria to design congressional districts, Justice Sandra Day O'Connor, writing for the court, seemed to suggest that what bothered her most about the case was that racial characteristics seemed to have been virtually the only thing that mattered to those doing the districting. Given that the Multiethnic Placement Act explicitly states that race may be used only in concert with other considerations, the court might uphold it.

26   The court, however, would be wrong in doing so. First, a compelling justification should be demanded whenever a racial distinction is drawn, which means that there should be no diminution of scrutiny simply because the Congress purports to authorize the use of a racial distinction along with other factors. Second, as everyone knows or should know, authorizing the use of racial criteria at all will mean in practice the authorization of racial matching—so long as social welfare bureaucrats who favor the practice take minimal steps to obscure the real basis of their decisions.

27   Some influential sectors of the civil rights community steer far clear of this controversy, particularly the argument advanced here, because they fear implications that might cast a shadow over affirmative action plans. Their fears are understandable; legitimating racial distinctions for purposes of affirmative action in higher education and employment do put a strain on the Equal Protection Clause and anti-discrimination statutes. But with respect to racial preferences in those contexts, it can at least be said that the aim is integrative: the purpose of preferring minority candidates is to speed

the process of racially integrating sectors of American life from which racial minorities have long been wrongly excluded. By contrast, there is no integrative purpose or effect to racial matching, even in the moderate form authorized by the Metzenbaum bill. To the contrary, its expressed purpose and obvious consequence is to maintain the racial status quo, at least in terms of constituting families.

Supporters of the Multiethnic Placement Act contend that 28 opponents of racial matching should nonetheless support this bill because it at least attacks the worst excesses of racial matching. Sometimes, however, half-steps in addressing a problem are more dangerous than inaction. The Multiethnic Placement Act will fail in its effort to prevent those lengthy delays which even proponents of racial matching recognize as hurtful. It will fail because, as the sponsors of the bill themselves recognize, there exists already a widespread and deeply-ingrained practice of discouraging trans-racial placements even when the cost of doing so is consigning children to lengthy or indefinite stays in institutional limbo. Attempting to make fine distinctions between acceptable and unacceptable delay will fail to uproot this pernicious practice. Indeed, the Multiethnic Placement Act will likely worsen the situation. At present, there exists no congressional authority for racial matching; if this bill is enacted, such authority will exist.

Conclusion

There is more at stake in the struggle over the Multiethnic 29 Placement Act than has been at stake in any bill involving race relations that the Congress has faced since the passage of the Civil Rights Act of 1964. That this year marks the 30th anniversary of the Civil Rights Act puts into sharp relief the significance of the pending legislation. That act constituted an effort to remove the color line from large areas of American life. It forbade discrimination on the basis of race in public accommodations and in much of the private employment market. It also authorized the cutting off of federal funds from any agency which discriminated on the basis of race. Yet, here we are, 30 years later, with racialist legislation proposed and sponsored by some of Congress's most distinguished liberal senators: Howard Metzenbaum of Ohio, Edward Kennedy of Massachusetts, Christopher Dodd of Connecticut.

30   The Multiethnic Placement Act looks down upon transracial placements, making them second-class arrangements to
be resorted to when all else fails. There was a time when
forward-looking people would have thought it praiseworthy
for prospective adoptive parents to have said to a state social
welfare agency, "We are willing to raise a parentless child
regardless of the child's race." Now we confront legislation
that openly denigrates such people, portraying them as a
mere fallback for parentless children of a different race than
they.

31   When Senator Metzenbaum introduced the Multiethnic
Placement Act, he ended his announcement by stating solemnly that his legislation "reaffirms the fundamental principle that our child welfare system should judge people by the
content of their character and not by the color of their skin."
But this is Orwellian double-speak. The stated aim of the bill
is to decrease the length of time that children wait to be
adopted. Yet it expressly permits delay for the purpose of
racial matching, prohibiting only "undue" delay. The bill's
stated aim is to prevent discrimination in the placement of
children on the basis of race, color, or national origin. Yet the
bill expressly permits an agency to "consider the race, color,
or national origin of a child as a factor in making a placement
decision." Metzenbaum states that the bill "reaffirms the fundamental principle that our child welfare system should judge
people by the content of their character and not by the color
of their skin." Yet the bill's language does just the opposite.

32   This state of affairs is, quite simply, a political disaster—at
least for integrationists like me who view the anti-racialist
impulse of the civil rights movement circa 1963 as the great
guiding sentiment around which struggles for racial justice
should continue to cohere. Whether or not they recognize it,
many liberals have abandoned their commitment to creating
a society in which racial difference withers away into moral
insignificance. Instead, often marching under the banner of
"diversity," they have acquiesced to measures that are moving
us toward a society in which one's racial background is
deemed to have a definite, positive, moral meaning that the
government officially recognizes, reinforces, and celebrates.

33   Many conservatives are also blameworthy. Some who
merely tolerate the changes wrought by the civil rights revolution, because they can effectively do nothing about them,
probably like the fact that racial matching is prevalent and
may soon receive congressional approval; after all, racial
matching validates to some degree the separatist intuitions

that animated *de jure* segregation. Others are simply indifferent to this issue. Not all are; Professor Charles Fried of Harvard Law School, Ronald Reagan's solicitor general, has been actively, eloquently, and rightly engaged in opposing the Multiethnic Placement Act. But he is unusual among conservatives, and the indifference shown by his ideological kin is itself noteworthy. Conservatives of various sorts unite in their attacks against racial preferences in educational and employment settings. But for the most part conservatives who loudly decry liberals' use of racial criteria in other settings have been noticeably quiet about the Multiethnic Placement Act.

Unfortunately, one plausible explanation for this is that while they care intensely about the disadvantage imposed upon whites by preferential treatment in education and employment, they care little about the burdens imposed by racial matching, burdens that hurt everyone but that hurt racial minority children in particular.   34

The only happy thing about this story is that an end to it has not yet been written. The Multiethnic Placement Act has not yet been enacted. Perhaps its objectionable aspects will be satisfactorily modified. Perhaps alternative legislation barring all race matching will supersede Metzenbaum's bill. Perhaps the president will veto the bill or the courts will invalidate it. But whatever happens, the fact that such a bill even exists in 1994—40 years after *Brown*, 30 years after the Civil Rights Act of 1964—is evidence that there is much to be done in order to create a more just, decent, and attractive society.   35

SHOULD SAME-SEX COUPLES
BE PERMITTED TO MARRY?

Anna Quindlen

Evan's Two Moms

Anna Quindlen (born 1955) for a number of years wrote a widely praised, syndicated column for the New York Times *and many other newspapers. She won a Pulitzer Prize for commentary in 1992. Her work has been collected in several books, including* Thinking Out Loud: On the Personal, the Political, the Public, and the Private *(1993). The following essay comes from that collection.*

1   Evan has two moms. This is no big thing. Evan has always had two moms—in his school file, on his emergency forms, with his friends. "Ooooh, Evan, you're lucky," they sometimes say. "You have two moms." It sounds like a sitcom, but until last week it was emotional truth without legal bulwark. That was when a judge in New York approved the adoption of a six-year-old boy by his biological mother's lesbian partner. Evan. Evan's mom. Evan's other mom. A kid, a psychologist, a pediatrician. A family.

2   The matter of Evan's two moms is one in a series of events over the last year that lead to certain conclusions. A Minnesota appeals court granted guardianship of a woman left a quadriplegic in a car accident to her lesbian lover, the culmination of a seven-year battle in which the injured woman's parents did everything possible to negate the partnership between the two. A lawyer in Georgia had her job offer withdrawn after the state attorney general found out that she and her lesbian lover were planning a marriage ceremony; she's brought suit. The computer company Lotus announced that the gay partners of employees would be eligible for the same benefits as spouses.

3   Add to these public events the private struggles, the couples who go from lawyer to lawyer to approximate legal pro-

tections their straight counterparts take for granted, the AIDS survivors who find themselves shut out of their partners' dying days by biological family members and shut out of their apartments by leases with a single name on the dotted line, and one solution is obvious.

Gay marriage is a radical notion for straight people and a   4 conservative notion for gay ones. After years of being sledge-hammered by society, some gay men and lesbian women are deeply suspicious of participating in an institution that seems to have "straight world" written all over it.

But the rads of twenty years ago, straight and gay alike,   5 have other things on their minds today. Family is one, and the linchpin of family has commonly been a loving commitment between two adults. When same-sex couples set out to make that commitment, they discover that they are at a disadvantage: No joint tax returns. No health insurance coverage for an uninsured partner. No survivor's benefits from Social Security. None of the automatic rights, privileges, and responsibilities society attaches to a marriage contract. In Madison, Wisconsin, a couple who applied at the Y with their kids for a family membership were turned down because both were women. It's one of those small things that can make you feel small.

Some took marriage statutes that refer to "two persons" at   6 their word and applied for a license. The results were court decisions that quoted the Bible and embraced circular argument: marriage is by definition the union of a man and a woman because that is how we've defined it.

No religion should be forced to marry anyone in violation   7 of its tenets, although ironically it is now only in religious ceremonies that gay people can marry, performed by clergy who find the blessing of two who love each other no sin. But there is no secular reason that we should take a patchwork approach of corporate, governmental, and legal steps to guarantee what can be done simply, economically, conclusively, and inclusively with the words "I do."

"Fran and I chose to get married for the same reasons that   8 any two people do," said the lawyer who was fired in Georgia. "We fell in love; we wanted to spend our lives together." Pretty simple.

Consider the case of *Loving* v. *Virginia*, aptly named. At the   9 time, sixteen states had laws that barred interracial marriage, relying on natural law, that amorphous grab bag for justifying prejudice. Sounding a little like God throwing Adam and Eve out of paradise, the trial judge suspended the

one-year sentence of Richard Loving, who was white, and his
wife, Mildred, who was black, provided they got out of the
State of Virginia.

10   In 1967 the Supreme Court found such laws to be unconstitutional. Only twenty-five years ago and it was a crime for
a black woman to marry a white man. Perhaps twenty-five
years from now we will find it just as incredible that two people of the same sex were not entitled to legally commit themselves to each other. Love and commitment are rare enough;
it seems absurd to thwart them in any guise.

Sidney Callahan

Why I Changed My Mind

Sidney Callahan is a regular columnist for Commonweal, *a
biweekly magazine of public affairs, religion, literature, and the
arts that is generally associated with Catholicism and liberal
politics. The following essay appeared in April 1994.*

1   Last month I came out of the closet and confessed at an
evening lecture that I believed that homosexuals should be
allowed to marry. The morning after I had second thoughts,
but I'm afraid my reconsiderations were mostly the result of
cowardice and churlishness.

2   First the cowardice. Yes, I undoubtedly dread getting into
arguments, especially with people I admire. I'm also distinctly uneager to be harassed by true believers playing punitive hardball—whether on the right or the left. Already I've
been denounced and disinvited for being a feminist, and been
greeted by banners unfurled to protest my acceptance of birth
control, this while delivering a prolife speech at a Catholic
conference. Yet in other venues I've been picketed, booed,
hissed, and raged at by abortion advocates. (At least the latter
episodes have the excitement of being thrown to the lions in
the arena.) Still, do I need to get into one more religious and
cultural donnybrook?

3   As for churlishness, I must say that as much as I hate being
disliked, I loathe even more being approved of by certain

groups. Who wants to end up on the same side with aggressively secular ideologues? And how unappetizing to aid and abet militant gay groups who engage in gross anti-Catholic tactics? Most of all I hate agreeing with those mindless religious types (I have my little list) who regularly seem to sell out their Christian birthright, along with the lives of the unborn, for a mess of PC pottage.

Unfortunately, flailing about and grinding one's teeth availeth naught, it gets you nowhere. The only way out of moral paralysis is to forget extrinsic political considerations and enter into the necessary struggle. If we want to bring forth a Christworthy, coherent sexual ethic for the twenty-first century then we must all think hard, pray hard, and seek God's Spirit of Love and Truth. Where? In all the familiar places: in Scripture, in tradition, in natural law reasoning, and in the signs and sciences of the times. So what is the gospel truth regarding homosexuality?   4

At this point I've read thousands of pages written by assorted experts and theologians giving their views on what constitutes an adequate moral, legal, scientific, and/or scriptural-theological approach to homosexuality (including recent *Commonweal* exchanges). But since I'm in the confessional mode let me own up to the fact that I also try to decide difficult moral dilemmas by praying, meditating, and naively imagining what Christ would have done and wants now. If the mind of Christ is in us, we must be transformed rather than being conformed to the world.   5

As I try to draw all these various strands of thought, imagination, and prayer into some order, I find myself diverging from official Vatican teaching. Yes, we are all told to look upon homosexuals as equal children of God who must be protected from assault, bigotry, and infringement of their civil rights. Indeed, Christ loves and includes the gay in his kingdom. And almost everyone on all sides agrees that homosexuality is not freely chosen but a given condition. So, too, all acknowledge that personal qualities and the call to holiness are not determined by sexual orientation. So far, so good.   6

But why is it intrinsically disordered for homosexuals and lesbians to act on their sexual orientation, even if they would fulfill all the same moral conditions required of heterosexual marital activity, such as commitment, love, and lifelong fidelity? After all, some heterosexual marriages need not, nor can be biologically procreative. I just cannot imagine Christ asking such an unequal sacrifice from homosexual persons with beloved partners who have not been called to vowed celibacy.   7

8   Those who do assign this burden in Christ's name describe
the deprivation as morally and religiously necessary. They
speak of maintaining the family for the common good, of
how gender complementarity is necessary for marital bonding across genders, of the importance of embodiment and
being a part of the ongoing procreative narrative. The pope
denounces "the false families" of homosexuals and lesbians.
Well, of course, I agree that a viable society must support and
privilege procreative families, but I don't see why this positive
support necessitates barring the marriage of gay couples.

9   Good Catholic parents of adult children I know welcome
their gay children's life long partners as "in-laws," who are
part of their family. Doesn't it seem a confirmation of the
Christian teaching on the goodness of monogamous marriage
that gay couples eschew promiscuity and desire to regularize
and ritualize their loving commitment to one another?

10   Assertions about the complementarity of the two genders
appear to be false to new psychological insights on the range
of gender variability and overlapping similarities, as well as
to the Christian call to transcend gender in Christian unity
where "there is neither male nor female." If the symbol of
Christ as male bridegroom in union with the church is used
too literally as the form for marriage, then could only females
(as brides) be church members? (Rigid overestimation of gender is also the fallacy that bans women from ordination.)

11   Any two persons must struggle to obtain loving unity, but
when you take into account the multitude of inevitable differences in temperament, intelligence, taste, talents, and moral
maturity, gender can be a minor consideration.

12   Affirming embodiment and respect for the symbolic language of the body is important, but I'd say the grammar book
includes a wider range of syntax and idiom than is officially
published. In fact I've come (finally) to see the rejection of
loving gay erotic expression as a rejection of embodiment,
and another form of resistance to the goodness of sexual
desire and pleasure. For most persons, gay or straight, chaste
friendships and general charity cannot produce the same
intense intimacy, bodily confirmation, mutual sanctification,
and fulfilling happiness that come from making love with a
faithful partner. (The inability of some celibates to accept the
importance of freely expressing sexual and erotic marital love
has produced the birth control impasse.)

13   Other rejections of the body also may be surfacing when
whatever homosexuals do together is considered especially
revolting and repugnant. Our stringent toilet, cleanliness, and

touch taboos enforced in infancy can linger on in the feeling that certain parts or functions of the body are intrinsically disgusting. Some of the anti-gay articles I've been dutifully perusing are revealing. They begin with warnings against the "gay conspiracy" and "homosexual cult" that aim "to seduce our children" into its diseased and perverted "clutches." Then follow references to "debased," "mutual self-gratifications," "through what very definitely and clearly is nothing but a deathhole...it yields only dead matter." Lesbians are absent from these phallocentric fulminations, presumably because they possess no "life giving or sharing organ" to end up in the wrong orifice.

Well, it has taken centuries to get over the ancient convic- 14
tions that menstruating females are unclean and ritually pol-
lute the altar. If, that is, we have gotten over it. When you see
some of the heated resistance to women's ordination, one
wonders. Oh Christ, if we could only take your words to heart
and learn what defiles a person and what doesn't.

Jean Bethke Elshtain

Accepting Limits

*Jean Bethke Elshtain is a professor of political science at
Vanderbilt University and the author of several books, including* Power Trips and Other Journeys *(1992). "Accepting Limits" makes use of several paragraphs from* Power Trips, *in
particular an essay titled "The Family and Civic Life." "Accepting Limits" was published in 1991 in* Commonweal, *the same
liberal biweekly review of public affairs, religion, and the arts
that carried the previous essay by Sidney Callahan. (For
another example of Elshtain's work see her article in the section on single parenthood, page 532.)*

Every society embraces an image of a body politic. This 1
complex symbolism incorporates visions and reflections on
who is inside and who is outside; on what counts as order and
disorder; on what is cherished and what is despised. This imagery is fluid but not, I will argue, entirely up for grabs. For without some continuity in our imagery and concern, we confront
a deepening nihilism. In a world of ever-more transgressive

enthusiasms, the individual—the self—is more, not less, in thrall to whatever may be the reigning ethos. Ours is a culture whose reigning ethic is surely individualism and freedom. Great and good things have come from this stress on freedom and from the insistence that there are things that cannot and must not be done for me and to me in the name of some overarching collective. It is, therefore, unsurprising that anything that comes before us in the name of "rights" and "freedom" enjoys a *prima facie* power, something akin to political grace.

2 But perhaps we have reached the breaking point. When Madonna proclaims, in all sincerity, that mock masturbation before tens of thousands is "freedom of expression" on a par, presumably, with the right to petition, assemble, and protest, something seems a bit out of whack—distorted, quirky, not-quite-right. I thought about this sort of thing a lot when I listened to the stories of the "Mothers of the Disappeared" in Argentina and to their invocation of the language of "human rights" as a fundamental immunity—the right not to be tortured and "disappeared." I don't believe there is a slippery slope from queasiness at, if not repudiation of, public sexual acts for profit, orchestrated masturbation, say, and putting free speech as a fundamental right of free citizens in peril. I don't think the body politic has to be nude and sexually voracious—getting, consuming, demanding pleasure. That is a symbolism that courts nihilism and privatism (however publicly it may be trumpeted) because it repudiates intergenerational, familial, and communal contexts and believes history and tradition are useful only to be trashed. Our culture panders to what social critic John O'Neill calls the "libidinal body," the body that titillates and ravishes and is best embodied as young, thin, antimaternal, calculating, and disconnected. Make no mistake about it: much of the move to imagery of the entitled self and the aspirations to which it gives rise are specifically, deeply, and troublingly antinatal—hostile to the regenerative female body and to the symbolism of social regeneration to which this body is necessarily linked and has, historically, given rise.

3 Don't get me wrong: not every female body must be a regenerative body. At stake here is not mandating and coercing the lives of individuals but pondering the fate of a society that, more and more, repudiates generativity as an animating image in favor of aspiration without limit of the contractual and "wanting" self. One symbol and reality of the latter is the search for intrusive intervention in human reproducing coming from those able to command the resources of genetic

engineers and medical reproduction experts, also, therefore, those who have more clout over what gets lifted up as our culture's dominant sense of itself. One finds more and more the demand that babies can and must be made whenever the want is there. This demandingness, this transformation of human procreation into a technical operation, promotes a project Oliver O'Donovan calls "scientific self-transcendence." The technologizing of birth is antiregenerative, linked as it is to a refusal to accept any natural limits. What technology "can do," and the law permits, we seem ready to embrace. Our ethics rushes to catch up with the rampant rush of our forged and incited desires.

These brief reflections are needed to frame my equally brief   4
comments on the legality, or not, of homosexual marriage. I have long favored domestic partnership possibilities—ways to regularize and stabilize commitments and relationships. But marriage is not, and never has been, primarily about two people—it is and always has been about the possibility of generativity. Although in any given instance, a marriage might not have led to the raising of a family, whether through choice or often unhappy recognition of, and final reconciliation to, the infertility of one or another spouse, the symbolism of marriage-family as social regenesis is fused in our centuries-old experience with marriage ritual, regulation, and persistence.

The point of criticism and contention runs: in defending the   5
family as framed within a horizon of intergenerationality, one privileges a restrictive ideal of sexual and intimate relations. There are within our society, as I already noted, those who believe this society can and should stay equally open to all alternative arrangements, treating "life-styles" as so many identical peas in a pod. To be sure, families in modernity coexist with those who live another way, whether heterosexual and homosexual unions that are by choice or by definition childless; communalists who diminish individual parental authority in favor of the preeminence of the group; and so on.

But the recognition and acceptance of plural possibilities   6
does not mean each alternative is equal to every other with reference to specific social goods. No social order has ever existed that did not endorse certain activities and practices as preferable to others. Ethically responsible challenges to our terms of exclusion and inclusion push toward a loosening but not a wholesale negation in our normative endorsement of intergenerational family life. Those excluded by, or who exclude themselves from, the familial intergenerational ideal, should not be denied social space for their own practices. And

it is possible that if what were at stake were, say, seeking out and identifying those creations of self that enhance an aesthetic construction of life and sensibility, the romantic bohemian or rebel would get higher marks than the Smith family of Remont, Nebraska. Nevertheless, we should be cautious about going too far in the direction of a wholly untrammeled pluralism lest we become so vapid that we are no longer capable of distinguishing between the moral weightiness of, say, polishing one's Porsche and sitting up all night with an ill child. The intergenerational family, as symbolism of social regenesis, as tough and compelling reality, as defining moral norm, remains central and critical in nurturing recognitions of human frailty, mortality, and finitude and in inculcating moral limits and constraints. To resolve the untidiness of our public and private relations by either reaffirming unambiguously a set of unitary, authoritative norms or eliminating all such norms as arbitrary is to jeopardize the social goods that democratic and familial authority, paradoxical in relation to one another, promise—to men and women as parents and citizens and to their children.

Barbara Findlen
Is Marriage the Answer?

Barbara Findlen is the executive editor of Ms. *magazine, the famous feminist publication that carried the following article in the May/June 1995 issue.*

1   In December 1990, Ninia Baehr and Genora Dancel applied for a marriage license at their local health department office in Honolulu. When the license was denied because they are both women, they—along with two other same-sex couples who applied for marriage licenses on the same day—sued the state of Hawaii on the grounds of discrimination. The three couples—two lesbian and one gay male—were well prepared: before applying for the licenses, they'd already determined that they might have a shot at changing Hawaii's marriage laws.

2   And indeed, by May 1993, the Hawaii Supreme Court ruled that prohibiting members of the same sex from marrying

constitutes sex discrimination and is therefore a violation of the state constitution, which includes an equal rights amendment. The supreme court then proceeded to send the case back to a lower court, ordering the state to show a "compelling interest" in maintaining the discrimination. Remarkably, most observers believe that, barring a change in the makeup of the court or some other extreme circumstance, the couples will triumph when the case is finally decided sometime within the next 18 months.

The case is significant, not just for the future of gay marriage, but also for the fate of domestic partnership agreements, which give benefits such as health insurance coverage to unmarried couples. Some activists are wondering, for example, what will become of the dozens of domestic partnership policies that have sprung up over the last decade, many of which also benefit unmarried heterosexual couples. If gay marriage were to become legal, entities that currently offer these policies might decide that since anyone can marry, benefits should be offered only to spouses. Domestic partnership policies would therefore be seen as unnecessary. Many of those who favor domestic partnership policies over marriage espouse the arguably radical notion that *no* rights or benefits should be based on marriage. Other critics would even prefer to see marriage, with its patriarchal trappings, abolished altogether.

While some people might view lesbian and gay marriage as a radical development because it would at last put homosexual relationships on a par with heterosexual ones, domestic partnership advocates view it as conservative because it upholds the basic primacy of marriage as the foundation of the family and marginalizes people who are outside that unit. Notes Paula L. Ettelbrick, a legislative counsel at New York's Empire State Pride Agenda: "The marriage campaign has moved our community to a more conservative, middle-of-the-road political perspective. It has taken people out of the broader, social justice view of family."

But there are different agendas among those who advocate domestic partnership, acknowledges Matt Coles, the director of the ACLU Lesbian and Gay Rights Project and coauthor of one of the first domestic partnership policies ever proposed in the U.S. (for the city of San Francisco in 1980). Some view domestic partnership as a straightforward equal-pay-for-equal-work issue: employment benefits that are offered to employees' legal spouses should be offered to partners of unmarried employees. For others, it's a way station en route to lesbian and gay marriage. Still others see it as a way to begin to fundamentally redefine the legal meaning of "family," thus undermining the power of the patriarchal nuclear family.

6   Melinda Paras, executive director of the National Gay and Lesbian Task Force (NGLTF), is aiming for the latter. "Part of our struggle," she says, "is to fight for a broader definition of families. Domestic partners shouldn't have to be gay or lesbian. They shouldn't have to be having sex. They can be two adults sharing a home and sharing commitment, responsible to each other."

7   Currently, about 35 municipalities and scores of private companies, educational institutions, and nonprofit organizations offer some kind of policy that bestows benefits on unmarried cohabiting couples—gay *and* straight. There are two kinds of domestic partnership policies—those offered by the private sector, which generally do not provide benefits to unmarried heterosexuals, and municipal policies created by city governments, which cover both same-sex and opposite-sex partners. A typical municipal policy might well define domestic partners in terms similar to those of Paras. In Madison, Wisconsin, for example, they can be any two unrelated adults "in a relationship of mutual support, caring, and commitment." In Seattle, the partners must "have a close and personal relationship" and share "basic living expenses." In many cities, more straight couples than gay couples register as domestic partners. Municipalities establish a registry, and city employees who file are usually given a certificate that validates their domestic partnership and often provides access to spousal equivalent benefits (health insurance, bereavement leave, and other benefits granted to married employees). People who don't work for the city may also receive a certificate. Though organizations in the private sector, such as auto clubs or health clubs, may honor this municipal certificate as a basis for providing benefits, it's strictly optional, and the benefits offered by the city to nonemployees are limited—perhaps access to family memberships at a museum or a gym, or the right to hospital or jail visitation.

8   Private sector policies tend to be much narrower than municipal policies. Most apply only to same-sex partners. The major benefit is usually health insurance, and some policies even stop short of that, offering only bereavement or family care leave, use of recreational facilities, access to married faculty or student housing—benefits that cost the institution little.

9   The rationale behind most private sector plans is: lesbian and gay employees can't marry, so as a matter of workplace

equity, they should have access to benefits they would have if they could marry. Nancy Polikoff, a law professor whose work has focused on lesbian and gay families, cites the policy at her own institution, American University, which applies only to same-sex domestic partners. "What happens when there's gay and lesbian marriage?" she says. "That's the end of domestic partnership benefits. We will be told, 'Get married.' What does that say about the notion that we can choose not to get married?"

What about a corporation like Levi Strauss & Co., which 10 offers benefits to unmarried heterosexual partners? It's hard to predict whether policies like that will disappear, but it seems likely that the possibility of same-sex marriage would remove a lot of the impetus behind the domestic partnership movement. Although the policies often benefit straight people, the initiative has mostly come from lesbians and gay men, who don't have access to marriage rights.

"My big fear," says Ettelbrick, "is that if gay people were 11 allowed to marry tomorrow, I know that we would lose a substantial part of our community that is working on domestic partner benefits. The point is that neither straight people nor gay people should have to get married in order to have some very basic protections for the families that they've chosen. I don't think we have a unified sense of social reform anymore. We have a piece-by-piece approach—we'll make change where we can. We no longer have bigger picture items on our agendas."

Domestic partnership, like many other issues that now concern this country, is curiously tied to health care. The word "benefit," after all, is often synonymous with health insurance. And why, many ask, is health insurance coverage tied to marital, couple, *or* employment status? "If universal health care were available, no one would be forced to say, 'I want to be able to get married to take advantage of my partner's health insurance benefits,'" says Polikoff. "What we ought to do is let every employee designate a person to receive co-benefits. That person could be your sexual partner, best friend, aunt, or sister. Why are we making people's sexual partners more important than others with whom they share their lives? This kind of arrangement would be my way station to uncoupling all of these benefits from marriage and creating a world in which the things that are now considered components of marriage become social entitlements or can be designated by individuals."

Adds Robin Kane, NGLTF's communications director: "We 13 could wait for universal health care coverage to be enacted by

Congress. We could wait for the Hawaii marriage ruling to come down and then for every state to battle out whether or not they'll recognize it. But in the meantime, there are people who are actually getting health insurance for their partners through domestic partner benefits."

14   But domestic partnership policies don't hold a candle to the entitlements that come with marriage. It is already possible to approximate some of the rights granted automatically to married people—inheritance can be addressed through wills, the right to make health care decisions through durable powers of attorney. Compare these with the rights that come with a marriage license and cannot be exercised by unmarried couples, no matter where they live or what agreements they have made: the right to joint parenting, through birth or adoption; the right to file joint income tax returns; legal immigration and residency for partners from other countries; benefits such as annuities, pensions, and Social Security for surviving spouses; wrongful death benefits for surviving partners; immunity from having to testify in court against a spouse.

15   Jane, a health club manager, and Beth, a teacher in suburban New York (not their real names), know the consequences of not having those rights. Five years ago, Jane gave birth to a daughter conceived via insemination by an anonymous donor. When a married couple have a baby in this way, the husband is automatically declared the father. Beth's application to legally adopt their daughter was denied on the grounds that the couple, who have been together for 18 years, were not married. "I'm considered her mother by our community, day care, school, and families," says Beth, "but I have no legal rights as her mother."

16   Whether or not lesbians and gay men should fight for the right to marry has been a subject of debate in the gay community for years. In 1989, the lesbian and gay magazine *Outlook* published opposing articles, "Since When Is Marriage a Path to Liberation?" by Paula Ettelbrick, and "Why Gay People Should Seek the Right To Marry," by Thomas B. Stoddard. Both authors are lawyers who were working for the Lambda Legal Defense and Education Fund at the time. "Marriage runs contrary to two of the primary goals of the lesbian and gay movement: the affirmation of gay identity and culture, and the validation of many forms of relationships," argued Ettelbrick. Answered Stoddard: "The issue is not the desirability of marriage, but rather the desirability of the right to marry."

Even Beth and Jane aren't sure they would exercise that 17
right. "It's for heterosexuals," says Jane. "Our union doesn't
need that ceremony. We would only do it for legal protection."

Feminists have long criticized the institution of marriage 18
as a place of oppression, danger, and drudgery for women.
Nineteenth-century feminists protested that a woman's legal
identity literally disappeared upon marriage. Even in 1969, a
New York City organization called the Feminists declared:
"All the discriminatory practices against women are patterned and rationalized by this slavery-like practice. We can't
destroy the inequities between men and women until we
destroy marriage." These days the uneasiness is due to marriage's power as the singular definer of family, a reinforcer of
sex roles, and an institution of heterosexual privilege. Karen
Lindsey has been thinking about different forms of family for
more than 15 years. Her 1981 book, *Friends as Family*, begins,
"The traditional family isn't working," and goes on to explore
workplace families, "honorary kin," and chosen families. "In
my ideal world, there would be no such thing as marriage,"
she says today. "What there would be is individuals choosing
to live together on whatever terms meet their needs, and then
appropriate legal connections to address those needs."

"People say that there are all these goodies that go with 19
being married and why shouldn't gay people get to have
them," agrees Polikoff. "My vision is one in which the goodies
are not tied to marriage."

As feminists, Ninia Baehr and Genora Dancel, two of the 20
Hawaii plaintiffs, are well aware of these arguments. But for
them, the decision to marry was an emotional, not a political,
one. Baehr, who was the codirector of the women's center at
the University of Hawaii when the suit was filed, says: "If I
had sat down and planned my career as a feminist years ago,
I would never have said, 'The most important thing I can do is
legalize marriage for lesbian and gay people.' But the reality
is that when I met Genora, I thought, 'My God, she's the one
that I've been dreaming about.' I wanted to get married. I
wanted to be able to say at the end of my life that I had loved
someone really well for a long time."

Hawaii state legislators meanwhile are doing whatever 21
they can to keep Baehr and Dancel and the other two couples
from legally tying the knot. Alarmed at the prospect of their
state being the first to allow gay marriage, they passed a law
last year that explicitly defines marriage as being between a
man and a woman. However, this legislation will presumably
be subject to the same "compelling interest" requirement as

the previous policy, so it's unlikely that the law will change the outcome of the case. A few legislators have proposed amending the state constitution to exclude same-sex marriage—the one sure way around the state supreme court—but these proposals have failed.

22   Although the Hawaii court ruling would apply only to marriages performed in that state, the decision could spark legal chaos all over the country. Lesbian and gay couples will likely flock to Hawaii to marry, then return to their home states and try to file joint tax returns, sign up for spousal health insurance coverage, or adopt children together. Currently every state recognizes marriages performed in other states. Couples who are denied recognition of their legal same-sex marriages granted in Hawaii will have grounds to sue their home states.

23   "There will be litigation in many states for years to come," says Evan Wolfson, cocounsel for the three Hawaii couples and director of the Lambda Legal Defense and Education Fund's Marriage Project. The dozens of expected cases could implicate even the federal government, which relies on the states to determine who is married for purposes of taxes, Social Security benefits, immigration, and other matters. And though all marriage laws are state laws, the question potentially could be settled by the U.S. Supreme Court. If that happened, lawyers for the couples would likely base their arguments on the provision of the U.S. Constitution that requires states to give "full faith and credit" to the lawful marriages of other states.

24   And these other states are keeping an anxious eye on Hawaii. The state legislature of Utah has passed legislation that would refuse recognition of any same-sex marriage performed in another state. South Dakota also tried, but failed, to pass such a law.

25   The ACLU's Matt Coles thinks one significant result of the pending Hawaii ruling will be a proliferation of domestic partnership protections for lesbians and gay men as states try—by offering spousal equivalent benefits—to avoid the need to recognize gay marriage.

26   NGLTF's Paras says: "I think we will end up with marriage and domestic partnership as simultaneously existing legal constructs. Marriage will be a huge battle that will mostly be lost for a long time. In the meantime, domestic partnership practices are expanding and will become a much larger body of law and policy. By the time equality finally gets won universally, we'll be in a whole other place about the definition of family, and gay marriage may become almost irrelevant."

V.

CIVIL LIBERTIES AND CIVIL RIGHTS

Introduction

A basic premise of this collection of readings is that writing typically emerges from other writing. As a demonstration of that premise, consider the very large body of writing that has emerged from some very basic texts in our political history. Consider, for instance, the words of the First Amendment to the Constitution:

> Congress shall make no law respecting an establishment of religion, or prohibiting the free exercise thereof; or abridging the freedom of speech, or of the press; or the right of the people peaceably to assemble, and to petition the Government for a redress of grievances.

Or consider section one of the Fourteenth Amendment, ratified in 1868:

> All persons born or naturalized in the United States, and subject to the jurisdiction thereof, are citizens of the United States and of the State wherein they reside. No State shall make or enforce any law which shall abridge the privileges or immunities of citizens of the United States; nor shall any State deprive any person of life, liberty, or property, without due process of law; nor deny to any person within its jurisdiction the equal protection of the laws.

Or this fragment from the Declaration of Independence:

> We hold these Truths to be self-evident, that all Men are created equal, that they are endowed by their Creator with certain inalienable Rights, that among these are Life, Liberty, and the Pursuit of Happiness. That to secure these rights, Governments are instituted among Men....

The readings in Part V explore some of the implications of these seminal passages.

Two sets of readings on the issue of censorship are included: one (on pornography) that picks up gender and language concerns from Part II; and another (the case of possible restrictions on electronic communications) that looks forward to Internet issues that are discussed in Part VII of this book.

Is pornography harmful? Should it be censored or restricted? Speaking for the affirmative, many women (as well as men) contend that pornography does indeed have harmful effects, that pornography provides a dangerous "theory" on how to treat women and rape or other forms of misogyny, the "practice." But other people see pornography as neutral in its effects or contend that the First Amendment protects all varieties of speech and writing from censorship. Did the framers of the Constitution intend to protect free speech and a free press in an absolute sense (as Hugo Black and William Douglas argued in a 1957 Supreme Court decision)? Or were the framers speaking only of political speech and writing (as the seven other Supreme Court justices agreed in that same 1957 case)? Is it indeed constitutional to restrict pornography? (After all, we do restrict libel, and we ban cigarette ads on TV and ads aimed at minors, on the grounds of their harmful effects and apolitical content.) And just what is pornography, anyway? Can it be defined in a way that makes restrictions practical, or would such definitions and restrictions undermine artistic and political freedom? The issue of pornography makes for strange bedfellows; it is an issue about which liberals and conservatives disagree among themselves, and it is an issue that has divided feminists. In fact, the argument among feminists is represented in this section by Susan Brownmiller and Andrea Dworkin, who find themselves arguing with Barbara Dority and Nadine Strossen.

Liberals and conservatives also break ranks over whether or not it would be wise to censor the Internet. Is the Internet being used to purvey pornography? Is pornography on the Internet readily available to children? Should hate speech on the Internet be a prosecutable offense, or is it speech protected by the First Amendment? If we restrict pornography and other forms of communication on the Internet, will that lead to further restrictions on a medium for communication that is apparently open and accessible now? This section of *Conversations* considers these questions by offering an exchange among many Internetters themselves, conducted mostly on the Internet, concerning the wisdom of laws that would censor pornography available through the computer.

The conflict between the individual and society, so apparent in discussions of censorship, is central to culture in the United States because we value both the dignity of the private individual and the importance of public institutions sanctioned through the democratic process. Faced with the dilemma of paying taxes to support a popular war, which he disagreed with, Henry David Thoreau proposed civil disobedience—a private act of personal conscience against "the tyranny of the majority." Later in history, Mahatma Gandhi and Martin Luther King Jr. refined civil disobedience into an effective tactic for achieving public justice and political equality. Were they right to do so? What is civil disobedience anyway? Is it a legitimate political tool or an invitation to anarchy that would destroy the principle of democratic rule? What should people do when "higher laws" put them in conflict with majority rule? What else can a democratic society do except be ruled by a majority? Can such a majority be a "tyranny," or is it the resistance to legitimate, democratic authority that is arrogant and tyrannical? Could civil disobedience even exist in a truly tyrannical society, one without a free press and trial by jury, one in which political minorities disappear in the middle of the night? The selections in this civil disobedience section articulate and debate the question of the legitimacy of civil disobedience, and they also offer a critical context for understanding a central document of civil disobedience and the U.S. civil rights movement: King's "Letter from Birmingham Jail."

Civil disobedience has been a common tactic since the mid-1950s, especially in connection with campaigns to expand the civil rights of African Americans and women. Civil disobedience has also been employed at times by pro-life groups eager to see the practice of abortion restricted in the United States; that is only one indication that the recognition of the right to abortion is inspiring probably the most heated discussion now taking place in our society. Since the Supreme Court in the *Roe* v. *Wade* decision of 1973 legalized abortions performed in the first three months of a pregnancy, a pitched battle has been fought between those absolutely committed to upholding the Supreme Court position and those just as absolutely constituted to overturning it. One camp, which sees the developing fetus as only a potential human being, is protective of women's right to privacy and personal freedom; the other camp, which sees the fetus as a human being with the rights of a human being, supports various restrictions on the right to abortion, if not an outright reversal of *Roe* v. *Wade*. In both camps, many people are convinced that only one side or the other can prevail in the abortion debate—that "victory" without substantial compromise can be achieved through the ballot box, rallies, and Supreme Court appointments. Those who seek absolute victory on either side are often so committed to their positions that they are unwilling to participate in reasoned discussions. They often produce more heat than light on the subject.

But other people are convinced that a resolution of the issue of abortion is not just possible but essential. Some pro-choice advocates understand abortion as a morally cloudy act and recognize that the Supreme Court has already placed some restrictions on abortion (i.e., abortion is restricted to the first months of pregnancy). On the other side, many pro-life advocates are confronting the apparent fact that our Constitution permits abortion, whether they like it or not, and are pursuing efforts to persuade people to avoid abortion not because it is illegal but because better contraceptive choices are usually available, if people would only seek them out. Members of both camps, in short, are seeking continuing discussion, reasoned exchange, and mutual respect; and they tend to hold out a hope for negotiated consensus on the matter—incremental progress toward national agreement. When does a fetus become a person? What circumstances justify abortion? Are there ways of reducing abortions and at the same time protecting women's right to privacy (e.g., through improved methods of contraception)? Are any additional restrictions on abortions (*Roe v. Wade* restricts abortions to the first three months of pregnancy) sensible? Can those restrictions protect the rights of everyone involved, even as those rights are also somewhat compromised? These matters are confronted in five readings in the section on abortion.

Five other readings follow on another matter of civil rights. In the past decade, members of another minority group—homosexuals—have clamored for additional civil rights, often quite publicly through marches and protests and other highly publicized tactics marshaled by organizations such as Act Up and Queer Nation. Should homosexuals be permitted to serve openly in the military? Should they be protected by fair housing and fair employment practices? Should gay couples be permitted to claim the rights enjoyed by married couples, such as the right to adopt children or share health benefits? Does the AIDS epidemic have implications for civil rights in this country? Those last two questions are taken up in greater detail in the section on same-sex marriage in Part IV, "Family Matters," and in the section on combating AIDS in Part VII, "Science and Society" (for AIDS is an issue that is certainly not limited to the gay community).

No doubt questions like the ones posed in the paragraphs above are being discussed on every American campus this year.

CENSORSHIP I: PORNOGRAPHY

*President's Commission on
Obscenity and Pornography*

Majority Report

In 1967, Congress by law established an eighteen-member special commission (appointed by President Nixon) to study the impact of obscenity and pornography on American life. After gathering testimony, reviewing research, and conferring at length, the commission in 1970 recommended against legislation that would restrain pornography. A minority of the members of the commission, feeling differently, submitted their own dissenting report. Excerpts from both follow.

1   Discussions of obscenity and pornography in the past have often been devoid of fact. Popular rhetoric has often contained a variety of estimates of the size of the "smut" industry and assertions regarding the consequences of the existence of these materials and exposure to them. Many of these statements, however, have had little anchoring in objective evidence. Within the limits of its time and resources, the Commission has sought, through staff and contract research, to broaden the factual basis for future continued discussion. The Commission is aware that not all issues of concern have been completely researched nor all questions answered. It also recognizes that the interpretations of a set of "facts" in arriving at policy implications may differ even among men of good will. Nevertheless, the Commission is convinced that on most issues regarding obscenity and pornography the discussion can be informed by important and often new facts. It presents its Report, hopeful that it will contribute to this discussion at a new level. . . .

2   Exposure to erotic stimuli appears to have little or no effect on already established attitudinal commitments regarding either sexuality or sexual morality. A series of four studies employing a large array of indicators found practically no significant differences in such attitudes before and after single

or repeated exposures to erotica. One study did find that after exposure persons became more tolerant in reference to other persons' sexual activities although their own sexual standards did not change. One study reported that some persons' attitudes toward premarital intercourse became more liberal after exposure, while other persons' attitudes became more conservative, but another study found no changes in this regard. The overall picture is almost completely a tableau of no significant change....

Statistical studies of the relationship between availability   3
of erotic materials and the rates of sex crimes in Denmark indicate that the increased availability of explicit sexual materials has been accompanied by a decrease in the incidence of sexual crime. Analysis of police records of the same types of sex crimes in Copenhagen during the past 12 years revealed that a dramatic decrease in reported sex crimes occurred during this period and that the decrease coincided with changes in Danish law which permitted wider availability of explicit sexual materials. Other research showed that the decrease in reported sexual offenses cannot be attributed to concurrent changes in the social and legal definitions of sex crimes or in public attitudes toward reporting such crimes to the police, or in police reporting procedures.

Statistical studies of the relationship between the avail-   4
ability of erotic material and the rates of sex crimes in the United States presents a more complex picture. During the period in which there has been a marked increase in the availability of erotic materials, some specific rates of arrest for sex crimes have increased (e.g., forcible rape) and others have declined (e.g., overall juvenile rates). For juveniles, the overall rate of arrests for sex crimes decreased even though arrests for nonsexual crimes increased by more than 100%. For adults, arrests for sex offenses increased slightly more than did arrests for nonsex offenses. The conclusion is that, for America, the relationship between the availability of erotica and changes in sex crime rates neither proves nor disproves the possibility that availability of erotica leads to crime, but the massive overall increases in sex crimes that have been alleged do not seem to have occurred....

I. Non-Legislative Recommendation

The Commission believes that much of the "problem"   5
regarding materials which depict explicit sexual activity

stems from the inability or reluctance of people in our society to be open and direct in dealing with sexual matters....

6   The Commission believes that accurate, appropriate sex information provided openly and directly through legitimate channels and from reliable sources in healthy contexts can compete successfully with potentially distorted, warped, inaccurate, and unreliable information about clandestine, illegitimate sources; and it believes that the attitudes and orientations toward sex produced by the open communication of appropriate sex information from reliable sources through legitimate channels will be normal and healthy, providing a solid foundation for the basic institutions of our society.

7   The Commission, therefore,...*recommends that a massive sex education effort be launched....* The Commission feels that such a sex education program would provide a powerful positive approach to the problems of obscenity and pornography. By providing accurate and reliable sex information through legitimate sources, it would reduce interest in and dependence upon clandestine and less legitimate sources. By providing healthy attitudes and orientations toward sexual relationships, it would provide better protection for the individual against distorted and warped ideas he may encounter regarding sex. By providing greater ease in talking about sexual matters in appropriate contexts, the shock and offensiveness of encounters with sex would be reduced....

II. Legislative Recommendation

8   *The Commission recommends that federal, state, and local legislation prohibiting the sale, exhibition, or distribution of sexual materials to consenting adults should be repealed....*

Our conclusion is based upon the following considerations:

9   1. Extensive empirical investigation, both by the Commission and by others, provides no evidence that exposure to or use of explicit sexual materials plays a significant role in causation of social or individual harms such as crime, delinquency, sexual or nonsexual deviancy or severe emotional disturbances.... Empirical investigation thus supports the opinion of a substantial majority of persons professionally engaged in the treatment of deviancy, delinquency and anti-social behavior, that exposure to sexually explicit materials has no harmful causal role in these areas. Studies show that a

number of factors, such as disorganized family relationships and unfavorable peer influences, are intimately related to harmful sexual behavior or adverse character development. Exposure to sexually explicit materials, however, cannot be counted as among these determinative factors.

2. On the positive side, explicit sexual materials are sought   10
as a source of entertainment and information by substantial numbers of American adults. At times, these materials also appear to serve to increase and facilitate constructive communication about sexual matters within marriage. The most frequent purchaser of explicit sexual materials is a college-educated, married male, in his thirties or forties, who is of above average socio-economic status. Even where materials are legally available to them, young adults and older adolescents do not constitute an important portion of the purchasers of such materials.

3. Society's attempts to legislate for adults in the area of   11
obscenity have not been successful. Present laws prohibiting the consensual sale or distribution of explicit sexual materials to adults are extremely unsatisfactory in their practical application. The Constitution permits material to be deemed "obscene" for adults only if, as a whole, it appeals to the "prurient" interest of the average person, is "patently offensive" in light of "community standards," and lacks "redeeming social value." These vague and highly subjective aesthetic, psychological and moral tests do not provide meaningful guidance for law enforcement officials, juries or courts. As a result, law is inconsistently and sometimes erroneously applied and the distinctions made by courts between prohibited and permissible materials often appear indefensible. Errors in the application of the law and uncertainty about its scope also cause interference with the communication of constitutionally protected materials.

4. Public opinion in America does not support the imposi-   12
tion of legal prohibitions upon the right of adults to read or see explicit sexual materials. While a minority of Americans favors such prohibitions, a majority of the American people presently are of the view that adults should be legally able to read or see explicit sexual materials if they wish to do so.

5. The lack of consensus among Americans concerning   13
whether explicit sexual materials should be available to adults in our society, and the significant number of adults who wish to have access to such materials, pose serious problems regarding the enforcement of legal prohibitions upon adults, even aside from the vagueness and subjectivity of

present law. Consistent enforcement of even the clearest prohibitions upon consensual adult exposure to explicit sexual materials would require the expenditure of considerable law enforcement resources. In the absence of a persuasive demonstration of damage flowing from consensual exposure to such materials, there seems no justification for thus adding to the overwhelming tasks already placed upon the law enforcement system. Inconsistent enforcement of prohibitions, on the other hand, invites discriminatory action based upon considerations not directly relevant to the policy of the law. The latter alternative also breeds public disrespect for the legal process.

14 6. The foregoing considerations take on an added significance because of the fact that adult obscenity laws deal in the realm of speech and communication. Americans deeply value the right of each individual to determine for himself what books he wishes to read and what pictures or films he wishes to see. Our traditions of free speech and press also value and protect the right of writers, publishers, and booksellers to serve the diverse interests of the public. The spirit and letter of our Constitution tell us that government should not seek to interfere with these rights unless a clear threat of harm makes that course imperative. Moreover, the possibility of the misuse of general obscenity statutes prohibiting distributions of books and films to adults constitutes a continuing threat to the free communication of ideas among Americans—one of the most important foundations of our liberties.

15 7. In reaching its recommendation that government should not seek to prohibit consensual distributions of sexual materials to adults, the Commission discussed several arguments which are often advanced in support of such legislation. The Commission carefully considered the view that adult legislation should be retained in order to aid in the protection of young persons from exposure to explicit sexual materials. We do not believe that the objective of protecting youth may justifiably be achieved at the expense of denying adults materials of their choice. It seems to us wholly inappropriate to adjust the level of adult communication to that considered suitable for children. Indeed, the Supreme Court has unanimously held that adult legislation premised on this basis is a clearly unconstitutional interference with liberty....

16 8. The Commission has also taken cognizance of the concern of many people that the lawful distribution of explicit sexual materials to adults may have a deleterious effect upon the individual morality of American citizens and upon the

moral climate in America as a whole. This concern appears to flow from a belief that exposure to explicit materials may cause moral confusion which, in turn, may induce antisocial or criminal behavior. As noted above, the Commission has found no evidence to support such a contention. Nor is there evidence that exposure to explicit sexual materials adversely affects character or moral attitudes regarding sex and sexual conduct. . . .

President's Commission on Obscenity and Pornography

Minority Report

Overview

The Commission's majority report is a Magna Carta for the pornographer. . . . The fundamental "finding" on which the entire report is based is: that "empirical research" has come up with "no reliable evidence to indicate that exposure to explicit sexual materials plays a significant role in the causation of delinquent or criminal behavior among youth or adults." The inference from this statement, i.e., pornography is harmless, is not only insupportable on the slanted evidence presented; it is preposterous. How isolate one factor and say it causes or does not cause criminal behavior? How determine that one book or one film caused one man to commit rape or murder? A man's entire life goes into one criminal act. No one factor can be said to have caused that act. 1

The Commission has deliberately and carefully avoided coming to grips with the basic underlying issue. The government interest in regulating pornography has always related primarily to the prevention of moral corruption and *not* to prevention of overt criminal acts and conduct, or the protection of persons from being shocked and/or offended. The basic question is whether and to what extent society may establish and maintain certain moral standards. If it is conceded that society has a legitimate concern in maintaining 2 moral standards, it follows logically that government has a legitimate interest in at least attempting to protect such standards against any source which threatens them....

3   Sex education, recommended so strongly by the majority, is the panacea for those who advocate license in media. The report suggests sex education, with a plaint for the dearth of instructors and materials. It notes that three schools have used "hard-core pornography" in training potential instructors. The report does not answer the question that comes to mind immediately: Will these instructors not bring the hard-core pornography into the grammar schools? Many other questions are left unanswered: How assure that the instructor's moral or ethical code (or lack of same) will not be communicated to children? Shouldn't parents, not children, be the recipients of sex education courses?

4   Children cannot grow in love if they are trained with pornography. Pornography is loveless; it degrades the human being, reduces him to the level of animal. And if this Commission majority's recommendations are heeded, there will be a glut of pornography for teachers and children.

5   In contrast to the Commission report's amazing statement that public opinion in America does not support the imposition of legal prohibitions upon the consensual distribution of pornography to adults, we find, as a result of public hearings conducted by two of the undersigned in eight cities throughout the country, that the majority of the American people favor tighter controls. Twenty-six out of twenty-seven witnesses at the hearing in New York City expressed concern and asked for remedial measures. Witnesses were a cross section of the community, ranging from members of the judiciary to members of women's clubs. This pattern was repeated in the cities of New Orleans, Indianapolis, Chicago, Salt Lake City, San Francisco, Washington, D.C., and Buffalo.... Additionally, law enforcement officers testifying at the Hill-Link hearings were unanimous in declaring that the problem of obscenity and pornography is a serious one.... We point also to the results of a Gallup poll, published in the summer of 1969. Eighty-five out of every 100 adults interviewed said they favored stricter state and local laws dealing with pornography sent through the mails, and 76 of every 100 wanted stricter laws on the sort of magazines and newspapers available on newsstands....

6   Some have argued that because sex crimes have apparently declined in Denmark while the volume of pornography has increased, we need not be concerned about the potential

effect in our country of this kind of material (because, essentially, of Denmark's benign experience). However two considerations must be noted. First we are a different culture with a greater commitment to the Judeo-Christian tradition; and secondly, we are actually only a year or so behind Denmark in the distribution and sale of pornography. Hardcore written pornography can be purchased anywhere in the U.S. now. Hardcore still pictures and movies can now be purchased over the counter in some cities. Anything can be purchased through the mails. And in a few cities people can attend hardcore pornographic movies. About the only thing we don't have, which Denmark has, are live sex shows. What is most relevant are sex crime statistics in this country, not Denmark ... :

Reported Rapes (verified)
   Up 116% 1960–69 (absolute increase)
   Up   93% 1960–69 (controlled for Pop. Growth)

Rape Arrests
   Up 56.6% all ages 1960–69
   Up 85.9% males under 18 1960–69

However, it should be stated that conclusively proving 7
causal relationships among social science type variables is extremely difficult if not impossible. Among adults whose life histories have included much exposure to pornography it is nearly impossible to disentangle the literally hundreds of causal threads or chains that contributed to their later adjustment or maladjustment. Because of the extreme complexity of the problem and the uniqueness of the human experience it is doubtful that we will ever have absolutely convincing scientific proof that pornography is or isn't harmful. And the issue isn't restricted to, "Does pornography cause or contribute to sex crimes?" The issue has to do with how pornography affects or influences the individual in his total relationship to members of the same as well as opposite sex, children and adults, with all of its ramifications.

Susan Brownmiller

Let's Put Pornography
Back in the Closet

Susan Brownmiller is a journalist, novelist, women's rights activist, and a founder of Women against Pornography. Her book Against Our Will: Men, Women, and Rape, *published in 1975, articulates a position on pornography that has been developed by later feminists. The following essay originally appeared in* Newsday, *a Long Island newspaper, in 1979 and a year later in* Take Back the Night, *a collection of essays against pornography.*

1   Free speech is one of the great foundations on which our democracy rests. I am old enough to remember the Hollywood Ten, the screenwriters who went to jail in the late 1940s because they refused to testify before a congressional committee about their political affiliations. They tried to use the First Amendment as a defense, but they went to jail because in those days there were few civil liberties lawyers around who cared to champion the First Amendment right to free speech, when the speech concerned the Communist Party.

2   The Hollywood Ten were correct in claiming the First Amendment. Its high purpose is the protection of unpopular ideas and political dissent. In the dark, cold days of the 1950s, few civil libertarians were willing to declare themselves First Amendment absolutists. But in the brighter, though frantic, days of the 1960s, the principle of protecting unpopular political speech was gradually strengthened.

3   It is fair to say now that the battle has largely been won. Even the American Nazi Party has found itself the beneficiary of the dedicated, tireless work of the American Civil Liberties Union. But—and please notice the quotation marks coming up—"To equate the free and robust exchange of ideas and political debate with commercial exploitation of obscene material demeans the grand conception of the First Amendment and its high purposes in the historic struggle for freedom. It is a misuse of the great guarantees of free speech and free press."

4   I didn't say that, although I wish I had, for I think the words are thrilling. Chief Justice Warren Burger said it in 1973, in the United States Supreme Court's majority opinion in *Miller* v. *California.* During the same decades that the right to political

free speech was being strengthened in the courts, the nation's obscenity laws also were undergoing extensive revision.

It's amazing to recall that in 1934 the question of whether   5
James Joyce's *Ulysses* should be banned as pornographic actually went before the Court. The battle to protect *Ulysses* as a work of literature with redeeming social value was won. In later decades, Henry Miller's *Tropic* books, *Lady Chatterley's Lover* and the *Memoirs of Fanny Hill* also were adjudged not obscene. These decisions have been important to me. As the author of *Against Our Will*, a study of the history of rape that does contain explicit sexual material, I shudder to think how my book would have fared if James Joyce, D. H. Lawrence and Henry Miller hadn't gone before me.

I am not a fan of *Chatterley* or the *Tropic* books, I should   6
quickly mention. They are not to my literary taste, nor do I think they represent female sexuality with any degree of accuracy. But I would hardly suggest that we ban them. Such a suggestion wouldn't get very far anyway. The battle to protect these books is ancient history. Time does march on, quite methodically. What, then, is unlawfully obscene, and what does the First Amendment have to do with it?

In the Miller case of 1973 (not Henry Miller, by the way, but   7
a porn distributor who sent unsolicited stuff through the mails), the Court came up with new guidelines that it hoped would strengthen obscenity laws by giving more power to the states. What it did in actuality was throw everything into confusion. It set up a three-part test by which materials can be adjudged obscene. The materials are obscene if they depict patently offensive, hard-core sexual conduct; lack serious scientific, literary, artistic or political value; and appeal to the prurient interest of an average person—as measured by contemporary community standards.

"Patently offensive," "prurient interest" and "hard-core"   8
are indeed words to conjure with. "Contemporary community standards" are what we're trying to redefine. The feminist objection to pornography is not based on prurience, which the dictionary defines as lustful, itching desire. We are not opposed to sex and desire, with or without the itch, and we certainly believe that explicit sexual material has its place in literature, art, science and education. Here we part company rather swiftly with old-line conservatives who don't want sex education in the high schools, for example.

No, the feminist objection to pornography is based on our   9
belief that pornography represents hatred of women, that pornography's intent is to humiliate degrade and dehumanize

the female body for the purpose of erotic stimulation and pleasure. We are unalterably opposed to the presentation of the female body being stripped, bound, raped, tortured, mutilated and murdered in the name of commercial entertainment and free speech.

10 ˙   These images, which are standard pornographic fare, have nothing to do with the hallowed right of political dissent. They have everything to do with the creation of a cultural climate in which a rapist feels he is merely giving in to a normal urge and a woman is encouraged to believe that sexual masochism is healthy, liberated fun. Justice Potter Stewart once said about hard-core pornography, "You know it when you see it," and that certainly used to be true. In the good old days, pornography looked awful. It was cheap and sleazy, and there was no mistaking it for art.

11   Nowadays, since the porn industry has become a multimillion dollar business, visual technology has been employed in its service. Pornographic movies are skillfully filmed and edited, pornographic still shots using the newest tenets of good design artfully grace the covers of *Hustler, Penthouse* and *Playboy,* and the public—and the courts—are sadly confused.

12   The Supreme Court neglected to define "hard-core" in the Miller decision. This was a mistake. If "hard-core" refers only to explicit sexual intercourse, then that isn't good enough. When women or children or men—no matter how artfully— are shown tortured or terrorized in the service of sex, that's obscene. And "patently offensive," I would hope, to our "contemporary community standards."

13   Justice William O. Douglas wrote in his dissent to the Miller case that no one is "compelled to look." This is hardly true. To buy a paper at the corner newsstand is to subject oneself to a forcible immersion in pornography, to be demeaned by an array of dehumanized, chopped-up parts of the female anatomy, packaged like cuts of meat at the supermarket. I happen to like my body and I work hard at the gym to keep it in good shape, but I am embarrassed for my body and for the bodies of all women when I see the fragmented parts of us so frivolously, and so flagrantly, displayed.

14   Some constitutional theorists (Justice Douglas was one) have maintained that any obscenity law is a serious abridgement of free speech. Others (and Justice Earl Warren was one) have maintained that the First Amendment was never intended to protect obscenity. We live quite compatibly with a host of free-speech abridgements. There are restraints against false and misleading advertising or statements—shouting

"fire" without cause in a crowded movie theater, etc.—that do not threaten, but strengthen, our societal values. Restrictions on the public display of pornography belong in this category.

The distinction between permission to publish and permis- 15 sion to display publicly is an essential one and one which I think consonant with First Amendment principles. Justice Burger's words which I quoted above support this without question. We are not saying "Smash the presses" or "Ban the bad ones," but simply "Get the stuff out of our sight." Let the legislatures decide—using realistic and humane contemporary community standards—what can be displayed and what cannot. The courts, after all, will be the final arbiters.

Barbara Dority

Feminist Morality, "Pornography," and Censorship

The following essay appeared in The Humanist *in late 1989.* The Humanist, *a product of the American Humanist Association, publishes clusters of articles on issues of public concern every month.*

The issue of "pornography" has engendered an intense 1 debate within the feminist movement. Will feminism, having achieved some significant gains, continue to capitulate to moralistic forces, or will it wake up and take a stand for the liberation of women in all domains, including the difficult and often contradictory domain of sexual expression?

Two separate issues are involved in this debate: first, the 2 moralistic feminist condemnation of "pornography"; and, second, the translation of that condemnation by nearly all feminist leaders into calls for various kinds of legislation which would effectively ban "pornographic" imagery and words. Both issues are alarming.

Literal Meanings

As a feminist secular humanist and a card-carrying member 3 of the American Civil Liberties Union, I believe the writers of the First Amendment meant every word exactly and literally: "Congress shall make no law...abridging the freedom of speech or of the press...." No law means *no law*.

4   The First Amendment does not say there is to be freedom of speech and press provided they are not sexually explicit, offensive, dangerous, or degrading. The authors of the Bill of Rights had learned firsthand why it was absolutely necessary to permit all manner of ideas to be expressed in the new republic. They knew this guarantee could not be confined to the expression of ideas that are conventional or shared by the majority but must include even those ideas considered repugnant or socially undesirable.

5   In the words of Justice William O. Douglas: "This demands that government keep its hands off all literature. There can be no freedom of expression unless all facets of life can be portrayed, no matter how repulsive these disclosures may be to some people." Justice Douglas later added that, in addition to freedom from government intervention, all manner of literature must remain available in the marketplace of ideas or the purpose of free expression is defeated. In other words, if we protect only the right to publish and then limit availability, we are still limiting freedom of speech.

6   The moralistic pro-censorship mind set has remained the same throughout the history of civilization. The censors aim at protecting us from the perceived harmful effects of what we read, see, and hear. Historically, they did this to protect our souls from blasphemy or society from alien political, social, or economic ideas. Today, it is being done to protect us from explicit sexual imagery and words. The justification, however, remains the same: it is best for us and best for society.

7   The highly subjective term *pornography* is grossly overused and abused. A wide range of materials has been so classified by feminists and summarily condemned, boycotted, picketed, and even banned.

8   The definition of *pornography* from Webster is: "The depiction of erotic behavior (as in pictures or writing) intended to cause sexual excitement." The blanket condemnation of all such materials is cause for grave concern. Obviously, this would include a great deal of advertising, network television, art, film, and a vast array of magazines, books, and videos. Indeed, many feminists have condemned most mainstream advertising and film as degrading and harmful to women. Most members of the feminist movement endorse and promote Minneapolis-style "antipornography" ordinances. Many feminists are committed full-time to these pursuits.

Despite their claims to a mandate, these women do not   9
speak for all feminists. Scores of women and men dropped
out (or were forced out) of the feminist movement when the
Equal Rights Amendment was defeated and attention shifted
to moralizing and "pornography." We will never know how
many feminists were lost to activism, or never activated, as a
result of this departure from our basic goals and principles.

Civil Liberties

Many of us believe that feminism and civil liberties are   10
inextricable. We remind our sisters that history has repeatedly
shown that censorship and suppression work directly against
feminist goals and are always used to limit women's rights in
the name of protection. If such censorship laws are passed, we
would create the illusion that something is being done to end
sexism and sexual violence—a harmful effect in itself.

We ask: whose definitions shall we use? Who will decide?   11
Who will make all the necessary individual judgments? Who
will distinguish "dehumanizing, objectifying, degrading"
materials from "erotica"?

All Sex Isn't Sexist

Many leaders in the feminist movement assert that the mes-   12
sage of all "pornography" even "soft-core," is that women are
slaves whose bodies are for sale and available to be used and
degraded. Again, this is not the only feminist view. For example, many feminists do *not* believe that *Playboy* and *Penthouse*
are sexist, or that the presentation of the naked female body,
whether or not in "inviting positions" is intrinsically sexist. We
do not believe that sexually explicit photos and words are
intrinsically exploitative, degrading, or objectifying.

Many feminist leaders tell us that "pornography" is sex dis-   13
crimination and hate literature against women—a violation
of women's civil rights. But the history and intent of civil
rights law and case law are clear: discrimination is not what
people say or write about other people; it is what people *do* to
other people. Individuals cannot be persecuted, censored, or
condemned for their ideas. In a free society, there are no
crimes of thought—only crimes of action.

Certainly some materials are offensive and degrading to   14
many women, and few would claim that sex discrimination

and oppression of women no longer exist in our culture. But many materials are offensive and degrading to *men,* blatantly promoting not only their oppression but their brutalization. There are aspects of our culture that oppress Indians, Hispanics, Asians, and homosexuals. Anti-Semitic literature is inarguably harmful to Jews, as is racist literature to blacks. Are we going to offer men and racial, ethnic, and religious minorities a civil right to suppress speech which they find objectionable? Many feminists tell us that "pornography" *causes* sexism and violence against women. But this claim draws on simplistic behaviorist psychology and has been repeatedly discredited by reputable specialists in sexual behavior. Even the notorious Meese commission reported that no such causal link can be substantiated. Sexist and violent materials are *symptoms* of a sexist and violent society—not the causes.

No Clear Danger

15   The claim that certain forms of expression are dangerous and an incitement to violence has been used time after time to try to prohibit speech that some people don't like. Although some of us do not support this exception to the First Amendment, the notion of "a clear and present danger" was evolved to address this threat. For "pornography" to be suppressed under this test, we would have to demonstrate that any viewer is likely to be provoked to sexual violence immediately upon seeing it.

16   Anecdotal stories of sex offenders who are found to possess "pornography" are often cited. As Sol Gordon has pointed out, a large percentage of these offenders are also found to possess milk in their refrigerators. Sporatic incidents do not prove a correlation, nor does a correlation prove causation.

17   Even if it is assumed that a small percentage of people are "encouraged" to engage in sexist behavior or commit violent acts after exposure to certain books or films, this still would not justify suppression. Such a "pervert's veto" would threaten a broad range of literature and film. A free society must accept the risks that come with liberty.

18   People receive different messages from sexually explicit material, and it is ridiculous and dangerous to conclude that a picture or an idea will have the same effect on all viewers or readers.

19   Charles Manson testified that he was inspired by the biblical Book of Revelation to commit multiple murders. Youths involved in interracial street fights have said that viewing

Roots led them to commit their crimes. John Hinckley testified that he knew he had to kill Ronald Reagan after reading *Catcher in the Rye.*

Worldwide Examples

If viewing and reading sexually explicit and violent materials caused people to become sex criminals, all the members of the Meese commission would now be dangerous sexual predators. The same would be true of the many sociologists who study this material, countless persons who create, publish, and disseminate it, mental health professionals who work with sex offenders, and all the moralists—on the right and the left—who pore over these materials as they analyze them for the rest of us.   20

In many repressive countries—whether in Central America, Asia, Africa, eastern Europe, or the Middle East—there is practically no "pornography." But there is a great deal of sexism and violence against women. In the Netherlands and Scandinavia, where there are almost no restrictions on sexually explicit materials, the rate of sex-related crime is much lower than in the United States. "Pornography" is virtually irrelevant to the existence of sexism and violence.   21

Nor does a causal relationship exist between an increase in the availability of "pornography" and inequality for women. While "pornography" has increased over the past fifty years, the rights of women have jumped dramatically.   22

Violence

"Violent pornography" is viewed by many as the most offensive form of expression. But it can be seen in two ways: as the depiction of consensual sadomasochism or as the depiction of actual coercion and violence against nonconsenting persons. If the latter, *the actual perpetrators of the violence or coercion* have broken the law and should be prosecuted to its full extent. However, not everyone sees the degradation of women in depictions of "violent" sexual activity. What some find degrading, others may find erotic.   23

Human sexual behavior is very complicated. In our society, and all over the world, consenting adults exist who like to engage in sadomasochistic activity and who do so of their own free will. They enjoy publications which depict or describe this behavior. For them, these activities are not   24 designed to degrade or promote violence against women *or men* but, rather, to satisfy a sexual need of the participants. It is not a crime or an issue subject to moral judgment to fantasize about rape, or even for two consenting adults to choose to enact a pretend rape. It is not anyone's right to judge the private sexual fantasies, inclinations, or activities of other consenting adults.

Freedom of Sex

25   We are told we must especially condemn materials depicting (usually simulated) violence to prove that we are opposed to violence against women. We must, many feminists say, condemn nearly all sexually explicit materials as degrading to women and label "pornography" a principal cause of women's oppression in order to retain our credentials as feminists.

26   Many feminist humanist women and men refuse to do this. We believe it is possible to be feminists dedicated to equal rights and the elimination of violence against women while defending the freedom of all kinds of sexual expression. It is a tragedy that the feminist movement has been drawn into an anti-sex stance, condemning "deviant" sexual representation and expression. We are horrified by the assertion of many feminists that male sexuality is inherently destructive, violent, and "pro-rape." We are appalled by the condemnation of men who enjoy "pornography" as sexist and anti-humanist or, in the case of women, by the assertion that they are "brainwashed by patriarchy."

27   This Victorian imagery—pure women controlling the vile, lustful impulses of men and being unable to think for themselves—is a feminine stereotype we should be working against. In this analysis, women cannot ever freely choose to have sex with men or use "male-identified" imagery in their sexual fantasies or practices. Certainly they cannot freely choose to earn their living by inviting the rapacious male gaze or providing sexual services to men.

28   Many feminist women and men believe it is moralistic, insulting, and inaccurate to maintain that no "normal" woman rationally chooses or consensually participates in the sex industry. This moralistic position alienates not only women in the sex industry but also women who create their own sexual pleasure without regard for its "political correctness."

29   We believe that this moralism and the attendant calls for censorship have seriously undermined the integrity of our

movement. Being a feminist means being against sexism—
not sex. In *Against Sadomasochism,* feminist Ti Grace Atkin-
son says, "I do not know any feminist worthy of that name
who, forced to choose between freedom and sex, would
choose sex." This is the choice being presented to feminist
women and men. In so doing, the movement betrays its principles and destroys its credibility.

   Many of us insist on the right to choose *both* freedom *and*   30
sexuality. We call upon other feminist humanists to do
likewise.

   Author's note: The access of minors to sexually explicit   31
material is a complex issue which would require another article for proper examination. The Supreme Court has held that
minors' access to legally "obscene" materials is not protected
by the First Amendment. The Court's nebulous and subjective
definition of *obscenity* raises even more definitional problems, and a vast array of materials are currently restricted on
the basis of this seriously flawed definition. These restrictions, instituted to protect minors, inevitably affect the freedom of adults. Legally, the burden of preventing the exposure
of children to offensive or "pornographic" materials *should*
rest with parents; as a *practical* matter, parents *must* assume
this responsibility.

John Irving

Pornography and
the New Puritans

If you saw the film The World According to Garp, *you have
had some experience with the work of John Irving (born 1942),
for he is the author of the novel on which the film was based as
well as six other novels. He contributed the following essay to
the* New York Times Book Review *in March 1992. Notice that
a response to the article, also printed in the* Times Book
Review, *is reprinted right after it.*

   These are censorial times. I refer to the pornography vic-   1
tims' compensation bill, now under consideration by the Senate Judiciary Committee—that same bunch of wise men who

dispatched such clearheaded, objective jurisprudence in the Clarence Thomas hearings. I can't wait to see what they're going to do with this maladroit proposal. The bill would encourage victims of sexual crimes to bring civil suits against publishers and distributors of material that is "obscene or constitutes child pornography"—*if* they can prove that the material was "a substantial cause of the offense," *and if* the publisher or distributor should have "foreseen" that such material created an "unreasonable risk of such a crime." If this bill passes, it will be the first piece of legislation to give credence to the unproven theory that sexually explicit material actually *causes* sexual crimes.

2   At the risk of sounding old-fashioned, I'm still pretty sure that rape and child molestation predate erotic books and pornographic magazines and X-rated videocassettes. I also remember the report of the two-year, $2 million President's Commission on Obscenity and Pornography (1970), which concluded there was "no reliable evidence . . . that exposure to explicit sexual material plays a significant role in the causation of delinquent or criminal sexual behavior." In 1986, not satisfied with that conclusion, the Meese commission on pornography and the Surgeon General's conference on pornography also failed to establish such a link. Now, here they go again.

3   This time, it's Republican Senators Mitch McConnell of Kentucky, Charles Grassley of Iowa and Strom Thurmond of South Carolina; I can't help wondering if they read much. Their charmless bill is a grave mistake for several reasons; for starters, it's morally reprehensible to shift the responsibility for any sexual crime onto a third party—namely, *away* from the actual perpetrator.

4   And then, of course, there's the matter of the bill running counter to the spirit of the First Amendment of the United States Constitution; this bill is a piece of back-door censorship, plain and simple. Moreover, since the laws on obscenity differ from state to state, and no elucidation of the meaning of obscenity is presented in the bill, how are the publishers or distributors to know in advance if their material is actionable or not? It is my understanding, therefore, that the true intent of the bill is to make the actual creators of this material think very conservatively—that is, when their imaginations turn to sex and violence.

5   I recall that I received a lot of unfriendly mail in connection with a somewhat explicit scene in my novel *The World*

According to Garp, wherein a selfish young man loses part of his anatomy while enjoying oral sex in a car. (I suppose I've always had a fear of rear-end collisions.) But thinking back about that particular hate mail, I don't recall a single letter from a young woman saying that she intended to rush out and *do* this to someone; and in the 14 years since that novel's publication, in more than 35 foreign languages, no one who actually *has done* this to someone has written to thank me for giving her the idea. Boy, am I lucky!

In a brilliant article on the Op-Ed page of *The New York* 6
Times, Teller, of those marvelous magicians Penn & Teller, had this to say about the pornography victims' compensation bill: "The advocates of this bill seem to think that if we stop showing rape in movies people will stop committing it in real life. Anthropologists call this 'magical thinking.' It's the same impulse that makes people stick pins in voodoo dolls, hoping to cripple an enemy. It feels logical, but it does not work." (For those of you who've seen these two magicians and are wondering which is Penn and which is Teller, Teller is the one who never talks. He *writes* very well, however.) "It's a death knell for creativity, too," Teller writes. "Start punishing make-believe, and those gifted with imagination will stop sharing it." He adds, "We will enter an intellectual era even more insipid than the one we live in."

Now *there's* a scary idea! I remember when the film version 7
of Günter Grass's novel *The Tin Drum* was banned in Canada. I always assumed it was the eel scene that offended the censors, but I don't know. In those days, a little naked sex—in the conventional position—was permissible, but unpleasant suggestiveness with eels was clearly going too far. But now, in the light of this proposed pornography victims' compensation bill, is there any evidence to suggest that there have been *fewer* hellish incidents of women being force-fed eels in Canada than in those countries where the film was available? Somehow, I doubt it. I know that they're out there—those guys who want to force-feed eels to women—but I suspect they're going to do what they're going to do, unaided by books or films. The point is: let's do something about *them,* instead of trying to control what they read or see.

It dismays me how some of my feminist friends are hot to 8
ban pornography. I'm sorry that they have such short memories. It wasn't very long ago when a book as innocent and valuable as *Our Bodies, Ourselves* was being banned by school boards and public libraries across the country. The idea of this good book was that women should have access to

detailed information about their bodies and their health, yet the so-called feminist ideology behind the book was thought to be subversive; indeed, it was (at that time) deplored. But many writers and writers' organizations (like PEN) wrote letters to those school boards and those public libraries. I can't speak to the overall effectiveness of these letters in regard to reinstating the book, but I'm aware that some of the letters worked; I wrote several of those letters. Now here are some of my old friends, telling me that attitudes toward rape and child molestation can be changed only if we remove the offensive *ideas*. Once again, it's ideology that's being banned. And although the movement to ban pornography is especially self-righteous, it looks like blacklisting to me.

9   Fascism has enjoyed many name changes, but it usually amounts to banning something you dislike and can't control. Take abortion, for example. I think groups should have to apply for names; if the Right to Life people had asked me, I'd have told them to find a more fitting label for themselves. It's morally inconsistent to manifest such concern for the poor fetus in a society that shows absolutely no pity for the poor child after it's born.

10   I'm also not so sure that these so-called Right to Lifers are as fired up about those fetuses as they say. I suspect what really makes them sore is the idea of women having sex and somehow not having to *pay* for it—pay in the sense of suffering all the way through an unwanted pregnancy. I believe this is part of the loathing for promiscuity that has always fueled those Americans who feel that a life of common decency is slipping from their controlling grasp. This notion is reflected in the unrealistic hope of those wishful thinkers who tell us that sexual abstinence is an alternative to wearing a condom. But I say how about *carrying* a condom, just in case you're moved to *not* abstain?

11   No one is coercing women into having abortions, but the Right to Lifers want to coerce women into having babies; that's why the pro-choice people are well named. It's unfortunate, however, that a few of my pro-choice friends think that the pornography victims' compensation bill is a good idea. I guess that they're really not entirely pro-choice. They want the choice to reproduce or not, but they *don't* want too broad a choice of things to read and see; they know what *they* want to read and see, and they expect other people to be content with what they want. This sounds like a Right to Life idea to me.

12   Most feminist groups, despite their vital advocacy of full enforcement of laws against violence to women and children,

seem opposed to Senate Bill 1521. As of this writing, both the National Organization for Women in New York State and in California have written to the Senate Judiciary Committee in opposition to the bill, although the Los Angeles chapter of NOW states that it has "no position." I admit it is perverse of me even to imagine what Tammy Bruce thinks about the pornography victims' compensation bill; I hope Ms. Bruce is not such a loose cannon as she appears, but she has me worried. Ms. Bruce is president of L.A. NOW, and she has lately distinguished herself with two counts of knee-jerk overreaction. Most recently, she found the Academy of Motion Picture Arts and Sciences to be guilty of an "obvious exhibition of sexism" in not nominating Barbra Streisand for an Oscar for best director. Well, maybe. Ms. Streisand's other talents have not been entirely overlooked; I meekly submit that the academy might have found *The Prince of Tides* lacking in directorial merit—it wouldn't be the first I've heard of such criticism. (Ms. Bruce says the L.A. chapter received "unrelenting calls" from NOW members who were riled up at the perceived sexism.)

Most readers will remember Tammy Bruce for jumping all over that nasty novel by Bret Easton Ellis. To refresh our memories: Simon & Schuster decided at the 11th hour not to publish *American Psycho* after concluding that its grisly content was in "questionable taste." Now please don't get excited and think I'm going to call that censorship; that was merely a breach of contract. And besides, Simon & Schuster has a right to its own opinion of what questionable taste is. *People* magazine tells us that Judith Regan, a vice president and senior editor at Simon & Schuster, recently had a book idea, which she pitched to Madonna. "My idea was for her to write a book of her sexual fantasies, her thoughts, the meanderings of her erotic mind," Ms. Regan said. The pity is, Madonna hasn't delivered. And according to Mitchell Fink, author of the Insider column for *People*, "Warner Books confirmed it is talking about a book—no word on what kind—with Madonna." I don't know Madonna, but maybe she thought the Simon & Schuster book idea was in questionable taste. Simon & Schuster, clearly, subscribes to more than one opinion of what questionable taste *is*.

But only two days after Mr. Ellis's book was dropped by Simon & Schuster, Sonny Mehta, president of Alfred A. Knopf and Vintage Books, bought *American Psycho*, which was published in March 1991. Prior to the novel's publication, Ms. Bruce called for a boycott of all Knopf and Vintage titles—except for books by feminist authors, naturally—until

American Psycho was withdrawn from publication (it wasn't), or until the end of 1991. To the charge of censorship, Ms. Bruce declared that she was *not* engaged in it; she sure fooled me.

15   But Ms. Bruce wasn't alone in declaring what *wasn't* censorship, nor was she alone in her passion; she not only condemned Mr. Ellis's novel—she condemned its availability. And not only the book itself *but its availability* were severely taken to task in the very pages in which I now write. In December 1990—three months *before American Psycho* was published, and at the urging of *The Book Review*—Roger Rosenblatt settled Mr. Ellis's moral hash in a piece of writing prissy enough to please Jesse Helms. According to Mr. Rosenblatt, Jesse Helms has never engaged in censorship, either. For those of us who remain improperly educated in regard to what censorship actually *is*, Mr. Rosenblatt offers a blanket definition. "Censorship is when a government burns your manuscript, smashes your presses and throws you in jail," he says.

16   Well, as much as I may identify with Mr. Rosenblatt's literary taste, I'm of the opinion that there are a few forms of censorship more subtle than that, and Mr. Rosenblatt has engaged in one of them. If you slam a book when it's published, that's called book reviewing, but if you write about a book three months in advance of its publication and your conclusion is "don't buy it," your intentions are more censorial than critical.

17   And it *is* censorship when the writer of such perceived trash is not held *as* accountable as the book's publisher; the pressure that was brought to bear on Mr. Mehta was totally censorial. *The Book Review* is at its most righteous in abusing Mr. Mehta, who is described as "clearly as hungry for a killing as Patrick Bateman." (For those of you who don't know Mr. Ellis's book, Patrick Bateman is the main character and a serial killer.) Even as reliable a fellow as the editorial director of *Publisher's Weekly*, John F. Baker, described *American Psycho* as a book that "does transcend the boundaries of what is acceptable in mainstream publishing."

18   It's the very idea of making or keeping publishing "acceptable" that gives *me* the shivers, because that's the same idea that lurks behind the pornography victims' compensation bill—making the *publisher* (not the perpetrator of the crime or the writer of the pornography) responsible for what's "acceptable." If you want to bash Bret Easton Ellis for what he's written, go ahead and bash him. But when you presume

to tell Sonny Mehta, or any other publisher, what he can or can't—or should or shouldn't—*publish,* that's when you've stepped into dangerous territory. In fact, that's when you're knee-deep in blacklisting, and you ought to know better—all of you.

Mr. Rosenblatt himself actually says, "No one argues that a   19
publishing house hasn't the right to print what it wants. We fight for that right. But not everything is a right. At some point, someone in authority somewhere has to look at Mr. Ellis's rat and call the exterminator." Now this is interesting, and perhaps worse than telling Sonny Mehta what he should or shouldn't publish—because that's exactly what Mr. Rosenblatt *is* doing while he's *saying* that he isn't.

Do we remember that tangent of the McCarran-Walter Act   20
of 1952, that finally defunct business about ideological exclusion? That was when we kept someone from coming into our country because we perceived that the person had *ideas* that were in conflict with the "acceptable" ideas of our country. Under this act of exclusion, writers as distinguished as Graham Greene and Gabriel Garcia Márquez were kept out of the United States. Well, when we attack what a publisher has the right to publish, we are simply applying the old ideological exclusion act at home. Of all people, those of us in the idea business should know better than that.

As for the pornography victims' compensation bill, the vote   21
in the Senate Judiciary Committee will be close. As of this writing, seven senators have publicly indicated their support of the bill; they need only one more vote to pass the bill out of committee. Friends at PEN tell me that the committee has received a lot of letters from women saying that support of the bill would in some way "make up for" the committee's mishandling of the Clarence Thomas hearings. Some women are putting the decision to support Justice Thomas alongside the decision to find William Kennedy Smith innocent of rape; these women think that a really strong antipornography bill will make up for what they perceive to be the miscarriage of justice in both cases.

The logic of this thinking is more than a little staggering.   22
What would these women think if lots of men were to write the committee and say that because Mike Tyson has been found guilty of rape, what we need is *more* pornography to make up for what's happened to Iron Mike? This would make a lot of sense, wouldn't it?

I conclude that these are not only censorial times; these are   23
stupid times. However, there is some hope that opposition to

Senate Bill 1521 is mounting. The committee met on March 12 but the members didn't vote on the bill. Discussion was brief, yet encouraging. Colorado Senator Hank Brown told his colleagues that there are serious problems with the legislation; he should be congratulated for his courageous decision to oppose the other Republicans on the committee, but he should also be encouraged not to accept any compromise proposal. Ohio Senator Howard Metzenbaum suggested that imposing third-party liability on producers and distributors of books, magazines, movies and recordings raises the question of whether the bill shouldn't be amended to cover the firearms and liquor industries as well.

24   It remains to be seen if the committee members will resist the temptation to *fix* the troubled bill. I hope they will understand that the bill cannot be fixed because it is based on an erroneous premise—namely, that publishers or distributors should be held liable for the acts of criminals. But what is important for us to recognize, even if this lame bill is amended out of existence or flat-out defeated, is that *new* antipornography legislation will be proposed.

25   Do we remember Nancy Reagan's advice to would-be drug users? ("Just say no.") As applied to drug use, Mrs. Reagan's advice is feeble in the extreme. But writers and other members of the literary community *should* just say no to censorship in any and every form. Of course, it will always be the most grotesque example of child pornography that will be waved in front of our eyes by the Good Taste Police. If we're opposed to censorship, they will say, are we in favor of filth like this?

26   No; we are not in favor of child pornography if we say no to censorship. If we disapprove of reinstating public hangings, that doesn't mean that we want all the murderers to be set free. No writer or publisher or *reader* should accept censorship in any form; fundamental to our freedom of expression is that each of us has a right to decide what is obscene and what isn't.

27   But lest you think I'm being paranoid about the iniquities and viciousness of our times, I'd like you to read a description of Puritan times. It was written in 1837—more than 150 years ago—and it describes a scene in a Puritan community in Massachusetts that you must imagine taking place more than 350 years ago. This is from a short story by Nathaniel Hawthorne called "Endicott and the Red Cross," which itself was written more than 10 years before Hawthorne wrote *The Scarlet Letter.* This little story contains the germ of the idea for that

famous novel about a woman condemned by Puritan justice
to wear the letter A on her breast. But Hawthorne, obviously,
had been thinking about the iniquities and viciousness of
early New England morality for many years.

Please remember, as you read what Nathaniel Hawthorne   28
thought of the Puritans, that the Puritans are not dead and
gone. We have many new Puritans in our country today; they
are as dangerous to freedom of expression as the old Puritans
ever were. An especially sad thing is, a few of these new Puritans are formerly liberal-thinking feminists.

"In close vicinity to the sacred edifice [the meeting-house]   29
appeared that important engine of Puritanic authority, the
whipping-post—with the soil around it well trodden by the
feet of evil doers, who had there been disciplined. At one corner of the meeting-house was the pillory, and at the other the
stocks;...the head of an Episcopalian and suspected Catholic
was grotesquely incased in the former machine; while a fel-
low-criminal, who had boisterously quaffed a health to the
king, was confined by the legs in the latter. Side by side, on the
meeting-house steps, stood a male and a female figure. The
man was a tall, lean, haggard personification of fanaticism,
bearing on his breast this label,—A WANTON GOSPELLER,—
which betokened that he had dared to give interpretations of
Holy Writ unsanctioned by the infallible judgment of the civil
and religious rulers. His aspect showed no lack of zeal...even
at the stake. The woman wore a cleft stick on her tongue, in
appropriate retribution for having wagged that unruly member against the elders of the church; and her countenance and
gestures gave much cause to apprehend that, the moment the
stick should be removed, a repetition of the offence would
demand new ingenuity in chastising it.

"The above-mentioned individuals had been sentenced to   30
undergo their various modes of ignominy, for the space of
one hour at noonday. But among the crowd were several
whose punishment would be life-long; some, whose ears had
been cropped, like those of puppy dogs; others, whose cheeks
had been branded with the initials of their misdemeanors;
one, with his nostrils slit and seared; and another, with a hal-
ter about his neck, which he was forbidden ever to take off, or
to conceal beneath his garments. Methinks he must have
been grievously tempted to affix the other end of the rope to
some convenient beam or bough. There was likewise a young
woman, with no mean share of beauty, whose doom to was to
wear the letter A on the breast of her gown, in the eyes of all
the world and her own children. And even her own children

knew what that initial signified. Sporting with her infamy, the lost and desperate creature had embroidered the fatal token in scarlet cloth, with golden thread and the nicest art of needlework; so that the capital A might have been thought to mean Admirable, or anything rather than Adulteress.

31   "Let not the reader argue, from any of these evidences of iniquity, that the times of the Puritans were more vicious than our own."

32   In my old-fashioned opinion, Mr. Hawthorne sure got that right.

Andrea Dworkin
Reply to John Irving

As she notes in the following reply, Andrea Dworkin (born 1947) has written (with University of Michigan law professor Catherine MacKinnon) antipornography ordinances for Minneapolis, Indianapolis, and other cities. (The ordinances later were overturned by the courts.) A successful and controversial essayist and fiction writer, she has also written Pornography: Men Possessing Women *(1988) and* Pornography and Civil Rights *(1988), both of which argue in favor of the kinds of laws that she advocates.*

To the Editor:

1   As a woman determined to destroy the pornography industry, a writer of 10 published books and someone who reads, perhaps I should be the one to tell John Irving ("Pornography and the New Puritans," March 29) who the new Puritan is. The old Puritans wouldn't like her very much; but then, neither does Mr. Irving.

2   I am 45 years old now. When I was a teen-ager, I baby-sat. In any middle-class home one could always find the dirty books—on the highest shelf, climbing toward God, usually behind a parched potted plant. The books themselves were usually "Ulysses," "Tropic of Cancer" or "Lady Chatterley's Lover." They always had as a preface or afterword the text of an obscenity decision in which the book was exonerated and art extolled. Or a lawyer would stand in for the court to tell us

that through his mighty efforts law had finally vindicated a persecuted genius.

Even at 15 and 16, I noticed something strange about the special intersection of art, law and sex under the obscenity rubric: some men punished other men for producing or publishing writing that caused arousal in (presumably) still other men. Although Mrs. Grundy got the blame, women didn't make these laws or enforce them or sit on juries to deliberate guilt or innocence. This was a fight among men—but about what? 3

Meanwhile, my life as a woman in prefeminist times went on. This means that I thought I was a human being with rights. But before I was much over 18, I had been sexually assaulted three times. Did I report these assaults (patriarchy's first question, because surely the girl must be lying)? 4

When I was 9, I told my parents. To protect me, for better or worse, they did not call the police. 5

The second time, beaten as well as raped, I told no one. I was working for a peace group, and I heard jokes about rape day in and day out. What do you tell the draft board when they ask you if you would kill a Nazi who was going to rape your sister? "I'd tell my sister to have a good time" was the answer of choice. 6

The third time, I was 18, a freshman in college, and I had been arrested for taking part in a sit-in outside the United Nations to protest the Vietnam War. It was February of 1965. This time, my experience was reported in *The New York Times*, newspapers all around the world and on television: girl in prison—New York's notorious Women's House of Detention—says she was brutalized by two prison doctors. Forced entry with a speculum—for 15 days I had vaginal bleeding, a vagina so bruised and ripped that my stone-cold family doctor burst into tears when he examined me. 7

I came out of the Women's House of Detention mute. Speech depends on believing you can make yourself understood: a community of people will recognize the experience in the words you use and they will care. You also have to be able to understand what happened to you enough to convey it to others. I lost speech. I was hurt past what I had words for. I lived out on the streets for several days, not having a bed of my own, still bleeding; and finally spoke because Grace Paley convinced me that she would understand and care. Then I spoke a lot. A grand jury investigated. Columnists indicted the prison. But neither of the prison doctors was charged with sexual assault or sexual battery. In fact, no 8 one ever mentioned sexual assault. The grand jury concluded that the prison was fine. In despair, I left the country—to be a writer, my human dream.

9   A year later I came back. I have since discovered that what happened to me is common: homeless, poor, still sexually traumatized, I learned to trade sex for money. I spent a lot of years out on the street, living hand to mouth, these New York streets and other streets in other hard cities. I thought I was a real tough woman, and I was: tough-calloused; tough-numb; tough-desperate; tough-scared; tough-hungry; tough-beaten by men often; tough-done it every which way including up. All of my colleagues who fight pornography with me know about this. I know about the lives of women in pornography because I lived the life. So have many feminists who fight pornography. Freedom looks different when you are the one it is being practiced on. It's his, not yours. Speech is different, too. Those sexy expletives are the hate words he uses on you while he is using you. Your speech is an inchoate protest never voiced.

10   In my work, fiction and nonfiction, I've tried to voice the protest against a power that is dead weight on you, fist and penis organized to keep you quiet. I would do virtually any-thing to get women out of prostitution and pornography, which is mass-produced, technologized prostitution. With pornography, a woman can still be sold after the beatings, the rapes, the pain, the humiliation have killed her. I write for her, on behalf of her. I know her. I have come close to being her.

11   I read a lot of books. None of them ever told me the truth about what happens to women until feminists started writing and publishing in this wave, over these last 22 years. Over and over, male writers consider prostituted women "speech"— their speech, their right. Without this exploitation, published for profit, the male writer feels censored. The woman lynched naked on a tree, or restrained with ropes and a ball gag in her mouth, has what? Freedom of what?

12   I lost my ability to speak—became mute—a second time in my life. I've written about being a battered wife: I was beaten and tortured over a period of a few years. Amnesty Interna-tional never showed up. Toward the end, I lost all speech. Words were useless to the likes of me. I had run away and asked for help—from friends, neighbors, the police—and had been turned away many times. My words didn't seem to mean anything, or it was O.K. to torture me.

13   Taken once by my husband to a doctor when hurt, I risked asking for help. The doctor said he could write me a prescrip-

tion for Valium or have me committed. The neighbors heard the screaming, but no one did anything. So what are words? I have always been good with them, but never good enough to be believed or helped. No, there were no shelters then.

But I am talking about speech: it isn't easy for me. I come   14
to speech from under a man, tortured and tormented. What he did to me took away everything; he was the owner of everything. He hurt all the words out of me, and no one would listen anyway. I come to speech from under the brutalities of thousands of men. For me, the violence of marriage was worse than the violence of prostitution; but this is no choice. Men act out pornography. They have acted it out on me. Women's lives become pornography. Mine did. And so for 20 years now I have been looking for the words to say what I know.

But maybe liberal men—so open-minded and intellectually   15
curious—can't find the books that would teach them about women's real lives. Maybe, while John Irving and PEN are defending *Hustler,* snuff films and *Deep Throat,* the direct product of the coercion of Linda Marchiano, political dissidents like myself are anathema—especially to the free-speech fetishists—not because the publishing industry punishes prudes but because dissenters who mean it, who stand against male power over women, are pariahs.

Maybe Mr. Irving and others do not know that in the world   16
of women, pornography is the real geography of how men use us and torment us and hate us.

With Catharine A. MacKinnon, I drafted the first civil law   17
against pornography. It held pornographers accountable for what they do: they traffic women (contravening the United Nations Universal Declaration of Human Rights and the Convention on the Elimination of All Forms of Discrimination Against Women); they eroticize inequality in a way that materially promotes rape, battery, maiming and bondage; they make a product that they know dehumanizes, degrades and exploits women; they hurt women to make the pornography, and then consumers use the pornography in assaults both verbal and physical.

Mr. Irving refers to a scene in *The World According to Garp*   18
in which a woman bites off a man's penis in a car when the car is accidentally rammed from behind. This, he says, did not cause women to bite off men's penises in cars. I have written (in my novels, *Ice and Fire* and *Mercy,* and in the story "The New Woman's Broken Heart") about a woman raped by two men sequentially, the first aggressor routed by the second

one, to whom the woman, near dead, submits; he bites viciously and repeatedly into her genitals. When I wrote it, someone had already done it—to me. Mr. Irving uses his imagination for violent farce. My imagination can barely grasp my real life. The violence, as Mr. Irving must know, goes from men to women.

19   Women write to me because of our shared experiences. In my books they find their lives—until now beyond the reach of language. A letter to me dated March 11 says in part: "The abuse was quite sadistic—it involved bestiality, torture, the making of pornography. Sometimes, when I think about my life, I'm not sure why I'm alive, but I'm always sure about why I do what I do, the feminist theory and the antipornography activism." Another letter, dated March 13, says: "It was only when I was almost [raped] to pieces that I broke down and learned to hate.... I have never stopped resenting the loss of innocence that occurred the day I learned to hate."

20   Male liberals seem to think we fight pornography to protect sexual innocence, but we have none to protect. The innocence we want is the innocence that lets us love. People need dignity to love.

21   Mr. Irving quoted Hawthorne's condemnation of Puritan orthodoxy in the short story "Endicott and the Red Cross"—a graphic description of public punishments of women: bondage, branding, maiming, lynching. Today pornographers do these things to women, and the public square is a big place— every newsstand and video store. A photograph shields rape and torture for profit. In defending pornography as if it were speech, liberals defend the new slavers. The only fiction in pornography is the smile on the woman's face.

Nadine Strossen

The Perils of Pornophobia

Nadine Strossen's essay on pornography appeared in The
Humanist *in the spring of 1995. Strossen, a member of the faculty at New York University Law School, is president of the
American Civil Liberties Union, an organization famous for
defending the constitutional rights of American citizens. Her
essay was adapted from her 1995 book* Defending Pornography: Free Speech, Sex, and the Fight for Women's Rights.

In 1992, in response to a complaint, officials at Pennsylva-   1
nia State University unceremoniously removed Francisco de
Goya's masterpiece, *The Nude Maja,* from a classroom wall.
The complaint had not been lodged by Jesse Helms or some
irate member of the Christian Coalition. Instead, the com-
plainant was a feminist English professor who protested that
the eighteenth-century painting of a recumbent nude woman
made her and her female students "uncomfortable."

This was not an isolated incident. At the University of Ari-   2
zona at Tucson, feminist students physically attacked a graduate student's exhibit of photographic self-portraits. Why?
The artist had photographed *herself* in her *underwear.* And at
the University of Michigan Law School feminist students who
had organized a conference on "Prostitution: From Academia
to Activism" removed a feminist-curated art exhibition held
in conjunction with the conference. Their reason? Conference speakers had complained that a composite videotape
containing interviews of working prostitutes was "pornographic" and therefore unacceptable.

What is wrong with this picture? Where have they come   3
from—these feminists who behave like religious conservatives, who censor works of art because they deal with sexual
themes? Have not feminists long known that censorship is a
dangerous weapon which, if permitted, would inevitably be
turned against them? Certainly that was the irrefutable lesson
of the early women's rights movement, when Margaret
Sanger, Mary Ware Dennett, and other activists were
arrested, charged with "obscenity" and prosecuted for distributing educational pamplets about sex and birth control.
Theirs was a struggle for freedom of sexual expression and

full gender equality, which they understood to be mutually reinforcing.

4   Theirs was also a lesson well understood by the second wave of feminism in the 1970s, when writers such as Germaine Greer, Betty Friedan, and Betty Dodson boldly asserted that women had the right to be free from discrimination not only in the workplace and in the classroom but in the bedroom as well. Freedom from limiting, conventional stereotypes concerning female sexuality was an essential aspect of what we then called "women's liberation." Women should not be seen as victims in their sexual relations with men but as equally assertive partners, just as capable of experiencing sexual pleasure.

5   But it is a lesson that, alas, many feminists have now forgotten. Today, an increasingly influential feminist procensorship movement threatens to impair the very women's rights movement it professes to serve. Led by law professor Catharine MacKinnon and writer Andrea Dworkin, this faction of the feminist movement maintains that sexually oriented *expression*—not sex-segregated labor markets, sexist concepts of marriage and family, or pent-up rage—is the preeminent cause of discrimination and violence against women. Their solution is seemingly simple: suppress all "pornography."

6   Censorship, however, is never a simple matter. First, the offense must be described. And how does one define something so infinitely variable, so deeply personal, so uniquely individualized as the image, the word, and the fantasy that cause sexual arousal? For decades, the U.S. Supreme Court has engaged in a Sisyphean struggle to craft a definition of *obscenity* that the lower courts can apply with some fairness and consistency. Their dilemma was best summed up in former Justice Potter Stewart's now famous statement: "I shall not today attempt further to define [obscenity]; and perhaps I could never succeed in intelligibly doing so. But I know it when I see it."

7   The censorious feminists are not so modest as Justice Stewart. They have fashioned an elaborate definition of *pornography* that encompasses vastly more material than does the currently recognized law of *obscenity*. As set out in their model law (which has been considered in more than a dozen jurisdictions in the United States and overseas, and which has been substantially adopted in Canada), pornography is "the sexually explicit subordination of women through pictures and/or words." The model law lists eight different crite-

ria that attempt to illustrate their concept of "subordination," such as depictions in which "women are presented in postures or positions of sexual submission, servility, or display" or "women are presented in scenarios of degradation, humiliation, injury, torture... in a context that makes these conditions sexual." This linguistic driftnet can ensnare anything from religious imagery and documentary footage about the mass rapes in the Balkans to self-help books about women's health. Indeed, the Boston Women's Health Book Collective, publisher of the now-classic book on women's health and sexuality, *Our Bodies, Ourselves,* actively campaigned against the MacKinnon-Dworkin model law when it was proposed in Cambridge, Massachusetts, in 1985, recognizing that the book's explicit text and pictures could be targeted as pornographic under the law.

Although the "MacDworkinite" approach to pornography 8 has an intuitive appeal to many feminists, it is *itself* based on subordinating and demeaning stereotypes about women. Central to the pornophobic feminists—and to many traditional conservatives and right-wing fundamentalists, as well—is the notion that *sex* is inherently degrading to women (although not to men). Not just sexual expression but sex itself—even consensual, nonviolent sex—is an evil from which women, like children, must be protected.

MacKinnon puts it this way: "Compare victims' reports of 9 rape with women's reports of sex. They look a lot alike.... The major distinction between intercourse (normal) and rape (abnormal) is that the normal happens so often that one cannot get anyone to see anything wrong with it." And from Dworkin: "Intercourse remains a means or the means of physiologically making a woman inferior." Given society's pervasive sexism, she believes, women cannot freely consent to sexual relations with men; those who do consent are, in Dworkin's words, "collaborators... experiencing pleasure in their own inferiority."

These ideas are hardly radical. Rather, they are a reincar- 10 nation of disempowering puritanical, Victorian notions that feminists have long tried to consign to the dustbin of history: woman as sexual victim; man as voracious satyr. The Mac-Dworkinite approach to sexual expression is a throwback to the archaic stereotypes that formed the basis for nineteenth-century laws which prohibited "vulgar" or sexually suggestive language from being used in the presence of women and girls.

In those days, women were barred from practicing law and 11 serving as jurors lest they be exposed to such language. Such "protective" laws have historically functioned to bar women from full legal equality. Paternalism always leads to exclusion, discrimination, and the loss of freedom and autonomy. And in its most extreme form, it leads to purdah, in which women are completely shrouded from public view.

12   The pro-censorship feminists are not fighting alone. Although they try to distance themselves from such traditional "family-values" conservatives as Jesse Helms, Phyllis Schlafly, and Donald Wildmon, who are less interested in protecting women than in preserving male dominance a common hatred of sexual expression and fondness for censorship unite the two camps. For example, the Indianapolis City Council adopted the MacKinnon-Dworkin model law in 1984 thanks to the hard work of former council member Beulah Coughenour, a leader of the Indiana Stop ERA movement. (Federal courts later declared the law unconstitutional.) And when Phyllis Schlafly's Eagle Forum and Beverly LaHaye's Concerned Women for America launched their "Enough Is Enough" anti-pornography campaign, they trumpeted the words of Andrea Dworkin in promotional materials.

13   This mutually reinforcing relationship does a serious disservice to the fight for women's equality. It lends credibility to and strengthens the right wing and its anti-feminist, anti-choice, homophobic agenda. This is particularly damaging in light of the growing influence of the religious right in the Republican Party and the recent Republican sweep of both Congress and many state governments. If anyone doubts that the newly empowered GOP intends to forge ahead with anti-woman agendas, they need only read the party's "Contract with America," which, among other things, reintroduces the recently repealed "gag rule" forbidding government-funded family-planning comes from even discussing abortion with their patients.

14   The pro-censorship feminists base their efforts on the largely unexamined assumption that ridding society of pornography would reduce sexism and violence against women. If there were any evidence that this were true, anti-censorship feminists—myself included—would be compelled at least to reexamine our opposition to censorship. But there is no such evidence to be found.

15   A causal connection between exposure to pornography and the commission of sexual violence has never been established. The National Research Council's Panel on Understanding and Preventing Violence concluded in a 1993 survey of laboratory

studies that "demonstrated empirical links between pornography and sex crimes in general are weak or absent." Even according to another research literature survey that former U.S. Surgeon General C. Everett Koop conducted at the behest of the staunchly anti-pornography Meese Commission, only two reliable generalizations could be made about the impact of "degrading" sexual material on its viewers: it caused them to think that a variety of sexual practices was more common than they had previously believed, and to more accurately estimate the prevalence of varied sexual practices.

Correlational studies are similarly unsupportive of the pro-censorship cause. There are no consistent correlations between the availability of pornography in various communities, states, and countries and their rates of sexual offenses. If anything, studies suggest an inverse relationship: a greater availability of sexually explicit material seems to correlate not with higher rates of sexual violence but, rather, with higher indices of gender equality. For example, Singapore, with its tight restrictions on pornography, has experienced a much greater increase in rape rates than has Sweden, with its liberalized obscenity laws.   16

There *is* mounting evidence, however, that MacDwor-kinite-type laws will be used against the very people they are supposed to protect—namely, women. In 1992, for example, the Canadian Supreme Court incorporated the MacKinnon-Dworkin concept of pornography into Canadian obscenity law. Since that ruling, in *Butler* v. *The Queen*—which MacKinnon enthusiastically hailed as "a stunning victory for women"—well over half of all feminist bookstores in Canada have had materials confiscated or detained by customs. According to the *Feminist Bookstore News*, a Canadian publication, "The *Butler* decision has been used . . . only to seize lesbian, gay, and feminist material."   17

Ironically but predictably, one of the victims of Canada's new law is Andrea Dworkin herself. Two of her books, *Pornography: Men Possessing Women* and *Women Hating*, were seized, customs officials said, because they "illegally eroticized pain and bondage." Like the MacKinnon-Dworkin model law, the *Butler* decision makes no exceptions for material that is part of a feminist critique of pornography or other feminist presentation. And this inevitably overbroad sweep is precisely why censorship is antithetical to the fight for women's rights.   18

The pornophobia that grips MacKinnon, Dworkin, and their followers has had further counterproductive impacts on   19 the fight for women's rights. Censorship factionalism within the feminist movement has led to an enormously wasteful diversion of energy from the real cause of and solutions to the ongoing problems of discrimination and violence against women. Moreover, the "porn-made-me-do-it" defense, whereby convicted rapists cite MacKinnon and Dworkin in seeking to reduce their sentences, actually impedes the aggressive enforcement of criminal laws against sexual violence.

20   A return to the basic principles of women's liberation would put the feminist movement back on course. We women are entitled to freedom of expression—to read, think, speak, sing, write, paint, dance, dream, photograph, film, and fantasize as we wish. We are also entitled to our dignity, autonomy, and equality. Fortunately, we can—and will—have both.

Maria Soto

Is It Pornography?

Maria Soto is a student at the University of Kentucky, where she wrote the following essay in a first-year writing course. Born in Panama, raised in Nicaragua, and a resident for a time in Brazil, she speaks a number of languages fluently; but English is of course not her first language. Just after this essay was completed, Calvin Klein responded to public pressure and removed the ads that Soto discusses.

1   During September of 1995 a major controversy arose about the printed ads of Calvin Klein that were exposed, publicly, on buses in New York City, as well as in advertisements in various magazines. Many people considered the ads to be child pornography because the pictures in the ads showed adolescents (apparently minors) in very seductive poses; those people felt that the ads shouldn't be on the streets or in any kind of magazine. However, before censoring something as pornographic, we have to determine if it is really pornographic or simply a use of sensuality to sell a product. In order to be able to make any judgment of that, we need first to determine what child pornography is. By reading and by discussing with other people what constitutes child pornography, I have concluded that

child pornography is any material that focuses on the sexuality of a child, that has the intention to be pornographic, and that humiliates those who view the material. Calvin Klein ads may be in poor taste, but they are not child pornography because they don't contain the elements of child pornography.

The first part of the definition states that child pornography is any material that focuses on the sexuality of a child, that is, material which drives the attention of the viewer to the sexual organs of the child and shows sexual activities. For example, a picture that shows a ten-year-old girl nude, and in which the camera takes a close-up of her sexual organs, can be defined as child pornography because it focuses on the sexual organs of the girl. On the other hand, a work of art in which a girl is nude but which drives the attention of the viewer not to her sexuality but to something else, is not child pornography. Edvuard Munch's "Puberty" for instance, portrays nudity, but it emphasizes the girl's suffering, so it is not pornography. Although no one can deny that the models in CK ads are posed in sensual positions, no sexual activity is portrayed, and no sexual organ is shown. A young girl in one of the ads, for instance, is pushing her jeans down as if to take them off, she is looking at the viewer in a challenging way, and her tiny T-shirt is barely covering her stomach; but while the picture is sexually suggestive, it does not depict sexual acts or focus on sexual organs. In another ad, a girl dressed in the same sort of tiny T-shirt is lying sideways on a bench, her jeans pulled down on her hips and an inch or two of her stomach showing. The picture could suggest the idea that she is not an innocent girl, and it undoubtedly focuses on her sensuality; but it doesn't amount to child pornography because it does not focus on her sexual organs or portray any sexual activity. Moreover, to me the girl looks like one of those teenagers that you see every day, walking on the street, wearing her jeans on her hips, and showing off her underwear. What is shown in the CK ads is not far away from the way many teens dress nowadays. Of course, sensuality is explicit in the ads and not on the streets, but judging something as pornographic because it is sensual is not legitimate.

Another important part of the definition of child pornography is the intention of the material. A pornographic item has as its main objective the provocation of sexual arousal; pornography provokes sexual desire. A picture of a ten-year-old girl who is bare and who is opening her legs in front of the camera is certainly material for a hard-core pornographic magazine because the purpose of the picture is to arouse

other people sexually. Determining the intention to be pornographic is of course difficult at times because not all material
that focuses on the sexuality of a child is intended for pornographic purposes. To use an obvious example, many medical
reports contain pictures that emphasize the sexual organs of
children, but the intention of those pictures is educational.
Nevertheless, for something sexually explicit to be considered
pornographic, it must have the intention of arousing sexual
desire. Otherwise, it could be considered a scientific or an
artistic work.

4   Calvin Klein ads are not meant to be pornographic; they
are meant to sell products. In order to sell their products, the
CK ads try to identify the models in the ads with adolescents
because adolescents are beginning to use their sexuality to
attract their peers. The models in the ads look very sensual, as
if they can seduce anyone, so that insecure adolescents will
think that "maybe if I wear Calvin Klein jeans, I'll be as seductive as that girl and maybe some boy will finally look at me."
Adolescents identify with the models and therefore buy CK
jeans: it's that simple. And it works. As Alan Millstein, editor
of the Fashion Network report, said in a recent issue of *Time,*
CK jeans are "flying out of the stores" as a result of the ads.
You can see the phenomenon yourself the next time you go to
a mall and see a group of teenagers all looking alike: with the
same jeans, the same hairstyle, the same shoes. And it's not
just any kind of jeans; they have to be produced by Guess? or
Calvin Klein. In short, for better or for worse, the sensuality
used in CK ads is just the expression of the patterns of behavior and beliefs of many American adolescents. The ads are
intended to sell jeans—it's that simple.

5   Finally, in cases of child pornography, humiliation is typically present; pornography degrades and exploits a person.
Although pornography includes humiliation, not all humiliating material is pornographic. For example, imagine a picture
of a prostitute working on the streets; the picture is humiliating because it shows the exploitation of human beings, but it is
not pornographic because it does not focus on the sexuality of
the prostitute and because its intention is not pornographic.
On the other hand, a young boy or girl in a porno movie is
being exploited because, undoubtedly, the movie is showing a
relationship of unequal power between a weak child and a
strong adult who can manipulate the actions of the child.

6   In Calvin Klein ads, no humiliation is present because they
are not being degraded or exploited. The pictures do not
imply a relationship of power and submission between the

person who took the picture and the persons depicted. Instead, as Calvin Klein himself affirmed in a statement published in the *New York Times* on August 28, the ads intend to show "the strength of character and independence" of the young people photographed. In other words, the ads try to demonstrate that adolescents can take care of themselves and make the right decisions (even, apparently, in the case of buying jeans). The ads I looked at while preparing this essay showed teenagers with confident faces and self-assured poses.

In spite of Calvin Klein's personal defense, many people persist in believing that the ads are instances of child pornography because young models are being posed seductively and suggestively; the ads seem to be sexualizing children. However, sexuality and sensuality are things natural to adolescence, not things unnatural. Whether people like it or not, it is normal and natural for a teenager to explore his or her sensuality. I'm not saying that showing the sexual parts of a teenager with the intention to arouse someone is not pornographic; it is. Nor am I saying that showing a picture of an eight-year-old in a sensual way is natural. It isn't. But the Calvin Klein ads are showing adolescents who really are using sensuality as a way to attract their peers, and, more important, the ads are intended to be commercial, not pornographic.   7

The only serious mistake that I can see in the ads is that they address a topic that is still taboo in our society, one that we continue to avoid confronting because it's easier to cheat ourselves into believing that adolescents are far away from being sexually active. Why is our society afraid to confront the sexuality of adolescents?   8

Will these ads cause adolescents to be more sexually active? I doubt it. It seems to me that the ads, more than playing with the sensuality of the models, are dealing with the social value of teenagers in our society. Although the main question around the Calvin Klein ads was whether or not they were pornographic, to me what needs to get the attention of the community is the social mores that the ads reflect. The ads seem to me to show us our adolescents—how they use things to attract people—things like cars, hairstyles, and clothing. It appears that we must have things in order to live and to be respected; we must have things in order to seem attractive or interesting human beings. Calvin Klein ads show how empty our culture is, how we value superficial things and attitudes. In that sense, the ads are discouraging indeed; frustrating indeed.   9

But they aren't pornographic.   10

CENSORSHIP II:
SHOULD ELECTRONIC
NETWORKS BE RESTRICTED?

Philip Elmer-Dewitt
Cyberporn

The following was a Time *magazine cover story on July 3, 1995. Philip Elmer-Dewitt is affiliated with* Time *and writes frequently about computers for the magazine. He also appeared on an ABC-TV* Nightline *segment with Ted Koppel concerning "cyberporn." After you read his article, be sure to read responses to it that appeared just after its publication on several Internet "chats"; some of them are reprinted here in* Conversations *just after Elmer-Dewitt's essay.*

1 Sex is everywhere these days—in books, magazines, films, television, music videos and bus-stop perfume ads. It is printed on dial-a-porn business cards and slipped under windshield wipers. It is acted out by balloon-breasted models and actors with unflagging erections, then rented for $4 a night at the corner video store. Most Americans have become so inured to the open display of eroticism—and the arguments for why it enjoys special status under the First Amendment—that they hardly notice it's there.

2 Something about the combination of sex and computers, however, seems to make otherwise worldly-wise adults a little crazy. How else to explain the uproar surrounding the discovery by a U.S. Senator—Nebraska Democrat James Exon—that pornographic pictures can be downloaded from the Internet and displayed on a home computer? This, as any computer-savvy undergrad can testify, is old news. Yet suddenly the press is on alert, parents and teachers are up in arms, and lawmakers in Washington are rushing to ban the smut from cyberspace with new legislation—sometimes with little regard to either its effectiveness or its constitutionality.

If you think things are crazy now, though, wait until the   3
politicians get hold of a report coming out this week. A
research team at Carnegie Mellon University in Pittsburgh,
Pennsylvania, has conducted an exhaustive study of online
porn—what's available, who is downloading it, what turns
them on—and the findings (to be published in the *Georgetown Law Journal*) are sure to pour fuel on an already explosive debate.

The study, titled *Marketing Pornography on the Information*   4
Superhighway, is significant not only for what it tells us about
what's happening on the computer networks but also for what
it tells us about ourselves. Pornography's appeal is surprisingly elusive. It plays as much on fear, anxiety, curiosity and
taboo as on genuine eroticism. The Carnegie Mellon study,
drawing on elaborate computer records of online activity, was
able to measure for the first time what people actually download, rather than what they say they want to see. "We now
know what the consumers of computer pornography really
look at in the privacy of their own homes," says Marty Rimm,
the study's principal investigator. "And we're finding a fundamental shift in the kinds of images they demand."

What the Carnegie Mellon researchers discovered was: 5

There's an awful lot of porn online.   In an 18-month study,   6
the team surveyed 917,410 sexually explicit pictures, descriptions, short stories and film clips. On those Usenet newsgroups where digitized images are stored, 83.5% of the
pictures were pornographic.

It is immensely popular.   Trading in sexually explicit imag-   7
ery, according to the report, is now "one of the largest (if not
the largest) recreational applications of users of computer
networks." At one U.S. university, 13 of the 40 most frequently visited newsgroups had names like *alt.sex.stories,*
rec.arts.erotica and *alt.sex.bondage.*

It is a big moneymaker.   The great majority (71%) of the   8
sexual images on the newsgroups surveyed originate from
adult-oriented computer bulletin-board systems (BBS) whose
operators are trying to lure customers to their private collections of X-rated material. There are thousands of these BBS
services, which charge fees (typically $10 to $30 a month) and
take credit cards; the five largest have annual revenues in
excess of $1 million.

9   *It is ubiquitous.* Using data obtained with permission
from **BBS** operators, the Carnegie Mellon team identified
(but did not publish the names of) individual consumers in
more than 2,000 cities in all 50 states and 40 countries, territories and provinces around the world—including some
countries like China, where possession of pornography can
be a capital offense.

10   *It is a guy thing.* According to the BBS operators, 98.9% of
the consumers of online porn are men. And there is some evidence that many of the remaining 1.1% are women paid to
hang out on the "chat" rooms and bulletin boards to make the
patrons feel more comfortable.

11   *It is not just naked women.* Perhaps because hard-core
sex pictures are so widely available elsewhere, the adult **BBS**
market seems to be driven largely by a demand for images
that can't be found in the average magazine rack: pedophilia
(nude photos of children), hebephilia (youths) and what the
researchers call paraphilia—a grab bag of "deviant" material
that includes images of bondage, sadomasochism, urination,
defecation, and sex acts with a barnyard full of animals.

12   The appearance of material like this on a public network
accessible to men, women and children around the world
raises issues too important to ignore—or to oversimplify. Parents have legitimate concerns about what their kids are being
exposed to and, conversely, what those children might miss if
their access to the Internet were cut off. Lawmakers must balance public safety with their obligation to preserve essential
civil liberties. Men and women have to come to terms with
what draws them to such images. And computer programmers
have to come up with more enlightened ways to give users control over a network that is, by design, largely out of control.

13   The Internet, of course, is more than a place to find pictures of people having sex with dogs. It's a vast marketplace of
ideas and information of all sorts—on politics, religion, science and technology. If the fast-growing World Wide Web ful-
fills its early promise, the network could be a powerful engine
of economic growth in the 21st century. And as the Carnegie
Mellon study is careful to point out, pornographic image files,
despite their evident popularity, represent only about 3% of
all the messages on the Usenet newsgroups, while the Usenet
itself represents only 11.5% of the traffic on the Internet.

14   As shocking and, indeed, legally obscene as some of the
online porn may be, the researchers found nothing that can't

be found in specialty magazines or adult bookstores. Most of the material offered by the private BBS services, in fact, is simply scanned from existing print publications.

But pornography is different on the computer networks. 15 You can obtain it in the privacy of your home—without having to walk into a seedy bookstore or movie house. You can download only those things that turn you on, rather than buy an entire magazine or video. You can explore different aspects of your sexuality without exposing yourself to communicable diseases or public ridicule. (Unless, of course, someone gets hold of the computer files tracking your online activities, as happened earlier this year to a couple dozen crimson-faced Harvard students.)

The great fear of parents and teachers, of course, is not that 16 college students will find this stuff but that it will fall into the hands of those much younger—including some, perhaps, who are not emotionally prepared to make sense of what they see.

Ten-year-old Anders Urmacher, a student at the Dalton 17 School in New York City who likes to hang out with other kids in the Treehouse chat room on America Online, got E-mail from a stranger that contained a mysterious file with instructions for how to download it. He followed the instructions, and then he called his mom. When Linda Mann-Urmacher opened the file, the computer screen filled with 10 thumbnail-size pictures showing couples engaged in various acts of sodomy, heterosexual intercourse and lesbian sex. "I was not aware that this stuff was online," says a shocked Mann-Urmacher. "Children should not be subjected to these images."

This is the flip side of Vice President Al Gore's vision of an 18 information superhighway linking every school and library in the land. When the kids are plugged in, will they be exposed to the seamiest sides of human sexuality? Will they fall prey to child molesters hanging out in electronic chat rooms?

It's precisely these fears that have stopped Bonnie Fell of 19 Skokie, Illinois, from signing up for the Internet access her three boys say they desperately need. "They could get bombarded with X-rated porn, and I wouldn't have any idea," she says. Mary Veed, a mother of three from nearby Hinsdale, makes a point of trying to keep up with her computer-literate 12-year-old, but sometimes has to settle for monitoring his phone bill. "Once they get to be a certain age, boys don't always tell Mom what they do," she says.

"We face a unique, disturbing and urgent circumstance, 20 because it is children who are the computer experts in our nation's families," said Republican Senator Dan Coats of

Indiana during the debate over the controversial anti-cyber-porn bill he co-sponsored with Senator Exon.

21   According to at least one of those experts—16-year-old David Slifka of Manhattan—the danger of being bombarded with unwanted pictures is greatly exaggerated. "If you don't want them you won't get them," says the veteran Internet surfer. Private adult BBSs require proof of age (usually a driver's license) and are off-limits to minors, and kids have to master some fairly daunting computer science before they can turn so-called binary files on the Usenet into high-resolution color pictures. "The chances of randomly coming across them are unbelievably slim," says Slifka.

22   While groups like the Family Research Council insist that online child molesters represent a clear and present danger, there is no evidence that it is any greater than the thousand other threats children face every day. Ernie Allen, executive director of the National Center for Missing and Exploited Children, acknowledges that there have been 10 or 12 "fairly high-profile cases" in the past year of children being seduced or lured online into situations where they are victimized. Kids who are not online are also at risk, however; more than 800,000 children are reported missing every year in the U.S.

23   Yet it is in the name of the children and their parents that lawmakers are racing to fight cyberporn. The first blow was struck by Senators Exon and Coats, who earlier this year introduced revisions to an existing law called the Communications Decency Act. The idea was to extend regulations written to govern the dial-a-porn industry into the computer networks. The bill proposed to outlaw obscene material and impose fines of up to $100,000 and prison terms of up to two years on anyone who knowingly makes "indecent" material available to children under 18.

24   The measure had problems from the start. In its original version it would have made online-service providers criminally liable for any obscene communications that passed through their systems—a provision that, given the way the networks operate, would have put the entire Internet at risk. Exon and Coats revised the bill but left in place the language about using "indecent" words online. "It's a frontal assault on the First Amendment," says Harvard law professor Laurence Tribe. Even veteran prosecutors ridicule it. "It won't pass scrutiny even in misdemeanor court," says one.

25   The Exon bill had been written off for dead only a few weeks ago. Republican Senator Larry Pressler of South Dakota, chairman of the Commerce committee, which has

jurisdiction over the larger telecommunications-reform act to which it is attached, told TIME that he intended to move to table it.

That was before Exon showed up in the Senate with his "blue book." Exon had asked a friend to download some of the rawer images available online. "I knew it was bad," he says. "But then when I got on there, it made *Playboy* and *Hustler* look like Sunday-school stuff." He had the images printed out, stuffed them in a blue folder and invited his colleagues to stop by his desk on the Senate floor to view them. At the end of the debate—which was carried live on C-SPAN—few Senators wanted to cast a nationally televised vote that might later be characterized as pornography. The bill passed 84 to 16.   26

Civil libertarians were outraged. Mike Godwin, staff counsel for the Electronic Frontier Foundation, complained that the indecency portion of the bill would transform the vast library of the Internet into a children's reading room, where only subjects suitable for kids could be discussed. "It's government censorship," said Marc Rotenberg of the Electronic Privacy Information Center. "The First Amendment shouldn't end where the Internet begins."   27

The key issue, according to legal scholars, is whether the Internet is a print medium (like a newspaper), which enjoys strong protection against government interference, or a broadcast medium (like television), which may be subject to all sorts of government control. Perhaps the most significant import of the Exon bill, according to EFF's Godwin, is that it would place the computer networks under the jurisdiction of the Federal Communications Commission, which enforces, among other rules, the injunction against using the famous seven dirty words on the radio. In a TIME/CNN poll of 1,000 Americans conducted last week by Yankelovich Partners, respondents were sharply split on the issue: 42% were for FCC-like control over sexual content on the computer networks; 48% were against it.   28

By week's end the balance between protecting speech and curbing pornography seemed to be tipping back toward the libertarians. In a move that surprised conservative supporters, House Speaker Newt Gingrich denounced the Exon amendment. "It is clearly a violation of free speech, and it's a violation of the right of adults to communicate with each other," he told a caller on a cable-TV show. It was a key defection, because Gingrich will preside over the computer-decency debate when it moves to the House in July. Meanwhile, two U.S. Representatives, Republican Christopher Cox   29

of California and Democrat Ron Wyden of Oregon, were putting together an anti-Exon amendment that would bar federal
regulation of the Internet and help parents find ways to block
material they found objectionable.

30   Coincidentally, in the closely watched case of a University of
Michigan student who published a violent sex fantasy on the
Internet and was charged with transmitting a threat to injure
or kidnap across state lines, a federal judge in Detroit last week
dismissed the charges. The judge ruled that while Jake Baker's
story might be deeply offensive, it was not a crime.

31   How the Carnegie Mellon report will affect the delicate
political balance on the cyberporn debate is anybody's guess.
Conservatives thumbing through it for rhetorical ammunition will find plenty. Appendix B lists the most frequently
downloaded files from a popular adult BBS, providing both
the download count and the two-line descriptions posted by
the board's operator. Suffice it to say that they all end in
exclamation points, many include such phrases as "nailed to
a table!" and none can be printed in TIME.

32   How accurately these images reflect America's sexual interests, however, is a matter of some dispute. University of Chicago sociologist Edward Laumann, whose 1994 *Sex in America*
survey painted a far more humdrum picture of America's sex
life, says the Carnegie Mellon study may have captured what
he calls the "gaper phenomenon." "There is a curiosity for
things that are extraordinary and way out," he says. "It's like
driving by a horrible accident. No one wants to be in it, but
we all slow down to watch."

33   Other sociologists point out that the difference between
the Chicago and Carnegie Mellon reports may be more apparent than real. Those 1 million or 2 million people who download pictures from the Internet represent a self-selected
group with an interest in erotica. The *Sex in America* respondents, by contrast, were a few thousand people selected to
represent a cross section of all America.

34   Still, the new research is a gold mine for psychologists,
social scientists, computer marketers and anybody with an
interest in human sexual behavior. Every time computer users
logged on to one of these bulletin boards, they left a digital
trail of their transactions, allowing the pornographers to com-
pile data bases about their buying habits and sexual tastes.
The more sophisticated operators were able to adjust their
inventory and their descriptions to match consumer demand.

35   Nobody did this more effectively than Robert Thomas,
owner of the Amateur Action BBS in Milpitas, California, and a

kind of modern-day Marquis de Sade, according to the Carnegie Mellon report. He is currently serving time in an obscenity case that may be headed for the Supreme Court.

Thomas, whose BBS is the online-porn market leader, discovered that he could boost sales by trimming soft- and hardcore images from his data base while frontloading his files with pictures of sex acts with animals (852) and nude prepubescent children (more than 5,000), his two most popular categories of porn. He also used copywriting tricks to better serve his customers' fantasies. For example, he described more than 1,200 of his pictures as depicting sex scenes between family members (father and daughter, mother and son), even though there was no evidence that any of the participants were actually related. These "incest" images were among his biggest sellers, accounting for 10% of downloads.   36

The words that worked were sometimes quite revealing. Straightforward oral sex, for example, generally got a lukewarm response. But when Thomas described the same images using words like choke or choking, consumer demand doubled.   37

Such findings may cheer antipornography activists; as feminist writer Andrea Dworkin puts it, "the whole purpose of pornography is to hurt women." Catharine MacKinnon, a professor of law at the University of Michigan, goes further. Women are doubly violated by pornography, she writes in *Vindication and Resistance,* one of three essays in the forthcoming *Georgetown Law Journal* that offer differing views on the Carnegie Mellon report. They are violated when it is made and exposed to further violence again and again every time it is consumed. "The question pornography poses in cyberspace," she writes, "is the same one it poses everywhere else: whether anything will be done about it."   38

But not everyone agrees with Dworkin and MacKinnon, by any means; even some feminists think there is a place in life— and the Internet—for erotica. In her new book, *Defending Pornography,* Nadine Strossen argues that censoring sexual expression would do women more harm than good, undermining their equality, their autonomy and their freedom.   39

The Justice Department, for its part, has not asked for new antiporn legislation. Distributing obscene material across state lines is already illegal under federal law, and child pornography in particular is vigorously prosecuted. Some 40 people in 14 states were arrested two years ago in Operation Longarm for exchanging kiddie porn online. And one of the leading characters in the Carnegie Mellon study—a former   40

Rand McNally executive named Robert Copella, who left book publishing to make his fortune selling pedophilia on the networks—was extradited from Tijuana, and is now awaiting sentencing in a New Jersey jail.

41   For technical reasons, it is extremely difficult to stamp out anything on the Internet—particularly images stored on the Usenet newsgroups. As Internet pioneer John Gilmore famously put it, "The Net interprets censorship as damage and routes around it." There are border issues as well. Other countries on the Internet—France, for instance—are probably no more interested in having their messages screened by U.S. censors than Americans would be in having theirs screened by, say, the government of Saudi Arabia.

42   Historians say it should come as no surprise that the Internet—the most democratic of media—would lead to new calls for censorship. The history of pornography and efforts to suppress it are inextricably bound up with the rise of new media and the emergence of democracy. According to Walter Kendrick, author of *The Secret Museum: Pornography in Modern Culture*, the modern concept of pornography was invented in the 19th century by European gentlemen whose main concern was to keep obscene material away from women and the lower classes. Things got out of hand with the spread of literacy and education, which made pornography available to anybody who could read. Now, on the computer networks, anybody with a computer and a modem can not only consume pornography but distribute it as well. On the Internet anybody can be Bob Guccione.

43   That might not be a bad idea, says Carlin Meyer, a professor at New York Law School whose *Georgetown* essay takes a far less apocalyptic view than MacKinnon's. She argues that if you don't like the images of sex the pornographers offer, the appropriate response is not to suppress them but to overwhelm them with healthier, more realistic ones. Sex on the Internet, she maintains, might actually be good for young people. "[Cyberspace] is a safe space in which to explore the forbidden and the taboo," she writes. "It offers the possibility for genuine, unembarrassed conversations about *accurate* as well as fantasy images of sex."

44   That sounds easier than it probably is. Pornography is powerful stuff, and as long as there is demand for it, there will always be a supply. Better software tools may help check the worst abuses, but there will never be a switch that will cut it off entirely—not without destroying the unbridled expres-

sion that is the source of the Internet's (and democracy's) greatest strength. The hard truth, says John Perry Barlow, cofounder of the EFF and father of three young daughters, is that the burden ultimately falls where it always has: on the parents. "If you don't want your children fixating on filth," he says, "better step up to the tough task of raising them to find it as distasteful as you do yourself."

The Aftermath of "Cyberporn"

Responses on the Internet

What follows is a sampling of the responses to Philip Elmer-Dewitt's article "Cyberporn." They appeared on Internet chat-lines just after his Time *essay hit the newsstands in the final days of June 1995. While some names have been edited out, otherwise the responses are printed here as they originally appeared.*

From: Jwarren@well.com
Date: June 29, 1995

If you liked NIGHTLINE's 6/27 Obscenity, You'll *Love*   1
TIME's Cover Story
Never one to be left behind in a sex feeding frenzy, last week's "July 3" issue of Time has an *amazingly* unbalanced sex cover story—complete with carefully posed wide-eyed child on the cover. To the outrage of many of us, its chief propagandist is Philip Elmer-DeWitt, whom many of us had believed until now was net-literate and a responsible reporter.
But this is a hatchet job—complete with biased, inflammatory reporting based on unrefereed, secret student "research" that is already being called seriously flawed in other periodicals such as the Washington Post. (It's the same inflammatory drivel foisted on a naive audience by Ted Koppel's staff.)
I keep thinking about the last century when various local politicos were frightened into passing ordinances requiring a bell-ringer to walk fifty paces ahead of any of those scary, terrifying gas buggies.
And I can't help but wonder, more and more . . . is this just a sex feeding frenzy by irresponsible, byline-seeking pack hacks

and circulation-pumping editors and TV show producers—or is someone feeding them this trash, and encouraging their wildly biased, wildly inaccurate-by-omission National Inquirer look-alike "reports"?

After all, what better way to stampede a systematically misinformed public into supporting censorship and suppression?

—jim

From: XXXX@XXXX.army.mil
Date: Fri, 30 Jun 95 9:38:48 EDT

2   Last night I found a set of FAQs that explained the pictures area on the newsgroups. From the explanation that they presented, it ain't easy to get pictures back, in fact it is a major pain in one's butt! Either todays kids are vastly more patient and resourceful than I was in my youth, and/or they have too much free time on their hands. Oh well, times change.

Date: Wed, 28 Jun 1995 22:57:10–0700
From: XXXX@XXXX.com
Subject: Indecent, Vile, Filthy

3   I am having the same experience as you, cruising the net for sex, not finding much. It takes lots of time.

A search with Yahoo gave me some titillating newsgroups, some recently posted pornographic fantasies in alt.sex.stories. I got an 800 number to phone, and reached a live woman in Dominican Republic. There are discussions about porn movies, and porn stars on the net, but they have been removed, with reference to fear of Exon. I found an interesting questionnaire for Bay Area Swingers which was really quite tastefully done . . .

But not much true filth. This file won't do too much harm.

Date: Tue, 4 Jul 1995 12:34:42–0400
From: "Brock N. Meeks" <brock@well.com>
CyberWire Dispatch // Copyright © 1995 //

4   Jacking in from the "Point-Five Percent Solution" Port:

Washington, DC—Time magazine's credibility is hemorrhaging.

The magazine's recent "Cyberporn" cover story has ignited a fire storm of criticism owing to its overblown coverage of a statistically inconsequential study, written by a university undergraduate.

Time's story is being assailed as "reckless," "shoddy work," and an outright "fraud" by academics and civil liberties groups.

Martin Rimm, who as an electrical engineering major at Carnegie Mellon University took 18 months to complete the study, says 90% of the criticism "is junk."

The writer of the Time story, Philip Elmer-Dewitt, characterized the attacks as "a lot of rhetoric from a professional lobbyist and a professor who called it reckless and criminal before she had read" the study.

Besides the pejoratives used to question how academically rigorous the Rimm study is, Time's critics also are chaffing at the veil of secrecy that has surrounded the study.

Time, the Georgetown Law Review (where the study was formally published, despite the fact that it only deals with points of law inside of footnotes) and ABC's Nightline, in a kind of media collusion, refused to let anyone outside those organizations do an independent review of the study before publication. Each cited secrecy and a prior arrangement with Rimm as the reason.

At least a week before publication, Time magazine was alerted to several potential problems in the study's methodology. "I raised what I thought were several red flags," said Donna Hoffman, an associate professor of management in the Owen School at Vanderbilt University, and one of the most respected researchers on Net access issues. "Those concerns were apparently ignored," she said.

Further, at least two legal experts, Mike Goodwin of the Electronic Frontier Foundation and Danny Weitzner of the Center for Democracy and Technology, were refused access to the study, despite being asked by Rimm to review the report's legal footnotes. Both declined to provide any legal analysis, issuing warnings that such analysis was impossible without seeing the footnotes in context.

Time magazine, aware of all this, ran its story without noting any of the criticism.

The 00.5 Percent Solution

One of the most egregious spin elements that Time used on the story was hyping Rimm's claim that 83.5% of all images on Usenet are "pornographic."

That 83.5% figure has already been seized upon by some members of Congress looking to bludgeon the First Amendment by placing unconstitutional constraints on Internet content. This figure is likely to become a rallying cry of the First Amendment impaired; it has already been trumpeted in at least one Senate floor speech.

Small problem: That figure—and the study which ejaculated its results to a select media group under the cloak of secrecy—is severely flawed, according to several academics and civil liberties groups that have since obtained and analyzed a copy.

By Rimm's own admission, the 83.5% figure is derived from a seven-day time slice of the postings to only 17 of some 32 Usenet groups that typically carry image files. Usenet is comprised of thousands of newsgroups, the vast majority of which are text based.

Further, Rimm's own figures show that his so-called "pornographic" images comprise merely ONE-HALF OF ONE PERCENT (00.5%) of all Internet traffic.

Time reporter Philip Elmer-DeWitt did report this fact. Sort of.

But readers of the Time story have to wade nearly 1,000 words into the story before stumbling across this passage:

> "As the Carnegie Mellon study is careful to point out, pornographic image files...represent only about 3 percent of all the messages on the Usenet newsgroups, while the Usenet itself represents only 11.5 percent of the traffic on the Internet."

Elmer-DeWitt would later claim during an online discussion on the WELL that he didn't finish the math, citing the .5% figure, because readers tend to get lost when more than two figures are cranked into a paragraph. (See, Time takes care of you!)

Cooking the Books

To juice the coverage, Time also cited that the study had "surveyed 917,410 sexually explicit pictures, descriptions, short stories and film clips."

These files, however, were dredged up from adult BBS systems; NOT from Internet newsgroups, a point that is not entirely clear when reading the article.

The 917K figure is further misleading because even Rimm admits in his paper that he winnowed out so many files that his analysis is based on merely 294,114 files. And that STILL doesn't tell the whole story.

"Naked Bitch with Mardi Gras Beads"

To analyze such a huge number of files, by visually verifying that something called "Naked Bitch with Mardi Gras Beads" is actually a woman and not a hoaxed picture of a female dog (as was actually the case), would have taken years. Instead, Rimm's analysis is based overwhelmingly on file *descriptions* only; not actual viewing, using an artificial intelligence program.

Yet a reader of Time's cover story gets none of this analysis.

Walking Back the Cat

How did a major magazine like Time get roped into reporting as "exhaustive," such an apparently flawed document? It was likely a combination of several factors, including errors in judgment, fatigue, and the need to scoop the competition on a hot button issue of the day.

The intelligence community often debriefs its operations through an exercise called "walking back the cat." During this exercise, the major players are gathered and the mission is examined in detail.

While not all the information surrounding the events that led up to the Time cover story are known, let's walk back the cat on what we do know.

Early 1994: Rimm assembles his "research team" to begin trolling some 68 adult BBSs. His team is instructed to try and obtain as much as possible data on the BBS customers through a kind of "social engineering."

Cyberwire Dispatch interviewed 15 major adult BBS operators to ask about their participation with Rimm. None of them remember ever having spoken to Rimm or a member of his "research team" about the study.

Dispatch asked Rimm; "Did your team go undercover, as it were, when getting permission from these [BBS operators] to use their information?" He replied only: "Discrete, ain't we?"

When asked how he was able to obtain detailed customer profiles from usually skeptical operators of adult BBSs he says: "If you were a pornographer, and you don't have fancy computers or Ph.D. statisticians to assist you, wouldn't you be just a wee bit curious to see how you could adjust your inventories to better serve your clientele? Wouldn't you want to know that maybe you should decrease the number of oral sex images and increase the number of bondage images? Wouldn't you want someone to analyze your logfiles to better serve the tastes of each of your customers?"

October 1994: Eight months before the "exclusive first look" that Time touts about its story on Rimm's findings, "people involved in the study were pitching it to the media," reports Michael C. Berch, editor of *INFOBAHN* magazine, in a posting to the alt.internet.media-coverage newsgroup.

Berch said he took a flyer on the story because he had "other coverage of Internet erotica" in the works.

Rimm says he has no knowledge of the exclusive offered to *INFOBAHN* or any other publication before shopping it to Time.

During this time, Rimm also shops a draft of his study to the CMU administration, according to a Time magazine report last year. Shocked at the findings, the school scurries to implement a full-scale censorship of alt.sex groups from the schools Usenet feed.

November 1994: All hell breaks loose. Word gets out that Carnegie Mellon University has decided to make public its policy to censor all alt.sex newsgroups from flowing into its computers.

The ensuing turmoil surrounding the CMU decision draws media attention and Time is there.

Time reporter Elmer-DeWitt hooks up with Rimm and, using sparse stats drawn from the Rimm paper, he writes in their November 21, 1994, issue a story headlined "Censoring Cyberspace."

In the story he refers to Rimm as only a "research associate." Elmer-DeWitt's story says the CMU administration acted on a draft of Rimm's study "about to be released." In actuality, the study doesn't see the light of day until some seven months later and only then under a secrecy agreement between Rimm and Time and the Georgetown Law Review.

Elmer-DeWitt writes in that November article that Rimm has, "put together a picture collection that rivaled Bob Guccione's (917,410 in all)."

In reality, Rimm had few, if any, actual images. The 917K figure then, as now, refers only to descriptions of images. And when the data was finally washed, only some 214K of those image *descriptions* were valid.

Fast Forward to March 1995:   Rimm finally finds a place to publish: the Georgetown Law Review. But he cuts a deal first: No one—absolutely no one—outside of the law review's immediate staff is allowed to read the full study.

David G. Post, a visiting associate professor of law at the Georgetown University Law Center, is approached "to help several of the student editors with questions that they had arising out of the study," he writes in a "Preliminary Discussion of Methodological Peculiarities in the Rimm Study of Pornography on the 'Information Superhighway,'" distributed after the Time article runs.

But when Post, who says he has "research interests in this area," asks to be shown a copy of the study before advising the students, he too is rebuffed "[T]hey were unable to do so because of a secrecy arrangement they had made with Mr. Rimm," he writes in his preliminary discussion.

Post also writes: "One would have, perhaps, more confidence in the results of the Rimm study had it been subjected to more vigorous peer review."

However, law review journals, unlike rigorous scientific journals, are not routinely peer reviewed.

But this study and its purported results were anything but "routine." The potential magnitude of the study—which was not lost on Rimm; he'd already seen the white-bread Administration at CMU rush to trample the First Amendment after reading an early draft—should have been enough for the Georgetown Law Review, not to mention the editors at Time, to *demand* outside review and Rimm be damned.

Professor Hoffman readily acknowledges that law reviews aren't subject to peer reviews. (Note: Maybe this is why the majority of lawyers can't write their way past a moderately bright 14-year-old.) However, she says quite bluntly and correctly: "A study like this belongs in a peer-reviewed journal if it's going to be used to impact public policies and stimulate public debate on an important societal issue."

June 1995:   Mike Godwin, online counsel for the Electronic Frontier Foundation and attorney Daniel Weitzner, deputy director of the Center for Democracy and Technology, are, at separate times, asked by Rimm to review the legal footnotes for accuracy.

Godwin and Weitzner say the task is impossible without seeing the full report. They are denied that request.

Weitzner fires off several critical concerns he has about the footnotes anyway, noting that any kind of real analysis is impossible.

Rimm later "thanks" Weitzner for his "participation," even though Weitzner clearly had denied the review request.

June 8–18, 1995: A copy of the study arrives at Time magazine where it sits idle. Elmer-DeWitt is up to his journalistic elbows trying to edit a major Time cover story on Estrogen. The story is complex and riding herd on it stresses Elmer-DeWitt.

The good news: Word filters down to him that his promotion, which has "been in the works for some time," he says, will be official in a couple of weeks, about the time of his vacation and right after he puts another major cover story to bed: the flash point "Cyberporn" story.

Four Time correspondents are assigned to the story to help with the research.

Time passes quickly. Rimm's story, like a forest fire, begins to create its own atmosphere, that rarefied air of "The Exclusive." In the unrelenting, brutalizing competition of the newsweeklies, the scoop is the ace in the hole.

The Time editors were convinced the Rimm study was their Ace. Somebody should have told them it was dealt from the bottom of the deck.

So now Elmer-DeWitt begins pushing for his story, citing its exclusive nature. But Elmer-DeWitt is negotiating the story's placement based on character flaw: He was already sold on the story, having used it back in November during the CMU censorship dust up. The story held up then, it should hold up on the cover. Besides, if it was good enough for the Georgetown Law Review, it was good enough for Time.

And Elmer-DeWitt plays the law review card, readily admitting: "If [Georgetown] hadn't accepted [Rimm's study] for publication, we wouldn't have done our story."

At this point, Elmer-DeWitt has too much invested in the story. Somehow he ignores the lingering doubts and presses forward with the writing. Later, on the WELL he will admit to be personally "pulling for" the validity of Rimm's study.

Meanwhile, one of his reporters, Hannah Bloch, is picking up some bad vibes from Professor Hoffman.

Hoffman and her husband/research partner Tom Novak have tagged-teamed some of the Net's trickiest usage based problems, developing some of the first quantitative models for accurate WEB "traffic accounting." And even from reading the abstract of Rimm's study, Hoffman smells sloppy research. "This is a nice example of bad research," she says.

After the Bloch-Hoffman telephone tag review finally ends, Hoffman says she still feels like Bloch "didn't get it." Hoffman e-mails Elmer-DeWitt directly with her concerns.

When Hoffman asks Elmer-DeWitt to see a copy of the study, he balks, citing the secrecy arrangement with Rimm. Hoffman lays out her concerns about Rimm's methodology and e-mails them to Elmer-DeWitt. Among those concerns, Hoffman notes that a study of such reported significance should have been subject to some kind of peer review.

But Elmer-DeWitt blows off Hoffman's concerns, not because of flawed logic or some perceived hidden agenda. Nope, Elmer-DeWitt decides to dismiss Hoffman out of hand when he discovers—quite suddenly—that law review journals are rarely peer reviewed. This somehow significantly lowers the credibility factor of Hoffman's concerns in Elmer-Dewitt's mind and, for whatever reason, he ignores them.

The concerns are never raised. Not in editorial meetings. Not in the text of the story. Nowhere. A Time reader is led to believe that the study was rigorous and without fault.

In truth, the story had been criticized on several levels and by several different people. The connection? None, save for their concern about sloppy research.

So Elmer-DeWitt presses on. Don't let facts stand in the way... he has a story to write; a vacation to get ready for. This is his baby, and he's under the gun to deliver.

June 19–23: With barely a chance to breathe after the work on Time's Estrogen cover story, as well as several other stories, Elmer-DeWitt wades into the reports from his other correspondents.

He fields editorial questions from higher up. There are still gaping, mawing [*sic*] holes in the story. By the end of the day Monday, the 19th, he knows he has to start writing come Tuesday morning. This is crunch time. There is no more slack in the schedule. Artwork has been commissioned. The cover slot secured. His vacation is looking better all the time...

Meanwhile, Time's public relations arm is cranking into high gear. They know they have a hot cover coming up. They want to get the most mileage out of it that they can. Where do they turn? Television.

They consult with Rimm. He's pitched the idea of giving the story to 20/20's Barbara Walters. Rejected. Too lightweight. Larry King Live is suggested. Good talk hype, high visibility, but not a serious enough venue.

Rejected. *Conan* and the *Late Show* were never considered.

Finally, the Time spin doctors decide on Ted Koppel and Nightline. "We thought Koppel would do a more balanced job," Elmer-DeWitt said.

Time calls ABC. "It's an exclusive and it's yours if you want it." Nobody mentions the fact that ABC was the third choice...

Another secrecy deal is cut. Nightline can't give the study to anyone else either. The article hits the stands on the 26th, but by that time Elmer-DeWitt will be vacationing. The ABC producers decide to tape him Friday, the 23rd.

Thursday hits and Elmer-DeWitt meets the 6 P.M. deadline. Researchers comb the story. Top editors read it, too. "Needs some work," they say and Elmer-DeWitt cranks up the computer to satisfy his bosses. The issue is put to bed.

Friday, June 23rd—It's Darkest Before the Dawn: At 22-hundred hours, 43 minutes, The Computer Underground Digest's Jim Thomas uploads to the WELL, under a new topic residing inside the "media" conference, an urgent message being sent through Cyberspace by Voters Telecom Watch.

The VTW alert puts the Net on notice: Time is ready to publish on Monday a study of porn on the Net. The VTW alert acts like an early warning flare: "The catch is that no one even knows if the study's methods are valid, because no one is being allowed to read it due to an exclusive deal between Time and the institution that funded the study."

Saturday, June 24th—Bad Moon Rising: Early in the morning, Hoffman logs on to the WELL and jolts the media conference, calling the Rimm study "reckless research" and noting how difficult it is to discuss porn on the Net without throwing fuel on the fire.

Elmer-DeWitt follows some five hours later with his own assessment of Hoffman's opening salvo. He says that Hoffman is right about fueling the fire. But he drops a bomb of his own: He wonders aloud how Hoffman can call the study reckless when she's never even read it.

However, he conveniently forgets to tell other WELL members that he denied several requests—Hoffman's among them—from people to see the full study before they commented on the record. He also fails to mention that it was a secret agreement with Rimm that made any independent review of the study impossible.

This early exchange, in a topic called merely "Newsweek-lies," set the stage for what would become a romp into "way new" journalism of the first degree.

Over the course of the next eight days, this topic on the WELL would ignite a grassroots investigative team held together with no particular agenda other than seeing all the facts about the Time story vetted.

Steven Levy, a writer for *Newsweek*, weighs in. He's also written something about Porn and the Net for his publication that will run on Monday. The Rimm study gets a single, dubious paragraph.

Levy would have missed the Rimm reference altogether, but Georgetown law professor David Post tips him to the fact that Time is running the story.

Levy scrambles himself to get a copy of the study. He gets shut out. The law review won't give him a copy, citing the secrecy arrangement with Rimm.

Levy tries to find out what Rimm or the Law Review are getting in return for all their secrecy. Each tells Levy to talk to the other. He gets no answer.

In the WELL conference he voices his concern about such secrecy arrangements, wondering if it was trade off for assurances that the story would get a cover.

What Levy doesn't know is that in the coming days, the mere mention of Rimm's study in his story causes the blood pressure to rise within the Time top editorial staff. Gone was their "exclusive," or so they thought, despite the fact that Levy had virtually no detailed knowledge of the Rimm paper. Elmer-Dewitt will be made to answer for "the leak," when Time does a postmortem on the story.

Elmer-DeWitt barks back at Levy, defending the secret agreement with Rimm. He says he's "much more comfortable" with that arrangement than with same that *Newsweek* has made made with top business executives. He drops Levy a compliment, calling him "one of the best," and then backhands him: "It's not my fault he works for the magazine that secured exclusive rights to Hitler's 'diaries.'"

He later takes back the remark about the Hitler diaries, admitting it was "a low blow," explaining he found it a bit ironic for Newsweek to be claiming the high moral ground.

A critical mass begins to form. WELLites begin to limber up, taking free shots at Time and Elmer-DeWitt...and all before anyone has seen the story.

EFF's Godwin weighs in, the voice of reason: "Let's hold off criticizing Time until we see what the story looks like." And yet, in the coming days, it will be Godwin that rises up as judge, jury, and executioner of Elmer-DeWitt and Time.

The fun has just begun and Elmer-DeWitt is about to step into a virtual home only the Menendez brothers could love.

June 25, 7:36 P.M.—The Feeding Begins: "The Time article is available on America Online right now," is the single line message posted to Newsweeklies on the WELL.

A feeding frenzy is about to take place and over the course of the next several days the WELL topic will resemble a great roiling, shark infested pool. Time and Elmer-Dewitt are the chum.

The events that shake out over the next few days, while localized on the WELL, are significant. First, the article's principal author has his virtual "home base" on the WELL. Second, the WELL becomes the focal point of the most intensive and extensive critiques of the Rimm study, a factor that proves invaluable, considering that Rimm was successful in bypassing this traditional academic gauntlet.

The early reviews of the Time story are horrendous. Someone suggests that the phrase "Rimm Job" will be used to identify overhyped undergraduate studies that masquerade as major newsmagazine cover stories.

Monday June 26, O-Dark-Thirty: Elmer-DeWitt logs in and posts a comment at 2:38 A.M. That prompts John Seabrook of the New Yorker magazine to query nearly 3 hours later: "You're up early. Trouble sleeping?"

At 2:39 P.M. Godwin's life for the next eight days is defined by this posting: "Philip's story is an utter disaster, and it will damage the debate about this issue because we will have to spend lots of time correcting misunderstandings that are directly attributable to the story."

Godwin proceeds to take huge, vicious chunks from the underbelly of the Time article by attacking its least defensible position: The infamous 83.5% figure.

Godwin will continue to feast at the table of Time for days to come, at times posting several devastating comments in a row. He is a machine. He admits to "obsessing" on the issue, but "I'm obsessing over what is the truth," he tells Dispatch about midnight.

He is on the edge of a day too far gone to care about, at the brink of the next too dark to foretell.

He has been unrelenting in his strategic dismantling of Elmer-DeWitt and the Rimm paper. Even his voice sounds tired. But all this takes its toll: Elmer-DeWitt had been a friend. "I feel like something has died," he will say later. And to a large extent, something has.

The packaging of the story gets hammered as well. The shock artwork, which includes a damn near pornographic image in its own right—what can only be described as a man fucking a computer terminal—is outrageously sensationalistic. Elmer-DeWitt even admits at one point that he agrees with views that the art is "over the top."

9:30 Monday Evening . . . : By now Elmer-DeWitt and Time are bloody if not bowed. A crack in Time's story begins to surface.

Elmer-Dewitt admits it himself, acknowledging that he should have had a "graph" in the story that referenced the advance criticism of the study that he knew about. "That was probably a screw up," he writes on the WELL. He says he "couldn't risk" giving anyone, such as Hoffman, an advance copy of the study for fear it would "leak."

Tuesday June 27th—The Plot Moistens: Virtually bleeding from a thousand cuts, Elmer-DeWitt acknowledges that the pressure got to him while writing the story. In fact, he says that if he and his team had had more time and "more presence of mind," they would have called in an "outside expert" to review the study.

But "presence of mind" was apparently lacking. Elmer-DeWitt admits that he had to go from editing one cover story to writing the next with only the weekend to rejuvenate. "Such is the life at a newsmagazine these days," he writes.

CuD's Jim Thomas surfs into a WEB site that is supposed to carry the Rimm study. What Thomas finds instead is a brief description of the study, a pointer to the law review article and a phone number were you can buy it—not download it.

And then he points out a curious note contained on the page: "Current plans for pages include the Introductory text from this article and the conspiracies which have reached the ears of the researchers." But there's no other explanation.

Nightline runs its exclusive-by-arrangement segment. Elmer-DeWitt has already been taped the previous Friday. Godwin goes head to head with Ralph Reed of the Christian Coalition.

Godwin becomes an instant hero: He jumps first into the discussion and is able to play the "family values" card before Reed. But Reed is tossing out facts and figures as if he has somehow been given an advance copy of the so-secret study.

When Rimm is asked if Reed had some kind of advance peek at the study, Rimm says: "Ralphy never saw the fucking study."

Wednesday, June 28th: Hoffman appears back on the WELL after a two day absence. She is shocked: In the media topic alone there have been 250 new posts.

Hoffman announces that she and her husband/partner, having finally obtained a copy of the study and are beginning a systematic critique of the Rimm report.

Six days later the Hoffman/Novak report is complete, all 9,000 words of it. It turns out to be devastating.

Professor David Post, from the Georgetown University Law center, cruises onto the Net with his own detailed critique of the Rimm study. Post deconstructs Rimm's report in the same manner as the Hoffman/Novak paper.

Thursday, June 29th: Hoffman discovers that the cryptic WEB page message alluding to "conspiracies" is aimed at her. On the WEB site, it seems Hoffman is being singled out for being a bit too vocal.

Hoffman fires off a nasty note to Rimm's faculty advisors at CMU. They answer quickly, apologizing for "conspiracy" language that "has no place in academic discourse," according to Marvin Sirbu, one of Rimm's advisors.

Rimm answers Hoffman, too. He apologizes for the WEB page, saying that the person who put it up had done so "accidentally."

The WEB page goes back to "normal."

Friday, June 30–Monday, July 3rd: There is not a minute's rest for Elmer-Dewitt. He is continuously hounded whenever he goes online. All this is very tiring for Elmer-DeWitt. Finally, after a long protracted battle on the WELL, Elmer-DeWitt seems to be inching nearer defeat, at least on certain points.

David Kline, a freelance writer and contributor to Wired magazine, logs in and writes that Elmer-DeWitt didn't conduct what he calls "journalistic due diligence" by investigating the study thoroughly and by not mentioning that other experts raised several doubts.

Kline's message has rung the brass bell.

The next time Elmer-DeWitt logs in, he cites Kline's message saying: "I think he's put his finger on precisely where I screwed up."

And yet, the story won't die. Going into Monday night (July 3), Rimm himself was preparing a detailed assault on the Hoffman/Novak critique.

I asked for an advance copy... Rimm said it was secret until he was ready to announce it.

Why am I not surprised?

Meeks (whew... finally) out...

July 10, 1995

An Open Letter to Phil Elmer-DeWitt and TIME's Responsible Editors (& T. Koppel)

Hi Phil—

It was sad and frustrating to see—and vigorously participate in—the net's flames that poured over you after you honchoed the cyberporn "report." I know you, and I know you are much, much better than that illustrates.   5

You and Time earned the flaming that you got, because you and your editors were the ones with the power to impact public and political opinion, and thus the responsibility to do it *very* carefully. Even under the insane pressure of a weekly deadline in the cutthroat newsweekly racket.

What's done's done. I'm writing about the immediate future—hopefully in time to make a difference. I know you and Time are planning a follow-up—which may be no more than the usual wee-tiny, "Oopps, we made a few little errors," quiblette, buried in some obscure corner of a week's prose.

I urge you: Please—don't do it that way. Such an approach—the press's usual approach to admitting errors—is simply not acceptable. Be assured that it will simply provoke another round of equally earned net-wide flames.

YOU, PHIL, AND TIME *CAN* RECEIVE WELL-EARNED APPLAUSE:

1. Do a second major article on cyberporn and its much more important issue, cybercensorship by government as opposed as to censorship via the delete button.

2. Bluntly, fully and in detail, rip apart the Rimm study with the same zeal that you or Time would put into a secret,

unrefereed procigarette tobacco study by an undergraduate student—if it had received the cover-story prominence and immediately been quoted on the floor of Congress.

3. Bluntly report and criticize your and Time's failings.

4. But most of all, present the other side of the censorship case—including emphasis on the alternatives that net-illiterate, now frightened, justifiably concerned parents, teachers and librarians can use to protect their children from doing what kids have always done . . . going where they're told not to go.

5. And have your p.r. department promote *this*, too, to Ted Koppel. Although Nightline's set-up piece was appalling, Ted himself—operating from unfortunate personal ignorance—*tried* to do an even-handed job of drawing out some of the issues . . . to the extent that he understood them. I am convinced that he will do a better job, with better research beforehand, if he takes the time to cover cybercensorship excused by the minority of *global* cyberporn that exists.

Soon, more and more print journalists will be doing their work online. The clear and present danger is that, by the time they and their publishers arrive online, the government will have established a long string of precedents for government-imposed content control.

Phil, over and over, we have seen that the net and the public have a great capacity for forgiveness—when national leaders have screwed up and promptly, bluntly and without excuses admitted it. Janet Reno after Waco is an example.

If you or your barricaded editors try to gloss this over, or give excuses, or whine forthwith, "We were imperfect, but . . ." scenarios, you will guarantee extensive, continuing, *earned* criticism.

If you—yourselves—rip the hell out of your own story, and present the other side as provocatively as you presented the Rimmtrash, (1) you will be doing a MUCH-needed service to the nation and the political process, and (2) you and Time will *earn* praise for correcting a mistake in an equally prominent, *responsible* manner.

Please Phil . . . do it. You are good enough and honorable enough to do so.

> Your friend (believe it or not),
> —jim
> Jim Warren, GovAccess list-owner/editor
> (jwarren@well.com)
> Advocate & columnist, MicroTimes,

Government Technology, BoardWatch, etc.
345 Swett Rd., Woodside CA 94062

Date: Fri, 7 Jul 1995 05:36:33 -0700
From: John Brueck <jbrueck@svpal.org>

Reading your articles [by Brock Meeks] on Time Warner 6
and Nightline on Internet "porn," it occurs to me that it is
interesting that Time in particular is raising this issue about
an area that essentially is controllable by choice or by parents.
What really offends me and others is the trash on daytime
talk shows and the gangsta rap on MTV.
The prime producer of gangsta rap is Time Warner. Are
they trying to divert attention from there [sic] own far less
controllable enterprise to the detriment of the internet?

Just a Paranoid Opinion

From: XXXXX.XXXX@compuserve.com
Date: 16 Jun 95 17:41:20 EDT

As a criminal defense lawyer generally concerned with the 7
"mundane" areas of homicide, drugs, and assorted sex crimes,
and aware of the hysteria in certain quarters re. "netcrime,"
the only benefit I see from the various proposed laws this
forum so vigorously posts is that my business will increase,
unfortunately at the expense of law-abiding and tax-paying
citizens who pose no danger to anybody, child or otherwise.
I truly hope that some reasonable minds recognize this for
the nonissue that it is and focus on real issues not so susceptible to pithy soundbites, i.e., the budget!
Cynic that I am, I have a horrible feeling that net regulation will become the Prohibition of the 90s. I hope that I am
wrong.

Date: Sun, 9 Jul 1995 11:51:19 -0400
From: farber@central.cis.upenn.edu (David Farber)

"Rimm, Martin (1995), 'The Pornographer's Handbook; 8
How to Exploit Women, Dupe Men, & Make Lots of Money,'
Carnegie, March (ISBN 0962547654)."

This seems real. Maybe there is a serious ethics issue that CMU and the ACM should face up to.

From: dave@xxxxxx.com
Date: Tue, 4 Jul 1995 12:22:34 -0500

9   You talk about someone orchestrating (?) a media indictment of porn. However, I think it's a lot simpler than that.
Remember the years of articles about the epidemic of strangers abducting kids? Notice how that story suddenly went
away.
       It's because, after years of hysteria, a reporter checked with
the FBI and found that nationwide they had (it was 7 or 70)
outstanding cases of children abducted by strangers. That
was it. And once the facts were out—it died down. Now it's
missing (custody disputes) and exploited (my parents made
me do chores) children.
       You have the same thing here. Look at Newsweek which
had a reasonably balanced series of articles. Why? I think it's
because their reporters [Steven Levy] are pretty net-wise
[very much so!] and so, when told to do a subscription-build-
ing piece, they were limited by their knowledge of the net [not
so—Elmer-Dewitt is quite knowledgeable of the net; just got
caught between eager-to-pander editors and questionable
"research," without enough time to perform the due diligence
that was needed—jim].
       While other magazines, with reporters who know nothing
about the subject, are therefore free to make more outlandish
claims—without violating their ethics. (News ethics say you
can't lie, but that ignorance is fine.)

Forwarded-by: xxxxxx@CS.Berkeley.EDU

10   The Cato Institute has released a study "New Age Com-
stockery: Exon vs. the Internet" by Robert Corn-Revere, dated
June 28, 1995, which goes into the history of decency laws in
the U.S.
       It seems that we had our first version of these with the
"Comstock law" of 1873, which was designed to keep people
from sending improper stuff through the postal service (snail-
mail). See, this guy Comstock noticed that people were sending pictures of Sally-next-door to the soldiers on the front.
This was bad and had to be stopped.

According to the study,

As is often the case, invention became the mother of repression. Congress reacted quickly to the postmaster's report, passing a law in 1865 making it a crime to send any "obscene book, pamphlet, picture, print, or other publication of vulgar and indecent character" through the U.S. mail.

That law was strengthened several years later at the insistence of Anthony Comstock, a former dry goods clerk who exerted broad influence as secretary of the New York Society for the Suppression of Vice. Under the popularly named "Comstock law," which prohibited use of the mails to send any "obscene, lewd, or lascivious book, pamphlet, picture, paper, print, or other publication of an indecent character," thousands of authors were jailed and literally tons of literature destroyed.

The full study is at http://www.cato.org/main/pa232.html.

Date: 06 Jul 95 08:27:59 EDT
From: xxxxx.2044@compuserve.com>

...the Comstock analogy is narrowly based on a U.S. 11
Postal Service metaphor, which captures very little of what goes on online.

We should also avoid aggrandizing this Exon amendment into all kinds of things it isn't. For instance, it is far from representative of "cybercensorship." That is a multidimensional subject growing daily, as more and more regulators and businesses gain their sea legs online. It's not just about porn, but everything else people would like to see controlled in their dispersion through the Net.

By the way, as hysteria over the Exon amendment grows, it's important to remember that a federal adult materials law can do some pretty cool things for online services, if properly drafted. First, it can extend the "safe harbor" treatment currently given to phone sex services to online services, meaning that if you do what the statute says, you know you'll stay out of trouble. Second, it can unify the law on a national level, so system operators don't have to tear their hair out wondering what the standards for adult materials are in each state where their users are located.

The broadest view of censorship online issues I have seen is still "Technologies of Freedom," by Ithiel de sola Pool. It lays out the historical structure of differential First Amendment protection in the major media in the U.S., pointing out how entirely different regulatory regimes arose in the different media, for various reasons. As "cyberspace" develops, it will have its own characteristic forms of regulation, taking its place alongside other media like newspapers, television, telephone and the postal system as a uniquely regulated kind of speech medium.

Date: Tue, 04 Jul 1995 12:34:49 GMT
From: xxxxxxdad@crecon.demon.co.uk>

12   As some of you will know, I'm dead set against the Exon Bill (so who isn't) and dead set against censorshit (so who in their right mind isn't). I've spoken out (online) against Net Nanny (based on its prerelease publicity including the press release its company placed on the Net). However, having had a chance to see it at a computer expo here in Birmingham UK last week, I offer the following comments:

Net Nanny is coming to the UK all set for Windows and DOS. I played with it a bit. The way it works is totally configurable by the parent or the system administrator or whatever. The in-charge person loads the program into a hidden directory on the hard drive and through whatever process (not worth describing, very easy) enters a "dictionary" of prohibited words. Anytime any of the words in the "dictionary" show up the program in which it shows (either having been typed from the keyboard or brought in via modem or in any way written to the screen), that specific program closes. And once closed it cannot be reopened until the machine is rebooted.

However, the in-charge person can get back into the program (apparently, the demoing sales person wasn't clear on it) and can do various other functions, because the key to the program lives on a floppy disk that the in-charge person keeps possession of. Logs of activity can be brought up and printed out, showing what words were accessed, how many times, in what programs, etc.

In other words, it is the only type of censorship I approve of, if censorship there has to be, i.e., the parent or teacher censoring what the child has access to rather than some government bureaucrat or anonymous corporate flak.

It arrives in the UK in two weeks in both DOS and Windows Versions.

If only they'd stop the scare mongering, sensationalist sales tactics.

Bruce

Date: Thu, 29 Jun 1995 07:21:40 +0000
From: xxxxxx@dircon.co.uk

I agree with you wholeheartedly that Exon's bill is ridiculous and unconstitutional, but I don't think there's any question about the easy availability of things on the net that a lot of parents wouldn't want their children to see. Such things as the alt.sex and the alt.binaries.pictures hierarchies spring to mind.

My personal opinion is that if my kid has the technical finesse to download and decode said binaries, more power to him/her, but I can understand that a lot of parents don't. The answer is, of course, more parental supervision and computer-savvy-ness, but it weakens our argument against Exon to say, "Oh no, there isn't easily accessible stuff that anyone would think pornographic..."

Date: Fri, 07 Jul 1995 11:18:41 -0500 (CDT)
From: hoffman@colette.ogsm.vanderbilt.edu
(Donna Hoffman)

Note that his advisor Sirbu doesn't put his name on the "rebuttal." I've heard that the CS department wanted to issue a statement saying it had nothing to do with it but that the department head refused, worrying it would look bad.

I've also heard that one of the advisors hasn't even seen the article and hasn't been involved with the project for over 6 months.

One of the "contributors" wrote a scathing critique (Sigel), and another who was acknowledged not only never saw the study but refused to make comments.

I've also heard the social science faculty are upset that the EE faculty won't just stand up and say this thing is a fraud and unethical.

But the CMU ADMINISTRATION is sending out press releases congratulating themselves for being on the cover of Time and Nightline, so there you have it.

Meanwhile, the Net community manages to stay informed about the debate, with posts as they occur, at http://www2000.ogsm.vanderbilt.edu/cyberporn.debate.cgi

Date: Thu, 13 Jul 1995 13:34:56 -0700
From: "Brock N. Meeks" <brock@well.com>
Subject: CWD—Porn-O-Plenty

15   Warning: This article contains sexually graphic language, funded in part by grants from Carnegie Mellon University. No, I'm not joking.

CyberWire Dispatch // Copyright © 1995 ///

Jacking in from the "Mr. Toad's Wild Ride" Port:

Washington, DC—If I were drunk or stoned or Hunter Thompson or a combination of any of those, maybe this past week would make sense.

But there is no empty Jack Daniels bottle on the floor, there is no drug residue dusting the desktop, and unless that wino on the street corner I can see from my office window, the one harassing the hooker, is Thompson—and you just never know—then I'm left all alone with a virtual Marty Rimm staring back at me from my Mac in the form of E-mail, inside a folder called "Rimm Job."

You know Marty. He's the current media lightning rod. Time magazine recently ran a cover story—"Cyberporn"—based on work he did while an undergraduate at Carnegie Mellon University. Marty's taken a lot of heat for that work... he's about to take a lot more, owing to a little moonlighting publishing venture he had going while conducting the study.

This story should write itself, but it doesn't. I've had phone calls, E-mail, and more phone calls. Each of them adds another small piece to the "Marty and Brock Show" to which I've been an unwitting dupe in for the past week. A fairly simple puzzle a week ago, it has now become a 10,000 piece jigsaw of the Milky Way.

Marty calls me "friend" for some reason and asks me questions via E-mail like "why do I like you, Brock?" Well, how the hell do I know?

And things just keep getting more and more bizarre. It's like I've stepped some kind of karmic black hole where a lot of good shit happens, but you can't tell anyone about it. At least not right away, because first you're bound to figure out "What It All Means."

But I can't. Maybe I'll never figure it out. Which means this is an ugly story, which means I have to write it ugly or it doesn't get written. So here goes and god help us all...

The same Marty that wrote the study on which Time magazine hung its June 26th "Cyberporn" cover story is the same Marty that wrote a dicey little paperback called the "Pornographer's Handbook: How to Exploit Women, Dupe Men and Make Lots of Money."

Somehow, somewhere, someone named "John Russel Davis" gets a hold of this porn handbook and begins to upload excerpts from it to the Internet.

It's 6:27 A.M. on July 11th and the only message I get from Marty is a one-liner: "Who is John Russel Davis?" I have no clue. This is the last I hear from Marty all day. He has gone into hiding, suddenly retreating from our E-mail tug-of-war.

The Marty has "gone dark."

Routine checks of E-mail reveal nothing. At 11:26 P.M. the "RimmSat" lights up. The Marty is back online.

He fires off this message to me: "Look, I'm pissed off about what Carolyn is spreading around certain Usenet newsgroups after I broke up with her. Someone named John Russel Davis from AOL appears to be helping her. If you don't know what newsgroups they are, I certainly am not going to be the one to tell you, but let's just say it's where bbs sysops hangout. Maybe then you'll know why I am so silent."

For those playing without a scorecard, "Carolyn" is "Carolyn Speranza" as in the person listed in "Books in Print" as the illustrator for Marty's "how to" porn marketing manual. She also happens to be listed as an advisor for his academic paper.

But Marty's outburst is a mystery to me. Having been wrapped in a regular reporting gig as Washington Bureau Chief for Interactive Week, I haven't been trolling the Usenet. When I tell him this, he gets insulting: "Brock, I thought you were more clever than this. If you were a bbs sysop, and you just got onto the Usenet for the first time... where would you go? But I've said too much, and I don't know what is the lesser of two evils: not to tell you (and hope it goes away), or you will eventually find out later anyway and be pissed off and nobody looks good."

The red flag has been waved and I call in the troops, posting a cryptic message on the WELL asking for assistance in tracking down messages from "John Russel Davis." Aaron Dickey, who toils away in the stock listings department for the Associated Press, takes up the challenge and delivers—in spads.

Into my mailbox flow excerpts of Marty's "how to" manual. Here is a sample of his turgid prose, taken from the Usenet posting, from a chapter on Anal Sex: "When searching for the best anal sex images, you must take especial care to always portray the woman as smiling, as deriving pleasure from being penetrated by a fat penis into her most tender crevice. The male, before ejaculation, is remarkably attuned to the slightest discrepancy; he is as much focused on her lips as on her anus. The slightest indication of pain can make some men limp."

The early returns on the excerpts are that they are a hoax. People castigate the anonymous "Davis" for having tried to foist such a laughable scam on the Net.

But Marty knows different and when I ask if these postings are authentic, he writes: "The excerpts circulating around the Usenet were stolen from my marketing book, Brock. You are the only one I am telling."

This would be the same "marketing book" that in another of these same Usenet excerpts says: "I spent two full years as a researcher at Carnegie Mellon University, where I received four grants to study adult materials on the Internet, Usenet, World Wide Web, and Adult BBS from around the world. Despite countless deprivations and temptations, I have examined this topic with great diligence, having obtained nearly one million descriptions of adult images which were downloaded by consumers more than eight million times. I developed linguistic parsing software to sort these images into 63 different classifications from oral to anal, from lesbian to bondage, from watersports to bestiality."

If that was your jaw hitting the floor, imagine what's happening at Carnegie Mellon about now.

Marty, at first, seemed unruffled by all this. When I asked him what kind of "damage control" he might be formulating to respond to the news of his little self-publishing venture, which, by the way, is listed as having the "Carnegie" imprint and which happens to have the same address in Pittsburgh as someone named "Martin Rimm," Marty replied: "What attention? I don't see it. This is just an oddity. Do you have reason to suspect otherwise?"

But by the night of July 13th, at virtually the 11th hour, he tries to cut a deal with me. He notes that people monitoring the Usenet groups think the excerpts "are a fraud." He says the only ones that know they are real are me and him (forgetting, I suppose, about Carolyn and "Davis"). He says he could essentially upload to the Net a kind of confession, "claiming authorship and you lose your scoop." In return for not blowing my scoop, he wants me to send him an advance copy of this article so he can review it.

He says I'm "close" on some things, but that I have missed "too much" of the story. We could work together, he promises. We could establish a "working relationship," something we obviously don't have now because my earlier article on this whole wretched debacle was "pathetically inaccurate," he claims.

If I comply with his deal, I would then know all, he says: "You will really understand what I did and did not do. If you want."

In case you're wondering, Marty is reading this for the first time along with the rest of you. He has never seen a word of it, other than his own E-mail messages reproduced here.

Not eight hours after he wanted to cut a deal, to "negotiate from the edge," as John Schwartz of the Washington Post characterizes such desperate ploys, he sends a message July 13 (Thursday) that is frantic and elusive: "The thing is about to blow, probably by Friday at noon. I am not happy about this. I don't like it. I don't want it. But I consider you the lesser of two evils. I am going away in about a half hour and will probably return next week."

I have no idea what "the thing" is. I have no idea what the "lesser of two evils" is.

Hell, right now, I'm not even sure he's telling me the truth.

Indeed, throughout this investigation, he has led me back and forth, playing games, trickling out information like some damn chinese water torture.

Mike Godwin, staff counsel for the Electronic Frontier Foundation, who has made the discrediting of the Time "Cyberporn" cover story and Marty's study something of a personal Jihad, sums up Marty like this: "The more you research Rimm, the more a portrait emerges of someone wily, subtle, glib, manipulative. Even when he tells you he's being totally honest, totally frank, you have this lurking feeling that below the surface he's calculating the precise effect his choice of words—both his admissions and his omissions—will have on you."

Godwin is dead bang on.

An old college classmate of Marty's, Bret Pettichord, surfaced during this whole affair. He and Marty went to the New College in Sarasota, Fla., in 1984. They were philosophy

majors. It was a small school, Petticort says, so "everyone
knew everyone." Marty was a loner. But Marty had a peculiar
quirk: He studied tapes of the Rev. Jerry Falwell. "Not for the
message," Petticort said, "Marty didn't buy into that." Instead,
Marty was "fascinated by how Falwell was able to sway people
with his rhetoric . . . and he studied that." But as far as Petticort knows, Marty never practiced it while in college. They
drifted apart, meeting briefly around 1986. When the "Marty
as Media Lightning Rod" emerged, Petticort got back in touch.
Marty's response: "I'm busy now."

Before the Great Usenet Excerpt incident, Marty was
already pacing back and forth across my computer screen.

When the listing of his porn book from "Books in Print" hit
the Net, it was like some one had lit Marty's fuse.

When I asked him to explain the book, he answered with
two questions: "[T]ell me (1) whether you actually have a
copy of the "Porn Handbook," and (2) where you got it."

I answered that I had sources in "low places" and that I
didn't appreciate having to "bargain" with him for information. His book "wasn't hard to track down," I told him.

His secret now blown, he goes ballistic: "It looks like that
bitch got a copy too," he wrote, complete with asterisks,
referring to Vanderbilt Professor Donna Hoffman, one of his
earliest critics. "To say I'm pissed is an understatement," he
wrote in E-mail. "They all agreed not to photocopy it—I'm
going to nail them for copyright violation." The "they" he
refers to there are the adult BBS operators.

I know, throughout this story you have to keep telling yourself: I am not in the Twilight Zone . . . I am *not* in the Twilight Zone. But I swear, I'm not making any of this up.

How did Marty pull this off? Adult BBS operators aren't
known for their openness and trusting attitudes, in general.
When I asked Marty how he was able to do what had taken
me years to do—develop sources inside this network of adult
BBS operators—he said: "[Y]ou didn't have powerful software which you could use to convince them that you indeed
had something to offer. What took you years I could do in
anywhere from five minutes to two months. You'll have to figure the rest out."

That software, of course, was the same software he mentions so prominently in his academic study, the one published
by the Georgetown Law Journal, the one that starts out telling how pornographers have started to use "sophisticated
software" to help them become better marketers.

Are you catching the trend here? It's the ultimate media hack. He's working both sides of the fence. On one hand, Marty is helping the porn operators better market their wares, enabling them to place the stuff more strategically online. And then he writes a study with which he reels in an "exclusive" Time magazine "Cyberporn" cover story decrying the fact that, oh-my-gawd, there's an ever increasing amount of porn online, due in part to better marketing tactics by adult BBS operators.

I tell Marty that I think it's "brilliant" that he was able to work the "acquisition of data" from BBS operators so that he could use it for his "how to" porn marketing manual and also crank it into his academic study.

His reply: "If I do say so myself."

It was so brilliant, in fact, that it almost backfired on him on the day the Time magazine story ran. You see, the BBS operators *didn't know* Marty was collecting their data for an academic study; they thought it was going to be used only by Marty, who would in turn, help them better market their porn.

Now, Marty didn't tell me that, directly, he made a game of it, making me ask questions and pose them to him in the form of a theory. So, when I ran the above theory by him, the one where he dupes the BBS operators and uses the data for both his porn book and the study, he wrote: "I'm somewhat impressed that you picked this up. Yes, I got about a dozen surprised calls this week [when the Time cover story ran] from sysops, but the academic study and BBS marketing manual were kept entirely separate...so they (the porn BBS operators) took no offense."

But the academic community has...except Carnegie Mellon University. To CMU Marty is the new "Media Darling."

Meanwhile, charges of unethical research practices are being launched and brought to the attention of the CMU administration.

Jim Thomas, a professor of sociology/criminal justice at Northern Illinois University, wrote a blistering attack challenging the ethics underlying Marty's study. Thomas's writing is brutal, written in the cold measured prose of an academic: "The most serious and explicit ethical violation is the deceptive nature in which Carnegie Mellon collected the data. Virtually every principle of informed consent was breached, because there is sufficient evidence to conclude that the research team gathered data deceptively, perhaps even fraudulently."

Marty's senior advisor, CMU professor Marvin Sirbu, is nowhere to be found. He has refused to answer questions E-mailed to him about whether he knew Marty was using university funds to gather data for a "how to" porn marketing book at the same time he was using the data for his academic study.

When Marty is asked whether Sirbu knew of his actions, he writes only: "Ask him."

Apparently Marty did run his methodology past George Duncan, a professor of statistics at the Heinz School at CMU. Marty says Duncan is a "privacy expert." However, Marty doesn't list Duncan among the many so-called advisors for his study. "In hindsight, I guess I should have listed him," he told me during our only phone interview.

When Duncan is asked about Marty's methodology he says he sees nothing wrong. When I ask him if he knows the data Marty was collecting was being used for the "Pornographer's Handbook" he says, "that's totally implausible." When I tell him that Marty has confirmed it and that I know for sure he used the data to help write the porn book, Duncan still says, "Well, that's just ridiculous."

What's not ridiculous is the fallout and the "collateral damage" as the military likes to say, in which they really mean "the number of innocent civilians that are murdered by a bomb meant only for a strategic target."

First there is the reputation of Time magazine. This can be summed up in one word: Toast. They will have to scramble big time to recover from having been spun by Marty "Mr. Porn Handbook" Rimm.

Then there is CMU. Your call here is as good as mine. The university, even as this article is grinding to a close, still refers to Marty's study as "the CMU study." They'll have to dodge a few bullets on this one now.

And then there is the Net itself. It will likely take some time to heal the damage here, too. Of course there is pornography on the Net, but it's not nearly as pervasive as recent events have made it out to be. And what's more encouraging, is that there is "real research," ironically enough, from Carnegie Mellon itself, that indicates that sexually oriented material, while available on the Net, isn't really that big a drawing point.

As CMU professor Sara Kiesler, one of the principles of a study called "HomeNet" says: "What's important is to look at how people use the Net and what they are actually looking at, as opposed to looking at what is actually on the Net itself."

Her study is finding that very few people access sexually oriented material, even when they know its readily available, she
said. And when they do access it, it's mostly out of curiosity.
She says, "There's not a high percentage of repeat access."

That should be the word that gets out; not the by now well-
debunked "83.5% of the Usenet is porn" figure that sadly
(thank you Time magazine) is becoming the sound bite of the
Religious Right and certain dense senators.

As for Marty? Well, he's been accepted by MIT's Technology
and Policy Program, where he'll go for his masters. I'm sure
he'll do just fine . . . after all, he does have this little publishing
venture to help him cover expenses.

Meeks out . . .

ON CIVIL DISOBEDIENCE

Henry David Thoreau
Civil Disobedience

Henry David Thoreau (1817–1862) is best known for his classic Walden *(1854), an autobiographical, satiric, spiritual, scientific, and naturalistic "self-help book" based on his two years' stay at Walden Pond, near Boston. A friend of Ralph Waldo Emerson and other transcendentalists, Thoreau expressed his idealism in a number of concrete ways, for example, in his opposition to slavery and the Mexican War. His refusal to pay taxes to support the Mexican War inspired his essay "Civil Disobedience" (1849). First delivered as a lecture in 1848, "Civil Disobedience" influenced the thinking of Mahatma Gandhi and Martin Luther King Jr.*

1   I heartily accept the motto,—"That government is best which governs least"; and I should like to see it acted up to more rapidly and systematically. Carried out, it finally amounts to this, which also I believe,—"That government is best which governs not at all"; and when men are prepared for it, that will be the kind of government which they will have. Government is at best but an expedient; but most governments are usually, and all governments are sometimes, inexpedient. The objections which have been brought against a standing army, and they are many and weighty, and deserve to prevail, may also at last be brought against a standing government. The standing army is only an arm of the standing government. The government itself, which is only the mode which the people have chosen to execute their will, is equally liable to be abused and perverted before the people can act through it. Witness the present Mexican war, the work of comparatively a few individuals using the standing government as their tool; for, in the outset, the people would not have consented to this measure.

2   This American government—what is it but a tradition, though a recent one, endeavoring to transmit itself unim-

paired to posterity, but each instant losing some of its integrity? It has not the vitality and force of a single living man; for a single man can bend it to his will. It is a sort of wooden gun to the people themselves. But it is not the less necessary for this; for the people must have some complicated machinery or other, and hear its din, to satisfy that idea of government which they have. Governments show thus how successfully men can be imposed on, even impose on themselves, for their own advantage. It is excellent, we must all allow. Yet this government never of itself furthered any enterprise, but by the alacrity with which it got out of its way. *It* does not keep the country free. *It* does not settle the West. *It* does not educate. The character inherent in the American people has done all that has been accomplished; and it would have done somewhat more, if the government had not sometimes got in its way. For government is an expedient by which men would fain succeed in letting one another alone; and, as has been said, when it is most expedient, the governed are most let alone by it. Trade and commerce, if they were not made of India-rubber, would never manage to bounce over the obstacles which legislators are continually putting in their way; and, if one were to judge these men wholly by the effects of their actions and not partly by their intentions, they would deserve to be classed and punished with those mischievous persons who put obstructions on the railroads.

But, to speak practically and as a citizen, unlike those who call themselves no-government men, I ask for, not at once no government, but *at once* a better government. Let every man make known what kind of government would command his respect, and that will be one step toward obtaining it. 3

After all, the practical reason why, when the power is once in the hands of people, a majority are permitted, and for a long period continue, to rule is not because they are most likely to be in the right, nor because this seems fairest to the minority, but because they are physically the strongest. But a government in which the majority rule in all cases cannot be based on justice, even as far as men understand it. Can there not be a government in which majorities do not virtually decide right and wrong, but conscience?—in which majorities decide only those questions to which the rule of expediency is applicable? Must the citizen ever for a moment, or in the least degree, resign his conscience to the legislator? Why has every man a conscience, then? I think that we should be men first, and subjects afterward. It is not desirable to cultivate a respect for the law, so much as for the right. The only 4

obligation which I have a right to assume is to do at any time
what I think right. It is truly enough said, that a corporation
has no conscience; but a corporation of conscientious men is
a corporation *with* a conscience. Law never made men a whit
more just; and, by means of their respect for it, even the well-
disposed are daily made the agents of injustice. A common
and natural result of an undue respect for law is, that you
may see a file of soldiers, colonel, captain, corporal, privates,
powder-monkeys, and all, marching in admirable order over
hill and dale to the wars, against their will, ay, against their
common sense and consciences, which makes it very steep
marching indeed, and produces a palpitation of the heart.
They have no doubt that it is a damnable business in which
they are concerned; they are all peaceably inclined. Now,
what are they? Men at all? or small movable forts and magazines, at the service of some unscrupulous man in power?
Visit the Navy-Yard, and behold a marine, such a man as an
American government can make, or such as it can make a
man with its black arts,—a mere shadow and reminiscence of
humanity, a man laid out alive and standing, and already, as
one may say, buried under arms with funeral accompani-
ments, though it may be,—

"Not a drum was heard, not a funeral note,
  As his corse to the rampart we hurried;
Not a soldier discharged his farewell shot
  O'er the grave where our hero we buried."[1]

5   The mass of men serve the state thus, not as men mainly,
but as machines, with their bodies. They are the standing
army, and the militia, jailers, constables, posse comitatus, etc.
In most cases there is no free exercise whatever of the judgment or of the moral sense; but they put themselves on a level
with wood and earth and stones; and wooden men can perhaps be manufactured that will serve the purpose as well.
Such command no more respect than men of straw or a lump
of dirt. They have the same sort of worth only as horses and
dogs. Yet such as these even are commonly esteemed good
citizens. Others—as most legislators, politicians, lawyers,
ministers, and office-holders—serve the state chiefly with
their heads; and, as they rarely make any moral distinctions,
they are as likely to serve the Devil, without *intending* it, as

---

[1]From "Burial of St. John Moore at Corunna" by Charles Wolfe (1817).

God. A very few, as heroes, patriots, martyrs, reformers in the great sense, and *men*, serve the state with their consciences also, and so necessarily resist it for the most part; and they are commonly treated as enemies by it. A wise man will only be useful as a man, and will not submit to be "clay," and "stop a hole to keep the wind away," but leave that office to his dust at least:—

"I am too high-born to be propertied,
To be a secondary at control,
Or useful serving-man and instrument
To any sovereign state throughout the world."[2]

6   He who gives himself entirely to his fellow-men appears to them useless and selfish; but he who gives himself partially to them is pronounced a benefactor and philanthropist.

7   How does it become a man to behave toward this American government to-day? I answer, that he cannot without disgrace be associated with it. I cannot for an instant recognize that political organization as *my* government which is the *slave's* government also.

8   All men recognize the right of revolution; that is, the right to refuse allegiance to, and to resist, the government, when its tyranny or its inefficiency are great and unendurable. But almost all say that such is not the case now. But such was the case, they think, in the Revolution of '75. If one were to tell me that this was a bad government because it taxed certain foreign commodities brought to its ports, it is most probable that I should not make an ado about it, for I can do without them. All machines have their friction; and possibly this does enough good to counterbalance the evil. At any rate, it is a great evil to make a stir about it. But when the friction comes to have its machine, and oppression and robbery are organized, I say, let us not have such a machine any longer. In other words, when a sixth of the population of a nation which has undertaken to be the refuge of liberty are slaves, and a whole country is unjustly overrun and conquered by a foreign army, and subjected to military law, I think that it is not too soon for honest men to rebel and revolutionize. What makes this duty the more urgent is the fact that the country so overrun is not our own, but ours is the invading army.

[2]The line before the quotation is from *Hamlet* V. i. 236–37; the quotation is from Shakespeare's *King John* V. ii. 79–82.

9   Paley,[3] a common authority with many on moral questions, in his chapter on the "Duty of Submission to Civil Government," resolves all civil obligation into expediency; and he
proceeds to say, "that so long as the interest of the whole society requires it, that is, so long as the established government
cannot be resisted or changed without public inconveniency,
it is the will of God that the established government be
obeyed, and no longer.... This principle being admitted, the
justice of every particular case of resistance is reduced to a
computation of the quantity of the danger and grievance on
the one side, and of the probability and expense of redressing
it on the other." Of this, he says, every man shall judge for
himself. But Paley appears never to have contemplated those
cases to which the rule of expediency does not apply, in which
a people, as well as an individual, must do justice, cost what it
may. If I have unjustly wrested a plank from a drowning man,
I must restore it to him though I drown myself. This, according to Paley, would be inconvenient. But he that would save
his life, in such a case, shall lose it. This people must cease to
hold slaves, and to make war on Mexico, though it cost them
their existence as a people.

10   In their practice, nations agree with Paley; but does any
one think that Massachusetts does exactly what is right at the
present crisis?

"A drab of state, a cloth-o'-silver slut,
To have her train borne up, and her soul trail in the dirt."

Practically speaking the opponents to a reform in Massachusetts are not a hundred thousand politicians at the South, but
a hundred thousand merchants and farmers here, who are
more interested in commerce and agriculture than they are in
humanity, and are not prepared to do justice to the slave and
to Mexico, *cost what it may.* I quarrel not with far-off foes, but
with those who, near at home, coöperate with, and do the
bidding of, those far away, and without whom the latter
would be harmless. We are accustomed to say, that the mass
of men are unprepared; but improvement is slow, because the
few are not materially wiser or better than the many. It is not
so important that many should be as good as you, as that
there be some absolute goodness somewhere; for that will
leaven the whole lump. There are thousands who are *in opin-*

[3]William Paley (1743–1805), English theologian.

ion opposed to slavery and to the war, who yet in effect do nothing to put an end to them; who, esteeming themselves children of Washington and Franklin, sit down with their hands in their pockets, and say that they know not what to do, and do nothing; who even postpone the question of freedom to the question of free-trade, and quietly read the prices-current along with the latest advices from Mexico, after dinner, and, it may be, fall asleep over them both. What is the price-current of an honest man and patriot to-day? They hesitate, and they regret, and sometimes they petition; but they do nothing in earnest and with effect. They will wait, well disposed, for others to remedy the evil, that they may no longer have it to regret. At most, they give only a cheap vote, and a feeble countenance and Godspeed, to the right, as it goes by them. There are nine hundred and ninety-nine patrons of virtue to one virtuous man. But it is easier to deal with the real possessor of a thing than with the temporary guardian of it.

All voting is a sort of gaming, like checkers or backgam-   11 mon, with a slight moral tinge to it, a playing with right and wrong, with moral questions; and betting naturally accompanies it. The character of the voters is not staked. I cast my vote, perchance, as I think right; but I am not vitally concerned that that right should prevail. I am willing to leave it to the majority. Its obligation, therefore, never exceeds that of expediency. Even voting *for the right* is *doing* nothing for it. It is only expressing to men feebly your desire that it should prevail. A wise man will not leave the right to the mercy of chance, nor wish it to prevail through the power of the majority. There is but little virtue in the action of masses of men. When the majority shall at length vote for the abolition of slavery, it will be because they are indifferent to slavery, or because there is but little slavery left to be abolished by their vote. *They* will then be the only slaves. Only *his* vote can hasten the abolition of slavery who asserts his own freedom by his vote.

I hear of a convention to be held at Baltimore, or else-   12 where, for the selection of a candidate for the Presidency, made up chiefly of editors, and men who are politicians by profession; but I think, what is it to any independent, intelligent, and respectable man what decision they may come to? Shall we not have the advantage of his wisdom and honesty, nevertheless? Can we not count upon some independent votes? Are there not many individuals in the country who do not attend conventions? But no: I find that the respectable man, so called, has immediately drifted from his position,

and despairs of his country, when his country has more reason to despair of him. He forthwith adopts one of the candidates thus selected as the only *available* one, thus proving that
he is himself *available* for any purposes of the demagogue.
His vote is of no more worth than that of any unprincipled
foreigner or hireling native, who may have been bought. O for
a man who is a *man*, and, as my neighbor says, has a bone in
his back which you cannot pass your hand through! Our statistics are at fault: the population has been returned too large.
How many *men* are there to a square thousand miles in this
country? Hardly one. Does not America offer any inducement
for men to settle here? The American has dwindled into an
Odd Fellow,—one who may be known by the development of
his organ of gregariousness, and a manifest lack of intellect
and cheerful self-reliance; whose first and chief concern, on
coming into the world, is to see that the Almshouses are in
good repair; and, before yet he has lawfully donned the virile
garb, to collect a fund for the support of the widows and
orphans that may be; who, in short, ventures to live only by
the aid of the Mutual Insurance company, which has promised to bury him decently.

13   It is not a man's duty, as a matter of course, to devote himself to the eradication of any, even the most enormous wrong;
he may still properly have other concerns to engage him; but it
is his duty, at least, to wash his hands of it, and, if he gives it no
thought longer, not to give it practically his support. If I devote
myself to other pursuits and contemplations, I must first see,
at least, that I do not pursue them sitting upon another man's
shoulders. I must get off him first, that he may pursue his
contemplations too. See what gross inconsistency is tolerated. I have heard some of my townsmen say, "I should like to
have them order me out to help put down an insurrection of
the slaves, or to march to Mexico;—see if I would go"; and yet
these very men have each, directly by their allegiance, and so
indirectly, at least, by their money, furnished a substitute.
The soldier is applauded who refuses to serve in an unjust
war by those who do not refuse to sustain the unjust government which makes the war; is applauded by those whose own
act and authority he disregards and sets at naught; as if the
state were penitent to that degree that it hired one to scourge
it while it sinned, but not to that degree that it left off sinning
for a moment. Thus, under the name of Order and Civil Government, we are all made at last to pay homage to and support our own meanness. After the first blush of sin comes its
indifference; and from immoral it becomes, as it were,

*un*moral, and not quite unnecessary to that life which we have made.

The broadest and most prevalent error requires the most   14
disinterested virtue to sustain it. The slight reproach to which the virtue of patriotism is commonly liable, the noble are most likely to incur. Those who, while they disapprove of the character and measures of a government, yield to it their allegiance and support are undoubtedly its most conscientious supporters, and so frequently the most serious obstacles to reform. Some are petitioning the state to dissolve the Union, to disregard the requisitions of the President. Why do they not dissolve it themselves,—the union between themselves and the state,—and refuse to pay their quota into its treasury? Do not they stand in the same relation to the state that the state does to the Union? And have not the same reasons prevented the state from resisting the Union which have prevented them from resisting the state?

How can a man be satisfied to entertain an opinion merely,   15
and enjoy *it*? Is there any enjoyment in it, if his opinion is that he is aggrieved? If you are cheated out of a single dollar by your neighbor, you do not rest satisfied with knowing that you are cheated, or with saying that you are cheated, or even with petitioning him to pay you your due; but you take effectual steps at once to obtain the full amount, and see that you are never cheated again. Action from principle, the perception and the performance of right, changes things and relations; it is essentially revolutionary, and does not consist wholly with anything which was. It not only divides states and churches, it divides families; ay, it divides the *individual,* separating the diabolical in him from the divine.

Unjust laws exist: shall we be content to obey them, or   16
shall we endeavor to amend them, and obey them until we have succeeded, or shall we transgress them at once? Men generally, under such a government as this, think that they ought to wait until they have persuaded the majority to alter them. They think that, if they should resist, the remedy would be worse than the evil. But it is the fault of the government itself that the remedy *is* worse than the evil. *It* makes it worse. Why is it not more apt to anticipate and provide for reform? Why does it not cherish its wise minority? Why does it cry and resist before it is hurt? Why does it not encourage its citizens to be on the alert to point out its faults, and *do* better than it would have them? Why does it always crucify Christ, and excommunicate Copernicus and Luther, and pronounce Washington and Franklin rebels?

17   One would think, that a deliberate and practical denial of its authority was the only offense never contemplated by government; else, why has it not assigned its definite, its suitable and proportionate penalty? If a man who has no property refuses but once to earn nine shillings for the state, he is put in prison for a period unlimited by any law that I know, and determined only by the discretion of those who place him there; but if he should steal ninety times nine shillings from the state, he is soon permitted to go at large again.

18   If the injustice is part of the necessary friction of the machine of government, let it go, let it go; perchance it will wear smooth,—certainly the machine will wear out. If the injustice has a spring, or a pulley, or a rope, or a crank, exclusively for itself, then perhaps you may consider whether the remedy will not be worse than the evil; but if it is of such a nature that it requires you to be the agent of injustice to another, then, I say, break the law. Let your life be a counter friction to stop the machine. What I have to do is to see, at any rate, that I do not lend myself to the wrong which I condemn.

19   As for adopting the ways which the state has provided for remedying the evil, I know not of such ways. They take too much time, and a man's life will be gone. I have other affairs to attend to. I came into this world, not chiefly to make this a good place to live in, but to live in it, be it good or bad. A man has not everything to do, but something; and because he cannot do *everything*, it is not necessary that he should do *something* wrong. It is not my business to be petitioning the Governor or the Legislature any more than it is theirs to petition me; and if they should not hear my petition, what should I do then? But in this case the state has provided no way; its very Constitution is the evil. This may seem to be harsh and stubborn and unconciliatory; but it is to treat with the utmost kindness and consideration the only spirit that can appreciate or deserves it. So is all change for the better, like birth and death, which convulse the body.

20   I do not hesitate to say, that those who call themselves Abolitionists should at once effectually withdraw their support, both in person and property, from the government of Massachusetts, and not wait till they constitute a majority of one, before they suffer the right to prevail through them. I think that it is enough if they have God on their side, without waiting for that other one. Moreover, any man more right than his neighbors constitutes a majority of one already.

21   I meet this American government, or its representative, the state government, directly, and face to face, once a year—no

more—in the person of its tax-gatherer; this is the only mode in which a man situated as I am necessarily meets it; and it then says distinctly, Recognize me; and the simplest, the most effectual, and, in the present posture of affairs, the indispensablest mode of treating with it on this head, of expressing your little satisfaction with and love for it, is to deny it then. My civil neighbor, the tax-gatherer, is the very man I have to deal with,—for it is, after all, with men and not with parchment that I quarrel,—and he has voluntarily chosen to be an agent of the government. How shall he ever know well what he is and does as an officer of the government, or as a man, until he is obliged to consider whether he shall treat me, his neighbor, for whom he has respect, as a neighbor and well-disposed man, or as a maniac and disturber of the peace, and see if he can get over this obstruction to his neighborliness without a ruder and more impetuous thought or speech corresponding with his action. I know this well, that if one thousand, if one hundred, if ten men whom I could name,—if ten *honest* men only,—ay, if *one* HONEST man, in this State of Massachusetts, *ceasing to hold slaves,* were actually to withdraw from this copartnership, and be locked up in the county jail therefor, it would be the abolition of slavery in America. For it matters not how small the beginning may seem to be; what is once well done is done forever. But we love better to talk about it: that we say is our mission. Reform keeps many scores of newspapers in its service, but not one man. If my esteemed neighbor, the State's ambassador, who will devote his days to the settlement of the question of human rights in the Council Chamber, instead of being threatened with the prisons of Carolina, were to sit down the prisoner of Massachusetts, that State which is so anxious to foist the sin of slavery upon her sister,—though at present she can discover only an act of inhospitality to be the ground of a quarrel with her,—the Legislature would not wholly waive the subject the following winter.

Under a government which imprisons any unjustly, the   22
true place for a just man is also a prison. The proper place to-day, the only place which Massachusetts has provided for her freer and less desponding spirits, is in her prisons, to be put out and locked out of the State by her own act, as they have already put themselves out by their principles. It is there that the fugitive slave, and the Mexican prisoner on parole, and the Indian come to plead the wrongs of his race should find them; on that separate, but more free and honorable ground, where the State places those who are not *with* her, but *against*

her,—the only house in a slave State in which a free man can abide with honor. If any think that their influence would be lost there, and their voices no longer afflict the ear of the State, that they would not be as an enemy within its walls, they do not know by how much truth is stronger than error, nor how much more eloquently and effectively he can combat injustice who has experienced a little in his own person. Cast your whole vote, not a strip of paper merely, but your whole influence. A minority is powerless while it conforms to the majority; it is not even a minority then; but it is irresistible when it clogs by its whole weight. If the alternative is to keep all just men in prison, or give up war and slavery, the State will not hesitate which to choose. If a thousand men were not to pay their tax-bills this year, that would not be a violent and bloody measure, as it would be to pay them, and enable the State to commit violence and shed innocent blood. This is, in fact, the definition of a peaceable revolution, if any such is possible. If the tax-gatherer, or any other public officer, asks me, as one has done, "But what shall I do?" my answer is, "If you really wish to do anything, resign your office." When the subject has refused allegiance, and the officer has resigned his office, then the revolution is accomplished. But even suppose blood should flow. Is there not a sort of blood shed when the conscience is wounded? Through this wound a man's real manhood and immortality flow out, and he bleeds to an everlasting death. I see this blood flowing now.

23   I have contemplated the imprisonment of the offender, rather than the seizure of his goods,—though both will serve the same purpose,—because they who assert the purest right, and consequently are most dangerous to a corrupt State, commonly have not spent much time in accumulating property. To such the State renders comparatively small service, and a slight tax is wont to appear exorbitant, particularly if they are obliged to earn it by special labor with their hands. If there were one who lived wholly without the use of money, the State itself would hesitate to demand it of him. But the rich man—not to make any invidious comparison—is always sold to the institution which makes him rich. Absolutely speaking, the more money, the less virtue; for money comes between a man and his objects, and obtains them for him; and it was certainly no great virtue to obtain it. It puts to rest many questions which he would otherwise be taxed to answer; while the only new question which it puts is the hard but superfluous one, how to spend it. Thus his moral ground is taken from under his feet. The opportunities of living are diminished in propor-

tion as what are called the "means" are increased. The best thing a man can do for his culture when he is rich is to endeavor to carry out those schemes which he entertained when he was poor. Christ answered the Herodians according to their condition. "Show me the tribute-money," said he;— and one took a penny out of his pocket;—if you use money which has the image of Caesar on it, and which he has made current and valuable, that is, *if you are men of the State,* and gladly enjoy the advantages of Caesar's government, then pay him back some of his own when he demands it. "Render therefore to Caesar that which is Caesar's, and to God those things which are God's,"—leaving them no wiser than before as to which was which; for they did not wish to know.

When I converse with the freest of my neighbors, I per-   24
ceive that, whatever they may say about the magnitude and seriousness of the question, and their regard for the public tranquillity, the long and the short of the matter is, that they cannot spare the protection of the existing government, and they dread the consequences to their property and families of disobedience to it. For my own part, I should not like to think that I ever rely on the protection of the State. But, if I deny the authority of the State when it presents its tax-bill, it will soon take and waste all my property, and so harass me and my children without end. This is hard. This makes it impossible for a man to live honestly, and at the same time comfortably, in outward respects. It will not be worth the while to accumulate property; that would be sure to go again. You must hire or squat somewhere, and raise but a small crop, and eat that soon. You must live within yourself, and depend upon yourself always tucked up and ready for a start, and not have many affairs. A man may grow rich in Turkey even, if he will be in all respects a good subject of the Turkish government. Confucius said: "If a state is governed by the principles of reason, poverty and misery are subjects of shame; if a state is not governed by the principles of reason, riches and honors are the subjects of shame." No: until I want the protection of Massachusetts to be extended to me in some distant Southern port, where my liberty is endangered, or until I am bent solely on building up an estate at home by peaceful enterprise, I can afford to refuse allegiance to Massachusetts, and her right to my property and life. It costs me less in every sense to incur the penalty of disobedience to the State than it would to obey. I should feel as if I were worth less in that case.

Some years ago, the State met me in behalf of the Church,   25
and commanded me to pay a certain sum toward the support

of a clergyman whose preaching my father attended, but never I myself. "Pay," it said, "or be locked up in the jail." I declined to pay. But, unfortunately, another man saw fit to pay it. I did not see why the schoolmaster should be taxed to support the priest, and not the priest the schoolmaster; for I was not the State's schoolmaster, but I supported myself by voluntary subscription. I did not see why the lyceum should not present its tax-bill, and have the State to back its demand, as well as the Church. However, at the request of the select-men, I condescended to make some such statement as this in writing:—"Know all men by these presents, that I, Henry Tho-reau, do not wish to be regarded as a member of any incorpo-rated society which I have not joined." This I gave to the town clerk; and he has it. The State, having thus learned that I did not wish to be regarded as a member of that church, has never made a like demand on me since; though it said that it must adhere to its original presumption that time. If I had known how to name them, I should then have signed off in detail from all the societies which I never signed on to; but I did not know where to find a complete list.

26   I have paid no poll-tax[4] for six years. I was put into jail once on this account, for one night; and, as I stood consider-ing the walls of solid stone, two or three feet thick, the door of wood and iron, a foot thick, and the iron grating which strained the light, I could not help being struck with the fool-ishness of that institution which treated me as if I were mere flesh and blood and bones, to be locked up. I wondered that it should have concluded at length that this was the best use it could put me to, and had never thought to avail itself of my services in some way. I saw that, if there was a wall of stone between me and my townsmen, there was still a more diffi-cult one to climb or break through before they could get to be as free as I was. I did not for a moment feel confined, and the walls seemed a great waste of stone and mortar. I felt as if I alone of all my townsmen had paid my tax. They plainly did not know how to treat me, but behaved like persons who are underbred. In every threat and in every compliment there was a blunder; for they thought that my chief desire was to stand the other side of that stone wall. I could not but smile to see how industriously they locked the door on my medita-tions, which followed them out again without let or hin-

[4]Tax assessed against a person (not property); payment was frequently prerequisite for voting.

drance, and *they* were really all that was dangerous. As they could not reach me, they had resolved to punish my body; just as boys, if they cannot come at some person against whom they have a spite, will abuse his dog. I saw that the State was half-witted, that it was timid as a lone woman with her silver spoons, and that it did not know its friends from its foes, and I lost all my remaining respect for it, and pitied it.

Thus the State never intentionally confronts a man's sense,   27
intellectual or moral, but only his body, his senses. It is not armed with superior wit or honesty, but with superior physical strength. I was not born to be forced. I will breathe after my own fashion. Let us see who is the strongest. What force has a multitude? They only can force me who obey a higher law than I. They force me to become like themselves. I do not hear of *men* being *forced* to live this way or that by masses of men. What sort of life were that to live? When I meet a government which says to me, "Your money or your life," why should I be in haste to give it my money? It may be in a great strait, and not know what to do: I cannot help that. It must help itself; do as I do. It is not worth the while to snivel about it. I am not responsible for the successful working of the machinery of society. I am not the son of the engineer. I perceive that, when an acorn and a chestnut fall side by side, the one does not remain inert to make way for the other, but both obey their own laws, and spring and grow and flourish as best they can, till one, perchance, overshadows and destroys the other. If a plant cannot live according to its nature, it dies; and so a man.

The night in prison was novel and interesting enough. The   28
prisoners in their shirt-sleeves were enjoying a chat and the evening air in the doorway, when I entered. But the jailer said, "Come, boys, it is time to lock up;" and so they dispersed, and I heard the sound of their steps returning into the hollow apartments. My room-mate was introduced to me by the jailer as "a first-rate fellow and a clever man." When the door was locked, he showed me where to hang my hat, and how he managed matters there. The rooms were whitewashed once a month; and this one, at least, was the whitest, most simply furnished, and probably the neatest apartment in the town. He naturally wanted to know where I came from, and what brought me there; and, when I had told him, I asked him in my turn how he came there, presuming him to be an honest man, of course; and, as the world goes, I believe he was. "Why," said he, "they accuse me of burning a barn; but I never did it." As near as I could discover, he had probably

gone to bed in a barn when drunk, and smoked his pipe there; and so a barn was burnt. He had the reputation of being a clever man, had been there some three months waiting for his trial to come on, and would have to wait as much longer; but he was quite domesticated and contented, since he got his board for nothing, and thought that he was well treated.

29   He occupied one window, and I the other; and I saw that if one stayed there long, his principal business would be to look out the window. I had soon read all the tracts that were left there, and examined where former prisoners had broken out, and where a grate had been sawed off, and heard the history of the various occupants of that room; for I found that even here there was a history and a gossip which never circulated beyond the walls of the jail. Probably this is the only house in the town where verses are composed, which are afterward printed in a circular form, but not published. I was shown quite a long list of verses which were composed by some young men who had been detected in an attempt to escape, who avenged themselves by singing them.

30   I pumped my fellow-prisoner as dry as I could, for fear I should never see him again; but at length he showed me which was my bed, and left me to blow out the lamp.

31   It was like traveling into a far country, such as I had never expected to behold, to lie there for one night. It seemed to me that I never had heard the town-clock strike before, nor the evening sounds of the village; for we slept with the windows open, which were inside the grating. It was to see my native village in the light of the Middle Ages, and our Concord was turned into a Rhine stream, and visions of knights and castles passed before me. They were the voices of old burghers that I heard in the streets. I was an involuntary spectator and auditor of whatever was done and said in the kitchen of the adjacent village-inn,—a wholly new and rare experience to me. It was a closer view of my native town. I was fairly inside of it. I never had seen its institutions before. This is one of its peculiar institutions; for it is a shire town. I began to comprehend what its inhabitants were about.

32   In the morning, our breakfasts were put through the hole in the door, in small oblong-square tin pans, made to fit, and holding a pint of chocolate, with brown bread, and an iron spoon. When they called for the vessels again, I was green enough to return what bread I had left; but my comrade seized it, and said that I should lay that up for lunch or dinner. Soon after he was let out to work at haying in a neighboring field, whither he went every day, and would not be back

till noon; so he bade me good-day, saying that he doubted if he should see me again.

When I came out of prison—for some one interfered, and   33
paid that tax,—I did not perceive that great changes had taken place on the common, such as he observed who went in a youth and emerged a tottering and gray-headed man; and yet a change had to my eyes come over the scene,—the town, and State, and country,—greater than any that mere time could effect. I saw yet more distinctly the State in which I lived. I saw to what extent the people among whom I lived could be trusted as good neighbors and friends; that their friendship was for summer weather only; that they did not greatly propose to do right; that they were a distinct race from me by their prejudices and superstitions, as the China-men and Malays are; that in their sacrifices to humanity they ran no risks, not even to their property; that after all they were not so noble but they treated the thief as he had treated them, and hoped, by a certain outward observance and a few prayers, and by walking in a particular straight though use-less path from time to time, to save their souls. This may be to judge my neighbors harshly; for I believe that many of them are not aware that they have such an institution as the jail in their village.

It was formerly the custom in our village, when a poor   34
debtor came out of jail, for his acquaintances to salute him, looking through their fingers, which were crossed to repre-sent the grating of a jail window, "How do ye do?" My neigh-bors did not thus salute me, but first looked at me, and then at one another, as if I had returned from a long journey. I was put into jail as I was going to the shoemaker's to get a shoe which was mended. When I was let out the next morning, I proceeded to finish my errand, and, having put on my mended shoe, joined a huckleberry party, who were impatient to put themselves under my conduct; and in half an hour,—for the horse was soon tackled,—was in the midst of a huckle-berry field, on one of our highest hills, two miles off, and then the State was nowhere to be seen.

This is the whole history of "My Prisons."   35

Mahatma Gandhi
Letter to Lord Irwin

*Mahatma Gandhi (Mahatma means "of great soul") was born
in India in 1869, studied law in London, and in 1893 went to
South Africa, where he opposed discriminatory legislation
against Indians, was exposed to the writing of Henry David
Thoreau, and carried on a famous correspondence with the
Russian novelist Leo Tolstoy concerning civil disobedience. In
1914, he returned to India, and in about 1920 began a lifetime
of committed support for India's independence from England—
notably through the practice and encouragement of nonviolent
resistance* (satyagraha). *After a decade of sporadic civil disobedience and periodic imprisonments, Gandhi in 1930 prepared
a Declaration of Independence for India and soon after led a
remarkable (and famous) 200-mile march to the sea to collect
salt in symbolic defiance of the English government's monopoly on that product; by the end of the year, more than 100,000
people were jailed in the campaign. India of course did finally
achieve independence, in 1947. The following year, while trying
to calm tensions between Hindus and Moslems, Gandhi was
assassinated.*

*The following letter was sent by Gandhi to the British vice-
roy in India, Lord Irwin, in March 1930, just ten days before
the salt march was to begin. It was sent from Satyagraha
Ashram, a community established to practice Gandhi's method
of nonviolent resistance.*

Satyagraha Ashram, Sabarmati,
March 2, 1930

Dear Friend,

1   Before embarking on civil disobedience and taking the risk
I have dreaded to take all these years, I would fain approach
you and find a way out.

2   My personal faith is absolutely clear. I cannot intentionally
hurt anything that lives, much less fellow human beings, even
though they may do the greatest wrong to me and mine.
Whilst, therefore, I hold the British rule to be a curse, I do not
intend harm to a single Englishman or to any legitimate
interest he may have in India.

3   I must not be misunderstood. Though I hold the British
rule in India to be a curse, I do not, therefore, consider
Englishmen in general to be worse than any other people on

earth. I have the privilege of claiming many Englishmen as dearest friends. Indeed much that I have learnt of the evil of British rule is due to the writings of frank and courageous Englishmen who have not hesitated to tell the unpalatable truth about that rule.

And why do I regard the British rule as a curse? 4

It has impoverished the dumb millions by a system of pro- 5 gressive exploitation and by a ruinously expensive military and civil administration which the country can never afford.

It has reduced us politically to serfdom. It has sapped the 6 foundations of our culture. And, by the policy of cruel disarmament, it has degraded us spiritually. Lacking the inward strength, we have been reduced, by all but universal disarmament, to a state bordering on cowardly helplessness.

In common with many of my countrymen, I had hugged the 7 fond hope that the proposed Round Table Conference might furnish a solution. But, when you said plainly that you could not give any assurance that you or the British Cabinet would pledge yourselves to support a scheme of full Dominion Status, the Round Table Conference could not possibly furnish the solution for which vocal India is consciously, and the dumb millions are unconsciously, thirsting.

It seems as clear as daylight that responsible British states- 8 men do not contemplate any alteration in British policy that might adversely affect Britain's commerce with India or require an impartial and close scrutiny of Britain's transactions with India. If nothing is done to end the process of exploitation India must be bled with an ever increasing speed. The Finance Member regards as a settled fact the 1/6 ratio which by a stroke of the pen drains India of a few crores.[1] And when a serious attempt is being made through a civil form of direct action, to unsettle this fact, among many others, even you cannot help appealing to the wealthy landed classes to help you to crush that attempt in the name of an order that grinds India to atoms.

Unless those who work in the name of the nation under- 9 stand and keep before all concerned the motive that lies behind the craving for independence, there is every danger of independence coming to us so changed as to be of no value to those toiling voiceless millions for whom it is sought and for whom it is worth taking. It is for that reason that I have been

---

[1] In Indian currency, a crore is equivalent to ten million rupees.

recently telling the public what independence should really mean.

10   Let me put before you some of the salient points.

11   The terrific pressure of land revenue, which furnishes a large part of the total, must undergo considerable modification in an independent India. Even the much vaunted permanent settlement benefits the few rich zamindars,[2] not the ryots.[3] The ryot has remained as helpless as ever. He is a mere tenant at will. Not only, then, has the land revenue to be considerably reduced, but the whole revenue system has to be so revised as to make the ryot's good its primary concern. But the British system seems to be designed to crush the very life out of him. Even the salt he must use to live is so taxed as to make the burden fall heaviest on him, if only because of the heartless impartiality of its incidence. The tax shows itself still more burdensome on the poor man when it is remembered that salt is the one thing he must eat more than the rich man both individually and collectively.

12   The iniquities sampled above are maintained in order to carry on a foreign administration, demonstrably the most expensive in the world. Take your own salary. It is over Rs. 21,000 per month, besides many other indirect additions. The British Prime Minister gets £ 5,000 per year, i.e., over Rs. 5,400 per month at the present rate of exchange. You are getting over Rs. 700 per day against India's average income of less than annas 2 per day. The Prime Minister gets Rs. 180 per day against Great Britain's average income of nearly Rs. 2 per day. Thus you are getting much over five thousand times India's average income. The British Prime Minister is getting only ninety times Britain's average income. On bended knees I ask you to ponder over this phenomenon. I have taken a personal illustration to drive home a painful truth. I have too great a regard for you as a man to wish to hurt your feelings. I know that you do not need the salary you get. Probably the whole of your salary goes for charity. But a system that provides for such an arrangement deserves to be summarily scrapped.

13   If India is to live as a nation, if the slow death by starvation of her people is to stop, some remedy must be found for immediate relief. The proposed Conference is certainly not the remedy. It is not a matter of carrying conviction by argu-

[2]A zamindar is a landowner.
[3]A ryot is a tenant farmer.

ment. The matter resolves itself into one of matching forces. Conviction or no conviction, Great Britain would defend her Indian commerce and interests by all the forces at her command. India must consequently evolve force enough to free herself from that embrace of death.

It is common cause that, however disorganized and, for the time being, insignificant it may be, the party of violence is gaining ground and making itself felt. Its end is the same as mine. But I am convinced that it cannot bring the desired relief to the dumb millions. And the conviction is growing deeper and deeper in me that nothing but unadulterated non-violence can check the organized violence of the British Government. Many think that non-violence is not an active force. My experience, limited though it undoubtedly is, shows that non-violence can be an intensely active force. It is my purpose to set in motion that force as well against the organized violent force of the British rule as [against] the unorganized violent force of the growing party of violence. To sit still would be to give rein to both the forces above mentioned. Having an unquestioning and immovable faith in the efficacy of non-violence as I know it, it would be sinful on my part to wait any longer. **14**

This non-violence will be expressed through civil disobedience, for the moment confined to the inmates of the Satyagraha Ashram, but ultimately designed to cover all those who choose to join the movement with its obvious limitations. **15**

I know that in embarking on non-violence I shall be running what might fairly be termed a mad risk. But the victories of truth have never been won without risks, often of the gravest character. Conversion of a nation that has consciously or unconsciously preyed upon another, far more numerous, far more ancient and no less cultured than itself, is worth any amount of risk. **16**

I have deliberately used the word "conversion." For my ambition is no less than to convert the British people through non-violence, and thus make them see the wrong they have done to India. I do not seek to harm your people. I want to serve them even as I want to serve my own. I believe that I have always served them. I served them up to 1919 blindly. But when my eyes were opened and I conceived non-cooperation, the object still was to serve them. I employed the same weapon that I have in all humility successfully used against the dearest members of my family. If I have equal love for your people with mine it will not long remain hidden. It will be acknowledged by them even as the members of my family **17** acknowledged it after they had tried me for several years. If the people join me as I expect they will, the sufferings they will undergo, unless the British nation sooner retraces its steps, will be enough to melt the stoniest hearts.

18   The plan through civil disobedience will be to combat such evils as I have sampled out. If we want to sever the British connection it is because of such evils. When they are removed the path becomes easy. Then the way to friendly negotiation will be open. If the British commerce with India is purified of greed, you will have no difficulty in recognizing our independence. I respectfully invite you then to pave the way for immediate removal of those evils, and thus open a way for a real conference between equals, interested only in promoting the common good of mankind through voluntary fellowship and in arranging terms of mutual help and commerce equally suited to both. You have unnecessarily laid stress upon the communal problems that unhappily affect this land. Important though they undoubtedly are for the consideration of any scheme of government, they have little bearing on the greater problems which are above communities and which affect them all equally. But if you cannot see your way to deal with these evils and my letter makes no appeal to your heart, on the 11th day of this month, I shall proceed with such co-workers of the Ashram as I can take, to disregard the provisions of the salt laws. I regard this tax to be the most iniquitous of all from the poor man's standpoint. As the independence movement is essentially for the poorest in the land the beginning will be made with this evil. The wonder is that we have submitted to the cruel monopoly for so long. It is, I know, open to you to frustrate my design by arresting me. I hope that there will be tens of thousands ready, in a disciplined manner, to take up the work after me, and, in the act of disobeying the Salt Act to lay themselves open to the penalties of a law that should never have disfigured the Statute-book.

19   I have no desire to cause you unnecessary embarrassment, or any at all, so far as I can help. If you think that there is any substance in my letter, and if you will care to discuss matters with me, and if to that end you would like me to postpone publication of this letter, I shall gladly refrain on receipt of a telegram to that effect soon after this reaches you. You will, however, do me the favour not to deflect me from my course unless you can see your way to conform to the substance of this letter.

20   This letter is not in any way intended as a threat but is a simple and sacred duty peremptory on a civil resister. There-

fore I am having it specially delivered by a young English
friend who believes in the Indian cause and is a full believer
in non-violence and whom Providence seems to have sent to
me, as it were, for the very purpose.

I remain,
Your sincere friend,
M. K. Gandhi

Martin Luther King Jr.
Love, Law, and Civil
Disobedience

*Born in Atlanta and educated at Morehouse College, Crozer
Theological Seminary (near Philadelphia), and Boston University, Martin Luther King Jr. (1929–1968) was the leader of the
civil rights movement of the 1960s. An ordained minister with
a doctorate in theology from Boston University, he worked
especially in the South and through nonviolent means to overturn segregation statutes, to increase the number of African
American voters, and to support other civil rights initiatives.
Reverend King won the Nobel Peace Prize in 1964. When he
was assassinated in 1968, all America mourned. The following
item is a transcript of a speech that Dr. King delivered in 1961
to the annual meeting of the Fellowship of the Concerned in
Atlanta. After you read the address, note how several passages
reappeared later (in a somewhat different form) in his "Letter
from Birmingham Jail," page 712.*

Members of the Fellowship of the Concerned, of the South-   1
ern Regional Council, I need not pause to say how very
delighted I am to be here today, and to have the opportunity
of being a little part of this very significant gathering. I certainly want to express my personal appreciation to Mrs. Tilly
and the members of the Committee, for giving me this
opportunity. I would also like to express just a personal word
of thanks and appreciation for your vital witness in this
period of transition which we are facing in our Southland,

and in the nation, and I am sure that as a result of this genuine concern, and your significant work in communities all across the South, we have a better South today and I am sure will have a better South tomorrow with your continued endeavor. And I do want to express my personal gratitude and appreciation to you of the Fellowship of the Concerned for your significant work and for your forthright witness.

2   Now, I have been asked to talk about the philosophy behind the student movement. There can be no gainsaying of the fact that we confront a crisis in race relations in the United States. This crisis has been precipitated on the one hand by the determined resistance of reactionary forces in the South to the Supreme Court's decision in 1954 outlawing segregation in the public schools. And we know that at times this resistance has risen to ominous proportions. At times we find the legislative halls of the South ringing loud with such words as interposition and nullification. And all of these forces have developed into massive resistance. But we must also say that the crisis has been precipitated on the other hand by the determination of hundreds and thousands and millions of Negro people to achieve freedom and human dignity. If the Negro stayed in his place and accepted discrimination and segregation, there would be no crisis. But the Negro has a new sense of dignity, a new self respect, and new determination. He has re-evaluated his own intrinsic worth. Now this new sense of dignity on the part of the Negro grows out of the same longing for freedom and human dignity on the part of the oppressed people all over the world; for we see it in Africa, we see it in Asia, and we see it all over the world. Now we must say that this struggle for freedom will not come to an automatic halt, for history reveals to us that once oppressed people rise up against that oppression, there is no stopping point short of full freedom. On the other hand, history reveals to us that those who oppose the movement for freedom are those who are in privileged positions who very seldom give up their privileges without strong resistance. And they very seldom do it voluntarily. So the sense of struggle will continue. The question is how will the struggle be waged.

3   Now there are three ways that oppressed people have generally dealt with their oppression. One way is the method of acquiescence, the method of surrender; that is, the individuals will somehow adjust themselves to oppression, they adjust themselves to discrimination or to segregation or colonialism or what have you. The other method that has been used in history is that of rising up against the oppressor with corrod-

ing hatred and physical violence. Now of course we know about this method in western civilization, because in a sense it has been the hallmark of its grandeur, and the inseparable twin of western materialism. But there is a weakness in this method because it ends up creating many more social problems than it solves. And I am convinced that if the Negro succumbs to the temptation of using violence in his struggle for freedom and justice, unborn generations will be the recipients of a long and desolate night of bitterness. And our chief legacy to the future will be an endless reign of meaningless chaos.

But there is another way, namely the way of non-violent 4 resistance. This method was popularized in our generation by a little man from India, whose name was Mohandas K. Gandhi. He used this method in a magnificent way to free his people from the economic exploitation and the political domination inflicted upon them by a foreign power.

This has been the method used by the student movement 5 in the South and all over the United States. And naturally whenever I talk about the student movement I cannot be totally objective. I have to be somewhat subjective because of my great admiration for what the students have done. For in a real sense they have taken our deep groans and passionate yearnings for freedom, and filtered them in their own tender souls, and fashioned them into a creative protest which is an epic known all over our nation. As a result of their disciplined, non-violent, yet courageous struggle, they have been able to do wonders in the South, and in our nation. But this movement does have an underlying philosophy, it has certain ideas that are attached to it, it has certain philosophical precepts. These are the things that I would like to discuss for the few moments left.

I would say that the first point or the first principle in the 6 movement is the idea that means must be as pure as the end. This movement is based on the philosophy that ends and means must cohere. Now this has been one of the long struggles in history, the whole idea of means and ends. Great philosophers have grappled with it, and sometimes they have emerged with the idea, from Machiavelli on down, that the end justifies the means. There is a great system of thought in our world today, known as Communism. And I think that with all of the weaknesses and tragedies of Communism, we find its greatest tragedy right here, that it goes under the philosophy that the end justifies the means that are used in the process. So we can read or we can hear the Lenins say that

lying, deceit, or violence, that many of these things justify the
ends of the classless society.

7   This is where the student movement and the non-violent
movement that is taking place in our nation would break with
Communism and any other system that would argue that the
end justifies the means. For in the long run, we must see that
the end represents the means in process and the ideal in the
making. In other words, we cannot believe, or we cannot go
with the idea that the end justifies the means because the end
is pre-existent in the means. So the idea of non-violent resistance, the philosophy of non-violent resistance, is the philosophy which says that the means must be as pure as the end,
that in the long run of history, immoral destructive means
cannot bring about moral and constructive ends.

8   There is another thing about this philosophy, this method
of non-violence which is followed by the student movement.
It says that those who adhere to or follow this philosophy
must follow a consistent principle of non-injury. They must
consistently refuse to inflict injury upon another. Sometimes
you will read the literature of the student movement and see
that, as they are getting ready for the sit-in or stand-in, they
will read something like this, "if you are hit do not hit back, if
you are cursed do not curse back." This is the whole idea,
that the individual who is engaged in a non-violent struggle
must never inflict injury upon another. Now this has an external aspect and it has an internal one. From the external point
of view it means that the individuals involved must avoid
external physical violence. So they don't have guns, they don't
retaliate with physical violence. If they are hit in the process,
they avoid external physical violence at every point. But it
also means that they avoid internal violence of spirit. This is
why the love ethic stands so high in the student movement.
We have a great deal of talk about love and non-violence in
this whole thrust.

9   Now when the students talk about love, certainly they are
not talking about emotional bosh, they are not talking about
merely a sentimental outpouring; they're talking something
much deeper, and I always have to stop and try to define the
meaning of love in this context. The Greek language comes to
our aid in trying to deal with this. There are three words in the
Greek language for love; one is the word Eros. This is a beautiful type of love, it is an aesthetic love. Plato talks about it a
great deal in his dialogue, the yearning of the soul for the
realm of the divine. It has come to us to be a sort of romantic
love, and so in a sense we have read about it and experienced

it. We've read about it in all the beauties of literature. I guess
in a sense Edgar Allan Poe was talking about Eros when he
talked about his beautiful Annabelle Lee, with the love surrounded by the halo of eternity. In a sense Shakespeare was
talking about Eros when he said "Love is not love which alters
when alteration finds, or bends with the remover to remove;
O, no! it is an ever fixed mark that looks on tempest and is
never shaken, it is the star to every wandering bark." (You
know, I remember that because I used to quote it to this little
lady when we were courting; that's Eros.) The Greek language
talks about Philia which was another level of love. It is an intimate affection between personal friends, it is a reciprocal love.
On this level you love because you are loved. It is friendship.

Then the Greek language comes out with another word   10
which is called the Agape. Agape is more than romantic love,
agape is more than friendship. Agape is understanding, creative, redemptive, good will to all men. It is an overflowing
love which seeks nothing in return. Theologians would say
that it is the love of God operating in the human heart. So
that when one rises to love on this level, he loves men not
because he likes them, not because their ways appeal to him,
but he loves every man because God loves him. And he rises
to the point of loving the person who does an evil deed while
hating the deed that the person does. I think this is what
Jesus meant when he said "love your enemies." I'm very
happy that he didn't say like your enemies, because it is pretty
difficult to like some people. Like is sentimental, and it is
pretty difficult to like someone bombing your home; it is
pretty difficult to like somebody threatening your children; it
is difficult to like congressmen who spend all of their time
trying to defeat civil rights. But Jesus says love them, and love
is greater than like. Love is understanding, redemptive, creative, good will for all men. And it is this idea, it is this whole
ethic of love which is the idea standing at the basis of the student movement.

There is something else: that one seeks to defeat the unjust 11
system, rather than individuals who are caught in that system. And that one goes on believing that somehow this is the
important thing, to get rid of the evil system and not the individual who happens to be misguided, who happens to be mis-
led, who was taught wrong. The thing to do is to get rid of the
system and thereby create a moral balance within society.

Another thing that stands at the center of this movement is   12
another idea: that suffering can be a most creative and powerful social force. Suffering has certain moral attributes

involved, but it can be a powerful and creative social force. Now, it is very interesting at this point to notice that both violence and non-violence agree that suffering can be a very powerful social force. But there is this difference: violence says that suffering can be a powerful social force by inflicting the suffering on somebody else; so this is what we do in war, this is what we do in the whole violent thrust of the violent movement. It believes that you achieve some end by inflicting suffering on another. The non-violent say that suffering becomes a powerful social force when you willingly accept that violence on yourself, so that self-suffering stands at the center of the non-violent movement and the individuals involved are able to suffer in a creative manner, feeling that unearned suffering is redemptive, and that suffering may serve to transform the social situation.

13   Another thing in this movement is the idea that there is within human nature an amazing potential for goodness. There is within human nature something that can respond to goodness. I know somebody's liable to say that this is an unrealistic movement if it goes on believing that all people are good. Well, I didn't say that. I think the students are realistic enough to believe that there is a strange dichotomy of disturbing dualism within human nature. Many of the great philosophers and thinkers through the ages have seen this. It caused Ovid the Latin poet to say, "I see and approve the better things of life, but the evil things I do." It caused even St. Augustine to say "Lord, make me pure, but not yet." So that that is in human nature. Plato centuries ago said that the human personality is like a charioteer with two headstrong horses, each wanting to go in different directions, so that within our own individual lives we see this conflict and certainly when we come to the collective life of man, we see a strange badness. But in spite of this there is something in human nature that can respond to goodness. So that man is neither innately good nor is he innately bad; he has potentialities for both. So in this sense, Carlyle was right when he said that "there are depths in man which go down to the lowest hell, and heights which reach the highest heaven, for are not both heaven and hell made out of him, everlasting miracle and mystery that he is?" Man has the capacity to be good, man has the capacity to be evil.

14   And so the non-violent resister never lets this idea go, that there is something within human nature that can respond to goodness. So that a Jesus of Nazareth or a Mohandas Gandhi can appeal to human beings and appeal to that element of

goodness within them, and a Hitler can appeal to the element of evil within them. But we must never forget that there is something within human nature that can respond to goodness, that man is not totally depraved, to put it in theological terms, the image of God is never totally gone. And so the individuals who believe in this movement and who believe in non-violence and our struggle in the South, somehow believe that even the worst segregationist can become an integrationist. Now sometimes it is hard to believe that this is what this movement says, and it believes it firmly, that there is something within human nature that can be changed, and this stands at the top of the whole philosophy of the student movement and the philosophy of non-violence.

It says something else. It says that it is as much a moral 15 obligation to refuse to cooperate with evil as it is to cooperate with good. Non-cooperation with evil is as much a moral obligation as the cooperation with good. So that the student movement is willing to stand up courageously on the idea of civil disobedience. Now I think this is the part of the student movement that is probably misunderstood more than anything else. And it is a difficult aspect, because on the one hand the students would say, and I would say, and all the people who believe in civil rights would say, obey the Supreme Court's decision of 1954 and at the same time, we would disobey certain laws that exist on the statutes of the South today.

This brings in the whole question of how can you be logi- 16 cally consistent when you advocate obeying some laws and disobeying other laws. Well, I think one would have to see the whole meaning of this movement at this point by seeing that the students recognize that there are two types of laws. There are just laws and there are unjust laws. And they would be the first to say obey the just laws, they would be the first to say that men and women have a moral obligation to obey just and right laws. And they would go on to say that we must see that there are unjust laws. Now the question comes into being, what is the difference, and who determines the difference, what is the difference between a just and an unjust law?

Well, a just law is a law that squares with a moral law. It is 17 a law that squares with that which is right, so that any law that uplifts human personality is a just law. Whereas that law which is out of harmony with the moral is a law which does not square with the moral law of the universe. It does not square with the law of God, so for that reason it is unjust and any law that degrades the human personality is an unjust law.

18   Well, somebody says that that does not mean anything to
me: first, I don't believe in these abstract things called moral
laws and I'm not too religious, so I don't believe in the law of
God: you have to get a little more concrete, and more practical. What do you mean when you say that a law is unjust, and
a law is just? Well, I would go on to say in more concrete
terms that an unjust law is a code that the majority inflicts on
the minority that is not binding on itself. So that this
becomes difference made legal. Another thing that we can say
is that an unjust law is a code which the majority inflicts on
the minority, which that minority had no part in enacting or
creating, because that minority had no right to vote in many
instances, so that the legislative bodies that made these laws
were not democratically elected. Who could ever say that the
legislative body of Mississippi was democratically elected, or
the legislative body of Alabama was democratically elected,
or the legislative body even of Georgia has been democratically elected, when there are people in Terrell County and in
other counties because of the color of their skin who cannot
vote? They confront reprisals and threats and all of that; so
that an unjust law is a law that individuals did not have a part
in creating or enacting because they were denied the right to
vote.

19   Now by the same token a just law would be just the opposite. A just law becomes sameness made legal. It is a code that
the majority, who happen to believe in that code, compel the
minority, who don't believe in it, to follow, because they are
willing to follow it themselves, so it is sameness made legal.
Therefore the individuals who stand up on the basis of civil
disobedience realize that they are following something that
says that there are just laws and there are unjust laws. Now,
they are not anarchists. They believe that there are laws
which must be followed; they do not seek to defy the law, they
do not seek to evade the law. For many individuals who would
call themselves segregationists and who would hold on to segregation at any cost seek to defy the law, they seek to evade
the law, and their process can lead on into anarchy. They seek
in the final analysis to follow a way of uncivil disobedience,
not civil disobedience. And I submit that the individual who
disobeys the law, whose conscience tells him it is unjust and
who is willing to accept the penalty by staying in jail until
that law is altered, is expressing at the moment the very highest respect for law.

20   This is what the students have followed in their movement.
Of course there is nothing new about this; they feel that they

are in good company and rightly so. We go back and read the *Apology* and the *Crito,* and you see Socrates practicing civil disobedience. And to a degree academic freedom is a reality today because Socrates practiced civil disobedience. The early Christians practiced civil disobedience in a superb manner, to a point where they were willing to be thrown to the lions. They were willing to face all kinds of suffering in order to stand up for what they knew was right even though they knew it was against the laws of the Roman Empire.

We could come up to our own day and we see it in many instances. We must never forget that everything that Hitler did in Germany was "legal." It was illegal to aid and comfort a Jew, in the days of Hitler's Germany. But I believe that if I had the same attitude then as I have now I would publicly aid and comfort my Jewish brothers in Germany if Hitler were alive today calling this an illegal process. If I lived in South Africa today in the midst of the white supremacy law in South Africa, I would join Chief Luthuli and others in saying break these unjust laws. And even let us come up to America. Our nation in a sense came into being through a massive act of civil disobedience, for the Boston Tea Party was nothing but a massive act of civil disobedience. Those who stood up against the slave laws, the abolitionists, by and large practiced civil disobedience. So I think these students are in good company, and they feel that by practicing civil disobedience they are in line with men and women through the ages who have stood up for something that is morally right. [21]

Now there are one or two other things that I want to say about this student movement, moving out of the philosophy of non-violence, something about what it is a revolt against. On the one hand it is a revolt against the negative peace that has encompassed the South for many years. I remember when I was in Montgomery, Ala., one of the white citizens came to me one day and said—and I think he was very sincere about this—that in Montgomery for all of these years we have been such a peaceful community, we have had so much harmony in race relations and then you people have started this movement and boycott, and it has done so much to disturb race relations, and we just don't love the Negro like we used to love them, because you have destroyed the harmony and the peace that we once had in race relations. And I said to him, in the best way I could say and I tried to say it in non-violent terms, we have never had peace in Montgomery, Ala., we have never had peace in the South. We have had a negative peace, which is merely the absence of tension; we've had [22] a negative peace in which the Negro patiently accepted his situation and his plight, but we've never had true peace, we've never had positive peace, and what we're seeking now is to develop this positive peace. For we must come to see that peace is not merely the absence of some negative force, it is the presence of a positive force. True peace is not merely the absence of tension, but it is the presence of justice and brotherhood. I think this is what Jesus meant when he said, I come not to bring peace but a sword. Now Jesus didn't mean he came to start war, to bring a physical sword, and he didn't mean, I come not to bring positive peace. But I think what Jesus was saying in substance was this, that I come not to bring an old negative peace, which makes for stagnant passivity and deadening complacency, I come to bring something different, and whenever I come, a conflict is precipitated, between the old and the new, whenever I come a struggle takes place between justice and injustice, between the forces of light and the forces of darkness. I come not to bring a negative peace, but a positive peace, which is brotherhood, which is justice, which is the Kingdom of God.

23   And I think this is what we are seeking to do today, and this movement is a revolt against a negative peace and a struggle to bring into being a positive peace, which makes for true brotherhood, true integration, true person-to-person relationships. This movement is also revolt against what is often called tokenism. Here again many people do not understand this; they feel that in this struggle the Negro will be satisfied with tokens of integration, just a few students and a few schools here and there and a few doors open here and there. But this isn't the meaning of the movement and I think that honesty impels me to admit it everywhere I have an opportunity, that the Negro's aim is to bring about complete integration in American life. And he has come to see that token integration is little more than token democracy, which ends up with many new evasive schemes and it ends up with new discrimination, covered up with such niceties of complexity. It is very interesting to discover that the movement has thrived in many communities that had token integration. So this reveals that the movement is based on a principle that integration must become real and complete, not just token integration.

24   It is also a revolt against what I often call the myth of time. We hear this quite often, that only time can solve this problem. That if we will only be patient, and only pray—which we must do, we must be patient and we must pray—but there are

those who say just do these things and wait for time, and time will solve this problem. Well, the people who argue this do not themselves realize that time is neutral, that it can be used constructively or destructively. At points the people of ill will, the segregationists, have used time much more effectively than the people of good will. So individuals in the struggle must come to realize that it is necessary to aid time, that without this kind of aid, time itself will become an ally of the insurgent and primitive forces of social stagnation. Therefore, this movement is a revolt against the myth of time.

There is a final thing that I would like to say to you, this movement is a movement based on faith in the future. It is a movement based on a philosophy, the possibility of the future bringing into being something real and meaningful. It is a movement based on hope. I think this is very important. The students have developed a theme song for their movement, maybe you've heard it. It goes something like this, "we shall overcome, deep in my heart, I do believe, we shall overcome," and then they go on to say another verse, "we are not afraid, we are not afraid today, deep in my heart I do believe, we shall overcome." So it is out of this deep faith in the future that they are able to move out and adjourn the councils of despair, and to bring new light in the dark chambers of pessimism. I can remember the times that we've been together. I remember that night in Montgomery, Ala., when we had stayed up all night, discussing the Freedom Rides, and that morning came to see that it was necessary to go on with the Freedom Rides, that we would not in all good conscience call an end to the Freedom Rides at that point. And I remember the first group got ready to leave, to take a bus for Jackson, Miss.; we all joined hands and started singing together. "We shall overcome, we shall overcome." And something within me said, now how is it that these students can sing this, they are going down to Mississippi, they are going to face hostile and jeering mobs, and yet they could sing, "We shall overcome." They may even face physical death, and yet they could sing, "We shall overcome." Most of them realized that they would be thrown into jail, and yet they could sing. "We shall overcome, we are not afraid." Then something caused me to see at that moment the real meaning of the movement. That students had faith in the future. That the movement was based on hope, that this movement had something within it that says somehow even though the arc of the moral universe is long, it bends toward justice. And I think this should be a challenge to all others who are struggling to transform the dangling discords of our Southland into a beautiful symphony of brotherhood. There is something in this student movement which says to us, that we shall overcome. Before the victory is won some may have to get scarred up, but we shall overcome. Before the victory of brotherhood is achieved, some will maybe face physical death, but we shall overcome. Before the victory is won, some will lose jobs, some will be called Communists, and reds, merely because they believe in brotherhood, some will be dismissed as dangerous rabblerousers and agitators merely because they're standing up for what is right, but we shall overcome. That is the basis of this movement, and as I like to say, there is something in this universe that justifies Carlyle in saying no lie can live forever. We shall overcome because there is something in this universe which justifies William Cullen Bryant in saying truth crushed to earth shall rise again. We shall overcome because there is something in this universe that justifies James Russell Lowell in saying, truth forever on the scaffold, wrong forever on the throne. Yet that scaffold sways the future, and behind the dim unknown standeth God within the shadows, keeping watch above His own. With this faith in the future, with this determined struggle, we will be able to emerge from the bleak and desolate midnight of man's inhumanity to man, into the bright and glittering daybreak of freedom and justice. Thank you.

On April 12, 1963, in order to have himself arrested on a symbolic day (Good Friday), Reverend Martin Luther King Jr. disobeyed a court injunction forbidding demonstrations in Birmingham, Alabama. That same day, eight leading white Birmingham clergymen (Christian and Jewish) published a letter in the Birmingham News *calling for the end of protests and exhorting protesters to work through the courts for the redress of their grievances. On the morning after his arrest, while held in solitary confinement, King began his response to these clergymen—his famous "Letter from Birmingham Jail." Begun in the margins of newspapers and on scraps of paper and finished by the following Tuesday, the letter was widely distributed and later became a central chapter in King's* Why We Can't Wait *(1964).*

Public Statement by Eight Alabama Clergymen

April 12, 1963

1   We the undersigned clergymen are among those who, in January, issued "An Appeal for Law and Order and Common Sense," in dealing with racial problems in Alabama. We expressed understanding that honest convictions in racial matters could properly be pursued in the courts, but urged that decisions of those courts should in the meantime be peacefully obeyed.

2   Since that time there had been some evidence of increased forbearance and a willingness to face facts. Responsible citizens have undertaken to work on various problems which cause racial friction and unrest. In Birmingham, recent public events had given indication that we all have opportunity for a new constructive and realistic approach to racial problems.

3   However, we are now confronted by a series of demonstrations by some of our Negro citizens, directed and led in part by outsiders. We recognize the natural impatience of people who feel that their hopes are slow in being realized. But we are convinced that these demonstrations are unwise and untimely.

4   We agree rather with certain local Negro leadership which has called for honest and open negotiation of racial issues in our area. And we believe this kind of facing of issues can best be accomplished by citizens of our own metropolitan area, white and Negro, meeting with their knowledge and experience of the local situation. All of us need to face that responsibility and find proper channels for its accomplishment.

5   Just as we formerly pointed out that "hatred and violence have no sanction in our religious and political traditions," we also point out that such actions as incite to hatred and violence, however technically peaceful those actions may be, have not contributed to the resolution of our local problems. We do not believe that these days of new hope are days when extreme measures are justified in Birmingham.

6   We commend the community as a whole, and the local news media and law enforcement officials in particular, on the calm manner in which these demonstrations have been handled. We urge the public to continue to show restraint should the demonstrations continue, and the law enforcement

officials to remain calm and continue to protect our city from violence.

7   We further strongly urge our own Negro community to withdraw support from these demonstrations, and to unite locally in working peacefully for a better Birmingham. When rights are consistently denied, a cause should be pressed in the courts and in negotiations among local leaders, and not in the streets. We appeal to both our white and Negro citizenry to observe the principles of law and order and common sense. Signed by:

C. C. J. Carpenter, D.D., LL.D.,
Bishop of Alabama
Joseph A. Durick, D.D.,
Auxiliary Bishop, Diocese of Mobile, Birmingham
Rabbi Milton L. Grafman,
Temple Emanu-El, Birmingham, Alabama
Bishop Paul Hardin,
Bishop of the Alabama-West Florida Conference
   of the Methodist Church
Bishop Nolan B. Harmon,
Bishop of the North Alabama Conference
   of the Methodist Church
George M. Murray, D.D., LL.D.,
Bishop Coadjutor, Episcopal Diocese of Alabama
Edward V. Ramage,
Moderator, Synod of the Alabama Presbyterian
   Church in the United States
Earl Stallings,
Pastor, First Baptist Church, Birmingham, Alabama

Martin Luther King Jr.
Letter from Birmingham Jail

April 16, 1963

My Dear Fellow Clergymen:

1   While confined here in the Birmingham city jail, I came across your recent statement calling my present activities "unwise and untimely." Seldom do I pause to answer criti-

cism of my work and ideas. If I sought to answer all the criticisms that cross my desk, my secretaries would have little time for anything other than such correspondence in the course of the day, and I would have no time for constructive work. But since I feel that you are men of genuine good will and that your criticisms are sincerely set forth, I want to try to answer your statement in what I hope will be patient and reasonable terms.

I think I should indicate why I am here in Birmingham, 2 since you have been influenced by the view which argues against "outsiders coming in." I have the honor of serving as president of the Southern Christian Leadership Conference, an organization operating in every southern state, with headquarters in Atlanta, Georgia. We have some eighty-five affiliated organizations across the South, and one of them is the Alabama Christian Movement for Human Rights. Frequently we share staff, educational and financial resources with our affiliates. Several months ago the affiliate here in Birmingham asked us to be on call to engage in a nonviolent direct-action program if such were deemed necessary. We readily consented, and when the hour came we lived up to our promise. So I, along with several members of my staff, am here because I was invited here. I am here because I have organizational ties here.

But more basically, I am in Birmingham because injustice 3 is here. Just as the prophets of the eighth century B.C. left their villages and carried their "thus saith the Lord" far beyond the boundaries of their home towns, and just as the Apostle Paul left his village of Tarsus and carried the gospel of Jesus Christ to the far corners of the Greco-Roman world, so am I compelled to carry the gospel of freedom beyond my own home town. Like Paul, I must constantly respond to the Macedonian call for aid.

Moreover, I am cognizant of the interrelatedness of all 4 communities and states. I cannot sit idly by in Atlanta and not be concerned about what happens in Birmingham. Injustice anywhere is a threat to justice everywhere. We are caught in an inescapable network of mutuality, tied in a single garment of destiny. Whatever affects one directly, affects all indirectly. Never again can we afford to live with the narrow, provincial "outside agitator" idea. Anyone who lives inside the United States can never be considered an outsider anywhere within its bounds.

You deplore the demonstrations taking place in Birming- 5 ham. But your statement, I am sorry to say, fails to express a similar concern for the conditions that brought about the demonstrations. I am sure that none of you would want to rest content with the superficial kind of social analysis that deals merely with effects and does not grapple with underlying causes. It is unfortunate that demonstrations are taking place in Birmingham, but it is even more unfortunate that the city's white power structure left the Negro community with no alternative.

6   In any nonviolent campaign there are four basic steps: collection of the facts to determine whether injustices exist; negotiation; self-purification; and direct action. We have gone through all these steps in Birmingham. There can be no gainsaying the fact that racial injustice engulfs this community. Birmingham is probably the most thoroughly segregated city in the United States. Its ugly record of brutality is widely known. Negroes have experienced grossly unjust treatment in the courts. There have been more unsolved bombings of Negro homes and churches in Birmingham than in any other city in the nation. These are the hard, brutal facts of the case. On the basis of these conditions, Negro leaders sought to negotiate with the city fathers. But the latter consistently refused to engage in good-faith negotiation.

7   Then, last September, came the opportunity to talk with leaders of Birmingham's economic community. In the course of the negotiations, certain promises were made by the merchants—for example, to remove the stores' humiliating racial signs. On the basis of these promises, the Reverend Fred Shuttlesworth and the leaders of the Alabama Christian Movement for Human Rights agreed to a moratorium on all demonstrations. As the weeks and months went by, we realized that we were the victims of a broken promise. A few signs, briefly removed, returned; the others remained.

8   As in so many past experiences, our hopes had been blasted, and the shadow of deep disappointment settled upon us. We had no alternative except to prepare for direct action, whereby we would present our very bodies as a means of laying our case before the conscience of the local and the national community. Mindful of the difficulties involved, we decided to undertake a process of self-purification. We began a series of workshops on nonviolence, and we repeatedly asked ourselves: "Are you able to accept blows without retaliating?" "Are you able to endure the ordeal of jail?" We decided to schedule our direct-action program for the Easter season, realizing that except for Christmas, this is the main shopping period of the year. Knowing that a strong economic-

withdrawal program would be the by-product of direct action, we felt that this would be the best time to bring pressure to bear on the merchants for the needed change.

Then it occurred to us that Birmingham's mayoral election   9
was coming up in March, and we speedily decided to postpone action until after election day. When we discovered that the Commissioner of Public Safety, Eugene "Bull" Connor, had piled up enough votes to be in the run-off, we decided again to postpone action until the day after the run-off so that the demonstrations could not be used to cloud the issues. Like many others, we waited to see Mr. Connor defeated, and to this end we endured postponement after postponement. Having aided in this community need, we felt that our direct action program could be delayed no longer.

You may well ask: "Why direct action? Why sit-ins,   10
marches and so forth? Isn't negotiation a better path?" You are quite right in calling for negotiation. Indeed, this is the very purpose of direct action. Nonviolent direct action seeks to create such a crisis and foster such a tension that a community which has constantly refused to negotiate is forced to confront the issue. It seeks so to dramatize the issue that it can no longer be ignored. My citing the creation of tension as part of the work of the nonviolent-resister may sound rather shocking. But I must confess that I am not afraid of the word "tension." I have earnestly opposed violent tension, but there is a type of constructive, nonviolent tension which is necessary for growth. Just as Socrates felt that it was necessary to create a tension in the mind so that individuals could rise from the bondage of myths and half-truths to the unfettered realm of creative analysis and objective appraisal, so must we see the need for nonviolent gadflies to create the kind of tension in society that will help men rise from the dark depths of prejudice and racism to the majestic heights of understanding and brotherhood.

The purpose of our direct-action program is to create a situ-   11
ation so crisis-packed that it will inevitably open the door to negotiation. I therefore concur with you in your call for negotiation. Too long has our beloved Southland been bogged down in a tragic effort to live in monologue rather than dialogue.

One of the basic points in your statement is that the action   12
that I and my associates have taken in Birmingham is untimely. Some have asked: "Why didn't you give the new city administration time to act?" The only answer that I can give to this query is that the new Birmingham administration must be prodded about as much as the outgoing one, before it

will act. We are sadly mistaken if we feel that the election of
Albert Boutwell as mayor will bring the millennium to Birmingham. While Mr. Boutwell is a much more gentle person
than Mr. Connor, they are both segregationists, dedicated to
maintenance of the status quo. I have hope that Mr. Boutwell
will be reasonable enough to see the futility of massive resistance to desegregation. But he will not see this without pressure from devotees of civil rights. My friends, I must say to
you that we have not made a single gain in civil rights without
determined legal and nonviolent pressure. Lamentably, it is
an historical fact that privileged groups seldom give up their
privileges voluntarily. Individuals may see the moral light and
voluntarily give up their unjust posture; but, as Reinhold Nie-
buhr has reminded us, groups tend to be more immoral than
individuals.

13   We know through painful experience that freedom is never
voluntarily given by the oppressor; it must be demanded by
the oppressed. Frankly, I have yet to engage in a direct-action
campaign that was "well timed" in the view of those who have
not suffered unduly from the disease of segregation. For years
now I have heard the word "Wait!" It rings in the ear of every
Negro with piercing familiarity. This "Wait" has almost
always meant "Never." We must come to see, with one of our
distinguished jurists, that "justice too long delayed is justice
denied."

14   We have waited for more than 340 years for our constitutional and God-given rights. The nations of Asia and Africa
are moving with jetlike speed toward gaining political independence, but we still creep at horse-and-buggy pace toward
gaining a cup of coffee at a lunch counter. Perhaps it is easy
for those who have never felt the stinging darts of segregation
to say, "Wait." But when you have seen vicious mobs lynch
your mothers and fathers at will and drown your sisters and
brothers at whim; when you have seen hate-filled policemen
curse, kick and even kill your black brothers and sisters;
when you see the vast majority of your twenty million Negro
brothers smothering in an airtight cage of poverty in the
midst of an affluent society; when you suddenly find your
tongue twisted and your speech stammering as you seek to
explain to your six-year-old daughter why she can't go to the
public amusement park that has just been advertised on television, and see tears welling up in her eyes when she is told
that Funtown is closed to colored children, and see ominous
clouds of inferiority beginning to form in her little mental sky,
and see her beginning to distort her personality by developing

an unconscious bitterness toward white people; when you have to concoct an answer for a five-year-old son who is asking: "Daddy, why do white people treat colored people so mean?"; when you take a cross-country drive and find it necessary to sleep night after night in the uncomfortable corners of your automobile because no motel will accept you; when you are humiliated day in and day out by nagging signs reading "white" and "colored"; when your first name becomes "nigger," your middle name becomes "boy" (however old you are) and your last name becomes "John," and your wife and mother are never given the respected title "Mrs."; when you are harried by day and haunted by night by the fact that you are a Negro, living constantly at tiptoe stance, never quite knowing what to expect next, and are plagued with inner fears and outer resentments; when you are forever fighting a degenerating sense of "nobodiness"—then you will understand why we find it difficult to wait. There comes a time when the cup of endurance runs over, and men are no longer willing to be plunged into the abyss of despair. I hope, sirs, you can understand our legitimate and unavoidable impatience.

You express a great deal of anxiety over our willingness to   15
break laws. This is certainly a legitimate concern. Since we so diligently urge people to obey the Supreme Court's decision of 1954 outlawing segregation in the public schools, at first glance it may seem rather paradoxical for us consciously to break laws. One may well ask: "How can you advocate breaking some laws and obeying others?" The answer lies in the fact that there are two types of laws: just and unjust. I would be the first to advocate obeying just laws. One has not only a legal but a moral responsibility to obey just laws. Conversely, one has a moral responsibility to disobey unjust laws. I would agree with St. Augustine that "an unjust law is no law at all."

Now, what is the difference between the two? How does   16
one determine whether a law is just or unjust? A just law is a man-made code that squares with the moral law or the law of God. An unjust law is a code that is out of harmony with the moral law. To put it in the terms of St. Thomas Aquinas: An unjust law is a human law that is not rooted in eternal law and natural law. Any law that uplifts human personality is just. Any law that degrades human personality is unjust. All segregation statutes are unjust because segregation distorts the soul and damages the personality. It gives the segregator a false sense of superiority and the segregated a false sense of inferiority. Segregation, to use the terminology of the Jewish philosopher Martin Buber, substitutes an "I–it" relationship

for an "I–thou" relationship and ends up relegating persons to the status of things. Hence segregation is not only politically, economically and sociologically unsound, it is morally wrong and sinful. Paul Tillich has said that sin is separation. Is not segregation an existential expression of man's tragic separation, his awful estrangement, his terrible sinfulness? Thus it is that I can urge men to obey the 1954 decision of the Supreme Court, for it is morally right; and I can urge them to disobey segregation ordinances, for they are morally wrong.

17   Let us consider a more concrete example of just and unjust laws. An unjust law is a code that a numerical or power majority group compels a minority group to obey but does not make binding on itself. This is *difference* made legal. By the same token, a just law is a code that a majority compels a minority to follow and that it is willing to follow itself. This is *sameness* made legal.

18   Let me give another explanation. A law is unjust if it is inflicted on a minority that, as a result of being denied the right to vote, had no part in enacting or devising the law. Who can say that the legislature of Alabama which set up that state's segregation laws was democratically elected? Throughout Alabama all sorts of devious methods are used to prevent Negroes from becoming registered voters, and there are some counties in which, even though Negroes constitute a majority of the population, not a single Negro is registered. Can any law enacted under such circumstances be considered democratically structured?

19   Sometimes a law is just on its face and unjust in its application. For instance, I have been arrested on a charge of parading without a permit. Now, there is nothing wrong in having an ordinance which requires a permit for a parade. But such an ordinance becomes unjust when it is used to maintain segregation and to deny citizens the First-Amendment privilege of peaceful assembly and protest.

20   I hope you are able to see the distinction I am trying to point out. In no sense do I advocate evading or defying the law, as would the rabid segregationist. That would lead to anarchy. One who breaks an unjust law must do so openly, lovingly, and with a willingness to accept the penalty. I submit that an individual who breaks a law that conscience tells him is unjust, and who willingly accepts the penalty of imprisonment in order to arouse the conscience of the community over its injustice, is in reality expressing the highest respect for law.

21   Of course, there is nothing new about this kind of civil disobedience. It was evidenced sublimely in the refusal of

Shadrach, Meshach and Abednego to obey the laws of Neb-uchadnezzar, on the ground that a higher moral law was at stake. It was practiced superbly by the early Christians, who were willing to face hungry lions and the excruciating pain of chopping blocks rather than submit to certain unjust laws of the Roman Empire. To a degree, academic freedom is a real-ity today because Socrates practiced civil disobedience. In our own nation, the Boston Tea Party represented a massive act of civil disobedience.

We should never forget that everything Adolf Hitler did in   22
Germany was "legal" and everything the Hungarian freedom fighters did in Hungary was "illegal." It was "illegal" to aid and comfort a Jew in Hitler's Germany. Even so, I am sure that, had I lived in Germany at the time, I would have aided and comforted my Jewish brothers. If today I lived in a Com-munist country where certain principles dear to the Christian faith are suppressed, I would openly advocate disobeying that country's antireligious laws.

I must make two honest confessions to you, my Christian   23
and Jewish brothers. First, I must confess that over the past few years I have been gravely disappointed with the white moderate. I have almost reached the regrettable conclusion that the Negro's great stumbling block in his stride toward freedom is not the White Citizen's Counciler or the Ku Klux Klanner, but the white moderate, who is more devoted to "order" than to justice; who prefers a negative peace which is the absence of tension to a positive peace which is the pres-ence of justice; who constantly says: "I agree with you in the goal you seek, but I cannot agree with your methods of direct action"; who paternalistically believes he can set the timetable for another man's freedom; who lives by a mythical concept of time and who constantly advises the Negro to wait for a "more convenient season." Shallow understanding from people of good will is more frustrating than absolute misunderstanding from people of ill will. Lukewarm acceptance is much more bewildering than outright rejection.

I had hoped that the white moderate would understand   24
that law and order exist for the purpose of establishing justice and that when they fail in this purpose they become the dan-gerously structured dams that block the flow of social progress. I had hoped that the white moderate would under-stand that the present tension in the South is a necessary phase of the transition from an obnoxious negative peace, in which the Negro passively accepted his unjust plight, to a substantive and positive peace, in which all men will respect

the dignity and worth of human personality. Actually, we who engage in nonviolent direct action are not the creators of tension. We merely bring to the surface the hidden tension that is already alive. We bring it out in the open, where it can be seen and dealt with. Like a boil that can never be cured so long as it is covered up but must be opened with all its ugliness to the natural medicines of air and light, injustice must be exposed, with all the tension its exposure creates, to the light of human conscience and the air of national opinion before it can be cured.

25   In your statement you assert that our actions, even though peaceful, must be condemned because they precipitate violence. But is this a logical assertion? Isn't this like condemning a robbed man because his possession of money precipitated the evil act of robbery? Isn't this like condemning Socrates because his unswerving commitment to truth and his philosophical inquiries precipitated the act by the misguided populace in which they made him drink hemlock? Isn't this like condemning Jesus because his unique God-consciousness and never-ceasing devotion to God's will precipitated the evil act of crucifixion? We must come to see that, as the federal courts have consistently affirmed, it is wrong to urge an individual to cease his efforts to gain his basic constitutional rights because the quest may precipitate violence. Society must protect the robbed and punish the robber.

26   I had also hoped that the white moderate would reject the myth concerning time in relation to the struggle for freedom. I have just received a letter from a white brother in Texas. He writes: "All Christians know that the colored people will receive equal rights eventually, but it is possible that you are in too great a religious hurry. It has taken Christianity almost two thousand years to accomplish what it has. The teachings of Christ take time to come to earth." Such an attitude stems from a tragic misconception of time, from the strangely irrational notion that there is something in the very flow of time that will inevitably cure all ills. Actually, time itself is neutral; it can be used either destructively or constructively. More and more I feel that the people of ill will have used time much more effectively than have the people of good will. We will have to repent in this generation not merely for the hateful words and actions of the bad people but for the appalling silence of the good people. Human progress never rolls in on wheels of inevitability; it comes through the tireless efforts of men willing to be co-workers with God, and without this hard work, time itself becomes an ally of the forces of social stag-

nation. We must use time creatively, in the knowledge that
time is always ripe to do right. Now is the time to make real
the promise of democracy and transform our pending
national elegy into a creative psalm of brotherhood. Now is
the time to lift our national policy from the quicksand of
racial injustice to the solid rock of human dignity.

You speak of our activity in Birmingham as extreme. At   27
first I was rather disappointed that fellow clergymen would
see my nonviolent efforts as those of an extremist. I began
thinking about the fact that I stand in the middle of two
opposing forces in the Negro community. One is a force of
complacency, made up in part of Negroes who, as a result of
long years of oppression, are so drained of self-respect and a
sense of "somebodiness" that they have adjusted to segregation; and in part of a few middle-class Negroes who, because
of a degree of academic and economic security and because
in some ways they profit by segregation, have become insensitive to the problems of the masses. The other force is one of
bitterness and hatred, and it comes perilously close to advocating violence. It is expressed in the various black nationalist
groups that are springing up across the nation, the largest
and best-known being Elijah Muhammad's Muslim movement. Nourished by the Negro's frustration over the continued existence of racial discrimination, this movement is
made up of people who have lost faith in America, who have
absolutely repudiated Christianity, and who have concluded
that the white man is an incorrigible "devil."

I have tried to stand between these two forces, saying that   28
we need emulate neither the "do-nothingism" of the compla-
cent nor the hatred and despair of the black nationalist. For
there is the more excellent way of love and nonviolent protest.
I am grateful to God that, through the influence of the Negro
church, the way of nonviolence became an integral part of
our struggle.

If this philosophy had not emerged, by now many streets   29
of the South would, I am convinced, be flowing with blood.
And I am further convinced that if our white brothers dismiss
as "rabble-rousers" and "outside agitators" those of us who
employ nonviolent direct action, and if they refuse to support
our nonviolent efforts, millions of Negroes will, out of frustration and despair, seek solace and security in black-nationalist
ideologies—a development that would inevitably lead to a
frightening racial nightmare.

Oppressed people cannot remain oppressed forever. The   30
yearning for freedom eventually manifests itself, and that is

what has happened to the American Negro. Something within has reminded him of his birthright of freedom, and something without has reminded him that it can be gained. Consciously or unconsciously, he has been caught up by the *Zeitgeist,* and with his black brothers of Africa and his brown and yellow brothers of Asia, South America and the Caribbean, the United States Negro is moving with a sense of great urgency toward the promised land of racial justice. If one recognizes this vital urge that has engulfed the Negro community, one should readily understand why public demonstrations are taking place. The Negro has many pent-up resentments and latent frustrations, and he must release them. So let him march; let him make prayer pilgrimages to the city hall; let him go on freedom rides—and try to understand why he must do so. If his repressed emotions are not released in nonviolent ways, they will seek expression through violence; this is not a threat but a fact of history. So I have not said to my people: "Get rid of your discontent." Rather, I have tried to say that this normal and healthy discontent can be channeled into the creative outlet of nonviolent direct action. And now this approach is being termed extremist.

31   But though I was initially disappointed at being categorized as an extremist, as I continued to think about the matter I gradually gained a measure of satisfaction from the label. Was not Jesus an extremist for love: "Love your enemies, bless them that curse you, do good to them that hate you, and pray for them which despitefully use you, and persecute you." Was not Amos an extremist for justice: "Let justice roll down like waters and righteousness like an ever-flowing stream." Was not Paul an extremist for the Christian gospel: "I bear in my body the marks of the Lord Jesus." Was not Martin Luther an extremist: "Here I stand; I cannot do otherwise, so help me God." And John Bunyan: "I will stay in jail to the end of my days before I make a butchery of my conscience." And Abraham Lincoln: "This nation cannot survive half slave and half free." And Thomas Jefferson: "We hold these truths to be self-evident, that all men are created equal..." So the question is not whether we will be extremists, but what kind of extremists we will be. Will we be extremists for hate or for love? Will we be extremists for the preservation of injustice or for the extension of justice? In that dramatic scene on Calvary's hill three men were crucified. We must never forget that all three were crucified for the same crime—the crime of extremism. Two were extremists for immorality, and thus fell below their

environment. The other, Jesus Christ, was an extremist for love, truth and goodness, and thereby rose above his environment. Perhaps the South, the nation and the world are in dire need of creative extremists.

I had hoped that the white moderate would see this need. 32 Perhaps I was too optimistic; perhaps I expected too much. I suppose I should have realized that few members of the oppressor race can understand the deep groans and passionate yearnings of the oppressed race, and still fewer have the vision to see that injustice must be rooted out by strong, persistent and determined action. I am thankful, however, that some of our white brothers in the South have grasped the meaning of this social revolution and committed themselves to it. They are still all too few in quantity, but they are big in quality. Some—such as Ralph McGill, Lillian Smith, Harry Golden, James McBride Dabbs, Ann Braden and Sarah Patton Boyle—have written about our struggle in eloquent and prophetic terms. Others have marched with us down nameless streets of the South. They have languished in filthy, roach-infested jails, suffering the abuse and brutality of policemen who view them as "dirty nigger-lovers." Unlike so many of their moderate brothers and sisters, they have recognized the urgency of the moment and sensed the need for powerful "action" antidotes to combat the disease of segregation.

Let me take note of my other major disappointment. I have 33 been so greatly disappointed with the white church and its leadership. Of course, there are some notable exceptions. I am not unmindful of the fact that each of you has taken some significant stands on this issue. I commend you, Reverend Stallings, for your Christian stand on this past Sunday, in welcoming Negroes to your worship service on a nonsegregated basis. I commend the Catholic leaders of this state for integrating Spring Hill College several years ago.

But despite these notable exceptions, I must honestly reiterate that I have been disappointed with the church. I do not 34 say this as one of those negative critics who can always find something wrong with the church. I say this as a minister of the gospel, who loves the church; who was nurtured in its bosom; who has been sustained by its spiritual blessings and who will remain true to it as long as the cord of life shall lengthen.

When I was suddenly catapulted into the leadership of the 35 bus protest in Montgomery, Alabama, a few years ago, I felt we would be supported by the white church. I felt that the white ministers, priests and rabbis of the South would be among our strongest allies. Instead, some have been outright opponents, refusing to understand the freedom movement and misrepresenting its leaders; all too many others have been more cautious than courageous and have remained silent behind the anesthetizing security of stained-glass windows.

36   In spite of my shattered dreams, I came to Birmingham with the hope that the white religious leadership of this community would see the justice of our cause and, with deep moral concern, would serve as the channel through which our just grievances could reach the power structure. I had hoped that each of you would understand. But again I have been disappointed.

37   I have heard numerous southern religious leaders admonish their worshipers to comply with a desegregation decision because it is the law, but I have longed to hear white ministers declare: "Follow this decree because integration is morally right and because the Negro is your brother." In the midst of blatant injustices inflicted upon the Negro, I have watched white churchmen stand on the sideline and mouth pious irrelevancies and sanctimonious trivialities. In the midst of a mighty struggle to rid our nation of racial and economic injustice, I have heard many ministers say: "Those are social issues, with which the gospel has no real concern." And I have watched many churches commit themselves to a completely otherworldly religion which makes a strange, un-Biblical distortion between body and soul, between the sacred and the secular.

38   I have traveled the length and breadth of Alabama, Mississippi and all the other southern states. On sweltering summer days and crisp autumn mornings I have looked at the South's beautiful churches with their lofty spires pointing heavenward. I have beheld the impressive outlines of her massive religious-education buildings. Over and over I have found myself asking: "What kind of people worship here? Who is their God? Where were their voices when the lips of Governor Barnett dripped with words of interposition and nullification? Where were they when Governor Wallace gave a clarion call for defiance and hatred? Where were their voices of support when bruised and weary Negro men and women decided to rise from the dark dungeons of complacency to the bright hills of creative protest?"

39   Yes, these questions are still in my mind. In deep disappointment I have wept over the laxity of the church. But be assured that my tears have been tears of love. There can be no deep disappointment where there is not deep love. Yes, I love

the church. How could I do otherwise? I am in the rather unique position of being the son, the grandson and the great-grandson of preachers. Yes, I see the church as the body of Christ. But, oh! How we have blemished and scarred that body through social neglect and through fear of being non-conformists.

There was a time when the church was very powerful—in   40
the time when the early Christians rejoiced at being deemed worthy to suffer for what they believed. In those days the church was not merely a thermometer that recorded the ideas and principles of popular opinion; it was a thermostat that transformed the mores of society. Whenever the early Christians entered a town, the people in power became disturbed and immediately sought to convict the Christians for being "disturbers of the peace" and "outside agitators." But the Christians pressed on, in the conviction that they were "a colony of heaven," called to obey God rather than man. Small in number, they were big in commitment. They were too God-intoxicated to be "astronomically intimidated." By their effort and example they brought an end to such ancient evils as infanticide and gladiatorial contests.

Things are different now. So often the contemporary church   41
is a weak, ineffectual voice with an uncertain sound. So often it is an arch-defender of the status quo. Far from being disturbed by the presence of the church, the power structure of the average community is consoled by the church's silent—and often even vocal—sanction of things as they are.

But the judgment of God is upon the church as never   42
before. If today's church does not recapture the sacrificial spirit of the early church, it will lose its authenticity, forfeit the loyalty of millions, and be dismissed as an irrelevant social club with no meaning for the twentieth century. Every day I meet young people whose disappointment with the church has turned into outright disgust.

Perhaps I have once again been too optimistic. Is orga-   43
nized religion too inextricably bound to the status quo to save our nation and the world? Perhaps I must turn my faith to the inner spiritual church, the church within the church, as the true *ekklesia* and the hope of the world. But again I am thankful to God that some noble souls from the ranks of organized religion have broken loose from the paralyzing chains of conformity and joined us as active partners in the struggle for freedom. They have left their secure congregations and walked the streets of Albany, Georgia, with us. They have gone down the highways of the South on tortuous rides for

freedom. Yes, they have gone to jail with us. Some have been dismissed from their churches, have lost the support of their bishops and fellow ministers. But they have acted in the faith that right defeated is stronger than evil triumphant. Their witness has been the spiritual salt that has preserved the true meaning of the gospel in these troubled times. They have carved a tunnel of hope through the dark mountain of disappointment.

44   I hope the church as a whole will meet the challenge of this decisive hour. But even if the church does not come to the aid of justice, I have no despair about the future. I have no fear about the outcome of our struggle in Birmingham, even if our motives are at present misunderstood. We will reach the goal of freedom in Birmingham and all over the nation, because the goal of America is freedom. Abused and scorned though we may be, our destiny is tied up with America's destiny. Before the pilgrims landed at Plymouth, we were here. Before the pen of Jefferson etched the majestic words of the Declaration of Independence across the pages of history, we were here. For more than two centuries our forebears labored in this country without wages; they made cotton king; they built the homes of their masters while suffering gross injustice and shameful humiliation—and yet out of a bottomless vitality they continued to thrive and develop. If the inexpressible cruelties of slavery could not stop us, the opposition we now face will surely fail. We will win our freedom because the sacred heritage of our nation and the eternal will of God are embodied in our echoing demands.

45   Before closing I feel impelled to mention one other point in your statement that has troubled me profoundly. You warmly commended the Birmingham police force for keeping "order" and "preventing violence." I doubt that you would have so warmly commended the police force if you had seen its dogs sinking their teeth into unarmed, nonviolent Negroes. I doubt that you would so quickly commend the policemen if you were to observe their ugly and inhumane treatment of Negroes here in the city jail; if you were to watch them push and curse old Negro women and young Negro girls; if you were to see them slap and kick old Negro men and young boys; if you were to observe them, as they did on two occasions, refuse to give us food because we wanted to sing our grace together. I cannot join you in your praise of the Birmingham Police Department.

46   It is true that the police have exercised a degree of discipline in handling the demonstrators. In this sense they have

conducted themselves rather "nonviolently" in public. But for what purpose? To preserve the evil system of segregation. Over the past few years I have consistently preached that nonviolence demands that the means we use must be as pure as the ends we seek. I have tried to make clear that it is wrong to use immoral means to attain moral ends. But now I must affirm that it is just as wrong, or perhaps even more so, to use moral means to preserve immoral ends. Perhaps Mr. Connor and his policemen have been rather nonviolent in public, as was Chief Pritchett in Albany, Georgia, but they have used the moral means of nonviolence to maintain the immoral end of racial injustice. As T. S. Eliot has said: "The last temptation is the greatest treason: To do the right deed for the wrong reason."

I wish you had commended the Negro sit-inners and dem-   47
onstrators of Birmingham for their sublime courage, their willingness to suffer and their amazing discipline in the midst of great provocation. One day the South will recognize its real heroes. They will be the James Merediths, with the noble sense of purpose that enables them to face jeering and hostile mobs, and with the agonizing loneliness that characterizes the life of the pioneer. They will be old, oppressed, battered Negro women, symbolized in a seventy-two-year-old woman in Montgomery, Alabama, who rose up with a sense of dignity and with her people decided not to ride segregated buses, and who responded with ungrammatical profundity to one who inquired about her weariness: "My feets is tired, but my soul is at rest." They will be the young high school and college students, the young ministers of the gospel and a host of their elders, courageously and nonviolently sitting in at lunch counters and willingly going to jail for conscience sake. One day the South will know that when these disinherited children of God sat down at lunch counters, they were in reality standing up for what is best in the American dream and for the most sacred values in our Judaeo-Christian heritage, thereby bringing our nation back to those great wells of democracy which were dug deep by the founding fathers in their formulation of the Constitution and the Declaration of Independence.

Never before have I written so long a letter. I'm afraid it is   48
much too long to take your precious time. I can assure you that it would have been much shorter if I had been writing from a comfortable desk, but what else can one do when he is alone in a narrow jail cell, other than write long letters, think long thoughts and pray long prayers?

49   If I have said anything in this letter that overstates the truth and indicates an unreasonable impatience, I beg you to forgive me. If I have said anything that understates the truth and indicates my having a patience that allows me to settle for anything less than brotherhood, I beg God to forgive me.

50   I hope this letter finds you strong in the faith. I also hope that circumstances will soon make it possible for me to meet each of you, not as an integrationist or a civil-rights leader but as a fellow clergyman and a Christian brother. Let us all hope that the dark clouds of racial prejudice will soon pass away and the deep fog of misunderstanding will be lifted from our fear-drenched communities, and in some not too distant tomorrow the radiant stars of love and brotherhood will shine over our great nation with all their scintillating beauty.

> Yours for the cause of Peace and Brotherhood,
> Martin Luther King Jr.

Lewis H. Van Dusen Jr.
Civil Disobedience: Destroyer of Democracy

Lewis H. Van Dusen Jr. (born 1910) has practiced law in Philadelphia since 1935. Decorated for valor during World War II, he also served with the State Department during his distinguished career. He has written many essays for professional journals; the following one appeared in 1969 in the American Bar Association Journal.

1   As Charles E. Wyzanski, Chief Judge of the United States District Court in Boston, wrote in the February 1968, *Atlantic:* "Disobedience is a long step from dissent. Civil disobedience involves a deliberate and punishable breach of legal duty." Protesters might prefer a different definition. They would rather say that civil disobedience is the peaceful resistance of conscience.

2   The philosophy of civil disobedience was not developed in our American democracy, but in the very first democracy of

Athens. It was expressed by the poet Sophocles and the philosopher Socrates. In Sophocles' tragedy, Antigone chose to obey her conscience and violate the state edict against providing burial for her brother, who had been decreed a traitor. When the dictator Creon found out that Antigone had buried her fallen brother, he confronted her and reminded her that there was a mandatory death penalty for this deliberate disobedience of the state law. Antigone nobly replied, "Nor did I think your orders were so strong that you, a mortal man, could overrun the gods' unwritten and unfailing laws."

Conscience motivated Antigone. She was not testing the   3
validity of the law in the hope that eventually she would be sustained. Appealing to the judgment of the community, she explained her action to the chorus. She was not secret and surreptitious—the interment of her brother was open and public. She was not violent; she did not trespass on another citizen's rights. And finally, she accepted without resistance the death sentence—the penalty for violation. By voluntarily accepting the law's sanctions, she was not a revolutionary denying the authority of the state. Antigone's behavior exemplifies the classic case of civil disobedience.

Socrates believed that reason could dictate a conscientious   4
disobedience of state law, but he also believed that he had to accept the legal sanctions of the state. In Plato's *Crito*, Socrates from his hanging basket accepted the death penalty for his teaching of religion to youths contrary to state laws.

The sage of Walden, Henry David Thoreau, took this philos-   5
ophy of nonviolence and developed it into a strategy for solving society's injustices. First enunciating it in protest against the Mexican War, he then turned it to use against slavery. For refusing to pay taxes that would help pay the enforcers of the fugitive slave law, he went to prison. In Thoreau's words, "If the alternative is to keep all just men in prison or to give up slavery, the state will not hesitate which to choose."

Sixty years later, Gandhi took Thoreau's civil disobedience   6
as his strategy to wrest Indian independence from England. The famous salt march against a British imperial tax is his best-known example of protest.

But the conscientious law breaking of Socrates, Gandhi,   7
and Thoreau is to be distinguished from the conscientious law testing of Martin Luther King, Jr., who was not a civil disobedient. The civil disobedient withholds taxes or violates state laws knowing he is legally wrong, but believing he is morally right. While he wrapped himself in the mantle of Gandhi and Thoreau, Dr. King led his followers in violation of

state laws he believed were contrary to the Federal Constitution. But since Supreme Court decisions in the end generally upheld his many actions, he should not be considered a true civil disobedient.

8   The civil disobedience of Antigone is like that of the pacifist who withholds paying the percentage of his taxes that goes to the Defense Department, or the Quaker who travels against State Department regulations to Hanoi to distribute medical supplies, or the Vietnam war protester who tears up his draft card. This civil disobedient has been nonviolent in his defiance of the law; he has been unfurtive in his violation; he has been submissive to the penalties of the law. He has neither evaded the law nor interfered with another's rights. He has been neither a rioter nor a revolutionary. The thrust of his cause has not been the might of coercion but the martyrdom of conscience.

Was the Boston Tea Party Civil Disobedience?

9   Those who justify violence and radical action as being in the tradition of our Revolution show a misunderstanding of the philosophy of democracy.

10   James Farmer, former head of the Congress of Racial Equality, in defense of the mass action confrontation method, has told of a famous organized demonstration that took place in opposition to political and economic discrimination. The protestors beat back and scattered the law enforcers and then proceeded to loot and destroy private property. Mr. Farmer then said he was talking about the Boston Tea Party and implied that violence as a method for redress of grievances was an American tradition and a legacy of our revolutionary heritage. While it is true that there is no more sacred document than our Declaration of Independence, Jefferson's "inherent right of rebellion" was predicated on the tyrannical denial of democratic means. If there is no popular assembly to provide an adjustment of ills, and if there is no court system to dispose of injustices, then there is, indeed, a right to rebel.

11   The seventeenth century's John Locke, the philosophical father of the Declaration of Independence, wrote in his *Second Treatise on Civil Government:* "Wherever law ends, tyranny begins... and the people are absolved from any further obedience. Governments are dissolved from within when the legislative [chamber] is altered. When the government

[becomes]...arbitrary disposers of lives, liberties and fortunes of the people, such revolutions happen...."

But there are some sophisticated proponents of the revolutionary redress of grievances who say that the test of the need for radical action is not the unavailability of democratic institutions but the ineffectuality of those institutions to remove blatant social inequalities. If social injustice exists, they say, concerted disobedience is required against the constituted government, whether it be totalitarian or democratic in structure.

Of course, only the most bigoted chauvinist would claim that America is without some glaring faults. But there has never been a utopian society on earth and there never will be unless human nature is remade. Since inequities will mar even the best-framed democracies, the injustice rationale would allow a free right of civil resistance to be available always as a shortcut alternative to the democratic way of petition, debate and assembly. The lesson of history is that civil insurgency spawns far more injustices than it removes. The Jeffersons, Washingtons, and Adamses resisted tyranny with the aim of promoting the procedures of democracy. They would never have resisted a democratic government with the risk of promoting the techniques of tyranny.

Legitimate Pressures and Illegitimate Results

There are many civil rights leaders who show impatience with the process of democracy. They rely on the sit-ins, boycott or mass picketing to gain speedier solutions to the problems that face every citizen. But we must realize that the legitimate pressures that won concessions in the past can easily escalate into the illegitimate power plays that might extort demands in the future. The victories of these civil rights leaders must not shake our confidence in the democratic procedures, as the pressures of demonstration are desirable only if they take place within the limits allowed by law. Civil rights gains should continue to be won by the persuasion of Congress and other legislative bodies and by the decision of courts. Any illegal entreaty for the rights of some can be an injury to the rights of others, for mass demonstrations often trigger violence.

Those who advocate taking the law into their own hands should reflect that when they are disobeying what they consider to be an immoral law, they are deciding on a possibly

immoral course. Their answer is that the process for democratic relief is too slow, that only mass confrontation can
bring immediate action, and that any injuries are the inevitable cost of the pursuit of justice. Their answer is, simply put,
that the end justifies the means. It is this justification of any
form of demonstration as a form of dissent that threatens to
destroy a society built on the rule of law.

16   Our Bill of Rights guarantees wide opportunities to use
mass meetings, public parades, and organized demonstrations to stimulate sentiment, to dramatize issues, and to
cause change. The Washington freedom march of 1963 was
such a call for action. But the rights of free expression cannot
be mere force cloaked in the garb of free speech. As the courts
have decreed in labor cases, free assembly does not mean
mass picketing or sit-down strikes. These rights are subject to
limitations of time and place so as to secure the rights of
others. When militant students storm a college president's
office to achieve demands, when certain groups plan rush-
hour car stalling to protest discrimination in employment,
these are not dissent, but a denial of rights to others. Neither is
it the lawful use of mass protest, but rather the unlawful use
of mob power.

17   Justice Black, one of the foremost advocates and defenders
of the right of protest and dissent, has said:

> ... Experience demonstrates that it is not a far step from
> what to many seems to be the earnest, honest, patriotic,
> kind-spirited multitude of today, to the fanatical, threaten-
> ing, lawless mob of tomorrow. And the crowds that press in
> the streets for noble goals today can be supplanted tomorrow
> by street mobs pressuring the courts for precisely opposite
> ends.[1]

18   Society must censure those demonstrators who would trespass on the public peace, as it must condemn those rioters
whose pillage would destroy the public peace. But more
ambivalent is society's posture toward the civil disobedient.
Unlike the rioter, the true civil disobedient commits no
violence. Unlike the mob demonstrator, he commits no
trespass on others' rights. The civil disobedient, while deliberately violating a law, shows an oblique respect for the law by

---

[1]In *Cox v. Louisiana*, 379 U.S. 536, 575, 584 (1965).

voluntarily submitting to its sanctions. He neither resists arrest nor evades punishment. Thus, he breaches the law but not the peace.

But civil disobedience, whatever the ethical rationaliza- 19 tion, is still an assault on our democratic society, an affront to our legal order and an attack on our constitutional government. To indulge civil disobedience is to invite anarchy, and the permissive arbitrariness of anarchy is hardly less tolerable than the repressive arbitrariness of tyranny. Too often the license of liberty is followed by the loss of liberty, because into the desert of anarchy comes the man on horseback, a Mussolini or a Hitler.

Violations of Law Subvert Democracy

Law violations, even for ends recognized as laudable, are 20 not only assaults on the rule of law, but subversions of the democratic process. The disobedient act of conscience does not ennoble democracy; it erodes it.

First, it courts violence, and even the most careful and lim- 21 ited use of nonviolent acts of disobedience may help sow the dragon-teeth of civil riot. Civil disobedience is the progenitor of disorder, and disorder is the sire of violence.

Second, the concept of civil disobedience does not invite 22 principles of general applicability. If the children of light are morally privileged to resist particular laws on grounds of conscience, so are the children of darkness. Former Deputy Attorney General Burke Marshall said: "If the decision to break the law really turned on individual conscience, it is hard to see in law how [the civil rights leader] is better off than former Governor Ross Barnett of Mississippi who also believed deeply in his cause and was willing to go to jail."[2]

Third, even the most noble act of civil disobedience 23 assaults the rule of law. Although limited as to method, motive and objective, it has the effect of inducing others to engage in different forms of law breaking characterized by methods unsanctioned and condemned by classic theories of law violation. Unfortunately, the most patent lesson of civil disobedience is not so much nonviolence of action as defiance of authority.

[2]"The Protest movement and the Law," *Virginia Legal Review* 51 (1965), 785.

24   Finally, the greatest danger in condoning civil disobedience as a permissible strategy for hastening change is that it
undermines our democratic processes. To adopt the techniques of civil disobedience is to assume that representative
government does not work. To resist the decisions of courts
and the laws of elected assemblies is to say that democracy
has failed.

25   There is no man who is above the law, and there is no man
who has a right to break the law. Civil disobedience is not
above the law, but against the law. When the civil disobedient
disobeys one law, he invariably subverts all law. When the
civil disobedient says that he is above the law, he is saying
that democracy is beneath him. His disobedience shows a
distrust for the democratic system. He is merely saying that
since democracy does not work, why should he help make it
work. Thoreau expressed well the civil disobedient's disdain
for democracy:

> As for adopting the ways which the state has provided for
> remedying the evil, I know not of such ways. They take too
> much time and a man's life will be gone. I have other affairs
> to attend to. I came into this world not chiefly to make this a
> good place to live in, but to live in it, be it good or bad.[3]

26   Thoreau's position is not only morally irresponsible but
politically reprehensible. When citizens in a democracy are
called on to make a profession of faith, the civil disobedients
offer only a confession of failure. Tragically, when civil disobedients for lack of faith abstain from democratic involvement, they help attain their own gloomy prediction. They
help create the social and political basis for their own despair.
By foreseeing failure, they help forge it. If citizens rely on
antidemocratic means of protest, they will help bring about
the undemocratic result of an authoritarian or anarchic state.

27   How far demonstrations properly can be employed to produce political and social change is a pressing question, particularly in view of the provocations accompanying the National
Democratic Convention in Chicago last August and the reaction of the police to them. A line must be drawn by the judiciary between the demands of those who seek absolute order,
which can lead only to a dictatorship, and those who seek
absolute freedom, which can lead only to anarchy. The line,

---

[3]Thoreau, "Civil Disobedience" (see page 637).

wherever it is drawn by our courts, should be respected on the college campus, on the streets, and elsewhere.

Undue provocation will inevitably result in overreaction, human emotions being what they are. Violence will follow. This cycle undermines the very democracy it is designed to preserve. The lesson of the past is that democracies will fall if violence, including the intentional provocations that will lead to violence, replaces democratic procedures, as in Athens, Rome, and the Weimar Republic. This lesson must be constantly explained by the legal profession.   28

We should heed the words of William James: 29

> Democracy is still upon its trial. The civic genius of our people is its only bulwark and . . . neither battleships nor public libraries nor great newspapers nor booming stocks: neither mechanical invention nor political adroitness, nor churches nor universities nor civil service examinations can save us from degeneration if the inner mystery be lost.
>
> That mystery, at once the secret and the glory of our English-speaking race, consists of nothing but two habits. . . . [O]ne of them is the habit of trained and disciplined good temper towards the opposite party when it fairly wins its innings. The other is that of fierce and merciless resentment toward every man or set of men who break the public peace.[4]

[4]James, *Pragmatism* (1907), pp. 127–28.

SHOULD ABORTION BE LEGAL?

Gwendolyn Brooks

The Mother

Gwendolyn Brooks (born 1917) is one of the most important American poets of this century. In her many books of poetry she often concentrates on the struggle of the individual against difficult circumstances, as in the following poem. "The Mother" first appeared in Brooks's first book A Street in Bronzeville *(1945), which takes the reader on a trip through the various facets of an African American community; most recently it was reprinted in her 1991 book* Blacks.

1   Abortions will not let you forget.
You remember the children you got that you did not get,
The damp small pulps with a little or with no hair,
The singers and workers that never handled the air.
You will never neglect or beat
Them, or silence or buy with a sweet.
You will never wind up the sucking-thumb
Or scuttle off ghosts that come.
You will never leave them, controlling your luscious sigh,
Return for a snack of them, with gobbling mother-eye.

2   I have heard in the voices of the wind the voices of my dim
    killed children.
I have contracted. I have eased
My dim dears at the breasts they could never suck.
I have said, Sweets, if I sinned, if I seized
Your luck
And your lives from your unfinished reach,
If I stole your births and your names,
Your straight baby tears and your games,
Your stilted or lovely loves, your tumults, your marriages,
    aches, and your deaths,
If I poisoned the beginnings of your breaths,
Believe that even in my deliberateness I was not deliberate.

Though why should I whine,
Whine that the crime was other than mine?—
Since anyhow you are dead.
Or rather, or instead,
You were never made.
But that too, I am afraid,
Is faulty: oh, what shall I say, how is the truth to be said?
You were born, you had body, you died.
It is just that you never giggled or planned or cried.

Believe me, I loved you all.   3
Believe me, I knew you, though faintly, and I loved, I loved
    you
All.

Sallie Tisdale

We Do Abortions Here

*A registered nurse and writer, Tisdale (born 1957) has pub-
lished two books about the nursing profession,* The Sorcerer's
Apprentice: Medical Miracles and Other Disasters *(1986) and*
Harvest Moon: Portrait of a Nursing Home *(1987), as well as*
Lot's Wife: Salt and the Human Condition *(1988). (She has
also published a book on the issue of pornography,* Talk Dirty
to Me, *and she writes frequently for* Tricycle, *a Zen Buddhist
publication.) In the following essay, published in 1987 in*
Harper's *magazine (a prestigious forum for discussions of
American culture and politics), Tisdale describes her experiences as a nurse in an abortion clinic. Does her essay take a
position on the abortion question?*

We do abortions here; that is all we do. There are weary,   1
grim moments when I think I cannot bear another basin of
bloody remains, utter another kind phrase of reassurance. So
I leave the procedure room in the back and reach for a new
chart. Soon I am talking to an eighteen-year-old woman pregnant for the fourth time. I push up her sleeve to check her
blood pressure and find row upon row of needle marks, neat
and parallel and discolored. She has been so hungry for her

drug for so long that she has taken to using the loose skin of her upper arms; her elbows are already a permanent ruin of bruises. She is surprised to find herself nearly four months pregnant. I suspect she is often surprised, in a mild way, by the blows she is dealt. I prepare myself for another basin, another brief and chafing loss.

2   "How can you stand it?" Even the clients ask. They see the machine, the strange instruments, the blood, the final stroke that wipes away the promise of pregnancy. Sometimes I see that too: I watch a woman's swollen abdomen sink to softness in a few stuttering moments and my own belly flip-flops with sorrow. But all it takes for me to catch my breath is another interview, one more story that sounds so much like the last one. There is a numbing sameness lurking in this job: the same questions, the same answers, even the same trembling tone in the voices. The worst is the sameness of human failure, of inadequacy in the face of each day's dull demands.

3   In describing this work, I find it difficult to explain how much I enjoy it most of the time. We laugh a lot here, as friends and as professional peers. It's nice to be with women all day. I like the sudden, transient bonds I forge with some clients: moments when I am in my strength, remembering weakness, and a woman in weakness reaches out for my strength. What I offer is not power, but solidness, offered almost eagerly. Certain clients waken in me every tender urge I have—others make me wince and bite my tongue. Both challenge me to find a balance. It is a sweet brutality we practice here, a stark and loving dispassion.

4   I look at abortion as if I am standing on a cliff with a telescope, gazing at some great vista. I can sweep the horizon with both eyes, survey the scene in all its distance and size. Or I can put my eye to the lens and focus on the small details, suddenly so close. In abortion the absolute must always be tempered by the contextual, because both are real, both valid, both hard. How can we do this? How can we refuse? Each abortion is a measure of our failure to protect, to nourish our own. Each basin I empty is a promise—but a promise broken a long time ago.

5   I grew up on the great promise of birth control. Like many women my age, I took the pill as soon as I was sexually active. To risk pregnancy when it was so easy to avoid seemed stupid, and my contraceptive success, as it were, was part of the promise of social enlightenment. But birth control fails, far more frequently than laboratory trials predict. Many of our clients take the pill; its failure to protect them is a shocking

realization. We have clients who have been sterilized, whose husbands have had vasectomies; each one is a statistical misfit, fine print come to life. The anger and shame of these women I hold in one hand, and the basin in the other. The distance between the two, the length I pace and try to measure, is the size of an abortion.

The procedure is disarmingly simple. Women are surprised, as though the mystery of conception, a dark and hidden genesis, requires an elaborate finale. In the first trimester of pregnancy, it's a mere few minutes of vacuuming, a neat tidying up. I give a woman a small yellow Valium, and when it has begun to relax her, I lead her into the back, into bareness, the stirrups. The doctor reaches in her, opening the narrow tunnel to the uterus with a succession of slim, smooth bars of steel. He inserts a plastic tube and hooks it to a hose on the machine. The woman is framed against white paper that crackles as she moves, the light bright in her eyes. Then the machine rumbles low and loud in the small windowless room; the doctor moves the tube back and forth with an efficient rhythm, and the long tail of it fills with blood that spurts and stumbles along into a jar. He is usually finished in a few minutes. They are long minutes for the woman; her uterus frequently reacts to its abrupt emptying with a powerful, unceasing cramp, which cuts off the blood vessels and enfolds the irritated, bleeding tissue. 6

I am learning to recognize the shadows that cross the faces of the women I hold. While the doctor works between her spread legs, the paper drape hiding his intent expression, I stand beside the table. I hold the woman's hands in mine, resting them just below her ribs. I watch her eyes, finger her necklace, stroke her hair. I ask about her job, her family; in a haze she answers me; we chatter, faces close, eyes meeting and sliding apart. 7

I watch the shadows that creep up unnoticed and suddenly darken her face as she screws up her features and pushes a tear out each side to slide down her cheeks. I have learned to anticipate the quiver of chin, the rapid intake of breath, and the surprising sobs that rise soon after the machine starts to drum. I know this is when the cramp deepens, and the tears are partly the tears that follow pain—the sharp, childish crying when one bumps one's head on a cabinet door. But a well of woe seems to open beneath many women when they hear that thumping sound. The anticipation of the moment has finally come to fruit; the moment has arrived when the loss is no longer an imagined one. It has come true. 8

9   I am struck with the sameness and I am struck every day
by the variety here—how this commonplace dilemma can so
display the differences of women. A twenty-one-year-old
woman, unemployed, uneducated, without family, in the fifth
month of her fifth pregnancy. A forty-two-year-old mother of
teenagers, shocked by her condition, refusing to tell her husband. A twenty-three-year-old mother of two having her seventh abortion, and many women in their thirties having their
first. Some are stoic, some hysterical, a few giggle uncontrol-
lably, many cry.

10   I talk to a sixteen-year-old uneducated girl who was raped.
She has gonorrhea. She describes blinding headaches, attacks
of breathlessness, nausea. "Sometimes I feel like two different
people," she tells me with a calm smile, "and I talk to myself."

11   I pull out my plastic models. She listens patiently for a time,
and then holds her hands wide in front of her stomach.

12   "When's the baby going to go up into my stomach?" she
asks.

13   I blink. "What do you mean?"

14   "Well," she says, still smiling, "when women get so big, isn't
the baby in your stomach? Doesn't it hatch out of an egg
there?"

15   My first question in an interview is always the same. As I
walk down the hall with the woman, as we get settled in
chairs and I glance through her files, I am trying to gauge her,
to get a sense of the words, and the tone, I should use. With
some I joke, with others I chat, sometimes fall into a brisk,
business-line patter. But I ask every woman, "Are you sure
you want to have an abortion?" Most nod with grim knowing
smiles. "Oh, yes," they sigh. Some seek forgiveness, offer
excuses. Occasionally a woman will flinch and say, "Please
don't use that word."

16   Later I describe the procedure to come, using care with my
language. I don't say "pain" any more than I would say
"baby." So many are afraid to ask how much it will hurt. "My
sister told me—" I hear. "A friend of mine said—" and the dire
expectations unravel. I prick the index finger of a woman for
a drop of blood to test, and as the tiny lancet approaches the
skin she averts her eyes, holding her trembling hand out to
me and jumping at my touch.

17   It is when I am holding a plastic uterus in one hand, a suction tube in the other, moving them together in imitation of
the scrubbing to come, that women ask the most secret question. I am speaking in a matter-of-fact voice about "the tissue"
and "the contents" when the woman suddenly catches my eye

and asks, "How big is the baby now?" These words suggest a quiet need for a definition of the boundaries being drawn. It isn't so odd, after all, that she feels relief when I describe the growing bud's bulbous shape, its miniature nature. Again I gauge, and sometimes lie a little, weaseling around its infantile features until its clinging power slackens.

But when I look in the basin, among the curdlike blood 18 clots, I see an elfin thorax, attenuated, its pencilline ribs all in parallel rows with tiny knobs of spine rounding upwards. The translucent arm and hand swim beside.

A sleepy-eyed girl, just fourteen, watched me with a slight 19 and goofy smile all through her abortion. "Does it have little feet and little fingers and all?" she'd asked earlier. When the suction was over she sat up woozily at the end of the table and murmured, "Can I see it?" I shook my head firmly.

"It's not allowed," I told her sternly, because I knew she 20 didn't really want to see what was left. She accepted this statement of authority, and a shadow of confused relief crossed her plain, pale face.

Privately, even grudgingly, my colleagues might admit the 21 power of abortion to provoke emotion. But they seem to prefer the broad view and disdain the telescope. Abortion is a matter of choice, privacy, control. Its uncertainty lies in specific cases: retarded women and girls too young to give consent for surgery, women who are ill or hostile or psychotic. Such common dilemmas are met with both compassion and impatience; they slow things down. We are too busy to chew over ethics. One person might discuss certain concerns, behind closed doors, or describe a particularly disturbing dream. But generally there is to be no ambivalence.

Every day I take calls from women who are annoyed that 22 we cannot see them, cannot do their abortion today, this morning, now. They argue the price, demand that we stay after hours to accommodate their job or class schedule. Abortion is so routine that one expects it to be like a manicure: quick, cheap, and painless.

Still, I've cultivated a certain disregard. It isn't negligence, 23 but I don't always pay attention. I couldn't be here if I tried to judge each case on its merits; after all, we do over a hundred abortions a week. At some point each individual in this line of work draws a boundary and adheres to it. For one physician the boundary is a particular week of gestation; for another, it is a certain number of repeated abortions. But these boundaries can be fluid too: one physician overruled his own limit to abort a mature but severely malformed fetus. For me, the limit is allowing my clients to carry their own burden, shoulder the responsibility themselves. I shoulder the burden of trying not to judge them.

24   This city has several "crisis pregnancy centers" advertised in the Yellow Pages. They are small offices staffed by volunteers, and they offer free pregnancy testing, glossy photos of dead fetuses, and movies. I had a client recently whose mother is active in the antiabortion movement. The young woman went to the local crisis center and was told that the doctor would make her touch the dismembered baby, that the pain would be the most horrible she could imagine, and that she might, after an abortion, never be able to have children. All lies. They called her at home and at work, over and over and over, but she had been wise enough to give a false name. She came to us a fugitive. We who do abortions are marked, by some, as impure. It's dirty work.

25   When a delivery man comes to the sliding glass window by the reception desk and tilts a box toward me, I hesitate. I read the packing slip, assess the shape and weight of the box in the light of its supposed contents. We request familiar faces. The doors are carefully locked; I have learned to half glance around at bags and boxes, looking for a telltale sign. I register with security when I arrive, and I am careful not to bang a door. We are a little on edge here.

26   Concern about size and shape seem to be natural, and so is the relief that follows. We make the powerful assumption that the fetus is different from us, and even when we admit the similarities, it is too simplistic to be seduced by form alone. But the form is enormously potent—humanoid, powerless, palm-sized, and pure, it evokes an almost fierce tenderness when viewed simply as what it appears to be. But appearance, and even potential, aren't enough. The fetus, in becoming itself, can ruin others: its utter dependence has a sinister side. When I am struck in the moment by the contents in the basin, I am careful to remember the context, to note the tearful teenager and the woman sighing with something more than relief. One kind of question, though, I find considerably trickier.

27   "Can you tell what it is?" I am asked, and this means gender. This question is asked by couples, not women alone. Always couples would abort a girl and keep a boy. I have been asked about twins, and even if I could tell what race the father was.

28   An eighteen-year-old woman with three daughters brought her husband to the interview. He glared first at me, then at his

wife, as he sank lower and lower in the chair, picking his teeth with a toothpick. He interrupted a conversation with his wife to ask if I could tell whether the baby would be a boy or a girl. I told him I could not.

"Good," he replied in a slow and strangely malevolent   29
voice, "'cause if it was a boy I'd wring her neck."

In a literal sense, abortion exists because we are able to ask   30
such questions, able to assign a value to the fetus which can shift with changing circumstances. If the human bond to a child were as primitive and unflinchingly narrow as that of other animals, there would be no abortion. There would be no abortion because there would be nothing more important than caring for the young and perpetuating the species, no reason for sex but to make babies. I sense this sometimes, this wordless organic duty, when I do ultrasounds.

We do ultrasound, a sound-wave test that paints a faint,   31
gray picture of the fetus, whenever we're uncertain of gestation. Age is measured by the width of the skull and confirmed by the length of the femur or thighbone; we speak of a pregnancy as being a certain "femur length" in weeks. The usual concern is whether a pregnancy is within the legal limit for an abortion. Women this far along have bellies which swell out round and tight like trim muscles. When they lie flat, the mound rises softly above the hips, pressing the umbilicus upward.

It takes practice to read an ultrasound picture, which is   32
grainy and etched as though in strokes of charcoal. But suddenly a rapid rhythmic motion appears—the beating heart. Nearby is a soft oval, scratched with lines—the skull. The leg is harder to find, and then suddenly the fetus moves, bobbing in the surf. The skull turns away, an arm slides across the screen, the torso rolls. I know the weight of a baby's head on my shoulder, the whisper of lips on ears, the delicate curve of a fragile spine in my hand. I know how heavy and correct a newborn cradled feels. The creature I watch in secret requires nothing from me but to be left alone, and that is precisely what won't be done.

These inadvertently made beings are caught in a twisting   33
web of motive and desire. They are at least inconvenient, sometimes quite literally dangerous in the womb, but most often they fall somewhere in between—consequences never quite believed in come to roost. Their virtue rises and falls outside their own nature: they become only what we make them. A fetus created by accident is the most absolute kind of surprise. Whether the blame lies in a failed IUD, a slipped

condom, or a false impression of safety, that fetus is a thing whose creation has been actively worked against. Its existence is an error. I think this is why so few women, even late in pregnancy, will consider giving a baby up for adoption. To do so means making the fetus real—imagining it as something whole and outside oneself. The decision to terminate a pregnancy is sometimes so difficult and confounding that it creates an enormous demand for immediate action. The decision is rejection; the pregnancy has become something to be rid of, a condition to be ended. It is a burden, a weight, a thing separate.

34   Women have abortions because they are too old, and too young, too poor, and too rich, too stupid, and too smart. I see women who berate themselves with violent emotions for their first and only abortion, and others who return three times, five times, hauling two or three children, who cannot remember to take a pill or where they put the diaphragm. We talk glibly about choice. But the choice for what? I see all the broken promises in lives lived like a series of impromptu obstacles. There are the sweet, light promises of love and intimacy, the glittering promise of education and progress, the warm promise of safe families, long years of innocence and community. And there is the promise of freedom: freedom from failure, from faithlessness. Freedom from biology. The early feminist defense of abortion asked many questions, but the one I remember is this: is biology destiny? And the answer is yes, sometimes it is. Women who have the fewest choices of all exercise their right to abortion the most.

35   Oh, the ignorance. I take a woman to the back room and ask her to undress; a few minutes later I return and find her positioned discreetly behind a drape, still wearing underpants. "Do I have to take these off too?" she asks, a little shocked. Some swear they have not had sex. Many do not know what a uterus is, how sperm and egg meet, how sex makes babies. Some late seekers do not believe themselves pregnant; they believe themselves *impregnable*. I was chastised when I began this job for referring to some clients as girls: it is a feminist heresy. They come so young, snapping gum, sockless and sneakered, and their shakily applied eyeliner smears when they cry. I call them girls with maternal benignity. I cannot imagine them as mothers.

36   The doctor seats himself between the woman's thighs and reaches into the dilated opening of a five-month pregnant uterus. Quickly he grabs and crushes the fetus in several

places, and the room is filled with a low clatter and snap of forceps, the click of the tanaculum,[1] and a pulling, sucking sound. The paper crinkles as the drugged and sleepy woman shifts, the nurse's low, honey-brown voice explains each step in delicate words.

I have fetus dreams, we all do here: dreams of abortions one after the other; of buckets of blood splashed on the walls; trees full of crawling fetuses. I dreamed that two men grabbed me and began to drag me away: "Let's do an abortion," they said with a sickening leer, and I began to scream, plunged into a vision of sucking, scraping pain, of being spread and torn by impartial instruments that do only what they are bidden. I woke from this dream barely able to breathe and thought of kitchen tables and coat hangers, knitting needles striped with blood, and women all alone clutching a pillow in their teeth to keep the screams from piercing the apartment-house walls. Abortion is the narrowest edge between kindness and cruelty. Done as well as it can be, it is still violence—merciful violence, like putting a suffering animal to death.   37

Maggie, one of the nurses, received a call at midnight not long ago. It was a woman in her twentieth week of pregnancy; the necessarily gradual process of cervical dilation begun the day before had stimulated labor, as it sometimes does. Maggie and one of the doctors met the woman at the office in the night. Maggie helped her onto the table, and as she lay down the fetus was delivered into Maggie's hands. When Maggie told me about it the next day, she cupped her hands into a small bowl—"It was just like a little kitten," she said softly, wonderingly. "Everything was still attached."   38

At the end of the day I clean out the suction jars, pouring blood into the sink, splashing the sides with flecks of tissue. From the sink rises a rich and humid smell, hot, earthy, and moldering; it is the smell of something recently alive beginning to decay. I take care of the plastic tub on the floor, filled with pieces too big to be trusted to the trash. The law defines the contents of the bucket I hold protectively against my chest as "tissue." Some would say my complicity in filling that bucket gives me no right to call it anything else. I slip the tissue gently into a bag and place it in the freezer, to be burned at another time. Abortion requires of me an entirely new set of assumptions. It requires a willingness to live with conflict,   39

[1]A type of sharp forceps used on bleeding arteries.

fearlessness, and grief. As I close the freezer door, I imagine a world where this won't be necessary, and then return to the world where it is.

Mary Meehan

A Pro-Life View from the Left

Mary Meehan has written many articles on various topics for respected newspapers and periodicals such as The Nation, The Washington Monthly, *and* The Washington Post. *In 1980, she contributed the following article to* The Progressive, *a monthly magazine that, true to its name, takes a liberal stance toward current public issues.*

1   The abortion issue, more than most, illustrates the occasional tendency of the Left to become so enthusiastic over what is called a "reform" that it forgets to think the issue through. It is ironic that so many on the Left have done on abortion what conservatives and Cold War liberals did on Vietnam: They marched off in the wrong direction, to fight the wrong war, against the wrong people.

2   Some of us who went through the anti-war struggles of the 1960s and early 1970s are now active in the right-to-life movement. We do not enjoy opposing our old friends on the abortion issue, but we feel that we have no choice. We are moved by what pro-life feminists call the "consistency thing"—the belief that respect for human life demands opposition to abortion, capital punishment, euthanasia, and war. We don't think we have either the luxury or the right to choose some types of killing and say that they are all right, while others are not. A human life is a human life; and if equality means anything, it means that society may not value some human lives over others.

3   Until the last decade, people on the Left and Right generally agreed on one rule: We all protected the young. This was not merely agreement on an ethical question: It was also an expression of instinct, so deep and ancient that it scarcely required explanation.

Protection of the young included protection of the unborn, 4
for abortion was forbidden by state laws throughout the
United States. Those laws reflected an ethical consensus, not
based solely on religious tradition but also on scientific evidence that human life begins at conception. The prohibition
of abortion in the ancient Hippocratic Oath is well known.
Less familiar to many is the Oath of Geneva, formulated by
the World Medical Association in 1948, which included these
words: "I will maintain the utmost respect for human life from
the time of conception." A Declaration of the Rights of the
Child, adopted by the United Nations General Assembly in
1959, declared that "the child, by reason of his physical and
mental immaturity, needs special safeguards and care, including appropriate legal protection, before as well as after birth."

It is not my purpose to explain why courts and parliaments 5
in many nations rejected this tradition over the past few
decades, though I suspect their action was largely a surrender
to technical achievement—if such inventions as suction aspi-
rators can be called technical achievements. But it is important to ask why the Left in the United States generally
accepted legalized abortion.

One factor was the popular civil-libertarian rationale for 6
freedom of choice in abortion. Many feminists presented it as
a right of women to control their own bodies. When the
objection was raised that abortion ruins *another person's*
body, they respond that a) it is not a body, just a "blob of pro-
toplasm" (thereby displaying ignorance of biology); or b) it is
not really a "person" until it is born. When it was suggested
that this is a wholly arbitrary decision, unsupported by any
biological evidence, they said, "Well, that's your point of view.
This is a matter of individual conscience, and in a pluralistic
society people must be free to follow their consciences."

Unfortunately, many liberals and radicals accepted this 7
view without further question. Perhaps many did not know
that an eight-week-old fetus has a fully human form. They did
not ask whether American slaveholders before the Civil War
were right in viewing blacks as less than human and as private property; or whether the Nazis were correct in viewing
mental patients, Jews, and Gypsies as less than human and
therefore subject to the final solution.

Class issues provided another rationale. In the late 1960s, 8
liberals were troubled by evidence that rich women could
obtain abortions regardless of the law, by going to careful
society doctors or to countries where abortion was legal.

Why, they asked, should poor women be barred from something the wealthy could have? One might turn this argument on its head by asking why rich children should be denied protection that poor children have.

9   But pro-life activists did not want abortion to be a class issue one way or the other; they wanted to end abortion everywhere, for all classes. And many people who had experienced poverty did not think providing legal abortion was any favor to poor women. Thus, in 1972, when a Presidential commission on population growth recommended legalized abortion, partly to remove discrimination against poor women, several commission members dissented.

10   One was Graciela Olivarez, a Chicana who was active in civil rights and anti-poverty work. Olivarez, who later was named to head the Federal Government's Community Services Administration, had known poverty in her youth in the Southwest. With a touch of bitterness, she said in her dissent, "The poor cry out for justice and equality and we respond with legalized abortion." Olivarez noted that blacks and Chicanos had often been unwanted by white society. She added, "I believe that in a society that permits the life of even one individual (born or unborn) to be dependent on whether that life is 'wanted' or not, all its citizens stand in danger." Later she told the press, "We do not have equal opportunities. Abortion is a cruel way out."

11   Many liberals were also persuaded by a church/state argument that followed roughly this line: "Opposition to abortion is a religious viewpoint, particularly a Catholic viewpoint. The Catholics have no business imposing their religious views on the rest of us." It is true that opposition to abortion is a religious position for many people. Orthodox Jews, Mormons, and many of the fundamentalist Protestant groups also oppose abortion. (So did the mainstream Protestant churches until recent years.) But many people are against abortion for reasons that are independent of religious authority or belief. Many would still be against abortion if they lost their faith; others are opposed to it after they *have* lost their faith, or if they never had any faith. Only if their non-religious grounds for opposition can be proven baseless could legal prohibition of abortion fairly be called an establishment of religion. The pro-abortion forces concentrate heavily on religious arguments against abortion and generally ignore the secular arguments—possibly because they cannot answer them.

12   Still another, more emotional reason is that so many conservatives oppose abortion. Many liberals have difficulty

accepting the idea that Jesse Helms can be right about *any-thing*. I do not quite understand this attitude. Just by the law of averages, he has to be right about something, sometime. Standing at the March for Life rally at the U.S. Capitol last year, and hearing Senator Helms say that "We reject the philosophy that life should be only for the planned, the perfect, or the privileged," I thought he was making a good civil-rights statement.

If much of the leadership of the pro-life movement is right-   13
wing, that is due largely to the default of the Left. We "little people" who marched against the war and now march against abortion would like to see leaders of the Left speaking out on behalf of the unborn. But we see only a few, such as Dick Gregory, Mark Hatfield, Jesse Jackson, Richard Neuhaus, Mary Rose Oakar. Most of the others either avoid the issue or support abortion. We are dismayed by their inconsistency. And we are not impressed by arguments that we should work and vote for them because they are good on such issues as food stamps and medical care.

Although many liberals and radicals accepted legalized   14
abortion, there are signs of uneasiness about it. Tell someone who supports it that you have many problems with the issue, and she is likely to say, quickly, "Oh, I don't think I could ever have one myself, but...." or "I'm really not pro-*abortion*; I'm pro-*choice*" or "I'm *personally* opposed to it, but...."

Why are they personally opposed to it if there is nothing   15
wrong with it?

Perhaps such uneasiness is a sign that many on the Left   16
are ready to take another look at the abortion issue. In the hope of contributing toward a new perspective, I offer the following points:

First, it is out of character for the Left to neglect the weak   17
and helpless. The traditional mark of the Left has been its protection of the underdog, the weak, and the poor. The unborn child is the most helpless form of humanity, even more in need of protection than the poor tenant farmer or the mental patient or the boat people on the high seas. The basic instinct of the Left is to aid those who cannot aid themselves—and that instinct is absolutely sound. It is what keeps the human proposition going.

Second, the right to life underlies and sustains every other   18
right we have. It is, as Thomas Jefferson and his friends said, self-evident. Logically, as well as in our Declaration of Independence, it comes before the right to liberty and the right to property. The right to exist, to be free from assault by others,

is the basis of equality. Without it, the other rights are meaningless, and life becomes a sort of warfare in which force
decides everything. There is no equality, because one person's
convenience takes precedence over another's life, provided
only that the first person has more power. If we do not protect
this right for everyone, it is not guaranteed for everyone,
because anyone can become weak and vulnerable to assault.

19   *Third,* abortion is a civil-rights issue. Dick Gregory and
many other blacks view abortion as a type of genocide. Confirmation of this comes in the experience of pro-life activists
who find open bigotry when they speak with white voters
about public funding of abortion. Many white voters believe
abortion is a solution for the welfare problem and a way to
slow the growth of the black population. I worked two years
ago for a liberal, pro-life candidate who was appalled by the
number of anti-black comments he found when discussing
the issue. And Representative Robert Dornan of California, a
conservative pro-life leader, once told his colleagues in the
House, "I have heard many rock-ribbed Republicans brag
about how fiscally conservative they are and then tell me that
I was an idiot on the abortion issue." When he asked why,
said Dornan, they whispered, "Because we have to hold them
down, we have to stop the population growth." Dornan elaborated: "To them, population growth means blacks, Puerto
Ricans, or other Latins," or anyone who "should not be having more than a polite one or two 'burdens on society.'"

20   *Fourth,* abortion exploits women. Many women are pressured by spouses, lovers, or parents into having abortions
they do not want. Sometimes the coercion is subtle, as when
a husband complains of financial problems. Sometimes it is
open and crude, as when a boyfriend threatens to end the
affair unless the woman has an abortion, or when parents
order a minor child to have an abortion. Pro-life activists who
do "clinic counseling" (standing outside abortion clinics, trying to speak to each woman who enters, urging her to have
the child) report that many women who enter clinics alone
are willing to talk and to listen. Some change their minds and
decide against abortion. But a woman who is accompanied
by someone else often does not have the chance to talk,
because the husband or boyfriend or parent is so hostile to
the pro-life worker.

2i   Juli Loesch, a feminist/pacifist writer, notes that feminists
want to have men participate more in the care of children,
but abortion allows a man to shift total responsibility to the
woman: "He can *buy* his way out of accountability by making

'The Offer' for 'The Procedure.'" She adds that the man's sexual role "then implies—exactly nothing: no relationship. How quickly a 'woman's right to choose' comes to serve a 'man's right to use.'" And Daphne de Jong, a New Zealand feminist, says, "If women must submit to abortion to preserve their lifestyle or career, their economic or social status, they are pandering to a system devised and run by men for male convenience." She adds, "Of all the things which are done to women to fit them into a society dominated by men, abortion is the most violent invasion of their physical and psychic integrity. It is a deeper and more destructive assault than rape. . . ."

Loesch, de Jong, Olivarez, and other pro-life feminists believe men should bear a much greater share of the burdens of child-rearing than they do at present. And de Jong makes a radical point when she says, "Accepting short-term solutions like abortion only delays the implementation of real reforms like decent maternity and paternity leaves, job protection, high-quality child care, community responsibility for dependent people of all ages, and recognition of the economic contribution of childminders." Olivarez and others have also called for the development of safer and more effective contraceptives for both men and women. In her 1972 dissent, Olivarez noted with irony that "medical science has developed four different ways for killing a fetus, but has not yet developed a safe-for-all-to-use contraceptive." 22

Fifth, abortion is an escape from an obligation that is owed to another. Doris Gordon, Coordinator of Libertarians for Life, puts it this way: "Unborn children don't cause women to become pregnant but parents cause their children to be in the womb, and as a result, they need parental care. As a general principle, if we are the cause of another's need for care, as when we cause an accident, we acquire an obligation to that person as a result. . . . We have no right to kill in order to terminate any obligation." 23

Sixth, abortion brutalizes those who perform it, undergo it, pay for it, profit from it, and allow it to happen. Too many of us look the other way because we do not want to think about abortion. A part of reality is blocked out because one does not want to see broken bodies coming home, or going to an incinerator, in those awful plastic bags. People deny their own humanity when they refuse to identify with, or even acknowledge, the pain of others. 24

With some it is worse: They are making money from the misery of others, from exploited women and dead children. 25

Doctors, businessmen, and clinic directors are making a great deal of money from abortion. Jobs and high incomes depend on abortion; it's part of the gross national product. The parallels of this with the military-industrial complex should be obvious to anyone who was involved in the anti-war movement.

26   And the "slippery slope" argument is right: People really do go from accepting abortion to accepting euthanasia and accepting "triage" for the world hunger problem and accepting "lifeboat ethics" as a general guide to human behavior. We slip down the slope, back to the jungle.

27   To save the smallest children, and to save its own conscience, the Left should speak out against abortion.

Sally Quinn

Our Choices, Ourselves

Sally Quinn (born 1941), a novelist, a writer for The Washington Post *since 1969, and a well-known and respected Washington "insider," contributed the following article to the* Post *in April 1992.*

1   When I was in college, a classmate told a group of us about a friend who had gotten pregnant and had been too scared to tell anyone. Now she was almost eight months along and showing. She had found someone to perform an abortion for her (illegal, of course; this was 1963) and was agonizing over what to do. She should definitely have the abortion, we all agreed. There was really no other choice.

2   When I think now how sanguine we all were about our position on aborting an 8-month-old, presumably normal, fetus it makes me shudder. A fetus, we figured, was just that— a fetus—until it came out of the mother's body; and up until that time, even at nine months, it was okay to abort it.

3   Thinking about that also makes me realize how far we've come in terms of our awareness of the complexity of the abortion issue. And thinking about it on a day like today, when tens of thousands of abortion rights advocates hold their

March for Women's Lives here, makes me realize how far we
have to go.

For me, today's protest, sponsored by the National Organi-   4
zation for Women and other groups, is a reminder that the
biggest problem with the abortion issue today is the nearly
absolute polarization of both sides. Like a marriage on the
rocks, the two sides have hardened their positions. The sad
thing is that most American women fall somewhere in
between but are driven by politics to adopt rigid views.

Part of the problem is the labels. Those who are against   5
abortion call themselves "pro-life" and refer to their opponents as "pro-abortion." On the other side are the abortion-
rights advocates who refer to those who oppose abortion as
"antiabortion" and "anti-choice."

The "label war" is out of balance. I can't understand how   6
people who oppose abortion rights managed to wrest away
the "pro-life" label. In the same way that conservatives
managed to appropriate the American flag, the position of
caring about human life has been virtually surrendered. But I
am for abortion rights, and I am as much—if not more—pro-
life as anyone. And I won't give that away.

The polarization gets intense because the antiabortion   7
people start with the position that abortion is murder. It's that
simple, they say. From the moment of conception, from the
second that the egg is fertilized by the sperm, it becomes a
human life. Period.

Of course, no one then acts as if the fetus is a human life.   8
The IRS does not let us count the fetus as a dependent. No
one to my knowledge has ever suggested that a fetus ought to
be baptized. And so on.

The fact is that most women are extremely conflicted about   9
the idea of abortion, particularly late-term abortions; even a
National Abortion Rights League spokeswoman will say, as
she did late last week, "We don't love abortion." Anyone who
has been pregnant can tell you that after you have felt that
quickening in your womb, after a fetus has kicked in your
belly, the very idea of abortion becomes painfully difficult.

Yet every woman who has amniocentesis or a chorionic vil-   10
lus sampling (a similar, but earlier test) does it because she at
least entertains the possibility of having an abortion if something is wrong with the fetus. One reason so many women opt
for the CVS (despite the greater risk of miscarriage) is that
they can't bear the idea of a late abortion. An amnio cannot
give you results until the fetus is almost five months old. At

five months, an abortion is, in effect, the delivery of a dead baby. You don't need the label "pro-life" to know that.

11 The single worst month of my life was the month between the time I had the amnio and the time I got the results. All the time, my child was kicking in my stomach. He was a part of me by then. I had invested so much in him that the idea of losing him was unthinkable.

12 All the choices were unthinkable. Modern-day tests like amnios and sonograms can tell you many abnormalities that could show up. They range in severity from anencephaly (being born without a brain, like the child in Florida last week), to Marfan syndrome, a connective tissue disorder that Abraham Lincoln may have had. Down syndrome is a major reason for an amnio, especially in older women. Spina bifida is revealed by a blood test. Both have varying degrees of severity.

13 As I lay in my bed each night, I was haunted by the idea of my child having any one of hundreds of possible defects. What would I do if.... If the diagnosed deformity were severe, the decision was obvious to me. In the case of less crippling defects, the decision would be heartwrenchingly confusing. None was easy.

14 Heart defects don't show up on the amnio, and my son was born with a heart defect. Most heart defects are easily repaired and the children go on to lead normal lives. Today, the defect is detectable by sonogram and women can choose to abort. Knowing what joy our son has brought to us, that would be unthinkable. And unbearable.

15 I had a friend whose amnio revealed that her baby would be born with severe defects. She decided to abort. She's never been the same since. And she never had another child.

16 The antiabortion people, meanwhile, have painted supporters of abortion rights as murderers, a bunch of sex-crazed women who don't want to suffer the consequences of their actions and don't give a damn about human life. But that is, of course, a fantasy. The reality is that favoring abortion rights is not the same as favoring abortion. It means you are concerned about privacy. It means you don't want someone else to impose his or her views—personal, political or religious—on you. According to the latest *Washington Post* survey, 57 percent of American women favor abortion rights—a figure that has been fairly consistent over the years.

17 At least half of my friends have had abortions at some time in their lives, and I'll bet that is not an unusual statistic for most American women of my age. It has always been scary

and sad. People are always surprised at how difficult emotionally it can be. And this is when it is safe and legal; there are about 1.6 million abortions performed each year in the United States.

In the days when abortion was unsafe and illegal (and the annual death rate was in the thousands), several of my mother's friends died from botched abortions. Some of these were already mothers—some with several children. I had friends who couldn't have children after badly botched abortions. I had a beautiful and brilliant friend in college who was afraid of an illegal abortion. She went to a home for unwed mothers and gave her baby up for adoption. She has been in and out of mental institutions ever since.   18

Even a few years ago, it was thought that only bad girls and actresses got pregnant out of wedlock. And not so long ago, I would have had an abortion if I'd gotten pregnant before marriage. There were times when I thought I was pregnant. The fear was indescribable. Even after abortion was legal, the fear was indescribable.   19

Though I believe in choice, it is perfectly understandable to me that some people do not believe that abortion is ever justified. Many Catholics hold this view. I have a Catholic friend who told me that they would not choose to have amniocentesis if his wife got pregnant because "I don't know whether or not I would have the strength to make the right decision if something turned out wrong."   20

Such people may even believe that abortion is akin to murder. But they're not prepared to accuse others whose opinions differ of committing murder.   21

Of course this "pro-life" position is not consistent. If it is murder, and it's premeditated, shouldn't the punishment be the same as for any murder conviction? And for those "pro-life" people in favor of the death penalty, shouldn't any mother who willingly aborts a child be put to death? Hanged by the neck until dead, fried in the chair, given an injection? And that goes for the doctor who performs the abortion, and anyone who aids it.   22

It's either murder or it ain't. You can't have it both ways.   23

Particularly specious are those who say abortion is murder but it's okay in the case of rape or incest.   24

Excuse me? The innocent "child" is murdered because it had the unfortunate luck of being conceived illegally? Does the manner of conception make the child any less human? By this reasoning, a 5-year-old who is discovered to have been conceived in incest could be put to death.   25

26   There are many reasons why someone may choose to abort. Rape or incest, birth defects, poverty, illness, a mother either too young or too old.

27   But there are other more subtle reasons too. If a mother feels unprepared, emotionally or psychologically or physically, whose decision should it be? Who, after all, will live with the consequences?

28   Often that decision to abort is nothing less than a pro-life decision. Anyone who has walked through a neo-natal ward in a hospital and seen the half-pound "babies" with dark glasses on and tubes coming out every pore, crack babies, AIDS babies, abandoned babies and babies who will grow up to be retarded or profoundly emotionally disturbed, can't help wondering about the quality of life these children will have.

29   It seems to me that those who are pro-choice may know what lies in store for these children—and care more about life than many of those who call themselves "pro-life."

30   If the abortion question had not so polarized America, the two "sides" might be better able to talk about such questions. But I get the impression that many antiabortion or "pro-life" advocates, for all their talk of "ethics" and "morality," have little concern for what happens to the babies after they are born. The mere fact of life is their only concern. But who will shoulder the financial and emotional burdens of these "lives"? Once it's a "life" they lose interest.

31   Meanwhile, a question haunts all of us who are in favor of abortion rights: When does life begin, anyway?

32   Under the *Roe* v. *Wade* ruling, a woman has virtually unrestricted access to abortion in the first trimester, may be subject to specific regulations in the second trimester and can be barred (except when it affects maternal health) in the third. This Solomon-like decision seems a proper way to look at it. On the one hand, I don't want anyone telling me what to do with my body; on the other, I have difficulty with the concept of aborting a 9-month-old fetus. I'm not ready to call it murder, but I have grave doubts.

33   But I don't like to admit any hesitancy or doubt. I fear being pounced on by those who will take my lack of conviction—my unwillingness to dig my heels in—as agreement with antiabortion advocates.

34   A 9-month-old fetus can certainly live independently. So, in some cases, can a 7-month-old fetus. Is it all right to kill the fetus inside the mother's body? I think not.

Catherine Stern aborted her 7-month-old fetus when she   35
learned it had no arms and legs and was possibly brain-dam-
aged. Would I have done that? Yes, devastating as it would
have been. But the consequences of not doing it would have
been worse.

In the future, science may allow us to know far more about   36
a fetus—from her IQ and height to the color of its hair. But
what if the fetus is projected to have an IQ of 80? Or if it were
homely? Would I allow an abortion if it were up to me? What
about choosing to abort if it's the "wrong" sex—already commonplace in some Third World countries, where female
babies are devalued? I find these notions reprehensible, yet
I'm unwilling to say where I would draw the line.

Meanwhile, some people are using abortion as a form of   37
birth control. I know a woman who brags that she's had eight
abortions rather than use contraceptives, which she derides
as "inconvenient." How do I feel about this? The way most
people do, regardless of where they stand on today's march:
Disgusted. Am I prepared to tell her that she can't have more
abortions? The answer is no.

That is how things have become polarized: Some antiabor-   38
tionists have poisoned the well to the point where they have
even made contraception and sex education controversial.
And by taking the position that abortion is murder, they have
forced those of us who believe in abortion rights to take an
equally hard-line position, no matter how bothered we are by
some of the results.

The fact is that you can't reduce this argument to simple   39
choices, and you can't avoid it by simple rules. There are a lot
of issues that women on both sides of the abortion issue
would agree on if they simply were able to admit their honest
doubts, but politics has made it even more divisive.

The First Amendment permits anyone to carry fetuses   40
around in bottles and say, "Is this what you want?" But the
black-and-white nature of the resulting argument destroys
any possibility of commonality of beliefs, or feelings, or emotions or interests.

If most women had the choice, they would acknowledge   41
that one group should not have the power to determine the
lives of another. And ultimately that has to be the way it is.
Ultimately, the debate is not about murder, or even choice,
but the most intimate kind of privacy.

If I got pregnant today, would I have an abortion? I know   42
the answer to that, and it's nobody's business but mine. And
that's the point.

Mike Royko
A Pox on Both Your Houses

Royko (born 1922), a syndicated columnist associated with the Chicago Tribune—*and with Chicago in general, since he worked as a reporter for several Chicago newspapers for many years—wrote the following commentary in July 1992, a few days after the Supreme Court upheld both* Roe v. Wade *and most parts of a controversial Pennsylvania law requiring women desiring an abortion to wait 24 hours, to receive written material on the medical procedure, and, if they are minors, to inform their parents. Mike Royko has won a Pulitzer Prize for social commentary.*

1   "Why are all those women so mad?" asked Slats Grobnik, gesturing at the TV set. "The old man stop for a few after work?"

2   No, it is far more serious than that. They are an anti-abortion group, furious because the Supreme Court has upheld the right of women to get abortions.

3   The TV switched to another angry group of women.

4   "Now what's this bunch mad about? They're yelling louder than the others."

5   They are a pro-abortion group, and they are furious because the Supreme Court has upheld a few restrictions.

6   "Like what?"

7   A 24-hour waiting period. Parental consent for teen-agers. And women being told what their options are, such as adoption, and what kind of medical and financial help is available if she has the baby.

8   "Wait a minute, I don't get it."

9   Get what?

10   "I can see how the anti-abortion crowd would be mad because abortions are still legal, right?"

11   That's what the court said.

12   "Then if they're legal, what's the other side got to beef about?"

13   They don't like any kind of restrictions. They feel it is a threat to their control over their own bodies.

14   "Waiting 24 hours? Nowadays, you got to wait 24 hours for everything. It takes longer than that to get a tooth drilled or your car tuned up. So what's the big rush? And what's wrong

with telling some girl about financial help or that there are people who want to adopt kids?"

They believe that is not society's business to intrude on their right to control their own bodies.   15

"Hey, when the draft board told me I was gonna go fight in Korea, that was messing with my right to control my body, because I guarantee you, I didn't want my body being shot up by no Chinese commies. So I wind up putting in two years with society, by way of the government, telling my body where it's going to go and what it's going to do. If I want to stick a needle in my arm and shoot up with dope, that's illegal. Even though that arm is part of my body right?"   16

Correct.   17

"See, that's what bothers me about this abortion fight. These people don't always make sense."   18

Which side?   19

"Both sides. They're not always, what'ya call it, consistent?"   20

In what way?   21

"Well, the one side says they are pro-life. Now, does that mean that they're against frying someone in the electric chair?"   22

I would doubt that.   23

"That's what I thought, because I know a few of the pro-life ladies and they want to hang 'em high. And were they against us dropping bombs and killing women and children in Iraq because we wanted to put this rich emir back on his throne in Kuwait?"   24

I would guess that they were part of the mainstream of public opinion that delighted in the triumphs of our heroic video war.   25

"That's what I think. So when they say they're pro-life, it all depends on what life, right?"   26

Yes, the unborn.   27

"And don't get me wrong. I don't have any trouble with that. Especially when I read that there's been 26 million abortions in the last 19 years. You know what that works out to on my pocket calculator?"   28

Lots.   29

"Yeah, more than 26,000 a week. About 3,700 a day. About 156 an hour. Almost three a minute. Think about it. Every 20 or 30 seconds, there's an abortion. Are there really that many people whose lives are gonna be ruined if they have a kid? I'm supposed to believe that it's a disaster if they gotta wait 24 hours? Or if someone talks to them about adoption?"   30

31   But it is a question of choice, which is why they call themselves pro-choice.

32   "They don't sound like they're in favor of a choice if they're in a flap because they don't want some young girl to wait 24 hours or to listen to what somebody's got to say about her options. Another thing—how do they feel about frying John Gacy, that serial killer who buried his victims under his house?"

33   What does he have to do with it?

34   "Well, I noticed something. Some women I know who are in favor of abortion are against the death penalty, and that don't make sense to me. How can you be in favor of killing some harmless little thing in a woman's tummy but you get all weepy when they pull the switch on some ax murderer? I don't see how you can be for one and not the other."

35   Well, maybe they believe that the decision as to whether John Gacy is executed should be made by his mother.

36   "Yeah, I guess that makes sense, kind of a pro-choice thing."

37   Right. So, where do you stand?

38   "On what?"

39   Abortion. Are you for it or against it?

40   "Forget it. If I say I'm against, then they'll say I'm in favor of killing women, right?

41   It wouldn't surprise me.

42   "And if I'm for it, they'll say I'm a baby-killer, right?"

43   Almost a certainty.

44   "So you're not gonna corner me. There's one thing I'm sure of, though. We got to check on the diets of American women."

45   What do their diets have to do with it?

46   "If there's been 26 million abortions over the last 19 years, they should try eating more brain foods."

GAY, LESBIAN, AND BISEXUAL RIGHTS

Michael Cunningham

Taking the Census
of Queer Nation

Michael Cunningham is a member of the gay rights group Act
Up. *A writer of fiction and nonfiction, he contributed the following essay to* Mother Jones *in the summer of 1992.* Mother
Jones, *published bimonthly, is a liberal, irreverent magazine of
commentary on current affairs. (Some of the names of people
in this essay—the ones identified by first name only—have
been changed.)*

Tim and I were walking home late from St. Vincent's Hos-   1
pital in New York City, where we'd been sitting with what
remained of a friend named John. We went every night,
although John had been unconscious for nearly a week. We
hoped that if we held his hand and spoke to him something
might still register. Doctors suspect that hearing is the last
sense to go. You should talk to the dying.

As Tim and I walked home through the streets of the West   2
Village, we talked about John's funeral. "Definitely something
glamorous," Tim said. "He'd hate anything morbid."

I agreed. When he was healthy, John had dyed his hair   3
platinum. He'd worn baggy shorts and purple high tops. Lam-
entation wasn't his style.

On the corner where we parted, I looked closely at Tim's   4
face. He was deeply pale, putty-colored, and his eyes looked
unnaturally large in his skull. He had AIDS too. He was still
working full-time and keeping two hospital vigils.

"What are you eating?" I asked. "You look like you've lost   5
weight."

He waved my question away. "I'm eating all the right   6
things," he said. "I'm taking perfect care of myself. Give it a
rest, Mom."

7   We said good-night, and he turned down Fourth Street, a scrawny, determined figure in oversized hoop earrings. I watched him for a moment, thinking about the workings of ordinary courage.

8   I'd just made it home and into bed when the phone rang. It was Tim.

9   "Hi," he said. "Guess where I'm calling from? St. Vincent's."

10   "Shit," I said. "Did John die right after we left?"

11   "No, it's not John," he said. His voice carried a thin, slightly blurred tone of good cheer, as if he'd been drugged. "It's me. I got beaten up. About five minutes after I left you. By three guys."

12   I went to get him with another friend of his, an English journalist named Karen. Tim was woozy and slightly manic from painkillers, and his fair hair was swathed in bandages. Karen asked him if he'd gotten a good look at the men who beat him.

13   "You know, I don't exactly remember them," he said in a chipper voice. "I know they were yelling 'faggot' at me. And I think I yelled back. Something like, 'You got it, sweethearts—who wants to be first?' Then I was in the emergency room, being stitched up. Poof. There one minute, here the next."

14   Karen and I got him back to his apartment and put him to bed. We sat with him until he fell asleep. Karen whispered, "He looks about fifteen, doesn't he?" He did look preternaturally young and wan, his blue-veined eyelids translucent, the bandage white around his head. He was a cheerful, domestically inclined boy from Indiana. He adored his friends, had a cat named Aretha, and always fell asleep before it was time to go out to the clubs. Someone had hit his frail, compromised body with a two-by-four. Someone, somewhere in the city, was congratulating himself at that moment. Someone was laughing and popping a beer.

15   To calm myself I laid my hand, gently, on Tim's scrawny chest. I felt the steady effort of his breathing. After a moment, Karen put her hand on top of mine. "This makes me crazy," I said to her. "This makes me want to hurt people." I was furious at myself for failing to watch out for Tim. And I was angry at Tim. Why did he have to talk back to those morons?

16   Karen shook her head disapprovingly, and I was suddenly, fiercely angry at her as well. Because she and her girlfriend are staunchly opposed to violence in any form. Because she refuses to have anything to do with activist groups like ACT UP (the AIDS Coalition to Unleash Power) or Queer Nation, the radical gay-rights organization spawned by ACT UP to

strike back at all the people who'd beat up an innocent gay kid like Tim. Because several weeks earlier, as we passed a series of posters announcing the homosexuality of some very big—and very closeted—Hollywood stars, she hissed: "The fascists who force other people to come out are doing us more harm than good."

If you're straight, it may be hard to understand the need for   17
an obstreperous, in-your-face organization like Queer Nation. It may be hard to imagine the intricate combination of rage and terror that constitutes the gay zeitgeist of 1992. There's a virus ticking its way through the arteries of people we love. That would be enough to make us crazy, right there. But what's driven some of us around the bend is the fact that, even as our friends keep dying, the hatred of homosexuals flourishes.

Gay-bashing is up all over the country. Homophobia is   18
thriving like mosquitoes in August, and it comes as often as not in relatively subtle, nonviolent packages. Take Magic Johnson, for instance. Shortly after announcing he was HIV-positive, he inspired wild applause on the Arsenio Hall show when he said, "I'm nowhere near homosexual." People cheered. If you're a person of color, try to imagine a celebrity telling an appreciative audience, "I thank God I'm white!" If you're Jewish, imagine the same audience clapping and whistling when a celebrity announces, "No way am I a Jew."

If you're gay and you're not angry, you're just not paying   19
attention.

I myself belong to ACT UP. I've helped engineer an on-   20
screen takeover of the *MacNeil/Lehrer Newshour* (you'd be surprised at how easy it is to get into a television studio). I've chained myself to the White House gates. I've committed these and other acts of civil disobedience in the company of people I consider heroes. I confess up front to deep affection and respect for Queer Nation, which was launched just over two years ago by a band of ACT UP members from New York City who wanted to concentrate on gay issues outside the realm of AIDS.

Queer Nation is a peculiar mix of outrage and wackiness—   21
you could call it the illegitimate child of Huey Newton and Lucy Ricardo. Male and female members go en masse to straight bars and hockey games, where they kiss their lovers passionately. They stage impromptu fashion shows in suburban shopping malls, featuring men in tutus and women in Harley-Davidson gear.

The name itself started as a joke of sorts. "Queer Nation"   22
was a temporary moniker, offered in jest. Once the founding

members got used to it, though, they didn't mind the idea of throwing a word like "queer" back in the faces of those who'd been spitting it at them for decades. They decided they could repossess the insult; they could cauterize it by taking it on themselves. Besides, the word emphasizes difference. Members aren't trying to say to the straight world, "Accept us, because we're just like you." That was the old tactic, which is now known disparagingly as assimilationism. Queer Nation's official tag line is "We're here. We're queer. Get used to it."

23   By the time it was a year old, Queer Nation existed in over sixty cities, from New York and San Francisco to Indianapolis and Shreveport. Now, just past its second anniversary, no one's quite sure how many chapters there are. The rise has been swift but chaotic, and established chapters have burned out nearly as quickly as new ones have appeared. Since I started writing this article, the Eugene and Houston chapters have taken off while the San Francisco chapter has dissolved.

24   Like ACT UP, Queer Nation is ferociously democratic and decentralized. Its founders were determined not to emulate what they called the "hierarchical, patriarchal" pecking order by which most groups—from the Young Republicans to the Crips and the Bloods—are run. At every chapter, anyone who shows up at a meeting is instantaneously a full member. Some chapters are run by consensus; some simply function as a forum for people who want to recruit others for demonstrations. The prevailing aim—you could call it an obsession—is to exclude no one.

25   It would be easy to play up Queer Nation's kind intentions and zany antics. But members can also be loudly confrontational. They've irritated a lot of people, including other lesbians and gay men. Gay opposition is wildly various, but I can offer a quintessential scenario. Say your parents are visiting from Michigan, and you've finally decided to come out to them. You're a relatively ordinary citizen with a nine-to-five job. In a quiet restaurant, over coffee, you say it: "Listen, I guess you may have suspected this. I don't want to keep secrets from you anymore. I'm gay." Your mother cries and tells you she loves you anyway. She says it with a certain forced conviction, which doesn't quite ring true. Your father is murderously silent. This is the hardest thing you've ever done. As you leave the restaurant, your mother is sniffling and your father is glacial. You're searching for something else to say, some way to make them understand that you haven't suddenly transformed yourself into an alien. As you struggle

for the right words, you walk out of the restaurant into a band of men and women carrying QUEER POWER signs. They're blowing whistles. Some wear nose rings and combat boots. Two of the men have on dresses, and one sports a Nancy Sinatra wig. As they pass, somebody slaps a Day-Glo sticker on your father's seersucker jacket. The sticker says Go GIRL.

Opposition to Queer Nation's tactics doesn't end with questions of style or demeanor. Last September, gay riots exploded in Los Angeles and San Francisco after California governor Pete Wilson vetoed AB 101, a bill that would have outlawed job discrimination on the basis of sexual orientation. After his veto, Queer Nationals and other gay activists hurled police barricades through windows. They set fires in the streets. And some of them threatened to expose gay members of Wilson's staff, further igniting the ongoing debate about outing, tactics, and propriety.   26

Gay activists face a fundamental question familiar to feminists and civil-rights leaders, among others. Do we play by the rules, court public sympathy, and push steadily but politely for recognition? Or do we make ourselves so unpleasant that yielding to our demands finally becomes easier than ignoring us? I myself favor the noisier alternatives. I believe the AIDS epidemic has taught us that nobody will listen unless we scream. But still, I'm plagued by doubts. At ACT UP meetings, when members talk about planning a new action that will "show our anger," I find myself asking, What exactly do we expect people to do with our anger once we've shown it to them? As I set out to visit Queer Nation chapters around the country, that question was on my mind. And on my first stop, in Atlanta, Georgia, a woman named Cheryl Summerville was pondering it too.   27

Cheryl Summerville may have been the best-behaved lesbian in the world. She lived outside Atlanta with her lover, Sandra Riley, in a house the two women helped build themselves. She and Riley were raising Summerville's son from a long-dissolved marriage and were thinking of having a child of their own. Summerville had a decent job as a cook at the local Cracker Barrel, one of a chain of country-style restaurants.   28

But in February of 1991, the associate manager of the restaurant, Marilee Gonzalez, called Summerville into her office. Gonzalez, who had been friendly with Summerville, told her in a nervous but formal tone that Cracker Barrel had decided to reexamine its policy about gay and lesbian employees. She asked, "Are you a lesbian?"   29

30   Summerville answered: "Marilee, you know I am. You
going to fire me for that?"

31   That day, Summerville received a pink slip on the orders of
Cracker Barrel district manager Jody Waller. The restaurant's
general manager filed a separation notice with the Georgia
Department of Labor, on which he wrote: "This employee is
being terminated due to violation of company policy. The
employee is gay."

32   Waller was complying with a memo sent to the managers
of all outlets by Cracker Barrel's main office in Lebanon, Tennessee. The memo said, in part: "It is inconsistent with our
concept and values, and is perceived to be inconsistent with
those of our customer base, to continue to employ individuals
in our operating units whose sexual preferences fail to demonstrate normal heterosexual values which have been the
foundation of families in our society."

33   In all, eighteen lesbians and gay men were fired from
Cracker Barrel's outlets. Some managers called the employees they suspected into their offices and formally asked if they
were homosexual. Others just convened staff meetings and
announced that certain employees were being terminated in
accordance with company policy.

34   Summerville simply didn't get it at first. In every respect
but one, she'd always been a model of conventional good
behavior. She'd received a "personal achievement award,"
given by Cracker Barrel to outstanding staff members, and
was up for another. She'd helped build a house with her own
hands, adored her parents and son, earned a living through
hard work. Her single transgression was to love another
woman and, even in that, she'd been modest and forthright.
She hadn't concealed her love for Sandra Riley, nor had she
flaunted it. Now she was out of work, for failing to display
normal values.

35   At first, Summerville assumed she could take Cracker Barrel to court. But only a few states and about sixty cities and
counties have barred discrimination on the basis of sexual
preference in both public and private employment. Atlanta
isn't among them. When Summerville learned she had no
legal recourse, she called ACT UP for help, but was told that it
worked only on issues relating directly to AIDS. She was
referred to the Atlanta chapter of Queer Nation.

36   Summerville was not a political person. She wasn't tortured by ideals or abstractions—she just wanted to live an
uncomplicated life. The idea of speaking to a group that
called itself Queer Nation gave her a kind of vertigo. "It took

me a week to get up the nerve," she says. She and Sandra Riley made a dry run in their car past the Five Points Community Center, where the group's next meeting was to take place. The center looked ordinary enough. But still.

On the night of the meeting, she and Riley were so nervous they arrived twenty minutes early. As the members started drifting in, Summerville was surprised to find that they looked like everybody else. "I didn't expect just normal-looking people," she says. "I thought we were in the wrong place. They were wearing just jeans and T-shirts. One of 'em came in in a suit, and I sure as hell didn't expect that." 37

Despite this, Summerville and Riley stood out, even among the conservatively dressed men. They are ample women, and they dress along suburban lines. Sandra Riley favors ruffles. She carries a pocketbook. "To start with, they ignored us," Summerville recalls. "They probably thought we'd stumbled into the wrong place or something." 38

But after the meeting was called to order, the first item of business was the firings at Cracker Barrel. "Somebody asked, 'What are we going to do about this?'" Summerville remembers. "And I said: 'Hey it was me. I'm one of 'em.'" Everyone turned to look at the short, stocky woman in a sweatshirt and jeans. "I want to know what we can do about it," she said. 39

The first demonstration against Cracker Barrel was held in a rainstorm. Thirty-plus people marched in front of the restaurant with signs, urging customers to stay away until the chain reversed its policy. It was, generally, a humiliating experience. "It was just kind of nasty," Summerville says. "It was pouring, and a few of us slipped in the mud. People laughed at us." 40

Before the picket lines started, members had been rebuffed when they tried to meet with the Cracker Barrel management to present their complaints. Soon after, the central office sent a memo to all Cracker Barrel outlets, claiming that its "recent position on the employment of homosexuals in a limited number of stores may have been a well-intentioned over-reaction to the perceived values of our customers and their comfort levels with these individuals." 41

If the firings themselves didn't qualify as national news, Cracker Barrel's subsequent change of heart apparently did. The controversy was reported in *The New York Times*, the *Wall Street Journal*, and the *Atlanta Journal & Constitution*, which also ran an editorial excoriating Cracker Barrel and asking how any discrimination could have possibly been "well-intentioned." 42

43   While it withdrew its chainwide policy about the discharge
of homosexuals, Cracker Barrel turned down Queer Nation's
demand that individual outlets be specifically forbidden from
practicing sexual discrimination in hiring. It also refused to
rehire the fired employees, and balked at Queer Nation's
request for a written apology.

44   In March of last year, Queer Nation started staging sit-ins
aimed at cutting Cracker Barrel's profits. The idea was simple: members filled as many tables as possible, ordered the
bare minimum, and sat there for two or three hours. When
they ordered their coffees or Cokes, the protesters at each
table gave their waitress a five-dollar tip wrapped in a note
that said: "We realize that you are not the source of the discriminatory policy of Cracker Barrel. We in no way want to
penalize you or make your life more difficult. On the contrary, we want to assure that YOU are not the next victim of
renegade bigotry at Cracker Barrel."

45   Every few weeks, Queer Nation hit a different Cracker Barrel
outlet, always on Sunday, after church. Last June, I went to the
ninth Cracker Barrel sit-in with Lynn Cothren, a thin blond
man wearing madras shorts and love beads. Cothren, a founding member of Queer Nation/Atlanta, is something of an anomaly. In an organization that eschews the very idea of leaders, he
boldly proclaimed himself chair of the Atlanta chapter. The
demonstrations against Cracker Barrel were largely his idea.

46   Nearly 120 people had gathered in a parking lot next to the
Cracker Barrel in Union City, about ten miles outside Atlanta.
They were a living monument to the notion that, aside from
some fundamental appetites, human beings have very little in
common. There were women in plaid flannel shirts, and
women with rouge and pink lipstick. There were middle-aged
men in sweat suits, bodybuilders, and reedy, acne-scarred
boys who still carried the mortified auras of their adolescent
torments.

47   Everyone was nervous. Most of the protesters had picketed
or participated in sit-ins before, but none had ever been
arrested for civil disobedience. Although the towers and
spires of Atlanta were visible on the horizon, Union City was
a conservative town. No one was sure what would happen or
how any of us would be treated when taken to jail.

48   Cheryl Summerville and Sandra Riley stood close together,
holding hands in the parking lot. Neither had slept the night
before. Riley, a large woman with long hair and a lovely, innocent face, looked as if she might cry at any moment. But
when Summerville told her that she thought she should

change her mind, Riley said: "What am I going to do while you're in jail? Sit outside worrying about you? No thanks." To be arrested, Riley wore heels and a blue flowered dress. She carried a white pocketbook.

After we all assembled, we filed into the restaurant. To 49 reach the dining room we passed through a gift shop that sold penny candy, stars-and-stripes decals, and plaster cherry pies with lattice crusts. The restaurant proper featured turn-of-the-century memorabilia screwed to its walls—farm implements and brown photographs of families. Hard shadowless light caromed off its acoustic ceiling.

I sat at a table with a fiftyish woman named Marty. She'd 50 come with her gay son and his lover and a young lesbian named Elizabeth, who'd been cut off by her family. Marty introduced her as "my adopted daughter." When I asked Marty how she felt about her son being gay, she drawled, "I've known he was gay since he was in the fourth grade, so I've had plenty of time to get used to it." When I asked if she'd rather he was straight, she said, "Well, he's a hell of a lot happier than one of his brothers, who's married with two kids."

A cheerful waitress brought us menus, and we told her we 51 were just having coffee. We gave her her five-dollar tip up front, wrapped in the note explaining what we were doing there. She smiled graciously, and pocketed the tip and the note without reading it. Slowly the restaurant filled with protesters. I drifted through, asking the few remaining nonmembers for reactions. A beige-faced woman in a biscuit-colored jumpsuit said: "I don't carry on about my sexuality in public. I don't know why you all have to carry on about yours." At another table, a man with a beard said: "Cracker Barrel was right to fire those people. What with AIDS and all, I don't want 'em touching food my kids are gonna eat."

Most of the waitresses didn't appear to mind. Some even 52 seemed to be having a good time. An older woman swept through the room periodically, filling coffee cups, and when she got to us she said to Marty: "Honey, I'm cuttin' you off. You're starting to shake the whole table."

I went to Cothren's table and asked him what, exactly, he 53 thought this protest was accomplishing. He looked at me as if he couldn't believe I would ask such a question. "We're putting direct pressure on them," he said. "We're cutting into their business."

"But so far," I said, "you've gotten only one minor conces- 54 sion. Obviously, their fundamental attitude hasn't changed. None of the people who were fired have their jobs back."

55   "We're going to win," Cothren answered in an impatient
tone, as if I simply didn't understand the righteousness of
Queer Nation's cause or the immensity of his will.

56   An hour passed before Jody Waller, the district manager,
appeared with two cops and began working his way through
the restaurant, table by table. Waller was a trim man with
glasses and a receding hairline, wearing a tie and a navy blazer.
At each table he announced: "I'm asking you to leave now. If
you don't leave, you'll be arrested. Do you understand?"

57   Eighteen people chose to stay and be arrested. The rest of us
went to the jail house to wait until they were released. We
marched in an orderly circle before the jail, which was located
in a town that seemed to consist only of the jail, a post office,
and several unprosperous-looking antique stores. We carried
signs that said THERE'S BIGOTRY IN MY BISCUIT and CRACKER BARREL
SERVES HATE. We displayed the signs to ourselves and to an
occasional passing car. In two hours, not a single person
walked by on the street.

58   At the end of two hours, several demonstrators were
released. We gathered around them expectantly, and they told
us they'd been treated with surprising respect. A court date
had been set for mid-August, when a judge would rule on
Cracker Barrel's trespassing charge. Summerville and Riley
stood close together, talking happily to their friends. Riley's
white shoes were unsmudged.

59   We started back to our cars, planning to meet at a bar in
Atlanta for a celebratory beer. But as we were dispersing, a
battered pickup truck roared toward us from down the street.
As it screamed past, a gang of shirtless teenage boys yelled,
"Faggots." They all wore their hair below their shoulders, a
minor cosmetic freedom won by others before they were
born. They turned around and passed us a second time, still
hollering insults.

60   They left a chill in the air. Any one of them could have been
Jody Waller's wild son, testing his limits before he grew up
and got his own job managing a Cracker Barrel. Cothren
didn't hesitate. He turned and marched back into the jail—a
skinny, wrathful twenty-eight-year-old man in Bermuda
shorts—to demand that his pot-bellied jailers track down the
boys and arrest them for verbal assault.

61   As I traveled around the country visiting other chapters of
Queer Nation, I kept thinking, God, these people are young. If
furious exuberance is the organization's most salient feature,
youth is a close second. I've just turned thirty-nine, and in my

travels I met only a handful of women and men my age or older. More often, I found myself among people who could literally have been my sons or daughters. The media liaison from the now-defunct San Francisco chapter tried to reassure me that the group's reputation for youth was exaggerated, saying proudly, "Some of us are in our late twenties and even our early thirties."

Youth, with its energy and its bottomless outrage, may   62
account for that fact that Queer Nation demonstrations are sometimes ignited by events that seem less than urgent. When the residents of Gay Court, in a suburban community east of San Francisco, petitioned to change the name of their street to High Eagle Road, a band of protesters from Queer Nation showed up with banners and bullhorns. In New York City, I went with about twenty activists to stage a "kiss-in" in a straight bar, where the patrons frankly couldn't have cared less. Looking for drama, I asked a straight-looking guy in a crewneck sweater what he thought about all this. "All *what?*" he asked.

"Those people over there," I said. "The ones who are kiss-   63
ing. The ones with the stickers that say 'Queer.'"

He looked calmly at a pair of tattooed men who were kiss-   64
ing passionately among a bevy of big-haired secretaries sipping margaritas. He shrugged. "Guess it means they're queer," he replied.

Youth, combined with Queer Nation's adamantly non-   65
hierarchical structure, may also partially account for the fact that the group is often disorganized nearly to the point of incoherence. In preparing to write this article, I made dozens of calls across the country and learned repeatedly that the person whose name I'd been given had left town for a few months, or moved away entirely, or fought with other members and quit. Members conceive passionate devotions and then burn out. They leave Queer Nation over philosophical differences, or because their grades are suffering, or because they've fallen in love with other members who don't return their affections.

When I called a contact person in Shreveport, Louisiana,   66
his mother answered the phone and told me, cordially, that her son had gone to live with his lover. When I reached him at his lover's house, he said that Queer Nation/Shreveport consisted entirely of himself and another man occasionally distributing literature on safer sex.

I had planned to attend a demonstration being held by   67
Queer Nation of Lincoln, Nebraska. Together with Queer

Nation/Iowa City, members were going to Iowa State University in Ames, where a heterosexual supremacist group—consisting of about a dozen people committed to fighting the very concept of gay rights—was campaigning for formal recognition by the university. Queer Nation was going to parade in front of the group leader's house, kissing and holding hands. I was looking forward to the demonstration. I'd made plane reservations. But when I called about some last-minute details, I learned that the action had been called off because a main organizer had set fire to another member's house.

68   I did go to Salt Lake City, because I'd heard Queer Nation was thriving there and because the woman I'd first contacted continued to answer her phone over a period of several months. Still, I arrived too late. By the time my plane landed, the group was in disarray. A splinter group had formed. Members were writing vicious lampoons of one another in the chapter's newsletter.

69   I admit it. I was beginning to feel a certain despair.

70   I also visited Queer Nation/San Francisco, which several months after I left degenerated into internecine battles and then disbanded entirely. In January of 1991, it was among the largest chapters in the country, attracting as many as four hundred to its weekly meetings. It carried out one of Queer Nation's most notorious protests, when bands of Queer Nationals did everything possible to disrupt the filming of *Basic Instinct,* a thriller about murderous lesbians and bisexual women.

71   By autumn, its numbers had dropped to the low twenties. Last December, the few remaining members agreed to dissolve the group. Some members there even call Queer Nation/San Francisco a "fad that fizzled out." Others say that it was done in by racism and sexism among the members themselves.

72   Tensions had flourished from the beginning. Soon after the San Francisco chapter was established, bands of women and people of color started LABIA (Lesbians and Bi-Women in Action) and United Colors. These organizations-within-the-organization were called "focus groups" and were meant to concentrate on issues that might escape the attention of the larger body.

73   As ever-increasing numbers packed themselves into the dour ochre-and-brown auditorium of San Francisco's Women's Building, members of LABIA and United Colors consistently felt that certain white men dominated. At one meeting last winter, several members came to the floor and asked the group at large to contribute a hundred dollars to a

march. They were turned down—no big deal. But after the meeting, a group of white male members started arguing about the march with a group of women. The argument grew so heated that the women left, with the men following them down the street, still shouting their opinions. The men's raucous voices brought faces to apartment windows; a passerby asked the women if they needed help.

Later, the men claimed they'd only been carrying on an 74 impassioned discourse. The women said they'd been terrorized. This was one of a number of incidents in which some of the white men told one version of a story and the women or people of color told another. Several months later, when a band of men from Queer Nation plastered stickers on the home of a lesbian city supervisor, LABIA pulled out altogether, claiming that the male "terrorism" could no longer be countenanced.

Christine Carraher, one of the founding members of the 75 bisexual focus group UBIQUITOUS, explains: "There's a wide gulf between a lot of lesbians and gay men. Sometimes I think it's worse than the one that exists between straight men and women."

"Some of these guys believe feminists are doing to men 76 what Big Nurse did to the warders in *One Flew Over the Cuckoo's Nest*," said a male member of the group.

As these tensions built, a big, noisy, politically savvy New 77 Yorker named Mitchell Halberstadt started showing up at meetings and shouting other members out of the room. Halberstadt is a classic New York activist, all bombast and aggression. When he arrived in San Francisco, he brought his swagger to a group that employed two "vibes watchers" at every meeting to make sure no one felt intimidated, and permitted members to stop the meeting and discuss their grievances every time they felt personally insulted. But now, if women or people of color stopped a meeting to complain of a racist or sexist remark, they were often shouted down by Halberstadt and several other men. Because there was no formalized code of behavior for the meetings, and no decision could be made without consensus, the abusive tirades had to be tolerated. More and more people left.

At a meeting in early November, there was another con- 78 frontation. When one of the few female members started to walk out of the room, Halberstadt barred the door, screaming, "How dare you try to leave!" Frank Herron, a physically imposing man, told Halberstadt he was out of line and that he would do anything to stop him from threatening the others.

And so the group that had pledged itself to banding together against homophobia was about to begin slugging it out over racism and sexism.

79   In an attempt to recover some sense of equilibrium, the members who stayed on—down to about twenty-five—held a special session in late November to discuss ways in which the general meetings could be better managed. At the session, John Woods of United Colors and a white member named Allen Carson proposed that the group agree to a ban on all sexist and racist language, although they did not offer a specific list of forbidden terms. Halberstadt blocked the proposal and later claimed: "My politics are antiauthoritarian. [This is] a power grab by wannabe bureaucrats."

80   Soon after that session, the handful of remaining members called a "hiatus" until March, at which time they would regroup and see what, if anything, they could get to rise from the ashes.

81   When I accepted the assignment to write about Queer Nation a year ago, I was full of zeal. I confess to ending my story in a state of confusion. I had expected to write a story about heroism, and I did, in fact, meet heroic people everywhere I went. I'd prefer to write only about their strength and solidarity. I don't like reporting about the squabbles, the naiveté, the self-destructive tendencies. I likewise don't quite know what to make of the fact that, of the chapters I visited, the only one that's holding together effectively—the group in Atlanta—is the only one with an old-fashioned leader. (Cheryl Summerville is now the chapter's cochair.) It's also the only one embroiled in a battle with a clear-cut villain, which may help account for its strength. Fighting homophobia, sexism, and racism, is, for most of us, a little like battling crabgrass. It's everywhere, so intricately stitched into the lawn that you can't quite tell where to begin.

82   My misgivings about Queer Nation stem mainly from its tendency toward self-destruction, and this criticism is shared by other lesbians and gay men. Becky Moorman, publisher of *The Bridge*, a lesbian and gay magazine based in Utah, says: "The [lesbian and gay] community's really divided about what Queer Nation is doing. Their protests aren't focused. They need to decide who they're speaking to and what they're trying to say." Anthony Christiansen, an openly gay Ph.D. candidate in Columbia University's clinical-psychology program, adds: "Queer Nation focuses so much on our difference [from heterosexuals], they lose track of our connectedness. There

are millions of complex situations out there—being gay isn't as cut-and-dried as they'd like to make out."

That may be the heart of the problem. We are probably the most diverse of all persecuted groups. A Martian field biologist sent to earth to capture two homosexual speci-mens could easily bring back a twenty-three-year-old white guy with an MBA from Yale and a sixty-five-year-old black lesbian separatist from Detroit. Queer Nation, fostered by people who've been unfairly excluded, is determined to be utterly inclusive. That's turning out to mean equal voice not only for women and men of all colors but also for the foolish, the prejudiced, and the outright deluded. 83

Perhaps Queer Nation is simply an early, flawed step toward a new kind of lesbian and gay militancy. Frank Herron of San Francisco insists that the city's chapter hasn't been a failure: "It's spawned a dozen groups doing different things. We've drawn a lot of people into activism." Herron sees the future of gay activism as a welter of small groups modeled on revolutionary cells. "Twelve people can reach a decision more easily than five hundred can," he says. "If these twelve need help, they work with another group of twelve. I don't know if we'll ever have a cohesive national gay activist organization." 84

Meanwhile, it's difficult not to feel panicky, because, as we argue over structure and focus, as we bicker among ourselves, our people are being attacked in increasing numbers. Since I was in Atlanta, Cheryl Summerville and Sandra Riley have become more famous and, simultaneously, more widely despised. After Summerville appeared on the Oprah Winfrey show in January, her sixteen-year-old son was so tormented by his classmates that she and Riley chose to move him to another school. There have been hate letters and threats. Riley has closed her sewing and alterations business so that she can be home when the boy gets back from school. 85

And as we struggle to set a coherent agenda, our people continue to die. My friend Tim, for one, died while I was working on this story. It was sudden, if that term can be applied to someone who'd had AIDS for almost three years. He was comparatively well and then he caught pneumonia and then he died. His parents, who hadn't spoken to him in years, didn't want his ashes. Karen is keeping them in a box in her apartment until we decide what to do with them. Another friend has taken Aretha, Tim's cat. 86

Just before Tim died, I found myself sitting with Karen at his bedside. He was unconscious, breathing noisily and steadily on a respirator. As Karen and I sat watching him, I 87 told her I was struggling to write an article about Queer Nation. She shrugged dismissively. "A bunch of thugs," she said.

88 "Right," I said. "That's right. And you've got a better idea, haven't you?" My voice was loud enough to surprise me.

89 "Honey, calm down," she said with a nervous smile.

90 "You've got a much better solution," I said. "It's very effective to be discreet in public and send a little money to the Gay Men's Health Crisis and write features about the ten best espresso bars in lower Manhattan. Thank you for your contribution."

91 A nurse put her head through the curtains and asked if everything was all right. We told her not to worry, to get on with her other business.

92 "You don't need to scream at me," Karen said quietly after the nurse had gone.

93 "I know," I said.

94 "I'm not the one you're really angry at."

95 "I know. Let's not talk about it, okay?"

96 Of course, she was right. But I couldn't calm myself. Later, after Tim died, I was able to see how stupid I'd been. How quickly I'd self-destructed. Karen had been there for me to scream at, and, even more important, she understood what I was screaming about. A man like Jody Waller, standing smugly with two cops behind him, doesn't get the point. There's no outward evidence that he suspects he's doing anything wrong.

97 Karen and I will never be friends. Now that Tim is gone, there's no reason for us to know each other. But during Tim's last days, she and I managed to act like compatriots. We had to. There was a funeral to plan, and, if we didn't do it, nobody would.

98 It's hard to know what to do sometimes. I wish I felt more certain about how to proceed. I wish I'd walked Tim home that night after we left St. Vincent's. I keep thinking I could have protected him.

Bruce Bawer

Notes on Stonewall

Bruce Bawer (born 1956 in New York City) is a professional writer with a background in literary studies. In addition to several books on one or another literary matter (his most recent is Prophets and Professors*), he has published a book of poems and a volume of film criticism. Bawer's 1993 book* A Place at the Table: The Gay Individual in American Society *was for several months the number one best-seller in gay bookstores. A former director of the National Book Critics Circle, Bawer reviews books frequently for the* New York Times Book Review *and the* Washington Post Book World *and has also published essays and reviews in* The American Scholar, The Nation, The Hudson Review, Newsweek, *and* The Advocate. *"Notes on Stonewall" appeared in* The New Republic, *a respected magazine on public affairs that once had a liberal slant but now occupies a middle position editorially.*

Twenty five years ago, in the early morning hours of June 28, 1969, several patrons at the Stonewall bar in Greenwich Village, many of them flamboyant drag queens and prostitutes, refused to go quietly when police carried out a routine raid on the place. Their refusal escalated into five days of rioting by hundreds of people. Though it wasn't the first time anyone had contested the right of the state to punish citizens just for being gay, that rioting marked a pivotal moment because news of it spread in every direction and sparked the imaginations of countless gay men and lesbians around the world. It made them examine, and reject, the silence, shame and reflexive compliance with prejudice to which most of them had simply never conceived a realistic alternative.   1

There is something wondrous about Stonewall, and it is this: that a mere handful of late-night bar patrons, many of them confused, lonely individuals living at the margins of society, started something that made a lot of lesbians and gay men do some very serious thinking of a sort they had never quite done before—thinking that led to action and to a movement. It was the beginning of a revolution in attitudes toward homosexuality. How odd it is to think that those changes could all be traced back to a drunken riot at a Greenwich Village bar on a June night in 1969. But they can. And that's why Stonewall deserves to be commemorated.   2

3   Today, however, Stonewall is not only commemorated but
mythologized. Many gay men and lesbians routinely speak of
it as if it was a sacred event that lies beyond the reach of
objective discourse. They talk as if there was no gay rights
activism at all before Stonewall, or else they mock pre-Stone-
wall activists as Uncle Toms. They recite the name "Stonewall" itself with the same reverence that American politicians
reserve for the names of Washington and Lincoln. And indeed
the word is perfectly suited to the myth, conjuring as it does
an image of a huge, solid barrier separating the dark ages
prior to the day that Judy Garland died from the out-loud-
and-proud present. Every year, on what has long since
become an all-purpose gay holiday—a combination of Independence Day, May Day, Mardi Gras and, since the advent of
HIV, Memorial Day as well—millions ritualistically revisit the
raucous, defiant marginality of Stonewall in marches around
the world. This year in New York, on the twenty-fifth anniversary, the ritual will reach a climax. For many, Stonewall has
already become a Platonic model of gay activism—and,
indeed, a touchstone of gay identity.

4   A few weeks ago, in a sermon about an entirely different
subject, the rector of the Episcopal church I belong to in
New York used the phrase "the politics of nostalgia." The
phrase has stuck in my mind, for it seems to me that both
sides of the gay rights struggle are trapped in what may well
be characterized as a politics of nostalgia. Many of those
who resist acceptance of homosexuality and reject equal
rights for gay men and lesbians know on some level that they
are wrong, but they cling to old thinking because a change,
however just, seems to them a drastic departure from the
comfortable world of "don't ask, don't tell." Some gay people,
likewise, cling to what might be called the Stonewall sensibility, reacting defensively and violently, as if to some horrendous blasphemy or betrayal, even to the hint that perhaps the
time has come to move in some way beyond that sensibility.
Such people often declare proudly that they have been "in
the trenches" for twenty-five years, which is to say that in a
way they have been reliving Stonewall every day since June
1969.

5   Yet every day *can't* be Stonewall—or shouldn't. And in fact
the time *has* come to move beyond the Stonewall sensibility.
For, thanks largely to developments that can trace their inspiration to that barroom raid, some things *have* changed since
1969. Levels of tolerance have risen; gay rights laws have
been passed; in the last quarter-century, and especially

recently, gay Americans have come out of the closet in increasing numbers. As a result, it has become clear to more and more heterosexuals that gay America is as diverse as straight America—that many of the people who were at the Stonewall bar on that night twenty-five years ago represent an anachronistic politics that largely has ceased to have salience for gay America today. To say this is not to condemn people who consider themselves members of that fringe or to read them out of the gay community. It is simply to say that for gay America to continue to be defined largely by its fringe is a lie, and that this lie, like all lies about homosexuality, needs to be countered vigorously. The Stonewall sensibility—like the Stonewall myth—has to be abandoned.

On May 6 *The New York Times* described the arguments   6
among gay leaders about the planning of Stonewall 25, the forthcoming New York event that will culminate in a march on the United Nations. Some of these leaders worried that Stonewall 25 wouldn't focus enough on the fact that many of the Stonewall heroes were transvestite and transsexual hustlers. One woman wanted, in her words, to "radicalize" Stonewall 25. "Stonewall," she told the *Times*, "was a rebellion of transgender people, and this event has the potential to reduce our whole culture to an Ikea ad."

It is strange to read the words of those who speak, on the   7
one hand, as if Stonewall, in and of itself, achieved something once and for all time that gay Americans are now free to celebrate, and, on the other, as if the kind of growing acceptance that is represented by the depiction of a middle-class gay couple in a furniture commercial on network t.v. is bad news, a threat to a Stonewall-born concept of gay identity as forever marginal. It would almost seem as if those leaders don't realize that Stonewall was only part of a long, complex process that is still proceeding, and that the best way to honor it is to build upon it by directing that process as wisely and responsibly as we can.

In the May 3 issue of the gay magazine *The Advocate*, activ-   8
ist Torie Osborn wrote that thirty-nine gay leaders, whom she described as "our community's best and brightest," had gathered recently to discuss the state of the movement and "retool [it] to match the changing times." The group, she wrote, "had a collective 750 years of experience in gay rights or other political work." But even as she wrote of seeking "common ground" and "common vision" among the gay leaders, Osborn reaffirmed the linking of gay rights to "other progressive movements with which many of us identify."

9   In other words, she embraced the standard post-Stonewall practice of indiscriminately linking the movement for gay equal rights with any left-wing cause to which any gay leader might happen to have a personal allegiance. That practice dates back to 1969, when radical activists, gay and straight, were quick to use the gay rights movement as a way to prosecute their own unrelated revolutionary agendas. Such linkages have been a disaster for the gay rights movement; not only do they falsely imply that most gay people sympathize with those so-called progressive movements, but they also serve to reinforce the idea of homosexuality itself as a "progressive" phenomenon, as something that is essentially political in nature. Osborn wrote further that she and the other gay leaders at the summit "talked about separating strategic thinking into two discrete areas: our short-term political fights and the long-term cultural war against systematic homophobia." And she added that "we have virtually no helpful objective data or clear strategy on the long-term war, which grapples with deep-seated sexphobia as well as heterosexism." Her conclusion (my emphasis): *"We need to start working on this problem."*

10   With all due respect to Osborn and her fellow gay leaders, it seems to me more than a bit astonishing that in spite of their collective 750 years of experience, at least some of them only now have begun to realize that homosexuals should be giving thought to something other than short-term political conflicts. At the same time, those leaders still can't quite understand the long-term challenge as anything other than, in Osborn's words, a "war." Nor can they see that achieving real and lasting equality is a matter not of changing right-wingers into left-wingers, or of emancipating Americans from "sexphobia," but of liberating people from their discomfort with homosexuality, their automatic tendency to think of homosexuals in terms of sex and their often bizarre notions of who gay people are, what gay people value and how gay people live.

11   Perhaps, at the threshold of the second generation of the post-Stonewall gay rights movement, it behooves us to recall that, as I've noted, there *was* at least some species of gay activism prior to Stonewall. Years before those patrons at the Stonewall bar hurled garbage, beer bottles, feces and four-letter words at the policemen who had come to arrest them, a few small groups of men in business suits and women in dresses staged sober, orderly marches at which they carried signs that announced their own homosexuality and that

respectfully demanded an end to anti-homosexual prejudice. Those people were even more radical than the rioters at Stonewall, and—dare I say it?—perhaps even more brave, given how few they were, how premeditated their protests and how much some of them had to lose by publicly identifying themselves as gay. They were heroes, too; they won a few legal battles and they might have won more. Sure, Stonewall was, without question, an important step—indeed, the biggest single step the gay rights movement has taken. But that's all it was: a step, the first big one in a long, difficult journey. It was a reaction to intolerance, and it set us on the road to tolerance. The next road leads to acceptance—acceptance not only of gay people by straight people, but an easier acceptance by young gay people of their own sexuality. It's a different road—and, in a way, a harder one.

First-generation post-Stonewall gay activists saw themselves as street combatants in a political war. Second generation activists would better see themselves as participants in an educational program of which the expressly political work is only a part. Getting America to accept homosexuality will first be a matter of education. The job is not to shout at straight Americans, "We're here, we're queer, get used to it." The job is to do the hard, painstaking work of *getting* straight Americans used to it. This isn't dramatic work; nor is it work that provides a quick emotional release. Rather, it requires discipline, commitment, responsibility.   12

In some sense, of course, most straight Americans *are* used to the idea of people being gay. The first generation of the post-Stonewall gay rights movement has accomplished that. At the same time, it has brought us to a place where many straight Americans are sick and tired of the very word "gay." They've heard it a million times, yet they don't understand it nearly well enough. They still feel uncomfortable, confused, threatened. They feel that the private lives of homosexuals have been pushed "in their faces," but they don't really *know* about those private lives.   13

And why should they be expected to? Yes, at Gay Pride Day marches, some gay men and lesbians, like the Stonewall rioters, have exposed America to images of raw sexuality—images that variously amuse, titillate, shock and offend while revealing nothing important about who most of those people really are. Why, then, do some people do such things? Perhaps because they've been conditioned to think that on that gay high holy day, the definitively gay thing to do is to be as   14 defiant as those heroes twenty-five years ago. Perhaps they do it because they can more easily grasp the concept of enjoying one day per year of delicious anarchy than of devoting 365 days per year to a somewhat more disciplined and strategically sensible demonstration designed to advance the causes of respect, dignity and equality.

15   And perhaps they do it because, frankly, it is relatively easy to do. Just as standing up at a White House press conference and yelling at the president can take less courage than coming out to your parents or neighbors or employers, so taking off your pants or your bra for a Gay Pride Day march in the company of hundreds of thousands of known allies can be easier than taking down your defenses for a frank conversation with a group of colleagues at an office lunch about how it was to grow up gay. For an insecure gay man or lesbian, moreover, explaining can feel awfully close to apologizing, and can open one up to charges of collaboration with the enemy by those who join the author Paul Monette in seeing America as the "Christian Reich" and themselves as members of the queer equivalent of the French resistance.

16   As a friend said to me recently, building acceptance of homosexuals is like teaching a language. When gays speak about themselves, they are speaking one language; when most straight people speak about gays, they are speaking another. Most heterosexuals look at gay lives the way I look at a page of German. I may be able to pick out a few familiar words, but I feel awkward when I use them, and if I try to put together a sentence I'm likely to find myself saying something I don't mean at all, perhaps even something offensive or hurtful. There's only one way to get past that feeling of confusion: tireless, meticulous dedication to study. You can't learn a foreign language overnight, and you can't teach it by screaming it at people. You teach it word by word, until, bit by bit, they feel comfortable speaking it and can find their way around the country where it's spoken. That's the job of the second generation of post-Stonewall gay activism: to teach those who don't accept us the language of who gay people are and where gay people live. Indeed, to the extent that professional homophobes have stalled progress in the movement toward legal and social parity for gay men and lesbians, it is not because those homophobes are so crafty, and certainly not because they are right. It is because they have spoken to straight America in its own language and addressed its concerns, whereas gay Americans, more often than not, out of an understandable fear and defensive self-righteousness, haven't.

Some reviewers in the gay press read the title of my book,   17
A Place at the Table: The Gay Individual in American Society, as
a sign that I, personally, long to sit at a dinner table with people like Pat Buchanan and Jerry Falwell—that this book is my
attempt to indicate to them that I'm a nice, well-mannered
gay man and that I, along with the other nice, well-mannered
gay men, should be allowed at the table while the "bad," ill-
mannered gays are excluded. Some other gay press reviewers
have understood that I don't mean that at all, and that I feel
everyone should be welcome at the American table, but they
have angrily rejected the idea: "Why," one critic wrote,
"should *I* want to sit at that table?" A writer for the gay magazine *Out* dismissed the book in one line: "Bruce Bawer has
written a book about the gay individual in American society
entitled *A Place at the Table.* Some will prefer take-out."

What these reactions signify to me is a powerful tendency   18
among some homosexuals to recoil reflexively from the vision
of an America where gays live as full and open members of
society, with all the rights, responsibilities and opportunities
of heterosexuals. Many gay people, indeed, have a deep, unar-
ticulated fear of that metaphorical place at the table. This is
understandable: gay people, as a rule, are so used to minimizing their exposure to homophobia, by living either in the
closet or on the margins of society, that for someone—even a
fellow gay person—to come along and invoke an image of gay
America sitting openly at a table with straight America can
seem, to them, like a hostile act. This sense of threat—this
devotion to the margin—may help explain the gay-activist
rancor toward the movie *Philadelphia.* But most gay men and
lesbians were happy to see a movie that showed homosexuality as part of the mainstream, just as most are pleased by the
new tendency to depict gay life, in everything from Ikea ads
to movies like *Four Weddings and a Funeral* in a matter-of-fact
way, as an integrated part of society.

Am I attacking radicalism? No. I'm saying that the word   19
"radical" must be defined anew by each generation. In the
late twentieth century, when radicalism has often been
viewed as a fashion choice, it's easy to lose sight of what real
radicalism is. It's not a matter of striking a defiant pose and
maintaining that pose over a period of years; it's not a matter
of signing on to a certain philosophy or program and adher-
ing to it inflexibly for the rest of your life. And it's not always
a matter of manning barricades or crouching in trenches. It's
a matter of honest inquiry, of waking up every morning and
looking at the social circumstances in which you find yourself

and having the vision to perceive what needs to be done and the courage to follow up on that vision, wherever it may take you. It's a matter of going to the *root* of the problem, wherever that root may lie.

20   And going to the root of this particular problem means going to the root of prejudice. It means probing the ignorance and fear that are responsible for the success of anti-gay crusaders. It means seriously addressing those opponents' arguments against gay rights, in which they combine a defense of morality and "family values" with attacks on homosexuality as anti-God, anti-American and anti-family. Too often, the first generation of the post-Stonewall gay movement has responded to such rhetoric by actually saying and doing things that have only reinforced the homophobes' characterization of homosexuality. The second generation of the movement would do well to respond not by attacking the American values and ridiculing the religious faith that these people claim as a basis for their prejudice, but by making it clear just how brutal, how un-American and how anti-religious their arguments and their prejudice are.

21   And there are a *lot* of untruths out there to overcome. More and more people understand that homosexuals are no more likely to be child molesters than heterosexuals are, but there remains on the part of many people a lingering discomfort about such notions, and anti-gay crusaders exploit that discomfort with ambiguous, dishonest rhetoric suggesting that homosexuals are (to quote a recent statement published in *The Wall Street Journal* by a group of religious figures calling itself the Ramsey Colloquium) a threat to the "vulnerabilities of the young." That's a lie. But how can homosexuals help heterosexuals understand it's a lie so long as some gay political leaders, in the best Stonewall tradition, feel more comfortable condemning the Log Cabin Republicans than they do condemning the North American Man-Boy Love Association?

22   Likewise, more and more people understand that homosexuals' lives are no more about sex than their lives are, but there are many who still *don't* understand that, and the anti-gay crusaders exploit their ignorance by saying (again in the words of the Ramsey Colloquium) that gay people "define" themselves by their "desires alone," that they seek "liberation from constraint," from obligations to the larger society and especially to the young, and from all human dignity. *That's* a lie. But how can gays help straights understand it's a lie so long as a few marchers on Gay Pride Day feel the best way to

represent all gay men and lesbians is to walk down the avenue in their underwear?

Anti-gay propagandists shrewdly exploit the fact that we   23
live in times when there's ample reason for concern about
children. American children today grow up in an often uncivil
and crime-ridden society, and with a pop culture that is at
best value-neutral and at worst aggressive and ugly. Altogether too many of those kids grow up inured to the sight of
beggars sleeping on the sidewalk, of condoms and hypoder-
mic needles in the gutter, of pornographic magazines on display at street-corner kiosks. Anti-gay propagandists routinely
link homosexuality to these phenomena, seeing homosexual
orientation, and gay people's openness about it, and gay people's desire for equal rights and equal respect, as yet more
signs of the decline of morals, of the family, of social cohesion
and stability and of civilization generally.

One of Stonewall's legacies is that gay leaders have too   24
often accepted this characterization of the conflict and see
any attempt to correct it as "sex-negative." The second generation of post-Stonewall gay activism has to make it clear that
that's not the way the sides break down at all, and that when
it comes to children, the real interests of parents and of gay
people (many of whom are themselves parents, of course) are
not unalterably opposed, but are, in fact, perfectly congruent.
Gay adults care about children, too; and they know from
experience something that straight parents can only strive to
understand—namely, what it's like to grow up gay.

Homosexuals, of course, are *not* a threat to the family;   25
among the things that threaten the family are parents' profound ignorance about homosexuality and their reluctance to
face the truth about it. In the second generation of the post-
Stonewall gay rights movement, gay adults must view it as an
obligation to ensure that parents understand that truth—and
understand, too, that according equal rights to homosexuals
and equal recognition to same-sex relationships (and creating
an atmosphere in which gay men and lesbians can live openly
without fear of losing their jobs or homes or lives) would not
threaten the institution of the family but would actually
strengthen millions of American families.

It is ironic that, to a large extent, what perpetuates Stone-   26
wall-style antagonism between gay and straight are not our
differences, really, but traits that we all share as human
beings. We all, for instance, fear the unknown. To most
straight people, homosexuality is an immense unknown; to
gay people, a society that would regard sexual orientation

indifferently and grant homosexuals real equality is also an immense unknown. But it is also our humanity that makes most of us long to know and live with the truth, even in the wake of a lifetime of lies. The greatest tribute we can pay to the memory of Stonewall is to work in our own homes and workplaces to dismantle, lie by lie, the wall of lies that has divided the families of America for too long.

John Berresford

Rights and Responsibilities, Not Freebies and Frolics

John Berresford does most of his writing as part of his job as an antitrust lawyer for the Federal Communications Commission in Washington, but he did find time to contribute the following article to The Washington Post *in June 1995. The* Post *is a politically moderate newspaper with a national as well as local readership, rather like* The New York Times.

1   I am gay and have been in the gay rights movement since I came out in 1981. I am also a conservative, a libertarian.

2   Sad to say, the gay rights movement has always been seen as being on the political left, as one more whining interest group claiming entitlement to all sorts of special treatment from the government. Or we are seen as having a simply fabulous time cavorting at Gay Pride parades and throwing condoms at Catholic services. Whether as crybabies or as Dionysian celebrants, we always appear outside the mainstream.

3   I cringe at both images. Most gay men and women do not go around demanding government favors or living a hedonistic "gay lifestyle." But just enough of us act out these images, or tolerate them, that they become real in the public mind. Middle America feels uncomfortable about this, at the very least. Our right-wing enemies love it, because it gives them someone to hate and someone to use as a foil for attracting mainstream support to their own causes. By accepting, and in

some cases cultivating, these images, we lose friends and help our enemies.

As a conservative, I wish such images would evaporate. If 4 there was ever a time when they made sense, on grounds of either truthfulness or usefulness, it ended when the Republicans took control of Congress. The waiting line for government benefits now leads nowhere, and public frolics now gain nothing but disapproval.

What can government give gays? Merely the form, not the 5 substance, of what we need and want. What we are really after is not merely legal rights but acceptance into the mainstream of American life—and acceptance is granted or withheld by the mainstream majority at its pleasure. If we want to be accepted, we must be welcomed. Lord knows it's easier to change the votes of a few legislators than the hearts and minds of millions of our fellow citizens. But politicians are weathervanes, they are not the wind.

So we should end some of our present practices: 6

We should loudly reject all "compensatory" agendas: hiring 7 quotas, affirmative action and group reparations—all of which I've heard advocated for "when we get our rights." The people who benefit most from such programs are the bureaucrats who administer them and the members of the "victim" groups with the best political connections.

We should stop pressing for "domestic partners" legis- 8 lation. It creates a special class of rights for a small class of people. The real beneficiaries would be the lawyers who would litigate the differences and similarities between domestic partnership and marriage.

We should not hate Jesse Helms, Pat Robertson and their 9 allies. Leave the hating to them. They will eventually destroy themselves, as Joe McCarthy and other haters did.

We should stop feeling sorry for ourselves. We may be vic- 10 tims, but frankly no one cares. This country's wellsprings of liberal guilt began running dry about 20 years ago, and by now they are flat empty.

Finally, we should stop seeing AIDS as anybody else's prob- 11 lem. The sad fact is that every gay man who got AIDS by sex got it from another gay man, and by doing something he chose to do. People with AIDS deserve sympathy, but it is the sympathy one extends to a chain smoker who comes down with lung cancer. It is not the same kind of sympathy one feels for someone who was struck by lightning or run down by a drunk driver.

12   But that's enough on the negative side. What positive actions can we take?

13   For starters, each of us should come out whenever it is reasonably safe. The best way to explode the myths about us is for each of us to become known as just another human being with the same needs, goals and drives as other human beings—except in a single respect that poses no threat to anyone else.

14   Our legislative goal should be for civil rights legislation with disclaimers of any quotas, guidelines, reparations or government-imposed and group-based remedies. It should emphasize private lawsuits for damages rather than enforcement of a bureaucracy.

15   In the legislatures, we should also lobby for the right to marry. Domestic-partners legislation makes us an officially sanctioned class of oddities and freaks. By seeking marriage, we demonstrate our wish to be part of the great American middle-class way of life.

16   Among ourselves, we must be willing to talk about morals, to impose them on ourselves and to do so conspicuously. As long as our primary image is one of gleeful promiscuity—an image promoted not only by our enemies but also by our own magazines and our own bars—we will be ostracized. Until we start imposing honesty, fidelity and emotion on our lives—in other words, until we are willing to talk about moral standards—we will make little real progress in social acceptance.

17   In a curious way, AIDS itself may be helping us find social acceptance. This terrible disease has brought to a screeching halt—at least in my generation of gay men—the manic boozing, drugging, and screwing of the '70s and '80s. It has forced us to attend more to friendships, stability and the consequences of our action. It has opened us to human suffering; one friend told me that caring for someone with AIDS was the first unselfish thing he had done in his adult life. AIDS has enabled us to show, to ourselves and to the mainstream, that we too are capable of great suffering, compassion, work and sacrifice. By our work with each other, we have shown mainstream society what we have to offer it, and how much it loses and wastes by excluding us.

18   The common theme of all this is simply facing the facts, working to bring out the best in ourselves and offering something admirable to the mainstream. All these views put me in odd company politically. But if you had to agree about everything with everyone else in an organization before you could join it, we'd have 260 million political parties in this country.

Conservatives are the people I happen to agree with most of the time. At least they are attempting to deal with the moral issues of our time (such as welfare dependency and violence) on a moral plane, and not as something for which the only remedy is another government program and more spending.

After I come out to them, I find that most conservatives are   19
perfectly tolerant (and not as cloyingly condescending as my liberal straight friends). The Helmses and Robertsons are in the minority. And it eventually dawns on the conservatives that if they want to keep the support of gays like me, they had better keep at least a distance between themselves and the haters.

Finally, moving in conservative circles permits me to ask   20
my conservative friends where this country would be without those great gays—Whittaker Chambers, J. Edgar Hoover, Walt Whitman and Cardinal Spellman. It's a polite way to remind them that we have been in their midst and doing good deeds from the beginning.

My liberal friends tend to employ three styles of attack on   21
my views. The first is ad hominem: How can you talk about morality when we all know that once you did this or that randy deed? My answer is that (a) the fact that your first response is to attack the messenger (me) shows that you can't repel the message; and (b) I had my adolescence like everyone else, and it's over.

My liberal friends' second attack is some variation on "Do   22
you mean that you're against all attempts to right the wrongs that have been done to us?" My answer is that I am as much in favor of basic civil rights for gays as they are. Where we differ is in the need for group-based remedies and in perceiving ourselves as victims whose main recourse should be coercion by the government.

The third attack from my liberal friends is usually some   23
form of "Well, you have a good point, but...." At that, I know I've made some progress.

I have a feeling there are many more conservative gays   24
than there seem to be. The time is ripe for us to leave the plantation of liberal government and start acting like what we are—a group of adults who want to live lives as normal and as healthy as everyone else in the mainstream. If we do, I think we will be on the path to my dream—an America in which being gay is no more remarkable than being left-handed.

Yale Kamisar

Drugs, AIDS, and the Threat to Privacy

Yale Kamisar is a prominent member of the faculty at the University of Michigan Law School. The author of Constitutional Law: Cases, Comments, Questions *and many other publications in academic law, he contributed the following analysis to* The New York Times Magazine, *a Sunday supplement to* The New York Times, *on September 13, 1987.*

1   "Time works changes, brings into existence new conditions and purposes," wrote Supreme Court Justice Joseph McKenna in 1910. "Therefore, a principle to be vital must be capable of wider application than the mischief which gave it birth.... [In interpreting] a constitution...our contemplation cannot be only of what has been but of what may be."

2   Few legal developments better illustrate these words than the history of the Fourth Amendment, which protects "the right of the people to be secure in their persons, homes, papers, and effects, against unreasonable searches and seizures."

3   The wording is succinct and majestic. But it is also vague and general. Whether and how to apply the Fourth Amendment to new conditions has generated great controversy— none of it greater than the current debate over mass drug testing and mandatory AIDS testing.

4   The two so-called plagues of the 1980's—what government officials have called the "national epidemic" of illicit drug use and the "global epidemic" of acquired immune deficiency syndrome—have put enormous pressure on the Fourth Amendment. Proposals that would require certain groups to submit to random urinalysis tests for drugs, or to blood tests for the AIDS virus, directly threaten the concept of "individualized suspicion" that lies at the heart of the amendment. In brief, this notion holds that the government should not be able to interfere with someone's liberty, or invade his privacy, unless officials can demonstrate that they have "probable cause" to believe that particular person is committing, or has committed, a crime. The amendment forbids the Government to issue search warrants unless officials can satisfy the "probable cause" requirement.

The concept of individualized suspicion would seem to be   5
incompatible—to put it mildly—with random drug tests or
"routine" blood tests for the AIDS virus. At the moment, drug
testing is being challenged in the courts; the directive for
"routine" AIDS testing is likely to challenged in the future.
Some day, I venture to say, Americans may look back on the
legal rulings about drug and AIDS testing as the most dramatic illustrations in history of how to apply the Fourth
Amendment to new conditions—or as the the most striking
examples of the failure to do so.

Until recently, the best example of the struggle to adapt the   6
Fourth Amendment to new developments was the Supreme
Court's consideration of wiretapping and electronic eavesdropping. In the first wiretapping case to reach the Court, in
1928, Chief Justice William Howard Taft, writing for a 5–4
majority, concluded that, so long as electronic surveillance
did not involve a physical entry into a person's home or office,
it fell outside the Fourth Amendment. Conversations, he reasoned, were not "things" to be "seized" within the meaning of
the amendment.

But as more and more sophisticated means of electronic   7
snooping emerged, it became increasingly clear that this
"property-trespass" theory of the Fourth Amendment could
not survive. In 1967, the Warren Court finally rejected it, noting that the Fourth Amendment "protects people, not places,"
and thus applies whenever the Government violates a person's "justifiable" expectation of privacy.

So the Court finally deemed tapping and bugging   8
"searches." It didn't necessarily follow, however, that all such
searches were inherently intrusive as to be *unreasonable*.
Today, law enforcement authorities may still conduct "electronic surveillance"—but only after having convinced a judge
that they have satisfied the "individualized suspicion"
requirement.

In the case of drug and mandatory AIDS testing, however,   9
the constitutional problems are much less clear-cut.

Last year, President Reagan signed an executive order   10
calling for widespread mandatory drug testing of some
Federal employees, and a growing number of state and
local agencies have followed suit. Last spring, the President
announced that the Federal Government would begin mandatory AIDS testing of selected groups—would-be immigrants,
illegal aliens seeking amnesty and Federal prisoners—who do
not enjoy the usual Fourth Amendment protections. The

President also called upon the states to provide what he called "routine" testing (which, according to some officials, seems to be a softer way of saying mandatory testing) for inmates in state and local prisons, patients at venereal disease clinics and drug-abuse centers, and couples applying for marriage licenses.

11   The battle over drug testing is already being waged in the state and Federal appellate courts and should reach the Supreme Court soon. Its outcome is bound to have an important bearing on AIDS testing.

12   Almost every court that has addressed the issue has rejected the Government's argument that because urinalysis does not involve a physical invasion, or even a touching, of the body, it does not constitute a search (an argument that might well have prevailed in the Taft Court). Instead, the courts have ruled that urinalysis falls under the Fourth Amendment because a person has a reasonable expectation of privacy with respect to personal information contained in his body fluids. Moreover, a urine test is often conducted under the close surveillance of a government representative— an embarrassing, if not humiliating, experience.

13   Many questions have been raised about the effectiveness of mass drug testing, and still more about that of mandatory AIDS testing. But even if the courts agree that mandatory testing is effective, effectiveness alone is still not sufficient justification to initiate a search. As one Federal court recently noted: "There is no doubt about it—searches and seizures can yield a wealth of information useful to the searcher. (That is why King George III's men so frequently searched the colonists.) That potential, however, does not make [a government search] a constitutionally reasonable one."

14   Sol Wachtler, Chief Judge of the New York State Court of Appeals, made this point last June, in the course of striking down a New York school district's requirement that all probationary teachers submit to urinalysis: "By restricting the government to reasonable searches, the State and Federal Constitutions recognize that there comes a point at which searches intended to serve the public interest, however effective, may themselves undermine the public's interest in maintaining the privacy, dignity and security of its members."

15   May the Government require those seeking public employment to submit to a drug test? No, answer civil-liberties lawyers, quickly invoking the doctrine of "unconstitutional

conditions," which says the Government may not condition employment on the surrender of constitutional rights.

Often this is the right answer, but not always. Under 16
certain circumstances, the Government may deprive pub- lic employees of some of the rights they would have as citizens—not on the simplistic theory that one is obliged to accept employment on the Government's terms, but on the ground that sometimes a citizen's full enjoyment of his constitutional rights may be demonstrably incompatible with the mission of the particular public agency employing him.

In April, for example, a Federal Court of Appeals in New 17
Orleans sustained a program requiring all Customs Service employees seeking transfers to certain jobs to submit to urine testing. The court underscored "the strong governmental interest in employing individuals for key positions in drug enforcement who themselves are not drug users."

On the other hand, a similar case last March, an intermedi- 18
ate New Jersey court, basing its decision exclusively on its State Constitution, reached the opposite conclusion. As this court saw it, a Newark police directive mandating that all members of the narcotics bureau submit to periodic drug tests authorized searches without individualized suspicion, despite the fact that the record "did not indicate that drug use within the narcotic bureau...is extensive." The court maintained that objective indications of drug use—such as absenteeism, chronic lateness, general deterioration of work habits—along with confidential information would be adequate to identify officers who might be using drugs.

The main targets of governmental drug testing so far have 19
been public employees, but proposed AIDS testing is likely to be far more widespread. In view of the Fourth Amendment's notion of individualized suspicion, how could the Government require all hospital patients or all marriage license applicants to submit to AIDS tests? After all, no court would ever approve a "dragnet" or "blanket" search of all people living in a high-crime neighborhood simply because such an operation would turn up evidence of criminal conduct on the part of some residents—as undoubtedly it would. (The requirement that marriage license applicants be tested for syphilis, still in force in many states, has apparently never been tested on Fourth Amendment grounds. The procedure's wide acceptance is likely to influence the courts when they address the AIDS question.)

20   But there are potential precedents. Although the Supreme Court has not specifically addressed these questions, in recent years lower Federal courts have consistently upheld what might be called "dragnet searches" of passengers at airport departure gates, and "blanket" metal-detector searches at the doors of courthouses and other government buildings.

21   In effect, the courts have carved out an exception to the traditional Fourth Amendment constraints that would allow what have been variously described as "regulatory searches," "administrative searches," or "inspections." (The original precedent involved granting government inspectors the power to examine residential and commercial buildings for possible violations of health, safety and sanitation standards.) The essence of this exception is that searches not conducted as part of a typical police investigation to secure criminal evidence but as part of a "general regulatory scheme"—one applying standardized procedures to minimize the potential for arbitrariness—need not be based on individualized suspicion.

22   The handiness of the administrative search concept has gladdened the hearts of many government lawyers. But it has alarmed other observers, including me. Today, potential administrative searches are buzzing around the Fourth Amendment like a swarm of bees. With drug and AIDS testing, the drone may soon be deafening.

23   As Wayne LaFave, a professor of law at the University of Illinois at Urbana and author of the leading treatise on search and seizure, points out: "Unless the administrative search is limited to truly extraordinary situation where rigorous application of typical Fourth Amendment standards would be *intolerable,* the amendment will largely disappear. The need to detect drug users is important, but hardly more so than the need to search for narcotics dealers, kidnappers and murderers. Yet we have never demanded 100 percent enforcement of the criminal law. Instead, we are committed to a philosophy of tolerating a certain level of undetected crime as preferable to an oppressive state."

24   Judge Benjamin Cardozo once observed that "the great tides and currents which engulf the rest of men do not turn aside in their course and pass judges by." The rulings upholding airport and courthouse searches—which were a response to the dramatic increase in airplane hijackings and the bombings of government buildings—illustrate Judge Cardozo's point. The danger today is that judges will be unduly influ-

enced by the contemporary tides and currents—by rising fears
of illicit-drug and AIDS "epidemics."

    Someday, the Supreme Court may rule that concerns about   25
physical safety are sufficiently compelling to justify random
drug testing of prison guards or other law-enforcement officers, or perhaps even other public employees who perform
dangerous tasks. But that is a long way from saying that
schoolteachers, or public employees generally, no matter
what the nature of their jobs, must submit to random drug
testing. Or that large groups of people must undergo "routine" AIDS testing.

    However great the threat posed by illicit drug use and the   26
AIDS virus, the "individualized suspicion" concept must
remain the heart of the Fourth Amendment. I believe we
should greet claims of "national interest," "emergency," or
"necessity" with considerable skepticism. Slogans like these
can be—and have been—a free people's most effective tranquilizers. As we mark the Constitution's 200th anniversary,
we would do well to remember that.

Dan Chaon

Transformations

*Dan Chaon lives in Cleveland, Ohio, and teaches at Cleveland
State University. He has published a number of short stories;
the one reprinted here appeared in 1991 in* Story, *a prestigious
quarterly that prints only short fiction.*

    The first time I saw my brother Corky in women's clothes,   1
I was eleven and he was fourteen. He came out of my parents'
bedroom in my mother's good dress, the one with bird of paradise flowers patterned on it, and her high heels and lipstick.
I thought he was kidding. He chased after me, talking in a
Southern accent, and I ran off laughing. Corky was always
pretending to be someone else, dressing up in clothes he'd
bought at the Catholic rummage house or found in the
garage, imitating the mannerisms of his math teacher, or

Uncle Evan, who drove semi trucks and stuttered, or some
disc jockey on the radio. I didn't realize then, not for years
and years actually, that he was gay and all.

2   He is still your brother, my father told me when he showed
me the picture. This was the second time I'd seen Corky in
women's clothes. In the photo, he was wearing a big red wig, a
blue-jean skirt, pumps, and a blouse with fringe. He looked
like a country singer. My father asked me: "Do you know who
this is?" All I said was, Yes, and, It figures.

3   My father shook his head at me. He liked to pretend that he
didn't care what Corky was, just so long as he was happy. That
was the official line. But I'd seen the kind of cloudy distance
that came into his eyes when he talked to Corky on the phone.
I'd noticed him, once, studying an old Polaroid of the three of
us, pheasant hunting, examining it as if looking for clues. I'd
seen his expression when one of his buddies from the electri-
cian's union asked: "So how's that boy of yours doing back
East?" My father shifted from foot to foot. "Oh, fine, fine," he
said quickly, and looked down.

4   But he looked me sternly in the eyes. "He is still your
brother," he said. He folded his thick hands, staring glumly at
the glossy black-and-white photo.

5   "My sister, you mean," I said.

6   He frowned. "You're getting pretty smart-mouthed," he
said. He laid the photo on the kitchen table between us, like
some important document I was supposed to sign. "He does
this as entertainment," my father said. The words "CABARET
BERLINER, New York," were printed on the bottom of the
picture.

7   "I'll bet," I said.

8   My brother worked at a bar in New York City. We'd known
that. We also knew he was gay. He'd told my parents over the
phone after he'd been away a year. I wasn't sure how they
reacted at first, though they seemed calm by the time they got
around to telling me. Corky had come to a decision, my father
said, and my mother nodded grimly. For a long time afterward, my father wouldn't refer to it at all except as "your
brother's decision," though he also pointed out to me that the
words "fag" and "queer" were worse than swearing as far as
he was concerned.

9   Corky was going to college in New York at the time, but he
dropped out shortly after to audition for plays and work in
bars at night. He hadn't been home since he told them.
Instead, he sent clippings, pictures, lists of productions he

was trying out for. "One thing about Corky," my father pointed out to me as he looked through the packets Corky sent. "At least he knows what he wants, and he's not afraid to go after it."

It was my senior year in high school, and my father thought   10
I had no ambition. Maybe that was true. In any case, I wasn't like Corky had been when he was in high school. His senior year, there was always something about him taped to the refrigerator—a certificate of merit, or a clipping from the local paper about a scholarship he'd won. He pinned the acceptance letters from colleges in neat rows on a bulletin board in our room, as if they were rare butterflies.

That was why I was surprised when he called to say he was   11
taking some time off to attend my high school graduation. I went to the Catholic school as Corky had, but there was no chance of me ending up valedictorian like him. For a while maybe people wondered whether I'd be a teacher's pet like Corky, and they even sometimes called me by his name. But it didn't take them long to find out that I wasn't going to leave any brilliant reputation in my wake. My father always said that I didn't "apply myself" like Corky did. Out of ninety-six seniors I was ranked forty-ninth. I would just be a vague, doughy face in the middle of the third row. There was no great cause for celebration. I hadn't found a job or a college to attend in the fall. But at least my parents had a son who could give them grandchildren, they could appreciate that. And as for that fat, mustached drama teacher, Sister Vincent, who continually remembered Corky's beautiful singing voice and his performance in *South Pacific*, well, I wished she could see his new song and dance at Cabaret Berliner.

Corky came home two days before graduation. My mother   12
and father and I went to pick him up at Stapleton Airport in Denver. The whole way there, I worried. I couldn't help but imagine Corky appearing to us in a feather boa and an evening gown or something, trotting down the ramp to meet us with a big lipstick grin. I told myself I was being low-minded and ugly, but that image of him kept popping into my mind. My face felt hot.

Meanwhile, my parents acted like everything was wonder-   13
ful. The full moon reflected off the early May snow that still lay on the fields, and my father kept howling like a wolf. It seemed to amuse my mother, because she chuckled every time he did it, and laughed aloud when he grabbed her around the waist and growled.

14   I was sitting in the back seat, watching the car drift toward
the center of the road while they horsed around. "I hope we
wreck," I said.

15   The three of us stood there in the waiting area, watching
the planes land. We didn't recognize Corky when he
approached us, but at least he was wearing normal clothes.
He'd dyed his hair bright red—it was shoulder-length, tied in
a ponytail. When he was close enough, I noticed the little
crease in his earlobe that meant it was pierced, but he didn't
have an earring. He hugged my mother, kissing her lightly.
Then he turned and kissed my father. My father always kissed
us on the lips, and wasn't even afraid to do it in public. He
puckered up like a cartoon character, and it would've been
funny if he wasn't so earnest about it. Here he was, this big,
middle-aged construction worker, smacking lips with his son.
He didn't even hesitate knowing Corky was gay, though I
looked around to see if people were staring.

16   When my brother turned to me, I stuck out my hand. I
didn't want him kissing on me. "So," he said, and squeezed
my palm, hard. "The graduate!"

17   I shrugged. "Yeah, well," I said. "I'm just glad it's over."

18   He kept holding my hand till I pulled back a little. He
grinned. "Congratulations," he said.

19   "Congratulations to you, too," I said, though I didn't know
why.

20   As we drove back to Mineral, I watched my brother suspiciously. Ever since we were little he'd always been the center
of things, and I doubted that he'd come all that way just to
congratulate me. I kept expecting him to take over at any
minute. I remembered how, when we were young, we had a
place behind the house, an old shed we'd furnished with lawn
chairs and cinder blocks and such. This became the plantation from *Gone with the Wind*—Corky was Rhett and Scarlett,
I was the slaves; or a rocket—Corky was the captain and the
alien invaders, I was the crew that got killed. Once, when I
was eleven and he was fifteen, and he was going to play the
lead in *South Pacific*, he got me all excited about trying out
for the part of his little Polynesian son. He gave me the music
and then made fun of me, standing by the bedroom door and
warbling like an old chicken.

21   Maybe, I thought, Corky had changed. It had been a long
time since I'd really spoken to him. It had been several years
since I'd seen him, and I seldom felt like talking to him on the
phone. Even when my father *did* put me on the line, I couldn't

think of what to say. "What's new," Corky would ask, and I'd shrug: "Nothing." Maybe he'd become a totally different person, and I hadn't known.

But I couldn't tell. He was so motionless as we drove that   22
he hardly seemed real. He just stared, like some stone idol, out toward the passing telephone poles and fields and the grasshopper oil wells nodding against the moonlit sky. His hands remained in his lap, except once, when he suddenly touched his hair with his fingertips as if adjusting a hat. When my parents asked him a question he leaned forward, smiling politely. "What? What did you say?"

It was late, nearly one in the morning, when we got home.   23
Corky went to the bedroom to unpack—our old room, my room now—and when I came in he was already stretched out on the upper bunk. It used to be that I slept in the bottom and he slept in the top, but since he'd left I'd been using the lower bunk to store papers and laundry and stuff. He looked down at me and smiled.

"That's my bed," I told him.   24

He sat up and his bare feet dangled over the edge, swinging   25
lightly. He was wearing silky-looking pajamas. We'd always just slept in our underwear, and I imagined that this was what he wore when he lay down next to another man. "That's rich," he said. "You know, all these years I wanted that bottom bunk. I suppose you always wanted the top."

"I didn't care one way or another," I said. I began to take   26
handfuls of dirty laundry from the bottom bunk and put them on the floor. "You can sleep there if you want."

He nodded and lay back. "It's been a long time since I've   27
heard any news from you."

"Yeah, well," I said. "My life isn't that exciting."   28

"You've really changed the room around," he said. He ges-   29
tured to a poster of a model in a white bikini who was holding a six-pack of beer. "She's sexy," he said.

"Yeah," I said. "I guess."   30

He looked from the poster to me, his lips puckered out a   31
little. "So," he said at last. "Do you have a girlfriend, Todd?"

"Yes," I said. "Sort of." I didn't. I had friends that were girls,   32
and one of them I took to most of the dances. But I wasn't like some of the guys in school, who'd been going steady with one girl since eighth grade. All the girls I liked had either paired off or weren't interested. The furtive gropes and kisses after dances hadn't amounted to much. I was afraid that even if I got a girl to do more, I'd be clumsy, and I couldn't stand the

thought of her laughing, maybe telling her friends. "You know," I told Corky. "I date around and stuff."

33   "Good for you," he said. He pulled his feet up onto the bed the way a fish would flip its tail. Then he laughed. I could feel my ears warming.

34   "What's so funny?" I said.

35   "Nothing," he said. "Just the way you said it." He deepened his voice to a macho swagger. "'I date around and stuff.'" He laughed again. "You used to be such a little high-voiced thing."

36   "Hm," I said. He leaned back and I turned off the light. I moved over near the closet, where it was darkest, so I could undress without him seeing me. The hangers made wind-chime sounds as I brushed them.

37   "It's so weird, being home," he said. His voice floated from the top bunk as I took off my shirt. I decided to sleep in my jeans. I didn't have any pajamas. "You can't believe how strange it is."

38   "Well, nothing has changed," I said. I groped across the dim room to my bed. I could see the lump where he was lying, a shadow bending toward me.

39   "No," he said, "no." And then, slowly: "So did you see the picture I sent?" The house was still. I could hear water whispering through the pipes in the walls; I could hear him breathing.

40   "I saw it." I tried to make my voice noncommittal. I sighed deeply, like I was already almost asleep.

41   He didn't say anything for a long time, and I thought he might have drifted off. When he spoke out of the dark, finally, his voice sounded odd, twittery, not like him, and it made my neck prickle. "Sometimes," he said, "I'm glad I sent it and other times not." I didn't say anything. "Todd?" he whispered.

42   I waited. I recalled the way we used to lie in our bunks when we were little and tell each other jokes and make up songs. I remembered how I would go to sleep to the sound of his murmuring, crooning. "What," I whispered back finally.

43   "How did Mom and Dad react?"

44   "How should I know?" I mumbled. "They don't tell me anything."

45   "What did they say?"

46   "What did you expect them to say?"

47   "I don't know," he said. "It's hard to explain."

48   But I didn't want him to explain. I didn't want to keep picturing him in that outfit, swishing and singing, maybe kissing a member of his audience, leaving a bright wing of lipstick on his forehead. "They didn't say much of anything," I told him. "They don't care what you do in your personal life."

"Do you?"   49

"Why should I?" I whispered. I rolled over, pretending to be   50
asleep.

When I woke, my brother was already up. I could hear him   51
talking in the kitchen, and the sound of eggs cracking on a
skillet. I went to the bathroom to shower and when I came
back to dress, I couldn't help but notice Corky's suitcase. It
was expensive-looking, dark strips of leather bound around
brick-red cloth. Through the walls I could hear the vague
whisper of conversation and I bent down, running my hands
along the sides, finding the zipper.

Most of the things had been taken out. He'd put them in   52
dresser drawers my mother had cleared out for him. But
there was a compartment along one side, and when I opened
it, I found what I figured I'd find. It gave me a fluttery feeling
in my stomach: a skirt, a flowered blouse, pantyhose, a box of
make-up with the colors arranged chromatically. Beneath
that were more photos—Corky gripping a fireman's pole, his
leg sliding along it, his eyes looking seductively away; being
lifted by a group of men in tuxedos, his head flung back, his
arms open wide, jeweled necklaces in his clenched fists.
There were two clippings of advertisements for Cabaret Berliner: a drawing of a man's hairy leg with a high heel on his
foot, and underneath, in small letters, the words: Corky
Petersen with Sister Mary Josephine—After Tea Dance Party.
Another had a photo of Corky in his cowgirl outfit. I wondered if he was planning to show us a sample of his act. I
closed the suitcase quickly.

They didn't look up when I came into the kitchen. They   53
were sitting at the table, eating toast and scrambled eggs.
Corky was telling my father that New York City was in a state
of collapse and had been ever since Reagan took office. He
said the homeless filled the streets, that a bag lady had died
on his doorstep. My father kept nodding very seriously,
frowning, "Mm-hmm," as if he were talking to a grownup. He
never spoke to me that way. Then Corky began to tell about
the semis that parked outside his apartment at night, and
how his whole place filled up with diesel fumes. He was
afraid to light a cigarette. In the middle of this, he looked up
and saw me standing there. "Well, hello, Sleeping Beauty," he
said, and cocked his hand on his hip.

I glared at him. "Mornin'," I said in my deepest voice. I slid   54
into the chair at the far end of the table.

"You hungry, punkin?" my mother asked brightly.   55

56   I looked sternly at her. I wanted to tell them that my name
was Todd, not Sleeping Beauty or pumpkin. But all I said
was, No. Then I looked at Corky. "So how come you live in
New York if you don't like it?"

57   Corky shrugged. "Frankly," he said, "there's no other place
I could stand." Then he leaned toward my father and lowered
his voice. "I'll tell you what's really scary," he said. "This
AIDS thing. Out here, I'm sure no one realizes, but it's really
terrifying."

58   My father blushed and we were all silent. "Well," my father
said, and cleared his throat. "I hope you're being careful." He
picked at his eggs.

59   "Careful?" Corky said. He gave a short laugh. "I can't even
tell you. The other night I was out with this guy." He stopped.
All of us were sitting stiffly, and my father had a pinched look
on his face. He touched his eyelids, as if to clear away the
image of Corky and this man, this lover.

60   "Well, anyway," Corky said. "He didn't even want to kiss.
He goes: 'I don't know you well enough yet.'" He took a bite of
toast, nervously, then looked over at me and winked. I kept
my face expressionless. He winked again. "So, Todd." He said
my name as if it were some ridiculously cheerful exclamation, like "gee whiz," or "wowee," the kind of thing he used to
say with mocking relish when he was in high school. "Tomorrow's the big day!" he said. "Graduation. Commencement.
The beginning of a new life."

61   "Right," I said. I didn't like to think about it that way. I
couldn't imagine myself working a regular job forty hours a
week, or leaving home for college or the service; it seemed
amazing to me that Corky lived alone, and paid his own bills,
got up in the morning without my mother waking him.

62   "Yes, Toddy," my mother said quickly. "We haven't seen you
in your cap and gown."

63   "Yeah, and you're not going to either," I said.

64   "What's the matter," my father said. I could see how it was
going to go. They'd do anything to escape more information
about Corky's sex life. "Are you ashamed of your cap and
gown?"

65   "I just don't want to put it on, that's all," I said. "What's the
big deal?"

66   "Oh, come on, Todd," my brother said. He grinned. I shook
my head at all of them. It figured—even with all of them looking at me, the focus was still on Corky underneath.

67   "I feel like a dancing dog," I said. I pushed away from the
table.

When I went into my bedroom, I just stood there for a 68
minute, staring at Corky's suitcase, then to the window. The
morning was warm and clear. Outside, the grass was a sickly
yellow-green in the patches that appeared where the snow
had drawn back. It made me think of a horror movie I'd seen
where the smooth, pale skin of a dead woman peeled away to
reveal a monster's face. At last, I went to the closet and took
the box out. The cap and gown were still wrapped in plastic,
and I tore it away roughly. I slid the gown over my head, the
silky cloth slick against my bare arms, my neck. I fit the cap
over my hair, and it fit snugly. It made me think of a wig. The
tassel dangled in front of my nose.

When I came into the kitchen my brother began to hum a 69
jazzy "Pomp and Circumstance," snapping his fingers. The
gown billowed around me, the cap tilted against my line of
vision, and I shambled forward, trying to imagine how Clint
Eastwood would walk in a cap and gown.

"You look real nice," my father nodded. 70
"Stand up straight," my mother said. 71

It would have been nice to say that I was going out that 72
night with a group of friends to some party out on somebody's farm where everyone was singing and carrying on
around a keg an older brother had bought. Some of my classmates were doing that, but not *my* friends. Jeanine's grandparents were coming in from California that night, Craig's
family was taking him out to dinner, Lisa and Jeff, both of
them too straight for their own good, were going to a special
Mass or wake or whatever it was for graduating seniors. I
remember Corky and the other seniors who were in plays had
a formal dinner for themselves. They'd sent out calligraphied
invitations, and dressed up in coats and ties. At the party,
they'd put parts of Corky's valedictorian speech to the music
of *My Fair Lady*. He'd come home late, singing in a Cockney
accent at the top of his lungs.

And what did I do? I sat around. Corky was busy provid- 73
ing the entertainment. As I sat after breakfast and read a
horror book, my brother helped with the dishes and told
my mother about Jacek, a Yugoslavian man he'd dated, a
man who made independent films and had done a video for
a rock group. Actually, Corky didn't say they'd dated. That
was only to be guessed from the careful description he'd
given. My mother drew various dishes out of the soapy
water, nodding as if she didn't quite understand what it all
meant.

74   After lunch, we went for a drive. Corky seemed excited. He
wanted to drive by Rattlesnake Knob, he said, and take pictures to show his friends in New York. I pictured him joking
about it at some cocktail party, showing his photos to a group
of lithe, smirking gay men, as they stood before the huge picture window of some penthouse, surrounding Corky, looking
at the pictures and then to the city lights that blurred to daz-
zles, to the Statue of Liberty with the moon hanging over her
head. "How quaint," they'd murmur.

75   The four of us squeezed into the cab of the pickup, with
Corky and me in the middle. We drove out toward the hills,
and when we passed the rock house, Corky made us stop.

76   The house stood in the middle of a field. It had been built
by pioneers and the sod roof had long since collapsed. The
rest of it had been built of pumice rock they'd gathered from
the hills, and from the smattering of trees they'd found by the
creek and cut down. It was still recognizable as a house, there
was still the frame of the doors and windows, though the
wood was mostly rotten and even the stone walls were crumbling. My father used to take us out here when we were little,
and tell us about pioneers. Corky wanted to take a picture.

77   He got out of the truck and strode purposefully through
the ditch to the fence. We followed after. He stretched the
lines of barbed wire apart so he could squeeze through, then
paused on the other side and looked closely at the wire. "Hey,
Dad," he said, as we came to the edge of the fence. "Look at
the strands of this wire. It's really intricate. Is that rare?"

78   My father bent over to look with Corky, so their foreheads
nearly touched, so they looked like mirror images of one
another, leaning over, hands on their knees. "No," my father
said. "No, not rare. Just old." He sighed, straightening up. It
used to be that, wherever we went, my father would be pointing things out, explaining things. As we'd drive up into the
hills, my father would tell us how the trickle of creek we'd
passed a mile back had made them; over millions of years a
valley was created with hills on either side. I remember imagining the gray hills with their jagged lace of pumice cliffs, rising up on either side, pushing slowly out of the flat prairie
like mushrooms. He taught us trivia that seemed amazing
then—how to tell a rattlesnake from a bullsnake; types of
barbed wire. Maybe he was remembering the same thing,
because he just stood there, touching his fingers to his eyelids, as Corky clicked his camera at the rusty barbed wire.

79   "So," my brother said to me as we walked across the pasture to the rock house. "Am I going to get to meet one of these

girlfriends of yours? Is one of them going to stop by the house tomorrow?"

"I don't know," I said. My parents looked at me. They didn't say anything, but it still made me feel like a failure. They knew I didn't have a girlfriend. Even in the one thing I had over Corky I was a flop. Corky stopped in front of the rock house, which was surrounded by tall dry weeds, and put his hands on his hips. He looked over his shoulder at me, and I sighed. My parents glanced at me, and I stared down at the sod. "They're not really girlfriends," I said. "They're just friend friends."

When I looked up, my eyes met Corky's. I couldn't tell what he was thinking. "Hey," he said. "Why don't you all stand in front of the place? That'll make a nice shot."

We arranged ourselves—my father stood behind my mother and me and pulled us close to him so he could hide his pot belly. He and Corky were the tall ones in the family, and I'd inherited my mother's shortness. We pressed together. "Smile," Corky called, and stepped back. I set my lips into one of those smiles I knew was crooked and silly, but I couldn't stop it. "That's great," Corky said. He aimed the camera at us. "It's one of those pictures you'll keep forever, you know?" We separated from our cluster. Corky took another picture.

As we walked back to the car, Corky put his arm around my shoulders. I stiffened, but I didn't shrug him off. "I think just plain friends are the best kind," he said.

"Yeah, right," I said. He tilted his head as if a cool breeze were blowing.

"I sing this song in my show called 'We're Only Friends.' It's really great. I've got this sort of Dietrich look, and the tune is a 30s German thing, you know." He began to sing softly, his voice raspy, deep, but strikingly like a woman's. His voice carried, wafting in the open air.

I didn't know what he was trying to prove. Maybe he was trying to get us used to the idea. Maybe he was just needling my parents. Maybe he was showing off. Whatever he thought, the Subject kept coming into our conversations. He had given a man my mother's recipe for fried chicken. He used "Blue Moon," my father's favorite song, as the closing number for his show. He kept at it, through dinner, after, as we were watching TV, tossing little bits out for our consideration. My father had gotten a glazed look, as if he could hear someone far away calling his name. My mother looked more and more bewildered.

87   As for me, I found myself thinking about the clothes I'd seen in his suitcase. I wondered if and when he was planning to put them on.

88   When he came into the bedroom late that night I was lying on the bottom bunk, reading my book. "Corky," I said. He was bent down, searching through his suitcase. "Do you—" I cleared my throat. I watched him collect a toothbrush and dental floss from his bag. "I mean you normally wear normal clothes, don't you?"

89   He looked up at me, not smiling. "I only dress for my act, if that's what you mean."

90   I nodded. I took a deep breath. "How come you packed women's clothes?"

91   His eyes narrowed. I remembered how he used to have his secret drawers, a scrapbook full of old clippings and things, the way he'd come in and found me looking through it. "Keep out of my stuff, you pig!" he'd shouted, and started punching me.

92   "What do you mean?" he said softly. He was looking me up and down, appraising me, and I watched him set the items in his hand back into the bag. He unzipped the compartment and pulled out the make-up kit, the photos. "This stuff?" he said fiercely. For a minute, I shrank back, as if he were my older brother again and I'd ruined another game. He stared at me, and then suddenly shook his head. "Todd," he said, as if remembering some other brother that wasn't me. "I thought maybe someone might have wanted to see my show." He shook his head. "People pay money to see it." He put the blouse to his face. "Here," he said, and threw it at me, hitting the book I was still holding in my hand. "Smell it."

93   It must have been the look on my face that made him laugh. I held it and sniffed the air. I had dark thoughts about what I was supposed to smell.

94   "Old Spice," he said. "For the manly man." It was my father's brand. "It's a joke," he said. He picked out the bunch of pictures and clippings and walked over to the bunks with them. He put them on top of the blouse. "If you want to look at this stuff, you can," he said. "I'm going to brush my teeth."

95   Before he got to the door, he turned. "What did you think?" he said. "I came home for the sole purpose of ruining your graduation by running around in drag?"

96   I looked down at the pictures of him. "Why *did* you come home?" I said.

97   He put his back to me. "Because I was stupid," he said.

At my graduation party, my relatives drank and gave me   98
money. Commencement was as long and dull as the past four
years of high school had been. In her speech, the valedictorian
kept referring to the future as a train, and I imagined myself
standing on the railroad tracks, watching it bear down on me.

The party made it even worse. There I was, in the middle of   99
the living room, holding a paper plate—melting ice cream, a
slice of chocolate cake—dabbing the frosting from the base of
the little wax graduate that had been in the center of the cake,
that my mother had insisted I take as a memento. After the
first time, when my uncle Evan had come up to me and
handed me an envelope, and asked me what my plans were,
and I tried to tell him I had a lot of options I was considering,
I gave up. The next time, when my aunt Susan handed me a
card and asked me the same question, I just shrugged.

Which of them had futures that were so wonderful? I   100
watched my great-aunt Birdie, already drunk even before
noon. She'd been married twice and now was living with
some man in Denver. Or my cousin David, who'd just gone
bankrupt. Or Grandpa Mitch, who a few months before had a
heart attack, who had to crawl from the bedroom, down the
hall to the phone. "Oh, he looks so thin, so pale," they whispered behind his back. "He shouldn't be in that old house
alone." Soon, he'd be in a rest home. My parents sat on the
couch near my grandfather, looking nervously at Corky. It
was sickening. They'd spent the better part of their lives raising us, and look what that got them.

Corky was across the room, sitting on a folding chair with   101
his legs crossed. He was right on the edge of the kitchen; people had to walk past him to get to the food and the beer. I
watched my relatives move slowly by, their eyes fixed on him.
They asked him how life was treating him in the Big Apple,
and tightened their smiles.

I stirred my ice cream and cake together. Even I couldn't   102
help staring at him. Aunt Birdie came weaving up to me, fid-
dling with the tab on her beer. A napkin was stuck to her shoe,
dragging behind her as she sidled up to me. "Congratulations,
precious," she said, and pushed her lips to my forehead, leaning against me for support. "What's in your future?" she
asked, and pushed a crumpled bill into my jacket pocket. I
shook my head. "Nothing." Corky had lit another cigarette
and was saying: "That sounds an awful lot like a play I auditioned for." Aunt Birdie kissed me on the eyelid, and I slid
away from her grasp. I decided I needed to go outside for a
while.

103   It was cold. I leaned against the side of the house and bunched my jacket together at the neck, staring out past the yard to the driveway, which was crowded with my relative's vehicles. I breathed slowly. For a minute I'd imagined I might spin out of control. I might have broken free of Aunt Birdie, lisping and sashaying, cooing: "My new play I auditioned for. Oh, how wonderful I am." I might have told everyone, in a loud voice, what hypocrites my parents were: "We're so proud of our Corky! How nice it is to have a son who's so glamorous and successful."

104   Corky came out a few moments later. He exhaled smoke as he poked his head out the door. "Todd," he said. "You're missing your party." He kept his body inside the house, so it looked like his head was disembodied, moving along the doorframe. He bent so he could look at me upside down. It was an old game from childhood. We used to practice miming around the edges of the doors, so from the other side it looked like we were floating, or being lifted by an invisible force. "Todd," he said, in a Donald Duck voice. "Why so glum, Todd?" His head vanished then, like a puppet yanked from a stage. He came out of the house, and stood beside me.

105   In the house, someone had turned on music, my father's Patsy Cline tape. It drifted mournfully in the stillness, wisping through the walls.

106   I sighed. "Did you ever," I said at last, "wonder what was going to happen to you?"

107   There was a flicker in his eyes, as if he'd forgotten something important. His smile wavered. "No," he said.

108   I considered this. Probably, he'd always known. "Well," I said. "What do you think will happen to me, then? Because I wonder. I wonder a lot."

109   He stared at me for a long time, and then put another cigarette to his lips. "You'll probably be miserable," he said. "Like everybody else." Our eyes met, and then we both looked down. His words hung there, with both of us considering them—as if he'd dropped a bowl at my feet, and we were both looking at the shards of broken glass. In the house, I could hear my father laughing.

110   "Thanks a lot," I said stiffly. "Sorry I asked."

111   He shrugged, and pulled a folded bill out of his pocket. He pushed it into my hand. "Maybe I will go squeeze into that dress," he whispered.

112   "Don't," I said through my teeth. I looked at the piece of paper in my hand. A hundred-dollar bill. "I can't take this," I said. "That's too much."

He lifted his eyebrows, and I watched him put it back in   113
his pocket. His hand slid out of his pocket holding a nickel,
which he flipped toward me. I fumbled, caught it. "There," he
said.

"Very funny," I said. He dragged deeply on his cigarette.   114
We stared at each other. "Go ahead," my brother whis-   115
pered. Smoke curled around his face as he breathed, and he
pushed his hands through his dyed hair, loosening his ponytail. "I know you're dying to. Say 'faggot.' Say 'cocksucker.'"
He smirked at me. But then as I watched, it seemed that some
awful transformation was coming over his face. It was trembling and contorting like there was something beneath it trying to escape. For a second I imagined that he must be seeing
something terrifying, a dark shape lunging at us, and I turned
quickly. But there was only the empty yard.

"Say it," he whispered. "Say it."   116

VI.

CRIME AND PUNISHMENT

Introduction

You've heard all the statistics.

According to the Department of Justice, a violent crime occurs somewhere in the United States every twenty seconds. A murder occurs every half hour (about 23,000 in 1990). Someone is raped every six minutes. Over fifteen million arrests were made in 1990, over a million of them for drug abuse violations. Many more Americans are in prison, per capita, than citizens in any other "developed" nation. The point is this: Crime has become an inescapable fact of American life. And what to do about it has become a perennial issue, as the selections in this part demonstrate.

The first set of readings, a sort of transition from the previous part on civil liberties and civil rights, discusses the question of gun control. Should the ownership and possession of firearms be restricted? An absolute "no" is the answer of those who wish to protect citizens' right to bear arms. They cite for support the Second Amendment to our Constitution: "A well regulated militia being necessary to the security of a free state, the right of the people to keep and bear arms shall not be infringed." On the other hand, a number of people (some of them included in this book) contend that the right to purchase and keep guns is not absolute, that we already restrict in certain reasonable ways "the right to bear arms" (e.g., you can't own rocket launchers or a tank; you can't own guns if you're a minor or a convicted felon or mentally incompetent). Faced with certain abuses—shocking assassinations; 25,000 shooting deaths each year—proponents of gun control simply argue for additional reasonable restrictions, particularly on the handguns that are so available in our society and so commonly employed in the conduct of violent crime. Just what is it about Americans and guns, anyway? Why do they figure so prominently in our society? Can anything be done about it? Should anything be done about it? Do guns cause crime, or are people responsible?

That brings up the question posed by the second set of readings in this part of *Conversations:* What is the source of crime, anyway? Is crime simply a manifestation of our human fallibility, our human sinfulness, that Americans are simply unwilling to face up to? Or do economic circumstances cause crime? Are most people driven to crime, desperate to meet their daily needs or determined to strike out against a system that keeps them attached permanently to an underclass? Is crime a blow against "the system"? Then again, if economic circumstances cause crime, why were crime rates lower during the Great Depression than during the economic boom years of the 1960s or 1980s? Or does crime have a broader social explanation? Is it an outgrowth of our society's rootlessness, or our fragmented families, or impersonal "value-free" schools? Is crime an inevitable by-product of a national identity that prizes nonconformity and anti-authoritarianism? (Think of Bonnie and Clyde and Thelma and Louise.) Or is crime glorified and perpetuated by the media—by violent movies and newspaper sensationalism and television shows? (In this connection, you may wish to read or reread earlier sections in this book on the effects of television and pornography.) Finally, two contributions to this part ask if some people are simply programmed to commit crime by their genetic disposition, their lack of intelligence, or their gender. Such arguments were dismissed after World War II because they had been promulgated by fascists responsible for horrible crimes against humanity, but in the past decade they have been put forward again by people who ask why men commit more crimes than women do and whether there is indeed a genetic predisposition to criminal behavior.

The third group of readings debate the justice and wisdom of capital punishment. From the mid-1960s to 1977 no executions were carried out in America as the nation debated the abuses in the application of capital punishment and the wisdom of carrying out such punishment at all; indeed, capital punishment has been outlawed in a great many nations. But in 1976, the Supreme Court by a 5–4 vote decided that capital punishment is constitutional under certain circumstances. Executions inevitably followed, and so the debate about capital punishment has been renewed: Is capital punishment an expression of justice, "an eye for an eye"? Is it a useful deterrent to other would-be murderers? Or does it feed one of our basest instincts—for revenge? Is the death penalty cruel and unusual punishment? Is it unfairly applied to minority criminals, especially for crimes against majority members? If so, is this an argument for abolition, or for improving our system of justice?

Part VI concludes with a discussion of whether illegal drugs should be regulated or made legal. As you know, former presidents Bush and Reagan made well-publicized declarations of war against illegal drugs, but the war remains unwon. In the face of persistent and debilitating drug use, some have proposed legalization—not because they see drugs as less than a menace, but because they trust in other measures than law to fight it. Those who would legalize drugs propose that we approach drug abuse as an economic and medical problem rather than as a legal one. Legalizers wish to minimize the effects of illegal drugs by eliminating black market profits; legislation would drive down drug prices, the argument goes, and therefore reduce secondary crime motivated by the need to finance the drug habit. Legalizers would regulate drugs and tax drug producers, as liquor is regulated and taxed; the revenues could be used for education and drug prevention campaigns, and for treatment of drug addicts. Those who would legalize drugs argue by analogy to the prohibition of alcohol in the 1920s, a prohibition that made average citizens into criminals, made gangsters and rumrunners into millionaires, and reduced respect for law throughout the land. But those against legalization also point to Prohibition—to the end of Prohibition in 1930, when alcohol use skyrocketed. They argue that legalizing drugs would result in an inevitable spread in the use of cocaine and heroin, and an inevitable increase in cocaine babies, child abuse, wrecked automobiles and airplanes, and wrecked lives. And they contend that it is against the American grain to legalize immoral acts, no matter how often the acts are being committed.

In any case, what to do about drugs—and what to do about crime and criminals in general—will continue to engage our national attention for the remainder of this century, if not beyond.

SHOULD GUNS BE REGULATED?

Leonard Kriegel

A Loaded Question: What Is It About Americans and Guns?

Leonard Kriegel (born 1933), a writer of fiction and essays, contributed the following piece to Harper's *magazine, a publication featuring contributions on American politics and culture, in mid-1992. The article itself will tell you more about him.*

I have fired a gun only once in my life, hardly experience 1
enough to qualify one as an expert on firearms. As limited as my exposure to guns has been, however, my failure to broaden that experience had nothing at all to do with moral disapproval or with the kind of righteous indignation that views an eight-year-old boy playing cops and robbers with a cap pistol as a preview of the life of a serial killer. None of us can speak with surety about alternative lives, but had circumstances been different I suspect I not only would have hunted but very probably would have enjoyed it. I might even have gone in for target shooting, a "sport" increasingly popular in New York City, where I live (like bowling, it is practiced indoor in alleys). To be truthful, I have my doubts that target shooting would really have appealed to me. But in a country in which grown men feel passionately about a game as visibly ludicrous as golf, anything is possible.

The single shot I fired didn't leave me with a traumatic 2
hatred of or distaste for guns. Quite the opposite. I liked not only the sense of incipient skill firing that shot gave me but also the knowledge that a true marksman, like a good hitter in baseball, had to practice—and practice with a real gun. Boys on the cusp of adolescence are not usually disciplined, but they do pay attention to the demands of skill. Because I immediately recognized how difficult it would be for me to

practice marksmanship, I was brought face to face with the
fact that my career as a hunter was over even before it had
started.

3   Like my aborted prospects as a major league ballplayer,
my short but happy life as a hunter could be laid at the
metaphorical feet of the polio virus which left me crippled at
the age of eleven. Yet the one thing that continues to amaze
me as I look back to that gray February afternoon when I discovered the temptation of being a shooter and hunter is that I
did not shoot one or the other of the two most visible targets—myself or my friend Jackie, the boy who owned the .22.

4   Each of us managed to fire one shot that afternoon. And
when we returned to the ward in which we lived along with
twenty other crippled boys between the ages of nine and thirteen, we regaled our peers with a story unashamedly embel-
lished in the telling. As the afternoon chill faded and the
narrow winter light in which we had hunted drifted toward
darkness, Jackie managed to hide the .22 from ward nurses
and doctors on the prowl. What neither of us attempted to
hide from the other boys was our brief baptism in the world
of guns.

5   Like me, Jackie was a Bronx boy, as ignorant about guns as
I was. Both of us had been taken down with polio in the summer of '44. We had each lost the use of our legs. We were currently in wheelchairs. And we had each already spent a year
and a half in the aptly named New York State Reconstruction
Home, a state hospital for long-term physical rehabilitation.
Neither of us had ever fired anything more lethal than a Daisy
air rifle, popularly known as a BB gun—and even that, in my
case at least, had been fired under adult supervision. But
Jackie and I were also American claimants, our imaginations
molded as much by Hollywood westerns as by New York
streets. At twelve, I was a true Jeffersonian who looked upon
the ownership of a six-shooter as every American's "natural"
right.

6   To this day I don't know how Jackie got hold of that .22. He
refused to tell me. And I still don't know how he got rid of it
after our wheelchair hunt in the woods. For months afterward I would try to get him to promise that he and I would go
hunting again, but, as if our afternoon hunt had enabled him
to come to terms with his own illusions about the future
(something that would take me many more years), Jackie
simply shook his head and said, "That's over." I begged, whee-
dled, cajoled, threatened. Jackie remained obdurate. A single
shot for a single hunt. It would have to be sufficient.

I never did find out whether or not I hit the raccoon. On   7
the ride back to the ward, Jackie claimed I had. After he
fired his shot, he dropped from his wheelchair and slid backward on his rump to the abandoned water pipe off the side
of the dirt road into which the raccoon had leaped at the
slashing crack of the .22. His hand came down on something
red—a bloodstain, he excitedly suggested, as he lifted himself into his wheelchair and we turned to push ourselves
back to the ward. It looked like a rust stain to me, but I
didn't protest. I was quite willing to take whatever credit I
could. That was around an hour after the two of us, fresh
from lunch, had pushed our wheelchairs across the hospital
grounds, turning west at the old road that cut through the
woods and led to another state home, this one ministering to
the retarded. The .22, which lay on Jackie's lap, had bounced
and jostled as we maneuvered our wheelchairs across that
rutted road in search of an animal—any animal would do—
to shoot. The early February sky hung above us like a charcoal drawing, striations of gray slate shadings feeding our
nervous expectation.

It was Jackie who first spotted the raccoon. Excited, he   8
handed the .22 to me, a gesture spurred, I then thought, by
friendship. Now I wonder whether his generosity wasn't simply self-protection. Until that moment, the .22 lying across
Jackie's dead legs had been an abstraction, as much an imitation gun as the "weapons" boys in New York City constructed
out of the wood frames and wood slats of fruit and vegetable
crates, nails, and rubber bands—cutting up pieces of discarded linoleum and stiff cardboard to use as ammunition. I
remember the feel of the .22 across my own lifeless legs, the
weight of it surprisingly light, as I stared at the raccoon who
eyed us curiously from in front of the broken pipe. Then I
picked up the gun, aimed, and squeezed the trigger, startled
not so much by the noise nor by the slight pull, but by the
fact that I had actually fired at something. The sound of the
shot was crisp and clean. I felt as if I had done something
significant.

Jackie took the gun from me. "Okay," he said eagerly. "My   9
turn now." The raccoon was nowhere in sight, but he aimed
in the direction of the water pipe into which it had disappeared and squeezed the trigger. I heard the crack again, a
freedom of music now, perhaps because we two boys had
suddenly been bound to each other and had escaped, for this
single winter afternoon moment, the necessary but mundane courage which dominates the everyday lives of crippled

children. "Okay," I heard him cry out happily, "we're god-
damn killers now."

10   A formidable enough hail and farewell to shooting. And
certainly better than being shot at. God knows what happened to that raccoon. Probably nothing; but for me, firing
that single shot was both the beginning and the end of my life
as a marksman. The raccoon may have been wounded, as
Jackie claimed. Perhaps it had crawled away, bleeding, to die
somewhere in the woods. I doubt it. And I certainly hope I
didn't hit it, although in February 1946, six months before I
returned to the city and to life among the "normals," I would
have taken its death as a symbolic triumph. For that was a
time I needed any triumph I could find, no matter how minor.
Back then it seemed natural to begin an uncertain future with
a kill—even if one sensed, as I did, that my career as a hunter
was already over. The future was hinting at certain demands
it would make. And I was just beginning to bend into myself,
to protect my inner man from being crushed by the knowledge of all I would never be able to do. Hunting would be just
another deferred dream.

11   But guns were not a dream. Guns were real, definitive,
stamped on the imagination of their functional beauty. A gun
was not a phallic symbol; a gun didn't offer me revenge on
polio; a gun would not bring to life dead legs or endow
deferred dreams with substance. I am as willing as the next
man to quarantine reality within psychology. But if a rose is
no more than a rose, then tell me why a gun can't simply be a
gun? Guns are not monuments to fear and aspiration any
more than flowers are.

12   I was already fascinated by the way guns looked. I was
even more fascinated by what they did and by what made
people use them. Like any other twelve-year-old boy, I was
absorbed by talk about guns. Six months after the end of the
Second World War, boys in our ward were still engrossed by
the way talking about guns entangled us in the dense under-
brush of the national psyche. And no one in that ward was
more immersed in weaponry than I. On the verge of adolescence, forced to seek and find adventure in my own imagination, I was captivated by guns.

13   It was a fascination that would never altogether die. A few
weeks ago I found myself nostalgically drifting through the
arms and armor galleries of the Metropolitan Museum of Art.
Years ago I had often taken my young sons there. A good part

of my pleasure now derived from memories pinned to the leisurely innocence of those earlier visits. As I wandered among those rich cabinets displaying ornate pistols and rifles whose carved wood stocks were embossed with gold and silver and ivory and brass, I was struck by how incredibly lovely many of these weapons were. It was almost impossible to conceive of them as serving the function they had been designed to serve. These were not machines designed to kill and maim. Created with an eye to beauty, their sense of decorative purpose was as singular as a well-designed eighteenth-century silver drinking cup. These guns in their solid display cases evoked a sense of the disciplined craftsmanship to which a man might dedicate his life.

Flintlocks, wheel locks, a magnificent pair of ivory pistols owned by Catherine the Great—all of them as beckoning to the touch of fingers, had they not been securely locked behind glass doors, as one of those small nineteenth-century engraved cameos that seem to force time itself to surrender its pleasures. I gazed longingly at a seventeenth-century wheel lock carbine, coveting it the way I might covet a drinking cup by Cellini or a small bronze horse and rider by Bologna. Its beautifully carved wooden stock had been inlaid with ivory, brass, silver, and mother-of-pearl, its pride of artisanship embossed with the name of its creator, Caspar Spät. I smiled with pleasure. Then I wandered through the galleries until I found myself in front of a case displaying eighteenth-century American flintlock rifles, all expressing the democratic spirit one finds in Louis Sullivan's buildings or Whitman's poetry or New York City playgrounds built by the WPA during the Great Depression. Their polished woods were balanced by ornately carved stag-antler powder horns, which hung like Christmas decorations beneath them. To the right was another display case devoted to long-barreled Colt revolvers; beyond that, a splendidly engraved 1894 Winchester rifle and a series of Smith & Wesson revolvers, all of them decorated by Tiffany.

And yet they were weapons, designed ultimately to do what weapons have always done—destroy. Only in those childlike posters of the 1970s did flower stems grow out of the barrel of a gun. People who shoot, like people who cook, understandably choose the best tools available. And if it is easier to hit a target with an Uzi than a homemade zip gun, chances are those who want to hit the target will feel few qualms about choosing the Uzi.

16   Nonetheless, these galleries are a remarkable testimony to
the functional beauty of guns. Nor am I the only person who
has been touched by their beauty. The problem is to define
where the killing ceases and the beauty begins. At what point
does a young boy's sense of adventure transform itself into
the terror of blood and destruction and pain and death? I
remember my sons' excitement when they toured these
splendid galleries with me. (Yes, doctor, I did permit them to
enjoy guns. And neither became a serial killer.) These weapons helped bring us together, bound father and sons, just
as going to baseball games or viewing old Chaplin movies
had.

17   Geography may not be the sole father of morality, but one
would have to be remarkably naive to ignore its claims
altogether. As I write this, I can see on the table in front of me
a newspaper headlining the most recent killings inflicted on
New York City's anarchic populace. Firearms now rule street
and schoolyard, even as the rhetoric of politicians demanding
strict gun control escalates—along with the body count.

18   And yet I recognize that one man's fear and suffering is
another man's freedom and pleasure. Here is the true morality of geography. Like it or not, we see the world against a
landscape of accommodation. Guns may be displayed behind
glass cases in that magnificent museum, but in the splendid
park in which that museum has been set down like a crowning jewel, guns have been known to create not art but terror.
Functional beauty, it turns out, does not alter purpose.

19   I have a friend who has lived his entire life in small towns
in Maine. My friend is both a hunter and a connoisseur of
guns. City streets and guns may be a volatile mix, but the
Maine woods and guns apparently aren't. Rifles and pistols
hang on my friend's living room wall like old family portraits.
They are lived with as comfortably as a family heirloom. My
friend speaks knowingly of their shape, describes each
weapon lovingly, as if it possessed its own substance. He is
both literate and civilized, but he would never deny that these
guns are more than a possession to him. They are an altar
before which he bends the knee, a right of ownership he considers inviolable, even sacrosanct. And yet my friend is not a
violent man.

20   I, too, am not a violent man. But I am a New Yorker. And
like most people who live in this city, I make certain assumptions about the value of the very indignities one faces by
choosing to live here. If I didn't, I probably couldn't remain in
New York. For with all of the problems it forces one to face,

the moral geography of New York also breeds a determination not to give in to the daily indignities the city imposes.

During the summer of 1977, I lived within a different   21
moral geography. I was teaching a graduate seminar on Manhood and American Culture at the University of New Mexico in Albuquerque, tracing the evolution of the American man from Ben Franklin's sturdy, middle-class acolyte to the rugged John Wayne of *Stagecoach*. Enchanted by the New Mexico landscape, I would frequently drive off to explore the small towns and brilliant canyons in whose silences ghosts still lingered. One day a friend volunteered to drive with me into the Manzano Mountains. I had announced my desire to look at the ruins of a seventeenth-century mission fort at Gran Quivira, while he wanted me to meet a man who had, by himself, built a house in those haunting, lovely mountains.

Tension between Anglos and Hispanics was strong in New   22
Mexico in the summer of 1977. Even a stranger could feel a palpable, almost physical, struggle for political and cultural hegemony. Coming from a New York in which the growing separation of black and white was already threatening to transform everyday life into a racial battlefield, I did not feel particularly intimidated by this. Instead of black and white, New Mexico's ethnic and racial warfare would be between Anglo, Hispanic, and Indian. Mountainair, where we were to visit my friend's friend, was considered an Anglo town. Chilili, some miles up the road, was Hispanic.

My friend's friend had built his house on the outskirts of   23
Mountainair, with a magnificent view of ponderosa pine. He was a man in his early sixties and had come to New Mexico from Virginia soon after World War II to take a job as a technical writer in a nuclear research laboratory in Albuquerque. Before the war he had done graduate work in literature at the University of Virginia, but the demands of fatherhood had decided him against finishing his doctorate. Like so many Americans before him, he had taken wife and young children to start over in the West.

In the warmth and generosity of his hospitality, however,   24
he remained a true Southerner. As we sat and talked and laughed in a huge sun-drenched living room that opened onto that magnificent view of the mountains and pines and long New Mexico sky, I could not help but feel that here was the very best of this nation—a man secure in himself, a man of liberal sympathies and a broad understanding of human behavior and a love of children and grandchildren and wife, a

man who spoke perceptively of Jane Austen's novels and
spoke sadly of the savage threat of drugs (his oldest son, a veteran of the war in Vietnam, was living with him, along with
wife and three-year-old daughter, trying to purge the heroin
addiction that threatened to wreck his life).

25   I remember him happily holding forth on Jane Austen's
Persuasion when his body suddenly seemed to freeze in mid-
sentence. I could hear a motor in the distance. Without
another word, he turned and crossed the room. Twin double-
barreled shotguns hung on the wall above the fireplace. He
took one, his right hand scooping shells from a canvas bag
hanging from a thong looped around a horseshoe nail banged
shoulder-high into the wall. His son, the ex-Marine, grabbed
the other gun and scooped shells from the same bag. Through
the glassed-in cathedral living room leading to the porch, I
watched the two of them stand side by side, shotguns pointed
at a pickup truck already out of range. "Those bastards!" I
heard my host snarl.

26   "We'll get 'em yet, Pop," his son said. "I swear it."

27   After we left to drive on to the ruins of Gran Quivira, I
asked the friend who had accompanied me to explain what
had happened. "A pickup truck from Chilili. Hispanics driving up the mountain to cut trees. It's illegal. But they do it
anyway."

28   "Do the trees belong to your friend?"

29   "Not his trees. Not his mountain." Then he shrugged.

30   "But it's his gun."

31   I angrily cast my eyes at the man and find myself staring
into the twin barrels of a shotgun loosely held but pointed
directly at me. It is that same summer in Albuquerque, three
weeks later, and I am sitting in the driver's seat of my car, my
ten-year-old son, Bruce, directly behind me. Alongside him is
the eleven-year-old daughter of the man who had invited me
to teach at the University of New Mexico. I have just backed
my car away from a gasoline pump to allow another car to
move out of the garage into the road. As the other car came
out of the gas station, the man with the shotgun adroitly cut
me off and maneuvered his rust-pocked yellow pickup ahead
of me in line before I could get back to the gas pump.

32   My first reaction is irritation with my car, as if the steel
and chrome were sentient and responsible. It is the same
ugly gold 1971 Buick in which, five summers earlier, I had
driven through a Spanish landscape remarkably similar to

the New Mexico in which I now find myself. Bruce had been with me then, too, along with his older brother and mother. But it is not the Buick that attracts men with guns. Nor is it that mythical violence of American life in which European intellectuals believe so fervently. In Spain we had been stopped at a roadblock, a sandbagged machine gun aimed by one of Franco's troops perusing traffic like a farmer counting chickens in a henhouse. The soldiers had asked for passports, scowled at the children, examined the Buick as if it were an armored tank, inspecting glove compartment and trunk and wedging their hands into the spaces between seat and back. At the hotel restaurant at which we stopped for lunch twenty minutes later, we learned that two *guardia civil* had been ambushed and killed by Basque guerrillas. During Franco's last years, such acts grew more and more frequent. Spain was filled with guns and soldiers. One was always aware of the presence of soldiers patrolling the vacation beaches of the Costa del Sol—and particularly aware of their guns.

As I am aware of the shotgun now. And as I am growing   33
aware of that same enraged sense of humiliation and helplessness that seized me as those Spanish soldiers examined car and sons and wife, their guns casually pointed at all I loved most in the world, these other lives that made my life significantly mine. "Guns don't kill, people do!" Offer that mind-deadening cliché to a man at a roadblock watching the faces of soldiers for whom the power of a gun is simply that it permits them to feel contempt for those without guns. Tell that to a man sitting in a car with two young children, contemplating doing what he knows he cannot do because the gun is in another man's hands. Both in Spain and in this New Mexico that Spain had planted in the New World like a genetic acorn breeding prerogatives of power, guns endowed men with a way to settle all questions of responsibility.

The man with the shotgun says nothing. He simply holds   34
the weapon in his beefy hand, its muzzle casually pointed in my direction. I toy with the notion of getting out of the car and confronting him. I am angry, enraged. I don't want to give in to his rude power. Only my son and my colleague's daughter are in the back of the car. Defensively, I turn to look at them. My colleague's daughter is wide-eyed and frightened. Bruce is equally frightened, but his eyes are on me. I am his father and he expects me to do something, to say something, to alter the balance of expectation and reality.

Our car was on line for gas first. To a ten-year-old, justice is a simple arithmetic.

35   To that ten-year-old's father it is not necessarily more complex. I could tell myself that it was insane to tell a man pointing a shotgun at me and these two children that he has broken the rules. Chances are he wouldn't have fired, would probably have responded with a shrug of the shoulders no more threatening than a confession of ignorance.

36   Obviously, none of this mattered. My growing sense of humiliation and rage had nothing to do with having to wait an extra minute or two while the station attendant filled the tank of the pickup. I was in no particular rush. I was simply returning home from a day-long excursion to a state park, where my son and his new friend had crawled through caves and climbed rocks splashed by a warm spring. But I was facing a man with a shotgun, a man who understood that people with guns define options for themselves.

37   The man with the gun decides whether or not to shoot, just as he chooses where to point his gun. It is not political power that stems from the barrel of a gun, as Maoists used to proclaim so ritualistically. It is individual power, the ability to impose one's presence on the world, simply because guns always do what language only sometimes does: Guns command! Guns command attention, guns command discipline, guns command fear.

38   And guns bestow rights and prerogatives, even to those who have read Jane Austen and engaged the world in their own comedy of manners. There is a conditional nature to all rights. And there are obligations that should not be shunted aside. Guns are many things, some symbolic, some all too real. But in real life they are always personal and rarely playful. They measure not capacity but the obligation the bearer of the gun has to believe that power belongs not to the gun but to him. And yet were I to tell this to my friend in Maine— that sophisticated, literate, humane man—I suspect he would turn to me and say, "That's right. There's always got to be somebody's finger on the trigger."

39   A confession, then: I may be as fascinated by guns as my gun-owning and gun-loving friend in Maine, but were it up to me, I would rid America of its guns. I would be less verbally self-righteous about gun control than I was in the past, for I think I have begun to understand those who, like my friend in Maine, have arguments of their own in defense of guns. They

are formidable arguments. Their fear matches mine, and I assume that their anguish over the safety of their children is also equal to mine. I, too, know the statistics. I can repeat, as easily as he can, that in Switzerland, where an armed citizenry is the norm, the homicide rate is far lower than in many countries that carefully control the distribution of guns to their populace. Laws are simply words on paper—unless they embody what a population wants.

There is no logic with which I can convince my gun-own-   40
ing friend in Maine. But there are images I wish I could get him to focus on. Like me, he is a writer. Only I write about cities, and my friend writes about the Maine woods. He is knowledgeable about animals and rocks and trees and silence, and I am knowledgeable about stubs of grass growing between cracks in a concrete sidewalk and the pitch and pull of conflicting voices demanding recognition. I wish I could explain to him the precise configuration of that double-barreled shotgun pointing at me and those two children. Maybe then I could convince him that truth is not merely a matter of geography. Yes, guns don't kill and people do—but in the America he and I share, those people usually kill with guns.

Four years after that incident at the gas station, I was sit-   41
ting with Bruce in a brasserie in Paris. It was a sunny July afternoon and we were eating lunch at a small outside table, the walls of the magisterial Invalides beckoning to us from across the street. Bruce was fourteen, and fifteen minutes earlier he had returned from his first trip alone on the Paris Metro. Suddenly a man approached, eyes menacing and bloodshot. He was short and thick, his body seemingly caked by the muscularity of a beaten-down club fighter or an unemployed stevedore. He stared at us, eyes filled with the rage of the insane. Then he flexed his muscles as if he were on exhibit as a circus strong man, cried out something—a sound I remember as a cross between gargling and choking—and disappeared just as suddenly down the street.

The incident still haunts me. The French, I suspect, are as   42
violent as they like to claim we Americans are. But in Paris it is difficult for a man filled with rage and craziness to get hold of a gun. Not impossible, mind you, just difficult. Somewhere along the line, the French have learned not that guns don't kill and people do but that people with guns can kill. And they know what we have yet to acknowledge—that when the Furies dance in the head it's best to keep the weapons in

display cases in the museum. For that, at least, I wish my friend in Maine could learn to be grateful. As I was, eating lunch with my son in Paris.

Roy Innis

Gun Control Sprouts
from Racist Soil

Roy Innis is the respected national chairman of the Congress of Racial Equality. Born in the Virgin Islands in 1934, as a youth he moved with his family to New York City and he has continued to make his home there. He contributed the following article to The Wall Street Journal *in November 1991.*

1   What irony. Most black leaders (as distinct from rank-and-file blacks) are supporters, at least in public, of the gun control—really, prohibition—movement. Do they realize that America's gun-control movement sprouted from the soil of Roger B. Taney, the racist chief justice who wrote the infamous *Dred Scott* decision of 1857?

2   In the early part of the 19th century, Dred Scott, a black slave, had been taken by his owner from Missouri, a slave state, to Illinois, a free state. From there he was taken into the Wisconsin territory, free territory above the 36° 30' latitude of the Missouri Compromise. After living in free territory for a while, he returned with his owner to Missouri.

3   When his owner died in 1846, Scott sued in the state courts of Missouri for his freedom, on the ground that he had lived in free territory. He won his case, but it was reversed in the Missouri Supreme Court. Scott appealed to the federal courts, since the person he was actually suing, John Sanford, the executor of the estate that owned Scott, lived in New York.

4   It was in that setting that Chief Justice Taney made his infamous rulings:

1. That black people, whether free or slave, were not citizens of the U.S.; therefore, they had no standing in court.
2. Scott was denied freedom.
3. The Missouri Compromise was ruled unconstitutional.

Well known to most students of race relations is the former attorney general and secretary of the Treasury's pre-civil war dictum that black people "being of an inferior order" had "no right which any white man was bound to respect." Much less known are his equally racist pronouncements denying black people, whether slave or free, specific constitutional protections enjoyed by whites.

In *Dred Scott* Chief Justice Taney, writing for the court's majority, stated that if blacks were "entitled to the privileges and immunities of citizens,... it would give persons of the negro race, who were recognized as citizens in any one state of the union, the right... to keep and carry arms wherever they went. And all of this would be done in the face of the subject race of the same color, both free and slaves, and inevitably producing discontent and insubordination among them, and endangering the peace and safety of the state...."

Although much of Justice Taney's overly racist legal reasoning was repudiated by events that followed—such as the Civil War and Reconstruction—the subliminal effects were felt throughout that era. In the post-Reconstruction period, when the pendulum swung back to overt racism, Justice Taney's philosophy resurfaced. It was during this period that racial paranoia about black men with guns intensified. It was potent enough to cause the infringement on the Second Amendment to the Constitution's "right... to keep and bear arms."

Under natural law, a freeman's right to obtain and maintain the implements of self-defense has always been sacred. This right was restricted or prohibited for serfs, peasants and slaves. Gun control was never an issue in America until after the Civil War when black slaves were freed.

It was this change in the status of the black man, from slave to freeman, that caused racist elements in the country (North and South) to agitate for restrictions on guns—ignoring long established customs and understanding of the Second Amendment. The specter of a black man with rights of a freeman, bearing arms, was too much for the early heirs of Roger Taney to bear.

10   The 14th and 15th Amendments to the Constitution, along
with the various Reconstruction civil rights acts, prevented
gun prohibitionists from making laws that were explicitly
racist and that would overtly deny black people the right to
bear arms. The end of Reconstruction signaled the return of
Taneyism—overtly among the masses and covertly on the
Supreme Court. Gun-control legislation of the late 19th and
early 20th centuries, enacted at the state and local levels, was
implicitly racist in conception. And in operation, those laws
invidiously targeted blacks.

11   With the influx of large numbers of Irish, Italian and Jewish immigrants into the country, gun laws now also targeted
whites from the underprivileged classes of immigrants. Eventually these oppressive gun laws were extended to affect all
but a privileged few. Throughout the history of New York
state's Sullivan law, enacted at the start of the 20th century,
mainly the rich and powerful have had easy access to licenses
to carry handguns. Some of the notables who have received
that privilege include Eleanor Roosevelt, John Lindsay,
Donald Trump, Arthur Sulzberger, Joan Rivers and disk
jockey Howard Stern.

12   Of the 27,000 handgun carry permits in New York City,
fewer than 2% are issued to blacks—who live and work in
high-crime areas and really are in need of protection.

13   And what of the origins of the National Rifle Association,
which is wrongly viewed as a racist organization by the black
supporters of gun prohibition? It was inspired and organized
by Union Army officers after the Civil War.

Elizabeth Swazey
Women and Handguns

*Elizabeth Swazey, an attorney, a certified firearms instructor,
and the director of the National Rifle Association's group on
women's issues, writes a column every other month for* American Rifleman *magazine (a publication of the NRA that is
devoted to articles of various kinds on various kinds of firearms and related issues). The following such column appeared
in 1992.*

James Michael Barnes failed to appear in court on March 1
8, 1991. He was dead.

According to New Jersey *Courier-Post* staff reporters Alan 2
Guenther and Renee Winkler, by February 1990 the relationship between Amy Gardiner and James Michael Barnes had
broken off. On February 9, he appeared on Gardiner's doorstep to return some of her things. Instead, he raped her. He
even photographed the event. Barnes pled guilty to assault
and was sentenced to two years probation. He also was
ordered to stay away from Gardiner and her relatives.

He didn't. According to court documents, Barnes broke 3
into Gardiner's home, stole from her, left a hot iron on her
carpet and smeared her walls and furniture with feces.

During this period, Barnes was charged with robbing and 4
intimidating another ex-girlfriend. Bail was set at $50,000
cash. Barnes stayed in jail until January 17. On that date,
prosecutors sought to have his opportunity for bail revoked
on grounds he was a threat to Gardiner. But the judge actually *reduced* Barnes' bail to $25,000. Barnes posted the 10%
required and was free that afternoon.

Free to look for Amy Gardiner. 5

But in the meantime, Gardiner had done three things. She 6
had filed harassment charges against Barnes; she had
changed her address; and she had purchased a shotgun. Two
weeks later at 9:30 in the evening, Gardiner's doorbell rang.
She was alone and didn't answer the door. Soon the telephone
rang. When she answered, the caller hung up. Sensing danger, Gardiner went to the bedroom to get the shotgun. Barnes,
armed with a revolver and a disturbed mind, kicked in the
front door and stormed into the bedroom, threatening to kill
her. Gardiner fired once. Barnes died. The terror was over.
But at what cost?

7   Taking the life of another human being, *no matter how justified*, carries a heavy burden. Why New Jersey Superior
Court Judge Joseph F. Green, Jr., allowed Barnes to buy temporary freedom for $2,500 is beyond me. Is that the price he
places on a woman's suffering, on the white-hot fear she felt
that night, alone, with a madman trying to kill her?

8   Amy Gardiner could be any of us, *You, Your wife, daughter
or friend*. According to the Dept. of Justice, three of four
American women will face crime in their lifetimes. And, as
has been held in another case, "...a government and its
agents are under no general duty to provide public services,
such as police protection, to any particular individual
citizen...." *Warren v. District of Columbia*, 444 A.2d 1
(D.C.App.181).

9   Or, put another way, "[T]here is no constitutional right to
be protected by the state against being murdered by criminals
or madmen." *Bowers v. DeVito*, 686 F.2d 616, at 618 (7th
Cir. 1982).

10   Amy Gardiner faced a criminal madman. Thankfully, the
innocent life prevailed. And while it is human nature to avoid
thinking about unpleasant topics, we must recognize that *any
one of us* could be violently attacked. Until our criminal justice system becomes a victims' justice system—and NRA is
helping turn the tide through our *CrimeStrike* program—violent criminals like James Michael Barnes will continue to be
routinely set free. We need to decide, in advance, how to
respond if you, I or a loved one is threatened.

11   Owning a gun, and whether to use it in lawful self-defense,
are *deeply personal choices* that each individual must make.
For those who decide in favor of gun ownership, NRA can
help. We offer introductory Personal Protection Seminars for
women across the country, and the intensive Personal Protection Program to men and women nationwide through a network of certified instructors. Information about both is
available by simply calling (800) 368-5714 or (202) 828-6224.

12   Handgun Control, Inc. (HCI) doesn't want women to have
this choice. The group's Chairman Emeritus Pete Shields
advises women faced with criminal attack to "give them what
they want." But what James Michael Barnes wanted was for
Amy Gardiner *to be dead.*

13   Sometimes HCI softens its message by expressing "concern" that if a woman tried to use a gun in self-defense, it
would be taken away and used against her. Why doesn't HCI
Chair Sarah Brady ever say this about men? Amy Gardiner
faced an armed attacker and prevailed. And the most recent

National Crime Survey by the Bureau of Justice Statistics found that in *less than 1%* of cases did criminals manage to turn guns against their owners.

HCI says one of its principal political goals this year is to conduct a "public information campaign" about "the extremist nature of the gun lobby and alert women...that they've been targeted as a new market...."   14

So the lines are drawn: NRA says defend your right to defend yourself. HCI says give criminals what they want. Now who's extreme?   15

National Rifle Association
Don't Edit the Bill of Rights

The ad printed on these two pages, developed and paid for by the National Rifle Association Institute for Legislative Action, appeared in USA Today *and many other newspapers in December 1991—on the 200th anniversary of the ratification of the Bill of Rights.*

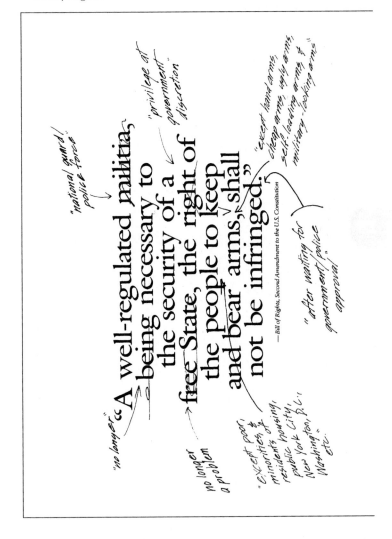

Paul Lawton

Constitutional Law and the Second Amendment

Paul Lawton was a student at the University of Texas at Austin when he wrote the following essay for a writing course there. He's pursuing a career in journalism.

In the end more than they wanted freedom, they wanted security. When the Athenians finally wanted not to give to society but for society to give to them, when the freedom they wished for was freedom from responsibility, then Athens ceased to be free.

—Edward Gibbon (1737–1794)

1   In 1994 Congress passed an outright ban on nineteen different types of assault weapons under the Schumer amendment to the Clinton Crime Bill. Representative John Dingell (D–MI) remarked when the bill passed that the ban was "obnoxious, offensive and contrary to the rights of all Americans." This, however, did not stop the representative from voting for the Crime Bill, in which the ban was contained. His reasoning was that he considered the remainder of the bill to be "smart and tough" (*Washington Times*, 8/26/94). While the representative seemed to have "voted his conscience" on the bill, one wonders if this ban circumvented the Second Amendment to satisfy the American public's need for safer streets.

2   The push against the assault weapons was extremely popular last year, and lawmakers were quick to jump on the bandwagon against weapons that are designed to "kill humans." Many argued that the weapons had no useful purpose for hunting and that the weapons were also impractical for defending the homestead. But even so, the federal government is supposed to amend the Constitution before they do something that is strictly prohibited by its own guidelines. For instance, to circumvent the First Amendment's right to burn the American flag, the bill would need, under Article Five of the Constitution, a two-thirds approval in both houses. The bill would then need to be approved by three-fourths of the state legislatures before burning the flag could not be considered protected speech under the First Amendment.

There is nothing inherently wrong or evil with this amend- 3
ment process. Indeed, Chief Justice John Marshall wrote in
the nineteenth century that the Constitution was "intended to
endure for ages to come, and, consequently, to be adapted to
the various crises of human affairs." Marshall presented the
very modern idea that the Constitution is meant to be
amended to fit the various needs of future generations. Thus,
many people gripped with fear from violent crime in America
would probably express a wish to ban weapons whose sole
purpose is the taking of human life.

However, many groups including the para-militaries which 4
have recently been labeled as promoters of hate, have
espoused the view that assault weapons are covered under the
Second Amendment and cannot, without amendment, be
legally banned by the federal government. The pro-gun control movement has argued quite the opposite, that the Second
Amendment does not guarantee, in fact, an individual right
and only refers to a state militia's right to bear arms.

In order to understand what the pro-gun control move- 5
ment believes about the Second Amendment's application to
individual rights, it is important to look at the actual text of
the amendment:

> A well-regulated Militia, being necessary for the security of a
> free State, the right of the people to keep and bear Arms,
> shall not be infringed.

One can clearly see the confusion that the word "Militia" 6
brings into the meaning of the amendment. Thus, the Pro-
Gun Control Movement, along with the American Bar Association, the ACLU, and texts such as Tribe's *American Constitutional Law,* have enunciated that the Second Amendment only
applies to state militias and makes no reference to an individual right.

From this interpretation, it has been assumed that, since 7
the right to bear arms is not an individual right, the extent to
which citizens may keep weapons can be limited by the federal government. To many so-called experts, the federal government was thus within its legal limits to ban assault
weapons. However, by taking a close look at the actual language of the Second Amendment and the legal precedent set
by the Supreme Court of the United States, it becomes obvious that the 102nd Congress passed a law that was entirely
unconstitutional and the very antithesis of what the past and
current interpretation of the amendment should allow.

8   The language of the Second Amendment can most clearly
be linked to the generation of the idea that only the militia has
the right to "keep and bear arms." However, Roy Copperud, a
leading legal expert who is impartial to the gun control
debate, was recently interviewed on the possible inter-preta-
tions of the amendment. Copperud concluded that the structure of the sentence indicates that existence of the right to
keep arms is assumed and that "the thrust of the sentence is
that the right shall be preserved inviolate for the sake of ensuring a militia." He also concluded that the language of the
amendment, although still acceptable in modern times, could
be rewritten as, "Since a well-regulated militia is necessary to
the security of a free state, the right of the people to keep and
bear arms shall not be abridged" (Schulman, Second Amendment Foundation). This clearly shows that the meaning of the
sentence is that all citizens need weapons to protect the state
and that the federal government should realize this fact and
not interfere with the natural right of the people to protect
themselves and their society.

9   The intent and belief in an armed populace is clearly
present in the Founding Father's rhetoric. Thomas Jefferson
wrote that "the strongest reason for the people to retain the
right to keep and bear arms is, as a last resort, to protect
themselves against tyranny in government." This Lockonian
philosophy that man has a natural justified right for self-protection was present in many of the leaders of the time and
reflects itself in the language of the Bill of Rights and consequently the Second Amendment.

10   This clearly shows that the language of the amendment
does not coincide with the contemporary interpretation of
the amendment. However, this is not the *coup de grace* of the
pro-gun control argument. Rather it presents only half a case
in a constitutional interpretation. The second half of the case
is the Supreme Court's judicial precedent on the Second
Amendment.

11   Judicial precedent is important because the Court is not
able to go back in time and ask the original framers what they
meant and how far the federal government can go before it is
infringing on the rights of the people. Thus, the Court looks at
its own past decisions to help decide if a law is in fact unconstitutional. Unfortunately for the pro-gun control movement,
the judicial precedent of the Court does not indicate a strong
agreement with the assault weapon ban of 1994.

12   Perhaps the first case the court talked about concerning
the right to bear arms is the 1856 *Scott* v. *Sandford* case, most

commonly referred to as the Dred Scott decision. Though the final decision was remarkably barbaric, the rhetoric used by the judges to defend their decision shows an opinion of the court that affirms the belief that the right to arms is a natural right of free men. In the opinion, the judges ruled that one of the criteria for Scott to be free would be the right of free speech and the right "to keep and carry arms wherever...[he] went" (LEXIS, 60 U.S. 393).

The next case, which dealt specifically with the Second [13] Amendment, was *United States* v. *Cruikshank* in 1876 where the court recognized that the right to keep and bear arms "is not a right granted by the Constitution ...[but n]either is it in any manner dependent upon that instrument for its existence" (LEXIS).

But perhaps the most stunning indictment against the [14] Assault Weapons Ban comes from *United States* v. *Miller* in 1939. Here the court devised a test to discern if a weapon is applicable under the Second Amendment clause. The weapon in question was a sawed-off shotgun and the court ruled that:

> In the absence of any evidence tending to show that possession or use of a "shotgun having a barrel of less than eighteen inches in length" at this time has some reasonable relationship to the preservation or efficiency of a well-regulated militia, we cannot say that the Second Amendment guarantees the right to keep and bear such an instrument. Certainly it is not within judicial note that this weapon is any part of the ordinary military equipment or that its use could contribute to the common defense.

Thus, the court ruled that the weapon must be of military use [15] to be protected under the Second Amendment, which clearly destroys the pro-gun opinion that assault weapons can be banned because they are neither hunting nor self-protection firearms. Here the Court ruled the opposite to be true. Only weapons used for military purpose are protected (153 U.S. 535).

The Court also issued an opinion in Miller that the militia [16] mentioned in the Second Amendment consists of "all males physically capable of acting in concert for the common defense." They further elaborated on the duties of this civilian militia by saying that "when called for service these men...[are] expected to appear bearing arms supplied by themselves and of the kind in common use at the time" (307

U.S. 174). More precisely, contrary to Miller, the Court declared that the people mentioned in the Second Amendment included all citizens of the United States and not just young males. The 1990 *United States* v. *Verdugo-Urquirdez* decision further clarified that the Second Amendment applies to all citizens and legal aliens in the United States (110 S. Ct. 3039).

17   Thus, the court decisions render a view of the Second Amendment that cannot possibly allow for the prohibition of any weapon that might be used for war. Since the Bill of Rights is the final say on whether the government has overstepped its boundaries, it becomes clear that the 1994 U.S. Congress overstepped its boundaries into the rights of its rulers. It seems incomprehensible that this bill would pass when a scant fourteen years ago the Subcommittee on the Constitution of the Committee on the Judiciary remarked that "The conclusion is thus inescapable that the history, concept, and wording of the Second Amendment to the Constitution of the United States, as well as its interpretation by every major commentator and court in the first half-century after its ratification, indicates that what is protected is an individual right of a private citizen to own and carry firearms in a peaceful manner." This careless disregard for both the limitations and rules of the Constitution certainly should make the federal government suspect to the American people. For in the end, the rights guaranteed in the amendments are the only protection against a tyrannical government the people have. Any attempt to erode these liberties should be inquired about to the fullest extent. Any attempt to circumvent this process should be considered inexcusable.

Robert Goldwin

Gun Control Is Constitutional

Goldwin is a scholar affiliated with the American Enterprise Institute, a conservative research institute. He contributed the following to The Wall Street Journal, *the conservative business-news daily, in December 1991. The letters published after it and responding to it appeared a few weeks later in the same newspaper.*

Congress has been dismayingly inconsistent in its voting 1
on gun-control legislation this year, first passing the Brady
Bill, then moving in the opposite direction by defeating a provision to ban certain assault weapons and ammunition. But
in one respect members of Congress are consistent: they
demand respect for our "constitutional right to own a gun."
They cite the Constitution's Second Amendment and argue it
prohibits effective national regulation of the private ownership of guns.

But there are strong grounds for arguing that the Second 2
Amendment is no barrier to gun-control legislation. In my
opinion, it even provides a solid constitutional basis for effective national legislation to regulate guns and gun owners.

The best clues to the meaning of the key words and phrases 3
are in debates in the First Congress of the United States. The
Members of that Congress were the authors of the Second
Amendment. A constitutional amendment calling for the prohibition of standing armies in time of peace was proposed by
six state ratifying conventions. Virginia's version, later copied
by New York and North Carolina, brought together three elements in one article—affirmation of a right to bear arms, reliance on state militia, and opposition to a standing army.

"That the people have a right to keep and bear arms; that a 4
well regulated militia, composed of the body of the people
trained to arms, is the proper, natural, and safe defense of a
free state; that standing armies, in times of peace, are dangerous to liberty, and therefore ought to be avoided. . . ."

The purpose was to limit the power of the new Congress to 5
establish a standing army, and instead to rely on state militias
under the command of governors. The Constitution was ratified without adopting any of the scores of proposed amendments. But in several states ratification came only with
solemn pledges that amendments would follow.

6   Soon after the First Congress met, James Madison, elected as a congressman from Virginia on the basis of such a pledge, proposed a number of amendments resembling yet different from articles proposed by states. These eventually became the Bill of Rights. In the version of the arms amendment he presented, Madison dropped mention of a standing army and added a conscientious objector clause.

7   "The right of the people to keep and bear arms shall not be infringed, a well armed and well regulated militia being the best security of a free country, but no person religiously scrupulous of bearing arms shall be compelled to render military service in person."

8   In this version, "bearing arms" must mean "to render military service," or why else would there have to be an exemption for religious reasons? What right must not be infringed? The right of the people to serve in the militia.

9   This militia amendment was referred to a congressional committee and came out of committee in this form:

10   "A well regulated militia, composed of the body of the people, being the best security of a free state, the right of the people to keep and bear arms shall not be infringed; but no person religiously scrupulous shall be compelled to bear arms."

11   Two significant changes had been made: first, the phrase "to render military service in person" was replaced by the phrase, "to bear arms," again indicating that they are two ways to say the same thing; second, an explanation was added that the "militia" is "composed of the body of the people."

12   The House then debated this new version in committee of the whole and, surprisingly, considering the subsequent history of the provision, never once did any member mention the private uses of arms, for self-protection, or hunting, or any other personal purpose. The debate focused exclusively on the conscientious objector provision. Eventually the committee's version was narrowly approved. The Senate in turn gave it its final form: briefer, unfortunately more elliptical, and with the exemption for conscientious objectors deleted:

13   "A well-regulated militia, being necessary to the security of a free state, the right of the people to keep and bear arms, shall not be infringed."

14   Certain explanations were lost or buried in this legislative process: that the right to bear arms meant the right to serve in the militia; that just about everybody was included in the militia; and that the amendment as a whole sought to minimize if not eliminate reliance on a standing army by empha-

sizing the role of the state militia, which would require that
everyone be ready to be called to serve.

But what about the private right "to keep and bear arms,"   15
to own a gun for self-defense and hunting? Isn't that clearly
protected by the amendment? Didn't just about everyone own
a gun in 1791? Wouldn't that "right" go without saying? Yes,
of course, it would go without saying, especially then when
there were no organized police forces and when hunting was
essential to the food supply.

But such facts tell us almost nothing relevant to our ques-   16
tion. Almost everyone also owned a dog for the same purposes. The Constitution nevertheless says nothing about the
undeniable right to own a dog. There are uncountable numbers of rights not enumerated in the Constitution. These
rights are neither denied nor disparaged by not being raised
to the explicit constitutional level. All of them are constitutionally subject to regulation.

The right to bear arms protected in the Second Amend-   17
ment has to do directly with "a well-regulated militia." More
evidence of the connection can be found in the Militia Act of
1792.

"Every free able-bodied white male citizen" (it was 1792,   18
after all) was required by the act to "enroll" in the militia for
training and active service in case of need. When reporting
for service, every militiaman was required to provide a prescribed rifle or musket, and ammunition.

Here we see the link of the private and public aspects of   19
bearing arms. The expectation was that every man would
have his own firearms. But the aspect that was raised to the
level of constitutional concern was the public interest in
those arms.

What does this mean for the question of gun control   20
today? Well, for example, it means that Congress has the constitutional power to enact a Militia Act of 1992, to require
every person who owns a gun or aspires to own one to
"enroll" in the militia. In plain 1990s English, if you want to
own a gun, sign up with the National Guard.

Requiring every gun owner to register with the National   21
Guard (as we require 18-year-olds to register with the
Selective Service) would provide the information about
gunowners sought by the Brady and Staggers bills, and much
more. Standards could be set for purchase or ownership of
guns, and penalties could be established.

Restoring a 200-year-old understanding of the Constitution   22
may be difficult, but there isn't time to dawdle. Americans

now own more than 200 million guns, and opinion polls show Americans want gun control. Why not avail ourselves of the Second Amendment remedy? Call in the militia, which is, after all, "composed of the body of the people."

Responses to Robert Goldwin: Letters to the Editor of the *Wall Street Journal*

1   In his "Gun Control Is Constitutional" the American Enterprise Institute's Robert A. Goldwin's principal concern, it seems, is to deny that the right to keep and bear arms precludes the power to regulate gun ownership and use. Few would disagree. Even activities protected by the First Amendment may be regulated when they threaten the rights of others.

2   But Mr. Goldwin also writes that "The right to bear arms protected in the Second Amendment has to do directly with 'a well regulated militia'"; thus, arguably, he continues, "if you want to own a gun, sign up with the National Guard." Clearly, this goes well beyond regulating to protect the rights of others. This would condition the "right" to keep and bear arms on joining the National Guard.

3   Mr. Goldwin's mistake stems from his having confused a necessary with a sufficient condition. The Second Amendment, in its language and its history, makes plain that the need for a well-regulated militia is a *sufficient* condition for the right to keep and bear arms. Yet Mr. Goldwin treats it as a *necessary* condition, which enables him to conclude that Congress could deny an individual the right to own a gun if he did not join the National Guard.

4   Mr. Goodwin makes this mistake, in turn, because he has misread Madison's original version of the Second Amendment, which exempted conscientious objectors from military service. Thus he says that "In this version, 'bearing arms' must mean 'to render military service,' or why else would there have to be an exemption for religious reasons? What right must not be infringed? The right of the people to serve in the militia."

Plainly, any conscientious objector provision would arise   5
not from a *right* but from a *duty* to serve in the militia. Yet Mr.
Goldwin believes the amendment means, as he later says,
"that the right to bear arms meant the right to serve in the
militia." Thus does he reduce the first of these rights to the
second, when clearly it is much broader.

Roger Pilon
Senior Fellow and Director
Center for Constitutional Studies
CATO Institute

The militia is not the National Guard but rather the people   1
of the original states. In Ohio, we have an Ohio militia that is
not a part of the National Guard. The fear of standing armies
and the control these armed men gave a central government
was foremost in the Framers' minds when writing the Bill of
Rights. Thomas Jefferson moved to prevent this type of power
in a few people's hands by the Second Amendment. He stated,
"No free man shall ever be debarred the use of arms."

The addition in the early drafts of a conscientious-objector   2
clause was added for the preservation of religious freedoms,
which the Colonists had not had in England. It is unfortunate
today's "scholars" seem to spend their time picking apart history and the great thoughts of the visionary men who formed
this country.

In my personal celebration of this 200-year-old document,   3
I have pledged the following: I will give up my freedom of
speech when they cut out my tongue; I will give up my right
to worship when they have slain my God and myself; I will
assemble with the people of my choice even when they are
imprisoned, and I will give up my rifle when they pry my cold
dead fingers from around it.

Samuel R. Bush III

Let those who want guns join the National Guard, says Mr.   1
Goldwin. Ah, the sanctimonious arrogance of it. What gives
Mr. Goldwin the right to deny mine when I abide by the laws?

He stresses the differences between the world of 1791 and   2
today to suit his prejudice. He studiously ignores other major
differences between 1791 and today.

3   In 1791, punishment was swifter and surer. Plea bargaining was not epidemic; judges did not provide revolving doors on prisons. There was no army of drug dealers and junkies preying on the public. If anything, the reasons for citizens to own weapons for self-defense are more compelling today than they were in 1791.

4   Let Mr. Goldwin show us how he would make us safer in our homes and we might understand his wish to strip away our only sure defense.

Carl Roessler

1   Mr. Goldwin suggests gun control via enlistment in the National Guard. Swell idea. Updating the right to bear arms from 1791 to 1991, when I report for service, I'll bring, as required, a few items consistent with the current infantryman's inventory: a Barett Light .50 semiautomatic sniper rifle, so I can reach out and touch people half a mile away; a Squad Automatic Weapon firing 5.56mm rounds at the rate of a whole lot per second out of 30-round clips or hundred-round belts; a 40mm grenade launcher...but you get the idea. Then, as a thoroughly modern, well-regulated militiaman, I'll take my weapons home, just as did Morgan's riflemen, and the musket bearers of Lexington and Concord, and the Colonial light artillerists.

Andrew L. Isaac

Daniel Polsby

The False Promise
of Gun Control

The following essay appeared in March 1994 in The Atlantic
Monthly, *a venerable, mildly left-of-center monthly magazine
that carries book and movie reviews, original poetry and fiction, and commentary on current events and issues. Daniel
Polsby (born 1945) has been a full-time professor of law at
Northwestern University for over two decades. He teaches
courses in criminal law and regularly writes on constitutional,
criminal, and family law for academic publications.*

During the 1960s and 1970s the robbery rate in the United   1
States increased sixfold, and the murder rate doubled; the rate
of handgun ownership nearly doubled in that period as well.
Handguns and criminal violence grew together apace, and
national opinion leaders did not fail to remark on the coincidence.

It has become a bipartisan article of faith that more hand-   2
guns cause more violence. Such was the unequivocal conclusion of the National Commission on the Causes and
Prevention of Violence in 1969, and such is now the editorial
opinion of virtually every influential newspaper and magazine, from *The Washington Post* to *The Economist* to the *Chicago Tribune.* Members of the House and Senate who have
not dared to confront the gun lobby concede the connection
privately. Even if the National Rifle Association can produce
blizzards of angry calls and letters to the Capitol virtually
overnight, House members one by one have been going public, often after some new firearms atrocity at a fast-food restaurant or the like. And last November they passed the Brady
bill.

Alas, however well accepted, the conventional wisdom   3
about guns and violence is mistaken. Guns don't increase
national rates of crime and violence—but the continued proliferation of gun-control laws almost certainly does. Current
rates of crime and violence are a bit below the peaks of the
late 1970s, but because of a slight oncoming bulge in the risk
population of males aged fifteen to thirty-four, the crime rate
will soon worsen. The rising generation of criminals will have
no more difficulty than their elders did in obtaining the tools
of their trade. Growing violence will lead to calls for laws still

more severe. Each fresh round of legislation will be followed by renewed frustration.

4   Gun-control laws don't work. What is worse, they act perversely. While legitimate users of firearms encounter intense regulation, scrutiny, and bureaucratic control, illicit markets easily adapt to whatever difficulties a free society throws in their way. Also, efforts to curtail the supply of firearms inflict collateral damage on freedom and privacy interests that have long been considered central to American public life. Thanks to the seemingly never-ending war on drugs and long experience attempting to suppress prostitution and pornography, we know a great deal about how illicit markets function and how costly to the public attempts to control them can be. It is essential that we make use of this experience in coming to grips with gun control.

5   The thousands of gun-control laws in the United States are of two general types. The older kind sought to regulate how, where, and by whom firearms could be carried. More recent laws have sought to make it more costly to buy, sell, or use firearms (or certain classes of firearms, such as assault rifles, Saturday-night specials, and so on) by imposing fees, special taxes, or surtaxes on them. The Brady bill is of both types: it has a background-check provision, and its five-day waiting period amounts to a "time tax" on acquiring handguns. All such laws can be called scarcity-inducing, because they seek to raise the cost of buying firearms, as figured in terms of money, time, nuisance, or stigmatization.

6   Despite the mounting number of scarcity-inducing laws, no one is very satisfied with them. Hobbyists want to get rid of them, and gun-control proponents don't think they go nearly far enough. Everyone seems to agree that gun-control laws have some effect on the distribution of firearms. But it has not been the dramatic and measurable effect their proponents desired.

7   Opponents of gun control have traditionally wrapped their arguments in the Second Amendment to the Constitution. Indeed, most modern scholarship affirms that so far as the drafters of the Bill of Rights were concerned, the right to bear arms was to be enjoyed by everyone, not just a militia, and that one of the principal justifications for an armed populace was to secure the tranquillity and good order of the community. But most people are not dedicated antiquitarians, and would not be impressed by the argument "I admit that my behavior is very dangerous to public safety, but the Second Amendment says I have a right to do it anyway." That would

be a case for repealing the Second Amendment, not respecting it.

Fighting the Demand Curve

Everyone knows that possessing a handgun makes it easier   8
to intimidate, wound, or kill someone. But the implication of this point for social policy has not been so well understood. It is easy to count the bodies of those who have been killed or wounded with guns, but not easy to count the people who have avoided harm because they had access to weapons. Think about uniformed police officers, who carry handguns in plain view not in order to kill people but simply to daunt potential attackers. And it works. Criminals generally do not single out police officers for opportunistic attack. Though officers can expect to draw their guns from time to time, few even in big-city departments will actually fire a shot (except in target practice) in the course of a year. This observation points to an important truth: people who are armed make comparatively unattractive victims. A criminal might not know if any one civilian is armed, but if it becomes known that a large number of civilians do carry weapons, criminals will become warier.

Which weapons laws are the right kinds can be decided   9
only after considering two related questions. First, what is the connection between civilian possession of firearms and social violence? Second, how can we expect gun-control laws to alter people's behavior? Most recent scholarship raises serious questions about the "weapons increase violence" hypothesis. The second question is emphasized here, because it is routinely overlooked and often mocked when noticed; yet it is crucial. Rational gun control requires understanding not only the relationship between weapons and violence but also the relationship between laws and people's behavior. Some things are very hard to accomplish with laws. The purpose of a law and its likely effects are not always the same thing. Many statutes are notorious for the way in which their unintended effects have swamped their intended ones.

In order to predict who will comply with gun-control laws,   10
we should remember that guns are economic goods that are traded in markets. Consumers' interest in them varies. For religious, moral, aesthetic, or practical reasons, some people would refuse to buy firearms at any price. Other people willingly pay very high prices for them.

11   Handguns, so often the subject of gun-control laws, are
desirable for one purpose—to allow a person tactically to
dominate a hostile transaction with another person. The
value of a weapon to a given person is a function of two factors: how much he or she wants to dominate a confrontation
if one occurs, and how likely it is that he or she will actually
be in a situation calling for a gun.

12   Dominating a transaction simply means getting what one
wants without being hurt. Where people differ is in how likely
it is that they will be involved in a situation in which a gun
will be valuable. Someone who *intends* to engage in a transaction involving a gun—a criminal, for example—is obviously
in the best possible position to predict that likelihood. Criminals should therefore be willing to pay more for a weapon
than most other people would. Professors, politicians, and
newspaper editors are, as a group, at very low risk of being
involved in such transactions, and they thus systematically
underrate the value of defensive handguns. (Correlative, perhaps, is their uncritical readiness to accept studies that
debunk the utility of firearms for self-defense.) The class of
people we wish to deprive of guns, then, is the very class with
the most inelastic demand for them—criminals—whereas the
people most likely to comply with gun-control laws don't
value guns in the first place.

Do Guns Drive Up Crime Rates?

13   Which premise is true—that guns increase crime or that
the fear of crime causes people to obtain guns? Most of the
country's major newspapers apparently take this problem to
have been solved by an article published by Arthur Kellermann and several associates in the October 7, 1993, *New
England Journal of Medicine.* Kellermann is an emergency-
room physician who has published a number of influential
papers that he believes discredit the thesis that private ownership of firearms is a useful means of self-protection. (An
indication of his wide influence is that within two months
the study received almost 100 mentions in publications and
broadcast transcripts indexed in the Nexis data base.) For
this study Kellermann and his associates identified fifteen
behavioral and fifteen environmental variables that applied
to a 388-member set of homicide victims, found a "matching"
control group of 388 non–homicide victims, and then ascer-
tained how the two groups differed in gun ownership. In

interviews Kellermann made clear his belief that owning a handgun markedly increases a person's risk of being murdered.

But the study does not prove that point at all. Indeed, as 14 Kellermann explicitly conceded in the text of the article, the causal arrow may very well point in the other direction: the threat of being killed may make people more likely to arm themselves. Many people at risk of being killed, especially people involved in the drug trade or other illegal ventures, might well rationally buy a gun as a precaution, and be willing to pay a price driven up by gun-control laws. Crime, after all, is a dangerous business. Peter Reuter and Mark Kleiman, drug-policy researchers, calculated in 1987 that the average crack dealer's risk of being killed was far greater than his risk of being sent to prison. (Their data cannot, however, support the implication that ownership of a firearm causes or exacerbates the risk of being killed.)

Defending the validity of his work, Kellermann has empha- 15 sized that the link between lung cancer and smoking was initially established by studies methodologically no different from his. Gary Kleck, a criminology professor at Florida State University, has pointed out the flaw in this comparison. No one ever thought that lung cancer causes smoking, so when the association between the two was established the direction of the causal arrow was not in doubt. Kleck wrote that it is as though Kellermann, trying to discover how diabetics differ from other people, found that they are much more likely to possess insulin than nondiabetics, and concluded that insulin is a risk factor for diabetes.

The New York Times, the *Los Angeles Times, The Washington* 16 *Post, The Boston Globe,* and the *Chicago Tribune* all gave prominent coverage to Kellermann's study as soon as it appeared, but none saw fit to discuss the study's limitations. A few, in order to introduce a hint of balance, mentioned that the NRA, or some member of its staff, disagreed with the study. But readers had no way of knowing that Kellermann himself had registered a disclaimer in his text. "It is possible," he conceded, "that reverse causation accounted for some of the association we observed between gun ownership and homicide." Indeed, the point is stronger than that: "reverse causation" may account for *most* of the association between gun ownership and homicide. Kellermann's data simply do not allow one to draw any conclusion.

If firearms increased violence and crime, then rates of 17 spousal homicide would have skyrocketed, because the stock of privately owned handguns has increased rapidly since the mid-1960s. But according to an authoritative study of spousal homicide in the *American Journal of Public Health*, by James Mercy and Linda Saltzman, rates of spousal homicide in the years 1976 to 1985 fell. If firearms increased violence and crime, the crime rate should have increased throughout the 1980s, while the national stock of privately owned handguns increased by more than a million units in every year of the decade. It did not. Nor should the rates of violence and crime in Switzerland, New Zealand, and Israel be as low as they are, since the number of firearms per civilian household is comparable to that in the United States. Conversely, gun-controlled Mexico and South Africa should be islands of peace instead of having murder rates more than twice as high as those here. The determinants of crime and law-abidingness are, of course, complex matters, which are not fully understood and certainly not explicable in terms of a country's laws. But gun-control enthusiasts, who have made capital out of the low murder rate in England, which is largely disarmed, simply ignore the counterexamples that don't fit their theory.

18   If firearms increased violence and crime, Florida's murder rate should not have been falling since the introduction, seven years ago, of a law that makes it easier for ordinary citizens to get permits to carry concealed handguns. Yet the murder rate has remained the same or fallen every year since the law was enacted, and it is now lower than the national murder rate (which has been rising). As of last November 183,561 permits had been issued, and only seventeen of the permits had been revoked because the holder was involved in a firearms offense. It would be precipitate to claim that the new law has "caused" the murder rate to subside. Yet here is a situation that doesn't fit the hypothesis that weapons increase violence.

19   If firearms increased violence and crime, programs of induced scarcity would suppress violence and crime. But—another anomaly—they don't. Why not? A theorem, which we could call the futility theorem, explains why gun-control laws must either be ineffectual or in the long term actually provoke more violence and crime. Any theorem depends on both observable fact and assumption. An assumption that can be made with confidence is that the higher the number of victims a criminal assumes to be armed, the higher will be the risk—the price—of assaulting them. By definition, gun-control laws should make weapons scarcer and thus more expensive. By our prior reasoning about demand among various

types of consumers, after the laws are enacted criminals should be better armed, compared with noncriminals, than they were before. Of course, plenty of noncriminals will remain armed. But even if many noncriminals will pay as high a price as criminals will to obtain firearms, a larger number will not.

Criminals will thus still take the same gamble they already 20
take in assaulting a victim who might or might not be armed. But they may appreciate that the laws have given them a freer field, and that crime still pays—pays even better, in fact, than before. What will happen to the rate of violence? Only a relatively few gun-mediated transactions—currently, five percent of armed robberies committed with firearms—result in someone's actually being shot (the statistics are not broken down into encounters between armed assailants and unarmed victims, and encounters in which both parties are armed). It seems reasonable to fear that if the number of such transactions were to increase because criminals thought they faced fewer deterrents, there would be a corresponding increase in shootings. Conversely, if gun-mediated transactions declined—if criminals initiated fewer of them because they feared encountering an armed victim or an armed good Samaritan—the number of shootings would go down. The magnitude of these effects is, admittedly, uncertain. Yet it is hard to doubt the general tendency of a change in the law that imposes legal burdens on buying guns. The futility theorem suggests that gun-control laws, if effective at all, would unfavorably affect the rate of violent crime.

The futility theorem provides a lens through which to see 21
much of the debate. It is undeniable that gun-control laws work—to an extent. Consider, for example, California's background-check law, which in the past two years has prevented about 12,000 people with a criminal record or a history of mental illness or drug abuse from buying handguns. In the same period Illinois's background-check law prevented the delivery of firearms to more than 2,000 people. Surely some of these people simply turned to an illegal market, but just as surely not all of them did. The laws of large numbers allow us to say that among the foiled thousands, some potential killers were prevented from getting a gun. We do not know whether the number is large or small but it is implausible to think it is zero. And, as gun-control proponents are inclined to say, "If only one life is saved..."

The hypothesis that firearms increase violence does pre- 22
dict that if we can slow down the diffusion of guns, there will

be less violence; one life, or more, *will* be saved. But the futility theorem asks that we look not simply at the gross number of bad actors prevented from getting guns but at the effect the law has on *all* the people who want to buy a gun. Suppose we succeed in piling tax burdens on the acquisition of firearms. We can safely assume that a number of people who might use guns to kill will be sufficiently discouraged not to buy them. But we cannot assume this about people who feel that they must have guns in order to survive financially and physically. A few lives might indeed be saved. But the overall rate of violent crime might not go down at all. And if guns are owned predominantly by people who have good reason to think they will use them, the rate might even go up.

23   Are there empirical studies that can serve to help us choose between the futility theorem and the hypothesis that guns increase violence? Unfortunately, no: the best studies of the effects of gun-control laws are quite inconclusive. Our statistical tools are too weak to allow us to identify an effect clearly enough to persuade an open-minded skeptic. But it is precisely when we are dealing with undetectable statistical effects that we have to be certain we are using the best models available of human behavior.

Sealing the Border

24   Handguns are not legally for sale in the city of Chicago, and have not been since April of 1982. Rifles, shotguns, and ammunition are available, but only to people who possess an Illinois Firearm Owner's Identification card. It takes up to a month to get this card, which involves a background check. Even if one has a FOID card there is a waiting period for the delivery of a gun. In few places in America is it as difficult to get a firearm legally as in the city of Chicago.

25   Yet there are hundreds of thousands of unregistered guns in the city, and new ones arriving all the time. It is not difficult to get handguns—even legally. Chicago residents with FOID cards merely go to gun shops in the suburbs. Trying to establish a city as an island of prohibition in a sea of legal firearms seems an impossible project.

26   Is a state large enough to be an effective island, then? Suppose Illinois adopted Chicago's handgun ban. Same problem again. Some people could just get guns elsewhere: Indiana actually borders the city, and Wisconsin is only forty miles away. Though federal law prohibits the sale of handguns in

one state to residents of another, thousands of Chicagoans with summer homes in other states could buy handguns there. And, of course, a black market would serve the needs of other customers.

When would the island be large enough to sustain a weapons-free environment? In the United States people and cargoes move across state lines without supervision or hindrance. Local shortages of goods are always transient, no matter whether the shortage is induced by natural disasters, prohibitory laws, or something else.   27

Even if many states outlawed sales of handguns, then, they would continue to be available, albeit at a somewhat higher price, reflecting the increased legal risk of selling them. Mindful of the way markets work to undermine their efforts, gun-control proponents press for federal regulation of firearms, because they believe that only Congress wields the authority to frustrate the interstate movement of firearms.   28

Why, though, would one think that federal policing of illegal firearms would be better than local policing? The logic of that argument is far from clear. Cities, after all, are comparatively small places. Washington, D.C., for example, has an area of less than 45,000 acres. Yet local officers have had little luck repressing the illegal firearms trade there. Why should federal officers do any better watching the United States' 12,000 miles of coastline and millions of square miles of interior? Criminals should be able to frustrate federal police forces just as well as they can local ones. Ten years of increasingly stringent federal efforts to abate cocaine trafficking, for example, have not succeeded in raising the street price of the drug.   29

Consider the most drastic proposal currently in play, that of Senator John Chafee, of Rhode Island, who would ban the manufacture, sale, and home possession of handguns within the United States. This proposal goes far beyond even the Chicago law, because existing weapons would have to be surrendered. Handguns would become contraband, and selling counterfeit, stolen, and contraband goods is big business in the United States. The objective of law enforcement is to raise the costs of engaging in crime and so force criminals to take expensive precautions against becoming entangled with the legal system. Crimes of a given type will, in theory, decline as soon as the direct and indirect costs of engaging in them rise to the point at which criminals seek more profitable opportunities in other (not necessarily legal) lines of work.   30

In firearms regulation, translating theory into practice will continue to be difficult, at least if the objective is to lessen the   31 practical availability of firearms to people who might abuse them. On the demand side, for defending oneself against predation there is no substitute for a firearm. Criminals, at least, can switch to varieties of law-breaking in which a gun confers little or no advantage (burglary, smash-and-grab), but people who are afraid of confrontations with criminals, whether rationally or (as an accountant might reckon it) irrationally, will be very highly motivated to acquire firearms. Long after the marijuana and cocaine wars of this century have been forgotten, people's demand for personal security and for the tools they believe provide it will remain strong.

32   On the supply side, firearms transactions can be consummated behind closed doors. Firearms buyers, unlike those who use drugs, pornography, or prostitution, need not recurrently expose themselves to legal jeopardy. One trip to the marketplace is enough to arm oneself for life. This could justify a consumer's taking even greater precautions to avoid apprehension, which would translate into even steeper enforcement costs for the police.

33   Don Kates Jr., a San Francisco lawyer and a much-published student of this problem, has pointed out that during the wars in Southeast and Southwest Asia local artisans were able to produce, from scratch, serviceable pot-metal counterfeits of AK-47 infantry rifles and similar weapons in makeshift backyard foundries. Although inferior weapons cannot discharge thousands of rounds without misfiring, they are more than deadly enough for light to medium service, especially by criminals and people defending themselves and their property, who ordinarily use firearms by threatening with them, not by firing them. And the skills necessary to make them are certainly as widespread in America as in the villages of Pakistan or Vietnam. Effective policing of such a cottage industry is unthinkable. Indeed, as Charles Chandler has pointed out, crude but effective firearms have been manufactured in prisons—highly supervised environments, compared with the outside world.

34   Seeing that local firearms restrictions are easily defeated, gun-control proponents have latched onto national controls as a way of finally making gun control something more than a gesture. But the same forces that have defeated local regulation will defeat further national regulation. Imposing higher costs on weapons ownership will, of course, slow down the weapons trade to some extent. But planning to slow it down in such a way as to drive down crime and violence, or to prevent motivated purchasers from finding ample supplies of

guns and ammunition, is an escape from reality. And like many another such, it entails a morning after.

Administering Prohibition

Assume for the sake of argument that to a reasonable degree of criminological certainty, guns are every bit the public-health hazard they are said to be. It follows, and many journalists and a few public officials have already said, that we ought to treat guns the same way we do smallpox viruses or other critical vectors of morbidity and mortality—namely, isolate them from potential hosts and destroy them as speedily as possible. Clearly, firearms have at least one characteristic that distinguishes them from smallpox viruses: nobody wants to keep smallpox viruses in the nightstand drawer. Amazingly enough, gun-control literature seems never to have explored the problem of getting weapons away from people who very much want to keep them in the nightstand drawer. 35

Our existing gun-control laws are not uniformly permissive and, indeed, in certain places are tough even by international standards. Advocacy groups seldom stress the considerable differences among American jurisdictions, and media reports regularly assert that firearms are readily available to anybody anywhere in the country. This is not the case. For example, handgun restrictions in Chicago and the District of Columbia are much less flexible than the ones in the United Kingdom. Several hundred thousand British subjects may legally buy and possess sidearms, and anyone who joins a target-shooting club is eligible to do so. But in Chicago and the District of Columbia, excepting peace officers and the like, only grandfathered registrants may legally possess handguns. Of course, tens or hundreds of thousands of people in both those cities—nobody can be sure how many—do in fact possess them illegally. 36

Although there is, undoubtedly, illegal handgun ownership in the United Kingdom, especially in Northern Ireland (where considerations of personal security and public safety are decidedly unlike those elsewhere in the British Isles), it is probable that Americans and Britons differ in their disposition to obey gun-control laws: there is reputed to be a marked national disparity in compliance behavior. This difference, if it exists, may have something to do with the comparatively marginal value of firearms to British consumers. Even before it had strict firearms regulation, Britain had very low rates of 37 crimes involving guns; British criminals, unlike their American counterparts, prefer burglary (a crime of stealth) to robbery (a crime of intimidation).

38   Unless people are prepared to surrender their guns voluntarily, how can the U.S. government confiscate an appreciable fraction of our country's nearly 200 million privately owned firearms? We know that it is possible to set up weapons-free zones in certain locations—commercial airports and many courthouses and, lately, some troubled big-city high schools and housing projects. The sacrifices of privacy and convenience, and the costs of paying guards, have been thought worth the (perceived) gain in security. No doubt it would be possible, though it would probably not be easy, to make weapons-free zones of shopping centers, department stores, movie theaters, ball parks. But it is not obvious how one would cordon off the whole of an open society.

39   Voluntary programs have been ineffectual. From time to time community-action groups or police departments have sponsored "turn in your gun" days, which are nearly always disappointing. Sometimes the government offers to buy guns at some price. This approach has been endorsed by Senator Chafee and the *Los Angeles Times*. Jonathan Alter, of *Newsweek*, has suggested a variation on this theme: youngsters could exchange their guns for a handshake with Michael Jordan or some other sports hero. If the price offered exceeds that at which a gun can be bought on the street, one can expect to see plans of this kind yield some sort of harvest—as indeed they have. But it is implausible that these schemes will actually result in a less-dangerous population. Government programs to buy up surplus cheese cause more cheese to be produced without affecting the availability of cheese to people who want to buy it. So it is with guns.

40   One could extend the concept of intermittent roadblocks of the sort approved by the Supreme Court for discouraging drunk driving. Metal detectors could be positioned on every street corner, or ambulatory metal-detector squads could check people randomly, or hidden magnetometers could be installed around towns, to detect concealed weapons. As for firearms kept in homes (about half of American households), warrantless searches might be rationalized on the well-established theory that probable cause is not required when authorities are trying to correct dangers to public safety rather than searching for evidence of a crime.

41   In a recent "town hall" meeting in California, President Bill Clinton used the word "sweeps," which he did not define, to

describe how he would confiscate firearms if it were up to him. During the past few years the Chicago Housing Authority chairman, Vincent Lane, has ordered "sweeps" of several gang-ridden public-housing projects, meaning warrantless searches of people's homes by uniformed police officers looking for contraband. Lane's ostensible premise was that possession of firearms by tenants constituted a lease violation that, as a conscientious landlord, he was obliged to do something about. The same logic could justify any administrative search. City health inspectors in Chicago were recently authorized to conduct warrantless searches for lead hazards in residential paint. Why not lead hazards in residential closets and nightstands? Someone has probably already thought of it.

Ignoring the Ultimate Sources of Crime and Violence

The American experience with prohibition has been that 42
black marketeers—often professional criminals—move in to profit when legal markets are closed down or disturbed. In order to combat them, new laws and law-enforcement techniques are developed, which are circumvented almost as soon as they are put in place. New and yet more stringent laws are enacted, and greater sacrifices of civil liberties and privacy demanded and submitted to. But in this case the problem, crime and violence, will not go away, because guns and ammunition (which, of course, won't go away either) do not cause it. One cannot expect people to quit seeking new weapons as long as the tactical advantages of weapons are seen to outweigh the costs imposed by prohibition. Nor can one expect large numbers of people to surrender firearms they already own. The only way to make people give up their guns is to create a world in which guns are perceived as having little value. This world will come into being when criminals choose not to use guns because the penalties for being caught with them are too great, and when ordinary citizens don't think they need firearms because they aren't afraid of criminals anymore.

Neither of these eventualities seems very likely without sub- 43
stantial departures in law-enforcement policy. Politicians' nostrums—increasing the punishment for crime, slapping a few more death-penalty provisions into the code—are taken seriously by few students of the crime problem. The existing

penalties for predatory crimes are quite severe enough. The problem is that they are rarely meted out in the real world. The penalties formally published by the code are in practice steeply discounted, and criminals recognize that the judicial and penal systems cannot function without bargaining in the vast majority of cases.

44   This problem is not obviously one that legislation could solve. Constitutional ideas about due process of law make the imposition of punishments extraordinarily expensive and difficult. Like the tax laws, the criminal laws are basically voluntary affairs. Our system isn't geared to a world of wholesale disobedience. Recalibrating the system simply by increasing its overall harshness would probably offend and then shock the public long before any of its benefits were felt.

45   To illustrate, consider the prospect of getting serious about carrying out the death penalty. In recent years executions have been running at one or two dozen a year. As the late Supreme Court Justice Potter Stewart observed, those selected to die constitute a "capriciously selected random handful" taken from a much larger number of men and women who, just as deserving of death, receive prison sentences. It is not easy to be exact about that much larger number. But as an educated guess, taking into account only the most serious murders—the ones that were either premeditated or committed in the course of a dangerous felony—there are perhaps 5,000 prisoners a year who could plausibly be executed in the United States: say, 100,000 executions in the next twenty years. It is hard to think that the death penalty, if imposed on this scale, would not noticeably change the behavior of potential criminals. But what else in national life or citizens' character would have to change in order to make that many executions acceptable? Since 1930 executions in the United States have never exceeded 200 a year. At any such modest rate of imposition, rational criminals should consider the prospect of receiving the death penalty effectively nil. On the best current evidence, indeed, they do. Documentation of the deterrent effect of the death penalty, as compared with that of long prison sentences, has been notoriously hard to produce.

46   The problem is not simply that criminals pay little attention to the punishments in the books. Nor is it even that they also know that for the majority of crimes, their chances of being arrested are small. The most important reason for criminal behavior is this: the income that offenders can earn in the world of crime, as compared with the world of work, all too often makes crime appear to be the better choice.

Thus the crime bill that Bill Clinton introduced last year,   47
which provides for more prisons and police officers, should
be of only very limited help. More prisons means that fewer
violent offenders will have to be released early in order to
make space for new arrivals; perhaps fewer plea bargains will
have to be struck—all to the good. Yet a moment's reflection
should make clear that one more criminal locked up does not
necessarily mean one less criminal on the street. The situation
is very like one that conservationists and hunters have always
understood. Populations of game animals readily recover
from hunting seasons but not from loss of habitat. Mean
streets, when there are few legitimate entry-level opportunities for young men, are a criminal habitat so to speak, in the
social ecology of modern American cities. Cull however much
one will, the habitat will be reoccupied promptly after its previous occupant is sent away. So social science has found.

Similarly, whereas increasing the number of police officers   48
cannot hurt, and may well increase people's subjective feelings of security, there is little evidence to suggest that doing
so will diminish the rate of crime. Police forces are basically
reactive institutions. At any realistically sustainable level of
staffing they must remain so. Suppose 100,000 officers were
added to police rosters nationwide, as proposed in the current crime bill. This would amount to an overall personnel
increase of about 18 percent, which would be parceled out
according to the iron laws of democratic politics—distributed
throughout states and congressional districts—rather than
being sent to the areas that most need relief. Such an
increase, though unprecedented in magnitude, is far short of
what would be needed to pacify some of our country's worst
urban precincts.

There is a challenge here that is quite beyond being met   49
with tough talk. Most public officials can see the mismatch
between their tax base and the social entropies they are being
asked to repair. There simply isn't enough money; existing
public resources, as they are now employed, cannot possibly
solve the crime problem. But mayors and senators and police
chiefs must not say so out loud: too-disquieting implications
would follow. For if the authorities are incapable of restoring
public safety and personal security under the existing ground
rules, then obviously the ground rules must change, to give
private initiative greater scope. Self-help is the last refuge of
nonscoundrels.

Communities must, in short, organize more effectively to   50
protect themselves against predators. No doubt this means

encouraging properly qualified private citizens to possess and carry firearms legally. It is not morally tenable—nor, for that matter, is it even practical—to insist that police officers, few of whom are at a risk remotely as great as are the residents of many city neighborhoods, retain a monopoly on legal firearms. It is needless to fear giving honest men and women the training and equipment to make it possible for them to take back their own streets.

51   Over the long run, however, there is no substitute for addressing the root causes of crime—bad education and lack of job opportunities and the disintegration of families. Root causes are much out of fashion nowadays as explanations of criminal behavior, but fashionable or not, they are fundamental. *The root cause of crime is that for certain people, predation is a rational occupational choice.* Conventional crime-control measures, which by stiffening punishments or raising the probability of arrest aim to make crime pay less, cannot consistently affect the behavior of people who believe that their alternatives to crime will pay virtually nothing. Young men who did not learn basic literacy and numeracy skills before dropping out of their wretched public schools may not have been worth hiring at the minimum wage set by George Bush, let alone at the higher, indexed minimum wage that has recently been under discussion by the Clinton Administration. Most independent studies of the effects of raising minimum wages show a similar pattern of excluding the most vulnerable. This displacement, in turn, makes young men free, in the nihilistic, nothing-to-lose sense, to dedicate their lives to crime. Their legitimate opportunities, always precarious in a society where race and class still matter, often diminish to the point of being for all intents and purposes absent.

52   Unfortunately, many progressive policies work out in the same way as increases in the minimum wage—as taxes on employment. One example is the Administration's pending proposal to make employer-paid health insurance mandatory and universal. Whatever the undoubted benefits of the plan, a payroll tax is needed to make it work. Another example: in recent years the use of the "wrongful discharge" tort and other legal innovations has swept through the courts of more than half the states, bringing to an end the era of "employment at will," when employees (other than civil servants) without formal contracts—more than three quarters of the work force— could be fired for good reason, bad reason, or no reason at all. Most commentators celebrated the loss of the at-will rule.

How could one object to a new legal tenet that prohibited only arbitrary and oppressive behavior by employers?

But the costs of the rule are not negligible, only hidden. At-will employment meant that companies could get out of the relationship as easily as employees could. In a world where dismissals are expensive rather than cheap, and involve lawyers and the threat of lawsuits, rational employers must become more fastidious about whom they hire. By raising the costs of ending the relationship, one automatically raises the threshold of entry. The burdens of the rule fall unequally. Worst hit are entry-level applicants who have little or no employment history to show that they would be worth their pay. 53

Many other tax or regulatory schemes, in the words of Professor Walter Williams, of George Mason University, amount to sawing off the bottom rungs of the ladder of economic opportunity. By suppressing job creation and further diminishing legal employment opportunities for young men on the margin of the work force, such schemes amount to an indirect but unequivocal subsidy to crime. 54

The solution to the problem of crime lies in improving the chances of young men. Easier said than done, to be sure. No one has yet proposed a convincing program for checking all the dislocating forces that government assistance can set in motion. One relatively straightforward change would be reform of the educational system. Nothing guarantees prudent behavior like a sense of the future, and with average skills in reading, writing, and math, young people can realistically look forward to constructive employment and the straight life that steady work makes possible. 55

But firearms are nowhere near the root of the problem of violence. As long as people come in unlike sizes, shapes, ages, and temperaments, as long as they diverge in their taste for risk and their willingness and capacity to prey on other people or to defend themselves from predation, and above all as long as some people have little or nothing to lose by spending their lives in crime, dispositions to violence will persist. 56

This is what makes the case for the right to bear arms, not the Second Amendment. It is foolish to let anything ride on hopes for effective gun control. As long as crime pays as well as it does, we will have plenty of it, and honest folk must choose between being victims and defending themselves. 57

WHAT CAUSES CRIME?

Clarence Darrow

Address to the Prisoners in the Cook County Jail

Clarence Darrow (1857–1928) was the most famous American lawyer of the early twentieth century. An eloquent speaker from Youngstown, Ohio, who practiced mostly in Chicago, Darrow defended Eugene V. Debs and other controversial labor leaders, Nathan Leopold and Richard Loeb (two notorious murderers), and John Scopes in the famous Monkey Trial of 1925. The following is a transcript of a speech that Darrow delivered to prisoners in Chicago in 1902.

1   If I looked at jails and crimes and prisoners in the way the ordinary person does, I should not speak on this subject to you. The reason I talk to you on the question of crime, its cause and cure, is that I really do not in the least believe in crime. There is no such thing as a crime as the word is generally understood. I do not believe there is any sort of distinction between the real moral conditions of the people in and out of jail. One is just as good as the other. The people here can no more help being here than the people outside can avoid being outside. I do not believe that people are in jail because they deserve to be. They are in jail simply because they cannot avoid it on account of circumstances which are entirely beyond their control and for which they are in no way responsible.

2   I suppose a great many people on the outside would say I was doing you harm if they should hear what I say to you this afternoon, but you cannot be hurt a great deal anyway, so it will not matter. Good people outside would say that I was really teaching you things that were calculated to injure society, but it's worth while now and then to hear something different from what you ordinarily get from preachers and the like. These will tell you that you should be good and then you

will get rich and be happy. Of course we know that people do not get rich by being good, and that is the reason why so many of you people try to get rich some other way, only you do not understand how to do it quite as well as the fellow outside.

There are people who think that everything in this world is an accident. But really there is no such thing as an accident. A great many folks admit that many of the people in jail ought to be there, and many who are outside ought to be in. I think none of them ought to be here. There ought to be no jails; and if it were not for the fact that people on the outside are so grasping and heartless in their dealings with the people on the inside, there would be no such institution as jails. 3

I do not want you to believe that I think all you people here are angels. I do not think that. You are people of all kinds, all of you doing the best you can—and that is evidently not very well. You are people of all kinds and conditions and under all circumstances. In one sense everybody is equally good and equally bad. We all do the best we can under the circumstances. But as to the exact things for which you are sent here, some of you are guilty and did the particular act because you needed the money. Some of you did it because you are in the habit of doing it, and some of you because you are born to it, and it comes to be as natural as it does, for instance, for me to be good. 4

Most of you probably have nothing against me, and most of you would treat me the same way as any other person would, probably better than some of the people on the outside would treat me, because you think I believe in you and they know I do not believe in them. While you would not have the least thing against me in the world, you might pick my pockets. I do not think all of you would, but I think some of you would. You would not have anything against me, but that's your profession, a few of you. Some of the rest of you, if my doors were unlocked, might come in if you saw anything you wanted —not out of any malice to me, but because that is your trade. There is no doubt there are quite a number of people in this jail who would pick my pockets. And still I know this—that when I get outside pretty nearly everybody picks my pocket. There may be some of you who would hold up a man on the street, if you did not happen to have something else to do, and needed the money; but when I want to light my house or my office the gas company holds me up. They charge me one dollar for something that is worth twenty-five cents. Still all these people are good people; they are pillars of society and support the churches, and they are respectable. 5

6   When I ride on the streetcars I am held up—I pay five cents for a ride that is worth two and a half cents, simply because a body of men have bribed the city council and the legislature, so that all the rest of us have to pay tribute to them.

7   If I do not want to fall into the clutches of the gas trust and choose to burn oil instead of gas, then good Mr. Rockefeller holds me up, and he uses a certain portion of his money to build universities and support churches which are engaged in telling us how to be good.

8   Some of you are here for obtaining property under false pretenses—yet I pick up a great Sunday paper and read the advertisements of a merchant prince—"Shirtwaists for 39 cents, marked down from $3.00."

9   When I read the advertisements in the paper I see they are all lies. When I want to get out and find a place to stand anywhere on the face of the earth, I find that it has all been taken up long ago before I came here, and before you came here, and somebody says, "Get off, swim into the lake, fly into the air; go anywhere, but get off." That is because these people have the police and they have the jails and the judges and the lawyers and the soldiers and all the rest of them to take care of the earth and drive everybody off that comes in their way.

10   A great many people will tell you that all this is true, but that it does not excuse you. These facts do not excuse some fellow who reaches into my pocket and takes out a five-dollar bill. The fact that the gas company bribes the members of the legislature from year to year, and fixes the law, so that all you people are compelled to be "fleeced" whenever you deal with them; the fact that the streetcar companies and the gas companies have control of the streets; and the fact that the landlords own all the earth—this, they say, has nothing to do with you.

11   Let us see whether there is any connection between the crimes of the respectable classes and your presence in the jail. Many of you people are in jail because you have really committed burglary; many of you, because you have stolen something. In the meaning of the law, you have taken some other person's property. Some of you have entered a store and carried off a pair of shoes because you did not have the price. Possibly some of you have committed murder. I cannot tell what all of you did. There are a great many people here who have done some of these things who really do not know themselves why they did them. I think I know why you did them—every one of you; you did these things because you were bound to do them. It looked to you at the time as if you had a chance to do them or not, as you saw fit; but still, after all,

you had no choice. There may be people here who had some money in their pockets and who still went out and got some more money in a way society forbids. Now, you may not yourselves see exactly why it was you did this thing, but if you look at the question deeply enough and carefully enough you will see that there were circumstances that drove you to do exactly the thing which you did. You could not help it any more than we outside can help taking the positions that we take. The reformers who tell you to be good and you will be happy, and the people on the outside who have property to protect—they think that the only way to do it is by building jails and locking you up in cells on weekdays and praying for you Sundays.

I think that all of this has nothing whatever to do with right conduct. I think it is very easily seen what has to do with right conduct. Some so-called criminals—and I will use this word because it is handy, it means nothing to me—I speak of the criminals who get caught as distinguished from the criminals who catch them—some of these so-called criminals are in jail for their first offenses, but nine tenths of you are in jail because you did not have a good lawyer and, of course, you did not have a good lawyer because you did not have enough money to pay a good lawyer. There is no very great danger of a rich man going to jail.

Some of you may be here for the first time. If we would open the doors and let you out, and leave the laws as they are today, some of you would be back tomorrow. This is about as good a place as you can get anyway. There are many people here who are so in the habit of coming that they would not know where else to go. There are people who are born with the tendency to break into jail every chance they get, and they cannot avoid it. You cannot figure out your life and see why it was, but still there is a reason for it; and if we were all wise and knew all the facts, we could figure it out.

In the first place, there are a good many more people who go to jail in the wintertime than in the summer. Why is this? Is it because people are more wicked in winter? No, it is because the coal trust begins to get in its grip in the winter. A few gentlemen take possession of the coal, and unless the people will pay seven or eight dollars a ton for something that is worth three dollars, they will have to freeze. Then there is nothing to do but to break into jail, and so there are many more in jail in the winter than in summer. It costs more for gas in the winter because the nights are longer, and people go to jail to save gas bills. The jails are electric-lighted. You may not know it, but these economic laws are working all the time, whether we know it or do not know it.

15   There are more people who go to jail in hard times than in good times—few people, comparatively, go to jail except when they are hard up. They go to jail because they have no other place to go. They may not know why, but it is true all the same. People are not more wicked in hard times. That is not the reason. The fact is true all over the world that in hard times more people go to jail than in good times, and in winter more people go to jail than in summer. Of course it is pretty hard times for people who go to jail at any time. The people who go to jail are almost always poor people—people who have no other place to live, first and last. When times are hard, then you find large numbers of people who go to jail who would not otherwise be in jail.

16   Long ago, Mr. Buckle, who was a great philosopher and historian, collected facts, and he showed that the number of people who are arrested increased just as the price of food increased. When they put up the price of gas ten cents a thousand, I do not know who will go to jail, but I do know that a certain number of people will go. When the meat combine raises the price of beef, I do not know who is going to jail, but I know that a large number of people are bound to go. Whenever the Standard Oil Company raises the price of oil, I know that a certain number of girls who are seamstresses, and who work night after night long hours for somebody else, will be compelled to go out on the streets and ply another trade, and I know that Mr. Rockefeller and his associates are responsible and not the poor girls in the jails.

17   First and last, people are sent to jail because they are poor. Sometimes, as I say, you may not need money at the particular time, but you wish to have thrifty forehanded habits, and do not always wait until you are in absolute want. Some of you people are perhaps plying the trade, the profession, which is called burglary. No man in his right senses will go into a strange house in the dead of night and prowl around with a dark lantern through unfamiliar rooms and take chances of his life, if he has plenty of the good things of the world in his own home. You would not take any such chances as that. If a man had clothes in his clothespress and beefsteak in his pantry and money in the bank, he would not navigate around nights in houses where he knows nothing about the premises whatever. It always requires experience and education for this profession, and people who fit themselves for it are no more to blame than I am for being a lawyer. A man

would not hold up another man on the street if he had plenty of money in his own pocket. He might do it if he had one dollar or two dollars, but he wouldn't if he had as much money as Mr. Rockefeller has. Mr. Rockefeller has a great deal better hold-up game than that.

The more that is taken from the poor by the rich, who have the chance to take it, the more poor people there are who are compelled to resort to these means for a livelihood. They may not understand it, they may not think so at once, but after all they are driven into that line of employment.   18

There is a bill before the legislature of this state to punish kidnaping children with death. We have wise members of the legislature. They know the gas trust when they see it and they always see it—they can furnish light enough to be seen; and this legislature thinks it is going to stop kidnaping children by making a law punishing kidnapers of children with death. I don't believe in kidnaping children, but the legislature is all wrong. Kidnaping children is not a crime, it is a profession. It has been developed with the times. It has been developed with our modern industrial conditions. There are many ways of making money—many new ways that our ancestors knew nothing about. Our ancestors knew nothing about a billion-dollar trust; and here comes some poor fellow who has no other trade and he discovers the profession of kidnaping children.   19

This crime is born, not because people are bad; people don't kidnap other people's children because they want the children or because they are devilish, but because they see a chance to get some money out of it. You cannot cure this crime by passing a law punishing by death kidnapers of children. There is one way to cure it. There is one way to cure all these offenses, and that is to give the people a chance to live. There is no other way, and there never was any other way since the world began; and the world is so blind and stupid that it will not see. If every man and woman and child in the world had a chance to make a decent, fair, honest living, there would be no jails and no lawyers and no courts. There might be some persons here or there with some peculiar formation of their brain, like Rockefeller, who would do these things simply to be doing them; but they would be very, very few, and those should be sent to a hospital and treated, and not sent to jail; and they would entirely disappear in the second generation, or at least in the third generation.   20

I am not talking pure theory. I will just give you two or three illustrations.   21

22   The English people once punished criminals by sending them away. They would load them on a ship and export them to Australia. England was owned by lords and nobles and rich people. They owned the whole earth over there, and the other people had to stay in the streets. They could not get a decent living. They used to take their criminals and send them to Australia—I mean the class of criminals who got caught. When these criminals got over there, and nobody else had come, they had the whole continent to run over, and so they could raise sheep and furnish their own meat, which is easier than stealing it. These criminals then became decent, respectable people because they had a chance to live. They did not commit any crimes. They were just like the English people who sent them there, only better. And in the second generation the descendants of those criminals were as good and respectable a class of people as there were on the face of the earth, and then they began building churches and jails themselves.

23   A portion of this country was settled in the same way, landing prisoners down on the southern coast; but when they got here and had a whole continent to run over and plenty of chances to make a living, they became respectable citizens, making their own living just like any other citizen in the world. But finally the descendants of the English aristocracy who sent the people over to Australia found out they were getting rich, and so they went over to get possession of the earth as they always do, and they organized land syndicates and got control of the land and ores, and then they had just as many criminals in Australia as they did in England. It was not because the world had grown bad; it was because the earth had been taken away from the people.

24   Some of you people have lived in the country. It's prettier than it is here. And if you have ever lived on a farm you understand that if you put a lot of cattle in a field, when the pasture is short they will jump over the fence; but put them in a good field where there is plenty of pasture, and they will be law-abiding cattle to the end of time. The human animal is just like the rest of the animals, only a little more so. The same thing that governs in the one governs in the other.

25   Everybody makes his living along the lines of least resistance. A wise man who comes into a country early sees a great undeveloped land. For instance, our rich men twenty-five years ago saw that Chicago was small and knew a lot of people would come here and settle, and they readily saw that if they had all the land around here it would be worth a good deal, so they grabbed the land. You cannot be a landlord

because somebody has got it all. You must find some other calling. In England and Ireland and Scotland less than five per cent own all the land there is, and the people are bound to stay there on any kind of terms the landlords give. They must live the best they can, so they develop all these various professions—burglary, picking pockets, and the like.

Again, people find all sorts of ways of getting rich. These are diseases like everything else. You look at people getting rich, organizing trusts and making a million dollars, and somebody gets the disease and he starts out. He catches it just as a man catches the mumps or the measles; he is not to blame, it is in the air. You will find men speculating beyond their means, because the mania of money-getting is taking possession of them. It is simply a disease—nothing more, nothing less. You cannot avoid catching it; but the fellows who have control of the earth have the advantage of you. See what the law is: when these men get control of things, they make the laws. They do not make the laws to protect anybody; courts are not instruments of justice. When your case gets into court it will make little difference whether you are guilty or innocent, but it's better if you have a smart lawyer. And you cannot have a smart lawyer unless you have money. First and last it's a question of money. Those men who own the earth make the laws to protect what they have. They fix up a sort of fence or pen around what they have, and they fix the law so the fellow on the outside cannot get in. The laws are really organized for the protection of the men who rule the world. They were never organized or enforced to do justice. We have no system for doing justice, not the slightest in the world.

Let me illustrate: Take the poorest person in this room. If the community had provided a system of doing justice, the poorest person in this room would have as good a lawyer as the richest, would he not? When you went into court you would have just as long a trial and just as fair a trial as the richest person in Chicago. Your case would not be tried in fifteen or twenty minutes, whereas it would take fifteen days to get through with a rich man's case.

Then if you were rich and were beaten, your case would be taken to the Appellate Court. A poor man cannot take his case to the Appellate Court; he has not the price. And then to the Supreme Court. And if he were beaten there he might perhaps go to the United States Supreme Court. And he might die of old age before he got into jail. If you are poor, it's a quick job. You are almost known to be guilty, else you would

not be there. Why should anyone be in the criminal court if
he were not guilty? He would not be there if he could be anywhere else. The officials have no time to look after all these
cases. The people who are on the outside, who are running
banks and building churches and making jails, they have no
time to examine 600 or 700 prisoners each year to see
whether they are guilty or innocent. If the courts were organized to promote justice the people would elect somebody to
defend all these criminals, somebody as smart as the prosecutor—and give him as many detectives and as many assistants
to help, and pay as much money to defend you as to prosecute you. We have a very able man for state's attorney, and he
has many assistants, detectives, and policemen without end,
and judges to hear the cases—everything handy.

29   Most all of our criminal code consists in offenses against
property. People are sent to jail because they have committed
a crime against property. It is of very little consequence
whether one hundred people more or less go to jail who ought
not to go—you must protect property, because in this world
property is of more importance than anything else.

30   How is it done? These people who have property fix it so
they can protect what they have. When somebody commits a
crime it does not follow that he has done something that is
morally wrong. The man on the outside who has committed
no crime may have done something. For instance: to take all
the coal in the United States and raise the price two dollars or
three dollars when there is no need of it, and thus kill thousands of babies and send thousands of people to the poor-
house and tens of thousands to jail, as is done every year in
the United States—this is a greater crime than all the people
in our jails ever committed; but the law does not punish it.
Why? Because the fellows who control the earth make the
laws. If you and I had the making of the laws, the first thing
we would do would be to punish the fellow who gets control
of the earth. Nature put this coal in the ground for me as well
as for them and nature made the prairies up here to raise
wheat for me as well as for them, and then the great railroad
companies came along and fenced it up.

31   Most all of the crimes for which we are punished are property crimes. There are a few personal crimes, like murder—
but they are very few. The crimes committed are mostly those
against property. If this punishment is right the criminals
must have a lot of property. How much money is there in this
crowd? And yet you are all here for crimes against property.
The people up and down the Lake Shore have not committed

crime; still they have so much property they don't know what to do with it. It is perfectly plain why these people have not committed crimes against property; they make the laws and therefore do not need to break them. And in order for you to get some property you are obliged to break the rules of the game. I don't know but what some of you may have had a very nice chance to get rich by carrying a hod for one dollar a day, twelve hours. Instead of taking that nice, easy profession, you are a burglar. If you had been given a chance to be a banker you would rather follow that. Some of you may have had a chance to work as a switchman on a railroad where you know, according to statistics, that you cannot live and keep all your limbs more than seven years, and you can get fifty dollars or seventy-five dollars a month for taking your lives in your hands; and instead of taking that lucrative position you chose to be a sneak thief, or something like that. Some of you made that sort of choice. I don't know which I would take if I was reduced to this choice. I have an easier choice.

32   I will guarantee to take from this jail, or any jail in the world, five hundred men who have been the worst criminals and law-breakers who ever got into jail, and I will go down to our lowest streets and take five hundred of the most abandoned prostitutes, and go out somewhere where there is plenty of land, and will give them a chance to make a living, and they will be as good people as the average in the community.

33   There is one remedy for the sort of condition we see here. The world never finds it out, or when it does find it out it does not enforce it. You may pass a law punishing every person with death for burglary, and it will make no difference. Men will commit it just the same. In England there was a time when one hundred different offenses were punishable with death, and it made no difference. The English people strangely found out that so fast as they repealed the severe penalties and so fast as they did away with punishing men by death, crime decreased instead of increased; that the smaller the penalty the fewer the crimes.

34   Hanging men in our county jails does not prevent murder. It makes murderers.

35   And this has been the history of the world. It's easy to see how to do away with what we call crime. It is not so easy to do it. I will tell you how to do it. It can be done by giving the people a chance to live—by destroying special privileges. So long as big criminals can get the coal fields, so long as the big criminals have control of the city council and get the public streets for streetcars and gas rights—this is bound to send

thousands of poor people to jail. So long as men are allowed to monopolize all the earth, and compel others to live on such terms as these men see fit to make, then you are bound to get into jail.

36   The only way in the world to abolish crime and criminals is to abolish the big ones and the little ones together. Make fair conditions of life. Give men a chance to live. Abolish the right of private ownership of land, abolish monopoly, make the world partners in production, partners in the good things of life. Nobody would steal if he could get something of his own some easier way. Nobody will commit burglary when he has a house full. No girl will go out on the streets when she has a comfortable place at home. The man who owns a sweatshop or a department store may not be to blame himself for the condition of his girls, but when he pays them five dollars, three dollars, and two dollars a week, I wonder where he thinks they will get the rest of their money to live. The only way to cure these conditions is by equality. There should be no jails. They do not accomplish what they pretend to accomplish. If you would wipe them out there would be no more criminals than now. They terrorize nobody. They are a blot upon any civilization, and a jail is an evidence of the lack of charity of the people on the outside who make the jails and fill them with the victims of their greed.

Richard J. Herrnstein and James Q. Wilson
Are Criminals Made or Born?

Richard J. Herrnstein was a professor of psychology at Harvard before he passed away in 1994. His colleague James Wilson, a professor of government at Harvard, also specializes in criminology. Together they published the book Crime and Human Nature *(1985); the following essay was adapted from that book and published in* The New York Times Magazine *in 1985.*

1   A revolution in our understanding of crime is quietly overthrowing some established doctrines. Until recently, criminologists looked for the causes of crime almost entirely in the offenders' social circumstances. There seemed to be no short-

age of circumstances to blame: weakened, chaotic or broken families, ineffective schools, antisocial gangs, racism, poverty, unemployment. Criminologists took seriously, more so than many other students of social behavior, the famous dictum of the French sociologist Emile Durkheim: Social facts must have social explanations. The sociological theory of crime had the unquestioned support of prominent editorialists, commentators, politicians and most thoughtful people.

Today, many learned journals and scholarly works draw a   2
different picture. Sociological factors have not been abandoned, but increasingly it is becoming clear to many scholars that crime is the outcome of an interaction between social factors and certain biological factors, particularly for the offenders who, by repeated crimes, have made public places dangerous. The idea is still controversial, but increasingly, to the old question "Are criminals born or made?" the answer seems to be: both. The causes of crime lie in a combination of predisposing biological traits channeled by social circumstance into criminal behavior. The traits alone do not inevitably lead to crime; the circumstances do not make criminals of everyone; but together they create a population responsible for a large fraction of America's problem of crime in the streets.

Evidence that criminal behavior has deeper roots than   3
social circumstances has always been right at hand, but social science has, until recent years, overlooked its implications. As far as the records show, crime everywhere and throughout history is disproportionately a young man's pursuit. Whether men are 20 or more times as likely to be arrested as women, as is the case in Malawi or Brunei, or only four to six times as likely, as in the United States or France, the sex difference in crime statistics is universal. Similarly, 18-year-olds may sometimes be four times as likely to be criminal as 40-year-olds, while at other times only twice as likely. In the United States, more than half of all arrests for serious property crimes are of 20-year-olds or younger. Nowhere have older persons been as criminal as younger ones.

It is easy to imagine purely social explanations for the   4
effects of age and sex on crime. Boys in many societies are trained by their parents and the society itself to play more roughly and aggressively than girls. Boys are expected to fight back, not to cry, and to play to win. Likewise, boys in many cultures are denied adult responsibilities, kept in a state of prolonged dependence and confined too long in schools that

many of them find unrewarding. For a long time, these factors were thought to be the whole story.

5   Ultimately, however, the very universality of the age and sex differences in crime have alerted some social scientists to the implausibility of a theory that does not look beyond the accidents of particular societies. If cultures as different as Japan's and Sweden's, England's and Mexico's, have sex and age differences in crime, then perhaps we should have suspected from the start that there was something more fundamental going on than parents happening to decide to raise their boys and girls differently. What is it about boys, girls and their parents, in societies of all sorts, that leads them to emphasize, rather than overcome, sex differences? Moreover, even if we believed that every society has arbitrarily decided to inculcate aggressiveness in males, there would still be the greater criminality among *young* males to explain. After all, in some cultures, young boys are not denied adult responsibilities but are kept out of school, put to work tilling the land and made to accept obligations to the society.

6   But it is no longer necessary to approach questions about the sources of criminal behavior merely with argument and supposition. There is evidence. Much crime, it is agreed, has an aggressive component, and Eleanor Emmons Maccoby, a professor of psychology at Stanford University, and Carol Nagy Jacklin, a psychologist now at the University of Southern California, after reviewing the evidence on sex differences in aggression, concluded that it has a foundation that is at least in part biological. Only that conclusion can be drawn, they said, from data that show that the average man is more aggressive than the average woman in all known societies, that the sex difference is present in infancy well before evidence of sex-role socialization by adults, that similar sex differences turn up in many of our biological relatives—monkeys and apes. Human aggression has been directly tied to sex hormones, particularly male sex hormones, in experiments on athletes engaging in competitive sports and on prisoners known for violent or domineering behavior. No single line of evidence is decisive and each can be challenged, but all together they convinced Drs. Maccoby and Jacklin, as well as most specialists on the biology of sex differences, that the sexual conventions that assign males the aggressive roles have biological roots.

7   That is also the conclusion of most researchers about the developmental forces that make adolescence and young adulthood a time of risk for criminal and other nonconven-

tional behavior. This is when powerful new drives awaken, leading to frustrations that foster behavior unchecked by the internalized prohibitions of adulthood. The result is usually just youthful rowdiness, but, in a minority of cases, it passes over the line into crime.

The most compelling evidence of biological factors for criminality comes from two studies—one of twins, the other of adopted boys. Since the 1920's it has been understood that twins may develop from a single fertilized egg, resulting in identical genetic endowments—identical twins—or from a pair of separately fertilized eggs that have about half their genes in common—fraternal twins. A standard procedure for estimating how important genes are to a trait is to compare the similarity between identical twins with that between fraternal twins. When identical twins are clearly more similar in a trait than fraternal twins, the trait probably has high heritability. 8

There have been about a dozen studies of criminality using twins. More than 1,500 pairs of twins have been studied in the United States, the Scandinavian countries, Japan, West Germany, Britain and elsewhere, and the result is qualitatively the same everywhere. Identical twins are more likely to have similar criminal records than fraternal twins. For example, the late Karl O. Christiansen, a Danish criminologist, using the Danish Twin Register, searched police, court and prison records for entries regarding twins born in a certain region of Denmark between 1881 and 1910. When an identical twin had a criminal record, Christiansen found, his or her co-twin was more than twice as likely to have one also than when a fraternal twin had a criminal record. 9

In the United States, a similar result has recently been reported by David Rowe, a psychologist at the University of Oklahoma, using questionnaires instead of official records to measure criminality. Twins in high school in almost all the school districts of Ohio received questionnaires by mail, with a promise of confidentiality as well as a small payment if the questionnaires were filled out and returned. The twins were asked about their activities, including their delinquent behavior, about their friends, and about their co-twins. The identical twins were more similar in delinquency than the fraternal twins. In addition, the twins who shared more activities with each other were no more likely to be similar in delinquency than those who shared fewer activities. 10

No single method of inquiry should be regarded as conclusive. But essentially the same results are found in studies of 11 adopted children. The idea behind such studies is to find a sample of children adopted early in life, cases in which the criminal histories of both adopting and biological parents are known. Then, as the children grow up, researchers can discover how predictive of their criminality are the family histories of their adopting and biological parents. Recent studies show that the biological family history contributes substantially to the adoptees' likelihood of breaking the law.

12   For example, Sarnoff Mednick, a psychologist at the University of Southern California, and his associates in the United States and Denmark have followed a sample of several thousand boys adopted in Denmark between 1927 and 1947. Boys with criminal biological parents and noncriminal adopting parents were more likely to have criminal records than those with noncriminal biological parents and criminal adopting parents. The more criminal convictions a boy's natural parents had, the greater the risk of criminality for boys being raised by adopting parents who had no records. The risk was unrelated to whether the boy or his adopting parents knew about the natural parents' criminal records, whether the natural parents committed their crimes before or after the boy was given up for adoption, or whether the boy was adopted immediately after birth or a year or two later. The results of this study have been confirmed in Swedish and American samples of adopted children.

13   Because of studies like these, many sociologists and criminologists now accept the existence of genetic factors contributing to criminality. When there is disagreement, it is about how large the genetic contribution to crime is and about how the criminality of biological parents is transmitted to their children.

14   Both the twin and adoption studies show that genetic contributions are not alone responsible for crime—there is, for example, some increase in criminality among boys if their adopted fathers are criminal even when their biological parents are not, and not every co-twin of a criminal identical twin becomes criminal himself. Although it appears, on average, to be substantial, the precise size of the genetic contribution to crime is probably unknowable, particularly since the measures of criminality itself are now so crude.

15   We have a bit more to go on with respect to the link that transmits a predisposition toward crime from parents to children. No one believes there are "crime genes," but there are two major attributes that have, to some degree, a heritable

base and that appear to influence criminal behavior. These are intelligence and temperament. Hundreds of studies have found that the more genes people share, the more likely they are to resemble each other intellectually and temperamentally.

Starting with studies in the 1930's, the average offender in broad samples has consistently scored 91 to 93 on I.Q. tests for which the general population's average is 100. The typical offender does worse on the verbal items of intelligence tests than on the nonverbal items but is usually below average on both.   16

Criminologists have long known about the correlation between criminal behavior and I.Q., but many of them have discounted it for various reasons. Some have suggested that the correlation can be explained away by the association between low socioeconomic status and crime, on the one hand, and that between low I.Q. and low socioeconomic status, on the other. These criminologists say it is low socioeconomic status, rather than low I.Q., that fosters crime. Others have questioned whether I.Q. tests really measure intelligence for the populations that are at greater risk for breaking the law. The low scores of offenders, the argument goes, betray a culturally deprived background or alienation from our society's values rather than low intelligence. Finally, it is often noted that the offenders in some studies have been caught for their crimes. Perhaps the ones who got away have higher I.Q.s.   17

But these objections have proved to be less telling than they once seemed to be. There are, for example, many poor law-abiding people living in deprived environments, and one of their more salient characteristics is that they have higher I.Q. scores than those in the same environment who break the law.   18

Then, too, it is a common misconception that I.Q. tests are invalid for people from disadvantaged backgrounds. If what is implied by this criticism is that scores predict academic potential or job performance differently for different groups, then the criticism is wrong. A comprehensive recent survey sponsored by the National Academy of Sciences concluded that "tests predict about as well for one group as for another." And that some highly intelligent criminals may well be good at eluding capture is fully consistent with the belief that offenders, in general, have lower scores than nonoffenders.   19

If I.Q. and criminality are linked, what may explain the link? There are several possibilities. One is that low scores on I.Q. tests signify greater difficulty in grasping the likely   20

consequences of action or in learning the meaning and significance of moral codes. Another is that low scores, especially
on the verbal component of the tests, mean trouble in school,
which leads to frustration, thence to resentment, anger and
delinquency. Still another is that persons who are not as skillful as others in expressing themselves verbally may find it
more rewarding to express themselves in ways in which they
will do better, such as physical threat or force.

21   For some repeat offenders, the predisposition to criminality may be more a matter of temperament than intelligence.
Impulsiveness, insensitivity to social mores, a lack of deep
and enduring emotional attachments to others and an appetite for danger are among the temperamental characteristics
of high-rate offenders. Temperament is, to a degree, heritable,
though not as much so as intelligence. All parents know that
their children, shortly after birth, begin to exhibit certain
characteristic ways of behaving—they are placid or fussy, shy
or bold. Some of the traits endure, among them aggressiveness and hyperactivity, although they change in form as the
child develops. As the child grows up, these traits, among others, may gradually unfold into a disposition toward uncon-
ventional, defiant or antisocial behavior.

22   Lee Robins, a sociologist at Washington University School
of Medicine in St. Louis, reconstructed 30 years of the lives of
more than 500 children who were patients in the 1920's at a
child guidance clinic in St. Louis. She was interested in the
early precursors of chronic sociopathy, a condition of antisocial personality that often includes criminal behavior as one
of its symptoms. Adult sociopaths in her sample who did not
suffer from psychosis, mental retardation or addiction, were,
without exception, antisocial before they were 18. More than
half of the male sociopaths had serious symptoms before they
were 11. The main childhood precursors were truancy, poor
school performance, theft, running away, recklessness, slov-
enliness, impulsiveness and guiltlessness. The more symptoms in childhood, the greater the risk of sociopathy in
adulthood.

23   Other studies confirm and extend Dr. Robins's conclusions.
For example, two psychologists, John J. Conger of the University of Colorado and Wilbur Miller of Drake University in Des
Moines, searching back over the histories of a sample of delinquent boys in Denver, found that "by the end of the third
grade, future delinquents were already seen by their teachers
as more poorly adapted than their classmates. They appeared

to have less regard for the rights and feelings of their peers; less awareness of the need to accept responsibility for their obligations, both as individuals and as members of a group, and poorer attitudes toward authority."

Traits that foreshadow serious, recurrent criminal behav-   24 ior have been traced all the way back to behavior patterns such as hyperactivity and unusual fussiness, and neurological signs such as atypical brain waves or reflexes. In at least a minority of cases, these are detectable in the first few years of life. Some of the characteristics are sex-linked. There is evidence that newborn females are more likely than newborn males to smile, to cling to their mothers, to be receptive to touching and talking, to be sensitive to certain stimuli, such as being touched by a cloth, and to have less upper-body strength. Mothers certainly treat girls and boys differently, but the differences are not simply a matter of the mother's choice—female babies are more responsive than male babies to precisely the kind of treatment that is regarded as "feminine." When adults are asked to play with infants, they play with them in ways they think are appropriate to the infants' sexes. But there is also some evidence that when the sex of the infant is concealed, the behavior of the adults is influenced by the conduct of the child.

Premature infants or those born with low birth weights   25 have a special problem. These children are vulnerable to any adverse circumstances in their environment—including child abuse—that may foster crime. Although nurturing parents can compensate for adversity, cold or inconsistent parents may exacerbate it. Prematurity and low birth weight may result from poor prenatal care, a bad diet or excessive use of alcohol or drugs. Whether the care is due to poverty, ignorance or anything else, here we see criminality arising from biological, though not necessarily genetic, factors. It is now known that these babies are more likely than normal babies to be the victims of child abuse.

We do not mean to blame child abuse on the victim by say-   26 ing that premature and low-birth-weight infants are more difficult to care for and thus place a great strain on the parents. But unless parents are emotionally prepared for the task of caring for such children, they may vent their frustration at the infant's unresponsiveness by hitting or neglecting it. Whatever it is in parent and child that leads to prematurity or low birth weight is compounded by the subsequent interaction between them. Similarly, children with low I.Q.s may have difficulty in understanding rules, but if their parents also have poor verbal skills, they may have difficulty in communicating rules, and so each party to the conflict exacerbates the defects of the other.

27   The statement that biology plays a role in explaining human behavior, especially criminal behavior, sometimes elicits a powerful political or ideological reaction. Fearful that what is being proposed is a crude biological determinism, some critics deny the evidence while others wish the evidence to be confined to scientific journals. Scientists who have merely proposed studying the possible effects of chromosomal abnormalities on behavior have been ruthlessly attacked by other scientists, as have those who have made public the voluminous data showing the heritability of intelligence and temperament.

28   Some people worry that any claim that biological factors influence criminality is tantamount to saying that the higher crime rate of black compared to white Americans has a genetic basis. But no responsible work in the field leads to any such conclusion. The data show that of all the reasons people vary in their crime rates, race is far less important than age, sex, intelligence and the other individual factors that vary within races. Any study of the causes of crime must therefore first consider the individual factors. Differences among races may have many explanations, most of them having nothing to do with biology.

29   The intense reaction to the study of biological factors in crime, we believe, is utterly misguided. In fact, these discoveries, far from implying that "criminals are born" and should be locked up forever, suggest new and imaginative ways of reducing criminality by benign treatment. The opportunity we have is precisely analogous to that which we had when the biological bases of other disorders were established. Mental as well as physical illness—alcoholism, learning disabilities of various sorts, and perhaps even susceptibilities to drug addiction—now seem to have genetic components. In each case, new understanding energized the search for treatment and gave it new direction. Now we know that many forms of depression can be successfully treated with drugs; in time we may learn the same of Alzheimer's disease. Alcoholics are helped when they understand that some persons, because of their predisposition toward addiction to alcohol, should probably never consume it at all. A chemical treatment of the predisposition is a realistic possibility. Certain types of slow

learners can already be helped by special programs. In time, others will be also.

Crime, admittedly, may be a more difficult program. So 30 many different acts are criminal that it is only with considerable poetic license that we can speak of "criminality" at all. The bank teller who embezzles $500 to pay off a gambling debt is not engaging in the same behavior as a person who takes $500 from a liquor store at the point of a gun or one who causes $500 worth of damage by drunkenly driving his car into a parked vehicle. Moreover, crime, unlike alcoholism or dyslexia, exposes a person to the formal condemnation of society and the possibility of imprisonment. We naturally and rightly worry about treating all "criminals" alike, or stigmatizing persons whom we think might become criminal by placing them in special programs designed to prevent criminality.

But these problems are not insurmountable barriers to 31 better ways of thinking about crime prevention. Though criminals are of all sorts, we know that a very small fraction of all young males commit so large a fraction of serious street crime that we can properly blame these chronic offenders for most such crime. We also know that chronic offenders typically begin their misconduct at an early age. Early family and preschool programs may be far better repositories for the crime-prevention dollar than rehabilitation programs aimed— usually futilely—at the 19- or 20-year-old veteran offender. Prevention programs risk stigmatizing children, but this may be less of a risk than is neglect. If stigma were a problem to be avoided at all costs, we would have to dismantle most special-needs education programs.

Having said all this, we must acknowledge that there is at 32 present little hard evidence that we know how to inhibit the development of delinquent tendencies in children. There are some leads, such as family training programs of the sort pioneered at the Oregon Social Learning Center, where parents are taught how to use small rewards and penalties to alter the behavior of misbehaving children. There is also evidence from David Weikart and Lawrence Schweinhart of the High/ Scope Educational Research Foundation at Ypsilanti, Mich., that preschool education programs akin to Project Head Start may reduce later delinquency. There is nothing yet to build a national policy on, but there are ideas worth exploring by carefully repeating and refining these pioneering experimental efforts.

33   Above all, there is a case for redirecting research into the causes of crime in ways that take into account the interaction of biological and social factors. Some scholars, such as the criminologist Marvin E. Wolfgang and his colleagues at the University of Pennsylvania, are already exploring these issues by analyzing social and biological information from large groups as they age from infancy to adulthood and linking the data to criminal behavior. But much more needs to be done.

34   It took years of patiently following the life histories of many men and women to establish the linkages between smoking or diet and disease; it will also take years to unravel the complex and subtle ways in which intelligence, temperament, hormonal levels and other traits combine with family circumstances and later experiences in school and elsewhere to produce human character.

Dorothy Nelkin and M. Susan Lindee
Elvis' DNA: The Gene
as a Cultural Icon

Dorothy Nelkin teaches sociology and law at New York University, and M. Susan Lindee is a historian of science at the University of Pennsylvania. The following excerpted article, adapted from their book The DNA Mystique: The Gene as a Cultural Icon *(1995), was published in* The Humanist *in the spring of 1995.*

1   In popular culture, Elvis Presley has become a genetic construct, driven by his genes to his unlikely destiny. In the 1985 biography *Elvis and Gladys,* for example, Elaine Dundy attributed Presley's success to the genetic characteristics of his mother's multiethnic family. "Genetically speaking," she wrote, "what produced Elvis was quite a mixture." To his "French Norman blood was added Scots-Irish blood," as well as "the Indian strain supplying the mystery and the Jewish strain supplying spectacular showmanship." All this combined with his "circumstances, social conditioning, and religious upbringing...[produced] the enigma that was Elvis."

Dundy traced Elvis' musical talents to his father (who "had a very good voice") as well as his mother (who had "the instincts of a performer"). His parents provided a musical environment, Dundy noted, but "even without it, one wonders if Elvis, with his biological musical equipment, would not still have become a virtuoso."

Another Elvis biographer, Albert Goldman, focused on his 2 subject's "bad" genes, describing him in *Elvis* as "the victim of a fatal hereditary disposition." Using language reminiscent of the stories of the Jukes and Kallikaks, the degenerate families of the early eugenics movement, Goldman attributed Elvis' character to ancestors who constituted "a distinctive breed of southern yeomanry" commonly known as hillbillies. A genealogy research organization, Goldman said, had traced Presley's lineage back nine generations to a nineteenth-century "coward, deserter, and bigamist." In Goldman's narrative, this genetic heritage explained Elvis' downfall: his addiction to drugs and alcohol, his emotional disorders, and his premature death were all in his genes. His fate was a readout of his DNA.

The idea that "good" and "bad" character traits (and destinies) are the consequence of "good" and "bad" genes appears 3 in a wide range of popular sources. In these works, the gene is described in moral terms and seems to dictate the actions of criminals, celebrities, political leaders, and literary and scientific figures. Films present stories of "tainted blood" and "born achievers," of success and failure, of kindness and cruelty, all written in the genes. The most complicated human traits are also blamed on DNA. Media stories (for example, Alan Wexler's article in the August 13, 1993, *Newsday*) feature various jokes about Republican genes, MBA genes, lawyer genes, and public-interest genes. Human behaviors linked to DNA in these accounts range from the trivial—a preference for flashy belt buckles—to the tragic—a desire to murder children.

Such popular constructions of behavior draw on the 4 increasing public legitimacy of the scientific field of behavioral genetics. Behavioral geneticists have been able to demonstrate that some relatively complicated behaviors— certainly in experimental animals and possibly in human beings—are genetically determined. Studies of animals reveal the genetic bases of survival instincts, mating rituals, and certain aspects of learning and memory. Border collies herd sheep in a unique characteristic way whether they have been trained or not, even if they have never seen sheep before. Some behaviors associated with particular hormones have been indirectly linked to genes: both aggressive and nurturing behaviors—in mice—can be manipulated with adjustments of hormone levels. Though such research highlights the biological events involved in some behaviors, it does not support the popular idea that genes determine human personality traits or such complex phenomena as success, failure, political leanings, or criminality.

5   Nonetheless, the claims that genes control human behaviors have received significant support from some behavioral geneticists who have positioned themselves as public scientists. Among the most cited and widely promoted scientists in this field is University of Minnesota psychologist Thomas Bouchard. Bouchard, a student of Arthur Jensen, has studied identical twins reared apart in order to determine the relationship between genetics and IQ, personality, and behavior. Bouchard's work has attracted significant popular attention since he began promoting his findings in 1982, but it has been controversial in the scientific community. Identical twins growing up in different families have long been seen as "natural experiments" in human genetics, even by the eugenicists of the 1920s. Bouchard, like others before him, has concluded that all similarities in identical twins reared apart are caused by their shared genes. But Bouchard's research subjects were self-selected (he advertised to find them) and interested in being twinlike. Some of them had also been reared together for several years before they were adopted into different families, therefore sharing at least an early environment. In addition, in any population a certain number of similarities will appear by chance. The fact that two people enjoy the same soft drink—in a culture in which soft drinks are widely consumed—is not evidence that they share a gene for the consumption of that soft drink.

6   For years Bouchard had problems getting his papers accepted for publication in scientific journals. Convinced of his work's importance, however, he submitted his findings to the press before they were peer-reviewed, or even when they had been rejected by scientific publications. The media responded with extraordinary interest, attracted to the drama in "the eerie world of re-united twins" and the potential for controversy over the sensitive issue of genes and IQ. *U.S. News and World Report* reported on the twin studies by describing the character traits that are "bred in our bones." Quirks such as wearing flashy belt buckles, liking particular television programs, or drinking coffee cold and problems such as addiction or eating disorders were all described as

originating in the genes. The "Donahue Show" began a program on the twin studies with films on animal behavior, suggesting that, like animals, we "get a push before the womb." *Time* magazine criticized the political liberals who explained crime and poverty as byproducts of destructive environments. An article in *Science Writer* magazine argued that the twin studies were "one more proof that parenting has its limits." And the *Boston Globe* announced that "geneticists now have ascendancy in the nature-nurture debate."

In October 1990, *Science* became the first major professional journal to publish Bouchard's work. There followed a media blitz. The *Philadelphia Inquirer* headlined its front-page story "Personality mostly a matter of genes" and welcomed the "landmark" study that proved that personality is put in place at the "instant" of conception. Even religiosity and church attendance, the article said, were determined by genes. Magazine articles touted Bouchard's research as part of the swelling tide of evidence for the importance of genes. 7

Since 1983, when behavioral genetics first appeared as a category in the *Reader's Guide to Periodical Literature*, hundreds of articles about the relationship between genetics and behavior have appeared in magazines, newspapers, and fictional accounts, often presented as the cutting edge of current science. Included among the traits attributed to heredity have been mental illness, aggression, homosexuality, exhibition, dyslexia, addiction, job and educational success, arson, tendency to tease, propensity for risk-taking, timidity, social potency, tendency to giggle or to use hurtful words, traditionalism, and zest for life. 8

Many of the stories of good and bad traits address a common and troubling contradiction. Why do some individuals, despite extremely difficult childhoods, become productive, even celebrated members of society, while other children, granted every opportunity and advantage, turn out badly? What accounts for the frequent disparity between achievement and hard work? Genetics appears to provide an explanation. Individuals succeed or fail not so much because of their efforts, their will, or their social circumstances but because they are genetically programmed for that fate. 9

Evil in the Genes

The existence of evil has posed problems for philosophers and theologians for much of human history. Religious systems 10 have personified evil as a supernatural being; folklore has located it in natural disaster, mythical beasts, or the "evil eye." Evil can be seen as the cosmic consequence of fate (the bad "luck of the draw") or the result of voluntary human action or moral failure. The agents invoked to explain the presence of evil are commonly powerful, abstract, and invisible— demons, gods, witches, a marked soul, and, today, the biochemistry of the brain. Environmental contingencies, similarly powerful and abstract—such as patterns of authority discussed by Stanley Milgram in "Behavioral Studies of Obedience" (*Journal of Abnormal and Social Psychology*) or social reinforcements advanced by B. F. Skinner in *Beyond Freedom and Dignity*—have also been seen as the sources of evil. But the belief that the "devil made me do it" does not significantly differ in its consequences from the belief that "my genes made me do it." Both seek to explain behavior that threatens the social contract; both locate control over human fate in powerful abstract entities capable of dictating human action in ways that mitigate moral responsibility and alleviate personal blame.

11   The response to research on the so-called criminal chromosome suggests the appeal of this view. In 1965 the British cytogeneticist Patricia Jacobs found that a disproportionate number of men in an Edinburgh correctional institution, instead of being XY (normal) males, were XYY males. Jacobs suggested that the extra Y chromosome "predisposes its carriers to unusually aggressive behavior." Other researchers later questioned whether XYY males were more aggressive, suggesting instead that they suffered from diminished intellectual functioning that made it more likely that they would be incarcerated. And the original estimate of the rate of XYY males occurring in the population in general was later revised upward, so that the difference in the prison population and the general population appeared to be less great than it had once seemed.

12   But the "criminal chromosome" had a remarkable popular life, first attracting the attention of the press in April 1968 when it was invoked to explain one of the most gruesome crimes of the decade. A *New York Times* reporter wrote that Richard Speck, then awaiting sentencing in the murder, one night, of nine student nurses, planned to appeal his case on the grounds that he was XYY. This story—which was incorrect (Speck was an XY male)—provoked a public debate about the causes of criminal behavior. *Newsweek* asked if criminals were "Born bad?" ("Can a man be born a criminal?") *Time*

headlined a story "Chromosomes and crime." By the early 1970s, at least two films had featured an XYY male criminal, and a series of crime novels had made their focus an XYY hero who struggled with his compulsion to commit crimes.

References to the criminal chromosome continued to   13 shape popular views of violence. In 1986, the *New York Times* asked, "Should such persons [XYY males] be held responsible for their crimes, or treated as victims of conditions for which they are not responsible, on a par with the criminally insane?" And in 1992, a PBS series on "The Mind" introduced a segment on violence: "Recent research suggests that even the acts of a serial killer may have a biological or genetic basis." Similarly, in February 1993 Phil Donahue advised his listeners on "how to tell if your child is a serial killer." His guest, a psychiatrist, described a patient who had been raised in a "Norman Rockwell" setting but then, driven by his extra Y chromosome, killed 11 women.

News reporters and talk-show hosts refer to "bad seeds,"   14 "criminal genes," and "alcohol genes." CBS talk-show host Oprah Winfrey found it meaningful to ask a guest whether her twin sister's "being bad" was "in her blood." In the movie *JFK*, one character tells another, "You're as crazy as your mama—goes to show it's in the genes." To *New York Times Magazine* writer Deborah Franklin, evil is "embedded in the coils of chromosomes that our parents pass to us at conception." And Camille Paglia described her theory of nature in *Sex, Art, and American Culture* as following Sade rather than Rousseau:

> Aggression and violence are primarily not learned but instinctual, nature's promptings, bursts of primitive energy from the animal realm that man has never left.... Dionysus, trivialized by Sixties polemicists, is not pleasure but pleasure-pain, the gross continuum of nature, the subordination of all living things to biological necessity.

Genetic or biological explanations of "bad" behavior are   15 sufficiently prevalent to serve as a common source of irony. A 1991 segment of the comic strip "Calvin and Hobbes" featured Calvin's perplexed father asking his son: "You've been hitting rocks in the house? What on earth would make you do something like that?" Calvin replied: "Poor genetic material." In another strip that same year, Calvin described a vicious "snow snake": "I suppose if I had two Y chromosomes I'd feel hostile, too!" And a barroom cartoon by Nick Downes (reprinted in the April 24, 1992, issue of *Science*) portrayed "Dead-Eye Dan, known far and wide for his fast gun, mean temper, and extra Y chromosome."

16   Bad genes have also become a facetious metaphor to describe national aggression. James O. Jackson's *Time* article, "The New Germany Flexes Its Muscles," described the nation as "a child of doubtful lineage adopted as an infant into a loving family; the child has been good, obedient, and industrious, but friends and neighbors are worried that evil genes may still lurk beneath a well-mannered surface." Christopher Lehmann-Haupt, in his *New York Times* article "Studying Soccer Violence by the Civilized British," blamed the violence on the "genetic drive to wage war against the outlander."

17   Some individuals, so the media imply, are "born to kill" and will do so despite environmental advantages. In December 1991, a 14-year-old high school boy was arrested for the murder of a schoolmate. The *New York Times* account of this event interpreted it as a key piece of evidence in "the debate over whether children misbehave because they had bad childhoods or because they are just bad seeds." The boy's parents had provided a good home environment, the reporter asserted; they had "taken the children to church almost every Sunday, and sacrificed to send them to a Catholic grammar school." Yet their son had been arrested for murder. This troubling inconsistency between the child's apparently decent background and his violent behavior called for explanation. The reporter resolved the mystery through the explanatory power of inheritance; the moral of the story was clearly stated in its headline: "Raising Children Right Isn't Always Enough." The implication? There are, indeed, "bad seeds.". . .

18   This same theme appeared in the news reports of a debate over the body and blood of Westley Allan Dodd, a serial killer of children who was hanged in January 1993. Dodd insisted that he could not be cured and that if he had the opportunity he would kill again and "enjoy it." His ordinary childhood offered no convincing explanation for his monstrous behavior. He had not been an abused child. After Dodd's execution, scientists attempted to obtain pieces of his brain and vials of his blood to determine whether his behavior could be attributed to neurological abnormalities or "gene oddities." Such stories arise from a conflict between childhood experience and adult behavior; when the two seem to conflict, biological predisposition seems to provide a plausible and appealing resolution.

19   Research that links criminal behavior to biological forces fuels the hope that genetic information will make possible the

prediction, and therefore the control, of deviant behavior. Certain scientists encourage such expectations. In a 1992 *Science* editorial, "Elephants, Monstrosities, and the Law," the journal's editor, biologist Daniel Koshland, told stories about acts of violence: "An elephant goes berserk at the circus, an elderly pillar of the community is discovered to be a child molester, a man admits to killing many young boys... a disgruntled employee shoots seven co-workers." Each crime, wrote Koshland, had a common origin—an abnormality of the brain....

Even when scientists emphasize the complexity of biologi-   20
cal and environmental conditions that could lead to violence, media accounts highlight the importance of genetics. The press coverage of the National Research Council's 1992 report, *Understanding and Preventing Violence,* is a case in point. The report said that violence arises from the "interactions among individuals' psychosocial development, neurological and hormonal differences, and social processes." It stressed the uncertain implications of research when it came to genetic influence on anti-social behavior: "These studies suggest at most a weak role for genetic processes in influencing potentials for violent behavior. The correlations and concordances of behavior in two of the three studies are consistent with a positive genetic effect, but are statistically insignificant." While not ruling out genetic processes, the NRC suggested: "If genetic predispositions to violence are discovered, they are likely to involve many genes and substantial environmental interaction rather than any simple genetic marker."

Only 14 of the 464 pages of the NRC report actually dealt   21
with the biological perspectives on violence, and less than two pages were about genetics. Nevertheless, Fox Butterfield's article on the report in the November 13, 1992, *New York Times* was headlined: "Study Cites Role of Biological and Genetic Factors in Violence." Genes appear far more newsworthy than social or economic circumstances as a source of anti-social behavior. While genetic theories of violence have been controversial, denounced as politically and racially motivated, some journalists have dismissed critiques as "politically correct." In an April 19, 1993, article in *Time,* Anastasia Toufexis, looking for the causes of "the savagery that is sweeping America," suggested that society's ills cannot fully be responsible, that violence may be caused by "errant genes." "Science could help shed light on the roots of violence and offer new solutions for society," she added, "but not if the research is suppressed."

22   Biological theories also appeal as explanations of group violence and war. A 1991 textbook, *Social Psychology*, uses "genetic similarity theory" to explain "the tendency to dislike members of groups other than our own." Discrimination against those who are different, say authors R. A. Baron and D. Byrne, is part of inherited human tendencies to defend those possessing similar genes. Extending this idea to explain war, Michael Ghiglieri, in a November 1987 *Discover* article, described a study of chimps and speculated whether war runs in our genes like baldness or diabetes." Such explanations extend the popular theories of the late 1960s and early 1970s, when a spate of books appeared explaining human behavior to a lay audience in evolutionary terms. These included Robert Ardrey's *The Territorial Imperative* (1966), Konrad Lorenz's *On Aggression* (1966), Desmond Morris' *The Naked Ape* (1967), and Lionel Tiger and Robin Fox's *The Imperial Animal* (1970). Promoting a biological model of organized human aggression, these authors explained it as a productive and necessary social activity. The books were fashionable, attracting a wide readership and extensive media coverage. Reviewing the response to aggression research, Temple University psychologist Jeffrey Goldstein found that the media systematically covered studies that offer evidence of genetic explanations of violence but were less interested in research on the influence of social and economic conditions.

23   Some biologists and social scientists have criticized research on the genetic predisposition to organized aggression for concealing inadequate methodologies behind quantitative data and for minimizing the influence of social, political, and economic factors on aggressive behavior. In May 1986, Jeffrey Goldstein helped assemble a group of these critics to discuss biological theories about the origin of warfare. Meeting in Spain, they produced the Seville Statement on Violence, which strongly repudiated the idea that war is biologically necessary or genetically controlled. "It is scientifically incorrect to say that war is caused by 'instinct' or any single motivation...scientifically incorrect to say that humans have a 'violent brain'...scientifically incorrect to say that in the course of human evolution there has been a selection for aggressive behavior more than for other kinds of behavior." The statement concluded that "biology does not condemn humanity to war. The same species who invented war is capable of inventing peace."

24   This brief but unambiguous text was signed by twenty well-known scholars from around the world and endorsed by

the American Psychological Association, the American Anthropological Association, the International Society for Research on Aggression, and Psychologists for Social Responsibility. Yet despite considerable efforts to publicize the statement, it attracted little media attention. A journalist responding to the efforts to disseminate the Seville material expressed the prevailing attitude: "Call me when you find the gene for war."

The interest in "bad genes"—the genes for deviance— 25 reflects a tendency to medicalize social problems. This is especially evident in scientific and social speculation about the nature and etiology of addiction. Definitions of alcoholism have shifted over time from sin to sickness, from moral transgression to medical disease, depending on prevailing social, political, and moral agendas. Debates over the etiology of alcoholism go back to ancient Rome, but the modern conception of alcoholism as a disease is usually attributed to the nineteenth-century theories of Benjamin Rush (1745–1813). Early leaders of the American temperance movement, likewise, defined alcoholism as a disease, but when the movement began to advocate outright prohibition, alcoholism was redefined, along with syphilis and opiate addiction, as a "vice"—a manifestation of immoral behavior. A moral concept of voluntary addiction replaced the model of disease, and the politics of prohibition in the 1920s turned alcoholism into a problem more legal than medical. At the same time, eugenicists were compiling family studies supposedly demonstrating its inherited nature.

In 1935, E. M. Jellinek, reviewing the biological literature 26 on alcoholism for a major Carnegie Foundation report, formulated a medical model that explained alcoholism in terms of the interaction of alcohol with an individual's physical and psychological characteristics and his or her social circumstances. This analysis, later republished by Jellinek as *The Disease Concept of Alcoholism*, focused attention on what made people susceptible. The same year, Alcoholics Anonymous was founded on the doctrine that alcoholism was a compelling biological drive that could be cured only by total abstinence and moral rectitude. AA's position contributed to the revival of the medical model, promoting the idea that alcoholics had "predisposing characteristics" that distinguished them from others. This view has persisted, in its contemporary form focusing on the genetic basis of alcoholism.

Common observation shows that alcoholism runs in fami- 27 lies. As in the case of violence, however, this in itself does not reveal the cause. Many traits run in families—poverty, for example, or poor manners—without being a consequence of heredity. The prevalence of alcoholism in certain families could reflect role models, the availability of alcohol, or the reaction to abuse. Nevertheless, a common perception was expressed by George Nobbe in his 1989 *Omni* article, "Alcoholic Genes": "Addicted to the bottle? It may be in your genes." The gene for alcoholism became a theme of the Oprah Winfrey and Phil Donahue shows. Shifra Diamond's August 1990 *Mademoiselle* article, "Drinking Habits May Be in the Family," asked: "Do you have a gene that makes you a designated drinker?" and suggested that "even if you have exceptional self-discipline, you could still be at high risk." And Nancy Reagan's famous anti-drug slogan, "Just Say No," provoked a 1991 *Christian Science Monitor* editorial about the "genes-impelled compulsion" to take drugs.

28   In the 1990 article "Scientists Pinpoint Brain Irregularities in Drug Addicts," *New York Times* reporter Daniel Goleman presented several cases to dramatize the genetic basis of alcoholism. A 26-year-old executive had been the class clown as a child and president of his high school class. Always extroverted and outgoing, he partied a lot and, as he matured, started taking drugs in order to stay high. Addiction appealed because of his "natural bent." Another young man had been anxious as a child until he discovered that alcohol made him relax. His father was an alcoholic, so he had easy access to liquor; Goleman, however, quoted sources that explained his addiction in terms of biological vulnerability.

29   Goleman's stories suggested one reason for the appeal of genetic explanations: they implied that biological markers will make it possible to identify those at risk of addiction. He quoted a scientist who optimistically claimed that genetic engineering will eventually eliminate the gene and therefore the problems of addiction. In effect, like genetic explanations of violence, identifying an "alcoholism gene" offers the hope that addiction can be controlled—not through the uncertain route of social reform but through biological manipulation....

30   To explain addictive behavior in absolute genetic or biological terms is to extract it from the social setting that defines and interprets behavior. There are no criminal genes or alcohol genes, only genes for the proteins that influence hormonal and physiological processes. And only the most general outline of social behavior can be genetically coded. Even behaviors known to be genetically inscribed, such as the

human ability to learn spoken language, do not appear if the environment does not promote them. Children do not learn to speak unless they hear spoken language, even though the ability to speak is genetic, a biological trait of the human species. In the case of alcoholism, for example, any biological or genetic predisposition that may exist can only become a full-blown pattern of behavior in an environment in which alcohol is readily available and socially approved. As this suggests, there are many interests at stake in the etiology of addiction, for causal explanations for addiction imply moral judgments about the responsibility and blame.

If defined as a sin, alcoholism represents an individual's   31
flaunting of social norms; if defined as a social problem, it represents a failure of the community environment; if defined as intrinsic to the product consumed, it represents the need for alcohol regulation. But if defined as a genetically determined trait, neither society nor the alcohol industry appears responsible. And if behavior is completely determined— either by genetics or environment—even the addicted individual cannot really be blamed. . . .

The appropriation of DNA—the good or bad gene—to   32
explain individual differences recasts common beliefs about the importance of heredity in powerful scientific terms. Science becomes a way to empower prevailing beliefs, justifying existing social categories and expectations as based on natural forces. The great, the famous, the rich and successful are what they are because of their genes. So, too, the deviant and the dysfunctional are genetically fated. Opportunity is less important than predisposition. Some are destined for success; others for problems or, at least, a lesser fate. The star— or the criminal—is not made but born.

This is a particularly striking theme in American society,   33
where the very foundation of the democratic experiment was the belief in the improvability—indeed, the perfectibility—of all human beings. Belief in genetic destiny implies there are natural limits constraining the possibilities for both individuals and for social groups. Humankind is not perfectible, because the species' flaws and failings are inscribed in an unchangeable text—the DNA—that will persist in creating murderers, addicts, the insane, and the incompetent, even under the most ideal social circumstances. In popular stories, children raised in ideal homes become murderers and children raised in difficult home situations become well-adjusted high achievers. The moral? No possible social system, no ideal nurturing plan can prevent the violent acts that seem to

threaten the social fabric of contemporary American life. Only biological controls, it seems, can solve such problems.

34   The idea of genetic predisposition encourages a passive attitude toward social injustice, an apathy about continuing social problems, and a reason to preserve the status quo. Genetic explanations, however, are malleable. They can be appropriated to justify prevailing stereotypes and maintain current social arrangements, but they can also be used to promote group identity or to celebrate human differences. The diverse social, political, and moral dimensions of such explanations become more transparent as they appear with growing frequency in stories and debates about the social meaning of sex, race, and sexual orientation.

Alison Bass

Why Aren't There More Women Murderers?

Bass is a staff writer for The Boston Globe *newspaper, where this article appeared in 1992.*

1   Accused serial killer Aileen Wuornos, who was recently sentenced to death in Florida, is the exception that doesn't prove the rule.

2   The rule is that women, unlike men, don't kill strangers or even casual acquaintances, except in very rare cases of self-defense. When women do kill—and they do so at astonishingly lower rates than men, who commit 85 percent of all homicides—the vast majority kill family members, usually men who have battered them for years.

3   As many as 90 percent of the women in jail today for murdering men have been battered by those men. A much smaller number—about 3 in 100,000—kill their children as a result of a postpartum psychosis that has gone untreated.

4   There is also a smattering of women with a history of mental disorders who kill in a psychotic rage. And then there is the rare woman who kills family members for money; according to historical accounts, Lizzie Borden was one.

Fewer than 3 percent of serial killers are female, according   5
to FBI statistics. No one knows why this disparity exists,
although many researchers believe that differences in brain
chemistry may be the primary reason why men are so much
more violent than women.

Usually, female multiple killers are caretakers—most often   6
nurses—who rationalize their crimes as mercy killings. Nurse
Genene Jones, for example, was suspected of killing as many
as 16 children in a Texas hospital with a lethal drug in an
attempt to prove to administrators that the hospital needed a
pediatric intensive care unit; she was convicted of killing one
infant and sentenced to 99 years in prison.

Another multiple killer, Velma Barfield, who was electro-   7
cuted in North Carolina in 1984 (the first woman to be executed in 26 years), admitted killing four family members after
years of sexual and physical abuse.

But Aileen Wuornos, who authorities say killed seven men,   8
is the first woman in FBI annals accused in a multiple killing
of strangers, a series of murders that spanned several years.
In many respects, Wuornos, a bisexual prostitute whose
alleged victims had picked her up for sex, fits the profile of a
male killer.

"She has the characteristics we see with our male killers,"   9
said John Douglas, unit chief of behavioral sciences for the
FBI at Quantico, Va. "Like many of our male killers, she
comes from a very dysfunctional background where she was
abused, physically and sexually. But usually women from that
kind of background internalize the abuse and their feelings.
While the men turn to aggression, the women turn to alcohol,
drugs, prostitution and suicide."

Women who have been badly abused as children also tend   10
to get involved with violent men who abuse them and their
children, perpetuating the cycle of violence into the next generation. One 1991 study by New York University researchers
found that 21 females who had been incarcerated for criminal behavior as teenagers did not—as many of their male
counterparts did—commit violent crimes as adults: instead
the majority became enmeshed in violent relationships,
abused or neglected their children, and lost custody of them
as a result.

Other research indicates that women who have been sexu-   11
ally abused as children—unlike men similarly abused—do
not commit sexual crimes.

"Women don't have sexual deviations—they don't make   12
obscene phone calls, they don't flash, they don't have

paraphilias [addictions to bizarre practices, such as having sex with a corpse]," says Ann Burgess, professor of psychiatric nursing at the University of Pennsylvania and an authority on sexual homicide. "It is rare for a woman to murder more than one person, and they never commit sexual crimes."

13   The big question is why.

14   While there is no definitive data on the subject, Burgess and other forensic experts believe there are sharp differences between men and women's brain chemistry, and that those differences are accentuated by cultural differences in the way males and females are raised.

15   "It must be a combination of things, but we know it can't be culture alone," says Angela Browne, a social psychologist at the University of Massachusetts Medical Center and a specialist on women who kill. "You can change environments across cultures, and across almost all cultures men are far more prone to homicide than women. Men are also more prone to socially sanctioned actions that lead to death, like civil strife and war."

16   "It makes sense to conclude that physiological rather than simply societal influences are at play," agrees Dr. Dorothy Otnow Lewis, professor of psychiatry at New York University and an authority on violence.

17   In detailed research, Lewis has found that men who have been horribly abused as children and suffer from a constellation of psychiatric and neurological disorders are much more likely than others to become extremely violent. But as Lewis notes, it takes the Y chromosome, i.e., maleness, to complete the picture.

18   Lewis and others believe male hormones such as testosterone and androgen play a key role in making men much more aggressive than women. But merely having a high level of testosterone does not make someone violent; many men with high levels are simply more competitive. They channel their hormonal drives into constructive pursuits.

19   It seems equally clear that culture plays a role.

20   "Men are brought up to fight and to defend themselves, and they are reinforced for engaging in those behaviors," says Robert Prentky, a forensic psychologist at New England Forensic Associates in Arlington and an authority on sexual violence. "When they are challenged by a bully at school, their fathers will teach them how to fight with their fists. But how many times do parents teach girls to defend themselves?"

21   Girls are taught to nurture and care for others; some psychologists believe females may be biochemically "wired" to

be more giving and nurturing. For whatever reason, women respond to conflict in ways very different than men do.

"Women may be emotionally abusive and damaging, 22 rather than physically abusive," says Browne, author of a book called *When Battered Women Kill.* "Even though women could theoretically equalize their lesser strength with a gun, they still don't perpetrate violence in very large numbers."

The statistics show that most women do not become vio- 23 lent unless they are in fear of their own lives or their children's. In research on battered women who kill their male partners, Browne found the majority of women were responding to threats against their children. And the rest had reason to believe that, after battering them for years, the men in their lives planned to kill them.

Browne also found that the rate of women who kill their 24 partners has fallen 25 percent since the mid-70s, when many shelters for battered women were opened and police started adopting tougher policies on domestic violence. There has been no comparable decrease in the rates of men who kill their female partners. (Of all the male-female partner killings in the United States, 61 percent of the victims were women.)

Research also shows that a small percentage of women kill 25 when their biochemistry goes haywire, as the result of drugs, alcohol, mental disease or pregnancy. The few female mass murderers had long histories of untreated severe mental disorders, such as paranoid schizophrenia and manic mood swings. Among them was Sylvia Seegrist, who in 1985 shot three people during a psychotic rampage at a Philadelphia area mall.

Perhaps the most preventable cause of lethal violence is 26 postpartum psychosis, which afflicts about one woman in 1,000. Fully 3 percent of women with this disorder kill their infants, according to Susan Hickman, a San Diego psychotherapist and specialist in postpartum psychiatric disorders.

"Women with postpartum psychiatric illnesses often expe- 27 rience sleep and appetite disturbances, and in the most extreme cases they hallucinate, hear voices and imagine things," she said. "Often there is some kind of delusional construct involving the infant; for example, a delusion about the baby's being the devil. These delusions often take a religious tone."

Hickman and others believe this psychosis is biochemical in 28 nature. During pregnancy, the placenta takes over some of the body's hormone production, and in most cases after delivery the pituitary gland, which regulates hormones, kicks back in. But in a few cases, Hickman speculates, the pituitary fails to kick back in and the woman's hormones become unbalanced, causing postpartum depression or psychosis.

29   "There is a neuroleptic medication that will control the symptoms very rapidly," Hickman says. "A woman can continue to nurse her baby and be restored to her normal functioning with the medication. And over time her body chemistry will level itself out and she should have no recurrence of symptoms, unless she has another pregnancy."

30   Aileen Wuornos, of course, was not pregnant. Nor, apparently, was she suffering from a serious mental disorder that clouded her judgment about right and wrong.

31   She had, however, experienced a brutal childhood. Her father was convicted of molesting a seven-year-old girl and implicated in the murder of another. When Wuornos was six months old, her mother handed her over to her grandparents, who physically abused her. Her grandfather also sexually abused her. At 13, she became pregnant after being raped by a stranger, according to psychiatrist Susan C. Vaughan of Columbia/New York State Psychiatric Institute, who has written about the case.

32   Thrown out of her grandparents' home when she became pregnant, Wuornos stayed in a home for unwed mothers until her baby was born and given up for adoption. After that, she lived on her own—in a neighbor's junked car or in a woods nearby—and turned to prostitution, drinking and drugs. She roamed the Midwest for years, supporting herself as a prostitute, and when she was 21, she tried to kill herself by shooting herself in the stomach, Vaughan wrote in the winter 1991 issue of the *American Academy of Psychoanalysis Forum.*

33   In the early 1980s, Wuornos was convicted of robbery. Florida police believe the murders did not begin until 1988, when Wuornos was living with another woman and supporting her through prostitution. After police caught up with her in January 1991, she admitted to killing two men who had picked her up for sex. She said she shot them repeatedly after they refused to pay her.

34   "Her motive may have been displaced rage motive—she just wanted to kill these men for revenge," Prentky speculates. "Other women may have her fantasies, but they don't act on it."

CAPITAL PUNISHMENT

George Orwell

A Hanging

Born Eric Arthur Blair in India in 1903, educated in England, and a member of the Imperial Police in Burma for five years, George Orwell was England's most prominent political writer in the decade before his death in 1950. A socialist but no communist, he wrote numerous books of fiction and nonfiction, but he is best remembered for Animal Farm *(1945) and* 1984 *(1948)—novels that contributed to our culture terms like* doublespeak *and* Big Brother. *His fictional description of "A Hanging" appeared in* Shooting an Elephant and Other Essays *(1950); it was first published in 1931.*

It was in Burma, a sodden morning of the rains. A sickly light, like yellow tinfoil, was slanting over the high walls into the jail yard. We were waiting outside the condemned cells, a row of sheds fronted with double bars, like small animal cages. Each cell measured about ten feet by ten and was quite bare within except for a plank bed and a pot for drinking water. In some of them brown, silent men were squatting at the inner bars, with their blankets draped round them. These were the condemned men, due to be hanged within the next week or two. 1

One prisoner had been brought out of his cell. He was a Hindu, a puny wisp of a man, with a shaven head and vague liquid eyes. He had a thick, sprouting mustache, absurdly too big for his body, rather like the mustache of a comic man on the films. Six tall Indian warders were guarding him and getting him ready for the gallows. Two of them stood by with rifles and fixed bayonets, while the others handcuffed him, passed a chain through his handcuffs and fixed it to their belts, and lashed his arms tight to his sides. They crowded very close about him, with their hands always on him in a careful, caressing grip, as though all the while feeling him to make sure he was there. It was like men handling a fish which 2 is still alive and may jump back into the water. But he stood quite unresisting, yielding his arms limply to the ropes, as though he hardly noticed what was happening.

3   Eight o'clock struck and a bugle call, desolately thin in the wet air, floated from the distant barracks. The superintendent of the jail, who was standing apart from the rest of us, moodily prodding the gravel with his stick, raised his head at the sound. He was an army doctor, with a gray toothbrush mustache and a gruff voice. "For God's sake, hurry up, Francis," he said irritably. "The man ought to have been dead by this time. Aren't you ready yet?"

4   Francis, the head jailer, a fat Dravidian in a white drill suit and gold spectacles, waved his black hand. "Yes sir, yes sir," he bubbled. "All iss satisfactorily prepared. The hangman iss waiting. We shall proceed."

5   "Well, quick march, then. The prisoners can't get their breakfast till this job's over."

6   We set out for the gallows. Two warders marched on either side of the prisoner, with their rifles at the slope; two others marched close against him, gripping him by arm and shoulder, as though at once pushing and supporting him. The rest of us, magistrates and the like, followed behind. Suddenly, when we had gone ten yards, the procession stopped short without any order or warning. A dreadful thing had happened—a dog, come goodness knows whence, had appeared in the yard. It came bounding among us with a loud volley of barks and leapt round us wagging its whole body, wild with glee at finding so many human beings together. It was a large woolly dog, half Airedale, half pariah. For a moment it pranced around us, and then, before anyone could stop it, it had made a dash for the prisoner, and jumping up tried to lick his face. Everybody stood aghast, too taken aback even to grab the dog.

7   "Who let that bloody brute in here?" said the superintendent angrily. "Catch it, someone!"

8   A warder detached from the escort charged clumsily after the dog, but it danced and gamboled just out of his reach, taking everything as part of the game. A young Eurasian jailer picked up a handful of gravel and tried to stone the dog away, but it dodged the stones and came after us again. Its yaps echoed from the jail walls. The prisoner, in the grasp of the two warders, looked on incuriously, as though this was another formality of the hanging. It was several minutes before someone managed to catch the dog. Then we put my handkerchief through its collar and moved off once more, with the dog still straining and whimpering.

It was about forty yards to the gallows. I watched the bare   9
brown back of the prisoner marching in front of me. He
walked clumsily with his bound arms, but quite steadily, with
that bobbing gait of the Indian who never straightens his
knees. At each step his muscles slid neatly into place, the lock
of hair on his scalp danced up and down, his feet printed
themselves on the wet gravel. And once, in spite of the men
who gripped him by each shoulder, he stepped lightly aside to
avoid a puddle on the path.

It is curious; but till that moment I had never realized what   10
it means to destroy a healthy, conscious man. When I saw the
prisoner step aside to avoid the puddle, I saw the mystery, the
unspeakable wrongness, of cutting a life short when it is in full
tide. This man was not dying, he was alive just as we are alive.
All the organs of his body were working—bowels digesting
food, skin renewing itself, nails growing, tissues forming—all
toiling away in solemn foolery. His nails would still be growing when he stood on the drop, when he was falling through
the air with a tenth-of-a-second to live. His eyes saw the yellow gravel and the gray walls, and his brain still remembered,
foresaw, reasoned—even about puddles. He and we were a
party of men walking together, seeing, hearing, feeling,
understanding the same world; and in two minutes, with a
sudden snap, one of us would be gone—one mind less, one
world less.

The gallows stood in a small yard, separate from the main   11
grounds of the prison, and overgrown with tall prickly weeds.
It was a brick erection like three sides of a shed, with plank-
ing on top, and above that two beams and a crossbar with the
rope dangling. The hangman, a gray-haired convict in the
white uniform of the prison, was waiting beside his machine.
He greeted us with a servile crouch as we entered. At a word
from Francis the two warders, gripping the prisoner more
closely than ever, half led, half pushed him to the gallows and
helped him clumsily up the ladder. Then the hangman
climbed up and fixed the rope round the prisoner's neck.

We stood waiting, five yards away. The warders had   12
formed in a rough circle round the gallows. And then, when
the noose was fixed, the prisoner began crying out to his god.
It was a high, reiterated cry of "Ram! Ram! Ram! Ram!" not
urgent and fearful like a prayer or cry for help, but steady,
rhythmical, almost like the tolling of a bell. The dog answered
the sound with a whine. The hangman, still standing on the
gallows, produced a small cotton bag like a flour bag and
drew it down over the prisoner's face. But the sound, muffled

by the cloth, still persisted, over and over again: "Ram! Ram! Ram! Ram! Ram!"

13   The hangman climbed down and stood ready, holding the lever. Minutes seemed to pass. The steady, muffled crying from the prisoner went on and on, "Ram! Ram! Ram!" never faltering for an instant. The superintendent, his head on his chest, was slowly poking the ground with his stick; perhaps he was counting the cries, allowing the prisoner a fixed number—fifty, perhaps, or a hundred. Everyone had changed color. The Indians had gone gray like bad coffee, and one or two of the bayonets were wavering. We looked at the lashed, hooded man on the drop, and listened to his cries—each cry another second of life; the same thought was in all our minds; oh, kill him quickly, get it over, stop that abominable noise!

14   Suddenly the superintendent made up his mind. Throwing up his head he made a swift motion with his stick. "Chalo!" he shouted almost fiercely.

15   There was a clanking noise, and then dead silence. The prisoner had vanished, and the rope was twisting on itself. I let go of the dog, and it galloped immediately to the back of the gallows; but when it got there it stopped short, barked, and then retreated into a corner of the yard, where it stood among the weeds, looking timorously out at us. We went round the gallows to inspect the prisoner's body. He was dangling with his toes pointed straight downwards, very slowly revolving, as dead as a stone.

16   The superintendent reached out with his stick and poked the bare brown body; it oscillated slightly. "*He's* all right," said the superintendent. He backed out from under the gallows, and blew out a deep breath. The moody look had gone out of his face quite suddenly. He glanced at his wristwatch. "Eight minutes past eight. Well, that's all for this morning, thank God."

17   The warders unfixed bayonets and marched away. The dog, sobered and conscious of having misbehaved itself, slipped after them. We walked out of the gallows yard, past the condemned cells with their waiting prisoners, into the big central yard of the prison. The convicts, under the command of warders armed with lathis, were already receiving their breakfast. They squatted in long rows, each man holding a tin pannikin, while two warders with buckets marched around ladling out rice; it seemed quite a homely, jolly scene, after the hanging. An enormous relief had come upon us now that the job was done. One felt an impulse to sing, to break into a run, to snigger. All at once everyone began chattering gaily.

The Eurasian boy walking beside me nodded towards the   18
way we had come, with a knowing smile: "Do you know sir,
our friend (he meant the dead man) when he heard his appeal
had been dismissed, he pissed on the floor of his cell. From
fright. Kindly take one of my cigarettes, sir. Do you not
admire my new silver case, sir? From the boxwallah, two
rupees eight annas. Classy European style."

Several people laughed—at what, nobody seemed certain.   19

Francis was walking by the superintendent, talking garru-   20
lously: "Well, sir, all has passed off with the utmost satisfacto-
riness. It was all finished—flick! Like that. It iss not always
so—oah, no! I have known cases where the doctor was
obliged to go beneath the gallows and pull the prisoner's legs
to ensure decease. Most disagreeable!"

"Wriggling about, eh? That's bad," said the superintendent.   21

"Ach, sir, it iss worse when they become refractory! One   22
man, I recall, clung to the bars of hiss cage when we went to
take him out. You will scarcely credit, sir, that it took six
warders to dislodge him, three pulling at each leg. We reasoned with him, 'My dear fellow,' we said, 'think of all the
pain and trouble you are causing to us!' But no, he would not
listen! Ach, he was very troublesome!"

I found that I was laughing quite loudly. Everyone was   23
laughing. Even the superintendent grinned in a tolerant way.
"You'd better all come out and have a drink," he said quite
genially. "I've got a bottle of whiskey in the car. We could do
with it."

We went through the big double gates of the prison into   24
the road. "Pulling at his legs!" exclaimed a Burmese magis-
trate suddenly, and burst into a loud chuckling. We all began
laughing again. At that moment Francis' anecdote seemed
extraordinarily funny. We all had a drink together, native and
European alike, quite amicably. The dead man was a hundred
yards away.

Edward I. Koch
Death and Justice

Outspoken and controversial, Edward I. Koch (born 1924) served as the Democratic mayor of New York City from 1978 to 1989. He has always been eager to engage in public debate on controversial issues in his three books, in his hundreds of speeches, and in his published articles. In 1985, he contributed the following essay to The New Republic, *an influential public affairs magazine generally considered middle-of-the-road in its outlook.*

1   Last December a man named Robert Lee Willie, who had been convicted of raping and murdering an 18-year-old woman, was executed in the Louisiana state prison. In a statement issued several minutes before his death, Mr. Willie said: "Killing people is wrong.... It makes no difference whether it's citizens, countries, or governments. Killing is wrong." Two weeks later in South Carolina, an admitted killer named Joseph Carl Shaw was put to death for murdering two teenagers. In an appeal to the governor for clemency, Mr. Shaw wrote: "Killing is wrong when I did it. Killing is wrong when you do it. I hope you have the courage and moral strength to stop the killing."

2   It is a curiosity of modern life that we find ourselves being lectured on morality by cold-blooded killers. Mr. Willie previously had been convicted of aggravated rape, aggravated kidnapping, and the murders of a Louisiana deputy and a man from Missouri. Mr. Shaw committed another murder a week before the two for which he was executed, and admitted mutilating the body of the 14-year-old girl he killed. I can't help wondering what prompted these murderers to speak out against killing as they entered the death-house door. Did their newfound reverence for life stem from the realization that they were about to lose their own?

3   Life is indeed precious, and I believe the death penalty helps to affirm this fact. Had the death penalty been a real possibility in the minds of these murderers, they might well have stayed their hand. They might have shown moral awareness before their victims died, and not after. Consider the tragic death of Rosa Velez, who happened to be home when a man named Luis Vera burglarized her apartment in Brook-

lyn. "Yeah, I shot her," Vera admitted. "She knew me, and I knew I wouldn't go to the chair."

During my 22 years in public service, I have heard the pros 4 and cons of capital punishment expressed with special intensity. As a district leader, councilman, congressman, and mayor, I have represented constituencies generally thought of as liberal. Because I support the death penalty for heinous crimes of murder, I have sometimes been the subject of emotional and outraged attacks by voters who find my position reprehensible or worse. I have listened to their ideas. I have weighed their objections carefully. I still support the death penalty. The reasons I maintain my position can be best understood by examining the arguments most frequently heard in opposition.

1. *The death penalty is "barbaric."* Sometimes opponents of 5 capital punishment horrify with tales of lingering death on the gallows, of faulty electric chairs, or of agony in the gas chamber. Partly in response to such protests, several states such as North Carolina and Texas switched to execution by lethal injection. The condemned person is put to death painlessly, without ropes, voltage, bullets, or gas. Did this answer the objections of death penalty opponents? Of course not. On June 22, 1984, *The New York Times* published an editorial that sarcastically attacked the new "hygienic" method of death by injection, and stated that "execution can never be made humane through science." So it's not the method that really troubles opponents. It's the death itself they consider barbaric.

Admittedly, capital punishment is not a pleasant topic. 6 However, one does not have to like the death penalty in order to support it any more than one must like radical surgery, radiation, or chemotherapy in order to find necessary these attempts at curing cancer. Ultimately we may learn how to cure cancer with a simple pill. Unfortunately, that day has not yet arrived. Today we are faced with the choice of letting the cancer spread or trying to cure it with the methods available, methods that one day will almost certainly be considered barbaric. But to give up and do nothing would be far more barbaric and would certainly delay the discovery of an eventual cure. The analogy between cancer and murder is imperfect, because murder is not the "disease" we are trying to cure. The disease is injustice. We may not like the death penalty, but it must be available to punish crimes of cold-blooded murder, cases in which any other form of punishment would be inadequate and, therefore, unjust. If we create a society in which

injustice is not tolerated, incidents of murder—the most fla-
grant form of injustice—will diminish.

7   *2. No other major democracy uses the death penalty.* No
other major democracy—in fact, few other countries of any
description—are plagued by a murder rate such as that in the
United States. Fewer and fewer Americans can remember the
days when unlocked doors were the norm and murder was a
rare and terrible offense. In America the murder rate climbed
122 percent between 1963 and 1980. During that same
period, the murder rate in New York City increased by almost
400 percent, and the statistics are even worse in many other
cities. A study at M.I.T. showed that based on 1970 homicide
rates a person who lived in a large American city ran a greater
risk of being murdered than an American soldier in World
War II ran of being killed in combat. It is not surprising that
the laws of each country differ according to differing conditions and traditions. If other countries had our murder problem, the cry for capital punishment would be just as loud as it
is here. And I daresay that any other major democracy where
75 percent of the people supported the death penalty would
soon enact it into law.

8   *3. An innocent person might be executed by mistake.* Consider the work of Adam Bedau, one of the most implacable
foes of capital punishment in this country. According to Mr.
Bedau, it is "false sentimentality to argue that the death penalty should be abolished because of the abstract possibility
that an innocent person might be executed." He cites a study
of the 7,000 executions in this country from 1893 to 1971, and
concludes that the record fails to show that such cases occur.
The main point, however, is this. If government functioned
only when the possibility of error didn't exist, government
wouldn't function at all. Human life deserves special protection, and one of the best ways to guarantee that protection is
to assure that convicted murderers do not kill again. Only the
death penalty can accomplish this end. In a recent case in
New Jersey, a man named Richard Biegenwald was freed
from prison after serving 18 years for murder; since his
release he has been convicted of committing four murders. A
prisoner named Lemuel Smith, who, while serving four life
sentences for murder (plus two life sentences for kidnapping
and robbery) in New York's Green Haven Prison, lured a
woman corrections officer into the chaplain's office and
strangled her. He then mutilated and dismembered her body.
An additional life sentence for Smith is meaningless. Because

New York has no death penalty statute, Smith has effectively been given a license to kill.

But the problem of multiple murder is not confined to the nation's penitentiaries. In 1981, 91 police officers were killed in the line of duty in this country. Seven percent of those arrested in the cases that have been solved had a previous arrest for murder. In New York City in 1976 and 1977, 85 persons arrested for homicide had a previous arrest for murder. Six of these individuals had two previous arrests for murder, and one had four previous murder arrests. During those two years the New York police were arresting for murder persons with a previous arrest for murder on the average of one every 8.5 days. This is not surprising when we learn that in 1975, for example, the median time served in Massachusetts for homicide was less than two-and-a-half years. In 1976 a study sponsored by the Twentieth Century Fund found that the average time served in the United States for first-degree murder is ten years. The median time served may be considerably lower. 9

4. *Capital punishment cheapens the value of human life.* On the contrary, it can be easily demonstrated that the death penalty strengthens the value of human life. If the penalty for rape were lowered, clearly it would signal a lessened regard for the victims' suffering, humiliation, and personal integrity. It would cheapen their horrible experience, and expose them to an increased danger of recurrence. When we lower the penalty for murder, it signals a lessened regard for the value of the victim's life. Some critics of capital punishment, such as columnist Jimmy Breslin, have suggested that a life sentence is actually a harsher penalty for murder than death. This is sophistic nonsense. A few killers may decide not to appeal a death sentence, but the overwhelming majority make every effort to stay alive. It is by exacting the highest penalty for the taking of human life that we affirm the highest value of human life. 10

5. *The death penalty is applied in a discriminatory manner.* This factor no longer seems to be the problem it once was. The appeals process for a condemned prisoner is lengthy and painstaking. Every effort is made to see that the verdict and sentence were fairly arrived at. However, assertions of discrimination are not an argument for ending the death penalty but for extending it. It is not justice to exclude everyone from the penalty of the law if a few are found to be so favored. Justice requires that the law be applied equally to all. 11

12   6. *Thou Shalt Not Kill.* The Bible is our greatest source of
moral inspiration. Opponents of the death penalty frequently
cite the sixth of the Ten Commandments in an attempt to
prove that capital punishment is divinely proscribed. In the
original Hebrew, however, the Sixth Commandment reads,
"Thou Shalt Not Commit Murder," and the Torah specifies
capital punishment for a variety of offenses. The biblical
viewpoint has been upheld by philosophers throughout history. The greatest thinkers of the 19th century—Kant, Locke,
Hobbes, Rousseau, Montesquieu, and Mill—agreed that natural law properly authorizes the sovereign to take life in
order to vindicate justice. Only Jeremy Bentham was ambivalent. Washington, Jefferson, and Franklin endorsed it. Abraham Lincoln authorized executions for deserters in wartime.
Alexis de Tocqueville, who expressed profound respect for
American institutions, believed that the death penalty was
indispensable to the support of social order. The United
States Constitution, widely admired as one of the seminal
achievements in the history of humanity, condemns cruel
and inhuman punishment, but does not condemn capital
punishment.

13   7. *The death penalty is state-sanctioned murder.* This is the
defense with which Messrs. Willie and Shaw hoped to soften
the resolve of those who sentenced them to death. By saying
in effect, "You're no better than I am," the murderer seeks to
bring his accusers down to his own level. It is also a popular
argument among opponents of capital punishment, but a
transparently false one. Simply put, the state has rights that
the private individual does not. In a democracy, those rights
are given to the state by the electorate. The execution of a
lawfully condemned killer is no more an act of murder than is
legal imprisonment an act of kidnapping. If an individual
forces a neighbor to pay him money under threat of punishment, it's called extortion. If the state does it, it's called taxation. Rights and responsibilities surrendered by the individual
are what give the state its power to govern. This contract is
the foundation of civilization itself.

14   Everyone wants his or her rights, and will defend them
jealously. Not everyone, however, wants responsibilities, especially the painful responsibilities that come with law enforcement. Twenty-one years ago a woman named Kitty Genovese
was assaulted and murdered on a street in New York. Dozens
of neighbors heard her cries for help but did nothing to assist
her. They didn't even call the police. In such a climate the
criminal understandably grows bolder. In the presence of

moral cowardice, he lectures us on our supposed failings and tries to equate his crimes with our quest for justice.

The death of anyone—even a convicted killer—diminishes   15
us all. But we are diminished even more by a justice system
that fails to function. It is an illusion to let ourselves believe
that doing away with capital punishment removes the murderer's deed from our conscience. The rights of society are
paramount. When we protect guilty lives, we give up innocent
lives in exchange. When opponents of capital punishment say
to the state: "I will not let you kill in my name," they are also
saying to murderers: "You can kill in your *own* name as long
as I have an excuse for not getting involved."

It is hard to imagine anything worse than being murdered   16
while neighbors do nothing. But something worse exists.
When those same neighbors shrink back from justly punishing the murderer, the victim dies twice.

Jacob Weisberg

This Is Your Death

The following account appeared in The New Republic *in July 1991.* The New Republic *is a weekly magazine of opinion about various public issues; it is considered to be middle-of-the-road in its general slant on things. In what way is Weisberg's article a contribution to the national discussion on the death penalty? Is Weisberg's own position on the death penalty apparent here?*

Thanks to the decision of a California district judge last   1
week, the American public has been spared the spectacle of
criminals being executed on television. But the lawsuit, filed
by KQED, the public television station in San Francisco, still
served a useful function. It reminded people not only that the
United States remains the only advanced democracy that exe-
cutes criminals, but that it is the only country in the world
with a grotesque array of execution techniques worth televising. A century ago Americans knew full well what it meant for
the state to hang someone from the end of a rope. Today,

thanks to the century-long search for a more "humane" method, we know little about the range of practices that would be featured on the execution channel.

2   Of the five means of execution still extant in the United States, the oldest is hanging, which was nearly universal before 1900. The gallows was last used in Kansas in 1965 and remains an option in Delaware, Montana, and Washington State. If a hanging were ever televised, viewers would see the blindfolded prisoner standing on a trap door with a rope fastened around his neck, the knot under his left ear. So long as he is hooded, it is impossible to know for how long after the trap door opens the victim suffers, or at what point he loses consciousness. But according to Harold Hillman, a British physiologist who has studied executions, the dangling person feels cervical pain, and probably suffers from an acute headache as well, a result of the rope closing off the veins of the neck.

3   In the opinion of Dr. Cornelius Rosse, the chairman of the Department of Anatomy at the University of Washington School of Medicine, the belief that fracture of the spinal cord causes instantaneous death is wrong in all but a small fraction of cases. The actual cause of death is strangulation or suffocation. In medical terms, the weight of the prisoner's body causes tearing of the cervical muscles, skin, and blood vessels. The upper cervical vertebrae are dislocated, and the spinal cord is separated from the brain, which causes death.

4   Clinton Duffy, the warden at San Quentin from 1942 to 1954, who participated in sixty hangings, described his first thus:

> The man hit bottom and I observed that he was fighting by pulling on the straps, wheezing, whistling, trying to get air, that blood was oozing through the black cap. I observed also that he urinated, defecated, and droppings fell on the floor, and the stench was terrible. I also saw witnesses pass out and have to be carried from the witness room. Some of them threw up.

It took ten minutes for the condemned man to die. When he was taken down and the cap removed, "big hunks of flesh were torn off" the side of his face where the noose had been, "his eyes were popped," and his tongue was "swollen and hanging from his mouth." His face had also turned purple. The annals of Walla Walla State Penitentiary in Washington, which was seeking to hire an executioner in 1988 when

Charles Campbell obtained a stay of execution, are filled with horror stories: prisoners partially decapitated by overlong drops, or pleading with hangmen to take them up and drop them again.

Almost as rare as hanging—but still around—is the firing squad. Gary Gilmore, who was shot in Utah in 1977, was the last to die by this method, which remains an option only there and in Idaho. Gilmore was bound to a chair with leather straps across his waist and head, and in front of an oval-shaped canvas wall. A black hood was pulled over his head. A doctor then located his heart with a stethoscope and pinned a circular white cloth target over it. Five shooters armed with .30-caliber rifles loaded with single rounds (one of them blank to spare the conscience of the executioners) stood in an enclosure twenty feet away. Each man aimed his rifle through a slot in the canvas and fired. 5

Though shooting through the head at close range causes nearly instantaneous death, a prisoner subjected to a firing squad dies as a result of blood loss caused by rupture of the heart or a large blood vessel, or tearing of the lungs. The person shot loses consciousness when shock causes a fall in the support of blood to the brain. If the shooters miss, by accident or intention, the prisoner bleeds to death slowly, as Elisio J. Mares did in Utah in 1951. It took Gilmore two minutes to die. 6

It was to mitigate the barbarism of these primitive methods that New York introduced the electric chair in 1890 as a humane alternative. Eighty-three people have been electrocuted since the Supreme Court reinstated capital punishment in 1976, making the method the most common one now in use. It is probably the most gruesome to watch. After being led into the death chamber, the prisoner is strapped to the chair with belts that cross his chest, groin, legs, and arms. Two copper electrodes are then attached: one to his leg, a patch of which will have been shaved bare to reduce resistance to electricity, and another to his shaved head. The electrodes are either soaked in brine or treated with gel (Electro-Creme) to increase conductivity and reduce burning. The prisoner will also be wearing a diaper. 7

The executioner gives a first jolt of between 500 and 2,000 volts, which lasts for thirty seconds. Smoke usually comes out of the prisoner's leg and head. A doctor then examines him. If he's not dead, another jolt is applied. A third and fourth are given if needed to finish the job. It took five jolts to kill Ethel Rosenberg. In the grisly description of Justice Brennan: 8

...the prisoner's eyeballs sometimes pop out and rest on [his] cheeks. The prisoner often defecates, urinates, and vomits blood and drool. The body turns bright red as its temperature rises, and the prisoner's flesh swells and his skin stretches to the point of breaking. Sometimes the prisoner catches on fire, particularly if [he] perspires excessively. Witnesses hear a loud and sustained sound like bacon frying, and the sickly sweet smell of burning flesh permeates the chamber.

An electrocuted corpse is hot enough to blister if touched. Thus autopsy must be delayed while internal organs cool. According to Robert H. Kirschner, the deputy chief medical examiner of Cook County, Illinois, "The brain appears cooked in most cases."

9   There is some debate about what the electrocuted prisoner experiences before he dies, but most doctors I spoke to believe that he feels himself being burned to death and suffocating, since the shock causes respiratory paralysis as well as cardiac arrest. According to Hillman, "It must feel very similar to the medieval trial by ordeal of being dropped in boiling oil." Because the energy of the shock paralyzes the prisoner's muscles, he cannot cry out. "My mouth tasted like cold peanut butter. I felt a burning in my head and my left leg, and I jumped against the straps," Willie Francis, a 17-year-old who survived an attempted execution in 1946, is reported to have said. Francis was successfully executed a year later.

10   Though all methods of execution can be botched, electrocutions go wrong frequently and dramatically, in part because the equipment is old and hard to repair. At least five have gone awry since 1983. If the electrical current is too weak, the prisoner roasts to death slowly. An instance of this was the May 4, 1990, killing of Jesse Joseph Tafero in Florida. According to witnesses, when the executioner flipped the switch, flames and smoke came out of Tafero's head, which was covered by a mask and cap. Twelve-inch blue and orange flames sprouted from both sides of the mask. The power was stopped, and Tafero took several deep breaths. The superintendent ordered the executioner to halt the current, then try it again. And again.

11   The affidavits presented for an internal inquiry into what went wrong describe the bureaucratization of the death penalty brilliantly. In the words of one of the officials:

... while working in the Death Chamber, proceeding with the execution as scheduled, I received an indication from Mr. Barton to close my electric breaker. I then told the executioner to close his electric breaker. When the executioner completed the circuit, I noticed unusual fire and smoke coming from the inmate's headpiece. After several seconds, I received an indication to open the electrical breaker to stop the electrical flow. At this time, I noticed the body move as if to be gasping for air. After several seconds, I received the indication to close the breaker the second time, which I did. Again, I noticed the unusual fire and smoke coming from the headpiece. After several seconds, I received the third indication to close the breaker, and again, the fire and smoke came from the headpiece...

And so on. Apparently a synthetic sponge, soaked in brine, had been substituted for the natural one applied to Tafero's head. This reduced the flow of electricity to as little as one hundred volts, and ended up torturing the prisoner to death. According to the state prison medical director, Frank Kligo, who attended, it was "less than aesthetically attractive."

Advanced technology does not always make the death penalty less painful to undergo or more pleasant to watch. The gas chamber, which was invented by an army medical corps officer after World War I, was first introduced as a humane alternative to the electric chair in 1924 in Nevada. The original idea, which proved impracticable, was to surprise the prisoner by gassing him in his cell without prior warning. Seven states, including California, still use the gas chamber. The most recent fatality was Leo Edwards, a 36-year-old who was killed in Jackson County, Mississippi, in 1989. 12

Had KQED won its suit, millions of viewers would have joined a dozen live witnesses in seeing Robert Alton Harris, who murdered two teenage boys in San Diego in 1978, led into a green, octagonal room in the basement of San Quentin Penitentiary. Inside the chamber are two identical metal chairs with perforated seats, marked "A" and "B." The twin chairs were last used in a double execution in 1962. If Harris's execution goes ahead this year or next, two orderlies will fasten him into chair A, attaching straps across his upper and lower legs, arms, groin, and chest. They will also affix a long stethoscope to Harris's chest so that a doctor on the outside can pronounce death. 13

14   Beneath the chair is a bowl filled with sulfuric acid mixed with distilled water, with a pound of sodium cyanide pellets suspended in a gauze bag just above. After the door is sealed, and when the warden gives the signal, an executioner in a separate room flicks a lever that releases the cyanide into the liquid. This causes a chemical reaction that releases hydrogen cyanide gas, which rises through the holes in the chair. Like most death row prisoners, Harris is likely to have been reduced to a state of passive acquiescence by his years on death row, and will probably follow the advice of the warden to breathe deeply as soon as he smells rotten eggs. As long as he holds his breath nothing will happen. But as soon as he inhales, according to the testimony of Duffy, the former warden, Harris will lose consciousness in a few seconds. "At first there is evidence of extreme horror, pain, and strangling. The eyes pop. The skin turns purple and the victim begins to drool. It is a horrible sight," he testified.

15   In medical terms, victims of cyanide gas die from hypoxia, which means the cut-off of oxygen to the brain. The initial result of this is spasms, as in an epileptic seizure. Because of the straps, however, involuntary body movements are restrained. Seconds after he first inhales, Harris will feel himself unable to breathe, but will not lose consciousness immediately. "The person is unquestionably experiencing pain and extreme anxiety," according to Dr. Richard Traystman of Johns Hopkins. "The pain begins immediately and is felt in the arms, shoulders, back, and chest. The sensation is similar to the pain felt by a person during a heart attack, where essentially the heart is being deprived of oxygen." Traystman adds: "We would not use asphyxiation, by cyanide gas or by any other substance, in our laboratory to kill animals that have been used in experiments."

16   Harris will stop wriggling after ten or twelve minutes, and the doctor will pronounce him dead. An exhaust fan then sucks the poison air out of the chamber. Next the corpse is sprayed with ammonia, which neutralizes traces of the cyanide that may remain. After about half an hour, orderlies enter the chamber, wearing gas masks and rubber gloves. Their training manual advises them to ruffle the victim's hair to release any trapped cyanide gas before removing him.

17   Thanks to these grotesqueries, states are increasingly turning to lethal injection. This method was imagined for decades (by Ronald Reagan, among others, when he was governor of California in 1973), but was technically invented in 1977 by

Dr. Stanley Deutsch, who at the time chaired the Anesthesiology Department at Oklahoma University Medical School. In response to a call by an Oklahoma state senator for a cheaper alternative to repairing the state's derelict electric chair, Deutsch described a way to administer drugs through an intravenous drip so as to cause death rapidly and without pain. "Having been anesthetized on several occasions with ultra short-acting barbiturates and having administered these drugs for approximately 20 years, I can assure you that this is a rapid, pleasant way of producing unconsciousness," Deutsch wrote to state senator Bill Dawson in February 1977. The method was promptly adopted in Oklahoma, and is now either the exclusive method or an option in half of the thirty-six states with death penalty laws. It is becoming the method of choice around the country because it is easier on both the witnesses and the prisoner.

A recent injectee was Lawrence Lee Buxton, who was killed   18 in Huntsville, Texas, on February 26. Buxton was strapped to a hospital gurney, built with an extension panel for his left arm. Technicians stuck a catheter needle into Buxton's arm. Long tubes connected the needle through a hole in a cement block wall to several intravenous drips. The first, which was started immediately, dispensed harmless saline solution. Then, at the warden's signal, a curtain went up, which permitted the witnesses—reporters and friends of the soon-to-be deceased—to view the scene. Unlike some prisoners, Buxton did not have a long wait before the warden received a call from the governor's office, giving the final go-ahead.

According to Lawrence Egbert, an anesthesiologist at the   19 University of Texas in Dallas who has campaigned against lethal injection as a perversion of medical practice, the first drug administered was sodium thiopental, a common barbiturate used as an anesthetic, which puts patients quickly to sleep. A normal dose for a long operation is 1,000 milligrams; Buxton got twice that. As soon as he lost consciousness, the executioner administered pavulon, another common muscle relaxant used in heart surgery. The dose was 100 milligrams, ten times the usual, which stops the prisoner's breathing. This would have killed him in about ten minutes; to speed the process, an equal dose of potassium chloride was subsequently administered. This is another drug commonly used in bypass surgery that relaxes the heart and stops it pumping. It works in about ten seconds. All witnesses heard was the prisoner take a deep breath, then a gurgling noise as his tongue dropped back in his mouth. Watt Espy, who has compiled a list of 17,718 executions in America, from the early period of drownings, burnings, sawings-in-half, pressings-to-death, and even the crucifixions of two mutinous Continental Army soldiers, compares lethal injection to the way a devoted owner treats "a faithful dog he's loved and cherished."

20   The only physical pain, if the killing is done correctly, "is the pain of the initial prick of the needle," according to Traystman. There are, however, some potential hitches. Since doctors are precluded by medical ethics from participating in executions, except to pronounce death, the injections are often performed by incompetent or inexperienced technicians. If a death worker injects the drugs into muscle instead of a vein, or if the needle becomes clogged, extreme pain can result. This is what happened when James Autry was killed in 1984 in Texas. *Newsweek* reported that he "took at least ten minutes to die and throughout much of that time was conscious, moving about, and complaining of pain." Many prisoners have damaged veins from injecting drugs intravenously, and technicians sometimes struggle to find a serviceable one. When Texas executed Stephen Morin, a former heroin addict, orderlies prodded his arms with catheters for forty-one minutes. Being strapped to a table for a lengthy period while waiting to die is a form of psychological torture arguably worse than most physical kinds. This is demonstrated by the fact that mock executions, which cause no physical pain, are a common method of torture around the world. The agony comes not from the prospect of pain, but from the expectation of death.

21   Televised executions would mark the reversal of the process described in Louis P. Masur's *Rites of Execution* and Robert Johnson's *Death Work*, whereby executions have been removed further and further from the community that compels them. Through the eighteenth century, executions were atavistic spectacles performed in full public view. In the nineteenth they were moved inside the prison yard and witnessed by only a few. In the twentieth century, executions moved deep inside the bowels of prisons, where they were performed ever more quickly and quietly to attract minimal notice. American death penalty opponents in the 1800s supported the abolition of public executions as a way-station to ending all executions. They thought that eliminating the grossest manifestations of public barbarism would inevitably lead to the end of capital punishment as an institution. The reform

had the opposite effect, however. Invisible executions shocked the sensibilities of fewer people, and dampened the momentum of the reform movement.

Those abolitionists who now support televising executions   22
have absorbed this historical lesson. They want to bring back the equivalent of public executions in order to shock the public into opposing all executions. They hope to accomplish with pictures what Arthur Koestler did with words in his 1955 tract *Reflections on Hanging*, the publication of which led to the abolition of the rope in Great Britain in 1969.

But advances in the art of killing may have deprived them   23
of that tactic. The prospect of televised executions is likely to accelerate the trend away from grisly methods and toward ever more hermetic ways of dispatching wrongdoers. Had the KQED suit been successful, Henry Schwarzschild, a retired ACLU death penalty expert, speculates that California would have responded by quickly joining the national trend toward lethal injection.

Michael Kroll of the Death Penalty Information Center   24
objects to televising executions for exactly this reason. He argues that a video camera would capture only a "very antiseptic moment at the end of a very septic process." With the advent of death by the needle, execution itself is becoming so denatured and mechanistic as to be unshocking even to most live witnesses. This throws death penalty opponents back upon a less vivid, but more compelling case: that it is punishing people with death, not the manner in which they are killed, that is the true issue here; that capital punishment is to be opposed not simply because it is cruel, but because it is wrong.

Doug Marlette

Doug Marlette, who won the Pulitzer Prize for editorial cartooning, draws for New York Newsday, *and his sometimes controversial work is regularly reprinted in* Newsweek, The Washington Post, *and elsewhere. Eleven collections of his work have been published, including* In Your Face: A Cartoonist at Work *(1991), where the following cartoon appeared. The cartoon was first published on Good Friday, as you might guess from the content, while Marlette worked for* The Charlotte *[North Carolina]* Observer.

SHOULD DRUGS BE LEGALIZED?

Kurt Schmoke

A War for the Surgeon General, Not the Attorney General

One of the most outspoken advocates of legalizing drugs has been Kurt Schmoke (born 1949), mayor of Baltimore since 1987. Previously, as Assistant U.S. Attorney and as State's Attorney for Baltimore, Schmoke was a highly visible prosecutor of drug cases. The following argument appeared in New Perspectives Quarterly, *a public affairs forum, in the summer of 1989. It was adapted from his testimony before a congressional committee on September 29, 1988.*

In the last ten years, the US has become absolutely awash in 1
illegal drugs. Tougher laws, greater efforts at interdiction, and stronger rhetoric at all levels of government and from both political parties have not and will not be able to stop the flow. That is why we must begin to consider what heretofore has been beyond the realm of consideration: decriminalization.

Addiction Is a Disease

The violence brought about by the black market in drugs is 2
attributable in large part to the fact that we have chosen to make criminals out of millions of people who have a disease. In the words of the American Medical Association, "It is clear that addiction is not simply the product of a failure of individual will-power.... It is properly viewed as a disease, and one that physicians can help many individuals control and overcome."

The nature of addiction is very important to the argument 3
in favor of decriminalization. The sad truth is that heroin and morphine addiction is, for most users, a lifetime affliction that is impervious to any punishment that the criminal-justice system could reasonably mete out.

4   Given the nature of addiction—whether to narcotics or cocaine—and the very large number of Americans using drugs (the National Institute on Drug Abuse estimates that one in six working Americans has a substance abuse problem), laws restricting their possession and sale have had predictable consequences—most of them bad.

Crimes Committed by Addicts

5   Addicts commit crimes in order to pay for their drug habits. According to the Justice Department, 90 percent of those who voluntarily seek treatment are turned away. In other words, on any given day, nine out of every ten addicts have no legal way to satisfy their addiction. And, failing to secure help, an untreated addict will commit a crime every other day to maintain his habit.

6   Whether one relies on studies, or on simple observation, it is indisputable that drug users are committing vast amounts of crime. Baltimore, the city with which I am most familiar, is no exception. According to James A. Inciardi, of the Division of Criminal Justice at the University of Delaware, a 1983 study of addicts in Baltimore showed that "... there were high rates of criminality among heroin users during those periods that they were addicted and markedly lower rates during times of nonaddiction." The study also showed that addicts committed crimes on a persistent day-to-day basis and over a long period of time. And the trends are getting worse. Thus, while the total number of arrests in Baltimore remained almost unchanged between 1983 and 1987, there was an approximately 40 percent increase in the number of drug-related arrests.

7   On the other hand, statistics recently compiled by the Maryland Drug and Alcohol Abuse Administration indicate that crime rates go down among addicts when treatment is available. Thus, for example, of the 6,910 Baltimore residents admitted to drug-abuse treatment in fiscal 1987, 4,386 or 63 percent had been arrested one or more times in the 24-month period prior to admission to treatment, whereas of the 6,698 Baltimore residents who were discharged from drug treatment in fiscal 1987, 6,152 or 91.8 percent were not arrested during the time of their treatment. These statistics tend to support the view that one way to greatly reduce drug-related crime is to assure addicts legal access to methadone or other drugs.

Overload of the Criminal-Justice System

We cannot prosecute our way out of the drug problem.   8
There are several reasons for this, but the most basic reason
is that the criminal-justice system cannot—without sacrific-
ing our civil liberties—handle the sheer volume of drug-
related cases.

Nationwide last year, over 750,000 people were arrested for   9
violating drug laws. Most of these arrests were for possession.
In Baltimore, there were 13,037 drug-related arrests in 1987.
Between January 1, 1988 and July 1, 1988, there were 7,981
drug-related arrests. Those numbers are large, but they
hardly reflect the annual total number of drug violations
committed in Baltimore. Should we, therefore, try to arrest
still more? Yes—as long as the laws are on the books. But as a
practical matter, we don't have any place to put the drug
offenders we are now arresting. The population in the Baltimore City Jail is currently 2,900 inmates, even though its
inmate capacity is only 2,700. This shortage of prison space
has led to severe overcrowding, and Baltimore is now under
court order to reduce its jail population.

Will more prisons help? Not in any significant way. We   10
simply cannot build enough of them to hold all of America's
drug offenders—which number in the millions. And even if
we could, the cost would far exceed what American taxpayers
would be willing to pay.

Decriminalization is the single most effective step we could   11
take to reduce prison overcrowding. And with less crowded
prisons, there will be less pressure on prosecutors to plea bargain and far greater chance that non-drug criminals will go to
jail—and stay in jail.

The unvarnished truth is that in our effort to prosecute and   12
imprison our way out of the drug war, we have allowed the
drug lords to put us exactly where they want us: wasting enormous resources—both in money and in personnel—attacking
the fringes of the problem (the drug users and small-time
pushers), while the heart of the problem—the traffickers and
their profits—goes unsolved.

Failed Supply-Side Policies

Not only can we not prosecute our way out of our   13
drug morass, we cannot interdict our way out of it either.
Lately, there have been calls for stepped-up border patrols,

increased use of the military and greater pressure on foreign governments.

14   Assuming these measures would reduce the supply of illegal drugs, that reduction would not alleviate the chaos in our cities. According to statistics recently cited by the American Medical Association, Latin American countries produced between 162,000 and 211,400 metric tons of cocaine in 1987. That is five times the amount needed to supply the US market. Moreover, we are probably only interdicting 10 to 15 percent of the cocaine entering this country. Thus, even if we quadrupled the amount of cocaine we interdict, the world supply of cocaine would still far outstrip US demand.

15   If the drug laws in the US simply didn't achieve their intent, perhaps there would be insufficient reason to get rid of them. But these laws are doing more than not working— they are violating Hippocrates' famous admonition: First, do no harm.

16   The legal prohibition of narcotics, cocaine and marijuana demonstrably increases the price of those drugs. For example, an importer can purchase a kilogram of heroin for $10,000. By the time that kilogram passes through the hands of several middlemen, its street value can reach $1,000,000. Such profits can't help but attract major criminal entrepreneurs willing to take any risk to keep their product coming to the American market.

Victimization of Children

17   Perhaps the most tragic victims of our drug laws are children. Many, for example, have been killed as innocent bystanders in gun battles among traffickers. Furthermore, while it is true that drug prohibition probably does keep some children from experimenting with drugs, almost any child who wants drugs can get them. Keeping drugs outlawed has not kept them out of children's hands.

18   Recent statistics in both Maryland and Baltimore prove the point: In a 1986–87 survey of Maryland adolescents, 13 percent of eighth graders, 18.5 percent of tenth graders and 22.3 percent of twelfth graders report that they are currently using drugs. In Baltimore, the percentages are 16.6, 16.5 and 20.3, respectively. It should be noted that these numbers exclude alcohol and tobacco, and that current use means at least once a month. It should also be noted that these numbers show a decrease from earlier surveys in 1982 and 1984.

Nevertheless, the fact remains that drugs are being widely used by students. Moreover, these numbers do not include the many young people who have left school or who failed to report their drug use.

A related problem is that many children, especially those living in the inner city, are frequently barraged with the message that selling drugs is an easy road to riches. In Baltimore, as in many other cities, small children are acting as lookouts and runners for drug pushers, just as they did for bootleggers during Prohibition. Decriminalization and the destruction of the black market would end this most invidious form of child labor. 19

As for education, decriminalization will not end the *Just Say No* and similar education campaigns. On the contrary, more money will be available for such programs. Decriminalization will, however, end the competing message of "easy money" that the drug dealers use to entice children. Furthermore, decriminalization will free up valuable criminal-justice resources that can be used to find, prosecute and punish those who sell drugs to children. 20

This said, if there has been one problem with the current drug-reform debate, it has been the tendency to focus on narrow problems and narrow solutions. That is, we talk about the number of people arrested, the number of tons of drugs entering our ports, the number of available treatment centers, and so on, but there is a bigger picture out there. We, as a nation, have not done nearly enough to battle the social and economic problems that make drug abuse an easy escape for the despairing, and drug trafficking an easy answer to a lack of education and joblessness. 21

Adolescents who take drugs are making a not-so-subtle statement about their confidence in the future. Children without hope are children who will take drugs. We need to give these children more than simple slogans. We need to give them a brighter tomorrow, a sense of purpose, a chance at economic opportunity. It is on that battlefield that the real war against drugs must be fought. 22

Spread of AIDS

The 1980s have brought another major public health problem that is being made still worse because of our drug laws: AIDS. Contaminated intravenous drug needles are now the principal means of transmission for the HIV infection. The 23 users of drug needles infect not only those with whom they share needles, but also their sex partners and their unborn children.

24   One way to effectively slow this means of transmission would be to allow addicts to exchange their dirty needles for clean ones. However, in a political climate where all illicit drug use is condemned, and where possession of a syringe can be a criminal offense, few jurisdictions have been willing to initiate a needle exchange program. This is a graphic example, along with our failure to give illegal drugs to cancer patients with intractable pain, of our blind pursuit of an irrational policy.

The Mixed Message of Tobacco and Alcohol

25   The case for the decriminalization of drugs becomes even stronger when illegal drugs are looked at in the context of legal drugs.

26   It is estimated that over 350,000 people will die this year from tobacco-related diseases. Last year the number was equally large. And it will be again next year. Why do millions of people continue to engage in an activity which has been proven to cause cancer and heart disease? The answer is that smoking is more than just a bad habit. It is an addiction. In 1988, Surgeon General C. Everett Koop called nicotine as addictive as heroin and cocaine. And yet, with the exception of taxes and labeling, cigarettes are sold without restriction.

27   By every standard we apply to illicit drugs, tobacco should be a controlled substance. But it is not, and for good reason. Given that millions of people continue to smoke—many of whom would quit if they could—making cigarettes illegal would be an open invitation to a new black market.

28   The certain occurrence of a costly and dangerous illegal tobacco trade (if tobacco were outlawed) is well understood by Congress, the Bush Administration and the criminal-justice community. No rationally thinking person would want to bring such a catastrophe down upon the US—even if it would prevent some people from smoking.

29   Like tobacco, alcohol is a drug that kills thousands of Americans every year. It plays a part in more than half of all automobile fatalities and is also frequently involved in suicides, non-automobile accidents, domestic disputes and crimes of violence. Millions of Americans are alcoholic, and alcohol costs the nation billions of dollars in health care

and lost productivity. So why not ban alcohol? Because, as almost every American knows, we already tried that. Prohibition turned out to be one of the worst social experiments this country has ever undertaken.

I will not review the sorry history of Prohibition except to   30
make two important points. The first is that in repealing Prohibition, we made significant mistakes that should not be repeated in the event that drug use is decriminalized. Specifically, when alcohol was again made legal in 1934, we made no significant effort to educate people as to its dangers. There were no (and still are no) *Just Say No* campaigns against alcohol. We allowed alcohol to be advertised and have associated it with happiness, success and social acceptability. We have also been far too lenient with drunk drivers.

The second point is that, notwithstanding claims to the   31
contrary by critics of decriminalization, there are marked parallels between the era of Prohibition and our current policy of making drugs illegal, and important lessons to be learned from our attempts to ban the use and sale of alcohol.

During Prohibition, the government tried to keep alcohol   32
out of the hands of millions of people who refused to give it up. As a result, our cities were overrun by criminal syndicates enriching themselves with the profits of bootleg liquor and terrorizing anyone who got in their way. We then looked to the criminal-justice system to solve the crime problems that Prohibition created. But the criminal-justice system—outmanned, outgunned and often corrupted by enormous black market profits—was incapable of stopping the massive crime wave that Prohibition brought, just as it was incapable of stopping people from drinking.

As a person now publicly identified with the movement to   33
reform our drug laws through the use of some form of decriminalization, I consider it very important to say that I am not soft on either drug use or drug dealers. I am a soldier in the war against drugs. As Maryland's State Attorney, I spent years prosecuting and jailing drug traffickers, and had one of the highest rates of incarceration for drug convictions in the country. And if I were still State's Attorney, I would be enforcing the law as vigorously as ever. My experience as a prosecutor did not in any way alter my passionate dislike for drug dealers, it simply convinced me that the present system doesn't work and cannot be made to work.

During the Revolutionary War, the British insisted on   34
wearing red coats and marching in formation. They looked very pretty. They also lost. A good general does not pursue a

strategy in the face of overwhelming evidence of failure. Instead, a good general changes from a losing strategy to one that exploits his enemy's weakness, while exposing his own troops to only as much danger as is required to win. The drug war can be beaten and the public health of the US can be improved if we are willing to substitute common sense for rhetoric, myth and blind persistence, and to put the war in the hands of the Surgeon General, not the Attorney General.

William Bennett

Should Drugs Be Legalized?

William Bennett (born 1943) studied and played football (and the guitar for a rock group) at Williams College. Later he earned a doctorate in philosophy at the University of Texas and a law degree at Harvard, and taught at Southern Mississippi, Boston University, and the University of Wisconsin. He joined the Reagan administration as chair of the National Endowment for the Humanities in 1981 and became Secretary of Education in 1985; in 1988, he was appointed as the nation's "drug czar"—in charge of waging President Bush's "war on drugs." He published the following argument in 1990 in Reader's Digest. *Note, too, the exchange between Bennett and Milton Friedman that is reprinted after this selection.*

1   Since I took command of the war on drugs, I have learned from former Secretary of State George Schultz that our concept of fighting drugs is "flawed." The only thing to do, he says, is to "make it possible for addicts to buy drugs at some regulated place." Conservative commentator William F. Buckley, Jr., suggests I should be "fatalistic" about the flood of cocaine from South America and simply "let it in." Syndicated columnist Mike Royko contends it would be easier to sweep junkies out of the gutters "than to fight a hopeless war" against the narcotics that send them there. Labeling our efforts "bankrupt," federal judge Robert W. Sweet opts for legalization, saying, "If our society can learn to stop using butter, it should be able to cut down on cocaine."

2   Flawed, fatalistic, hopeless, bankrupt! I never realized surrender was so fashionable until I assumed this post.

Though most Americans are overwhelmingly determined   3
to go toe-to-toe with the foreign drug lords and neighborhood
pushers, a small minority believe that enforcing drug laws
imposes greater costs on society than do drugs themselves.
Like addicts seeking immediate euphoria, the legalizers want
peace at any price, even though it means the inevitable proliferation of a practice that degrades, impoverishes and kills.

I am acutely aware of the burdens drug enforcement   4
places upon us. It consumes economic resources we would
like to use elsewhere. It is sometimes frustrating, thankless
and often dangerous. But the consequences of *not* enforcing
drug laws would be far more costly. Those consequences
involve the intrinsically destructive nature of drugs and the
toll they exact from our society in hundreds of thousands of
lost and broken lives...human potential never realized...
time stolen from families and jobs...precious spiritual and
economic resources squandered.

That is precisely why virtually every civilized society has   5
found it necessary to exert some form of control over mind-
altering substances and why this war is so important. Americans feel up to their hips in drugs now. They would be up to
their necks under legalization.

Even limited experiments in drug legalization have shown   6
that when drugs are more widely available, addiction sky-
rockets. In 1975 Italy liberalized its drug law and now has one
of the highest heroin-related death rates in Western Europe.
In Alaska, where marijuana was decriminalized in 1975, the
easy atmosphere has increased usage of the drug, particularly
among children. Nor does it stop there. Some Alaskan school-
children now tout "coca puffs," marijuana cigarettes laced
with cocaine.

Many legalizers concede that drug legalization might   7
increase use, but they shrug off the matter. "It may well be
that there would be more addicts, and I would regret that
result," says Nobel laureate economist Milton Friedman. The
late Harvard Medical School psychiatry professor Norman
Zinberg, a longtime proponent of "responsible" drug use,
admitted that "use of now illicit drugs would certainly
increase. Also, casualties probably would increase."

In fact, Dr. Herbert D. Kleber of Yale University, my deputy   8
in charge of demand reduction, predicts legalization might
cause "a five-to-sixfold increase" in cocaine use. But legalizers regard this as a necessary price for the "benefits" of legalization. What benefits?

9   1. *Legalization will take the profit out of drugs.* The result supposedly will be the end of criminal drug pushers and the big foreign drug wholesalers, who will turn to other enterprises because nobody will need to make furtive and dangerous trips to his local pusher.

10   But what, exactly, would the brave new world of legalized drugs look like? Buckley stresses that "adults get to buy the stuff at carefully regulated stores." (Would you want one in *your* neighborhood?) Others, like Friedman, suggest we sell the drugs at "ordinary retail outlets."

11   Former City University of New York sociologist Georgette Bennett assures us that "brand-name competition will be prohibited" and that strict quality control and proper labeling will be overseen by the Food and Drug Administration. In a touching egalitarian note, she adds that "free drugs will be provided at government clinics" for addicts too poor to buy them.

12   Almost all the legalizers point out that the price of drugs will fall, even though the drugs will be heavily taxed. Buckley, for example, argues that somehow federal drugstores will keep the price "low enough to discourage a black market but high enough to accumulate a surplus to be used for drug education."

13   Supposedly, drug sales will generate huge amounts of revenue, which will then be used to tell the public not to use drugs and to treat those who don't listen.

14   In reality, this tax would only allow government to *share* the drug profits now garnered by criminals. Legalizers would have to tax drugs heavily in order to pay for drug education and treatment programs. Criminals could undercut the official price and still make huge profits. What alternative would the government have? Cut the price until it was within the lunch-money budget of the average sixth-grade student?

15   2. *Legalization will eliminate the black market.* Wrong. And not just because the regulated prices could be undercut. Many legalizers admit that drugs such as crack or PCP are simply too dangerous to allow the shelter of the law. Thus criminals will provide what the government will not. "As long as drugs that people very much want remain illegal, a black market will exist," says legalization advocate David Boaz of the liberatarian Cato Institute.

16   Look at crack. In powdered form, cocaine was an expensive indulgence. But street chemists found that a better and far less expensive—and far more dangerous—high could be achieved by mixing cocaine with baking soda and heating it.

Crack was born, and "cheap" coke invaded low-income communities with furious speed.

An ounce of powdered cocaine might sell on the street for $1200. That same ounce can produce 370 vials of crack at $10 each. Ten bucks seems like a cheap hit, but crack's intense ten- to 15-minute high is followed by an unbearable depression. The user wants more crack, thus starting a rapid and costly descent into addiction.   17

If government drugstores do not stock crack, addicts will find it in the clandestine market or simply bake it themselves from their legally purchased cocaine.   18

Currently crack is being laced with insecticides and animal tranquilizers to heighten its effect. Emergency rooms are now warned to expect victims of "sandwiches" and "moon rocks," life-threatening smokable mixtures of heroin and crack. Unless the government is prepared to sell these deadly variations of dangerous drugs, it will perpetuate a criminal black market by default.   19

And what about children and teen-agers? They would obviously be barred from drug purchases, just as they are prohibited from buying beer and liquor. But pushers will continue to cater to these young customers with the old, favorite come-ons—a couple of free fixes to get them hooked. And what good will anti-drug education be when these youngsters observe their older brothers and sisters, parents and friends lighting up and shooting up with government permission?   20

Legalization will give us the worst of both worlds: millions of *new* drug users *and* a thriving criminal black market.   21

3. *Legalization will dramatically reduce crime.* "It is the high price of drugs that leads addicts to robbery, murder and other crimes," says Ira Glasser, executive director of the American Civil Liberties Union. A study by the Cato Institute concludes: "Most, if not all, 'drug-related murders' are the result of drug prohibition."   22

But researchers tell us that many drug-related felonies are committed by people involved in crime *before* they started taking drugs. The drugs, so routinely available in criminal circles, make the criminals more violent and unpredictable.   23

Certainly there are some kill-for-a-fix crimes, but does any rational person believe that a cut-rate price for drugs at a government outlet will stop such psychopathic behavior? The fact is that under the influence of drugs, normal people do not act normally, and abnormal people behave in chilling and horrible ways. DEA agents told me about a teen-age addict in   24

Manhattan who was smoking crack when he sexually abused
and caused permanent internal injuries to his one-month-old
daughter.

25   Children are among the most frequent victims of violent,
drug-related crimes that have nothing to do with the cost of
acquiring the drugs. In Philadelphia in 1987 more than half
the child-abuse fatalities involved at least one parent who was
a heavy drug user. Seventy-three percent of the child-abuse
deaths in New York City in 1987 involved parental drug use.

26   In my travels to the ramparts of the drug war, I have seen
nothing to support the legalizers' argument that lower drug
prices would reduce crime. Virtually everywhere I have gone,
police and DEA agents have told me that crime rates are highest where crack is cheapest.

27   4. *Drug use should be legal since users only harm themselves.* Those who believe this should stand beside the medical examiner as he counts the 36 bullet wounds in the
shattered corpse of a three-year-old who happened to get in
the way of his mother's drug-crazed boyfriend. They should
visit the babies abandoned by cocaine-addicted mothers—
infants who already carry the ravages of addiction in their
own tiny bodies. They should console the devastated relatives
of the nun who worked in a homeless shelter and was stabbed
to death by a crack addict enraged that she would not stake
him to a fix.

28   Do drug addicts only harm themselves? Here is a former
cocaine addict describing the compulsion that quickly draws
even the most "responsible" user into irresponsible behavior:
"Everything is about getting high, and any means necessary
to get there becomes rational. If it means stealing something
from somebody close to you, lying to your family, borrowing
money from people you know you can't pay back, writing
checks you know you can't cover, you do all those things—
things that are totally against everything you have ever
believed in."

29   Society pays for this behavior, and not just in bigger insurance premiums, losses from accidents and poor job performance. We pay in the loss of a priceless social currency as
families are destroyed, trust between friends is betrayed and
promising careers are never fulfilled. I cannot imagine sanc-
tioning behavior that would increase that toll.

30   I find no merit in the legalizers' case. The simple fact is
that drug use is wrong. And the moral argument, in the end,
is the most compelling argument. A citizen in a drug-induced
haze, whether on his back-yard deck or on a mattress in a

ghetto crack house, is not what the founding fathers meant by the "pursuit of happiness." Despite the legalizers' argument that drug use is a matter of "personal freedom," our nation's notion of liberty is rooted in the ideal of a self-reliant citizenry. Helpless wrecks in treatment centers, men chained by their noses to cocaine—these people are slaves.

Imagine if, in the darkest days of 1940, Winston Churchill   31
had rallied the West by saying, "This war looks hopeless, and besides, it will cost too much. Hitler can't be *that* bad. Let's surrender and see what happens." That is essentially what we hear from the legalizers.

This war *can* be won. I am heartened by indications that   32
education and public revulsion are having an effect on drug use. The National Institute on Drug Abuse's latest survey of current users shows a 37-percent *decrease* in drug consumption since 1985. Cocaine is down 50 percent; marijuana use among young people is at its lowest rate since 1972. In my travels I've been encouraged by signs that Americans are fighting back.

I am under no illusion that such developments, however   33
hopeful, mean the war is over. We need to involve more citizens in the fight, increase pressure on drug criminals and build on antidrug programs that have proved to work. This will not be easy. But the moral and social costs of surrender are simply too great to contemplate.

Milton Friedman

Prohibition and Drugs

When he was on the faculty of the University of Chicago, Milton Friedman won the Nobel Prize for his "monetarist" school of economics, one that stresses stable growth in the supply of money and credit in an economy. A conservative who influenced the policies of Ronald Reagan and George Bush, he enjoys writing about a range of public issues. Now a senior research fellow at the Hoover Institute at Stanford University, he wrote the two following essays on the legalization of drugs—one for Newsweek *(1972) and one for* The Wall Street Journal *(1989).*

The Wall Street Journal *article, which contains a reference in paragraph five to the* Newsweek *essay, is an "open letter" to William Bennett, the nation's "drug czar" (i.e., director of the Office of National Drug Policy) under former President Bush. Bennett is the author of the previous essay in this section as well as the response to Milton Friedman that is reprinted after Friedman's two essays. Friedman's own counter-response follows that, on page 939.*

1   "The reign of tears is over. The slums will soon be only a memory. We will turn our prisons into factories and our jails into storehouses and corncribs. Men will walk upright now, women will smile, and the children will laugh. Hell will be forever for rent."

2   That is how Billy Sunday, the noted evangelist and leading crusader against Demon Rum, greeted the onset of Prohibition in early 1920. We know now how tragically his hopes were doomed. New prisons and jails had to be built to house the criminals sprawned by converting the drinking of spirits into a crime against the state. Prohibition undermined respect for the law, corrupted the minions of the law, created a decadent moral climate—but did not stop the consumption of alcohol.

3   Despite this tragic object lesson, we seem bent on repeating precisely the same mistake in the handling of drugs.

Ethics and Expediency

4   On ethical grounds, do we have the right to use the machinery of government to prevent an individual from becoming an alcoholic or a drug addict? For children, almost everyone would answer at least a qualified yes. But for responsible adults, I, for one, would answer no. Reason with the potential addict, yes. Tell him the consequences, yes. Pray for and with him, yes. But I believe that we have no right to use force, directly or indirectly, to prevent a fellow man from committing suicide, let alone from drinking alcohol or taking drugs.

5   I readily grant that the ethical issue is difficult and that men of goodwill may well disagree. Fortunately, we need not resolve the ethical issue to agree on policy. *Prohibition is an attempted cure that makes matters worse—for both the addict and the rest of us.* Hence, even if you regard present policy toward drugs as ethically justified, considerations of expediency make that policy most unwise.

Consider first the addict. Legalizing drugs might increase   6
the number of addicts, but it is not clear that it would. Forbidden fruit is attractive, particularly to the young. More
important, many drug addicts are deliberately made by pushers, who give likely prospects their first few doses free. It pays
the pusher to do so because, once hooked, the addict is a cap-
tive customer. If drugs were legally available, any possible
profit from such inhumane activity would disappear, since
the addict could buy from the cheapest source.

Whatever happens to the number of addicts, the individual   7
addict would clearly be far better off if drugs were legal.
Today, drugs are both incredibly expensive and highly uncertain in quality. Addicts are driven to associate with criminals
to get the drugs, become criminals themselves to finance the
habit, and risk constant danger of death and disease.

Consider next the rest of us. Here the situation is crystal-   8
clear. The harm to us from the addiction of others arises
almost wholly from the fact that drugs are illegal. A recent
committee of the American Bar Association estimated that
addicts commit one-third to one-half of all street crime
in the U.S. Legalize drugs, and street crime would drop dramatically.

Moreover, addicts and pushers are not the only ones cor-   9
rupted. Immense sums are at stake. It is inevitable that some
relatively low-paid police and other government officials—
and some high-paid ones as well—will succumb to the temptation to pick up easy money.

Law and Order

Legalizing drugs would simultaneously reduce the amount   10
of crime and raise the quality of law enforcement. Can you
conceive of any other measure that would accomplish so
much to promote law and order?

But, you may say, must we accept defeat? Why not simply   11
end the drug traffic? That is where experience under Prohibition is most relevant. We cannot end the drug traffic. We may
be able to cut off opium from Turkey—but there are innumerable other places where the opium poppy grows. With French
cooperation, we may be able to make Marseilles an unhealthy
place to manufacture heroin—but there are innumerable
other places where the simple manufacturing operations
involved can be carried out. So long as large sums of money
are involved—and they are bound to be if drugs are illegal—it

is literally hopeless to expect to end the traffic or even to reduce seriously its scope.

12   In drugs, as in other areas, persuasion and example are likely to be far more effective than the use of force to shape others in our image.

Milton Friedman
An Open Letter to Bill Bennett

Dear Bill:

1   In Oliver Cromwell's eloquent words, "I beseech you, in the bowels of Christ, think it possible you may be mistaken" about the course you and President Bush urge us to adopt to fight drugs. The path you propose of more police, more jails, use of the military in foreign countries, harsh penalties for drug users, and a whole panoply of repressive measures can only make a bad situation worse. The drug war cannot be won by those tactics without undermining the human liberty and individual freedom that you and I cherish.

2   You are not mistaken in believing that drugs are a scourge that is devastating our society. You are not mistaken in believing that drugs are tearing asunder our social fabric, ruining the lives of many young people, and imposing heavy costs on some of the most disadvantaged among us. You are not mistaken in believing that the majority of the public share your concerns. In short, you are not mistaken in the end you seek to achieve.

3   Your mistake is failing to recognize that the very measures you favor are a major source of the evils you deplore. Of course the problem is demand, but it is not only demand, it is demand that must operate through repressed and illegal channels. Illegality creates obscene profits that finance the murderous tactics of the drug lords; illegality leads to the corruption of law enforcement officials; illegality mono-polizes the efforts of honest law forces so that they are starved for resources to fight the simpler crimes of robbery, theft and assault.

4   Drugs are a tragedy for addicts. But criminalizing their use converts that tragedy into a disaster for society, for users and

non-users alike. Our experience with the prohibition of drugs is a replay of our experience with the prohibition of alcoholic beverages.

I append excerpts from a column that I wrote in 1972 on "Prohibition and Drugs." The major problem then was heroin from Marseilles; today, it is cocaine from Latin America. Today, also, the problem is far more serious than it was 17 years ago: more addicts, more innocent victims; more drug pushers, more law enforcement officials; more money spent to enforce prohibition, more money spent to circumvent prohibition. [5]

Had drugs been decriminalized 17 years ago, "crack" would never have been invented (it was invented because the high cost of illegal drugs made it profitable to provide a cheaper version) and there would today be far fewer addicts. The lives of thousands, perhaps hundreds of thousands of innocent victims would have been saved, and not only in the U.S. The ghettos of our major cities would not be drug-and-crime-infested no-man's lands. Fewer people would be in jails, and fewer jails would have been built. [6]

Colombia, Bolivia and Peru would not be suffering from narco-terror, and we would not be distorting our foreign policy because of narco-terror. Hell would not, in the words with which Billy Sunday welcomed Prohibition, "be forever for rent," but it would be a lot emptier. [7]

Decriminalizing drugs is even more urgent now than in 1972, but we must recognize that the harm done in the interim cannot be wiped out, certainly not immediately. Postponing decriminalization will only make matters worse, and make the problem appear even more intractable. [8]

Alcohol and tobacco cause many more deaths in users than do drugs. Decriminalization would not prevent us from treating drugs as we now treat alcohol and tobacco: prohibiting sales of drugs to minors, outlawing the advertising of drugs and similar measures. Such measures could be enforced, while outright prohibition cannot be. Moreover, if even a small fraction of the money we now spend on trying to enforce drug prohibition were devoted to treatment and rehabilitation, in an atmosphere of compassion not punishment, the reduction in drug usage and in the harm done to the users could be dramatic. [9]

This plea comes from the bottom of my heart. Every friend of freedom, and I know you are one, must be as revolted as I am by the prospect of turning the United States into an armed camp, by the vision of jails filled with casual drug users and of [10] an army of enforcers empowered to invade the liberty of citizens on slight evidence. A country in which shooting down unidentified planes "on suspicion" can be seriously considered as a drug-war tactic is not the kind of United States that either you or I want to hand on to future generations.

William Bennett

A Response to Milton Friedman

Dear Milton:

1   There was little, if anything, new in your open letter to me calling for the legalization of drugs (*The Wall Street Journal,* Sept. 7). As your 1972 article made clear, the legalization argument is an old and familiar one, which has recently been revived by a small number of journalists and academics who insist that the only solution to the drug problem is no solution at all. What surprises me is that you would continue to advocate so unrealistic a proposal without pausing to consider seriously its consequences.

2   If the argument for drug legalization has one virtue it is its sheer simplicity. Eliminate laws against drugs, and street crime will disappear. Take the profit out of the black market through decriminalization and regulation, and poor neighborhoods will no longer be victimized by drug dealers. Cut back on drug enforcement, and use the money to wage a public health campaign against drugs, as we do with tobacco and alcohol.

Counting Costs

3   The basic premise of all these propositions is that using our nation's laws to fight drugs is too costly. To be sure, our attempts to reduce drug use do carry with them enormous costs. But the question that must be asked—and which is totally ignored by the legalization advocates—is, what are the costs of *not* enforcing laws against drugs?

In my judgment, and in the judgment of virtually every serious scholar in this field, the potential costs of legalizing drugs would be so large as to make it a public policy disaster. 4

Of course, no one, including you, can say with certainty what would happen in the U.S. if drugs were suddenly to become a readily purchased product. We do know, however, that wherever drugs have been cheaper and more easily obtained, drug use—and addiction—has skyrocketed. In opium and cocaine producing countries, addiction is rampant among the peasants involved in drug production. 5

Professor James Q. Wilson tells us that during the years in which heroin could be legally prescribed by doctors in Britain, the number of addicts increased forty-fold. And after the repeal of Prohibition—an analogy favored but misunderstood by legalization advocates—consumption of alcohol soared by 350%. 6

Could we afford such dramatic increases in drug use? I doubt it. Already the toll of drug use on American society—measured in lost productivity, in rising health insurance costs, in hospitals flooded with drug overdose emergencies, in drug caused accidents, and in premature death—is surely more than we would like to bear. 7

You seem to believe that by spending just a little more money on treatment and rehabilitation, the costs of increased addiction can be avoided. That hope betrays a basic misunderstanding of the problems facing drug treatment. Most addicts don't suddenly decide to get help. They remain addicts either because treatment isn't available or because they don't seek it out. The National Drug Control Strategy announced by President Bush on Sept. 5 goes a long way in making sure that more treatment slots are available. But the simple fact remains that many drug users won't enter treatment until they are forced to—often by the very criminal justice system you think is the source of the problem. 8

As for the connection between drugs and crime, your unswerving commitment to a legalization solution prevents you from appreciating the complexity of the drug market. Contrary to your claim, most addicts do not turn to crime to support their habit. Research shows that many of them were involved in criminal activity before they turned to drugs. Many former addicts who have received treatment continue to commit crimes during their recovery. And even if drugs were legal, what evidence do you have that the habitual drug user wouldn't continue to rob and steal to get money for clothes, food or shelter? Drug addicts always want more drugs than 9

they can afford, and no legalization scheme has yet come up
with a way of satisfying that appetite.

10   The National Drug Control Strategy emphasizes the
importance of reclaiming the streets and neighborhoods
where drugs have wrought havoc because, I admit, the price
of having drug laws is having criminals who will try to subvert them. Your proposal might conceivably reduce the
amount of gang- and dealer-related crime, but it is fanciful to
suggest that it would make crime vanish. Unless you are willing to distribute drugs freely and widely, there will always be
a black market to undercut the regulated one. And as for the
potential addicts, for the school children and for the pregnant
mothers, all of whom would find drugs more accessible and
legally condoned, your proposal would offer nothing at all.

11   So I advocate a larger criminal justice system to take drug
users off the streets and deter new users from becoming more
deeply involved in so hazardous an activity. You suggest that
such policies would turn the country "into an armed camp."
Try telling that to the public housing tenants who enthusiastically support plans to enhance security in their buildings, or
to the residents who applaud police when a local crack house
is razed. They recognize that drug use is a threat to the individual liberty and domestic tranquility guaranteed by the
Constitution.

12   I remain an ardent defender of our nation's laws against
illegal drug use and our attempts to enforce them because I
believe drug use is wrong. A true friend of freedom understands that government has a responsibility to craft and
uphold laws that help educate citizens about right and wrong.
That, at any rate, was the Founders' view of our system of
government.

Liberal Ridicule

13   Today this view is much ridiculed by liberal elites and
entirely neglected by you. So while I cannot doubt the sincerity of your opinion on drug legalization, I find it difficult to
respect. The moral cost of legalizing drugs is great, but it is a
cost that apparently lies outside the narrow scope of libertarian policy prescriptions.

14   I do not have a simple solution to the drug problem. I
doubt that one exists. But I am committed to fighting the
problem on several fronts through imaginative policies and
hard work over a long period of time. As in the past, some of

these efforts will work and some won't. Your response, however, is to surrender and see what happens. To my mind that
is irresponsible and reckless public policy. At a time when
national intolerance for drug use is rapidly increasing, the
legalization argument is a political anachronism. Its recent
resurgence is, I trust, only a temporary distraction from the
genuine debate on national drug policy.

Milton Friedman

A Response to William Bennett

William Bennett is entirely right (editorial page, Sept. 19)   1
that "there was little, if anything, new in" my open letter
to him—just as there is little, if anything, new in his proposed
program to rid this nation of the scourge of drugs. That is
why I am so disturbed by that program. It flies in the face of
decades of experience. More police, more jails, more-stringent
penalties, increased efforts at interception, increased publicity about the evils of drugs—all this has been accompanied by
more, not fewer, drug addicts; more, not fewer, crimes and
murders; more, not less, corruption; more, not fewer, innocent victims.

Like Mr. Bennett, his predecessors were "committed to   2
fighting the problem on several fronts through imaginative
policies and hard work over a long period of time." What evidence convinces him that the same policies on a larger scale
will end the drug scourge? He offers none in his response to
me, only assertion and the conjecture that legalizing drugs
would produce "a public policy disaster"—as if that is not
exactly what we already have.

Legalizing drugs is not equivalent to surrender in the fight   3
against drug addiction. On the contrary, I believe that legalizing drugs is a precondition for an effective fight. We might
then have a real chance to prevent sales to minors; get drugs
out of the schools and playgrounds; save crack babies and
reduce their number; launch an effective educational campaign on the personal costs of drug use—not necessarily conducted, I might add, by government; punish drug users guilty

of harming others while "under the influence"; and encourage large numbers of addicts to volunteer for treatment and rehabilitation when they could do so without confessing to criminal actions. Some habitual drug users would, as he says, "continue to rob and steal to get money for clothes, food or shelter." No doubt also there will be "a black market to undercut the regulated one"—as there now is bootleg liquor thanks to high taxes on alcoholic beverages. But these would be on a far smaller scale than at present. Perfection is not for this world. Pursuing the unattainable best can prevent achievement of the attainable good.

4   As Mr. Bennett recognizes, the victims of drugs fall into two classes: those who choose to use drugs and innocent victims—who in one way or another include almost all the rest of us. Legalization would drastically reduce the number of innocent victims. That is a virtual certainty. The number of self-chosen victims might increase, but it is pure conjecture that the number would, as he asserts, skyrocket. In any event, while both groups of victims are to be pitied, the innocent victims surely have a far greater claim on our sympathy than the self-chosen victims—or else the concept of personal responsibility has been emptied of all content.

5   A particular class of innocent victims generally overlooked is foreigners. By what right do we impose our values on the residents of Colombia? Or, by our actions undermine the very foundations of their society and condemn hundreds, perhaps thousands, of Colombians to violent death? All because the U.S. government is unable to enforce its own laws on its own citizens. I regard such actions as indefensible, entirely aside from the distortions they introduce into our foreign policy.

6   Finally, he and I interpret the "Founders' view of our system of government" very differently. To him, they believed "that government has a responsibility to...help educate citizens about right and wrong." To me, that is a totalitarian view opening the road to thought control and would have been utterly unacceptable to the Founders. I do not believe, and neither did they, that it is the responsibility of government to tell free citizens what is right and wrong. That is something for them to decide for themselves. Government is a means to enable each of us to pursue our own vision in our own way so long as we do not interfere with the right of others to do the same. In the words of the Declaration of Independence, "all Men are...endowed by their Creator with certain unalienable Rights, that among these are Life, Liberty, and the pursuit of Happiness. That to secure these Rights Governments are insti-

tuted among Men, deriving their just powers from the consent of the Governed." In my view, Justice Louis Brandeis was a "true friend of freedom" when he wrote, "Experience should teach us to be most on our guard to protect liberty when the government's purposes are beneficial. Men born to freedom are naturally alert to repel invasions of their liberty by evil-minded rulers. The greater dangers to liberty lurk in insidious encroachment by men of zeal, well meaning, but without understanding."

Milton Friedman
Hoover Institution
Stanford, Calif.

VII.

SCIENCE AND
SOCIETY

Introduction

No one doubts that science and technology have become central enterprises in our culture. Some scientists would like to have it otherwise, actually; they would like to insulate science as much as possible from social pressures. But that would be impossible: Not only is it impossible to keep scientific developments in medicine, genetic engineering, evolutionary biology, supercolliders, space exploration, and environmental science away from public scrutiny, it is also not in our interest to do so. For ultimately science and technology are themselves social creations, carried out through very human means for human purposes; that has already been made quite clear in the discussion of gender and the human brain in Part III of this book and in the controversies over abortion and censoring the internet in Part V. To try to dehumanize science and technology is to diminish them. Nevertheless, as science and technology become more central to our society, it is inevitable that conflicts between science and technology (on the one hand) and society (on the other) will become more important and more complicated. The scientific enterprise will inevitably involve ethical and rhetorical dimensions.

The first readings in this part establish that very clearly. Over the past decade many people have wondered about the ethics of "using" animals, whether for clothing or cosmetics, or for food or laboratory experiments. Do animals really have rights? If so, what are they? Do people have any rights that animals do not have? Is it legitimate to put people before animals—or animals before people? Do animals compose another kind of American minority in need of protection from a stronger and exploitative majority? Is it a form of discrimination—"speciesism"—to exploit animals, or do human beings by virtue of their special attributes have the right to do just that? Do the benefits of using animals for food, clothing, and medical science outweigh the liabilities? Does the controversy come down to a conflict of rights that pits the rights of animals against the rights of people—including the rights of scientists to pursue their work? Should the animal rights movement be less focused on abstract rights and more concerned about treating animals decently while they are "used"? According to some estimates, 50 million animals—cats, dogs, pigs, frogs, turtles, mice, rats, chimpanzees, rabbits, the proverbial guinea pigs, and more—are experimented on each year, very probably some of them on your own campus. And very probably the use of animals is an issue someplace on your campus as well.

The second section of this part of *Conversations* takes up the vexing question of AIDS: How should we fight this terrible, worldwide epidemic that has already claimed many millions of people throughout the world? (By the year 2000, as many as 20 million people are likely to have the disease; in the United States alone, half a million people had contracted the disease by the end of 1992.) First recognized in the United States early in the 1980s, AIDS (or acquired immune deficiency syndrome) seems to be caused by the human immunodeficiency virus—the HIV virus—that is spread through sexual contact, through the reuse of infected needles (especially by drug users), through childbirth (when the mother is infected), or through the transfusion of contaminated blood. Since the causes of the AIDS epidemic are well understood, the question arises: How should we fight it? Should citizens reconsider the sexual mores that have become conventional in the past few decades? Should health-care workers or other citizens have to undergo regular testing for the HIV virus? Should laws be passed requiring HIV carriers to inform their sexual partners that they carry the virus? Can health-care workers be required to treat AIDS patients? Will ingrained cultural practices need to be modified if AIDS is to be checked? This section mirrors a debate about a public health issue that is on everyone's mind these days.

The third section discusses one of the most controversial questions related to science and society today: the matter of euthanasia. Again, the question comes up because of advances in technology—because medical science has extended life expectancies and because medical technology can extend the life of the grievously ill and injured. But what are society's responsibilities to the very ill and incapacitated? Under what circumstances is it permissible to deny or remove medical treatment from a patient? And is it ever permissible to use medical technology actively to end a life—when someone is suffering, for example? Who should decide when euthanasia is permissible—family or physicians? Will an acceptance of euthanasia bring out our worst prejudices toward the aged, toward the mentally disadvantaged, toward the insane or deviant? Questions like these are taken up daily because of legal cases involving the "right to die" with dignity, because of highly publicized "right to die" organizations such as the Hemlock Society, and because some physicians have been quite public about assisting terminally ill patients to commit suicide.

This part and this book end appropriately with a look at one of the most important political and social developments of our times: the computer. Many people are convinced that computer technology has been an unqualified blessing for our society—that its use in speeding up routine operations and making information available with breathtaking ease is one of the great technological improvements of our day. They look forward to further applications of computer technology that we cannot begin to imagine, and they envision a more democratic society emerging from computer technology. But others aren't so sure, especially when it comes to Internet communications. What happens to our sense of community in the Computer Age? What happens to political institutions in the United States? Is the Internet making the fruits of technology available to more people, or is it simply offering even more advantages to the wealthy at the expense of the poor? And what of the other cultural effects of the computer: Will it smooth over differences? Will it fragment us into semiautonomous collections of special interest groups? How can we ensure that all Americans have access to the benefits of computers? What should the government's role be in promoting the "information highway"?

The advances brought by science and technology solve many human problems, but with these advances come a number of perplexing ethical dilemmas. This is the lesson of this final part of *Conversations,* and this is the challenge to all citizens, whether or not they are scientists, in this last decade of the twentieth century.

DO ANIMALS HAVE RIGHTS?

Tom Regan
Religion and Animal Rights

Tom Regan, a philosopher and educator who teaches at North Carolina State University, is president of the Culture and Animals Foundation in Raleigh, North Carolina. The author of many books on animal rights, he presented the following argument before the Conference on Creation Theology and Environmental Ethics at the World Council of Churches in Annecy, France, in 1988. It was reprinted in The Animals' Voice *magazine, which is devoted to animal rights.*

In its simplest terms the animal rights position I uphold maintains that such diverse practices as the use of animals in science, sport and recreational hunting, the trapping of fur-bearing animals for vanity products, and commercial animal agriculture are categorically wrong—wrong because these practices systematically violate the rights of the animals involved. Morally, these practices ought to be abolished. That is the goal of the *social* struggle for animal rights. The goal of our *individual* struggle is to divest ourselves of our moral and economic ties to these injustices—for example, by not wearing the skins of dead animals and by not eating their decaying corpses.   1

Not a few people regard the animal rights position as extreme, calling, as it does, for the abolition of certain well-entrenched social practices rather than for their "humane" reform. And many seem to imagine that once this label ("extreme") is applied, the need for further refutation evaporates. After all, how can such an "extreme" moral position be correct?   2

I addressed this question in a recent speech, reminding my audience of a few "extreme" moral positions we all accept: 3
Rape is *always* wrong.   4
Child pornography is *always* wrong.   5
Racial and sexual discrimination are *always* wrong.   6

7   I went on to note that when an injustice is absolute, as is true of each of the examples just cited, then one must oppose it absolutely. It is not reformed, more humane child pornography that an enlightened ethic calls for; it is its abolition that is required—it is this *extreme* position we must uphold. And analogous remarks apply in the case of the other examples.

8   Once this much is acknowledged, it is evident (or at least it should be) that those who oppose or resist the animal rights position will have to do better than merely attach the label "extreme" to it. Sometimes "extreme" positions about what is wrong are right.

9   Of course, there are two obvious differences between the animal rights position and the other examples of extreme views I have given. The latter views are very generally accepted, whereas the former position is not. And unlike these very generally accepted views, which concern wrongful acts done to human beings, the animal rights position concerns the (alleged) wrongfulness of treating animals (nonhuman animals, that is) in certain ways. Those who oppose or resist the animal rights position might seize upon these two differences in an effort to justify themselves in accepting extreme positions regarding rape and child abuse, for example, while rejecting the "extremism" of animal rights.

10   But neither of these differences will bear the weight of justification. That a view (whether moral or otherwise) is very generally accepted is not a sufficient reason for accepting it as true. There was a time when the shape of the earth was very generally believed to be flat, and when the presence of physical and mental handicaps was very generally thought to make the people who bore them morally inferior. That very many people believed these falsehoods obviously did not make them true. We won't discover or confirm what's true by taking a vote.

11   The reverse of the preceding also can be demonstrated. That a view (moral or otherwise) is not generally accepted is not a sufficient reason for judging it to be false. When those lonely few first conjectured that the earth is round and that women are the moral equals of men, they conjectured truly, notwithstanding how grandly they were outnumbered. The solitary person who, in Thoreau's enduring image, marches to a different drummer, may be the only person to apprehend the truth.

12   The second difference noted above is more problematic. That difference cites the fact that child abuse and rape, for example, involve evils done to human beings, while the ani-

mal rights position claims that certain (alleged) evils are done to nonhuman animals. Now, there is no question that this does constitute a difference. The question is, is this a *morally relevant difference*—a difference, that is, that would justify us in accepting the extreme opposition we judge to be appropriate in the case of child abuse and rape, for example, but which most people resist or abjure in the case of, say, vivisection. For a variety of reasons I do not myself think that this difference is a morally relevant one. Permit me to explain why.

Viewed scientifically, this second difference succeeds only   13 in citing a biological difference: The victims of rape and child abuse belong to one species (the species *Homo sapiens*) whereas the (alleged) victims of vivisection and trapping belong to other species (the species *Canis lupus*, for example). But biological differences *inside* the species *Homo sapiens* do not justify radically different treatment among those individual humans who differ biologically (for example, in terms of sex, or skin color, or chromosome count). Why, then, should biological differences *outside* our species count morally? If having one eye or deformed limbs does not disqualify a human being from moral consideration equal to that given to those humans who are more fortunate, how can it be rational to disqualify a rat or a wolf from equal moral consideration because, unlike us, they have paws and a tail?

Some of those who resist or oppose the animal rights posi-   14 tion might have recourse to "intuition" at this point. They might claim that one either "sees" that the principal biological difference at issue (namely, species membership) *is* a morally relevant one, or does *not* see this. No *reason* can be given as to why belonging to the species *Homo sapiens* gives one a superior moral status, just as no *reason* can be given as to why belonging to the species *Canis lupus* gives wolves an inferior moral status (if wolves have a moral status at all). This difference in moral status can only be grasped immediately, without making an inference, by an exercise of intuitive reason. This moral difference is "self-evident"—or so it will be claimed by those who claim to "intuit" it.

However attractive this appeal to intuition may seem to   15 some, it woefully fails to bear the weight of justification. The plain fact is, people have claimed to "intuit" differences in the comparative moral standing of individuals and groups *inside* the human species, and these alleged "intuitions," we all would agree, are painful symptoms of unquestioned and unjustifiable prejudice. Over the course of history, for example, many men have "intuited" the moral superiority of men when compared with that of women, and many white-skinned humans have "intuited" the moral superiority of white-skinned humans when compared with humans having different skin colors. If this is a matter of intuition, then no reason can be given for this superiority. No inference is (or can be) required, no evidence adduced. One either "sees" it, or one doesn't. It's just that those who do "see" it (or so they will insist) apprehend the truth, while those whose deficient intuitive faculties prevent them from "seeing" it fail to do so.

16   I cannot believe that any thoughtful person will be taken in by this ruse. Appeals to "intuition" in these contexts are symptomatic of unquestioned and unjustifiable moral prejudices. What prompts or encourages men to "see" their moral superiority over women are the sexual prejudices men bring with them, not what is to be found in the existence of sexual differences themselves. And the same is true, *mutatis mutandis,* of "seeing" moral superiority in racial or other biological differences between humans.

17   That much established, the weakness of appeals to intuition in the case at hand should be apparent. Since intuition is not to be trusted when questions of the comparative moral standing of biologically different individuals *inside* the species *Homo sapiens* are at issue, it cannot be rational to assume or insist that such appeals can or should be trusted when questions of the comparative moral standing of individuals *outside* the species are at issue. Moreover, since appeals to intuition in the former case turn out to be symptomatic of unquestioned and unjustifiable moral prejudices, rather than being revelatory of some important moral truth, it is not unreasonable to suspect that the same diagnosis applies to appeals to intuition in the latter case. If true, then those who "intuit" the moral superiority of all members of the species *Homo sapiens* over all members of every other species also emerge as the unwitting victims or the willful perpetrators of an unquestioned and unjustifiable moral prejudice.

18   "Speciesism" is the name given to this (alleged) prejudice. This idea has been characterized in a variety of ways. For present purposes let us begin with the following twofold characterization of what I shall call "categorical speciesism."

19   Categorical speciesism is the belief that (1) the inherent value of an individual can be judged solely on the basis of the biological species to which that individual belongs, and that (2) all the members of the species *Homo sapiens* have equal inherent value, while all the members of every other species

lack this kind of value, simply because all and only humans are members of the species *Homo sapiens*.

In speaking of inherent value, both here and throughout   20
what follows, I mean something that coincides with Kant's famous idea of "end-in-itself." Individuals who have inherent value, in other words, have value in their own right, apart from their possible utility for others; as such, these individuals are never to be treated in ways that reduce their value to their possible usefullness for others; they are always to be treated as "ends-in-themselves," not as "means merely." Categorical speciesism, then, holds that all and only humans have this kind of value precisely because all and only humans belong to the species *Homo sapiens*.

I have already indicated why I believe that appeals to intu-   21
ition cannot succeed in establishing the truth of categorical speciesism as so characterized. How, then, might the prejudicial character of speciesism be established?

Part of that answer is to be found when we pause to con-   22
sider the nature of the animals we humans hunt, trap, eat and use for scientific purposes. Any person of common sense will agree that these animals bring the mystery of consciousness to the world. These animals, that is, not only are *in* the world, they are aware *of it*—and also of their "inner" world. They see, hear, touch and feel; but they also desire, believe, remember and anticipate.

If anyone questions my assessment of the common sense   23
view about these animals, then I would invite them to speak with people who share their lives with dogs or cats or horses, or others who know the ways of wolves or coyotes, or still others who have had contact with any bird one might wish to name. Common sense clearly is on the side of viewing these animals as unified psychological beings, individuals who have a biography (a psychological life-story), not merely a biology. And common sense is not in conflict with our best science here. Indeed, our best science offers a scientific corroboration of the common sense view.

That corroboration is to be found in a set of diverse but   24
related considerations. One is evolutionary theory, which implies that (1) the more complex has evolved from the less complex, that (2) members of the species *Homo sapiens* are the most complex life form of which we are aware, that (3) members of our species bring a psychological presence to the world, that (4) the psychological capacities we find in humans have evolved over time, and that (5) these capacities would not have evolved at all and would not have been passed

on from one generation to the next if they (that is, these capacities) failed to have adaptive value—that is, if they failed to offer advantages to our species in its ongoing struggle to survive in an ever-changing environment.

25   Given these five points, it is entirely consistent with the main thrust of evolutionary theory, and is, indeed, required by it, to maintain that the members of some species of non-human animals are like us in having the capacity to see and hear and feel, for example, as well as to believe and desire, to remember and anticipate.

26   Certainly this is what Darwin thinks, as is evident when he writes of the animals we humans eat and trap, to use just two instances, that they differ psychologically (or mentally) from us in degree, not in kind.

27   A second, related consideration involves comparative anatomy and physiology. Everything we know about nature must incline us to believe that a complex structure has a complex reason for being. It would therefore be an extraordinary lapse of form if we humans had evolved into complicated psychological creatures, with an underlying anatom-ical and physiological complexity, while other species of animals had evolved to have a more or less complex anatomy and physiology, very much like our own in many respects, and yet lacked—*totally* lacked—any and every psychological capacity. If nature could respond to this bizarre suggestion, the verdict we would hear would be, "Nonsense!"

28   Thus it is, then, that both common sense and our best science speak with one voice regarding the psychological nature we share with the nonhuman animals I have mentioned—those, for example, many people stew, roast, fry, broil and grill for the sake of their gustatory desires and delights. When the dead and putrefying bodies of these animals are eaten, our psychological kin are consumed.

29   Recall the occasion for this review of relevant scientific considerations. Categorical speciesism, which I characterized earlier, is not shown to be a moral prejudice merely because those who accept it are unable to prove its truth. This much has been conceded and, indeed, insisted upon. What more, then, would have to be established before the charge of moral prejudice could be made to stick? Part of that answer is to be found in the recent discussion of what common sense and our best science contribute to our understanding of the nonhuman animals we have been discussing. Both agree that these animals are fundamentally like ordinary human beings—like you and me. For, like us, these animals

have a unified psychological presence in the world, a life-story that is uniquely their own, a separate biography. In the simplest terms *they are somebody, not something*. Precisely because this similarity is so well established, grounded in the opinions, as Aristotle would express this, of both "the many and the wise," any substantive moral position at odds with it seems dubious to say the least.

And categorical speciesism, as I have characterized it, *is* at   30
odds with the joint verdict of common sense and our best science. For once the appeal to intuition is denied (and denied for good reasons), the onus of justification must be borne by the speciesist to cite some unique feature of being human that would ground the attribution of inherent value exclusively to human beings, a task that we now see is all but certain to end in failure, given the biological status humans share with those nonhuman animals to whom I have been referring. Rationally considered, we must judge similar cases similarly. This is what the principle of formal justice requires, what respect for logical consistency demands. Thus, since we share a biographical presence in the world with these animals, it seems arbitrary and prejudicial in the extreme to insist that all humans have a kind of value that every other animal lacks.

In response to this line of argument people who wish to   31
retain the spirit of speciesism might be prompted to alter its letter. This position I shall call modified speciesism. According to this form of speciesism those nonhuman animals who, like us, have a biographical presence in the world have *some* inherent value, it's just that the degree of inherent value they have *always is less* than that possessed by human beings. And if we ask why this is thought to be so, the answer modified speciesism offers is the same as categorical speciesism: The degree of value differs because humans belong to a particular species to which no other animal belongs—the species *Homo sapiens*.

I think it should be obvious that modified speciesism is   32
open to many of the same kinds of damaging criticisms as categorical speciesism. What, we may ask, is supposed to be the basis of the alleged superior value of human beings? Will it be said that one simply "intuits" this? Then all the same difficulties this appeal faced in the case of categorical speciesism will resurface and ultimately swamp modified speciesism. To avoid this, will it be suggested that the degree of inherent value an individual possesses depends on the relative complexity of that individual's psychological repertoire—the greater the complexity, the greater the value? Then modified

speciesism simply will not be able to justify the ascription of superior inherent value to all human beings when compared with every nonhuman animal. And the reason it will not be able to do this is simple: Some nonhuman animals bring to their biography a degree of psychological complexity that far exceeds what is brought by some human beings. One need only compare, say, the psychological repertoire of a healthy two year old chimp, or dog, or hog, or robin to that of a profoundly handicapped human of any age, to recognize the incontrovertible truth of what I have just said. Not all human beings have richer, more complex biographies than every nonhuman animal.

33   How are speciesists to get around this fact—for get around it they must, because fact it is. There is a familiar theological answer to this question; at least it is familiar to those who know something of the Judeo-Christian religious traditions, as these traditions sometimes have been interpreted. That answer states that human beings—all of us—are inherently more valuable than any other existing individual because we are spiritually different and, indeed, unique. This uniqueness stems from our having been created in the image of God, a status we share with no other creature. If, then, it is true that all humans uniquely image God, then we are able to cite a real (spiritual) difference between every member of our species and the countless numbers of the millions of other species of creaturely life. And, if, moreover, this difference is a morally relevant one, then speciesists might seem to be in a position to defend their speciesism (and this is true whether they are categorical or moderate speciesists) in the face of the demands of formal justice. After all, that principle requires that we judge similar cases similarly, whereas any two individuals—the one human, the other of some other species— will not be relevantly similar, given the hypothesis of the unique spiritual worth of all human beings.

34   Now I myself am not ill-disposed to the idea of there being something about us humans that gives us a unique spiritual worth, nor am I ill-disposed to the idea that the ground of this worth is to be found or explicated in the idea that we humans uniquely "image" God. Not surprisingly, therefore, the interpretation of these ideas I favor, while it concedes this (possible) difference between humans and the rest of creation, does not yield anything like the results favored by speciesism, whether categorical or moderate. Let me explain.

35   The position I favor is the one that interprets our divine "imaging" in terms of our moral responsibility. By this I mean

that we are expressly chosen by God to be God's vice-regent in the day-to-day affairs of the world; we are chosen by God, that is, to be as loving in our day-to-day dealings with the created order as God was in creating that order in the first place. In *this* sense, therefore, there *is* a morally relevant difference between human beings and every other creaturely expression of God. For it is only members of the human species who are given the awesome freedom and responsibility to be God's representative within creation. And it is, therefore, only we humans who can be held morally blameworthy when we fail to do this, and morally praiseworthy when we succeed.

Within the general context of this interpretation of our 36 unique "imaging" of God, then, we find a morally relevant difference between God's creative expression in the human and God's creative expression in every other aspect of creation. But—as should be evident—this difference *by itself* offers neither aid nor comfort to speciesism, of whatever variety. For to agree that only humans image God, in the sense that only humans have the moral responsibility to be loving toward God's creation, in no way entails either that all and only humans have inherent value (so-called categorical speciesism) or that all and only humans have a superior inherent value (modified speciesism, as I have called it). It is perfectly consistent with our unique status as God's chosen representative within creation that *other* creatures have inherent value and possess it to a degree equal to that possessed by human beings. Granted, our uniqueness lies in our moral responsibility to God and to God's creation, including, of course, all members of the human family. But this fact, assuming it to be a fact, only answers the question, "Which among God's creatures are capable of acting rightly or wrongly (or, as philosophers might say, 'are moral agents')?" What this fact, assuming it to be one, does not answer are the questions, "To which creatures can we act rightly or wrongly?" and "What kind of value do other creatures have?"

Every prejudice dies hard. Speciesism is no exception. 37 That it is a prejudice and that, by acting on it, we humans have been, and continue to be, responsible for an incalculable amount of evil, an amount of truly monumental proportions, is, I believe, as true as it is regrettable. In my philosophical writings over the past fifteen years I have endeavored to show how this tragic truth can be argued for on wholly secular grounds. On this occasion I have looked elsewhere for support—have in fact looked to the original saga of creation we find in *Genesis*—in the hope that we

might there find a religious or theological account that reso-
nates with the secular case for animal rights. Neither case—
not the secular and not the religious—has, or can have, the
conclusiveness of a proof in, say, geometry. I say "can have"
because I am reminded of Aristotle's astute observation, that
it is the mark of an educated person not to demand "proof"
that is inappropriate for a given subject matter. And whatever
else we might think of moral thought, I believe we at least can
agree that it is importantly unlike geometry.

38   It remains true, nonetheless, that my attempt to explain
and defend as egalitarian this view of the inherent value of
humans and other animals must face a number of important
challenges. For reasons of length, if for no other, I cannot on
this occasion characterize or respond to all these challenges,
not even all the most fundamental ones. The best I can do,
before concluding, is describe and defuse two of them.

39   The first begins by observing that, within the traditions of
Judaism and Christianity, *every form of life*, not simply
humans and other animals, is to be viewed as expressive of
God's love. Thus, to attempt to "elevate" the value of nonhuman animals, as I might be accused of having done, could be
viewed as having the unacceptable consequence of negating
or reducing the value of everything else.

40   I think this objection misses the mark. There is nothing in
the animal rights philosophy (nothing, that is, in the kind of
egalitarianism I have endeavored to defend) that either
denies or diminishes the value of fruits, nuts, grains and
other forms of vegetative life, or that refuses to accept the
possibility that these and the rest of creation are so many
ways in which God's loving presence is manifested. Nor is
there anything in this philosophy that disparages the wise
counsel to treat all of creation gently and appreciatively. It is
an arrogant, unbridled anthropocentrism, often aided and
abetted in our history by an arrogant, unbridled Christian
theology, not the philosophy of animal rights, that has
brought the earth to the brink of ecological disaster.

41   Still, this philosophy does find in humans and other animals, because of our shared biographical status in creation, a
kind of value—inherent value—which other creatures fail to
possess, either not at all or at least not to the degree in which
humans and other animals possess it. Is it possible to defend
this view? I believe it is, both on the grounds of a purely secular moral philosophy and by appeal to Biblical authority. The
secular defense I have attempted to offer elsewhere and will
not repeat here. As for the Christian defense, I shall merely

reaffirm the vital importance (in my view) of *Genesis 1,* as well as (to my mind) the more than symbolic significance of the covenant, and note that in both we find biblical sanction for viewing the value of animals to be superior to that of vegetables. After all, we do not find carrots and almonds included in the covenant, and we do find God expressly giving these and other forms of vegetative life to us, as our food, in *Genesis'* first creation saga. In a word, then, vegetative life was meant to be used by us, thus giving it utility value for us (which does not mean or entail that we may use these life forms thoughtlessly or even irreverently).

So much for the first challenge. The second one emanates 42 from quite a different source and mounts a quite different objection. It begins by noting the large disparities that exist in the quality of life available to those who are affluent (the "haves") and those who are poor (the "have-nots"), especially those who live in the so-called "Third World." "It is all fine and good to preach the gospel of animal rights to those people who have the financial and other means to practice it, if they choose to do so," this objection states, "but please do spare us your self-righteous denunciation of the struggling (and often starving) masses of people in the rest of the world, who really have no choice but to eat animals, wear their skins, and use them in other ways. To condemn these people is to value animal life above human life. And this is misanthropy at its worst."

Now, this particular variation on the familiar theme of 43 misanthropy (at least this is familiar to advocates of animal rights) has a point, up to a point. The point it has, is that it would be self-righteous to condemn the people in question for acting as they do, especially if we are acting worse than they are (as well we may be). But, of course, nothing in what I have argued supports such a condemnation, and this for the simple reason that I have nowhere argued that people who eat animals, or who hunt and trap them, or who cut their heads off or burst their intestines in pursuit of "scientific knowledge," either are or must be *evil* people. The position I have set forth concerns the moral wrongness of what people do, not the *vileness of their character.* In my view, it is entirely possible that good people sometimes do what is wrong, and evil people sometimes do what is right.

Indeed, not only is this possible, it frequently happens, and 44 among those circumstances in which it does, some concern the actions performed by people in the Third World. At least this is the conclusion we reach if we take the philosophy of animal rights seriously. To make my meaning clearer, consider the following example. Suppose we chance upon a tribe of hunter-gatherers who annually, on a date sacred to their tradition, sacrifice the most beautiful female child to the gods, in the hope that the tribe will prosper in the coming year. In my view this act of human sacrifice is morally wrong and ought to be stopped (which does *not* mean that we should invade with tanks and flame-throwers to stop it!). From this moral assessment of what these human beings do, however, it does not follow that we should judge them to be evil, vicious people. It could well be that they act from only the best intentions and with nothing but the best motives. Nevertheless, what they do, in my judgment, is morally wrong.

45   What is true of the imaginary case of this tribe is no less true of real-life cases where people in the Third World raise and kill animals for food, cruelly subject other animals to forced labor, and so on. Anytime anyone reduces the inherent value of a nonhuman animal to that animal's utility value for human beings, what is done, in my view, is morally wrong. But it does not follow from this that we should make a negative moral judgment about the character of the human moral agents involved, especially if, as is true in the Third World, there are mitigating circumstances. For it often happens that people who do what is morally wrong should be *excused* from moral blame and censure. A person who shoots a family member, for example, in the mistaken belief that there is a burglar in the house, does what is wrong and yet may well *not* be morally blameworthy. Similarly, those people in the Third World who act in ways that are prohibited by respect for the rights of animals, do what is wrong. But because of the harsh, uncompromising exigencies of their life, where they are daily faced with the demand to make truly heroic sacrifices, where indeed it often is a matter of their life or their death that hangs in the balance, the people of the Third World in my view should be excused from our harsh, uncompromising judgments of moral blame. The circumstances of their life, one might say, are as mitigating as any circumstances can be.

46   In light of the preceding remarks, I hope it is clear why it would be a bad reading of the philosophy of animal rights, to charge its proponents with a hearty appetite, if not for animal flesh then at least for self-righteousness. When we understand the difference between morally assessing a person's act and that person's character, and when we take cognizance of the appropriateness of reducing or erasing moral blame in the face of mitigating circumstances, then the proponents of ani-

mal rights should be seen to be no more censorious or "self-righteous" than the proponents of any other moral philosophy.

The challenge to lead a good, respectful, loving life just in   47
our dealings within the human family is onerous and
demanding. How much more onerous and demanding must
it be, therefore, if we widen the circle of the moral community to include the whole of creation. How might we begin to
meet this enlarged challenge? Doubtless there are many possible places to begin, some of which will be more accessible
to some than to others. For my part, however, I cannot help
believing that an appropriate place to begin is with the food
on our plates. For here we are faced with a direct personal
choice, over which we exercise absolute sovereign authority.
Such power is not always within our grasp. How little influence we really have, you and I, on the practices of the World
Bank, the agrarian land-reform movement, the call to reduce
armed conflicts, the cessation of famine and the evil of abject
poverty! These large-scale evils stand beyond the reach of our
small wills.

But not the food on our plates. Here we are at liberty to   48
exercise absolute control. And here, then, we ought to be asking ourselves, "Which of those choices I can make are most in
accord with the idea of the integrity of creation?"

When we consider the biographical and, I dare say, the   49
spiritual kinship we share with those billions of animals
raised and slaughtered for food, when, further, we inform
ourselves of the truly wretched conditions in which most of
these animals are raised, not to mention the deplorable methods by which they are transported and the gruesome, blood-
soaked reality of the slaughterhouse; and when, finally, we
take honest stock of our privileged position in the world, a
position that will not afford us the excuse from moral blame
shared by the desperately poor who, as we say, "really have no
choice"—when we consider all these factors, then the case for
abstaining from animal flesh has the overwhelming weight of
both impartial reason and a spiritually-infused compassion
on its side.

True, to make this change will involve some sacrifices—in   50
taste perhaps, in convenience certainly. And yet the whole
fabric of Christian *agape* is woven from the threads of sacrificial acts. To abstain, on principle, from eating animals, therefore, although it is not the end-all, can be the begin-all of our
conscientious effort to journey back to (or toward) Eden, can
be one way (among others) to re-establish or create that relationship to the earth which, if *Genesis 1* is to be trusted, was

part of God's original hopes for and plans in creation. It is the integrity of this creation we seek to understand and aspire to honor. In the choice of our food, I believe, we see, not in a glass darkly, but face to face, a small but not unimportant part of both the challenge and the promise of Christianity and animal rights.

Vicki Hearne

What's Wrong with Animal Rights

Hearne is an animal trainer, a writer, and a contributing editor at Harper's *magazine, the public and cultural affairs magazine where this essay was published in September 1991. The letters that follow it were published a few months later in* Harper's.

1   Not all happy animals are alike. A Doberman going over a hurdle after a small wooden dumbbell is sleek, all arcs of harmonious power. A basset hound cheerfully performing the same exercise exhibits harmonies of a more lugubrious nature. There are chimpanzees who love precision the way musicians or fanatical housekeepers or accomplished hypochondriacs do; others for whom happiness is a matter of invention and variation—chimp vaudevillians. There is a rhinoceros whose happiness, as near as I can make out, is in needing to be trained every morning, all over again, or else he "forgets" his circus routine, and in this you find a clue to the slow, deep, quiet chuckle of his happiness and to the glory of the beast. Happiness for Secretariat is in his ebullient bound, that joyful length of stride. For the draft horse or the weight-pull dog, happiness is of a different shape, more awesome and less obviously intelligent. When the pulling horse is at its most intense, the animal goes into himself, allocating all of the educated power that organizes his desire to dwell in fierce and delicate intimacy with that power, leans into the harness, and MAKES THAT SUCKER *MOVE*.

2   If we are speaking of human beings and use the phrase "animal happiness," we tend to mean something like "crea-

ture comforts." The emblems of this are the golden retriever rolling in the grass, the horse with his nose deep in the oats, the kitty by the fire. Creature comforts are important to animals—"Grub first, then ethics" is a motto that would describe many a wise Labrador retriever, and I have a pit bull named Annie whose continual quest for the perfect pillow inspires her to awesome feats. But there is something more to animals, a capacity for satisfactions that come from work in the fullest sense—what is known in philosophy and in this country's Declaration of Independence as "happiness." This is a sense of personal achievement, like the satisfaction felt by a good wood-carver or a dancer or a poet or an accomplished dressage horse. It is a happiness that, like the artist's, must come from something within the animal, something trainers call "talent." Hence, it cannot be imposed on the animal. But it is also something that does not come *ex nihilo*. If it had not been a fairly ordinary thing, in one part of the world, to teach young children to play the pianoforte, it is doubtful that Mozart's music would exist.

Happiness is often misunderstood as a synonym for plea- 3
sure or as an antonym for suffering. But Aristotle associated happiness with ethics—codes of behavior that urge us toward the sensation of getting it right, a kind of work that yields the "click" of satisfaction upon solving a problem or surmounting an obstacle. In his *Ethics*, Aristotle wrote, "If happiness is activity in accordance with excellence, it is reasonable that it should be in accordance with the highest excellence." Thomas Jefferson identified the capacity for happiness as one of the three fundamental rights on which all others are based: "life, liberty, and the pursuit of happiness."

I bring up this idea of happiness as a form of work because 4
I am an animal trainer, and work is the foundation of the happiness a trainer and an animal discover together. I bring up these words also because they cannot be found in the lexicon of the animal-rights movement. This absence accounts for the uneasiness toward the movement of most people, who sense that rights advocates have a point but take it too far when they liberate snails or charge that goldfish at the country fair are suffering. But the problem with the animal-rights advocates is not that they take it too far; it's that they've got it all wrong.

Animal rights are built upon a misconceived premise that 5
rights were created to prevent us from unnecessary suffering. You can't find an animal-rights book, video, pamphlet, or rock

concert in which someone doesn't mention the Great Sentence, written by Jeremy Bentham in 1789. Arguing in favor of such rights, Bentham wrote: "The question is not, Can they *reason?* nor, can they *talk?* but, can they suffer?"

6   The logic of the animal-rights movement places suffering at the iconographic center of a skewed value system. The thinking of its proponents—given eerie expression in a virtually sado-pornographic sculpture of a tortured monkey that won a prize for its compassionate vision—has collapsed into a perverse conundrum. Today the loudest voices calling for—demanding—the destruction of animals are the humane organizations. This is an inevitable consequence of the apotheosis of the drive to relieve suffering: Death is the ultimate release. To compensate for their contradictions, the humane movement has demonized, in this century and the last, those who made animal happiness their business: veterinarians, trainers, and the like. We think of Louis Pasteur as the man whose work saved you and me and your dog and cat from rabies, but antivivisectionists of the time claimed that rabies increased in areas where there were Pasteur Institutes.

7   An anti-rabies public-relations campaign mounted in England in the 1880s by the Royal Society for the Prevention of Cruelty to Animals and other organizations led to orders being issued to club any dog found not wearing a muzzle. England still has her cruel and unnecessary law that requires an animal to spend six months in quarantine before being allowed loose in the country. Most of the recent propaganda about pit bulls—the crazy claim that they "take hold with their front teeth while they chew away with their rear teeth" (which would imply, incorrectly, that they have double jaws)—can be traced to literature published by the Humane Society of the United States during the fall of 1987 and earlier. If your neighbors want your dog or horse impounded and destroyed because he is a nuisance—say the dog barks, or the horse attracts flies—it will be the local Humane Society to whom your neighbors turn for action.

8   In a way, everyone has the opportunity to know that the history of the humane movement is largely a history of miseries, arrests, prosecutions, and death. The Humane Society is the pound, the place with the decompression chamber or the lethal injections. You occasionally find worried letters about this in Ann Landers's column.

9   Animal-rights publications are illustrated largely with photographs of two kinds of animals—"Helpless Fluff" and "Agonized Fluff," the two conditions in which some people seem

to prefer their animals, because any other version of an animal is too complicated for propaganda. In the introduction to his book *Animal Liberation*, Peter Singer says somewhat smugly that he and his wife have no animals and, in fact, don't much care for them. This is offered as evidence of his objectivity and ethical probity. But it strikes me as an odd, perhaps obscene, underpinning for an ethical project that encourages university and high school students to cherish their ignorance of, say, great bird dogs as proof of their devotion to animals.

I would like to leave these philosophers behind, for they are inept connoisseurs of suffering who might revere my Airedale for his capacity to scream when subjected to a blowtorch but not for his wit and courage, not for his natural good manners that are a gentle rebuke to ours. I want to celebrate the moment not long ago when, at his first dog show, my Airedale, Drummer, learned that there can be a public place where his work is respected. I want to celebrate his meticulousness, his happiness upon realizing at the dog show that no one would swoop down upon him and swamp him with the goo-goo excesses known as the "teddy-bear complex" but that people actually got out of his way, gave him room to work. I want to say, "There can be a six-and-a-half-month-old puppy who can care about accuracy, who can be fastidious, and whose fastidiousness will be a foundation for courage later." I want to say, "Leave my puppy alone!" 10

I want to leave the philosophers behind, but I cannot, in part because the philosophical problems that plague academicians of the animal-rights movement are illuminating. They wonder, do animals have rights or do they have interests? Or, if these rightists lead particularly unexamined lives, they dismiss that question as obvious (yes, of course, animals have rights, prima facie) and proceed to enumerate them, James Madison style. This leads to the issuance of bills of rights—the right to an environment, the right not to be used in medical experiments—and other forms of trivialization. 11

The calculus of suffering can be turned against the philosophers of festering flesh, even in the case of food animals, or exotic animals who perform in movies and circuses. It is true that it hurts to be slaughtered by man, but it doesn't hurt nearly as much as some of the cunningly cruel arrangements meted out by "Mother Nature." In Africa, 75 percent of the lions cubbed do not survive to the age of two. For those who make it to two, the average age at death is ten years. Asali, the 12 movie and TV lioness, was still working at age twenty-one. There are fates worse than death, but twenty-one years of a close relationship with Hubert Wells, Asali's trainer, is not one of them. Dorset sheep and polled Herefords would not exist at all were they not in a symbiotic relationship with human beings.

13   A human being living in the "wild"—somewhere, say, without the benefits of medicine and advanced social organization—would probably have a life expectancy of from thirty to thirty-five years. A human being living in "captivity"—in, say, a middle-class neighborhood of what the Centers for Disease Control call a Metropolitan Statistical Area—has a life expectancy of seventy or more years. For orangutans in the wild in Borneo and Malaysia, the life expectancy is thirty-five years; in captivity, fifty years. The wild is not a suffering-free zone or all that frolicsome a location.

14   The questions asked by animal-rights activists are flawed, because they are built on the concept that the origin of rights is in the avoidance of suffering rather than in the pursuit of happiness. The question that needs to be asked—and that will put us in closer proximity to the truth—is not, do they have rights? or, what are those rights? but rather, what is a right?

15   Rights originate in committed relationships and can be found, both intact and violated, wherever one finds such relationships—in social compacts, within families, between animals, and between people and nonhuman animals. This is as true when the nonhuman animals in question are lions or parakeets as when they are dogs. It is my Airedale whose excellencies have my attention at the moment, so it is with reference to him that I will consider the question, what is a right?

16   When I imagine situations in which it naturally arises that A defends or honors or respects B's rights, I imagine situations in which the relationship between A and B can be indicated with a possessive pronoun. I might say, "Leave her alone, she's my daughter" or, "That's what she wants, and she is my daughter. I think I am bound to honor her wants." Similarly, "Leave her alone, she's my mother." I am more tender of the happiness of my mother, my father, my child, than I am of other people's family members; more tender of my friends' happiness than your friends' happinesses, unless you and I have a mutual friend.

17   Possession of a being by another has come into more and more disrepute, so that the common understanding of one person possessing another is slavery. But the important detail

about the kind of possessive pronoun that I have in mind is reciprocity: If I have a friend, she has a friend. If I have a daughter, she has a mother. The possessive does not bind one of us while freeing the other; it cannot do that. Moreover, should the mother reject the daughter, the word that applies is "disown." The form of disowning that most often appears in the news is domestic violence. Parents abuse children; husbands batter wives.

Some cases of reciprocal possessives have built-in limita- 18 tions, such as "my patient/my doctor" or "my student/my teacher" or "my agent/my client." Other possessive relations are extremely limited but still remarkably binding: "my neighbor" and "my country" and "my president."

The responsibilities and the ties signaled by reciprocal pos- 19 session typically are hard to dissolve. It can be as difficult to give up an enemy as to give up a friend, and often the one becomes the other, as though the logic of the possessive pronoun outlasts the forms it chanced to take at a given moment, as though we were stuck with one another. In these bindings, nearly inextricable, are found the origin of our rights. They imply a possessiveness but also recognize an acknowledgment by each side of the other's existence.

The idea of democracy is dependent on the citizens' hav- 20 ing knowledge of the government; that is, realizing that the government exists and knowing how to claim rights against it. I know this much because I get mail from the government and see its "representatives" running about in uniforms. Whether I actually have any rights in relationship to the government is less clear, but the idea that I do is symbolized by the right to vote. I obey the government, and, in theory, it obeys me, by counting my ballot, reading the *Miranda* warning to me, agreeing to be bound by the Constitution. My friend obeys me as I obey her; the government "obeys" me to some extent, and, to a different extent, I obey it.

What kind of thing can my Airedale, Drummer, have 21 knowledge of? He can know that I exist and through that knowledge can claim his happiness, with varying degrees of success, both with me and against me. Drummer can also know about larger human or dog communities than the one that consists only of him and me. There is my household—the other dogs, the cats, my husband. I have had enough dogs on campuses to know that he can learn that Yale exists as a neighborhood or village. My older dog, Annie, not only knows that Yale exists but can tell Yalies from townies, as I learned while teaching there during labor troubles.

22   Dogs can have elaborate conceptions of human social structures, and even of something like their rights and responsibilities within them, but these conceptions are never elaborate enough to construct a rights relationship between a dog and the state, or a dog and the Humane Society. Both of these are concepts that depend on writing and memoranda, officers in uniform, plaques and seals of authority. All of these are literary constructs, and all of them are beyond a dog's ken, which is why the mail carrier who doesn't also happen to be a dog's friend is forever an intruder—this is why dogs bark at mailmen.

23   It is clear enough that natural rights relations can arise between people and animals. Drummer, for example, can insist, "Hey, let's go outside and do something!" if I have been at my computer several days on end. He can both refuse to accept various of my suggestions and tell me when he fears for his life—such as the time when the huge, white flapping flag appeared out of nowhere, as it seemed to him, on the town green one evening when we were working. I can (and do) say to him either, "Oh, you don't have to worry about that" or, "Uh oh, you're right, Drum, that guy looks dangerous." Just as the government and I—two different species or organism—have developed improvised ways of communicating, such as the vote, so Drummer and I have worked out a number of ways to make our expressions known. Largely through obedience, I have taught him a fair amount about how to get responses from me. Obedience is reciprocal; you cannot get responses from a dog to whom you do not respond accurately. I have enfranchised him in a relationship to me by educating him, creating the conditions by which he can achieve a certain happiness specific to a dog, maybe even specific to an Airedale, inasmuch as this same relationship has allowed me to plumb the happiness of being a trainer and writing this article.

24   Instructions in this happiness are given terms that are alien to a culture in which liver treats, fluffy windup toys, and miniature sweaters are confused with respect and work. Jack Knox, a sheepdog trainer originally from Scotland, will shake his crook at a novice handler who makes a promiscuous move to praise a dog, and will call out in his Scottish accent, "Eh! Eh! Get back, get BACK! Ye'll no be abusin' the dogs like that in my clinic." America is a nation of abused animals, Knox says, because we are always swooping at them with praise, "no gi'ing them their freedom." I am reminded of

Rainer Maria Rilke's account in which the Prodigal Son leaves—has to leave—because everyone loves him, even the dogs love him, and he has no path to the delicate and fierce truth of himself. Unconditional praise and love, in Rilke's story, disenfranchise us, distract us from what truly excites our interest.

In the minds of some trainers and handlers, praise is dishonesty. Paradoxically, it is a kind of contempt for animals that masquerades as a reverence for helplessness and suffering. The idea of freedom means that you do not, at least not while Jack Knox is nearby, helpfully guide your dog through the motions of, say, herding over and over—what one trainer calls "explainy-wainy." This is rote learning. It works tolerably well on some handlers, because people have vast unconscious minds and can store complex pre-programmed behaviors. Dogs, on the other hand, have almost no unconscious minds, so they can learn only by thinking. Many children are like this until educated out of it.   25

If I tell my Airedale to sit and stay on the town green, and someone comes up and burbles, "What a pretty thing you are," he may break his stay to go for a caress. I pull him back and correct him for breaking. Now he holds his stay because I have blocked his way to movement but not because I have punished him. (A correction blocks one path as it opens another for desire to work; punishment blocks desire and opens nothing.) He holds his stay now, and—because the stay opens this possibility of work, new to a heedless young dog—he watches. If the person goes on talking, and isn't going to gush with praise, I may heel Drummer out of his stay and give him an "Okay" to make friends. Sometimes something about the person makes Drummer feel that reserve is in order. He responds to an insincere approach by sitting still, going down into himself, and thinking, "This person has no business pawing me. I'll sit very still, and he will go away." If the person doesn't take the hint from Drummer, I'll give the pup a little backup by saying, "Please don't pet him, he's working," even though he was not under any command.   26

The pup reads this, and there is a flicker of a working trust now stirring in the dog. Is the pup grateful? When the stranger leaves, does he lick my hand, full of submissive blandishments? This one doesn't. This one says nothing at all, and I say nothing much to him. This is a working trust we are developing, not a mutual-congratulation society. My backup is praise enough for him; the use he makes of my support is praise enough for me.   27

28   Listening to a dog is often praise enough. Suppose it is just after dark and we are outside. Suddenly there is a shout from the house. The pup and I both look toward the shout and then toward each other: "What do you think?" I don't so much as cock my head, because Drummer is growing up, and I want to know what he thinks. He takes a few steps toward the house, and I follow. He listens again and comprehends that it's just Holly, who at fourteen is much given to alarming cries and shouts. He shrugs at me and goes about his business. I say nothing. To praise him for this performance would make about as much sense as praising a human being for the same thing. Thus:

A. What's that?
B. I don't know. [Listens] Oh, it's just Holly.
A. What a goooooood human being!
B. Huh?

29   This is one small moment in a series of like moments that will culminate in an Airedale who on a Friday will have the discrimination and confidence required to take down a man who is attacking me with a knife and on Saturday clown and play with the children at the annual Orange Empire Dog Club Christmas party.

30   People who claim to speak for animal rights are increasingly devoted to the idea that the very keeping of a dog or a horse or a gerbil or a lion is in and of itself an offense. The more loudly they speak, the less likely they are to be in a rights relation to any given animal, because they are spending so much time in airplanes or transmitting fax announcements of the latest Sylvester Stallone anti-fur rally. In a 1988 *Harper's* forum, for example, Ingrid Newkirk, the national director of People for the Ethical Treatment of Animals, urged that domestic pets be spayed and neutered and ultimately phased out. She prefers, it appears, wolves—and wolves someplace else—to Airedales and, by a logic whose interior structure is both emotionally and intellectually forever closed to Drummer, claims thereby to be speaking for "animal rights."

31   She is wrong. I am the only one who can own up to my Airedale's inalienable rights. Whether or not I do it perfectly at any given moment is no more refutation of this point than whether I am perfectly my husband's mate at any given moment refutes the fact of marriage. Only people who know Drummer, and

whom he can know, are capable of this relationship. PETA and the Humane Society and the ASPCA and the Congress and NOW—as institutions—do have the power to affect my ability to grant rights to Drummer but are otherwise incapable of creating conditions or laws or rights that would increase his happiness. Only Drummer's owner has the power to obey him—to obey who he is and what he is capable of—deeply enough to grant him his rights and open up the possibility of happiness.

Responses to Vicki Hearne: Letters to the Editor of *Harper's*

Vicki Hearne is so wrapped up in defining happiness for Drummer, her Airedale, that she neglects to examine the most crucial argument advanced by proponents of animal rights. Despite Hearne's complaint, it is only the most extreme animal-rights activists who suggest that domestic pets be "phased out." The remainder of those concerned with the plight of animals, like myself, focus instead on what Hearne only alludes to: suffering.   1

Few would agree that training a show dog or putting a horse to work is cruel. Surely Hearne takes good care of her own dog, as do most pet owners. Countless acts of animal neglect do exist, however, and are preventable. The wanton destruction of laboratory rats to test cosmetics or the obsessive shooting of cats to study gunshot wounds *is* cruel and unusual. These blatant abuses outrage the majority of animal-rights activists and fuel their sympathies. Much as it may surprise Hearne, these activists are not losing sleep over her playing fetch with her loyal Drummer.   2

Furthermore, Hearne twists logic when she suggests that since the Humane Society destroys animals, the entire animal-rights movement is rotten to the core. This is old, tired rhetoric. The Humane Society destroys unwanted animals so that they will not suffer. Moreover, by writing that "the wild is not a suffering-free zone," Hearne infers that any pain an animal incurs in a domestic situation (home or laboratory) is somehow, in her view, legitimated. Here, she fails to isolate intention from her clever "calculus of suffering." Does Mother Nature *intend* to hurt, maim, and kill, or are these   3 effects simply part of a larger cyclical design? Clearly the answer is the latter. The wolf tears apart the frail and sick caribou not only to ensure its own survival but to maintain the balance of nature. Humankind, however, is not compelled to shock the monkey. Must we infect, injure, and inject in our quest for luscious lipstick, thicker eyelashes, more efficient handguns? Does this research ensure our survival? Although some animal experimentation does provide useful data, much of it provides only superfluous pain for animals.

4 True, the notion of animal rights per se is troubling: Who really knows what animals desire or need? Although Hearne pretends to possess the secrets of the animal world, the truth is that we will never know the true essence of animal happiness. No human is Doctor Doolittle. No one, not even the dog lovers among us, can speak to or for animals' sensibilities. But does this insurmountable communication gap permit us to act without empathy? To disregard decency and common sense? If animal suffering can be prevented, without significant detriment to whatever useful scientific knowledge animal testing purports to produce, then perhaps our own species will have progressed.

Ethan Gilsdorf
Baton Rouge, La.

1 In order for a human or an animal to have rights, says Vicki Hearne, that human or animal must be involved in a reciprocal relationship with the source of the right and must be able to have a knowledge of the reciprocal character of the relationship. Animals, she argues, can never understand rights and responsibilities to the degree necessary for them to be rights-holders. If we accept this theory, however, we must then reject rights for very young children and the mentally deranged or incompetent, because they, too, cannot have sufficiently elaborate conceptions of rights and responsibilities. Hearne is unable to admit that we might include children or incompetents among rights-holders simply because they are human, because that begs the question of whether we are morally justified in denying rights to nonhumans only because they happen to belong to a different species.

2 Hearne also argues that the animal-rights movement is built upon the misconceived premise that rights were intended to prevent animals from unnecessary suffering. In truth, the basis of animal-rights theory has less to do with the

prevention of suffering than with the recognition of the inherent value of the animal's life irrespective of whether that life is of any benefit to anyone other than the animal.

Gary L. Francione
Professor of Law and Director,
Animal Rights Law Clinic
Rutgers University
Newark

Happiness, as dog trainer Vicki Hearne defines it, comes to 1
animals in the course of being trained and "getting it right."
Thus, the draft horse is happy only when it strains against an unbearable weight, and the trained rhino is happy only when it perches on a tiny stool and mimics ballet steps. What Hearne has recognized, and then twisted, is the very real desire of some animals to please humans. Rowlf, in Richard Adams's *The Plague Dogs*, puzzles about why the whitecoats drown and revive him over and over again. He finally hits upon an explanation: He was trying to "get it right," but he just couldn't. Hearne's hellish, whitecoat logic is as follows: Animals like to please humans. Therefore, animals are happiest when they are fulfilling humans' whims, however cruel. Therefore, in order to contribute to animals' happiness, humans should force animals to fulfill human whims. If it pleases a vivisector to pour oven cleaner into a rabbit's eye, the rabbit is happiest with oven cleaner in his eye. If it pleases a deep-sea fishing guide to use a live kitten for bait, the kitten is happiest impaled on a fishing hook.

Hearne concludes by revealing the philosophical underpin- 2
nings of her theory: "Only [an animal's] owner has the power...to grant him his rights...." Jefferson, whose name Hearne blasphemously evokes in support of a theory that would sicken him, knew better. He recognized that rights are inalienable, their existence self-evident. A rabbit's right not to have oven cleaner poured in its eye is inherent. It exists whether the state recognizes it or not. If our government repeals the Thirteenth Amendment tomorrow, slavery may once again be legal, but it will still be wrong. Pouring oven cleaner in rabbits' eyes is wrong. It always has been; it always will be. One day, the law will conform to this truth.

Elizabeth L. DeCoux
Jackson, Miss.

Alexis Dorn

Animal Rights, Vegetarianism, and Saving the Planet

Alexis Dorn (born 1973) was raised near Philadelphia. At the age of fourteen she could no longer bring herself to eat meat and committed herself to vegetarianism. She plans to join the Peace Corps and then to become a high school social studies teacher. She wrote the following essay for a first-year college composition course in 1991.

1   Why should we expect anyone to think that there is something wrong with eating meat? A belief has developed in our culture, over many years, that to be truly an "All-American," one should enjoy barbecues, cold cuts, and fast food. We mark our year off with appropriate meat dishes—the fourth of July with the smokey smell of grilled hot dogs and hamburgers; the late summer with picnics, checkered blankets, and fried chicken; the age-old tradition of roasting the decorated turkey for the day of giving thanks. And don't forget the garnished ham for Christmas or New Years.

2   In festive surroundings, who stops to wonder what went into the process of acquiring the animal and preparing it to be consumed? Or when driving through a Burger King, who realizes that thousands of miles away a lush rain forest is turning into a desert because of the demand for hamburgers in America? People have remained ignorant of the horrifying consequences of their eating habits, but now is the time for everyone to become more aware. Otherwise the earth will no longer be able to handle everything that Americans continue to dish out.

3   Becoming aware may be a monumental task for the American public because certainly the beef industry does not advertise the destruction that occurs when animals are bred and slaughtered. Instead, the industry concentrates on spending its time and cash (more than $45 million a year) to announce that for McDonald's, "Billions are served" and that "BEEF...It's what's for dinner," or that beef is "Real food for real people." (Apparently the people who care about the animals and the earth are somehow not real.) Never will it be advertised that 55 square feet of rain forest are being destroyed for each hamburger that is being enjoyed. And never will it be publicly announced that because of the destruction of the Amazon for cattle grazing, thousands of

species are becoming extinct. We must find information like this ourselves, in books such as the *Rain Forest Book* and *Diet for a New America*, written by John Robbins, the vegetarian king who rejected his position at the top of the lucrative Baskin-Robbins business.

Just as the meat-related industries will not admit to the 4 harm being done to supply Americans with meat, people in general will not admit that they alone can make a positive change. But everyone must realize that by refusing to purchase any meat, we can dramatically help preserve the natural balance of the entire earth. People now must become sensitive to all of the outcomes of every action every day. They must see animal rights in direct relation to humans, to the balance of the ecosystems, and to the preservation of not only the animals being slaughtered but also thousands of various species of life. As a corollary of animal rights, vegetarianism questions not just the morality of medical research or even the frivolousness of fur coats on humans; it underscores how the negative energy that we are putting into the slaughtering of innocent animals is killing us too. Now, with new compassion, we all must save the earth and ourselves by sparing the animals from a death they do not deserve.

As for "real people" and what they eat: remember that Tho- 5 reau, Einstein, and Gandhi were all vegetarians; all are among the most respected thinkers in history. Vice President Al Gore also knows the consequences of meat eating; he has written about them in his book *Earth In The Balance*. Gore speaks about how the rain forest is being burned to create fast pasture for fast-food beef: "More than one Tennessee's worth of rain forest [is] being slashed and burned each year." Those who listen to Gore's words, or read his writings, are aware of the fact that thousands of species are about to perish because of the slashing and burning.

What exactly can be done? Is it feasible for our govern- 6 ment to discourage America's lucrative beef industry in order for animals to survive? Must we continue to allow this destruction to occur, even though these species are dying out one thousand times faster now than at any time in the past 65 million years? We are starting to worry about letting the plants that could hold cures for our worst diseases just slip away. We are becoming angry that the rain forests are turning into deserts. We are feeling guilty that because of our desire to satisfy our superficial hunger for wealth and convenience, we are slaughtering countless animals and endangering the future of all life on earth.

7   If the destruction in the Amazon is too far away for the
people of the United States to become compassionate, think
about the destruction that is occurring in our own country.
From *Diet for a New America*, we learn that the cattle raised in
the United States use up in one way or another more than
50% of the precious water resources of our nation—a circumstance that could cause all of the water left over from the ice
age to vanish in less than 30 years. John Robbins explains
that the production of cattle is polluting the environment as
well as taking from it: "The livestock of the United States produce twenty times as much excrement as the entire human
population of the country." Those livestock also produce 12%
of the harmful methane gas that is released into the atmosphere, methane gas that helps contribute to global warming.

8   Supporters of the beef industry will say, "Well, kill them
and eat them and there won't be that problem!" But it is the
continuing cycle of destruction that is the problem. Without
human intervention, cows would be roaming in herds in their
natural balance with the earth. Instead, they are placed in
unnatural, man-made environments where they are kept
immobile and restricted from freedom. The cost of satisfying
our unnecessary desires is the lives of countless innocent animals. If humans would be humane enough to let the animals
live, rather than gruesomely to kill and barbarically eat them,
the earth could restore its peace and perhaps a healthy future
would not be such an impossible feat.

9   Please realize that every purchase of meat contributes to
the cycle of destruction, and that only by stopping the consumption of animals can the earth have a chance for balance
again. Know that it is the casual life-style of the American
humans that has knocked the ecosystem of the entire world
out of whack. And believe that as long as meat is consumed,
tranquility will never be restored. Until the time that respect
is given to the earth, the environment and all its critters, creatures, plants and animals are struggling for survival.

Foundation for Biomedical Research

It's the Animals You Don't See
That Really Helped

This ad was developed by the Foundation for Biomedical Research, an organization whose self-described aim is articulated in the fine print on the ad. The copy at the bottom reads, "Recently a surgical technique perfected on animals was used to remove a malignant tumor from a little girl's brain. We lost some lab animals. But look what we saved." The ad appeared in many publications from 1990 to 1992.

Garry B. Trudeau
Doonesbury

The following excerpts from Garry B. Trudeau's "Doonesbury" appeared around Christmas 1989. For more of his work, and more on Trudeau, see pages 94, 95, and 161.

Doonesbury   BY GARRY TRUDEAU

Doonesbury   BY GARRY TRUDEAU

Doonesbury   BY GARRY TRUDEAU

HOW SHOULD WE FIGHT AIDS?

Hanna Rosin

The Homecoming

*Hanna Rosin published the following account of AIDS in the
African American community in the June 5, 1995, issue of* The
New Republic, *a middle-of-the-road magazine of political and
cultural affairs. (The essay reprinted after this one, by Ann
Louise Bardach, was in the same issue.)*

A middle-aged black man named Otis is about to reveal his   1
most intimate secret to a perfect stranger. He checks to make
sure nobody's lurking around the corner (lst and M, southeast
Washington, D.C., a block full of prostitutes and addicts). He
hears a dealer hawking "face" (heroin), and waits, tugging
anxiously at his faded blue sweatshirt, until the man skulks
away. Then he leans over to this stranger, an outreach worker
from the local AIDS clinic, and whispers that he has, "Well,
you know, the disease."

Otis says he found out he was HIV-positive in 1986,   2
during a wave of infections that alerted AIDS researchers
they had been wrong about the virus. At first, they predicted
it would shift away from white gay men to terrorize the broad
population, mutating into an equal-opportunity killer. Instead,
it found people like Otis—poor, addicted and black. Blacks,
12 percent of the population, account for one-third of all
AIDS cases. Three out of five new AIDS victims now are
black, up from one in five in 1986. Black women are now fifteen times more likely to have AIDS than white women, and
their children, eighteen times more likely. By now, AIDS
should be familiar, yet Otis can't bring himself to mention it
by name.

Otis's story helps explain how HIV has been able to make   3
such inroads in poor black America. He found out he was
positive by a fluke. When he was in prison on possession
charges, nurses from the National Institutes of Health offered
$15 to anyone who would agree to be tested, and Otis volun-

teered because he needed the money. (It took the nurse fifteen tries to find a live vein.) He's not sure where he got the virus—either from his girlfriend, whose husband was a junkie (now dead), or from his cousin, who once stole his works and lent them to a "small, skinny guy who had that look, you know, like he was a homo."

4   Each time Otis tells the truth, he becomes a pariah. He says his wife left him when people found out he was positive and started calling her a "diseased bitch." His 14-year-old niece, visiting from Georgia with her son, "freaked when she found out, started screaming, 'He's been using the same bathroom, he touched my baby.'" When he confided in his minister, the man pointed at him the next day in church and preached about the sins of bad living. Otis won't go to an AIDS clinic, even for a prescription: "Nope. No way in hell. That's, you know...a homo place, and your mama or your cousin or anybody could see you go in and then you're branded for life." What about medicine? "Somebody told me it makes your hair fall out," he says defensively. Only once does Otis let down his defenses, when he talks about the night he went to a support group at a local church. Most of the people were in advanced stages, looked sickly and could barely move, and "it tore me down. I thought, 'This is my future.'"

5   Wayne Greaves has been chief of Howard University's AIDS clinic since before it existed, when nine patients with a mystery disease were crammed into a corner of the hospital. A wiry, wound-up man, he is as apt to lash out at his no-show patients as at "bigots" at the NIH. Three years ago he co-authored a study that is perhaps the best clue to the virus's surge among blacks, although it remains buried in the *Journal of AIDS*. Greaves and two colleagues reviewed autopsy reports of seventy HIV-positive inner-city patients. What they found surprised even Greaves: about half had been diagnosed *after death*, even though most showed obvious symptoms of AIDS-related diseases. The shame around AIDS in black America makes prevention almost impossible and treatment widely refused, and it keeps infection on an increasingly upward curve. "There are some people who would rather not know," Greaves says angrily. "A lot, actually, would rather not know."

6   One reason they'd rather not know is the uneasiness in the community about open homosexuality, still closely associated with the disease. "There's an enormous hidden population," says Frank Oldham, former director of Washington's Agency for HIV/AIDS, "a huge number of bisexual men who don't

identify as gay. It's fascinating: they go to church, to the park with their families, then at night you'll see them cruising the gay bars." Many see nothing wrong with this way of living. "Open homosexuality is viewed as something imposed on us by the gay white culture," explains Alonzo Fair, from a group called URBAN, which has widely polled Washington's blacks about AIDS. "The black community has always accepted homosexuality. There is always a gay person in church or who lives down the street or a cousin, and that's perfectly fine. It's only when that person defines himself as gay, you know, adopts the gay white culture, like doing the rainbow flag thing, that the community reacts negatively. For a black man, family comes first."

This devotion to family can end up destroying it. Men who   7
do risky things but don't consider themselves at risk are the virus's welcome mat into the black home. Black men are twice as likely as white men to be bisexual, according to a recent study of 65,000 HIV-positive men published in *American Journal of Public Health*. Black drug users, who sometimes double as male prostitutes, are four times as likely. This makes black America vulnerable to the kind of heterosexual break-out that white America has so far avoided and that is the norm in other parts of the world. Half the black bisexual men in the study were married when they died. It's likely their wives didn't know: in a California AIDS study, only one-fifth of the black women responding were aware that their partners were bisexual. As a result, AIDS is now the leading killer of young black women.

Race itself does not affect one's chances of contracting   8
HIV, as in, say, sickle-cell anemia. But inner-city ills do. For example, one-quarter of all black men in their 20s, and 15 percent of adult males, rotate through prison. Among inmates, unprotected anal sex is common. Prison is thus a place where the virus can spread to men who may have sex with men while in jail and with women when they get out. In 1990, doctors at Riker's Island conducted what is called a blind seroprevalence test. They took the name tags off blood samples used in mandatory syphilis tests and checked them for HIV. A quarter of both male and female samples tested positive, a result since replicated in other big city prisons. A study of long-term inmates in the Florida jail system found that 20 percent had contracted HIV while in prison. The confessionals in *Angoli*, the best of the prison magazines, tell all. One Louisiana inmate who tested positive in 1989 admitted that he and his cellmate did "every unsafe thing you could do."

Another, who knew he was positive yet still had sex with other inmates, mused, "Maybe I shouldn't do it no more . . . but if the guy is willing to go for it. . . . We all have to die sooner or later."

9   At the same time, suspicion and mistrust of mainstream medical institutions make it harder to mount an effective, communal response. It's easy to see this phenomenon at work in east Washington, D.C., not far from Otis's block, at a place called Paradise Manor. Here, identical new swing sets perch on every trimmed lawn, and each tidy brick housing complex bears a name like Harmony, Freedom or Justice. Occupying four units of Miracle is the Abundant Life Clinic, a center for alternative therapies specializing in AIDS and run by Dr. Abdul Alim Muhammed, health minister for the Nation of Islam. Walk inside and the waiting room exudes none of the menacing air you find at Nation rallies; to the background accompaniment of a Whitney Houston tape, the staff chats flirtatiously, the women tossing back their brightly patterned veils. If not for the blown-up portrait of Louis Farrakhan and the Lyndon LaRouche pamphlets ("WHO OWNS HENRY KISS-INGER?"), you might mistake this for any other AIDS clinic.

10   Muhammed sweeps into the room, tall and striking in his crisp white lab coat and mint-striped shirt, and greets me cheerfully. He has reason to be upbeat. Mayor Marion Barry has appointed him co-director of the AIDS transition team, elevating him to unofficial AIDS czar for the black commu-nity in Washington, D.C. Add that to an award in 1993 from then-Mayor Sharon Pratt Kelly and $500,000 in federal grants over the last two years, and he's the most prominent black anti-AIDS figure in the capital. We move into his office and he takes a seat behind his glass-topped desk. In this sterile, pleasant room, it's hard to picture him as he was a year ago, fulminating to a Baltimore crowd about AIDS being "the per-fect genocidal weapon" manufactured by the white govern-ment against black people, issuing death threats to Baltimore Mayor Kurt Schmoke.

11   Muhammed's latest initiative is convincing Mayor Barry to divert a $2 million grant from the city's largest AIDS clinic, run by, as he sees it, white homosexuals, to his own. With that money, he'll be closer to achieving his mission to "save the world." This mission includes widespread mandatory testing, followed by treatment with his miracle drug, Kemron. The drug was discovered by Joseph Cummins, a white veterinarian in Amarillo, Texas, the only white man

whose photo will ever grace the walls of the Abundant Life Clinic. In 1989, Cummins trekked to the Kenyan Medical Research Institute with his discovery, a protein-like drug called alpha interferon, which is used to treat a rare form of leukemia. There, doctors fed their patients wafers laced with low doses of the drug. After three months of a study with no control group, the doctors breathlessly announced a miracle. Ninety-nine of 101 patients bounded back to health, they claimed. "Fifty AIDS victims have already been cured!" cheered Kenyan President Daniel Arap Moi. On the other side of the world, his euphoria provided an occasion for New York's *Amsterdam News* to blast the "racist white press" for "cabalistically ignoring this amazing discovery."

It was hardly ignored. In 1991, the World Health Org-   12
anization conducted a study of 150 patients in Zambia and concluded that Kemron produced no benefits. In an effort to settle the question, the National Institutes of Health in 1992 reviewed thirteen clinical trials from around the world. Their study concluded that alpha interferon "is not recommended for persons of HIV infection" and that patients using it should immediately switch to other drugs.

The news failed to squelch interest in Kemron. In March   13
1992, Farrakhan announced that the Abundant Life Clinic would market the drug aggressively in the United States. Ads ran every week in *The Final Call*, the group's paper, and the marketing campaign proved a smashing success. Thousands of patients, by the NIH's estimate, most of whom were poor and without insurance, shelled out money for the miracle drug. And at a premium: the Nation sells Kemron for $150 to $250 for a one-month supply, depending on the brand, and charges a $1,000 initiation fee. Other vendors price the drug at $65 for a thirty-day supply. It's clearly a profitable business.

At its worst, the story of Kemron is about the Nation's   14
shameless manipulation of scared proselytes. There is also, however, a less scandalous, if ultimately more disturbing point here: so widespread are fears of government institutions and white doctors among African Americans, that they will take any alternative over conventional medical treatment.

One study attempted to quantify these fears. In 1990,   15
researchers from the Southern Christian Leadership Conference (SCLC) handed out surveys to 1,000 black churchgoers in five cities: Atlanta, Charlotte, Detroit, Kansas City and Tuscaloosa. More than one-third agreed that AIDS was a form of genocide against blacks; another third were unsure. And more

than a third believed HIV was produced in a germ-warfare lab, a theory shared by 40 percent of black college students enrolled in Washington, D.C.

16   Consider these musings on the origin of the virus, solicited from passersby in one random inner-city block in Albany one afternoon last December. They are set to a Public Enemy soundtrack in *HIV and Genocide: Responding to African American Community Concerns,* a New York State Health Department training video: "It came from Vietnam. It started with chemical warfare, and then the government put it out into the population." "It was an experiment, OK. It was an experiment and then someone spread it on one group of people, onto one nationality. I'm not saying I'm prejudiced because I'm not. But that's my opinion, and everyone has a right to an opinion." "I don't know if it was the government or some secret organization outside the government but I believe the government had a hand into it or the secret organization had a hand into it." "I think first it was some kind of laboratory experiment. Then they perpetrated it on people of color in Africa and Haiti and places that the powers that we think of as throwaway people. Now people like me—and I don't consider myself a throwaway person—now I have the virus."

17   "If it looks like a duck, and walks like a duck, well then?" says Ron Simmons, director of Us Helping Us: People Into Living, the only group in Washington, D.C., founded by gay black men to support their own. Bundled in a black hooded sweatshirt, surrounded by photos of black men in zebra-print thongs and a stern portrait of Malcolm X, he puts his feet up on his desk and expounds on the origin of the HIV virus. "My thinking is they're killing black and brown folks, and the reason they gave it to white folks first is because it was too soon after the Atlanta child murders in '78, and there would have been riots."

18   Under the Centers for Disease Control and Prevention's new community initiative, Simmons's group was recently awarded a $50,000 federal grant. It will use the money to expand an already-thriving network of support groups for black men through which group leaders promote a philosophy of holistic healing: herbs, vitamins, Chinese teas, breathing exercises and absolutely no AZT, or any other of the standard chemical drugs. Simmons says he never tells members not to take AZT; he just guides them toward an "informed decision": "One thing about corporate medicine is they find a way to make money off you until you're in your grave," he jeers, holding up a copy of his bible, *Poison by Pre-*

scription: The AZT Story. "Black folks have what I call a healthy paranoia. After all, they did it once, so they can do it again."

"They" is the U.S. government—specifically, the Public 19
Health Service. What they did was the Tuskegee Syphilis Study, a forty-year experiment on untreated syphilis in 400 black sharecroppers in Alabama which followed them to "end point," or death. Researchers carried on with the experiment until 1972, twenty years after penicillin became the standard treatment for the disease, and could have been used to cure the men under study.

Long considered this country's worst large-scale violation 20
of medical ethics, Tuskegee has become the parable by which many blacks understand their relationship to public health services. From Los Angeles to Atlanta, groups such as Us Helping Us preach the virtues of healthy paranoia. "Tuskegee has taken on a life of its own as a disaster myth," says Stephen Thomas, a professor at Emory University who conducted the SCLC conspiracy study and has since polled 6,000 blacks around the country. "It has transcended being a historical event and turned into an urban legend, a personification of medical abuses and racism."

The result has been a lot of refused treatment. Dr. Joe Tim- 21
pone, director of D.C. General Hospital's AIDS Unit, estimates that about one-fifth of his 800 black patients will not take AZT. It's hard enough, he complains, to persuade people with no money for bus fare or a babysitter, who miss an average of half their appointments, to stick to a regimen of bimonthly visits and fifteen pills a day. Add in chronic suspicion and his job becomes "almost impossible." A study by the AIDS Research Consortium in Atlanta found that 80 percent of women who should have been taking AZT or other antiretroviral drugs weren't. "If an AIDS vaccine came out tomorrow," warns Thomas, "a significant number of blacks would not take it."

Not even if it were free. Wayne Greaves from Howard Uni- 22
versity spends his days convincing people to enroll in clinical trials, studies of experimental medicine, where patients receive free care and medication. Most of his efforts are fruitless. "Even here, where we are mostly black, they won't come near us. We go out and recruit, and they say, 'Yeah, yeah, the money's coming from the NIH, right, so who are you trying to kid?'" Mary Lynn, the outreach worker for the program, who hikes around Washington seeing hundreds of people a week, says that around 70 percent ask about Tuskegee. "They're

completely convinced they'll be used as guinea pigs for some
evil agenda."

23   In adults, AZT only slows HIV's progression; it doesn't cure
anyone. But in the case of babies born HIV-positive, the drug
actually can be a cure. In February 1994, a joint French-
American study found that giving AZT to a pregnant woman
and her infant child dramatically reduces the baby's chances
of contracting the virus from 25.5 percent to 8.3 percent—"by
far the most important and helpful news to come out of the
epidemic," says Elaine Abrams, director of Harlem Hospital's
AIDS Pediatric Clinic. But the news would be better if women
who heard it believed it. "They just say no," says Abrams,
almost all of whose 200 patients are black. "Plenty of women
refuse to get tested, to have their infants tested or to take
medicine. Maybe they're afraid, or they see a healthy-looking
baby in their arms and it all doesn't make sense." In a recent
focus group on maternal transmission of HIV, conducted by
the New York State Health Department, two groups of pregnant women split evenly by race, with black mothers-to-be
refusing to "take that poison," as one put it.

24   Black clergy, the community's natural leaders, only feed the
paranoia. When a clean-needles program was first proposed
in New York City in 1989, Calvin O. Butts of the Abyssinian
Baptist Church decreed he was "not in favor of cooperating
with the devil," meaning those who might perpetuate addiction. Leading the national charge was Reverend Graylan Ellis-
Hagler, who now presides over the Plymouth Congregational
Church in Washington. "First, the white establishment pushes
drugs in to the community," he told the *Atlantic* in 1993. "They
cripple the community politically and economically with the
drugs. They send the males to jail. Then someone hands us
needles to maintain the dependency."

25   Religious opposition killed needle-exchange programs in
every city except New York, which squeezed through a trial
program in 1991. The result is the only unqualified success
story in the prevention war. In a city where half of intravenous drug users test positive, the program cut infection rates
by 50 to 75 percent, according to a study of its 2,500 participants. Now, Ellis-Hagler is willing to relent, he says, "because
there aren't strong enough feelings from the community to
create a hysteria," although he still finds the program "a pitiful last resort, and racist." It may be too late. By now, momentum has died down. Washington, for example, has only

enough money for a tiny pilot program inconveniently located in a downtown federal building.

The vacuum has been filled by a kind of generic sermonizing, drained of any urgency. Ten years ago, ministers routinely refused to preside over funerals of people who died of AIDS, and funeral homes refused to bury them. That kind of disgust has mostly been replaced by evasive homilies, expressed by a scattered few, such as Washington's Reverend Pervis "Fireball" McKenna, who takes pride in insisting, "I preach against all sin and that's one of them. I'm with the Bible on sin, and all of it is against God, period, whether it be homosexuals or whatever." In milder forms, ministers presiding over funerals will say "this person was a sinner, but he renounced that world at the end of his life," or they won't mention how the person died.   26

A typical example is the Metropolitan Baptist Church, a favorite of Washington, D.C.'s, black gay community. On a recent Sunday, the pews were packed with men in crisp wool suits and women in white gloves with straightened hair, their well-behaved children in tow. The choir, 100 strong, seemed to be the refuge for many of the single, and some obviously gay men. The imposing Reverend H. Beecher Hicks Jr., draped in purple velvet vestments, presided. In his trembling baritone, he admonished his flock of "black bourgeoisie" to remember their roots, to exercise compassion outside the church walls.   27

The church has had an AIDS ministry for two years and its director has been instructed never to use the word "gay," says a former adviser. Mostly it educates congregation members that it's OK to shake hands with the HIV-positive, to "love the sinner but not the sin," says Hicks. Its mission is the same as the dozens of other help ministries run by the church. "I don't make a lot out of it," explains Hicks. "It's like Alcoholics Anonymous, Narcotics Anonymous, like people who are depressed or divorced. We find a way to meet everyone's personal needs, and don't lift one up over the other."   28

As of January, some 84,568 young African Americans had died of AIDS.   29

Ann Louise Bardach
The White Cloud

Ann Louise Bardach is a writer who contributes to Vanity Fair *and other magazines that examine contemporary culture. The following essay appeared in* The New Republic *in June 1995, in the same issue as the previous item by Hanna Rosin.*

1   Freddie Rodriguez is discouraged. He has just come from his afternoon's activity of trying to stop men from having unprotected sex in Miami's Alice Wainwright Park, a popular gay cruising spot. Rodriguez, 29, is a slim, handsome Cuban-American with a pale, worried face who works for Health Crisis Network. "I take a bag of condoms to the park with me and I try talking to people before they duck in the bushes and have sex," he explains. "I tell them how dangerous it is. Sometimes I beg them to use a condom. Sometimes they listen to me. Today, no one was interested." Most of the men, he says, are Latinos and range in age from 16 to 60. Many are married and would never describe themselves as gay. "Discrimination is not really the issue here. Most Latinos do not identify themselves as gay, so they're not discriminated against," he says, his voice drifting off. "Ours is a culture of denial."

2   To understand why the second wave of AIDS is hitting Latinos particularly hard, one would do well to start in Miami. Once a mecca for retirees, South Beach today is a frenzy of dance and sex clubs, for hetero- and homosexual alike. "We have the highest rate of heterosexual transmission in the country, the second-highest number of babies born with AIDS and we are number one nationwide for teen HIV cases," says Randi Jenson, reeling off a litany that clearly exhausts him. Jenson supervises the Miami Beach HIV/AIDS Project and sits on the board of the Gay, Lesbian and Bisexual Community Center. "And we have the highest rate of bisexuality in the country." When I ask how he knows this, he says, "Trust me on this one, *we know....* The numbers to watch for in the future will be Hispanic women—the wives and girlfriends."

3   Already, AIDS is the leading cause of death in Miami and Fort Lauderdale for women ages 25 to 44, four times greater than the national average. According to the Centers for Disease Control and Prevention (CDC), AIDS cases among Hispanics have been steadily rising. But any foray into the Latino subculture shows that the numbers do not tell the whole

story, and may not even tell half. CDC literature notes that "it is believed that AIDS-related cases and deaths for Latinos are understated by at least 30 percent. Many Hispanics do not and cannot access HIV testing and health care." Abetted by widespread shame about homosexuality, a fear of governmental and medical institutions (particularly among undocumented immigrants) and cultural denial as deep as Havana Harbor, AIDS is moving silently and insistently through Hispanic America. It is the stealth virus.

"No one knows how many Latino HIV cases are out there," Damian Pardo, an affable Cuban-American, who is president of the board of Health Crisis Network, tells me over lunch in Coral Gables. "All we know is that the numbers are not accurate—that the actual cases are far higher. Everyone in the community lies about HIV." Everyone, according to Pardo, means the families, the lovers, the priests, the doctors and the patients. "The Hispanic community in South Florida is far more affluent than blacks. More often than not, people see their own family doctor who simply signs a falsified death certificate. It's a conspiracy of silence and everyone is complicitous."   4

Freddie Rodriguez—smart, affluent, urbane—didn't learn that Luis, his Nicaraguan lover, was HIV-positive until it was too late to do anything about it. "He was my first boyfriend. He would get sick at times but he refused to take a blood test. He said that it was impossible for him to be HIV-positive. I believed him. One day, he disappeared. Didn't come home, didn't go to work—just disappeared." Frantic, Rodriguez called the police and started phoning hospitals. Finally, Luis turned up at Jackson Memorial Hospital. He had been discovered unconscious and rushed to intensive care. When Rodriguez arrived at the hospital, he learned that his lover was in the AIDS wing. Even then, Luis insisted it was a mistake. Two weeks later, he was dead. "I had to tell Luis's family that he was gay," Rodriguez says, "that I was his boyfriend and that he had died of AIDS. They knew nothing. He lived a completely secret life."   5

Although Rodriguez was enraged by his lover's cowardice, he understood his dilemma all too well. He remembered how hard it was to tell his own family. "When I was 22, I finally told my parents that I was gay. My mother screamed and ran out of the room. My father raised his hands in front of his eyes and told me, 'Freddie do you see what's in front of me? It's a big, white cloud. I do not hear anything, see anything and I cannot remember anything because it is all in this big   6 white cloud.' And then he left the room." One of Rodriguez's later boyfriends, this one Peruvian, was also HIV-positive, but far more duplicitous. "He flat out lied to me when I asked him. He knew, but he only told me after we broke up, *after* we had unsafe sex," says Rodriguez, who remains HIV-negative. "Part of the *machismo* ethic," Rodriguez explains, "is not wearing a condom."

7   Miami's Body Positive, which provides psychological and non-clinical services to AIDS patients, is housed in a pink concrete bubble off Miami's Biscayne Boulevard. The building and much of its funding are provided by founder Doris Feinberg, who lost both her sons to AIDS during the late 1980s. The gay Cuban-American star of MTV's "The Real World," Pedro Zamora, worked here for the last five years of his life and started its P.O.P. program—Peer Outreach for Persons Who Are Positive. Ernie Lopez, a 26-year-old Nicaraguan who has been Body Positive's director for the last five years, estimates that 40 percent of the center's clients are Latino, in a Miami population that is 70 percent Hispanic. On the day I visit, I see mostly black men at the facility. Lopez warns me not to be fooled. "The Latino numbers are as high as the blacks, but they are not registered," he says. "Latinos want anonymity. They come in very late—when they are desperate and their disease is very progressed. Often it's too late to help them."

8   "*Soy completo,*" is what they often say in Cuba, meaning, "I'm a total human being." It is the preferred euphemism for bisexuality and in the *machista* politics of Latino culture, bisexuality is a huge step up from being gay. It is this cultural construct that prevents many Latin men from acknowledging that they could be vulnerable to HIV, because it is this cultural construct that tells them they are not gay. Why worry about AIDS if only gay men get AIDS? "To be bisexual is a code," says Ernesto Pujol, a pioneer in Latino AIDS education. "It means, 'I sleep with men but I still have power.' I think there is a legitimate group of bisexuals, but for many bisexuality is a codified and covered homosexuality." Self-definitions can get even more complex. "I'm not gay," a well-known intellectual told me in Havana last year. "How could I be gay? My boyfriend is married and has a family."

9   Without putting too fine a point on it, what defines a gay man in some segments of the Latino world is whether he's on the top or the bottom during intercourse. "The salient property of the *maricon*," my Cuban friend adds, "is his passivity. If you're a 'top,'—*el bugaron*—you're not a faggot." Moreover, there are also many heterosexual Latino men who do not

regard sex with another man as a homosexual act. "A lot of heterosexual Latinos—say, after a few drinks—will fuck a transvestite as a surrogate woman," says Pujol, "and that is culturally acceptable—absolutely acceptable." Hence the potential for HIV transmission is far greater than in the mainstream Anglo world.

According to Pujol, "only Latinos in the States are inter- 10 ested in other gay men. They have borrowed the American liberated gay model. In Latin America, the hunt is for 'straight' men. Look at the transvestites on Cristina's (the Spanish-language equivalent of "Oprah") talk show. Their boyfriends are always some macho hunk from the *bodega*." Chino, a Cuban gay now living in Montreal, typifies the cultural divide. "I don't understand it here," he says scornfully. "It's like girls going out with girls."

"If you come out," says Jorge B., a Cuban artist in Miami 11 Beach, "you lose your sex appeal to 'straight' men" (straight in this context meaning married men who have sex with other men). The Hispanic preference for "straight men" is so popular that bathhouses such as Club Bodycenter in Coral Gables are said to cater to a clientele of older married men who often pick up young lovers after work before joining their families for dinner. Some men will not risk going to a gay bar, says Freddie Rodriguez. "They go to public restrooms where they can't be identified." While many gay Hispanics do eventually "come out," they do so at a huge price—a shattering loss of esteem within their family and community. "The priest who did Mass at my grandfather's funeral denied communion to me and my brother," recalls Pardo. "He knew from my mother's confession that we were gay."

Latino attitudes here are, of course, largely imported, their 12 cultural fingerprints lifted straight out of Havana, Lima or Guatemala City. Consider Chiapas, Mexico, where gay men were routinely arrested throughout the 1980s; many of their bodies were later found dumped in a mass grave. Or Ecuador, where it is against the law to be a homosexual, and effeminate behavior or dress can be grounds for arrest. Or Peru, where the Shining Path has targeted gays for assassination. Or Colombia, where death squads do the same, characteristically mutilating their victims' genitals.

While Latino hostility to homosexuals in the United States 13 tends to be less dramatic, it can also be virulent, particularly when cradled in reactionary politics. In Miami, right-wing Spanish-language stations daily blast their enemies as "communists, traitors and Castro puppets." But the epithet reserved for the most despised is "homosexual" or *"maricon."* When Nelson Mandela visited Miami in 1990, he was denounced daily as a *"marijuanero maricon"*—a pot-smoking faggot—for having supported Fidel Castro.

14   On the other side of the country, AIDS Project Los Angeles is the second-largest health provider for AIDS patients in the United States (after Gay Men's Health Crisis in New York). It's a sparkling facility with a food bank, a dental program and all manner of support services. Housed in the David Geffen Building at the corner of Fountain and Vine, it is well-provided for by a generous Hollywood community. Currently, AIDS Project Los Angeles attends to the needs of more than 4,500 clients, 60 percent of whom are gay men. Roughly one-fourth of the total are Latinos, and the majority of those are Mexican. Thirty-two-year-old Troy Fernandez is one of the project's senior aides on public policy. Born in Yonkers and of Puerto Rican descent, Fernandez is a caramel-colored black man with long dreadlocks streaming down his back. Dressed in crisp white jeans, he's as slim and elegant as a fountain pen. He's also HIV-positive—part of the second wave.

15   Although Fernandez "did the downtown dance scene and Fire Island," in his 20s, he didn't go to the bathhouses, and he was never on the front line of the party scene. Even when the political equation of the gay revolution—"the more promiscuous, the more liberated"—still had currency, Fernandez was warier than his peers. By 1981, friends of his had started to die of the mysterious illness then known as the gay plague. Fernandez got himself checked out as soon as HIV testing became available, and came up negative year after year while he continued to practice safe sex. Then he moved to Los Angeles and met Rodrigo.

16   Rodrigo was a well-educated Mexican-American, a high-level insurance executive, a Republican conservative and "completely closeted." Among Rodrigo's tightly knit family, only one of his brothers—also gay—knew his secret. When Fernandez asked his partner if he was HIV-positive, he said no. He'd never been tested, but he knew he wasn't. He also insisted he was monogamous. "It's all about what risks you are willing to take," says Fernandez slowly. "I understand why people stop practicing safe sex. One is always renegotiating the risk factors at some level. You see, you want to believe that your lover is telling you the truth."

17   In 1990, Rodrigo got sick. By then Fernandez had become suspicious, and pressed his partner to be tested. "I told him

he had to do it for my sake," he says, "if nothing else." When Rodrigo learned he was positive "it was a double whammy," says Fernandez. "He had to admit that he was sick and dying and worse—he had to admit that he was gay." Within the year, Fernandez learned that he, too, had the virus. Remembering, he lets loose a long sigh. "I don't have an answer for why I took a chance. I knew better, but it only takes one time." Fernandez surmises on the basis of personal anecdotal experience that as many as "90 percent [of gay] Latinos are closeted. Many may have self-identified but tell no one else." He bases his estimate on the number of married men who come into AIDS Project Los Angeles. "They always say they need the information for their brother or brother-in-law."

Rarely visible in the statistics are the wives and girlfriends 18 of these men—the group that experts predict will soar to the top of the AIDS charts by the end of the decade. Currently, blacks and Latinas make up 77 percent of all AIDS cases among women; the number of Latina cases is seven times higher than that of Anglo women. Researchers have long known that the "receptive partner," is at greater risk of contracting not only HIV but all sexually transmitted diseases. For reasons generally unknown, women tend to get sicker sooner and die faster. Moreover, for many Latinas striving to be good Catholic wives in a culture where church and family are the co-pillars of the community, contracting HIV is an unfathomable betrayal and an irredeemable disgrace.

Ernesto Pujol remembers a Salvadoran housewife in her 19 mid-50s, then living in Brooklyn. "She had just tested positive. She was crying. She was so bitter—so angry at her husband and the waste of her life. She had bought the whole Latina martyrdom of being the faithful wife." The husband was a drunk who had battered her, belittled her, and who would finally kill her. Still, she maintained that her husband had been infected by female prostitutes—and never looked at the evidence that he had had sex with men. "None of the women I worked with ever admitted that their spouses were gay or bisexual," says Pujol. "They would say, 'He drinks, you know.' They would rather blame prostitutes than consider the culturally unacceptable possibility of other men."

Wanda Santiago, 36, has lived much of her life as a pariah. 20 A Puerto Rican lesbian, born and raised in Brooklyn, Santiago learned in 1989 that she was HIV-positive. At 13, she started doing drugs when her family moved to a rough neighborhood in Williamsburg. At 16, she was pregnant and married and drinking. After three years, her husband left. "I knew I was gay since I was 8," she says, "but I thought getting married would cure me." In 1978, Santiago came out and turned the care of her young son over to her mother.

21   Santiago suspects she contracted HIV during her romance with an Ecuadoran woman who was stationed with the Navy in Virginia. "I was crazy about her," says Santiago, who lived with the woman for three years. "Every now and then, she would bring a man to our bed," says Santiago. "It could have been one of them, or maybe I got it from a needle." A few years after her relationship hit the skids, Santiago sobered up for good, but by then she was feeling tired all the time. "For a week after I tested positive, I refused to believe it," she says. "Total denial."

22   Until 1991, Santiago worked for the Health & Rehabilitation Service screening Latinas with sexually transmitted diseases for HIV. "A lot of them refused to be tested," she says. "If they did test positive, they wouldn't believe it. The fear overwhelmed them. They would say, 'Don't talk about it,' 'I don't have it' and 'Don't tell my husband.' Many were in denial about their husbands screwing around. They thought they would get blamed for getting the disease. It's much worse in Hispanic culture than it is for whites or blacks because Hispanics won't even talk about it. A lot of the women were afraid to use condoms because they would get beat up by their husbands. See, if you're infected by a man, you're a whore. If you're infected by drugs, then you deserve it. But it's OK for a man to have HIV because it's OK for a man to whore around."

23   Mary Lou Duran has been working with the community in East Los Angeles for twenty-one years, the last three and a half of them as a case manager for the HIV patients at Altamed Services. Her clients are women: primarily Mexican-American or Central American refugees, both legal and undocumented, ranging in age from 17 to 56, and including "several grandmothers." A few of the older women may have gotten the virus from blood transfusions during surgery in Mexico, before the availability of HIV testing. But the overwhelming majority were infected by spouses or lovers. "One woman, from Guatemala, died in October," Duran says. "She had a very aggressive virus and died in less than three and a half years. She got it from a boyfriend and left a child behind. I feel the majority of the women I see are innocent victims— wives and girlfriends who have no idea what is going on." Duran then relates a more personal experience: "In my own

family, there have been three deaths—three nephews who were gay. But my family says, 'No one has died of AIDS.' They call it cancer. We can't comfort each other because we can't discuss it. 'They weren't gay,' they say, and 'They didn't have AIDS.'"

By coincidence, one of Duran's ailing nephews ran into her 24 at a clinic where she was working. "He was shocked to see me," she remembers. "He was sick—very progressed by the time he came in for help." They chatted briefly, awkwardly. It was her only personal contact with the tragedy in her family. "I have always been a community worker and my family has come to me when they have a need of sorts, but never while I do this work. They have never asked for my help. They have no interest or curiosity in my work. They never ask any questions. Nothing is ever said. The entire community is in denial. They just don't believe it is happening. They think that AIDS is about gay white males."

When not manning the AIDS project, Troy Fernandez 25 makes the rounds of Hollywood bathhouses, doing what amounts to "interventions"—foisting condoms on men before they have sex. "The culture of the bathhouses has changed," he says, his voice brightening. "Some people sit around and talk. Sure, it's still mainly sex but there's some talk." Fernandez doesn't believe closing the bathhouses serves any purpose. "If you close the Hollywood Spa or the Compound, people will simply go to Plummer Park or the restroom at the Beverly Center. My friends in New York say the bathrooms at Juilliard are very busy these days. Face it, we are not going to stop people from having sex."

What then are the prospects of halting the second wave? 26 Fernandez is initially speechless, and it takes a few minutes for him to get pumped up again. "We should get real that what we're doing is not working." He sings the praises of another program he's involved in—*Saber es Poder* (Knowledge is Power), which enables him and others to go into heavily Hispanic schools and talk to kids in grades seven through twelve. "But I can't say 'dick' to a kid in a school program without losing funding," he complains. "The truth is, Joycelyn Elders was right. We have to start talking to kids when they're young, not when it's too late or the second wave will keep rolling along and then the third wave and then the fourth wave."

As for Ernesto Pujol, he says he will never forget Carla, a 27 soft-spoken, graceful Puerto Rican he met during his days running the Brooklyn AIDS unit of New York's Crisis Intervention Services. Happily married to a Brazilian man, Carla was at work on her doctorate. "The entire family got sick about the same time," says Pujol. "Her husband, she and their 2-year-old daughter. He died first, then the baby. I remember the day in the hospital that she told her family that she had AIDS and of course they became hysterical. It was very sad. She was a devout Catholic and AIDS caused her a great crisis of faith—like a slap in the face. As a couple, they had everything going for them—white upper-middle-class Latinos who could pass, educated and charming. Her husband had told her that he got it from an old girlfriend who was an addict but I suspected that he had had prior bisexual behavior. She chose to believe what her husband told her and I wasn't about to take that away from her. He was a very terrific, wonderful guy who was also working on his doctorate. But he was haunted by his past—and HIV is a past that won't ever let go of you."

AIDS Public Education Ads

The ads on the following pages were developed as a part of AIDS-education campaigns. The first, from the United States Department of Health and Human Services, began appearing about 1990. The second, a product of the American Red Cross targeted at the Hispanic American community, began appearing in 1988.

Talk About AIDS

How About Dinner, A Movie, And A Talk About AIDS?

Marie: That's not exactly my idea of a great date.

Why?

Marie: Because it's kind of depressing.

When you think about AIDS and being single, what's the first thing that comes to mind?

Marie: Be careful!

AIDS scares you?

Marie: Sure. But, it's something I have to think about.

When you say you think about it, what do you mean?

Marie: I ask myself questions I never thought about before.

Do you ask guys?

Marie: I'm starting to.

How is that working out?

Marie: Actually, not so bad.

AMERICA
RESPONDS
TO AIDS
1-800-342-AIDS
1-800-AIDS-TTY

U.S. DEPARTMENT OF HEALTH AND HUMAN SERVICES • PUBLIC HEALTH SERVICE • CENTERS FOR DISEASE CONTROL   CDC

¿Qué les espera en el futuro?

¡Protéjalos! Infórmese acerca del SIDA. Llame a la Cruz Roja en su comunidad.

Con nuestro agradecimiento a La Cruz Roja Colombiana, Seccional Caldas

 **American Red Cross**

Marcia Angell

A Dual Approach to the AIDS Epidemic

In May 1991, Marcia Angell—a physician and the executive editor of the prestigious New England Journal of Medicine*— wrote the following editorial concerning methods of containing the AIDS epidemic. Note that several responses to Dr. Angell's argument, as well as her own reply to those responses, are printed following her essay.*

Ten years ago five homosexual men in Los Angeles were reported to have acquired a mysterious and profound immune deficiency associated with pneumocystis pneumonia and other opportunistic infections. The report on these men, published in the *Morbidity and Mortality Weekly Report* on June 5, 1981, marked the beginning of the AIDS epidemic.[1] Within weeks, similar cases were being described elsewhere.[2-5] Even before the isolation of the causative virus in 1983 and the introduction of serologic testing in 1985, it was clear that a major epidemic had begun.

Now, a decade later, well over 100,000 Americans have died of AIDS and an estimated 1 million are currently infected with the virus, of whom more than 125,000 are thought to have clinical AIDS.[6] Women and children are affected, as well as both heterosexual and homosexual men. Although the rate of spread in the homosexual community has slowed, the reservoir is now huge, and we can therefore expect to see the number of cases continue to grow. Thus, AIDS is no longer an obscure disease known only to the medical and homosexual communities; it is now a household word, of concern to most Americans and frightening to many. Not since the polio outbreaks of the early 1950s have we been faced with so threatening an epidemic. Furthermore, with the advent of expensive treatments that extend the lives of persons infected with the human immunodeficiency virus (HIV) for many years, the cost of this epidemic has become a troubling issue in a time of shrinking resources.

In addition to the medical and economic issues surrounding AIDS, there are social issues unique to this epidemic that have greatly complicated our response to it. Unlike the polio epidemic of the 1950s or the influenza pandemic of 1918, AIDS tends to afflict people who are for one reason or

1

2

3

another the objects of discrimination. Although increasingly a disease of inner-city black and Hispanic intravenous drug abusers of both sexes and their sexual partners, AIDS was at first almost exclusively a disease of homosexual men. It therefore carried the stigma of any sexually transmitted disease, but unlike syphilis or gonorrhea, it also carried the stigma of homosexuality—a double burden. Members of the homosexual community, articulate and well educated and accustomed to injustice, mobilized to protect themselves from a discriminatory backlash more effectively than the politically powerless drug abusers could possibly have done. Concerned that identification of those with AIDS would lead to loss of employment, housing, and medical insurance, as well as to social ostracism, they and others sensitive to civil rights issues argued successfully for confidentiality and against screening and efforts to trace sexual partners. Thus, although AIDS is reportable in all states, HIV infection is not, nor are contacts systematically traced. Instead, testing for infection is by and large voluntary, as is the notification of sexual partners.

4   We are now seeing growing opposition to this policy of strict confidentiality, as described by Bayer in this issue of the *Journal*.[7] With recent reports of the transmission of AIDS from patients to health care providers and, more recently, from a provider to patients,[8] we hear calls for the routine screening of both groups—all patients admitted to hospitals and all doctors and nurses. There are also calls for the routine screening of pregnant women and newborns in response to the growing number of infants who contract AIDS from their mothers perinatally. Requiring the notification of sexual partners is less emphasized, perhaps because it is so difficult, but it, too, is receiving renewed attention.

5   Debates about these issues, it seems to me, too often confuse the social with the epidemiologic problems. To be sure, both sets of issues are closely enmeshed, but there seems to have been little effort to sort them out. Many of those who believe that controlling the epidemic should be our most important priority recommend draconian methods for doing so, including not only widespread screening, but also the removal of infected children from their schools, infected adults from their jobs, and both from the neighborhood. On the other hand, those moved primarily by compassion for AIDS sufferers and concern for civil rights are likely to resist the usual methods for monitoring and containing an epidemic—methods that might spare more people suffering.

  I believe we need a dual approach that attempts to distin- 6
guish social from epidemiologic problems and that deals with
both, simultaneously but separately. Clearly, HIV-infected
persons need to be protected against discrimination and hysteria, but doing so requires social and political measures, not
epidemiologic ones. Jobs, housing, and insurance benefits, for
example, should be protected by statute. The economic consequences of HIV infection require additional attention, since
they go far beyond the possible loss of employment and ordinary insurance benefits. Treating AIDS is expensive, and the
disease lasts for the rest of a patient's life, during much of
which he or she may be unable to work. Even the most generous medical insurance is unlikely to cover all the health care
needs of a patient with AIDS; thus, as patients grow sicker
they also stand to become destitute.

  We as a society should deal more systematically with the 7
devastating economic consequences of HIV infection. I suggest we establish a nationally funded program, analogous to
the end-stage renal disease program, for the medical care of
HIV-infected persons. The end-stage renal disease program,
established by Congress in 1972, extends Medicare coverage
to all patients with kidney failure.[9] This is a response to the
development of effective but extremely expensive treatments
for end-stage renal disease—namely, long-term dialysis and
renal transplantation. Handling the AIDS epidemic in the
same way would probably cost society no more than it spends
on HIV infection now. Increases in costs due to expanded
access would probably be offset by the elimination of the
expensive practice of attempting to shift costs. Under the
present patchwork system, each potential payer (employers
as well as federal, state, municipal, and private insurers) naturally wishes to pass the costs to another. Thus, for example,
a health care institution that finds itself possibly liable for the
care of an employee who becomes infected with HIV takes an
adversarial stance, asserting that there is no proof the infection was work-related. Whatever the outcome of any such dispute, some element in the system, often Medicaid, eventually
must assume the costs. A nationally funded program would
have the advantage of uniformity, simplicity, and efficiency. It
would also give those at risk an incentive to be tested, thus
allowing for earlier treatment and the protection of sexual
partners. The present system, in contrast, is filled with disin-
centives for being tested.

  If by such measures we can soften the social and economic 8
burdens on people with HIV infection, perhaps we will be

freer to address the epidemiologic problems more rigorously. Concern about social issues now creates a reluctance to deal effectively with the epidemiologic problems. For example, systematic tracing of the sexual partners of HIV-infected persons is generally resisted because of the threat to confidentiality, although contact tracing makes sense from an epidemiologic standpoint and is officially required for other sexually transmitted diseases. Similarly, there is resistance to a screening program for all pregnant women and newborns,[10–12] although such a program would be reasonable, given the accuracy of new confirmatory tests and the fact that perinatally acquired HIV infection is now more common than congenital syphilis or phenylketonuria, both of which are tested for routinely. Infected women could make more-informed choices about family planning, and infected newborns could be treated earlier.

9   Testing health care providers and hospitalized patients is also controversial,[13] although it makes sense from several standpoints. Screening patients on admission would identify those with whom health care providers must be most alert; it is unrealistic to expect them to maintain the highest level of vigilance continuously. Similarly, because it is remotely possible that there could be an exchange of blood during a medical procedure, patients have a right to know whether a doctor or nurse who performs invasive procedures is infected with HIV. If necessary, retraining in noninvasive areas or early retirement could be provided for by special insurance programs for health care professionals. Screening both patients and health care providers would also, of course, identify those for whom treatment could be begun early and whose sexual partners could be protected.

10   I believe that, on balance, systematic tracing and notification of the sexual partners of HIV-infected persons and screening of pregnant women, newborns, hospitalized patients, and health care professionals are warranted. These populations are, after all, relatively accessible to the health care system and at some special risk. Attempting to screen the entire population would simply be impractical; on the other hand, targeting only high-risk groups would be unworkable, in part because it would entail making distinctions that are often impossible as well as invidious. With any increase in screening, however, the specter of discrimination arises once a person is known to be infected. Only if such discrimination, at least in its more tangible expressions, is countered by statute and if those with HIV infection are assured of

receiving all the medical care they need, can we pursue the basic elements of infection control more resolutely and so spare others the tragedy of this disease.

References

1. Gottlieb MS, Schanker HM, Fan PT, Saxon A, Weisman JD. *Pneumocystis* pneumonia—Los Angeles, MMWR 1981; 30:250–2.
2. Friedman-Kien A, Laubenstein L, Marmor M. et al. Kaposi's sarcoma and *Pneumocystis* pneumonia among homosexual men—New York City and California. MMWR 1981; 30:305–8.
3. Gottlieb MS, Schroff R, Schanker HM, et al. *Pneumocystis carinii* pneumonia and mucosal candidiasis in previously healthy homosexual men: evidence of a new acquired cellular immunodeficiency, N Engl J Med 1981; 305:1425–31.
4. Masur H, Michelis MA, Greene JB, et al. An outbreak of community-acquired *Pneumocystis carinii* pneumonia: initial manifestation of cellular immune dysfunction. N Engl J Med 1981; 305:1431–8.
5. Siegal FP, Lopez C, Hammer GS, et al. Severe acquired immunodeficiency in male homosexuals, manifested by chronic perianal ulcerative herpes simplex lesions. N Engl J Med 1981; 305:1439–44.
6. Karon JM, Dondero TJ Jr. HIV prevalence estimates and AIDS case projections for the United States: report based upon a workshop. MMWR 1990; 39(RR-16): 1–31.
7. Bayer R. Public health policy and the AIDS epidemic—an end to HIV exceptionalism? N Engl J Med 1991; 324:1500–4.
8. Update: transmission of HIV infection during an invasive dental procedure—Florida. JAMA 1991; 265:563–8.
9. Levinsky N, Rettig RA. The Medicare end-stage renal disease program: a report from the Institute of Medicine. N Engl J Med 1991; 324:1143–8.
10. Hardy LM, ed. HIV screening of pregnant women and newborns. Washington, D.C.: National Academy Press, 1991.
11. Working Group on HIV Testing of Pregnant Women and Newborns. HIV infection, pregnant women, and newborns: a policy proposal for information and testing. JAMA 1990; 264:2416–20.
12. Nolan K. Ethical issues in caring for pregnant women and newborns at risk for human immunodeficiency virus infection. Semin Perinatol 1989; 13:55–65.
13. Brennan TA. Transmission of the human immunodeficiency virus in the health care setting—time for action. N Engl J Med 1991; 324:1504–9.

Responses to Marcia Angell: Letters to the Editor of the *New England Journal of Medicine* (and a Counter-Response by Marcia Angell)

To the Editor:

1   Angell proposes a nationally funded program for the care of all persons infected with the human immunodeficiency virus (HIV). Although the provision of adequate medical care to all persons, including the HIV-infected, should be a social goal, it is silly to think that it is a reality, or will soon be. Divorced from her utopian promise of care, Angell's recommendation is little more than a stick with no carrot.

2   There is, however, an alternative course between, on the one hand, Angell's proposal that millions of people should be subjected to mandatory testing in exchange for an elusive promise of free treatment and, on the other hand, the current situation, in which too few have access to confidential HIV testing, education and counseling, prophylactic therapies, and associated services, such as substance-abuse treatment and legal services for discrimination problems. That middle path would increase the incentive for voluntary, confidential HIV testing by funding HIV-testing programs fully, enacting or strengthening guarantees of confidentiality and nondiscrimination, expanding Medicaid eligibility and coverage to ensure medical treatment for all, adopting a national standard of care for that treatment, and providing a full range of substance-abuse treatment for those who need it. Indeed, if people are confident that testing will result in life-sustaining treatment, that their substance abuse will receive compassionate care, and that their jobs, housing, and families will be safeguarded, few would decline opportunities for voluntary, confidential HIV testing and counseling. By contrast, forced testing without such guarantees is worse than useless: it is counterproductive in that it drives people away from the systems of health care and support.

3   The middle path is also more consistent with our political and moral culture, which demands that before we resort to coercion, all possible alternatives that are less restrictive be tried and proved insufficient. A decade into the HIV epidemic,

some, like Angell, are apparently convinced that a disease-control strategy based on voluntarism—voluntary testing, voluntary treatment, and voluntary preventive behavior—has been a failure. The truth, however, is that given the meager Medicaid coverage and coverage for uninsured people in most states, the lack of frank, explicit information on HIV prevention, the lack of assurances of confidentiality and non-discrimination, and the lack of substance-abuse treatment, voluntarism has not yet been given a decent chance to work.

William B. Rubenstein, Esq.
AIDS Project
American Civil Liberties Union

David A. Hansell, Esq.
Gay Men's Health Crisis

Evan Wolfson, Esq.
Lambda Legal Defense
and Education Fund, Inc.

To the Editor: I have always thought it peculiarly irrational   1
that the American medical and political establishments embrace an entitlement program for a single condition, end-stage renal disease. Thus, people with this disease enjoy the benefits of a national health care program for the manage-ment of their renal failure. Angell advocates creating a similar program for persons infected with HIV. I submit that persons with any serious, progressive illness are at similar risk of cat-astrophic medical expenses and consequent indigence. Why are the victims of end-stage renal disease and the acquired immunodeficiency syndrome (AIDS) more worthy of entitle-ment programs than, say, patients with cancer or multiple sclerosis? If we are going to have national health care, should it not be for all Americans, not just the relative few with a spe-cific diagnosis?

David C. Dodson, M.D.

To the Editor: Angell's contention that it is "unrealistic to   1
expect [health care providers] to maintain the highest level of vigilance continuously" seems defeatist and is, in my experience, unduly pessimistic. We minimize our risk of

occupational exposure to HIV by assuming that every patient is infected. Once that premise is internalized, knowing a patient's HIV status does not influence which precautions are implemented.

2   Angell also supports the right of patients to know the HIV status of their health care providers—by mandatory testing, I infer. But the question of mandatory testing of health care providers presupposes that such testing could convert a currently very low risk to a zero risk. Although the consequences of HIV transmission are tragic, it is not clear that mandatory testing of practitioners can reduce the risk to patients below what it now appears to be. The enzyme-linked immunosorbent assay for HIV antibody is being continuously improved but is known to give false negative results both during the "window" between infection and the production of detectable antibody[1] and in people who remain antibody-negative for years while harboring HIV.[2] Even with a perfect HIV test, we could never be entirely certain that a given person was uninfected.

3   The logistics and costs of such an effort are also formidable. Who would be tested? The number of health care providers in the United States who perform invasive procedures may well exceed a million. And given the window, how frequently would testing need to be done in order to provide the degree of certainty that patients want? Yearly, monthly, daily? Repeated testing of such a large, low-prevalence population is an expensive proposition, and at this point the potential gain is not apparent.

Because transmission to patients is possible, the obligations of practitioners who know themselves to be infected does merit further discussion. However, in developing policies to protect our patients and ourselves, we cannot afford to be unclear about the limits of our technology or the level of certainty that can be attained.

Barbara E. Berger, M.S., R.N.

1. Nakamura RM, Bylund DJ, Rooney KE. Current status of clinical laboratory tests for the human immunodeficiency virus. J Clin Lab Anal 1990; 4:295–306.
2. Imagawa DT, Lee MH, Wolinsky SM, et al. Human immunodeficiency virus type 1 infection in homosexual men who remain seronegative for prolonged periods. N Engl J Med 1989; 320: 1458–62.

To the Editor: The institution of widespread HIV testing for   1
health care workers or their patients will not have a substantial effect on the rate of accidentally acquired HIV infection
in either group. The rates of transmission are exceedingly low
and become even lower when attention is paid to the use of
universal precautions. A real tragedy will result not from the
lack of widespread HIV testing but from the misallocation of
health care resources away from larger health problems. It
would be ironic if extensive HIV-screening programs for health
care workers and their patients reduced even further the
health care resources available to inner-city patients, the very
group most affected by the AIDS epidemic. Although rare
unfortunate cases of nosocomial HIV infection command
public attention, let us not forget the millions of Americans
whose lives can be threatened through the lack of adequate
health care.

Real safety in health care delivery comes from appropriate   2
routine work practices, such as universal precautions, that
protect against many infectious diseases, not just HIV. There
are far greater risks to patients from exposure to health care
workers impaired by alcoholism and drug abuse. Perhaps the
greatest risk to patients results from travel to and from medical facilities. Moreover, as a nation we seem to overlook many
serious problems while trying to avoid unlikely ones. It was
not until last year that the number of deaths from AIDS finally
exceeded that of deaths from injuries involving firearms in the
United States. We need rational public policies concerning
health care that address major health problems so that
resources can be allocated fairly to all Americans. There is a
greater good that can be achieved with the acceptance by
health care workers and their patients of the extremely minimal risk of accidental HIV infection, so that the health care
system as a whole can function more effectively for everyone.

Edward C. Klatt, M.D.

To the Editor: Angell assumes that "patients have a right to   1
know whether a doctor or nurse who performs invasive procedures is infected with HIV," since it is "remotely possible"
that blood-to-blood contact could occur. This position is
inconsistent with the principles and practice of informed
consent, in that it sets an untenable standard for the required
disclosure of remote risks to patients.

2   The Centers for Disease Control (CDC) has estimated that the risk of HIV transmission from an infected health care worker to a patient is 2.4 to 24 per million procedures.[1] In fact, except for one dentist whom the CDC has documented to have used substandard infection-control technique,[2] such transmission remains undocumented. Yet a consistent application of Angell's "right to know" would require the disclosure of all such risks in health care delivery—remote, undocumented, or both. Thus, health care workers could be required to inform patients of many individual disabilities or conditions affecting themselves, such as side effects of continuing medications, chronic conditions, sleeplessness, psychiatric conditions, even surgeon-specific postoperative and perioperative mortality rates and surgeon-specific rates of wound infection. All are arguably much more relevant to patients' safety than a health worker's HIV infection.

3   The law of informed consent has long held that only "material" or "significant" risks need to be disclosed to patients before treatment.[3, 4] The materiality or significance of the risk is determined in turn by the standard of a "reasonable patient" or, in some states, by the customary practice of the medical community. Although many and perhaps most patients would probably like to know such information, the medical, legal, and public health communities must bring their professional judgment to bear on the reasonableness of that desire. These communities should be mindful of their obligation to distinguish between how much of that desire can be attributed to overreaction and how much to a rational apprehension of harm. I also question whether, if disclosure is mandated, the information disclosed should concern the individual practitioner's record and practice of infection control, rather than his or her known serologic status with regard to blood-borne pathogens.

4   If improving the safety and choice afforded to patients is our goal, we should not begin by singling out HIV infection of health workers, from which the aggregate harm to patients is truly remote.

Nancy M. Louden
Ad Hoc Committee on AIDS
Association of the Bar of the
City of New York

1. Centers for Disease Control. Estimates of the risk of endemic transmission of HBV and HIV to patients by the percutaneous

route during invasive surgical and dental procedures. Atlanta: Centers for Disease Control, January 30, 1991.

2. Update: transmission of HIV infection during an invasive dental procedure—Florida. MMWR 1991; 40:21, 25-7.

3. Information that need not be disclosed. In: Rozovsky FA. Consent to treatment: a practical guide. 2nd ed. Boston: Little, Brown, 1990:59-64.

4. The legal requirements for disclosure and consent: history and current status. In: Appelbaum PS, Lidz CW, Meisel A. Informed consent: legal theory and clinical practice. New York: Oxford University Press, 1987:50-4.

Editor's reply: In my editorial I proposed a dual approach 1 to the AIDS epidemic: on the one hand, I advocated stronger measures to protect those with HIV infection from social and economic deprivation; on the other, I recommended the routine screening of certain population groups that are accessible to the health care system. Rubenstein et al. imply that I believe the two elements of this dual approach can be separated; I do not.

I find it puzzling that some of the correspondents whose 2 letters appear here seem to object to my proposals because they do not represent perfect solutions to problems. Thus, they object to funding the treatment of HIV infection because we do not fund the care of everyone. They see the fact that screening would yield a small number of false negative results as a reason to remain ignorant about the status of the great majority in whom the test would be accurate. (Somehow, the issue of false negative results does not stop them from calling for more widespread voluntary screening.) As is too often the case in this epidemic, the rights of sexual partners are all but overlooked.

It is particularly disturbing that some doctors seem to 3 focus disproportionately on resisting proposals to test health care providers. To be sure, the risk of HIV transmission from doctors to patients is exceedingly small—much smaller than the risk of transmission from patients to doctors. But there are two reasons for testing doctors that have nothing to do with the magnitude of the risk. First, agreeing to routine screening would give doctors the moral leadership necessary to ask for reciprocity from their patients: they would in effect not be asking anything of them that they were not willing to do themselves. Second, the public overwhelmingly believes that certain groups of health care providers should be screened for HIV infection, and there is no overriding reason not to do so. Some believe it "draconian" to divert HIV-positive doctors to noninvasive professional pursuits, but the CDC and the American Medical Association think otherwise, and I agree. The further admonition that a screening program would make doctors reluctant to care for patients with AIDS is odd: it suggests that doctors would be more worried about having to retrain than about contracting a lethal disease.

4   The best approach to containing the spread of a transmissible disease is to find out who is infected and who is at risk and to treat the former and try to protect the latter. The system I proposed is not perfect, but it is better than our current nonsystem. We should not make the perfect the enemy of the good.

Marcia Angell, M.D.

Andrew Holleran

Trust

"Trust" is one essay in Andrew Holleran's book of essays Ground Zero, *published in 1988. "Ground Zero" is Manhattan, an island blasted by AIDS, which is depicted as a plague in the midst of writers and artists and talented others, and so* Ground Zero *documents the hopes and fears of the gay community in the face of the catastrophe. It is a funny and tragic, hopeful and frightening book about doctors, sex, fear, and despair. Holleran has also written the novels* Dancer from the Dance *(1978) and* Nights in Aruba *(1983), both examinations of gay life.*

1   We were sitting on a porch in Florida this afternoon leafing through the portfolio of photographs a friend had brought over, half watching the butterflies in the geraniums, when I came to the portrait of a handsome man and asked who this was. A man in San Francisco, my friend replied, who had just walked out on his lover. "And you know what his exit line

was?" he said. "'When you get the night sweats, you'll know you've got it.'"

"What do you mean?" I said. 2

"He has AIDS," my friend said of the good-looking man 3 with the mustache and wavy hair. "He had it when he began the relationship, but he told his lover if they kept a positive attitude, they wouldn't get it. Now, of course, the boyfriend's got it, and when it happened," he said, pointing to the photograph, "he packed his bags and walked out, saying, 'When you get the night sweats, you'll know you've got it.'"

"But—but—" I said, incredulous, dumbfounded, staring at 4 this handsome man in the photograph, "who is he?"

"He's smart," said my friend. "He's a psychologist. He 5 wanted to get AIDS."

"Wanted to?" I said. 6

"He went out to the baths, just when it began, when he 7 knew it was dangerous, and put his ass up in the air," he said. "He wanted to get it."

"But how does the lover feel?" I said, pointing to the adja- 8 cent photograph, a man with a dark beard and friendly eyes. "The one he gave it to?"

"He has chronic hepatitis," my friend said. "His stomach is 9 swelled out to here," he said, drawing a potbelly in the air. "He just thinks it's one more version of being dumped on by life."

When I first heard stories—like this one—I didn't believe 10 them; they belonged to that realm of rumor in which the gossip is made up out of whole cloth, merely because it's so dramatic. No one would do that in real life, I thought. It just isn't believable. The first story I heard—about five years ago—involved the death of a decorator in New York whose brother flew east from California to attend the wake and stayed with a man I'll call Bob. The brother was attractive, and one evening after the wake, talking things over before the fireplace, Bob and the brother ended up having sex. When the sex was over, talking once more, Bob asked the brother what he would do with all the money he'd inherit from the decorator; the brother replied, "Spend it. I have AIDS, too."

Surely this was made up, I thought; no one could possibly 11 do that. It's certainly true, as Scott Fitzgerald wrote, that a sense of the fundamental decencies is parceled out unequally at birth, but I could not even imagine the person who would knowingly expose another person to the virus. I had trouble with people who littered; I wanted them arrested and given the electric chair. I knew the junk that clogged the mangroves in which gay men cruised at Virginia Key in Miami, soiled the dunes at the gay beach south of Jacksonville, was proof that gay people, yes, *even gay people*, were slobs. But I had perhaps a rather exalted vision of homosexuals; I suspected, in some chamber of my heart, that they were, well, neater, nicer, more sensitive than the rest. Mayor Lindsay used to say, "The trouble with New York is that there are too many slobs." But I didn't include the gay community in that; I found it hard to believe—and very discouraging—that they even littered.

12   But then a few years of the plague, and more stories of this sort, passed, and the next one I heard about someone I knew sounded a little more imaginable: A young man just out of the hospital after a bout of pneumocystic pneumonia went to the Saint to celebrate, met someone, and took him home. Hmmmm. One *would* go to the Saint to celebrate, perhaps, that was not unlikely, and perhaps in the mood created by the place, the dancing, one might meet someone, and . . . but there it stopped. People do not murder other people casually. Surely he would have told the person he had just got out of the hospital, and so on.

13   And then, shortly after hearing this story, I read about Fabian Bridges. Fabian Bridges was just a newspaper article at first—about a male prostitute shunted back and forth between two cities that didn't want him, because he had AIDS and the judge thought the only solution was to put him on a bus out of town. Put this way, I felt sorry for Fabian Bridges; then I saw him in a documentary on television. On television Fabian Bridges was seen haunting the seedier parts of cities (those blocks that look exactly alike in Pittsburgh, Houston, Jacksonville, New York: the dirty bookstores, the theaters, the parking lots), after being asked by a doctor in the most patient, cajoling, restrained manner, to stop having sex. Stop having sex was what Fabian somehow seemed unable to do— though he voiced a mild regret at having ejaculated inside a customer (a man he'd come to like). This wistful regret was the only one Fabian Bridges evinced; friends who saw the film explained him away with brain infection—the virus had already destroyed his ability to act morally. But I wasn't so sure; it seemed possible to me Fabian Bridges was just one of those horrors—a morally inert succubus drifting through life without much will to do right or wrong. Who knows? The gay community in Texas did what the courts and police could not—took Fabian in, got him off the street—and then death took him off the planet. But not before, one assumes, he had taken others with him.

We read daily now of prostitutes of both sexes who refuse   14
to stop working, even though they have AIDS. There is an ex-
American army sergeant being tried in Germany right now
for having had sex with three men and not telling them he
had the virus; the case has been clouded by the fact that one
of them, a Spaniard, also had AIDS at the time. My, my. It just
goes on and on. Admit the principle, and there is no end to
the permutations.

I was watching TV with a friend the evening the death of   15
Rock Hudson was announced. After asking me in a curious
voice why gay men were so promiscuous, my friend then
inquired, "Why did you *trust* one another?" The question gave
me a moment's pause; I had never thought of it in those terms
before—terms of trust. I said, "Because there was no reason
not to. Everything could be cured with some form of penicillin." Yet now that I reflect on it all, it seems to me that not
antibiotics but trust was the thing that made that life possible: the assumption that the person you slept with would not
knowingly infect you with anything vile. Trust was the basis
of the whole system—the Visa card that sent you to Brazil,
Berlin, or California with the prospect of romance. (The thing
that impelled people to go there, soon after the plague
appeared in New York, in fact, on the assumption that It
hadn't arrived in these places yet.) There were exceptions to
all this, of course. I got crabs in those days more times than I
could count; by the twentieth time, I was less strict about
waiting a few days after dousing myself with A-200 before
going out again. I got amoebas and learned, after the fact, I'd
been exposed to hepatitis; but I considered most of these just
occupational hazards, germs swimming in the community
pool, and not the malicious, much less lethal, act of any particular person. True, there were nights when, at the baths, I
would see a man leave someone's room and the door to that
room open a moment later to take on a new visitor—and I
would think, *The fat, lazy cow. Can't even go downstairs and
shower between encounters.* And in my disgust I would eventually walk past that open door to see who the slob was. He
was always someone ordinary, I mean, without any distinguishing marks that set him apart from everyone else at the
baths; and that, of course, is the trouble with trust now.

The rumor that AIDS had been spread by an airline stew-   16
ard had been around several years; the version I heard featured an Australian on Air Qantas. The airline steward, of
course, has always personified a certain aspect of gay life—
the most complete version of the fantasy; to be a new face in

Rome, Paris, Cairo, London, Madrid—all in the same week, to sleep not with everyone in your gym, but with the whole world. It seemed, at a certain age, the only thing to do; an adventure one would be a fool not to spend at least a year on. Promiscuity and jet travel were somehow twins—synergistic. How else to get It from a green monkey in the interior of Africa to a penthouse in New York? The tracing of Patient Zero in Randy Shilts's new book on AIDS is not only a dramatic case of mystery solving; it's the culmination of all those stories about this person—this gay person in whom I could not quite believe—that have been floating around for years now. No wonder the mainstream press picked up on it. It finally gives a face to what has been so far faceless. It crystallizes all the anger and moral outrage that have been gathering without an object. The steward from Air Canada reduces a force, a vast dilemma, to what even an age accustomed to institutional power hungers for—the story of a single human being making a choice between right and wrong, good and evil. Gaetan Dugas apparently, made the wrong choice. Gaetan personifies, in what we've read of him so far, a recognizable type in gay life: the vain and careless Queen. The Pretty Boy with the not-so-pretty value system. The Moral Slob. The Femme, oh very, Fatale. Flying from place to place, the man at the baths who—I presume—opened his door a moment after the last man had left and did not bother to go downstairs to shower; who, when the lights came up, if what we read is true, commented casually on his Kaposi's sarcoma as "the new gay cancer. Perhaps you'll get it, too."

17   A friend with AIDS gave some advice about having sex nowadays that still seems excellent: "Have sex," he said, "as if everyone is infected." What better guide? Standing in the Jewel in New York, watching the men go up and down the aisle, I can easily imagine now that some have AIDS. (In fact, someone told me last week that people with AIDS go there.) Why not? What else would you do if you had AIDS? Would you not more than ever have to be there, to cruise, to forget, to feel alive? Fabian Bridges, Patient Zero, are only extreme versions of something in many of us; we have all fudged reality a bit in the past five years, I suspect—behaved with standards that now seem to us lax and self-deluded. Indeed, the longer the plague goes on, and the more pervasive our exposure to it, the more unappetizing sex becomes—sex that seems risky, that is. But this psychological barrier, this distaste, was not always there; it took years to coalesce and solidify. The trouble is we know now that a person can give

someone AIDS in several moral states—not knowing he has it, knowing he has it but not thinking what he does is dangerous ("Just keep a positive attitude!"), knowing he has it and passing it on out of despair, revenge, indifference, hatred, selfishness, or sheer amorality; having a hole where the conscience should be, or a vengeful feeling that what the community gave to him, he can give back. It's the same principle, after all—the man who goes out with crabs and the man who goes out with AIDS. Only crabs can be killed with A-200; the virus cannot. And with that fact, all trust dissolves.

The truth is most people are not amoral, most of them care 18 very much about not endangering someone they have sex with, but the fact that some are, is enough to shut down the whole system. It's a bit like the Tylenol scare—most of the bottles on the shelf were surely safe, but the possibility that one of them might contain poison was enough to make the manufacturer withdraw the product. AIDS destroys trust. We cannot possibly investigate, much less be responsible for, what the man we are attracted to has done with the past five or seven years of his life. We can't guarantee ourselves. This limits sex with each passing year. It shuts down a whole system of behavior, a community; it builds a wall between each of us. AIDS is a form of pollution; in this case, polluted semen and blood. We've spoiled even that. AIDS is a form of terrorism—sex becomes Paris the summer the bombs went off. Nobody goes. Like Central Park—empty at night because everyone's afraid of muggers—homosexual life becomes a vast empty space from which everyone has withdrawn. We look at one another not merely as appetizing possibilities, possible boyfriends, fantasies, pleasure—we look at each other as lethal instruments, threats, dangers, obstacle courses, things one would have to sift through a whole host of tests in order to eat. Sodomy—the central ritual from which all else proceeded—is out of the question. Kissing, fellatio, all must be weighed. The tree of sex shrivels up. When I go to the Jewel in New York, or the baths in Jacksonville, I see what I've come to call the Same Nine People. They're not exactly nine, and they're not always the same, but almost, and you get the point. The fact is, there does not have to be a lot of Patient Zeros out there to destroy the way of life we had evolved; there just has to be one. As long as a friend writes me from San Diego that a man he knows in an AZT program out there called to ask him if he had any ethyl chloride for the march in Washington, because he thought it the greatest cruising opportunity ever—well, that's enough.

19   One afternoon last spring we took a walk down to the Morton Street pier and found a wire-mesh fence along its perimeter to keep people away from the rotting timbers at the edge. Not in New York, of course: There were still people sunbathing along the margin, beyond the concrete divider and the silver fence. One in particular was nude; the sun gleamed on every pore of his bare back and buttocks, the tiny hairs on his forearm and neck—and I stood there for a moment staring at him, wondering which one of us was confined. The nude and the chicken wire fence was one of those images that expresses the whole dilemma. Or the nude and the Plexiglas panel, in the bookstore off Times Square a friend of mine repairs to after an exhausting day at work—the individual booths are all separated by transparent walls, like a handball court one can see into, and the men stand in their separate cells, jerking off to one another. Or the dance floor at Track's. It's filled with people dancing; the handsome men take their shirts off at a certain point, as they used to formerly, observing rituals practiced by a court that no longer exists. It is all muted, a ghost of itself, all difficult to explain, till I see a muscular man beating a stick against a gourd while a woman dances to his syncopation and, as she whirls around, read what the sweatshirt she's wearing says: CHOOSE LIFE. That is the caption that explains the dance now, and our whole community. You've heard of postmodern. This is post-trust.

EUTHANASIA

Anonymous

It's Over, Debbie

In 1988, the Journal of the American Medical Association *published the following anonymous contribution to its "A Piece of My Mind" opinion column. Nothing ever published there has been more controversial.*

The call came in the middle of the night. As a gynecology resident rotating through a large, private hospital, I had come to detest telephone calls, because invariably I would be up for several hours and would not feel good the next day. However, duty called, so I answered the phone. A nurse informed me that a patient was having difficulty getting rest, could I please see her. She was on 3 North. That was the gynecologic-oncology unit, not my usual duty station. As I trudged along, bumping sleepily against walls and corners and not believing I was up again, I tried to imagine what I might find at the end of my walk. Maybe an elderly woman with an anxiety reaction, or perhaps something particularly horrible. 1

I grabbed the chart from the nurses station on my way to the patient's room, and the nurse gave me some hurried details: a 20-year-old girl named Debbie was dying of ovarian cancer. She was having unrelenting vomiting apparently as the result of an alcohol drip administered for sedation. Hmm, I thought. Very sad. As I approached the room I could hear loud, labored breathing. I entered and saw an emaciated, dark-haired woman who appeared much older than 20. She was receiving nasal oxygen, had an IV, and was sitting in bed suffering from what was obviously severe air hunger. The chart noted her weight at 80 pounds. A second woman, also dark-haired but of middle-age, stood at her right, holding her hand. Both looked up as I entered. The room seemed filled with the patient's desperate effort to survive. Her eyes were hollow, and she had suprasternal and intercostal retractions with her rapid inspirations. She had not eaten or slept in two 2 days. She had not responded to chemotherapy and was being given supportive care only. It was a gallows scene, a cruel mockery of her youth and unfulfilled potential. Her only words to me were, "Let's get this over with."

3   I retreated with my thoughts to the nurses station. The patient was tired and needed rest. I could not give her health, but I could give her rest. I asked the nurse to draw 20 mg of morphine sulfate into a syringe. Enough, I thought, to do the job. I took the syringe into the room and told the two women I was going to give Debbie something that would let her rest and to say good-bye. Debbie looked at the syringe, then laid her head on the pillow with her eyes open, watching what was left of the world. I injected the morphine intravenously and watched to see if my calculations on its effects would be correct. Within seconds her breathing slowed to a normal rate, her eyes closed, and her features softened as she seemed restful at last. The older woman stroked the hair of the now-sleeping patient. I waited for the inevitable next effect of depressing the respiratory drive. With clocklike certainty, within four minutes the breathing rate slowed even more, then became irregular, then ceased. The dark-haired woman stood erect and seemed relieved.

4   It's over, Debbie.

Name Withheld by Request

Charles Colson
It's Not Over, Debbie

Charles Colson (born 1931) was converted to Christianity while serving a prison term for his role in the Watergate scandal of the Nixon administration. He has written five books on Christian topics and contributes regularly to the evangelical publication Christianity Today, *where the following column appeared in 1988.*

1   The scene is a darkened hospital ward. An intern stands over Debbie, a young woman with terminal cancer. Her breathing is labored as she struggles for oxygen. She weighs 80 pounds. She is in horrible pain.

The doctor has never seen Debbie before, but a glance at   2
her chart confirms she is not responding to treatment. He
leans down to hear her whisper, "Let's get this over with."

Most doctors would have hurried to give relief against the   3
pain, or tried to offer some solace to the anguished relative
standing near the bed. But this intern measured out 20 milligrams of morphine into a syringe—enough, he wrote later, "to
do the job"—and injected it. Four minutes later, Debbie was
dead. The doctor's only comment: "It's over, Debbie."

Stories like this, publicized a few months back, are shock-   4
ing but should not surprise us. While no one likes to admit it,
active euthanasia is not uncommon. It has been closeted in
hospital ethics committees, cloaked in euphemisms spoken to
grieving relatives. It is the unnamed shadow on an unknown
number of death certificates—of handicapped newborns;
sickly, aged parents; the terminally ill in critical pain.

No, Debbie's case is something new only because of the pub-   5
lic nature of both its telling and the debate that has followed.

This story was first written, anonymously but without   6
apology, by the intern himself, and published in the *Journal of
the American Medical Association* (JAMA)—one of the most
respected medical journals in the world.

Following the article's publication, the commentary came   7
fast and furious. Some experts dismissed the incident as
fictional. Others believed it, but focused their criticism on
the young doctor's lack of familiarity with Debbie's medical
history.

But the article's greatest effect was to yank euthanasia out   8
of the closet and thrust it into the arena of national debate. On
the surface that might seem healthy, getting the whole ugly
issue into the open. But there's a subtle danger here: The JAMA
article and the impassioned discussion it provoked offer a case
study of a recurring process in American life by which the
unthinkable in short order becomes the unquestionable.

Usually it works like this: Some practice so offensive that it   9
could scarcely be discussed in public is suddenly advocated
by a respected expert in a respected forum. The public is
shocked, then outraged. The very fact that such a thing could
be publicly debated becomes the focus of the debate.

But in the process, the sheer repetition of the shocking grad-   10
ually dulls its shock effect. No longer outraged, people begin to
argue for positions to moderate the extreme; or they accept the
premise, challenging instead the means to achieve it. (Note
that in Debbie's debate, many challenged not the killing, but
the intern's failure to check more carefully into the case.)

11   And gradually, though no one remembers quite how it all happened, the once unspeakable becomes tolerable and, in time, acceptable.

12   An example of how this process works is the case of homosexuality. Not long ago it was widely regarded, even in secular society, as a perversion. The gay-rights movement's first pronouncements were received with shock; then, in the process of debate, the public gradually lost its sense of outrage. Homosexuality became a cause—and what was once deviant is today, in many jurisdictions, a legally protected right. All this in little more than a decade.

13   Debbie's story appears to have initiated this process for euthanasia. Columnist Ellen Goodman welcomed the case as "a debate that should be taking place."

14   So what was once a crime becomes a debate. And, if history holds true, that debate will usher the once unmentionable into common practice.

15   Already the stage is set. In a 1983 poll, 63 percent of Americans approved of mercy killing in certain cases. In a 1988 poll, more than 50 percent of lawyers favored legal euthanasia. The Hemlock Society is working to put the issue on the ballot in several states.

16   I don't intend to sound alarmist: legal euthanasia in this country is still more a threat than a reality. But 20 years ago, who would have thought abortion would one day be a constitutional right, or that infanticide would be given legal protection?

17   The path from the unmentionable to the commonplace is being traveled with increasing speed in medical ethics. Without some concerted resistance, euthanasia is likely to be the next to make the trip. As Ellen Goodman concluded her column, "The Debbie story is not over yet, not by a long shot."

18   Indeed.

19   Novelist Walker Percy, in *The Thanatos Syndrome*, offers one vision of where such compromising debates on the value of life might take us.

20   The time is the 1990s. Qualitarian Life Centers have sprung up across the country after the landmark case of *Doe* v. *Dade* "which decreed, with solid scientific evidence, that the human infant does not achieve personhood until 18 months." At these centers one can conveniently dispose of unwanted young and old alike.

21   An old priest, Father Smith, confronts the narrator, a psychiatrist, in this exchange:

"You are an able psychiatrist. On the whole a decent, gener-   22
ous humanitarian person in the abstract sense of the word.
You know what is going to happen to you."

"What?"   23

"You are a member of the first generation of doctors in   24
the history of medicine to turn their backs on the oath of
Hippocrates and kill millions of old, useless people, unborn
children, born malformed children, for the good of mankind—and to do so without a single murmur from one of
you. Not a single letter of protest in the august *New England
Journal of Medicine*. And do you know what you are going to
end up doing?"

"No," I say...   25

The priest aims his azimuth squarely at me and then   26
appears to lose his train of thought....

"What is going to happen to me, Father?" I ask before he   27
gets away altogether.

"Oh," he says absently, appearing to be thinking of some-   28
thing else, "you're going to end up killing Jews."

James Rachels

Active and Passive Euthanasia

*James Rachels (born 1941), a philosopher and teacher at New
York University, University of Miami, and the University of
Alabama at Birmingham (where he currently works), is particularly interested in ethics. He contributed the following essay
to the* New England Journal of Medicine *in 1975.*

The distinction between active and passive euthanasia is   1
thought to be crucial for medical ethics. The idea is that it is
permissible, at least in some cases, to withhold treatment and
allow a patient to die, but it is never permissible to take any
direct action designed to kill the patient. This doctrine seems
to be accepted by most doctors, and it is endorsed in a statement adopted by the House of Delegates of the American
Medical Association on December 4, 1973:

> The intentional termination of the life of one human being by another—mercy killing—is contrary to that for which the medical profession stands and is contrary to the policy of the American Medical Association.
>
> The cessation of the employment of extraordinary means to prolong the life of the body when there is irrefutable evidence that biological death is imminent is the decision of the patient and/or his family. The advice and judgment of the physician should be freely available to the patient and/or his immediate family.

However, a strong case can be made against this doctrine. In what follows I will set out some of the relevant arguments, and urge doctors to reconsider their views on this matter.

2   To begin with a familiar type of situation, a patient who is dying of incurable cancer of the throat is in terrible pain, which can no longer be satisfactorily alleviated. He is certain to die within a few days, even if present treatment is continued, but he does not want to go on living for those days since the pain is unbearable. So he asks the doctor for an end to it, and his family joins in the request.

3   Suppose the doctor agrees to withhold treatment, as the conventional doctrine says he may. The justification for his doing so is that the patient is in terrible agony, and since he is going to die anyway, it would be wrong to prolong his suffering needlessly. But now notice this. If one simply withholds treatment, it may take the patient longer to die, and so he may suffer more than he would if more direct action were taken and a lethal injection given. This fact provides strong reason for thinking that, once the initial decision not to prolong his agony has been made, active euthanasia is actually preferable to passive euthanasia, rather than the reverse. To say otherwise is to endorse the option that leads to more suffering rather than less, and is contrary to the humanitarian impulse that prompts the decision not to prolong his life in the first place.

4   Part of my point is that the process of being "allowed to die" can be relatively slow and painful, whereas being given a lethal injection is relatively quick and painless. Let me give a different sort of example. In the United States about one in 600 babies is born with Down's syndrome. Most of these babies are otherwise healthy—that is, with only the usual pediatric care, they will proceed to an otherwise normal infancy. Some, however, are born with congenital defects such as intestinal obstructions that require operations if they

are to live. Sometimes, the parents and the doctor will decide
not to operate, and let the infant die. Anthony Shaw describes
what happens then:

> ...When surgery is denied [the doctor] must try to keep the
> infant from suffering while natural forces sap the baby's life
> away. As a surgeon whose natural inclination is to use the
> scalpel to fight off death, standing by and watching a sal-
> vageable baby die is the most emotionally exhausting experi-
> ence I know. It is easy at a conference, in a theoretical
> discussion, to decide that such infants should be allowed to
> die. It is altogether different to stand by in the nursery and
> watch as dehydration and infection wither a tiny being over
> hours and days. This is a terrible ordeal for me and the hos-
> pital staff—much more so than for the parents who never set
> foot in the nursery.

I can understand why some people are opposed to all euthanasia, and insist that such infants must be allowed to live. I
think I can also understand why other people favor destroying these babies quickly and painlessly. But why should anyone favor letting "dehydration and infection wither a tiny
being over hours and days"? The doctrine that says that a
baby may be allowed to dehydrate and wither, but may not be
given an injection that would end its life without suffering,
seems so patently cruel as to require no further refutation.
The strong language is not intended to offend, but only to put
the point in the clearest possible way.

My second argument is that the conventional doctrine   5
leads to decisions concerning life and death made on irrelevant grounds.

Consider again the case of the infants with Down's syn-   6
drome who need operations for congenital defects unrelated
to the syndrome to live. Sometimes, there is no operation,
and the baby dies. But when there is no such defect, the baby
lives on. Now, an operation such as that to remove an intestinal obstruction is not prohibitively difficult. The reason why
such operations are not performed in these cases is, clearly,
that the child has Down's syndrome and the parents and doctor judge that because of that fact it is better for the child to
die.

But notice that this situation is absurd, no matter what   7
view one takes of the lives and potential of such babies. If the
life of such an infant is worth preserving, what does it matter
if it needs a simple operation? Or, if one thinks it better that

such a baby should not live on, what difference does it make that it happens to have an unobstructed intestinal tract? In either case, the matter of life and death is being decided on irrelevant grounds. It is the Down's syndrome, and not the intestines, that is the issue. The matter should be decided, if at all, on that basis, and not be allowed to depend on the essentially irrelevant question of whether the intestinal tract is blocked.

8   What makes this situation possible, of course, is the idea that when there is an intestinal blockage, one can "let the baby die," but when there is no such defect there is nothing that can be done, for one must not "kill" it. The fact that this idea leads to such results as deciding life or death on irrelevant grounds is another good reason why the doctrine should be rejected.

9   One reason why so many people think that there is an important moral difference between active and passive euthanasia is that they think killing someone is morally worse than letting someone die. But is it? Is killing in itself worse than letting die? To investigate this issue, two cases may be considered that are exactly alike except that one involves killing whereas the other involves letting someone die. Then it can be asked whether this difference makes any difference to the moral assessments. It is important that the cases be exactly alike, except for this one difference and not some other that accounts for any variation in the assessments of the two cases. So, let us consider this pair of cases:

10   In the first, Smith stands to gain a large inheritance if anything should happen to his six-year-old cousin. One evening while the child is taking his bath, Smith sneaks into the bathroom and drowns the child, and then arranges things so that it will look like an accident.

11   In the second, Jones also stands to gain if anything should happen to his six-year-old cousin. Like Smith, Jones sneaks in planning to drown the child in his bath. However, just as he enters the bathroom Jones sees the child slip and hit his head, and fall face down in the water. Jones is delighted; he stands by, ready to push the child's head back under if it is necessary. With only a little thrashing about, the child drowns all by himself, "accidentally," as Jones watches and does nothing.

12   Now Smith killed the child, whereas Jones "merely" let the child die. That is the only difference between them. Did either man behave better, from a moral point of view? If the difference between killing and letting die were in itself a morally important matter, one should say that Jones's behavior was

less reprehensible than Smith's. But does one really want to say that? I think not. In the first place, both men acted from the same motive, personal gain, and both had exactly the same end in view when they acted. It may be inferred from Smith's conduct that he is a bad man, although that judgment may be withdrawn or modified if certain further facts are learned about him—for example, that he is mentally deranged. But would not the very same thing be inferred about Jones from his conduct? And would not the same further considerations also be relevant to any modification of this judgment? Moreover, suppose Jones pleaded, in his own defense, "After all, I didn't do anything except just stand there and watch the child drown. I didn't kill him; I only let him die." Again, if letting die were in it-self less bad than killing, this defense should have at least some weight. But it does not. Such a "defense" can only be regarded as a grotesque perversion of moral reasoning. Morally speaking, it is no defense at all.

Now, it may be pointed out, quite properly, that the cases   13
of euthanasia with which doctors are concerned are not like this at all. They do not involve personal gain or the destruction of normal healthy children. Doctors are concerned only with cases in which the patient's life is of no further use to him, or in which the patient's life has become or will soon become a terrible burden. However, the point is the same in these cases: the bare difference between killing and letting die does not, in itself, make a moral difference. If a doctor lets a patient die, for humane reasons, he is in the same moral position as if he had given the patient a lethal injection for humane reasons. If his decision was wrong—if, for example, the patient's illness was in fact curable—the decision would be equally regrettable no matter which method was used to carry it out. And if the doctor's decision was the right one, the method used is not in itself important.

The AMA policy statement isolates the crucial issue very   14
well; the crucial issue is "the intentional termination of the life of one human being by another." But after identifying this issue, and forbidding "mercy killing," the statement goes on to deny that the cessation of treatment is the intentional termination of a life. This is where the mistake comes in, for what is the cessation of treatment, in these circumstances, if it is not "the intentional termination of the life of one human being by another"? Of course it is exactly that, and if it were not, there would be no point to it.

Many people will find this judgment hard to accept. One   15
reason, I think, is that it is very easy to conflate the question

of whether killing is, in itself, worse than letting die, with the very different question of whether most actual cases of killing are more reprehensible than most actual cases of letting die. Most actual cases of killing are clearly terrible (think, for example, of all the murders reported in the newspapers), and one hears of such cases every day. On the other hand, one hardly ever hears of a case of letting die, except for the actions of doctors who are motivated by humanitarian reasons. So one learns to think of killing in a much worse light than of letting die. For it is not the bare difference between killing and letting die that makes the difference in these cases. Rather, the other factors—the murderer's motive of personal gain, for example, contrasted with the doctor's humanitarian motivation—account for the different reactions to the different cases.

16   I have argued that killing is not in itself any worse than letting die; if my contention is right, it follows that active euthanasia is not any worse than passive euthanasia. What arguments can be given on the other side? The most common, I believe, is the following:

17   "The important difference between active and passive euthanasia is that in passive euthanasia, the doctor does not do anything to bring about the patient's death. The doctor does nothing, and the patient dies of whatever ills already afflict him. In active euthanasia, however, the doctor does something to bring about the patient's death: he kills him. The doctor who gives the patient with cancer a lethal injection has himself caused his patient's death; whereas if he merely ceases treatment, the cancer is the cause of the death."

18   A number of points need to be made here. The first is that it is not exactly correct to say that in passive euthanasia the doctor does nothing, for he does do one thing that is very important: he lets the patient die. "Letting someone die" is certainly different in some respects, from other types of action—mainly in that it is a kind of action that one may perform by way of not performing certain other actions. For example, one may let a patient die by way of not giving medication, just as one may insult someone by way of not shaking his hand. But for any purpose of moral assessment, it is a type of action nonetheless. The decision to let a patient die is subject to moral appraisal in the same way that a decision to kill him would be subject to moral appraisal: it may be assessed as wise or unwise, compassionate or sadistic, right or wrong. If a doctor deliberately let a patient die who was suffering from a routinely curable illness, the doctor would

certainly be to blame for what he had done, just as he would be to blame if he had needlessly killed the patient. Charges against him would then be appropriate. If so, it would be no defense at all for him to insist that he didn't "do anything." He would have done something very serious indeed, for he let his patient die.

Fixing the cause of death may be very important from a legal point of view, for it may determine whether criminal charges are brought against the doctor. But I do not think that this notion can be used to show a moral difference between active and passive euthanasia. The reason why it is considered bad to be the cause of someone's death is that death is regarded as a great evil—and so it is. However, if it had been decided that euthanasia—even passive euthanasia—is desirable in a given case, it has also been decided that in this instance death is no greater an evil than the patient's continued existence. And if this is true, the usual reason for not wanting to be the cause of someone's death simply does not apply. ¹⁹

Finally, doctors may think that all of this is only of academic interest—the sort of thing that philosophers may worry about but that has no practical bearing on their own work. After all, doctors must be concerned about the legal consequences of what they do, and active euthanasia is clearly forbidden by law. But even so, doctors should also be concerned with the fact that the law is forcing upon them a moral doctrine that may well be indefensible, and has a considerable effect on their practices. Of course, most doctors are not now in the position of being coerced in this matter, for they do not regard themselves as merely going along with what the law requires. Rather, in statements such as the AMA policy statement that I have quoted, they are endorsing this doctrine as a central point of medical ethics. In that statement, active euthanasia is condemned not merely as illegal but as "contrary to that for which the medical profession stands," whereas passive euthanasia is approved. However, the preceding considerations suggest that there is really no moral difference between the two, considered in themselves (there may be important moral differences in some cases in their consequences, but, as I pointed out, these differences may make active euthanasia, and not passive euthanasia, the morally preferable option). So whereas doctors may have to discriminate between active and passive euthanasia to satisfy the law, they should not do any more than that. In particular, they should not give the distinction any added authority and weight by writing it into official statements of medical ethics. ²⁰

Sidney Hook

In Defense of
Voluntary Euthanasia

Sidney Hook (1902–1989) studied philosophy under John Dewey and became an outspoken, controversial, daring social thinker. A prolific essayist who also published some thirty books, a champion of Marx in the 1930s but of individual freedoms as well, Hook remained iconoclastic and independent throughout his career, which he chronicled in his 1987 autobiography, Out of Step: An Unquiet Life in the 20th Century. *He wrote the following essay for* The New York Times *in 1987.*

1   A few short years ago, I lay at the point of death. A congestive heart failure was treated for diagnostic purposes by an angiogram that triggered a stroke. Violent and painful hiccups, uninterrupted for several days and nights, prevented the digestion of food. My left side and one of my vocal cords became paralyzed. Some form of pleurisy set in, and I felt I was drowning in a sea of slime. At one point, my heart stopped beating; just as I lost consciousness, it was thumped back into action again. In one of my lucid intervals during those days of agony, I asked my physician to discontinue all life-supporting services or show me how to do it. He refused and told me that someday I would appreciate the unwisdom of my request.

2   A month later, I was discharged from the hospital. In six months, I regained the use of my limbs, and although my voice still lacks its old resonance and carrying power I no longer croak like a frog. There remain some minor disabilities and I am restricted to a rigorous, low sodium diet. I have resumed my writing and research.

3   My experience can be and has been cited as an argument against honoring requests of stricken patients to be gently eased out of their pain and life. I cannot agree. There are two main reasons. As an octogenarian, there is a reasonable likelihood that I may suffer another "cardiovascular accident" or worse. I may not even be in a position to ask for the surcease of pain. It seems to me that I have already paid my dues to death—indeed, although time has softened my memories they are vivid enough to justify my saying that I suffered enough to warrant dying several times over. Why run the risk of more?

Secondly, I dread imposing on my family and friends another grim round of misery similar to the one my first attack occasioned.

My wife and children endured enough for one lifetime. I know that for them the long days and nights of waiting, the disruption of their professional duties and their own familial responsibilities counted for nothing in their anxiety for me. In their joy at my recovery they have been forgotten. Nonetheless, to visit another prolonged spell of helpless suffering on them as my life ebbs away, or even worse, if I linger on into a comatose senility, seems altogether gratuitous.

But what, it may be asked, of the joy and satisfaction of living, of basking in the sunlight, listening to music, watching one's grandchildren growing into adolescence, following the news about the fate of freedom in a troubled world, playing with ideas, writing one's testament of wisdom and folly for posterity? Is not all that one endured, together with the risk of its recurrence, an acceptable price for the multiple satisfactions that are still open even to a person of advanced years?

Apparently those who cling to life, no matter what, think so. I do not.

The zest and intensity of these experiences are no longer what they used to be. I am not vain enough to delude myself that I can in the few remaining years make an important discovery useful for mankind or can lead a social movement or do anything that will be historically eventful, no less event-making. My autobiography, which describes a record of intellectual and political experiences of some historical value, already much too long, could be posthumously published. I have had my fill of joys and sorrows and am not greedy for more life. I have always thought that a test of whether one had found happiness in one's life is whether one would be willing to relive it—whether, if it were possible, one would accept the opportunity to be born again.

Having lived a full and relatively happy life, I would cheerfully accept the chance to be reborn, but certainly not to be reborn again as an infirm octogenarian. To some extent, my views reflect what I have seen happen to the aged and stricken who have been so unfortunate as to survive crippling paralysis. They suffer, and impose suffering on others, unable even to make a request that their torment be ended.

I am mindful too of the burdens placed upon the community, with its rapidly diminishing resources, to provide the adequate and costly services necessary to sustain the lives of those whose days and nights are spent on mattress graves of pain. A better use could be made of these resources to increase the opportunities and qualities of life for the young. I am not denying the moral obligation the community has to look after its disabled and aged. There are times, however, when an individual may find it pointless to insist on the fulfillment of a legal and moral right.

11   What is required is no great revolution in morals but an enlargement of imagination and an intelligent evaluation of alternative uses of community resources.

12   Long ago, Seneca observed that "the wise man will live as long as he ought, not as long as he can." One can envisage hypothetical circumstances in which one has a duty to prolong one's life despite its costs for the sake of others, but such circumstances are far removed from the ordinary prospects we are considering. If wisdom is rooted in the knowledge of the alternatives of choice, it must be reliably informed of the state one is in and its likely outcome. Scientific medicine is not infallible, but it is the best we have. Should a rational person be willing to endure acute suffering merely on the chance that a miraculous cure might presently be at hand? Each one should be permitted to make his own choice—especially when no one else is harmed by it.

13   The responsibility for the decision, whether deemed wise or foolish, must be with the chooser.

Leon R. Kass

Why Doctors Must Not Kill

A physician and professor at the University of Chicago, Leon R. Kass published the following in 1991 in a special issue of Commonweal on euthanasia. Commonweal is a biweekly review of public affairs, religion, the arts, and literature (it publishes many book reviews). It has a generally liberal outlook and is associated with Catholicism.

1   Do you want your doctor licensed to kill? Should he or she be permitted or encouraged to inject or prescribe poison? Shall the mantle of privacy that protects the doctor-patient relationship, in the service of life and wholeness, now also

cloak decisions for death? Do you want *your* doctor deciding, on the basis of his own private views, when you still deserve to live and when you now deserve to die? And what about the other fellow's doctor—that shallow technician, that insensitive boor who neither asks nor listens, that unprincipled money-grubber, that doctor you used to go to until you got up the nerve to switch: do you want *him* licensed to kill? Speaking generally, shall the healing profession become also the euthanizing profession?

Common sense has always answered, "No." For more than two millennia, the reigning medical ethic, mindful that the power to cure is also the power to kill, has held as an inviolable rule, "Doctors must not kill." Yet this venerable taboo is now under attack. Proponents of euthanasia and physician-assisted suicide would have us believe that it is but an irrational vestige of religious prejudice, alien to a true ethic of medicine, which stands in the way of a rational and humane approach to suffering at the end of life. Nothing could be further from the truth. The taboo against doctors killing patients (even on request) is the very embodi-ment of reason and wisdom. Without it, medicine will have trouble doing its proper work; without it, medicine will have lost its claim to be an ethical and trustworthy profession; without it, all of us will suffer—yes, more than we now suffer because some of us are not soon enough released from life.   2

Consider first the damaging consequences for the doctor-patient relationship. The patient's trust in the doctor's wholehearted devotion to the patient's best interests will be hard to sustain once doctors are licensed to kill. Imagine the scene: you are old, poor, in failing health, and alone in the world; you are brought to the city hospital with fractured ribs and pneumonia. The nurse or intern enters late at night with a syringe full of yellow stuff for your intravenous drip. How soundly will you sleep? It will not matter that your doctor has never yet put anyone to death; that he is legally entitled to do so will make a world of difference.   3

And it will make a world of psychic difference too for conscientious physicians. How easily will they be able to care whole-heartedly for patients when it is always possible to think of killing them as a "therapeutic option"? Shall it be penicillin and a respirator one more time, or, perhaps, this time just an overdose of morphine? Physicians get tired of treating patients who are hard to cure, who resist their best efforts, who are on their way down—"gorks," "gomers," and "vegetables" are only some of the less than affectionate names   4 they receive from the house officers. Won't it be tempting to think that death is the best "treatment" for the little old lady "dumped" again on the emergency room by the nearby nursing home?

5   It is naive and foolish to take comfort from the fact that the currently proposed change in the law provides "aid-in-dying" only to those who request it. For we know from long experience how difficult it is to discover what we truly want when we are suffering. Verbal "requests" made under duress rarely reveal the whole story. Often a demand for euthanasia is, in fact, an angry or anxious plea for help, born of fear of rejection or abandonment, or made in ignorance of available alternatives that could alleviate pain and suffering. Everyone knows how easy it is for those who control the information to engineer requests and to manipulate choices, especially in the vulnerable. Paint vividly a horrible prognosis, and contrast it with that "gentle, quick release": which will the depressed or frightened patient choose, especially in the face of a spiraling hospital bill or children who visit grudgingly? Yale Kamisar asks the right questions: "Is this the kind of choice, assuming that it can be made in a fixed and rational manner, that we want to offer a gravely ill person? Will we not sweep up, in the process, some who are not really tired of life, but think others are tired of them; some who do not really want to die, but who feel that they should not live on, because to do so when there looms the legal alternative of euthanasia is to do a selfish or cowardly act? Will not some feel an obligation to have themselves 'eliminated' in order that funds allocated for their terminal care might be better used by their families or, financial worries aside, in order to relieve their families of the emotional strain involved?"

6   Euthanasia, once legalized, will not remain confined to those who freely and knowingly elect it—and the most energetic backers of euthanasia do not really want it thus restricted. Why? Because the vast majority of candidates who merit mercy-killing cannot request it for themselves: adults with persistent vegetative state or severe depression or senility or aphasia or mental illness or Alzheimer's disease; infants who are deformed; and children who are retarded or dying. All incapable of requesting death, they will thus be denied our new humane "assistance-in-dying." But not to worry. The lawyers and the doctors (and the cost-containers) will soon rectify this injustice. The enactment of a law legalizing mercy killing (or assisted suicide) on voluntary

request will certainly be challenged in the courts under the equal-protection clause of the Fourteenth Amendment. Why, it will be argued, should the comatose or the demented be denied the right to such a "dignified death" or such a "treatment" just because they cannot claim it for themselves? With the aid of court-appointed proxy consenters, we will quickly erase the distinction between the right to choose one's own death and the right to request someone else's—as we have already done in the termination-of-treatment cases.

Clever doctors and relatives will not need to wait for such changes in the law. Who will be around to notice when the elderly, poor, crippled, weak, powerless, retarded, uneducated, demented, or gullible are mercifully released from the lives their doctors, nurses, and next of kin deem no longer worth living? In Holland, for example, a recent survey of 300 physicians (conducted by an author who supports euthanasia) disclosed that over 40 percent had performed euthanasia *without the patient's request,* and over 10 percent had done so in more than five cases. Is there any reason to believe that the average American physician is, in his private heart, more committed than his Dutch counterpart to the equal worth and dignity of every life under his care? Do we really want to find out what he is like, once the taboo is broken? 7

Even the most humane and conscientious physician psychologically needs protection against himself and his weaknesses, if he is to care fully for those who entrust themselves to him. A physician-friend who worked many years in a hospice caring for dying patients explained it to me most convincingly: "Only because I knew that I could not and would not kill my patients was I able to enter most fully and intimately into caring for them as they lay dying." The psychological burden of the license to kill (not to speak of the brutalization of the physician-killers) could very well be an intolerably high price to pay for the physician-assisted euthanasia. 8

The point, however, is not merely psychological: it is also moral and essential. My friend's horror at the thought that he might be tempted to kill his patients, were he not enjoined from doing so, embodies a deep understanding of the medical ethic and its intrinsic limits. We move from assessing consequences to looking at medicine itself. 9

The beginning of ethics regarding the use of power generally lies in nay-saying. The wise setting of limits on the use of power is based on discerning the excesses to which the power, unrestrained, is prone. Applied to the professions, 10 this principle would establish strict outer boundaries—indeed, inviolable taboos—against those "occupational hazards" to which each profession is especially prone. *Within* these outer limits, no fixed rules of conduct apply; instead, prudence—the wise judgment of the man-on-the-spot—finds and adopts the best course of action in the light of the circumstances. But the outer limits themselves are fixed, firm, and non-negotiable.

11   What are those limits for medicine? At least three are set forth in the venerable Hippocratic Oath: no breach of confidentiality; no sexual relations with patients; no dispensing of deadly drugs. These unqualified, self-imposed restrictions are readily understood in terms of the temptations to which the physician is most vulnerable, temptations in each case regarding an area of vulnerability and exposure that the practice of medicine requires of patients. Patients necessarily divulge and reveal private and intimate details of their personal lives; patients necessarily expose their naked bodies to the physician's objectifying gaze and investigating hands; patients necessarily expose and entrust the care of their very lives to the physician's skill, technique, and judgment. The exposure is, in all cases, one-sided and asymmetric: the doctor does not reveal his intimacies, display his nakedness, offer up his embodied life to the patient. Mindful of the meaning of such nonmutual exposure, the physician voluntarily sets limits on his own conduct, pledging not to take advantage of or to violate the patient's intimacies, naked sexuality, or life itself.

12   The prohibition against killing patients, the first negative promise of self-restraint sworn to in the Hippocratic Oath, stands as medicine's first and most abiding taboo: "I will neither give a deadly drug to anybody if asked for it, nor will I make a suggestion to this effect.... In purity and holiness I will guard my life and my art." In forswearing the giving of poison, the physician recognizes and restrains a god-like power he wields over patients, mindful that his drugs can both cure and kill. But in forswearing the giving of poison, *when asked for it,* the Hippocratic physician rejects the view that the patient's choice for death can make killing him—or assisting his suicide—right. For the physician, at least, human life in living bodies commands respect and reverence—*by its very nature.* As its respectability does not depend upon human agreement or patient consent, revocation of one's consent to live does not deprive one's living body of respectability. The deepest ethical principle restraining the physician's power is not the autonomy or freedom of the patient; neither

is it his own compassion or good intention. Rather, it is the dignity and mysterious power of human life itself, and, therefore, also what the oath calls the purity and holiness of the life and art to which he has sworn devotion. A person can choose to be a physician, but he cannot simply choose what physicianship means.

The central meaning of physicianship derives not from medicine's powers but from its goal, not from its means but from its end: to benefit the sick by the activity of healing. The physician as physician serves only the sick. He does not serve the relatives or the hospital or the national debt inflated due to Medicare costs. Thus he will never sacrifice the well-being of the sick to the convenience or pocketbook or feelings of the relatives or society. Moreover, the physician serves the sick not because they have rights or wants or claims, but because they are sick. The healer works with and for those who need to be healed, in order to help make them whole. Despite enormous changes in medical technique and institutional practice, despite enormous changes in nosology and therapeutics, the center of medicine has not changed: it is as true today as it was in the days of Hippocrates that the ill desire to be whole; that wholeness means a certain well-working of the enlivened body and its unimpaired powers to sense, think, feel, desire, move, and maintain itself; and that the relationship between the healer and the ill is constituted, essentially even if only tacitly, around the desire of both to promote the wholeness of the one who is ailing. 13

Can wholeness and healing ever be compatible with intentionally killing the patient? Can one benefit the patient as a whole by making him dead? There is, of course, a logical difficulty: how can any good exist for a being that is not? But the error is more than logical: to intend and to act for someone's good requires his continued existence to receive the benefit. 14

To be sure, certain attempts to benefit may in fact turn out, unintentionally, to be lethal. Giving adequate morphine to control pain might induce respiratory depression leading to death. But the intent to relieve the pain of the living presupposes that the living still live to be relieved. This must be the starting point in discussing all medical benefits: no benefit without a beneficiary. 15

Against this view, someone will surely bring forth the hard cases: patients so ill-served by their bodies that they can no longer bear to live, bodies riddled with cancer and racked with pain, against which their "owners" protest in horror and from which they insist on being released. Cannot the person 16 "in the body" speak up against the rest, and request death for "personal" reasons?

17   However sympathetically we listen to such requests, we must see them as incoherent. Such person-body dualism cannot be sustained. "Personhood" is manifest on earth only in living bodies; our highest mental functions are held up by, and are inseparable from, lowly metabolism, respiration, circulation, excretion. There may be blood without consciousness, but there is never consciousness without blood. Thus one who calls for death in the service of personhood is like a tree seeking to cut its roots for the sake of growing its highest fruit. No physician, devoted to the benefit of the sick, can serve the patient as person by denying and thwarting his personal embodiment.

18   To say it plainly, to bring nothingness is incompatible with serving wholeness: one cannot heal—or comfort—by making nil. The healer cannot annihilate if he is truly to heal. The physician-euthanizer is a deadly self-contradiction.

19   But we must acknowledge a difficulty. The central goal of medicine—health—is, in each case, a perishable good: inevitably, patients get irreversibly sick, patients degenerate, patients die. Healing the sick is *in principle* a project that must at some point fail. And here is where all the trouble begins: How does one deal with "medical failure"? What does one seek when restoration of wholeness—or "much" wholeness—is by and large out of the question?

20   Contrary to the propaganda of the euthanasia movement, there is, in fact, much that can be done. Indeed, by recognizing finitude yet knowing that we will not kill, we are empowered to focus on easing and enhancing the *lives* of those who are dying. First of all, medicine can follow the lead of the hospice movement and—abandoning decades of shameful mismanagement—provide truly adequate (and now technically feasible) relief of pain and discomfort. Second, physicians (and patients and families) can continue to learn how to withhold or withdraw those technical interventions that are, in truth, merely burdensome or degrading medical additions to the unhappy end of a life—including, frequently, hospitalization itself. Ceasing treatment and allowing death to occur when (and if) it will seem to be quite compatible with the respect life itself commands for itself. Doctors may and must allow to die, even if they must not intentionally kill.

21   Ceasing medical intervention, allowing nature to take its course, differs fundamentally from mercy killing. For one

thing, death does not necessarily follow the discontinuance of treatment; Karen Ann Quinlan lived more than ten years after the court allowed the "life-sustaining" respirator to be removed. Not the physician, but the underlying fatal illness becomes the true cause of death. More important morally, in ceasing treatment the physician need not *intend* the death of the patient, even when the death follows as a result of his omission. His intention should be to avoid useless and degrading medical *additions* to the already sad end of a life. In contrast, in active, direct mercy killing the physician must, necessarily and indubitably, intend *primarily* that the patient be made dead. And he must knowingly and indubitably cast himself in the role of the agent of death. This remains true even if he is merely an assistant in suicide. A physician who provides the pills or lets the patient plunge the syringe after he leaves the room is *morally* no different from one who does the deed himself. "I will neither give a deadly drug to anybody if asked for it, nor will I make a suggestion to this effect."

Once we refuse the technical fix, physicians and the rest of us can also rise to the occasion: we can learn to act humanly in the presence of finitude. Far more than adequate morphine and the removal of burdensome machinery, the dying need our presence and our encouragement. Dying people are all too easily reduced ahead of time to "thinghood" by those who cannot bear to deal with the suffering or disability of those they love. Withdrawal of contact, affection, and care is the greatest single cause of the dehumanization of dying. Not the alleged humaneness of an elixir of death, but the humanness of connected living-while-dying is what medicine—and the rest of us—most owe the dying. The treatment of choice is company and care.   22

The euthanasia movement would have us believe that the physician's refusal to assist in suicide or perform euthanasia constitutes an affront to human dignity. Yet one of their favorite arguments seems to me rather to prove the reverse. Why, it is argued, do we put animals out of their misery but insist on compelling fellow human beings to suffer to the bitter end? Why, if it is not a contradiction for the veterinarian, does the medical ethic absolutely rule out mercy killing? Is this not simply inhumane?   23

Perhaps *inhumane*, but not thereby *inhuman*. On the contrary, it is precisely because animals are not human that we must treat them (merely) humanely. We put dumb animals to sleep because they do not know that they are dying, because   24 they can make nothing of their misery or mortality, and, therefore, because they cannot live deliberately—i.e., humanly—in the face of their own suffering and dying. They cannot live out a fitting end. Compassion for their weakness and dumbness is our only appropriate emotion, and given our responsibility for their care and well-being, we do the only humane thing we can. But when a conscious human being asks us for death, by that very action he displays the presence of something that precludes our regarding him as a dumb animal. Humanity is owed humanity, not humaneness. Humanity is owed the bolstering of the human, even or especially in its dying moments, in resistance to the temptation to ignore its presence in the sight of suffering.

25   What humanity needs most in the face of evils is courage, the ability to stand against fear and pain and thoughts of nothingness. The deaths we most admire are those of people who, knowing that they are dying, face the fact frontally and act accordingly: they set their affairs in order, they arrange what could be final meetings with their loved ones, and yet, with strength of soul and a small reservoir of hope, they continue to live and work and love as much as they can for as long as they can. Because such conclusions of life require courage, they call for our encouragement—and for the many small speeches and deeds that shore up the human spirit against despair and defeat.

26   Many doctors are in fact rather poor at this sort of encouragement. They tend to regard every dying or incurable patient as a failure, as if an earlier diagnosis or a more vigorous intervention might have avoided what is, in truth, an inevitable collapse. The enormous successes of medicine these past fifty years have made both doctors and laymen less prepared than ever to accept the fact of finitude. Doctors behave, not without some reason, as if they have godlike powers to revive the moribund; laymen expect an endless string of medical miracles. Physicians today are not likely to be agents of encouragement once their technique begins to fail.

27   It is, of course, partly for these reasons that doctors will be pressed to kill—and many of them will, alas, be willing. Having adopted a largely technical approach to healing, having medicalized so much of the end of life, doctors are being asked—often with thinly veiled anger—to provide a final technical solution for the evil of human finitude and for their own technical failure: If you cannot cure me, kill me. The last gasp of autonomy or cry for dignity is asserted against a medicalization and institutionalization of the end of life that robs

the old and the incurable of most of their autonomy and dignity: intubated and electrified, with bizarre mechanical companions, once proud and independent people find themselves cast in the roles of passive, obedient, highly disciplined children. People who care for autonomy and dignity should try to reverse this dehumanization of the last stages of life, instead of giving dehumanization its final triumph by welcoming the desperate goodbye-to-all-that contained in one final plea for poison.

The present crisis that leads some to press for active euthanasia is really an opportunity to learn the limits of the medicalization of life and death and to recover an appreciation of living with and against mortality. It is an opportunity for physicians to recover an understanding that there remains a residual human wholeness—however precarious—that can be cared for even in the face of incurable and terminal illness. Should doctors cave in, should doctors become technical dispensers of death, they will not only be abandoning their posts, their patients, and their duty to care; they will set the worst sort of example for the community at large—teaching technicism and so-called humaneness where encouragement and humanity are both required and sorely lacking. On the other hand, should physicians hold fast, should doctors learn that finitude is no disgrace and that human wholeness can be cared for to the very end, medicine may serve not only the good of its patients, but also, by example, the failing moral health of modern times.

Elizabeth Martinez

Is Rightful Death
a Feminist Issue?

Elizabeth Martinez is a Mexican American activist and a teacher of Women's Studies and Chicano Studies. She frequently writes on Latino issues, and placed the following essay in Ms. *magazine in July/August 1993.*

1   A little after midnight the nurse called to say that my mother had just died. I had expected it to take much longer, and earlier in the day she seemed perhaps a little weaker but no more than that. When my daughter and I arrived at the nursing home in Oakland, the night nurse merely nodded as she unlocked the front door. Her lack of comment seemed unusual at the time, though not unwelcome.

2   It was hard to walk into my mother's room and I lingered in the doorway, feeling lost. Finally I walked to her bed. Her face was very beautiful. The puffiness of her cheeks had gone, perhaps because the feeding tube had been removed five days before; so, too, the lines of strain in her face. She looked handsome again for the first time in many months, a 92-year-old lady of grace and presence. Bending to kiss her forehead, I heard myself think: "It must have been the right thing to do."

3   We asked to talk to the nurse who had found her dead. From another patient's darkened room Virginia came striding out into the light of the corridor: tall, angular, strong. When I asked if she thought my mother had died in her sleep, her face became thoughtful and she said nothing. I persisted anxiously, "Do you think she died in a peaceful way?" Then Virginia understood and opened her long arms wide to wrap them around me, murmuring, yes yes, it was all right.

4   After the arrangements to have my mother's body removed to a mortuary had been completed, we could leave. The night nurse, Georgia, short and round-faced, walked us to the door. In a strong voice she called out across the moonless night: "Drive carefully. Drive carefully!"

5   That was her way: What else could Georgia have said? What does anyone say to a person whose mother has just died when it was that person who made it happen? Had I somehow wished Georgia would say the usual words, "I'm so sorry"?

This question was just one of many mysteries on a long   6
and wondrous journey.

Since 1987 my mother had been in "a persistent vegetative   7
state," as they say, kept alive by artificial means. In building
machines that can breathe, feed, and clean out wastes for
people, we have generated a host of anguishing, Faustian
questions: When should life-support measures be taken? If a
person's mind and spirit are gone, should these measures be
abandoned? If so, when, and who decides? Today we also
hear nationwide debate about doctor-induced death, largely
as a result of Dr. Jack Kevorkian's suicide devices.

Whether the issue is refusing to prolong life mechanically,   8
facilitating suicide, or more active euthanasia—in Greek, the
"easy death"—we eventually confront this society's attitude
toward death itself. The dominant U.S. culture breeds fear
(and with it, dread of aging). To recognize a timely death as
part of planet life, as nature, and sometimes as a friend, does
not come easy for most of the Western world.

Defining medical care as a mystery only they can fathom,   9
many physicians disempower patients who might otherwise
decide their own life-or-death treatment. Health professionals
may also act out ageist attitudes toward the elderly. At the
same time patients and their relatives, conditioned by paternalism or perhaps fear of guilt, may *want* the physician to
make crucial decisions. Since U.S. doctors tend to be men,
who often regard female patients as "immature," "overemo-
tional," or even "hysterical," sexism can play a crucial role.
This is a major reason why the National Organization for
Women supports death with dignity as a feminist issue. NOW
notes that the courts have upheld 60 percent of the male
requests to die and only 14 percent of the female requests.

Issues of class, race, and culture further complicate the   10
debate. If you live in a violence-ridden urban area, the right
to die must seem a ludicrous middle-class hang-up. When
you have no health insurance (up to 36 million Americans in
1992), you're not likely to worry about excessive use of life-
support technology. People of color, especially if they have
recently immigrated, may consider "the right to die" strange
or untrustworthy. There is a sinister side to the picture, too:
the right to die may be supported for very wrong reasons
by government cost-cutters who note the millions put out
for care of the indigent, and by hospital administrators worried about making money under Medicare's reimbursement
system.

11   I knew nothing of such debates when my mother suffered a
series of strokes in the early 1980s that left her almost comatose and requiring total care around the clock. Eventually her
house had to be sold to pay the nursing home bills. Packing
up her papers, I found a one-page typed living will written on
her birthday in 1967 and renewed 12 years later. In fact, cop-
ies surfaced all over the house. The paper said: "If a time
should come when my body can be kept alive only by artificial means which preserve the *breath* of life, but in no way
preserve life's *spirit*, I do not want artificial stimuli used. This
is my strict direction and my request."

12   It was no surprise: she had watched her own mother die
that way and hated it. The paper also signaled how she had
often been ahead of her time. She was an innovative high
school teacher of Spanish, a tennis champion without professional training, an astute social critic and supporter of liberal
causes, amateur pianist, world traveler, short story writer,
and bridge enthusiast. She took special pleasure in dancing
with my father until his death and later with a 78-year-old
boyfriend who wrote poetry at 3 A.M. and then called her to
read it over the telephone ("Do you think it's all right for me
to be seeing a younger man?" she asked at the age of 83). She
liked to be around hustle and bustle, young people, the unpredictable, anything that seized her imagination. Few people
love life more than she did.

13   This was the person we had seen over recent years grow
progressively incontinent and unable to walk, eat, talk, or see.
When she turned 90, still semialert, we celebrated in the nursing home with a big lunch on the sunny veranda, other relatives, and a mariachi band. On her next birthday she lay in
bed diapered and with a feeding tube, speechless and staring
open-eyed at the ceiling. Could she possibly want such an
existence?

14   Yet even after finding her living will, I snatched at the most
fragile sign of "life." If she uttered two words, as happened
every few weeks, I was thrilled. The desire for her to "stay
alive" tugged at one end of my feelings; at the other stood the
knowledge of her desire to die with dignity. Visiting her
became an encounter with reprimand, real or imagined; her
face seemed to ask me crossly, Why haven't you done what I
requested? Didn't you notice that it was my *strict* direction?
And I asked myself: Am I afraid of what people will think?

15   In recent years public opinion has been both liberal and
cautious about the right to die. A 1990 Gallup poll found that

84 percent of U.S. residents would want treatment withheld if they were on life-support systems with no hope of recovering. The poll also found that 66 percent believe someone in great and hopeless pain had a moral right to commit suicide. Another 1990 poll showed that 53 percent favor allowing a doctor's help in committing suicide.

At the same time voters rejected a 1991 Washington State   16
initiative that would have allowed doctors to end a person's life if two gave written opinions that death would naturally occur within six months. Last year a California "Death with Dignity" initiative would have given mentally competent, terminally ill adults the right to issue a directive requesting physician-aid-in-dying; it too was voted down, by a 54–46 margin. In both cases most voters apparently saw the act as lacking adequate safeguards against abuse or too vague on key requirements. On the other hand, many—like this writer—voted for the California initiative as being basically sound. Many "no" votes in that state must have stemmed from uninformed fear; the Catholic church and the medical establishment waged an almost $4 million opposition campaign against the initiative's $700,000. Future initiative-makers need to draw lessons from the weaknesses of these two.

Antiabortion forces have argued that "*Roe* v. *Wade* was a   17
precedent for killing people," and from there it's a "slippery slope" downhill to euthanasia. Thus they negate the right to control one's own body in matters of dying as in birthing. According to a 1990 *New York Times* report, antiabortion groups have blocked legislation in at least three states that would allow withholding of nutrients, which they see as "forced starvation" (they do not usually oppose disconnecting respirators).

Opposition has sometimes come from members of the dis-   18
abled community, who hear echoes of genocide in the idea that life may not be worth living for the so-called unfit. African Americans and Latinos have supported the right to die much less enthusiastically than other sectors of the population. History, of course, gives all people of color reason to suspect any law that grants power over their lives to mostly white strangers. Advocates of death with dignity as a right respond that the rich have usually been able to have it by virtue of their influence over doctors and their ability to travel if necessary. The poor—which includes so many people of color—should be guaranteed the same right to choose. Death with dignity is the final civil right.

19   In time it did become clear that I wasn't worried about disapproval from friends or relatives if I ended my mother's life.
The battle lay within, between two kinds of love—one that
wanted her still on this planet, for me, and one that affirmed
respect for her personhood, from me. When she contracted
pneumonia after a year of being inert, her doctor said: "It's
the old folks' friend, a quick and easy way to go. If you want
the antibiotics stopped, let me know." Three long days passed
of articulating the decision as: "Today I have to decide
whether to kill my mother or not." I finally gave the order, but
she had already taken enough medication to recover.

20   More months passed and the living will would not go away.
After another consultation the doctor reduced her fluids, as
this might diminish her physical resistance. She showed no
effects. The battle resumed in my head: perhaps she doesn't
want to die, after all. Or, in better moments: Is she just laughing at me? The doctor refused to do any more. I assumed,
based on reading newspaper stories about such cases, that
the law gave him no choice.

21   Struggles for the legal right to die present a long, sad, and
often surreal parade of cases like that of Karen Ann Quinlan,
the young New Jersey woman in a coma whose parents finally
got her respirator turned off by a historic court order. The parents of Nancy Cruzan, who existed on a feeding tube, went all
the way to the U.S. Supreme Court. In 1990 the court issued a
double-edged ruling. On one hand it upheld an individual's
constitutional right to the discontinuance of life-support treatment. On the other hand the court maintained the right of a
state—in this case, Missouri—to demand "clear and convincing evidence" of a patient's desire to avoid life-support measures. As a result the Cruzan family had to produce new
witnesses before Nancy could finally die.

22   Galvanized into action by the court decision, Congress
passed the Patient Self-Determination Act. It requires health
care facilities that receive Medicare or Medicaid funds (95
percent of such centers) to inform new patients about their
legal right to write a living will or choose a proxy to represent
their wishes about medical treatment. The Supreme Court's
decision also made thousands of people put their wishes in
writing to evidence them.

23   Today all 50 states authorize some form of advance directive from a patient—either a living will or a durable power of
attorney, which is the preferred method. (Doing both is best,
some say: the first establishes your wishes, the second facili-

tates their implementation.) Legal uncertainty or conflict continues where the patient has given no directive and where the procedure contemplated—for instance, feeding tube removal—is not authorized. Only one state, Kentucky, specifically prohibits termination of tube-feeding. Others stand silent on the issue and therefore implicitly allow it. It's a legal crazy quilt.

Not knowing California was one of those states that implicitly allowed feeding tube removal at the time, I continued to do nothing about my mother. But the feeling became inescapable: it isn't right to be waiting for the easy or legal way out.   24

One Sunday, walking on the beach alongside the Pacific with a friend, we talked about my paralysis. She was a nurse, and over the afternoon hours she demystified the steps to be taken and their physical consequences. By sunset I could see the decision—huge and relentless, like waves rolling in. But also quieting. That evening I talked with a woman who had helped her own mother to die, and she told me what I might expect to feel along with the practical problems. Then she commented, "Perhaps you can think of this as an opportunity."   25

Until that moment I had thought of having accepted a painful necessity at last. But here was a chance to make my mother a gift: something worthy of the boundless devotion she had given me and my daughter for so many years, something I knew she wanted, something only I could give. Thinking this way, the weight of double guilt—for not carrying out my mother's will and then for wanting to carry it out—floated away. In its place rose an enormous and simple gratitude that she had endowed us with certainty about her wishes.   26

One large problem remained: no doctor to remove the feeding tube.   27

The American Hospital Association estimates that 70 percent of the deaths in the United States are somehow negotiated with patients, family, and doctors quietly agreeing not to use life-support technology. In 1986 the American Medical Association declared that all life-prolonging medical treatment could be ethically disconnected when a patient's coma is irreversible. Nevertheless, my mother's doctor had refused to do anything active.   28

In retrospect I imagine his position then was a matter of personal preference or morality. Health policy expert and practicing physician Dr. Thomas Bodenheimer of San Francisco   29 spoke to me about why doctors sometimes encourage life-support measures. "It is uncomfortable and time-consuming to talk to the family or patient about death. Also, docs may fear malpractice suits, if we don't 'do everything.' And we are trained to save life, not assist death—it's not easy to change our ways. A few unscrupulous doctors think about the fees they don't collect on a dead body, but mostly I think it is a matter of benign neglect. Docs will automatically put more time and thought into acutely ill patients."

30   An old friend, a doctor, agreed to remove the tube. "I agree with what you're doing," he said immediately. We wanted it done in the nursing home where my mother had received exceptional care for five years. But the social worker there told me, "They think you are doing the right thing, they just couldn't handle it emotionally after taking care of her so long."

31   Without my asking, she quickly found another facility. The nursing director there, Jane—I have changed her name like others in this story—assured me that the staff would relieve any discomfort that lack of food caused my mother. They were required to offer nourishment and fluids by hand; if somehow my mother took them, this could prolong her life.

32   But that was the only legal issue that Jane mentioned; her time and heart went into other matters. "In cases like this," she explained, "I call a special meeting of the whole staff and explain the situation to them. I have to be sure that they feel clear about it and some will disagree with what you're doing. Then I ask for volunteers to take care of the person." Jane spoke without hesitation; it would never occur to her just to assign workers, as if they had no feelings. I nodded, wordless. "One more thing," Jane told me. "You should tell your mother what's going to happen. It doesn't matter if she seems not to hear you or understand. I think she will."

33   On the day of the transfer from the old nursing home to the new one, I sat down by her bed and said that the tube would be taken out in a few hours. That I was doing what she wished, at last. For all my belief in the rightness of this act, I couldn't make my words more direct than that. Nothing showed in her face and her eyes stared straight ahead.

34   At the new place, after she was settled, my daughter and I stood outside in the sun waiting for the doctor who would remove the tube. Last-minute doubts and fears started to batter me: Was this really what she wanted? Why didn't she refer specifically to feeding tubes in her living will? Maybe she only meant to reject a respirator?

The doctor arrived, listened to my worries. "You know her,   35
you know how she lived, what she wanted," he said. "In the
end, what you are doing is right not just because of the living
will but because you know what kind of person she is." Then
he went in and, with Jane's help, removed the tube. When he
came back, he smiled and just said, "This is an amazing nursing home."

The next day, returning to visit, I found my mother asleep   36
in bed. On the pillow next to her head lay the miniature teddy
bear that I had left on the bedside cabinet, and a fresh flower
perched in her hair. The nurse walked in then, a woman
named Frances, who looked at me and explained. "I always
sleep with my teddy bear so I thought she might like it too,
bless her heart."

Five days later my mother died. "Five days—so quick for   37
such a strong person," friends and relatives commented. "She
must have been ready." A few asked, "Why did it take you so
long to do what she wanted?" I had no answer to that except
it took both of us a long, long time—but then we did meet.

WHAT DO YOU MAKE
OF THE INTERNET?

John Perry Barlow

Is There a There in Cyberspace?

John Barlow ran a cattle ranch in Wyoming for seventeen years while writing songs for The Grateful Dead. Forced to sell his ranch in 1988, he began writing and speaking about computer-mediated communication. He is a cofounder of the Electronic Frontier Foundation and is on the board of directors of WELL (Whole Earth 'Lectronic Link). Barlow frequently discusses Internet issues in interviews and in his own writing. The essay below appeared in the March/April issue of the Utne Reader, *a left-of-center magazine that publishes articles on issues of public interest, including several of the others in this section of* Conversations.

1   I am often asked how I went from pushing cows around a remote Wyoming ranch to my present occupation (which *The Wall Street Journal* recently described as "cyber-space cadet"). I haven't got a short answer, but I suppose I came to the virtual world looking for community.

2   Unlike most modern Americans, I grew up in an actual place, an entirely nonintentional community called Pinedale, Wyoming. As I struggled for nearly a generation to keep my ranch in the family, I was motivated by the belief that such places were the spiritual home of humanity. But I knew their future was not promising.

3   At the dawn of the 20th century, over 40 percent of the American workforce lived off the land. The majority of us lived in towns like Pinedale. Now fewer than 1 percent of us extract a living from the soil. We just became too productive for our own good.

4   Of course, the population followed the jobs. Farming and ranching communities are now home to a demographically insignificant percentage of Americans, the vast majority of whom live not in ranch houses but in more or less identical

split-level "ranch homes" in more or less identical suburban "communities." Generica.

In my view, these are neither communities nor homes. I believe the combination of television and suburban population patterns is simply toxic to the soul. I see much evidence in contemporary America to support this view. 5

Meanwhile, back at the ranch, doom impended. And, as I watched community in Pinedale growing ill from the same economic forces that were killing my family's ranch, the Bar Cross, satellite dishes brought the cultural infection of television. I started looking around for evidence that community in America would not perish altogether. 6

I took some heart in the mysterious nomadic City of the Deadheads, the virtually physical town that follows the Grateful Dead around the country. The Deadheads lacked place, touching down briefly wherever the band happened to be playing, and they lacked continuity in time, since they had to suffer a new diaspora every time the band moved on or went home. But they had many of the other necessary elements of community, including a culture, a religion of sorts (which, though it lacked dogma, had most of the other, more nurturing aspects of spiritual practice), a sense of necessity, and, most importantly, shared adversity. 7

I wanted to know more about the flavor of their interaction, what they thought and felt, but since I wrote Dead songs (including "Estimated Prophet" and "Cassidy"), I was a minor icon to the Deadheads, and was thus inhibited, in some socially Heisenbergian way, from getting a clear view of what really went on among them. 8

Then, in 1987, I heard about a "place" where Deadheads gathered where I could move among them without distorting too much the field of observation. Better, this was a place I could visit without leaving Wyoming. It was a shared computer in Sausalito, California, called the Whole Earth 'Lectronic Link, or WELL. After a lot of struggling with modems, serial cables, init strings, and other computer arcana that seemed utterly out of phase with such notions as Deadheads and small towns, I found myself looking at the glowing yellow word "Login:" beyond which lay my future. 9

"Inside" the WELL were Deadheads in community. There were thousands of them there, gossiping, complaining (mostly about the Grateful Dead), comforting and harassing each other, bartering, engaging in religion (or at least exchanging their totemic set lists), beginning and ending love affairs, praying for one another's sick kids. There was, it 10 seemed, everything one might find going on in a small town, save dragging Main Street and making out on the back roads.

11   I was delighted. I felt I had found the new locale of human community—never mind that the whole thing was being conducted in mere words by minds from whom the bodies had been amputated. Never mind that all these people were deaf, dumb, and blind as paramecia or that their town had neither seasons nor sunsets nor smells.

12   Surely all these deficiencies would be remedied by richer, faster communications media. The featureless log-in handles would gradually acquire video faces (and thus expressions), shaded 3-D body puppets (and thus body language). This "space," which I recognized at once to be a primitive form of the cyberspace William Gibson predicted in his sci-fi novel *Neuromancer*, was still without apparent dimensions or vistas. But virtual reality would change all that in time.

13   Meanwhile, the commons, or something like it, had been rediscovered. Once again, people from the 'burbs had a place where they could encounter their friends as my fellow Pinedalians did at the post office and the Wrangler Cafe. They had a place where their hearts could remain as the companies they worked for shuffled their bodies around America. They could put down roots that could not be ripped out by forces of economic history. They had a collective stake. They had a community.

14   It is seven years now since I discovered the WELL. In that time, I cofounded an organization, the Electronic Frontier Foundation, dedicated to protecting its interests and those of other virtual communities like it from raids by physical government. I've spent countless hours typing away at its residents, and I've watched the larger context that contains it, the Internet, grow at such an explosive rate that, by 2004, every human on the planet will have an e-mail address unless the growth curve flattens (which it will).

15   My enthusiasm for virtuality has cooled. In fact, unless one counts interaction with the rather too large society of those with whom I exchange electronic mail, I don't spend much time engaging in virtual community at all. Many of the near-term benefits I anticipated from it seem to remain as far in the future as they did when I first logged in. Perhaps they always will.

16   Pinedale works, more or less, as it is, but a lot is still missing from the communities of cyberspace, whether they be places like the WELL, the fractious newsgroups of USENET,

the silent "auditoriums" of America Online, or even enclaves
on the promising World Wide Web.

What is missing? Well, to quote Ranjit Makkuni of Xerox   17
Corporation's Palo Alto Research Center, "the *prāna* is missing," *prāna* being the Hindu term for both breath and spirit. I
think he is right about this and that perhaps the central question of the virtual age is whether or not *prāna* can somehow
be made to fit through any disembodied medium.

Prāna is, to my mind, the literally vital element in the holy   18
and unseen ecology of relationship, the dense mesh of invisible life, on whose surface carbon-based life floats like a thin
film. It is at the heart of the fundamental and profound difference between information and experience. Jaron Lanier has
said that "information is alienated experience," and, that
being true, *prāna* is part of what is removed when you create
such easily transmissible replicas of experience as, say, the
evening news.

Obviously a great many other, less spiritual, things are also   19
missing entirely, like body language, sex, death, tone of voice,
clothing, beauty (or homeliness), weather, violence, vegeta-
tion, wildlife, pets, architecture, music, smells, sunlight, and
that ol' harvest moon. In short, most of the things that make
my life real to me.

Present, but in far less abundance than in the physical   20
world, which I call "meat space," are women, children, old
people, poor people, and the genuinely blind. Also mostly
missing are the illiterate and the continent of Africa. There is
not much human diversity in cyberspace, which is populated,
as near as I can tell, by white males under 50 with plenty of
computer terminal time, great typing skills, high math SATS,
strongly held opinions on just about everything, and an
excruciating face-to-face shyness, especially with the opposite
sex.

But diversity is as essential to healthy community as it is to   21
healthy ecosystems (which are, in my view, different from
communities only in unimportant aspects).

I believe that the principal mason for the almost universal   22
failure of the intentional communities of the '60s and '70s was
a lack of diversity in their members. It was a rare commune
with any old people in it, or people who were fundamentally
out of philosophical agreement with the majority.

Indeed, it is the usual problem when we try to build some-   23
thing that can only be grown. Natural systems, such as
human communities, are simply too complex to design by the
engineering principles we insist on applying to them. Like Dr.

Frankenstein, Western civilization is now finding its rational skills inadequate to the task of creating and caring for life. We would do better to return to a kind of agricultural mind-set in which we humbly try to re-create the conditions from which life has sprung before. And leave the rest to God.

24   Given that it has been built so far almost entirely by people with engineering degrees, it is not so surprising that cyberspace has the kind of overdesigned quality that leaves out all kinds of elements nature would have provided invisibly.

25   Also missing from both the communes of the '60s and from cyberspace are a couple of elements that I believe are very important, if not essential, to the formation and preservation of real community: an absence of alternatives and a sense of genuine adversity, generally shared. What about these?

26   It is hard to argue that anyone would find losing a modem literally hard to survive, while many have remained in small towns, have tolerated their intolerances and created entertainment to enliven their culturally arid lives simply because it seemed there was no choice but to stay. There are many investments—spiritual, material, and temporal—one is willing to put into a home one cannot leave. Communities are often the beneficiaries of these involuntary investments.

27   But when the going gets rough in cyberspace, it is even easier to move than it is in the 'burbs, where, given the fact that the average American moves some 12 times in his or her life, moving appears to be pretty easy. You can not only find another bulletin board service (BBS) or newsgroup to hang out in, you can, with very little effort, start your own.

28   And then there is the bond of joint suffering. Most community is a cultural stockade erected against a common enemy that can take many forms. In Pinedale, we bore together, with an understanding needing little expression, the fact that Upper Green River Valley is the coldest spot, as measured by annual mean temperature, in the lower 48 states. We knew that if somebody was stopped on the road most winter nights, he would probably die there, so the fact that we might loathe him was not sufficient reason to drive on past his broken pickup.

29   By the same token, the Deadheads have the Drug Enforcement Administration, which strives to give them 20-year prison terms without parole for distributing the fairly harmless sacrament of their faith. They have an additional bond in the fact that when their Microbuses die, as they often do, no one but another Deadhead is likely to stop to help them.

30   But what are the shared adversities of cyberspace? Lousy user interfaces? The flames of harsh invective? Dumb jokes?

Surely these can all be survived without the sanctuary provided by fellow sufferers.

One is always free to yank the jack, as I have mostly done.   31
For me, the physical world offers far more opportunity for
prāna-rich connections with my fellow creatures. Even for
someone whose body is in a state of perpetual motion, I feel I
can generally find more community among the still-embodied.

Finally, there is that shyness factor. Not only are we trying   32
to build community here among people who have never experienced any in my sense of the term, we are trying to build
community among people who, in their lives, have rarely
used the word *we* in a heartfelt way. It is a vast club, and
many of the members—following Groucho Marx—wouldn't
want to join a club that would have them.

And yet...   33

How quickly physical community continues to deteriorate.   34
Even Pinedale, which seems to have survived the plague of
ranch failures, feels increasingly cut off from itself. Many of
the ranches are now owned by corporate types who fly their
Gulfstreams in to fish and are rarely around during the many
months when the creeks are frozen over and neighbors are
needed. They have kept the ranches alive financially, but they
actively discourage their managers from the interdependence
my former colleagues and I require. They keep agriculture on
life support, still alive but lacking a functional heart.

And the town has been inundated with suburbanites who   35
flee here, bringing all their terrors and suspicions with them.
They spend their evenings as they did in Orange County,
watching television or socializing in hermetic little enclaves of
fundamentalist Christianity that seem to separate them from
us and even, given their sectarian animosities, from one
another. The town remains. The community is largely a
wraith of nostalgia.

So where else can we look for the connection we need to   36
prevent our plunging further into the condition of separateness Nietzsche called sin? What is there to do but to dive further into the bramble bush of information that, in its
broadcast forms, has done so much to tear us apart?

Cyberspace, for all its current deficiencies and failed prom-   37
ises, is not without some very real solace already.

Some months ago, the great love of my life, a vivid young   38
woman with whom I intended to spend the rest of it, dropped
dead of undiagnosed viral cardiomyopathy two days short of
her 30th birthday. I felt as if my own heart had been as shredded as hers.

39   We had lived together in New York City. Except for my daughters, no one from Pinedale had met her. I needed a community to wrap around myself against colder winds than fortune had ever blown at me before. And without looking, I found I had one in the virtual world.

40   On the WELL, there was a topic announcing her death in one of the conferences to which I posted the eulogy I had read over her before burying her in her own small town of Nanaimo, British Columbia. It seemed to strike a chord among the disembodied living on the Net. People copied it and sent it to one another. Over the next several months I received almost a megabyte of electronic mail from all over the planet, mostly from folks whose faces I have never seen and probably never will.

41   They told me of their own tragedies and what they had done to survive them. As humans have since words were first uttered, we shared the second most common human experience, death, with an openheartedness that would have caused grave uneasiness in physical America, where the whole topic is so cloaked in denial as to be considered obscene. Those strangers, who had no arms to put around my shoulders, no eyes to weep with mine, nevertheless saw me through. As neighbors do.

42   I have no idea how far we will plunge into this strange place. Unlike previous frontiers, this one has no end. It is so dissatisfying in so many ways that I suspect we will be more restless in our search for home here than in all our previous explorations. And that is one reason why I think we may find it after all. If home is where the heart is, then there is already some part of home to be found in cyberspace.

43   So...does virtual community work or not? Should we all go off to cyberspace or should we resist it as a demonic form of symbolic abstraction? Does it supplant the real or is there, in it, reality itself?

44   Like so many true things, this one doesn't resolve itself to a black or a white. Nor is it gray. It is, along with the rest of life, black/white. Both/neither. I'm not being equivocal or wishy-washy here. We have to get over our Manichean sense that everything is either good or bad, and the border of cyberspace seems to me a good place to leave that old set of filters.

45   But really it doesn't matter. We are going there whether we want to or not. In five years, everyone who is reading these words will have an e-mail address, other than the determined Luddites who also eschew the telephone and electricity.

When we are all together in cyberspace we will see what   46
the human spirit, and the basic desire to connect, can create
there. I am convinced that the result will be more benign if
we go there open-minded, open-hearted, and excited with the
adventure than if we are dragged into exile.

And we must remember that going to cyberspace, unlike   47
previous great emigrations to the frontier, hardly requires us
to leave where we have been. Many will find, as I have, a
much richer appreciation of physical reality for having spent
so much time in virtuality.

Despite its current (and perhaps in some areas permanent)   48
insufficiencies, we should go to cyberspace with hope.
Groundless hope, like unconditional love, may be the only
kind that counts.

M. Kadi

Welcome to Cyberia

*M. Kadi is a pseudonym for the author, who works as a con-
sultant in the computer industry in the San Francisco Bay
Area of California but who wishes to write about computer
issues anonymously. She contributed this essay to the Winter/
Spring 1994–95 issue of* H2SO4, *which, as its name implies, is
an inexpensively produced, avant garde, irreverent, small-
circulation magazine based in San Francisco that publishes
literary and political commentaries, both serious and not-so-
serious, and tries to bring together both academic and nonacademic writers and readers. It publishes works from many political and cultural perspectives. The essay published here also
appeared in truncated form in the* Utne Reader *(which often
republishes items from the alternative press) along with several
other selections in this section of* Conversations, *by Barlow,
Rheingold, and Saige.*

*Computer networking offers the soundest basis for world peace
that has yet been presented. Peace must be created on the bulwark of understanding. International computer networks will*

*knit together the peoples of the world in bonds of mutual
respect; its possibilities are vast, indeed.*
                                    —*Scientific American,* June 1994

*Cyberspace is a new medium. Every night on Prodigy, Com-
puServe, GEnie and thousands of smaller computer bulletin
boards, people by the hundreds of thousands are logging on to
a great computer-mediated gabfest, an interactive debate that
allows them to leap over barriers of time, place, sex and social
status.*
                                              —*Time* Magazine

*The Internet is really about the rise of not merely a new tech-
nology, but a new culture—a global culture where time, space,
borders and even personal identity are radically redefined.*
                                    —*OnLine Access* Magazine

1   Computer bulletin board services offer up the glories of
e-mail, the thought provocation of Newsgroups, the sharing
of ideas implicit in public posting, and the interaction of real-
time chats. The fabulous, wonderful limitless world of Communication is just waiting for you to log on. Sure. Yeah.
Right.

2   I confess, I am a dedicated cyber-junkie. It's fun. It's interesting. It takes me places where I've never been before. I sign
on once a day, twice a day, three times a day, more and more;
I read, I post, I live. Writing an article on the ever-expanding,
ever-entertaining, ever-present world of online existence
would have been easy for me. But it would have been familiar,
perhaps dull and it might have been a lie. The world does not
need another article on the miracle of online reality; what we
need, what I need, what this whole delirious, inter-connected,
global-community of a world needs, is a little reality check.

3   To some extent the following scenario will be misleading.
There *are* flat rate online services (Netcom for one) which
offer significant connectivity for a measly 17 dollars a month.
But I'm interested in the activities and behavior of the private
service users who will soon comprise a vast majority of online
citizens. Furthermore, let's face facts. The U.S. government
by and large foots the bill for the Internet, through maintaining the structural (hardware) backbone, including, among
other things, funding to major universities. As surely as the
Department of Defense started this whole thing, AT&T or Ted
Turner is going to end up running it, so I don't think it's too
unrealistic to take a look at the Net as it exists in its commer-

cial form in order to expose some of the realities lurking behind the regurgitated media rhetoric and the religious fanaticism of net junkies.

The average person, J. Individual, has an income. How   4
much of J. Individual's income is going to be spent on computer connectivity? Does $120 a month sound reasonable? Well, you may find that a bit too steep for your pocketbook, but the brutal fact is that $120 is a "reasonable" monthly amount. The major on-line services have a monthly service charge of approximately $15. Fifteen dollars to join the global community, communicate with a diverse group of people, and access the world's largest repository of knowledge since the Alexandrian library doesn't seem unreasonable, does it? But don't overlook the average per-hour connection rate of $3 (which can skyrocket upwards of $10, depending on your modem speed and service). You might think that you are a crack whiz with your communications software—that you are rigorous and stringent and never, ever respond to e-mail or a forum while you're on-line—but let me tell you that no one is capable of logging on efficiently every time. Thirty hours per month is a realistic estimate.

In case you think 30 hours a month is an outrageous esti-   5
mate, think of it in terms of television. (OK, so you don't own a television, well, goody-for-you—imagine that you do!) 30 hours, is, quite obviously, one hour a day. That's not so much. 30 hours a month in front of a television is simply the evening news plus a weekly Seinfeld/Frazier [sic] hour. 30 hours a month is less time than the average car-phone owner spends on the phone while commuting. Even a conscientious geek, logging on for e-mail and the up-to-the-minute news that only the net services can provide is probably going to spend 30 hours a month online. And, let's be truthful here, 30 hours a month ignores shareware downloads, computer illiteracy, real-time chatting, interactive game playing and any serious forum following, which by nature entail a significant amount of scrolling and/or downloading time.

If you are really and truly going to use the net services to   6
connect with the global community, the hourly charges are going to add up pretty quickly. Take out a piece of paper, pretend you're writing a check, and print out "One hundred and twenty dollars—" and tell me again, how diverse is the on-line community?

That scenario aside, let's pretend that you're single, that   7
you don't have children, that you rarely leave the house, that you don't have a TV and that money is not an issue. Meaning,

pretend for a moment that you have as much time and as much money to spend online as you damn-well want. What do you actually do online?

8   Well, you download some cool shareware, you post technical questions in the computer user group forums, you check your stocks, you read the news and maybe some reviews—Hey, you've already passed that 30 hour limit! But, of course, since "computer networks make it easy to reach out and touch strangers who share a particular obsession or concern," you are participating in the online forums, discussion groups, and conferences.

9   Let's review the structure of forums. For the purposes of this essay, we will examine the smallest of the major user-friendly commercial services—America OnLine (AOL). There is no precise statistic available (at least none that the company will reveal—you have to do the research by HAND!!!) on exactly how many subject-specific discussion areas (folders) exist on AOL. Any online service is going to have zillions of posts pertaining to computer usage (e.g., the computer games area of AOL breaks into five hundred separate topics with over 100,000 individual posts), so let's look at a less popular area: the "Lifestyles and Interests" department.

10   For starters, there are 57 initial categories within the Lifestyles and Interests area. One of these categories is Ham Radio. Ham Radio? How can there possibly be 5,909 separate, individual posts about Ham Radio? 5,865 postings in the Biking (and that's just bicycles, not motorcycles) category. Genealogy—22,525 posts. The Gay and Lesbian category is slightly more substantial—36,333 posts. There are five separate categories for political and issue discussion. The big catch-all topic area, The Exchange, has over 100,000 posts. Basically, service wide (on the smallest service, remember) there are over a million posts.

11   So, you want to communicate with other people, join the online revolution, but obviously you can't wade through everything that's being discussed—you need to decide which topics interest you, which folders to browse. Within The Exchange alone (one of 57 subdivisions within one of another 50 higher divisions) there are 1,492 separate topic-specific folders—each containing a rough average of 50 posts, but with many containing close to 400...

12   So there you are, J. Individual, ready to start interacting with folks, sharing stories and communicating. You have narrowed yourself into a single folder, three tiers down in the AOL hierarchy, and now you must choose between nearly fif-

teen hundred folders. Of course, once you choose a few of these folders, you will then have to read all the posts in order to catch up, be current, and not merely repeat a previous post.

A polite post is no more than two paragraphs long (a screenful of text which obviously has a number of intellectually negative implications). Let's say you choose ten folders (out of 1,500). Each folder contains an average of 50 posts. Five hundred posts, at, say, one paragraph each, and you're now looking at the equivalent of a two hundred page book. 13

Enough with the stats. Let me back up a minute and present you with some very disturbing, but rational, assumptions. J. Individual wants to join the online revolution to connect and communicate. But, J. Individual is not going to read all one million posts on AOL. (After all, J. Individual has a second online service.) Exercising choice is J. Individual's god-given right as an American, and, by gosh, J. Individual is going to make some decisions. So J. is going to ignore all the support groups—after all, J. is a normal, well-adjusted person and all of J.'s friends are normal, well-adjusted people; what does J. need to know about alcoholism or incest victims? J. Individual is white. So J. Individual is going to ignore all the multicultural folders. J. couldn't give a hoot about gender issues and does not want to discuss religion or philosophy. Ultimately, J. Individual does not engage in topics that do not interest J. Individual. So who is J. meeting? Why, people who are *just like* J. 14

J. Individual has now joined the electronic community. Surfed the Net. Found some friends. *Tuned in, turned on, and geeked out.* Traveled the Information Highway and, just a few miles down that great democratic expressway, J. Individual has settled into an electronic suburb. 15

Are any of us so very different? It's my time and my money and I am not going to waste any of it reading posts by disgruntled Robert-Bly drum-beating men's-movement boys who think that they should have some say over, for instance, whether or not I choose to carry a child to term simply because a condom broke. I know where I stand. I'm an adult. I know what's up and I am not going to waste my money arguing with a bunch of neanderthals. 16

Oh yeah; I am so connected, so enlightened, so open to the opposing viewpoint. I'm out there, meeting all kinds of people from different economic backgrounds (who have $120 a month to burn), from all religions (yeah, right, like anyone actually discusses religion anymore from a user standpoint), 17 from all kinds of different ethnic backgrounds and with all kinds of sexual orientations (as if any of this ever comes up outside of the appropriate topic folder).

18   People are drawn to topics and folders that interest them and therefore people will only meet people who are interested in the same topics in the same folders. Rarely does anyone venture into a random folder just to see what others (the Other?) are talking about.

19   Basically, between the monetary constraints and the sheer number of topics and individual posts, the great Information Highway is not a place where you will enter an "amazing web of new people, places, and ideas." One does not encounter people from "all walks of life" because there are too many people and too many folders. Diversity might be out there (and personally I don't think it is), but the simple fact is that the average person will not encounter it because with one brain, one job, one partner, one family, and one life, no one has the time!

20   Just in case these arguments based on time and money aren't completely convincing, let me bring up a historical reference. Please take another look at the opening quote of this essay, from *Scientific American*. It was featured in their 50 Years Ago Today column. Where you read "computer networking," the quote originally contained the word *television*. Amusing, isn't it?

21   Finally, for me, there is a subtle and terrible irony lurking within the Net: the Net, despite its speed, its exchange, ultimately reeks of stasis. In negating physical distance, the immediacy of electronic transfers devalues movement and the journey. In one minute a thought is in my head, and the next minute it is typed out, sent, read, and in your head. The exchange may be present, but the journey is imperceptible. The Infobahn hype would have us believe that this phenomenon is a fast-paced dynamic exchange, but the feeling, when you've been at it long enough, is that this exchange of ideas lacks movement. Lacking movement and the journey, to me it loses all value.

22   Maybe this is prejudice. Words are not wine, they do not necessarily require age to improve them. Furthermore, I have always hated the concept that Art comes only out of struggle and suffering. So, to say that e-mail words are weaker somehow because of the nature, or lack, of their journey, is to romanticize the struggle. I suppose I am anthropomorphising text too much—but I somehow sense that one works harder to endow one's handwritten words with a certain strength, a

certain soul, simply because those things are necessary in order to survive a journey. The ease of the e-mail journey means that your words don't need to be as well-prepared, or as well-equipped.

Electronic missives lack time, space, embodiment and his-   23
tory (in the sense of a collection of experiences). Lacking all these things, an electronic missive is almost in complete opposition to my existence and I can't help but wonder what, if anything, I am communicating.

Howard Rheingold
The Virtual Community

This essay, excerpted from Rheingold's book The Virtual Community *(1993), first appeared in the* Utne Reader *with several other essays reprinted in this section of* Conversations.

In the summer of 1986, my then-2-year-old daughter   1
picked up a tick. There was this blood-bloated *thing* sucking on our baby's scalp, and we weren't quite sure how to go about getting it off. My wife, Judy, called the pediatrician. It was 11 o'clock in the evening. I logged onto the WELL, the big Bay Area infonet, and contacted the Parenting conference (a conference is an on-line conversation about a specific subject). I got my answer on-line within minutes from a fellow with the improbable but genuine name of Flash Gordon, M.D. I had removed the tick by the time Judy got the callback from the pediatrician's office.

What amazed me wasn't just the speed with which we   2
obtained precisely the information we needed to know, right when we needed to know it. It was also the immense inner sense of security that comes with discovering that real people—most of them parents, some of them nurses, doctors, and midwives—are available, around the clock, if you need them. There is a magic protective circle around the atmosphere of the Parenting conference. We're talking about our sons and daughters in this forum, not about our computers or our opinions about philosophy, and many of us feel that this tacit understanding sanctifies the virtual space.

3   The atmosphere of this particular conference—the attitudes people exhibit to each other in the tone of what they say in public—is part of what continues to attract me. People who never have much to contribute in political debate, technical argument, or intellectual gamesmanship turn out to have a lot to say about raising children. People you knew as fierce, even nasty, intellectual opponents in other contexts give you emotional support on a deeper level, parent to parent, within the boundaries of this small but warmly human corner of cyberspace.

4   In most cases, people who talk about a shared interest don't disclose enough about themselves as whole individuals on-line to inspire real trust in others. But in the case of the subcommunity called the Parenting conference, a few dozen of us, scattered across the country, few of whom rarely if ever saw the others face to face, have a few years of minor crises to knit us together and prepare us for serious business when it comes our way. Another several dozen read the conference regularly but contribute only when they have something important to add. Hundreds more read the conference every week without comment, except when something extraordinary happens.

5   Jay Allison and his family live in Massachusetts. He and his wife are public-radio producers. I've never met them face to face, although I feel I know something powerful and intimate about the Allisons and have strong emotional ties to them. What follows are some of Jay's postings on the WELL:

6   "Woods Hole. Midnight. I am sitting in the dark of my daughter's room. Her monitor lights blink at me. The lights used to blink too brightly so I covered them with bits of bandage adhesive and now they flash faintly underneath, a persistent red and green, Lillie's heart and lungs.

7   "Above the monitor is her portable suction unit. In the glow of the flashlight I'm writing by, it looks like the plastic guts of a science-class human model, the tubes coiled around the power supply, the reservoir, the pump.

8   "Tina is upstairs trying to get some sleep. A baby monitor links our bedroom to Lillie's. It links our sleep to Lillie's too, and because our souls are linked to hers, we do not sleep well.

9   "I am naked. My stomach is full of beer. The flashlight rests on it, and the beam rises and falls with my breath. My daughter breathes through a white plastic tube inserted into a hole in her throat. She's 14 months old."

10   Sitting in front of our computers with our hearts racing and tears in our eyes, in Tokyo and Sacramento and Austin, we

read about Lillie's croup, her tracheostomy, the days and nights
at Massachusetts General Hospital, and now the vigil over
Lillie's breathing and the watchful attention to the mechanical
apparatus that kept her alive. It went on for days. Weeks. Lillie
recovered, and relieved our anxieties about her vocal capabilities after all that time with a hole in her throat by saying the
most extraordinary things, duly reported on-line by Jay.

Later, writing in *Whole Earth Review,* Jay described the   11
experience:

"*Before this time, my computer screen had never been a place*   12
to go for solace. Far from it. But there it was. Those nights sit-
ting up late with my daughter, I'd go to my computer, dial up
the WELL, and ramble. I wrote about what was happening that
night or that year. I didn't know anyone I was "talking" to. I had
never laid eyes on them. At 3:00 a.m. my "real" friends were
asleep, so I turned to this foreign, invisible community for sup-
port. The WELL was always awake.

"*Any difficulty is harder to bear in isolation. There is nothing*   13
to measure against, to lean against. Typing out my journal
entries into the computer and over the phone lines, I found fel-
lowship and comfort in this unlikely medium."

Many people are alarmed by the very idea of a virtual com-   14
munity, fearing that it is another step in the wrong direction,
substituting more technological ersatz for yet another natural
resource or human freedom. These critics often voice their
sadness at what people have been reduced to doing in a civilization that worships technology, decrying the circumstances
that lead some people into such pathetically disconnected
lives that they prefer to find their companions on the other
side of a computer screen. There is a seed of truth in this fear,
for communities at some point require more than words on a
screen if they are to be other than ersatz.

Yet some people—many people—who don't do well in spon-   15
taneous spoken interaction turn out to have valuable contributions to make in a conversation in which they have time to
think about what to say. These people, who might constitute a
significant proportion of the population, can find written
communication more authentic than the face-to-face kind.
Who is to say that this preference for informal written text is
somehow less authentically human than opting for audible
speech? Those who critique computer-mediated communication because some people use it obsessively hit an important
target, but miss a great deal more when they don't take into
consideration people who use the medium for genuine human

interaction. Those who find virtual communities cold places point at the limits of the technology, its most dangerous pitfalls, and we need to pay attention to those boundaries. But these critiques don't tell us how the Allisons, my own family, and many others could have found the community of support and information we found in the WELL when we needed it. And those of us who do find communion in cyberspace might do well to pay attention to the way the medium we love can be abused.

16   Although dramatic incidents are what bring people together and stick in their memories, most of what goes on in the Parenting conference and most virtual communities is informal conversation and downright chitchat. The model of the WELL and other social clusters in cyberspace as "places" emerges naturally whenever people who use this medium discuss its nature. In 1987, Stewart Brand quoted me in his book *The Media Lab* about what tempted me to log onto the WELL as often as I did: "There's always another mind there. It's like having the corner bar, complete with old buddies and delightful newcomers and new tools waiting to take home and fresh graffiti and letters, except instead of putting on my coat, shutting down the computer, and walking down to the corner, I just invoke my telecom program and there they are. It's a place."

17   I've changed my mind about a lot of aspects of the WELL over the years, but the sense of place is still as strong as ever. As Ray Oldenburg proposes in his 1989 book *The Great Good Place*, there are three essential places in people's lives: the place we live, the place we work, and the place we gather for conviviality. Although the casual conversation that takes place in cafés, beauty shops, pubs, and town squares is universally considered to be trivial, idle talk, Oldenburg makes the case that such places are where communities can come into being and continue to hold together. These are the unacknowledged agoras of modern life. When the automobilecentric, suburban, fast-food, shopping-mall way of life eliminated many of these "third places" from traditional towns and cities around the world, the social fabric of existing communities started shredding.

18   Oldenburg puts a name and a conceptual framework on a phenomenon that every virtual community member knows instinctively, the power of informal public life:

19   *"Third places exist on neutral ground and serve to level their guests to a condition of social equality. Within these places, conversation is the primary activity and the major vehicle for the display and appreciation of human personality and individ-*

uality. Third places are taken for granted and most have a low profile. Since the formal institutions of society make stronger claims on the individual, third places are normally open in the off hours, as well as at other times. The character of a third place is determined most of all by its regular clientele and is marked by a playful mood, which contrasts with people's more serious involvement in other spheres. Though a radically different kind of setting for a home, the third place is remarkably similar to a good home in the psychological comfort and support that it extends.

"Such are the characteristics of third places that appear to be   20
universal and essential to a vital informal public life....

"The problem of place in America manifests itself (in a sorely   21
deficient informal public life. The structure of shared experience beyond that offered by family, job, and passive consumerism is small and dwindling. The essential group experience is being replaced by the exaggerated self-consciousness of individuals. American lifestyles, for all the material acquisition and the seeking after comforts and pleasures, are plagued by boredom, loneliness, alienation, and a high price tag....

"Unlike many frontiers, that of the informal public life does   22
not remain benign as it awaits development. It does not become easier to tame as technology evolves, as governmental bureaus and agencies multiply, or as population grows. It does not yield to the mere passage of time and a policy of letting the chips fall where they may as development proceeds in other areas of urban life. To the contrary, neglect of the informal public life can make a jungle of what had been a garden while, at the same time, diminishing the ability of people to cultivate it."

It might not be the same kind of place that Oldenburg had   23
in mind, but many of his descriptions of third places could also describe the WELL. Perhaps cyberspace is one of the informal public places where people can rebuild the aspects of community that were lost when the malt shop became a mall. Or perhaps cyberspace is precisely the *wrong* place to look for the rebirth of community, offering not a tool for conviviality but a life-denying simulacrum of real passion and true commitment to one another. In either case, we need to find out soon.

Because we cannot see one another in cyberspace, gender,   24
age, national origin, and physical appearance are not apparent unless a person wants to make such characteristics public. People whose physical handicaps make it difficult to form new friendships find that virtual communities treat them as

they always wanted to be treated—as thinkers and transmitters of ideas and feeling beings, not carnal vessels with a certain appearance and way of walking and talking (or not walking and not talking).

25   One of the few things that enthusiastic members of virtual communities in places like Japan, England, France, and the United States all agree on is that expanding their circle of friends is one of the most important advantages of computer conferencing. It is a way to *meet* people, whether or not you feel the need to affiliate with them on a community level. It's a way of both making contact with and maintaining a distance from others. The way you meet people in cyberspace puts a different spin on affiliation: In traditional kinds of communities, we are accustomed to meeting people, then getting to know them; in virtual communities, you can get to know people and *then* choose to meet them. Affiliation also can be far more ephemeral in cyberspace because you can get to know people you might never meet on the physical plane.

26   How does anybody find friends? In the traditional community, we search through our pool of neighbors and professional colleagues, of acquaintances and acquaintances of acquaintances, in order to find people who share our values and interests. We then exchange information about one another, disclose and discuss our mutual interests, and sometimes we become friends. In a virtual community we can go directly to the place where our favorite subjects are being discussed, then get acquainted with people who share our passions or who use words in a way we find attractive. In this sense, the topic is the address: You can't simply pick up a phone and ask to be connected with someone who wants to talk about Islamic art or California wine, or someone with a 3-year-old daughter or a 40-year-old Hudson; you can, however, join a computer conference on any of those topics, then open a public or private correspondence with the previously unknown people you find there. Your chances of making friends are increased by several orders of magnitude over the old methods of finding a peer group.

27   You can be fooled about people in cyberspace, behind the cloak of words. But that can be said about telephones or face-to-face communication as well; computer-mediated communications provide new ways to fool people, and the most obvious identity swindles will die out only when enough people learn to use the medium critically. In some ways, the medium will, by its nature, be forever biased toward certain kinds of obfuscation. It will also be a place where people often end up

revealing themselves far more intimately than they would be
inclined to do without the intermediation of screens and
pseudonyms.

Point of view, along with identity, is one of the great vari-   28
ables in cyberspace. Different people in cyberspace look at
their virtual communities through differently shaped key-
holes. In traditional communities, people have a strongly
shared mental model of the sense of place—the room or village or city where their interactions occur. In virtual communities, the sense of place requires an individual act of
imagination. The different mental models people have of the
electronic agora complicate the question of why people seem
to want to build societies mediated by computer screens. A
question like that leads inexorably to the old fundamental
questions of what forces hold any society together. The roots
of these questions extend farther than the social upheavals
triggered by modern communications technologies.

When we say "society," we usually mean citizens of cities in   29
entities known as nations. We take those categories for
granted. But the mass-psychological transition we made to
thinking of ourselves as part of modern society and nation-
states is historically recent. Could people make the transition
from the close collective social groups, the villages and small
towns of premodern and precapitalist Europe, to a new form
of social solidarity known as society that transcended and
encompassed all previous kinds of human association? Ferdi-
nand Tönnies, one of the founders of sociology, called the premodern kind of social group *gemeinschaft,* which is closer to
the English word *community,* and the new kind of social
group he called *gesellschaft,* which can be translated roughly
as *society.* All the questions about community in cyberspace
point to a similar kind of transition, for which we have no
technical names, that might be taking place now.

Sociology student Marc Smith, who has been using the   30
WELL and the Net as the laboratory for his fieldwork,
pointed me to Benedict Anderson's *Imagined Communities,* a
study of nation-building that focuses on the ideological labor
involved. Anderson points out that nations and, by extension,
communities are imagined in the sense that a given nation
exists by virtue of a common acceptance in the minds of the
population that it exists. Nations must exist in the minds of
their citizens in order to exist at all. "Virtual communities
require an act of imagination," Smith points out, extending
Anderson's line of thinking to cyberspace, "and what must be
imagined is the idea of the community itself."

Franklin Saige
Mega Buys

"Mega Buys," originally included in the Utne Reader *in the same issue as several other essays in this section (by Barlow, Rheingold, and Kadi), is excerpted from a longer essay that appeared in* Plain. *As its name implies,* Plain *is a journal built around the concept of simple living.*

1   A television ad for MCI reportedly features a child star chanting, "There will be a road. It will not connect two points. It will connect all points. It will not go from here to there. There will be no there. We will all only be here." Maybe this is actually a profound utterance, if we listen carefully, rather than the baloney it appears to be. Because even though the rumble of the bulldozers clearing the way for the information superhighway is fairly distant, perhaps it's time to listen, and then ask just where exactly is this "here" where we will all be?

2   One of the perils of modern technology is that it is invented to be sold, as opposed to most earlier inventions, which were made to be used by the inventor, the inventor's patron, or the community. Modern technology comes clothed in seductive imagery in order to make the sale, but it can take away our freedom once we buy into it. It takes away our freedom by reducing our ability to choose—our ability to choose not to think in terms of "organization" or having our schedules "managed," for example. It takes away our freedom by narrowing our options to a set of preprogrammed choices. It removes the sensory complexity that is the most obvious characteristic of the lived world.

3   Of course, there is another school of thought on this question: Most people believe that technology barely influences how we live our lives. "It's what we *do* with technology that counts," they say. In other words, it depends on our moral fitness, our will to master the machine.

4   I suppose that even the most seductive forms of technology can be resisted, at least for a while. People resisted using automobiles at first. Many people thought the automobile would be too noisy, too fast, too pretentious, and just too expensive to fit the existing social fabric. Initially, most people did not buy one. But even though their fears about the automobile were quickly realized, soon everyone who could afford to own one, did. Then these automobiles were used in ways that grad-

ually led to the weakening of the family and the community, not to mention the destruction of the landscape.

If hundreds of millions of car owners supposedly could 5 choose how they would use this technology, what happened to make them choose destructive rather than supportive uses? Did they simply change their values on a whim? Or could something inherent in the technology have pulled them in a particular direction?

What does the automobile do *best:* pull families apart, 6 cause urban sprawl, distort our sense of distance, or make travel more convenient? Only the last—convenience—is proven false every morning at rush hour, yet the car was sold to us on metaphors of speed and convenience. If we want to know where the information superhighway is leading us, maybe we should ask ourselves what *it* will do best.

To follow this road, we need to know that the term "infor- 7 mation superhighway" is strictly the creation of the advertising muse. It was coined to piggyback onto the prestige of the "information highway" of interactive (meaning two-way) networked computers sharing text and data known as the Internet. What makes the superhighway super is that it will be a commercially run interactive video network put together by the mega telecommunication and cable television industries. "Interactive pay TV" would be a more accurate name for it, though the Internet and similar data networks will undoubtedly be incorporated and offered as incidental services. A true definition of the information superhighway would focus on its somewhat less lofty pursuits: video shopping, pay-per-view movies on demand (presently a $10 billion annual market for video rental stores), and two-way videophones.

Once the billions of dollars to build the system have been 8 spent, every marketer will be in your living room and inside your head; your entertainment viewing choices, and especially your video shopping buying preferences, will be monitored and analyzed so that advertisers can turn around and market to you in a very targeted manner. Imagine one day using your television to purchase cloth diapers from the Virtual Wal-Mart. Then you switch to an entertainment program and *voilà!* the commercials are all for Pampers, piped to your household as a result of your latest purchasing profile. That is the commercial dream, very interactive, though not exactly in the poetic way it is being portrayed.

Whatever the specific route the superhighway takes, it is 9 obviously going to be *best* at invading your private life. Ultimately, its best use will be driving up consumption, which appeals to marketers more than to me, concerned as I am about the condition of the planet and my soul. I don't know about you, but I need less temptation to buy things, not more. And I don't want to be constantly sold to.

10   In *In the Absence of the Sacred,* Jerry Mander lists "Ten Recommended Attitudes About Technology." Along with number one ("Since most of what we are told about new technology comes from its proponents, be deeply skeptical of all claims") and number two ("Assume all technology guilty until proven innocent"), my favorite is number five: "Never judge a technology by the way it benefits you personally. Seek a holistic view of its impacts. The operative question is not if it benefits you, but who benefits most? And to what end?"

11   Since people appear to be more enslaved in their work and home lives than ever before, we could ask whether the problems their computers and electronic media seem to alleviate can be traced to the advent of computers themselves. Have computers and television speeded up economic life and undermined the social fabric?

12   None of the electronic technologies would be here if not for their utility as pillars of the consuming society. An ambulance is a "good" use for an internal combustion engine, but it takes a whole society of energy-guzzling car buyers addicted to mobility and speed to provide commercial reasons to make an internal combustion engine industry happen.

13   We are presently being assured that stepping into the virtual reality of the information superhighway and opening our minds to it is a good thing. Doubtless there will be many examples of this good: Grandparents will be able to see the grandkids on the videophone. The disabled will have more opportunities to be included.

14   And we will hear more and more about "virtual communities"—an exciting concept because, after all, the real ones have nearly disappeared. Perhaps almost-real ones will suffice, but I am unwilling to be part of a technology that can only exist if it drives me to consume more, which drains my will to seek out real community.

15   A woman at an organic farming conference I attended told the program speaker, who was against most new technologies, that even though she, too, thought these technologies might be harmful to the social fabric, still she felt she had to keep up with them: "Since this is what's going on in the world, don't we have to participate, just to survive?" No one could answer her then, and I have only part of the answer myself. I can only say I'm unwilling to drive the superhighway, and I sense that many others are deciding whether to continue on this ride or find an

exit. On the other hand, the people I glimpse in their cubicles, or sitting around their TV hearths at home, don't seem too dissatisfied. What will wake them up? How can I help them reverse direction and get back out of the machine?

I have no interest in being part of a "movement" to "ban" or "boycott." To do that, I would have to become like my friends in the ecology movement, *connected* to computer networks in order to *exchange information* and get *organized*. I see the technology encouraging in them precisely the way of relating to lived experience that has brought about the crises they seek to alleviate.   16

My strategy for exiting the information superhighway is simply never to enter it. The only "direct action" I can take is to live a real life, in real time, without viewing or networking or overconsuming anything. No input, no output. And I am going to tell anyone who will listen that real life, in a real community, in real reality, is better than the virtual reality of the information superhighway any day of the week.   17

Susan Herring

Gender Differences
on the Internet

Bringing Familiar Baggage
to the New Frontier

Susan Herring teaches linguistics at the University of Texas at Arlington. Her special interests are language and gender and the study of computer-mediated communication, so the following presentation came naturally to her. She offered it first as a talk at the annual meeting of the American Library Association, and then she made the talk available through the computer via the World Wide Web.

1. Introduction

Although research on computer-mediated communication (CMC) dates back to the early days of computer network technology in the 1970s, researchers have only recently begun to take the gender of users into account.[1] This is perhaps not   1 surprising considering that men have traditionally dominated the technology and have comprised the majority of users of computer networks since their inception, but the result is that most of what has been written about CMC incorporates a very one-sided perspective. However, recent research has been uncovering some eye-opening differences in the ways men and women interact "on-line," and it is these differences that I will address in my talk today.

2   My basic claim has two parts: first, that women and men have recognizably different styles in posting electronic messages to the Internet, contrary to claims that CMC neutralizes distinctions of gender, and second, that women and men have different communication ethics—that is, they value different kinds of on-line interactions as appropriate and desirable. I illustrate these differences—and some of the problems that arise because of them—with specific reference to the phenomenon of "flaming."

2. Background

3   Since 1991 I've been lurking (or what I prefer to call "carrying out ethnographic observation") on various computer-mediated discussion lists, downloading electronic conversations and analyzing the communicative behaviors of participants. I became interested in gender shortly after subscribing to my first discussion list, LINGUIST-L, an academic forum for professional linguists. Within the first month after I began receiving messages, a conflict arose on the list (what I would later learn to call a "flame war") in which the two major theoretical camps within the field became polarized around an issue of central interest. My curiosity was piqued by the fact that very few women were contributing to this important professional event; they seemed to be sitting on the sidelines while men were airing their opinions and getting all the attention. In an attempt to understand the women's silence, I made up an anonymous survey which I sent to LINGUIST-L asking subscribers what they thought of the discussion and if they hadn't contributed, why not.

3. Initial Observations

4   The number one reason given by both men and women for not contributing to the LINGUIST discussion was "intimidation"—as one respondent commented, participants were "rip-

ping each other's lungs out." Interestingly, however, men and women responded differently to feeling intimidated. Men seemed to accept such behavior as a normal feature of academic life, making comments to the effect that "Actually, the barbs and arrows were entertaining, because of course they weren't aimed at me." In contrast, many women responded with profound aversion. As one woman put it:

> That is precisely the kind of human interaction I committedly avoid. (...) I am dismayed that human beings treat each other this way. It makes the world a dangerous place to be. I dislike such people and I want to give them WIDE berth.

When I analyzed the messages in the thread itself, another gender difference emerged, this time relating to the linguistic structure and rhetoric of the messages. A daunting 68% of the messages posted by men made use of an adversarial style in which the poster distanced himself from, criticized, and/or ridiculed other participants, often while promoting his own importance. The few women who participated in the discussion, in contrast, displayed features of attenuation—hedging, apologizing, asking questions rather than making assertions— and a personal orientation, revealing thoughts and feelings and interacting with and supporting others.

It wasn't long before I was noticing a similar pattern in other discussions and on other lists. Wherever I went on mixed-sex lists, men seemed to be doing most of the talking and attracting most of the attention to themselves, although not all lists were as adversarial as LINGUIST. I started to hear stories about the witness men taking over and dominating discussions even of women-centered topics on women-centered lists.[2] In contrast, on the few occasions when I observed women attempting to gain an equal hearing on male-dominated lists, they were ignored, trivialized, or criticized by men for their tone or the inappropriateness of their topic.[3] It wasn't until I started looking at lists devoted to women's issues, and to traditionally "feminized" disciplines such as women's studies, teaching English as a second language, and librarianship, that I found women holding forth in an amount consistent with their numerical presence on the list. I also found different interactional norms: little or no flaming, and cooperative, polite exchanges.

4. Different Styles

6   As a result of these findings, I propose that women and men have different characteristic on-line styles. By characteristic styles, I do not mean that all or even the majority of users of each sex exhibit the behaviors of each style, but rather that the styles are recognizably—even stereotypically—gendered. The male style is characterized by adversariality: put-downs, strong, often contentious assertions, lengthy and/or frequent postings, self-promotion, and sarcasm. Below are two examples, one from an academic list (LINGUIST) and the other from a non-academic list (POLITICS).[4]

1) [Jean Linguiste's] proposals towards a more transparent morphology in French are exactly what he calls them: a farce. Nobody could ever take them seriously—unless we want to look as well at pairs such as *pe`re-me`re*, *coq-poule* and defigure the French language in the process.

[strong assertions ("exactly," "nobody"), put-downs ("JL's proposals…are a farce"; implied: "JL wants to defigure the French language")]

2) >yes, they did…This is why we must be allowed to remain >armed…who is going >to help us if our government >becomes a tyranny? no one will.

oh yes we *must* remain armed. anyone see day one last night abt charlestown where everyone/s so scared of inform-ing on murderers the cops have given up? where the reply to any offense is a public killing? knowing you/re not gonna be caught cause everyone/s to affraid to be a witness?

yeah, right, twerp.

>   —[Ron] "the Wise"—

what a joke.

[sarcasm, name calling, personal insults]
The second example would be characterized as a "flame" by most readers because of its personally offensive nature.

7   Less exclusively male-gendered but still characteristic of male postings is an authoritative, self-confident stance whereby men are more likely than women to represent them-selves as experts, e.g., in answering queries for information. The following example is from NOTIS-L.

3) The NUGM Planning meeting was canceled before all of this came up. It has nothing to do with it. The plans were simply proceeding along so well that there was no need to hold the meeting. That is my understanding from talking to NOTIS staff last week.

[authoritative tone, strong assertions ("nothing," "simply," "just")]

The female-gendered style, in contrast, has two aspects which typically co-occur: supportiveness and attenuation. "Supportiveness" is characterized by expressions of appreciation, thanking, and community-building activities that make other participants feel accepted and welcome. "Attenuation" includes hedging and expressing doubt, apologizing, asking questions, and contributing ideas in the form of suggestions. The following examples from a non-academic list (WOMEN) and an academic list (TEST-L) illustrate each aspect:

4) >[Aileen],
    >
    >I just wanted to let you know that I have really enjoyed all your posts about
    >Women's herstory. They have been extremely informative and I've learned alot
    >about the women's movement. Thank you!
    >
    >-[Erika]
    DITTO!!!! They are wonderful!
    Did anyone else catch the first part of a Century of Women? I really enjoyed it.
    Of course, I didn't agree with everything they said...but it was really informative.
    [Roberta]~~~~~~~~~~~~~~~~~~~~~~~~~~

[appreciates, thanks, agrees, appeals to group]

5) [...] I hope this makes sense. This is kind of what I had in mind when I realized I couldn't give a real definitive answer. Of course, maybe I'm just getting into the nuances of the language when it would be easier to just give the simple answer.

    Any response?

[hedges, expresses doubt, appeals to group]

9   The female style takes into consideration what the sociologist Erving Goffman called the "face" wants of the addressee—specifically, the desire of the addressee to feel ratified and liked (e.g., by expressions of appreciation) and her desire not to be imposed upon (e.g., by absolute assertions that don't allow for alternative views). The male style, in contrast, confronts and threatens the addressee's "face" in the process of engaging him in agonistic debate.

10   Although these styles represent in some sense the extremes of gendered behavior, they have symbolic significance above and beyond their frequency of use. For example, other users regularly infer the gender of message posters on the basis of features of these styles, especially when the self-identified gender of a poster is open to question. Consider the following cases, the first involving a male posting as a female, the second a suspected female posting as a male:

11   (i) A male subscriber on SWIP-L (Society for Women in Philosophy list) posted a message disagreeing with the general consensus that discourse on SWIP-L should be non-agonistic, commenting "there's nothing like a healthy denunciation by one's colleagues every once in a while to get one's blood flowing, and spur one to greater subtlety and exactness of thought." He signed his message with a female pseudonym, however, causing another (female) subscriber to comment later, "I must confess to looking for the name of the male who wrote the posting that [Suzi] sent originally and was surprised to find a female name at the end of it." The female subscriber had (accurately) inferred that anyone actively advocating "denunciation by one's colleagues" was probably male.

12   (ii) At a time when one male subscriber had been posting frequent messages to the WOMEN list, another subscriber professing to be a man posted a message inquiring what the list's policy was towards men participating on the list, admitting "I sometimes feel guilty for taking up bandwidth." The message, in addition to showing consideration for the concerns of others on the list, was very attenuated in style and explicitly appreciative of the list: "I really enjoy this list (actually, it's the best one I'm on)." That prompted another (female) subscriber to respond, "now that you've posed the question...how's one to know you're not a woman posing this question as a man?" Her suspicion indicates that on some level she recognized that anyone posting a message expressing appreciation and consideration for the desires of others was likely to be female.

*   *   *

The existence of gendered styles has important implica- 13
tions, needless to say, for popular claims that CMC is anonymous, "gender-blind," and hence inherently democratic. If
our on-line communicative style reveals our gender, then gender differences, along with their social consequences, are
likely to persist on computer-mediated networks.[5]

Entire lists can be generated in their style as well. It is tac- 14
itly expected that members of the non-dominated gender will
adapt their posting style in the direction of the style of the
dominant gender. Thus men on women's special interest lists
tend to attenuate their assertions and shorten their messages,
and women, especially on male-dominated lists such as LIN-
GUIST and PAGLIA-L, can be contentious and adversarial.
Arguably, they *must* adapt in order to participate appropriately in keeping with the norms of the local list culture. Most
members of the non-dominant gender on any given list, however, end up style-mixing, that is, taking on some attributes of
the dominant style while preserving features of their native
style, e.g., with men often preserving a critical stance and
women a supportive one at the macro-message level. This suggests that gender communication styles are deeply rooted—
not surprising, since they are learned early in life—and that
some features are more resistant to conscious reflection and
modification than others.

5. Different Communication Ethics

The second part of this talk concerns the value systems 15
that underlie and are used to rationalize communicative
behavior on the net. In particular, I focus on the phenomenon
of flaming, which has been variously defined as "the expression of strong negative emotion," use of "derogatory, obscene,
or inappropriate language," and "personal insults." A popular
explanation advanced by CMC researchers[6] is that flaming is
a by-product of the medium itself—the decontextualized and
anonymous nature of CMC leads to "disinhibition" in users
and a tendency to forget that there is an actual human being
at the receiving end of one's emotional outbursts. However,
until recently CMC research has largely overlooked gender as
a possible influence on behavior, and the simple fact of the
matter is that it is virtually only men who flame. If the
medium makes men more likely to flame, it should have a
similar effect on women, yet if anything the opposite appears
to be the case. An adequate explanation of flaming must
therefore take gender into account.

16   Why do men flame? The explanation, I suggest, is that women and men have different communication ethics, and flaming is compatible with male ethical ideals. I stumbled upon this realization recently as a result of a survey I conducted on politeness on the Internet. I originally hypothesized that the differences in the extremes of male and female behavior on-line—in particular, the tendency for women to be considerate of the "face" needs of others while men threaten others' "face"—could be explained if it turned out that women and men have different notions of what constitutes appropriate behavior. In other words, as a woman I might think adversarial behavior is rude, but men who behave adversarially might think otherwise. Conversely, men might be put off by the supportive and attenuated behaviors of women.

17   In the survey, I asked subscribers from eight Internet discussion lists to rank their like or dislike for 30 different on-line behaviors, including "flaming," "expressing thanks and appreciation," and "overly tentative messages," on a scale of 1 (like) to 5 (dislike). The survey also asked several open-ended questions, including most importantly: What behaviors bother you most on the net?

18   My initial hypothesis turned out to be both correct and incorrect. It was incorrect in that I found no support whatsoever for the idea that men's and women's value systems are somehow reversed. Both men and women said they liked expressions of appreciation (avg. score of 2), were neutral about tentative messages (avg. about 3), and disliked flaming (although women expressed a stronger dislike than men, giving it a score of 4.3 as compared with only 3.9 for men). This makes male flaming behavior all the more puzzling; should we conclude then that men who flame are deliberately trying to be rude?

19   The answers to the open-ended questions suggest a different explanation. These answers reveal a gender contrast in values that involves politeness but cannot be described in terms of politeness alone. It seems women place a high value on consideration for the wants and needs of others, as expressed in the following comment by a female net user:

> If we take responsibility for developing our own sensitivities to others and controlling our actions to minimize damage—
> we will each be doing [good deeds] for the whole world constantly.

Men, in contrast, assign greater value to freedom from censorship (many advocate absolute free speech), forthright and open expression, and agonistic debate as a means to advance the pursuit of knowledge. Historically, the value on absolute freedom of speech reflects the civil libertarian leanings of the computing professionals who originally designed the net and have contributed much of the utopian discourse surrounding it; the value on agonistic debate is rooted in the Western (male) philosophical tradition.

These ideals are stirringly evoked in the following quote from R. Hauben (1993) praising the virtues of the Usenet system, on which 95% of the contributors are estimated to be male: 20

> The achievement of Usenet News demonstrates the importance of facilitating the development of uncensored speech and communication—there is debate and discussion—one person influences another—people build on each other's strengths and interests, differences, etc.

One might think that uncensored speech if abused could cause problems, but M. Hauben (1993) explains that there is a democratic way of handling this eventuality:

> When people feel someone is abusing the nature of Usenet News, they let the offender know through e-mail. In this manner. . . people fight to keep it a resource that is helpful to society as a whole.

In daily life on the Internet, however, the ideal of "people fight[ing] to keep [the net] a resource that is helpful to society as a whole" often translates into violent action. Consider, for example, the response of a male survey respondent to the question: "What behaviors bother you most on the net?" (typos are in the original):

> As much as I am irritated by [incompetent posters], I don't want imposed rules. I would prefer to "out" such a person and let some public minded citizen fire bomb his house to imposing rules on the net. Letter bombing an annoying individual's feed is usually preferable to building a formal hierarchy of net cops.

Another net vigilante responds graphically as follows:

I'd have to say commercial shit. Whenever someone adver-
tises some damn get-rich-quick scheme and plasters it all
over the net by crossposting it to every newsgroup, I reach
for my "gatling gun mailer crasher" and fire away at the
source address.

These responses not only evoke an ideal of freedom from
external authority, they provide an explicit justification for
flaming—as a form of self-appointed regulation of the social
order, a rough and ready form of justice on the virtual frontier. Thus a framework of values is constructed within which
flaming and other aggressive behaviors can be interpreted in
a favorable (even prosocial) light. This is not to say that all or
even most men who flame have the good of net society at
heart, but rather that the behavior is in principle justifiable
for men (and hence tolerable) in ways that it is not for most
women.

6. Netiquette

21   Further evidence that flaming is tolerated and justified
within a system of male values comes from the content of
written rules of network etiquette, or "netiquette," such as are
available on many public FTP sites and in introductory messages to new members of some discussion lists. I analyzed the
content of netiquette rules from six lists, along with those
found in the guidelines for Usenet and in the print publication *Towards an Ethics and Etiquette for Electronic Mail* by
Shapiro and Anderson (1985). What do netiquette rules have
to say about flaming?

22   The answer is: remarkably little, given that it is one of the
most visible and frequently complained about "negatives"
cited about the Internet. One might even say there is a striking lack of proscription against flaming, except on a few
women-owned and women-oriented lists. And in the rare
instances where flaming is mentioned, it is implicitly authorized. Thus the guidelines for new subscribers to the POLI-
TICS list prohibit "flames of a personal nature," and Shapiro
and Anderson advise "Do not insult or criticize third parties
without giving them a chance to respond." While on the surface appearing to oppose flaming, these statements in fact
implicitly authorize "flames other than of a personal nature"
(for example, of someone's ideas or values) and "insulting or
criticizing third parties" (provided you give them a chance to

respond!). Normative statements such as these are compatible with male values and male adversarial style; the intimidating rhetoric on LINGUIST and many other lists is not a violation of net etiquette according to these rules.[7] Yet these are behaviors that female survey respondents say intimidate them and drive them away from lists and newsgroups. Can the Internet community afford to tolerate behaviors that intimidate and silence women? This is a question that urgently needs to be raised and discussed net-wide.

7. Conclusions

To sum up, I have argued that women and men constitute 23 different discourse communities in cyberspace—different cultures, if you will—with differing communicative norms and practices. However, these cultures are not "separate but equal" as recent popular writing on gender differences in communication has claimed. Rather, the norms and practices of masculine net culture, codified in netiquette rules, conflict with those of the female culture in ways that render cyberspace—or at least many "neighborhoods" in cyberspace—inhospitable to women. The result is an imbalance whereby men control a disproportionate share of the communication that takes place via computer networks.

This imbalance must be redressed if computer-mediated 24 communication is ever to live up to its much-touted democratic potential. Fortunately, there are ways in which women can promote their concerns and influence the discourse of the net;[8] I will mention three here. First and foremost is to participate, for example, in women-centered lists. Such lists provide supportive fora for women on-line, and are frequently models of cooperative discourse whose norms can spread if subscribers participate in other lists as well. But separatism has its disadvantages, among them the risk of ghettoization. Women must not let themselves be driven by flame throwers away from mainstream, mixed-sex fora, but rather should also actively seek to gain influence there, individually and collectively, especially in fora where metadiscourse about the net itself takes place.

The second way to promote women's interests net-wide is 25 to educate on-line communities about the rhetorical strategies used in intimidating others, and to call people on their behavior and its consequences when they use such strategies.[9] This is already happening on some women-centered lists such as WMST-L and SWIP-L—aware of the tendency for a single man or group of men to dominate discussions, female subscribers call attention to this behavior as soon as they realize it is happening; interestingly, it is happening less and less often on these lists. Group awareness is a powerful force for change, and it can be raised in mixed-sex fora as well.

26   Finally, women need to contribute in any way they can to the process that leads to the encoding of netiquette rules. They need to instigate and participate persuasively in discussions about what constitutes appropriate and inappropriate behavior on-line—seeking to define in concrete terms what constitutes "flaming," for instance, since women and men are likely to have different ideas about this. They must be alert to opportunities (or make their own opportunities) to write out guidelines for suggested list protocol (or modifications to list protocol if guidelines already exist) and post them for discussion. No greater power exists than the power to define values, and the structure of the Internet—especially now, while it is still evolving and seeking its ultimate definition—provides a unique opportunity for individual users to influence the normative process.

27   Indeed, it may be vital that we do so if women's on-line communication styles are to be valued along with those of men, and if we are to insure women the right to settle on the virtual frontier on their own—rather than on male-defined—terms.

Notes

1. A notable exception to this generalization is the work of Sherry Turkle in the 1980s on how women and men relate to computers.
2. For an extreme example of this phenomenon that took place on the soc.feminism Usenet newsgroup, see Sutton (1994).
3. Herring, Johnson, and DiBenedetto (1992, in press).
4. All names mentioned in the messages are pseudonyms.
5. This problem is discussed in Herring (1993a).
6. For example, Kiesler et al. (1984), Kim and Raja (1990), and Shapiro and Anderson (1985).
7. The discussion of politeness and communication ethics here is an abbreviated version of that presented in Herring (In press a, In press b).
8. For other practical suggestions on how to promote gender equality in networking, see Kramarae and Taylor (1993).
9. Cases where this was done, both successfully and unsuccessfully, are described in Herring, Johnson, & DiBenedetto (In press).

References

Hauben, Michael. 1993. "The social forces behind the development of Usenet News." Electronic document. (FTP weber.ucsd.edu, directory/pub/usenet.hist)

Hauben, Ronda. 1993. "The evolution of Usenet News: The poor man's ARPANET." Electronic document. (FTP weber.ucsd.edu, directory/pub/usenet.hist)

Herring, Susan. 1992. "Gender and participation in computer-mediated linguistic discourse." Washington, DC: ERIC Clearinghouse on Languages and Linguistics, document no. ED345552.

Herring, Susan. 1993a. "Gender and democracy in computer-mediated communication." *Electronic Journal of Communication* 3(2), special issue on Computer-Mediated Communication, T. Benson, ed. Reprinted in R. Kling (ed.), *Computerization and Controversy*, 2nd edition. New York: Academic (In press).

Herring, Susan. 1993b. "Men's language: A study of the discourse of the Linguist list." In A. Crochetière, J.-C. Boulanger, and C. Ouellon (eds.), *Les Langues Menacées: Actes du XVe Congrès International des Linguistes*, Vol. 3. Québec: Les Presses de l'Université Laval, 347–350.

Herring, Susan. In press a. "Politeness in computer culture: Why women thank and men flame." In M. Bucholtz, A. Liang and L. Sutton (eds.), *Communicating In, Through, and Across Cultures: Proceedings of the Third Berkeley Women and Language Conference*. Berkeley Women and Language Group.

Herring, Susan. In press b. "Posting in a different voice: Gender and ethics in computer-mediated communication." In C. Ess (ed.), *Philosophical Perspectives on Computer-Mediated Communication*. Albany: SUNY Press.

Herring, Susan. Forthcoming. "Two variants of an electronic message schema." In S. Herring (ed.), *Computer-Mediated Communication: Linguistic, social, and cross-cultural perspectives*. Amsterdam/Philadelphia: John Benjamins.

Herring, Susan; Deborah Johnson; and Tamra DiBenedetto. 1992. "Participation in electronic discourse in a 'feminist' field." In M. Bucholtz, K. Hall, and B. Moonwomon, eds., *Locating Power: Proceedings of the Second Berkeley Women and Language Conference*. Berkeley Women and Language Group.

Herring, Susan; Deborah Johnson; and Tamra DiBenedetto. In press. "'This discussion is going too far!' Male resistance to female participation on the Internet." In M. Bucholtz and K. Hall (eds.), *Gender Articulated: Language and the Socially-Constructed Self*. New York: Routledge.

Kiesler, Sara; Jane Seigel; and Timothy W. McGuire. 1984. "Social psychological aspects of computer-mediated communication." *American Psychologist*, 39, 1123–1134.

Kim, Min-Sun and Narayan S. Raja. 1990. "Verbal aggression and self-disclosure on computer bulletin boards." ERIC document (ED334620).

Kramarae, Cheris and H. Heanie Taylor. 1993. "Women and men on electronic networks: A conversation or a monologue?" In Taylor, Kramarae and Ebben, eds., *Women, Information Technology and Scholarship*, 52–61. Urbana, IL: Center for Advanced Study.

Rheingold, Howard. 1993. *The Virtual Community: Homesteading on the Electronic Frontier*. Reading, MA: Addison-Wesley.

Seabrook, John. 1994. "My first flame." *The New Yorker,* June 6, 1994, 70–79.

Shapiro, Norman Z. and Robert H. Anderson. 1985. *Toward an Ethics and Etiquette for Electronic Mail*. The Rand Corporation.

Sutton, Laurel. 1994. "Using USENET: Gender, power, and silencing in electronic discourse." *Proceedings of the 20th Annual Meeting of the Berkeley Linguistics Society (BLS-20)*. Berkeley: Berkeley Linguistics Society, Inc.

Turkle, Sherry, 1984. *The Second Self: Computers and the Human Spirit*. London: Granada.

Credits

Credits

Pages 909–917: From Jacob Weisberg, "This Is Your Death," *The New Republic*, July 1, 1991. Reprinted by permission of *The New Republic*.

Page 918: From *In Your Face*, by Doug Marlette. Boston: Houghton Mifflin. Copyright © 1991 by Doug Marlette. Reprinted by permission of Doug Marlette.

Pages 919–926: From Kurt Schmoke, "A War for the Surgeon General, Not the Attorney General," *New Perspectives Quarterly* (Summer 1989), vol. 6, no. 2. Reprinted by permission of the author.

Pages 926–931: From William Bennett, "Should Drugs Be Legalized?" Reprinted with permission from the March 1990 Reader's Digest. Copyright © 1990 by The Reader's Digest Assn., Inc.

Pages 931–934: From Milton Friedman, "Prohibition and Drugs," *Newsweek*, 1972. Reprinted by permission of the author.

Pages 934–936: From Milton Friedman, "An Open Letter to Bill Bennett," *The Wall Street Journal*, September 7, 1989. Reprinted with permission of the author and The Wall Street Journal, © 1989, Dow Jones & Company, Inc. All rights reserved.

Pages 936–939: From William Bennett, "A Response to Milton Friedman," *The Wall Street Journal*, September 19, 1989. Reprinted with permission of the author and The Wall Street Journal, © 1989, Dow Jones & Company, Inc. All rights reserved.

Pages 939–941: From Letters to the Editor, "Bennett Fears 'Public Policy Disaster'—It's Already Here," *The Wall Street Journal*, September 29, 1989. Reprinted by permission.

PART VII

Pages 947–960: From Tom Regan, *The Animal's Voice Magazine*. Reprinted from *The Animal's Voice Magazine*, 1989. PO Box 341347, Los Angeles, CA 90034 / 1–800–82–VOICE.

Pages 960–969: From Vicki Hearne, "What's Wrong with Animal Rights," *Harper's Magazine*, September 1991. Copyright © 1991 by *Harper's Magazine*. All rights reserved. Reprinted from the September issue by special permission.

Pages 969–971: From "Letters to the Editor About 'Animal Rights, Wronged,'" *Harper's Magazine*, December 1991. Copyright © 1991 by *Harper's Magazine*. All rights reserved. Reprinted from the December issue by special permission.

Pages 972–974: From Alexis Dorn, "Animal Rights, Vegetarianism, and the American Effort to Save the Planet." Reprinted by permission of Alexis Dorn.

Page 975: Advertisement reprinted by permission of the Foundation for Biomedical Research.

Pages 977–985: From Hanna Rosin, "The Homecoming," *The New Republic*, June 5, 1995. Reprinted by permission of *The New Republic*.

Pages 985–994: Ann Louise Bardach, "The White Cloud," *The New Republic*, June 5, 1995. Reprinted by permission of *The New Republic*.

Pages 997–1001: From Marcia Angell, "A Dual Approach to the AIDS Epidemic," *The New England Journal of Medicine* (May 23, 1991), vol. 234, pp. 1498–1500. Reprinted by permission of *The New England Journal of Medicine*.

Pages 1002–1008: From Letters to the Editor, "Responding to the AIDS Epidemic," *The New England Journal of Medicine* (September 12, 1991), vol. 235, pp. 809–811. Reprinted by permission of *The New England Journal of Medicine*.

Author/Title Index